THE BEST PUBLIC
GOLF COURSES
IN THE UNITED STATES,
CANADA,
THE CARIBBEAN AND
MEXICO

THE BEST PUBLIC
GOLF COURSES
IN THE UNITED STATES,
CANADA,
THE CARIBBEAN AND
MEXICO

ROBERT McCORD

RANDOM HOUSE
NEW YORK

This is a revised and updated edition of *The 479 Best Public Golf Courses in the United States, Canada, the Caribbean and Mexico* by Robert McCord, which was published by Random House, Inc., in 1993.

Library of Congress Cataloging-in-Publication Data

McCord, Robert R.
The Best Public Golf Courses in the United States, Canada, the Caribbean and Mexico/
Robert McCord—2nd ed.

Includes index.
ISBN: 0-679-76903-X
1. Golf courses—United States—Directories. 2. Golf courses—Canada—Directories.
3. Golf courses—Caribbean Area—Directories. 4. Golf courses—Mexico—Directories.
I. Title. II. Title: The best public golf courses in the United States, Canada, the Caribbean and Mexico.

GV981.M33 1996 796.352'08'873—cc20 92-56832

The Best Public Golf Courses in the United States, Canada, the Caribbean and Mexico is available at special discounts for bulk purchases for resale, sales promotions or premiums. A special edition, including a personalized cover, excerpts and corporate imprints, can be created in large quantities for special needs. For further information, write to Special Markets, Random House, Inc., 201 East 50th Street, New York, NY 10022.

Page Design: Bob Feldgus, New York
Desktop Publishing: Harwood Publishing & Design, New York
Printed in the United States of America on acid-free paper
Random House website address: http://www.randomhouse.com/
98765432

Second Edition

For Nancy, my valentine of a lifetime

Acknowledgments

I would like to thank the many people who have helped make this book possible. These include my editor, Joe Fox, whose idea this book was and who has provided me with encouragement and helpful criticism along the way. Joe Fox died at work in his office at Random House in late 1995. A superb editor and good friend, Joe is missed by myself and many others. Thanks to my current editor, Lawrence LaRose, and the Random House staff. Thanks to the many golf professionals, golf-course managers, golf-resort managers and other personnel who took the time to discuss their golf courses with me and provided me with a variety of written material to facilitate the writing of this book; representatives of state, provincial, county and municipal tourist bureaus, chambers of commerce and libraries who provided me with golf and general tourist information related to their territories; the American Automobile Association; the United States Golf Association; the National Golf Foundation; and state and regional golf associations; Bob Feldgus, who designed the interior of the book; and Barbara Harkins and Larry Harkins of Harwood Publishing, who handled the desktop publishing work. I would especially like to thank my wife, Nancy, who has provided me with encouragement and helpful suggestions on this project and many others.

Contents

Introduction xiii

I. THE UNITED STATES
ALABAMA
Mobile Area 3
Montgomery Area 6
ALASKA 13
ARIZONA
Flagstaff Area 15
Phoenix Area 16
Tucson Area 35
ARKANSAS 47
CALIFORNIA
Northern 50
San Francisco Area 54
Monterey Peninsula Area 60
Santa Barbara/San Luis Obispo Area 71
Los Angeles Area 78
Palm Springs Area 86
San Diego Area 98
COLORADO
Denver and North Central Area 110
Northwestern Area 118
South Central Area 126
Pueblo Area 129
Southwestern Area 131
CONNECTICUT 134
DELAWARE 137
FLORIDA
Southeastern 139
Orlando Area/Central 154
Daytona Area/East Coast 174
Jacksonville Area/Northeastern 178
Northwestern 186
Tampa/St. Petersburg Area 190
Southwestern 197
GEORGIA
Atlanta Area 207
Augusta Area 218
Columbus 223
Savannah/St. Simons Island Areas 225
HAWAII
Hawaii 236
Kauai 247
Lanai 256

Maui 25
Oahu 26

IDAHO
Boise Area 27
Lewiston Area 27
Pocatello Area 27

ILLINOIS
Bloomington/Normal Area 28
Chicago Area 28
Northern 29
Southern 30
Springfield Area 30

INDIANA
Indianapolis Area 30
South Bend Area 31
Southern Indiana 31
Terre Haute 31

IOWA 32
KANSAS 32
KENTUCKY 33
LOUISIANA 33
MAINE 33
MARYLAND 34

MASSACHUSETTS
Cape Cod Area 35
Springfield Area/Western 35
Western Area 35

MICHIGAN
Detroit/Southeastern Area 36
Northeast/Bay City and North 36
Northwestern 37
Southwestern/Middle Western 38
MINNESOTA 39

MISSISSIPPI 4
MISSOURI 4
MONTANA 4
NEBRASKA 4

NEVADA
Las Vegas Area 4
Reno/Tahoe Area 4

NEW HAMPSHIRE
Northern 4
Southern 4

NEW JERSEY
Northern 4
Central 4
Atlantic City Area 4

NEW MEXICO 455
NEW YORK
  New York City/Long Island 467
  Hudson River Valley 471
  Catskills 473
  South Central 476
  Central 478
  Western 481
  Northern 482
NORTH CAROLINA
  Greensboro Area 492
  Pinehurst Area 498
  Raleigh/Durham Area 510
  Western Area 513
  Wilmington Area 515
NORTH DAKOTA 520
OHIO 524
OKLAHOMA 536
OREGON
  Bend Area 541
  Eugene Area 545
  Portland Area 546
PENNSYLVANIA
  Allentown/Lancaster/Philadelphia Area 556
  Harrisburg Area 558
  State College 562
  Western/Pittsburgh Area 564
RHODE ISLAND 571
SOUTH CAROLINA
  Charleston Area 572
  Hilton Head Area 580
  Myrtle Beach Area 591
SOUTH DAKOTA 606
TENNESSEE 611
TEXAS
  Austin Area 619
  Dallas/Fort Worth Area 625
  Houston Area 632
  San Antonio Area 637
UTAH 645
VERMONT 652
VIRGINIA
  Northeastern and Washington, D.C. Area 661
  Richmond Area 663
  Western Virginia Area 663
  Williamsburg Area 672

WASHINGTON
  Bellingham/Northwestern Area 68
  Seattle/Tacoma Area 68
  Spokane Area/Eastern 69
  Wenatchee/Central Area 70
WEST VIRGINIA 70
WISCONSIN
  Southern 71
  Central 72
WYOMING 72

II. CANADA
ALBERTA 73
BRITISH COLUMBIA 74
MANITOBA 76
NEW BRUNSWICK 76
NEWFOUNDLAND AND LABRADOR 76
NOVA SCOTIA 76
ONTARIO 76
PRINCE EDWARD ISLAND 77
QUEBEC 78
SASKATCHEWAN 78

III. BAHAMAS, BERMUDA, CARIBBEAN
BAHAMAS 79
BERMUDA 79
DOMINICAN REPUBLIC 79
JAMAICA 79
PUERTO RICO 80
U.S. VIRGIN ISLANDS 80
WEST INDIES 80

IV. MEXICO
BAJA SUR 8
COLIMA 8
GUERRERO 8
JALISCO 8

Index 8

Introduction

This is a collection of the best public, resort and semiprivate golf courses that you can play in the United States, Canada, the Caribbean, the Bahamas, Bermuda and Mexico. The selection is a result of over 100,000 miles of travel, hundreds of interviews with golf professionals and managers at hundreds of golf courses and a careful review of the recommendations of leading golf periodicals and guides.

The featured golf courses in this book provide a grand tour for golfers who wish to play quality golf courses that present a variety of golf challenges on terrain ranging from the mountains of an Apache Indian reservation in New Mexico to beautiful seaside golf courses such as Pebble Beach in California, Highland Links in the Cape Breton Highlands of Nova Scotia, and the Teeth of the Dog at the Casa de Campo Resort in the Dominican Republic.

Represented in these pages are the masterpieces of many of golf's greatest architects, including Harry Shapland Colt, Alice and Pete Dye, Henry Chandler Egan, Devereaux Emmet, Tom Fazio, Arthur Hills, Rees Jones, Robert Trent Jones, Sr., Robert Trent Jones, Jr., Joe Lee, Charles Blair MacDonald, Alister MacKenzie, Jack Nicklaus, Seth J. Raynor, Donald Ross, Stanley Thompson, A. W. Tillinghast, Dick Wilson and many others. Some of their best work and that of other fine golf architects is represented in this book.

In addition to featured write-ups of 617 courses in North America, the Caribbean and Mexico, more than an additional 2,000 courses are recommended as excellent tests of golf. In many instances, there is a very thin line between being a featured course and being a recommended one. Among the featured courses in the United States are virtually all the most recently highly rated public, resort, semiprivate and daily fee courses from *Golf Digest* and *Golf* magazines. The featured and recommended lists for Canada include the most highly rated courses by *Score* magazine, Canada's leading golf publication. Also, virtually all of *Meetings and Conventions* magazine's Gold Tee Award winners for excellent golf and conference facilities are included in this book—most of them featured. Should there be a publicly accessible golf course (public, resort, semiprivate, or daily fee) that you think should be included in the next edition of this book, or if there is some oversight or error that you feel should be corrected, please submit your recommendations to the publisher, and every effort will be made to review and act upon your request.

There are over 15,000 golf courses in North America, the Caribbean and Mexico. My intention with this book is to provide the best choice of 617 golf courses accessible to the public and several additional recommended courses that provide quality golf in a variety of interesting and challenging settings. I hope that this book will be of use to you on your own golf odyssey and that on that adventure you will fully experience all the joys, frustrations and wonders of a truly intricate and fascinating game.

Robert McCord
New York City

THE UNITED STATES

Mobile Area

Course Name: KIVA DUNES GOLF CLUB

Course Type: Public
Address: 815 Plantation Drive
Gulf Shores, AL 36542
Phone: (334) 540–7000
Fax: (334) 540–7003

GOLF COURSE

Director of Golf: Mark Stillings
Head Professional: Glen Clem
Course Length/Par (All Tees): Back
7092/72, Blue 6464/72, White 5849/72,
Forward 4994/72
Course Slope/Rating (All Tees): Back
132/73.9, Blue 129/70.8, White
119/67.8, Ladies' Red 115/68.5
Course Architect: Jerry Pate (1995)
Golf Facilities: Full Pro Shop X, Snack
Bar X, Lounge X, Restaurant X,
Locker Room X, Showers X, Club
Rental X, Club Repair No, Cart Rental
X, Instruction X, Practice Green X,
Driving Range X, Practice Bunker X,
Club Storage No
Tee-Time Reservation Policy: Up to 3
days in advance
Ranger: Yes
Tee-off-Interval Time: 8 min.
Time to Play 18 Holes: 4 hrs. 15 min.
Course Hours/Earliest Tee-off: 7:32 a.m.
Green and Cart Fees: $59 for 18 holes
Credit Cards: All major cards
Season: Year round. Busiest May to mid-
Sept.
Course Comments: Can walk anytime at
full fee
Golf Packages: Inquire at pro shop or call
Gulf Shores Golf (800) 745-SAND
Discounts: Seasonal. Lower rates early
Sept. to late May
Places to Stay Nearby: Gulf Shores
Plantation (334) 540–2291, (800) 554–
0344; Holiday Inn on the Beach (334)
948–6191, (800) HOLIDAY; Quality Inn
Beachside (334) 948–6874. MOBILE:
Radisson Admiral Semmes Hotel (334)
432–8000, (800) 333–3333
Local Attractions: Bon Secour National
Wildlife Refuge, Fort Morgan Historic
Site, seasonal festivals, boating, fishing,
beaches. Mobile. Gulf Coast Chamber
of Commerce, 3150 Gulf Shores Pkwy.,
P.O. Box 457, Gulf Shores, AL 36547
(334) 968–7511
Directions: From I-10 go south on Hwy.
59 to Gulf Shores. Proceed to 4th light
and take a right on Hwy. 180. Proceed
13 miles to golf course on left
Closest Commercial Airports: Mobile
Regional (1 hr.); New Orleans
International (3 hrs.)

KIVA DUNES GOLF CLUB

Kiva Dunes is a new Jerry Pate–
designed golf course built within a 250-
acre residential real estate development
bordered by Mobile Bay to the north and
the Gulf of Mexico to the south. This links-
style dunesland course has natural wetland
areas, dunes, manmade water hazards, and
sweeping winds that can exceed 30 miles
per hour. Most holes on the course run in
an east and west direction and variable
winds can change how the course plays
with unexpected suddenness. The fairway
landing areas at Kiva Dunes are generous,
but forced carries and hazards are more of
a consideration from the back two tee positions. The large greens are firm, fast, and
undulating. An ability to hit below the
wind and run the ball up onto these putting
surfaces is helpful at Kiva Dunes.

There are many memorable holes on
this course including the 175-yard par-3
thirteenth whose tee shot must negotiate
several yards of marsh grass, myrtle, and
scrub oaks in order to reach an elevated,
two-tiered green surrounded by bunkers.
The prevailing southeast wind usually
comes into the golfer's face from right to
left requiring you to add one club to your
tee shot selection. A tall pine guards the
left side of the kidney-shaped green creating the illusion that it is directly in front of
a pin placed to the rear left on the green.
Water from a marshy area can come into
play on this hole and water borders eight
other holes at Kiva Dunes.

A good par 5 on the back nine is the
540-yard fifteenth which usually has the
benefit of a tailwind. The generous tee shot

landing area is bordered by natural brush and oak trees to the left. The approach is to a slightly elevated green with two bunkers towards its front and a large bunker at the base of the rear of the green ten feet below the putting surface. The strategy is to hit a high approach shot that will benefit from the tailwind, yet stay clear of brush to the right of the approach area and a waste bunker that begins 170 yards from the green and ends approximately 100 yards from the target on the right side.

Kiva Dunes is just west of the Bon Secour National Wildlife Refuge—4500 acres of coastal land with sand dunes, woodlands, and wildlife such as beaver, alligator, ducks, heron, and many other varieties. Kiva Dunes was rated one of the best new public golf courses of 1995 by *Golf Digest*.

Course Name: LAKEWOOD GOLF CLUB
Azalea, Dogwood Courses

Course Type: Resort
Resort: Marriott's Grand Hotel
Address: Scenic Highway 98
Point Clear, AL 39564
Phone: (334) 990–6312 (Golf Course)
(800) 544–9933, (800) 228–9290 (Resort)
Fax: (334) 990–6327 (Golf Course)
(334) 928–1149 (Resort)

GOLF COURSE

Director of Golf: David Clark
Head Professional: David Clark
Course Length/Par (All Tees): Azalea: Back 6770/72, White 6292/72, Orange 5833/72, Forward 5307/72. Dogwood: Back 6676/71, White 6331/71, Forward 5532/72
Course Slope/Rating (All Tees): Azalea: Back 128/72.5, White 124/70.3, Orange 120/68.2, Ladies' Forward 118/71.3. Dogwood: Back 124/72.1, White 121/70.5, Ladies' Forward 122/72.6
Course Architects: Azalea: Perry Maxwell (9 holes, 1947), Ron Garl (9 holes, 1986). Dogwood: Perry Maxwell with James Maxwell (9 holes, 1947), Joe Lee (9 holes, 1967)

Golf Facilities: Full Pro Shop X, Snack Bar X, Lounge X, Restaurant X, Locker Room X, Showers X, Club Rental X, Club Repair X, Cart Rental X, Instruction X, Practice Green X, Driving Range X, Practice Bunker X, Club Storage X
Tee-Time Reservation Policy: At time of confirmed resort reservation up to 1 yr. in advance. Must be a resort guest, member, or guest of a member to play the course
Ranger: Yes
Tee-off-Interval Time: 10 min.
Time to Play 18 Holes: 4 hrs.
Course Hours/Earliest Tee-off: 7:30 a.m.
Green Fees: $48.87 for 18 holes, $29.79 for 9 holes
Cart Fees: $13.20 for 18 holes per person
Credit Cards: All major cards
Season: Year round
Course Comments: Cart mandatory
Golf Packages: Available through resort. Lowest rates Nov. to Feb.
Discounts: Seasonal (Nov. to Feb.)
Places to Stay Nearby: Golf courses available to members and resort guests only. MOBILE: Drury Inn (334) 344–7700; Stouffer Riverview Plaza (334) 438–4000; Shoney's Inn of Mobile (334) 660–1520; Holiday Inn I–10 (334) 666–5600, (800) HOLIDAY; Radisson Admiral Semnes Hotel (334) 432–8000. ORANGE BEACH: Perdido Ranch Hilton Resort (334) 981–9811, (800) 634–8001. BED AND BREAKFASTS: Stickney's Hollow (334) 456–4556, Church St. Inn (334) 438–3107
Local Attractions: MOBILE AREA: Bragg-Mitchell Mansion, Carlen House, and Mobile's historic districts, Oakleigh Garden district, Fine Arts Museum of the South, Conde-Charlotte Museum House, Oakleigh Mansion, Old Dauphin Way, Spring Hill, Bellingrath Gardens, Gulf Coast beaches, Fort Morgan, *USS Alabama*, greyhound dog track, shopping, Jubilee Fish Theatre, fishing, boat cruises and charters. Mobile Visitor Information Center (334) 968–7511, (800) 252–3862. Alabama Bureau of Tourism and Travel (800) ALABAMA

Directions: From Mobile Airport: Left (east) on Airport Blvd., to I–65 south, I–65 south to I-10 east, I–10 east to Hwy. 98, right on Hwy. 98 east to Alt. 98. Turn right on Alt. 98 to Scenic Hwy. 98 (in Fairhope). Follow Scenic Hwy. 98 to the resort

Closest Commercial Airport: Mobile Regional (25 mi.)

RESORT

Date Built: 1847

No. of Rooms: 307 guest rooms, including 21 suites, 8 cottages

Meeting Rooms: 12. Capacity of Largest: 10,000 sq. ft. Meeting Space: 22,000 sq. ft.

Room Price Range: $89 to $159 for regular rooms. Highest rates March to late May, lowest rates late Oct. to mid-March. Golf and other packages including seasonal discounts available

Lounges: Birdcage Lounge, Pavilion Bar

Restaurants: Grand Dining Room, Bay View, Lakewood Club Room, Pelican's Nest

Entertainment: Live music, dancing

Credit Cards: All major cards

General Amenities: Children's programs for ages 5 to 12, including a camp (Memorial Day to Labor Day) and counselors; shopping arcade, tennis shop, golf shop, photographic services, beauty salon; business-conference center with complete audiovisual, secretarial, food-service support; babysitting, movies, games

Recreational Amenities: 10 tennis courts, instruction; swimming pool, boating, horseback riding, bicycling, croquet, badminton, volleyball, horseshoes, aerobics classes, shuffleboard, fishing, surfing, sauna; health club with Universal weight equipment, free weights, Life Cycles, treadmill, exercise bikes, rowing machine; outdoor hot tub

Reservation and Cancellation Policy: Cancellations must be made 5 days in advance by 9 p.m. to avoid penalties. Credit card, cash, or check deposit required to hold a reservation. Deposit forfeited if adequate cancellation notification not given

Comments and Restrictions: No pets. Local kennels available. Taxes additional to basic rates

LAKEWOOD GOLF CLUB

The Grand Hotel resort is beautifully situated on 550 acres on the Point Clear peninsula, which juts out from the eastern shore of Mobile Bay, 23 miles southeast of Mobile, Alabama. The Grand Hotel has a rich history going back to 1847, when F. H. Chamberlain bought 400 acres of prime waterfront property and began the construction of the 40-room Point Clear Hotel. During the Civil War the hotel suspended business but served as a hospital for Confederate soldiers. Destroyed by fire, the hotel was restored and reopened in 1875 as the Grand Hotel. In 1981, the Marriott Corporation acquired the property with the commitment to restore it to its original splendor. Having since added eighteen holes of golf to its original 18-hole layout designed by Perry Maxwell in the 1940s, the Grand Hotel is now considered by *Golf* magazine to be one of the best golf resorts in America.

Maxwell designed the original Dogwood Course, which opened in 1947. His original first through fifth and fifteenth through eighteenth holes have been integrated into the Azalea Course, with holes six through fourteen designed by Ron Garl and opened in 1986. Maxwell was born in 1879 in Princeton, Kentucky, and became a banker after graduating from the University of Kentucky. He took up golf when he was in his late twenties and laid out a rudimentary nine-hole golf course with his wife on their farm in Ardmore, Pennsylvania. This course later became the Dornick Hills Golf and Country Club.

Maxwell retired from banking soon after his wife's death in 1919 and began to design and build golf courses full-time. He gained such stature that he was asked to rebuild greens at Augusta National and Pine Valley and he designed and remodeled well over 100 golf courses, including the Ohio State University golf courses in Columbus, Ohio, with Alister MacKenzie, and the Southern Hills Country Club in Tulsa,

Oklahoma. Maxwell was a charter member of the American Society of Golf Course Architects. Maxwell's son, James Press Maxwell, who has become an excellent golf architect in his own right, helped complete Dogwood when his father became ill. Perry Maxwell died in 1952.

The back nine of the 6676-yard par-71 Dogwood Course has all original Maxwell-designed holes and is considered to be the toughest nine at the Lakewood Golf Club. Challenging par 4s make this stretch of holes difficult and include the 438-yard number-1-handicap fourteenth, which plays relatively straight but long down a well-treed fairway to a medium-sized, tiered green that slopes forward from a shelf in the back. A large trap to the right and a smaller trap to the left guard the green. A difficult par-3 on this side is the 236-yard thirteenth, which plays to a green well protected by five traps. Wide-spreading old oaks and pines can make the Dogwood Course especially difficult. Well-placed tee shots are especially important on this layout.

The Azalea Course plays 6770 yards from the back tees and also demands accurate tee shots to avoid the omnipresent trees. Many pros use long irons off the tees and in the fairways to avoid trouble.

Azalea starts out with a 580-yard dogleg-right par 5, one of the most difficult holes on the course. Two long, accurate shots are required to be around the green in two, and few golfers get in a position to putt for an eagle here. The green is hourglass-shaped, deep, and slopes a bit from the front into a little valley in the center. Two traps and an overhanging tree protect the green on the left, and there is a trap on the right. The number-1-handicap hole is the 428-yard par-4 eighth, which is straight but has a blind tee shot up to a plateau. The second shot is to an undulating green that slopes slightly forward from a tier in the back.

The signature hole on Azalea is the 521-yard par-5 fourteenth, whose tee shot has to negotiate bunkers on the left and a tree-lined fairway to the right. The second shot forces you to decide whether to go for a large island green with one huge bunker or

to play up to a landing area. Both the green and landing area are obscured by a slight rise in the fairway.

The golf-shop facilities are excellent at Lakewood, having been ranked in the Top 100 pro shops by *Golf Shop Operations* magazine. Casual lunches and dinners are served at the Lakewood Golf Club, and a variety of group and individual golf packages are available through the resort. The course is open to members and resort guests only, and you are advised to arrange your tee times when you make your reservation.

The resort itself offers a variety of recreational activities ranging from tennis, swimming, and horseback riding to aerobic dancing and the amenities of a health club. Dining facilities include the elegant Grand Dining Room which has won the coveted American Automobile Association's Four-Diamond Award. Children's services, including babysitting and complete camp programs, add to the diversity of this resort. The beautiful environs, especially the beaches and Gulf Coast, can be seen from many vantage points at this well-restored resort whose tallest structure is three stories.

Montgomery Area

Course Name:　**CAMBRIAN RIDGE GOLF CLUB Canyon, Loblolly, Sherling, Short Courses**

Course Type:　Public
Address:　　　101 Sunbelt Parkway
　　　　　　　Greenville, AL 36037
Phone:　　　　(334) 382–9787,
　　　　　　　(800) 949–4444
Fax:　　　　　(334) 382–9343

GOLF COURSE

Director of Golf: Kenny Szuch
Head Professional: T. R. Bowser
Course Length/Par (All Tees): Canyon: Back 9/3746/36, Orange 9/3940/36, White 9/3058/36, Forward 9/2422/36. Loblolly: Back 9/3551/36, Orange 9/3295/36, White 9/3078/36, Forward 9/2350/36. Sherling: Back 9/3681/36, Orange 9/3423/36, White 9/3028/36,

Forward 9/2435/36. Short Course: Back
9/1640/27, Orange 9/1415/27, White
9/1116/27, Forward 9/745/27

Course Slope/Rating (All Tees):
Sherling/Canyon: Back 142/75.4,
Orange 137/73.2, White 132/70.7,
Forward 127/68.1. Canyon/Loblolly:
Back 140/74.6, Orange 135/72.5, White
131/70.5, Forward 126/67.8. Sherling/
Loblolly: Back 133/73.9, Orange
128/71.6, White 123/69.4, Forward
119/67.0. Short Course: NA/NA

Course Architect: Robert Trent Jones, Sr.
and Roger Rulewich (1993, 1994)

Golf Facilities: Full Pro Shop X, Snack
Bar X, Lounge X, Restaurant X,
Locker Room X, Showers X, Club
Rental X, Club Repair Off Site, Cart
Rental X, Instruction X, Practice
Green X, Driving Range X, Practice
Bunker X, Club Storage No

Tee-Time Reservation Policy: Up to 1 yr.
in advance for groups. Up to 45 days in
advance with additional $2 service
charge. Up to 7 days in advance without
service charge. Contact: (800) 949–4444

Ranger: Yes

Tee-off-Interval Time: 8 min.

Time to Play 18 Holes: 4½ hrs.

Course Hours/Earliest Tee-off: 6:30 a.m.
until daylight savings time

Green Fees: Championship courses: $32
for 18 holes Fri., Sat., Sun., holidays;
$24 weekdays. Short Course: $15 for 9
holes Fri., Sat., Sun., holidays; $12.50
for 9 holes weekdays

Cart Fees: Championship courses: $15 for
18 holes, $6 for 9 holes. Short Course:
$10 per cart

Credit Cards: All major cards

Season: Year round. Busiest Feb. through
Apr.

Course Comments: Walking allowed
Mon.–Thurs., after 3 p.m. Fri.–Sun.

Golf Packages: Inquire at pro shop

Discounts: Twilight, Robert Trent Jones
Trail Pass (800) 949–4444

Places to Stay Nearby: Best Western Inn
(334) 382–9200, (800) 528–1234;
Econo Lodge (334) 382–3118, (800)
446–6900; Holiday Inn (334) 382–2651,
(800) HOLIDAY

Local Attractions: MONTGOMERY: Hank
Williams Memorial, Alabama State
Capitol, Alabama War Memorial,
Alabama Shakespeare Festival, Dexter
Avenue King Memorial Baptist Church,
Executive Mansion, First White House
of the Confederacy, Jasmine Hill Gar-
dens and Outdoor Museum, Mont-
gomery Museum of Fine Arts, W. A.
Gayle Planetarium, Montgomery Zoo,
Scott and Zelda Fitzgerald Museum,
State Archives and History Museum,
Victoryland Greyhound Racing Park.
Montgomery Visitor Information Center,
401 Madison Ave., Montgomery, AL
36014 (334) 240–9400

Directions: From I–65 take Exit 130/Hwy.
263 in Greenville. Proceed west on
Hwy. 263 approximately 4 mi. to Hwy.
44. Turn left on Hwy. 44 and travel 1
mi. to golf course on the right

Closest Commercial Airports: Dannelly
Field/Montgomery (45 min.); Hartsfield
Atlanta International, GA (3½ hrs.)

CAMBRIAN RIDGE GOLF CLUB

Cambrian Ridge, 130 miles northeast of
Mobile and 32 miles south of Montgomery,
is located in the small town of Greenville,
the "Camellia City." The Championship
Course features three nines, the Canyon,
Loblolly, and Sherling. The Canyon is a
target-style layout carved from a former
hunting grounds. It presents dramatic elevation changes, beginning with the 301-yard
par 4 opening hole that drops over 200
feet, crowned fairways, meandering creeks,
and severely contoured greens. The Sherling has holes that run along the top of
Cambrian Ridge, a geologic feature that
dissects the course, which also has abrupt
elevation changes and a large reservoir.
Sherling's 636-yard eighth, a 3-shot par 5,
is made very difficult by its length, heavily
bunkered fairway, and a green well-protected by water. This nine concludes with a
371-yard par 4 that climbs uphill past a
deep ravine to a double green shared with
the ninth on the Canyon course. Overlooking this hole is the clubhouse with its wraparound veranda, exposed-beamed ceilings
inside, cut stone fireplace, leather chairs

and sofas, green tartan carpeting, and other country club-like features such as louvered wooden lockers and memorabilia displays. It is hard to believe that this is a publicly funded daily fee golf course.

The Canyon/Sherling course is rated the best public course in the state of Alabama by *Golf Digest*. The Loblolly nine, carved out of giant loblolly pines, is an excellent layout that can be played in combination with the Sherling or Canyon. The Loblolly offers rolling fairways framed by mature trees, and many of its greens are guarded by water. It includes the 182-yard par-3 fourth which plays to a 3-tiered 70-yard-deep target. Another golf option at Cambrian Ridge is to play its excellent short course, a standard feature of all seven Robert Trent Jones Trail locations which include either three championship nines and a 9-hole short course or two 18-hole championship courses and an 18-hole short course.

At Cambrian Ridge, the clubhouse provides 30-mile views of woodlands. A walk through these golfing woods will acquaint you with dogwood, azaleas, magnolia, and four-footed creatures such as deer and bobcat. You can stroll over to the 48-acre giant horseshoe amphitheatre practice facility that has seven target greens and several practice bunkers. Public golf doesn't get any better than this.

Course Name: GRAND NATIONAL GOLF CLUB Lake, Links, Short Courses

Course Type: Public
Address: 3000 Sunbelt Parkway
             Opelika, AL 36801
Phone: (334) 749–9042,
             (800) 949–4444
Fax: (334) 749–8479

GOLF COURSE

Director of Golf: Bucky Ayers
Head Professional: Mike McClellan
Course Length/Par (All Tees): Lake: Back 7089/72, Orange 6488/72, Yellow 5948/72, Forward 4910/72. Links: Back 7311/72, Orange 6539/72, White 6070/72, Forward 4843/72. Short Course: Back 3328/54, Orange 2798/54, White 2476/54, Forward 1715/54
Course Slope/Rating (All Tees): Lake: Back 138/74.9, Orange 134/72.3, Yellow 129/69.9, Forward 123/66.8. Links: Back 141/74.9, Orange 136/72.7, White 131/70.2, Forward 125/67.4. Short Course: NA/NA
Course Architect: Robert Trent Jones, Sr. and Roger Rulewich (Lake: 1992, Links: 1993, Short Course: 1993)
Golf Facilities: Full Pro Shop X, Snack Bar X, Lounge X, Restaurant X, Locker Room X, Showers X, Club Rental X, Club Repair Minor, Cart Rental X, Instruction X, Practice Green X, Driving Range X, Practice Bunker X, Club Storage No
Tee-Time Reservation Policy: Up to 1 yr. in advance for large groups. Up to 45 days in advance with $2 per person reservation fee. Up to 7 days in advance without reservation fee. Contact: (800) 949–4444
Ranger: Yes
Tee-off-Interval Time: 8 min.
Time to Play 18 Holes: 5 hrs.
Course Hours/Earliest Tee-off: 7 a.m.
Green Fees: Lake, Links: $32 for 18 holes Fri., Sat., Sun., holidays; $24 for 18 holes weekdays. Short Course: $15 for 18 holes Fri., Sat., Sun., holidays; $12.50 for 18 holes weekdays
Cart Fees: Lake, Links: $15 for 18 holes per person. Short Course: $9.68 for 18 holes, $6.45 for 9 holes per person
Credit Cards: All major cards
Season: Year round. Busiest Mar. through May, Sept. through Nov.
Course Comments: Walking allowed Mon. through Thurs., after 3 p.m. Fri. through Sun.
Golf Packages: Group packages. Inquire at pro shop
Discounts: Twilight rates, Robert Trent Jones Trail Pass (800) 949–4444
Places to Stay Nearby: Auburn University Hotel and Conference Center (334) 821–8200; The Crenshaw Guest House (334) 821–1131; Hampton Inn (334) 821–4111, (800) 426–7866

Local Attractions: AUBURN: Auburn University, Auburn Historic District. OPELIKA: Historic Downtown District, Salem-Shotwell Covered Bridge. TUSKEGEE: Tuskegee National Historic Site–Carver Museum, The Oaks, Tuskegee National Forest, Bankhead National Forest. Montgomery. Auburn/Opelika Convention and Visitors Bureau, 714 E. Glenn Ave., P.O. Box 2216, Auburn, AL 36831, (334) 887–8747, (800) 321–8880

Directions: From Hwy. 280 proceed north on Lee County Hwy. 97. Travel 2.5 miles to golf course entrance on the right

Closest Commercial Airports: Dannelly Field/Montgomery (1 hr.); Columbus Metropolitan, GA (45 min.); Hartsdale Atlanta International, GA (2 hrs.)

GRAND NATIONAL GOLF CLUB

The Robert Trent Jones Trail is a $100 million project funded by the state of Alabama's retirement system. Designed by Robert Trent Jones, Sr., the dean of American golf course architects, The Trail includes 18 golf courses at seven locations extending from Huntsville to Mobile. Each facility has a country club-quality clubhouse, practice facility and at least 36 holes of public golf. Grand National, built on over 650 acres of rolling timberland around Lake Saugahatchee, offers 54 holes of golf including the championship Lake Course, Links Course and the Short Course, an excellent par-3 layout. Thirty-two of these holes border the 600-acre lake.

Both *Golfweek* and *Golf Digest* rank both the Lake and the Links among the best courses in Alabama. These layouts are long and difficult with a variety of elevation changes, large bentgrass greens, massive sand bunkers, and an abundance of water hazards. The Lake front nine loops back to the stunning clubhouse overlooking the ninth. The back nine then ventures out and loops back. The finishing nine features the 230-yard fifteenth which plays to a deep, island green that protrudes out into the lake. The next hole is a 334-yard par-4 dogleg right that plays from an elevated tee. A drive to the left-center of the fairway will set up a finesse shot over water to a forward-sloping green with a bunker to its right. The seventeenth is a 205-yard par 3 bordered by pines to the right and the lake to the left. A left-to-right wind off the lake makes it difficult to reach this plateaued green on the tee shot. The 429-yard par-4 finishing hole is one of the most difficult on the course. The second shot is uphill to a large green with a shelf to its left rear and a trap guarding its right front side. The links course offers an equally stunning display of tough golf holes including the 471-yard par-4 finishing hole where a drive must carry the corner of the lake. The approach shot is to a shallow, slightly elevated green shored up by boulders. The par-3 short course is an 18-hole delight with tee distances ranging from 154 to 254 yards from the back tees.

All the courses at Grand National provide a choice of four tee distances. It is especially important to play from a distance that suits your game or you will be in for a very long and frustrating day. Just down the hill from the clubhouse is a spacious practice facility including several target greens, practice bunkers, and a putting green.

The Robert Trent Jones Trail was established to attract more retirees to Alabama, bolster tourism, and bring new industry to the state. More than half of Grand National's play comes from outside Alabama. Many golfers purchase discounted Trail Passes that enable them to play all the Trail courses. Each site is within a two hour drive of another Robert Trent Jones Trail location.

Course Name: LAGOON PARK GOLF COURSE

Course Type: Public
Address: 2855 Lagoon Park Drive
              Montgomery, AL 36109
Phone: (334) 271–7000

GOLF COURSE

Head Professional: Nick Gettys
Course Length/Par (All Tees): Back 6773/72, Middle 6413/72, Forward 5342/72

Course Slope/Rating (All Tees): Back 124/72.1, Middle 121/70.3, Forward 113/64.6

Course Architect: Charles Graves (1978)

Golf Facilities: Full Pro Shop X, Snack Bar X, Lounge Beer only, Restaurant No, Locker Room X, Showers X, Club Rental X, Club Repair Minor, Cart Rental X, Instruction X, Practice Green X, Driving Range X, Practice Bunker X, Club Storage X

Tee-Time Reservation Policy: Reserved tee times weekends and major holidays. Call from 7:30 a.m. Thurs.; first come, first served otherwise. Normally a 15- to 30-min. wait. Large groups should call in advance

Ranger: Yes

Tee-off-Interval Time: 8 min.

Time to Play 18 Holes: 4 hrs., 15 min.

Course Hours/Earliest Tee-off: 7 a.m.

Green Fees: $20 for 18 holes Sat., Sun., holidays; $15 for 18 holes weekdays

Cart Fees: $20 for 18 holes per cart Pull Carts: $2 for 18 holes

Credit Cards: Discover, MasterCard, Visa

Season: Year round, closed every Tues.

Course Comments: Can walk anytime. Annual-fee membership (various plans). Yardage book available

Golf Packages: No

Discounts: Only through annual-fee rates

Places to Stay Nearby: Marriott Courtyard (334) 272–5533, (800) 321–2211; Ramada Inn (334) 277–2200, (800) 272–6232; Hampton Inn (334) 277–2400, (800) 426–7866; Holiday Inn East (334) 272–0370, (800) HOLIDAY; La Quinta Motor Inn (205) 271–1620; Madison Hotel (334) 264–2231; Days Inn-South (334) 281–8000, (800) 329–7466; Residence Inn by Marriott (334) 265–0741, (800) 331–3131. BED AND BREAKFAST: Bed and Breakfast Montgomery (334) 264-0056

Local Attractions: Alabama Archives and State History Museum, Alabama Shakespeare Festival, Alabama State Capitol, Civil Rights Memorial, First White House of the Confederacy, Fort Toulose/Jackson Park, Hank Williams Memorial, Old Alabama Town, Montgomery Zoo, Victoryland greyhound racing, Montgomery Museum of Fine Arts, Montgomery Zoo, Scott and Zelda Fitzgerald Museum. Montgomery Visitor Information Center (334) 240–9437

Directions: From I-85/eastern bypass Rte. 82: 3 mi. north on Rte. 82, exit left to Lagoon Park, follow signs

Closest Commercial Airport: Dannelly Field/Montgomery (15 mi.)

LAGOON PARK

Located in a 410-acre municipal park, the Lagoon Park Golf Course is a well-maintained, flat, eighteen-hole layout designed by Charles Graves and opened in 1978 after four years of planning and construction. One of the first to specialize in parks and recreation planning, Graves planned several city, county, and state parks. In the 1960s he began to incorporate golf courses into some of his projects, and Lagoon Park was opened shortly before he retired in 1979.

To maintain its high standards for golf-course maintenance, Lagoon Park is closed on Tuesdays, an unusual policy for public golf courses. The 6773-yard (back tees) course wends its way through a rich variety of foliage, including pines, bay, gum and dogwood trees and azaleas. Lagoon Park requires accurate drives and solid putting on its large, medium-fast, undulating greens. The entire course is Bermuda grass overseeded with rye grass in the winter.

One of the most difficult holes at Lagoon Park is the number-1-handicap 435-yard par-4 fourth hole, a dogleg right with water to the left and right. The tee shot must be well placed to the left center of the fairway to avoid having to contend with large pines on the right. The approach shot flies onto a large, forward-sloping green. The number-2-handicap 546-yard par-5 fifteenth hole is a double dogleg that requires accurate placement of the first two shots to each corner of the doglegs. Often this requires a long iron or 3-wood to avoid hitting through the fairway into the water on the right or into trees on the left. The third shot is straight to a medium-sized green.

Many of the par 4s at Lagoon Park are lengthy challenges of 400 yards or more from the back tees. Par 3s, such as the 201-yard sixteenth hole over water, make the course play more difficult than it at first might seem.

Rated as one of America's top 75 public golf courses by *Golf Digest,* Lagoon Park has hosted the Southern Collegiate Invitational, the National Public Links Qualifier, and various other tournaments. However, its policy is not to hold many tournaments because the public golfer is its main customer.

Surrounding the golf course are ample park facilities for tennis, softball, jogging, picnicking and other outdoor activities. For example, the Pete Peterson Lodge, located in the northwest corner of the park, is surrounded by picnic shelters and can be rented for family reunions and company outings. A 400-meter jogging paracourse is adjacent to the golf complex. This facility includes a jogging track and 10 exercise stations. There is an elaborate softball complex with lighting, food concessions, a batting range and press facilities. The Lagoon Park Tennis Center includes 17 courts with lighting, a tennis shop, snack bar, and locker room and shower facilities.

Recommended Golf Courses in Alabama

Within 1 Hour of Birmingham:

Bent Brook Golf Club, Bessemer, (205) 424–2368, Public. Windmill/Brook: 18/6964/72. Graveyard/Windmill: 18/6877/71. Brook/Graveyard: 18/7053/71

Eagle Point Golf Club, Birmingham, (205) 991–9070, Public, 18/6454/71

Mountain View Golf Club, Graysville, (205) 674–8362, Public, 18/6004/72

Oxmoor Valley Golf Club (Robert Trent Jones Trail), Birmingham, (205) 942–1177, (800) 949–4444, Public, Ridge: 18/7053/72. Valley: 18/7240/72. Short Course: 18/3154/54

Timber Ridge Golf Club, Talladega, (205) 362–0346, Semiprivate, 18/6700/71

Within 1 Hour of Dothan:

Highland Oaks Golf Club, Dothan, (334) 712–2820, (800) 949–4444, Public.

Highlands/Marshwood: 18/7704. Marshwood/Magnolia: 18/7591/72. Highlands/Magnolia: 18/7511/72

Lakepoint Resort Golf Course, Eufaula, (334) 687–6676, 800 (544) 544–5253, Resort, 18/6752/72

Olympia Resort, Dothan, (334) 677–3326, Resort, 18/7242/72

Within 1 Hour of Florence:

Deer Run Golf Course, Moulton, (205) 974–7384, Public, 18/6745/72

Glen Lakes Country Club, Foley, (334) 943–8000, (800) 796–4853, Resort, Semiprivate, 18/6635/71

Within 1 Hour of Gadsden:

Silver Lakes Golf Course, Glencoe, (205) 892–3268, Public. Mindbreaker/Heartbreaker: 18/7407/72. Heartbreaker/Backbreaker: 18/7674/72. Mindbreaker/Backbreaker: 18/7425/72

Terrapin Hills Golf Club, Fort Payne, (205) 845–4624, Public, 18/6696/71

Within 1 Hour of Huntsville:

Goose Pond Colony Golf Course, Scottsboro, (205) 574–5353, (800) 268–2884, Public, 18/6843/72

Hampton Cove Golf Club (Robert Trent Jones Trail), Huntsville, (205) 551–1818, (800) 949–4444, Public, Highlands: 18/7262/72. River: 18/7507/72. Short Course: 18/3140/54

Lake Guntersville Golf Club, Guntersville, (205) 582–0379, Public, 18/6785/72

Point Mallard Golf Club, Decatur, (205) 351–7776, Public, 18/7113/72

Within 1 Hour of Mobile:

Azalea City Golf Course, Mobile, (205) 342–4221, Public, 18/6765/72

Cotton Creek Club, Gulf Shores, (334) 968–7766, Semiprivate, East/North: 18/7028/72. North/West: 18/6971/72. East/West: 18/6975/72

Craft Farms, Gulf Shores, (334) 968–4133, (800) 327–2657, Public. The Woodlands: 18/6484/72

Gulf State Park Golf Course, Gulf Shores, (334) 948–4653, Public, 18/6563/72

Isle Dauphin Golf Club, Dauphin Island, (334) 861–2433, Public, 18/6620/72

Linksman Golf Club, Mobile, (334) 661–0018, Public, 18/6275/72

Magnolia Grove Golf Club (Robert Trent Jones Trail) , Semmes, (334) 645–0075, (800) 949–4444, Public, Crossings: 18/7150/72. Falls: 18/7240/72. Short Course: 18/3140/54

Rock Creek Golf Club, Fairhope, (334) 928–4223, Semiprivate, 18/6920/72

Timbercreek Golf Club, Daphne, (334) 621–9900, Dogwood/Magnolia: 18/7062/72. Magnolia/Pines: 18/6928/72. Dogwood/Pines: 18/7090/72

Within 1 Hour of Montgomery:

Auburn Links, Auburn, (334) 887–5151, Public, 18/7145/72

Oak Hills, Montgomery, (334) 281–3344, Semiprivate, 18/7115/72

Still Waters Resort, Dadeville, (205) 825–7021, (800) 687–3732, Resort, 18/6407/72

Alabama: Useful Information

Alabama Bureau of Tourism and Travel, 401 Adams Ave., Montgomery, AL 36104, (800) ALABAMA

Division of Parks, Department of Conservation and Natural Resources, 64 N. Union St., Montgomery, AL 36130, (334) 242–3333 (recreation information), (800) ALAPARK (for reservations)

Division of Fish and Game, Department of Conservation, 64 N. Union St., Montgomery, AL 36130, (334) 242–3465 (fishing and hunting regulations)

U.S. Forest Service, 2946 Chestnut St., Montgomery, AL 36107, (334) 832–4470 (national forest information)

Course Name: EAGLEGLEN GOLF COURSE

Course Type: Public
Address: Boniface and Glenn Highways (Main Gate) Anchorage, AK 99506-2530
Phone: (907) 552–3821

GOLF COURSE

Head Professional: Albert Fry (Manager)
Course Length/Par (All Tees): Back 6689/72, Middle 6024/72, Forward 5457/72
Course Slope/Rating (All Tees): Back NA/71.6, Middle NA/68.5, Ladies' Forward NA/70.4
Course Architect: Robert Trent Jones, Jr. (1969)
Golf Facilities: Full Pro Shop X, Snack Bar X, Lounge X, Restaurant No, Locker Room X, Showers No, Club Rental X, Club Repair X, Cart Rental X, Instruction X, Practice Green X, Driving Range X, Practice Bunker X, Club Storage X
Tee-Time Reservation Policy: 1 day in advance
Ranger: Yes
Tee-off-Interval Time: 8 min.
Time to Play 18 Holes: 4 hrs., 15 min.
Course Hours/Earliest Tee-off: Dawn to dusk
Green Fees: $28 daily fee
Cart Fees: $19 for 18 holes per cart
Credit Cards: MasterCard, Visa
Season: End of May to Oct.
Course Comments: Can walk anytime. Yardage book available. Military has priority. 18-hole fee is a daily fee
Golf Packages: None
Discounts: Military, seniors, juniors
Places to Stay Nearby: Sheraton Anchorage (907) 276–8700; Clarion Hotel Anchorage (907) 243–2300, (800) 544–0553; Holiday Inn (907) 279–8671; Anchorage Hotel (907) 272–4553, (800) 544–0988; Quality Inn Tower Suites (907) 976–0110; Westmark Anchorage (907) 276–7676

Local Attractions: Chugach State Park, bird watching, University of Alaska, ballooning, bicycle trails, boating, camping, glacier and other cruises, fishing and hunting charters, hiking, Anchorage Museum of History and Art, skiing, dog-sledding, Alaska Center for Performing Arts, Alaska Zoo, Fort Richardson Fish and Wildlife Center. Anchorage Chamber of Commerce (907) 272–2401. Alaska Division of Tourism (907) 465–2010
Directions: Glenn Hwy., Boniface Gate (at Elmendorf Air Force Base), left on Second, golf course on left
Closest Commercial Airport: Anchorage International (20 min.)

EAGLEGLEN GOLF COURSE

The Eagleglen Golf Course, designed by Robert Trent Jones, Jr., and opened in 1969 is located near Anchorage, Alaska, at the Elmendorf Air Force Base.

Eagleglen starts out with a challenging 535-yard par 5 ranked as the number-1-handicap hole from the middle tees. A lateral water hazard is on the right side of the fairway 200 to 275 yards from the tee, and water cuts across the fairway approximately 200 yards from the green. The second shot is into a somewhat narrow landing area protected by two traps on the right and a stream running parallel to the fairway on the left. The approach is to a large green protected by four sand traps, one front left, another front right, and two in back

The number-1-handicap hole from the back tees is the 438-yard par-4 seventh hole, which is long and straight to a large green protected by three traps, one to the left, one to the rear, and one to the right of the green. The 438-yard par-4 tenth hole rates a number 2 handicap from the back tees and is similar in layout to the seventh, with traps protecting a large green on either side.

The eighteenth hole provides an interesting finish. This 521-yard par-5 dogleg right has a relatively narrow fairway beginning approximately 150 yards from the tee. On the right is a stream that borders the fairway until it cuts in front of the green approximately 65 yards from the putting surface, which is large and protected by traps on the left and right. The tee shot should be left center and the second shot straight up the left side to a landing area in front of the green.

There are 65 traps and bunkers at Eagleglen, most of which protect the predominantly large greens. A variety of hole layouts, distances, and doglegs make it an interesting course. This is one of the first that Robert Trent Jones, Jr., designed after ending his apprenticeship with his famous father, Robert Trent Jones, Sr., in the 1960s. The greens vary in size and shape depending on shot-making strategy required for the hole. For example, the short 368-yard par-4 ninth hole is a dogleg right with a 72-foot-deep skull-shaped green angled left to right. This target is well protected by four traps, almost requiring the approach shot to be flown in. The 544-yard par-5 fifteenth has a very deep rectangular-shaped green with four traps protecting the green, including one front right, making it difficult to roll the second shot onto the putting surface.

Eagleglen is recognized as one of the best golf courses in the state of Alaska and provides a fine opportunity to play one of Robert Trent Jones, Jr.'s, earlier efforts.

Recommended Golf Courses in Alaska

Anchorage Golf Course, Anchorage, (907) 522–3363, Public, 18/6616/72

Chena Bend Golf Course, Ft. Wainwright, (907) 353–6223, Public, 18/6646/72

Moose Run Golf Course, Ft. Richardson, (907) 428–056, Public, 18/6499/72

North Star Golf Course, Fairbanks, (907) 457–4653, Semiprivate, 18/6852/72

Palmer Municipal Golf Course, Palmer, (907) 745–4653, Public, 18/7195/72

Settler's Bay Golf Club, Wasila, (907) 376–5466, Public, 18/6830/72

Alaska: Useful Information

Alaska Division of Tourism, 333 Willoughby Ave., Floor 9, P.O. Box E–1503 MS 1503–VG, Juneau, AK 99811, (907) 465–2012, Fax: (907) 586–8399

National Parks, Alaska Area Office, 2525 Gambell, Anchorage, AK 99502, (907) 762–2617 (state parks information)

U.S. Forest Service, P.O. Box 21628, Juneau, AK 99802 (national forest information)

Alaska Department of Fish and Game, P.O. Box 3-2000, Juneau, AK 99802, (907) 344–0541 (fishing and hunting information)

Alaska Public Lands Information Center, 605 W. Fourth Ave., Juneau, AK 99501, (907) 271–2737

Alaska State Parks, P.O. Box 107001, Anchorage, AK 99510–7001, (907) 762–2617

Course Name: SEDONA GOLF RESORT

Course Type: Resort
Address: 7256 Highway 179
P.O. Box 20337
Oak Creek, AZ 86341
Phone: (520) 284–9355 (Golf Course)
Fax: (520) 258–1443 (Golf Course)

GOLF COURSE

Head Professional: John Benzel
Course Length/Par (All Tees): Back 6642/71, White 6126/71, Gold 5637/71, Forward 5040/71
Course Slope/Rating (All Tees): Back 130/70.4, White 124/68.1, Gold 120/67.7, Forward 119/67.3
Course Architect: Gary Panks (1988)
Golf Facilities: Full Pro Shop X, Snack Bar X, Lounge X, Restaurant X, Locker Room No, Showers No, Club Rental X, Club Repair Minor, Cart Rental X, Instruction X, Practice Green X, Driving Range X, Practice Bunker X, Club Storage Limited
Tee-Time Reservation Policy: Up to 2 wks. in advance from 7:30 a.m.
Ranger: Yes
Tee-off-Interval Time: 9 min.
Time to Play 18 Holes: 4 hrs., 15 min.
Course Hours/Earliest Tee-off: 7 a.m.
Green and Cart Fees: $68.50 for 18 holes with cart, $60 for 18 holes walking
Credit Cards: American Express, Master-Card, Visa
Season: Year round. Busiest season Sept. to Nov.
Course Comments: Can walk anytime. Hospitality cart on course. 10-round pass and 1-yr. range passes on sale
Golf Packages: Available through local hotels
Discounts: Twilight rate from 2 p.m.
Places to Stay Nearby: Inn at Bell Rock (520) 282–4161; Los Abrigados (520) 282–1777; Enchantment Resort (520) 282–2900; Junipine Resort (520) 282–3375, (800) 542–8484; Le Auberge de Sedona (520) 282–7131, (800) 272–6777

Local Attractions: Grand Canyon, hiking, hot-air ballooning, Slide Rock State Park, Shrine of the Red Rocks, Sedona Arts Center, camping, Chapel of the Holy Cross, Page Springs Hatchery, Oak Creek Canyon. Sedona. Sedona-Oak Creek Canyon Chamber of Commerce (520) 282–7722, (800) 288–7336
Directions: From Phoenix (90 mi.), I–17 north toward Flagstaff, take exit 298 (Sedona-Oak Creek Canyon) onto Hwy. 179 north, approximately 7 mi. north to Sedona Golf Resort entrance (large water fountain left-hand side of hwy.), turn left, follow signs
Closest Commercial Airports: Flag-staff/Pulliam Municipal (1 hr.); Skyharbor International, Phoenix (2 hrs.)

SEDONA GOLF RESORT

The highest point in Arizona is 12,633 feet, near Flagstaff, and the lowest point is 70 feet, near Yuma. The village of Oak Creek and the Sedona Golf Resort are 45 miles south of Flagstaff at approximately 4200 feet and feature some of the stunted woodlands of the upper Sonoran vegetation zone, which begins at approximately 4500-foot elevations. These include juniper, oak, and piñon pine, as well as manzanita and other bushes. Around the golf course, which borders the Coconino National Forest, you might also see javelina, jackrabbits, deer, coyote, ducks, roadrunners and other creatures.

The Sedona Golf Resort course, designed by Gary Panks and opened in 1988, is the centerpiece of a future resort and residential real-estate development. It was awarded an honorable mention by *Golf Digest* magazine as the best new resort course of 1989 and, with its four tee distances, has attracted low and high handicappers alike. Surrounding the course are the magnificent towering pinnacles and sheer red sandstone canyon walls of the red rock country of Sedona. Oak Creek nestles in an area that attracts artists, retired people and nature lovers.

The course plays 6642 yards from the back tees, with the 623-yard uphill par-5 fifth being one of its most formidable holes. A slight dogleg right over rolling fairways, two strong, straight shots are required to leave a short iron to the target, which is a large double green shared with the eighth hole. Most of the bentgrass greens at Sedona are large, undulating, fast, and well protected by traps.

Sedona also features some long, difficult par 4s, including the 449-yard fifteenth, which plays straight to a large, kidney-shaped green protected by four pot bunkers on the right and a large waste bunker to the left. These obstacles make it difficult to roll the ball onto the green. The 448-yard par-4 eighth is another long, straight journey to a large, three-tiered green with a pot bunker on the right and two traps, including a large waste bunker, to the left. The front side is par 37, has three par 5s, and plays 3585 yards. The back nine is much shorter at 3057 yards and a par 34, with three par 3s and one par 5. The signature hole is the tough 210-yard par-3 tenth, which plays from an elevated tee to a large left-to-right sloping green trapped to the left, right and rear.

Gary Panks earned a B.S. degree in landscape architecture from Michigan State University, where he was captain of the golf team. He began his own golf-architecture business in 1991 and has remodeled and built a variety of golf courses in the Southwest and elsewhere. With Geoffry Cornish he remodeled the Paradise Valley Country Club in Scottsdale, Arizona, and he designed the Sedona Golf Resort course.

Instruction is available at the Sedona Golf Resort, and walking is allowed anytime. Both the course and the beauty of the surrounding countryside make a visit well worthwhile. Golf packages are offered through a number of local hotels and motels. Inquire at the golf shop for current information.

Recommended Golf Courses Within 1 Hour of Flagstaff:

Antelope Hills Golf Club, Prescott, (602) 344–4653, Public, North: 18/6771/72. South: 18/7014/72

Elden Hills Golf Club, Flagstaff, (520) 527–7999, Public, 18/6023/73

Elephant Rocks Golf Club, Williams, 635–4935, Public, 18/5937/70 (nine holes)

Oak Creek Country Club, Sedona, (520) 284–1660, Semiprivate, 18/6854/72

Prescott Country Club, Dewey, (602) 772–8984, Semiprivate, 18/6783/72

Silver Creek Golf Club, White Mountain Lake, (520) 537–2744, Public, 18/6813/72 (2½ hrs. from Flagstaff)

Phoenix Area

**Course Name: THE BOULDERS
North, South Courses**

Course Type: Resort
Resort: The Boulders
Address: 34631 N. Tom Darlington Drive, Carefree, AZ 85377
Phone: (602) 488–9028 (Golf Course) (602) 488–9009, (800) 553–1717 (Resort)
Fax: (602) 488–4118 (Resort)

GOLF COURSE

Director of Golf: Stu Stubbs
Course Length/Par (All Tees): North: Back 6950/72, Blue 6717/72, White 6277/72, Gold 5440/72, Forward 4893/72. South: Back 7000/71, Blue 6589/71, White 6073/71, Gold 5141/71, Forward 4715/71
Course Slope/Rating (All Tees): North: Back 144/73.4, Blue 135/72.3, White 130/70.2, Ladies' Gold 120/70.6, Forward 111/68.2. South: Back 146/73.3, Blue 137/71.4, White 127/69.2, Ladies' Gold 118/70.8, Forward 114/68.1
Course Architects: Robert F. Lawrence (9 holes, 1969), Jack Snyder (9 holes, 1974; remodeled 18 holes, 1978), Jay Morrish (remodeled 18 holes, 1984; added 9 holes, 1986; added 9 holes, 1991)
Golf Facilities: Full Pro Shop X, Snack Bar X, Lounge X, Restaurant X, Locker Room X, Showers X, Club Rental X, Club Repair X, Cart Rental X, Instruction X, Practice Green X, Driving Range X, Practice Bunker X, Club Storage X

Tee-Time Reservation Policy: At time of reservation at Boulders. Must be a resort guest, member or guest of member to play the courses

Ranger: Yes

Tee-off-Interval Time: 10 min.

Time to Play 18 Holes: 4½ hrs.

Course Hours/Earliest Tee-off: 7 a.m.

Green and Cart Fees: $135 for 18 holes with cart

Credit Cards: Major cards

Season: Year round. Resort closed July and Aug.

Course Comments: Cart mandatory. Yardage book available. North and South Course play rotated between members and resort guests daily. Busiest Nov. through May

Golf Packages: Available through resort

Discounts: Seasonal. Peak season Jan. 16 to May 9, Dec. 24 to 31. Three seasonal rate schedules

Places to Stay Nearby: Scottsdale Princess (602) 585–4848, (800) 344–4758; Hyatt/Gainey Ranch (602) 948–5050, (800) 233–1234; Marriott Suites Hotel (602) 945–1550, (800) 228–9290; Desert Suites (602) 585–5000, (800) 541–5203; Holiday Inn (602) 945–4392, (800) HOLIDAY

Local Attractions: Scottsdale Center for the Arts, Taliesin West, shopping, restaurants, ballooning, horseback riding, white-water rafting, seasonal festivals, professional sports. PHOENIX: Arizona State Museum, Mission San Xavier del Bac, Desert Botanical Garden, Heard Museum of Anthropology and Primitive Art, Saguaro National Monument, Tucson Mountain Park, professional football, basketball, major league baseball spring training. Scottsdale Chamber of Commerce (602) 945–8481, (800) 877–1117. Phoenix Visitors Bureau (602) 254–6500

Directions: From Rte. 17: Carefree Hwy. exit, east approximately 10 mi. to resort on right

Closest Commercial Airports: Skyharbor International, Phoenix (45 min.); Flagstaff/Pulliam Municipal (4 hrs.)

RESORT

Date Built: 1985

No. of Rooms: 136 guest casitas

Meeting Rooms: 6. Capacity of Largest: 200 persons. Meeting Space: 2000 sq. ft.

Room Price Range: $230 to $465 per day, single, without meals. Modified American Plan (breakfast and dinner available). Inquire for seasonal rates and packages

Lounge: Discovery Lounge

Restaurants: Latilla, Palo Verde, Boulders Club, Bakery Cafe, Contina del Pedregal

Entertainment Music nightly from 5 p.m.

Credit Cards: All major cards

General Amenities: Shopping marketplace (El Pedregal), babysitting, massage, beauty/facial appointments, tour arrangements; meeting and conference facilities including audiovisual, banquet and secretarial services

Recreational Amenities: 6 tennis courts, 2 swimming pools, exercise and fitness center, Jacuzzi, hot-air ballooning, riding trails, nature paths; bicycling, walking and jogging trails; helicopter flights, soaring

Reservation and Cancellation Policy: 2 nights' deposit or half of a package is required to confirm reservations. Early departure penalty. Reservation must be canceled 3 weeks in advance to ensure full refund. All package plans must be paid 30 days prior to arrival. No refunds on unused portions. Refunds issued only if the cancellation is received 3 wks in advance of arrival date

Comments and Restrictions: Resort closed June 21 to Sept. 3. There is a tax on all accommodations, a tax on food and beverage charges, $15 per night service charge in lieu of cash gratuities for all resort personnel excluding food and beverage. European plan (no meals) seasonally available. Back-to-back packages not allowed

THE BOULDERS

The Boulders North Course, designed by Jay Morrish, is a 6731-yard layout combining the Lake and Saguaro nines from a previous 27-hole layout. The 6543-yard South Course, also designed by Morrish, combines the preexisting Boulders nine and a new nine to round out a 36-hole championship complex that is part of this 1300-acre, $50 million resort situated in the Sonora Desert 16 miles northeast of Phoenix. Both the resort complex and its residential real-estate development have been designed to harmonize with this magnificent desert setting, which includes elaborate boulder rock formations, giant cacti, and a variety of plants such as palo verde trees, snakeweed, yucca, wild buckwheat, desert lavender, mesquite, and sweet acacia.

From the moment you tee up at The Boulders, you know you are in a special place and another world as you look out at buttes, the desert, magnificent mountains in the distance, and ribbons of well-manicured Bermuda fairways and bentgrass greens. The North Course leads off with the number-1-handicap hole, a 485-yard par 5 that plays over a panoply of desert vegetation to a fairway edged by rough and the surrounding desert. On the second shot the fairway narrows radically, then opens up to a landing area approximately 75 yards from the green and in front of a wide barranca (gully). The option is to lay up to this plateau or to go for the green, which is slightly elevated with three traps on the right. The putting surface slopes forward and is banked in back. The combination of desert fronting and surrounding almost every fairway, well-placed fairway bunkers guarding landing areas and large, undulating, well-trapped greens makes shot placement and strategy crucial. Many of the greens have difficult, well-trapped entrances, and some of the traps are quite deep.

Another tough hole on the front nine, which is almost 300 yards shorter than the back nine from the back tees, is the 548-yard par-5 third hole, a dogleg left. A drive of at least 150 yards is required to carry the desert terrain in front of the tee and to reach the wide, rolling fairway. The second shot is uphill, with no view of the green unless a strong tee shot has been hit. The fairway narrows severely from 175 yards into a green that has a small pool in front. A wash is to the left of the pool, and approximately 10 to 20 yards of bailout room are to the rear, left and right before the desert begins. The second shot can easily run down the sloping fairway into the pool. The green is large and forward-sloping, with a shelf to its rear left.

The second nine plays longer and more difficult than the front nine on the North Course, largely because of five lengthy par 4s.

One of my favorite holes on the North Course is the 405-yard par-4 thirteenth, which is a blind dogleg left. The tee shot plays to a plateaued landing area looking down 30 to 40 feet to an amphitheater green protected in front by desert, a trap to the left, and a boulder to the left. The barranca in front of the green is approximately 25 yards wide. There is some margin for error around the green, but don't be short.

The 175-yard par-3 fourteenth is a beautiful hole that plays over water to a right-to-left-sloping tiered green with two traps on the left and another to the right front. The 420-yard par-4 finishing hole is a great way to end this desert adventure. The tee shot is blind on this dogleg right and has to carry over approximately 150 yards of desert to a wide landing area looking down on a deep, forward-sloping green protected by water and a bunker on the left. It is best to stay to the right on the tee shot and come into this hole through the narrowing entrance way to the green.

The South Course, which plays about the same length on each nine, is a 7000-yard par-71 layout beautifully woven through desert and upscale residential real estate that unobtrusively complements the topography. As with the North, most of the tees are slightly elevated, with a view over desert terrain to rolling fairways strategically bounded by landing-area bunkers and backed by beautiful mountains and bouldered geological wonders in the distance. The 421-yard par-4 first hole is a beautiful one whose second shot is dramatically downhill to a green protected by huge boulders back and front. The wide but shallow green is flat, with boulders 25 to 30 yards wide and water guarding the front of the putting surface. A well-placed tee shot is essential to set up a good score on this hole.

Robert F. "Red" Lawrence originally designed nine holes of The Boulders, which opened in 1969. Arthur Jack Snyder added another nine in 1974 and remodeled the course in 1978. Jay Morrish was then brought in to do another remodeling, which was completed in 1984. He added another nine, completed in 1986, and finally, still another nine in 1991 to provide 36 holes of golf. Morrish, a native of Grand Junction, Colorado, has worked with Robert Trent Jones, Jr., George Fazio, and Jack Nicklaus. At present most of his work is done with Tom Weiskopf, including excellent courses at the Tournament Players Club and Troon in Scottsdale, as well as the Shadow Glen Course in Kansas City.

Morrish first saw the Sonora Desert, where the future Boulders site would be, when he was working with Jones on the golf course at the Wigwam in Litchfield Park, Arizona. He designed The Boulders course on his own before teaming up with Weiskopf. He was influenced by Frank Lloyd Wright's philosophy that the desert landscape is a series of dots formed by trees and rocks. In designing and remodeling The Boulders he envisioned the tees, bunkers and greens as part of that interrelated landscape.

The guest accommodations at The Boulders include 136 guest rooms housed in Southwestern-styled casitas, individually sited with a special view and relationship to the rocks and landscape nearby. The casitas are decorated with natural wood and Mexican tile, and feature private patios, fireplaces, fully stocked minibars and a large bath and dressing area.

The separate lodge houses two restaurants, a cocktail lounge, ballroom, gift shop, concierge, reception and guest service areas. The pool and dining pavilion are also located on the terrace level at the lodge. Both The Boulders Golf Club and the tennis park, which features 6 plexi-cushioned courts, have complete pro shops and instruction. All of these amenities are within walking distance of the lodge and casitas. Conference and seminar facilities are also available at The Boulders. It also recently added a $3.7 million fitness center, which features aerobics, a lap swimming pool, Jacuzzi, exercise equipment and a fitness director.

The Boulders has won many conference, hospitality, and architectural awards. *Golf* magazine has ranked it among the twelve best golf resorts in America (gold medal winner), and *Golf Digest* includes it in its 75 best resort courses in America list and ranks it among the top 10 golf courses in the state of Arizona. As an added bonus, The Boulders has a resident horticulturist, Dave Hutchinson, who nurtures the subtle foliage on the resort's 1300 acres. The quality of his work is immediately evident when you visit The Boulders.

Course Name: GAINEY RANCH GOLF CLUB Arroyo, Dunes, Lakes Courses

Course Type: Resort
Resort: Hyatt Regency Scottsdale Resort at Gainey Ranch
Address: 7500 E. Doubletree Ranch Road Scottsdale, AZ 85258
Phone: (602) 951–0022 (Golf Course) (602) 991–3388, (800) 233–1234 (Resort)

GOLF COURSE

Director of Golf: Mike Franko

Course Length/Par (All Tees): Arroyo/Lakes: Back 6800/72, Green 6252/72 White 5790/72, Forward 5330/72. Dunes/Arroyo: Back 6662/72, Green 6133/72, White 5681/72, Forward 5169/72. Lakes/Dunes: Back 6614/72 Green 6019/72, White 5529/72, Forward 4993/72

Course Slope/Rating (All Tees): Arroyo/Lakes: Men's Back 128/71.9, Green 123/69.2, Ladies' White 130/75.3, Forward 120/69.9. Dunes/Arroyo: Back 124/70.7, Green 120/68.2, Ladies' White 118/71.6, Forward 113/68.9. Lakes/Dunes: Back 126/71.1, Green 118/67.7, Ladies' White 128/74.3, Forward 117/68.3

Course Architects: Bradford Benz and J. Michael Poellot (1986)

Golf Facilities: Full Pro Shop X, Snack Bar X, Lounge X, Restaurant X, Locker Room X, Showers X, Club Rental X, Club Repair X, Cart Rental X, Instruction X, Practice Green X, Driving Range X, Practice Bunker X, Club Storage X

Tee-Time Reservation Policy: At time of registration at hotel. Must be a resort guest, member or guest of member to play the courses

Ranger: Yes

Tee-off-Interval Time: 7 min.

Time to Play 18 Holes: 4 hrs.

Course Hours/Earliest Tee-off: 7 a.m.

Green and Cart Fees: $123 for 18 holes with cart, $85 for 9 holes with range balls, bag storage

Credit Cards: All major cards

Season: Year round

Course Comments: Cart mandatory

Golf Packages: Various options including McCormick Ranch, Stone Creek. Inquire at resort

Discounts: Seasonal. Peak season Nov.1 to May 31. Off-season rates available

Places to Stay Nearby: Must be a resort guest at the Hyatt, member or guest of member to play the courses

Local Attractions: PHOENIX: Heard Museum of Anthropology and Primitive Art, Heritage Square, Desert Botanical Garden, Pioneer Arizona, zoo, Frank Lloyd Wright architecture, Phoenix Symphony, Champlin Fighter Museum, Arizona State University, professional football, basketball. AREA: Scottsdale Center for the Arts, Grand Canyon, archeological sites. Phoenix Convention and Visitors Bureau (602) 254-6500

Directions: From I–10: 44th St. exit, 44th St. north into McDonald heading east to Scottsdale Rd., left, 2½ mi. to Doubletree Ranch Rd.; right to resort on left. From I-17: B–ll Rd. exit east (12 to 15 mi.) to Scottsdale Rd., right to Doubletree Ranch Rd., left on Doubletree to resort

Closest Commercial Airport: Skyharbor International, Phoenix (25 min.)

RESORT

Date Built: 1986

No. of Rooms: 493 guest rooms, including 25 suites, 7 casitas

Meeting Rooms: 24. Capacity of Largest: 1500 persons. Meeting Space: 37,000 sq. ft.

Room Price Range: $325 to $2600 for suite peak season (Jan. through May), meals not included. Golf and other packages available year round

Lounge: Lobby Bar

Restaurants: Golden Swan, Squash Blossom, Sandolo

Entertainment: Live entertainment in Lobby Bar and other areas, Andiamo! night club

Credit Cards: All major cards

General Amenities: Children's day camp, meeting and conference facilities with audiovisual and food services

Recreational Amenities: 8 tennis courts; bicycling, jogging, walking, horseback riding; 10 interconnected pools and adjoining Jacuzzis; hot-air balloon rides; 4500 sq. ft. health spa with exercise equipment, aerobic and exercise classes, 2 sauna rooms, fitness evaluation and counseling programs

Reservation and Cancellation Policy: 1-night's deposit required within 10 days of booking. 72-hr. cancellation notice required for full refund

Comments and Restrictions: No pets. Children 18 and under can stay in parents' room with no additional charge. Room tax and sales tax additional to base rates

GAINEY RANCH GOLF CLUB

The Gainey Ranch Golf Club is situated in a 560-acre residential development within walking distance of the Hyatt Regency Scottsdale, a 493-room resort hotel.

The 27-hole golf course includes the 3424-yard Arroyo, the 3238-yard Dunes and the 3376-yard Lakes courses, which can be played in any combination. The Arroyo/Lakes course, which plays 6800 yards from the back tees, has been recognized by *Golf Digest* as one of America's 75 Best Resort Courses. More than 3 million yards of dirt were brought in to create the courses, which were designed by Bradford Benz and J. Michael Poellot.

Benz attended Iowa State University where he received bachelor's and master's degrees in landscape architecture. Poellot received a B.S. degree in landscape architecture from Iowa State and teamed up with Benz in 1980, after serving as the senior architect planner with the Robert Trent Jones II Group. They have developed courses in the Far East, including the first private country club in Communist China, in Beijing, as well as numerous others in the United States. Benz and Poellot now have their own firm based in California.

The Dunes Course features a variety of hills, dunes, and desert. Although at 3238 yards from the back tees this nine is somewhat short, there are many blind shots that make it seem longer. The 550-yard par-5 finishing hole is a tough dogleg right that few golfers reach in two. The first shot is to an open landing area, but on the second you either have to clear an arroyo that cuts the fairway approximately 150 yards from the green or lay up and play a mid iron to a small, elevated target protected by pot bunkers in front and back.

The Arroyo Course is considered the most difficult of the three layouts, with a winding, dry river bed and two lakes. The 555-yard par-5 finishing hole is the most difficult hole on Arroyo and is considered the best par 5 at Gainey Ranch. The first shot has to negotiate a bunker on the right near the landing area, and the second is into a large, highly contoured green with traps in front. To the left of the green is a large lake that begins well down the left fairway. The golfer has to decide whether to go for it or lay up and pitch onto a green that has various levels and is not easy to read.

The Lakes Course has five lakes, and water comes into play on seven of the holes. The 492-yard par-5 ninth, for example, is a dogleg left to a green well protected by water from 150 yards in and to the right. Some golfers try to clear trees on the left and play the second shot from the adjacent fairway to reach the green in two. It is always possible to land in the water on the second or third

shot, however, depending on how you elect to play this hole.

The golf facilities at the Hyatt Regency include an excellent pro shop that has been ranked among the best in America by *Golf Shop Operations* magazine. Locker rooms, showers, a restaurant, and bar service are available. Nearby is a two-tiered driving range, practice bunkers, two chipping greens, and a putting green. Instruction is available from the staff of PGA professionals, and golf packages are available through the resort.

In addition to golf, recreation and meeting facilities, the Hyatt offers a choice of three restaurants and has live entertainment at Andiamo!, a high-energy night club. The resort has received a Golden Tee Award from *Meetings and Conventions* magazine in recognition of its excellent golf and meeting facilities.

Course Name: GRAYHAWK GOLF CLUB

Course Type: Public
Address: 19600 N. Pima Rd.
             Scottsdale, AZ 85255
Phone: (602) 502–1800
Fax: (602) 502–1600

GOLF COURSE

Director of Golf: Joe Shershenovich
Course Length/Par (All Tees): Back: 7001/72, Palo Verde 6408/72, Terra Cotta 5884/72, Forward 5143/72
Course Slope/Rating (All Tees): Back: 141/74.3, Palo Verde 121/70.3, Terra Cotta 116/67.9, Ladies' Terra Cotta 133/74.2, Forward 121/70.0
Course Architects: David Graham and Gary Panks (1994)
Golf Facilities: Full Pro Shop X, Snack Bar X, Lounge X, Restaurant X, Locker Room X, Showers X, Club Rental X, Club Repair X, Cart Rental X, Instruction X, Practice Green X, Driving Range X, Practice Bunker X, Club Storage X
Tee-Time Reservation Policy: Up to 30 days in advance
Ranger: Yes
Tee-off-Interval Time: 9 min.
Time to Play 18 Holes: 4½ hrs.

Course Hours/Earliest Tee-off: 7:06 a.m.

Green and Cart Fees: $155 for 18 holes with cart if reservation made more than 5 days in advance

Credit Cards: All major cards

Season: Year round. Busiest months Jan. through May

Course Comments: Can walk but must pay full fee. Yardage book

Discounts: Seasonal (Jun. to early Sept. low season)

Places to Stay Nearby: Marriott Suites Scottsdale (602) 945–1550, (800) 228–9290; The Phoenician (602) 941–8200, (800) 888–8234; Residence Inns by Marriott (602) 948–8666, (800) 331–3131; Scottsdale Princess (602) 585–4848, (800) 223–1818

Local Attractions: See page 25

Directions: From Sky Harbor Airport (35 min.): Take 44th St. north to Camelback Rd. Turn right on Camelback to Scottsdale Rd. then turn left. Proceed north on Scottsdale 20 min. to light (Bell Rd.). Take a right and proceed to second light (Pima Rd.) then proceed north on Pima 3½ miles to the golf course on the left

Closest Commercial Airport: SkyHarbor International, Phoenix (35 min.).

GRAYHAWK GOLF CLUB

Perched at 1700 feet overlooking the Phoenix Valley with a view of the McDowell Mountains to the east is the Grayhawk Golf Club Talon course, site of the 1995 Anderson Consulting World Championship of Golf. This David Graham and Gary Panks–designed layout is beautifully landscaped with mesquite, palo verde, ironwood, barrel cactus, saguaro, and other vegetation. There are few forced carries over this native terrain, but strayed shots easily find bunkers, canyons, or native foliage. Length and accuracy off the tee enable you to accurately approach the large, contoured, fast Crenshaw bentgrass greens. Wind can affect play on the first four holes on both nines where incoming winds prevail. Crosswinds are likely on Nos. 14 and 15, and tailwinds tend to be present on the other eight holes. There are a variety of

elevation changes on the course, and deep bunkers and mounded areas surrounding the greens sometimes make it difficult to see the target if you are poorly positioned.

The final four holes at the Talon provide a challenging conclusion to the round. The 450-yard dogleg left par-4 fifteenth, which plays 419, 393, and 324 yards from the other tee positions, requires a tee shot that must avoid being stymied by a large tree protecting the left side of the fairway 156 yards from the green. The 416-yard par-4 sixteenth, called "Deception," has an approach to a deep green that is guarded by a sprawling bunker that begins 80 yards in front of the green and meanders up to its front edge. Talon's signature hole is the 126-yard par-3 seventeenth, "Devil's Drink," which plays to an island green that provides no room for error. The 588-yard par-5 finishing hole, "Five Falls," is bordered by a series of bunkers to the right of the tee shot landing area. The second shot can easily catch a long waste bunker bordering the left side of the fairway. The approach is to a deep, undulating green guarded by water to its left.

The Grayhawk Golf Club is the centerpiece of a 1600-acre planned community. Near the finishing hole is a sumptuous 40,000 square-foot clubhouse and a spacious practice area featuring a golf learning center headed by Peter Kostis and Gary McCord. The Talon is rated one of the best courses in golf-rich Arizona by *GolfWeek* magazine. A new 18-hole Tom Fazio layout will be ready for play by 1996.

Course Name: LOS CABALLEROS GOLF CLUB

Course Type: Resort
Resort: Rancho de los Caballeros
Address: Vulture Mine Road
               Wickenburg, AZ 85358
Phone: (520) 684–2704 (Golf Course)
               (520) 684–5484 (Resort)
Fax: (520) 684–2267 (Resort)

GOLF COURSE

Head Professional: Van Batchelder

Course Length/Par (All Tees): Back 6965/72, Middle 6577/72, Ladies' Forward 5896/73

Course Slope/Rating (All Tees): Back 134/72.5, Middle 122/70.6, Ladies' Forward 123/73.5

Course Architects: Greg Nash and Jeff Hardin (1980)

Golf Facilities: Full Pro Shop X, Snack Bar X, Lounge X, Restaurant X, Locker Room X, Showers X, Club Rental X, Club Repair X, Cart Rental X, Instruction X, Practice Green X, Driving Range X, Practice Bunker X, Club Storage X

Tee-Time Reservation Policy: Resort guest or member: 1 mo. in advance. Public: 2 days in advance from 7:30 a.m.

Ranger: Yes

Tee-off-Interval Time: 7 and 8 min.

Time to Play 18 Holes: 4 hrs.

Course Hours/Earliest Tee-off: 7 a.m. to 9 a.m. depending on season

Green and Cart Fees: Peak-season rates: $95 for 18 holes with cart, $55 for 9 holes with cart

Credit Cards: MasterCard, Visa

Season: Course open year round. Resort open Oct. to May. Busiest season Feb. to May

Course Comments: Cart mandatory. Must be resort guest, member or guest to get priority tee times. Nonguests can play the course at higher rates any time of year

Golf Packages: Available through resort

Discounts: June to Sept.

Places to Stay Nearby: Best Western, Rancho Grande (520) 684–5445, (800) 528–1234; Flying E Ranch (520) 684–2690; Wickenburg Tennis and Guest Ranch (520) 684–7811, (800) 942–5362

Local Attractions: Hassayampa River Preserve, Desert Caballeros Western Museum, ghost towns, Wickenberg sites, Joshua Forest, Grand Canyon. PHOENIX: Heard Museum of Anthropology and Primitive Art, Heritage Square, Desert Botanical Garden, Champlin Fighter Museum, Frank Lloyd Wright architecture, professional sports. Wickenberg Chamber of Commerce (520) 684–5479. Phoenix Convention and Visitors Bureau (602) 254–6500

Directions: From Phoenix (58 mi.): I–60/89 west, left on Vulture Mine to resort. From California: I–60/89 east, right on Vulture Mine to resort

Closest Commercial Airport: Skyharbor International, Phoenix (1 hr.)

RESORT

Date Built: 1947

No. of Rooms: 73 rooms and suites

Meeting Rooms: 10. Capacity of Largest: 275 persons. Meeting Space: 4500 sq. ft.

Room Price Range: $160 to $325 per person including American plan, 3 meals per day. Golf packages available

Lounge: Bar patio

Restaurants: Main dining room, golf-club restaurants

Entertainment: Cookouts, country-western singer, other music

Credit Cards: None—cash or check only

General Amenities: Movies, children's program at no charge, social hostess for tour planning, games, photo albums depicting history of the ranch, meeting and conference facilities with audio-visual and food services

Recreational Amenities: 4 acrylic tennis courts, trap and skeet shooting, horse-back riding, swimming pool, jogging, horseshoes, billiards, square dancing

Reservation and Cancellation Policy: 1-day's rate by check advance deposit. 30-day cancellation notice required for full refund

Comments and Restrictions: No pets. Boarding facilities nearby, inquire. In lieu of tipping, 15% of daily room rate; corral, skeet, transportation fees; and bar charges added to bill. State sales tax additional. Ranch is open to guests Oct. through May only

LOS CABALLEROS GOLF CLUB

Because of an inadvertent gold discovery by Henry Wickenburg in 1863, Wickenburg, located 58 miles northwest of Phoenix, became Arizona's third largest city a few years later. Eventually more than 80 mines were operating in the Wickenburg area, but today it is "the Dude Ranch Capital of the World." Rancho de los Caballeros, a friendly, low-key, 150-guest resort, is owned by the family of Dallas Gant, originally from Altus, Oklahoma. Gant came to Wickenburg as a young man and first worked as an assistant at Jack and Sophie Burden's Remuda Ranch, then one of the top guest ranches in the state. He met Edith Courteen of Milwaukee, Wisconsin, in the late 1930s in Santa Fe, New Mexico, where she went to school. They married in 1941, and by 1947 the Gants formed the Los Caballeros Ranch Company with two partners. Today, the ranch is a working cattle ranch consisting of 1200 acres of deeded land and 16,000 acres of land leased from the state of Arizona and the Federal Bureau of Land Management. Dallas Gant, Sr., passed away in 1968, but his son Rusty runs the business, following the same philosophy emphasizing personal service that his parents refined over the years.

Plans for the golf course began in the spring of 1978, and the 6965-yard par-72 layout was completed in 1980. Designed by Greg Nash and Jeff Hardin of Phoenix, the course has been named one of the best golf courses in the state of Arizona and one of the Top 75 resort courses in the United States by *Golf Digest* magazine. Featuring lush Bermuda fairways overseeded with perennial rye grass, the course encircles the ranch and is a favorite of many golfers in the Phoenix area, who enjoy its quiet desert splendor and natural design compatibility with its environment.

Each hole is an individual experience unto itself, with the fairways running straight from the tee box to greens that are generally medium fast, hard to read, and small to medium sized. Fourteen of the holes have elevated greens, and desert etches the sides of each fairway. Most of the traps around the greens are placed in front. The wind can be a factor on some holes; for example, the 598-yard par-5 thirteenth has never been reached in two because the golfer plays directly into the wind.

The sixteenth is probably the most difficult hole at Los Caballeros. A 444-yard par 4, the first shot is straight, and the second is onto a narrow green with a trap on the right and a drop-off to the left. This green, with its subtle undulations, is considered to be one of the most difficult to read on the course. The number-1-handicap hole is the 569-yard par-5 seventh, which plays from a hilltop to a hilltop landing area, then down and up to a two-tiered, forward-sloping green. Two traps are to the left of the green, and the desert is on the immediate right. The eighth hole is a tough, long, 210-yard par 3 that usually plays into the wind. Traps are on the left, right and in front. The green is large and usually requires a fairway wood to hold it from this distance.

The clubhouse has a pro shop, locker rooms, and a complete bar and grill seating 75 persons. The club is owned by its membership but is open to guests of the ranch and the public year round. Rancho de los Caballeros has a variety of amenities and activities ranging from horseback riding, cookout rides, skeet and trap shooting, and tennis to children's programs. The American plan includes 3 meals a day, and tables are assigned in the friendly dining area. The on-site Palo Verde Conference Center includes its own kitchen and various meeting room options with audiovisual support from the ranch staff. Groups of 150 can comfortably be accommodated.

Situated at 2400 feet, Rancho de los Caballeros, with its superb views of rugged Vulture Peak and the desert, is well worth the visit.

Course Name: STONECREEK GOLF CLUB

Course Type: Public
Address: 4435 East Paradise Village Parkway South, Paradise Valley, AZ 85032
Phone: (602) 953–9110

GOLF COURSE

Director of Golf: Gregg Lindquist
Course Length/Par (All Tees): Back 6836/71, Forest 6280/71, Tan 5909/71, Forward 5098/71
Course Slope/Rating (All Tees): Back 134/72.6, Forest 127/69.8, Tan 122/68.4,

Forward 118/68.4, Ladies' Tan 130/73.3, Forward 118/69.2

Course Architects: Roy Dye and Gary Grandstaff (1983), Arthur Jack Snyder (1983), Greg Nash (1984), Arthur Hills (1988)

Golf Facilities: Full Pro Shop X, Snack Bar X, Lounge X, Restaurant X, Locker Room X, Showers X, Club Rental X, Club Repair No, Cart Rental X, Instruction X, Practice Green X, Driving Range X, Practice Bunker X, Club Storage X

Tee-Time Reservation Policy: Members: 1 wk. in advance, hotel packages. Public: 3 days in advance from 7 a.m.

Ranger: Yes

Tee-off-Interval Time: 7 and 8 min.

Time to Play 18 Holes: 4 hrs., 15 min.

Course Hours/Earliest Tee-off: 8 a.m.

Green and Cart Fees: $98 plus tax for 18 holes with cart weekends, $69 plus tax for 18 holes with cart Mon. through Thurs.

Credit Cards: All major cards

Season: Year round. Busiest season Jan. 1 to mid-April

Course Comments: Carts mandatory. Yardage book available

Golf Packages: Available through local hotels

Discounts: Seasonal

Places to Stay Nearby: Embassy Suites Camelhead (602) 244–8800, (800) 362–2779; Pointe Hilton Resort at Tapatio Cliffs (602) 866 7500, (800) 934–1000; Pointe Hilton Resort at Squaw Peak (602) 997–2626, (800) 934–1000; Wyndham Paradise Valley Resort (602) 947–5400, (800) 822–4200

Local Attractions: PHOENIX: Heard Museum of Anthropology and Primitive Art, Heritage Square, Desert Botanical Garden, Pioneer Arizona, zoo, Frank Lloyd Wright architecture, Phoenix Symphony, Champlin Fighter Museum, Arizona State University, horseback riding. Area: ruins, Grand Canyon, hiking. Phoenix Visitors Bureau (602) 254–6500

Directions: From Skyharbor International Airport (30 min.): 44th St. north to Tatum, golf course straddles Tatum Blvd., follow signs

Closest Commercial Airport: Skyharbor International, Phoenix (30 min.)

STONECREEK GOLF CLUB

In the late 1980s the Westcor group bought what used to be the Anasazi Golf Club. Westcor had Arthur Hills and Associates redesign the course to make it more playable by reducing the penal aspects of the course. The Anasazi, who mysteriously disappeared in the fourteenth century, are ancestors of the local Hopi Indians.

Golf magazine included Stonecreek in its "50 Best Bangs for a Buck in Public Golf" list in 1989. The 6836-yard par 71 is a Scottish links style course with four tee positions to accommodate various golf strategies and abilities. The greens are fast and undulating and vary in depth from a narrow 16 yards on the 609-yard par-5 sixteenth to 46 yards on the par-4 seventeenth. The fairways are relatively open, with hidden moguls and bunkers dotting the rolling, somewhat flat terrain that often plays to elevated greens.

The front side is a relatively short 3273 yards from the back tees, with the 389-yard par-4 sixth ranked as the number-1-handicap hole. The tee shot plays to a landing area to the left of a huge trap paralleling the right fairway, beginning 215 yards from the green. The second shot must avoid water both left and right to reach a long green bordered on the right by water and protected on the left by two traps. In addition to a well-placed tee shot, this hole requires an extremely accurate second shot to this tricky, undulating green.

Another difficult hole on the front nine is the 399-yard par-4 second, a slight dogleg to the right with hardpan running down the right side from tee to green. The landing area is protected on the left by three bunkers beginning 160 yards from a long and somewhat narrow green. The combination of well-placed traps, water and moguls makes the front nine a bit more difficult than it would seem.

The back nine features the number-2-handicap 609-yard par-5 sixteenth. The first two shots should be played center or left-center to avoid the hardpan of Stonecreek, which runs from tee to green on the right. From 100 yards in to a long, narrow green that tilts right to left are a pond on the right and three traps on the left beginning from 55 yards out to the back of the green. Three well-struck shots are required to reach this relatively flat green that slopes from the rear right to front left.

Water comes into play on three other holes on the back nine, including the picturesque 227-yard par-3 fifteenth, which features a lake on the right from 170 yards in and around to the back of a deep green protected by a huge, long trap on the right. This hole is less onerous from the 166-yard championship tee but still requires an extremely well-placed tee shot.

Stonecreek emphasizes golf instruction and provides a variety of junior programs, beginner clinics, ladies' programs, and private instruction. Full practice facilities, an excellent golf shop, and food and beverage facilities are available at this service- and customer-oriented facility.

Course Name: SUPERSTITION SPRINGS GOLF CLUB

Course Type: Public
Address: 6542 E. Baseline Road Mesa, AZ 85206
Phone: (602) 985–5555 (Reservation System)

GOLF COURSE

Head Professional: Jim Tuttle
Course Length/Par (All Tees): Back 7005/72, Middle 6405/72, Forward 5328/72
Course Slope/Rating (All Tees): Back 135/74.1, Middle 132/71.2, Ladies' Forward 120/70.9
Course Architect: Greg Nash (1986)
Golf Facilities: Full Pro Shop X, Snack Bar X, Lounge X, Restaurant X, Locker Room X, Showers X, Club Rental X, Club Repair Minor, Cart Rental X, Instruction X, Practice Green X, Driving Range X, Practice Bunker X, Club Storage X
Tee-Time Reservation Policy: 7 days in advance from 7 a.m. Reservations may be made up to 60 days in advance for a surcharge of $7 per player
Ranger: Yes
Tee-off-Interval Time: 7 and 8 min.
Time to Play 18 Holes: 4½ hrs.
Course Hours/Earliest Tee-off: Sunrise
Green and Cart Fees: $105 plus tax for 18 holes with cart Fri., Sat., Sun., holidays, $95 weekdays; $50 plus tax for 9 holes with cart
Credit Cards: American Express, MasterCard, Visa
Season: Year round. Busiest season mid-Jan. to mid-April
Course Comments: Cart mandatory. Yardage book available
Golf Packages: Available through area hotels
Discounts: Seasonal. Periodic special offers
Places to Stay Nearby: Sheraton Mesa (602) 898–8300, (800) 325–3535; Courtyard by Marriot (800) 321–2211; Hilton Pavilion (602) 833–5555, (800) HILTONS; Dobson Ranch Inn and Resort (602) 831–7000, (800) 528–1356; Lexington Hotel Suites (602) 964–2897. Valley of the Sun Accommodation Information (800) 992–6005 (AZ), (800) 528–0483 (outside AZ)
Local Attractions: Apache trail, water sports, Mesa Southwest Museum, Arizona Museum for Youth, Arizona Temple (Mormon), Champlin Fighter Museum, Arizona Farm and Heritage Museum, horseback riding, sporting events, festivals. Phoenix: Mesa Visitor Information (602) 969-1307, Phoenix Convention and Visitors Bureau (602) 254–6500
Directions: Superstition Springs Hwy. east to Superstition Springs Blvd. exit
Closest Commercial Airport: Skyharbor International, Phoenix (30 min.)

SUPERSTITION SPRINGS GOLF CLUB

The Superstition Springs Golf Club, situated in a 1700-acre planned development called Superstition Springs, was originally developed by Western Savings and Loan and, after a brief stint with the Resolution Trust Corporation, is now privately owned again. The overall complex is a mixed-land-use development designed to include resort hotels, office plazas, retail centers and industrial parks. The club itself opened in November 1986 and caters to the high-end public golfer who likes resort level conditions. A large clubhouse serves the golf course and includes meeting rooms, locker rooms and showers; a restaurant and lounge and a large full-service golf shop that has been selected by *Golf Shop Operations* magazine as one of America's 100 best facilities.

The 7005-yard par-72 layout has undulating fairways, expansive bunkers, strategic mounding, and water on half its holes. A variety of doglegs, long and short par 4s and 5s and some beautiful, challenging par 3s make Superstition Springs a memorable golf experience. The front nine starts out with a 391-yard par 4, which is a slight dogleg right with fairway bunkers to the left and right from 100 to 190 yards into the green. The putting surface is deep, narrow, and protected on the left by a trap. The second hole is a straight 432-yard par 4 to a narrow green with sand on the left and grass bunkers to the right. The third is a 205-yard par 3 to a two-tiered green with sand on the right and pot bunkers to the left. The next hole is a relatively short 332-yard par 4, but water guards the front and right side of a narrow, deep green from 70 yards in. The par-4 fifth is another possible "layup" hole playing 325 yards to a very small green that is protected in front by water and traps, with a huge bunker in back. Six is the number-1-handicap hole and, at 610 yards, is a very formidable par 5 aptly called "Apache Tears." The tee shot has to avoid a long pond on the right, and the second shot must negotiate a large pond on the left. The green is very long and narrow and is backed by a huge bunker with palm trees behind it.

The par-3 seventh plays 228 yards to a long, narrow green with sand traps left and grass bunkers right. Also to the right is a water hazard. The par-5 eighth is a long and tough 597 yards with fairway bunkers both left and right of the tee-shot landing area. The second shot can catch the bunkers on the right beginning 170 yards from the green or hit large traps to the front left and right of the putting surface. The last hole on the front nine is a beautiful but intimidating 425-yard par 4 that plays over a lake that runs to within 70 yards of the green. The fairway is to the right, so you can opt for how much distance you can bite off. The second shot is toward a large green protected in front by a large trap and to the left by another large sand area. There are two shelves to the back left and right on the 47-yard-deep green. Pin placement can be a big factor on this hole.

On the back nine the 231-yard par-3 fifteenth is a tough hole that plays from an elevated tee with water front and right to within 20 yards of a deep green heavily trapped on the right. The number-2-handicap hole is the dramatic 537-yard par-5 "Treasure Island" seventeenth, which is a definite risk/reward hole with its peninsula green etched by water beginning on the right 150 yards from the tee. The tee shot is ideally placed left of center, and then you can go for it or lay up as the fairway narrows into the neck of the peninsula holding the green. There is some room for error to the right of the green, but any shot to the left will be in the water.

The finishing hole at Superstition Springs is a tough 455-yard par 4 with a pond directly in front of the tee, then narrowing to a stream on the right beginning approximately 150 yards from the tee and meandering through the fairway up to the right side of the green. The putting surface is protected by huge traps to the right and rear. To the left is out of bounds, so two straight, long shots are required for a chance at par.

The full-service clubhouse at Superstition Springs is distinguished by its southern plantation design and provides scenic views of the golf course and the nearby Superstition Mountains. *Golf* magazine has placed Superstition Springs on its "50 Best Bangs for a Buck in Public Golf" list, and the course was nominated by

Golf Digest as one of the best new public golf courses opened in 1987. The plan under the new ownership is to keep the course public. Outings and tournaments are welcome.

Course Name: **TOURNAMENT PLAYERS CLUB (TPC) OF SCOTTSDALE Stadium, Desert Courses**

Course Type: Public
Resort: Scottsdale Princess
Address: 17020 N. Hayden Road
              Scottsdale, AZ 85255
Phone: (602) 585–3939 (Golf Course)
              (602) 585–3600,
              (602) 585–4848,
              (800) 223–1818 (Resort)
Fax: (602) 585–0086 (Resort)

GOLF COURSE

Director of Golf: Ray Dznowski, Jr.

Head Professional: Desert Course: Tim Eleeson. Stadium Course: Jim Klufa

Course Length/Par (All Tees): Stadium: Back 6992/71, Championship 6508/71, Regular 6049/71, Forward 5567/71. Desert: Back 6552/71, Championship 5908/71, Regular 5339/71, Forward 4715/71

Course Slope/Rating (All Tees): Stadium: Back 130.7/73.9, Championship 124/71, Regular 120/68.9, Ladies' Forward 122.3/71.6. Desert: Back 112/71.4, Championship 109/68.4, Regular 103/67.4, Ladies' Forward 106/66.3

Course Architects: Jay Morrish and Tom Weiskopf (1986)

Golf Facilities: Full Pro Shop X, Snack Bar X, Lounge X, Restaurant X, Locker Room X, Showers X, Club Rental X, Club Repair X, Cart Rental X, Instruction X, Practice Green X, Driving Range X, Practice Bunker X, Club Storage X

Tee-Time Reservation Policy: 7 days in advance, major credit card guarantee, 48-hr. cancellation policy. Single players accepted daily on first-come, first-served basis

Ranger: Yes

Tee-off-Interval Time: 8 min.

Time to Play 18 Holes: 4½ hrs.

Course Hours/Earliest Tee-off: 6 a.m.

Green Fees: Stadium: $125 plus tax for 18 holes, $72 plus tax for 9 holes (twilight) with cart. Desert: $20 plus tax for 18 holes

Cart Fees: $13 per person for 18 holes on Desert Course. Cart fee included in green fee at Stadium Course

Credit Cards: American Express, Master-Card, Visa

Season: Year round. Busiest season Jan. 1 to April 30

Course Comments: Cart mandatory on Stadium Course

Golf Packages: Available through Scottsdale Princess, Resort Suites

Discounts: Seasonal (May to Dec.), juniors, Scottsdale residents, seniors (weekdays). Twilight rates. 3 rate schedules apply depending on the season

Places to Stay Nearby: Holiday Inn Sunapee Resorts Scottsdale (602) 991–2400, (800) 852–5205; Inn at the Citadel (602) 585–6133, (800) 927–8367; Residence Inns by Marriott (602) 948–8666, (800) 331–3131; Fairfield Inn (602) 483–0042, (800) 228–2800; Radisson Resort (602) 991–3800, (800) 333–3333

Local Attractions: Scottsdale Center for the Arts, Taliesin West, shopping, restaurants, ballooning, horseback riding, white-water rafting, seasonal festivals, professional sports. PHOENIX: Arizona State Museum, Mission San Xavier del Bac, Desert Botanical Garden, Heard Museum, Saguaro National Monument, Tucson Mountain Park; professional football, basketball, major league baseball spring training. Scottsdale Chamber of Commerce (602) 945-8481, (800) 877–1117. Phoenix Convention and Visitors Bureau (602) 254–6500

Directions: From airport (21 mi.): 44th St. to Town Blvd. to Bell Rd., right on Bell to Pima, left on Pima, 3/4 mi. to golf course

Closest Commercial Airport: Skyharbor International, Phoenix (30 min.)

RESORT

Date Built: 1987

No. of Rooms: 600, including 400 in main building, 125 casitas, 75 villas

Meeting Rooms: 28. Capacity of Largest: 2250 persons banquet style. Meeting Space: 58,000 sq. ft.

Room Price Range: $225 to $2000 for suite peak season (Jan. to mid-May), meals not included. Golf packages - available

Lounges: 6 bars and lounges, including Cazadores

Restaurants: Las Ventanas, Marquessa, La Hacienda, Grill at the Tournament Players Club, Cabana Café

Entertainment: Club Caballo Bayo with live dance band

Credit Cards: All major cards

General Amenities: Complete meeting facilities including 58,000 sq. ft. of space, audiovisual and food services; beauty salon, spa, shopping, sightseeing, babysitting, tour arrangements

Recreational Amenities: 9 tennis courts (6 lighted), 3 heated swimming pools; racquetball and squash court; health club including exercise equipment such as Universal weight-training machines, cycles, rowers; dry saunas, whirlpools, steam baths, jogging, bicycling, croquet, volleyball, basketball, horseback riding

Reservation and Cancellation Policy: Credit card guarantee or check to hold reservation. 3 days' advance notice of cancellation required to receive full refund

Comments and Restrictions: No pets. No room charge for children 12 and under when sharing room with 2 adults. Maximum 2 children per room. Local room tax and sales tax added to base rates

TPC OF SCOTTSDALE

TPC of Scottsdale has two 18-hole layouts designed by Jay Morrish and Tom Weiskopf. The Desert Course, which opened in 1987, plays 6552 yards from the back tees and, at least according to its slope and USGA ratings, is the easier of the two. It has less water and is shorter than the 6992-yard Stadium Course, which is the site of the Phoenix Open in January and is recognized by *Golf Digest* as one of the best public golf courses in America. The entire complex is situated on 450 acres of land.

A desert gem nestled beneath the McDowell Mountains, the Stadium Course is adorned with grassy knolls, spectator mounds, picturesque lakes and amphitheater-type seating for golf events. The front nine has very little water but includes long and difficult par 4s, including the 453-yard fifth and the number-2-handicap 470-yard eighth. The eighth requires two long, accurate shots to reach a relatively small green. An inbound wind usually makes this hole extremely difficult.

The back nine has water on six of its holes including the number-1-handicap 469-yard par-4 eleventh hole, which has a two-tiered, crowned green with a large pot bunker to the right and two larger bunkers on the left. It is better to play to the right side of the fairway on this hole and come in through an opening to the green.

The fifteenth hole is a 501-yard par 5 that has a somewhat small island green and is protected by traps both left and right. In the Phoenix Open, this is the closest-to-the-pin green that awards $10,000 for the best shot. The eighteenth is a 438-yard par 4 whose fairway is edged by water on the left. The object is to cut the water to reduce the distance for the second shot, which comes onto a small green with a bunker on the right. The predominant wind on this hole is generally from left to right.

The TPC Desert Course, also designed by Morrish and Weiskopf, is adjacent to the Stadium Course and is well worth playing. The 6552-yard par-71 layout has many of the same features as the Stadium Course: undulating fairways, well-placed traps and mounds, especially around the greens, and somewhat large putting surfaces that are medium-fast, with moderate undulation. Desert surrounds each fairway, with water present on only two holes. The Desert Course opens with the number-2-handicap 521-yard par 5, which requires two straight shots to an area in front of an elongated green that is trapped in back. The number-

1-handicap hole on this course is the long 465-yard par-4 seventeenth, which plays straight from tee to a green sloped right to left with a trap in back.

The Scottsdale Princess is only 2 minutes from the golf course and has all the amenities one could want in a resort hotel, including state-of-the-art conference and meeting facilities and a range of fitness and athletic facilities. Among its excellent restaurants is the Marquessa, which features Spanish Catalan cuisine and an excellent Spanish wine selection. Both the restaurant and the resort have won the prestigious American Automobile Association Five-Diamond Award.

The TPC of Scottsdale is a public facility owned by the city of Scottsdale and managed by PGA Tour Investments. You can walk the Desert Course, and there is a complete pro shop with a wide range of instructional options including daily golf clinics, private lessons, playing lessons, lessons with video analysis, and individual, group, and clinic game improvement plans. Food and beverage facilities are available at both courses, and golf outings (minimum of 16 players) can be booked up to 90 days in advance and must be prepaid at that time. Catering through the Princess Hotel is also available as are a variety of golf packages.

Course Name: TROON NORTH

Course Type: Public
Address: 10370 E. Dynamite Blvd.
Scottsdale, AZ 85255
Phone: (602) 585–7700 (Reservations), (602) 585–5300 (Pro Shop)

GOLF COURSE

Head Professional: Scott Heideman
Course Length/Par (All Tees): Back 7028/72, Gold 6690, Silver 6247/72, Copper 5901/72, Forward 5050/72
Course Slope/Rating (All Tees): Back 147/73.3, Gold 133/71.0, Silver 129/69.8, Copper 126/68.3, Forward 118/64.8. Ladies' Copper 128/74.4, Forward 116/69.0
Course Architects: Jay Morrish and Tom Weiskopf (1990)

Golf Facilities: Full Pro Shop X, Snack Bar X, Lounge X, Restaurant X, Locker Room X, Showers X, Club Rental X, Club Repair X, Cart Rental X, Instruction X, Practice Green X, Driving Range X, Practice Bunker X, Club Storage X
Tee-Time Reservation Policy: Up to 5 days in advance from 7 a.m. Credit card guarantee. Groups of 16 or more 90 days in advance
Ranger: Yes
Tee-off-Interval Time: 9 min.
Time to Play 18 Holes: 4½ hrs.
Course Hours/Earliest Tee-off: 7 a.m.
Green and Cart Fees: Peak season (Sept. to Memorial Day): $145 for 18 holes with cart, $85 for 9 holes with cart
Credit Cards: American Express, Master-Card, Visa
Season: Year round. Busiest season Dec. 1 to April 30
Course Comments: Cart mandatory. Yardage book provided
Golf Packages: Contact pro shop
Discounts: Seasonal. Lowest rates June through Aug.
Places to Stay Nearby: Scottsdale Princess (602) 585–4848, (800) 344–4758; Hyatt/Gainey Ranch (602) 948–5050, (800) 233–1234; Courtyard by Marriott (602) 995–5200, (800) 321–2211; Orange Tree Golf Resort (602) 948–6100, (800) 228–0386; Holiday Inn Sunapee Resort (602) 991–2400, (800) HOLIDAY
Local Attractions: Scottsdale Center for the Arts, Taliesin West, shopping, restaurants, ballooning, horseback riding, white-water rafting, seasonal festivals, professional sports. PHOENIX: Arizona State Museum, Mission San Xavier del Bac, Desert Botanical Garden, Heard Museum of Anthropology and Primitive Art, Saguaro National Monument, Tucson Mountain Park, professional football, basketball, major league baseball spring training. Scottsdale Chamber of Commerce (602) 945–8481, (800) 877–1117. Phoenix Convention and Visitors Bureau (602) 254-6500
Directions: 2 mi. east of Pima Rd. on Dynamite Rd.

Closest Commercial Airport: Skyharbor International, Phoenix (45 min.)

TROON NORTH

Troon North is the centerpiece of an 1800-acre planned golf community located in a picturesque desert setting northeast of Phoenix. Designed by Tom Weiskopf and Jay Morrish, the 7028-yard par-72 layout is situated near the base of Pinnacle Peak Mountain and provides an enjoyable and challenging golfing adventure through arroyos, natural washes, saguaro cactus and the stunning vegetation and topography of the high Sonora Desert.

It's a bit of a drive in a golf cart from the clubhouse to the first tee. This serves to put you in a Scottish-links style world. Troon North opens with a 444-yard par 4, with two well-placed left fairway bunkers 220 yards from the tee. The desert is to your left and right, with a drop-off on the right that catches many balls. I found 6 within 5 minutes after fading a tee shot in that direction, and thought I was going to be in for a long day. The course is fair, however, with a variety of tee positions and no gimmick holes. The second shot on the first hole is to a long green, tilted left to right, with large traps protecting it on the front left and right. Typically, the bentgrass greens are undulating, medium-fast, medium-large, and very true.

One of my favorite holes on the front nine is the third, the 554-yard par-5 dogleg right "Monument" hole, which has a huge boulder monument at the bend of the dogleg approximately 275 yards from the back tee. Two huge traps are along the left fairway beginning 275 yards from the tee; a good strategy is to play the right center of the fairway so that the second shot catches a downward slope to a level area 50 to 100 yards from the green. The number-1-handicap hole on the front side is the 464-yard par-4 fifth, which plays straight and long to a left-to-right-sloping, deep, undulating green protected by mounds.

The back nine begins with a 392-yard par-4 dogleg left that, from the tee, appears like a desert obstacle course. Desert is to the left and right of the fairway, of course,

and approximately 175 yards of desert vegetation are between you and the beginning of the landing area. Two right-side fairway bunkers are situated 150 yards from the green. Seventy-five yards from the green is a 30-yard-wide, heavily bouldered gully, backed by a large fairway sand trap. The putting surface itself is large, kidney shaped, forward sloping from left to right and surrounded by grass mounds. The critical tee shot has to negotiate the two fairway bunkers on the right to a relatively narrow landing area to score on this hole.

The toughest hole on the course is the 604-yard number-2-handicap par-5 fourteenth, a slight dogleg to the right requiring a tee shot that avoids a right fairway bunker. The green is long, left-to-right-tilting and dog-bone shaped. Two large traps are on the right, and a left fairway trap is 30 yards from the dance floor. Most mortals are grateful to reach this green in three. The back nine includes a picturesque 140-yard par 3, the sixteenth, which is appropriately called "the Postage Stamp" because of its small green well protected by huge traps both left and right, with a smaller one in front. There is virtually no bailout on this hole because a small lake is to the right and front of the green. There are also boulders and desert in front of the small target.

The finishing hole at Troon North is a 444-yard par-4 dogleg left, with two fairway bunkers beginning on the right 250 yards from the tee. The tee shot should be hit left-center, cutting off some of the distance to a large, well-protected green framed by two huge traps to the left and right.

Tom Weiskopf, whose 72-hole total of 276 scored at Troon in the British Open in 1973 (along with Arnold Palmer's identical score in 1962) is still the lowest Open score at Troon, has fond memories of that course and has modeled Troon North after the great Scottish layout. *Golf Digest* gave it an honorable mention in its best new resort course category in 1991, and it is now considered one of the best golf courses in the United States.

Course Name: THE WIGWAM
Gold, Blue, Red Courses

Course Type: Resort
Resort: The Wigwam Resort
Address: 451 Litchfield Road
               Litchfield Park, AZ 85340
Phone: (602) 272–4653 (Golf Course)
               (602) 935–3811,
               (800) 327–0396 (Resort)
Fax: (602) 935–3737 (Resort)

GOLF COURSE

Director of Golf: Keith Kalny
Head Professional: Craig Allen
Course Length/Par (All Tees): Gold:
Back 7021/72, Middle 6428/72, Forward
5673/72. Blue: Back 6030/70, Forward
5235/70. Red: Back 6867/72, Middle
6297/72, Forward 5821/72
Course Slope/Rating (All Tees): Gold:
Back 129/73.6, Middle 124/70.6, La-
dies' Middle 129/NA, Forward 120/70.2.
Blue: Back 115/67.9, Ladies' Forward
112/69.8. Red: Back 118/71.8, Middle
113/69.9, Ladies' Middle 121/NA, For-
ward 115/71.9
Course Architects: Gold: Robert Trent
Jones, Sr. (renovation, 1965). Blue:
Robert Trent Jones, Sr. (1965). Red:
Robert "Red" Lawrence (1973)
Golf Facilities: Full Pro Shop X, Snack
Bar X, Lounge X, Restaurant X,
Locker Room X, Showers X, Club
Rental X, Club Repair X, Cart Rental
X, Instruction X, Practice Green X,
Driving Range X, Practice Bunker X,
Club Storage X
Tee-Time Reservation Policy: Resort
guests: At time of reservation on -ad-
vanced reservations course, 1 month
prior for specific course. Members: 1
wk. in advance. Public: 5 days in ad-
vance with credit card guarantee, 2
days without
Ranger: Yes
Tee-off-Interval Time: 8 and 9 min.
Time to Play 18 Holes: 4 hrs., 15 min.
Course Hours/Earliest Tee-off: 7 a.m. to
8 a.m. depending on season
Green and Cart Fees: Gold Course:
$117.75 for 18 holes with cart. Blue,
Red Courses: $96.98 for 18 holes with

cart. Peak season rates for outside play
early Jan. to late Apr.
Credit Cards: All major cards
Season: Year round. Busiest season Jan. 1
through April
Course Comments: Cart mandatory. Yard-
age book available
Golf Packages: Available through resort
Discounts: Hotel guests, replays. Seasonal.
Lowest rates late Apr. to early Jan.
Places to Stay Nearby: Arizona Biltmore,
Phoenix (602) 955–6600, (800) 528–
3696; The Boulders, Carefree (602) 488–
9009; Los Caballeros, Wickenberg (520)
684–5484; Embassy Suites West Side
(602) 279–3211, (800) 362–2779; Hyatt
Regency Phoenix (602) 252–1234, (800)
233–1234; BED AND BREAKFAST: Bed
and Breakfast in Arizona (602) 995–2831
Local Attractions: SEDONA: Grand Can-
yon. WICKENBERG: Desert Caballeros
Western Museum, Hassayampa River
Preserve. PHOENIX: Heard Museum of
Anthropology and Primitive Art, Heritage Square, Champlin Fighter Museum,
Arizona State Capitol Museum, Desert
Botanical Garden, zoo, Phoenix Art Mu-
seum, professional sports. Sedona-Oak
Creek Canyon Chamber of Commerce
(800) 288–7336. Wickenberg Chamber
of Commerce (520) 684–5479. Phoenix
Convention and Visitors Bureau (602)
254–6500
Directions: From Skyharbor International
Airport, Phoenix (30 min.): I–17 north
to I–10 west, I–10 west to exit 128/Litch-
field Rd. Litchfield Rd. north to resort
Closest Commercial Airport: Skyharbor
International, Phoenix (30 min.)

RESORT

Date Built: 1918
No. of Rooms: 241 casita guest rooms,
including 68 suites, villas
Meeting Rooms: 14. Capacity of Largest:
1160 persons. Meeting Space: 16,000
sq. ft.
Room Price Range: $380 to $430 for suite
peak season (Jan. to mid-April), meals
not included. Modified American plan
rate available on request. Golf packages
and other special rates available

Lounges: Piano Lounge, Arizona Bar

Restaurants: Terrace Dining Room, Arizona Kitchen, Grille on the Greens

Entertainment: Live music, dancing nightly

Credit Cards: All major cards

General Amenities: Shopping, sightseeing tours, meeting facilities with audiovisual and banquet services

Recreational Amenities: 9 Plexi-pave courts with lighting, horseback riding; health clubs for men and women with sauna, whirlpools, complete exercise facilities; 2 heated swimming pools, croquet, shuffleboard, bicycling, trap and skeet shooting, volleyball

Reservation and Cancellation Policy: 1 night's deposit required in the form of credit card guarantee or personal check. Deposit must be received within 14 days of reservation. 14-day cancellation notice required or deposit is forfeited

Comments and Restrictions: Children 12 yrs. and under are free when occupying parents' room. Room tax and sales tax added to base rates

THE WIGWAM

The Wigwam is located 17 miles west of Phoenix and is considered one of the finest and most exclusive desert resorts in the United States. The resort is situated on 75 acres featuring orange and palm trees, jasmine, bougainvillea, and well-manicured grounds. The Wigwam began as a private resort in 1918 and first opened to the public in 1929. A recent $30-million restoration and expansion program adds luster to this fine old resort, which has 241 standard and premier casitas.

Golf facilities at the Wigwam include three golf coursesthe Gold and the Blue courses, designed by Robert Trent Jones, Sr., and the Red Course, designed by Robert "Red" Lawrence. Jones also designed the nearby Village of Oak Creek Country Club with Robert Trent Jones, Jr., in the early 1970s. Lawrence, who died in 1976, designed numerous Arizona golf courses including the Padre Course at Camelback in Scottsdale, the original Boul-

ders nine in Carefree, and the Desert Forest Golf Course in Carefree.

The Gold Course, which plays 7021 yards from the back tees, has often been on *Golf Digest*'s America's 75 best resort courses list. And *Golf* magazine has ranked the Wigwam among its prestigious silver medal winners as one of the best golf resorts in America. The greens on the Gold Course are somewhat large, and elevated, well bunkered, moderately fast, and somewhat undulating. Trees including eucalyptus, willows, Aleppo pine, mesquite, orange and palm can come into play as well as oleander more than 20 feet high. Five holes have water hazards.

The toughest hole on the front side is the 441-yard par-4 eighth, which is a slight dogleg right to an undulating green with two traps on the left and that slopes toward the fairway. A canal crosses in front of the green and can catch short second shots as they attempt to reach the putting surface. The double-dogleg 593-yard par-5 tenth is another challenging hole. A long, straight shot is required to the corner of each dogleg, and the approach shot is to a deep, forward-sloping green protected by a small pond to the front left.

A memorable par 3 is the 179-yard eleventh, which plays over water to a large, well-bunkered green. The seventeenth, a dogleg left 405-yard par 4, is a good test of golf, requiring the second shot to avoid a small lake to the right of the green and traps to the left of the narrow putting surface.

The par-70 Blue Course plays 6030 yards from the back tees, with the 426-yard par-4 eighth the toughest hole. This is a long dogleg right with the green well protected by traps both left and right. Water comes into play on four holes on this course.

The Red Course plays 6887 yards from the back tees, with water coming into play on half the holes. The number-1-handicap hole is the 568-yard par-5 sixth, which plays long and relatively straight down a fairway bordered most of the way by a stream and a small pond as you approach the green. The 382-yard par-4 fourteenth is straight, but the second shot is to a green well protected by water to the front and side.

The pro shop has been recognized by *Golf Shop Operations* magazine as one of the best in the United States. Breakfast, lunch and dinner are served at the Grille on the Greens restaurant, which overlooks the golf course. The Wigwam has won numerous hospitality awards, including the American Automobile Association Five-Diamond and the *Mobil Travel Guide*'s Five-Star awards. The resort has been recognized as a premier conference center by *Conventions and Meetings* magazine (Gold Tee Award). The resort courses can be played by nonguests, but a stay at the Wigwam resort itself is highly recommended.

Recommended Golf Courses in Arizona

Within 1 Hour of Phoenix:

Arizona Biltmore Country Club, Phoenix, (602) 955–9655, Resort. Adobe: 18/6783/72. Links: 18/6397/71

Arizona Golf Resort and Conference Center, Mesa, (602) 832–1661, (800) 528–8282, Resort, 18/6572/71

Arrowhead Ranch Country Club, Glendale, (602) 561–9625, Semiprivate, 18/7001/72

Club Terravita, Scottsdale, (602) 488–1333, Semiprivate, 18/7186/72

Club West Golf Club, Phoenix, (602) 460–4400, Public, 18/7057/72

Coyote Lakes Golf Club, Surprise, (602) 566–2323, Public, 18/6159/72

Eagle's Nest Country Club at Pebble Creek, Goodyear, (602) 935–6750, (800) 795–4663, Semiprivate, 18/6860/72

El Dorado Lakes Golf Club, Gilbert, (602) 926–9589, (800) 468–7918, 18/6716/72

The 500 Club, Glendale, (602) 492–9500, Public, 18/6543/72

The Foothills Golf Club, Phoenix, (602) 460–4653, Public, 18/6958/72

Foothills Club West, Phoenix, (602) 460–4400, Public, 18/7057/72

Fountain Hills Golf Club, Fountain Hills, (602) 837–1173, Semiprivate, 18/6087/71

Gold Canyon Golf Club, Apache Junction, (602) 982–9449, (800) 624–6445, Resort, 18/6400/71

Happy Trails Golf Resort, Surprise, (602) 584–6000, Semiprivate, 18/6646/72

Hillcrest Golf Club, Sun City West, (602) 584–1500, Public, 18/6960/72

Karsten Golf Course at Arizona State University, Tempe, (602) 921–8070, Public, 18/7057/72

Las Sendas Golf Club, Mesa, (602) 396–4000, Public, 18/6836/72

The Legend Golf Resort at Arrowhead, Glendale, (602) 561–1902, (800) 468–7918, Public, 18/7005/72

Marriott's Camelback Inn Resort and Golf Club, Scottsdale, (602) 948–6770, (800) 242–2635, Resort. Padre: 18/6559/71. Indian Bend: 18/7014/72

McCormick Ranch Golf Club, Scottsdale, (602) 948–0260, (800) 243–1332, Resort. Pine: 18/7013/72. Palm: 18/7032/72

Ocotillo Country Club, Chandler, (602) 220–9000, Public. Blue: 9/3325/30. White: 9/3208/35. Gold: 9/3404/36

Orange Tree Golf Resort, Scottsdale, (602) 948–3730, (800) 228–0386, Resort, 18/6762/72

Palm Valley Golf Club, Goodyear, (602)935–2500, Semiprivate, 18/7015/72

Papago Golf Course, Phoenix, (602) 275–8428, Public, 18/7063/72

Phoenician Resort, Scottsdale, (602) 423-2449, (800) 888–8234, Resort, 18/6487/71

Pointe Golf Club at Lookout Mountain, Phoenix, (602) 866–6356, (800) 876–4683, Resort, 18/6617/72

Red Mountain Ranch Country Club, Mesa, (602) 985–0285, Semiprivate, 18/6726/72

San Marcos Golf & Country Club, Chandler, (602) 963–3358, Semiprivate, 18/6501/72

Scottsdale Country Club, Scottsdale, (602) 948–2535, Semiprivate. North: 9/3021/35. South: 9/3064/35. East: 9/3381/35

Tatum Ranch Golf Club, North Phoenix, (602) 587–2399, (800) 468–7918, Public, 18/6870/72

Tonto Verde Golf Club, Rio Verde, (602) 471–2710, Semiprivate, 18/6736/72

Westbrook Village Golf Club, Peoria, (602) 933–0174, Semiprivate, 18/6412/72

Tucson Area

Course Name: LA PALOMA
              COUNTRY CLUB
              Hill, Ridge,
              Canyon Courses

Course Type: Resort
Resort: The Westin La Paloma
Address: 3800 E. Sunrise Drive
              Tucson, AZ 85718
Phone: (520) 299–1500 (Golf Course)
              (520) 742–6000,
              (800) 876–3683 (Resort)
Fax: (520) 577–5887 (Resort)

GOLF COURSE

Director of Golf: Keith Pope
Course Length/Par (All Tees): Hill/Ridge: Back 7017/72, Blue 6464/72, White 5984/72, Green 5714/72, Forward 4878/72. Ridge/Canyon: Back 7088/72, Blue 6635/72, White 6011/72, Green 5731/72, Forward 5075/72. Canyon/Hill: Back 6996/72, Blue 6453/72, White 5955/72, Green 5505/72, Forward 5057/72
Course Slope/Rating (All Tees): Hill/Ridge: Back 155/74.4, Blue 150/72.0, White 140/69.9, Green 138/68.7, Forward 115/67.8. Ladies' Forward 124/71.8. Ridge/Canyon: Back 155/75.4, Blue 149/72.3, White 138/69.9, Green 136/68.8, Forward 116/68.9. Ladies' Forward 127/72.1. Canyon/Hill: Back 155/75.4, Blue 152/72.2, White 140/70.0, Green 135/67.7, Forward 118/69.0. Ladies' Forward 123/70.9
Course Architect: Jack Nicklaus (1986)

Golf Facilities: Full Pro Shop X, Snack Bar X, Lounge X, Restaurant X, Locker Room X, Showers X, Club Rental X, Club Repair Minor, Cart Rental X, Instruction X, Practice Green X, Driving Range X, Practice Bunker X, Club Storage X
Tee-Time Reservation Policy: Resort guests: Up to 60 days in advance. Golf-package participants: 1 yr. in advance. Public: 24 hrs. in advance
Ranger: Yes
Tee-off-Interval Time: 10 min.
Time to Play 18 Holes: 4½ hrs.
Course Hours/Earliest Tee-off: 7 a.m. Later in peak season
Green and Cart Fees: Resort guests: $125 for 18 holes with cart, range balls. Public/members of other clubs: $150 for 18 holes with cart. Peak season rates early Jan. to late May
Credit Cards: All major cards
Season: Year round. Busiest season Sept. to Nov., Feb. to May
Course Comments: Cart mandatory. Yardage book available
Golf Packages: Available through resort
Discounts: Lowest rates after May 23 to Sept.
Places to Stay Nearby: Sheraton Tucson El Conquistador (520) 544–5000, (800) 325–7832; the Tucson National Golf and Conference Resort (520) 297–2271, (800) 528–4856; Best Western Inn Suites–Catalina Foothills (520) 297–8111, (800) 842–4242; Arizona Inn (520) 325–1541, (800) 933–1093
Local Attractions: Old Tucson, Reid Park Zoo, Kitt Peak National Observatory, Colossal Cave, Mission San Xavier, Arizona State Museum, Arizona-Sonora Desert Museum, horseback riding, University of Arizona, Del Bac, Pima Air Museum, Titan Missile Museum, Tucson Mountain Park, Saguaro National Monument, Tucson Museum of Art, Arizona Historical Society/Tucson, Chiricahua National Monument, professional sports, shopping, theater, concerts, restaurants. Tombstone, AZ. Mexico. Metropolitan Tucson Convention and Visitors Bureau (602) 624–1817

Directions: I–10 to Orange Grove exit, east on Orange Grove to Skyline, right at Skyline, right at Via Palametta into resort

Closest Commercial Airport: Tucson International (30 min.)

RESORT:

Date Built: 1986

No. of Rooms: 487, including 41 suites, 2 presidential suites

Meeting Rooms: 20. Capacity of Largest: 2100 persons. Meeting Space: 42,000 sq. ft.

Room Price Range: From $280 peak season (Jan. to May 23). From $89 during the lowest season (May 23 to early Sept.) Golf and other packages available

Lounges: Desert Garden Lounge, Cactus Club

Restaurants: Desert Garden, La Paloma Dining Room, La Villa, Sabinos, Courtside Deli, 19th Hole

Entertainment: Music in Desert Garden Lounge, various other areas

Credit Cards: All major cards

General Amenities: Complete meeting facilities with audiovisual and food services, therapeutic-massage and skin-care services, children's lounge, theme cookout areas, shopping arcade

Recreational Amenities: 12 tennis courts (10 with lights), pro shop, instruction; health club with Nautilus and Life Cycle equipment; aerobics classes, bicycling, croquet, table tennis, jogging, swimming pool, volleyball court, 3 therapy pools; 2 racquetball courts, horseback riding

Reservation and Cancellation Policy: 1 night's deposit required to hold reservation. Fully refundable if notice of cancellation received 15 days prior to arrival date

Comments and Restrictions: No pets. Room tax and sales tax additional to base rate

LA PALOMA COUNTRY CLUB

La Paloma, a Spanish word meaning "the Dove," is a 790-acre master-planned community, luxury resort, golf course, and country club situated at approximately 2500 feet in the high desert country in Tucson. The 27-hole Jack Nicklaus–designed golf course is a natural desert golf course without any water hazards.

The golf course itself is a target golf course that includes the Hill, Ridge and Canyon nines, whose names reflect their topography. These can be played in any combination, with the most difficult considered to be the Ridge/Canyon Course, which has a slope rating of 155 and a USGA rating of 75.4 from the back tees. The ability to select five possible tee distances on all of La Paloma's nines provides ample opportunity for any golfer to find his or her comfortable playing level. The Ridge starts off with a 381-yard par 4 straight over desert to a landing area protected by fairway bunkers on the right beginning 150 yards from the green, which is deep, narrow and protected by traps to the left and right. The tee shot provides a beautiful view of the Santa Catalina Mountains and the desert, which includes a variety of cacti with vivid names such as hedgehog, pincushion and prickly pear. From a golfer's point of view, you'll probably want to keep these at a distance.

The 411-yard par-4 second is a dogleg right playing from an elevated tee over mature vegetation to a landing area. The approach is to a contoured, hillside green angled right to left and protected by a large sand bunker and grassy hollows on the right. The 517-yard par-5 third can be reached in two with two big shots to a long, narrow green angled left to right and protected both left and right by traps. The 199-yard par-3 fourth begins a string of tough holes. Considered the most picturesque par 3 on the entire layout, it plays over a canyon floor to a large, long green protected left and right by traps. The 420-yard par-4 fifth hole is a dogleg left that challenges you to cut the dogleg guarded by a huge, long bunker.

The next hole is the number-1-handicap hole and a long par-4 dogleg left that plays 459 yards from the back tees. The fairway begins 225 yards from the tee, so consider it an achievement if you reach the landing area. The second shot is toward a deep green guarded on the right by a huge, long bunker that begins 130 yards from the green. The 171-yard par-3 seventh plays across a valley to a small hillside green, and the 436-yard par-4 eighth is a dogleg left guarded on the left by a long bunker running up the fairway to a green protected both left and right by traps. The closing hole on the front side is a 560-yard par 5 through a beautiful valley to a straight fairway and a green surrounded by deep, grassy mounds and hollows.

The Canyon Course presents several long, tough par 4s, with the last three holes providing a good test of golf. The 445-yard par-4 seventh is a dogleg right requiring 200 yards just to reach the fairway guarded by a major wash to the left and a sloping hill to the right. The second shot is toward a contoured green cut sharply into a hill-side and protected in front by a trap. The 211-yard par-3 eighth requires a long tee shot over natural vegetation and a huge bunker to a long green angled perpendicular to the tee, thus providing a shallow landing area. The closing hole is a 418-yard par-4 dogleg right protected by two left fairway bunkers 160 yards from a green protected by mounds and grass bunkers.

The Hill Course's toughest hole is the 467-yard par-4 fifth, which is a dogleg right requiring two excellent shots to reach the green in regulation. A trap and grassy hollows protect the green in front and to the right. A grassy swale guards the left side. The 419-yard par-4 sixth is downhill to an open landing area, leaving a scenic second shot across a native desert swale to a long, narrow green. Next is the number-2-handicap 538-yard par-5 seventh, which requires a 225-yard tee shot over native terrain to reach the fairway and an accurate second shot to leave a 75-yard wedge over a wash to a relatively small green. The finishing hole is a 415-yard par-4 dogleg right that has a long bunker beginning 200 yards from the tee and running along the landing area. The second shot is over a deep valley to a small green guarded by deep, grassy hollows.

La Paloma has been designated by *Golf Digest* as one of the best golf-resort courses in America, and it has won awards from *Golf Shop Operations* magazine, *Meetings and Conventions* magazine, and others. The 487 guest rooms at the resort are spread among 27 two-story complexes conveying a village-style atmosphere, and the architectural style is southwestern-mission-revival. Each guest room has a private exterior entrance and a private patio or balcony, and the 6 restaurants and snack bars provide a wide range of cuisine.

The 35,000-square-foot golf clubhouse is within easy walking distance of guest-room buildings and includes a pro shop, guest golf-bag storage area, men's and women's locker rooms, and the 19th Hole Lounge.

Course Name: LOEWS VENTANA CANYON RESORT
Canyon Course

Course Type: Resort
Resort: Loews Ventana Canyon Resort
Address: 7000 N. Resort Drive
Tucson, AZ 85715
Phone: (520) 577–1400 (Golf Course)
(520) 299–2020,
(800) 235–6397 (Resort)
Fax: (520) 299–6832 (Resort)

GOLF COURSE

Director of Golf: Steve Friedlander
Course Length/Par (All Tees): Back 6818/72, Gold 6282/72, Silver 5756/72, Forward 4919/72
Course Slope/Rating (All Tees): Back 136/74, Gold 129/71.3, Silver 124/68.9, Forward 120/69.3, Ladies' Silver NA/NA, Ladies' Forward 121/69.2
Course Architect: Tom Fazio (1988)
Golf Facilities: Full Pro Shop X, Snack Bar X, Lounge X, Restaurant X, Locker Room X, Showers X, Club Rental X, Club Repair X, Cart Rental X, Instruction X, Practice Green X, Driving Range X, Practice Bunker X, Club Storage X
Tee-Time Reservation Policy: Resort guests: 30 days in advance with groups of 8 or less. Public: 7 days in advance on space-available basis
Ranger: Yes

Tee-off-Interval Time: 10 min.
Time to Play 18 Holes: 4½ hrs.
Course Hours/Earliest Tee-off: 7:30 a.m.
Green and Cart Fees: Resort guests: $118 for 18 holes with cart. Public: $150 for 18 holes with cart
Credit Cards: American Express, Master-Card, Visa
Season: Year round. Busiest season Jan. through April
Course Comments: Cart mandatory. Yardage book available. Groups of 10 or more can arrange tournaments. Contact (520) 299-2020
Golf Packages: Available through resort
Discounts: Seasonal. Peak season Jan. through April. Lowest rates May to Sept.
Places to Stay Nearby: Courtyard by Marriott (520) 573–0000, (800) 321–2211; Sheraton Tucson El Conquistador Golf and Tennis Resort (520) 544–5000, (800) 325–7832; Westward Look Resort (520) 297–1151, (800) 722–2500; Doubletree Hotel (520) 881–4200, (800) 522–8733
Local Attractions: Old Tucson, Reid Park Zoo, Kitt Peak National Observatory, Colossal Cave, Mission San Xavier, Arizona State Museum, Arizona-Sonora Desert Museum, horseback riding, University of Arizona, Del Bac, Pima Air Museum, Titan Missile Museum, Tucson Mountain Park, Saguaro National Monument, Tucson Museum of Art, Arizona Historical Society/Tucson, Chiricahua National Monument, professional sports, shopping, theater, concerts, restaurants. Tombstone, AZ. Mexico. Metropolitan Tucson Convention and Visitors Bureau (520) 624-1817
Directions: I-10 to Ina Rd. exit, east on Ina Rd. to Skyline, which becomes Sunrise, to Kolb Rd. Turn left, follow Kolb Rd. to resort
Closest Commercial Airport: Tucson International (30 min.)

RESORT:

Date Built: 1984
No. of Rooms: 398, including 366 guest rooms, 24 suites

Meeting Rooms: 18. Capacity of Largest: 1000 persons. Meeting Space: 37,000 sq. ft.
Room Price Range: From $295 peak season from Jan. through May. From $125 lowest season from June through to Sept. A variety of golf, tennis, fitness and other packages available at lower rates
Lounge: Cascade Lounge
Restaurants: Canyon Cafe, Cascade, Flying V Bar and Grill, Ventana Room, Bill's Grill
Entertainment: Live music
Credit Cards: All major cards
General Amenities: Tennis pro shop, massage therapy, beauty-salon services for men and women, golf pro shop; meeting and conference facilities with full audiovisual, food service and secretarial-support capabilities
Recreational Amenities: Lakeside Spa and Tennis Club, jogging trail, heated lap pool, wet and dry saunas, Universal weight and cardiovascular exercise equipment, aerobics salon, 10 lighted tennis courts, tennis lessons, 2½-mile fitness trail, bicycling, hiking, walking, jogging
Reservation and Cancellation Policy: Credit card guarantee required. 48-hr. cancellation notice for full refund
Comments and Restrictions: No pets. State sales tax and room tax additional to base rates

LOEWS VENTANA CANYON RESORT

In the heart of Ventana Canyon overlooking Tucson, Loews Ventana Canyon is a 1000-acre luxury resort 3000 feet above sea level in the high Sonora Desert. The 330,000-square-foot 398-room hotel has been harmoniously designed to be compatible with the spectacular 9000-foot Santa Catalina Mountains nearby and the stunning desert, which features giant saguaro cacti, hackberry shrubs, brittle-brush, jumping cholla, prickly pear, squirrels, roadrunners, white-tailed deer, cottontail rabbits, and over 130 species of birds. An 80-foot canyon waterfall is also on the property.

There are two Tom Fazio–designed eighteen-hole championship golf courses at Loews Ventana, but only one, the Canyon, is accessible to those staying at Loews Ventana Canyon. The Mountain Course can be played by members and by those staying at the Ventana Golf and Racquet Club, which is also on the property. The Canyon Course was nominated in 1988 by *Golf Digest* as one of the best new golf resort courses in America, and *Meetings and Conventions* magazine has awarded the resort and course its Gold Tee Award as an outstanding golf conference resort. Loews Ventana has also won *Golf* magazine's Silver Medal Award as one of America's best golf resorts.

The par-72 Canyon Course plays 6818 yards from the back tees through the canyons, flats and crevasses of the Catalina foothills. The native desert borders most of the holes, which are unique and challenging tests of your game. The first hole is a 408-yard straight par 4 requiring a left-of-center tee shot, leaving a mid-iron to a flat green with trees to the right and a trap in back. The 483-yard par-5 second is a dogleg right reachable in two, but a grass bunker protects the green in front. The next three holes run through the canyon, beginning with a 401-yard downhill par 4 whose second shot is to a green that is deep and narrow but runs downhill to the rear. The 290-yard par-4 fourth hole has a tee shot over desert and a second shot that requires a deft wedge to a round, smallish green. The 148-yard par-3 fifth is short, beautiful and a potential nightmare if you miss to the left, right or rear, where desert and traps await you. The green is narrow, forward-sloping and almost 50 yards deep. The 464-yard par-4 sixth is long but downhill, requiring a right-of-center tee shot, then a well-struck second shot downhill to a deep green with a trap on the left.

The number-1-handicap 552-yard par-5 seventh is well protected down the left side by desert and bunkers, with mounds and bunkers protecting the right. A tee shot of approximately 225 yards or more is required to reach the fairway over desert terrain. The second shot should be straight toward a small, forward-sloping green protected to the right and rear by trees and bunkers. The par-3 eighth plays 182 yards downhill to a shallow, wide green squeezed in front by a huge trap and trees. The closing hole on this side is a 416-yard par 4 that plays straight over desert to a landing area protected by bunkers on the right, then uphill to a deep, narrow green trapped on the right and front.

The 336-yard par-4 tenth is downhill and should be played slightly left from the tee to enable you to come into a long, two-tiered, narrow green framed by a giant rock on the left, a large trap on the right and two smaller traps in front. The 463-yard par-4 eleventh plays downhill, with a second shot into a long, narrow, forward-sloping green trapped to the left. The next hole, a 574-yard par-5, is the number-2-handicap hole and requires two straight, long shots on an uphill and undulating fairway, with the third to another long, narrow green trapped to the left and right. Thirteen is a spectacular 158-yard par 3 overlooking the entire valley, with a tee shot over desert to a deep, two-tiered green with some room for error right and short, but desert, traps and trouble abound everywhere else. The 303-yard downhill par-4 fourteenth can be driven, but a shallow, extremely wide, radically sloping green can give you problems when you get there.

The fifteenth begins a run of four tough finishing holes. This 474-yard par 4 is downhill and should be played right-of-center off the tee to avoid a large left-fairway bunker beginning 175 yards from a deep, narrow green well protected to the left and rear by traps. The 221-yard par-3 sixteenth has desert, traps and trees to the left, right and rear, with a bailout area short of the deep green. The par-4 seventeenth plays 442 yards from the back tees over desert to a landing area flanked by fairway bunkers. The second shot is to a narrow green over 50 yards long and protected by trees both left and right, with a huge trap along its right flank.

The finishing hole is spectacular. This 503-yard par 5 requires a straight tee shot to a landing area flanked by desert. If you have a long tee shot and decide to go for the green you'll be looking at a wide, shallow target edged by water both back and right. A bunker is to the left and a gully is in front. Most players hit the second shot to a landing area 75 to 125 yards from the green. The next shot still leaves plenty of room for heroics or disaster. The green itself is two-tiered, with the lower tier located in the front part of the putting surface.

The nineteenth hole features the Flying V Bar and Grill, which is adjacent to the award-winning pro shop and overlooks the golf course. Private lessons, video lessons and clinics are available, and a complete practice facility is on site. The resort has a wide range of meeting facilities and amenities, including a variety of golf packages for groups. Loews Ventana Canyon Resort has won numerous hospitality awards including a *Mobil Travel Guide* Four-Star rating and the American Automobile Association's Four-Diamond Award. The Ventana Room restaurant has received an Award of Excellence from the *Wine Spectator* magazine. Given that it was opened only in 1986, Loews Ventana Canyon Resort has come a long way quickly, with critical acclaim in the areas of hospitality, golf, tennis, cuisine, meetings facilities, architecture, and environmental responsibility.

Course Name: **LOEWS VENTANA GOLF AND RACQUET CLUB Canyon, Mountain Courses**

Course Type: Resort
Resort: Ventana Golf and Racquet Club
Address: 6200 N. Clubhouse Lane
                     Tucson, AZ 85715
Phone: (520) 577–6258 (Golf Course)
                     (800) 828–5701 (Resort)
Fax: (520) 299–0256 (Resort)

GOLF COURSE

Director of Golf: Steve Friedlander
Course Length/Par (All Tees): Canyon: Back 6818/72, Gold 6282/72, Silver 5756/72, Forward 4919/72. Mountain: Back 6948/72, Gold 6356/72, Silver 5061/72, Forward 4789/72.

Course Slope/Rating (All Tees): Canyon: Back 136/74.0, Gold 129/71.3, Silver 124/68.9, Forward 120/69.3, Ladies' Forward 121/69.2. Mountain: Back 149/73.6, Gold 139/71.2, Silver 135/69.1, Forward 125/64.2, Ladies' Silver 129/73.7, Ladies' Forward 117/68.8

Course Architect: Mountain: Tom Fazio (1984), Canyon: Tom Fazio (1988)

Golf Facilities: Full Pro Shop X, Snack Bar X, Lounge X, Restaurant X, Locker Room X, Showers X, Club Rental X, Club Repair X, Cart Rental X, Instruction X, Practice Green X, Driving Range X, Practice Bunker X, Club Storage X

Tee-Time Reservation Policy: Canyon: 30 days in advance for guests, 7 days in advance for public. Mountain: 7 days in advance for members and their guests only

Ranger: Yes
Tee-off-Interval Time: 10 min.
Time to Play 18 Holes: 4½ hrs.
Course Hours/Earliest Tee-off: 6:30 a.m. summer (June through Aug.), 7 a.m. Sept. to May, 7:30 a.m. Oct.; 8 a.m. Nov. to Feb.

Green and Cart Fees: Guests: $118 for 18 holes with cart. Nonguests: $150 for 18 holes with cart

Credit Cards: American Express, Master-Card, Visa

Season: Year round. Busiest season Jan. to April 1

Course Comments: Cart mandatory. Yardage books available

Golf Packages: Available through resort

Discounts: Seasonal. Peak season Jan. to June. Lowest rates May to Sept. Group rates available

Places to Stay Nearby: Must be a Ventana Golf and Racquet Club guest to play the Mountain Course. Courtyard by Marriott (520) 573–0000, (800) 321–2211; Sheraton Tucson El Conquistador Golf and Tennis Resort (520) 544–5000, (800) 325–7832; Westward Look Resort (520) 297–1151, (800) 722–2500; Doubletree Hotel (520) 881–4200, (800) 222–8733

Local Attractions: Old Tucson, Reid Park Zoo, Kitt Peak National Observatory, Colossal Cave, Mission San Xavier, Arizona State Museum, Arizona-Sonora Desert Museum, horseback riding, University of Arizona, Del Bac, Pima Air Museum, Titan Missile Museum, Tucson Mountain Park, Saguaro National Monument, Tucson Museum of Art, Arizona Historical Society/Tucson, Chiricahua National Monument, professional sports, shopping, theater, concerts, restaurants. Tombstone, AZ. Mexico. Metropolitan Tucson Convention and Visitors Bureau (520) 624–1817

Directions: I–10, to Ina Rd. exit, east on Ina Rd. to Skyline, which becomes Sunrise, to Kolb Rd. Turn left, follow Kolb Rd. to resort

Closest Commercial Airport: Tucson International (30 min.)

RESORT:

Date Built: 1985
No. of Rooms: 48 luxury suites
Meeting Rooms: 2. Capacity of Largest: 70 persons. Meeting Space: 3000 sq. ft.
Room Price Range: Rates from $295 for 1 bedroom to $410 for 2 bedroom peak season. Rates from $115 for 1 bedroom to $175 for 2 bedroom lowest season. Various packages and seasonal rates available
Lounge: Fireside Lounge
Restaurants: Clubhouse Dining Room, Terrace Lounge and Patio, Flying V Restaurant (golf course)
Entertainment: At Loews Ventana resort
Credit Cards: All major cards
General Amenities: Beauty salon, nursing, babysitting services, executive and club meeting rooms, in-suite refreshment center stocked daily, golf and tennis sports shops
Recreational Amenities: 12 lighted, hard-surface tennis courts; heated swimming pool, children's wading pool; exercise room with Paramount equipment and Heartmate stationary cycles; sauna, steam, whirlpool, jogging/exercise course
Reservation and Cancellation Policy: Credit card guarantee required to hold reservation. 48-hr. cancellation policy to avoid penalty charges
Comments and Restrictions: No pets. 5 suites minimum per night for group rates. Room tax and sales tax additional to room rates. Children age 17 and under are free when sharing adult's room

LOEWS VENTANA GOLF AND RACQUET CLUB

The Ventana Golf and Racquet Club, which provides access to two Tom Fazio–designed championship golf courses, is situated on 1100 acres in the high Sonora Desert. The Santa Catalina Mountains form a dramatic background for this club, which has 48 luxurious rental suites available to individual, golf-package and conference guests. All Loews Ventana facilities are open to in-house guests because they are considered short-term members. *Golf* magazine has named both the Ventana Canyon Golf and Racquet Club and, separately, the 398-room Loews Ventana Canyon Resort, which is also on the property, winners of its Silver Medal Award for best golf resorts in America. The club has also received a Gold Tee Award as a premier golf conference center from *Meetings and Conventions* magazine. *Golf Shop Operations* has selected the Sports Shop at Ventana Canyon Golf and Racquet Club as one of the top 100 resort golf shops in America.

The 6818-yard par-72 Canyon Course opened in 1989 and is available to club members, resort guests, and the public. The course was named by *Golf Digest* as one of the top 5 new resort courses of 1988/89. (See Loews Ventana, pages 37–40, for description.)

Ventana Canyon takes its name from Canyon de la Ventana (Canyon of the Window), an opening in a large rock outcropping near the head of the canyon. On this course you will see a variety of plants and wildlife, including prickly pear, pincushion cactus, mesquite, coyote, deer, quail, rabbit, owl and many others. If you are a club member or club-suite guest, you have the option to play the Mountain Course, which was opened in 1984 and has been ranked among the best in the state of Arizona by

Golf Digest. This 6948-yard par-72 layout has also been the site of various PGA events.

The front nine features some tough par 4s, including the 454-yard seventh, which is the number-1-handicap hole. The tee shot plays 200 yards over desert to a narrow landing area. The approach is to a deep, narrow green protected by traps both left and right. This hole is sandwiched among four tough holes. The par-4 fifth plays 403 yards over water to a dogleg left fairway, then to a long, narrow green protected by trees and traps both left and right. The ideal is to place the tee shot to the right, but water awaits you in that area. The 249-yard par-3 sixth is just plain long, to a deep green tilting left to right, with a huge bunker to its left. The eighth is a 517-yard par-5 that plays straight to a medium-sized green, with a 40-yard wide hazard cutting the fairway from 150 yards into the green. The ninth is a 414-yard par 4 that is straight to a shallow green. One of the most beautiful holes on the front side is the 107-yard par-3 third, which Fazio calls "the shortest and most expensive par 3 I've ever designed." The desert view is spectacular, the green is small, and there is virtually no bailout from the desert engulfing this hole.

You'd better be accurate coming into the greens on the back nine because most of them are less than 20 yards wide. An accurate tee shot is required to set up approach shots that will take advantage of the depth of the putting surfaces. Pin position, of course, is another factor. The last two holes are challenging finishing holes, starting with the number-2-handicap 403-yard par-4 seventeenth. The second shot is into a left-to-right-angled, narrow green with a huge trap behind it. The fairway is lined with trees and desert all the way, as is the 589-yard par-5 finishing hole, which requires a long shot down the middle, a second shot to the left, and a third shot that avoids a huge, long, right-side bunker beginning 85 yards from the deep, narrow green.

There are few parallel fairways at Ventana Canyon, and the distances from green to the next tee give you complete privacy on these beautiful and challenging

desert golf courses. Complete practice facilities are available within walking distance of the suites. Individual and group instruction are available. Various golf packages are provided, with rates varying according to season.

The suites themselves have 1 or 2 bedrooms, each with its own living and dining area, full kitchen and private patio or balcony. The suites are rented like rooms in the nearby resort hotel, usually to guests of members, conference attendees or leisure-travel groups as part of golf or tennis packages.

The clubhouse, with its gigantic windows framing views of the mountains, the desert and golf course, contains lounge areas, card rooms, meeting and banquet facilities, men's and women's locker rooms and fine dining in the Clubhouse Dining Room.

All the amenities of the Loews Ventana Canyon Resort, described previously, are available to Ventana Golf and Racquet Club guests. The combination of these conference, recreation, and dining amenities set in a beautiful desert setting is a unique experience.

Course Name: STARR PASS GOLF CLUB

Course Type: Public
Address: 3645 W. Starr Pass Blvd.
               Tucson, AZ 85745
Phone: (520) 670–0400

GOLF COURSE

Director of Golf: Scott McGeachin

Course Length/Par (All Tees): Gold 6910/71, Blue 6193/71, White 5665/71, Forward 5071/71

Course Slope/Rating (All Tees): Gold 139/74.6, Blue 127/71.3, White 122/68.7, Ladies' Forward 121/70.7

Course Architects: Robert Cupp and Craig Stadler (1986)

Golf Facilities: Full Pro Shop X, Snack Bar X, Lounge X, Restaurant X, Locker Room X, Showers X, Club Rental X, Club Repair X, Cart Rental X, Instruction X, Practice Green X,

Driving Range X, Practice Bunker X, Club Storage X

Tee-Time Reservation Policy: Up to 30 days with credit card from 6:30 a.m. Group outings of 16 players or more anytime in advance

Ranger: Yes

Tee-off-Interval Time: 8 min.

Time to Play 18 Holes: 4½ hrs.

Course Hours/Earliest Tee-off: 6 a.m.

Green and Cart Fees: Peak season (Jan. to mid-April): $99 plus tax for 18 holes with cart. Lowest season June through Sept.

Credit Cards: American Express, Discover, MasterCard, Visa

Season: Year round. Busiest season Jan. to April

Course Comments: Cart mandatory. Golf academy on site. Clubhouse casitas on site (800) 503-2898

Golf Packages: Available

Discounts: Seasonal. Lowest rates mid-April to end of Sept.

Places to Stay Nearby: Best Western Inn at the Airport (520) 746–0271, (800) 528–1234; Courtyard by Marriott (520) 573–0000, (800) 321–2211; Doubletree Hotel (520) 881–4200, (800) 222–8733; Radisson Suite Hotel Tucson (520) 721–7100, (800) 333–3333; Sheraton Tucson El Conquistador Golf and Tennis Resort (520) 544–5000, (800) 325–7832

Local Attractions: Old Tucson, Reid Park Zoo, Kitt Peak National Observatory, Colossal Cave, Mission San Xavier, Arizona State Museum, Arizona-Sonora Desert Museum, horseback riding, University of Arizona, Del Bac, Pima Air Museum, Titan Missile Museum, Tucson Mountain Park, Saguaro National Monument, Tucson Museum of Art, Arizona Historical Society/Tucson, Chiricahua National Monument, professional sports, shopping, theater, concerts, restaurants. Tombstone, AZ. Mexico. Metropolitan Tucson Convention and Visitors Bureau (520) 624–1817

Directions: From I–10: Exit 259 to Starr Pass Blvd. Proceed 4 mi. west of I–10 on Starr Pass to golf course

Closest Commercial Airport: Tucson International (20 min.)

STARR PASS GOLF CLUB

Starr Pass Golf Club, formerly the TPC at Starr Pass, is a 6193-yard par-71 Robert Cupp–designed golf course situated on rolling terrain just a 20-minute drive from Tucson International Airport. Each fairway on this beautiful desert layout is an oasis in a sea of sand and desert foliage. Few people play the back tees; the blue tees, which measure 6193 yards over 18 holes, are enough to challenge anyone. Robert Cupp used PGA Tour player Craig Stadler as a consultant on Starr Pass.

The bentgrass greens at Star Pass are large, fast, and undulating. Inevitably they are protected by desert sand and strategically placed sand bunkers. The number-1-handicap hole on the course is the 506-yard par-5 fifth hole. The tee shot plays to a fairway bordered by desert, and the second shot is toward a deep green guarded by two traps on the left and a huge trough of desert that cuts down the right side of the green and across the fairway. If you go for the green in two shots, all kinds of trouble arises if you miss. Many golfers lay up to a plateau in front of the desert trough and hit a pitching wedge to the green on the third shot.

The signature hole at Starr Pass is the 350-yard par-4 fifteenth, which plays straight to a horseshoe-shaped green filled in front by a trap and backed with another one. The fairway narrows severely on the tee shot, so many golfers use long irons off the tee. If the approach shot is long, there is a sharp drop-off and desert trouble. This hole typifies the accuracy and strategic club selection required at Starr Pass.

Starr Pass Golf Club has a fully stocked golf shop; junior-Olympic pool with spa, locker-room facilities that include spas for both men and women, an exercise room, dining and banquet facilities, and a practice area that includes putting greens, practice bunkers and a driving range. Individual and group instruction are available from the staff of professionals and assistants. Group outings (minimum of 16 players) may be booked anytime in advance. The busiest season here is from January through April, and reduced seasonal rates are available at other times of the year.

Golf Digest rates Starr Pass one of the best courses in the state of Arizona. The Northern Telecom Tucson Open, a PGA Tour event, is played there every year. Nestled in the mountain foothills with beautiful views of the city of Tucson and the surrounding mountains, Starr Pass, with its etching of cactus, wildflowers and sagebrush, is an excellent public facility with championship playing conditions.

**Course Name: TUCSON NATIONAL
                  Orange, Gold,
                  Green Courses**

Course Type: Resort
Resort: Tucson National Golf
              Resort and Spa
Address: 2727 W. Club Drive
              Tucson, AZ 85741
Phone: (520) 297–2271 (Golf Course)
              (520) 297–2271,
              (800) 528–4856 (Resort)
Fax: (520) 742–2452 (Resort)

GOLF COURSE

Director of Golf: Paul Nolen
Course Length/Par (All Tees): Orange/ Gold: Back 7108/73, Middle 6549/73, Forward 5647/73. Gold/Green: Back 6860/73, Middle 6388/73, Forward 5442/73. Green/Orange: Back 6692/72, Middle 6215/72, Forward 5371/72
Course Slope/Rating (All Tees): Orange/Gold: Back 136/74.9, Middle 122/71, Ladies' Forward 123/72.4. Gold/Green: Back 135/74.7, Middle 121/70.9, Ladies' Forward 118/71. Green/Orange: Back 134/74.6, Middle 120/70.2, Ladies' Forward 117/70.3
Course Architects: Robert Bruce Harris (18 holes, 1963), Bruce Devlin and Robert von Hagge (remodeled 18 holes, added 9 holes, 1979)
Golf Facilities: Full Pro Shop X, Snack Bar X, Lounge X, Restaurant X, Locker Room X, Showers X, Club Rental X, Club Repair Minor, Cart Rental X, Instruction X, Practice Green X, Driv-

ing Range X, Practice Bunker X, Club Storage X
Tee-Time Reservation Policy: Resort guests: Up to 30 days in advance. Public: Up to 2 days in advance
Ranger: Yes
Tee-off-Interval Time: 8 min.
Time to Play 18 Holes: 4 hrs., 15 min.
Course Hours/Earliest Tee-off: 7 a.m.
Green and Cart Fees: Peak season rates Jan. through April: Resort guests: $125 for 18 holes with cart. Nonguests: $150 for 18 holes with cart
Credit Cards: All major cards
Season: Year round. Busiest season Jan. to mid-May
Course Comments: Cart mandatory. Golf school on site
Golf Packages: Available through resort
Discounts: Resort guests. Seasonal. 9-hole rates discounts
Places to Stay Nearby: Courtyard by Marriott (520) 573–0000, (800) 321–2211; Sheraton Tucson El Conquistador Golf and Tennis Resort (520) 544–5000, (800) 325–7832; Westward Look Resort (520) 297–1151, (800) 722–2500; Doubletree Hotel (520) 881–4200, (800) 222–8733
Local Attractions: Tucson Children's Museum, Arizona Historical Society Museum, horseback riding, skiing, theater and concerts, sporting events, Old Tucson, Reid Park Zoo, Kitt Peak National Observatory, Colossal Cave, Mission San Xavier, Tucson Museum of Art, Arizona Historical Society/Tucson, Chiricahua National Monument. Tombstone, AZ. Mexico. Metropolitan Tucson Convention and Visitors Bureau (520) 624–1817
Directions: I–10 to exit 246/Cortaro Rd., east on Cortaro 3½ mi. to Shannon, left on Shannon. North on Shannon to resort on the right
Closest Commercial Airport: Tucson International (30 min.)

RESORT:

Date Built: 1961
No. of Rooms: 167 villas and suites, including 24 executive casitas

Meeting Rooms: 13. Capacity of Largest: 350 persons. Meeting Space: 15,000 sq. ft.

Room Price Range: $275 to $350 per night peak season (Jan. through Apr.). Golf packages available year round

Restaurants: Fiesta Dining Room, Poolside Cabana, Legends Bar and Grille, Catalina Grille

Lounges: Fiesta Dining Room Lounge, Cabana

Entertainment: Piano or other live music

Credit Cards: All major cards except Discover

General Amenities: Babysitting services, meeting and conference facilities including audiovisual and food services

Recreational Amenities: Tennis center with 4 lighted tennis courts, 2 heated swimming pools, fully equipped gymnasium with exercise equipment, sand volleyball court, Jacuzzi; 14,000-sq.-ft. health spa with gymnasium, physical-fitness evaluation and body-composition analysis; massage, facials, weight-training programs, manicures, pedicures, make-up consultation and other amenities

Reservation and Cancellation Policy: Credit card guarantee required to hold reservation. 72-hr. cancellation notice required to avoid penalties

Comments and Restrictions: No pets allowed. Taxes additional to base rates

TUCSON NATIONAL

Tucson National's first 18 holes were designed by Robert Bruce Harris and built in the early 1960s, when Tucson National was a private club. Bruce Devlin and Robert von Hagge remodeled the original course and added another 9 in the late 1970s. Now Tucson National is open to the public but also has slightly more than 300 private members.

Tucson National's nines are the Orange, Gold, and Green courses. The Orange and Gold combination plays 7108 yards (par 73) from the back tees and has been rated one of America's 75 best resort courses by *Golf Digest.* Seven lakes dot this layout, which features fast, well-bunkered bentgrass greens. The putting surfaces

vary in size from small to more than 40 yards deep, depending on the length, design and strategy required for the hole. The courses are traditionally laid out, with no native desert in front of the tee boxes, but water hazards and well-placed fairway bunkers add to the difficulty of Tucson National.

The finishing holes on the Orange and Gold nines are among the most difficult and memorable on this course. The 438-yard par-4 ninth on the Orange Course requires an accurate tee shot to a small landing area to the left of a lake and to the right of a row of trees. The approach shot is to a large green that slopes from back right to front left and has a bunker directly in front.

The 439-yard par-4 ninth on the Gold Course plays very long because it is uphill and the wind is usually in the golfer's face. The tee shot is over the edge of a lake to the right. The second shot is to a large green with bunkers left, rear and to the right.

The Green Course flows through hills above the resort. It has narrower fairways and is more of a position golf course than the other two nines. The 374-yard dogleg left par-4 sixth hole plays to a narrow fairway landing area with out-of-bounds to the left and right off the tee. The approach is severely uphill to a deep green. If the pin is placed to the rear of the green, the flag is not visible when hitting your second shot to the target. Another tough hole on this nine is the 542-yard par-5 third, the number-1-handicap hole. The fairway is narrow on this hole, requiring you to hit two back-to-back long, accurate shots to be around the green. The putting surface is well-guarded by traps to the right and left.

The clubhouse at Tucson National has a pro shop, restaurant, bar and snack bar. Resort guests have access to locker rooms and showers. The public can use the locker room and shower facilities at the nearby spa for a minor fee. The practice facilities at Tucson National are excellent. Individual and group instruction is available from the staff of PGA professionals. Golf packages are available year round, with peak season from early January to May.

A separate 14,000-square-foot European-style luxury spa facility includes a fully-equipped gymnasium in both the men's and women's spas, aerobics classes, Finnish saunas, massages, hydrotherapy pools and other amenities. Swimming, tennis, volley-ball and other recreational activities are also available. On site is a 15,000-square-foot conference center with a variety of meeting rooms in theater-style, banquet, board-room and classroom configurations. *Meetings and Conventions* magazine has awarded Tucson National a Golden Tee Award for its excellent golf and conference facilities.

The resort has 167 deluxe villa suites, each with a private balcony or patio overlooking the golf course. Its Fiesta Dining Room features a variety of dishes ranging from steak and seafood to Mexican cuisine. The resort is situated on 650 acres of high chaparral desert, with magnificent views of the Santa Catalina Mountains. It has received a Four-Star Award from the *Mobil Travel Guide.*

Recommended Golf Courses in Arizona

Within 1 Hour of Tucson:

Canoa Hills Golf Course, Green Valley, (520) 648–1880, Semiprivate, 18/6610/72

Fred Enke Golf Course, Tucson, (520) 296–8607, Public, 18/6807/72

Pueblo del Sol Golf Course, Sierra Vista, (520) 378–6444, Public, 18/6880/72

Randolph Park Golf Course, Tucson, (520) 325–2811, Public. North: 18/6902/72, South 18/6229/70

Rio Rico Country Club, Rio Rico, Resort, (520) 281–8567, (800) 288–4746, 18/7119/72

San Ignacio Golf Club, Green Valley, (520) 648–3468, Public, 18/6704/72

Sheraton Tucson El Conquistador Golf and Tennis Resort, Tucson, (520) 544–1800, (800) 325–7832, Resort, Sunrise: 18/6819/72. Sunset: 18/6723/72

Tubac Golf Resort, Tubac, (520) 398–2211, (800) 848–7893, Resort, 18/6957/72

Fort Mohave:

Desert Lakes Golf Course, Fort Mohave, (602) 768–1000, Public, 18/6537/72

Lake Havasu City Area:

Emerald Canyon Golf Course, Parker, (602) 667–3366, Public, 18/6657/72

London Bridge Golf Course, Lake Havasu City, (602) 855–2719, Public. London Bridge: 18/6618/71. Stonebridge: 18/6166/71

Nautical Inn, Lake Havasu City, (602) 855–2141, Resort, 18/4022/61

Yuma:

Desert Hills Municipal Golf Course, Yuma, (602) 344–4653, Public, 18/6853/72

Arizona: Useful Information

Arizona Office of Tourism, 2702 N. Third St., Phoenix, AZ 85204, (602) 248–1480, (800) 842–8257

Phoenix and Valley of the Sun Convention and Visitors Bureau, 1 Arizona Center, 400 East Van Buren St., Phoenix, AZ 85004–2290, (602) 254-6500

Metropolitan Tucson Convention and Visitors Bureau, 130 S. Scott Ave., Tucson, AZ 85701, (520) 624–1817

Grand Canyon Visitor Center, (520) 638-7888

Grand Canyon National Park Lodges, Box 699, Grand Canyon, AZ 86023, (520) 638–2401

National Forest Service, Southwestern Region, Public Affairs Office, 517 Gold Ave. SW, Albuquerque, NM 87102, (505) 842–3292 (national forest information)

Game and Fish Commission, 222 W. Greenway Rd., Phoenix, AZ 85023, (602) 942–3000 (fishing and hunting regulations)

Arizona State Parks, 800 W. Washington St., Ste. 415, Phoenix, AZ 85007, (602) 542–4174 (recreation information)

Course Name: MOUNTAIN RANCH
GOLF COURSE

Course Type: Resort
Resort: Fairfield Bay Resort
Address: P.O. Box 3008
Fairfield Bay, AR 72088
Phone: (501) 884–3400 (Golf Course)
(501) 884–3333 (Resort)
Fax: (501) 884–3345 (Resort)

GOLF COURSE

Head Professional: Tim Jenkins
Course Length/Par (All Tees): Back
6780/72, White 6280/72, Gold
5760/72, Forward 5325/72
Course Slope/Rating (All Tees): Back
134/71.8, White 126/69.6, Gold
NA/NA, Ladies' Forward 121/69.8
Course Architect: Edmund B. Ault (1984)
Golf Facilities: Full Pro Shop X, Snack
Bar X, Lounge X, Restaurant X,
Locker Room X, Showers X, Club
Rental X, Club Repair X, Cart Rental
X, Instruction X, Practice Green X,
Driving Range X, Practice Bunker X,
Club Storage X
Tee Time Reservation Policy: 14 days in
advance unless conference group.
Tournament 1 yr. in advance
Ranger: Yes
Tee-off-Interval Time: 7 and 8 min.
Time to Play 18 Holes: 4½ hours
Course Hours/Earliest Tee-off: 7 a.m.
Green Fees: Peak rates May to Aug.: $28
for 18 holes, $17.50 for 9 holes
Cart Fees: $20 for 18 holes per cart
Pull Carts: Not rented. Allowed when
walking
Credit Cards: All major cards except Diners
Club
Season: Year round. Busiest season May to
Aug.
Course Comments: Can walk after 2 p.m.,
but due to elevation changes carts usu-
ally desirable. Yardage book available
Golf Packages: Available through resort
Discounts: Memberships through property,
time-share ownership. Seasonal discounts
Places to Stay Nearby: HEBER SPRINGS:
Lake and River Inn (501) 362–3161;
Colonial Motor Inn (501) 362–5846;
Red Apple Inn and Country Club (501)
362–3111; MOUNTAIN VIEW: Lodge at
Ozark Folk Center (501) 264–3871
Local Attractions: Indian rock house, boating, fishing, horseback riding, Blanchard
Springs Caverns, Greers Ferry dam and
fish hatchery, Little Red River, Ozark
Mountain Folk Center, Wiederkehr wine
cellars. Fairfield Bay Chamber of Com-
merce (501) 884-3324. Clinton Chamber
of Commerce (501) 745–8110. Greers
Ferry Chamber of Commerce (501) 825–
7188
Directions: From Little Rock (85 mi.
north): Hwy. 65 north 40 mi. to Hwy.
16, turn right, follow Hwy. 16 east to
entrance of resort at Fairfield Bay
Closest Commercial Airports: Little Rock
Regional (90 min.); Memphis International, TN (3 hrs.)

RESORT

Date Built: 1966
No. of Rooms: 220 time-share condomini-
ums, 45 rental units
Meeting Rooms: 10. Capacity of Largest:
550 persons. Meeting Space: 6500 sq. ft.
Room Price Range: $59 for 1 bedroom.
Villas also available for rent. Busiest
season Apr. through Oct.
Lounges: Country Club, Racquet Club
Restaurants: Bogies (Country Club), mall
restaurants (6 eating establishments),
Racquet Club, Grandma's Oven
Entertainment: Live entertainment
Credit Cards: All major cards
General Amenities: Tennis pro shop,
shopping mall with 35 retail outlets
Recreational Amenities: Tennis center
with 12 tennis courts, instruction; 5
swimming pools, fishing, water-skiing,
fishing guides, bowling alley, horseback
riding, marina, scuba diving, miniature
golf, volleyball, health club (3000 sq.
ft.) with sauna
Reservation and Cancellation Policy:
Advance deposit of 1 night's lodging
required and should accompany reservation requests. Cancellations received 10
days before scheduled arrival date subject to a refund

Comments and Restrictions: No pets allowed. Taxes additional to base rates

MOUNTAIN RANCH GOLF COURSE

Mountain Ranch is an Edmund B. Ault–designed golf course within a time-share and rental resort real-estate development, Fairfield Bay, approximately 85 miles north of Little Rock. Nearby is 40,000-acre Greers Ferry Lake in this recreational area in the foothills of the beautiful Ozark Mountains. Fairfield Bay has a population of over 3000 residents from most of the fifty states. Approximately 60,000 people annually visit the resort area, which features fishing, swimming and a variety of boating activities on Greers Ferry Lake as well as tennis, horseback riding, camping, hiking and other activities. Hunting and fishing are popular at the lake, where some of the best walleye fishing in North America can be found. Other fish prevalent here are black bass, rock bass, crappie, catfish, white bass, bream, trout, striped bass, and smallmouth bass. Game includes deer, dove, quail, rabbit, squirrel and turkey. There are over 1250 campsites around the lake.

But if it's golf you're after, Mountain Ranch Golf Course is the place. The front nine is somewhat open, with rolling fairways, rock outcroppings, and the course's only water hazard. The back nine is tightly treed with Southern pine and hardwood trees including dogwoods, which are especially beautiful in the spring. The greens are somewhat large, and many of them are tiered. There are over 70 bunkers on Mountain Ranch, which places a premium on accuracy and club selection.

The number-1-handicap hole on the course is the 405-yard par-4 fifth, a dogleg to the left, which plays uphill to a deep, two-tiered green with a trap on the left and right. Two well-placed fairway bunkers are to the left of the landing area, and the fairway, because of its uphill slope, makes this hole play very long. The fifth hole is considered one of the best holes in the state of Arkansas, as is the 395-yard par-4 fifteenth, which plays straight up a tree-lined fairway to a wide, shallow, two-

tiered green guarded by three traps in front and one in back. The tee shot is uphill, and club selection on the second shot is crucial because of the shallow, well-protected target. The higher shelf on the green is to the right and is approximately 4 feet higher than the lower shelf, so pin position can make a big difference here.

Elevation changes can be very dramatic at Mountain Ranch, a factor in its beauty and in its difficulty. The 560-yard par-5 fourteenth is a dogleg right with a drop of 150 feet from the tee to the fairway below. The fairway slopes from left to right, so chances are you'll be trying to hit a fade with the ball above your feet on the second shot. The deep, narrow green is not easy to see because it is up on a higher slope to your right.

A tough par 3 at Mountain Ranch is the 200-yard sixteenth, which plays over a gorge to a multitiered cloverleaf green protected by five traps. There are three distinct, flat shelves on this beautiful green, making it easy to three-putt. The seventeenth hole is a 440-yard par 4 that plays slightly right to a shallow, wide, two-tiered green guarded by three traps in front. Three fairway bunkers are to the right of the landing area on this well-treed hole. The finishing hole is a 540-yard par 5 with a blind tee shot that has to avoid four bunkers left and right of the landing area. The second shot is down toward a two-tiered green well guarded by two traps on its left front and two traps to its right.

There are three tee distances on the Mountain Ranch Golf Course, and Gold tees whose distance will be 5760 yards are due to be completed soon. The resort conference center offers a variety of group and other golf packages. Mountain Ranch also has very low seasonal discounts. The course is open to the public, and you can rent a condominium or house here or stay at a variety of motels or campsites in the area.

A recommended local attraction is the Ozark Mountain Folk Center, which offers examples of authentic crafts and features dance and various musical events in its

1043-seat auditorium. The Mountain Ranch Golf Course has a full service restaurant, Bogies, as well as a full pro shop, men's and women's locker rooms, club rental, and full practice facilities including individual instruction from the staff of professionals. The golf course is ranked by *Golf Digest* as one of the top 5 in the state of Arkansas.

Recommended Golf Courses in Arkansas

Within 1½ Hours of Little Rock:

Belvedere Country Club, Hot Springs, (501) 623–2305, Semiprivate, 18/6770/72

Degray State Park Golf Course, Bismarck, (501) 865–2807, Public, 18/6930/72

Hindman Park Golf Course, Little Rock, (501) 565–6450

Hot Springs Golf and Country Club, Hot Springs, (501) 623–4981, Resort. Majestic: 18/6715/72. Arlington: 18/6646/72. Pineview: 9/2929/34

Longhills Golf Club, Benton, (501) 794–9907, 18/6539/72

Red Apple Inn and Country Club, Heber Springs, (501) 362–3111, (800) 255–8900, Resort, 18/6450/71

Within 1½ Hours of Fort Smith:

Ben Geren Golf Course, Ft. Smith, (501) 646–5301, Public, 18/6782/72

Dawn Hill Golf and Racquet Club, Siloam Springs, (501) 524–4838, Resort, 18/6852/72

Paradise Valley Athletic Club, Fayetteville, (501) 521–5841, Semiprivate, 18/6950/71

Prairie Creek Country Club, Rogers, (501) 925–2414, Semiprivate, 18/6707/72

Within 1 Hour of Jonesboro:

Cherokee Village Golf Club, Cherokee Village, North: (501) 257–3430, South: (501) 257–2555, Resort. North: 18/6687/72. South: 18/7058/72

Arkansas: Useful Information

Arkansas Department of Parks and Tourism, 1 Capitol Mall, Little Rock, AR 72201, (800) 643–8383

Little Rock Convention and Visitors Bureau, Statehouse Plaza, P.O. Box 3232, Little Rock, AR 72203, (501) 376–4781

Game and Fish Commission, 2 Natural Resources Dr., Little Rock, AR 72205, (501) 223–6300 (fishing and hunting regulations)

U.S. Forest Service, Southern Region, 1720 Peachtree St. NW, Atlanta, GA 30367, (404) 347–2384 (U.S. Forest Service information)

Course Name: ANCIL HOFFMAN

Course Type: Public
Address: 6700 Tarshes
Carmichael, CA 95608
Phone: (916) 482–5660

GOLF COURSE

Head Professional: Steve Price
Course Length/Par (All Tees): Back 6794/72, Middle 6434/72, Ladies' Forward 5954/73
Course Slope/Rating (All Tees): Back 128/72.8, Middle 119/71.0, Ladies' Forward 123/73.4
Course Architect: William F. Bell (1965)
Golf Facilities: Full Pro Shop X, Snack Bar X, Lounge X, Restaurant X, Locker Room No, Showers No, Club Rental X, Club Repair X, Cart Rental X, Instruction X, Practice Green X, Driving Range X, Practice Bunker X, Club Storage X
Tee-Time Reservation Policy: 1 wk. in advance from Mon., 6:30 a.m. for weekend tee times
Ranger: Yes
Tee-off-Interval Time: 7 min.
Time to Play 18 Holes: 4½ hrs.
Course Hours/Earliest Tee-off: Sunrise to sunset
Green Fees: Non-residents: $23.75 for 18 holes Sat., Sun., holidays; $20 for 18 holes weekdays
Cart Fees: $20 for 18 holes Sat., Sun., holidays; $11 for 9 holes
Credit Cards: Cash or local checks for golf fees. MasterCard, Visa for merchandise only
Season: Year round
Course Comments: Can walk anytime
Golf Packages: None
Discounts: Seniors (county senior card only), juniors
Places to Stay Nearby: SACRAMENTO: Sheraton (Rancho Cordova) (916) 638–1100; Red Lion's Sacramento Inn (916) 922–8041; Holiday Inn Capitol Plaza (916) 446–0100, (800) HOLIDAY; Hyatt Regency (916) 443–1234; Hotel El Rancho Resort (916) 371–6731, (800) 952–5566; Best Western Harbor Inn and Suites (916) 371–2100, (800) 528–1234
Local Attractions: University of California —Davis; state fair, Crocker Art Museum, state capitol building, Old Sacramento, State Indian Museum, California State Railroad Museum, Sutter's Fort, Napa Valley wine tours. Lake Tahoe. Old Sacramento Visitors Center (916) 442–7644. Sacramento Convention and Visitors Bureau (916) 449–6711
Directions: Take Business 80 to El Camino, east on El Camino to California St., left to golf course
Closest Commercial Airports: Sacramento Metropolitan (40 min.), Oakland International (1½ hrs.), San Francisco International (2 hrs.)

ANCIL HOFFMAN

Ancil Hoffman Golf Course is a 6794-yard par-72 layout situated on the American River near Sacramento. The rolling, well-treed course is in a picturesque river-valley park setting with a bluff surrounding the course. Ancil Hoffman was designed by William F. Bell, a native Californian, who designed many municipal golf courses in the state, including both the North and South courses at Torrey Pines in La Jolla, the Palo Alto Golf Course, and the Victoria Golf Course in Carson. Ancil Hoffman was named after a longstanding local resident and member of the county board of supervisors. At one time, the late Ancil Hoffman managed Max Baer, the heavyweight boxing champion.

Huge oak trees and pine trees protect many of the fairways on Ancil Hoffman, which is former farmland. The greens tend to be medium sized or small, with subtle undulations and strategically placed traps. It is important to be accurate off the tee because of these obstacles. On most holes, it is possible to run the ball up onto the greens which are not heavily trapped in front. This is a traditional golf course with no gimmick holes.

On the front side, one of the tougher holes is the 438-yard par-4 sixth, which plays straight down a tightly treed fairway to a forward-sloping, medium-sized green protected on the left, back and right front by traps. The tee shot has to carry over 200 yards to avoid a deep swale in the fairway. The 583-yard par-5 seventh is the number-1-handicap hole, requiring two long, straight shots down a well-treed, flat fairway. This leaves a wedge to a wide-open green. The finishing hole on this side is a 197-yard par 3 that plays to a forward-sloping, large green trapped left front.

The most difficult hole on the course is the 449-yard par-4 sixteenth, which has a huge oak tree in the left fairway 200 yards from the tee. Some golfers go over the top of the tree with a three wood and hit a long iron to the forward-sloping, well-trapped green. The 440-yard twelfth hole is another difficult par 4; it is a slight dogleg left, has a heavily treed right, and is intermittently treed along the left side. This hole sometimes plays into the wind, especially during the winter months, making it difficult to reach the green, trapped left and right, in regulation.

Ancil Hoffman is regularly ranked among the top 75 public golf courses in America by *Golf Digest*, and its pro shop has been listed among the top 100 public golf course pro shops several times by *Golf Shop Operations* magazine. The course is heavily played, partly due to the dearth of quality public golf facilities in the Sacramento area. The first tee-off is at sunrise, and you can walk anytime. A driving range, practice green, practice bunker and professional instruction are available. Events such as the Sacramento County Championships and the USGA Women's Mid-Amateur qualifying events have been held here, attesting to the quality of the layout.

Course Name: PLUMAS LAKE

Course Type: Semiprivate
Address: 1551 Country Club Road
            Marysville, CA 95901
Phone: (916) 742–3201

GOLF COURSE

Head Professional: Pat Gould
Course Length/Par (All Tees): Back 6400/71, Middle 6153/71, Forward 5759/72

Course Slope/Rating (All Tees): Back 122/70.5, Middle 120/69.3, Ladies' Forward 126/73.2
Course Architects: Donald McKee (9 holes, 1928), Bob Baldock (added 9 holes and redesigned 9 holes, 1962)
Golf Facilities: Full Pro Shop X, Snack Bar X, Lounge X, Restaurant X, Locker Room X, Showers Men, Club Rental X, Club Repair X, Cart Rental X, Instruction X, Practice Green X, Driving Range X, Practice Bunker X, Club Storage Members
Tee-Time Reservation Policy: Up to 7 days in advance from 7 a.m. Members have reserved tee times Sat., Sun., holidays 7:30 to 11 a.m. If tee times not filled, public can play
Ranger: Yes
Tee-off-Interval Time: 8 min.
Time to Play 18 Holes: 4½ hrs.
Course Hours/Earliest Tee-off: Sunrise to sunset
Green Fees: $20 for 18 holes Fri., Sat., Sun., holidays; $15 for 18 holes Mon. to Thurs. $11 for 9 holes Fri., Sat., Sun., holidays; $8 for 9 holes Mon. to Thurs.
Cart Fees: $18 for 18 holes, $10 for 9 holes. Pull Carts: $2 for 18 holes
Credit Cards: Cash or check for golf fees. MasterCard, Visa for merchandise
Season: Year round
Course Comments: Can walk anytime. Open year round
Golf Packages: None
Discounts: Twilight rate from 1 p.m. winter, 3 p.m. summer
Place to Stay Nearby: GRASS VALLEY: Murphy's Inn (916) 273–6873. SACRAMENTO: Holiday Inn Capital Plaza (916) 446–0100, (800) HOLIDAY; Hyatt Regency (916) 443–1234, (800) 233–1234; Hotel El Rancho Resort (916) 371–6731, (800) 952–5566. YUBA CITY: Best Western (916) 674–8824, (800) 528–1234
Local Attractions: Sutter's Buttes, fishing, rodeo, camping, boating, Mary Aaron Museum. SACRAMENTO: California State Railroad Museum, Old Sacramento, Crocker Art Museum, State Indian Museum, state capitol building, Sutter's Fort, Napa Valley wine tours. Lake Tahoe. Mendocino.

Yuba-Sutter Chamber of Commerce (916) 743–6501. Sacramento Convention and Visitors Bureau (916) 449–6711

Directions: From Sacramento (35 min.): I–5 to Hwy. 70 exit (Marysville/Yuba City), north on Hwy. 70, about 4 mi. north of East Nicholas, over bridge to Feather River Blvd., left on Feather River Blvd. 6.3 mi. to Country Club Rd. to golf course

Closest Commercial Airports: Sacramento Metropolitan (35 min.), Oakland International (2½ hrs.), San Francisco International (3 hrs.)

PLUMAS LAKE

The Plumas Lake Golf and Country Club is a 6400-yard par-71 traditional, strategic golf course located 40 minutes north of Sacramento, near Yuba City. The original nine was designed by Donald McKee and completed in 1928. Bob Baldock redesigned an 18-hole course in 1962, integrating the old course with the new nine. Plumas Lake is heavily treed, with small, fast, flat, well-conditioned greens. Most holes on this flat layout are trapped around the greens, but there are few fairway bunkers.

The course starts out with a 421-yard par 4 straight to a medium-sized green trapped both left and right. The succeeding holes are straightforward until you reach a run of difficult holes from the number-1-handicap eighth to the difficult fourteenth. The eighth is a 408-yard par-4 dogleg left with a huge live oak in the fairway 100 yards from the green. A poorly placed drive forces you to go over this tree to reach a small green trapped on the left and right. The ninth is a straight, 340-yard par 4, but three oak trees in the middle of the fairway can stymie the golfer's second shot.

The 486-yard par-5 tenth is straight, with a large ditch running along the right side and across the fairway near a tight, small green trapped on the left and right. Trees guard the left side of the fairway, and it is often difficult to reach the green in two. Placement of the tee shot and avoiding the ditch crossing the fairway on the second shot is critical. The 374-yard par-4 eleventh is a dogleg left uphill to a green

with a trap to the right front. The tee shot should be hit to the right center of the fairway to avoid the overhanging trees on the left. The par-4 twelfth is the most difficult hole on the back nine. It plays 433 yards straight to a large green protected by traps on both sides. Two long, accurate shots are required to reach this green in regulation.

The 219-yard par-3 thirteenth plays longer than it seems because it is uphill to a green that has to be reached on the fly. The 424-yard par-4 fourteenth is straight down a corridor of trees to a green trapped both left and right. The back nine concludes with a straight 501-yard par 5, a 162-yard par 3, a 335-yard straight par 4, and a slight dogleg-left 332-yard par 4.

Baldock, Plumas Lake's designer, born in Omaha, Nebraska, in 1908, became a Class A PGA golfer and worked for golf architect William P. Bell before starting his own design firm. He designed or remodeled more than 350 golf courses and built several in California, including many with his son, Robert L. Baldock. A few of his designs are Horse Thief Golf and Country Club in Tehachapi with Robert L. Baldock; Swallow's Nest, a par-3 golf course in Sacramento; Valley Gardens Country Club in Santa Cruz with Robert L. Baldock, and Heather Farms in Walnut Creek.

The California State Amateur qualifier was held at Plumas Lake in 1992. It is a popular golf facility providing a solid, traditional golf challenge on a mature, well-designed layout. You can walk the golf course anytime. The green fees are reasonable, and *Golf* magazine has recommended the course among its "50 Best Bangs for The Buck in Public Golf" courses in the United States.

Course Name: SQUAW CREEK GOLF CLUB

Course Type: Resort
Resort: Resort at Squaw Creek
Address: 400 Squaw Creek Road
Squaw Valley, CA 94616
Phone: (916) 583–6300 (Golf Course)
(800) 327–3353 (Resort)
Fax: (916) 581–5407 (Resort)

GOLF COURSE

Director of Golf: Mancil Davis

Head Professional: Bob Hickam

Course Length/Par (All Tees): Back: 6931/71, Blue 6453/71, White 6010/71, Forward 5297/71

Course Slope/Rating (All Tees): Back 140/72.9, Blue 132/70.9, White 129/69.1, Forward 127/68.9

Course Architect: Robert Trent Jones, Jr. with Kyle Phillips (1992)

Golf Facilities: Full Pro Shop X, Snack Bar X, Lounge X, Restaurant X, Locker Room X, Showers X, Club Rental X, Club Repair X, Cart Rental X, Instruction X, Practice Green X, Driving Range X, Practice Bunker X, Club Storage X

Tee-Time Reservation Policy: At time of confirmed resort reservations. The public may call anytime to arrange a tee time. 48-hr. cancellation policy

Ranger: Yes

Tee-off-Interval Time: 10 min.

Time to Play 18 Holes: 4½ hrs.

Course Hours/Earliest Tee-off: 7 a.m.

Green and Cart Fees: $110 for 18 holes Fri., Sat., Sun., holidays; $100 for 18 holes weekdays with or without cart

Credit Cards: All major cards

Season: May through Oct. Busiest July through Labor Day

Course Comments: Walking permitted. Caddies available. Yardage book

Golf Packages: Through resort

Discounts: Twilight rates from 3:30 p.m. Seasonal discounts prior to July and after Labor Day

Places to Stay Nearby: Northstar-at-Tahoe (916) 562–1010, (800) GO–NORTH; Squaw Valley Inn (916) 583–1576, (800) 323–7666

Local Attractions: See page 425

Directions: From Reno-Tahoe International, NV (42 mi.): Take I–80 west to Rte. 89 South Exit. Proceed south on Rte. 89 ten mi. to resort entrance

Closest Commercial Airport: Reno-Tahoe International, NV (45 min.)

RESORT

Date Built: 1990

No. of Rooms: 405 rooms including 200 suites

Meeting Rooms: 26. Capacity of Largest: 950 persons reception-style. Meeting Space: 33,000 sq. ft.

Room Price Range: Regular room rates from $250, suite rooms from $350. Golf and other packages available

Lounges: Bullwhackers Pub

Restaurants: Cascades, Glissandi, Ristorante Montagna, Sun Plaza Deck, Sweet Potatoes Deli

Entertainment: Live music

Credit Cards: All major cards

General Amenities: Promenade boutiques, gambling, and nightlife at nearby Reno, Nevada's north and south shores; children's program for ages 3 to 13

Recreational Amenities: Hiking, camping, fishing, boating, Peter Burwash International Tennis Center with 2 Har-tru courts, 3 swimming pools, waterslide, executive fitness center with stationary bicycles, weights, Stairmasters, indoor spa and sauna; croquet, arcade games, horseback riding, year-round ice skating, water sports at Lake Tahoe, winter skiing, and other activities

Reservation and Cancellation Policy: For reservations made 14 or more days in advance, 1 day deposit is required. Children 18 years of age and under stay free. A 7-day cancellation policy is in effect during golf season

Comments and Restrictions: No pets allowed

SQUAW CREEK

Beautifully situated at 6200 feet in the High Sierras, Squaw Creek's Robert Trent Jones, Jr.–designed layout has been meticulously interwoven among delicate wetlands alive with bald eagles, red-winged blackbirds, and an array of wildflowers including lupine, yarrow, aster, columbine, and Indian paintbrush. The golf course is located on only 81 acres of land in a horseshoe-shaped meadow surrounded by mountains on three sides. Five holes navigate steep terrain and the rest meander across the valley floor. Squaw Creek is a target golf course that rewards accuracy, course management, and strategic thinking. If you stray the ball it is likely to be lost to the wetlands or thick foliage protecting the landing areas.

The most difficult hole on the front nine, the par-4 eighth, measures only 338 yards from the back tees, but an aerial view of the hole makes it seem like miniscule drops of fairway, tee box, and putting surface green were painted into the omnipresent wetlands. The tee shot must avoid the wetlands and bunkers guarding the landing area. Should your approach miss the small green you will need another ball. The back nine concludes with another two difficult holes. The tee shot on the 429-yard par-4 seventeenth must avoid the wetlands skirting the left side. A bunker protects the right side of the landing area. The approach is over wetlands and a creek that fronts a small green with two bunkers guarding its left side. The 484-yard par-4 finishing hole thankfully offers three other pin distances to chose from. A dead solid perfect tee shot is required to stay out of the wetlands and pond on both sides of the narrow fairway. The forward-sloping green is guarded by water to its front and left. A pair of bunkers squeeze the front entranceway to the putting surface and another protects its rear.

After matching wits with this picturesque but potentially treacherous wildlife preserve, there are other diversions on site or at nearby Lake Tahoe. At the resort are four restaurants including Glissandi which specializes in French haute cuisine. Or you might want to try Bullwhackers Pub which offers an interesting array of regional beers. Squaw Creek was rated among the "Top 10 You Can Play" for 1992 by *Golf* magazine and has received numerous hospitality awards including *Meeting and Convention* magazine's Golden Tee Award. A year round resort, Squaw Creek is a premiere downhill and cross-country skiing destination.

Recommended Golf Courses in Northern California

Sacramento Area and North:

Alta Sierra Golf and Country Club, Grass Valley, (916) 273–2010, (800) 358–GOLF, Semiprivate, 18/6537/72

Beau Pre Golf Club, McKinleyville, (707) 839–2342, (800) 931–6690, Semiprivate, 18/5910/71

Canyon Oaks Country Club, Chico, (916) 343–2582, Semiprivate, 18/6804/72

Diamond Oaks Golf Course, Roseville, (916) 783–4947, Public, 18/6283/72

Fall River Valley Golf and Country Club, Fall River Mills, (916) 336–5555, Public, 18/7365/72

Graeagle Meadows Golf Course, Graeagle, (916) 836–2323, Public, 18/6668/72

Haggin Oaks Golf Course, Sacramento, (916) 481–4507, Public. North: 18/6631/72. South: 18/6602/72

Lake Shastina Golf Course, Weed, (916) 938–3205, (800) 358–4653, Resort, 18/6969/72, 9/3009/36

Lake Tahoe Golf Course, South Lake Tahoe, (916) 577–0788, Public, 18/6685/72

North Star-at-Tahoe Golf Course, Truckee, (916) 562–2490, (800) 466–6784, Resort, 18/6897/72

Plumas Pines Country Club, Blairsden, (916) 836–1420, 18/6504/72

Rancho Murietta Country Club, Rancho Murietta, (916) 354–3400, (800) 852–GOLF (Northern CA), Resort. North: 18/6839/72. South: 18/6886/72

Southridge Golf Club, Sutter, (916) 755–4653, Semiprivate, 18/7047/72

Tahoe Donner Golf and Country Club, Truckee, (916) 587–9440, Resort, 18/6961/72

San Francisco Area

Course Name: PASATIEMPO

Course Type: Public
Address: 18 Clubhouse Road
                      P.O. Box 535
                      Santa Cruz, CA 95061
Phone: (408) 459–9155

GOLF COURSE

Head Professional: Shawn McEntee

Course Length/Par (All Tees): Back 6483/71, Middle 6154/71, Forward 5647/71

Course Slope/Rating (All Tees): Back 138/72.9, Middle 134/71.4, Ladies' Forward 133/72.9

Course Architect: Alister MacKenzie (1929)

Golf Facilities: Full Pro Shop X, Snack Bar X, Lounge X, Restaurant X, Locker Room No, Showers No, Club Rental X, Club Repair X, Cart Rental X, Instruction X, Practice Green X, Driving Range X, Practice Bunker X, Club Storage No

Tee-Time Reservation Policy: From 1 wk. in advance for Mon. to Fri., call from 10 a.m. Mon. for weekends (Sat., Sun., holidays)

Ranger: Yes

Tee-off-Interval Time: 8 min.

Time to Play 18 Holes: 4½ hrs.

Course Hours/Earliest Tee-off: 6:45 a.m. to dark

Green Fees: $100 for 18 holes. Twilight rate $60

Cart Fees: $32 for 18 holes per cart Pull Carts: $5 for 18 holes

Credit Cards: American Express, MasterCard, Visa

Season: Year round

Course Comments: Can walk anytime. Yardage book available. Memberships available. Private Sat., holidays until 10:30 a.m., Sun. until 9:30 a.m.

Golf Packages: None

Discounts: Seasonal, twilight

Place to Stay Nearby: Inn at Pasatiempo (408) 423–5000; Dream Inn (408) 426–4330; Holiday Inn (408) 426–7100, (800) HOLIDAY; Best Western All Suites Inn (408) 458–9898, (800) 334–7234; Riverside Garden Inn (408) 458–9660. BED AND BREAKFAST: Babbling Brook Bed and Breakfast Inn (408) 427–2437

Local Attractions: University of California—Santa Cruz, Begonia Nurseries, wineries, Santa Cruz Art League galleries, Performing Arts Center, Mission Santa Cruz, National Bridges State Beach, Roaring Camp and Big Trees

narrow-gauge railroad, beaches, boating, restaurants. Carmel. Monterey. San Francisco. Santa Cruz Tourist Bureau (408) 425–1234

Directions: From north on Hwy. 17: Exit Pasatiempo Dr., left (follow signs, 1 mi.). From south on Hwy. 17: Exit Pasatiempo Dr., straight (follow signs, 1 mi.)

Closest Commercial Airports: San Jose International (45 min.), Monterey (1 hr., 15 min.), San Francisco International (2 hrs.)

PASATIEMPO

To know much about Pasatiempo, you have to know something about Marion Hollins, because it was her dream. Hollins was born into a wealthy family on Long Island in 1893, and in the parlance of the day she was a tomboy, and then a great athlete. By 1921 she had won the U.S. Women's Amateur, and in 1932 she became the first captain of the United States Curtis Cup Team. Marion was also the first woman to enter the Vanderbilt Cup automobile races on Long Island.

Hollins eventually moved west in the 1920s, and at Del Monte, on the Monterey peninsula in California, she met Samuel Morse, who had already established his Pebble Beach Golf Course and was planning to build Cypress Point. They immediately hit it off, and he offered her the position of athletic director of his enterprises. She accepted and secured the services of the noteworthy golf architect Alister MacKenzie of Scotland to design Cypress Point. Later, in 1927, while riding on horseback along the Carbonero Ridge in the rolling foothills north of Santa Cruz, she could see Monterey Bay and the Monterey Peninsula in the distance, and below her she could see the land that would eventually be Pasatiempo. Her plan was to build a fine golf course surrounded by homes, a clubhouse, tennis courts, swimming pool, a steeplechase course, bridle paths, roads, a park area and a beach club on Monterey Bay. She had no money to finance the project, however.

Hollins soon made $2.5 million in a successful oil investment in the Kettleman Hills northeast of Bakersfield; formed a partnership with F. W. Baker, an expatriate British financier; and purchased 570 acres of Ranch Carbonero land above Santa Cruz. MacKenzie, who was the official advisor to Prestwick, Troon and Royal St. Georges as well as St. Andrews, was hired to design the golf course. The golf course formally opened on September 8, 1929, and the first foursome included Hollins, Glenna Collett (winner of several U.S. Amateurs), British champion Cyril Tolley and Bobby Jones. Jones would later work with MacKenzie to design Augusta National.

Originally the golf course was a 6845-yard par 73. Today it is a 6483-yard par-71 layout from the back tees with a slope rating of 138. You start off with a 504-yard par 5, handicapped as the easiest hole on the course, downhill to a green flanked by traps right and left. The most difficult hole on the front side is the 217–yard par-3 third hole, which when the course first opened had a distance of 243 yards. The tee shot is uphill to a green with four traps and tricky undulations that are difficult to read. Before this hole was revised, it was considered one of the most difficult par-3 holes in the United States. Among its obstacles were 13 separate sand traps.

The 391-yard par-4 sixteenth hole is the number-1-handicap hole and was MacKenzie's favorite. The first shot on this dogleg left is a blind shot that plays downhill. The second shot is across a barranca (ravine) to a three-tiered green. With a creek on the right and a bunker to the left and to the back of the green, this is a difficult hole to par. The finishing hole is a 173-yard par 3 that plays across a cavernous ravine.

MacKenzie retired to his home along the sixth fairway after completing Pasatiempo and remained a consultant. He and Hollins had agreed that changes in the topography of the original land were to be kept to a minimum, and the layout reflects this.

MacKenzie designed numerous courses, including a par-3 nine-hole course on Charlie Chaplin's estate in Beverly Hills; the Ohio State University Golf Club (Gray Course), Columbus, Ohio; the University of Michigan Golf Club, Ann Arbor, with Perry Maxwell; the Adirondack Club, Lake Placid, New York; Augusta National Golf Club with Robert Tyre Jones, Jr.; and the Cypress Point Club, Pebble Beach, California, with Robert Hunter. He died after a sudden heart attack at Pasatiempo in 1934.

During the Depression the pace of home construction and real-estate sales slowed, and eventually Marion Hollins and her partners had to sell Pasatiempo. She moved back to Monterey to work for Samuel Morse and died in 1944. Pasatiempo reached its nadir during World War II but has gradually come back over the years under new investment and management. Currently it is ranked by *Golf Digest* as one of the top 100 golf courses, public or private, in the United States. In 1986 the 86th U.S. Women's Amateur Championship, won by Kay Cockerill, was held here, and the Western Intercollegiate Championship is held here regularly.

Pasatiempo has golf memberships but is open to the public. The high architectural landscaping and environmental standards of Marion Hollins are reflected in the beauty of the buildings and grounds at Pasatiempo today. She wanted only the best and spent $2.5 million of her own money in Depression era dollars to attain it. Your visit to Pasatiempo will be a unique golf experience.

**Course Name: SILVERADO
                         COUNTRY CLUB
                         North, South Courses**

Course Type: Resort
Resort: Silverado Country Club
                     and Resort
Address: 1600 Atlas Peak Road
                     Napa, CA 94558
Phone: (707) 257–0200 (Golf Course)
                     (707) 257–0200,
                     (800) 532–0500 (Resort)
Fax: (707) 257–5400 (Resort)

GOLF COURSE

Head Professional: Jeff Goodwin
Course Length/Par (All Tees): North:
    Back 6896/72, Middle 6351/72, Forward

5857/72. South: Back 6632/72, Middle 6213/72, Forward 5672/72

Course Slope/Rating (All Tees): North: Back 131/73.4, Middle 126/70.9, Ladies' Forward 124/73.9. South: Back 127/72.1, Middle 123/70.4, Ladies' Forward 123/71.8

Course Architects: North: Johnny Dawson (1955), Robert Trent Jones, Jr. (renovation, 1964). South: Robert Trent Jones, Jr. (1965)

Golf Facilities: Full Pro Shop X, Snack Bar X, Lounge X, Restaurant X, Locker Room X, Showers X, Club Rental X, Club Repair X, Cart Rental X, Instruction X, Practice Green X, Driving Range X, Practice Bunker X, Club Storage X

Tee-Time Reservation Policy: At time of confirmed room reservation. Must be a resort guest, member or guest of member to play the courses

Ranger: Yes

Tee-off-Interval Time: 8 min.

Time to Play 18 Holes: 4½ hrs.

Course Hours/Earliest Tee-off: 7 a.m., 6:30 a.m. weekends in summer

Green and Cart Fees: Resort guests: $105 for 18 holes with cart; Public: $120 for 18 holes with cart

Credit Cards: All major cards

Season: Year round

Course Comments: Cart mandatory. Yardage book available. Reciprocal play with members of private clubs

Golf Packages: Available through resort

Discounts: Twilight

Places to Stay Nearby: NAPA: Clarion Inn (707) 253–7433; Inn at Napa Valley (707) 253–9540, (800) 433–4600; La Residence (707) 235–0337; CALISTOGA: Brannan Cottage Inn (707) 942–4200; RUTHERFORD: Auberge du Soleil (707) 963–1211; ST. HELENA: Harvest Inn (707) 963–9463, (800) 950–8466; SANTA ROSA: Fountaingrove Inn (707) 578–6101, (800) 222–6101; Vintners Inn (707) 575–7350, (800) 421–2584; SONOMA: Sonoma Mission Inn (707) 938–9000, (800) 358–9022. BED AND BREAKFAST: Bed and Breakfast Exchange (707) 967–7756

Local Attractions: Winery tours, Napa Valley Wine Library, Silverado Museum, Robert Louis Stevenson State Park, Luther Burbank Memorial Gardens, Mission San Francisco Solano. Calistoga, CA. Napa Chamber of Commerce (707) 226–7455

Directions: From San Francisco Bay Bridge (50 min.): Hwy. 80 east toward Sacramento, to Hwy. 37 west exit (Vallejo). 2 mi. to Hwy. 29 north, 12 mi. to Napa, follow signs to Lake Berryessa, turn left onto Atlas Peak Rd. Follow signs to resort

Closest Commercial Airports: Oakland International (60 min.), San Francisco International (75 min.), Sacramento Metropolitan (75 min.)

RESORT

Date Built: 1966

No. of Rooms: 270 studio, 1-, 2-, and 3-bedroom condominium suites

Meeting Rooms: 13. Capacity of Largest: 500 persons. Meeting Space: 12,000 sq. ft.

Room Price Range: $120 to $465. High season Mar. through late Nov.

Lounge: Main Bar

Restaurants: Vintner's Court, Royal Oak, Silverado Bar and Grill

Entertainment: Music, dancing

Credit Cards: All major cards

General Amenities: Meeting facilities with audiovisual and food services, helicopter tours, racquetball and health center (10 min. away)

Recreational Amenities: Bicycling, boating, glider rides, horseback riding, hot-air ballooning, tennis (20 courts, 3 lighted for night play), 8 swimming pools, saunas, tennis camps and clinics

Reservation and Cancellation Policy: Reservation deposit required to hold reservation. 3-day advance cancellation notice to avoid penalties

Comments and Restrictions: No pets. Taxes additional to base rates

SILVERADO COUNTRY CLUB

The Silverado Country Club is located in Napa Valley, California, the seat of the

American wine industry, approximately 1 hour northeast of San Francisco. The Silverado story began when General John Franklin Miller, a Civil War veteran, purchased several parcels of land that became the 1200-acre Silverado property. The living room of the original Miller mansion is now the club's lounge, measuring 84 by 20 feet with high ceilings. The estate passed from the Miller family to a Mrs. Vesta Peak Maxwell in 1932, and she in turn sold the property to the Silverado Land Company in 1953, retaining 1 acre for her own future residence. The converted mansion became a golf clubhouse. Shortly thereafter the resort's first eighteen-hole golf course was built, later to be redesigned by Robert Trent Jones, Jr., in 1966. This is now the North Course. The South Course, also designed by Jones, was built at the same time.

The North and South courses were the first golf courses that Robert Trent Jones, Jr., designed as an individual golf architect, newly independent from his famous father's practice. Since that time he has designed many golf courses, establishing himself as one of the preeminent golf-course architects. Among his California golf courses are the Links at Spanish Bay, Pebble Beach, with Sandy Tatum and Tom Watson; the Lake Shastina Resort (two courses); and the Links at Monarch Beach in Laguna Niguel. He also designed Edinburgh USA in Brooklyn Park, Minnesota; the Cochiti Golf Course in Cochiti Lake, New Mexico; the Sugarloaf Golf Club in Carrabasset Valley, Maine; the Arrowhead Golf Club in Roxborough Park, Colorado, and many others.

The North Course of Silverado plays 6896 yards from the back tees and has flatter, smaller greens and less water than the South Course. Mature trees, especially oak, grace these rolling layouts, and generally you can see the pin from tee to green, enabling you to conceptualize how to play the hole. There are no gimmicks on these traditional courses, and there is some forgiveness if you miss. The number-1-handicap hole on the North Course is the very first hole, a par 4, which plays 436 yards slightly uphill to a green well protected by traps to the left, front right and back. The

green slopes from front to back and right to left, with occasional ridges that make it difficult to read.

The par-5 fifth hole is a 536-yard double dogleg right, then left to a crowned green. Three traps guard the front of the green, which can be reached in two by going straight over the right edge of the fairway that is guarded by trees and water to the far right on the tee shot. The second shot has to negotiate left and right fairway bunkers beginning 150 yards from the green.

The par 3s on both the front and back sides are difficult from the back tees. The 183-yard eleventh plays over the edge of a lake on the right to a tiered green backed by two traps. At one time Johnny Miller lived in the house to the right of this hole but has since moved to a nearby residence out of harm's way. The 195-yard fifteenth is a tee shot over the edge of a stream and lake on the right to a small, two-tiered undulating green that has two traps in back.

The South Course has large, rolling greens and a plethora of sizeable traps in the Robert Trent Jones, Jr. style. It plays 6632 yards from the back tees and requires you to cross water several times. The number-1-handicap eighth hole is a slight dogleg right par 4 that plays 422 yards to a shallow, wide green protected in front by a huge trap. This hole has made the top 10 most difficult list on the Senior Tour, which stages a regular tour event in October at Silverado. The fairway slopes left on this dogleg right, so one may be hitting a second shot from a sidehill, downhill, or uphill lie.

The ninth hole is a 512-yard par-5 dogleg right, with fairway bunkers on the left and a large evergreen to the right pinching the fairway halfway to a deep, narrow green flanked by water on the left and a huge trap and trees on the right. The temptation is to ignore these obstacles and go for the green in two. The eleventh hole is probably the most difficult hole on the course for the average golfer. A par 5 measuring 569 yards from the back tees, the fairway wraps left around a long lake that begins 350 yards from the green. The fairway narrows coming into the green on the second shot, with trees bordering the right side. Often the wind is in your face on this hole, and because of the way the fairway angles to the left, it is not easy to calibrate distance. The green is shallow, wide, and undulating, with a variety of plateaus.

The 185-yard par-3 fifteenth plays over water to a shallow, wide green that must be played at least to the middle, or the ball will roll back into the water hazard. If you are long, however, your ball will likely end up in one of two traps in back, leaving you a tricky pitch toward the water. The 500-yard par-5 finishing hole is a dogleg left with a large bunker to the right at the knee of the dogleg halfway to the hole. A high hook over the corner will put you in a position to reach the green in two, but a sea of bunkers beginning 50 yards from the front of the green can give you fits if you're short.

Ample practice facilities and PGA golf instruction are available to you at Silverado, which also has a new 12,000-square-foot conference center. The 1200-acre grounds, which include the 360-acre golf complex, have received recognition for their horticultural beauty. Facilities also include a tennis club, excellent restaurants, and wines from the surrounding vineyards and beyond. Silverado has been ranked among America's 75 best resort courses by *Golf Digest*, and *Golf* magazine has placed it on its best golf resorts in America list.

The Wappo Indians called the region of Napa "Talahussi" or "beautiful land." The first European settler did not appear here until 1850, and only since the 1960s has the valley emerged as one of the most attractive tourist attractions in the United States. This was just about the time that Robert Trent Jones, Jr., wove his magic among the rolling hills, streams and lakes of Silverado.

Recommended Golf Courses in California

Within 1 Hour of San Francisco: Napa Valley and Coastal Region:

Adobe Creek Golf Club, Petaluma, (707) 765–3000, Public, 18/6825/72

Bennett Valley Golf Course, Santa Rosa, (707) 528–3673, Public, 18/6600/72

Bodega Harbour Golf Links, Bodega Bay, (707) 875–3538, Semiprivate, 18/6220/70

Chardonnay Golf Club, Napa, (707) 257–8950, Semiprivate. Club Shakespeare: 18/7001/72. Vineyards: 18/6811/71

Fountaingrove Country Club, Santa Rosa, (707) 579–4653, Semiprivate, 18/6797/72

Hidden Valley Golf and Country Club, Middletown, (707) 787–3035, Semiprivate, 18/6590/72

Las Positas Golf Course, Livermore, (510) 443–3122, Public, 18/6725/72

Napa Municipal Golf Club, Napa, (707) 255–4333, Public, 18/6730/72

Oakmont Golf Course, Santa Rosa, (707) 539–0415, Semiprivate. West: 18/6417/72. East: 18/4293/63

Paradise Valley Golf Course, Fairfield, (707) 426–1600, Public, 18/6993/72

Pine Mountain Lake Country Club, Groveland, (209) 962–8620, Semiprivate, 18/6358/70

Rancho Solano Golf Course, Fairfield, (707) 429–4653, Public, 18/6705/72

San Geronimo Golf Club, San Geronimo, (415) 488–4030, Semiprivate, 18/6801/72

Sea Ranch Golf Links, Sea Ranch, (707) 785–2468, Public, 9/3370/36, 18/6740/72

Sonoma Golf Club, Sonoma, (707) 996–0300, (800) 956–4653, Public, 18/7069/72

Windsor Golf Club, Windsor, (707) 838–7888, Public, 18/6650/72

San Francisco Area/East Bay South to Stockton:

Alameda Municipal Golf Course, Alameda, (510) 522–4321, Public. Fry: 18/6141/72. Clark: 18/6559/71

Canyon Lakes Country Club, San Ramon, (510) 735–6511, Public, 18/6731/71

Dry Creek Golf Course, Galt, (209) 745–4653, Public, 18/6707/72

Franklin Canyon Golf Course, Rodeo, (510) 799–6191, Public, 18/6776/72

La Contenta Golf Club, Valley Springs, (209) 772–1081, (800) 446–5321, Semiprivate, 18/6409/72

Mountain Springs, Sonora, (209) 532–1000, Public, 18/6665/72

Oakhurst Country Club, Clayton, (510) 672–9737, Semiprivate, 18/6739/72

Santa Teresa Golf Club, San Jose, (408) 225–2650, Public, 18/6742/72

Tilden Park Golf Course, Berkeley, (510) 848–7373, Public, 18/6294/70

Willow Park Golf Club, Castro Valley, (510) 537–8989, Public, 18/6227/71

San Francisco and South to Santa Cruz:

Aptos Seascape Golf Course, Aptos, (408) 688–3213, Public, 18/6116/72

Delaveaga Golf Club, Santa Cruz, (408) 423–7214, Public, 18/6010/72

Half Moon Bay Golf Links, Half Moon Bay, (415) 726–4438, Public, 18/7116/72

Harding Park Golf Course, Daly City, (415) 664–4690, Public, 18/6637/72, 9/2316/32

Lincoln Park Golf Course, San Francisco, (415) 221–9911, Public, 18/5149/68

Palo Alto Golf Club, Palo Alto, (415) 856–0881, Public, 18/6814/72

Presidio Golf Club, San Francisco, (415) 751–0562, Public, 18/6589/72

Monterey Peninsula Area

Course Name: CARMEL VALLEY RANCH

Course Type: Resort
Resort: Carmel Valley Ranch
Address: One Old Ranch Road
Carmel, CA 93923
Phone: (408) 625–9500,
(800) 422–7635 (Resort)
Fax: (408) 624–2858 (Golf Course)

GOLF COURSE

Director of Golf: Andy Cude

Course Length/Par (All Tees): Back 6234/70, White 5563/70, Red 5046/70, Forward 4337/70

Course Slope/Rating (All Tees): Back 134/70.5, White 126/67.6, Ladies' Red 120/68.6, Ladies' Forward 112/64.7

Course Architect: Pete Dye (1980, remodeled 1995)

Golf Facilities: Full Pro Shop X, Snack Bar X, Lounge X, Restaurant X, Locker Room X, Showers X, Club Rental X, Club Repair X, Cart Rental X, Instruction X, Practice Green X, Driving Range X, Practice Bunker X, Club Storage X

Tee-Time Reservation Policy: At time of confirmed reservation at the resort. You must be a resort guest, member, or guest of a member to play the course

Ranger: Yes

Tee-off-Interval Time: 7 and 8 min.

Time to Play 18 Holes: 4 hrs.

Course Hours/Earliest Tee-off: 7 a.m.

Green and Cart Fees: $100 for 18 holes for resort guests

Credit Cards: All major cards

Season: Year round. Busiest July through late Oct.

Course Comments: Walking allowed Mon. through Thurs. after 3 p.m. Golf schools and individual instruction on site

Golf Packages: Available through resort

Discounts: Inquire at resort for special rates

Places to Stay Nearby: PEBBLE BEACH: The Lodge at Pebble Beach (408) 649–2711, (800) 654–9300. CARMEL: Adobe Inn (408) 624–3933; Cobblestone Inn (408) 625–5222. CARMEL VALLEY VILLAGE: Quail Lodge (408) 624–1561, (800) 538–9516

Local Attractions: Big Sur, Laguna Seca Raceway, 17-Mile Drive, Point Lobos State Wildlife Reserve, Monterey Bay Aquarium, whale watching, hang gliding, hot air ballooning, ocean kayaking, boating, beaches, horseback riding, restaurants, shopping

Directions: Take Hwy. 1 to Carmel Valley Rd. Drive east (inland) on Carmel

Valley Rd. approximately 5 min. Resort is on the right

Closest Commercial Airports: Monterey Peninsula Airport (20 min.); San Jose International (1½ hrs.); San Francisco International (2½ hrs.)

RESORT

Date Built: 1980
No. of Rooms: 100 Suites
Meeting Rooms: 8. Capacity of Largest: 200 persons. Meeting Space: Approximately 8500 sq. ft. including heated outdoor deck
Room Price Range: From $255 to $700. Packages and other special offers available
Lounges: Lounge area with fireplace
Restaurants: Golf Clubhouse Grill, The Oaks, Tennis Clubhouse
Entertainment: Pianist weekends
Credit Cards: All major cards
General Amenities: Business services including banquet, typing, word processing, photocopying, facsimile transmission, translation and presentation services; dry cleaning, car rental, concierge
Recreational Amenities: 10 hard-court, 2 clay tennis courts, 2 swimming pools, 6 whirlpool spas, hiking, jogging, bicycling, horseback riding, fishing, windsurfing, boating
Reservation and Cancellation Policy: 72-hour cancellation policy
Comments and Restrictions: No pets allowed

CARMEL VALLEY RANCH

The Carmel Valley Ranch resort is nestled on 1700 lush acres of former ranchland just six miles inland from Carmel and the Pacific Ocean. When you step into the ranch-style lodge to register, the specially woven floral rugs, native stone fireplace, local art displays, and tasteful decor convey the private tranquility of this award-winning destination that has recently undergone a multi-million dollar restoration.

The Pete Dye-designed golf course is served by a large clubhouse perched on a hill overlooking the golf course with views of the Santa Lucia Mountains. The front nine is mildly undulating with a series of short par 3s and par 4s. One of my favorite holes on the front side is the 172-yard par-3 fifth which plays over the edge of a pond to a wide green guarded by bunkers on each side. The putting surface has a series of mounds and swales making it very difficult to read. One of the more difficult holes on this side is the 548-yard par-5 sixth which plays straight to a deep, two-tiered green guarded by bunkers to its front right and left sides. A stream borders the left side of the fairway, and heavy rough can catch balls to the right of the landing areas. The back nine meanders up the side of a mountain then flows back down to the clubhouse. A difficult hole on this side is the 438-yard par-4 eleventh. This scenic hole plays from an elevated tee down to a landing area guarded by a long fairway bunker on the left. The second shot is up thirty feet to a flat green cut out of the side of a hill. Recent renovations have modified this hole and others at Carmel Valley ranch to make them a bit less penal. For example, hole No. 12's fairway originally was vertically split into two levels by signature Pete Dye railroad ties. Another beautiful hole on this side is the 150-yard par-3 thirteenth that provides you a view of the entire valley.

Carmel Valley, under the ownership and management of Carefree Resorts, proprietors of The Boulders in Carefree, Arizona and The Peaks at Telluride, Colorado, now offers a variety of golf packages and golf school options at this resort. Carmel Valley's practice facility includes a driving range, four greens, and two practice bunkers. Guest suites at this award-winning destination are tucked into the hillsides and offer cathedral ceilings, working fireplaces, wraparound decks, handcrafted quilts, and other amenities. The Oaks restaurant is in the main lodge, and the Golf Clubhouse Grill and Tennis Clubhouse are convenient for light meals. Nearby are the scenic attractions of Big Sur, Carmel, Point Lobos, Monterey, and the Pacific.

Course Name: THE LINKS AT
**   SPANISH BAY**

Course Type: Resort
Resort: The Inn at Spanish Bay
Address: 2700 Seventeen-Mile Drive
               P.O. Box 567
               Pebble Beach, CA 93953
Phone: (408) 624–3811,
               (800) 654–9300 (Golf
               Course) (408) 647–7500,
               (800) 654–9300 (Resort)
Fax: (408) 624–6357 (Resort)

GOLF COURSE

Head Professional: Rich Cosand
Course Length/Par (All Tees): Back
  6820/72, Middle 6078/72, Forward
  5287/72
Course Slope/Rating (All Tees): Back
  142/74.7, Middle 133/70.8, Forward
  129/70.6
Course Architects: Robert Trent Jones, Jr.,
  Tom Watson and Frank Tatum (1987)
Golf Facilities: Full Pro Shop X, Snack
  Bar X, Lounge X, Restaurant X,
  Locker Room No, Showers No, Club
  Rental X, Club Repair X, Cart Rental
  X, Instruction X, Practice Green X,
  Driving Range X, Practice Bunker No,
  Club Storage X
Tee-Time Reservation Policy: Guests: At
  time of registration up to 18 mos. in ad-
  vance. Public: 60 days in advance for 2
  or more players
Ranger: No
Tee-off-Interval Time: 10 min.
Time to Play 18 Holes: 5 hrs.
Course Hours/Earliest Tee-off: 20 min.
  after sunrise
Green and Cart Fees: Guests: $135 for 18
  holes with cart. Public: $165 for 18
  holes with cart
Credit Cards: American Express, Diners
  Club, MasterCard, Visa
Season: Year round. Busiest season late
  summer/early fall
Course Comments: Can walk anytime.
  Yardage book available. Caddies $40
  per bag
Golf Packages: Available through resort
Discounts: Residents, twilight, replays

Places to Stay Nearby: PEBBLE BEACH:
  The Lodge at Pebble Beach (408) 647–
  7500, (800) 654–9300. MONTEREY: Monterey Plaza (408) 646–1700, (800) 631–
  1339; Spindrift Inn (408) 646–8900,
  (800) 528–0444; Hotel Pacific (408)
  373–5700, (800) 554–5542. CARMEL:
  Colonial Terrace Inn (408) 624–2741,
  (800) 345–1818 (CA); Cypress Inn
  (408) 624–3871, (800) 443–7443;
  Adobe Inn (408) 624–3933. CARMEL
  VALLEY VILLAGE: Quail Lodge (408)
  624–1561, (800) 538–9516; Carmel Valley Ranch Resort (408) 625–9500, (800)
  4 CARMEL
Local Attractions: MONTEREY: Whale
  watching, Monterey Bay Aquarium,
  Fisherman's Wharf, Cannery Row,
  beaches, boating, Steinbeck House,
  Hearst Castle (San Simeon), Monterey
  Peninsula Museum of Art, galleries,
  restaurants, seasonal events. CARMEL:
  Carmel Mission, Point Lobos State
  Reserve, shopping. Monterey Peninsula
  Chamber of Commerce (408) 649–1770
Directions: Hwy. 101 to Monterey Peninsula turnoff, Rte. 156 west to Hwy. 1
  south to 17-Mile Dr./Pebble Beach exit;
  a guard at the entrance provides direc-
  tions to the resort
Closest Commercial Airports: Monterey
  Peninsula (15 min.), San Francisco International (2½ hrs.), San Jose International
  (1½ hrs.)

RESORT

Date Built: 1987
No. of Rooms: 270, including 13 executive
  suites, 1 hospitality suite, 1 governor's
  suite, 1 presidential suite
Meeting Rooms: 16. Capacity of Largest:
  1000 persons. Meeting Space: 14,000
  sq. ft.
Room Price Range: $295 to $1650 for
  suites
Lounges: Traps, Lobby Lounge
Restaurants: Roy's, Bay Club, Clubhouse
  Bar and Grill (breakfast, lunch)
Entertainment: Live band in Roy's
Credit Cards: American Express, Visa
General Amenities: Women's boutique,
  meeting and banquet facilities with

audiovisual and banquet services, Lodge at Pebble Beach facilities

Recreational Amenities: Swimming pool, wading pool, tennis pavilion (8 courts, 2 lighted) with professional instructors; fitness center with weight room, sauna, aerobics; hiking trails, equestrian center and riding trails, bicycling

Reservation and Cancellation Policy: Reservations must be secured by an advance deposit within 14 days from date of booking. 72-hr. cancellation notice required for deposit refund

Comments and Restrictions: No pets. $17 gratuity per night per room. Golf reservations should be made immediately following confirmation of room reservation. Taxes additional to base rates

THE LINKS AT SPANISH BAY

As Frank "Sandy" Tatum, the co-designer of the Links at Spanish Bay, explains it, the Links at Spanish Bay were designed to link golf played in the setting of this beautiful bay to golf as it is played on the seaside links courses in Scotland. As the game developed on those courses, holes were laid out among the dunes, playing surfaces were firm and undulating and the low, running shot was a requirement to manage the prevailing seaside winds that swept over the links. The setting at Spanish Bay has all the characteristics of the places that make those links in Scotland so special. The designers of this course, each a lover of links golf in Scotland, have used this setting to provide the extraordinary experience of playing links golf on the Monterey Peninsula.

The trees, greens and fairways are planted with fescue grasses, the same strain of grass that grew naturally on the links of Scotland, to provide the smooth, firm playing surfaces that add so much to the distinctive pleasure of links golf. The approaches to the green were designed, wherever the terrain would permit, to accommodate the low, running shot. The tees, fairways and greens were located on and among the dunes to give the course the aesthetic flavor that makes playing links golf so specially satisfying.

The 6820-yard par-72 layout borders the Pacific Ocean, with the inn situated in the center within walking distance of the first tee. The 459-yard par-4 fifth hole is one of the more difficult holes on the course. A slight dogleg right, the tee shot must negotiate three bunkers in the right center of the fairway that begin approximately 200 yards from the front of the green for 40 yards. The second shot is into a large, deep green with a trap to the left front. Another challenging hole at Spanish Bay is the 571-yard par-5 fourteenth hole, with a relatively straight tee shot to a narrow landing area. On the second shot the golfer is faced with four bunkers that begin 140 yards from the front of the green. Two are on the left edge, a large, long bunker is in the center of the fairway and another is slightly to the right. The green is set sideways and is protected on the right front by a bunker.

The third hole, a 405-yard par-4 dogleg left, provides a spectacular view of the Pacific Ocean from an elevated tee. You have to negotiate four bunkers on the left on the tee shot. On the second shot, you come into a typically large, undulating green with the ocean on the horizon all the way. The fifth hole doglegs right toward the ocean after the 190-yard par-3 fourth. The brave try to cut a drive over the three bunkers on this 459-yard par 4.

The two finishing holes at Spanish Bay are a wonderful golf experience. The seventeenth runs parallel to the ocean on the right, with the wind sweeping from right to left. A 414-yard par 4, the tee shot has to avoid six right-side bunkers that begin 248 yards from the green and run for approximately 100 yards toward the hole. The second shot is into a 35-yard-deep, undulating, kidney-shaped green with a long trap on the left.

The 571-yard par-5 eighteenth plays back inland toward the clubhouse with the ocean behind you and three left-fairway bunkers awaiting you approximately 250 yards from the back tee. If you're long off the tee, you can try to reach the green by flying a huge wetlands protected in front by a large pot bunker that runs on the left fairway from 95 yards into a deep, undulating green protected by two traps on the right. Or you can play up the right side of the fairway and hit a lofted club on your third shot into the green, which has a natural redwinged-blackbird sanctuary on the left. (This might provide a welcome distraction, depending on your score.) Jones and his associates have taken what was once a 195-acre tract of barren waste and converted it into a remarkable layout. With its thousands of cubic yards of sand, 100-foot Monterey pines; natural wildlife habitats; tricky, undulating greens; rolling fairways; dunes; bunkers and the panorama of the Pacific Ocean, this is truly one of golf's newer shrines.

The Inn at Spanish Bay is a three- and four-level luxury hotel with 270 guest rooms, 145 of which have ocean views. The rest have beautiful forest views. Situated on 236 acres of land within a grove of Monterey pines, the inn is approximately 1000 feet from the Pacific Ocean and is a short walk to the golf course. Also nearby are 80 luxury townhouse residences on a private 20-acre ocean-front enclave and the 24,000-square-foot clubhouse that stands between the inn and the residences. Breakfast and lunch are served in the clubhouse, with first-fairway and ocean views while dining. The inn itself has two restaurants and two lounges with a number of other amenities, including a 5700-square-foot ballroom and extensive meeting and banquet facilities totaling 14,000 square feet.

Carmel and downtown Monterey are within a few miles of the resort, as are Pebble Beach, Spyglass, and Poppy Hills. The Inn at Spanish Bay is recognized by *Golf* and *Golf Digest* magazines as one of America's best golf resorts.

Course Name: PEBBLE BEACH
**   GOLF LINKS**

Course Type: Resort
Resort: The Lodge at Pebble Beach
Address: Seventeen-Mile Drive
              Pebble Beach, CA 93953
Phone: (408) 624–3811,
              (800) 654–9300
              (Golf Course) (408) 647–
              7500, X60;

(800) 654–9300 (Resort)
(408) 624–3811 (Restaurants)
Fax: (408) 624–6357 (Resort)

GOLF COURSE

Head Professional: R. J. Harper
Course Length/Par (All Tees): Back 6799/72, Middle 6357/72, Front 5197/72
Course Slope/Rating (All Tees): Back 144/75, Middle 139/72.7, Front 130/71.9
Course Architect: Jack Neville (1919)
Golf Facilities: Full Pro Shop X, Snack Bar X, Lounge X, Restaurant X, Locker Room X, Showers X, Club Rental X, Club Repair Minor, Cart Rental X, Instruction X, Practice Green X, Driving Range X, Practice Bunker X, Club Storage X
Tee-Time Reservation Policy: Public: 24 hrs. in advance from 7 a.m. Guests: Up to 18 mos. in advance
Ranger: Yes
Tee-off-Interval Time: 12 min.
Time to Play 18 Holes: 5 hrs., 15 min.
Course Hours/Earliest Tee-off: 7 a.m.
Green and Cart Fees: Guests: $195 for 18 holes with cart. Public: $245 for 18 holes with cart
Credit Cards: All major cards
Season: Year round. Busiest season Oct., slowest season Nov. and Dec.
Course Comments: Can walk anytime. Yardage book available. Caddies available. Executive 9-hole Peter Hay Course
Golf Packages: Available through resort
Discounts: Twilight, replays
Place to Stay Nearby: PEBBLE BEACH: Inn at Spanish Bay (408) 647–7500, (800) 654–9300. MONTEREY: Monterey Plaza (408) 646–1700, (800) 631–1339; Spindrift Inn (408) 646–8900, (800) 528–0444; Doubletree Inn (408) 649–4511, (800) 528–0444; Hotel Pacific (408) 373–5700, (800) 554–5542. CARMEL: Adobe Inn (408) 624–3933. CARMEL VALLEY VILLAGE: Quail Lodge (408) 624–1561, (800) 538–9516; Carmel Valley Ranch Resort (408) 625–9500, (800) 4 CARMEL
Local Attractions: MONTEREY: Whale watching, Monterey Bay Aquarium, Fisherman's Wharf, Cannery Row,

beaches, boating, Steinbeck House, Hearst Castle (San Simeon), Monterey Peninsula Museum of Art, galleries, restaurants, seasonal events. CARMEL: Carmel Mission, Point Lobos State Reserve, shopping. Monterey Peninsula Chamber of Commerce (408) 649–1770

Directions: Hwy. 101 to Monterey Peninsula turnoff, Rte. 156 west to Hwy. 1 south to 17–Mile Dr./Pebble Beach exit; a guard at the entrance provides directions to the resort

Closest Commercial Airports: Monterey Peninsula (15 min.), San Jose International (1½ hrs.), San Francisco International (2½ hrs.)

RESORT

Date Built: 1919

No. of Rooms: 161, including 11 in main building, 150 in separate low-rise building. 140 rooms with fireplaces

Meeting Rooms: 9. Capacity of Largest: 400 persons. Meeting Space: 8000 sq. ft.

Room Price Range: $295 to $450 per night

Lounges: Terrace Lounge, Tap Room

Restaurants: Cypress Room, Club XIX, Gallery

Entertainment: Terrace Lounge, music in Tap Room, dancing

Credit Cards: American Express, JCB, MasterCard, Visa

General Amenities: Shopping promenade with post office, banks, travel agency; library, card room, meeting and conference facilities, access to Inn at Spanish Bay amenities

Recreational Amenities: Heated swimming pool, hiking, bicycling, Beach and Tennis Club with 14 tennis courts, equestrian center with 34 mi. of bridle paths throughout Del Monte Forest, health and fitness center

Reservation and Cancellation Policy: Reservations must be secured by an advance deposit within 14 days from date of booking. 72-hr. cancellation notice required for deposit refund

Comments and Restrictions: $15 gratuity per night per room. Golf reservations should be made at time of room reservation

PEBBLE BEACH GOLF LINKS

Until after World War II, few but the rich came to Pebble Beach because of its relative inaccessibility 120 miles south of San Francisco. In the late 1800s the Hotel Del Monte, destroyed by fire in 1917, was built there by a holding company owned by Charles Crocker (of Southern Pacific Railroad fame), Leland Stanford, Collings P. Huntington and Mark Hopkins. In 1919, the hotel was rebuilt and a new owner, Samuel F. B. Morse, grandnephew of the telegraph inventor, acquired the Hotel Del Monte and the Del Monte Forest, and formed Del Monte Properties. Jack Neville, a California State Amateur champion and 1923 Walker Cup player, was hired by Morse to build an ocean-front golf course along Seventeen-Mile Drive. Neville laid out the course and then brought in Douglas Grant, another former California Amateur champion, to bunker it. By 1919, one of the best golf courses in the world was completed.

Eventually, as America became more affluent, golf became more popular and television tournament coverage of "The Crosby," and the U.S. Open in particular, publicized Pebble Beach. The course became well known internationally. It was here that Bobby Jones, playing in the first U.S. Amateur held west of the Mississippi, was eliminated by Johnny Goodman in the first round in 1924. It was the only amateur tournament during the last seven years of his active career where he failed to reach the final round. Jack Nicklaus won the U.S. Amateur and U.S. Open at Pebble Beach and most golf aficionados remember Tom Watson's incredible final two birdies to edge Nicklaus in the 1982 Open.

Many weather-related disaster stories have emerged from wind-swept Pebble Beach. Bing Crosby, a scratch golfer himself, liked to call it "mollusk country." Arnold Palmer spent some time in that vicinity in the 1964 Crosby on the 218-yard par-3 seventeenth, which is usually into the wind and has a large two-level green with the sea to the left and behind it. Palmer took a nine when he hit his tee shot too hard and had to try to get back to the green from the wave-swept rocks.

The Pebble Beach Golf Links is a 6799-yard par-72 layout with a 144 slope rating from the back tees and eight holes directly on the ocean. A stretch of seaside holes begins at the 327-yard par-4 fourth and runs through the tenth hole. The vistas of the golf course and the ocean are magnificent from here, especially the 516-yard par-5 sixth, which plays directly down toward the ocean. This number-2-handicap hole has a large bunker in the left fairway approximately 270 yards from the back tee. At this point the ocean bluffs begin to cut into the right fairway, which narrows the fairway all the way to a typically small, 29-yard deep, elongated green protected by two traps to the right and one to the left.

The 107-yard par-3 seventh hole has ocean wrapping around the right fairway and the green, which is 25 yards deep and surrounded by six traps. The combination of wind and these hazards can make this hole very difficult. The 431-yard par-4 eighth is a dogleg right with water right all the way. This is the first of three notoriously difficult par-4 holes. A 240-yard uphill drive leaves you with a mid-iron over a huge ocean-filled chasm to a small 21-yard deep green that slopes severely from back to front and is protected by two rear traps, one to the right and one front left. With an absolute carry of about 180 yards across this bay to the small green, many pros reach the green in three.

The 464-yard ninth runs all the way downhill to the green, and the fairway slopes right toward the sea. The tendency is to keep the ball left, but this lengthens the hole, and the second shot is often from a sidehill lie if the tee shot is to the left. A deep gully left and short of the small green will punish a timid approach shot. This is considered the most difficult hole on the course. The 426-yard tenth has similar challenges, with the ocean on the right and the fairway sloping in that direction. A large fairway bunker begins on the left 209 yards from the left-to-right sloping green, which is 26 yards deep, with a trap left and a huge trap wrapping around the back. The second shot has to have enough distance to carry the inlet that etches into the fairway on the right.

The 565-yard par-5 fourteenth is the number-1-handicap hole, playing inland with the ocean to your back. This dogleg right generally takes three shots for anyone to reach a small green protected by a huge frontal bunker and a trap on the right. The par-5 548-yard finishing hole is dramatically lined by ocean to the left all the way from tee to a small green trapped to the left, right and front. A huge bunker runs into the green along the left side of the fairway about 133 yards out. The temptation for the pros is to reach the green in two by cutting the left corner. Some players have been known to start the ball out over the ocean and have the wind bring it back in. Most mortals reach this green in three or more. The second shot should be placed on the left side of the fairway to avoid the tree on the right that overhangs the green. At this point, regardless of what you scored, you've played what many consider the best golf course in the world.

The Lodge at Pebble Beach is the original 1919-rebuilt Del Monte but renovated with all modern conveniences. There are 161 guest rooms and suites with 3 restaurants, a promenade of shopping boutiques, and 8000 square feet of conference facilities. A beach and tennis club has a heated fresh-water swimming pool, 12 tennis courts, a complete pro shop and a fully equipped exercise center. Most of the rooms are located in rambling low-rise buildings with private patio or balcony and views of flowering gardens, seaside fairways and sunsets over Carmel Bay.

The grounds at Pebble Beach are beautiful. Each year 200,000 seedlings of indigenous plants are cultivated and planted throughout the property, and at least 15,000 of these are trees. A pygmy tree forest can be found in the Morse Preserve, and of course there is the famous Lone Cypress. Species such as the Monterey cypress and Gowen cypress have been grown as part of the resort's reforestation program.

Pebble Beach is one of those shrines of golf that anyone in love with the game must visit or play.

Course Name: POPPY HILLS

Course Type: Public
Address: 3200 Lopez Road
P.O. Box 1157
Pebble Beach, CA 93953
Phone: (408) 625-2154 (Golf Shop)
(408) 625-2035 (Reservations)

GOLF COURSE

Head Professional: John R. Geertsen, Jr.
Course Length/Par (All Tees): Back 6865/72, Middle 6288/72, Forward 5252/72
Course Slope/Rating (All Tees): Back 143/74.8, Middle 135/72.0, Ladies' Forward 131/72.1
Course Architect: Robert Trent Jones, Jr. (1986)
Golf Facilities: Full Pro Shop X, Snack Bar X, Lounge X, Restaurant X, Locker Room X, Showers X, Club Rental X, Club Repair Offsite, Cart Rental X, Instruction X, Practice Green X, Driving Range X, Practice Bunker X, Club Storage Groups
Tee-Time Reservation Policy: Individuals, 2 foursomes or less: 1 mo. in advance. Group reservation, confirmation, 3 or more foursomes (80 players max): 1 yr. in advance. Group reservation requests: 3 yrs. in advance. Credit card guarantee/deposit requirements
Ranger: Yes
Tee-off-Interval Time: 10 min.
Time to Play 18 Holes: 5 hrs.
Course Hours/Earliest Tee-off: 6:30 a.m. Fri., Sat., holidays; 6:50 a.m. Mon., Wed., Thurs.; 8 a.m. Tues.
Green Fees: $105 for 18 holes
Cart Fees: $30 for 18 holes per cart
Credit Cards: MasterCard, Visa

Season: Year round. Busiest Mar. through Nov.
Course Comments: Can walk anytime. Yardage book available
Golf Packages: Available through hotels
Discounts: Guest of member, Northern California Golf Association member
Places to Stay Nearby: PEBBLE BEACH: The Lodge at Pebble Beach (408) 647-7500, (800) 654-9300; Inn at Spanish Bay (408) 647-7500, (800) 654-9300. MONTEREY: Monterey Plaza (408) 646-1700, (800) 631-1339; Hotel Pacific (408) 373-5700, (800) 554-5542. CARMEL VALLEY VILLAGE: Quail Lodge (408) 624-1561, (800) 538-9516; Carmel Valley Ranch Resort (408) 625-9500, (800) 4 CARMEL. CARMEL: Adobe Inn (408) 624-3933; Cypress Inn (408) 624-3871, (800) 443-7443; Colonial Terrace Inn (408) 624-2741, (800) 345-1818 (CA)
Local Attractions: MONTEREY: Whale watching, Monterey Bay Aquarium, Fisherman's Wharf, Cannery Row, beaches, boating, Steinbeck House, Hearst Castle (San Simeon), Monterey Peninsula Museum of Art, galleries, restaurants, seasonal events. CARMEL: Carmel Mission, Point Lobos State Reserve, shopping. Monterey Peninsula Chamber of Commerce (408) 649-1770
Directions: Rte. 101 to Rte. 156 exit, 156 west to Hwy. 1 south, 17-Mile Dr./Pebble Beach exit to Pebble Beach gate for instructions and a map, to stop number 3 on the Drive and golf course
Closest Commercial Airports: Monterey Peninsula (15 min.), San Jose International (1½ hrs.), San Francisco International (2½ hrs.)

POPPY HILLS

Poppy Hills, home of the Northern California Golf Association, is located within the Seventeen-Mile Drive Pebble Beach complex on California's Monterey Peninsula. The facility, the first to be built by a regional golf association, was opened in 1986 after 14 years of planning and development.

Situated on 166 acres of land within the Del Monte Forest and designed by Robert Trent Jones, Jr., the 6865-yard (back tees) Poppy Hills course is a fine test of golf from any of its four tee distances. The course's rolling fairways wind through forest and require strategic shot positioning to avoid the large bunkers, well-placed trees and occasional water hazards. The Pacific Ocean winds are often a major factor here.

Poppy Hills' first hole is a slight dogleg right 413-yard par-4 that plays uphill, then down, to a large, fast two-tiered green. If you are too far right your ball will slide into a hazard quaintly called "Riparian Corridor." Trees protect the left side of the fairway and three bunkers guard the right side of the fairway 200 yards from the tee. Three traps protect the front and right sides of the green.

The 560-yard par-5 fourth is the number-1-handicap hole. A double dogleg that swings to the right and then back to the left, this hole is well protected by trees to the left and right. Three bunkers guard a narrowing fairway from approximately 270 yards to 230 yards from the green. Two relatively straight and long shots are required to get within a pitching wedge of a 53-yard deep green protected by four traps beginning 115 yards from the putting surface.

The number-2-handicap hole is the 393-yard thirteenth hole, an uphill dogleg right to an elevated green. The fairway is lined by trees on the right but is open on the left side with no bunkers. The second shot is to a large, shallow green, protected by two traps on the right.

One of my favorite holes on this course is the par-5 tenth hole, which plays 515 yards from the back tees and adds at least two or three clubs when the wind is blowing toward the golfer from the north. The tee shot is blind and uphill, with trees on both sides and five fairway bunkers protecting the landing area. The next shot should be hit down the right side of the fairway to come into an elongated green, protected front and back by traps and on the left by a large pond. Any shot to the left of the green, which lies slightly downhill and

slopes from right to left, will be in the water.

Many golfers walk Poppy Hills, and it takes about 5 hours to play. Each hole is unique, and the tees are well distanced from the previous green. The clubhouse is a large, modern facility with a fully equipped pro shop, dining area, locker rooms and administrative offices for the Northern California Golf Association. *USA Today* named Poppy Hills one of the top golf courses built in the United States over the past two decades, and *Golf Digest* has listed it among the top 20 courses, public and private, in California.

Course Name: SPYGLASS HILL GOLF COURSE

Course Type: Resort
Resorts: The Lodge at Pebble Beach and the Inn at Spanish Bay
Address: Stevenson Drive and Spyglass Hill/P.O. Box 658
               Pebble Beach, CA 93953
Phone: (408) 625–8563 (Golf Course)
               (408) 649–2711,
               (800) 654–9300 (Resort)
Fax: (408) 647–7496 (Resort)

GOLF COURSE

Head Professional: Laird Small
Course Length/Par (All Tees): Back 6810/72, Middle 6277/72, Forward 5556/72
Course Slope/Rating (All Tees): Back 141/76.1, Middle 135/73.1, Forward 131/72.8, Ladies' Forward 133/73.7
Course Architect: Robert Trent Jones, Sr. (1966)
Golf Facilities: Full Pro Shop X, Snack Bar X, Lounge Wine/Beer, Restaurant No, Locker Room No, Showers No, Club Rental X, Club Repair Minor, Cart Rental X, Instruction X, Practice Green X, Driving Range X, Practice Bunker X, Club Storage Minor
Tee-Time Reservation Policy: Guests: 18 mos. in advance. Public: 60 days in advance with 2 or more players
Ranger: Yes
Tee-off-Interval Time: 10 min.
Time to Play 18 Holes: 5 hrs.

Course Hours/Earliest Tee-off: 6:45 a.m. summer

Green and Cart Fees: Guests: $150 for 18 holes with cart. Public: $195 for 18 holes with cart

Credit Cards: All major cards except Discover

Season: Year round

Course Comments: Can walk anytime. Yardage book available. Caddies available

Golf Packages: Available through resort

Discounts: Twilight rate 3 hrs. before sunset

Place to Stay Nearby: PEBBLE BEACH: The Lodge at Pebble Beach (408) 647–7500, (800) 654–9300. MONTEREY: Monterey Plaza (408) 646–1700, (800) 631–1339; Spindrift Inn (408) 646–8900, (800) 528–0444; Hotel Pacific (408) 373–5700, (800) 554–5542. CARMEL: Adobe Inn (408) 624–3933. CARMEL VALLEY VILLAGE: Quail Lodge (408) 624–1561, (800) 538–9516; Carmel Valley Ranch Resort (408) 625–9500, (800) 4 CARMEL

Local Attractions: MONTEREY: Whale watching, Monterey Bay Aquarium, Fisherman's Wharf, Cannery Row, beaches, boating, Steinbeck House, Hearst Castle (San Simeon), Monterey Peninsula Museum of Art, Big Sur, galleries, restaurants, seasonal events. CARMEL: Carmel Mission, Point Lobos State Reserve, shopping. Monterey Peninsula Chamber of Commerce (408) 649–1770

Directions: From Hwy. 1: Pebble Beach exit, to Pebble Beach gate for map and instruction

Closest Commercial Airports: Monterey Peninsula (15 min.), San Jose International (1½ hrs.), San Francisco International (2½ hrs.)

SPYGLASS HILL GOLF COURSE

The Pebble Beach Co. owns the 5300-acre Del Monte Forest on California's Monterey Peninsula, including the Inn at Spanish Bay; The Links at Spanish Bay; The Spanish Bay Club, which includes a heated outdoor fresh-water swimming pool, a tennis pavilion with 8 championship courts, including 2 lighted for night play, and a fully equipped pro shop; the Resi-

dences at Spanish Bay, including 80 luxury townhouses; the Pebble Beach Equestrian Center, with 34 miles of forest and beach trails; the Seventeen-Mile Drive with spectacular sites such as the Lone Cypress, Seal Rock and Pescadero Point; and the Lodge and courses at Pebble Beach, which include the Beach and Tennis Club with a heated outdoor swimming pool, 12 tennis courts, a complete pro shop and fully equipped exercise center, as well as the Pebble Beach Golf Links, Del Monte Golf Course, and Spyglass Hill.

Spyglass Hill was opened March 11, 1966, after six years of planning, as a part of S.F.B. Morse's master plan for the entire Pebble Beach ocean front. The founder of the Pebble Beach Company and chairman of the board for Del Monte Properties wanted to build golf courses around the Del Monte Forest's shoreline, a task that was completed with the opening of the Links at Spanish Bay in 1987. Spyglass Hill was financed by $626,000 from the members of the Northern California Golf Association, with Del Monte Properties providing the land free of charge.

Six names were originally proposed for the course, and Spyglass Hill was selected as a compromise after a committee deadlock. Named after Robert Louis Stevenson's classic novel Treasure Island, Spyglass' holes are named after characters in Stevenson's books. Robert Trent Jones, Sr., designed the course, which is intended to reward good shot making and to allow little room for error. Jones's son Robert Trent Jones, Jr., designed the nearby Poppy Hills Golf Course and the Links at Spanish Bay.

Jones, Sr. says of the course, "The first five holes were designed with Pine Valley in mind, and the remainder are designed like Augusta National with its majestic pines, lofty ocean views, challenging bunkers protecting landing areas, lakes to grab the errant shot, well-bunkered greens and a challenging putting surface." According to Jones, all pars should be difficult and bogeys should be easy on Spyglass. The PGA has rated hole number eight as the second toughest, number sixteen as the fifth toughest, and number six as the tenth most difficult on the tour. Spyglass Hill is one of the toughest courses in the world from the championship tees, and *Golf Digest* recently rated the course among the best of all golf courses in America, public and private.

"Treasure Island" is the number-1-handicap 600-yard dogleg-left par-5 first hole, which plays downhill to a kidney-shaped, backward-sloping green protected by three large traps left, front and back. It almost always takes at least three shots to reach this green. The 415-yard par-4 dogleg-right sixth begins a string of four difficult finishing holes on the front nine. This hole plays long and uphill and is tree-lined all the way. Two bunkers squeeze the fairway 160 yards from the green, which is skull shaped, slopes severely forward, and has a narrow entrance between two traps right and front, and rear left.

The seventh hole is a 515-yard par 5 straight down a tightly treed fairway to a long, narrow, right-to-left sloping green. A long pond parallel to the fairway protects the green from 80 yards to the front left of the putting surface. The 395-yard par-4 eighth plays straight down a tree-lined fairway that slopes to the right. The second shot is severely uphill to a long, kidney-shaped green protected by a long trap to its right and slightly front. Two or three extra clubs are often needed to reach this green in regulation. The final hole on the front side is the 425-yard par-4 "Captain Smollett." The tee shot must negotiate trees on the left and a fairway bunker 200 yards from the green. The second shot is to a slightly angled deep green with a narrow throat flanked by traps left and right.

A tough par 3 on the back nine is the 180-yard twelfth hole, aptly called "Skeleton Island." The deep, narrow green is angled slightly left to right and paralleled on the left by a large pond approximately 65 yards long. A large trap is to the right and in front of the green, and another trap is on the right. The farther back the pin, the more the water comes into play. "Tom Morgan," the 440-yard par-4 thirteenth hole, is a slight dogleg left uphill to a deep, forward-sloping green flanked by two traps. Trees line the fairway from tee to green,

and a fairway bunker protects the right side 250 yards from the tee. Not many golfers reach this green in two because the second shot is uphill.

The 465-yard par-4 sixteenth is a dogleg right through a treed fairway to one of the smallest greens on the course. A large tree guards the right side of the fairway 215 yards from the green, and two traps protect the front left of the left-to-right sloping putting surface, making it difficult to bounce the ball on in two. This hole, called "Black Dog," is regularly listed as one of the PGA Tour's toughest.

The combination of treed fairways, well-placed bunkers, and strategically shaped and angled greens makes Spyglass quite formidable. For example, the 555-yard par-4 fourteenth, or "Long John Silver," is the number-2-handicap hole and plays up a treed fairway to a landing area squeezed by two large trees. A big hitter might go for the green on the second shot, but most golfers will play up to a narrowing opening to the green, which is shallow, wide, and guarded front-right by a long pond parallel to the fairway 65 yards from the green. Trees guard the back of the putting surface, and two small traps guard the green to the left and right front. The green slopes from left to right. This hole is a wonderful test of golf.

The amenities of the Lodge at Pebble Beach and the Inn at Spanish Bay are nearby and available. See pages 62–67 for details. A snack bar serves breakfast and lunch at the course itself, but there are no locker-room facilities. Spyglass Hill hosts the annual AT&T Pebble Beach National Pro-Am.

Recommended Golf Courses in California

Monterey Peninsula Area:

Fort Ord Golf Course, Fort Ord, (408) 899–2351, Public, Bayonet: 18/6982/72. Blackhorse: 18/6396/72

Golf Club at Quail Lodge, Carmel, (408) 624–1581, Private (must stay at resort to play course), 18/6515/71

Laguna Seca Golf Course, Monterey, (408) 373–3701, Public, 18/6125/71

Old Del Monte Golf Course, Monterey, (408) 373–2436, Public, 18/6278/72

Pacific Grove Municipal Golf Course, Monterey, (408) 648–3175, Public, 18/5732/70

Pajaro Valley Golf Course, Watsonville, (408) 724–3851, Public, 18/6234/72

Rancho Canada Golf Course, Carmel, (408) 624–0111, Public. East: 18/6113/71. West: 18/6229/72

Ridgemark, Hollister, (408) 637–8151, Semiprivate. Diablo: 18/6603/72. Galiban: 18/6771/72

Salinas Fairways Golf Course, Salinas, (408) 758–7300, Public, 18/6587/72

Santa Barbara/San Luis Obispo Area

Course Name: HUNTER RANCH GOLF COURSE
Course Type: Public
Address: 4041 Highway 46 East
Paso Robles, CA 93446
Phone: (805) 237–7444
Fax: (805) 237–7430

GOLF COURSE

Director of Golf: Michael McGinnis
Head Professional: Jeff Vanderhoof
Course Length/Par (All Tees): Back 6741/72, Middle 6293/72, Forward 5639/72
Course Slope/Rating (All Tees): Back 128/72.2, Middle 124/70.4, Ladies' Forward 125/71.1
Course Architect: Kenneth Hunter, Jr. and Michael McGinnis (1995)
Golf Facilities: Full Pro Shop X, Snack Bar X, Lounge X, Restaurant X, Locker Room X, Showers No, Club Rental X, Club Repair X, Cart Rental X, Instruction X, Practice Green X, Driving Range X, Practice Bunker X, Club Storage For Outings
Tee-Time Reservation Policy: Up to 7 days in advance
Ranger: Yes

Tee-off-Interval Time: 10 min.
Time to Play 18 Holes: 4½ hrs.
Course Hours/Earliest Tee-off: 6:00 a.m. Sat., Sun., holidays; 7:00 a.m. weekdays
Green Fees: $40 for 18 holes Fri., Sat., Sun., holidays; $30 for 18 holes Mon. through Thurs.
Cart Fees: $24 for 18 holes per cart
Credit Cards: MasterCard, Visa
Season: Year round. Busiest months Sept. through Nov., Apr. through June
Course Comments: You can walk anytime
Golf Packages: No
Discounts: Twilight
Places to Stay Nearby: PASO ROBLES: Adelaide Inn (805) 238–2770; Travelodge (805) 238–0078; (800) 578–7878. CAMBRIA: Blue Whale Bed and Breakfast (805) 927–4647; Castle Inn by the Sea (805) 927–8605; Fog Catcher Inn (805) 927–1400; Sand Pebbles Inn (805) 927–5600. SAN LUIS OBISPO: Apple Farm Inn (805) 544–2040, (800) 255–2040; Garden Street Inn Bed and Breakfast (805) 545–9802; Madonna Inn (805) 543–3000, (800) 543–9666; Pacific Suites Hotel (805) 549–0800. MORRO BAY: Inn at Morro Bay (805) 772–5651, (800) 321–9566. SAN SIMEON: Greentree Inn Best Western (805) 927–4691; (800) 992–9240
Local Attractions: Morro Rock, Leffingwell's Landing. PASO ROBLES: Arciero Winery, Eberle Winery, Helen Moe's Antique Doll Museum. SAN SIMEON: The Hearst Castle. SAN LUIS OBISPO: Mission Plaza, California Polytechnic State University, Apple Farm, Farmer's Market, San Luis Obispo County Historical Museum, Mission San Luis Obispo, seasonal festivals. CAMBRIA: restaurants, the beach, shops, art galleries. San Simeon Chamber of Commerce (805) 927–3500. Cambria Chamber of Commerce (805) 927–3624. San Luis Obispo Chamber of Commerce (805) 543–1323
Directions: From Hwy. 101 turn east onto Hwy. 46 and proceed 3½ miles to the golf course
Closest Commercial Airports: San Luis Obispo (30 min.), Santa Barbara (2 hrs.), Los Angeles International (3½ hrs.)

HUNTER RANCH GOLF COURSE

Hunter Ranch is a 6741 yard layout built on 227 acres of former ranchland just north and inland from St. Luis Obispo off the Pacific coast. This gently rolling terrain has fast, undulating bentgrass greens that are well protected by bunkers. Water hazards in the form of creeks and ponds can come into play on ten holes including the first hole, a challenging 405-yard par 4 whose tee shot landing area is bordered by a bunker to the left. The approach is to a heavily contoured green with a pronounced left-to-right slope. A creek runs along its left side.

A good par 3 at Hunter Ranch is the 186-yard fourteenth which plays over a canyon to a large, three-tiered green perched on a peninsula with severe drop-offs on three sides and bunkers to its rear. If you miss the target the penalties are severe. One of the most difficult par 5s at Hunter Ranch is the 544-yard seventeenth, a dogleg right whose tee shot has to avoid a creek on the right side and a bunker to the left of the landing area. The second shot provides a choice of whether to play to the right or to the left side of a double fairway. Should you elect to lay up rather than go for the green on your second shot, it is likely to rest on an uneven lie. A creek bordering the green adds to the difficulty of approach shots.

Hunter Ranch is a strategic course on the front side and a more penal course on the back nine which features ravines and a lake that comes into play on Nos. 11, 12, and 15. The course, with its distinctive Australian outback-designed clubhouse, is easy to walk and has no housing on the property. One of the designers of this fine layout is Michael McGinnis, the Director of Golf here and at two other sites, La Purisima in Lompoc and Sandpiper in Goleta, owned by limited partnerships headed by Kenneth H. Hunter, Jr., codesigner of Hunters Ranch. Another course, Huerhuero Creek, a few minutes from Hunters Ranch, is being built by the Hunter group and should open in 1997.

Course Name: LA PURISIMA GOLF COURSE

Course Type: Public
Address:　　　3455 State Highway 246
　　　　　　　　Lompoc, CA 93436
Phone:　　　　(805) 735–8395

GOLF COURSE

Director of Golf: Michael McGinnis
Head Professional: Jim DeLaby
Course Length/Par (All Tees): Back 7105/72, Middle 6657/72, Forward 5763/72
Course Slope/Rating (All Tees): Back 142/75.5, Middle 132/72.8, Forward 118/68.1, Ladies' Forward 131/74.3
Course Architect: Robert Muir Graves (1986)
Golf Facilities: Full Pro Shop X, Snack Bar X, Lounge Beer/Wine, Restaurant X, Locker Room No, Showers No, Club Rental X, Club Repair X, Cart Rental X, Instruction X, Practice Green X, Driving Range X, Practice Bunker X, Club Storage No
Tee-Time Reservation Policy: Up to 7 days in advance from 7 a.m. for weekdays; up to 7 days in advance from 6 a.m. for Sat., Sun., holiday tee times
Ranger: Yes
Tee-off-Interval Time: 7 and 8 min.
Time to Play 18 Holes: 4 hrs., 15 min.
Course Hours/Earliest Tee-off: 6 a.m. Sat., Sun., holidays; 7 a.m. Mon. to Fri.
Green Fees: $40 for 18 holes Fri., Sat., Sun., holidays; $30 for 18 holes Mon. to Thurs. $30.00 for 9 holes Fri., Sat., Sun., holidays; $20 for 9 holes Mon. to Thurs.
Cart Fees: $24 for 18 holes, $15 for 9 holes. Pull Carts: $2 for 18 holes
Credit Cards: MasterCard, Visa
Season: Year round
Course Comments: Can walk anytime. Yardage book available
Golf Packages: Reduced room rates at local hotels
Discounts: Twilight, seniors, juniors (members only)
Places to Stay Nearby: LOMPOC: (5 min.): Motel 6 (805) 736–6514, (800) 437–7468; Days Inn (800) 329–7466, (805)

735–7744; Embassy Suites (805) 735–8311, (800) 362–2779; Quality Inn and Executive Suites (805) 735–7444, (800) 228–5151. SOLVANG: Alisal (805) 688–6411; Chimney Sweep Inn (805) 688–2111; Royal Copenhagen Motel (805) 688–5561; Danish Country Inn (805) 688–2018, (800) 44RELAX; Peterson Village Inn (805) 688–3121, (800) 321–8985; Kronborg Inn (805) 688–2383. BUELLTON: Holiday Inn (805) 688–1000, (800) HOLIDAY; Ramada Inn (805) 688–8448, (800) 272–6232

Local Attractions: Santa Barbara County wine tours, Lompoc Museum, La Purisima Mission State Historic Park. SOLVANG: Old Mission Santa Ines. Santa Barbara. Ojai. Ojai Chamber of Commerce (805) 646–8126. Santa Barbara Visitors Bureau (805) 966–9222. Solvang Visitors Bureau (805) 688–6144. Buellton Visitors Information Center (805) 688–7829

Directions: From Los Angeles (3 hrs.): Hwy. 101 north to Hwy. 246 exit Buellton, west on Hwy. 246 (12 mi.), course on right. From Santa Barbara (37 mi.): Same directions

Closest Commercial Airports: Santa Barbara Municipal (1 hr.); Burbank/Glendale/Pasadena (2 hrs.); Los Angeles International (3½ hrs.)

LA PURISIMA GOLF COURSE

Located approximately 1 hour north and west of Santa Barbara in the Santa Ynez Valley, near Lompoc, California, La Purisima is situated on 300 acres of former ranch land with rolling hills, lakes, ravines and oak forests. The 7105-yard par-72 layout, which was designed by Robert Muir Graves and opened in 1986, is a challenge to any golfer, as suggested by its slope rating of 142 and USGA rating of 75.5 from the back tees.

The front nine is hilly and relatively open, with lakes and streams coming into play on five holes. The course starts out with a 542-yard par-5 dogleg left, which has a small lake on the right beginning 275 yards from an elevated, deep, narrow green protected by two traps to the front and one on the right. Ideally

the first two shots are straight and to the center of the fairway, leaving a wedge or a nine iron on the approach shot.

The second hole is my favorite on the front nine. This is a sharp 432-yard par-4 dogleg left from an elevated tee, with water to the left and right. The tee shot is through a narrow opening to a wide fairway. The first shot should be center or left-center, leaving 150 to 175 yards to the green, which has water front left and behind beginning from 100 yards away. A poorly positioned tee shot forces you to lay up on your second shot. The green is relatively large, concave and forward-sloping, and is protected by a large trap on the right.

The number-1-handicap hole at La Purisima is the 433-yard par-5 fifth hole, which is uphill all the way to a shallow, wide green protected to the front and left by traps. On the tee shot, the right fairway is guarded by a stream. Two bunkers pinch the fairway 160 yards away from the forward-sloping, slick green. The next hole is considered by many to be unreachable in two. A 566-yard par-5 with an elevated tee, left-sloping fairway and two traps to the left of the landing area, this hole often plays into the wind. The second shot is to a target area between two large stands of oak approximately 100 yards from a shallow, forward-sloping, rectangular green protected to the right front and back by large traps. This hole reflects the difficulties of La Purisima: wind, strategically placed trees and bunkers, and greens that require you to fly the ball in rather than bump and run.

The 427-yard par-4 seventh is a dogleg left with a severe drop. The two-tiered green, which is 30 to 40 feet above you on your approach, has a large trap in front. If you hit the ball straight on your tee shot, you have to avoid hitting through the fairway at the dogleg. If you try to go over the top on the left, trees and four fairway bunkers await you. Then there is the wind, which constantly affects club selection and strategy on this hole. The finishing hole on the front nine is a tough 227-yard par 3 protected by eucalyptus trees to the right and left. Beyond and over a creek bed is a deep, skull-shaped green protected by traps on the left and right.

The back nine at La Purisima is somewhat tighter than the front, with water coming into play on five of the holes. The four finishing holes provide a challenge to any golfer. My favorite is the 532-yard par-5 fifteenth, which begins with a narrow tee shot through a chute of oaks to a wide fairway. If you hit straight and long, your ball will catch a slope and roll into deep brush. If you are left and long, you will catch the fairway bunkers approximately 250 yards from the tee. The ideal tee shot is approximately 250 yards and to the right of these bunkers, with your second shot over an unnerving brush-covered canyon to a landing area within pitching range of a deep, narrow green that tilts left to right toward three nearby traps. Shot making on this hole requires accuracy rather than distance, and many frustrated golfers spend time hacking at balls in the brush.

A handsome white stucco Spanish-style clubhouse overlooks the golf course and the surrounding hills. Complete practice facilities, an attractive, high-ceilinged snack bar and restaurant, and a full pro shop are available.

Course Name: OJAI VALLEY INN AND COUNTRY CLUB

Course Type: Resort
Resort: Ojai Valley Inn
Address: Country Club Road
          Ojai, CA 93024–1866
Phone: (805) 646–5511 (Golf Course)
        (800) 422–OJAI (Resort)
Fax: (805) 646–7969 (Resort)

GOLF COURSE

Director of Golf: Scott Flynn
Head Professional: Mark Greenslit
Course Length/Par (All Tees): Back 6252/70, Middle 5909/70, Ladies' Forward 5242/71
Course Slope/Rating (All Tees): Back: 123/70.6, Middle 117/68.9, Ladies' Forward 121/70.0
Course Architects: George C. Thomas, Jr., and William F. Bell (1923); Jay Morrish (renovation, 1988)

Golf Facilities: Full Pro Shop X, Snack Bar X, Lounge X, Restaurant X, Locker Room X, Showers X, Club Rental X, Club Repair Minor, Cart Rental X, Instruction X, Practice Green X, Driving Range X, Practice Bunker X, Club Storage X
Tee-Time Reservation Policy: Guests: 3 mos. in advance. Public: 3 days from 6:30 a.m.
Ranger: Yes
Tee-off-Interval Time: 10 min.
Time to Play 18 Holes: 4 hrs.
Course Hours/Earliest Tee-off: 6:30 a.m.
Green Fees: Resort guests: $80 for 18 holes. Public: $95 for 18 holes
Cart Fees: $15 for 18 holes per rider
Credit Cards: All major cards
Season: Year round
Course Comments: Can walk anytime. Yardage book available. Golf academy on site
Golf Packages: Available through resort
Discounts: Available
Places to Stay Nearby: SANTA BARBARA: El Encanto Hotel & Garden Villas (805) 687–5000, (800) 346–7039; Four Seasons Biltmore (805) 969–2261, (800) 332–3442; San Ysidro Ranch (805) 969–5046, (800) 368–6788; Fess Parker's Red Lion Resort (805) 564–4333, (800) 879–2929; Old Yacht Club Inn (805) 962–1277, (800) 676–1676 (USA), (800) 549–1676 (CA); Santa Barbara Inn (805) 966–2285, (800) 231–0431; Motel 6 (805) 564–1392. VENTURA: Harbortown Marina Resort (805) 658–1212, (800) 622–1212; the Country Inn at Ventura (805) 653–1434, (800) 44RELAX; Inn on the Beach (805) 652–2000
Local Attractions: Shopping, Ojai Valley Museum, Ojai Art Center, Ojai Music Festival, wineries, Los Padres National Forest, Wheeler Hot Springs, Lake Casitas, boating, fishing, hiking, mountain climbing. Santa Barbara. Los Angeles. Ojai Chamber of Commerce (805) 646–8126. Santa Barbara Visitors Bureau (805) 966–9222
Directions: Hwy. 101 to Rte. 133 to Ojai. Golf course and inn on the right approximately 30 min. after exiting onto 133

Closest Commercial Airports: Santa Barbara (45 min.), Burbank/Glendale/Pasadena (80 min.), Los Angeles International (2 hrs.)

RESORT

Date Built: 1923
No. of Rooms: 218 units, including 16 suites with fireplaces
Meeting Rooms: 8. Capacity of Largest: 550 persons. Meeting Space: 8500 sq. ft.
Room Price Range: $195 for rooms to $850 for villas, meals not included. Golf and other packages available
Lounges: Club, Neff Lounge
Restaurants: Oak Grill and Terrace, Vista Dining (Vista Horizon and Buena Vista dining rooms for private parties)
Entertainment: Music in main dining room
Credit Cards: All major cards
General Amenities: Shopping in Ojai, tennis pro shop, golf pro shop, meeting facilities with audiovisual-support capabilities, boutique, babysitter, children's playground
Recreational Amenities: 8 tennis courts (4 lighted), 2 heated swimming pools including a lap pool, sauna, steam rooms, whirlpool, exercise facilities, table tennis, jogging, hiking, horseback riding, croquet, bicycling
Reservation and Cancellation Policy: 1 night's deposit on a major credit card guarantee. 72-hr. cancellation notice required for a full refund
Comments and Restrictions: Small pets only. Pet kennel nearby. Children of any age sharing the same room with their parents stay free. Taxes additional to base rate

OJAI VALLEY INN AND COUNTRY CLUB

One might call the Ojai Valley Inn and Country Club Shangri-La. In 1937 Hollywood film director Frank Capra actually decided to film *Lost Horizon* in Ojai because it reminded him of the Shangri-La described in James Hilton's novel. The 200-acre resort is situated 30 minutes inland from the Pacific and 73 miles northeast of Los Angeles in a little valley surrounded by the Topa Topa Mountains. The native American Indians called the valley Ojai (pronounced Oh-hi), meaning "the Nest." This rural retreat with a sunny mild climate nurtures oak, bright blue lupine, citrus groves and fields of golden poppies. It attracted several wealthy families in the early 1900s, including that of Edward Drummond Libby, a millionaire glass manufacturer from Toledo, Ohio. Inspired by Spanish architecture and culture, Libby wanted to create an Andalusian-style community, which he called Arbolada, and part of this project was the Ojai Valley Inn and Country Club.

Wallace Neff, a renowned architect from Pasadena, designed the clubhouse and inn. The $200,000 golf course, an extravagant sum at the time, was designed by George C. Thomas, Jr., who also designed the Riviera and Bel-Air Country Club golf courses, as well as the North Course of the Los Angeles Country Club. William F. Bell supervised the construction and later became a leading golf architect in his own right. He later formed a successful partnership with his son, William F. Bell., Jr. In designing the Ojai course, which was completed in 1923, Thomas had two major considerations, namely, "that the average golfer could enjoy his round without too great a penalty," and second, that "a test must be offered requiring the low handicap man to play fine golf in order to secure pars."

The inn and the country club attracted the rich and famous, including many from the movie colony, but fell on hard times until a recent $35-million renovation under the ownership of the Crown family of Chicago and the management of Hilton International. Jay Morrish, designer of the excellent Troon courses in Scottsdale, Arizona, among others, was brought in to spearhead the $2-million golf-course renovation project, which is now complete. As a result, Ojai has been recognized by *Golf* magazine as one of the premier resort golf courses in the United States, and its other resort facilities, including accommodations and an excellent tennis facility, have added to the original lustre of Libby's Arbolada without destroying the architectural and design continuity.

Ojai's 6252-yard par-70 golf course is relatively open, with rolling fairways on the front side. The 442-yard par-4 fourth is the number-1-handicap hole and doglegs to the left downhill from an elevated tee. Trees border the fairway on the left, and the right side is relatively open. The second shot is uphill through a tree-lined entrance to a large, skull-shaped green whose opening is well protected by two large traps. The second shot usually has to be flown onto this green with a mid-iron or long iron.

The two long par 3s on this side are a challenge to any golfer. The 203-yard second hole plays to a large right-to-left angled, deep green protected by traps both left and right. The 227-yard eighth hole has a large, deep green that slopes slightly forward and backward from a crest situated toward the front of the green. A huge trap on the left is a popular landing area for many tee shots. The combination of strategically placed trees, well-placed traps and difficult par 3s makes this side play tougher than its distance would indicate.

The back nine has more doglegs and dramatic elevation changes, starting with the 412-yard par-4 dogleg-right tenth hole that plays from an elevated tee to a fairway well protected by a hillside and trees on the right but relatively open on the left. A long left-to-right tee shot to the center of the sloping fairway leaves you with an uphill second shot to a left-to-right angled, forward-sloping green with a trap and a huge oak overhanging on the left. One of my favorite holes is the 358-yard par-4 eleventh, a dogleg right over a gully located 75 yards from a wide but shallow green protected by two traps on the right. The tee shot is from a scenic elevated tee and should be placed left-center for you to have a view to the tree-protected green on your second shot. As with most holes at Ojai, strategic placement rather than distance is essential.

The 115-yard par-3 twelfth is over a gully with a 75- to 100-foot drop to a plateaued green with the beautiful Topa Topa Mountains in the background. Traps protect the forward-sloping green left- and right-front. There is little margin for error on this hole because of trees, a ravine and downward slopes from the medium-sized green. The same is true of the 128-yard par-3 seventeenth, which is protected by trees, a bank and a large trap on the right, a drastically sloped downward drop-off on the left, and trees and a bank to the rear.

The 392-yard par-4 dogleg-right sixteenth is the number-2-handicap hole on the course. The tee shot is uphill over a crest that begins a downward slope 200 yards from the hole. A good tee shot that runs down the hill leaves you with a clear shot to the elevated green, but if you are on the right side, you have to fly the well-placed trap in front of the putting surface. The finishing hole is a 517-yard par 5 that plays straight to a deep green protected by one trap on the left and three traps on the right. These traps can easily catch a second or third shot to the green. The green slopes forward, with a shelf covering 40 percent of the rear putting surface.

The bentgrass greens putt true and are moderately fast at Ojai. There are no dramatic undulations, but a number of greens have one or two tiers, making pin placement a key factor in playing each hole. Ojai is a beautifully situated golf course that presents a fair challenge to any golfer. The inn itself is Spanish-mission architecture, with many rooms overlooking the golf course. During the recent multimillion dollar renovation, a 375-seat Topa conference center was added to accommodate meetings and groups. Hotel facilities, including swimming pool, tennis courts, full golf pro shop and restaurants are all within walking distance of the first tee, which is scenically situated on a hill overlooking the golf course.

Course Name: SANDPIPER GOLF CLUB

Course Type: Public
Address: 7925 Hollister Avenue
                      Goleta, CA 93117
Phone: (805) 968–1541

GOLF COURSE

Director of Golf: Mike McGinnis
Head Professional: John Hughes
Course Length/Par (All Tees): Back 7067/72, Middle 6672/72, Ladies' Forward 5723/73
Course Slope/Rating (All Tees): Back 135/75, Middle, 126/72.5, Forward 108/67.4, Ladies' Forward 117/72.6
Course Architect: William F. Bell, Jr. (1972)
Golf Facilities: Full Pro Shop X, Snack Bar X, Lounge Beer/Wine, Restaurant X, Locker Room No, Showers No, Club Rental X, Club Repair Sent out, Cart Rental X, Instruction X, Practice Green X, Driving Range X, Practice Bunker X, Club Storage No
Tee-Time Reservation Policy: Up to 1 wk. in advance, after 6 a.m. for weekend tee times; 1 wk. in advance after 7 a.m. for weekday tee times
Ranger: Yes
Tee-off-Interval Time: 7 and 8 min.
Time to Play 18 Holes: 5 hrs.
Course Hours/Earliest Tee-off: 7 a.m.
Green Fees: $80 for 18 holes Fri., Sat., Sun., holidays, $40 for 9 holes; $60 for 18 holes weekdays, $30 for 9 holes
Cart Fees: $24 for 18 holes per cart, $15 for 9 holes
Pull Carts: Available
Credit Cards: MasterCard, Visa
Season: Year round
Course Comments: Can walk anytime. Yardage book available
Golf Packages: None
Discounts: Twilight
Places to Stay Nearby: GOLETA: Holiday Inn (800) HOLIDAY. Montecito: San Ysidro Ranch (805) 969–5046, (800) 368–6788. SANTA BARBARA: Harbor View Inn (805) 963–0780, (800) 755–0222; Old Yacht Club Inn (805) 962–1277, (800) 676–1676 (USA), (800) 549–1676 (CA); Four Seasons Biltmore (805) 969–2261, (800) 332–3442; The Sandman Inn (800) 350–8174, (800) 687–2468; Fess Parker's Red Lion Resort (805) 564–4333, (800) 879–2929;

Santa Barbara Inn (805) 966–2285, (800) 231–0431
Local Attractions: Andre Clark Bird Refuge, El Presidio State Historic Park, Santa Barbara County wineries, Santa Barbara Zoo, antiques, Mission Santa Barbara, County Courthouse, Santa Barbara Museum of Art, Historical Museum, Historical Society Museum, Museum of Natural History, beaches. Solvang, CA. Ojai, CA. Montecito, CA. Santa Barbara Visitors Bureau (805) 966–9222
Directions: From Hwy. 101 north: Winchester Canyon Rd. turnoff, first left turn west over freeway, follow signs. From Hwy. 101 south: Winchester Canyon/Hollister Ave. exit, straight to stop, right to golf course
Closest Commercial Airports: Santa Barbara (15 min.), Burbank/Glendale/Pasadena (1 hr.), Los Angeles International (2 hrs.)

SANDPIPER GOLF CLUB

Sandpiper Golf Club, with its beautiful setting along the Pacific Ocean in Goleta, on the north end of Santa Barbara, has sometimes been compared to Pebble Beach. Bordered by the Santa Ynez Mountains and the ocean, Sandpiper is one of the few seaside courses between San Diego and Monterey. The layout, which was opened in 1972, was designed by William F. Bell, the son of golf architect William Bell, who designed the nearby Ojai Valley Inn and Country Club with George C. Thomas, Jr., the Arizona Biltmore Golf Course (Adobe Course) in Phoenix and many other fine courses in the West.

Bell, Jr., a past president of the American Society of Golf Architects, trained and worked with his father after graduating from the University of Southern California. He took over the practice when his father died in 1953. Mr. Bell went on to lay out over 200 courses before he died in 1984. Some of his California courses include Industry Hills Golf Club (Eisenhower and Zaharias courses), City of Industry; Ancil Hoffman Golf Course, Sacramento; Bonita Golf Course, Bonita; Rancho Bernardo Inn and Country Club (West Course), San Diego; and Torrey Pines Municipal (North and South courses), La Jolla. He also designed several other courses in the West and the Pacific.

Sandpiper is a 7067-yard par-72 Bermudagrass layout with large, sweeping fairways and large, fast, undulating greens with subtle breaks. Six of the holes play close to the ocean, including the number-2-handicap 446-yard par-4 fourteenth, whose right fairway parallels the water that pounds against the bluffs below. On the left is gorse, so you have to hit two strong, straight shots to reach the green, which is kidney-shaped and is surrounded by four large traps.

The number-1-handicap hole is the 471-yard par-4 second hole, which usually plays directly into the wind toward the ocean. For approximately 150 yards from the tee there is a narrow chute through eucalyptus trees to the landing area. The second shot is often off a downhill lie to a slightly elevated 36-yard-deep green sloping right to left and also back to front. A huge trap is in back of the green and a smaller one on the right. Few golfers reach this green in two, and when they do, it is difficult to putt.

The 197-yard par-3 sixth hole plays along the ocean, with beautiful views and tricky winds generally blowing left to right across the playing area. The green is large and is protected by three traps. The thirteenth is a 516-yard par 5 that is a relatively straight hole whose right fairway borders the ocean bluffs. For the average golfer the third shot is over a deep canyon and down to a wide, shallow green protected by two traps to the left and right front, and one in back.

With the exception of the wind, the front nine at Goleta plays like an inland golf course, with relatively open fairways. The wind, however, makes many holes play much more difficult than it would first appear. The back nine is more spectacular because of several dramatic ocean holes, including numbers ten through fourteen. The eleventh, for example, is a beautiful and difficult 224-yard par 3 that plays from an elevated tee directly toward the

ocean and a deep, narrow green protected by two traps on the right and one to the left. The finishing hole, also a par 3, is 174 yards over a small lake from an elevated tee to a green protected front, right and left by traps.

In the background are the modern clubhouse and the Santa Ynez Mountains. The clubhouse has a complete pro shop and snack bar with eating areas outside, including a barbecue area used for groups and outings. The views of the ocean and the golf course from this vantage point are spectacular.

Recommended Golf Courses in California

Within 1 Hour of Santa Barbara:

Alisal Ranch Golf Course, Solvang, (805) 688–4215, Resort, 18/6396/72

Black Lake Golf Resort, Nipomo, (805) 481–4204, (800) 423–0981, Resort, 18/6425/72

Horse Thief Country Club, Tehachapi, (805) 822–5581, Semiprivate, 18/6678/72

Rio Bravo Resort, Bakersfield, (805) 871–4653, Private, 18/7018/72

River Ridge Golf Course, Oxnard, (805) 983–4653, Public, 18/6543/72

Simi Hills Golf Course, Simi Valley, (805) 522–0803, Public, 18/6509/71

Soule Park Golf Course, Ojai, (805) 646–5633, Public, 18/6381/72

Within 1 Hour of St. Luis Obispo:

Avila Beach Resort Golf Course, Avila Beach, (805) 595–2307, Public, 18/6443/71

Chalk Mountain Golf Club, Atascadero, (805) 446–8848, Public, 18/6299/72

Morro Bay Golf Course, Morro Bay, (805) 772–4341, Public, 18/6360/71

Los Angeles Area

Course Name: INDUSTRY HILLS Dwight D. Eisenhower, Babe Didrikson Zaharias Courses

Course Type: Public

Resort:	Industry Hills and Sheraton Resort
Address:	One Industry Hills Parkway City of Industry, CA 91744
Phone:	(818) 810–GOLF (Golf Course), (818) 810–4455, (800) 325–3535 (Resort)
Fax:	(818) 854–2425 (Golf Course) (818) 964–9535 (Resort)

GOLF COURSE

Head Professional: Richard Stegall

Course Length/Par (All Tees): Eisenhower: Back 7181/72, Blue 6735/72, White 6262/72, Forward 5589/72. The Babe: Back 6778/71, Blue 6600/71, White 6124/71, Forward 5363/71

Course Slope/Rating (All Tees): Eisenhower: Back 149/76.6, Blue 138/73.5 White 130/70.9, Ladies' Forward 124/72.4. The Babe: Back 144/74.2, Blue 137/72.9, White 130/70.3, Ladies' Forward 123/71.8

Course Architect: William F. Bell, Jr. (1979)

Golf Facilities: Full Pro Shop X, Snack Bar X, Lounge X, Restaurant X, Locker Room X, Showers X, Club Rental X, Club Repair X, Cart Rental X, Instruction X, Practice Green X, Driving Range X, Practice Bunker X, Club Storage X

Tee-Time Reservation Policy: At time of hotel reservation, or 3 days in advance from 8 a.m. to 4 p.m. Sun. to Thurs.; 6 a.m. to 4:30 p.m. for Fri., Sat., holidays

Ranger: Yes

Tee-off-Interval Time: 8 min.

Time to Play 18 Holes: 5 hrs.

Course Hours/Earliest Tee-off: Sunrise

Green and Cart Fees: $60 for 18 holes Fri., Sat., Sun., holidays with cart; $45 for 18 holes Mon. to Thurs. with cart

Credit Cards: All major cards

Season: Year round

Course Comments: Can walk anytime but must pay cart fee

Golf Packages: Available through Sheraton only

Discounts: Twilight, seniors (the Babe Course only)

Places to Stay Nearby: On site: Sheraton Hotel (818) 965–0861, (800) 325–3535. CITY OF INDUSTRY: Courtyard by Marriott (818) 965–1700, (800) 321–2211. LOS ANGELES AREA: Biltmore, Los Angeles (213) 624–1011, (800) 245–8673; Los Angeles Airport Marriott (213) 641–5700, (800) 228–9290; Newporter Resort (714) 644–1700; Anaheim Marriott (714) 750–0800, (800) 228–9290; Westin Bonaventure Hotel (213) 624–1000, (800) 228–3000; Ritz Carlton Huntington (818) 568–3900, (800) 241–3333. LAGUNA NIGUEL: Ritz Carlton (714) 240–2000, (800) 241–3333

Local Attractions: LOS ANGELES AREA: Norton Simon Museum of Art, the Music Center, El Pueblo State Historic Park, Natural History Museum of Los Angeles County, Armand Hammer Museum, Los Angeles Zoo, Chinatown, Little Tokyo, Huntington Library, Art Gallery and Botanical Gardens; El Pueblo de Los Angeles Historical Monument, Griffith Park, professional and college sporting events, restaurants, shopping, Hollywood studios, Olivera St., L.A. County Museum, J. Paul Getty Museum, California Museum of Science and Industry, Craft and Folk Art Museum. Catalina Island. Malibu. Newport. ANAHEIM: Disneyland, professional sports. Los Angeles Visitor and Convention Bureau (213) 689–8822

Directions: From Los Angeles: Rte. 10 east to 60 east, Azusa exit, left on Azusa to Industry Hills Pkwy, left to resort and golf course; or Rte. 10 east to Azusa exit, right on Azusa to Industry Hills Pkwy., right to resort and golf course

Closest Commercial Airports: Ontario (30 min.), Burbank/Glendale/Pasadena (30 min.), Los Angeles International (55 min.), John Wayne/Orange County (55 min.)

RESORT

Date Built: 1982

No. of Rooms: 296

Meeting Rooms: 17. Capacity of Largest: 1200 persons banquet style. Meeting Space: 23,256 sq. ft.

Room Price Range: $89 to $350. Golf packages and other packages, and seasonal rates available

Lounges: Lounge, Putter Cup Bar and Grille

Restaurants: Putter Cup Bar and Grille, Top o' the Brae Restaurant, St. Andrews Snack Bar

Entertainment: Jazz on the Hill, live entertainment in lounge

Credit Cards: All major cards

General Amenities: Meeting and conference facilities with audiovisual and food services

Recreational Amenities: 17 tennis courts, volleyball, horseshoes, equestrian center, Ralph W. Miller Golf Library, Olympic swimming pool, Jacuzzi, sauna

Reservation and Cancellation Policy: Reservation deposit required. Cancellation required before 4 p.m. on day of stay to be fully refunded a deposit

Comments and Restrictions: No pets. Taxes additional to base rates

INDUSTRY HILLS

Besides having two excellent eighteen-hole golf courses, an equestrian center, tennis complex, Olympic swimming facility, and hotel conference center, Industry Hills has the distinction of winning the Outstanding Civil Engineering Achievement Award (1981). The City of Industry was incorporated in 1957 and is dedicated in its charter to the primary goal of creating and maintaining an ideal setting for manufacturing, distribution, and industrial facilities. Situated just 22 miles from downtown Los Angeles, the city now has over 600 firms and is expected to employ over 100,000 people in the 1990s.

The Industry Hills plan of development provided for the transformation of fallow, badly scarred, unsightly land into a recreation and conservation area for the enjoyment of corporate and neighboring residents. As a result, the current 600-acre site, which is situated on a hill with magnificent views of the San Gabriel and San Bernardino mountains, is one of the best recreation and conservation areas in the Los Angeles vicinity.

If you are staying at the 300-room Sheraton conference center hotel, the pro shop, practice area and starting tee are only an elevator ride and a short walk away. The Eisenhower Course, which was designed by William F. Bell, Jr., and opened in 1979, is a demanding 7181-yard par-72 layout from the back tees. The course, set in hilly terrain with a variety of well-placed bunkers, trees, ponds and large, undulating bentgrass greens, gives you the option to play from four different tee placements.

The first hole is a 539-yard par-5 dogleg right with a pond on the left 260 yards from the green. The tee shot should be center or left-center to avoid being stymied by trees along the right side. The second shot is onto or in front of the gently undulating green protected left, right-front and rear by traps. The 369-yard par-4 second hole is my favorite on the front nine. The tee shot is from an elevated tee, with wonderful views of the mountains. Below is a large, forward-sloping green protected in front by a pond and to the right and back left by traps. The first shot is down to a flat landing area. The approach is over the pond to an elevated green trapped to the left, and is out of bounds to the rear. Because of the steep slope of the green, it is not wise to be above the hole when putting or chipping.

The number-1-handicap hole on the Eisenhower is the extremely long 499-yard par-4 sixth, which has two strategically placed left-side bunkers 260 yards from a long, forward-sloping green and protected to the left front by a large trap. Two long, straight shots are required to reach this green in regulation. The 470-yard fourth and the 467-yard seventh are two other long, difficult par 4s on the front nine.

The back nine opens with a tricky par 5 with a blind tee shot downhill to a green 558 yards away. The second shot usually has to be played to the left of a large pond that begins on the right 122 yards from a long green which is angled downhill and sloping from right to left to the top of the pond.

The number-2-handicap hole is the long 474-yard par-4 twelfth, which is protected both left and right by fairway traps beginning 220 yards from the green. The second shot is even tougher, to a right-to-left-sloping long green protected on all sides by five traps. The eighteenth is a huge, 651-yard par 5, with water to the left 275 yards from a deep, three-tiered green with two traps to the right and a huge trap on the left. The first two shots should be played down the left side of the fairway to avoid traps and pine trees on the right.

The Babe Didrikson Zaharias Course, named in honor of one of the greatest female golfers and athletes of all time, is another 18-hole William F. Bell, Jr.- designed layout. The course is par-71 and plays 6778 yards from the back tees. It should also be played if you have the opportunity. Industry Hills also features the excellent Ralph W. Miller Golf Library and Museum that includes more than 5000 books and 1500 bound periodicals, as well as equipment, videos, artwork and other golf memorabilia. An added bonus at Industry Hills is the cable railway built to transport golfers and their equipment up a steep incline from the ninth and eighteenth holes of the Eisenhower and Babe courses. At the top is St. Andrews Station, whose plaza includes the railway coach that transported the body of the late British prime minister Winston Churchill to his funeral procession.

The golf shop at Industry Hills has been listed among the best in the United States by *Golf Shop Operations* magazine, and the Eisenhower Course has been selected as one of the top 75 public golf courses in the United States by *Golf Digest* magazine.

The Ralph W. Miller Golf Museum and Library

The Ralph W. Miller Golf Museum has recently moved to new quarters at Industry Hills, one of the finest public golf courses in southern California. Miller, who died in 1974, was a well-known golfer and golf historian in southern California who contributed his excellent collection of periodicals, books, photographs and golf memorabilia to the museum. There are now more than 7000 golf journals and books (including *The Goff*, published in 1743), as well as displays of golf art, equipment and memorabilia professionally maintained by a capable full-time staff. The museum and library are located in the Sheraton Hotel adjacent to the golf courses. Ralph W. Miller Museum and Library, Industry Hills Golf Club, 1 Industry Hills Parkway, City of Industry, CA 91744, (818) 854–2354.

Course Name: **MORENO VALLEY RANCH GOLF CLUB Lake, Mountain, Valley Courses**

Course Type: Public
Address: 28095 John F. Kennedy Dr.
Moreno Valley, CA 92555
Phone: (909) 924–4444

GOLF COURSE

Head Professional: Hank Schiller
Course Length/Par (All Tees): Valley/ Mountain: Back 6680/72, Blue 6338/72, White 5833/72, Forward 5196/72. Mountain/Lake: Back 6684/72, Blue 6361/72, White 5830/72, Forward 5108/72. Lake/Valley: Back 6898/72, Blue 6453/72, White 5907/72, Forward 5246/72
Course Slope/Rating (All Tees): Valley/ Mountain: Back 137/74.2, Blue 125/70.9, White 118/68.5, Ladies' Forward 112/69.7. Lake/Mountain: Back 135/73.1, Blue 125/70.9, White 118/68.5, Ladies' Forward 112/69.1. Lake/Valley: Back 138/74.4, Blue 126/71.5, White 119/68.9, Ladies' Forward 114/69.8
Course Architect: Pete Dye (1988)
Golf Facilities: Full Pro Shop X, Snack Bar X, Lounge X, Restaurant X, Locker Room X, Showers X, Club Rental X, Club Repair X, Cart Rental X, Instruction X, Practice Green X, Driving Range X, Practice Bunker X, Club Storage No
Tee-Time Reservation Policy: 7 days in advance from 6:30 a.m.
Ranger: Yes
Tee-off-Interval Time: 7 and 8 min.
Time to Play 18 Holes: 4½ hrs.
Course Hours/Earliest Tee-off: 6:30 a.m.

Green and Cart Fees: $53 for 18 holes Sat., Sun., holidays; $38 for 18 holes Mon. to Fri.

Credit Cards: American Express, MasterCard, Visa

Season: Year round

Course Comments: Cart mandatory. Yardage book available. Banquet facilities up to 300 people

Golf Packages: None

Discounts: Seniors, ladies (inquire Mon.), twilight, passbooks

Places to Stay Nearby: MORENO VALLEY: Best Western Image Suites (909) 924–4546, (800) 528–1234; Ramada Inn (909) 243–0088. RIVERSIDE: Holiday Inn (909) 682–8000, (800) HOLIDAY; Sheraton Hotel (909) 784–8000, (800) 325–3535. TEMECULA: Doubletree Suites (909) 676–5656, (800) 528–0444. SAN BERNARDINO: Hilton (909) 889–0133, (800) 445–8667; Maruko Hotel and Convention Center (909) 381–6181, (800) 472–3353

Local Attractions: RIVERSIDE: University of California—Riverside, Riverside Art Museum, Sherman Indian Museum. Big Bear Ski Resort. Lake Perris with water sports, fishing and camping. Palm Springs. Los Angeles. Anaheim. Los Angeles Tourism (213) 624–7300, Anaheim Tourism (714) 999–8999, Moreno Valley Chamber of Commerce (909) 697–4404, Riverside Chamber of Commerce (909) 683–7100, Palm Springs Tourism (800) 347–7746

Directions: Hwy. 60, exit Moreno Beach Dr., south 2 mi. to JFK Dr., left to golf course

Closest Commercial Airports: Ontario (30 min.), Palm Springs Municipal (1 hr.), Los Angeles International (1½ hrs.)

MORENO VALLEY RANCH

Moreno Valley Ranch offers 27 holes of golf within its 4000 acres that include working ranch land. The Valley/Mountain layout totals 6880 yards from the back tees with a 137 slope rating. The many traps and bunkers along some strategically placed water hazards make the Valley nine the toughest on the golf course.

The number-1-handicap hole is the 465-yard par-4 first, which has four fairway bunkers, two to the left and two to the right, on the way to a large, fast, undulating green flanked by a trap on the right, water on the left, and is backed by a huge bunker. The 463-yard par-4 sixth hole winds up a mountain canyon. If you miss to the right on your second shot, which is usually a long iron uphill on this straight hole, the ball will slide downhill and into trouble. The green itself is a difficult, four-tiered putting surface with a trap on the left.

The 547-yard par-5 seventh hole is also challenging, with a huge bunker running all the way from the tee to the beginning of the fairway approximately 180 yards away. A well-placed left-fairway bunker is approximately 250 yards from the green, which is small, protected on the left and right front by traps and in the back and right by a large pond.

The Mountain nine has no water but has mountains, rocks, sagebrush and waste areas to supplement the challenging Dye contingent of bunkers and traps. Somewhat shorter than the Valley nine, this layout places a premium on accuracy. The 453-yard par-4 fifth hole is the number-1-handicap hole. It is relatively straight, is bordered by mountains on the left and has bunkers running down the right side of the fairway. The green is deep, three-tiered and slopes from left to right.

The seventh hole is truly a signature par 3. It plays from an elevated tee to an egg-shaped, unbunkered green on a mountain 180 yards away. Little else is in between except rock, sagebrush, the forward tees and the cart path. Should you miss your shot, there is always the consolation of the view of Big Bear Mountain, St. Andrews Mountain and the city of Moreno Valley below.

The Lake Course is tight, and well-integrated with the surrounding terrain. However, this means there are few expanses and little margin for error because of the abundance of rough, bunkers, rocks and other obstacles. The 428-yard par-4 fifth hole is the number-1-handicap hole, with mountains out of bounds on the left and three well-placed bunkers lining the fairway from the beginning of the landing area to 185 yards from the green, which is protected by a huge trap on the right.

Each of the three nine-hole layouts can be played in any combination. As with all Pete Dye-designed golf courses, this is a very demanding layout requiring well-placed shots and good golf-course management. Therefore, before your round you might want to take advantage of the 14-acre driving range that is part of this impressive facility.

Course Name: **PELICAN HILL GOLF CLUB**
Links, Ocean Courses

Course Type: Public
Address: 22651 Pelican Hill Road South
Newport Coast, CA 92057
Phone: (714) 760–0707

GOLF COURSE

Director of Golf: Jay Colliate
Head Professional: Robert Ford
Course Length/Par (All Tees): Links: Back 6836/71, Blue 6416/71, White 6150/71, Red 5800/71, Forward 4950/71. Ocean: Back 6634/70, Blue 6305/70, White 5883/70, Red 5409/70, Forward 4743/70
Course Slope/Rating (All Tees): Links: Back 142/74.3, Blue 133/72.0, White 122/69.8, Ladies' Red 125/73.0, Forward 111/67.5. Ocean: Men: Back 130/72.1, Blue 125/70.3, White 119/68.1, Ladies' Red 124/72.5, Forward 116/68.7
Course Architect: Ocean: Tom Fazio (1991), Links: Tom Fazio (1993)
Golf Facilities: Full Pro Shop X, Snack Bar X, Lounge Beer, Restaurant No, Locker Room X, Showers X, Club Rental X, Club Repair No, Cart Rental X, Instruction X, Practice Green X, Driving Range X, Practice Bunker X, Club Storage No
Tee-Time Reservation Policy: 6 days in advance with credit card prepayment. Automated reservations accepted 24 hrs.

a day. $20 per player charge to make reservations more than 6 days in advance
Ranger: Yes
Tee-off-Interval Time: 10 min.
Time to Play 18 Holes: 4½ hrs.
Course Hours/Earliest Tee-off: 7 a.m.
Green and Cart Fees: $158 for 18 holes with cart Wed. to Sun., holidays; $129 for 18 holes with cart Mon. and Tues.
Credit Cards: American Express, Diners Club, J.C.B., MasterCard, Visa
Season: Year round
Course Comments: Cart mandatory. Yardage book available
Golf Packages: None
Discounts: Twilight
Places to Stay Nearby: NEWPORT BEACH: The Little Inn on the Bay (714) 673–8800, (800) 438–4466, (800) 438–4466 (CA); Four Seasons, Newport (714) 759–0808, (800) 332–3442; Hyatt Regency, Irvine (714) 863–3111, (800) 233–1234; Sheraton Newport Beach (714) 833–0570, (800) 325–3535; Le Meridien Newport Beach (714) 476–2001; Marriott Hotel and Tennis Club (714) 640–4000, (800) 228–9290; Newporter Resort (714) 644–1700; Pana Point Resort (714) 661–5000. LAGUNA BEACH: Inn at Laguna Beach (714) 497–9722. LAGUNA NIGUEL: Ritz Carlton (714) 640–2000, (800) 241–3333
Local Attractions: Disneyland, Briggs Cunningham Automotive Museum, Movieland Wax Museum, Sherman Library and Gardens, Anaheim Stadium, Mission San Juan Capistrano, Newport Harbor Art Museum, harbor cruises, shopping, restaurants. Corona Del Mar. Laguna Beach. Balboa Island. Newport Conference and Visitors Bureau (714) 644–1190
Directions: I–5 to Rte. 55 (Newport Beach Freeway) to Hwy. 73 to McArthur. Left onto Newport Coast Dr., to Pelican Hill Rd., right on Pelican Hill Rd. to the golf course on the left
Closest Commercial Airports: John Wayne/Orange County (15 min.), Los Angeles International (1 hr.)

PELICAN HILL GOLF CLUB

Situated in the rolling hills and canyons overlooking the Pacific Ocean on the north side of Newport, Pelican Hill's Ocean Course is a beautiful eighteen-hole 6647-yard par-70 layout. Designed by Tom Fazio, the Ocean Course appropriately has ocean views from all eighteen holes. Fazio, who began as an assistant project director in the suburban Philadelphia office of the Fazio family golf course design firm, has designed many excellent golf courses, including Wild Dunes in Charleston, South Carolina; Ventana Canyon Golf and Racquet Club (with George Fazio), Tucson, Arizona; Barton Creek Club (Fazio Course), Austin, Texas; Pelican's Nest, Naples, Florida; and many others.

The Ocean Course is the cornerstone of an affluent residential real-estate development surrounding the golf course. On site is the Fazio-designed Links Course. At present a temporary clubhouse is in place with full pro shop and a snack bar. A driving range and putting area are down the road, and PGA Class A instruction is available at the Pelican Hill Practice and Teaching Center which offers individual, group, junior, women's, corporate and other programs.

The Ocean Course was sodded with drought-tolerant, hybrid Bermuda grass developed in Georgia and tested at a nearby University of California agricultural station to reassure designers of its ability to resist climate changes. Nearly 5000 trees and 40,000 shrubs were planted on the course, including pines, eucalyptus, sequoias, corals and other varieties selected from throughout the United States. The principal source of water is reclaimed water stored in two man-made lakes. Two weather stations on the course measure the rate of water loss through evaporation and absorption into plants (evapotranspiration), while three computers monitor these rates and regulate irrigation flows accordingly. To conserve water, irrigating is done in the evening, when the least amount of evaporation occurs and when it won't disrupt play.

The greens on this course are large, tricky and fast, with a tendency to break toward the ocean. The fairways are relatively wide, with generous slopes into the fairway. It is necessary to hit the greens below the hole because they are tricky to read and three putts are not uncommon. On some holes, such as the eighteenth, the greens are well over 30 yards deep. Pin placement is obviously a factor here, but the wind is not as much of a handicap as one would expect at an oceanside course. The hills surrounding the course modify the breeze, and the gentle trade winds from the ocean don't compare to winds at Pebble Beach or Sandpiper farther north.

The holes at the Ocean Course have colorful and sometimes ominous names like "the Chute," "On the Rocks," "Ocean Bound," "Entrapment," "Deep Canyon" and "Double Cross." The first hole, "The Long," a 443-yard par 4, is straight down the coastline with a grand view of Newport Harbor. The tee shot is downhill to a flat landing area, and the second shot requires extreme accuracy through eucalyptus trees that front a right-to-left-sloping green protected on the left front by a deep bunker.

The front side finishes with four tough holes, beginning with the 403-yard par-4 "Cross Canyon" sixth, which plays from an elevated tee over Los Trancos Canyon to a broad fairway guarded by large bunkers on the left side. The second shot is to an elevated green, which makes the hole play extremely long.

The 195-yard par-3 seventh, called "On the Rocks," is a beautiful hole that plays across a lake to a green set into the rocks and etched by the horizon of the Pacific Ocean beyond. The large green is protected by a bunker on the right and often demands skill with long putts once you get there. Next is "the Alley," the only par 5 on the front nine. This hole plays 563 yards from the back tees and is a true three-shot par 5. Three straight, accurate shots are required to reach a right-to-left running green with a trap on the front left protecting it. The second shot has to negotiate a tightly treed alleyway. The ninth is the 456-yard number-

1-handicap par-4 "Twisted Pine," which usually plays into the wind, making it extremely difficult to reach in regulation. The elevated green also adds to this hole's length and challenge.

The signature hole at Pelican Hill is the spectacular 212-yard par-3 twelfth, which plays to a large green nestled among rock outcroppings, with a large waste area in front. Called "Pelican's Nest," required distance can vary by as much as 40 yards for the tee shot depending on pin placement, but it is better to be long than short. The four finishing holes are tough, concluding with the magnificent 442-yard par-4 "Double Cross," so named because you have to cross a canyon twice on your way down toward the green from an elevated tee carved out of the hillside.

The combination of long par 4s; large, difficult and often elevated greens; and the demands for strategic shot making and awareness of pin position makes the Ocean Course a bright new light on the public golf horizon.

Not to be outdone is The Links Course which offers a stunning variety of holes such as "Postage Stamp," "Cliff Hanger," "Forced Carry," "Gut Check," and "Double Down." "Gut Check," the 543-yard, dogleg right, par-5 seventeenth requires an accurate tee shot to avoid a bunker and water to the right. A Toyon tree to the left of a deep green and the ocean on the horizon tend to create an optical illusion that makes club selection important on the approach. The round concludes with the 426-yard par-4 "Double Down," a dogleg right whose tee shot landing area is framed by huge bunkers. The approach is to a deep, narrow green guarded by large bunkers to its right.

This Newport Coast resort and residential community will ultimately include up to 2600 homes along with a 1300-room conference hotel and a 450-room resort hotel. More than 75 percent of the community has been preserved as permanent open space. When you tee it up on these courses be certain to play from the proper tee distance, perhaps one tee closer than you normally would play. It is unlikely you will find two better or more beautiful courses anywhere.

Recommended Golf Courses in California

Los Angeles Area:

Anaheim Hills Golf Course, Anaheim, (714) 998–3041, Public, 18/6218/71

Brookside Golf Course, Pasadena, (818) 796–8151, Public. C.W. Coiner: 18/6977/72. E.O.Nay: 18/6046/70

Catalina Island Golf Club, Avalon, (310) 510–0530, Public, 9/2167/32

Cypress Golf Club, Los Alamitos, (714) 527–1800, Public, 18/6510/71

Elkins Ranch Golf Course, Fillmore, (805) 524–1440, Public, 18/6302/71

El Rivino Country Club, Riverside, (909) 684–8905, Public, 18/6466/73

Griffith Park Golf Course, Los Angeles, (213) 664–2255, Public. Harding: 18/6536/72. Wilson: 18/6942/72

Hesperia Golf and Country Club, Hesperia, (619) 244–9301, Semiprivate, 18/6996/72

Links at Monarch Beach, Laguna Niguel, (714) 240–8247, Resort, 18/6072/70

Los Robles Golf and Country Club, Thousand Oaks, (805) 495–6171, Public, 18/6264/70

Los Serranos Golf and Country Club, Chino Hills, (909) 597–1711, Public. South: 18/7007/74. North: 18/6292/71

Los Verdes Golf and Country Club, Rancho Palos Verdes, (310) 377–0338, Public, 18/6651/71

Malibu Country Club, Malibu, (818) 889–6680, Public, 18/6740/72

Marshall Canyon Golf Course, La Verne, (714) 593–6914, Public, 18/6068/71

Menifee Lakes Country Club, Menifee, (909) 672–3090, Semiprivate, 18/6472/72

Mountain Meadows, Pomona, (714) 623–3704, Public, 18/6499/72, 9/1981/31

Oak Valley Golf Club, Beaumont, (909) 769–7200, Public, 18/7003/72

Palos Verdes Golf Club, Palos Verdes Estates, (310) 375–2759, Semiprivate, 18/6206/71

Rancho Park, Los Angeles, (310) 839–4374, Public, 18/6585/71

Recreation Park Golf Course, Long Beach, (310) 494–5000, Public, 18/6324/72

Rio Hondo Golf Club, Downey, (310) 927–2329, Public, 18/6344/71

San Dimas Canyon Golf Club, San Dimas, (909) 599–2313, Public, 18/6314/72

Shandin Hills Golf Club, San Bernardino, (909) 886–0669, Public, 18/6517/72

Tijeras Creek Golf Club, Rancho Santa Margarita, (714) 589–9793, Public, 18/6601/72

Palm Springs Area

Course Name: DESERT DUNES

Course Type: Public
Address: 19300 Palm Drive Desert Hot Springs, CA 92240
Phone: (619) 329–2941
Fax: (619) 351–5371

GOLF COURSE

Director of Golf: Todd Connelly
Course Length/Par (All Tees): Back 6876/72, Blue 6614/72, White 6205/72 Forward 5359/72
Course Slope/Rating (All Tees): Back 135/74.1, Blue 129/72.1, White 121/69.3, Ladies' Forward 119/70.7
Course Architect: Robert Trent Jones, Jr. (1989)
Golf Facilities: Full Pro Shop X, Snack Bar X, Lounge X, Restaurant X, Locker Room X, Showers X, Club Rental X, Club Repair X, Cart Rental X, Instruction X, Practice Green X, Driving Range X, Practice Bunker X, Club Storage X
Tee-Time Reservation Policy: 7 days in advance from 6:30 a.m.
Ranger: Yes
Tee-off-Interval Time: 7 min.
Time to Play 18 Holes: 4½ hrs.

Course Hours/Earliest Tee-off: 6:30 a.m. to dark
Green and Cart Fees: $105 for 18 holes Sat., Sun., holidays; $95 for 18 holes weekdays
Credit Cards: All major cards except Discover
Season: Year round. Busiest season Nov. to April
Course Comments: Cart mandatory
Golf Packages: Available through course
Discounts: Seasonal (May to Sept.)
Places to Stay Nearby: PALM SPRINGS: La Quinta Resort (619) 564–4111, (800) 598–3828; Wyndham Palm Springs (619) 322–6000, (800) 346–7308; Ingleside Inn (619) 325–0046, (800) 772–6655; Courtyard by Marriott (619) 322–6100, (800) 321–2211; Hyatt Grand Champions, Indian Wells (619) 341–1000, (800) 882–1234; Ritz Carlton Rancho Mirage (619) 321–8282, (800) 241–3333; Orchard Tree Inn (619) 325–2791, (800) 733–3435
Local Attractions: PALM SPRINGS: shopping, dining, bicycling, tennis, hiking, aerial tramway, Village Green Heritage Center, Desert Museum, Moorten Botanical Garden, Indian Canyons, Living Desert Reserve, Joshua Tree National Monument. City of Palm Springs Tourist Division (800) 347–7746
Directions: From I–10: Palm Dr., Gene Autry Trail exit, north toward Desert Hot Springs, 2 mi., course on right side
Closest Commercial Airports: Palm Springs Municipal (20 min.), Ontario (1 hr.), Los Angeles International (2 hrs.)

DESERT DUNES

In 1989, Desert Dunes was nominated as one of the best new public golf courses in the United States and currently it is considered one of the top 75 public golf courses in America by *Golf Digest*. Designed by Robert Trent Jones, Jr., after Scotland's Troon and Portmarnoch links courses, Desert Dunes is situated on a 174-acre site in the San Gorgonio Pass near Desert Hot Springs, California. Wind is a factor while playing this 6876-yard par-72 layout that is dotted with mounds, moguls and rolling fairways that lead to well-trapped, large, undulating, medium-fast greens. The entrances to the greens are relatively open, so you can bump and run the ball to combat the wind. The four tee positions on the course provide a fair test and enjoyable golf experience regardless of your handicap.

The first hole is a relatively straight 544-yard par 5 that should be played up the left side, because a shot to a valley on the right will leave you with an obstructed view of the green, which is large, tiered and forward sloping, with two traps on the left and one in front. The 417-yard par-4 number-2-handicap second hole is straight, with magnificent views of the San Jacinto Mountains and desert on the left and the clubhouse in the distance. The first shot should be hit to the right of two left-fairway bunkers 160 yards from the green. The second shot is into a 40-yard long, skull-shaped green that slopes left and forward, with one trap on the left and two to the right front.

My favorite hole on the front nine is the beautiful 181-yard par-3 eighth, which plays from an elevated tee to a long green etched by a lake on the right and banked in back with traps to the left front and rear. The front half of the green is terraced, and the right half slopes toward the water. Depending on the wind and pin position, this can be a very tough hole.

The back nine at Desert Dunes has some tamarisk trees, but the Scottish links-style atmosphere prevails. The beautiful 386-yard par-4 tenth hole is lined with trees leading to a deep, forward-sloping green protected by two traps on the right, one trap to the left and a variety of grass bunkers. The tee shot has to negotiate tamarisk trees, which narrow the entrance to the fairway to less than 30 yards. The number-3-handicap 431-yard par-4 fifteenth starts a strong run of finishing holes. The tee shot should be kept right-center to avoid two fairway bunkers and mesquite. The second shot is into a long, narrow green slightly angled left to right, with a huge trap to the right and left front.

The 530-yard par-5 sixteenth is a spectacular hole, with its fairway bending right around fairway bunkers and a large lake that begins 180 yards from the green. The putting surface is trapped on the left and to the right rear, and slopes toward the water. The landscaped area around the green is like a desert rock garden, with a waterfall dropping into the lake on the right. Because the long green is bordered by water on its right, it provides a shallow target, especially from the center and right side of the fairway.

The 192-yard par-3 seventeenth is often into the wind to a deep, kidney-shaped green that has two traps on the left and one on the right. The green is relatively flat, with a landing area in front for short hitters. The closing hole is a challenging 443-yard par 4 requiring a long tee shot that should be hit to the center or left to avoid sliding down the right slope of the fairway. The second shot is into a huge but narrow double green shared with the ninth hole. The green slopes left to right, with plenty of trouble to the right front in the form of traps and grass bunkers.

The clubhouse is a spacious, modern facility with a complete pro shop, restaurant and snack bar facilities, locker rooms and practice facilities nearby. As you drive up the long, palm-lined entrance way to the clubhouse, which looms like a monument, you sense that you aren't about to have an average golf experience. Playing this beautiful, well-designed Robert Trent Jones, Jr., layout bears this out.

Course Name: **DESERT SPRINGS**
Palms, Valley, Greens Courses

Course Type: Resort
Resort: Marriott's Desert Springs
Address: 74855 Country Club Drive
Palm Desert, CA 92260
Phone: (619) 341–1756 (Golf Course)
(619) 341–2211,
(800) 228–9290 (Resort)
Fax: (619) 341–1872

GOLF COURSE

Director of Golf: Tim Skogen
Head Professional: Steve Schaller

Course Length/Par (All Tees): Palms: Back 6679/72, Blue 6381/72, White 6143/72, Forward 5492/72. Valley: Back 6679/72, Blue 6377/72, White 6063/72, Forward 5330/72. The Greens: 1464/54

Course Slope/Rating (All Tees): Palms: Back 124/72, Blue 118/70.2, White 114/69, Ladies' Forward 116/70.8. Valley: Back 124/72.1, Blue 121/70.4, White 109/68.5, Ladies' Forward 110/69.6. The Greens: NA/NA

Course Architects: Palms: Ted Robinson (1985); Valley: Ted Robinson (1986); The Greens: Ted Robinson (1989)

Golf Facilities: Full Pro Shop X, Snack Bar X, Lounge X, Restaurant X, Locker Room X, Showers X, Club Rental X, Club Repair X, Cart Rental X, Instruction X, Practice Green X, Driving Range X, Practice Bunker X, Club Storage X

Tee-Time Reservation Policy: Resort guests: 1 mo. in advance. Public: Up to 3 days in advance guaranteed with a major credit card. No reservation required for the Greens Putting Course

Ranger: Yes

Tee-off-Interval Time: 7 and 8 min.

Time to Play 18 Holes: 4 hrs., 30 min.

Course Hours/Earliest Tee-off: 6:30 a.m. summer

Green and Cart Fees: Resort guests: $125 Sat., Sun. holidays, $115 weekdays for 18 holes with cart. Public: $135 Sat., Sun., holidays, $125 weekdays for 18 holes with cart. The Greens: $10, $5 for children

Credit Cards: All major cards

Season: Year round. Busiest season Nov. to April

Course Comments: Cart mandatory. Computer yardage guide on carts

Golf Packages: Available through resort

Discounts: Seasonal (June to Sept.), twilight

Places to Stay Nearby: PALM DESERT: Embassy Suites Hotel (619) 340–6600, (800) 362–3779; Shadow Mountain Resort and Racquet Club (619) 346–6123, (800) 472–3713; Vacation Inn (619) 340–4441, (800) 231–8675. RANCHO MIRAGE: Rancho Las Palmas (619) 568–2727, (800) 228–9290; Ritz Carlton Rancho Mirage (619) 321–8282, (800) 241–3333. PALM SPRINGS: Ingleside Inn (619) 325–0046, (800) 772–6655; Courtyard by Marriott (619) 322–6100, (800) 325–3535; Wyndham Palm Springs (619) 322–6000, (800) 872–4335; Hyatt Grand Champions, Indian Wells (619) 341–1000, (800) 882–1234; Orchard Tree Inn (619) 325–2791, (800) 733–3435

Local Attractions: Bicycling, hiking, tennis, shopping, restaurants, aerial tramway, Village Green Heritage Center, Desert Museum, Moorten Botanical Garden, Indian Canyons, Living Desert Reserve, Joshua Tree National Monument. City of Palm Springs Tourist Division (800) 347–7746

Directions: I–10, Monterey Ave. exit, south to Country Club Dr., take left to resort

Closest Commercial Airports: Palm Springs Municipal (15 min.), Ontario (1½ hrs.), Los Angeles International (2 hrs.)

RESORT

Date Built: 1987

No. of Rooms: 891

Meeting Rooms: 33. Capacity of Largest: 2000 persons. Meeting Space: 20,000 sq. ft.

Room Price Range: $280 low season to $425 peak season (late Dec. through May), European plan. Golf and other packages available

Lounges: Costas, Lake View Lounge, Atrium Lounge

Restaurants: Mikado, Sea Grille, Club Room Restaurant, Lake View Restaurant, Tuscany's, Oasis, The Springs

Entertainment: Music in Lake View Restaurant, various music/live bands in Costa's

Credit Cards: All major cards

General Amenities: Retail shops, convention and meeting facilities with audiovisual and food services, babysitting, beauty salon

Recreational Amenities: 21 tennis courts, swimming pools and fresh-water lake, exercise facilities, hiking, horseback riding, 27,000-sq.-ft. health spa

Reservation and Cancellation Policy: 1 night's advance deposit. 10-day cancellation notice required to obtain full refund

Comments and Restrictions: No pets allowed. Local pet facilities available. Taxes additional to base rates

DESERT SPRINGS

Situated 13 miles east of Palm Springs, Desert Springs covers 375 acres, employs over 2000 people, is surrounded by 23 acres of private lakes and waterways, has over 5000 trees, and features two eighteen-hole Ted Robinson-designed golf courses and a unique 350-yard eighteen-hole putting course, the Greens. The Greens includes fairways, doglegs, double doglegs, lakes, sand traps, roughs, trees, and challenging greens. The holes range from 70 to 135 yards and are par 2, 3, or 4. It is also lighted for night play.

The 6679-yard par-72 Palms Course wraps around the 891-room hotel complex, which features beautiful landscaping, pools and waterfalls and magnificent views of the Santa Rosa, San Jacinto and Little San Bernardino mountains. The first four holes start you out gradually, beginning with the 528-yard par-5 first hole, which is straight, with a rolling fairway and mounds taking you to a medium-sized green protected on its right front by a large trap and in back by a small trap. Water is to your left all the way to the green, which is banked in back and edged with large palm trees. As you play the Palms Course you will find the greens medium sized, with average speed and subtle undulations. Traps are not abundant, but they are well placed, and the rolls and mounds on the fairways can leave you with tricky lies that require an overall knowledge of the terrain and an ability to cope with it.

The 429-yard fifth hole is the number-1-handicap hole, a par 4 playing straight to a forward-sloping green protected on the left and right by traps. The tee shot should be slightly to the right over a mound and down a chute to a flat area 150 to 175 yards from the hole. Knowing where to land the ball on tee shots is crucial to managing the Palms Course even though it isn't a target course and does provide a reasonable margin for error. This particular hole, as a posted sign attests, has been rated the best fifth hole in the Coachella Valley by *Palm Springs Life* magazine.

One of my favorite holes on the front nine is the 162-yard par-3 third hole, which plays all the way over water to a deep green backed by a huge bunker and bordered by palm trees. To the left is a marvelous landscaped waterfall, with flowers planted on islands in the stream.

The back nine features four strong finishing holes with strategically placed water and bunkers. The 373-yard par-4 fifteenth plays as a slight dogleg left to an oval green located on a peninsula, protected on the left by a trap and sloping forward and slightly left to right. The first shot should be hit to the right fairway, leaving 125 to 150 yards through a narrow neck to the green. The number-4-handicap 409-yard par-4 sixteenth requires a well-placed drive over water from an elevated tee to a landing area between two fairway bunkers. The next shot is generally a mid-iron over water to a forward-sloping, undulating green protected by two traps on the left and a large trap to the right. The next hole is a 160-yard par 3 over pools and waterfalls to an island green backed by mountains in the distance. A huge trap and palm-treed banks back the medium-sized, oval green that is guarded by two traps in front. Many golf balls lie under the surface of the water surrounding this hole.

The eighteenth, a 423-yard par-4 dogleg left, is bordered by water on the left all the way to a right- and forward-sloping green protected by traps to the left and rear in an amphitheaterlike setting. The tee shot should be to hit the left of a right-side fairway bunker, leaving a mid-iron to the green.

Another option at Desert Springs is to play the 6679-yard par-72 Valley Course, which is within walking distance of the hotel. It also has a dramatic finishing hole, a 403-yard par 4 that plays to a landing area straddled by five fairway bunkers, leaving a mid-iron over water to a green banked with palms to the rear.

The rest of the resort has all the amenities ranging from practice ranges and golf instruction from PGA professionals to tennis courts, shopping arcades, an elaborate spa and 10 restaurants, snack bars and lounges. The logo for Desert Springs is a hummingbird, chosen because it represents motion, energy, color and a positive attitude. Golf packages are available through the resort year round.

Course Name: INDIAN WELLS
West, East Courses

Course Type: Resort
Resort: Hyatt Grand Champions Resort
Address: 44–600 Indian Wells Lane
Indian Wells, CA 92210
Phone: (619) 346–4653 (Golf Course)
(619) 341–1000,
(800) 882–1234 (Resort)
Fax: (619) 773–9032 (Golf Course),
(619) 568–2236 (Resort)

GOLF COURSE

Director of Golf: John Darrah
Course Length/Par (All Tees): West: Back 6478/72, Middle 6115/72, Forward 5387/72. East: Back 6662/72, Middle 6227/72, Forward 5521/72
Course Slope/Rating (All Tees): West: Back 116/70.4, Middle 109/68.7, Ladies' Forward 111/70.0. East: Back 118/71.6, Middle 110/69.4, Ladies' Forward 113/70.7
Course Architect: Ted Robinson (1986)
Golf Facilities: Full Pro Shop X, Snack Bar X, Lounge X, Restaurant X, Locker Room X, Showers X, Club Rental X, Club Repair X, Cart Rental X, Instruction X, Practice Green X, Driving Range X, Practice Bunker X, Club Storage X
Tee-Time Reservation Policy: Resort guests: At time of reservation. Public: 3 days in advance from 6 a.m.
Ranger: Yes
Tee-off-Interval Time: 7 and 8 min.
Time to Play 18 Holes: 4½ hrs.
Course Hours/Earliest Tee-off: Sunrise

Green and Cart Fees: Resort Guests: $110 for 18 holes with cart Fri., Sat., Sun.; $100 for 18 holes with cart Mon. to Thurs. Public: $120 for 18 holes with cart Fri., Sat., Sun.; $110 for 18 holes with cart Mon. to Thurs.
Credit Cards: American Express, MasterCard, Visa
Season: Year round. Busiest season Jan. to April
Course Comments: Cart mandatory
Golf Packages: Available through resort
Discounts: Seasonal (May to Dec.), twilight
Places to Stay Nearby: The following hotels have golf packages with Indian Wells golf courses: Stouffer Esmeralda (619) 773–4444, (800) 552–4386; Erawan Garden Hotel (619) 346–8021, (800) 237–2926. Inquire at pro shop for current hotels with package agreements with Indian Wells
Local Attractions: Bob Hope Cultural Center/McCallum Theatre, Desert Museum, Living Desert Reserve, Eldorado Polo Club, horseback riding, desert jeep tours, hot-air ballooning, aerial tramway. City of Palm Springs Tourist Division (800) 347–7746
Directions: I–10 to Washington Ave. exit, south on Washington Ave. to Rte. 111; right on Washington Ave. (2 mi.) to Indian Wells Ln,, right to golf courses
Closest Commercial Airports: Palm Springs Municipal (20 min.), Ontario (1½ hrs.), Los Angeles International (2½ hrs.)

RESORT

Date Built: 1986
No. of Rooms: 336 guest rooms, including suites and villas
Meeting Rooms: 15. Capacity of Largest: 1000 persons. Meeting Space: 17,000 sq. ft.
Room Price Range: $265 to $970 peak season (mid-Dec. to end of May). Golf, tennis, fitness and other packages available year round
Lounge: Pianissimo

Restaurants: Charlie's, Trattoria California, Grand View Lounge (golf clubhouse)

Entertainment: Pianissimo Lounge has music

Credit Cards: All major cards

General Amenities: Meeting facilities with audiovisual and banquet services, business center with secretarial support, gift shop, children's program

Recreational Amenities: 12 tennis courts (8 hard, 2 grass, 2 clay), 5500-sq.-ft. health and fitness club, 4 swimming pools, 2 whirlpool spas, aerobics classes, massage therapists, walking, jogging, bicycling

Reservation and Cancellation Policy: 1 night's deposit required within 10 days of booking. 1 night's deposit will be retained if the cancellation is received less than 48 hrs. in advance

Comments and Restrictions: Complimentary accommodations extended to children under 18 yrs. of age if sharing a room with parents. Maximum 3 adults per room. No pets. Taxes additional to base rates

INDIAN WELLS

The Hyatt Grand Champions Resort is located 16 miles from Palm Springs, near the beautiful San Jacinto Mountains. The five-story hotel itself cost $120 million and was completed in 1986. It is luxuriously appointed with European furniture, Carrara marble from Italy, silk fabric and original artwork. The resort is a blend of traditional European elegance and casual California style. The Grand Champions provides a variety of business conference facilities and capabilities, as well as recreational facilities, including two 18-hole Ted Robinson-designed golf courses with complete practice and instructional services, a tennis club that has 12 courts, instructional programs and a 10,500-seat stadium for special events, and a complete health club. A variety of golf, tennis and fitness packages are available, including the Indian Wells Golf School program.

The first tee on both the West or East course is within easy walking distance of the hotel, whose facilities are on 34 well-manicured acres of desert land. The West Course plays 6478 yards and the East 6662 yards from the back tees. Both courses have rolling fairways with relatively small, undulating, elevated greens. Water and well-placed bunkers make the course play more difficult than it would first seem. Out of bounds comes into play on fourteen of the holes, and pin placement can add to the challenge of the golf course. Both courses demand course management and accuracy, because if you miss plateaued fairway-landing areas, you are likely to have a sidehill or downhill lie, and if you miss around the greens, you're likely to be chipping off a grassy mound or from a trap.

The West Course has more elevation changes than the East Course. It begins with a 501-yard par 5 that is a slight uphill climb to a deep green protected by traps on the left and right. The tee shot must avoid a left-fairway bunker. The second shot is played between a pond on the left and a large bunker on the right. Generally three shots are needed to reach the three-tiered green, which should be approached from the right.

Both par 3s on this side are interesting and difficult from the back tees. The 189-yard third is to a forward-sloping green trapped front, left and right rear, allowing little margin for error. The 211-yard eighth plays uphill to another well-trapped, undulating green. The traps are to the front, right front and left rear with the left side the only bailout area.

Probably the most difficult hole on this side is the 399-yard par-4 sixth, which is a slight dogleg right with water protecting the fairway on the right and left. The second shot is to a forward-sloping, deep, narrow green that has a large trap to the right front and water on the right.

The back nine leads off with a straight 413-yard par 4 whose tee shot must negotiate two fairway bunkers framing a wide landing area. The second shot is uphill to a medium-sized green protected by large traps to the rear and right. The course's signature hole is the beautiful 466-yard par-5 dogleg-right sixteenth, whose tee shot has to negotiate fairway bunkers and out-of-bounds stakes on the left and right. The second shot leaves you with the choice of trying to carry a lake, which runs to the green on the right beginning 75 yards from the putting surface, or playing up and then pitching to the right to a left-angled, forward-sloping green that has a large trap to the right front.

The East Course is a bit longer and rated slightly more difficult than the West. The last four holes on the front side are a good golf challenge, beginning with the 496-yard par-5 sixth, a dogleg left. The tee shot must negotiate a narrow opening bunkered at the turn 180 yards from the back tees. The second shot is toward a forward-sloping, medium-sized green trapped both left and right. The 196-yard par-3 seventh plays to a two-tiered, deep green protected by a large trap on the right and a smaller one to the front and left. An incoming wind often makes this hole play longer than it would appear, and pin position further complicates its problems.

The 536-yard dogleg-right par-5 eighth plays slightly downhill to a deep double green protected left and front by traps. Because of a lake to the right, on the tee shot you are advised to hit the ball left-center while avoiding a fairway bunker 240 yards away. The second shot has to avoid a bunker on the left and a lake to the right. The ninth hole, a par 4, plays 423 yards from the back tees straight to a medium-sized green protected by small traps to the front and rear. The drive has to avoid the hilly left side and the two right-fairway bunkers beginning 200 yards away.

The 370-yard par-4 thirteenth is beautiful and potentially maddening because you have an island fairway to contend with. On this dogleg-right hole, the tee shot has to reach a fairway protected left and right by bunkers at the 150-yard stakes. The second shot is again over water and uphill to a green trapped front and back. The finishing hole is a beautiful dogleg-right 511-yard par 5 with lots of water. The tee shot is to a wide fairway with a large, parallel fairway

bunker and a lake to the right. The second shot tempts you to go for the green, which is shallow and wide. This approach is over water that begins 90 yards from the putting surface. Or you can lay up to the left as most mortals do. The green is three-tiered, with traps both left and front.

You won't be disappointed playing either of these courses. *Golf* magazine has recognized Hyatt Grand Champions as one of the best resort golf facilities in the United States. *World Tennis* magazine has placed the resort on its top tennis resorts list, and it has won many hospitality awards, including the American Automobile Association's Four-Diamond Award.

Course Name: LA QUINTA
**   Dunes, Mountain Courses**

Course Type: Resort
Resort: La Quinta Resort & Club
Address: 49–499 Eisenhower Drive
                        P.O. Box 69
                        La Quinta, CA 92253
Phone: (619) 564–7610 (Golf Course)
                        (619) 564–4111, (800) 472–
                        4316 (CA), (800) 854–1271
                        (Continental U.S.) (Resort)

GOLF COURSE

Director of Golf: Scott Delecio
Head Professional: Alan Deck
Course Length/Par (All Tees): Dunes:
    Back 6747/72, Championship 6230/72
    Middle 5405/72, Forward 5010/72.
    Mountain: Back 6758/72, Championship
    6230/72, Middle 5932/72, Forward
    5405/72
Course Slope/Rating (All Tees): Dunes:
    Back 137/73.1, Championship 124/70.1,
    Middle 114/67.1, Ladies' Middle
    124/72.7, Forward 114/68.0. Mountain:
    Back 140/74.1, Championship 130/71.5,
    Middle 113/67.0, Ladies' Middle
    126/71.3, Forward 120/68.4
Course Architect: Pete Dye (Dunes, 1982;
    Mountain, 1980)
Golf Facilities: Full Pro Shop X, Snack
    Bar X, Lounge X, Restaurant X,
    Locker Room X, Showers X, Club
    Rental X, Club Repair X, Cart Rental
    X, Instruction X, Practice Green X,

Driving Range X, Practice Bunker X, Club Storage X

Tee-Time Reservation Policy: Guests: Up to 120 days in advance. Outside Guests: May book 4 to 30 days in advance at a pre-book rate or may book 3 days in advance at the regular outside rate

Ranger: Yes

Tee-off-Interval Time: 7 and 8 min.

Time to Play 18 Holes: 4½ hrs.

Course Hours/Earliest Tee-off: 7 a.m. peak season

Green and Cart Fees: Dunes: $105 to $140 for 18 holes with cart, range balls. Mountain: $175 to $210 for 18 holes

Credit Cards: American Express, Diners Club, J.C.B., MasterCard, Visa

Season: Year round. Peak season Nov. through April

Course Comments: Cart mandatory. Members and guests have tee-time priority

Golf Packages: Available through resort

Discounts: Seasonal (May to Sept.)

Places to Stay Nearby: PALM SPRINGS: Ingleside Inn (619) 325–0046, (800) 772–6655; Courtyard by Marriott (619) 322–6100, (800) 321–2211; Ritz Carlton, Rancho Mirage (619) 321–8282, (800) 241–3333; Embassy Suites, Palm Desert (619) 340–6600, (800) 362–2779

Local Attractions: Living Desert Reserve, restaurants, shopping, balloon flights, Desert Museum, Oasis Water Park, Palm Springs Aerial Tramway, Moorten Botanic Garden, McCallum Theatre, Joshua Tree National Monument, Empire Equestrian Park, Indian Canyons. City of Palm Springs Tourist Division (800) 347–7746

Directions: I–10 to Washington St. exit, drive south 5 mi. on Washington St. past Hwy. 111 to 50th Ave., turn right, continue past Eisenhower Dr. to security gate and follow road to the club

Closest Commercial Airports: Palm Springs Municipal (20 min.), Ontario (1½ hrs.), Los Angeles International (2½ hrs.)

RESORT

Date Built: 1926

No. of Rooms: 640 guest rooms and suites in hotel, 56 guest casitas

Meeting Rooms: 23. Capacity of Largest: 1800 persons. Meeting Space: 66,000 sq. ft.

Room Price Range: $109 off season (July 1 to Sept. 29) to $2600 hacienda suite peak season (Jan. 17 to May 31). Various golf, tennis, seasonal and other packages available

Lounges: Montañas Bar, Santa Rosa Lobby Lounge

Restaurants: Morgans, Adobe Grill, Golf Clubhouse, Tennis Clubhouse, Montañas

Entertainment: Music in Montañas, plaza area, Adobe Grill

Credit Cards: All major cards

General Amenities: Beauty parlor, business center, plaza shopping arcade, La Quinta Resort Kids Club, babysitting; meeting and convention facilities, including audiovisual, banquet and secretarial services

Recreational Amenities: 25 pools and 38 hot spas, bicycle rental, 30 tennis courts (3 different surfaces) including instruction, Olympic–sized pool, jogging trails

Reservation and Cancellation Policy: Reservations confirmed by deposit of 1 night's room rate. This deposit nonrefundable if the reservation is canceled within 48 hrs. of arrival date, or 30 days for group registrants

Comments and Restrictions: Additional flat fee for small pets. Inquire regarding policy. Kennel arrangements can be made through concierge

LA QUINTA

La Quinta Resort & Club is situated 125 miles east of Los Angeles in the Coachella Valley at the base of the Santa Rosa Mountains. The resort was the brainchild of Walter H.Morgan, the youngest son of a San Francisco oyster magnate. Morgan came to the desert in 1921 for health reasons and purchased 1400 acres of "Happy Hollow," so named by the Cahuilla Indians who originally inhabited the area. Gordon Kaufman, who later designed the Los Angeles Times Building and Santa Anita Raceway, was the architect for the resort which opened in 1926 as a small, secluded retreat. Kaufman received a certificate of honor from the American Institute of Architects "in appreciation of the merit in design and execution of work in the building of La Quinta," whose construction cost was $150,000, a hefty amount for the times.

Morgan had a nine-hole golf course designed by Norman Beth constructed on the grounds, and introduced the sport to the Coachella Valley for a green fee of 1 dollar. Because of his social connections, education, wit and charm, Morgan attracted business, political, social and Hollywood celebrities to La Quinta, a tradition that has remained to this day. Some of these guests have included the William Crockers of San Francisco, Greta Garbo, Bette Davis, Frank Capra, the Vanderbilts, Dwight Eisenhower, Johnny Carson, Governor Edmund "Pat" Brown and many others.

As a result of financial setbacks, Morgan committed suicide in 1931. The resort shut down during World War II, and the United States Army requisitioned the property. After the war, La Quinta again became a celebrity favorite, and in the late 1950s, under the ownership of Chicago attorney Leonard Ettelson, golf was revived at the resort. The La Quinta Country Club was built across the street, and eventually, as the country club became less accessible to hotel guests, Ettelson invested with Landmark Land Company, Inc., to create 54 holes of golf between the resort and the Santa Rosa Mountains. In 1977, Landmark purchased Ettelson's interest in the property, including the La Quinta Resort.

Pete Dye was retained to design all three golf courses, including the Mountain Course and the Dunes courses, which are open to members, guests and the public. The Citrus course is private.

La Quinta has been the site of the PGA Club Professional Championship, PGA Tour Qualifying School, and the California State Open Championship. It has also won many golf, tennis and hospitality awards from the American Automobile Association, *Meetings and Conventions* magazine,

the La Quinta Historical Society, the *Wine Spectator*, *Golf* magazine and *Golf Digest*.

The Dunes Course is a 6861-yard par-72 layout that is a relatively open, target golf course. Water in the form of lakes comes into play on eight holes. Most of the Bermuda-grass greens, which are overseeded with rye in the winter, are elevated and vary in size and shape. The greens tend to be moderate to fast, depending on the season, and are undulating and well trapped. Few fairways parallel each other, and the ninth hole does not come back to the clubhouse as the course winds its way through a real-estate development of Spanish-style structures.

The Dunes front nine is a bit easier than the back nine. The number-1-handicap hole is the 592-yard par-5 seventh, which plays long and straight to a relatively small, gently sloping green, protected by front and side bunkers. The 190-yard par-3 eighth is a beautiful but potentially dangerous hole, with water to the right and front. A bunker is to the left and behind the forward-sloping green. The opening hole on this side is a difficult 384-yard par 4 that plays from an elevated tee to a landing area with a bunker and lakes to the right. The second shot is to an elevated green with traps left, front and right, making the green difficult to hold. Because the greens are well protected by traps, shots coming onto the green on this course usually have to be flown in.

The most noteworthy hole on the back nine is the 436-yard par-4 seventeenth, which has been named one of the eighteen toughest golf holes in America (1986) by the PGA of America. This is a dogleg left with a lake on the left running up to the green, which has railroad-tie buttressing in the Dye tradition. The green, which slopes toward the lake, is framed by the water on the left and bunkers on the right. Two well-placed shots are required to reach this green in regulation. A tee shot too far right leaves too much distance to the well-protected green, and a shot too far left puts you in the water or in a bunker protecting the left fairway.

One of the more picturesque holes on this side is the 147-yard par-3 thirteenth, which plays over water to a small green with a trap in back and water on the left. A date-palm grove can be seen beyond the green, as can the beautiful Santa Rosa Mountains.

The 30,000-square-foot clubhouse includes a restaurant that is open daily, offering full-service breakfast, lunch and cocktails. The golf shop has been selected Best Resort Shop of the Year by *Golf Shop Operations* magazine and golf instruction is available from PGA professionals. The resort also has 30 tennis courts at its on-site tennis club, which has been highly rated by *Tennis* and *World Tennis* magazines.

The Mountain Course requires accuracy in order to avoid an abundance of grass, sand and pot bunkers and water hazards that guard four holes. The greens on this course are usually elevated and well protected by bunkers. A tough and memorable hole on the front side is the 436-yard par-4 ninth whose tee shot must reach a plateaued area for an optimum approach to a deep green framed by bunkers. A water hazard guards the left side of the fairway. The round concludes with a 508-yard par 5, a severe dogleg left that requires to well-positioned shots to afford you the opportunity to finish with a birdie. Whether you play the Dunes or Mountain course, you will have a challenging and enjoyable golf experience.

A $45-million expansion and renovation project completed in 1989 enhanced La Quinta with the addition of two new restaurants, a 17,000-square-foot meeting and banquet-space area called the Salon de Fiesta, and 20,000 square feet of resort retail space. La Quinta now has 640 guest rooms, 25 swimming pools, and 38 hot spas on 45 beautifully landscaped acres. There are also 5 restaurants and a recent addition is the Salon de Flores Ballroom. It has been a long time since Walter Morgan built his desert dream, but today it still glows stylishly in the desert.

Course Name: **PGA WEST JACK NICKLAUS RESORT, TPC STADIUM COURSES**

Course Type: Resort
Resort: PGA West
Address: 56–150 PGA Boulevard La Quinta, CA 92253
Phone: (619) 564–7170, (619) 564–6666
Fax: (619) 771–3105

GOLF COURSE

Director of Golf: John Miller
Head Professional: Billy Neal
Course Length/Par (All Tees): Nicklaus: Back 7126/72, Championship 6546/72, Regular 6037/72, Gold 5612/72, Forward 5043/72. TPC Stadium: Back 7261/72, Championship 6753/72, Regular 6164/72, Gold 5675/72, Forward 5087/72
Course Slope/Rating (All Tees): Niclaus: Back 138/75.5, Championship 129/72, Regular 122/69.2, Gold 124/72.1, Forward 116/69. TPC Stadium: Back 151/77.3, Championship 139/74.4, Regular 130/71.2, Gold 126/72.3, Forward 119/69.0
Course Architect: Nicklaus: Jack Nicklaus (1987), TPC Stadium: Pete Dye (1986)
Golf Facilities: Full Pro Shop X, Snack Bar X, Lounge X, Restaurant X, Locker Room X, Showers X, Club Rental X, Club Repair X, Cart Rental X, Instruction X, Practice Green X, Driving Range X, Practice Bunker X, Club Storage X
Tee-Time Reservation Policy: La Quinta guests: Up to 120 days in advance. Outside guests may book 4 to 30 days in advance at a pre-book rate or may book 3 days in advance at the regular outside rate
Ranger: Yes
Tee-off Interval Time: 8 min.
Time to Play 18 Holes: 4½ hrs.
Course Hours/Earliest Tee-off: 6:30 a.m. summer
Green and Cart Fees: Guests: receive reduced rates. Public: Nicklaus: Peak season rates $205 Sat., Sun., holidays

for 18 holes with cart, range balls. $190 weekdays. TPC Stadium: $210 Sat., Sun., holidays for 18 holes. $195 weekdays

Credit Cards: All major cards except Discover

Season: Year round

Course Comments: Cart mandatory

Golf Packages: Available

Discounts: Seasonal (April to Nov.)

Places to Stay Nearby: La Quinta Resort (619) 564–4111, (800) 854–1271 (outside CA), (800) 472–4316 (CA); Ritz Carlton Rancho Mirage (619) 321–8282, (800) 241–3333 PALM SPRINGS: Wyndham Palm Springs (619) 322–6000, (800) 872–4335; Courtyard by Marriott (619) 322–6100, (800) 321–2211; Ingleside Inn (619) 325–0046, (800) 772–6655; Orchard Tree Inn (619) 325–2791, (800) 733–3435; Marriott Rancho Las Palmas, Rancho Mirage (619) 568–2727, (800) 458–8786; Hyatt Grand Champions, Indian Wells (619) 341–1000, (800) 882–1234; Doubletree Resort (619) 322–7000, (800) 528–0444; Best Western Royal Sun (800) 334–7234, (800) 338–1188

Local Attractions: Desert Museum, Living Desert Reserve, shopping, aerial tramway, Eldorado Polo Club, Oasis Water Park, celebrity home tour, Agua Caliente Indian Reservation, Andreas Canyon, Moorten Botanical Garden, horseback riding, bicycle tours, hot-air ballooning, McCallum Theatre. City of Palm Springs Tourist Division (800) 347–7746, Desert Resorts Bureau (619) 770–9000

Directions: I–10, Washington St. exit, Washington St. south to Rte. 111, left on Rte. 111 to Jefferson St., right on Jefferson St. to end and golf course

Closest Commercial Airports: Palm Springs Municipal (45 min.), Ontario (1½ hrs.), Los Angeles International (2½ hrs.)

PGA WEST

PGA West's golf facilities include a 45,000-square-foot clubhouse, driving ranges, putting and chipping facilities, and PGA professional instruction. PGA West has hosted the Skins Game, Bob Hope Chrysler Classic, PGA Club Professional Championship, PGA Tour Qualifying School and the Wilson/PGA Club Professional Classic.

The Jack Nicklaus Resort Course is a target golf course that plays 7126 yards from the back tees. Water comes into play on seven holes on this course, and there is a variety of fairway mounding, depressions and lipped bunkers that can add strokes to your score. The bentgrass greens are large and moderately fast, with varying undulations. Accuracy is rewarded, errant shots can be severely penalized, and it often takes a good poke just to reach the fairways from the tees.

Each hole has a name, from the opening hole, called "Jack's or Better," to the finishing hole, "Bear Trap." The first five holes on the front nine ease the golfer into the golf course, with the 357-yard par-4 fifth, "Wishbone," being one of the more interesting ones. On this hole, you are faced with a choice of two fairways divided by a waste area, making pin placement critical in plotting your strategy. The green is wide but only 20 yards deep, with sand to the left, front and rear. Positioning off the tee is of obvious importance here.

The final four holes on the front nine are tough, beginning with the 457-yard par-4 "Jagged Edge," which plays straight to a deep green with a trap on the left. The 520-yard par-5 "Desert Valley" seventh provides some relief, but a huge, 65-yard-long waste bunker runs up the left side beginning 130 yards from a green that is deep, slopes back to front and left to right, and is protected by traps on the front left and right. The beautiful 164-yard par-3 "Lily Pad" follows. The tee shot is over water to a long, narrow green with swales to the right front and rear. The trap behind the green cannot be seen from the tee.

The ninth, a 470-yard par 4, is the number-1-handicap hole and is aptly named "Jack's Revenge." A large lake protects the fairway and double green beginning 360 yards from the tee. If the drive is to the left, you'll be hitting over water to a deep green protected by a trap to the left and rear.

The back nine features three strong finishing holes, beginning with the 436-yard par-4 "Cattail," which is straight and long. The tee shot must be long and left to carry water that begins at the tee and runs on the right side for 220 yards. The second shot is toward a small, forward-sloping, left-to-right angled green guarded by a large bunker to the front left. The 210-yard par-3 seventeenth plays to a deep flat green angled left to right and protected by traps to the rear, right front and left front. The par-4 eighteenth, "Bear Trap," plays 458 yards over desert to a landing area bordered by a large lake on the right that runs up to the green. The second shot is to a deep double green shared with the ninth hole. It will probably take three shots to reach the putting surface safely.

The TPC Stadium Course is a typical Pete Dye target course, which is extremely difficult, with a 77.3 USGA rating and a 151 slope from the back tees. The layout was carved from flat, irrigated agricultural land, and over 2 million cubic yards of earth were moved to create undulating fairways, deep bunkers, elevation changes and mounds, and to form lakes, which come into play on half the holes. The bentgrass greens are often large but vary in size and undulation, depending on the overall design and strategy for the hole. For example, the par-3 sixth hole has a huge, 55-yard-deep green, while the 390-yard par-4 fourteenth has a green less than half that size. A good short game and course management are required here or you'll put some big numbers on the board and lose a load of golf balls.

For starters, the par-3 sixth hole, aptly called "Amen," plays 255 yards over water from the back tees to a deep green protected by water on the right. The tee shot should be kept to the left, where there is some bailout room. The PGA rated this hole one of the 18 toughest in America in 1986. The 450-yard par-4 ninth hole, "Reflection," has been rated by *Golf* magazine as one of the 100 greatest golf holes in America. This long dogleg right is considered by many to be the most difficult hole on the course. Water guards the right side all the way from the tee to a two-tiered green, which is totally surrounded by bunkers. The number-1-handicap hole is the 557-yard par-5 eighth, which is probably going to take three shots to reach the green. The tee shot has to negotiate a large bunker on the right and smaller ones to the left. The next shot is through a narrow-necked fairway bordered by an elongated, parallel bunker on the left to a left-to-right tilting egg-shaped green with a large trap in front and left. Needless to say, shot placement is more important than distance on this hole.

The 414-yard par-4 tenth hole is charmingly called "Quarry." The left side is water from tee to green, which is deep and angled left to right, with traps both to the left and front. The tee shot, which probably should be a long iron or a 3-wood, must carry the water to a well-bunkered fairway. Then there are the three finishing holes, which will test any golfer. The 571-yard par-5 sixteenth, "San Andreas Fault," is a slight dogleg left and a true three-shot par 5. The tee shot must get by a huge, deep bunker on the left, and the second shot, if hit to the left, will be in a 20-foot-deep lateral bunker. The green is flat and deep, with the huge lateral bunker protecting it on the left.

Next comes "Alcatraz," a 166-yard par 3 that has no bailout because water surrounds the 31-yard-deep green. Lee Trevino aced this hole in the 1987 Skins Game. Club selection is the key here. The finishing hole is the 440-yard par-4 "Coliseum," which plays over water running from the tee to an elongated green protected by traps to the rear and front right. The tee shot has to be straight to the fairway and must avoid the right fairway bunkers, which begin 230 yards from the back tees.

You can now head straight for the bar or one of the practice facilities, which are among the best in the United States. When you've played a Pete Dye course, you know you've met a golf challenge.

Recommended Golf Courses in California

Palm Springs Area:

Desert Falls Country Club, Palm Desert, (619) 341–4020, Semiprivate, 18/7017/72

Desert Princess Country Club, Cathedral City, (619) 322–2280, (800) 637–0557, Resort. La Vista/El Cielo: 18/6764/72. El Cielo/Los Lagos: 18/6636/72. La Vista/Los Lagos: 18/6667/72

Lawrence Welk's Desert Oasis, Palm Springs, (619) 328–6571, Semiprivate. Lakeview: 9/3197/36. Mountainview: 9/3308/36. Resort: 9/3169/36

Marriott's Rancho Las Palmas Resort, Rancho Mirage, (619) 568–2727, (800) 228–9290, Resort. North/South: 18/6019/71. South/West: 18/5567/69. West/North: 18/5558/70

Mesquite Golf and Country Club, Palm Springs, (619) 323–1502, Public, 18/6328/72

Mission Hills North Golf Course, Rancho Mirage, (619) 328–3198, (800) 358–2211, Resort, 18/7062/72

Mission Lakes Country Club, Desert Hot Springs, (619) 329–8061, Semiprivate, 18/6737/71

Palm Desert Country Club, Palm Desert, (619) 345–2525, Semiprivate, 18/6678/72

Palm Desert Resort and Country Club, Palm Desert, (619) 345–2791, Resort, 18/6571/72

Soboba Springs Country Club, San Jacinto, (909) 654–9354, Semiprivate, 18/6826/73

Sun City Palm Springs Golf Club, Bermuda Dunes, (619) 772–2200, Resort, 18/6720/72

Sun Lakes, Banning, (909) 845–2135, Semiprivate, 18/6997/72

San Diego Area

Course Name: FOUR SEASONS RESORT AVIARA

Course Type: Public

Address: 7447 Batiquitos Drive
               Carlsbad, CA 92009
Phone: (619) 929–0077

GOLF COURSE

Director of Golf: Jim Bellington
Head Professional: Bill Crist
Course Length/Par (All Tees): Palmer 7007/72, Back 6591/72, Middle 6054/71 Forward 5007/72
Course Slope/Rating (All Tees): Palmer 137/74.2, Back 130/71.8, Middle 121/68.9, Ladies Forward 119/69.1
Course Architect: Arnold Palmer (1991)
Golf Facilities: Full Pro Shop X, Snack Bar X, Lounge X, Restaurant X, Locker Room X, Showers X, Club Rental X, Club Repair X, Cart Rental X, Instruction X, Practice Green X, Driving Range X, Practice Bunker X, Club Storage X
Tee-Time Reservation Policy: 6 days in advance from 6:30 a.m.
Ranger: Yes
Tee-off-Interval Time: 9 min.
Time to Play 18 Holes: 4 hrs., 15 min.
Course Hours/Earliest Tee-off: 7 a.m.
Green and Cart Fees: $115 Sat., Sun., holidays for 18 holes with cart, $95 weekdays
Credit Cards: American Express, Diners Club, MasterCard, Visa
Season: Year round
Course Comments: Cart mandatory. Yardage book available
Golf Packages: Available through resort
Discounts: Twilight rates (year round)
Places to Stay Nearby: CARLSBAD: Embassy Suites (619) 453–0400, (800) 362–2779; La Costa Hotel and Spa (619) 438–9111, (800) 854–5000. LA JOLLA: Sheraton Grande Torrey Pines (619) 558–1500, (800) 325–3535; La Valencia Hotel (619) 454–0771, (800) 451–0772; La Jolla Cove Motel (619) 459–2621, (800) 248–COVE; Hyatt Regency La Jolla (619) 552–1234, (800) 233–1234; La Jolla Marriott (619) 587–1414, (800) 228–9290
Local Attractions: Beaches, La Valencia Hotel, Scripps Institute of Oceanography, shopping, restaurants. SAN DIEGO:

San Diego Museum of Contemporary Art, Old Town, fishing, professional baseball, football; Balboa Park, Mission Bay and Sea World, Point Loma, San Diego Zoo, Maritime Museum of San Diego, Coronado Island, Embarcadero, whale watching, shopping, restaurants, harbor tours. San Diego International Tourist Information Center (619) 236–1212

Directions: From I–5 (5 min.): Poinsettia exit, east to Alga, Alga to Batiquitos Dr., Right to golf course

Closest Commercial Airports: San Diego International/Lindbergh Field (30 min.), John Wayne/Orange County (1 hr.), Los Angeles International (2 hrs.)

FOUR SEASONS RESORT AVIARA

The Four Seasons Resort Aviara golf course is an Arnold Palmer-designed 7007-yard par-72 layout. It covers 180 acres and encompasses three valleys and the beautiful Batiquitos Lagoon approximately 45 minutes north of San Diego. Opened in 1991, the golf course is the centerpiece of a resort that will include a sports club and luxury hotel, scheduled to be completed in 1997. *Golf Digest* and *Golf* magazine declared the Four Seasons Aviara one of the top 10 new resort golf courses of 1991. The tees, fairways and rough at the Four Seasons are Bermuda grass, and the large, undulating greens are bentgrass.

Water comes into play on nine of the holes, seven of them on the back nine. The course is relatively open, but a combination of length, well-placed bunkers, wind and challenging, large greens gives the course a 137 slope rating and 74.2 USGA rating from the Palmer tees. One of the more interesting holes on the front nine is the 149-yard par-3 third, which plays to a deep green guarded by a stream and a lake to the front and left, a stream on the right, and traps behind. there is little room for a mistake on this hole, especially if winds are gusting off the pacific ocean, which can be seen from the clubhouse.

The number-1-handicap hole is the 543-yard dogleg-right uphill par-5 fifth. The tee shot has to avoid a long, parallel bunker on

the right. The second shot must negotiate a narrowing fairway with a long, right, parallel bunker beginning 175 yards from the green, and two large left bunkers, one 75 yards from the green, the other to the front left of the putting surface. the green tilts to the right, making it seem deep if you approach from the left but shallow if you come in from the right. The 536-yard par-5 eighth is a slight dogleg left with an open tee shot. The second shot is a character builder because you are faced with water to the left of the green beginning 135 yards from the putting surface. There is also more water in front and to the right of the dance floor. Large traps guard the green on the left and right. Most players would be wise to lay up to the right side on the second shot.

The back nine is tougher, wetter, longer and more interesting than the front side. The 515-yard par-5 dogleg-left tenth has a long lake on the left running from the tee to a deep green protected by huge traps on the left and right. The tee-shot landing area is bordered on the left by a bunker, and the water to the right. The second shot has to pass between the water on the left and a long, parallel fairway bunker that begins 120 yards from the green, which tilts slightly left to right and has an open entrance if you are coming in from the right side.

The five finishing holes will get your golf adrenalin flowing. The 201-yard par-3 fourteenth is a beautiful downhill hole. A huge trap is set to the left of the shallow but wide green, which is protected by water to the right front. The 473-yard par-4 fifteenth requires two accurate, long shots to a deep green well trapped on the right and behind. The tee shot must avoid a series of bunkers beginning approximately 225 yards from the back tees.

The 418-yard par-4 sixteenth is a slight dogleg left down an unbunkered fairway to a green protected by a long pond that begins 110 yards from the putting surface. There is also a large trap to the rear. Club selection on the second shot is determined by pin placement on the extremely deep, narrow green that runs 192 feet from front to rear. The 585–yard seventeenth is a straight, par-5 hole requiring a tee shot and second shot through stands of eucalyptus trees. The deep, narrow green is protected by grass bunkers and a trap in the back.

The eighteenth, a 443-yard par 4, is a great finishing hole. The landing area on this dogleg right is protected by two large bunkers beginning 195 yards from the green and a long pond that runs from 200 yards out to the back of the green on the right. The second shot has to negotiate a long, parallel bunker to the left that begins approximately 45 yards from the green and runs up to its left front side. The green itself is 150 feet deep, angled right to left, and backed by a large trap. An oncoming wind can often make this hole play longer.

Awaiting you at the end of your round is a 32,000-square-foot clubhouse overlooking the Batiquitos Lagoon. On the first level are a fully equipped pro shop, men's and women's locker facilities, with showers, saunas and dressing areas. The Argyle Restaurant and Bar is on the second level. Group tournaments, pro lessons, video analysis, and group instruction can be arranged for all levels of skills from beginner to pro.

The soon-to-be-completed 336-room Four Seasons Resort is part of a 1000-acre master-planned resort and residential community. These facilities will be set on Batiquitos Lagoon, a wildlife preserve and the longest lagoon in California. The hotel is designed in the grand Spanish colonial style, and the major areas will include the main building, guest wing, meeting space, a fine-dining restaurant, cafe, bar and grill, reflective pond, villa and sports center in addition to the completed golf course and clubhouse facilities.

The guest quarters will provide a wide choice of style in the main building and villa, all within walking distance of the first tee. The rooms will range from 625-square-foot standard kings to a 6746-square-foot villa. Dining facilities will include 3 restaurants and a lounge. The meeting facility and amphitheater will encompass 39,000 square feet of space, with capacity for up to 1300 persons.

The resort will also have an 8000-square-foot European-style spa, a swimming pool, and a sports center with 2 pools, an indoor track, 12 tennis courts, racquet sports, fitness rooms, sauna, massage, and child-care area.

The Four Seasons Aviara, situated among hills and valleys with views to the mountains and the nearby Pacific, is an ideal place to play golf and promises to be a world-class resort.

Course Name: RANCHO LA COSTA North, South Courses

Course Type: Resort
Resort: La Costa Resort and Spa
Address: Costa del Mar Road
                    Carlsbad, CA 92009
Phone: (619) 438–9111,
                    (800) 729–4772 (Spa)
                    (619) 438–9111
                    (800) 854–5000 (Resort)
Fax: (619) 438–5866 (Resort)

GOLF COURSE

Head Professional: Gary Glaser
Course Length/Par (All Tees): North: Back 6987/72, Blue 6608/72, White 6269/72, Forward 5939/72. South: Back 6894/72, Blue 6524/72, White 6198/72, Ladies' Forward 5612/74
Course Slope/Rating (All Tees): North: Back 137/74.8, Blue 128/72.1, White 121/69.9, Forward 114/67.9, Ladies' Forward 127/74. South: Back 138/74.4, Blue 129/72.0, White 121/69.8, Forward 114/66.7, Ladies' Forward 123/72.1
Course Architects: North: Dick Wilson (9 holes, 1965), Joe Lee et. al. (9 holes, 1985). South: Dick Wilson (9 holes, 1965), Joe Lee (9 holes, 1972)
Golf Facilities: Full Pro Shop X, Snack Bar X, Lounge X, Restaurant X, Locker Room X, Showers X, Club Rental X, Club Repair X, Cart Rental X, Instruction X, Practice Green X, Driving Range X, Practice Bunker X, Club Storage X

Tee-Time Reservation Policy: At time of registration at resort. Public: Up to 6 days in advance

Ranger: Yes

Tee-off-Interval Time: 7 and 8 min.

Time to Play 18 Holes: 4½ hrs.

Course Hours/Earliest Tee-off: 7:30 a.m.

Green Fees: Guests: $110 for 18 holes. Public: $170

Cart Fees: $20 for 18 holes per person. Caddies Available

Credit Cards: All major cards

Season: Year round. Busiest seasons Jan., Feb., July, Aug.

Course Comments: Cart or caddy mandatory. Yardage Book available. $32 for single, $55 for double caddy in addition to green fees. Must be a registered guest of the resort, member or guest of a member to play the golf courses

Golf Packages: Available through resort

Discounts: Twilight

Places to Stay Nearby: Sheraton Grande Torrey Pines (619) 558–1500, (800) 325–3535; La Valencia Hotel (619) 454–0771, (800) 451–0772; La Jolla Cove Motel (619) 459–2621, (800) 248–COVE; Colonial Inn (619) 454–2181, (800) 832–5525; La Jolla Marriott (619) 587–1414, (800) 228–9290; Hyatt Regency La Jolla (619) 552–1234, (800) 233–1234; Embassy Suites (619) 453–0400, (800) 362–2779

Local Attractions: Beaches, La Valencia Hotel, Scripps Institute of Oceanography, shopping, restaurants. SAN DIEGO· San Diego Museum of Contemporary Art, Old Town, fishing; professional baseball, football; Balboa Park, Mission Bay and Sea World, Point Loma, San Diego Zoo, Maritime Museum of San Diego, Coronado Island, Embarcadero, whale watching, shopping, restaurants, harbor tours. San Diego International Tourist Information Center (619) 236–1212

Directions: I–5 to La Costa Ave. Exit, La Costa Ave. East to El Camino Real Rd., Right to Costa del Mar Rd.

Closest Commercial Airports: San Diego International/Lindbergh Field (30 min.), John Wayne/Orange County (1 hr.), Los Angeles International (2 hrs.)

RESORT

Date Built: 1965

No. Of Rooms: 478 guest rooms, suites, residences

Meeting Rooms: 16. Capacity of Largest: 660 persons banquet style. Meeting Space: 50,000 sq. Ft.

Room Price Range: $225 to $3000 per person per night. Golf, tennis, spa and other packages available

Lounges: Tournament of Champions Lounge, Lobby Lounge, International Saloon

Restaurants: Spa Dining Room, Champagne Room, Brasserie La Costa, Center Court Restaurant, Ristorante Figaro

Entertainment: Live bands in Tournament of Champions Lounge, movie theater

Credit Cards: All major cards

General Amenities: Meeting and conference facilities including audiovisual and food services; retail shopping arcade, La Costa Salon, playground

Recreational Amenities: Racquet Club with 23 tennis courts (4 clay, 19 hard court), pro shop, instruction; men's and women's spas with sauna, steam, massage, facials and gymnasiums with Life circuit, Life Rower, Lifecycle, Stairmaster, Ube and other equipment; La Costa Lifestyle Clinic, medical and fitness evaluations, nutrition center, life fitness and longevity center; 2 heated swimming pools, jogging track, bicycling

Reservation and Cancellation Policy: 1 night's deposit required to guarantee reservation. 48-hr. cancellation in advance of scheduled arrival required for full refund

Comments and Restrictions: No pets allowed. Guests must be registered at hotels or be members or guest of members to play the golf courses or use the spa. Beauty salon and restaurants open to the public. Taxes additional to base rates

RANCHO LA COSTA

Opulent is the word that comes to mind when describing La Costa. Situated on 1000 acres of prime real estate just 30 minutes north of San Diego, the resort includes two eighteen-hole PGA Championship golf courses; a 23-court racquet club with grass, clay and composition surfaces; 6 restaurants; a 50,000-square-foot conference center and a complete spa and health center. The *Mobile Travel Guide* Four-Star and American Automobile Association Four-Diamond resort has recently undergone a $100-million addition and renovation and now comprises 478 luxurious rooms, suites and executive homes; heated swimming pools; a jogging trail and even a 180-seat movie theater featuring first-run films nightly.

The North Course at La Costa is a 6984-yard par-72 layout designed by Dick Wilson and Joe Lee. The first nine was part of the championship course originally built by Wilson in 1965. Lee added another nine in 1972. The North Course is the site of the PGA Mercedes Tournament of Champions. Water comes into play on seven of its holes, and most of them have a liberal supply of strategically placed bunkers and trees. The first hole is a straight, 412-yard par 4, with two fairway bunkers straddling the tee-shot landing area. The second shot is to a medium-sized, circular green with a narrow opening guarded by two deep traps. Another trap protects the back right.

The second hole is the number-3-handicap 526-yard par 5, which is a slight dogleg right to a green surrounded by four traps and guarded by a large pond on the right from 100 yards in. The third is a 187-yard par 3 to a forward-sloping, acorn-shaped green protected by four traps. The fourth is a 382-yard par 4 protected left and right by fairway bunkers 170 yards from a tiered green that is 35 yards deep and well protected by large traps left, right and center. The second shot has to carry the front trap to the green.

The 392-yard par-4 fifth hole tee-shot landing area is protected by three left- and right-fairway bunkers. The approach is to a deep, tiered green protected by two traps on each side. The sixth is the number-1-handicap hole, a 545-yard par-5 dogleg left. The first shot should be played left of center and the second down the left side to cut some of the distance to the green, which is large, deep and has traps to the left, right and front. This hole plays long because the approach to the green is uphill and the golfer is generally playing into the wind.

The seventh is 463 yards and par 4, downhill and downwind to a large green protected on the left front and right by traps. Two fairway traps are on the left beginning 220 yards from the green, with a large right-fairway trap opposite. The front nine finishes with two of my favorite holes. The 201-yard par-3 eighth plays over water that runs from tee to green on the right side. The tee shot is usually downwind to a 27-yard deep, oval, forward-sloping green protected by two traps in back. The ninth is a 412-yard par-4 dogleg right whose tee shot has to negotiate water on the right and three fairway bunkers to the left and at the knee of the dogleg. The second shot is uphill and into the wind to a large green protected both left-front and right by large traps.

The number-2-handicap hole is the 446-yard par-4 fourteenth, whose fairway is cut twice by a stream. The tee shot has to be hit straight to a landing area protected by fairway bunkers on the right and a stream on the left. The second shot requires extreme accuracy onto a small, heart-shaped green protected left, front and back by huge traps, with trees edging the fairway on the right from 75 yards out to the green. The finishing hole is a 538-yard par 5 that is into the wind and requires two long, straight shots to be around the green in two. Fairway bunkers are clustered 220 yards from the tee and 150 yards from the green, with a stream crossing the fairway 70 yards from a long foot-shaped green protected left, right rear and front by large traps.

The 6894-yard par-72 South Course is also well guarded by a stream, bunkers and a large pond. The slope rating from the back tees is 138 and the USGA rating is 74.4. A total of four tee positions enables you to fit your game to the course. The last four holes on the South Course are called "golf's longest mile" because the golfer is usually hitting into the wind. The 569-yard par-5 seventeenth often requires three woods to reach a well-protected, deep green with traps to the left and rear and water on the right.

If you feel beat up after playing Rancho La Costa, the various spa facilities await you. Everything from life-fitness and longevity programs to herbal wraps, hot-oil-conditioning treatments, nutrition programs, facials and a variety of other options are available. As for golf, complete practice facilities, pro shop and the latest video-based instructional programs are available from PGA professionals. Various golf and other packages are available through the resort. Caddies are also available on the golf course should you wish to walk and benefit from the advice of someone who knows the course.

Course Name: **SINGING HILLS COUNTRY CLUB AND LODGE Oak Glen, Pine Glen Willow Glen Courses**

Course Type: Resort
Address: 3007 Dehesa Road
El Cajon, CA 92019
Phone: (619) 442–3425 (Golf Course)
(619) 442–3423 (Lodge)

GOLF COURSE

Director of Golf: Tom Addiss III
Head Professional: Devin Thomas
Course Length/Par (All Tees): Willow Glen: Back 6605/72, Middle 6247/72, Forward 5585/72. Oak Glen: Back 6597/71, Middle 6489/71, Forward 6044/71. Pine Glen: Back 2508/54, Forward 2253/54
Course Slope/Rating (All Tees): Willow Glen: Back 124/72.0, Middle 113/69.5. Ladies' Middle 130/76.3, Ladies' Forward 122/72.8. Oak Glen: Back 121/70.7, Middle 107/68.3, Ladies' Forward 124/71.4. Pine Glen: NA/NA

Course Architect: Ted Robinson (1967)
Golf Facilities: Full Pro Shop X, Snack Bar X, Lounge X, Restaurant X, Locker Room No, Showers No, Club Rental X, Club Repair X, Cart Rental X, Instruction X, Practice Green X, Driving Range X, Practice Bunker X, Club Storage X
Tee-Time Reservation Policy: At time lodge Reservations are booked. Public: 1 wk. In advance
Ranger: Yes
Tee-off-Interval Time: 8 min.
Time to Play 18 Holes: 4½ hrs.
Course Hours/Earliest Tee-off: Daylight
Green Fees: Willow Glen, Oak Glen: $35 for 18 holes Sat., Sun., Holidays; $29 for 18 holes weekdays. Pine Glen: $12 for 18 holes
Cart Fees: $20 for 18 holes per cart
Credit Cards: All major cards
Season: Year round. Busiest Jan., June through Aug.
Course Comments: Can walk anytime except when some group tournaments are underway
Golf Packages: Available through hotel
Discounts: Twilight, seniors (par 3 course), juniors
Places to Stay Nearby: Singing Hills Lodge (on premises) (619) 442–3423. SAN DIEGO: U.S. Grant Hotel (619) 232–3121, (800) 237–5029; Le Meridien Hotel (619) 435–3000, (800) 543–4300; Horton Grand Hotel (619) 544–1886, (800) 542–1886. LA JOLLA: La Valencia Hotel (619) 454–0771, (800) 451–0772; La Jolla Cove Motel (619) 459–2621, (800) 248–COVE
Local Attractions: Beaches, La Valencia Hotel, Scripps Institute of Oceanography, shopping, restaurants. SAN DIEGO: San Diego Museum of Contemporary Art, Old Town, fishing, professional baseball, football; Balboa Park, Mission Bay and Sea World, Point Loma, San Diego Zoo, Maritime Museum of San Diego, Coronado Island, Embarcadero, whale watching, shopping, restaurants, harbor tours. San Diego International Tourist Information Center (619) 236–

1212. El Cajon Chamber of Commerce (619) 440–6161.

Directions: From I–5 or I–805: I–8 east to El Cajon Blvd. exit, continue to second stop light, turn right on Washington, through series of stop lights to four-way stop intersection. Continue 2.2 mi. from stop to club

Closest Commercial Airports: San Diego International/Lindbergh Field (30 min.), John Wayne/Orange County (1 hr.), Los Angeles International (2 hrs.)

SINGING HILLS COUNTRY CLUB AND LODGE

Situated on 720 acres in a picturesque river valley in El Cajon, Singing Hills Country Club and Lodge is just 30 minutes east of San Diego. Opened in 1967, the Ted Robinson-designed layout now includes 54 holes of golf, including the 6608-yard par-72 Willow Glen Course, the 6597-yard par-71 Oak Glen layout and the 2508-yard par-54 Pine Glen executive course. The natural terrain, featuring hills, rock outcroppings, water and beautiful old sycamores and oaks, adds considerable character to Singing Hills, which has hosted a variety of PGA, USGA and Southern California Golf Association events.

The number four 323-yard par-4 hole on Willow Glen is one of my favorite holes on the course. The first shot is from an elevated tee with a drop of 100 to 150 feet to a flat fairway featuring a lake on the right and in front of the green from 90 yards in. The tee shot should be placed left of center to leave a wedge to the forward-sloping green, which is well protected by four traps, one on each side. Water—including the Sweetwater River, which runs through the entire course—ponds and lakes come into play on half the holes on Willow Glen.

The number-1-handicap hole is the 544-yard par-5 eighth hole, which has the highest stroke average on the course. This hole is long, straight and well protected by trees. The first shot is through a tight corridor of trees to a relatively flat fairway. The second shot is slightly uphill toward a deep, forward-sloping, undulating green with a

large oak tree and water to the right. This is a great three-shot par-5 hole.

The par 3s on Willow Glen are all challenging, with my favorite being the 169-yard twelfth, which plays to a deep, two-tiered green with a trap in back. From the tee, on the left are trees and beautiful flower beds, and on the right is a pond that lines the fairway and with the dulcet sounds of a waterfall culminates at the green. The finishing hole is also a par 3 that plays 167 yards to a deep, three-tiered green protected on the right and front by a huge trap and on the left by another trap. The most difficult hole on this side is the 413-yard par-4 sixteenth, which plays straight but often long because of an incoming wind and an elevated green that usually makes the second shot to the pin blind.

Oak Glen is well worth playing, as is the executive course. Oak Glen also has water on half its holes, mostly on the front nine. The 149-yard par-3 fourth hole is extremely tough because water runs along the left fairway and around the back of a long, forward-sloping green. A huge tree stands 50 yards from the green midway between the water and the cart path. There is no bail-out on this hole, and hitting the tree or the water is all too easy. I also like the 488-yard par-5 seventh hole, which is long, straight and protected on the left by trees and out-of-bounds markers. More trees are on the right. The elevated tee shot is through a narrow opening. On the second shot, the fairway begins to narrow from 180 yards into a deep green that slopes from back to front.

Within walking distance of the well-appointed golf shop and the first tees at Singing Hills is a motel-style lodge with 103 rooms. Additional facilities such as conference rooms, hospitality rooms, and banquet amenities are available for groups ranging from 15 to 300 persons. An adjacent tennis club has 11 courts, a clubhouse, pro shop and instruction. Business conferences and group-tournament outings are heavily promoted at Singing Hills, and if you are visiting for more than a day or two, there are several excellent, accessible golf courses within easy driving distance of this well-run, well-maintained golf destination.

Course Name: STEELE CANYON
GOLF CLUB
Canyon, Meadow,
Ranch Courses

Course Type: Semiprivate
Address: 3199 Stonefield Drive
Jamul, CA 91935
Phone: (619) 441–6900
Fax: (619) 441–6809

GOLF COURSE

Director of Golf: Jeff Johnson
Head Professional: John Rathbun
Course Length/Par (All Tees): Canyon/Ranch: Back 6741/71, White 6220/71, Gold 5657/71, Forward 4656/71. Canyon/Meadow: Back 6672/71, White 6196/71, Gold 5522/71, Forward 4814/71. Ranch/Meadow: Back 7001/72, White 6484/72, Gold 5821/72, Forward 5026/72
Course Slope/Rating (All Tees): Canyon/Ranch: Back 135/72.2, White 112/69.7, Gold 107/66.2, Ladies' Gold 124/72.6, Forward 112/66.6. Canyon/Meadow: Back 134/72.2, White 122/69.2, Gold 110/65.8, Ladies' Gold 126/72.6, Forward 118/67.9. Ranch/Meadow: Back 137/74.0, White 125/70.7, Gold 118/67.5, Ladies' Gold 135/74.2, Forward 124/69.5
Course Architect: Gary Player (1991)
Golf Facilities: Full Pro Shop X, Snack Bar X, Lounge X, Restaurant No, Locker Room No, Showers No, Club Rental X, Club Repair X, Cart Rental X, Instruction X, Practice Green X, Driving Range X, Practice Bunker No, Club Storage No
Tee-Time Reservation Policy: 7 days in advance from 6:00 a.m.
Ranger: Yes
Tee-off-Interval Time: 10 min.
Time to Play 18 Holes: 4½ hrs.
Course Hours/Earliest Tee-off: Sunrise
Green and Cart Fees: $60 for 18 holes with cart Sat., Sun., holidays; $46 for 18 holes with cart weekdays

Credit Cards: American Express, MasterCard, Visa
Season: Year round
Course Comments: Can walk, but cart fee must be paid
Golf Packages: None
Discounts: Twilight
Places to Stay Nearby: Singing Hills Lodge (619) 442–3423. SAN DIEGO: U.S. Grant Hotel (619) 232–3121, (800) 237–5029; Le Meridian Hotel (619) 435–3000, (800) 543–4300. LA JOLLA: La Valencia Hotel (619) 454–0771, (800) 451–0772; La Jolla Cove Motel (619) 459–2621, (800) 248–COVE
Local Attractions: Beaches, La Valencia Hotel, Scripps Institute of Oceanography, shopping, restaurants. SAN DIEGO: San Diego Museum of Contemporary Art, Old Town, fishing, professional baseball, football; Balboa Park, Mission Bay and Sea World, Point Loma, San Diego Zoo, Maritime Museum of San Diego, Coronado Island, Embarcadero, whale watching, shopping, restaurants, harbor tours. San Diego International Tourist Information Center (619) 236–1212. El Cajon Chamber of Commerce (619) 440–6161.
Directions: From San Diego (30 min.): Rte. 94 east, becomes Rte. 54, right on Willow Glen Rd., first right on Steele Canyon Rd., first left on Jamul at light, course on left at Stonefield Dr.
Closest Commercial Airports: San Diego International/Lindbergh Field (30 min.), John Wayne/Orange County (1 hr.), Los Angeles International (2 hrs.)

STEELE CANYON GOLF CLUB

Steele Canyon is situated on a former cattle ranch 17 miles inland from the Pacific Ocean and 30 minutes from downtown San Diego. The three nine-hole courses, designed by Gary Player, are the centerpiece of a real-estate development begun in the mid-1980s. The Canyon, Ranch and Meadow nines are descriptive of their locales, with magnificent views of the beautiful hills and valley in the area.

The 6741-yard par-71 Canyon/Ranch layout is a wonderful combination of up-

and downhill holes over rolling fairways carved out of hilly ranch land, with magnificent views of valleys and hills beyond. The Canyon Course begins within walking distance of the clubhouse. The first hole, a par-4 dogleg left, plays 409 yards from an elevated tee down to a fairway, which then runs uphill to a forward-sloping, deep green with a large trap to the right and a banked hill to the left. The second hole is a links-style, treeless 552-yard par 5, an uphill dogleg-left requiring a strong tee shot over rough to reach the fairway. The second shot is toward a relatively small green situated on a flat plateau with a hillside bank behind and right and a drop-off to the left. This is the number-1-handicap hole on the front nine, and the uphill topography of the hole requires of most golfers at least three shots to reach the green.

The third hole is a beautiful, 182-yard par 3 that plays from a plateaued tee over a barranca to a hillside green with a bank on the right and a drop-off to the left. The 524-yard par-5 fourth has spectacular vistas of the surrounding valley and hills, and a 100- to 150-foot drop to a fairway bunker on the right and a relatively flat area on the left. The second shot is toward a right-to-left-sloping, slightly elevated green with a terrace on the right third of the putting surface.

As you reach the fifth tee of the 214-yard par 3 you might feel like a mountain goat or a hang glider because over 100 feet below you is a large green with water to the far right and three traps on the left and two traps right-rear, with a hillside on the left sloping down to the green. The 360-yard par-4 sixth plays uphill, with water on the left, a banked, rough-covered hillside along the right and fairway bunkers 125 to 150 yards from the long, undulating, forward-sloping green that has an abrupt drop-off to the left. The second shot to the green allows little margin for error. The seventh hole is the third par 3 on the Canyon nine and plays 171 yards over a gully from a plateaued tee to a plateaued green banked to the rear, with a severe drop-off in front. Though wide, the green is relatively shallow and slopes forward. Putting or chipping from above the hole toward the gully can be very unnerving.

The 390-yard par-4 eighth plays from an elevated tee downhill to a fairway protected by a hillside to the right and gorse and rocks to the left. The second shot is over a narrowing fairway with water on the left and a hillside to the right. The green is in an amphitheater setting with water toward the front and left and three traps in the banked, knolled hillside to the rear. The par-4 finishing hole plays 404 yards straight down a bunkered fairway to a large, forward-sloping green with traps left, right and rear.

The Ranch nine is longer than the Canyon and features two tough par 3s, the 189-yard fourth and the 230-yard eighth. The number-1-handicap hole on this side is the 441-yard par-4 third, which has a scenic view from an elevated tee down to a flat landing area, with five left-side fairway bunkers 150 to 200 feet below. The second shot is to a green banked back and right, and with two traps on the left. The par-5 finishing hole plays 542 yards downhill from a dramatic elevated tee to a fairway with pasture left and a drop-off to the right. Three bunkers, two to the right and one to the left, flank the landing area, and on the second shot the fairway slopes down and is squeezed by water left and right approximately 125 to 225 yards from the green.

These golf courses provide a challenging variety of memorable golf holes. Be sure to play this layout when you are in the San Diego area. There are four tee positions, ranging from 6741 to 4656 yards. Golf instruction is available from the staff of PGA professionals.

Course Name: TORREY PINES
**   North, South Courses**

Course Type: Public
Address: 11480 N. Torrey Pines Road
                       La Jolla, CA 92037
Phone: (619) 452–3226

GOLF COURSE

Head Professional: Joe DeBock
Course Length/Par (All Tees): North:
  Back 6659/72, Middle 6375/72, Ladies'

Forward 6104/74. South: Back 7021/72, Middle 6706/72, Ladies' Forward 6447/76.

Course Slope/Rating (All Tees): North: Back 129/71.3, Middle 119/69.6, Ladies' Forward 111/73.6. South: Back 130/74, Middle 126/72.2, Ladies' Forward 121/75.8.

Course Architect: William F. Bell, Jr. (1955)

Golf Facilities: Full Pro Shop X, Snack Bar X, Lounge X, Restaurant X, Locker Room No, Showers No, Club Rental X, Club Repair X, Cart Rental X, Instruction X, Practice Green X, Driving Range X, Practice Bunker X, Club Storage No

Tee-Time Reservation Policy: 7 days in advance (619) 570–1234, from 5 a.m.

Ranger: Yes

Tee-off-Interval Time: 7 min.

Time to Play 18 Holes: 5 hrs.

Course Hours/Earliest Tee-off: 7:30 a.m.

Green Fees: $49.50 for 18 holes Sat., Sun., holidays, $42 for 18 holes weekdays. $21 for 9 holes

Cart Fees: $25 for 18 holes

Credit Cards: MasterCard, Visa

Season: Year round

Course Comments: Can walk anytime. Yardage book available. Cart mandatory for tournament play

Golf Packages: Golf-school package available through golf shop (619) 452–3226

Discounts: Twilight, city and county residents

Places to Stay Nearby: Sheraton Grande (619) 558–1500, (800) 762–6100; La Valencia Hotel (619) 454–0771, (800) 451–0772; La Jolla Cove Motel (619) 459–2621, (800) 248–COVE; Torrey Pines Inn (619) 453–4420; Colonial Inn (619) 454–2181, (800) 832–5525; La Jolla Marriott (619) 587–1414, (800) 228–9290; Hyatt Regency La Jolla (619) 552–1234, (800) 233–1234; Embassy Suites (619) 453–0400, (800) 362–2779

Local Attractions: Beaches, La Valencia Hotel, Scripps Institute of Oceanography, shopping, restaurants. SAN DIEGO: San Diego Museum of Contemporary Art, Old Town, fishing; professional baseball, football; Balboa Park, Mission Bay and Sea World, Point Loma, San Diego Zoo, Maritime Museum of San Diego, whale watching, shopping, restaurants, harbor tours. Coronado Island. Embarcadero. San Diego International Tourist Information Center (619) 236–1212

Directions: From San Diego (5 min.): I–5, Gennessee exit, west to North Torrey Pines Rd., turn north to golf course (follow signs)

Closest Commercial Airports: San Diego International/Lindbergh Field (45 min.), John Wayne/Orange County (1 hr.), Los Angeles International (2½ hrs.)

TORREY PINES

The Torrey Pines North and South golf courses are municipal facilities run by the City of San Diego Park and Recreation Department. These courses have consistently been listed by *Golf Digest* in its top 75 public golf courses in America rankings. Torrey Pines is the annual host to the Buick Invitational and Shearson-Lehman Hutton Open. Beautifully situated adjacent to the 1100-acre Torrey Pines State Preserve and above the Pacific Ocean north of La Jolla, the courses have been played by many of the best golfers in the world, including Tom Watson, Arnold Palmer, Gary Player and Jack Nicklaus. The courses are relatively open and graced with cypress, torrey pines and eucalyptus, and visited by a rich variety of birds and other creatures such as deer and an occasional bobcat. They are also swept by some unpredictable winds from the ocean.

The greens are bentgrass and small to medium in size, moderately fast and relatively flat. Both courses were designed by William F. Bell, a native Californian who designed many excellent courses in the Golden State, including Industry Hills (Eisenhower Course, Zaharias Course), City of Industry; Ancil Hoffman Golf Club, Carmichael; Palo Alto Municipal with his father, William Park Bell; Singing Hills Country Club (Willow Glen Course); El Cajon with William P. Bell and William H. Johnson; and many others.

At 7021 yards from the back tees the Torrey Pines' South Course plays slightly harder than the 6659-yard North Course, but either layout is a fine test of golf. Fog, rain and chilling winds can further complicate your golf game at Torrey Pines. The westerly ocean wind is usually a factor in the afternoon.

The North Course leads off with a straight, 520-yard par 5 with intermittent fairway trees to a deep, narrow green protected to the front, left and rear by traps. Two fairway bunkers straddle the tee-shot landing area. A picturesque hole on this front side is the 160-yard par-3 sixth, which plays from an elevated tee down toward the ocean and a medium-sized green protected on the left front, right front, and rear by traps. A crosswind can blow your tee shot into a canyon on the left, and the forward-sloping green can be tricky. The eighth hole, a 436-yard par 4, is the number-1-handicap hole and plays straight to a large green protected by large traps on the right. The ocean is behind you on your tee shot, so you might get some help from the wind.

The back nine begins with a straight 416-yard par 4 to a large green with two traps in front and one to the left rear. The eleventh is a tough 437-yard par-4 dogleg left that has a canyon on the left and a relatively small green protected by a trap on the right. The tee shot should be hit right-center but not into the fairway bunker 225 yards from the tee. The second shot can be rolled onto the open front of the green. The 421-yard par-4 thirteenth plays away from the ocean and is a sharp dogleg left, tempting the long hitter to go over the top. A good tee shot to the bend of the dogleg will leave a mid-iron to a right-to-left-angled green protected on the right front and left by traps. Another scenic hole is the 172-yard par-3 seventeenth, which plays downhill to a green protected by a large trap on the right and a pond on the left. The tee shot is usually into the wind, making club selection crucial.

The long South Course starts out with a difficult 453-yard straight par 4 with a fairway trap on the right, midway to the green. The putting surface is protected on the left and right front by traps, which makes rolling the second shot onto the green difficult. The seventh hole, a 454-yard par 4, has been voted one of the toughest holes on the PGA Tour. It is a long dogleg right that bends slightly toward the ocean to a right-to-left-angled green protected both left front and right by traps. The number-1-handicap hole is the 447-yard par-4 fourth, which plays straight to a deep green protected by traps on the left and right.

The twelfth and thirteenth holes are the most noteworthy holes on the back nine. Twelve, a straight par 4, plays 469 yards from the back tees and 457 yards from the regular tees to a deep green with a trap on the left. The next hole is a 533-yard par 5 that plays straight to a wide, shallow green guarded on the left and right front by traps. The finishing hole, a 499-yard par 5, provides ample birdie opportunity if you hit two long, straight shots while avoiding two fairway bunkers midway to the green and a large pond to the left front of the putting surface. The green is small and straddled by two traps.

At Torrey Pines, a full-service golf shop serves both courses and a restaurant and snack bar are in a separate building. A driving range and putting and chipping facilities are available, along with PGA instruction.

La Jolla was originally called La Hoya (meaning "the cave") because of the caves that dot the shoreline here. The Spaniards then called it La Jolla, "the Jewel," and the two golf courses, along with the surrounding nature preserves and coastline, are part of this natural legacy. These courses are heavily played, so call in advance. You can walk on if you show up before the 7:30 a.m. reservation tee-off schedule begins, but you will have a lot of company.

Recommended Golf Courses in California

Within 1 Hour of San Diego:

Carlton Oaks Country Club and Lodge, Santee, (619) 448–8500, Public, 18/7088/72

Carmel Highlands Doubletree Golf and Tennis Resort, San Diego, (619) 672–9100, (800) 622–9223, Resort, 18/6501/72

Carmel Mountain Ranch Country Club, San Diego, (619) 487–9224, Public, 18/6669/72

Coronado Golf Course, Coronado, (619) 435–3121, Public, 18/6633/72

Eastlake Country Club, Chula Vista, (619) 482–5757, Public, 18/6608/72

Eagle Crest Golf Club, Escondido, (619) 737–9762, Public, 18/6417/72

Monarch Beach Golf Links, Dana Pointe, (714) 240–8247, Resort, 18/6227/72

Mount Woodson Country Club, Ramona, (619) 788–3555, Semiprivate, 18/6017/70

Palo Mesa Resort, Fallbrook, (619) 728–5881, Resort, 18/6528/72

Rams Hill Country Club, Borrego Springs, (619) 767–5125, (800) 722–4700, Resort, 18/6866/72

Rancho Bernardo Inn and Country Club, San Diego, (619) 675–8470, (800) 662–6439, Resort, 18/6388/72

Rancho San Diego Golf Course, El Cajon, (619) 442–9891, Public. Ivanhoe: 18/7011/72. Monte Vista: 18/6036/71

Red Hawk Golf Club, Temecula, (909) 695–1222, (800) 451–4295, Public, 18/7139/72

Southern California Golf Association Member's Course at Rancho California, Murietta, (909) 677–7446, (800) 752–9724, Public, 18/7059/72

Temecula Creek Inn, Temecula, (909) 676–2405, (800) 962–7335, Resort. Creek/Oaks: 18/6784/72. Oaks/Stonehouse: 18/6693/72. Creek/Stonehouse: 18/6605/72

Death Valley: Furnace Creek Golf Course, Death Valley, (619) 786–2301 (Pro Shop), (619) 786–2345 (Resort), Resort, 18/6036/70

Fresno Area: Fresno West Golf & Country Club, Kerman, (209) 846–8655, Public, 18/6959/72

California: Useful Information

California Office of Tourism, P.O. Box 9278, T 98, Dept. 1003, Van Nuys, CA 91409, (800) 862–2543

Department of Fish and Game, 1416 9th St., Sacramento, CA 95814, (916) 445–3531 (fishing and hunting regulations)

California State Park System, Dept. of Parks and Recreation, P.O. Box 942896, Sacramento, CA 94296–0001, (916) 445–6477 (recreation information)

National Forests, Pacific-Southwest Region, U.S. Forest Service, 630 Sansome St., Rm. 527, San Francisco, CA 94111, (415) 556–0122 (recreation information)

National Park Service, Fort Mason, Bldg. 201, Bay and Franklin Sts., San Francisco, CA 94123, (415) 556–0560 (recreation information)

Los Angeles Convention and Visitors Bureau, 685 S. Figueroa St., Los Angeles, CA 90017, (213) 689–8822

Los Angeles Chamber of Commerce, 404 S. Bixel St., Los Angeles, CA 90017, (213) 629–0602

San Diego International Visitors Information Center, 11 Horton Plaza, San Diego, CA 92101, (619) 230–1212; or 2688 E. Mission Bay Dr., San Diego, CA 92109, (619) 276 8200

San Francisco Visitor Information Center, 900 Market St., San Francisco, CA, (415) 391–2000

Redwood Empire Association Visitor Information Center, 785 Market St., San Francisco, CA 94103, (415) 543–8334 (information on Northern California)

Denver and North Central Area

Course Name: ARROWHEAD GOLF CLUB

Course Type: Public
Address: 10850 W. Sundown Trail
Littleton, CO 80125
Phone: (303) 973–9614

GOLF COURSE

Head Professional: Gordon Tolbert
Course Length/Par (All Tees): Back 6682/70, Middle 6249/70, Forward 5521/70
Course Slope/Rating (All Tees): Back 134/70.9, Middle 129/68.9, Ladies' Forward 124/71.4
Course Architect: Robert Trent Jones, Jr. (1972, reopened 1982)
Golf Facilities: Full Pro Shop X, Snack Bar X, Lounge X, Restaurant X, Locker Room No, Showers No, Club Rental X, Club Repair X, Cart Rental X, Instruction X, Practice Green X, Driving Range X, Practice Bunker No, Club Storage No
Tee-Time Reservation Policy: Up to 7 days in advance
Ranger: Yes
Tee-off-Interval Time: 8 min.
Time to Play 18 Holes: 5 hrs.
Course Hours/Earliest Tee-off: 6 a.m. to dark (seasonal)
Green and Cart Fees: Non-Colorado residents: $90 for 18 holes with cart. Colorado residents: $80 for 18 holes with cart 7 days a week
Credit Cards: All major cards
Season: March throug Nov.
Course Comments: Cart mandatory. Yardage book available
Golf Packages: Available through some local hotels
Discounts: Twilight rates, American Golf Club discounts. Seasonal prior to June and after Sept.
Places to Stay Nearby: Embassy Suites Denver Tech Center South (303) 792–0433, (800) EMBASSY; Denver Hilton South (303) 779–6161, (800) 445–8667; Hyatt Regency Tech Center (303) 779–1234, (800) 233–1234; Holiday Inn (303) 695–1700, (800) 962–7672; Sheraton Denver Tech Center (303) 779–1100, (800) 552–7030; Denver Marriott Southeast (303) 758–7000, (800) 228–9290. BED AND BREAKFAST: Bed and Breakfast Colorado Ltd. (303) 494–4994, (800) 373–4995 (statewide reservation service)
Local Attractions: LITTLETON: Littleton Historical Museum. DENVER: Denver Art Museum, Museum of Western Art, Trianon Museum and Art Gallery, Children's Museum of Denver, Mile High Flea Market, Colorado state capitol, Coors Brewing Co. tours, Rocky Mountain Arsenal Wildlife tours, Black American West and Heritage Center, Buffalo Bill's Museum and grave, Byer-Evans House, Colorado History Museum, Colorado Railroad Museum, Denver Fire Fighters Museum, Denver Museum of Miniature Dolls and Toys, Denver Museum of Natural History, Molly Brown House Museum, buffalo herd, Denver Botanical Gardens, Denver Zoo, dog racing; professional soccer, baseball, basketball; river rafting, horseback riding, shopping, restaurants, art galleries, concerts, theater, night clubs, University of Denver. Denver Metro Convention and Visitors Bureau (303) 892–1112, (800) 283–2754, Fax: (303) 892–1636
Directions: From Denver (25 mi.): Santa Fe Ave. South to Titan Rd. and right on Titan Rd. Stay on Titan Rd. until you see signs for golf course
Closest Commercial Airport: Denver International (1 hr.)

ARROWHEAD GOLF CLUB

The Arrowhead Golf Club is backed by a spectacular wall of red-rock typically found in nearby Red Rocks Park, the Garden of the Gods and Roxborough Park, which form the eastern slope of the Rocky Mountains. This area is inhabited by more than 300 species of birds and animals, including falcons, eagles, deer, elk, fox and some 235 varieties of wildflowers and plants. The Ute and Arapaho Indians once populated this area, but eventually settlers took over, introducing a mixture of oil exploration, railroading, ranching and other mercantile activities. The golf course, whose construction began in 1970 under the direction of Robert Trent Jones, Jr., went through numerous financial stops and starts before being reopened in 1982. Since that time it has come to be rated one of the top 75 public golf courses in America by *Golf Digest*.

Arrowhead's 6682-yard layout has water on half its holes; large, fast, undulating greens well protected by traps; and fairway bunkers in key spots near strategic landing areas. Red sandstone rocks are regular features of the golf landscape, including the 199-yard par-3 third, which is backed entirely by these giant wonders. The large, left-to-right angled green, which is 154 feet wide and 73 feet deep, is also guarded by traps to the front, left and right. The red-rock backdrop is somewhat like the Green Monster at Fenway Park—something to ponder while teeing up.

The number-1-handicap hole on the course is the 436-yard par-4 fourth, which is a dogleg right to a right-to-left-tilted green protected by a gully on the left front, rocks to the left, a trap on the right, and water to the right front. The tee shot has to negotiate four fairway bunkers to the left and right of the landing area. The approach shot is to a slightly elevated green that requires more club than one would think.

Another tough hole is the 393-yard seventh, which plays straight to a side-angled, wide, shallow green with huge traps to the left, front and rear. A large pond is on the right, and another large one to the left. There is no bailout on the second shot. The 207-yard par-3 ninth hole offers a beautiful view of a large green protected by two large traps to the left and in front, with a lake to the right.

The back nine plays a bit shorter than the 3435-yard front nine but it is just as spectacular. The elevated tenth tee provides you with a magnificent view of towering, jagged red sandstone rocks and Roxborough State Park. A string of right-fairway bunkers begins 185 yards from the green on this 418-yard par 4. The green is angled left to right and protected by a huge trap to the left and forward. A

smaller trap guards the right rear of the putting surface. The 180-yard par-3 thirteenth plays from an elevated tee to a wide, shallow green 90 feet below. A lake backs the green, and two huge traps guard the front of it. Beautiful rocks and oak trees are on the left and right below the tee.

The finishing hole is a 543-yard par 5 that plays straight to a medium-sized green protected by three traps to the right and one on the left. Beginning 230 yards from the green is a lake that runs all the way to the left rear of the putting surface. The fairway narrows severely where this water hazard begins, then opens up a little as you approach the hole. The combination of water and sand makes it difficult to roll your second shot onto the green.

Recently over $2 million has been invested in course and clubhouse improvements at Arrowhead. Tournaments, meetings and outings are welcome here, and group and individual instruction is available. Memberships are available at this club, but the public is welcome. Arrowhead is only 45 min. south of Denver, and it is a golf experience you won't forget.

Course Name: **FOX HOLLOW AT LAKEWOOD**
Canyon, Links, Meadows

Course Type: Public
Address: 13410 West Morrison Road
Lakewood, CO 80228
Phone: (303) 986–7888
Fax: (303) 986–9990

GOLF COURSE

Head Professional: Craig Parzybok
Course Length/Par (All Tees): Canyon/Meadow: Back 6808/71, Blue 6558/71, White 6154/71, Red 5203/71, Forward 4449/71. Links/Meadow: Back 6888/72, Blue 6639/72, White 6295/72, Red 5396/72, Forward 4801/72. Canyon/Links: Back 7030/71, Blue 6745/71, White 6347/71, Red 5461/71, Forward 4802/71
Course Slope/Rating (All Tees): Canyon/Meadow: Back 138/71.2, Blue 134/70.0, White 128/68.0, Red 121/69.9, Forward 107/65.3. Links/Meadow: Back

132/71.9, Blue 127/70.7, White 122/69.0, Red 119/71.5, Forward 107/66.6. Canyon/Links: Back 134/72.3, Blue 128/70.9, White 124/69.0, Red 124/71.6, Forward 112/67.5

Course Architect: Denis Griffiths (1993)

Golf Facilities: Full Pro Shop X, Snack Bar X, Lounge No, Restaurant X, Locker Room No, Showers No, Club Rental X, Club Repair No, Cart Rental X, Instruction X, Practice Green X, Driving Range X, Practice Bunker X, Club Storage No

Tee-Time Reservation Policy: Up to 6 days in advance

Ranger: Yes

Tee-off-Interval Time: 9 min.

Time to Play 18 Holes: 4 hrs. 40 min.

Course Hours/Earliest Tee-off: 6:30 a.m.

Green Fees: $27 for 18 holes

Cart Fees: $10 per rider for 18 holes

Credit Cards: MasterCard, Visa

Season: Year round. Busiest July and Aug.

Course Comments: Can walk anytime. Residents of Jefferson and Lakewood counties have tee time reservation priority

Golf Packages: No

Discounts: Junior and senior rates Mon. through Thurs. Lower green fees for local residents

Places to Stay Nearby: Doubletree Club Hotel (303) 969–9900; Holiday Inn Denver Lakewood (303) 980–9200, (800) HOLIDAY; Sheraton Denver West Hotel and Conference Center (303) 987–2000, (800) 325–3535. DENVER: See page 113

Local Attractions: LAKEWOOD: Belmar Museum. DENVER: See page 113

Directions: From downtown Denver (35 min. southwest): Take Sixth Ave. west to Kipling, then take Kipling south to Morrison Rd. Turn right (west) on Morrison and proceed 1/2 mile to golf course

Closest Commercial Airport: Denver International (1 hr.)

FOX HOLLOW AT LAKEWOOD GOLF COURSE

Just southwest of Denver is a collection of three nine-hole courses that were rated among the best new layouts of 1993 by

Golf Digest. The Canyon, Links, and Meadows venues at Fox Hollow provide five tee distances and can accomodate any level of golfer. The Canyon offers a mix of elevation changes and level holes framed by trees. A challenging hole on this side is the 445-yard par-4 fourth which plays to a sloping fairway from the tee. The second shot must carry a canyon downhill to a deep green framed by trees.

The Meadow course is a rolling, open layout with cottonwood and other varieties bordering some holes. The 425-yard par-4 fifth is the most difficult hole on this nine. The tee shot must carry a small ravine and avoid trees to the left and right. This first shot should be positioned far enough left to provide a clear approach to a green well-bunkered to its left. The Canyon/Meadow combination is considered the most difficult eighteen at Fox Meadow, but the Links course, with water protecting some of its holes, is not a pushover. Its dogleg 574-yard par-4 sixth hole is the longest hole at Fox Hollow. Water can come into play on the second shot, and mounds to the left of the green can kick approach shots in strange directions.

Deer, coyote, hawks, and other creatures visit this scenic parkland course designed by Denis Griffiths, a native of Marshalltown, Iowa, who has designed Pole Creek in Colorado, Chateau Elan in Georgia, and other fine layouts.

Course Name: **THE GOLF COURSES AT HYLAND HILLS Gold, Blue, South, North Courses**

Course Type: Public

Address: 9650 N. Sheridan Boulevard Westminster, CO 80030

Phone: (303) 428–6526

GOLF COURSE

Director of Golf: Marv Mazone

Course Length/Par (All Tees): Gold: Back 7021/72, Blue 6693/72, White 6171/72, Ladies' Forward 5654/73. Blue: Back 3498/37, White 3286/37, Forward 3097/37. South: 1060/27. North: 712/21

Slope/Rating (All Tees): Gold: Back 132/71.9, Blue 127/70.2, White 119/67.8, Ladies' Forward 120/71.9. Other courses: NA/NA

Course Architects: Gold: Henry Hughes (1964), Frank Hummel (renovation, 1984). Blue: Henry Hughes (1964). South: NA. North: NA

Golf Facilities: Full Pro Shop X, Snack Bar X, Lounge X, Restaurant X, Locker Room X, Showers X, Club Rental X, Club Repair Minor, Cart Rental X, Instruction X, Practice Green X, Driving Range X, Practice Bunker X, Club Storage No

Tee-Time Reservation Policy: Weekday reservations are taken at 7 a.m. up to one day in advance. Weekend reservations are taken from 11 a.m. from Wed. for Sat. reservation, from Fri. for Sun. play. District golf annual and reservation permit holders may call earlier. 9-hole Blue Course reservations are taken one day in advance. Par-3 North and South course reservations first-come, first-served

Ranger: Yes, prime season

Tee-off-Interval Time: 8 min.

Time to Play 18 Holes: 4 hrs., 45 min.

Course Hours/Earliest Tee-off: 5:45 a.m. to dark

Green Fees: Nondistrict residents: Gold: $19 for 18 holes. Blue: $12 for 9 holes. South: $6 for 9 holes. North: $3 for 7 holes

Cart Fees: $17 for 18 holes, $9 for 9 holes

Pull Carts: $3.25 for 18 holes, $2.25 for 9 holes

Credit Cards: American Express, Master-Card, Visa. MasterCard, Visa for pro shop

Season: Year round. Busiest season May to Sept.

Course Comments: Can walk anytime. Yardage books available

Golf Packages: None

Discounts: Residents, seniors

Places to Stay Nearby: WESTMINSTER: La Quinta Inn-Westminster Mall (303) 425–9099, (800) 531–5900; Ramada Hotel Denver/Boulder (303) 427–4000, (800) 272–6232. DENVER: Brown Palace Hotel (303) 297–3111, 321–2599; Embassy Suites Hotel—Downtown (303) 297–8888, (800) EMBASSY. BED AND BREAKFAST: Queen Anne Inn Luxury Bed and Breakfast (303) 269–6666

Local Attractions: DENVER: U.S. Mint, Denver Art Museum, Museum of Western Art, Trianon Museum and Art Gallery, Children's Museum of Denver, Mile-High Flea Market, Colorado state capitol, Coors Brewing Co. tours, Rocky Mountain Arsenal Wildlife tours, Black American West and Heritage Center, Buffalo Bill's Museum and grave, Byer-Evans House, Colorado History Museum, Colorado Railroad Museum, Denver Fire Fighters Museum, Denver Museum of Miniature Dolls and Toys, Denver Museum of Natural History, Molly Brown House Museum, buffalo herd, Denver Botanical Gardens, Denver Zoo, dog racing; professional soccer, baseball, basketball; river rafting, horseback riding, shopping, restaurants, art galleries, concerts, theater, night clubs, University of Denver. Denver Metro Convention and Visitors Bureau (303) 892–1112, (800) 283–2754, Fax: (303) 892–1636

Directions: From Denver International Airport: Take Tower Rd. north to 104th St. Turn left on 104th to Sheriden Blvd. Turn left on Sheriden to 96th and the golf course

Closest Commercial Airport: Denver International (45 min.)

THE GOLF COURSES AT HYLAND HILLS

Henry Hughes, the original architect of Hyland Hills, was the son of Henry T. Hughes, a construction superintendent for Donald Ross at the Broadmoor in Colorado Springs, Colorado. After working on his father's construction crew and serving as greenskeeper at the Cherry Hills course in Denver, the younger Hughes later developed golf courses while serving as greens superintendent at the Green Gables Country Club in Denver. In the 1960s he became a full-time golf architect and designed Hyland Hills. Later, T. Frank Hummel, a native of La Junta, Colorado, designed holes seven through sixteen on the Gold Course at Hyland Hills. A trained engineer and golf professional, Hummel designed several courses in the Rockies including the U.S. Air Force Academy, the Gleneagle Country Club in Colorado Springs and others.

The Hyland Hills golf complex has an 18-hole regulation course (Gold), a Hughes-designed 9-hole regulation course (Blue), two in-house-designed par-3 courses (South, North), and a lighted practice area, including an 1800-square-foot practice green and the 36-hole Adventure Golf Putt-Putt facility. The Gold Course is ranked among the best public golf courses in the United States by *Golf Digest*. The National Women's Public Links Championship was held here in 1990.

The Gold Course is an open layout with rolling fairways and a considerable amount of water in the form of lakes and creeks. The number-1-handicap 478-yard par-4 sixth hole is considered to be the most difficult hole on the course. The fairway for the first shot is intermittently treed and relatively open, but the approach shot is usually a long iron or a wood over a rough-filled ditch to a medium-sized green. A large tree, approximately 75 yards to the left and front of the green, can block an incoming shot from the left, and a trap protects the green on the right-front side. A creek runs parallel to the right fairway close to the green from 75 yards in.

The number-2-handicap 398-yard par-4 seventeenth hole is a dogleg right requiring a tee shot over a small lake. The second shot comes into a small, tiered green situated 20 yards behind a ditch that runs across the fairway. The green is protected on the right by a trap. The finishing hole is a 346-yard par-4 dogleg left. Ideally, the tee shot is hit to the left center of the fairway, and the second shot must be lofted over a creek that runs in front of a wide, shallow green, banked in back. The creek, trees and out of bounds run down the left side from tee to green.

Annual and resident permit holders have a slight priority in reserving tee times at Hyland Hills. Private and group lessons for all levels of play are available from PGA professionals and their staff. The clubhouse includes 6 racquetball courts and a full-service dining facility that serves breakfast, lunch and dinner. Hyland Hills welcomes groups and tournaments. During peak season, the course averages 1 tournament group per day.

Course Name: MARIANNA BUTTE GOLF COURSE

Course Type: Public
Address: 701 N. Clubhouse Road
                 Loveland, CO 80537
Phone: (970) 663–3483 (Golf Shop),
                 (970) 669–5800 (Tee Times)

GOLF COURSE

Head Professional: Kent Heusinkveld

Course Length/Par (All Tees): Back 6572/72, White 5956/72, Red 5420/72, Forward 5067/72

Course Slope/Rating (All Tees): Back 130/70.6, White 116/67.1, Ladies' Red 121/70.2, Ladies' Forward 117/68.1

Course Architect: Dick Phelps (1992)

Golf Facilities: Full Pro Shop X, Snack Bar X, Lounge X, Restaurant No, Locker Room No, Showers No, Club Rental X, Club Repair Minor, Cart Rental X, Instruction X, Practice Green X, Driving Range X, Practice Bunker No, Club Storage No

Tee-Time Reservation Policy: Up to 5 days in advance starting at 7 p.m., up to 2 days in advance for annual pass holders. 24-hour-a-day call-in reservation system for three Loveland municipal courses (970) 669–5800

Ranger: Yes

Tee-off-Interval Time: 8 min.

Time to Play 18 Holes: 41/2 hrs.

Course Hours/Earliest Tee-off: Sunrise

Green Fees: $28 for 18 holes Fri., Sat., Sun., holidays; $18 for 9 holes. $22 for 18 holes weekdays, $12 for 9 holes

Credit Cards: All major cards

Season: Year round weather permitting. Busiest June through Aug.

Course Comments: No-shows will be charged for their tee times. Can walk anytime

Golf Packages: No

Discounts: Annual passes available for golf, driving range. Twilight, junior, senior, multiple round passes, annual cart passes

Places to Stay Nearby: Best Western Coach House Resort (970) 667–7810, (800) 528–1234; Budget Host Exit 254 Inn (970) 667–5202. LYONS: The Inn at Rock'N River (970) 443–4611. BOULDER: Boulderado Hotel (970) 442–4344, (800) 321–8444. DENVER: See page 113

Local Attractions: Loveland Museum and Gallery, Rocky Mountain National Park. BOULDER: Boulder Museum of History, Celestial Seasonings Tour of Tea, Chataqua Park, Flagstaff Scenic Highway, University of Colorado, hiking, fishing, hunting, boating. Loveland Tourism, P.O. Box 7058A, Loveland, CO 80537, (970) 667–6311

Directions: From Denver (50 miles north): Take Hwy. 70 west to I–25 north to Hwy. 402 (Exit 255). Proceed west 6 miles on Hwy. 402 to golf course

Closest Commercial Airport: Denver International (75 min.)

MARIANNA BUTTE GOLF COURSE

Marianna Butte, located in Loveland at the mouth of Big Thompson Canyon, was named one of the best new golf courses of 1993 by *Golf Digest*. Built around a butte that serves as its hub, Marianna Butte is an easy walking course and has breathtaking views of Longs Peak and the Rockies to the west, the Devil's Backbone rock formation to the north, and a sweeping vista of plains to the east. The course features seven lakes, 55 bunkers and some severe elevation changes including the 90-foot drop from tee to green on the 126-yard par-3 fourteenth. Rivers and creeks connecting the lakes on this course serve notice that a golfer will be penalized if he misses landing areas.

Marianna Butte has a mature look accentuated by an array of 100-feet-tall mature pine and other trees. The front nine is a bit more forgiving, but the back nine exacts its revenge, especially on the last four holes. The 410-yard fifteenth is a tight par 4 with fairway bunkers and trees providing an obstacle course to the green. The 561-yard double-dogleg par-5 sixteenth requires a drive of more than 220 yards from the back tees to clear the Big Thompson River which borders this hole. The next shot is down a well-treed fairway towards a well-bunkered green guarded by cottonwoods. The 376-yard par-4 seventeenth requires a precise drive to the right-center in order to negotiate overhanging trees on the left and a bunker guarding the landing area. The par-4 finishing hole plays 358 yards to an elevated green perched 80 feet above the fairway. A solid drive must be followed by a well-calculated approach shot to have any chance for a par on this hole.

Marianna's temporary clubhouse with an excellent pro shop sits on the butte that dominates the property. Considered one of the best golf bargains in Colorado, you can experience a great round of golf here at a reasonable price.

Course Name: RIVERDALE Dunes, Knolls Courses

Course Type: Public

Address: 13300 Riverdale Road Brighton, CO 80601

Phone: (303) 659–6700

GOLF COURSE

Director of Golf: Bob Doyle

Course Length/Par (All Tees): Dunes: Back 7027/72, Blue 6354/72, White 5830/72, Forward 4902/72. Knolls: Back 6756/71, Middle 6426/71, Ladies' Forward 5933/72

Course Slope/Rating (All Tees): Dunes: Back 124/71.9, Blue 118/68.7, White 110/66.3, Forward NA/67.5, Ladies' White NA/72.2, Ladies' Forward NA/67.5. Knolls: Back 114/70.6, Middle 111/68.7, Ladies' Forward 117/72.2

Course Architects: Dunes: Pete Dye and Perry Dye (1986). Knolls: Henry B. Hughes (1965)

Golf Facilities: Full Pro Shop X, Snack Bar X, Lounge X, Restaurant X,

Locker Room X, Showers Men only, Club Rental X, Club Repair X, Cart Rental X, Instruction X, Practice Green X, Driving Range X, Practice Bunker X, Club Storage No

Tee-Time Reservation Policy: 2 days in advance for weekdays, from 5:30 p.m. Mon. for Sat. tee times, from 5:30 p.m. Tues. for Sun. tee times

Ranger: Yes

Tee-off-Interval Time: 9 and 10 min.

Time to Play 18 Holes: 4½ hrs. to 5 hrs.

Course Hours/Earliest Tee-off: 5 a.m. until dark

Green Fees: Residents: $23 for 18 holes, $13 for 9 holes. Nonresidents: $26 for 18 holes, $14 for 9 holes

Cart Fees: $20 for 18 holes, $11 for 9 holes

Credit Cards: MasterCard, Visa

Season: Year round, weather permitting. Busiest season March 1 to Nov. 1

Course Comments: Can walk. Cart required for outings. Yardage book available

Golf Packages: None

Discounts: Volume discount cards, residents

Places to Stay Nearby: NORTHGLENN: Holiday Inn (303) 452–4100, (800) HOLIDAY; Sheraton (303) 451–1002, (800) 325–3535. DENVER NORTH: La Quinta Inn—Central (303) 458–1222, (800) 531–5900; Ramada Hotel Denver/Boulder (303) 427–4000, (800) 228–2828; Regency Hotel (303) 458–0808, (800) 531–5900; Travelodge Hotel Denver North (303) 296–4000, (800) 255–3050

Local Attractions: LITTLETON: Littleton Historical Museum. DENVER: U.S. Mint, Denver Art Museum, Museum of Western Art, Trianon Museum and Art Gallery, Children's Museum of Denver, Mile High Flea Market, Colorado state capitol, Coors Brewing Co. tours, Rocky Mountain Arsenal Wildlife tours, Black American West and Heritage Center, Buffalo Bill's Museum and grave, Byer-Evans House, Colorado History Museum, Colorado Railroad Museum, Denver Fire Fighters Museum, Denver Museum of Miniature Dolls and Toys, Denver Museum of Natural History, Molly Brown House Museum, buffalo herd, Denver Botanical Gardens, Denver Zoo, dog racing; professional soccer, baseball, basketball; river rafting, horseback riding, shopping, restaurants, art galleries, concerts, theater, night clubs, University of Denver. Denver Metro Convention and Visitors Bureau (303) 892–1112, (800) 283–2754, Fax: (303) 892–1636

Directions: From Denver (25 min.): I–25 north to 120th Ave., east on 120th to north on Colorado Blvd. to 128th Ave., east (right) to Riverdale Rd., turn left, follow signs

Closest Commercial Airport: Denver International (20 min.)

RIVERDALE

Riverdale is a municipal facility in Brighton, in Adams County, 20 minutes northeast of Denver. The county owns both the 6756-yard par-71 Knolls Course and the new 7027-yard Perry and Pete Dye-designed Dunes Course, which opened in 1986. This is Perry Dye's first public course west of the Mississippi that features a stadium-style design. In 1993 it will be the site for the men's USGA National Public Links, and it was runner up on *Golf Digest*'s 1986 list of the best new public golf courses. Dye describes his approach to the Dunes as follows:

Building a public course in this agricultural zone was a challenge I had to accept. The elevation of that flat, alluvial farming field dropped a mere foot from what is now the clubhouse to the banks of the Platte River. Thousands of cubic meters of dirt were moved to create a links course, which, by venerable Scottish tradition, runs along a body of water and is characterized by dunes, rolling mounds, and bunkers. . . . Undulating fairways, gracefully dipping greens, swales and dunes now outline a horizon on that far-reaching flatness and melt with contours of the outlying landscape.

. . . In accepting the challenge of this course, I accepted the responsibility of improving public courses, of upgrading their standing and of making their players more demanding.

The Dunes Course is characterized by big landing areas, with trees coming into play on only two holes. The entire course is bentgrass, and the greens are large, fast, undulating and very difficult. There is some room for error around the greens, but water, sand traps and grass pot bunkers can help you rack up strokes.

The number-1-handicap hole is the 639-yard par-5 third, which plays straight to a small green with two pot bunkers to the right. Three straight, accurate shots are required to reach this green in three. The blue tees play 538 yards on this hole. A picturesque hole on the front side is the 153-yard par-3 eighth, which plays over water to a wide, shallow green guarded by a lake to its left and two traps in front.

The number-2-handicap hole is the 544-yard par-5 eleventh, which is a slight dogleg right to a medium-sized green. A series of four small ponds runs from 300 yards out all the way to the front right of the green. The fifteenth hole is a beautiful 426-yard par-4 dogleg left that wraps around a large lake from tee to green. The second shot is over water to a deep green guarded on the left by water and buttressed by Dye-signature railroad ties.

The 204-yard par-3 seventeenth is considered to be one of the best holes in the Denver area. The tee shot is to a long, narrow green with a huge trap to the right and water on the right from the tee to the back of the green. The finishing hole is a 363-yard par 4 over water to a fairway that begins approximately 200 yards away. You can hit the ball left to a fairway that begins to the left of the water, but that will leave you a long, difficult second shot to the deep, narrow green.

The Knolls Course at Riverdale was designed by Henry B. Hughes, who was born in Chillicothe, Missouri, and is the son of Henry T. Hughes, the construction superintendent for Donald Ross at the Broadmoor in Colorado Springs. The Knolls is one of the first public courses developed outside of the city and county of Denver. Water comes into play on more than half the holes at the Knolls. This course, which is more forgiving than the Dunes, is also worth playing when you visit Riverside. Henry B. Hughes designed many courses in Colorado, including the Hyland Hills Country Club in Bloomfield, the Aurora Hills Golf Club in Aurora, and the Paradise Valley Country Club in Englewood.

Perry Dye, the older son of the noted golf course architects Pete and Alice Dye, worked in the family business after earning a degree in real-estate marketing from the University of Denver. He formed his own firm in 1982, concentrating on real-estate-development golf courses. Dye Designs designed the Copper Creek Golf Course in Copper Mountain, Colorado, and Perry jointly designed the TPC at Plum Creek, Castle Rock with his father.

The Dunes Course is now ranked in *Golf Digest*'s America's 75 best public golf courses. A variety of clientele ranging from juniors to seniors and group outings frequent both the Dunes and the Knolls courses. An award-winning pro shop serves the public golfer from a modern clubhouse with food, banquet and locker-room facilities.

Recommended Golf Courses Within North Central Area

Within 1 Hour of Boulder:

Indian Peaks Golf Club, Lafayette, (303) 666–4706, Public, 18/7083/72

Ft. Collins:

Ptarmigan Golf and Country Club, Ft. Collins, (303) 226–6600, Public, 18/7201/72

Within 1 Hour of Denver:

Boomerang Links, Greeley, (303) 351–8934, (800) 266–6371, Public, 18/7214/72

Coal Creek Golf Course, Louisville, (303) 666–7888, Public, 18/6957/72

Eagles Nest Golf Course, Silverthorne, (303) 468–0681, Public, 18/6605/72

Inverness Golf Club, Englewood, (303) 799–9660, Resort, 18/6948/70

Legacy Ridge Golf Course, Westminster, (303) 438–8997, Public, 18/7251/72

Loveland Golf Club, Loveland, (303) 667–5256, Public, 18/6827/72

The Meadows, Littleton, (303) 972–8831, Public, 18/6995/72

Meadow Hills Golf Course, Aurora, (303) 690–2500, Public, 18/6717/70

Plum Creek Golf Course, Castle Rock, (303) 688–2611, Public, 18/7138/72

Raccoon Creek Golf Course, Littleton, (303) 373–4653, Public, 18/7013/72

Wellshire Golf Course, Denver, (303) 757–1352, Public, 18/6620/72

Northwestern Area

Course Name: BRECKENRIDGE

Course Type: Public
Address: 200 Clubhouse Drive
              P.O. Box 7965
              Breckenridge, CO 80424
Phone: (303) 453–9104

GOLF COURSE

Head Professional: Erroll Miller
Course Length/Par (All Tees): Back 7279/72, Tournament 6570/72, Regular 5980/72, Forward 5066/72
Course Slope/Rating (All Tees): Back 146/73.1, Tournament 138/69.9, Regular 128/66.9, Ladies' Forward 128/67.7
Course Architect: Jack Nicklaus (1985)
Golf Facilities: Full Pro Shop X, Snack Bar X, Lounge X, Restaurant X, Locker Room No, Showers No, Club Rental X, Club Repair X, Cart Rental X, Instruction X, Practice Green X, Driving Range X, Practice Bunker X, Club Storage X
Tee-Time Reservation Policy: 2 days in advance, or through hotel packages
Ranger: Yes
Tee-off-Interval Time: 10 min.
Time to Play 18 Holes: 4½ hrs.
Course Hours/Earliest Tee-off: 7:30 a.m. to dark
Green Fees: $57 for 18 holes, $35 for 9 holes

Cart Fees: $12 for 18 holes per person, $7 for 9 holes per person. Pull Carts: $2 for 18 holes
Credit Cards: American Express, Master-Card, Visa
Season: Memorial Day to mid-Oct.
Course Comments: Can walk the course (limited on weekends). Seasonal passes available
Golf Packages: Available
Discounts: None
Places to Stay Nearby: River Mountain Lodge (303) 453–4711, (800) 325–2342 (outside CO), (800) 553–4456 (CO); Breckenridge Spa (303) 453–9300, (800) 736–1607; Hilton (303) 453–4500, (800) 321–8444; Beaver Run Resort and Conference Center (303) 453–6000, (800) 525–2253 (US and Canada); Village of Breckenridge Resort (303) 453–2000, (800) 800–STAY. Breckenridge Resort Chamber (800) 221–1091
Local Attractions: Shopping, skiing, concerts, art galleries, hiking, fishing, Arapaho National Forest, camping, bicycling, Breckenridge recreation center, historical tours. Breckenridge Chamber of Commerce (303) 453–6018
Directions: From Denver (86 mi.): I-70 west to Hwy. 9, south to Breckenridge, follow the signs
Closest Commercial Airports: Denver International (2 hrs.), Colorado Springs Municipal (2 hrs.)

BRECKENRIDGE

The Breckenridge Golf Club is west of Denver in the Rocky Mountains. The 7279-yard par-72 layout, which winds through mountains, valleys, forests and streams, is ranked among the best golf courses in Colorado by *Golf Digest* magazine. At 9300 feet altitude, the golf course plays a bit shorter than the yardage would suggest, but its 146 slope and 73.1 USGA rating from the back tees indicates that it's not that easy. This public facility is owned by the town of Breckenridge and is the only municipally owned Nicklaus-designed golf course in the world.

As everyone knows, Jack Nicklaus is one of the greatest golfers of all time.

Born in Columbus, Ohio, in 1940, he has won 20 major championships, including 6 Masters, 5 PGAs, 4 U.S. Opens, 3 British Opens, and 2 U.S. Amateurs. He has long been interested in golf-course design, partly due to his meticulous play, and started design-consulting before he was 30. He has worked with Pete Dye and Desmond Muirhead, and in 1974 started his own golf-course-architecture business, with Robert Cupp and Jay Morrish as full-time designers. Nicklaus and his group have designed many noteworthy courses, including Rancho Mirage with Jay Morrish, Bob Cupp and Scott Miller in California; the Bear Course of Grand Traverse with Bob Cupp in Acme, Michigan; the Harbour Town Golf Links with Pete and Alice Dye in Hilton Head, South Carolina; and many others.

Water comes into play on more than half the holes at Breckenridge, and the sand traps tend to be few but well placed. Nicklaus starts you out gradually with a 403-yard straight par 4. The tee shot is over streams to a fairway protected by two bunkers to the right of the landing area. The second shot is onto a right-to-left-angled green protected by two traps on the right and one to the left. The bentgrass greens at Breckenridge tend to be medium speed, medium sized and mildly undulating.

The 554-yard par-5 second plays straight to a deep green flanked by three traps on the left and one to the right. The third hole is a tough 403-yard dogleg right, with a lake running on the right side from fairway to green. The tee shot should be played over the left edge of the water to a landing area on the left side of a narrowing fairway. The next shot is onto a deep green angled almost perpendicular to the tee and protected by a large trap to the front right and one in back. A tee shot to the right can force you to come into this green over the trap in front, making the hole much more difficult.

The number-1-handicap hole on the course is the long 473-yard par-4 ninth, which requires two long, accurate shots to a deep green protected by two traps on the left and one in back. A large fairway

bunker on the right, halfway to the green, can be trouble.

The 423-yard par-4 eighteenth is an excellent finishing hole. The first shot is to a landing area with a long, large fairway bunker to the right. The second shot is over a stream to a long green protected front, right and back by traps. A large lake guards the green and the left fairway on this approach shot.

From the new clubhouse with a complete dining facility and a golf shop that has been recognized by *Golf Shop Operations* magazine as one of the best in the country, you can enjoy views of the Ten-Mile Range and the nearby Breckenridge Ski Area. Complete practice facilities and instruction are available.

The town of Breckenridge is the oldest continuously occupied community on Colorado's western slope. Founded in 1859, it was originally a gold-mining town. It contains over 250 Victorian buildings registered in the Breckenridge Historic District, which is one of the largest historic districts in Colorado. Homes, condominiums, and other accommodations can be rented through Breckenridge Central Reservations at the Breckenridge Resort Chamber (303) 453–2918, (800) 221–1091 (U.S. and Canada). Breckenridge was named after John C. Breckinridge, James Buchanan's vice president, in hopes of improving the town's chances of being awarded a post office. But when Mr. Breckinridge joined the Confederate side as a soldier in the Civil War, the Union-leaning town changed the spelling of its name by dropping an "i" and adding an "e."

Course Name: KEYSTONE RANCH GOLF COURSE

Course Type: Resort
Resort: Keystone Resort
Address: Keystone Ranch Road
off Highway 6/Box 38
Keystone, CO 80435
Phone: (303) 468–4250 (Golf Course)
(303) 468–4250,
(800) 222–0188 (Resort)
Fax: (303) 468–4343 (Resort)

GOLF COURSE

Head Professional: Mike Dahlheim

Course Length/Par (All Tees): Back 7090/72, Middle 6521/72, Forward 5720/72

Course Slope/Rating (All Tees): Back 130/71.4, Middle 120/68.9, Ladies' Forward 120/70.7

Course Architects: Robert Trent Jones, Jr., and Don Knott (1980)

Golf Facilities: Full Pro Shop X, Snack Bar X, Lounge X, Restaurant X, Locker Room X, Showers X, Club Rental X, Club Repair X, Cart Rental X, Instruction X, Practice Green X, Driving Range X, Practice Bunker X, Club Storage X

Tee-Time Reservation Policy: Resort guests: 7 days in advance. At time of reservation if on a golf package. Public: 4 days in advance

Ranger: Yes

Tee-off-Interval Time: 10 min.

Time to Play 18 Holes: 4 hrs., 15 min.

Course Hours/Earliest Tee-off: 7:20 a.m.

Green and Cart Fees: Peak season: Guests: $86 for 18 holes with cart. Public: $96 for 18 holes with cart

Credit Cards: All major cards

Season: Late May to early Oct. Busiest late June to early Sept.

Course Comments: Cart mandatory. Yardage book available. Golf school on site. Walking after 5 p.m. at half the regular rate

Golf Packages: Available through resort

Discounts: Seasonal (late May to late June, mid-Sept. to closing). Twilight rate from 2:30 p.m. 9 holes from 5 p.m.

Places to Stay Nearby: Inn at Keystone (303) 468–1334, (800) 443–2280; Keystone Lodge (303) 468–2316; Ski Tip Lodge (303) 468–4202. DILLON: Best Western Ptarmigan Lodge (303) 468–2341, (800) 842–5939; Summit Inn and Conference Center (303) 468–6111. Keystone area central hotel reservation service (303) 468–4123, (800) 222–0188

Local Attractions: Camping, hiking, fishing, boating, hunting, winter skiing. BRECKEN-RIDGE: National historic district. DILLON: Dillon Reservoir, Summit Historical Society Museum, White River National Forest, Arapaho National Forest. ASPEN/SNOWMASS: Aspen Art Museum, Wheeler Opera House, Aspen Historical Society, ghost towns, rodeos, seasonal festivals, restaurants. Keystone Tourist Information (303) 468–4123, (800) 222–0188. Aspen Visitors Center (303) 925–5656

Directions: From Dillon: Hwy. 6 east 5 mi. to Keystone Ranch Rd., south on Keystone Ranch Rd. to golf course

Closest Commercial Airport: Denver International (2 hrs.)

RESORT

Date Built: 1969

No. of Rooms: 152 hotel rooms, 800 studio to 4-bedroom condominium suites and homes

Meeting Rooms: 45. Capacity of Largest: 1350 persons banquet style. Meeting Space: 77,500 sq. ft.

Room Price Range: $125 single occupancy in Keystone condominium suites to $220 per night for a 3-bedroom mountain condominium (summer specials). Golf packages available mid-June through mid-Sept.

Lounges: Tenderfoot Lounge, Last Lift Bar, Keysters, and others

Restaurants: Garden Steak House, Bighorn Southwestern Grill, Keystone Ranch House, Alpenglow Stube, and others

Entertainment Live music, storyteller, Keystone Music Festival, barn dances, hayrides

Credit Cards: All major cards

General Amenities: Supervised children's programs and day care, historic tours, chairlift ride, nature hikes, meeting and conference facilities with audiovisual and banquet services, petting farm, village arcade, video rentals, Lake Dillon sailboat cruises

Recreational Amenities: Sailing, fishing, horseback riding, hot-air ballooning; 14 tennis courts at Tennis and Fitness Center with 5-station weight system, pro shop, lessons; 11 heated swimming pools, sauna and Jacuzzi areas, bicycling, kayaking, jogging trails, winter skiing, boating, fly-fishing lessons and guided fly fishing, horseback riding and trail rides, llama treks

Reservation and Cancellation Policy: 1 night's deposit required within 14 days of reservation or 30 days prior to arrival. Cancellation within 30 days of arrival subject to forfeiture of deposit. Cancellation outside 30 days of arrival subject to processing fee. Changes within 30 days of arrival subject to charge. Final payment due on arrival

Comments and Restrictions: No pets. Additional adults in room/condominium suites (up to 2) $15 per person per night. Surcharge and state and local taxes additional to base rates. Children under 18 stay free. Special discount summer value offers. Reductions on certain hotel rates when you book within 7 days of arrival

KEYSTONE RANCH GOLF COURSE

The Keystone Resort is a year-round resort community situated at 9300 feet elevation in the Rocky Mountains 75 miles west of Denver, Colorado, near the Continental Divide. A major attraction at Keystone is the 7090-yard par-72 Keystone Ranch Golf Course designed by Robert Trent Jones, Jr., and Don Knott. This golf course is included among America's 75 best resort courses by *Golf Digest*.

The Keystone Ranch Golf Course begins with holes carved out of the woods, including the 433-yard par-4 second which plays down a tree-lined fairway to a medium-sized green protected by a large bunker to the left and framed by trees. Most of the bentgrass greens at Keystone are medium sized, heavily bunkered, undulating, and moderately fast.

Holes four through eight are designed after Scottish linksland courses and have elevated tees, target-fairway landing areas, and sage-covered mounds and banks. This sequence of holes includes the 564-yard par-5 seventh, whose tee shot is to a landing area protected by a pond on the left and a bunker to the right. The second shot is over a stream that cuts the fairway 160 yards from the green to a landing area guarded by the stream along the left fair-

way. The approach is to a deep green framed by the stream on the left and a series of three bunkers beginning from in front of the green on the right.

A memorable hole on the front nine is the 368-yard dogleg-right par-4 ninth, which plays over a lake completely guarding the right side of the fairway from tee to green. From the back tees a drive of 225 yards or more puts you within 100 yards of a wide, shallow green protected by large bunkers to the left and rear, with water to the right but cutting into the fairway in front of the green. A well-placed tee shot and an accurate approach are required on this beautiful hole. Because of the high altitude, the ball will carry approximately 10 to 15 percent farther than it would at sea level.

The next eight holes wend their way through a valley, beginning with a 463-yard par 4 that plays uphill to a deep green guarded by one bunker on the right and another 60 yards to the left and in front of the green. The tee shot is to a landing area guarded by a large bunker on the right. The approach shot is likely to be from a sidehill lie, making this one of the most difficult holes at Keystone Ranch.

The finishing hole is a beautiful, challenging 585-yard par 5 bordered on the left by a lake from tee to green. The tee shot is to a landing area flanked by a bunker to the right and a bunker and the lake to the left. The second shot is to a landing area just beyond a bunker on the right, approximately 100 yards from the green. The approach shot is to a green bordered by water on the left and a trap front left, and another trap to the right. There is a trap farther right that will catch errant second shots.

The combination of varied landscape with woods, streams, a 9-acre lake, rolling valleys, meadows, and views of the mountains beyond makes this a beautiful and memorable golf experience. At the ranch-style wood-and-stone clubhouse you will find a complete pro shop, locker rooms, showers, living room, dining room and bar. The Keystone Ranch House restaurant at this restored 1930s ranch homestead is one of the best of more than 20 eating establishments within this resort community. Gourmet meals are served here and at the Garden Room, overlooking Keystone Lake and Ski Tip Lodge near the ski slopes. There are a variety of family dining spots at Keystone.

Choices of accommodations include condominium suites, all near Keystone Mountain, in Keystone Village, and in wooded areas throughout the resort. The Keystone Lodge is AAA Four-Diamond rated and is a member of Preferred Hotels Worldwide. The Ski Tip Lodge is a historic bed and breakfast, and the Keystone Mountain Inn also offers hotel accommodations. A range of studios, hotel rooms, 1- to 4-bedroom homes and other amenities such as kitchens, fireplaces, swimming pools, saunas and Jacuzzis are among the options at these housing sites. Rental homes are also available throughout the Keystone Valley.

In the winter, Keystone turns into a major ski area with Keystone, North Peak and Arapaho Basin providing a venue for downhill and cross-country skiing. Sleigh rides, snowmobiling, helicopter skiing and ice skating are other popular winter activities at this year-round resort.

Keystone Resort provides excellent golf facilities and a wide range of conference, dining and recreational activities, making it an ideal spot to visit. Golf packages are available through the resort.

Course Name: POLE CREEK GOLF CLUB

Course Type: Public
Address: Golf Club Road/Box 3348
Winter Park, CO 80482
Phone: (303) 726–8847

GOLF COURSE

Head Professional: Kim Anders
Course Length/Par (All Tees): Back 7107/72, White 6413/72, Forward 5006/72
Course Slope/Rating (All Tees): Back 133/72.5, White 127/69.6, Ladies' White 129/74.9, Ladies' Forward 119/69.9
Course Architects: Ron Kirby and Gary Player (9 holes, 1981; 9 holes, 1983)

Golf Facilities: Full Pro Shop X, Snack Bar X, Lounge X, Restaurant X, Locker Room X, Showers X, Club Rental X, Club Repair X, Cart Rental X, Instruction X, Practice Green X, Driving Range X, Practice Bunker X, Club Storage X
Tee-Time Reservation Policy: Up to 5 days in advance without credit card guarantee. Anytime in advance with credit card guarantee (includes surcharge)
Ranger: Yes
Tee-off-interval Time: 9 min.
Time to Play 18 Holes: 4½ hrs.
Course Hours/Earliest Tee-off: 8 a.m.
Green Fees: $60 for 18 holes Fri., Sat., Sun., holidays; $55 for 18 holes weekdays. $40 for 9 holes Fri., Sat., Sun., holidays; $35 for 9 holes weekdays
Cart Fees: $25 for 18 holes, $15 for 9 holes
Pull Carts: $4 for 18 holes, $2 for 9 holes
Credit Cards: Discover, MasterCard, Visa
Season: Mid-May through Oct. Busiest season mid-June to mid-Sept.
Course Comments: Can walk anytime. Yardage book available
Golf Packages: Available
Discounts: Seasonal (usually early June and after mid-Sept.)
Places to Stay Nearby: Iron Horse Resort (303) 726–8851, (800) 621–8190; Silverado II Resort and Conference Center (303) 726–9451, (800) 654–7157; Winter Park Resort (303) 726–8801, (800) 472–7017; Vintage Hotel (303) 726–8801, (800) 472–7017 (USA). For inn, hotel, lodge, bed-and-breakfast, condominium, chalet and cabin information: Winter Park Central Reservations (800) 453–2525
Local Attractions: Rocky Mountain National Park, fishing, bicycling, boating, music festivals, white-water rafting, rodeos, horseback riding, winter skiing, Arapaho National Forest, Rocky Mountain National Park. Winter Park/Fraser Valley Chamber of Commerce (303) 726–4118, (800) 722–4118
Directions: From Denver (70 mi.): I–70 west to exit 232, Hwy. 40 to Winter

Park. From Winter Park follow Hwy. 40 for 10 mi., turn left on Golf Course Rd. (after Tavernash) to golf course (follow signs)

Closest Commercial Airport: Denver International (2 hrs.)

POLE CREEK GOLF CLUB

Winter Park, the home of the Pole Creek Golf Club, is a major ski and summer resort area 70 miles northwest of Denver. A haven for skiers in the winter, Winter Park averages over 350 inches of snowfall at altitudes in excess of 11,000 feet. In the summer, the area is popular for fishing, rodeo, music festivals, hiking, bicycling, camping and other outdoor sports. Several rental condominiums are available at various resort properties, and there are many lodges and hotels in the area.

Pole Creek was honored by *Golf Digest* in 1985 as the best new public golf course in America. Pole Creek meanders through the 6900-yard layout, which was designed by Ron Kirby and Gary Player. The stream is fed by the melting snows from atop the nearby Continental Divide. Beautifully situated at 8900 feet, the rolling fairways wind through thick pine forests towered over by majestic snow-capped peaks. Wildlife such as elk, deer, porcupine, badgers, beaver, and hawks often visit the golf course, sometimes to the chagrin of the course superintendent.

The combination of trees, water and well-placed bunkers requires the golfer to manage his or her game, think strategically and place shots accurately. The rough can be thick, similar to Scottish rough, and, oddly enough some holes have a Scottish appearance. A great deal of the course runs through a valley that was formerly ranch land, and water comes into play on eleven holes. The bentgrass greens are slow to medium speed, medium sized and undulating. Because of the altitude, the ball tends to carry about 10 to 15 percent farther than it would at sea level. As a result, club selection requires considerable thought at Pole Creek.

The number-1-handicap hole on the course is the 584-yard par-5 seventh, which is a beautiful dogleg left. The first shot is downhill toward a left-side fairway bunker guarding the landing area. The second shot is over a lake cutting into the left side of the fairway to a landing area just before Pole Creek, which crosses the fairway. The next shot is uphill to a green that is well trapped on the left.

Another scenic and difficult hole is the 212-yard par-3 sixteenth, whose tee shot is often into the wind to a shallow but wide green surrounded front, right and rear by the creek. Traps protect the green on the left. The 551-yard par-5 finishing hole is long and straight with a right-side bunker protecting the landing area on the tee shot. The second shot, if you are going for it, has to reach the green on the fly because traps protect it to the left, front and rear. Most golfers play up and reach the green with a short iron.

It takes approximately 4½ to 5 hours to play Pole Creek, and walking is allowed. Memberships are available for residents and nonresidents, and tournaments or groups of 10 or more players are welcome. Green fees include unlimited driving-range use, and private and group instruction is available. Golf packages are available, and Pole Creek's restaurant and bar affords you a spectacular view of the Continental Divide. Pole Creek is ranked by *Golf Digest* among the top 75 public golf courses in America.

Course Name: SONNENALP GOLF CLUB

Course Type: Resort
Resort: Sonnenalp Hotel and Golf Club
Address: 20 Vail Road
Vail, CO 81657
Phone: (303) 926–3533 (Golf Course) (303) 476–5656, (800) 654–8312 (Resort)
Fax: (303) 926–3551 (Golf Course) (303) 476–1639 (Resort)
Telex: 287599

GOLF COURSE

Head Professional: Doug Wall
Course Length/Par (All Tees): Back 7059/71, Yellow 6423/71, Grey 5907/71, Forward 5293/71

Course Slope/Rating (All Tees): Back 136/72.7, Yellow 132/69.8, Grey 126/67.5, Ladies' Forward 115/70

Course Architects: Golf Force (Jack Nicklaus, Robert Cupp, Jay Morrish, 1981)

Golf Facilities: Full Pro Shop X, Snack Bar X, Lounge X, Restaurant X, Locker Room X, Showers X, Club Rental X, Club Repair X, Cart Rental X, Instruction X, Practice Green X, Driving Range X, Practice Bunker X, Club Storage X

Tee-Time Reservation Policy: Resort guests: At time of registration. Public: Day of play

Ranger: Yes

Tee-off-Interval Time: 10 min.

Time to Play 18 Holes: 4 hrs., 15 min.

Course Hours/Earliest Tee-off: 6:30 a.m.

Green and Cart Fees: Resort guests: $90 for 18 holes with cart. Public: $112 for 18 holes with cart

Credit Cards: American Express, Master-Card, Visa

Season: Mid-March to mid-Nov.

Course Comments: Cart mandatory. Yardage book available. 9-hole play available

Golf Packages: Available through resort

Discounts: Seasonal discount (up to late May). Twilight rate after 4 p.m.

Places to Stay Nearby: Antlers at Vail (303) 476–2471, (800) 258–8619; Best Western Vailglo Lodge (303) 476–5506, (800) 541–9423; Hyatt Regency Beaver Creek (303) 949–1234, (800) 233–1234; Marriott's Mark Resort (303) 476–4444, (800) 223–8245; Beaver Creek Lodge (303) 845–9800, (800) 732–6777; Westin Resort–Vail (303) 476–7111, (800) 228–3000. Central reservations system for over 80 properties: Vail Resort Association (303) 476–1000, (800) 525–3875

Local Attractions: Seasonal art and music festivals, winter skiing, fishing, hiking, camping, bicycling, boating, horseback riding, ballooning, art galleries, Colorado Ski Museum, tennis, river rafting, Holy Cross Wilderness Area, Vail Nature Cen-ter, White River National Forest. Vail Valley Tourist Bureau (303) 476–1000

Directions: From Denver (100 mi.): I–70 west, Edwards exit 163, follow signs

Closest Commercial Airport: Denver International (2 hrs.)

RESORT

Date Built: 1980 (first building), 1986 (Swiss Chalet, Bavarian House)

No. of Rooms: 160 rooms and suites

Meeting Rooms: 13. Capacity of Largest: 300 persons banquet style. Meeting Space: 9700 sq. ft.

Room Price Range: Double occupancy from $105 off season (mid-April to mid-Nov.), with breakfast; to $660 penthouse peak season (Christmas-New Year's), with breakfast. Golf, music-lovers' and other packages available

Lounges: Clubhouse Bar, Bully III Pub

Restaurants: Singletree Restaurant, Chalet Bar and Restaurant, Gourmet Room, Ludwig's

Entertainment: Live music in Austria House

Credit Cards: Diners Club, MasterCard, Visa

General Amenities: Plays, musical activi-ties, art galleries, children's programs, day care, seasonal festivals, meeting and conference facilities with audiovisual and banquet services

Recreational Amenities: 4 tennis courts, 2 outdoor heated swimming pools, skiing, sledding, winter skiing, fishing, horseback riding, river rafting, bicy-cling, ski school, sauna, Jacuzzi

Reservation and Cancellation Policy: 1 night's deposit due 14 days after reser-vation made. Suites and penthouses require deposit of $500 within 10 days of booking. Final payment, in full, due 30 days prior to arrival. Holiday-season reservations require full payment 60 days prior to arrival. All cancellations subject to an automatic cancellation fee. Cancellations made less than 30 days (60 days for holiday season) forfeit all monies on account if room not resold

Comments and Restrictions: No pets allowed. Taxes additional to base rates.

All rates based on 2 persons per bedroom. $20 additional for each person. Summer: Children 12 yrs. and under stay free in their parents' room. Winter: Children 5 yrs. and under stay free in their parents' room. Maximum of 3 persons per room

SONNENALP

The Sonnenalp Golf Club is part of the Sonnenalp Hotel and Resort. This 7059-yard par-71 layout is located in the Vail Valley ski resort area approximately 2 hrs. west of Denver in the Rocky Mountains. Singletree was designed by the Jack Nicklaus, Robert Cupp and Jay Morrish team and opened in 1981.

The front nine at Sonnenalp is somewhat flat, and wind can be a factor, as it usually is on the more rolling front nine. The landing areas at Sonnenalp are generous, but the fast, small, bentgrass greens are usually well protected by traps and water, making the approach shot and short game essential. The course is situated at more than 8000 feet, so you are going to get approximately 10 percent more carry here. This adds to the importance of club selection and the management of the course.

The 467-yard par-4 twelfth hole is one of the most difficult holes on the course. The tee shot, usually into the prevailing wind, has to be straight and long to set up a reasonable approach shot to a small, two-tiered green. The tee shot must also steer clear of a large fairway bunker on the right. Another difficult par 4 on this side is the 443-yard ninth hole, which bends slightly to the left. The first shot must avoid a fairway bunker to the left of the landing area. The approach shot is to a small green with three large ponds with waterfalls to its right and front and bunkers to its rear. Anything short on the approach shot will roll back into the water. This hole used to be the finishing hole, but the nines were reversed a few years ago.

The last two holes on the front nine are excellent tests of golf. The 199-yard par-3 seventeenth plays into a left-to-right crosswind to a wide, shallow green with several bunkers virtually surrounding it. A choice of six different tee distances is provided on this hole. Club selection is everything on this hole. The eighteenth hole is a 594-yard par 5 whose narrowing fairway bends left then slightly right to a deep green protected by a trap on the left. Recent renovations have made this a true three-shot par 5. A bunker has been added to the left, 30 yards in front of the green, and six bunkers have been added on the right from 130 yards in. Also, mounds and swales have been added to make this a strong finishing hole.

The Sonnenalp Golf Club has a full pro shop, locker rooms and showers, restaurant, and instruction from the staff of professionals. Individual and group instruction are available at the on-site driving range, practice bunker and practice green. There are also a variety of golf packages and seasonal discounts. Peak-season rates for normal resort facilities are charged during the ski season. The lowest resort room rates are offered during the golf season, which generally runs from mid-March to mid-November. Seasonal golf discounts are often available up until mid- to late May.

The Sonnenalp, German for "sun on the mountains," is a Bavarian-style family-owned operation, with Rosana and Johannes Fassler your hosts. There are 160 rooms and suites situated in three buildings—Austria House, Swiss Chalet and the completely rebuilt Bavarian House. Food ranges from continental cuisine at Ludwig's to informal meals in the Bully III Pub and Swiss raclette and fondue at the Chalet Bar and Restaurant. Piano, harp and other live music is generally heard in Austria House, which has the atmosphere of an Old World inn. The resort prides itself on New World efficiency and Old World charm.

The golf course, rated one of America's 75 best resort courses by *Golf Digest* magazine, is now completely owned by the Sonnenalp so it can guarantee its guests tee times and a quality golf experience. Because of its location, Sonnenalp has the benefit of milder weather and a longer season than most courses in this area. The course has excellent, fast greens and is a well maintained layout in a beautiful setting with Rocky Mountain views.

Recommended Golf Courses in Northwestern Area

Within 1 Hour of Aspen:

Aspen Municipal Golf Course, Aspen, (303) 925–2145, Public, 18/7165/71

Beaver Creek Golf Club, Avon, (303) 845–5775, Resort, 18/6752/70

The Club at Cordillera, Edwards, (303) 926–5100, Semiprivate, 18/7444/72

Copper Creek Golf Club, Copper Mountain, (303) 968–2339, (800) 458–8386, Resort, 18/6094/70

Dos Rios Country Club, Gunnison, (303) 641–1482, Semiprivate, 18/6535/72

Eagle Vail Country Club, Avon, (303) 949–5267, Resort, 18/6819/72

Grand Lake Golf Course, Grand Lake, (303) 627–8008, Public, 18/6542/70

Skyland Country Club, Crested Butte, (303) 349–6131, Resort, 18/7208/72

Snowmass Club Golf Links, Snowmass, (303) 923–3148 (Pro Shop), (800) 525–6200 (Resort), Semiprivate, 18/6890/71

Vail Golf Club, Vail, (303) 479–2660, (800) 332–3666 (CO), Public, 18/7048/71

Within 1 Hour of Grand Junction:

Battlement Mesa, Parachute, (303) 285–7274, Public, 18/7309/72

Rifle Creek Golf Course, Rifle, (303) 625–1093, Public, 18/6241/72

Steamboat Springs:

Sheraton Steamboat Springs Resort, Steamboat Springs, (303) 879–1391, (800) 848–8848, Resort, 18/6906/72

South Central Area

Course Name: THE BROADMOOR GOLF CLUB
East, West, South Courses

Course Type: Resort
Resort: The Broadmoor

Address: Lake Avenue and Lake Circle
                   P.O. Box 1439
                   Colorado Springs, CO
                   80901–1439
Phone: (719) 634–7711 (Golf Course)
                   (719) 577–5775,
                   (800) 634–7711 (Resort)
Fax: (719) 577–5779 (Golf Course)
                   (719) 577–5700 (Resort)

GOLF COURSE

Director of Golf: Dow Finsterwald

Course Length/Par (All Tees): East: Back 7218/72, Middle 6555/72, Ladies' Forward 5920/73. West: Back 6937/72, Middle 6109/72, Ladies' Forward 5505/73. South: Back 6781/72, White 6108/72, Ladies' Red 5609/72, Ladies' Forward 5834/70

Course Slope/Rating (All Tees): East: Back 129/73.0, Middle 121/70.6, Ladies' Forward 126/74.1. West: Back 133/73.4, Middle 127/69.5, Ladies' Forward 122/71.6. South: Back 135/72.1, White 125/69.1, Ladies' Red 127/72.5, Ladies' Forward 117/68.4

Course Architects: East and West: Donald Ross (1918), Robert Trent Jones, Sr., (9 holes, 1950; 9 holes, 1965). South: Arnold Palmer/Ed Seay (1976)

Golf Facilities: Full Pro Shop X, Snack Bar X, Lounge X, Restaurant X, Locker Room X, Showers X, Club Rental X, Club Repair X, Cart Rental X, Instruction X, Practice Green X, Driving Range X, Practice Bunker X, Club Storage X

Tee-Time Reservation Policy: At time of reservation, up to 1 yr. in advance. Must be a resort guest, member or guest of member to play the East, West courses. Public may reserve tee time at South up to 24 hrs. in advance

Ranger: Yes

Tee-off-Interval Time: 8 min.

Time to Play 18 Holes: 4 hrs., 15 min.

Course Hours/Earliest Tee-off: 7:30 a.m. summer

Green Fees: $83 for 18 holes daily fee

Cart Fees: $15 for 18 holes per person. Caddies available

Credit Cards: All major cards

Season: Year round, weather permitting. Busiest season May to Sept.

Course Comments: East or West: Caddy or cart prior to 3 p.m., can walk afterward. South: Can walk anytime. Must be a resort guest, member or guest of member to play East, West courses. South open to the public

Golf Packages: Available through resort

Discounts: Seasonal

Places to Stay Nearby: Antler's Doubletree (719) 473–5600, (800) 528–0444; Embassy Suites (719) 599–9100, (800) EMBASSY; Sheraton Colorado Springs (719) 576–5900, (800) 325–3535; Marriott Residence Inn (719) 574–0370, (800) 331–3131; Colorado Springs Marriott (719) 260–1800, (800) 962–6982; Holiday Inn North (719) 633–5541, (800) HOLIDAY

Local Attractions: U.S. Air Force Academy, U.S. Olympic Training Center, Cheyenne Mountain Zoo, Pike's Peak, Royal Gorge, Garden of the Gods, Cave of the Winds, Will Rogers's Shrine of the Sun, Seven Falls, Manitou mineral springs, Helen Hunt Falls, Cripple Creek, Colorado Springs minor league baseball, historic gold camps and mining tours, Fine Arts Center, Colorado College, Pioneer Museum, river rafting, fishing, camping, hiking, skiing, Pro Rodeo Hall of Fame, pottery, arts and crafts, World Figure Skating Hall of Fame and Museum, Children's Museum. Colorado Springs Chamber of Commerce (719) 635–1551

Directions: From Denver (1 hr., 15 min.): I–25 to exit 138, right turn, 2 mi. at end of Lake Ave.

Closest Commercial Airports: Colorado Springs Municipal (15 min.), Denver International (1 hr., 15 min.)

RESORT

Date Built: 1918 (main building), 1961 (Broadmoor South), 1976 (Broadmoor West)

No. of Rooms: 550

Meeting Rooms: 36. Capacity of Largest: 1600 persons banquet style. Meeting Space: 100,000 sq. ft.

Room Price Range: From $145 per person off season (mid-Oct. to May) to $1,700 suite peak season (mid-May to mid-Oct.). Golf, tennis, spring, Easter and other packages available year round

Lounges: Terrace Lounge, Golden Bee, Tavern, Golf Club (South, Main) Rendezvous, Penrose Lounge

Restaurants: Penrose Room, Tavern, Garden Room, Mayan Room, Main Dining Room, Charles Court, Golden Bee, Expresso's, Julie's Sidewalk Cafe

Entertainment: Theater, orchestra entertainment in the Tavern

Credit Cards: Diners Club, MasterCard, Visa

General Amenities: Babysitting, photographer, supervised children's program, 17 boutiques for shopping, movie theater, sightseeing tours, meeting and conference facilities in theater, classroom, banquet, reception, conference formats with audiovisual and food services

Recreational Amenities: Spa with fitness center, hydrotherapy, dry therapeutic treatment, steam sauna, whirlpool, plunge pools, aerobics dance studio; 16 tennis courts, pro shop, instruction; skeet and trap shooting, bicycling, boating, ice skating, horseback riding, winter skiing, 3 squash courts, 4 heated swimming pools, hiking trails, river rafting

Reservation and Cancellation Policy: 1 night's deposit required within 2 wks. (14 days) of the booking being made. Credit card or check acceptable. Reservations may be canceled or stays may be shortened up to 7 days prior to arrival without penalty

Comments and Restrictions: Taxes additional to base rates

THE BROADMOOR GOLF CLUB

In 1916 Spencer Penrose and his associate Charles L. Tutt decided to build one of the world's most fashionable hotels. New York City architects drew up plans for an Italian Renaissance structure that would be "permanent and perfect." The decor of all of the Broadmoor buildings is Mediterranean in motif, and many of the hotel's adornments were purchased from art centers all over the world. After various additions and a recent multimillion-dollar renovation, the Broadmoor reigns supreme over 3000 acres of land at the foot of Cheyenne Mountain in the Colorado Rockies.

The Broadmoor is a must visit for anyone serious about golf. Many tournaments have been played here, beginning in 1921, just after Donald Ross built the East Course. The Trans-Mississippi Championship, Western Amateur, NCAA, U.S. Amateur, Curtis Cup, U.S. Women's Amateur, Ducks Unlimited Pro Am and the World's Seniors Golf Tournament, as well as the Broadmoor Men's and Ladies' Invitationals, have been held here. In 1995 the East Course was the site of the U.S. Women's Open.

Originally opened in 1918, the East Course is a 7218-yard par-72 layout sculpted from 135 acres of underbrush, scrub oaks and rolling terrain on the lower slopes of Cheyenne Mountain. Robert Trent Jones, Sr., added an additional eighteen holes in stages from 1950 to 1964, and the Jones and Ross layouts were combined to make Broadmoor's East and West courses. The Ross holes are numbers one through three and thirteen through eighteen, or everything on the hotel side of Cheyenne Mountain Blvd.

The East Course has large, fast greens with some undulation. They are well protected by bunkers, and once you get there, you are likely to have some monster putts that, counter to your perception, always break away from the mountains—unless there is water nearby, of course; then it breaks in that direction. The combination of length, large and tricky greens, and strategically placed sand bunkers make this a difficult golf course.

When Jack Nicklaus won his first major title, the U.S. Amateur, here in 1959, the current fifteenth hole on the East Course was then the eighteenth under the old golf course configuration. Nicklaus made a birdie three to defeat Charlie Coe one up in the 36-hole match play final. This 421-yard par-4 is a dogleg right with a tee shot to a flat landing area. The second shot is over water to an elevated green guarded by a large trap to the right and forward.

The East Course has several long, par-4 holes that are a challenge to anyone's game. The pros' advice here is to add 10 percent to your normal distance calculations because of the high altitude. The 471-yard par-4 seventh is the number-1-handicap hole on the course. This dogleg left plays to a green well guarded by traps left- and right-front of the putting surface. The tee shot has to negotiate a pond and bunker on the left side of the fairway, as the fairway bends left toward the putting surface.

The West Course plays 6937 yards from the back tees and was opened in 1965. The first nine was built in 1950. The greens are fast and undulating but smaller than those of the East Course, and they are very well protected by sand bunkers. A key to scoring is to manage holes seven through twelve, which are tight and farther up into the mountains. The twelfth, for example, is a tough 460-yard par-4 dogleg right that has a deep green protected by traps left- and right-front. The right corner of the dogleg is well bunkered, making the landing area more difficult to hit.

The most difficult hole on the front side is the 455-yard dogleg-left par-4 sixth, which is a gradual uphill climb to a deep green guarded by a huge bunker on the left. Another fairway bunker awaits you to the left of the tee-shot landing area. The West Course has a variety of significant elevation changes, but most of the time you will have a reasonably flat lie.

Both the East and West courses are served by a clubhouse at the main hotel. The main clubhouse is the oldest building in the Broadmoor complex, designed and constructed in 1891 to be a Monte Carlo-type casino. Originally it was located where the Broadmoor now stands but was moved to its present location when the hotel was constructed. The clubhouse has locker rooms and showers, a full pro shop, cocktail bar, dining room, squash courts, a tennis shop, and instruction available from PGA professionals and staff. Upstairs are private rooms for dining and dancing, and a swimming pool. Nearby is a driving range, practice green and practice bunkers. Memberships are available at the Broadmoor, and only members, their guests, and resort guests can play the courses. Caddies are available, or you may take a cart. Walking is allowed on the East and West courses after 3 p.m. and any time on the South course, which was designed by Arnold Palmer and Ed Seay, built on 260 acres south of the East and West courses, and opened in 1976.

The South Course is somewhat open and works its way along the side of the mountain. It has small to medium-sized greens compared to the East Course, and a variety of elevation changes, including some shots over ravines. One of the more famous holes on the South Course is the 157-yard par-3 thirteenth, which plays from an elevated tee over water to a deep green fronted by water and surrounded by traps. The number-1-handicap hole is the 439-yard dogleg-right par-4 fifth. The tee shot is to a landing area just in front of a ravine that cuts the fairway. The approach shot is to an elevated green with a bunker to the rear.

The South Course has its own clubhouse with complete dining, pro shop and locker-room facilities. Individual or group lessons are available from Broadmoor's PGA professionals and assistants. Golf packages are available through the Broadmoor year round. Weather permitting, the golf courses are always open for play. Average daytime temperatures in winter are approximately 50 degrees. Golf package rates are lowest during the winter months.

The original Broadmoor was built in 1918 in the Italian Renaissance style. Since then, various renovations and additions have been made, and there are now three separate buildings—the Main, Broadmoor South and Broadmoor West. There are 550 rooms and 8 different restaurants, ranging from the main dining area, adorned with Toulouse-Lautrec originals, to the Golden Bee, an authentic eighteenth-century English pub. The Broadmoor has won numerous hospitality awards, including the *Mobil Travel Guide* Five-Star and AAA Five-Diamond awards.

Meetings and Conventions magazine has awarded the Broadmoor its Gold Tee Award as an outstanding conference center and golf resort. There are over 100,000 sq. ft. of meeting and conference space at the Broadmoor. Audiovisual, banquet and a range of other support services are available for meetings of up to 2500 persons. The Broadmoor even has a 100-by-40-foot stage with a hydraulic-lift orchestra pit. Custom events, ranging from theatrical productions to a complete private ice-skating revue, can be arranged by the staff of professionals here.

The Broadmoor is a world-class golf facility and an excellent resort. *Golf* magazine has awarded it a gold medal as one of the 12 best golf resorts in America, and *Golf Digest* rates the East Course among America's 75 best resort courses. Both the East and West courses are ranked among the 10 best public or private golf courses in the state of Colorado by *Golf Digest*.

Recommended Golf Courses in South Central Colorado

Colorado Springs Area:

Cheyenne Conference Mountain Resort (Country Club of Colorado), Colorado Springs, (719) 576–4600, (800) 428–8886, Resort, 18/7078/72

Fujiki Golf and Country Club, Woodland Park, (719) 687–7587, Semiprivate, 18/6747/72

Pine Creek Golf Course, Colorado Springs, (719) 594–9999, Public, 18/6980/72

Pueblo Area

Course Name: **GRANDOTE GOLF AND COUNTRY CLUB**

Course Type: Public
Address: 5540 Highway 12
              P.O. Box 506
              La Veta, CO 81055
Phone: (719) 742–3122,
              (800) 762–9513
Fax: (719) 742–3393

GOLF COURSE

Head Professional: NA
Course Length/Par (All Tees): Back 7085/72, Blue 6630/72, White 6315/72, Forward 5608/72

Course Slope/Rating (All Tees): Back 133/72.8, Blue 127/70.8, White 124/69.4, Ladies' Forward 117/70.7

Course Architect: Jay Morrish and Tom Weiskopf (1987)

Golf Facilities: Full Pro Shop X, Snack Bar X, Lounge X, Restaurant X, Locker Room No, Showers No, Club Rental X, Club Repair Outside, Cart Rental X, Instruction X, Practice Green X, Driving Range X, Practice Bunker X, Club Storage X

Tee-Time Reservation Policy: Call anytime

Ranger: Yes

Tee-off-Interval Time: 10 min.

Time to Play 18 Holes: 41/2 hrs.

Course Hours/Earliest Tee-off: 7 a.m.

Green Fees: $45 for 18 holes Fri., Sat., Sun., Holidays, $30 weekdays

Cart Fees: $20 for 18 holes per cart

Credit Cards: All major cards

Season: Mid-Apr. through Nov. Busiest in July

Course Comments: Can walk anytime. Yardage book available

Golf Packages: Inquire at pro shop for packages, local accomodations

Discounts: Seasonal specials

Places to Stay Nearby: PUEBLO: Abriendo Inn (719) 544–2703; Best Western Inn at Pueblo West (719) 547–2111, (800) 448–1972; Holiday Inn (719) 543–8050, (800) HOLIDAY. WALSENBERG: Best Western Rambler (719) 738–1121, (800) 448–1972

Local Attractions: LA VETA: Fort Francisco Museum, Goemmer Butte, La Veta Pass, Oakview Watch Tower, Wahatoga and Daigre Lakes. La Veta Chamber of Commerce (719) 742–3676. PUEBLO: Colorado State Fair, El Pueblo Museum, Pueblo Aircraft Museum, Lake Pueblo State Recreational Area, Sangre de Cristo Arts and Conference Center, San Isabel National Forest, Union Avenue Historic District. Pueblo Chamber of Commerce (719) 542–1704. WALSENBERG: Lathrop State Park, Lily Lake, Mount Blanca, Sharp's Trading Post. Walsenberg Chamber of Commerce (719) 738–1065.

Directions: From Pueblo (45 miles): Take Hwy. 25 south to Walsenberg. Proceed west 16 miles on Hwy. 160 to Hwy. 12 to golf course

Closest Commercial Airports: Pueblo (1 hr.); Colorado Springs Municipal (2 hrs.); Denver International (3 hrs.)

GRANDOTE GOLF AND COUNTRY CLUB

Grandote Golf and Country Club is an all bentgrass Tom Weisfkopf and Jay Morrish layout situated at 7000 feet in the Cuchara Valley in southern Colorado. The front nine runs through a rolling meadow, but the tougher back nine has more elevation changes. Wildlfe including bear, deer, mink, coyote, and other varieties roam this area which is treed with oak, pine, aspen, and others.

Grandote spreads over 280 acres. Water can come into play on seven holes. The greens tend to be large, somewhat undulating, and quick. Large, sculpted bunkers protect the putting surfaces, but there are few bunkers around the fairways. The signature hole on the course is the 386–yard par-4 twelfth whose tee is at the highest point on the golf course. From here you can see the surrounding mountains and the blind, dogleg right fairway below. The second shot is to an undulating green well-protected by bunkers.

The practice area at Grandote has an ample driving range with target flags, chipping and putting greens, and a practice bunker. You can walk the course anytime, but it is quite a hike. In 1995 *Golf Digest* rated Grandote the third best public or private course in Colorado.

Recommended Golf Courses Within 1½ Hours of Pueblo:

Great Sand Dunes Country Club, Mosca, (719) 378–2357, (800) 284–9213, Public, 18/6816/72

Pueblo West Golf Course, Pueblo West, (719) 547–2280, Public, 18/7368/72

Walking Stick Golf Club, Pueblo, (719) 584–3400, Public, 18/7210/72

Southwestern Area

Course Name: TAMARRON: THE CLIFFS

Course Type: Resort
Resort: Tamarron
Address: Highway 550
P.O. Drawer 3131
Durango, CO 81302–3131
Phone: (970) 259–2000 (Golf Course)
(970) 259–2000,
(800) 678–1000 (Resort)
Fax: (970) 259–0745 (Resort)

GOLF COURSE

Director of Golf: Steve Nichols
Course Length/Par (All Tees): Back 6885/72, Middle 6340/72, Forward 5380/72
Course Slope/Rating (All Tees): Back 142/73.0, Middle 135/70.5, Ladies' Forward 126/71.9
Course Architect: Arthur Hills (1975)
Golf Facilities: Full Pro Shop X, Snack Bar X, Lounge X, Restaurant X, Locker Room X, Showers X, Club Rental X, Club Repair X, Cart Rental X, Instruction X, Practice Green X, Driving Range X, Practice Bunker X, Club Storage X
Tee-Time Reservation Policy: Resort guests: From time of reservation. Public: Call to check availability
Ranger: Yes
Tee-off-Interval Time: 8 min.
Time to Play 18 Holes: 4½ hrs.
Course Hours/Earliest Tee-off: 7:45 a.m.
Green Fees: $95 for 18 holes with cart peak season June to late Sept.
Cart Fees: Included in green fees. Reduced rates for repeat rounds
Credit Cards: American Express, Master-Card, Visa
Season: May to Nov. 1. Busiest season mid-June to mid-Sept.
Course Comments: Cart mandatory. Yardage book available. Golf package and instructional schools available. For other information, call resort
Golf Packages: Available through resort
Discounts: Seasonal

Places to Stay Nearby: DURANGO AREA: Strater Hotel (970) 247–4431, (800) 247–4431; Iron Horse Inn (970) 259–1010, (800) 748–2990; General Palmer Hotel (970) 247–4747; Best Western Rio Grande Inn (970) 385–4980, (800) 245–4466; Days Inn Durango (970) 259–1430, (800) 325–2525; Holiday Inn (970) 247–5393, (800) HOLIDAY; Jarvis Suite Hotel (970) 259–6190; Red Lion Inn (970) 259–6580, (800) 547–8010. Purgatory-Durango Central Reservations for most area accommodations (970) 247–8900, (800) 525–0892. BED AND BREAKFASTS: Blue Lake Ranch (970) 385–4537; Damn Yankee Bed and Breakfast (800) 845–7512
Local Attractions: Mesa Verde National Park, Durango and Silverton Narrow Gauge Railroad, Diamond Circle Theater, Heritage Tours of Durango, Animas River Railway, Purgatory Ski Area, Silverton, Wininuche Wilderness area, Trimble Hot Springs, Vallecito Lake, Durango Pro Rodeo, fishing, camping, hiking, water skiing, boating, horseback riding, hunting, antiques, nature hikes, bicycling, seasonal festivals, San Juan Skyway. Mesa Verde National Park (970) 529–4421. Durango Chamber of Commerce (970) 247–0312, (800) 525–8855
Directions: From Durango (18 mi.): North on Hwy. 550
Closest Commercial Airports: Durango/La Plata County (45 min.); Albuquerque International, NM (4 hrs.); Denver International (6½ hrs.); Salt Lake City International, UT (8 hrs.)

RESORT

Date Built: 1974
No. of Rooms: 304 deluxe guest rooms, executive suites, suites, 2- and 3-bed-room townhouses
Meeting Rooms: 17. Capacity of Largest: 240 persons banquet style. Meeting Space: 14,000 sq. ft.
Room Price Range: $130 to $185 deluxe guest room to $425 2-bedroom deluxe peak season (June-Sept.). Golf, tennis, family and other packages available

Lounge: San Juan Lounge

Restaurants: San Juan Club, Kokopeui Deli, San Juan Terrace, Remington's

Entertainment: Live entertainment in San Juan Lounge, dancing

Credit Cards: All major cards

General Amenities: Supervised children's programs for ages 4 to 12, babysitting services, massage therapy, jeep tours, glider rides, western sunset cookout, hayrides, specialty shops; meeting and conference facilities in theater, classroom, conference, banquet and reception settings with audiovisual and food services

Recreational Amenities: Horseback riding, river rafting, fishing, 3 outdoor tennis courts, pro shop, instruction; health club with weight and exercise rooms, sauna, steam; indoor/outdoor pool and spa, basketball, volleyball, winter skiing, sleigh rides

Reservation and Cancellation Policy: Credit card guarantee or check required to hold reservations. Cancellation must be made 14 days prior to scheduled arrival. No penalties except $10 processing fee

Comments and Restrictions: No pets allowed. No-tipping policy. A service charge is included to cover all services. Taxes additional to base rates

TAMARRON

The Tamarron Golf Course is a 6885-yard par-72 layout cut through oak, aspen, and ponderosa pines at 7600 feet in the San Juan Mountains just north of Durango. This layout has rolling fairways and large, undulating bentgrass greens protected by large sand traps. There are water hazards on eight holes, and the combination of high altitude, elevation changes, doglegs, difficult greens, strategically placed bunkers and water hazards make Tamarron one of the toughest golf courses in the state of Colorado.

The front nine starts out with two of the most difficult holes on the course. The 445-yard first hole is a dogleg left to a deep, narrow green protected by a large bunker on the right. A sloping fairway and large pine in the landing area require a very accu-

rate tee shot. The second hole is a 555-yard par-5 dogleg right with a tee shot to an open landing area. The rolling, tree-lined fairway begins to narrow on the second shot, which has to avoid a huge trap on the left and another beginning on the right, approximately 30 yards in front of a deep green. The putting surface is also guarded on the left by a large sand trap.

At this stage you are working your way up to one of the highest points on the course; then Tamarron rolls down into a broad meadow running through the middle of the 750-acre property. Another tough hole on the front nine is the 440-yard ninth, which is a dogleg right to a deep, elevated, narrow green with bunkers on both sides. A large pond on the right side of the fairway guards the tee-shot landing area, especially if you try to cut the corner. The golfer has to favor the left side of the fairway on this hole.

The back nine begins its climb through corridors of rock, oaks and pines at over 8000 feet in altitude and affords you spectacular views of the surrounding 10,000-feet-high Hermosa Cliffs. The 440-yard par-4 sixteenth is a severe dogleg left that plays to a well-treed landing area on the tee shot. The approach is over a ravine to a deep, narrow green protected by a drop-off and water on the left and a trap on the right. The tee shot is critical to set up the crucial approach shot on this hole.

The 400-yard par-4 seventeenth is a sharp dogleg right. The fairway is guarded by a pond on the left and a stream on the right. The tee shot should be kept left-center, leaving a 125- to 175-yard approach shot over the stream to a deep but narrow green. The finishing hole is a beautiful 440-yard par 4 that plays to a deep, narrow green completely surrounded by three huge traps. Surrounding the green are stands of beautiful birch and aspen in a cathedral-like setting. The fairway is bordered by a stream on the left from tee to green.

Tamarron offers a variety of golf packages. The lowest rates tend to be in May and October. One program, the preferred golf plan, offers a 3-day and 3-night stay in a deluxe guest room, breakfast, 3 days of golf, golf cart, unlimited use of the practice range, daily golf clinics and other amenities for just over $100 per person per night, double occupancy, during the off season. The peak season is July and August when package rates can be 50 percent higher

There is also a Tamarron Instructional Plan, which offers an individualized instructional format designed to improve any skill level, while covering all the fundamentals of the game as well as allowing one to play the resort's championship course. This program includes 5 days and 4 nights at Tamarron with 6 hrs. of instruction with drills and exercise, and a variety of other features including a 4-to-1 student-to-teacher ratio. Other packages, including family, tennis and others are offered by the resort year round. Tamarron Instructional Clinics and Executive Golf Retreat are also held here.

Accommodations at Tamarron range from deluxe guest rooms, most of which have kitchenettes or kitchens, to 2-bedroom deluxe suites which are ideal for large families or groups. Accommodations are available in the main lodge or condominiums nearby. Within driving distance of Tamarron are many impressive sights, including the San Juan Skyway, historic Durango, Mesa Verde National Park, Box Canyon Falls, the deserted ancient homes of the Anasazi Indians, and the Durango and Silverton Narrow Gauge Railroad, which was once used to bring ore from the mining town of Silverton to Durango. Near the Four Corners, where New Mexico, Arizona, Utah and Colorado meet, the area surrounding Tamarron offers a combination of national beauty and a sense of the western frontier.

The Tamarron Golf Course is ranked among America's 75 best resort courses by *Golf Digest*. Just over the state line in

Farmington, New Mexico, is the new Piñon Hills Golf Course, which is ranked number one in that state. Quality golf is alive and well in this part of the world, and is well worth exploring.

Recommended Golf Courses Within 1 Hour of Durango:

Dalton Ranch and Golf Club, Durango, (970) 247–8774, Semiprivate, 18/7040/72

Fairfield Pagosa Golf Club, Pagosa Springs, (970) 731–4755, Resort. Pines: 18/6748/71. Meadows: 9/3732/36

Colorado: Useful Information

Colorado Tourism Board, 1677 Wadsworth Rd., Lake Wood, CO 80202, (303) 232–1500, (800) 608–4748, (303) 592–5510 (information), (800) 433–2656 (vacation planning kit)

Colorado Ski Country, 1560 Broadway, Ste. 1440, Denver, CO 80202, (303) 837–0793

Colorado Parks and Outdoor Recreation, 1313 Sherman St., Rm. 618, Denver, CO 80203, (303) 866–3437 (recreation information)

U.S. Forest Service, 740 Simms, Lakewood, CO 80225, (303) 275–5350 (national forest information and reservations) (800) 280–CAMP

Colorado Division of Wildlife, 6060 Broadway, Denver, CO 80216, (303) 297–1192 (fishing and hunting regulations)

Course Name: RICHTER PARK

Course Type: Public
Address: 100 Aunt Hack Road
Danbury, CT 06811
Phone: (203) 792–2552

GOLF COURSE

Head Professional: Bob Rogers
Course Length/Par (All Tees): Back 6741/72, White 6307/72, Gold 5519/72, Forward 5200/72
Course Slope/Rating (All Tees): Back 134/73.3, White 128/71.6, Ladies' Gold 122/72.8, Ladies' Forward NA/NA
Course Architect: Edward Ryder (1971)
Golf Facilities: Full Pro Shop X, Snack Bar X, Lounge X, Restaurant X, Locker Room X, Showers X, Club Rental X, Club Repair X, Cart Rental X, Instruction X, Practice Green X, Driving Range No, Practice Bunker No, Club Storage No
Tee-Time Reservation Policy: First come first served. Weekend reservations for residents first 2 hrs. of each day by lottery
Ranger: Yes
Tee-off-Interval Time: 8 min.
Time to Play 18 Holes: 4½ hrs.
Course Hours/Earliest Tee-off: 6:30 a.m. weekends, 7 a.m. weekdays
Green Fees: $44 for 18 holes
Cart Fees: $22 for 18 holes
Pull Carts: $3 for 18 holes
Credit Cards: MasterCard, Visa
Season: March 15 to Dec. 1
Course Comments: Can walk anytime (not easy to walk). Yardage book available
Golf Packages: None
Discounts: Twilight, resident seniors, juniors
Places to Stay Nearby: SOUTHBURY: Heritage Inn and Conference Center (203) 264–8200. DANBURY: Hilton (203) 794–0600, (800) HILTONS; Ethan Allan Inn (203) 744–1776, (800) 742–1776; Ramada Inn (203) 792–3800, (800) 228–2828. NEW MILFORD: Homestead Inn (203) 354–4080

Local Attractions: Access to the Berkshire Mountains and leaf tours, music festivals and other seasonal events, shopping, antiquing, Military Museum of Southern New England, Scott-Fanton Museum. Danbury Chamber of Commerce (203) 743–5565
Directions: I–84 from the west, to exit 2, left at bottom ramp to light, right, take 2nd left, follow signs up the hill to golf course. I–84 from east, take exit 2B, take right at bottom of ramp, go to the light, right turn, take 2nd left, follow signs to golf course
Closest Commercial Airports: Stewart International, Newburgh, NY (1 hr.); LaGuardia, NY (1 hr.); Bradley International, Hartford (1 hr., 20 min.)

RICHTER PARK

Richter Park is a beautiful wooded, hilly golf course in western Connecticut. The facility is situated in Stanley Lasker Richter Memorial Park, land that was donated to the city of Danbury by Mrs. Irene Myers Richter, his widow. The park contains other amenities such as hiking trails, tennis courts, an arts center, fishing ponds and an activity center. The golf course has regularly received recognition from *Golf Digest* as one of the top 75 public golf courses in America, and over 50,000 rounds of golf are played here during a season that runs from mid-March through November. The course has bentgrass greens that are moderately fast, large and undulating. The fairways and tees are Kentucky bluegrass. The Richter Park layout is well maintained with beautiful oak, maple and other varieties of trees gracing its rolling hills. Water hazards, often in the form of beautiful lakes and ponds, are found on almost every hole. You can walk the course anytime, but it is somewhat difficult to do so because of the terrain.

Most of the sand bunkers at Richter Park are around the greens, and some holes have no sand bunkers at all. The 413-yard par-4 sixth, for example, is a straight hole whose tee-shot landing area has water on the left. The second shot is to a deep, narrow green with no bunkers. This is the number-1-handicap hole on the course. Both par 3s on this side play almost completely over water. The 183-yard par-3 third has a deep green with three bunkers to the left and one to the right. The 174-yard fifth has a large green flanked by two large traps. A difficult par 4 on the front side is the 430-yard fourth, which plays straight to a deep green with large bunkers to the left and right. The tee shot must avoid bunkers protecting the landing area.

The most difficult hole on the back nine is the 527-yard dogleg-right par-5 twelfth, which has a blind uphill tee shot. The fairway slopes from left to right, so the ball should be kept on the left side of the fairway. The second shot is also likely to be uphill and blind. The approach shot is down to a beautiful green on a small peninsula edged by a large lake. A huge bunker looms behind the green, and water cuts in front and to the right of the green. You are likely to have a downhill, sidehill lie on the approach shot, and wind can be a factor coming into the hole. The twelfth is considered the signature hole at Richter Park.

The finishing hole is a tough, beautiful 437-yard par-4 dogleg right. If your tee shot isn't left of center and far enough, large, mature trees on the right will stymie your approach shot, which is uphill to a deep green protected by a large bunker to the left and another to the right.

Richter Park is an example of a well-maintained, well-designed public golf facility. The beautiful natural terrain was used by the golf-course architect Edward Ryder to create a variety of interesting and challenging holes that include dramatic uphill and downhill slopes, streams, ponds, lakes and mature trees. Ryder became a golf-course architect after studying landscape architecture, engineering and business at Hofstra University on Long Island, New York. After working with the golf-course contracting firm of C. B. Carlson and Sons, he formed a golf-course design partnership in the 1960s and later formed his own firm in Florida. Some of his designs include the Harry Brownson Country Club in Shelton, Connecticut, with Val Carlson; and the

Salem Golf Club in North Salem, New York, also with Carlson.

The clubhouse at Richter Park has a snack bar/restaurant, locker rooms, showers, and a golf shop. The practice facilities are limited to a small warmup area and 2 putting greens. Instruction is available, however, and a variety of golf clinics for young people are given here. Richter Park has hosted the Metropolitan Public Links Championship, the Northeast Public Links Tournament, the Ladies State Amateur and the annual Fran McCarthy Junior Golf Tournament. The number of rounds played on the course has increased significantly from 35,878 in 1984 to over 50,000 rounds in 1991. Approximately one-third of these rounds are played by nonresidents who come from far and wide to play this excellent golf course.

Recommended Golf Courses in Connecticut

Within 1 Hour of Danbury:

Crestbrook Golf Course, Watertown, (203) 945–5249, Public, 18/6376/71

Heritage Inn (Heritage Village Country Club), Southbury, (203) 264–8200 (Resort), (203) 264–8081 (Tee Times) Resort, 18/6266/72

H. Smith Richardson Golf Course, Fairfield, (203) 255–6094, Public, 18/6676/72

Pequabuck Golf Club, Pequabuck, (203) 583–7307, Semiprivate, 18/6015/69

Ridgefield Golf Course, Ridgefield, (203) 748–7008, Public, 18/6380/70

Whitney Farms Golf Course, Monroe, (203) 268–0707, Public, 18/6600/72

Within 1 Hour of Hartford:

Bel Compo Golf Club, Avon, (203) 678–1679, Public, 18/7028/72

Blackledge Country Club, Hebron, (203) 228–0250, Public, 18/6853/72

Cedar Knob Golf Club, Somers, (203) 749–3550, Public, 18/6734/72

Lyman Orchards Golf Club, Middlefield, (203) 349–8055, Semiprivate. Gary Player: 18/6600/71. Robert Trent Jones: 18/7011/72

Minnechang Golf Course, Glastonbury, (203) 643–9914, Public, 18/6510/70

Pine Valley Country Club, Southington, (203) 628–0879, Public, 18/6325/71

Portland Golf Course, Portland, (203) 342–6107, Public, 18/6213/71

Portland Golf Club West, Portland, (203) 342–4043, Public, 18/3620/60

Simsbury Farms Golf Club, West Simsbury, (203) 658–6246, Public, 18/6421/72

Tallwood Country Club, Hebron, (203) 646–3437, Public, 18/6366/72

Timberlin Golf Course, Kensington, (203) 828–3228, Public, 18/6733/72

Tunxis Plantation Country Club, Farmington, (203) 677–1367, Public. White: 18/6638/72. Red/Green: 18/6647/72

Within 1 Hour of New London:

Norwich Golf Course, Norwich, (203) 889–6973, Public, 18/6221/71

Shennecossett Country Club, Groton, (203) 445–0262, Public, 18/6491/72

Willimantic Country Club, Willimantic, (203) 456–1971, Semiprivate, 18/6300/71

Within 1 Hour of Stamford:

Sterling Farms, Stamford, (203) 329–7888, Public, 18/6401/72

Tashua Knolls, Trumbull, (203) 261–5989, Public, 18/6502/72

Connecticut: Useful Information

State of Connecticut Department of Economic Development, 865 Brook St., Rocky Hill, CT 06067–3405, (800) 282–6863 (tourist information)

State of Connecticut Department of Environmental Protection, State Office Bldg., 165 Capitol Ave., Hartford, CT 06106, (203) 566–2304 (recreation information)

Connecticut Historical Commission, 59 S. Prospect St., Hartford, CT 06106, (203) 566–3005 (historic sites)

Connecticut Commission on the Arts, 227 Lawrence St., Hartford, CT 06106, (203) 566–4770 (cultural events)

DELAWARE

Course Name: RON JAWORSKY'S GARRISON'S LAKE GOLF CLUB

Course Type: Public
Address: Route 13/101 Fairways Circle
Smyrna, DE 19977
Phone: (302) 653–9847

GOLF COURSE

Head Professional: Jim Matthias
Course Length/Par (All Tees): Back 7028/72, Middle 6595/72, Ladies' Forward 5760/74
Course Slope/Rating (All Tees): Back 123/73.5, Middle 118/71.4, Ladies' Forward 123/72.8
Course Architect: Edmund B. Ault (front 9, 1962; back 9, 1964)
Golf Facilities: Full Pro Shop X, Snack Bar X, Lounge X, Restaurant X, Locker Room X, Showers X, Club Rental X, Club Repair X, Cart Rental X, Instruction X, Practice Green X, Driving Range X, Practice Bunker X, Club Storage X
Tee-Time Reservation Policy: Up to 7 days in advance
Ranger: As needed
Tee-off-Interval Time: 8 min.
Time to Play 18 Holes: 4½ hrs.
Course Hours/Earliest Tee-off: 7 a.m. to dark
Green Fees and Cart Fees: $25 for 18 holes Sat., Sun., holidays with cart, $23 for 18 holes weekdays. $20 for 18 holes Sat., Sun. holidays walking, $18 for 18 holes weekdays
Credit Cards: All major cards except Discover
Season: Year round
Course Comments: Can walk anytime. Yardage book available
Golf Packages: None
Discounts: Twilight rates after 2:30
Places to Stay Nearby: DOVER: Sheraton (302) 678–8500, (800) 325–3535; Holiday Inn (302) 734–5701, (800) HOLIDAY
Local Attractions: DOVER: Delaware Agricultural Museum, Delaware State Museum, state house of legislature, John Dickinson Plantation, Longwood Gardens, Kennett Square, PA; Winterthur Museum and Gardens; Brandywine River Museum, Chadds Ford, PA; Hagley Museum; New Castle historic buildings. Delaware Tourism Office (800) 282–8667 (DE), (800) 441–8846 (outside DE)
Directions: I–95 south to Rte. 13 south, to Smyrna, 5 mi. south of Smyrna on Rte. 3, golf course on the right
Closest Commercial Airports: Dover (20 min.), Philadelphia International, PA (1 hr., 15 min.)

RON JAWORSKY'S GARRISON'S LAKE GOLF CLUB

Garrison's Lake Golf Club is approximately 20 minutes north of Dover, Delaware, and 1 hour and 15 minutes south of Philadelphia. The 7028-yard layout was designed by Edmund B. Ault. The front nine was opened in 1962 and the eighteen was completed and opened in 1964. Born in nearby Washington, D.C., in 1908, Edmund B. Ault started out in construction engineering after studying at the Columbia (Maryland) Technical Institute. He became interested in golf-course design and worked with golf architect Fred Findlay before starting his own design business in 1946. Ault became a prolific designer, remodeling and designing numerous courses in the Washington, D.C., area and as far away as Switzerland. He designed Delcastle Farms Golf Course, Wilmington, the Dover Air Force Base Golf Course (9 holes) with Al Johnson; the Pike Creek Valley Golf Course; the Shawnee Country Club (9 holes); and the Sussex Pines Country Club in Delaware. Ault was a one-time low-handicap golfer who played in the U.S. Amateur. He was a strong advocate of flexibility in golf courses and pioneered the systematic coordination of pin placements with tee-marker locations.

Garrison's Lake is a relatively flat course that used to be prime farmland. Dorothy and Charles Ewing originally developed the land as recreational and ran a landscaping business on the property. Mrs.

Ewing sold the property to club members in the 1970s, and today it is open to the public during the week. The course is well treed and has large, medium-speed bent-grass greens with slight undulation. Each green is well protected by two or three traps, and there are very few fairway bunkers. Water comes into play only on the back nine, but to a significant degree on four holes.

The fifth hole, a 444-yard par-4 slight dogleg left, is the number-1-handicap hole on the course. The first shot is down a narrow, well-treed fairway, and the second has to be straight to a large green with traps to the left and right and trees surrounding it. A tough par 3 on this side, the 201-yard eighth, is rated the number-5-handicap hole on the course. It plays to a circular green with two traps to the right and front and one trap to the left. Trees surround the green, leaving little margin for error. The eleventh hole, which plays 222 yards to a green flanked on the left and right by large traps, is another difficult par 3. There is enough room in front to bounce the ball onto the green, however.

The par 5s at Garrison's Lake tend to be somewhat short, and the par 4s tend to be the most difficult holes. The 454-yard par-4 thirteenth, for example, plays long and straight to a green protected left and right by traps. The tee-shot landing area is flanked by water on the left and two bunkers on the right. The 406-yard fifteenth is a slight dogleg to the right to a medium-sized green protected by three traps—two to the left and front and one on the right. The finishing hole is another long par 4 playing 422 yards to an oval-shaped green with traps to the left and right.

The combination of length, well-placed traps protecting the greens and the tightness of this course, which has more than 10,000 trees, makes Garrison's Lake a good challenge. The course is open year round, weather permitting.

Recommended Golf Courses in Delaware

Delcastle Golf Club, Wilmington, (302) 995–1990, Public, 18/6628/72

Ed "Porky" Oliver Golf Club, Wilmington, (302) 571–9041, Public, 18/6115/69

Rock Manor Golf Club, Wilmington, (302) 652–4083 (Club), (302) 654–2237 (Pro Shop), Semiprivate, 18/5779/69

Three Little Bakers, Wilmington, (302) 737–1877, Semiprivate, 18/6609/71

Delaware: Useful Information

Delaware State Travel Service, Delaware Tourism Office, 99 Kings Hwy., P.O. Box 1401, Dover, DE 19903, (800) 282–8667 (in DE), (800) 441–8846 (outside DE)

Division of Fish and Wildlife, P.O. Box 1401, Dover, DE 19903, (302) 739–4431 (fishing and hunting regulations)

**Course name: THE CHAMPIONS AT
                 SUMMERFIELD**

Course Type: Public
Address: 3400 S.E. Summerfield Way
              Stuart, FL 34997
Phone: (407) 283–1500
Fax: (407) 283–7849

GOLF COURSE

Head Professional: David Scull
Course Length/Par (All Tees): Back
   6899/72, Blue 6335/72, White 5614/72,
   Forward 4941/72
Course Slope/Rating (All Tees): Back
   131/72.8, Blue 125/70.5, White
   117/68.7, Ladies' White 125/73.9,
   Ladies' Forward 116/69.4
Course Architect: Tom Fazio (1994)
Golf Facilities: Full Pro Shop X, Snack
   Bar X, Lounge X, Restaurant X,
   Locker Room X, Showers X, Club
   Rental X, Club Repair X, Cart Rental
   X, Instruction X, Practice Green X,
   Driving Range X, Practice Bunker No,
   Club Storage No
Tee-Time Reservation Policy: Up to 4
   days in advance peak season (Nov.
   through Apr.), up to 7 days in advance
   otherwise
Ranger: Yes
Tee-off-Interval Time: 10 min.
Time to Play 18 Holes: 4 hrs. 15 min.
Course Hours/Earliest Tee-off: 7 a.m.
Green and Cart Fees: $57 for 18 holes
   peak season (Nov. through Feb.)
Credit Cards: MasterCard, Visa
Season: Year round. Busiest Nov. through
   Apr.
Course Comments: Cart required unless
   annual member. Yardage book
Golf Packages: No
Discounts: Seasonal (May through Oct.),
   Florida residents, multiple play
Places to Stay Nearby: Holiday Inn–
   Downtown (407) 287–6200, (800)
   HOLIDAY; Indian River Plantation
   Beach Resort (407) 225–3700, (800)
   444–1432. BED AND BREAKFAST: The
   Homeplace (407) 220-9148. JUPITER:
   The Jupiter Beach Resort (407) 746–

2511, (800) 228–8811. PORT ST. LUCIE:
Club Med Sandpiper (407) 335–4400,
(800) 258–2633. VERO BEACH:Guest
Quarters Suite Hotel (407) 231–5666,
(800) 742–5388
Local Attractions: Coastal Science Center,
   Eliot Museum, Gilbert's Bar House of
   Refuge Museum, fishing, boating,
   beaches, major league baseball spring
   training at Port St. Lucie, Hobe Sound
   National Wildlife Refuge, Jupiter Island.
   Stuart/Martin County Chamber of Com-
   merce, 1650 S.W. Kanner Hwy., Stuart,
   FL 34994 (407) 287–1088
Directions: Take I–95 to Exit 61. Proceed
   approximately 5 miles east on Hwy. 76
   to Cove Rd. Take a right on Cove Rd. to
   U.S. 1. Turn right to golf course
Closest Commercial Airports: Palm
   Beach International (30 min.); Fort Lauderdale–Hollywood International (1½
   hrs.); Daytona Beach Regional (4 hrs.)

THE CHAMPIONS CLUB AT SUMMERFIELD

The Champions Club wends its way
through more than 240 acres of wetlands,
upland preserves, and lakes on the southeast coast of Florida in Stuart. A member
of the National Audubon Society Signature
Cooperative Sanctuary Program, The Champions layout is rife with wood storks, sand
bill cranes, pied-billed grebes, and other
varieties. Bunkers, water, and foliage including palmetto, pine, and cinnamon ferns
penalize shots that miss the well-manicured
landing areas.

The Champions builds to a crescendo
with three of its most difficult holes concluding your wetland round. The 434-yard
par-4 sixteenth is a dogleg right with three
bunkers guarding the left edge of the turn.
Woods border the right side, forcing you to
carefully position the ball between these
obstacles. The approach is to a two-tiered
green guarded by bunkers on both sides.
The 210-yard par-3 seventeenth usually
requires a 2- or 3-iron from the back tees
to reach a putting surface well protected by
bunkers to its left and water to its right.
The eighteenth, a 557-yard par 5, is straight
and long with woods on the left and water

on the right. Heavily guarded by bunkers, this narrow finishing hole is especially difficult when the wind blows in.

The Champions Club is part of a master-planned 550-acre community. The Tom Fazio-designed layout was rated among the best new courses of 1994 by *Golf Digest*. The course is owned and operated by a company headed by golf analyst Steve Melnyk.

Course Name: COLONY WEST

Course Type: Public
Address: 6800 N.W. 88th Avenue
                      Tamarac, FL 33321
Phone: (305) 721–7710

GOLF COURSE

Directors of Golf: Eddie Rack, Norm Rack
Course Length/Par (All Tees): Back 7271/71, Blue 6864/71, White 6461/71, Red 5422/71, Forward 4810/71
Course Slope/Rating (All Tees): Back 138/75.8, Blue 135/73.9, White 130/71.8, Red 127/71.6, Ladies' Forward 127/71.6
Course Architects: Bruce Devlin and Robert von Hagge (1970)
Golf Facilities: Full Pro Shop X, Snack Bar X, Lounge X, Restaurant X, Showers X, Club Rental X, Club Repair Sent out, Cart Rental X, Instruction X, Practice Green X, Driving Range No, Practice Bunker No, Club Storage X
Tee-Time Reservation Policy: 3 days in advance from 7 a.m.
Ranger: Yes
Tee-off-Interval Time: 8 min.
Time to Play 18 Holes: 4 hrs., 20 min.
Course Hours/Earliest Tee-off: 7:30 a.m.
Green and Cart Fees: $70 for 18 holes with cart peak season (Nov. to May); $40 low season
Credit Cards: American Express, MasterCard, Visa
Season: Year round. Busiest season Dec. to April
Course Comments: Cart mandatory. Yardage book available. Summer memberships available
Golf Packages: Available
Discounts: Seasonal (May 1 to Nov. 1). Summer memberships (May 1 to Nov.

15). Twilight rate after 3 p.m. (May 1 to Nov. 1)
Places to Stay Nearby: TAMARAC: Wellesley Inn (305) 484–6909; Budgetel Inn (305) 485–7900; Holiday Inn (305) 472–5600, (800) HOLIDAY. FT. LAUDERDALE: Marriott's Harbor Beach Resort (305) 525–4000, (800) 228–9290; Pier 66 Resort and Marina (305) 525–6666, (800) 432–1956; Riverside Hotel (305) 467–0671, (800) 325–3280; Carriage House Resort Motel (305) 427–7670
Local Attractions: Hugh Taylor Birch State Recreation Area, Bonnet House Museum of Art, River Walk, Arts and Science District, Historic District/ Entertainment Center, Broward Center for the Performing Arts, Discovery Center Museum, New World Aquarium, Ocean World, Swimming Hall of Fame, horse racing, spring-training baseball, fishing, boating, dog racing, shopping, Seminole native village, Flamingo Gardens. Greater Ft. Lauderdale Convention and Visitors Bureau (305) 765–4466
Directions: From I–95: Proceed west on Cypress Creek Rd. to N.E. 62nd St., which then becomes McNab Rd., to Pine Island Rd. Make left at Pine Island Rd. to golf course
Closest Commercial Airport: Ft. Lauderdale–Hollywood International (20min.), Miami International (30 min.), Palm Beach International (50 min.)

COLONY WEST

Colony West, centrally located between Palm Beach and Miami on Florida's Gold Coast, bills itself as "a public golf course with a country club atmosphere," and it certainly is that. Rated as one of the top public golf courses in America by *Golf Digest*, Colony West was designed by Bruce Devlin and Robert von Hagge, and it opened in 1970. Originally built to be the home of the Jackie Gleason Tournament, the 36-hole facility is now owned by the Rack family, which also owns a golf course in the Pittsburgh area. Eddie Rack, his son Norm, and Norm's son Craig are all professionals and manage the business. Another layout, the adjacent 3827-yard par-65 Glades Course, is especially popular as a walking course.

Cut out of cypress trees and featuring water on most of its holes, this 18-hole championship course measures 7271 yards from the back tees. Four tee positions are available. Sloped at 138 from the back tees, the Championship Course starts out with the number-1-handicap 621-yard par 5, which requires three long, straight shots to reach a green protected on the right by a trap and measuring 42 yards from front to back. This Tifdwarf Bermuda-grass green, typical of Colony West, is large, somewhat fast, and relatively flat.

The number-2-handicap par-4 twelfth hole plays 452 yards and is a dogleg to the left. The green is deep and protected by traps to the left and right. The tee shot has to be in a position to enable the golfer to fly a water hazard in front of the green yet still stay on the putting surface.

The eighteenth hole is another tough par 4. It is 452 yards long and well protected by trees on the left and two fairway bunkers to the right. A water hazard cuts across the fairway 76 yards from a deep, elongated green protected by a large trap to the rear left and a smaller trap to the right and forward. Eight par 4s on the course play close to 400 yards or more from the back and blue tees, and the par 3s also play relatively long. Accuracy is at a premium on the 220-yard par-3 eighth hole, which has five traps protecting a 52-yard-deep oblong green. The 202-yard par-3 thirteenth green is also oblong, 50 yards in depth, and protected by four traps and water on the right.

Colony West caters to private and corporate golf outings and has a variety of facilities, including a large, modern clubhouse; an elevator for the handicapped; a swimming pool; locker rooms; lounge; banquet-catering facilities; complete pro shop and a variety of other amenities. The practice area is limited at present, including only a putting green.

Course Name: **DORAL GOLF RESORT AND SPA**
Blue, Red, Gold, White, Silver, Green Courses

Course Type: Resort
Resort: Doral Golf Resort and Spa
Address: 4400 N.W. 87th Avenue
Miami, FL 33178
Phone: (305) 592–2000,
(800) 71–DORAL (Tee Times)
(305) 594–0954 (Silver Course Only)
Fax: (305) 594–4682 (Resort)
Telex: 518 928 M1A M1A13

GOLF COURSE

Head Professional: Randy Cahall
Course Length/Par (All Tees): Blue: 6939/72, Middle 6597/72, Forward 5786/72. Red: Back 6120/71, Middle 5681/71, Forward 5204/71. Gold: Back 6602/70, Blue 6209/70, White 5747/70, Forward 5179/70. White: Back 6208/72, Middle 5913/72, Forward 5286/72. Silver: Back 6801/72, Blue 6383/72, White 6016/72, Forward 5064/72. Green: Back 1085/27

Course Slope/Rating (All Tees): Blue: Back 127/73.2, Middle 122/70.4, Ladies' Forward 124/71.8. Red: Back 118/69.9, Middle 114/67.6, Ladies' Forward 118/70.6. Gold: Back 127/73.3, Middle 124/70.7, Ladies' Forward 123/71.7. White: Back 122/71.6, Middle 113/68.4, Ladies' Forward 116/69.3. Silver: Back 129/72.0, Blue 122/70.5, White 118/68.6, Forward 108/63, Ladies' White 126/73.45, Ladies' Forward 113/67.12

Course Architects: Blue Course: Dick Wilson with Robert von Hagge (1961), Robert von Hagge and Bruce Devlin (renovation, 1971). Red Course: Robert von Hagge (1961), Robert von Hagge and Bruce Devlin (renovation, 1985, 1989). Gold Course: Robert von Hagge and Bruce Devlin (1968, renovation, 1982); Raymond Floyd (1996, renovation). White Course: Robert von Hagge (1965). Silver Course: Robert von Hagge (1984). Green Course: Robert von Hagge (1961)

Golf Facilities: Full Pro Shop X, Snack Bar X, Lounge X, Restaurant X, Locker Room X, Showers X, Club Rental X, Club Repair X, Cart Rental X, Instruction X, Practice Green X, Driving Range X, Practice Bunker X, Club Storage X

Tee-Time Reservation Policy: Resort guests: at time of reservation. Public: Up to 24 hrs. in advance.

Ranger: Yes

Tee-off-Interval Time: 7 to 9 min.

Time to Play 18 Holes: 4½ hrs.

Course Hours/Earliest Tee-off: 7 a.m.

Green and Cart Fees: Outside play (peak season Fri., Sat., Sun. holidays) Blue: $185 for 18 holes with cart. Red, Gold: $135; White $95. Silver: $63 for 18 holes with cart. Green: $40 for 9 holes with cart, $25 walking. Weekday rates slightly less for 18 hole courses

Credit Cards: All major cards

Season: Year round. Busiest season late Nov. to March

Course Comments: Can walk Green Course. Cart mandatory on other courses. Silver Course at nearby Doral Park Golf and Country Club. Doral practice range opens at 6:30 a.m. Golf learning center on site

Golf Packages: Available through resort. Inquire about packages and guest rates

Discounts: Seasonal (May to early Sept.) Resort guests get reduced rates. Twilight rates

Places to Stay Nearby: See recommended list for Miami on page 153

Local Attractions: For information, call Greater Miami Convention and Visitors Bureau (800) 283–2707

Directions: From Miami International Airport (15 min.): Hwy. 836 west 2 mi. north on N.W. 87th Ave. to resort

Closest Commercial Airports: Miami International (15 min.), Fort Lauderdale–Hollywood International (45 min.), Palm Beach International (1 hr., 15 min.)

RESORT

Date Built: 1961

No. of Rooms: 649 rooms and 48 suites in 8 separate lodges

Meeting/Exhibit Rooms: 35. Capacity of Largest: 1000 persons. Meeting Space: 75,000 sq. ft.

Room Price Range: $250 standard to $350 deluxe peak season (mid-Nov. to mid-May). Golf and other packages available

Lounges: Rousseau's Lounge, Pool Bar and Snacks, Champions Sports Bar

Restaurants: Celebrations at the Spa, Champions Sports Bar, Splash, Terrazza, Windows

Entertainment: Disc jockey, dancing

Credit Cards: All major cards

General Amenities: Children's playground, activity center and programs; meeting and conference facilities for small groups to banquets for 1000 persons with audiovisual, food service, and secretarial support

Recreational Amenities: 15-court tennis complex with pro shop and instructional programs, Olympic-sized swimming pool, 24-stable equestrian center, bass and tarpon fishing in 18 lakes, bicycling paths, jogging trail, basketball and volleyball courts, game rooms, Aqua Sports Club with certified instruction and rentals for catamaran sailing, windsurfing, parasailing, wave riding, kayaking, snorkeling, scuba diving, and banana rides; fitness center and health clubs with aerobic equipment, Universal machines, steam rooms, massage, saunas, Jacuzzis, water aerobics, rowing machines, whirlpools; adjacent Doral Saturnia International Spa Resort, a 148,000-sq. ft. complex with nutrition, fitness, stress management, image-making, weight reduction, and other programs

Reservation and Cancellation Policy: Credit card guarantee required or 1 night's deposit 14 days prior to arrival. 3-day cancellation policy to avoid penalties

Comments and Restrictions: Taxes, service charge per person per night additional

DORAL RESORT AND COUNTRY CLUB

The Doral is one of those places that you have to go to if you are serious about golf. The name Doral is the melding of Alfred

Kaskel's name with that of his wife Doris. Kaskel was a veteran hotelier and real-estate developer who opened the Carillon Hotel on Miami Beach in 1958. He was also a golf enthusiast who had the foresight to buy 2400 acres of swampland just west of Miami International Airport. By then he had decided to build "the finest golf resort the world has ever seen." A lavish clubhouse and the first three of his 6 golf courses were built before any modern expressway was completed. By 1962, Kaskel brought PGA golf to southern Florida with the first Doral Open and the largest PGA prize pool of that time, $50,000. Kaskel died in 1968. The Doral has every conceivable recreation facility including horseback riding; fishing on 18 private lakes; boating and water sports at the resort swimming pools or at the resort's nearby Aqua Sports Club on the Atlantic Ocean; the 48-suite Doral Saturnia International Spa with full spa services from nutritional and fitness programs to massage and skin treatments; the new Saturnia Fitness Center with Nautilus equipment, sauna, hot tubs, aerobics classes, whirlpool steam room, Jacuzzis and much more. There is also a 15-court Arthur Ashe, Jr., Tennis Center. New facilities and renovations to existing amenities at the Doral are the result of a recent multimillion-dollar expansion and renovation program.

The most acclaimed golf course at the Doral is "the Blue Monster," or Blue Course, which is the home of the Doral–Ryder Open. It was designed by Dick Wilson with Robert von Hagge and opened in 1961. The Blue Course has been rated among the top 100 courses in America since *Golf Digest* began the list in 1966. This 6939-yard par-72 layout has rich tropical landscaping, 8 man-made lakes, a network of streams and canals, and over 125 sand bunkers. The unpredictable Atlantic Coast wind can also add to the difficulty of this demanding golf course. The greens are Bermuda grass, moderately fast, and, as you can imagine, well protected by sand and water. Mature trees guarding the tight fairways also add to the complexity of "the Blue Monster." Billy Casper won the first

Doral in 1962. Greg Norman holds the course record with a 62, which he shot on the last day of the tournament in 1990 when he went on to win by holing a chip shot in a sudden-death playoff.

The Blue Course has an interesting and demanding array of par-3 holes that also reflect the variety of shapes and sizes of the greens here. The 237-yard fourth hole plays over the corner of a lake to a deep green guarded by two traps front and left, a trap to the right and water further right. The 163-yard ninth plays over water to another deep green with a trap and water to the left. The 246-yard thirteenth plays to a significantly raised green that is difficult to hold. The green is medium sized with traps both left and right. This hole plays a lengthy 228 yards from the middle tees. The 174-yard fifteenth plays to a wide, shallow green guarded by two traps in front and one to the rear. The wind is generally across or against the golfer's tee shot on this hole.

The finishing hole on the Blue Course, a 425-yard par 4 hole, is considered to be one of the most difficult on the tour. It is a slight dogleg left, completely bordered by water on the left from tee to green. The left-to-right-angled green is deep, narrow and protected by two traps on the right and the lake on the left. Trees and water guard the tee-shot landing area. You have to avoid pulling your approach shot into the water. Pin position is also a major factor on this great finishing hole.

Doral's Red Course has recently gone through a major renovation under the direction of the original course architect Robert von Hagge. The 6120 yardage remains unchanged, but the original flat fairways are now rolling and narrower. The grass on the fairways has been replaced by a new hybrid strain of Bermuda that is both disease and pest resistant. Greens have been replanted with Tifdwarf, also a hybrid Bermuda, which tends to create a faster putting surface. The new grass and elevated fairways will also improve the drainage and make the course easier to maintain. The elevation of many greens has also been changed.

The Red Course is also well bunkered, with water hazards on every hole except two. The 141-yard par-3 fifteenth, which has been significantly redesigned, is likely to be one of the more memorable on the course. The tee shot is completely over water to a 150-foot-long, narrow, three-tiered "island" green, which drops a total of 7 feet from back to front. A rock wall surrounds this excellent golf hole.

The Gold Course, also designed by von Hagge with Bruce Devlin, is considered to be the most difficult course at Doral after "the Blue Monster." Like all the courses here, the Gold Course is well bunkered, with water coming into play on every hole. There are many interesting doglegs on this layout, which was opened in 1968 and remodeled in 1982. Raymond Floyd just completed another extensive renovation of this course in 1996. The number-1-handicap hole is the long, 440-yard par-4 second, a dogleg left to a deep green straddled by two large bunkers. Water and large bunkers on the left protect the tee-shot landing area. The front side of the Gold Course plays almost 300 yards longer than the back nine, which has three par 3s, including the 153-yard twelfth, which plays over water to a wide, shallow green with two traps to the rear and water front, left and behind.

The 6208-yard White Course was designed by von Hagge and opened in 1965. Its rolling fairways meander along around clusters of challenging bunkers. Water comes directly into play on nine holes, including the number-2-handicap third, a 368-yard par-4 dogleg right that plays over water on the approach shot to a green protected by water front, right and rear. The 540-yard par-5 thirteenth is considered to be one of the most difficult holes at Doral. This straight hole is guarded by water on the left and to the front of a deep green. The White Course has an excellent 411-yard par-4 finishing hole that plays over water on the approach shot to a large, well-bunkered green.

The Robert von Hagge–designed 6801-yard par-72 Silver Course is at nearby Doral Park. This layout has water hazards on every hole, severe mounding along the fairways, and well over 75 sand bunkers.

The most difficult hole on the Silver Course is the 446-yard par-4 thirteenth, whose tee shot has to avoid an obstacle course of fairway bunkers. The second shot is to a green well protected by traps on the left and water on the right.

The 1085-yard par-3 nine hole Green Course was designed by Robert von Hagge and opened in 1961. This is an excellent layout for a beginner or anyone wishing to work on his or her short game. The longest hole is the 159-yard third, and the shortest is only 79 yards.

The main clubhouse at the Doral Resort includes an impressive pro shop boutique that covers more than 8100 sq. ft. on four different levels. Here you can find golf, tennis and other apparel, and a separate equipment center has a full line of golf equipment. Golf lessons are available through the staff of PGA professionals and assistants, and a variety of golf workshops are conducted under the auspices of Director of Golf Instruction Jim McLean. Lessons are available to all levels of players on the extensive driving-range, chipping, practice bunker and putting facilities of Doral. A variety of golf and other packages are available through the resort year round. Golf-package rates are lowest from May to early September. Non-guests can play the course but pay higher green and cart fees.

The Doral has won a number of hospitality awards, including the American Automobile Association Four-Diamond and the *Mobil Travel Guide* Four-Star designations. *Meetings and Conventions*, *Successful Meetings*, and *Corporate and Incentive Travel* magazines have all recognized the Doral as an outstanding meeting resort. There are numerous meeting and conference rooms here, totaling more than 75,000 sq. ft. This includes a new state-of-the-art conference wing with full audiovisual, banquet and secretarial-support capabilities.

Golf Digest has rated the Blue Course at the Doral one of the best resort courses in the United States. *Golf* magazine has awarded the Doral its silver medal as one of the best golf resorts in America.

Course Name: EMERALD DUNES

Course Type: Resort
Address: 2100 Emerald Dunes Drive
West Palm Beach, FL 33411
Phone: (407) 684–4653
Fax: (407) 684–2730

GOLF COURSE

Head Professional: Rob Young
Course Length/Par (All Tees): Back
7006/72, Blue 6558/72, White 6120/72,
Green 5593/72, Forward 4676/72
Course Slope/Rating (All Tees): Back
133/73.8, Blue 129/71.7, White
125/69.7, Green 120/67.3, Ladies' Green
126/72.2, Ladies' Forward 115/67.1
Course Architect: Tom Fazio (1990)
Golf Facilities: Full Pro Shop X, Snack
Bar X, Lounge X, Restaurant X,
Locker Room X, Showers X, Club
Rental X, Club Repair X, Cart Rental
X, Instruction X, Practice Green X,
Driving Range X, Practice Bunker X,
Club Storage X
Tee-Time Reservation Policy: Up to 30
days in advance. Must be secured with a
credit card. Additional advance required
to hold tee times more than 30 days in
advance. Penalties for cancellations less
than 18 hrs. in advance
Ranger: Yes
Tee-off-Interval Time: 8 to 10 min.
Time to Play 18 Holes: 4 hrs. 15 min.
Course Hours/Earliest Tee-off: 7 a.m.
Green and Cart Fees: $130 for 18 holes
Fri., Sat., Sun., holidays; $120 for 18
holes weekdays
Credit Cards: All major cards
Season: Year round. Busiest Nov. through
Apr.
Course Comments: Walking allowed any-
time but you must pay full golf fee. Pull
carts available
Golf Packages: Seasonal and hotel golf
packages. Inquire at pro shop
Discounts: Seasonal. Lowest rates July and
Aug.
Places to Stay Nearby: BOCA RATON: Boca
Raton Hotel and Resort (407) 997–8205,
(800) 327–0101. MANALAPAN: Ritz-
Carlton (407) 533–6000, (800) 241–
3333. PALM BEACH: Brazilian Court

(407) 655–7740, (800) 522–0335; The
Breakers (407) 655–6611, (800) 833–
3141; Four Seasons Ocean Grand Hotel
(407) 582–2800, (800) 432–2335. PALM
BEACH GARDENS: Radisson Suites (407)
622–1000, (800) 333–3333. WEST PALM
BEACH: Holiday Inn (407) 659–3880,
(800) HOLIDAY; Omni Hotel (407)
689–6400
Local Attractions: PALM BEACH: The
Henry Morrison Flagler Museum, Hibel
Museum of Art, Society of the Four
Arts, restaurants, shopping. WEST PALM
BEACH: Dreher Park Zoo, Lion Country
Safari, Norton Gallery of Art, South
Florida Science Museum, Planetarium
and Aquarium, major league baseball
spring training, greyhound races. Palm
Beach County Convention & Visitors
Bureau, 1555 Palm Beach Lakes Blvd.,
Suite 204, West Palm Beach, FL 33401
(407) 471–3995
Directions: Take Florida Turnpike to Exit
99 in West Palm Beach. Proceed 1/4
mile west on Okeechobee Blvd. to golf
course
Closest Commercial Airport: Palm Beach
International (10 min.)

EMERALD DUNES GOLF COURSE

Emerald Dunes, one of the best public
golf courses in the state of Florida, is a
collection of water holes in the heart of the
Palm Beaches. The centerpiece of Vista
Center, an upscale corporate office park,
Emerald Dunes was elected one of the
"Top Ten You Can Play" by *Golf* magazine
in 1991. The course, which has water and
an abundance of bunkers on virtually every
hole, is intimidating at first. The landing areas tend to be generous, but the wind can
be a factor, especially during the blustery
winter months. Fazio, a part owner of
Emerald Dunes, strove to make the course
a challenge to all levels of golfer. He did
not incorporate penal water hazards, unfair
rough, or hidden hazards on this layout. As
a result, you have a variety of shot strategies, and you will finish an enjoyable
round in less than 4½ hours.

Two of the best holes at Emerald Dunes
are the finishing holes on each side. The

474-yard par-4 ninth, titled the "Green Monster," is a dogleg right bordered by water on the right. A long, well-placed drive is required to leave a lofted approach to a deep green framed by two small bunkers. The five tee distances of 474, 420, 393, 370, and 293 yards accomodate all levels of golfer on this hole. The 436-yard par-4 finishing hole, "Super Dune," is a dogleg left with water bordering most of the right side. Bunkers skirt the right side from 130 yards in to a gigantic 60-yard-deep target with three more bunkers to its left. A series of cascading waterfalls to the right add to the elegance of this target. An incoming wind often makes this hole more formidable. The elevated tee at "Super Dune" provides a clear view of a memorable conclusion to your round at Emerald Dunes. Along the way there have been a surprising number of elevation changes on a scenic course dotted with large oaks and palms, and graced with heron, egret, and other wildlife.

The capacious mission-style clubhouse, with its Emerald Grille overlooking the eighteenth hole, provides you with an ideal forum to review your round. Emerald Dunes has an excellent pro shop and a quality golf learning center and practice facility. In the near future a hotel, conference center, and corporate headquarters sites will be added to the property.

Course Name:　**THE LINKS AT KEY BISCAYNE**

Course Type:　Public
Address:　Crandon Boulevard
　　　　　Key Biscayne, FL 33149
Phone:　(305) 361–9139
Fax:　(305) 361–1032

GOLF COURSE

Director of Golf: Jerry Castigliano
Course Length/Par (All Tees): Back 7099/72, Middle 6457/72, Forward 5662/73
Course Slope/Rating (All Tees): Back 139/72.7, Middle 125/71, Ladies' Forward 129/74
Course Architects: Robert von Hagge and Bruce Devlin (1972)

Golf Facilities: Full Pro Shop X, Snack Bar X, Lounge X, Restaurant X, Locker Room X, Showers X, Club Rental X, Club Repair No, Cart Rental X, Instruction X, Practice Green X, Driving Range X, Practice Bunker X, Club Storage X
Tee-Time Reservation Policy: Up to 7 days in advance
Ranger: Yes
Tee-off-Interval Time: 7 and 8 min.
Time to Play 18 Holes: 4½ hrs.
Course Hours/Earliest Tee-off: 7 a.m.
Green and Cart Fees: Peak season (Nov. through April): $76 for 18 holes with cart for nonresidents of Dade County
Pull Carts: $4.50 for 18 holes
Credit Cards: American Express, MasterCard, Visa
Season: Year round. Busiest season Dec. to April
Course Comments: Can walk after 1 p.m. at a reduced fee. Bring own towels, toiletries for locker room
Golf Packages: None
Discounts: Seasonal (May to Nov.). Twilight (time varies by season). Dade County residents pay lower golf fees
Places to Stay Nearby: Sonesta Beach Hotel and Tennis Club (305) 361–2021, (800) SONESTA; Sheraton Royal Biscayne Beach Resort and Racquet Club (305) 361–5775, (800) 325–3535
Local Attractions: Miami Marine Stadium, Miami Seaquarium, Virginia Key beach, Bill Baggs Cape Florida State Recreation Area, Cape Florida lighthouse, boating, fishing, swimming, International Tennis Center. Key Biscayne Chamber of Commerce (305) 361–5207
Directions: From Miami: Rickenbacker Causeway, 4½ miles east and south from causeway along Crandon Blvd. to golf course on the right
Closest Commercial Airports: Miami International (20 min.), Ft.Lauderdale–Hollywood International (45 min.)

THE LINKS AT KEY BISCAYNE

The Links at Key Biscayne is a short drive east from Miami. Key Biscayne is the site of the Senior Tour Royal Caribbean

Classic and has long been rated one of the best public golf courses in the country by *Golf Digest* magazine. This 7099-yard layout is a Robert von Hagge/Bruce Devlin design with fast, medium- to large-sized undulating, Bermuda-grass greens. Water hazards are found on 13 holes, and an abundance of sand bunkers, and palm, mangrove and other trees test your shot-making and golf-course-management skills. Five of the holes on this beautiful course play near or along Biscayne Bay.

Most of the holes at Key Biscayne are varied and memorable. The number-1-handicap hole is the gargantuan 642-yard fourth, with a slight dogleg left to a large, deep green protected by a trap on the left. But many consider the most difficult hole to be the 434-yard par-4 seventh, a dogleg right whose tee shot has to be far enough to have a good angle onto a deep green protected by water on both sides. The approach shot is over water and must avoid a trap to the right of the green. An excellent par 3 on the front side is the 187-yard third hole, which plays over Biscayne Bay on the right all the way to a large green with traps left and to the rear.

The back nine starts off with its two toughest holes. The 561-yard par-5 tenth is a double dogleg with little margin for error. The tee shot is to a landing area guarded by a large pond on the right and traps on the left. The second shot has to avoid water left and right, and the approach shot is to a large green flanked by bunkers. The 427-yard par-4 eleventh is a dogleg right. The tee-shot landing area is generous but guarded by bunkers to the left and a large pond to the right. The second shot is over water to a deep green bracketed by traps, with water to the rear and to the right. A great par 3 on this side is the 185-yard twelfth, which plays over water to a large green backed by traps.

The total distance between the back tees and the middle tees on the Links at Key Biscayne is a hefty 642 yards. By playing the middle tees, some of the holes seem less onerous. Because of the sand bunkers, water, tricky doglegs and varying wind conditions, the men might start with the 6457-

yard distance. The ladies have a par-73 5662-yard layout to contend with.

Key Biscayne has a two-story clubhouse with full pro shop, bar, snack bar and two restaurants, one downstairs and a more elaborate one upstairs. Lockers are taken up by local residents and members, so bring your own towel and toiletries if you plan to use the facilities. A driving range, chipping green, putting green, and sand bunkers are available. You can arrange a lesson through the resident PGA professional. Nearby are the bright lights of Miami, or you can spend a more relaxed visit on Key Biscayne.

Course Name: **PGA NATIONAL GOLF CLUB**
Champion, Haig, Squire, General, Estate Courses

Course Type: Resort
Resort: PGA National Resort & Spa
Address: 400 Avenue of The Champions Palm Beach Gardens, FL 33418–3698
Phone: (407) 627–1804 (Golf Course Tee Times)
(407) 627–1800 (Golf Shop)
(407) 627–2000 (Resort),
(800) 633–9150 (Resort)
Fax: (407) 622–0261 (Resort)

GOLF COURSE

Director of Golf: John Gardner
Head Professionals: Jane Broderick, Jim Kroll, Jerry Thompson
Course Length/Par (All Tees): Champion: Back 7022/72, Gold 6742/72, Blue 6373/72, White 6023/72, Forward 5377/72. Haig: Back 6806/72, Middle 6352/72, Forward 5645/72. Squire: Back 6498/72, Middle 6025/72, Forward 5114/72. General: Back 6768/72, Middle 6270/72, Forward 5324/72. Estate: Back 6784/72, Middle 6328/72, Forward 4955/72
Course Slope/Rating (All Tees): Champion: Back 142/74.7, Gold 134/73.2, Blue 129/71.1, White 124/69.1, Ladies' Forward 123/71.1. Haig: Back 130/73.0, Middle 125/70.6, Ladies' Forward 121/72.5. Squire: Back 127/71.3, Middle

122/69.8, Ladies' Forward 123/69.8.
General: Back 130/73.0, Middle
125/70.4, Ladies' Forward 122/71.0.
Estate: Back 131/73.4, Middle 124/70.7,
Ladies' Forward 118/68.4

Course Architects: Champion: Tom Fazio
and George Fazio (1981), Jack Nicklaus
(renovation, 1990). Haig: Tom Fazio
and George Fazio (1980); Fazio Golf
Course Design (renovation, 1993).
Squire: Tom Fazio and George Fazio
(1981). General: Arnold Palmer (1984).
Estate: Karl Litten (1984)

Golf Facilities: Full Pro Shop X, Snack
Bar X, Lounge X, Restaurant X,
Locker Room X, Showers X, Club Rent-
al X, Club Repair X, Cart Rental X,
Instruction X, Practice Green X, Driv-
ing Range X, Practice Bunker X, Club
Storage X

Tee-Time Reservation Policy: Resort
guests: 1 yr. in advance with confirmation number. Must be a resort guest,
member, or PGA professional to play
courses

Ranger: Yes

Tee-off-Interval Time: 7½ min. for all
courses except Champion, which is 8
min.

Time to Play 18 Holes: 4½ hrs.

Course Hours/Earliest Tee-off: 7 a.m.
peak season

Green Fees: Peak season (late Dec. to
early May): Champion: $135 for 18
holes. Haig, Squire, General, Estate: $92
for 18 holes

Cart Fees: $19 for 18 holes per person per
cart

Credit Cards: American Express, Master-
Card, Visa

Season: Year round. Busiest season Jan. to
April

Course Comments: Cart mandatory. Yardage book available

Golf Packages: Available through resort.
Lowest rates June through Sept. Call
(800) 633–9150. Academy of Golf
Packages available (800) 832–6235

Discounts: Seasonal (mid-April to mid-
Oct.). Must be a resort guest, club
member or PGA professional to play the
courses

Places to Stay Nearby: PALM BEACH GAR-
DENS: Palm Beach Gardens Marriott
(407) 622–8888; Radisson Suite Hotel
(407) 622–1000; Economy Inns of America (407) 624–7186. PALM BEACH: The
Breakers (407) 655–6611; Ocean Grand
(407) 582–2800; Palm Beach Hilton
(407) 586–6542.

Local Attractions: Jai alai, polo, thoroughbred harness racing, dog racing, horseback riding, charter fishing boats,
shopping on Worth Ave. in Palm Beach
and other areas, Jupiter Theatre, West
Palm Beach night clubs, Flagler Museum. Palm Beach Visitor's Bureau
(407) 471–3995

Directions: From Palm Beach International
Airport (15 mi.): North on Florida Turn-
pike to exit 109 (Palm Beach Gardens
Interchange), PGA Blvd. west to resort.
From I–95: PGA Blvd. exit, west to re-
sort

Closest Commercial Airports: Palm
Beach International (30 min.), Fort
Lauderdale–Hollywood International (1
hr.), Miami International (1 hr., 15 min.)

RESORT

Date Built: 1981

No. of Rooms: 339 rooms and 80 cottage
suites

Meeting/Exhibit Rooms: 23. Capacity of
Largest: 840, ballroom seating. Meeting
Space: 33,900 sq. ft.

Room Price Range: $289 single to $995
presidential suite peak season late Dec.
to mid-April. Golf, tennis, spa and other
packages available year round

Lounges: Explorer's, 19th Hole

Restaurants: Explorers' Club, Arezzo,
Citrus Tree, CrabCatcher, Breakaway
Sports Pub & Eatery, 19th Hole

Entertainment: Pianist at Lounge

Credit Cards: American Express, Diners
Club, Discover, MasterCard, Visa

General Amenities: Meeting and conference
facilities with theater-style, classroom,
banquet and reception areas with
audiovisual and food services; 240-acre
wilderness preserve

Recreational Amenities: 19 tennis courts
(12 lighted for night play), 26-acre sail-

ing lake with private beach, 7 mi. of nature trails; 26,000-sq. ft. fitness center with 32 Nautilus machines, treadmills, Lifecycles, Monark Cycles, Life Rowers, StairMasters, NordicTrack, recumbent bikes, free weights, aerobic studio; croquet, volleyball, 3 indoor racquetball courts, tropical swimming pool, large pool, boating, health, fitness and therapy programs; spa programs for men and women, with massage, hydrotherapy, mud treatments, facials, manicures, 6 mineral pools; billiards, darts, video games

Reservation and Cancellation Policy: Credit card guarantee or deposit required to hold reservation. 48-hr. notice prior to arrival time required for full refund

Comments and Restrictions: No pets allowed. Tax and gratuities additional to base rates. Unused portions of packages not refundable

PGA NATIONAL GOLF CLUB

PGA National, headquarters of the Professional Golfers Association of America, is a 2340-acre resort located just west of I–95 and 60 minutes north of Miami. PGA National is an excellent golf facility with a country-club ambience. There are 90 holes of championship golf here, including the Champion, Haig and Squire courses designed by Tom and George Fazio. The Championship Course was redesigned by Jack Nicklaus and completed in 1990. The General Course was designed by Arnold Palmer, and Karl Litten designed the Estate Course. This range of golf courses and the varying degrees of difficulty of their tee distances should accommodate any golfer's game.

Golf magazine has awarded PGA National its Silver Medal Award as one of the top golf resorts in the United States. If you had to choose among the 5 courses at PGA National, you probably would want to play the Champion Course, which is rated one of the top 75 resort golf courses in America by *Golf Digest* magazine. This 7022-yard layout was the site of the 1983 Ryder Cup Matches, the 1987 PGA Championship and many other

important PGA events. It is currently the site of the PGA of America Seniors' Championships. Nicklaus's redesign made the course more playable and enjoyable for all skill levels because it now has five sets of tees from the 5377-yard forward tees to the 7022-yard back tees. The fairways and greens were redesigned to be concave containing areas for golf shots, and gallery mounds were constructed to accommodate spectator viewing and media coverage throughout the course.

The Champion Course has water hazards on every hole except two. This course is dedicated to Jack Nicklaus in honor of his commitment to the game and high standard of play. The greens vary in size from 20 yards deep on the 422-yard par-4 eighth to the sizeable 43-yard-deep green on the 463-yard par-4 fourteenth. The greens are Tifdwarf hybrid Bermuda overseeded with bentgrass October through December. The Champion Course has slightly over 50 sand bunkers, but water serves to add major obstacles along the fairways and around the moderately fast, undulating greens.

The number-1-handicap hole on the Champion is the 444-yard par-4 eleventh, whose tee shot has to avoid a lake on the left side. The approach shot is onto a small, right-to-left-angled green with water on the immediate right, a trap to the left and water farther left. This hole plays 419, 381, 345, and 156 yards from the other four tee positions. Another difficult hole is the 484-yard par-5 sixth, which has a somewhat narrow fairway leading to a sizeable green with traps on each side. The tee shot must carry some water, which then runs all the way up to the left side of the green. A series of bunkers guard the right fairway in the tee-shot landing area.

A difficult par 4 on the back side is the 463-yard fourteenth, which is bordered on the right by water from the beginning of the fairway to a large green guarded on the right by three sand bunkers and water and on the left by grass bunkers. The finishing hole is a double-dogleg 545-yard par 5. The tee-shot landing area is protected by sand bunkers and water left and right. The approach shot has to avoid more traps on the left and water on the right as the fairway snakes left and then right back to a medium-sized green with traps left- and right-front, water right and rear and another trap to the rear.

The Haig and Squire courses were designed by Tom and George Fazio. The 6806-yard Haig was the first course open for play at PGA National (March 4, 1980) and is dedicated to Walter Hagen, who won 5 PGA Championships among his many titles. The 150-yard markers here are rosebushes, because Hagen was always advising people to "stop and smell the roses." The most challenging hole on the Haig Course is the 413-yard par-4 eighth, which plays straight to a deep green protected by traps to the left and right. There are more than 65 sand bunkers on this course, and water comes into play on almost every hole, including the 210-yard par-3 sixteenth, which begins a string of strong finishing holes. The sixteenth has water on the right, and the large green is flanked by two sand bunkers. The 532-yard par-5 seventeenth has a large trap to the left and water to the right on the tee shot. The approach shot has to avoid water just in front of the green and to the left as well as traps to the right and rear. The final hole is a 456-yard par-4 dogleg right with water on the left from tee to a large green straddled by bunkers. A series of large fairway bunkers is on the right, halfway to the hole.

The Squire Course, true to form, has more than 60 sand bunkers, water on 17 holes, and medium to large, moderately fast, undulating hybrid Bermuda greens overseeded with bentgrass in the winter. This course is dedicated to Gene Sarazen, "the Squire," who was the first to win the professional Grand Slam—the U.S. Open, the British Open, the PGA Championship and the Masters. Tom and George Fazio refer to the Squire as "the thinking man's course," requiring the golfer to test his or her accuracy with fairway woods off many tees and with precise short irons to approach the greens on this 6498-yard par-72 layout.

A scenic hole on the Squire is the number-1-handicap 506-yard par-5 fifth, which is bordered by water on the left and comes into a deep green with traps left, right and right-forward. A difficult par 4 on this side is the 396-yard eighth, with water on the right and a large fairway trap to the left on the tee shot. The approach shot is to a sizeable green with a trap to the left and one to the right, with water a factor if you push the ball to the right. The finishing hole, a 494-yard par 5, is an excellent test of golf. A pond guards the left side of the fairway on the tee shot, and the approach shot has to clear a large water hazard in front of the green, which is surrounded by three traps. More water is to the left of the green.

All of the courses at PGA National are well worth playing. The General Course was designed by Arnold Palmer and dedicated to him as the charismatic "general" who has led many an army of followers on his legendary charges. The average golfer who wanted to compete and sometimes grew frustrated trying to do so could identify with Palmer's attacking style as he chased the demons and gods of this difficult game. The General plays 6768 yards from the back tees and has undulating fairways, numerous grass bunkers, and water hazards on sixteen holes. The Bermudagrass greens are large, moderately fast and rolling, and are well protected by sand and water. The 429-yard par-4 seventeenth is considered by many to be the most challenging hole on the course. The tee shot is over a small stream, and the approach shot is to a green guarded by a trap to the front and right, forcing the golfer to fly the ball onto the putting surface. The 567-yard par-5 eighteenth is a beautiful finishing hole. The right side is protected by water from halfway down the fairway to the green. The approach shot must avoid water to the front and left of the green.

The 6784-yard Estate Course, which is approximately 5 miles from the resort, was originally opened in 1984 as the Stonewal Golfe Club. This Karl Litten–designed layout was purchased by PGA National in 1988, and the PGA of America used it as the primary site for their Club Professional

Winter Tournament Program in 1991. The Estate Course has its own practice range, practice bunker, practice putting green, pro shop, locker room and restaurant. The course has moderately fast, Tifdwarf Bermuda greens, water hazards on every hole except one and more than 85 sand bunkers on 120 acres, which feature lush, green fairways winding through open meadows lined with Florida pines and rich subtropical foliage.

The Champion, General, Haig and Squire courses also have an outstanding pro shop. There are over 3,000 sq. ft. of merchandising space here, and complete locker-room facilities as well. The 19th Hole sports lounge overlook the golf course. The practice area includes two driving ranges, and a variety of chipping, putting and sand bunker facilities.

A variety of golf packages are offered at PGA National, with the lowest rates being available from mid-April to mid-December.

Individual and group lessons are available through the contingent of PGA professionals and assistants on PGA National's permanent staff. The resort runs its own Academy of Golf, which offers excellent instructional programs.

Tennis magazine has rated PGA National one of the best tennis resorts in the country. The resort has received a variety of meetings and hospitality awards, including *Mobil Travel Guide* Four Star, American Automobile Association Four Diamond, and *Meetings and Conventions* magazine's Gold Tee awards.

The PGA National has just gone through a multimillion-dollar expansion and renovation program, bringing you excellent golf facilities with all the resort and recreational trimmings.

Course Name: WEST PALM BEACH COUNTRY CLUB

Course Type: Public
Address: 7001 Parker Avenue
                West Palm Beach, FL 33405
Phone: (407) 582–2019

GOLF COURSE

Director of Golf: Dub Pagan

Course Length/Par (All Tees): Back 6800/72, Middle 6523/72, Forward 5871/72

Course Slope/Rating (All Tees): Back 114/71.2, Middle NA/69.6, Ladies' Forward 121/71.4

Course Architect: Dick Wilson (1947)

Golf Facilities: Full Pro Shop X, Snack Bar X, Lounge X, Restaurant X, Locker Room X, Showers X, Club Rental X, Club Repair X, Cart Rental X, Instruction X, Practice Green X, Driving Range X, Practice Bunker X, Club Storage X

Tee-Time Reservation Policy: Lottery system, at 7 p.m. night before; from 6 p.m. Wed. for Sat., Thurs. for Sun. tee times

Ranger: No

Tee-off-Interval Time: 7 min.

Time to Play 18 Holes: 4 hrs.

Course Hours/Earliest Tee-off: 6:58 a.m.

Green Fees: $30 for 18 holes peak season

Cart Fees: $10 for 18 holes per person

Pull Carts: $2 for 18 holes

Credit Cards: MasterCard, Visa

Season: Year round. Busiest season Dec. to March

Course Comments: Restricted walking. Memberships available. Annual fee for residents, nonresidents

Golf Packages: None

Discounts: Golf cards. Summer (April to Nov. 1)

Places to Stay Nearby: Heart of Palm Beach Hotel (407) 655–5600; Palm Beach Airport Hilton (407) 684–9400, (800) HILTONS; Courtyard by Marriott (407) 640–9000, (800) 321–2211; Holiday Inn Palm Beach Airport (407) 659–3880, (800) HOLIDAY

Local Attractions: Beaches, fishing, diving, baseball spring training, equestrian sports, Jupiter Dinner Theater, Flagler Museum, Palm Beach Jai Alai, Children's Museum, zoo, lion country safari, shopping. Palm Beach County Convention and Visitors Bureau (407) 471–3995, (800) 242–1774. West Palm Beach Chamber of Commerce (407) 833–3711

Directions: I–95, exit Forest Hill Blvd., east to Parker, right to golf course at dead end

Closest Commercial Airports: Palm Beach International (3 mi.), Fort Lauderdale–Hollywood International (1 hr.), Miami International (1½ hrs.)

WEST PALM BEACH COUNTRY CLUB

The West Palm Beach Country Club was originally part of what later became the West Palm Beach International Airport. It was moved to its current location, and the new golf course designed by Dick Wilson was opened in 1947. The course is administered by a five-member commission and has memberships, but it is run like a public golf course in that tee times are assigned by lottery to everyone. Or you can call the same day after each lottery to get an open time if one is available. The course itself is self-funded, and steady improvements have recently been made by replacing greens, planting new trees, upgrading irrigation facilities and improving management.

Wilson was born in Philadelphia and educated at the University of Vermont. His interest in golf architecture began while he was working at the Merion Golf Club, which he later remodeled. He moved to Florida in the early 1930s to construct the Indian Creek Club in Miami. Later he designed LaCosta (Gold Course), Carlsbad, California, with Joe Lee; Bay Hill, Orlando, Florida, with Joe Lee, Robert von Hagge and Bob Simmons; Cog Hill Nos. 3 and 4, Lemont, Illinois, with Joe Lee; and the Greenbrier (Lakeside Course), White Sulphur Springs, West Virginia, with Robert Simmons. He died in 1965 at age 61. Ward Northrop, another designer with whom Wilson frequently worked, has served as a consultant on the recent improvements at the West Palm Beach Country Club.

West Palm Beach is an older, traditional 6789-yard par-72 layout beautifully situated on 200 acres of rolling land with Australian pines, cabbage palms, coconut palms, bottle brush trees and a variety of other foliage protecting the fairways and greens. Situated on a large dune line that runs 60 miles up the east coast of Florida, the course has no water hazards but has many strategically placed traps, especially around the typically elevated greens. Wind from the nearby Atlantic Ocean can be a factor on the course, with crosswinds affecting at least three holes on the back nine.

West Palm Beach starts out with a 505-yard par-5 dogleg left that is reachable in two shots. The green is protected by traps left and right. Another par 5, 501 yards and straight from tee to green, follows, with a straight, 184-yard par 3 protected by three traps around the green next. The fourth is the number-1-handicap par 4, which plays a long 461 yards downhill then a bit uphill from approximately 125 yards to the green. Because the green has a drop-off slope right to left, it is best to keep your tee shot left and then come onto the green with a mid-iron. The fifth is a short, 315-yard par 4, but the green is protected left, front and right by traps. The sixth is another long 422-yard par 4, and the seventh is a difficult, 204-yard par 3 that plays down a tree-lined fairway into the wind to a two-tiered green sitting behind a huge sand bunker. The eighth is a 403-yard par 4 straight to a green that is well trapped on the right. The ninth is a 414-yard dogleg left to a green protected left and right by traps.

The back nine begins with a short, 488-yard par 5 that doglegs right and usually plays downwind to a green protected both left and right by traps. The next hole is a 143-yard par 3 to a deep green protected by traps to the left and right. The 444-yard par-4 twelfth hole is flanked by tall trees all the way downhill to the green. This is the number-2-handicap hole on the course. The thirteenth is a straight par 4 playing 398 yards, and the fourteenth is a 205-yard par 3 whose green is protected left and right by traps. The 398-yard par-4 fifteenth has a roundish green protected in front by a large trap. The par-4 sixteenth plays 391 yards straight to a kidney-shaped green trapped on the right, and the seventeenth is a 355-yard par-4 dogleg left to a green trapped on both sides. The finishing hole is a 555-yard par 5 that usually plays straight into the wind to a large green protected by traps both to the left and right.

The West Palm Beach Country Club has a well-established clubhouse with full pro shop, ladies' and men's locker rooms, bag storage, dining room, bar and grill. A staff of professionals and assistants can provide group or individual lessons. Lessons are given on the nearby driving range, and chipping and putting areas.

Places to Stay in Miami

Biscayne Bay Marriott Hotel and Marina (305) 374–3900, (800) 228–9290; Omni International Hotel (305) 374–0000, (800) THE–OMNI; Courtyard by Marriott—Miami Lakes (305) 556–6665, (800) 321–2211; Courtyard by Marriott—Miami West (305) 477–8118, (800) 321–2211; Doubletree Hotel at Coconut Grove (305) 858–2500, (800) 222–TREE; Holiday Inn—University of Miami (305) 667–5611, (800) HOLIDAY; Mayfair House Hotel (305) 441–0000, (800) 341–0809; Radisson Mart Plaza Motel (305) 261–3800, (800) 333–3333; Residence Inn by Marriott—Miami (305) 591–2211, (800) 331–3131; Miami River Inn (305) 325–0045

Places to Stay in Miami Beach

Fontainebleau Hilton Resort and Spa (305) 538–2000, (800) 548–8886; Holiday Inn—Ocean Side Convention Center (305) 534–1511, (800) HOLIDAY; Sheraton Bal Harbour (305) 865–7511, (800) 999–9898; Turnberry Isle Resort and Club (305) 932–6200, (800) 327–7028; Alexander Hotel (305) 865–8500, (800) 327–6211

Places to Stay in Coral Gables

Colonnade Hotel (305) 441–2600 (Coral Gables); Biltmore Hotel (305) 445–1926, (800) 228–3000 (Coral Gables); Hyatt Regency Coral Gables (305) 441–1234, (800) 233–1234

Local Attractions in Miami and Miami Beach

The American Police Hall of Fame and Museum, Gold Coast Railroad Museum, Metro–Dade Cultural Center, Metro Zoo, Museum of Science and Space Transit Planetarium, Parrot Jungle and Gardens, Vizcaya, harbor cruises, restaurants, shopping, boating, fishing; water sports, including water-skiing, skin diving and surfing; tennis, hiking, bicycling, horseback riding, horse racing; professional football, basketball and baseball; night clubs, Miami Seaquarium, Jackie Gleason Center for the Performing Arts, concerts, theater, opera, ballet, Spanish Theater, Biscayne National Park, Everglades National Park, Historical Museum of Southern Florida, Center for Fine Arts, Bass Museum of Art, Little Havana, University of Miami, Little Haiti. Coral Gables. Coconut Grove. Virginia Key. Key Biscayne. Biscayne National Park Tour Boats (305) 247–2400; Everglades National Park Boat Tours (813) 695–2591, (800) 445–7724 (FL). Greater Miami Chamber of Commerce, 1601 Biscayne Blvd., Miami, FL 33132, (305) 350–7700. Miami Beach Chamber of Commerce, 1920 Meridian Ave., Miami Beach, FL 33139, (305) 672–1270. Greater Miami Convention and Visitors Bureau, 701 Brickell Ave., Ste. 2700, Miami, FL 33131, (305) 539–3000, (800) 283–2707.

Recommended Golf Courses in Florida

Within 1½ Hours of Fort Lauderdale:

Atlantis Country Club, Atlantis, (407) 968–1300, Semiprivate, 18/6477/72

Binks Forest Golf Course, Wellington, (407) 795–0595, Semiprivate, 18/7065/72

Biltmore Golf Course, Coral Gables, (305) 460–5366, Public, 18/6652/71

Boca Raton Resort and Club, Boca Raton, (407) 395–3000, (800) 321–0101, Resort, 18/6682/71

Bonaventure Country Club, Ft. Lauderdale, (305) 389–2100, Resort. East: 18/7011/72. West: 18/6189/70

Breakers West Golf Club, West Palm Beach, (407) 653–6320, Semiprivate, 18/7028/71

Club Med Sandpiper, Port St. Lucie, (407) 337–6615, Resort. Saints: 18/6557/72. Sinners: 18/6896/72

Crystal Lake Country Club, Pompano Beach, (305) 942–1900, Semiprivate. North: 18/6390/70. South: 18/6610/72

Deer Creek Golf and Country Club, Deerfield Beach, (305) 421–5550, Semiprivate, 18/6732/72

Delray Beach Golf Club, Delray Beach, (407) 243–7380, Public, 18/7040/72

Don Shula's Hotel and Golf Club, Miami Lakes, (305) 821–1150, Resort, 18/7055/72, 18/2080/54

Fairwinds Golf Course, Fort Pierce, (407) 466–4653, (800) 894–1781, Public, 18/6783/72

Golf Club of Miami, Miami, (305) 829–4700, Public. East: 18/6553/70. South: 18/4420/62. West: 18/7017/72

Habitat Golf Course, Valkaria, (407) 952–6312, Public, 18/6836/72

Harbour Ridge, Stuart, (407) 336–0400, Private (playing privileges to those who rent units at the golf courses). Golden Marsh: 18/6607/72. River Ridge: 18/6702/72

Indian River Plantation, Stuart, (407) 225–3700, Resort, 18/4042/61

Indianwood Golf and Country Club, Indiantown, (407) 597–3794, (800) 521–3223, Semiprivate, 18/6047/70

Jacaranda Country Club, Plantation, (305) 472–5836, Semiprivate. West: 18/6680/72. East: 18/7164/72

Key West Resort, Key West, (305) 294–5232, Public, 18/6526/70

The Links at Polo Trace, Delray Beach, (407) 495–5300, Semiprivate, 18/7096/72

Lost Lake Golf Club, Hobe Sound, (407) 220–6666, Semiprivate, 18/6850/72

North Palm Beach Country Club, North Palm Beach, (407) 626–4345, Public, 18/6275/72

Ocean Village, Fort Pierce, (407) 489–0300, Resort, 9/1250/27

Palm Aire Spa Resort, Pompano Beach, (305) 972–3300, (800) 272–5624, Resort.

Pines: 18/6610/72. Palms: 18/6932/72. Sabals: 18/3401/60

Palm Beach Lakes Golf Club, West Palm Beach, (407) 683–2701, Public, 18/5244/68

Palm Beach Polo and Country Club, West Palm Beach, (407) 798–7401, Resort. Cypress: 18/7116/72. Dunes: 18/7050/72. Olde: 9/3461/36

Pompano Beach Golf Course, Pompano Beach, (305) 786–4141, Public. Palms: 18/6050/71. Pines: 18/6573/72

Raintree Golf Club, Pembroke Pines, (305) 432–4400, (800) 346–5332, Semiprivate, 18/6761/72

Rolling Hills Golf Resort, Ft. Lauderdale, (305) 475–0400, (800) 327–7735. Resort, 18/6905/72, 9/3147/35

Royal Palm Beach Country Club, Royal Palm Beach, (407) 798–6430, Public, 18/7100/72

St. Lucie West Country Club, Port St. Lucie, (407) 340–1911, Semiprivate, 18/6801/72

Sand Ridge Golf Club, Vero Beach, (407) 770–5000, Public. Dunes: 18/6900/72. Lakes: 18/6200/72

Turnberry Isle Yacht and Country Club, North Miami Beach, (305) 932–6200, (800) 327–7028, Resort. North: 18/6323/70. South: 18/7003/72

Westminster Golf and Country Club, Boynton Beach, (407) 734–6300, Semiprivate, 18/6760/72

Winston Trails Golf Club, Lake Worth, (407) 439–3700, Public, 18/6835/72

Orlando Area/Central

Course Name: ARNOLD PALMER'S
               BAY HILL CLUB
               Challenger, Champion,
               Charger Courses

Course Type: Resort
Resort: Bay Hill Club and Lodge
Address: 9000 Bay Hill Boulevard
              Orlando, FL 32819–4899

Phone: (407) 876–2429 (Golf Course)
        (800) 523–5999 (Resort)
Fax: (407) 876–1035 (Resort)

GOLF COURSE

Head Professional: Jim Deaton

Course Length/Par (All Tees): Challenger/Champion: Back 7114/72, Regular 6547/72, Seniors 6184/72, Forward 5214/72. Charger: Back 3090/36, Regular 2957/36, Seniors 2787/36, Forward 2476/36

Course Slope/Rating (All Tees): Challenger/Champion: Back 141/74.6, Regular 127/71.8, Seniors 124/70.2, Ladies' Forward 133/70.3. Charger: Back NA/NA, Regular NA/NA, Seniors NA/NA, Ladies' Forward NA/NA

Course Architects: Dick Wilson, Joe Lee, Robert von Hagge (1961); Arnold Palmer (renovation, 1980)

Golf Facilities: Full Pro Shop X, Snack Bar X, Lounge X, Restaurant X, Locker Room X, Showers X, Club Rental X, Club Repair X, Cart Rental X, Instruction X, Practice Green X, Driving Range X, Practice Bunker X, Club Storage X

Tee-Time Reservation Policy: At time of reservation, up to 6 mos. in advance. Members only Sat. before noon. Ladies' day Thurs. 8 to 10 p.m.

Ranger: Yes

Tee-off-Interval Time: 8 min.

Time to Play 18 Holes: 4½ hrs.

Course Hours/Earliest Tee-off: 7 a.m.

Green Fees: Peak Season: $150 for 18 holes

Cart Fees: $15 for 18 holes

Credit Cards: American Express, MasterCard, Visa

Season: Year round. Busiest season mid-Dec. to mid-March

Course Comments: Cart or caddy mandatory. Must be resort guest, member or guest of member to play the courses

Golf Packages: Available through resort. Lowest rates May to Sept.

Discounts: Seasonal (May to Dec.)

Places to Stay Nearby: SEE ORLANDO LISTINGS ON PAGE 173

Local Attractions: SEE ORLANDO LISTINGS ON PAGE 173

Directions: From Orlando International Airport (20 min.): Bee Line Expressway (Hwy. 582) west to I–4. I–4 east to exit 29 (State Rd. 482/Sand Lake Rd.), west on Sand Lake to Apopka–Vineland Rd., right on Apopka–Vineland, go ½ mi. to Bay Hill entrance (Bay Hill Blvd.) on left, follow Bay Hill Blvd. to club on right

Closest Commercial Airports: Orlando International (20 min.), Tampa International (1½ hrs.)

RESORT

Date Built: 1961

No. of Rooms: 70

Meeting/Exhibit Rooms: 4. Capacity of Largest: 100 persons. Meeting Space: 5000 sq. ft.

Room Price Range: From $225 peak season (Jan. through Apr.), with breakfast; from $160 May to Jan. Golf packages available year round

Lounge: Members' Lounge

Restaurants: Grille Room, Bay Window

Entertainment: Piano in Bay Window, live music for special occasions

Credit Cards: American Express, MasterCard, Visa

General Amenities: Babysitting can be arranged, meeting and conference facilities available

Recreational Amenities: Marina, fishing, water-skiing, boating, 6 tennis courts, tennis instruction, pro shop, junior-Olympic swimming pool

Reservation and Cancellation Policy: Credit card registration or deposit required to hold reservation. 72-hr. cancellation notice prior to arrival date required to avoid 1 night's rate penalty

Comments and Restrictions: No pets allowed. Taxes and gratuities additional to base rates

ARNOLD PALMER'S BAY HILL CLUB

Arnold Palmer is the owner of the Bay Hill Club, site of the PGA Tour Bay Hill Invitational. He redesigned the course in 1980, having purchased it in the 1960s after he exploded onto the golf scene with dramatic nationally televised victories in the U.S. Open and Masters. Palmer won the U.S. Open at Cherry Hill in Denver after he made up 7 strokes on the last round to shoot a 65, with a 30 on the front nine. Earlier in the year he finished with two birdies to win the Masters. Feats such as these captured the national imagination and contributed significantly to the ascendance of golf, especially on national television. Arnie's Army has been marching ever since—this son of a professional and greenskeeper at Latrobe (PA) Country Club is as popular as ever. And you can play his golf course.

Dick Wilson along with Joe Lee and Robert von Hagge originally designed Bay Hill. Before he redesigned it, Palmer had gained considerable experience as a golf-course architect, working as a design consultant with Francis Duane from 1969 to 1974 and then joining with Ed Seay to found Palmer Course Design Co. Among the many courses that Palmer has designed are Grenelefe Golf and Racquet Club (East Course) with Ed Seay and Bob Walker in Haines City, Florida; PGA National Golf Club (General Course) with Ed Seay, Palm Beach Gardens, Florida; Wildcat Run Country Club with Ed Seay, Estero, Florida; Shanty Creek Golf Club (Legend Course) with Ed Seay and Bob Walker, Bellaire, Michigan; and many others. In 1984 Palmer's company built the first golf course ever opened in Communist China.

Bay Hill has been the site of many dramatic golf tournaments. One of the most spectacular tour finishes occurred in 1990, when Robert Gamez, then the 21-year-old PGA Rookie of the Year, dropped a 176-yard 7-iron on the last hole for a finishing eagle and a win over Greg Norman and Larry Mize in the Nestlè Invitational. This 441-yard par-4 finishing hole was ranked the most difficult finishing hole on the tour that year. It is a slight dogleg right, with the tee shot rolling over the ridge to set up a long approach to a deep green protected by three traps on the left and water on the

right. Pin placements to the rear and right can make this hole especially difficult.

Bay Hill has three nines, the 3580-yard Challenger, the 3534-yard Champion, and the 3090-yard Charger. The Challenger/Champion combination is used for the Bay Hill Invitational, and this layout is considered one of the best resort courses in America by *Golf Digest*. The course is long, with water hazards on more than half its holes. Traps, and in many cases water, guard every green, forcing you to fly the ball into most of the target areas. For example, the 467-yard par-4 ninth, the number-1-handicap hole on the course, plays to a deep green with two traps squeezing the entranceway. Another trap is to the left rear. The 218-yard par-3 second plays from an elevated tee to a wide, shallow green with two traps in front and a large trap in back. The dramatic par-5 sixth hole plays 543 yards to the left around a lake to a deep green with traps on the right and water on the left. To get home in two, you have to try to cut off as much of the dogleg as possible, but the water awaits you. The greens at Bay Hill tend to be large, moderately fast and somewhat undulating, so three putts are always a possibility.

The back nine on the Challenger/Champion course has a variety of difficult holes, especially the par 4s. The 428-yard par-4 eleventh is a dogleg left bordered by water on the left from 150 yards out to the green. The tee shot has to avoid two fairway bunkers on the right. The second shot is to a deep, narrow green with two traps on the right and water on the left. A great par 3 on this side is the 219-yard seventeenth, which plays over water to medium-sized green almost completely surrounded by three traps and water. The wind can be a factor on this hole, which is Palmer's favorite at Bay Hill.

Bay Hill is a club with the Grille Room Restaurant, Bay Window Restaurant and the Members' Lounge. There are 70 guest rooms, and only guests or members and their guests can play the courses. Registered guests can reserve tee times up to 6 months in advance, but the number of tee times are limited, because only members can play before noon on Saturday, and Ladies' Day is from 8 to 10 a.m. on Thursdays. Caddies are available if advance notice is given to the staff at the pro shop. A complete pro shop, locker room and showers, and restaurant facilities are available at Bay Hill. Group and individual instruction is available, and the Arnold Palmer Golf Academy offers programs for beginners, intermediates, advanced, professionals, senior citizens, juniors, parents and their children, and disabled golfers.

Arnold Palmer has been very active in formulating and monitoring these programs. His philosophy is evident from the description in the promotional literature for the Arnold Palmer Golf Academy:

Dear Fellow Golfer,

My father stressed two things when he taught me to play golf—fundamentals and attitude. When you rely on those, he would say, golf is really pretty simple and a whole lot of fun. I agree.

Today, you hear talk about golf's mechanics and complexities. Much of it is confusing and, I believe, takes away from the game.

That's the reason I began this Golf Academy.

In addition to golf instruction, a variety of golf vacation packages are offered at Bay Hill. The packages generally include accommodations overlooking the course and club, 27 holes of championship golf with cart, locker-room access and club storage, range balls, and club breakfast. You also have access to the club's restaurants and lounge, a private marina for fishing/cruising the nearby Butler chain lakes, swimming pool, lighted clay and hard tennis courts, and meeting and banquet facilities.

Course Name: GOLDEN OCALA GOLF AND COUNTRY CLUB

Course Type: Public
Address: 7300 U.S. Highway 27
              Ocala, FL 34482
Phone: (904) 622–0198 (Information)
              (904) 622–0100 (Tee Times)
              (904) 622–5344 (Business Office)

GOLF COURSE

Director of Golf: Chip Hierlihy

Course Length/Par (All Tees): Back 6755/72, Middle 6247/72, Forward 5591/72

Course Slope/Rating (All Tees): Back 122/72.1, Middle 117/69.8, Ladies' Forward 119/71.7

Course Architect: Ron Garl (1986)

Golf Facilities: Full Pro Shop Limited, Snack Bar Limited, Lounge No, Restaurant No, Locker Room No, Showers No, Club Rental X, Club Repair No, Cart Rental X, Instruction X, Practice Green X, Driving Range X, Practice Bunker No, Club Storage No

Tee-Time Reservation Policy: Up to 2 weeks in advance

Ranger: Yes

Tee-off-Interval Time: 8 min.

Time to Play 18 Holes: 4½ hrs.

Course Hours/Earliest Tee-off: 7:02 a.m.

Green and Cart Fees: $40 for 18 holes with cart peak season. Call for current rates

Credit Cards: MasterCard, Visa

Season: Year round. Busiest season Dec. to April

Course Comments: Cart mandatory

Golf Packages: None

Discounts: Unscheduled replays, twilight rates, Florida residents

Places to Stay Nearby: Ramada Steinbrenner's Yankee Inn (904) 732–3131; Ocala Hilton (904) 854–1400; Radisson Inn (904) 629–0091; Holiday Inn (904) 629–0831, (800) HOLIDAY. BED AND BREAKFAST: Seven Sisters Inn (904) 867–1170

Local Attractions: OCALA: Camping, fishing, jai alai, Museum of Dog Racing. SILVER SPRINGS: Jungle cruise, glass bottom boats, Jeep safari, annual shows, Wild Waters Family Water Park. Ocala–Marion County Chamber of Commerce (904) 629–8051

Directions: I–75 exit 70 (Hwy. 27), Hwy. 27 north 3.5 mi., golf course on left past stop light

Closest Commercial Airports: Ocala (10 min.), Jacksonville International (1½ hrs.), Tampa International (1½ hrs.), Orlando International (1½ hrs.)

GOLDEN OCALA GOLF AND COUNTRY CLUB

It is truly a unique experience to play the Golden Ocala Golf and Country Club. The course was conceived as part of a 2000-acre real-estate development, and arrangements were made with the Castro family of Castro Convertible Bed fame to purchase the land. A magnificent 200-acre golf course was developed, and $1 million was spent to refurbish a former private school building that was to be the development's administrative and sales offices but now houses the pro shop and eating facilities. The idea was to have a golf course with replica holes of great golf courses such as Royal Troon, Muirfield, Augusta, St. Andrews and Baltusrol. From Brian Morgan's research and photography of the original courses, Ron Garl designed the course, which opened in 1986. The real-estate project has had financial problems, hence no clubhouse, so the former school serves that purpose, and the starting hole is the seventh hole instead of the first.

But don't let that deter you. The seventh is the number-1-handicap 537-yard par 5, a slight dogleg left bordered completely by trees. The first shot is from an elevated tee to a fairway that slopes down then gradually rises to a slightly elevated green. The tee shot has to negotiate two large traps on the left and must be far enough, more than 250 yards, that you can see the green on your second shot. The green is tucked left around a corner and protected by a tall stand of trees on the left and six traps beginning from 100 yards in and wrapping themselves around the green to the rear and left.

The first of the eight replica holes is the eleventh, which duplicates the twelfth hole at Augusta, popularly known as "the Golden Bell." This 156-yard par 3 plays from an elevated tee over a stream that runs in front of a wide, shallow green protected by one trap front-center and two traps in back. The thirteenth hole is a 444-yard par 4 that replicates the famous "Road" hole (no. 17) at St. Andrews.

Other replica holes include the 483-yard par-5 twelfth, modeled after the Azalea hole at Augusta (no. 13); the 351-yard par-4 fourteenth, which duplicates the first hole at St. Andrews; the 109-yard par-3 fifteenth, which imitates the fourth hole at Baltusrol; the 129-yard par-3 fourth modeled after the eighth hole at Royal Troon, affectionately called "the Postage Stamp"; the 508-yard par-5 fifth hole, which emulates the ninth at Muirfield; and the sixth hole, which is a 179-yard par 3 patterned after the number-6, "Juniper," hole at Augusta.

The eighteenth hole is a fine finishing hole, a dogleg to the left and well protected by trees. The first 100 yards of a rolling fairway are flat, then drop off to an invisible landing area. Beginning approximately 220 yards from the pin, the fairway rolls uphill to a green protected in front by a boulder-filled ditch that crosses the fairway directly in front. Three traps almost completely surround the rest of the green, which has an upper and lower shelf and slopes back to front. Most golfers play up to within 100 yards and attempt to drop a pitching wedge below the hole.

Although amenities are limited and no locker rooms or showers are available, Golden Ocala, ranked one of the best public courses in America by *Golf Digest*, is a well-maintained layout and a unique golf experience. It is worthwhile to make a visit to this interesting course, which is located midway between Tampa and Orlando.

**Course Name: GRAND CYPRESS
                 GOLF CLUB
                 North, South, East,
                 New Courses**

Course Type: Resort
Resort: The Villas of Grand Cypress,
              Hyatt Regency Grand
              Cypress
Address: N. Jacaranda
              Orlando, FL 32836
Phone: (407) 239–4700
              (407) 239–1975, (407) 239–
              4700 (Academy of Golf),
              (800) 835–7377 (Resort),
              (800) 835–7377 (Villas of
              Grand Cypress)
              (407) 239–1234,

(800) 233–1234 (Hyatt Hotel and Resorts)

Fax: (407) 239–7219 (Villas)
(407) 239–3800 (Hyatt)
Telex: 441–931 (Hyatt Regency)

GOLF COURSE

Head Professional: Brad Doyle

Course Length/Par (All Tees): North/South: Back 6993/72, Blue 6355/72, White 5823/72, Forward 5328/72. South/East: Back 6906/72, Blue 6363/72, White 5790/72, Forward 5126/72. East/North: Back 6937/72, Blue 6357/72, White 5820/72, Forward 5158/72. New: Back 6773/72, Middle 6181/72, Forward 5314/72. Grand Cypress Golf Academy (3 holes): Back 1104/12, Blue 981/12, White 840/12, Forward 755/12

Course Slope/Rating (All Tees): North/South: Back 130/73.9, Blue 123/70.7, White 121/68.5, Ladies' Forward 119/70.1. South/East: Back 132/74.4, Blue 126/71.6, White 123/69.3, Ladies' Forward 123/70.2. East/North: Back 130/73.9, Blue 124/70.9, White 121/68.8, Ladies' Forward 114/69.1. New: Back 126/72.1, Middle 117/69.4, Ladies' Forward 117/69.8. Grand Cypress Golf Academy: NA/NA

Course Architects: North: Jack Nicklaus with Robert Cupp (1984). South: Jack Nicklaus with Robert Cupp (1984). East: Jack Nicklaus with Robert Cupp (1985). New: Jack Nicklaus (1987). Grand Cypress Golf Academy: Jack Nicklaus with Robert Cupp (1985)

Golf Facilities: Full Pro Shop X, Snack Bar X, Lounge X, Restaurant X, Locker Room X, Showers X, Club Rental X, Club Repair X, Cart Rental X, Instruction X, Practice Green X, Driving Range X, Practice Bunker X, Club Storage X

Tee-Time Reservation Policy: Resort guests: 60 days in advance

Ranger: Yes

Tee-off-Interval Time: 10 min.

Time to Play 18 Holes: 4½ hrs.

Course Hours/Earliest Tee-off: New: 8 a.m. North, South, East Jan. to March: 7:30 a.m.

Green and Cart Fees: Peak season Jan. to May: Resort Guests (must be a resort guest to play): $125 for 18 holes with cart

Credit Cards: All major cards

Season: Year round. Busiest season Jan. to April

Course Comments: Cart or caddy mandatory. Caddies available only on New Course. Putting course on site in addition to Grand Cypress Academy of Golf

Golf Packages: Available year round through resort

Discounts: Seasonal (mid-May to mid-Sept.)

Places to Stay Nearby: SEE ORLANDO LISTINGS ON PAGE 173

Local Attractions: SEE ORLANDO LISTINGS ON PAGE 173

Directions: From Orlando International Airport (25 min.): Beeline Expressway to I–4, west on I–4 (toward Tampa) to exit 27 (Kissimmee/Lake Buena Vista/State Rd. 535), take State Rd. 535 north ½ mi., turn left at second traffic light. Proceed 1 mi. north and follow signs to Villas of Grand Cypress

Closest Commercial Airports: Orlando International (20 min.); TampaInternational (1½ hrs.)

RESORT

The Villas of Grand Cypress

Date Built: 1986

No. of Rooms: 146 club suites, 1- to 4-bedroom villas

Meeting/Exhibit Rooms: 7. Capacity of Largest: 200 persons. Meeting Space: 7000 sq. ft.

Room Price Range: $300 for club suite to $1400 for 4-bedroom villa peak season (mid-Jan. to mid-April). Various golf packages and other special offers available. Lowest rates mid-May to Sept.

Lounge: Pool Bar, Fairways Lounge

Restaurants: Black Swan, Fairways (in golf clubhouse)

Entertainment: Piano music in Black Swan

Credit Cards: All major cards

General Amenities: Babysitting, children's activities; meeting and conference facilities for as many as 150 persons with audiovisual, banquet, secretarial services available

Recreational Amenities: Hyatt Regency facilities and amenities available to Villas of Grand Cypress guests, putting course

Reservation and Cancellation Policy: Credit card or deposit required to hold reservation. 72-hr. cancellation notice required to avoid penalties

Comments and Restrictions: Gratuities and taxes additional to base rates

RESORT

Hyatt Regency Grand Cypress

Date Built: 1984

No. of Rooms: 750 with 74 suites, including 42 executive suites, 13 VIP suites, 14 hospitality suites, 5 luxury suites

Meeting/Exhibit Rooms: 27. Capacity of Largest: 1800 persons banquet style. Meeting Space: 57,000 sq. ft.

Room Price Range: $240 for standard room, double occupancy, up to 5 persons, to $2200 for 2-bedroom presidential suite, peak season (mid-Jan. to mid-April). Golf, honeymoon, recreation and other packages available

Lounges: Trellises, On Rocks, Papillon, Hurricane

Restaurants: La Coquina, Hemingway's, Cascades, White Horse Saloon, Palm Cafe

Entertainment: Piano music in Trellises; country and western band in White Horse Saloon

Credit Cards: All major cards

General Amenities: Child-care center including a Camp Hyatt program for ages 5 to 15; helipad, nature area and Audubon walk, shuttle service, meeting and conference facilities with more than 57,000 sq. ft. of space with audiovisual, food, secretarial services

Recreational Amenities: Racquet club with 12 Har-Tru tennis courts (5 lighted) with instruction, equestrian center, pitch-and-putt golf course, windsurfing, bicycling, volleyball, shuffleboard, boating, fitness/exercise/jogging trail, swimming pool, game room; complete health club with Lifecycles, treadmills, StairMasters, Universal weight equipment, free weights and aerobics classes with instruction, aqua-aerobic classes, sauna, steam, massage; 21-acre Lake Windsong, with beach, canoes, sailboats, paddleboats; 2 racquet ball courts. Villas of Grand Cypress facilities and amenities available to Hyatt Regency guests

Reservation and Cancellation Policy: Credit card guarantee or 1 night's prepayment within 14 days of arrival. 72-hour cancellation notice required to avoid penalties

Comments and Restrictions: No pets allowed. Concierge can arrange kennel facilities. Taxes and gratuities in addition to base rates

GRAND CYPRESS GOLF CLUB

Grand Cypress Golf Club is one of the most elegant resorts in the southeastern United States, with a 750-room hotel (the Hyatt); 146 club suites (the Villas of Grand Cypress); 48 holes of Jack Nicklaus–designed golf; a 21-acre recreational lake; a racquet club; an equestrian center; racquetball courts; a complete health club; fitness and jogging trails; shuffleboard; bicycling; boating; a swimming pool; whirlpools; and water slides on its 1500-acre property. A professionally staffed child care center is available.

There are 7 restaurants to choose from at both the Hyatt and the villas, ranging from the elegant La Coquina, a 118-seat formal dining room serving such delicacies as poached filet of pompano with avocado mousse and macadamia nut creme, to the White Horse Saloon, which serves specially aged black angus prime rib, free-range chicken, and other frontier delights. For those interested in a health-oriented menu, Hemingway's and the Cascades offer specially developed "cuisine naturelle" dishes. The resort regularly receives the *Mobil Travel Guide* Four Star Award and has received the prestigious

American Automobile Association Five Diamond Award for the past 5 years.

Because of its careful attention to quality landscape design and excellence, Grand Cypress has received many honors including the Environmental Improvement Merit Award from the Associated Landscape Contractors of America, the American Land Development Association Design Award, highest honors for resort development, and the Award of Excellence by the American Society of Landscape Architects.

During the 1980s Jack Nicklaus designed 48 holes of golf, including a unique, three-practice-hole facility for golf instruction. The three nine-hole courses, North, South and East, as well as the 1104-yard practice layout, were designed with Robert Cupp, who later developed his own golf-course architectural design firm. The 6993-yard par-72 North/South layout has been ranked among America's 75 best resort courses by *Golf Digest* since the course opened in 1985. The resort's Mediterranean-style clubhouse has won a number of architectural awards, including the Award for Excellence in Architecture from the Georgia Association of the American Institute of Architects and the SARC Design Award for Excellence in Architecture from the American Institute of Architects.

These Jack Nicklaus courses were designed to reward good shot making. His three design constants are that golf should be more a game of precision than power, that a course reward the player who uses the mind ahead of the muscles, and that little as possible of what Mother Nature has made available is disturbed. The North/South has generous landing areas but demanding approach shots onto small, well-protected undulating greens that are usually flanked by Scottish-style mounding, pot bunkers, and grassy hollows. The wind can be a factor on these open layouts, and water hazards are found on thirteen of the holes.

This includes the two most difficult holes on the front (North) side. The 423-yard par-4 seventh is a dogleg right with a lake running from tee to green on the right. The tee shot should be played to the right

of center, but there is a large bunker and long lake to contend with there. The approach shot is over the water to a deep, narrow green that becomes more difficult to hit because of the angle from which the shot has to be played. The green actually seems wide and shallow when you play from the right side of the fairway. The 435-yard par-4 ninth hole has a narrow, mounded fairway that flows to a deep, narrow green flanked by water on the left and two traps on the right. A lake borders the left fairway from tee to green, and the green curls to the left and around the water, making the approach shot very difficult.

The most challenging hole on the back (South) nine is the 570-yard par-5 fifteenth (the sixth hole on the South Course), which is a long, narrow dogleg to the left. Water borders the fairway to the left on the tee shot, and the fairway is squeezed by pot bunkers beginning 275 yards from the back tees and 245 yards from the blue tees. The next shot has more water on the left and a large fairway bunker on the right, 100 yards from the green, as the fairway begins to curl left. The green is small, plateaued and protected by water on the left, with a large trap bordering its right side. The finishing hole mirrors the ninth on the North Course and shares its green. This 463-yard dogleg right has a waste bunker running from 250 yards out to the green on the right side, which is also bordered by a lake from tee to green. The tee shot has to be long and accurate to a narrowing fairway to have a decent approach to a narrow, deep, two-tiered green. The putting surface is protected by a waste bunker and water on the right, a large trap to the rear and mounds to the left. This is typical of the demanding approach shots required by this course.

The East Course plays 3434 yards from the back tees and can be played in combination with either of the other two nine-hole courses. A picturesque hole on the East Course is the 153-yard par-3 fifth, which plays to an island green protected by a large trap to the rear and a smaller one to the right. The wind can make this hole exceedingly difficult.

Within walking distance of the clubhouse are the Grand Cypress Villa accommodations, the Grand Cypress Golf Academy, the Executive Meeting Center, and complete practice facilities separate from the three-hole Golf Academy layout. A shuttle service makes it very easy to get back and forth to the Hyatt, which offers additional amenities on a somewhat larger scale.

In addition to individual and group instruction provided by the able staff of professionals and assistants at Grand Cypress, the Grand Cypress Academy of Golf provides sophisticated instruction, including swing analysis and practice utilizing biomechanical research data, video, computer graphics and professional instruction. The 3- and 4-day academy sessions feature full-swing, short-game and on-course-swing analysis and club fitting; a take-home computer video analysis that includes the instructor's comments; a leather-bound Academy of Golf instruction notebook; unlimited use of academy holes and range practice; club cleaning and storage; a leather golf glove; complimentary beverages; and a round of golf on the Grand Cypress courses. Enrollment is limited to 16 students per group. Also offered are 2- and 4-day schools, as well as specialty schools that include minischools with 3 half-day sessions, the Phil Rogers (one of the instructors) series, junior programs for golfers ages 12 to 17 and custom-designed schools for corporate groups. Annual membership is also available.

The three-hole Academy golf layout includes a par-3, par-4, and par-5 hole, with the total course distance ranging from 1104 yards (back tees) to 755 yards (forward tees). As with the regular courses, there are four tee distances to accommodate the style and ability of each golfer as he or she practices the game.

The New Course, which opened in 1987, is fast becoming a favorite among professionals and nonprofessionals alike. The design was inspired by the Old Course at St. Andrews, Scotland, and features tree-less, wide-open fairways; more than 140 pot bunkers; 7 large, double greens; winding creeks spanned by stone bridges and rolling duneslike mounds. This course was ranked number 2 by *Golf Digest* in its best new resort course category in 1988 and it has been rated among the best golf courses, public or private, in Florida by *GolfWeek* and *Golf Digest*.

Fees are slightly reduced if you elect to walk the New Course, and caddies are available if you request one at least 24 hours in advance. A nice touch on the first tee is a practice putting area similar to that at St. Andrews.

The New Course plays 6773 yards from the back tees, 6181 yards from the middle and 5314 yards from the forward. The two finishing holes provide a great way to end your round. The 485-yard par-5 seventeenth is a replica of the famous "Road" hole at St. Andrews. This is a rolling, slight dogleg right to a narrow, large green that is shared with the first hole. Should your ball stray onto the adjacent shell-rock road, you are obliged to play it from there, just like in the old country. There is also a St. Andrews-like stone wall behind the green, and should your ball find that area, you have to play it as it lies. The finishing hole is a 371-yard par 4 that plays straight to a green with a drop-off in front ("the Valley of Sin") like St. Andrews. You should really make plans to play this course.

The award-winning clubhouse at Grand Cypress has all the amenities. The full-service pro shop is rated one of the best in the country by *Golf Shop Operations* magazine. There are complete locker-room and shower facilities for men and women, with the elegant Black Swan and less formal Fairways Restaurant and Lounge in the clubhouse. And more than 20 PGA professionals and assistants are there to meet your instructional needs. Payne Stewart, Corey Pavin, Mark O'Meara and many other PGA tour professionals who live in the Orlando area practice at Grand Cypress.

Meeting and conference facilities are available in the on-site Hyatt Regency, which has a wide array of conference configurations ranging from ballrooms to executive board rooms in its 57,000-square-foot space. The Villas of Grand Cypress has a separate, smaller, 7000-square-foot facility that can accommodate as many as 200 persons. *Meetings and Conventions, Successful Meetings, Corporate and Incentive Travel* and *Corporate Meetings and Incentives* magazines have consistently ranked Grand Cypress among the best meeting and conference facilities in the United States. *World Tennis* magazine has recognized Grand Cypress as a Five Star Tennis Resort. The British Horse Society has approved the Grand Cypress Equestrian Center for livery and training. This is the first U.S. facility to be so honored. The resort has recently received the Gold Medal Resort Award from *Golf* magazine which has ranked it as one of the twelve best golf resorts in America. Whether you are coming here for golf, a business outing or a family vacation, there is something for everyone.

Course Name: GRENELEFE
West, East, South Courses

Course Type: Resort
Resort: Grenelefe Resort and Conference Center
Address: 3200 State Road 546 Haines City, FL 33844–9732
Phone: (813) 422–7511 (Golf Course) (813) 422–7511, (800) 282–7875 (FL), (800) 237–9549, (Outside FL) (Resort)
Fax: (813) 421–5000 (Resort)

GOLF COURSE

Director of Golf: Howie Barrow
Course Length/Par (All Tees): West: Back 7325/72, Light Green 6898/72, White 6199/72, Forward 5398/72. East: Back 6802/72, Light Green 6368/72, White 6156/72, Forward 5114/72. South: Back 6869/71, Light Green 6333/71, White 5939/71, Ladies' Forward 5174/71
Course Slope/Rating (All Tees): West: Back 130/75, Light Green 126/73.1, White 122/70.5, Ladies' Forward 118/70.9. East: Back 123/72.5, Light Green 120/NA, White 114/69.6, Ladies' Forward 114/NA. South: Back 124/72.6, Light Green 119/70.3, White 116/68.4, Ladies' Forward 115/69.5
Course Architects: West: Robert Trent Jones and David Wallace (1965). East: Ed Seay and Arnold Palmer (1976). South: Ron Garl and Andy Bean (1983)
Golf Facilities: Full Pro Shop X, Snack Bar X, Lounge X, Restaurant X, Locker Room X, Showers X, Club Rental X, Club Repair X, Cart Rental X, Instruction X, Practice Green X, Driving Range X, Practice Bunker X, Club Storage X
Tee-Time Reservation Policy: At time of reservation, up to 1 yr. in advance on deluxe packages
Ranger: Yes
Tee-off-Interval Time: 7 min.
Time to Play 18 Holes: 4½ hrs.
Course Hours/Earliest Tee-off: 7:30 a.m.
Green and Cart Fees: Peak Season: West: $110 for 18 holes with cart. East, South: $95 for 18 holes with cart
Credit Cards: All major cards except Discover
Season: Year round. Busiest season mid-Jan. to mid-April
Course Comments: Cart mandatory. Yardage book available. Second rounds of golf subject to availability
Golf Packages: Available year round through resort
Discounts: Seasonal (May 1 to Sept.)
Places to Stay Nearby: Must be resort guest, member or guest of member to play the courses. HAINES CITY: Best Western Lake Hamilton (813) 421–6929, (800) 528–1234. ALSO SEE ORLANDO LISTINGS ON PAGE 173
Local Attractions: SEE ORLANDO LISTINGS ON PAGE 173
Directions: From Orlando or Tampa: I–4 to U.S. Hwy. 27, south on Hwy. 27 (12 mi.) to State Rd. 544, east on State Rd. 544 (7 mi.) to resort entrance
Closest Commercial Airports: Orlando International (45 min.), Tampa International (1½ hrs.), Jacksonville International (3½ hrs.)

RESORT

Date Built: 1974

No. of Rooms: 950 suites and villas

Meeting/Exhibit Rooms: 32. Capacity of Largest: 1500 persons banquet style. Meeting Space: 70,000 sq. ft.

Room Price Range: $180 deluxe room to $385 2-bedroom villa for 2 persons peak season (mid-Jan. to mid-April). Golf and other packages available as well as lower rates off season. Lowest rates mid-May to Oct.

Lounges: Forest Pub, Lancelot's Lounge

Restaurants: Grene Heron, Camelot Restaurant, Forest Pub

Entertainment: Live music in Lancelot's Lounge, piano music in Grene Heron

Credit Cards: All major cards except Discover

General Amenities: Supervised children's programs, video games, TV/VCR room; meeting and conference facilities in theater-style, banquet, classroom, conference configurations with audiovisual, food service, secretarial services; florist, convenience store, beauty shop, barber shop, shopping excursions

Recreational Amenities: Fitness center, 20 tennis courts (11 lighted for night play), volleyball, basketball court (lighted), table tennis, 18-hole miniature golf course, softball, bicycling, croquet, marina, 4 swimming pools, 2 whirlpools and saunas; jogging, fitness and nature trails; fishing, horseshoes, badminton, outdoor Jacuzzis, bicycling, bird watching, 6400-acre lake with marina

Reservation and Cancellation Policy: Credit card guarantee or cash deposit required. Cancellation required 14 days mid-Jan. to mid-April prior to arrival to avoid penalties; 7-day cancellation notice otherwise

Comments and Restrictions: No pets. Modified American plan available. Taxes and gratuities in addition to base rates. Children under 18 yrs. free when sharing accommodations with parents (European plan only). Package rates not available to groups. Golf-package fees apply to South and East courses. Additional fee for play on West Course

GRENELEFE

Grenelefe is a 1000-acre resort located just 45 minutes southeast of Orlando. Unlike some of the flatter, open golf venues in Florida, Grenelefe has rolling fairways and an abundance of mature pines and oaks on its 54 holes. The centerpiece of the golf amenities at Grenelefe is the 7325-yard West Course, designed by Robert Trent Jones, Sr., and built by David Wallace. This layout is very difficult because of its length, tight fairways, small greens and well-placed sand bunkers. There are water hazards on only four holes, and these hazards are not a major factor on the golf course. *Golf Digest* ranks the West Course one of the best resort courses in America.

The most difficult hole on the West Course is the 479-yard par-4 fourteenth. This dogleg left plays downhill on the tee shot, then somewhat straight to a small, narrow undulating green with a trap in front and another to the left and to the rear. The distance and the small, tree-protected target make this hole difficult. There are four tee distances at Grenelefe, and it would probably be a more enjoyable golf experience not to play from the back tees.

The par 3s are long and difficult on the West Course—from any distance. The 230-yard fourth plays to a deep green protected by two large traps, one on each side of the putting surface. The 206-yard seventh plays to another deep green with traps left, right and to the rear. The 204-yard thirteenth plays to a large, skull-shaped green protected by three traps, and the 210-yard sixteenth has a roundish, medium-sized green with two traps to the left and rear.

The finishing hole, a 561-yard double-dogleg par 5, is another challenging hole on the West Course. The tee shot and second shot are to narrow landing areas, and the approach shot is to a well-guarded green with a trap to the left front and another to the right.

The West Course has its own clubhouse with pro shop, locker rooms and showers, and a restaurant. The East and South courses are served by one clubhouse, which has a pro shop and restaurant but no locker-room facility. Over 35 percent of the tee times at Grenelefe are reserved for members, although those times become available to resort guests if the members elect not to use them. Only resort guests, members and guests of members can play the course, whose busiest months are January through April. A variety of golf packages are available through the resort year round, and the best prices are generally available during the summer months.

The East and South courses are excellent golf courses too. The 6802-yard East Course was designed by Ed Seay with Arnold Palmer and opened in 1976. This course is shorter and tighter than the West Course but also has small to medium-sized greens that are well protected by sand bunkers. Water hazards are found on four holes, including the 429-yard par-4 sixth, one of the more difficult holes on the course. The tee shot is out of a chute of trees and somewhat uphill to a plateaued landing area. The approach shot is downhill to a deep green with water on its left and large sand traps both left and right.

The four lake holes are critical holes on the Ron Garl/Andy Bean–designed South Course. The 185-yard par-3 seventh plays from an elevated tee to a wide, shallow green fronted by a large pond and protected in back by traps. The 520-yard par-5 double-dogleg eighth plays over a small stream to a landing area bordered by a lake on the right and fairway bunkers on the left. You can either play over a second lake to the green on the second shot or play up to the right of the lake to reach the large green in three. The 403-yard par-4 ninth plays straight to a very deep, left-to-right-angled green with a large trap and a lake in front and another trap to the rear. The approach shot, which plays over water, is the key on this hole. The 408-yard par-4 tenth plays over water to a somewhat open fairway, but the approach shot has to clear a huge trap directly in front of a large green that has two additional bunkers to its left and right.

Grenelefe has 2 driving ranges with adjoining golf instructional studios, 5 practice greens and 4 practice bunkers for your own individual practice convenience. A variety of golf instruction is available from the professionals at Grenelefe in addition to individual and group instruction on demand.

Various other recreational activities are offered at Grenelefe. The 20-court tennis complex has been rated among the best resort facilities in America by *World Tennis, Tennis* and *Racquet* magazines. *Meetings and Conventions* magazine has awarded the resort its Gold Tee Award for having one of the best golf conference resorts in America. Groups of up to 2000 persons can easily be accommodated here.

Grenelefe has consistently won a variety of hospitality awards including a *Mobil Travel Guide* Four-Star rating and an American Automobile Association Four-Diamond rating. A variety of eating facilities are found at the resort, including the Grene Heron, a somewhat formal gourmet restaurant featuring American and Continental cuisine ranging from jumbo-shrimp cocktail to baked grouper au homard. There is also an on-site convenience store should you wish to bring food to your villa.

Renovations have recently been completed on Grenelefe's 950 1- and 2-bedroom guest villas and suites, all of which have golf-course views. The accommodations available at Grenelefe range from club-suite/efficiency rooms, which include 2 double beds with full bath, kitchenette, dressing room, patios and outside entrance, to more spacious 1- and 2-bedroom villa suites. Modified and full American meal plan options are available.

Golf packages are available, as are tennis, fishing, Thanksgiving, New Year's, honeymoon and numerous other year-round packages and special rates.

Course Name: HUNTER'S CREEK

Course Type: Public
Address: 14401 Sports Club Way
               Orlando, FL 32837
Phone: (407) 240–4653

GOLF COURSE

Director of Golf: Danny Boswell
Course Length/Par (All Tees): Back 7432/72, Blue 6905/72, White 6521/72, Forward 5755/72

Course Slope/Rating (All Tees): Back 127/75.2, Blue 122/72.8, White 118/71, Ladies' Forward 120/72.5

Course Architect: Lloyd Clifton (1986)

Golf Facilities: Full Pro Shop X, Snack Bar X, Lounge No, Restaurant No, Locker Room X, Showers X, Club Rental X, Club Repair X, Cart Rental X, Instruction X, Practice Green X, Driving Range X, Practice Bunker X, Club Storage No

Tee-Time Reservation Policy: 3 days in advance from 7 a.m.

Ranger: Yes

Tee-off-Interval Time: 7 min.

Time to Play 18 Holes: 4 hrs., 15 min.

Course Hours/Earliest Tee-off: 7:20 a.m.

Green and Cart Fees: $60 for 18 holes with cart peak season (Jan.-Mar.)

Credit Cards: MasterCard, Visa

Season: Year round. Busiest season Jan. through March

Course Comments: Cart mandatory

Golf Packages: None

Discounts: Seasonal (May to Dec.)

Places to Stay Nearby: Residence Inn (407) 396–2056, (800) 648–7408 (FL), (800) 468–3027 (outside FL); Casa Rosa Inn (407) 396–2020. SEE ORLANDO LISTINGS ON PAGE 173

Local Attractions: SEE ORLANDO LISTINGS ON PAGE 173

Directions: From Orlando International Airport (20 min.): Beeline Expressway west to Hwy. 423, south on Hwy. 423 to Hunter's Creek, follow signs to golf course

Closest Commercial Airports: Orlando International (20 min.), Tampa International (1½ hrs.)

HUNTER'S CREEK

Hunter's Creek is a lengthy, 7432-yard par-72 layout designed by Lloyd Clifton and opened in 1986. The course is the centerpiece of a 6-square-mile master planned community being developed by the Newland Group, a San Diego–based real estate-investment firm. The long-range plan is for 9624 single- and multifamily units with a town center that will contain 100 acres of commercial property. The golf course covers more than 160 acres, is somewhat open and flat, and has water hazards on every hole. More than 70 sand bunkers appear on this layout, and the greens tend to be large, fast and somewhat undulating.

You might have the suspicion that you are in for a long and challenging test of golf when you notice that the number-15-handicap hole on the course, the par-5 second, is 615 yards long. This hole is a double dogleg to a large green with three large bunkers protecting it left, right and rear. The hole can be shortened by cutting the doglegs, but it will still take you three shots to get there, especially if the wind is blowing, which it often is on this open golf course. The number-1-handicap hole is the 428-yard par-4 fourth, which is long, straight and paralleled by water on the right. The tee shot has to avoid the water and a bunker on the right and out of bounds to the left. The approach shot is to a very deep, three-tiered green with traps left and right. Depending on the wind and pin position, four or five different clubs could be selected for this shot. Another demanding hole on the front side is the dogleg-left, 457-yard par-4 ninth, which has a large bunker at the left knee of the dogleg. The fairway slopes to the right in this area and is likely to kick the ball into the right rough. The second shot is toward a large, flat green with a huge trap to the right and forward, another to the left and a third to the rear.

The two finishing holes at Hunter's Creek are fine tests of golf. The 425-yard par-4 seventeenth is a slight dogleg left to a medium-sized green with traps both left and rear, and a huge bunker on the right. The tee shot is squeezed by a fairway bunker on the right, halfway to the hole. The approach shot not only has to negotiate the traps, but it must also avoid a small lake on the left. The 450-yard par-4 eighteenth is another slight dogleg left with a huge bunker at the left corner. The tee shot is to a landing area to the right of this bunker, and the second shot is to a large, deep green with a huge bunker in front and to the left, and another trap to the right. There is also water to the right, which can come into play if you slice or push the ball.

The distance, wind, water and traps make Hunter's Creek very difficult. The course plays 6905 yards from the blue tees and 6521 yards from the white. The forward tees are 5755 yards, with a ladies' USGA rating of 72.5 and slope of 120. On the seventeenth, the tee distances are 425, 409, 390, and 339 yards respectively from back to front, and on the eighteenth the distances are 450, 434, 424 and 332. No matter which tees you play from, you'll be challenged.

Hunter's Creek has a driving range, practice green, and practice bunker on site, and instruction is available from the staff of professionals. The green fees are very reasonable considering the quality of the course, and the busiest months here are January through March. Lower rates are available after that.

Golf Digest rates Hunter's Creek among the best public courses in America, and various college tournaments, PGA qualifiers, U.S. Open qualifiers, and Florida Ladies' Amateur qualifiers have been played here.

Course Name: **WALT DISNEY WORLD Palm, Magnolia, Lake Buena Vista, Osprey Ridge, Eagle Pines, Oak Trail Courses**

Course Type: Resort
Resort: Walt Disney World
Address: P. O. Box 10000
Lake Buena Vista, FL
32830–0040
Phone: (407) 824–2270 (Tee Times, Tournaments)
(407) W DISNEY (Reservations)
(407) 824–4321 (Information)
Fax: (407) 824–3704 (Golf Courses)
(407) 354–0261 (Reservations), (407) 827–5149 (Information)

GOLF COURSE

Head Professional: Kevin Prentice

Operating Manager: Mike Beaver
Course Length/Par (All Tees): Palm: Back 6957/72, White 6461/72, Gold 6029/72, Ladies' Forward 5398/74. Magnolia: Back 7190/72, White 6642/72, Gold 6091/72, Ladies' Forward 5232/74. Lake Buena Vista: Back 6819/72, White 6642/72, Gold 5917/72, Ladies' Forward 5194/73. Osprey Ridge: Back 7101/72, Crest 6680/72, Wings 6103/72, Forward 5402/72. Eagle Pines: Back 6772/72, Crest 6309/72, Wings 5520/72, Forward 4838/72. Oak Trail: Back 2913/36, Forward 2532/36

Course Slope/Rating (All Tees): Palm: Back 133/73.0, White 129/70.7, Gold 124/68.7, Ladies' Forward 124/70.4. Magnolia: Back 133/73.9, White 128/71.6, Gold 123/69.1, Ladies' Forward 123/70.5. Lake Buena Vista: Back 128/72.7, White 123/70.1, Gold 120/68.2, Ladies' Forward 120/69.4. Osprey Ridge: Back 135/73.9, Crest 128/71.8, Wings 121/68.9, Ladies' Forward 124/70.4. Eagle Pines: Back 131/72.3, Crest 125/69.9, Wings 115/66.3, Ladies' Forward 111/68.0. Oak Trail: Back NA/NA, Forward NA/NA

Course Architects: Palm: Joe Lee (1971). Magnolia: Joe Lee (1972). Lake Buena Vista: Joe Lee (1970). Osprey Ridge: Tom Fazio (1992). Eagle Pines: Pete Dye (1992). Oak Trail: Ron Garl (1980, renovation and additional 3 holes, 1990)

Golf Facilities: Full Pro Shop X, Snack Bar X, Lounge X, Restaurant X, Locker Room X, Showers X, Club Rental X, Club Repair X, Cart Rental X, Instruction X, Practice Green X, Driving Range X, Practice Bunker X, Club Storage X

Tee-Time Reservation Policy: Resort guests: Can make tee times 30 days in advance with a confirmed reservation number in a Walt Disney World Resort. Day guests: Can make tee times up to 4 days in advance Jan.-Apr., up to 7 days in advance May-Dec.

Ranger: Yes

Tee-off-Interval Time: Buena Vista, Magnolia, Palm: 8 min. Eagle Pines, Osprey Ridge: 10 min.

Time to Play 18 Holes: 4½ hrs.

Course Hours/Earliest Tee-off: 7:15 a.m.

Green and Cart Fees: Peak rates (Jan.-Apr.) on Palm, Magnolia, Lake Buena Vista: $95 for 18 holes with cart. Osprey Ridge, Eagle Pines: $120 for 18 holes with cart. Oak Trail: $24 for 9 holes with pull cart, $32 for 18 holes with pull cart

Credit Cards: American Express, MasterCard, Visa

Season: Year round. Busiest season Jan. to April

Course Comments: Cart mandatory except for executive Oak Trail Course

Golf Packages: Available year round through resort. Lowest rates May to Dec. Extensive corporate outing and tournament programs

Discounts: Resort guest rate. Replays half regular rate on space-available basis on regular courses (excluding Oak Trail). Twilight rate after 3 p.m. Junior 9-hole rate on Oak Trail for youths 17 and under

Places to Stay Nearby: SEE ORLANDO LISTINGS ON PAGE 173

Local Attractions: SEE ORLANDO LISTINGS ON PAGE 173

Directions: Southwest of Orlando, off I–4. Take I–4 west from I–95 or Hwy. 1 to resort exit. Take I–4 east from I–75 to resort exits. Traveling northbound on Florida Turnpike, use Kissimmee–St. Cloud interchange and Hwy. 192 to resort

Closest Commercial Airport: Orlando International (30 min.)

RESORT

Date Built: 1971, with subsequent additions and renovations

No. of Rooms: MAGIC KINGDOM RESORT AREA: Grand Floridian Beach Resort, 900 guest rooms and suites; Disney Inn, 288 guest rooms; Polynesian Resort, 853 rooms and suites; Contemporary Resort, 1041 guest rooms and suites; Fort Wilderness Resort and Campground,

407 rooms. EPCOT RESORT AREA: Yacht and Beach Club Resort, 1213 guest rooms and suites; Disney World Dolphin, 1510 rooms and suites with 6 concierge floors; Disney World Swan, 758 rooms and suites; Boardwalk Resort, 924 rooms and villas; Caribbean Beach Resort, 2112 rooms. DISNEY VILLAGE RESORT AREA: Dixie Landings Resort, 2048 rooms; Port Orleans Resort, 1008 rooms; Vacation Club Resort, 197 luxury villas; Village Resort, 709 villas. HOTEL PLAZA AREA: Buena Vista Palace, 1014 rooms and suites; Grosvenor Resort, 626 rooms; Travelodge Hotel, 325 rooms; Guest Quarters Suite Resort, 229 suites; Hotel Royal Plaza, 396 rooms; Hilton, 813 rooms; Courtyard by Marriott, 323 rooms; Doubletree Guest Suites, 229 suites; Villas at Disney Institute, 585 suites and villas

Meeting/Exhibit Rooms: 84. Capacity of Largest: 3648 persons banquet style. Meeting Space: 230,000 sq. ft.

Room Price Range: $69 for All-Star resorts to $780 for Boardwalk Resort Villas. Golf and vacation packages available year round

Lounges: 48 throughout the resort

Restaurants: 87 restaurants, buffets and snack bars featuring everything from American fast food to international and ethnic cuisine such as Chinese, Moroccan, Caribbean, Creole, Japanese, Mexican, Hawaiian/Polynesian, Norwegian, French, Italian, German, Cajun and others. Also themed restaurants such as Planet Hollywood, Rainforest Cafe and House of Blues (1997). Kosher and special diet meals are available

Night Clubs: Adventures Club, Cage, Comedy Warehouse, Rock and Roll Beach Club, ESPN World, 8 TRAX, and others

Entertainment: Singers, dancers, jesters, comedians, musical revues, theme parks, character breakfasts and dinner shows, Disney Professional Development and Learning programs

Credit Cards: American Express, MasterCard, Visa

General Amenities: Child care and babysitting, supervised children's programs for ages 3 through 12, barber and beauty shops, guided tours, camera rental and film developing; shopping at more than 120 locations offering character merchandise, vacation wear, sundries, apparel, jewelry, crafts and collectibles, and more; disabled guest assistance, laundry and dry cleaning; meeting and conference facilities with audiovisual, banquet, secretarial and other full-support services; theme parks and attractions at Magic Kingdom, Epcot Center, Disney Village Marketplace, Disney MGM Studios, Pleasure Island

Recreational Amenities: Boating, jogging trails, horseback riding; fully equipped health clubs with personal-fitness trainers at Contemporary Resort, Village Resort, Disney Inn, Boardwalk Inn, Grand Floridian, Yacht and Beach Club; bicycling, movie theaters, petting farm, more than 20 swimming pools, 15 lighted tennis courts, zoological park

Reservation and Cancellation Policy: Vary, depending on booking date and package plans. Personal checks, money orders, American Express, MasterCard and Visa accepted. Vacation plans require 48 hrs. cancellation notice for full refund

Comments and Restrictions: Pets not allowed at Disney resorts or theme parks. There are a limited number of campsites that will allow pets. Four air-conditioned kennels available. Taxes additional to base rates. Children under 18 stay free in rooms with parents. Extra charges per additional adults in rooms and at campsites. Food may not be brought into theme parks

WALT DISNEY WORLD

When people think of Orlando, they almost automatically think of Walt Disney World and its multitude of cartoon characters, rides, exhibits, hotels, restaurants and recreational activities. Over 28,000 acres of land were quietly purchased before the full plan for Walt Disney World was presented by Disney in late 1965. Based on prior experience with Disneyland in California, the Disney organization felt it had to acquire

more land to create and control a total family-entertainment environment. The Magic Kingdom, which covers 100 acres, was opened on October 1, 1971. The Magic Kingdom includes 45 major adventures encompassed in 7 lands, such as Fantasyland, Tomorrowland, and Frontierland. EPCOT Center opened on October 1, 1982, and covers 260 acres. It features Future World, with theme areas focusing on discovery and scientific achievements. World Showcase covers 11 nations in a display area surrounding World Showcase Lagoon. Disney MGM Studios was fully opened by 1989. It covers 135 acres and is a working TV and film studio as well as a theme park. Attractions include Jim Henson's Muppets, Indiana Jones and many others. Pleasure Island is a 6-acre nightclub theme park featuring 7 nightclubs as well as shops and restaurants. This is adjacent to Disney Village Marketplace, which includes more than 2-dozen shops and dining locations.

The theme resorts at Disney World have 24 hotels, a campground and vacation villas totalling more than 23,000 vacation club accommodations. An astounding 600,000 square feet of modern meeting space are also located throughout the resort areas. Disney-owned and -operated hotels have 230,000 sq. ft. of space, with major function space available at the Contemporary Resort, Grand Floridian Beach Resort, Yacht and Beach Club Resort, Disney Village Resort Area, Disney World Dolphin, Disney World Swan, Buena Vista Palace, the Hilton, Hotel Royal Plaza and Grosvenor Resort.

Today Walt Disney world property covers 29,000 acres with 5900 developed acres and a wilderness preserve of over 8000 acres. More than 36,000 people are employed at Walt Disney World. Whether you like oversized mice, ducks and other creatures with perpetual smiles or not, this resort is a phenomenal achievement.

Recognized as a Gold Medal Resort by *Golf* magazine, golf at Walt Disney World is appropriately referred to as the"Magic Linkdom." Featured are 99 holes of golf, including the Palm and Magnolia courses, which are ranked among the best resort golf courses in the United States. The Palm Course, also a site for the Disney World/Oldsmobile Classic, is rated one of *Golf Digest's* top 75 resort courses and is considered as difficult as the Magnolia Course by 1983 Disney World/Oldsmobile Classic winner Payne Stewart. This course was also designed by Lee and has his signature elevated tees and greens as well as a considerable amount of sand and water. Water comes into play on 9 holes, and there are 95 sand traps on this layout. The greens are moderately fast, medium sized to large, undulating and well protected by sand traps and water.

The number-1-handicap hole on the Palm Course is the 412-yard par-4 sixth. The tee shot has to avoid water, which lines the left fairway, and trees to the right. The second shot is over water to a two-tiered, deep green with water front and right and a huge trap to the rear. The par-4 holes continue to be tough as you make the turn to the back nine. The 450-yard tenth has a tee shot that must carry water approximately 200 yards from the back tees and avoid a bunker on the right and trees on either side of the landing area. The approach shot is to a small, right-sloping green with traps left-front, left and rear.

The finishing hole is another challenging par 4. This 454-yard finale has often been included on the PGA tour's toughest-hole list. The first shot is down a tree-lined fairway with bunkers guarding the left side. The second shot is all carry to a small, forward-sloping green with traps front, left and rear. A shot pushed too far right will land in water.

The Magnolia Course plays 7190 yards from the back tees and is the longest of the courses. This Joe Lee-designed layout has water hazards on more than half its holes; has moderately fast, medium sized to large, undulating greens; and is well bunkered, especially around the greens. Trees and fairway bunkers are strategically placed, making the course a challenge to any golfer from the appropriate choice of four tee distances.

One of my favorite holes is the 448-yard par-4 fifth, which is a dogleg to the right.

Trees guard the right side of the fairway, and two bunkers border the tee-shot landing area on the left. The second shot is to a narrow, deep, forward-sloping green with two large bunkers to the right and another to the left. PGA tour professional Raymond Floyd's advice in the yardage book is:

I play this hole with a cut driver. Downwind I use a 3-wood.... [It is] important to be in [the] fairway, which makes [the] approach shot straight-forward to a well-bunkered green.

A scenic par-3 is the 195-yard sixth, which plays over water to a deep, side-angled green surrounded by three sand bunkers. The front bunker is shaped like Mickey Mouse, seemingly a metaphor for weak tee shots. This bunker is also called the "mouse trap."

An excellent par 5 on the back nine is the 595-yard dogleg-right fourteenth, which is bordered by water to the right on the tee shot. The first shot should be played to the left corner of the dogleg, and the second shot will most likely be laid up to the right of a large pond bordering the fairway on the left and cutting in front of a large green bordered by traps right, rear and left.

Lanny Wadkins calls the 427-yard par-4 seventeenth one of the most dangerous holes on the course. This dogleg left is bordered by water both right and left on the tee shot, which has to carry water to the fairway. The second shot is to a deep, forward sloping green with two large traps to the left and a trap and water to the right. This has been rated one of the toughest holes on the PGA tour.

The Magnolia is named after the more than 1500 magnolia trees that are planted on the course. The final round of the Walt Disney World/Oldsmobile Golf Classic has been played on the Magnolia Course since 1971. The combination of water hazards, 97 sand traps, length, challenging greens and well-designed golf holes make The Magnolia Course a beautiful and memorable test of golf.

The third Joe Lee course at Disney World is the 6829-yard Lake Buena Vista Course. This is a tighter course and has less water and slightly smaller (but well-bunkered) greens than the other courses. Lake Buena Vista has recently been remodeled. New tee boxes, redesigned fairways, and an abundance of sand and water—including an island green—highlight these changes. Six of the layout's eighteen holes have been realigned, and the front and back nines have been flip-flopped so that old number ten is now the first tee and the former ninth is the new finishing hole.

The three finishing holes at Lake Buena Vista begin with the 157-yard par-3 sixteenth, which plays to the new island green fronted on the left by a large trap and guarded by another one to the rear. The 542-yard par-5 seventeenth plays down a narrowing tree-lined fairway to a deep, two-tiered green well guarded in front by two traps and flanked on the left by another one. The tee shot is over water to a landing area bordered by bunkers. The second shot has to avoid a left fairway bunker that begins 115 yards from the green.

The 448-yard par-4 finishing hole is a tree-lined dogleg left to a deep green with traps both left and rear and with a banked drop-off to the right. Fairway bunkers straddle the tee-shot landing area. Two long, well-placed shots are required to reach this green in regulation.

Lake Buena Vista is the third course used in the Walt Disney World/Oldsmobile Golf Classic. Located at the new Disney Institute, it is served by a new clubhouse, which includes locker room, showers, health club, restaurant, snack bar and pro shop. The Magnolia, Palm and nine-hole par-36 Oak Trail executive golf course are served by the clubhouse at the Shades of Green Resort. The executive course was called the Wee Links when it was a six-hole layout and was intended to be a model for encouraging junior golf. It was re-opened as a nine-hole course in 1991 after renovations. Originally the course had artificial turf tees and greens; it is now entirely Bermuda grass. Oak Trail plays 2913 yards from the back tees, with holes ranging from 517 to 132 yards in length. This is an excellent course for beginning golf, family play and practice. Most greens and tees are elevated.

The latest members of Disney's Magic Linkdom are the Tom Fazio–designed 7101-yard par-72 Osprey Ridge Course and the 6772-yard par-72 Pete Dye–designed Eagle Pines layout. Both of these courses opened in 1992 and are serviced by a futuristic clubhouse designed by Gwathmey Siegal Associates of New York. The striking exterior has a variety of geometric shapes and colors ranging from purple to green to yellow. One of the more memorable design elements is a sculpture made of giant silver golf tees ranging in size from 6 to 10 feet high that awaits you at the entrance to the clubhouse. Inside is a functionally designed space with pro shop, restaurant and bar facilities, locker rooms and showers. There is also the 2000-square foot Tournament Room, which can be used for meetings and golf outings. The entire facility is called the Bonnet Creek Golf Club and is easily accessible within the Disney World Complex. Both golf courses are close to Disney's Fort Wilderness Campground and the new Dixie Landings and Port Orleans Resorts.

The Osprey Ridge Course has four sets of tees ranging from 7101 yards to 5402 yards in total distance. It features medium-sized to large, undulating Bermuda-grass greens that are currently moderate in speed. Water comes into play on ten holes, and there are a variety of strategically placed large sand traps. Mounds and a meandering ridge that runs through the course provide interesting obstacles, banking and elevation changes. Lush Florida vegetation abounds on many holes. For example, the first hole, a 353-yard par 4, is flanked by two wetland areas. But most of the holes convey a sense of openness with unintimidating landing areas. The links-style layout has generous distances between greens and the next tees, plenty of shelters and restroom facilities, and friendly people at refreshment carts who will keep you fortified in the Florida sun.

Osprey Ridge has an abundance of beautiful and sometimes golf-threatening foliage, including pine, scrub oak, palmetto, bay trees, cypress and other varieties. Wildlife including ospreys, wild turkeys, tortoises, armadillos, deer, rabbits and others populate the course, its woodlands and wetlands. Wind is another element on this layout that can change the character of play. Often the winds here are swirling and unpredictable, and make it a challenge to manage your golf game.

The front nine starts out with some of the easier holes on the course but includes two long par 3s before you reach the 582-yard par-5 seventh, which is the number-1-handicap hole, largely due to distance. One of my favorite holes on this side is the 193-yard par-3 third, which plays from an elevated tee to a large, wide green bordered by banked hills on the left and fronted on the right by a huge sand wasteland. If your tee shot strays to the right, you could get more sand bunker practice than you would care to have.

The course gets more difficult on the back nine. The 453-yard par-4 fourteenth is a dogleg left wrapped around a small lake. Woods border a narrow landing area, and it is very easy to cut the corner the wrong way and put the tee shot in the water or through the fairway and into the woods. The approach shot is to a large green fronted on the left by a large sand bunker.

The three finishing holes at Osprey Ridge are excellent tests of golf. The 542-yard par-5 sixteenth is a question-mark-shaped dogleg left with water protecting the fairway on the left from 260 yards out to a large, elevated green surrounded by sizeable bunkers. This hole is usually played by keeping the ball slightly right on the first two shots and hitting a wedge onto the green. The front of the green drops off dramatically, making pin placement and angle of approach a major factor. The seventeenth is a 216-yard par 3 that plays over the edge of a lake to a huge green banked on the right and bordered by a lake on the left. There is not much fairway to work with in front of the green, so it is better to be a bit long on this one.

The 454-yard par-4 eighteenth bends dramatically to the right and is bordered by a stream to the right. On the left is a continuous ridge that frames the left side from tee to green. The tee-shot landing area is framed by bunkers both left and right. It is possible to cut the corner on the right, but sand and water await you. The approach shot is to a very deep, narrow green with gallery banking left and rear. To the right is a large trap and water. Another trap squeezes the front of the green on the left.

Dye's Eagle Pines Course is a 6772-yard par-72 layout with four tee distances ranging down to 4838 yards. Water can come into play on more than half the holes, which are framed by pine straw, giving the course a desert-golf-course look. The Bermuda grass greens are medium sized, moderately fast, and slightly undulating. The sand bunkers are strategically placed but relatively sparse; however, there are many large waste bunkers on this unusual-looking Dye course. A variety of interesting native grasses such as wiregrass, cordgrass, chalky bluestem and others punctuate this layout. The fairways on the course are slightly concave rather than crowned, ensuring proper drainage while maintaining the surrounding wetlands and natural areas.

Eagle Pines has a wide variety of distances and hole designs. For example, the par-4 holes range from 296 yards to 463 yards from the back tees. The number-1-handicap hole is the 463-yard par-4 fifth, a dogleg to the right. The first shot should be to the center or right of center at the knee of the dogleg. The next shot is to a small, undulating green with water to the rear, left and slightly left-front. You'll be happy to reach this green in regulation.

The 414-yard par-4 eighteenth is an excellent finishing hole. This dogleg left is bordered by water on the left and has a deep, banana-shaped green protected by water, which cuts into the fairway closer to the green. A series of bunkers are to the left, rear and right. Shot making and course management rather than length are important on this course. By the end of the round, you will have used every club in your bag, but it will be helpful to bring along your short game.

Each of the three clubhouse facilities serving the Disney courses has restaurant, bar, locker-room, shower and pro-shop amenities. PGA and LPGA teaching staff are available to provide individual private lessons, playing lessons and group lessons. A golf studio is available for video swing analysis and other forms of instruction.

A variety of golf packages are available year round at Disney's Magic Linkdom. The lowest rates are usually available in the May to late December period. The highest rates are charged from January through late April. Depending on the courses you wish to play, you can stay at a convenient Disney hotel or villa.

There are more than 85 Walt Disney World eating establishments ranging from character meals that include guests such as Mary Poppins, Mickey Mouse and the White Rabbit to more formal restaurants such as the Victoria & Albert's, which has earned the American Automobile Association 4-Diamond Rating. Cajun, Creole, Japanese, Norwegian, Moroccan, Chinese, Polynesian, Mexican, French, Italian, Japanese and a range of other cuisines including basic American hot dogs and hamburgers can be found at Disney World. Meals for special diets and kosher food, and nonsmoking eateries are on the premises. The golf clubs each have restaurants, including the Garden Gallery or Evergreens at the Palm and Magnolia Clubhouse, Seasons Dining Room and Lounge at Lake Buena Vista, and the Sand Trap Grill and Bar at the Bonnet Creek Golf Club.

Information about golf packages, seasonal specials, and Disney facilities and events can be obtained from your travel agency or the resort directly. Vacation packages range from bed and breakfast plans to all-inclusive deluxe packages at the resorts. Whether it is quality golf or family entertainment that you are seeking, the Walt Disney World Resort has it all.

Orlando Places to Stay and Attractions

(See Disney World Resort for Disney-related accommodations)

Grand Cypress Resort (407) 239–1234, (800) 233–1234; Hyatt Orlando Hotel (407) 396–1234, (800) 233–1234; Marriott's Orlando World Center (407) 239–4200, (800) 621–0638. ORLANDO/INTERNATIONAL DRIVE AREA: Peabody Orlando

(407) 352–4000, (800) PEABODY; Westgate Lakes Hotel (407) 345–0000, (800) 424–0708; Stouffer Orlando Resort (407) 351–5555, (800) 327–6677, (800) HOTELS–1; Embassy Suites Hotel at Plaza International (407) 352–1400, (800) 362–2779; Radisson Inn (407) 345–0505, (800) 304–8000; Vistana Resort (407) 239–3376, (800) 877–8787. WINTER PARK: Park Plaza Hotel (407) 647–1072, (800) 228–7220

Local Attractions in Orlando

WALT DISNEY WORLD: Magic Kingdom, Epcot Center, Disney MGM and other attractions; Central Florida Zoological Park, Mystery Fun House, Universal Studios Florida, Wet 'n Wild, Fun 'n Wheels, Gatorland Zoo, Sea World, Xanadu, Alligatorland Safari Zoo, Cypress Gardens, Bok Tower Gardens, Kennedy Space Center, Spaceport USA, Citrus World, Kissimmee Livestock Market, Inc., Lake Wales Museum, Slocum Water Gardens, Water Ski Museum and Hall of Fame, shopping including factory outlets, bicycling, fishing, horseback riding, tennis, water sports, jai alai, dog racing; professional baseball, basketball, football; restaurants, Rollins College, music, theater, art galleries and museums including the Cornell Fine Arts Museum, Cartoon Museum, Central Florida Railroad Museum, Maitland Art Center, Charles Hosmer Morse Museum of American Art, Orlando Museum of Art, Winter Park, Elvis Presley Museum. Greater Orlando Chamber of Commerce (407) 425–1234. Fax: (407) 839–5020. Tourist Information Center (407) 363 5871. Orlando/Orange County Convention and Visitors Bureau (407) 363–5831. Fax: (407) 363–5899

Recommended Golf Courses in Florida

Within 1 Hour of Orlando:

Bay Tree National Golf Links, Melbourne, (407) 259–9060, Semiprivate, 18/7043/72

Big Cypress Country Club, Lakeland, (813) 859–6871, Semiprivate, 18/6650/72

Cocoa Beach Golf Club, Cocoa Beach, (407) 868–3351, Public, River/Dolphin:

18/6367/71. Dolphin/Lakes: 18/6370/71.
Lakes/River: 18/6691/72

Country Club at Mount Dora, Mt. Dora,
(904) 735–2263, Semiprivate, 18/6612/72

Country Club at Silver Springs Shores,
Ocala, (904) 687–2828, Semiprivate,
18/6616/72

Country Club of Sebring, Sebring,
(813) 382–3500, Semiprivate, 9/3272/36

Deer Island Golfers Club, Taveres, (904)
343–7550, Semiprivate, 18/6676/72

Debary Golf and Country Club, Debary,
(407) 668–2061, Semiprivate, 18/6776/72

Deltona Hills Golf and Country Club,
Deltona, (904) 489–3911, Semiprivate,
18/6850/72

Diamondback Golf Club, Haines City,
(813) 421–0437, Semiprivate, 18/6776/72

Dodger Pines Country Club, Vero Beach,
(407) 569–4400, Semiprivate, 18/6692/73

Eastwood Golf Club, Orlando, (407) 281–
4653, Public, 18/7176/72

Ekana Golf and Country Club, Oviedo,
(407) 366–1211, Semiprivate, 18/6683/72

Falcon's Fire Golf Club, Kissimmee, (407)
239–5445, Public, 18/6901/72

Golf Course at Cypress Head, Port Orange,
(904) 756–5449, Public, 18/6814/72

Indigo Lakes Resort, Daytona Beach, (904)
254–3607, (800) 874–9918, Semiprivate,
18/7123/72

Marriott's Orlando World Center Golf
Course, Orlando, (407) 239–5659, Resort,
18/6265/71

Metro West Golf Course, Orlando, (407)
299–1099, Semiprivate, 18/7051/72

Mission Inn Golf and Tennis Resort,
Howey-in-the-Hills, (904) 324–3885, (800)
874–9053, Resort. El Campeon:
18/6852/72. Las Colinas: 18/6867/72

Palisades Golf Club, Clermont, (904) 394–
0085, Semiprivate, 18/6988/72

Pelican Bay Country Club, Daytona Beach,
(904) 788–6496, Public, 18/6829/72

Poinciana Golf and Racquet Resort, Kissimmee, (407) 933–5300, (800) 331–7743,
Semiprivate, 18/6701/72

Ridgewood Lakes Golf Club, Davenport,
(813) 424–8688, Semiprivate, 18/7016/72

River Bend Golf Club, Ormond Beach,
(904) 673–6000, (800) 334–8841, Semiprivate, 18/6821/72

Riviera Country Club, Ormond Beach,
(904) 677–2464, Semiprivate, 18/6302/71

Rolling Hills Golf and Country Club, Wildwood, (904) 748–4200, Semiprivate,
18/6425/71

Rosemont Golf and Country Club, Orlando, (407) 298–1230, Resort, 18/6788/72

Royal Oak Resort and Golf Club, Titus-
ville, (407) 269–4500, Resort, 18/6709/71

Sabal Pointe Country Club, Longwood,
(407) 869–4622, Semiprivate, 18/6603/72

Seven Hills Golfers Club, Spring Hill,
(904) 688–8888, Semiprivate, 18/6750/72

Southern Dunes Golf and Country Club,
Haines City, (813) 421–4653, (800) 632–
6400, Public, 18/7200/72

Spruce Creek, Daytona Beach, (904) 756–
6114, Semiprivate, 18/6833/72

Sugar Mill Country Club, New Smyrna
Beach, (904) 426–5211, Semiprivate. Blue:
9/3339/36. White: 9/3410/36. Red:
9/3356/36

Timacon Golf and Country Club, Lake
Mary, (407) 321–0010, Semiprivate,
18/7019/72

Viera East Golf Club, Viera, (407) 639–
6500, Public, 18/6720/72

Wekiva Golf Club, Longwood, (407) 862–
5113, Semiprivate, 18/6640/72

Daytona Area/East Coast

Course Name: LPGA INTERNATIONAL

Course Type: Public
Address: 300 Champions Drive
                    Daytona Beach, FL 32114
Phone: (904) 274-3880
Fax: (904) 274-3880

GOLF COURSE

Director of Golf: Pam Phipps

Course Length/Par (All Tees): Back 7088/72, Blue 6664/72, White 6225/72, Gold 5744/72, Forward 5131/72

Course Slope/Rating (All Tees): Back 134/74, Blue 130/72, White 124/70.1, Ladies' White 146/75.6, Gold 118/67.1, Ladies' Gold 131/72.4, Ladies' Forward 122/68.9

Course Architect: Rees Jones (1994)

Golf Facilities: Full Pro Shop X, Snack Bar X, Lounge X, Restaurant X, Locker Room No, Showers No, Club Rental X, Club Repair X, Cart Rental X, Instruction X, Practice Green X, Driving Range X, Practice Bunker X, Club Storage No

Tee-Time Reservation Policy: Up to 7 days in advance

Ranger: Yes

Tee-off-Interval Time: 8 min.

Time to Play 18 Holes: 4½ hrs.

Course Hours/Earliest Tee-off: 7:30 a.m.

Green and Cart Fees: $65 for 18 holes

Credit Cards: All major cards

Season: Year round. Busiest Dec. through Apr.

Course Comments: Walking allowed after 2 p.m. Yardage book available

Golf Packages: Through local hotels. Inquire at pro shop

Discounts: Daytona Beach residents, twilight. Lowest seasonal rates May through Oct. Discounts Nov. through Dec.

Places to Stay Nearby: Adams Mark (904) 254–8200, (800) 228–9290; Daytona Beach Hilton Resort (904) 767–7350, (800) 525–7350; Indigo Lakes Holiday Inn (904) 258–6333, (800) HOLIDAY; Howard Johnson Hotel (904) 255–4471, (800) 767–4471

Local Attractions: Daytona International Speedway, Halifax Historical Society and Museum, Klassix Auto Museum, Marineland of Florida, Museum of Arts and Sciences, Southeast Museum of Photography. Destination Daytona, 126 E. Orange Ave., Daytona Beach, FL 32114 (904) 255–0415, (800) 854–1234

Directions: Located 2 miles west of I–95 and north of I–92 (International Speedway Blvd.). Take Hwy. 92 west then turn north on LPGA Blvd. to Champions Drive and the golf course

Closest Commercial Airports: Daytona Regional (20 min.); Orlando International (1 hr.); Jacksonville International (1½ hrs.); Palm Beach International (3½ hrs.)

LPGA INTERNATIONAL

Home of the Ladies Professional Golfers Association and site of the LPGA Sprint Championship, one of the richest on the LPGA Tour, LPGA International was named one of "The Top 10 You Can Play" by *Golf* magazine for 1994. Built in a wetland area a few miles inland from Daytona's beach, architect Rees Jones strove to make this layout a challenge for the best women players as well as lesser mortals. An open windswept course with an abundance of sculpted mounds, bunkers, and water hazards, Jones provides a variety of shot angles and distances depending on which of the five tee distances you select. After the golfer navigates the shifting winds to reach the ample, undulating, Bermuda grass greens, it is easy to three-putt because of the size and subtle breaks on the putting surface. Approach shots must be executed properly to have reasonable putting opportunites on this course.

The most difficult part of LPGA International begins at No. 13, a 576-yard par 5 that is likely to have an incoming wind. A 213-yard tee shot is required to carry a large pond fronting the fairway landing area which is bordered by a huge bunker on the right. A series of mounds and swales make the adjacent rough especially difficult should you stray your shots. The second shot is toward an elevated 34-yard-deep green that is protected by a bunker to its right front, water farther right, and a larger bunker to its left. When the wind blows in at more than 40 miles per hour, it takes many golfers three wood shots to reach this monster.

LPGA International sprawls over 360 acres, making a cart mandatory. A full service clubhouse will soon be built, a hotel is planned for 1997, and an 18-hole Arthur Hills-designed course is in the works. Within easy walking distance of the clubhouse are a driving range, three practice holes, chipping greens with practice bunkers, and a putting green. This is an outstanding new addition to Rees Jones's growing oeuvre of excellent golf courses.

Course Name: PALM COAST RESORT Cypress Knoll, Matanzas Woods, Palm Harbor, Pine Lakes Courses

Course Type: Resort
Resort: ITT Sheraton Palm Coast Resort
Address: 300 Clubhouse Drive Palm Coast, FL 32151–0001
Phone: (904) 437–5807 (Cypress Knoll)
(904) 446–6330 (Matanzas Woods)
(904) 445–0845 (Palm Harbor)
(904) 445–0852 (Pine Lakes)
(904) 445–3000,
(800) 654–6538 (Resort)
Fax: (904) 445–9685

GOLF COURSE

Director of Golf: Cypress Knoll: Joe Gutterman. Matanzas Woods: Jim Crosbee. Palm Harbor: Bud Burkley. Pine Lakes: Ken Van Leuven

Course Length/Par (All Tees): Cypress Knoll: Back 6591/72, Middle 6261/72, Forward 5386/72. Matanzas Woods: Back 6985/72, White 6514/72, Forward 5336/72. Palm Harbor: Back 6572/72, Middle 6013/72, Forward 5346/72. Pine Lakes: Back 7074/72, White 6122/72, Gold 5526/72, Forward 5166/72

Course Slope/Rating (All Tees): Cypress Knoll: Back 130/71.6, Middle 127/70.0, Forward 117/69.3. Matanzas Woods: Back 132/73.2, Middle 127/71, Ladies' Forward 126/72.1. Palm Harbor: Back 127/71.8, Middle 121/69.2, Ladies' Forward 128/71.2. Pine Lakes: Back 126/73.5, White 121/70, Gold 117/68.9, Ladies' Forward 124/71.4

Course Architects: Cypress Knoll: Gary Player (1991). Matanzas Woods: Arnold Palmer and Ed Seay (1985). Palm Harbor: Bill Amick (1972). Pine Lakes: Arnold Palmer and Ed Seay (1982)

Golf Facilities: Full Pro Shop X, Snack Bar X, Lounge X, Restaurant X, Locker Room X, Showers No, Club Rental X, Club Repair X, Cart Rental X, Instruction X, Practice Green X, Driving Range X, Practice Bunker X, Club Storage X

Tee-Time Reservation Policy: Up to 6 days in advance

Ranger: Yes

Tee-off-Interval Time: Cypress Knoll, Matanzas Woods Palm Harbor, Pine Lakes: 7 min.

Time to Play 18 Holes: 4 to 4½ hrs.

Course Hours/Earliest Tee-off: 7 a.m.

Green and Cart Fees: Cypress Knoll, Matanzas Woods, Palm Harbor, Pine Lakes: $50 for 18 holes with cart

Credit Cards: MasterCard, Visa

Season: Year round. Busiest season Jan. through April

Course Comments: Cart mandatory. Yardage book available for Palm Harbor

Golf Packages: Available through resort

Discounts: Seasonal. Peak season golf fees Jan. through April

Places to Stay Nearby: DAYTONA BEACH: Daytona Beach Marriott (904) 254–8200, (800) 228–9290; Indigo Lakes Resort and Conference Center (904) 258–6333, (800) 223–4161. FLAGLER BEACH: Topaz Motel/Hotel (904) 439–3301. ST. AUGUSTINE: Casa Solana (904) 824–3555; Colony's Ponce de Leon Golf and Conference Resort (904) 824–2821; Kenwood Inn (904) 824–2116

Local Attractions: DAYTONA BEACH: Daytona Beach Kennel Club (greyhound racing), Daytona International Speedway, Marineland of Florida, Museum of Arts and Sciences, Daytona outlet mall, Halifax Historical Society and Museum. ST. AUGUSTINE: Lightner Museum, Museum Theater, oldest house, historical tours. Flagler Beach. Daytona Visitor Tourist Information (904) 255–0415, (800) 854–1234. Augustine Visitor Information Center (904) 824–3334

Directions: From I–95, Exit 91C, turn east off exit ramp on Palm Coast Pkwy. to last right (Palm Harbor Pkwy.) before toll bridge. Make right on Palm Harbor Pkwy. to Sheraton and resort

Closest Commercial Airports: Daytona Beach International(30 min.), Orlando International (1½ hrs.), Jacksonville International (2 hrs.)

RESORT

Date Built: 1969

No. of Rooms: 154 rooms in 4 guest lodges, 68 luxurious fully furnished 2-bedroom villas

Meeting/Exhibit Rooms: 11. Capacity of Largest: 350 persons banquet style. Meeting Space: 13,000 sq. ft.

Room Price Range: $89 for standard to $330 for villa. Golf and other packages available year round

Lounges: Sunspot Beach Club, Henry's Lounge

Restaurants: Champions, Fibber's (at Pine Lakes Country Club), Chip-In (Palm Harbor Golf Club), Par-Tee Room (Matanzas Woods), Players' Grille (Cypress Knoll), Players Cafe (Palm Coast Players Club), Flagler's restaurant, Henry's Good Spirits

Entertainment: Henry's Lounge

Credit Cards: All major cards

General Amenities: Organized children's programs, meeting and conference facilities with support services

Recreational Amenities: Palm Coast Players Club with 18 tennis courts (12 clay [6 lighted], 4 hard [lighted], 2 grass), racquetball, swimming pool, tennis shop, instruction, locker room and showers. Belle Terre Swim and Racquet Club with swimming pool, baby pool, 4 hard surface tennis courts; fitness center with Nautilus, 3 Biocycles, Liferower, treadmills, Life Step machine, locker room and showers, snack bar; 80-slip marina, fishing, water sports, bowling, bicycling, miniature golf, jogging paths, volley ball, billiards, paddle tennis

Reservation and Cancellation Policy: 48-hr. cancellation notice required to avoid penalties

Comments and Restrictions: Taxes and gratuities additional to base rates

PALM COAST RESORT

Palm Coast is a planned community situated on 42,000 acres of land near the Intracoastal Waterway between Daytona Beach and St. Augustine and just over 1 hour from Orlando. The resort features a variety of recreational activities, including fishing, boating, swimming, tennis, bicycling, health club amenities and much more. Four eighteen-hole golf courses, including the private Hammock Dunes Links Course, are within a short distance of the 154-room Sheraton Hotel. An additional 68 2-bedroom villas are also available for rent.

The Matanzas Woods Golf Club is an Arnold Palmer and Ed Seay-designed layout that plays 6985 yards from the back tees. Water can come into play on half the holes on this course, which is exceptionally well maintained. The fairways are mounded, generous and bordered by pines, oaks and cypress. The greens are large, well trapped and medium speed. A challenging run of holes at Matanzas Woods includes numbers thirteen through fifteen. The 179-yard par-3 thirteenth is completely bordered by water on the left, as is the 548-yard par-5, dogleg-right fourteenth that also features Lake Success along the right fairway. The tee shot is to a landing area fronted by water, and the second shot is toward a deep green trapped on both sides. The fifteenth is a formidable 466-yard par 4 that plays to a large, deep green. To the right of the fairway is Lake Success. If you manage these three holes, it is likely you will have a good day at Matanzas Woods. *Golf Digest* rated this course one of the best new resort courses of 1986.

The 7074-yard Pine Lakes Course was also designed by Palmer and Seay. This layout is the longest and most open golf course at the resort and features expansive fairways, generous well-trapped greens, and water can come into play on more than half the holes. A memorable par 3 is the 206-yard eighth that has a two-tiered green with two large traps in front and another to the rear. The other tee distances are a more forgiving 149 and 109 yards. The 530-yard par-5 eighteenth at Pine Lakes is an excellent finishing hole. The first two shots are down a narrow fairway bordered by trees on the left and lakes on the right. Water and three traps protect the green which must be reached on the fly. This course usually requires strong long-iron play.

Cypress Knoll was designed by Gary Player and plays 6591 yards from the back tees. This links-style layout wends its way through pines, hardwood forests, wetlands and features medium-sized greens that enable you to roll the ball on from the fairway. However, if you play from the back tees, the landing areas can be narrow, and water can be a factor on thirteen holes. This course requires accuracy and course management rather than length. This is evident on the first hole, a par-5 number-1-handicap, which plays 546 yards from the back tees. The tee shot must negotiate a narrow fairway and carry water. The second shot is to a wider landing area, but the approach will be buried in traps or deep rough if too much club is used coming into the target.

The 6572-yard Palm Harbor Golf Club was designed by Bill Amick and, having been built in the early 1970s, is the oldest course at Palm Coast. This layout features moderately fast, small- to medium-sized greens with little undulation. All of the greens were recently renovated on Palm Harbor, and the course is in excellent condition. The demanding, tree-lined, narrow fairways at Palm Harbor will most likely put demands on your entire golf game.

All of the golf courses at Palm Coast have practice ranges, instruction and dining facilities available. Golf packages are available through the resort. For a full range of golf, tennis, boating, fishing and other outdoor amenities, Palm Coast is a great place to visit. And there are ample facilities for meetings in over 13,000-square-feet of space that includes ballroom, theater-style, classroom and small meeting room venues. A staff of professional meeting planners is here to assist you.

Jacksonville Area/Northeastern

Course Name: **AMELIA ISLAND PLANTATION Amelia Links: Oakmarsh, Oceanside, Oysterbay, Long Point Courses**

Course Type: Resort
Resort: Amelia Island Plantation
Address: Highway A1A South
Amelia Island, FL 32034
Phone: (800) 874–6878 (Golf Course)
(904) 261–6161, (800) 342–6841 (FL), (800) 874–6878 (Outside FL) (Resort)
Fax: (904) 277–5159 (Resort)

GOLF COURSE

Director of Golf: Ed Tucker
Head Professionals: Long Point: Paul Venditti
Course Length/Par (All Tees): Amelia Links Oakmarsh/Oceanside: Back 6140/71, White 5550/71, Green 5186/71, Forward 4791/71. Oysterbay/Oceanside: Back 6026/71, White 5404/71, Green 5111/71, Forward 4729/71. Oakmarsh/Oysterbay: Back 6502/72, White 5810/72, Green 5521/72, Forward 5058/72. Long Point: Back 6775/72, White 6068/72, Green 5539/72, Forward 4927/72
Course Slope/Rating (All Tees): Amelia Links: Oakmarsh/Oceanside: Back 120/69.3, White 114/66.6, Green 109/65.2, Ladies' Forward 116/68. Oysterbay/Oceanside: Back 117/68.6, White 111/65.8, Green 105/64.3, Ladies' Forward 115/67.6. Oakmarsh/Oysterbay: Back 127/70.7, White 121/67.6, Green 117/66.4, Ladies' Forward 123/69.7. Long Point: Back 127/72.5, White 121/69.5, Green 116/67, Ladies' Forward 121/69.1
Course Architects: Oakmarsh: Pete Dye (1975, renovation, 1989). Oceanside:

Pete Dye (1975). Oysterbay: Pete Dye (1975). Long Point: Tom Fazio (1987)

Golf Facilities: Full Pro Shop X, Snack Bar X, Lounge X, Restaurant X, Locker Room X, Showers X, Club Rental X, Club Repair X, Cart Rental X, Instruction X, Practice Green X, Driving Range X, Practice Bunker X, Club Storage X

Tee-Time Reservation Policy: At time of confirmed reservation at resort

Ranger: Yes

Tee-off-Interval Time: 8 min. at Links; 8 and 9 min. at other courses

Time to Play 18 Holes: 4½ hrs.

Course Hours/Earliest Tee-off: 8 a.m.

Green and Cart Fees: Peak season (mid-Feb. to May): Amelia Links: $87 for 18 holes, $50 for 9 including cart, range balls, club storage. Long Point: $102 for 18 holes, $60 for 9 including cart, range balls, club storage

Credit Cards: MasterCard and Visa

Season: Year round. Busiest season Feb. to May

Course Comments: Cart mandatory. Yardage book available. Must be a guest of Amelia Island Plantation to play the courses

Golf Packages: Availabile year round through resort. Lowest rates mid-Sept. to mid-Nov.

Discounts: Seasonal. Lowest rates June to mid-Feb.

Places to Stay Nearby: Must be a guest of resort or a member to play any of the courses

Local Attractions: Amelia Island Museum of History, walking tour of Fernandina Beach Historic District, shopping, Jacksonville Landing, Little Talbot Island State Park. Amelia Island–Fernandina Beach Chamber of Commerce (904) 261–3248

Directions: I–95 to Fernandina Beach/Callahan exit, turn east on Hwy. A1A, follow signs to Amelia Island Pkwy., which leads to the resort

Closest Commercial Airports: Jacksonville International (45 min.), Savannah International, GA (2½ hrs.), Orlando International (3 hrs.)

RESORT

Date Built: 1972

No. of Rooms: 1100 rooms, suites, villas

Meeting/Exhibit Rooms: 21. Capacity of Largest: 750 persons. Meeting Space: 43,000 sq. ft.

Room Price Range: $191 for lowest 1-bedroom, $722 for highest 3-bedroom villa per night peak season (mid-March to May), based on maximum occupancy of 2 adults per bedroom. Golf and other packages available

Lounges: Admiral's Lounge, Paddle Loft, Sports Bar

Restaurants: Amelia Inn, Veranda at Racquet Park, Beach Club Bar and Grill, Coop, Golf Shop Restaurant, Dunes Club Bar and Grill, Putter Club

Entertainment: Occasional disco at Beach Club Bar and Grill, live music at Admiral's Lounge

Credit Cards: All major cards

General Amenities: Youth recreation program, babysitting, meeting and conference facilities with audiovisual, banquet, secretarial support

Recreational Amenities: Racquet Park with 23 tennis courts, 3 lighted for night play, with pro shop and instruction; health and fitness center with full-service spa, racquet ball, heated indoor lap pool; aerobic, aquadynamic and conditioning classes; fitness consultations, Jacuzzi, workout room with Keiser progressive-resistance strength-training machines, exercycles, treadmill and ski simulator, saunas, steam rooms, whirlpools, massage; fishing, sailing, horseback riding, bicycling, jogging, 20 outdoor pools

Reservation and Cancellation Policy: 10-day cancellation notice required for refund. 1 night's rate required as a deposit to confirm reservations for stays up to 5 nights. 2 nights' rate required for stays over 5 nights. Reservations made for arrival within 10 days must be guaranteed by a major credit card

Comments and Restrictions: Taxes not included in room rates. Daily housekeeping and service fee included in rates

AMELIA ISLAND PLANTATION

Amelia Island Plantation is beautifully situated on 1250 acres of palmetto, pine and live oak forests 30 miles northeast of Jacksonville off the coast of Florida. This is the southernmost of the famed Golden Isles, and it is lush, with expansive marshlands, ocean frontage, rolling terrain, dense forests and natural lagoons. Amelia Links, a 27-hole layout, includes three Pete Dye–designed 9-hole courses. Also located on Amelia Island is the 18-hole Tom Fazio–designed Long Point Course, which traverses woods, marsh, ocean shores, water and natural dune ridges. *Golf Digest* rates the Oakmarsh/Oceanside Course among America's 75 best resort courses, and *Golf* magazine ranks Amelia Island Plantation one of the top 12 golf resorts in America. *Golfweek* ranks Long Point among the best courses in Florida.

At 3308 yards, Oakmarsh is the longest of Dye's three nines. This course is framed by beautiful stands of ancient live oaks and tall pines, which line every fairway. Originally opened in 1975 and redesigned in 1989 by Dye, this new layout is now considered the most demanding nine at Amelia Links. The hole rated most difficult at Oakmarsh is the 540-yard par-5 second, which plays down a corridor of trees to a large green with a large bunker to the right, 80 yards from the putting surface, and another large bunker to the left and in front of it. A large tree blocks the left of the green, making the entrance extremely narrow. The tee-shot landing area has a bunker on the left, and another large fairway bunker is 150 yards from the green. Accuracy and club selection are important on this hole, especially because the approach shot has to be flown onto the green.

The eighth hole is a challenging and memorable 342-yard par 4 that plays over a marsh on the tee shot to a fairway bordered by trees on the left and water on the right. The second shot is back over water to a large green bordered by water to the left and rear. Two traps are on the right. Again, the approach shot has to be very accurate on this hole.

Oceanside is the back nine and plays 2832 yards from the championship tees. Three of the holes on this side are on huge dunes providing a wonderful view of the ocean. One of these is the 341-yard par-4 fourth, which plays to a medium-sized green framed by two traps. The ocean is to the right and a cluster of palm trees is in the landing area from 150 to 100 yards into the green. Tee-shot placement is critical to have a clear second shot at the green. And the ocean wind is always a factor. The seventh is a testing par 5 that has water running along the left side of the fairway to beyond the green, which is very narrow. The fairway is also narrow and is guarded by trees and water on the left and trees and a series of bunkers on the right. Again, accuracy and strategic shot placement are mandatory to score on this golf course.

The 504-yard par-5 finishing hole is bordered from tee to green by water on the left. A slight dogleg left, the tee shot is over water to a landing area bracketed by palm trees. The second shot is toward a very small green backed by trees and protected by a huge trap on the left and slightly to the front. Another fairway bunker is on the left, approximately 80 yards from the green, and on the far right is water that shouldn't come into play.

Both Oakmarsh and Oysterbay have been the site of the Seniors' Tournament and the U.S. Women's Mid-Amateur Tournament. However, many members and guests of Amelia Island Plantation regard Oceanside as the premier track at the Links courses.

Oysterbay plays 3194 yards from the back tees, with marsh coming directly into play on four of the nine holes. The most difficult and possibly most memorable hole on the Oysterbay nine is the 441-yard par-4 eighth, whose tee shot has to carry 150 yards of marsh to reach a fairway protected by marsh on the left and trees on the right, all the way to the green. The small green, which curls to the left in a slight dogleg, is protected left and front by a long bunker. Another smaller bunker is to the right and approximately 30 yards from the green.

Most of the greens at the Amelia Links courses are small and well protected by traps and water. Water hazards and marshes are found on more than half the holes. There is an average of only three sand bunkers per hole, but the tight fairways, water hazards, wind, and small greens make it difficult to score. No matter which combination of nines you play, however, you'll enjoy golfing here. The Amelia Links has its own pro shop, snack bar, restaurant, driving range and putting area. There is a changing room but no locker-room and shower facilities.

Dye was brought to Amelia by Charles Fraser, who began the development of Amelia Plantation in 1972. Dye had previously worked for Fraser at Sea Pines Plantation, creating the highly rated Harbour Town Golf Links. The three Amelia Links nines designed by Dye are remarkably classical in that they are natural and simple compared to some of his later work. You still have to negotiate the narrow fairways to reach relatively small greens, however. Fazio also used the natural contours of Amelia to build the 6775-yard Long Point Course, which opened in 1987. He claims, "There was so much variety there. Any one of those things—ocean, marsh, woods, water, natural dune ridges—make for a good golf course." Because Fazio didn't have to drastically alter the landscape, Long Point looked like a mature golf course from the day it first opened.

The front nine at Long Point is shorter and tighter than the back nine. The most challenging holes are back-to-back par 3s that play along the coastline. The 166-yard sixth plays straight to a deep green with two traps on the right and one to the rear. The ocean is to the right. The 158-yard seventh is also bordered by the ocean on the right and is paralleled by low-lying vegetation on the left. The green is not trapped and is large and surrounded by scraggly dunes. Depending on the wind, anything from a 1-iron to an 8-iron can be used off the tee on these holes.

Wind also makes many of the holes on the more open but longer back nine extremely difficult to reach in regulation. The 440-yard par-4 eighteenth plays straight to a deep green protected by traps to the left and right front of the green. These are very likely to catch the approach shot, especially if a strong wind is blowing. One of the few doglegs on the Long Point Course is the number-1-handicap 540-yard par-5 second hole. The tee shot on this hole plays to a narrow fairway guarded by a large trap on the left. The fairway then bends left and is bordered by marsh. A small green is flanked by a large trap on the left and a long bunker on the right. It is an extremely tight shot to the putting surface because of the small target, well-placed bunkers and nearby marsh, which wraps around the back of it. This is considered to be the signature hole on the course, and justifiably so.

Play on all the courses at Amelia Island Plantation is reserved exclusively for resort guests and club members. Long Point also has its own pro shop, changing room, snack bar and practice facilities. The Amelia Links Golf Shop has received recognition by *Golf Shop Operations* magazine as one of the Best Resort Golf Shops in America. The staff of PGA professionals and assistants can provide individual and group instruction to meet your needs. Both Amelia Links and the Long Point Club provide complete instructional services throughout the year. A variety of golf, tennis and other packages are always available. The lowest-rate season is early September to mid-November, and the highest is mid-March to mid-May.

A golf academy is centered at the Long Point Teaching Pavilion and is conducted for 2- or 3-day sessions by the professional teaching staff at Amelia Island. These sessions are conducted for players of all abilities. Tournament services including customized clinics with Amelia's resident LPGA or PGA tour pro are available. Many meetings can be accommodated by Amelia Island Plantation's 43,000 sq. ft. of meeting space. *Successful Meetings*, *Meetings and Conventions* and *Corporate Meetings and Incentives* magazines have recognized Amelia Island Plantation as a premiere site for conferences.

Tennis magazine rates Amelia one of the top 50 tennis resorts in the United States, and *World Tennis* magazine calls it a five-star tennis resort. Golf, tennis and other packages are offered throughout the year. *Family Circle* magazine has named Amelia Plantation the "Family Beach Resort of the Year," and the resort is rated a Four-Diamond resort by the American Automobile Association and a Four-Star resort by the *Mobil Travel Guide.*

**Course Name: SAWGRASS RESORT
TPC Stadium, TPC Valley,
East, West, South, Marsh
Landing, Oak Bridge
Courses**

Course Type: Resort
Resort: Marriott at Sawgrass Resort
Address: 1000 TPC Boulevard
Ponte Vedra Beach, FL
32082–8118
Phone: (904) 273–3235 (Tournament
Players Club)
(904) 287–2261(Sawgrass
Country Club)
(904) 285–6469 (Marsh
Landing)
(904) 285–7777 (Oak
Bridge)
(800) 457–GOLF (Resort)
Fax: (904) 285–0906 (Resort)

GOLF COURSE

Directors of Golf: TPC: Chuck Bombard. Sawgrass Country Club: Joe Burch. Oak Bridge: Tom Aycock. Marsh Landing: Dewey Arnett

Head Professional: Mark Barlow

Course Length/Par (All Tees): TPC Stadium: Back, 6857/72, Blue 6394/72, White 5761/72, Forward 5034/72. TPC Valley: Back 6838/71, Blue 6491/71, White 6027/71, Forward 5114/71. East/West: Back 6900/72, Blue 6438/72, White 6019/72, Forward 5128/72. West/South: Back 6864/72, Blue 6461/72, White 6023/72, Forward 5118/72. South/East: Back 6916/72, Blue 6503/72, White 6062/72, Forward 5176/72. Marsh Landing: Back 6841/72, Blue 6443/72, White 6001/72, Ladies'

Forward 4985/72. Oak Bridge: Back 6383/70, White 6031/70, Green 5504/70, Forward 4869/70

Course Slope/Rating (All Tees): TPC Stadium: Back NA/74, Blue NA/71.9, White NA/68.7, Forward NA/64.7. TPC Valley: Back NA/72.6, Blue NA/70.9, White NA/69.0, Forward NA/63.8. East/West: Back 136/73.8, Blue 132/71.8, White 126/70.0, Ladies' Forward 118/70.5. West/South: Back 134/73.1, Blue 131/71.3, White 126/69.3, Ladies' Forward 115/69.5. South/East: Back 136/73.8, Blue 132/72.0, White 127/70.0, Ladies' Forward 118/69.9. Marsh Landing: Back 131/72.7, Blue 128/70.8, White 123/68.6, Ladies' Forward 120/68.6. Oak Bridge: Back 126/70.3, White 123/68.8, Green 119/66.4, Ladies' Forward 117/67.8

Course Architects: TPC Stadium: Pete Dye (1982). TPC Valley: Pete Dye with Bobby Weed (1987). East/West/South: Ed Seay (1974), Gardner Dickinson (renovation, 1977), Ed Seay (renovation, 1991). Marsh Landing: Arnold Palmer, Ed Seay and Harrison Minchew (1986). Oak Bridge: Ed Seay (1973)

Golf Facilities: Full Pro Shop X, Snack Bar X, Lounge X, Restaurant X, Locker Room X, Showers X, Club Rental X, Club Repair X, Cart Rental X, Instruction X, Practice Green X, Driving Range X, Practice Bunker X, Club Storage X

Tee-Time Reservation Policy: At time of reservation at resort up to 30 days in advance

Ranger: Yes

Tee-off-Interval Time: TPC courses: 8 and 9 min. Other courses: 7 and 8 min.

Time to Play 18 Holes: 4½ hrs.

Course Hours/Earliest Tee-off: 7:30 a.m. to 8 a.m. depending on season

Green Fees: Peak season (March to mid-May): TPC Stadium: $135 for 18 holes. TPC Valley: $80 for 18 holes. East/West/South: $120 for 18 holes. Marsh Landing: $156 for 18 holes with cart. Oak Bridge: $80 for 18 holes with cart

Cart Fees: Peak Season: TPC courses: $21 for 18 holes, East/West/South: $22 for 18 holes

Credit Cards: All major cards

Season: Year round. Busiest season March to May

Course Comments: Cart mandatory, except can walk East/West/South after 4:30 p.m. Yardage book available

Golf Packages: Available through resort

Discounts: Seasonal. Peak season generally March through May

Places to Stay Nearby: PONTE VEDRA BEACH: Lodge at Ponte Vedra Beach (904) 273–9500, (800) 243–4304. JACKSONVILLE: Jacksonville Omni (904) 355–6664, (800) 843–6664; Marina at St. Johns Place (904) 396–5100; Comfort Suites Hotel (904) 739–1155, (800) 228–5150. ST. AUGUSTINE: Sheraton Palm Court (904) 445–3000, (800) 325–3535; Casa Solana (904) 824–3555; Colony's Ponce de Leon Golf and Conference Resort (904) 824–2821, (800) 228–2821

Local Attractions: St. Augustine, Marineland, Jacksonville Landing, deep-sea fishing. JACKSONVILLE: Florida Performing Arts Center, Jacksonville Symphony Orchestra, Cummer Gallery of Art, Jacksonville Zoo, Kingsley Plantation (Fort St. George Island), Alhambra Dinner Theater, Class AA Southern League baseball, Fort Caroline National Memorial, Gator Bowl, Jacksonville Art Museum, Jacksonville Museum of Science and Industry. Fernandina Beach. Amelia Island. Jacksonville and Jacksonville Beaches Convention and Visitors Bureau (904) 353–9736

Directions: I-95, exit at J. Turner Butler Blvd. (State Rd. 202), continue east 14 mi. across Intracoastal Waterway to the beach, south on A1A (3 mi.) to resort on the right

Closest Commercial Airports: Jacksonville International (1 hr.), Orlando International (3 hrs.)

RESORT

Date Built: 1987

No. of Rooms: 520, including hotel rooms, suites and guest rooms in villas

Meeting Rooms: 18. Capacity of Largest: 550 persons banquet style. Meeting Space: 35,000 sq. ft.

Room Price Range: $185 for hotel room to $235 for suites double occupancy (peak season mid-Mar. to mid-May). Golf packages available

Lounges: Champ's Lounge, Cascades

Restaurants: Augustine Grill, Cafe on the Green, 100th Hole

Entertainment: Piano bar, live band or disc jockey in Changes Lounge

Credit Cards: All major cards

General Amenities: Supervised children's programs, Sawgrass Village retail stores, meeting and convention facilities with audiovisual and food services

Recreational Amenities: 19 clay, grass, hard courts with instruction, pro shop available; 3 outdoor swimming pools, fishing in 350 acres of fresh-water lakes and ponds, or sea fishing; 2 fitness centers with Universal workout system, rowing machines, aerobics, sauna, and other facilities; horseback riding, nature and bicycling trails, Wellness Center for advanced corporate conditioning, beaches, boating, snorkeling, swimming

Reservation and Cancellation Policy: Credit card registration required to hold room. Cancellation notice required 2 days prior to scheduled arrival date to avoid penalties

Comments and Restrictions: Taxes additional to base rates

SAWGRASS RESORT

Sawgrass is definitely a place for the golfing gourmand. There are 99 holes of golf here, including the famous Pete Dye–designed Tournament Players Club (TPC) Stadium Course. This 6857-yard par-72 layout opened in 1980 to mixed reviews. The professionals didn't particularly like the small, contoured greens; mounds and depressions in some fairways; steep slopes around some of the greens; and the condition that the heavily played layout is in when the pros show up to play the Players Championship in March. The PGA Tour, which owns the course, has spent several million dollars in the past 10 years to modify it. Meanwhile, *Golf Digest* and *Golf* magazines rank TPC Sawgrass among the best golf courses in the country. Many people don't like Pete Dye's courses, partly because they are difficult and have their various quirks, and partly because some of his designs seem to make more of a fashion statement than a golf statement. However this is one of the best golf courses open to the public in the United States.

Water and numerous bunkers of every size and configuration are found on this demanding test of golf. You have a choice of four distances ranging from 6857 to 5034 yards. Possibly the most difficult par 5 at the TPC Stadium Course is the 454-yard par-4 fifth, which plays over water and waste bunkers to a tee-shot landing area guarded by a waste bunker on the right and another waste bunker ahead, and a pond to the left. The approach is to a medium-sized green fronted on the right by a huge waste bunker and guarded on the left by three more bunkers and trees.

The three finishing holes at the TPC Stadium Course will make your visit here especially memorable. The tee shot of the 497-yard par-5 sixteenth is to a landing area guarded by a huge waste bunker to the right. The next shot is toward a deep green with a large pond running up to and in back of it on the right. To the left of the green are a few small pot bunkers. The big hitter will be tempted to go for the green in two, but the approach shot is a potential disaster if it strays.

The 132-yard par-3 seventeenth is the ultimate target hole on a target golf course. The tee shot is all carry to an island green with a bunker to the front right. With a bit of wind, this hole tests any golfer's nerves. The 440-yard par-4 finishing hole is bordered by water on the left from tee to green. This slight dogleg left requires a well-positioned, long drive to leave a mid-iron approach to a medium-sized green guarded left and rear by five bunkers. The water is very close to the green on the left.

The TPC Stadium Course and the slightly easier Dye–designed TPC Valley Course, part of the Tournament Players Club which is accessible to Marriott guests, are served by the same clubhouse, with all the amenities. The Sawgrass Country Club has its own clubhouse and three excellent nines designed by Ed Seay. These courses, the East, West and South, are just across Route A1A and used to be the site of the Tournament Players Championship before the TPC Stadium Course opened. The East/West combination was used for that tournament, and this 6900-yard layout is ranked among the best resort golf courses in America by *Golf Digest*. These layouts feature water hazards on most of the holes, an abundance of strategically placed bunkers, and medium-sized to large, fast, undulating greens. These are more traditional courses and can be very difficult from the back tees, especially during the windy winter months. Seay returned in 1991 to remodel some of the holes on this layout, which he considers his signature golf course.

There are many memorable holes at the Sawgrass Country Club. The 210-yard par-3 sixth hole on the West nine, for example, is almost all carry over water to a wide, shallow green well protected by bunkers to the front and rear and water to the left. You have a choice of four tee distances on these layouts, and you can walk the courses after 4:30 p.m. The Sawgrass Country Club, like the TPC, has its own clubhouse, with complete practice facilities and instruction available.

There are two more Seay-designed golf courses: the Oak Bridge Golf Club and the Marsh Landing Country Club. You can stay at the Lodge at Ponte Vedra Beach and play these courses, or you can stay at the Marriott. Marsh Landing is laid out near the Intracoastal Waterway in marshlands rich with birds and other wildlife. Playing this course will give you the feeling of being in a beautiful nature preserve. These courses have their own complete clubhouse and practice facilities.

Golf packages are available through the Marriott, which has complete resort amenities. It has swimming pools, 2½ miles of beach with various water sports ranging from snorkeling to water-skiing; horseback riding, Har-Tru tennis courts with professional instruction, restaurants and children's activity programs. There is also a fitness center with sauna, steam room, Jacuzzi and spa facilities.

The Marriott is a favorite meeting and conference spot, with over 35,000 sq. ft. of meeting space. The resort has won the Gold Tee Award from *Meetings and Conventions* magazine for its outstanding golf and meeting capabilities. It has also been rated a Four-Diamond resort by the American Automobile Association. It is a *Mobil Travel Guide* Four-Star Resort. *Golf* magazine awarded the Marriott at Sawgrass a Silver Medal Award as one of the best golf resorts in America. *Better Homes and Gardens* has rated the Marriott at Sawgrass one of America's top 50 favorite family resorts.

Course Name: WINDSOR PARKE GOLF CLUB

Course Type: Semiprivate
Address: 4747 Hodges Boulevard
Jacksonville, FL 32224
Phone: (904) 223-4653

GOLF COURSE

Head Professional: Tim Mervosh
Course Length/Par (All Tees): Back 6740/72, Blue 6435/72, White 6043/72, Forward 5206/72
Course Slope/Rating (All Tees): Back 133/71.9, Blue 130/70.5, White 126/68.7, Ladies' White 133/74, Ladies' Forward 123/69.4
Course Architect: Arthur Hills (1990)
Golf Facilities: Full Pro Shop X, Snack Bar X, Lounge X, Restaurant X, Locker Room X, Showers X, Club Rental X, Club Repair X, Cart Rental X, Instruction X, Practice Green X, Driving Range X, Practice Bunker X, Club Storage X
Tee-Time Reservation Policy: Members: Up to 7 days in advance. Public: Up to 5 days in advance
Ranger: Yes
Tee-off-Interval Time: 10 min.
Time to Play 18 Holes: 4 hrs., 15 min.
Course Hours/Earliest Tee-off: 7 a.m.

Green and Cart Fees: $55 for 18 holes with cart Sat., Sun., holidays; $47 with cart weekdays. $27.50 for 9 holes with cart Sat., Sun., holidays; $24.50 for 9 holes with cart weekdays
Credit Cards: American Express, MasterCard, Visa
Season: Year round. Busiest season March to May
Course Comments: Can walk after 4 p.m. Pull carts not allowed. Memberships available
Golf Packages: Available through golf course
Discounts: Seasonal. Residents
Places to Stay Nearby: Marriott at Sawgrass (904) 285-7777, (800) 457-GOLF; Holiday Inn Bay Meadows, (904) 737-1700, (800) HOLIDAY; Comfort Suites Hotel (904) 739-1155, (800) 228-5150; Omni (904) 355-6664, (800) 843-4664; Lodge at Ponte Vedra Beach (904) 273-9500, (800) 243-4304; Residence Inn—Bay Meadows by Marriott (904) 733-8088, (800) 331-3131
Local Attractions: St. Augustine, Marineland, Jacksonville Landing, deep-sea fishing. JACKSONVILLE: Florida Performing Arts Center, Jacksonville Symphony Orchestra, Cummer Gallery of Art, Jacksonville Zoo, Kingsley Plantation (Fort St. George Island), Alhambra Dinner Theater, Class AA Southern League baseball, NFL football, Fort Caroline National Memorial, Gator Bowl, Jacksonville Art Museum, Jacksonville Museum of Science and Industry. Fernandina Beach. Amelia Island. Jacksonville and Jacksonville Beaches Convention and Visitors Bureau (904) 353-9736
Directions: From downtown Jacksonville. I-95 south to J. Turner Butler Blvd., east 8 to 10 mi. to Hodges Blvd. exit, first right off Hodges
Closest Commercial Airports: Jacksonville International (45 min.), Orlando International (2½ hrs.)

WINDSOR PARKE

Windsor Parke is an Arthur Hills-designed 6740-yard par-72 layout on what used to be a tree farm in Jacksonville, Florida. The golf course features medium-sized, fast Bermuda grass greens with some undulation. Water hazards appear on half the holes, but most of them parallel somewhat straight fairways. Each hole is an individual experience, and the few parallel holes on the course are well-separated by majestic oaks and pines. Because of the many stands of mature trees, Windsor Parke is reminiscent of a North Carolina golf course. The terrain on this layout is rolling, with marshes and inland waterways adding to its beauty and challenge. Windsor Parke was rated the best new public course in the Southeast in 1991 and fourth nationally by *Golf Digest* magazine in 1991.

The number-1-handicap hole on the course is the 457-yard par-4 seventh hole, which plays straight to a deep green protected by a large bunker and a stream on the left. Water crosses in front of the tee and runs up the left side of the fairway. The right side is completely bordered by trees.

Windsor Parke is an extremely well maintained golf course. The entire course including the rough is overseeded in the winter. The tee-off intervals are a generous 10 min. (partly because the second hole is a traffic-stopping par 3), and the current policy is to keep the number of rounds played at approximately 40,000 per year. Because of the quality of the golf course and its maintenance, U.S. Open Qualifiers, Mid-Amateur events, the National Junior Golf Association Tournament and Public Links events have been held here.

Windsor Parke started out as part of a mixed-use development but has been sold to a separate limited partnership. Memberships in the club are available, with the target being 300 members. A residential development is near the course, and hotels have been constructed in the area.

The clubhouse has full amenities, including locker rooms, a restaurant, dining room and complete pro shop. Instruction is available from the staff of professionals at the nearby driving range, practice chipping and bunker area, and at the putting green. The official tee-time reservation policy for non-members is 5 days in advance, but golfers

coming in from out of town can get more lead time.

Recommended Golf Courses in Florida

Within 1 Hour of Jacksonville:

Cimarrone Golf & Country Club, Jacksonville, (904) 287–2000, Semiprivate, 18/6891/72

Deerfield Lakes Golf Course, Callahan, (904) 879–1210, Public, 18/6700/72

Eagle Harbor Golf Club, Orange Park, (904) 269–9300, Semiprivate, 18/6840/72

The Golf Club at Amelia Island, Amelia Island, (904) 277–8015, Resort, 18/6681/72

Haile Plantation Golf and Country Club, Gainesville, (904) 335–0555, Semiprivate, 18/6526/72

Halifax Plantation Golf Club, Ormond Beach, (904) 676–9600, 18/7128/72

Meadowbrook Golf Club, Gainesville, (904) 332–0577, Semiprivate, 18/6289/72

Ponce de Leon Resort, St. Augustine, (904) 829–5314, (800) 228–2821, Resort, 18/6925/72

Ponte Vedra Inn and Club, Ponte Vedra Beach, (904) 285–6911, Resort. Ocean: 18/6515/72. Lagoon: 18/5574/70

Ravines Golf and Country Club, Middleburg, (904) 282–7888, 18/6784/72

St. Johns Country Club Course, St. Augustine, (904) 825–4900, Public, 18/6949/72

Northwestern

Course Name:	**BAY POINT YACHT AND COUNTRY CLUB Lagoon Legend, Club Meadows Courses**
Course Type:	Resort
Resort:	Marriott's Bay Point Resort
Address:	100 Delwood Beach Road Panama City Beach, FL 32411–7207
Phone:	(904) 235–6909 (Golf Course) (904) 234–3307, (800) 874–7105 (Resort)
Fax:	(904) 233–1308 (Resort)

GOLF COURSE

Director of Golf: Tom Weaver

Course Length/Par (All Tees): Lagoon Legend: Back 6942/72, Blue 6469/72, White 6079/72, Gold 5614/72, Forward 4949/72. Club Meadows: Back 6913/72, White 6372/72, Red 5634/72, Forward 4999/72

Course Slope/Rating (All Tees): Lagoon Legend: Back 152/75.3, Blue 148/73, White 144/70.7, Ladies' Gold 135/74, Ladies' Forward 127/69.8. Club Meadows: Back 120/72.5, White 116/70.1, Red 116/69.1, Forward 113/68

Course Architects: Lagoon Legend: Bruce Devlin and Robert von Hagge (1985). Club Meadows: Willard Byrd (1971)

Golf Facilities: Full Pro Shop X, Snack Bar X, Lounge X, Restaurant X, Locker Room X, Showers X, Club Rental X, Club Repair X, Cart Rental X, Instruction X, Practice Green X, Driving Range X, Practice Bunker X, Club Storage X

Tee-Time Reservation Policy: Resort Guests: Up to 60 days in advance. Public: Up to 2 weeks in advance

Ranger: Yes

Tee-off-Interval Time: 8 min.

Time to Play 18 Holes: 4½ hrs.

Course Hours/Earliest Tee-off: 6:46 a.m.

Green and Cart Fees: Public: $75 for 18 holes with cart peak season (mid-Apr. to mid-June). Resort guests slightly lower

Credit Cards: American Express, Master-Card, Visa

Season: Year round. Busiest season Feb. to April

Course Comments: Cart mandatory. Yardage book available for Lagoon Legend

Golf Packages: Available year round through resort. Lowest rates Nov. to Feb.

Discounts: Seasonal (Mid-June to mid-Apr.). Juniors. Resort guests

Places to Stay Nearby: Edgewater Beach Resort (904) 235–4044, (800) 874–8686; Sandestin Beach Resort (904) 267–8000, (800) 277–0800; Village Inn (904) 837–7413; Summer Breeze (904) 837–4853, (800) 874–8914

Local Attractions: Shipwreck Island Water Park, Ebro greyhound racing, bicycling, boating, diving, fishing, sailing, tennis, Miracle Strip Amusement Park, St. Andrews State Recreation Area, Shell Island, Falling Waters State Recreation Area. Destin. Pensacola. Fort Walton Beach. Panama City Beach Convention and Visitors Bureau (904) 233–6583, (800) PCBEACH

Directions: I–10 to Hwy. 231 south, to 23rd St., take right on Hwy. 98 to Thomas Dr., left on Thomas Dr. to Magnolia, left on Magnolia, follow the signs to the resort

Closest Commercial Airports: Bay County, Panama City (15 min.), Tallahassee Municipal (2 hrs.), Pensacola Municipal (2 hrs.), Mobile Regional, AL (3 hrs.); Montgomery, AL (4 hrs.), Orlando International (7 hrs.)

RESORT

Date Built: 1986

No. of Rooms: 355 guest rooms and suites, including 155 1- and 2-bedroom lake and fairway suites

Meeting/Exhibit Rooms: 14. Capacity of Largest: 650 persons banquet style. Meeting Space: 25,000 sq. ft.

Room Price Range: $94 to $294 for 2-bedroom suite double occupancy. Peak season (mid-Apr. to mid-June.). Golf and other packages available

Lounges: Circe's, Terrace Court, Bay Breeze Pool Bar, 19th Hole, Dockers

Restaurants: Fiddler's Green, Stormy's, Teddy's Terrace Court, Greenhouse, Sunset Grill and Pub, 19th Hole, Dockers

Entertainment: Band at Bay Breeze Pool Bar, live entertainment and dancing at Circe's, piano music in Magnolia Court

Credit Cards: All major cards except Discover

General Amenities: Children's programs (ages 5 to 12), Bay Town shops and 5 resort specialty shops, riverboat excursions, meeting and conference facilities with audiovisual and banquet services

Recreational Amenities: Club Meadows Health Club with sauna, steam room, massage, Jacuzzi, workout room; stocked fishing pond; Bay Point Sports Park with croquet court, bumper boats, arcade, miniature golf, batting cages; tennis center with 12 courts; hotel health club with Jacuzzis, massage; bicycling, beach volleyball, game room, sailing, snorkeling, parasailing, 145-slip marina, 6 swimming pools (1 indoor), beaches on Gulf of Mexico, motor scooters

Reservation and Cancellation Policy: 1 night's deposit or major credit card to hold room. 10-day cancellation notice prior to arrival to cancel without risk of penalty

Comments and Restrictions: Golf packages require 2-night minimum stay and are for 2 persons. 3-night minimum on holiday weekends. Taxes additional to base rates

BAY POINT YACHT AND COUNTRY CLUB

Marriott's Bay Point Resort is beautifully situated on 1100 acres of land amid a wildlife sanctuary. It boasts 2.6 miles of waterfront, 3.1 miles of winding canals, and 32 ponds along the white sands of the Gulf of Mexico just south of Pensacola, Florida. This resort has been named one of the top resorts in America by *World Tennis* and *Golf Illustrated* magazines. *Better Homes and Gardens* rates it one of America's favorite family resorts.

Bay Point is located on a private peninsula nestled between the Grand Lagoon and St. Andrews Bay. The golf facilities at Bay Point include the Bruce Devlin and Robert von Hagge–designed 6942-yard Lagoon Legend, which at 152 has one of the highest slope ratings in the country. This beautiful and difficult test of golf has water hazards on almost every hole, is well bunkered and is often affected by winds coming off the Gulf. The Bermuda greens, which are overseeded with a rye/bentgrass/pampas mixture in winter, are large, moderately fast and somewhat undulating. The number-1-handicap hole on the Lagoon Legend is the 450-yard par-4 third hole, which plays straight to a medium-sized green surrounded by traps. There tends to be a crosswind on this hole, and the green is somewhat plateaued and difficult to hold, making it a very difficult par 4.

The back nine starts out with a tricky 376-yard par-4 dogleg right. The tee shot has to avoid water on the right, and the second shot is over water to a small green with water front, right and rear. A large sand trap guards the left side of the putting surface, which slopes a bit forward and has a small terrace to the back and left.

The two most difficult holes on this side are the fourteenth and fifteenth, both par 4s. The 434-yard fourteenth is a dogleg right, with a water hazard and huge waste bunker on the right from in front of the tee to approximately 125 yards from the green. The narrow, deep putting surface is guarded by a large trap in back and a pond to the right and front. The tee shot has to avoid the water and sand on the right. The approach shot has very little margin for error, especially if the pin is to the rear and tucked between the water and the trap. The front of the green has a higher tier than the back, and the wind often makes the hole play longer. The 454-yard fifteenth plays over water, and the tee shot has to clear a series of fairway mounds to have a reasonable approach shot to the green. The approach shot is to a side-angled, narrow, deep green with a trap to the rear and a huge bunker to the left and forward. If the pin position is to the rear and left, the approach shot is extremely difficult. Lagoon Legend is ranked among the 20 best public and private golf courses in Florida by *Golf Digest.*

The Club Meadows Course was designed by William Byrd and is more tightly treed than is Lagoon Legend, with many doglegs and small but flat, well-bunkered greens. Water comes into play on only a few holes, including the 421-yard par-4 finishing hole. This is a slight dogleg right that plays over a marsh to a landing area flanked by two traps. The approach shot is to a green protected by two traps and marshes left and right. Another difficult par 4 on Club Meadows is the 443-yard tenth, which is probably the toughest hole on the course. This hole plays straight to a narrow, deep green with a large trap to the left. The wind is often into the golfer's face, making this hole play much longer than the yardage would indicate.

There is a clubhouse for each golf course at Marriott's Bay Point Resort. Each has a pro shop, restaurant and a putting green nearby. Only the Club Meadows has locker rooms, showers and a driving range. Instruction is available on an individual or group basis. Golf clinics are offered by the staff of professionals and assistants. A variety of golf packages are offered year round, with the lowest rates available November through February. The public can play the course anytime and resort guests can reserve tee times up to 60 days in advance. Your best bet, however, is one of reasonable golf packages at Bay Point.

Bay Point's Yacht Club has 145 slips and berths sized for yachts to 120 feet in a 12-acre protected cove. A major fishing event here is the Bay Point Billfish Invitational held every July. Tournament, and the Panama City Beach Fishing Rodeo. King, mackerel, bluefish, red snapper, tuna, dolphin, sailfish and marlin are some of the popular sporting fish pursued here. Sailing charters, fishing charters and sunset cruises can easily be arranged at Bay Point.

Meeting and conference facilities at the resort have earned a Gold Tee Award from *Meetings and Conventions* magazine. Bay Point's 25,000-square-foot meeting space can accommodate banquets for as many as 650 persons. It is the largest meeting and convention complex on Florida's northern Gulf Coast.

For excellent golf and family recreation at a reasonable price, Marriott's Bay Point Resort is a place to consider.

Course Name: **SANDESTIN BEACH HILTON GOLF AND TENNIS RESORT Baytowne, Burnt Pine, Links Courses**

Course Type: Resort
Resort: Sandestin Beach Hilton Golf and Tennis Resort
Address: 9300 Highway 98 West Destin, FL 32541

Phone: (904) 267–8155 (Baytowne), (904) 267–6500 (Burnt Pine), (904) 267–8144 (Links), (800) 277–0800 (Resort)
Fax: (904) 267–6505 (Burnt Pine), (904) 267–8222 (Resort)

GOLF COURSE

Director of Golf: Bruce Gerlander

Head Professionals: Dave Lebarre (Baytowne), Mathew Lindley (Burnt Pine), J. D. Schlotterback (Links)

Course Length/Par (All Tees): Baytowne: Troon/Dunes: Back 7185/72, Blue 6537/72, White 5969/72, Forward 5158/72. Dunes/Harbor: Back 6891/72, Blue 6270/72, White 5729/72, Forward 4862/72. Harbor/Troon: Back 6891/72, Blue 6417/72, White 5780/72, Forward 4884/72. Burnt Pine: Back 7046/72, Three 6524/72, Two 5950/72, Forward 5096/72. Links: Back 6710/72, Blue 6265/72, White 5777/72, Forward 4969/72

Course Slope/Rating (All Tees): Baytowne: Troon/Dunes: Back 128/74.6, Blue 123/72.2, White 118/69.1, Forward 115/69.1. Dunes/Harbor: Back 127/73.4, Blue 121/71.1, White 116/68.1, Forward 114/68.5. Harbor/Troon: Back 127/73.9, Blue 122/71.7, White 118/64.1, Forward 113/68.2. Burnt Pine: Back 135/74.1, Three 130/71.5, Two 124/68.3, Forward 122/69.4. Links: Back 124/72.8, Blue 120/70.8, White 116/68.7, Forward 115/69.2

Course Architects: Baytowne: Tom Jackson (18, 1985, 9, 1987). Burnt Pine: Rees Jones (1994). Links: Tom Jackson (1976)

Golf Facilities: Full Pro Shop X, Snack Bar X, Lounge X, Restaurant X, Locker Room No, Showers No, Club Rental X, Club Repair X, Cart Rental X, Instruction X, Practice Green X, Driving Range X, Practice Bunker X, Club Storage X

Tee-Time Reservation Policy: Up to 7 days in advance for Sandestin guests with confirmed reservations. Up to 24

hours for the public. Package guests and owners, anytime

Ranger: Yes

Tee-off-Interval Time: 10 min.

Time to Play 18 Holes: 4 hrs.

Course Hours/Earliest Tee-off: 7:30 a.m.

Green and Cart Fees: Burnt Pines: $105 plus tax for 18 holes for the public; Bay-towne, Links: $75 plus tax for 18 holes for the public, peak season

Credit Cards: All major cards

Season: Year round. Highest rates early March to early Aug., lowest early Nov. to late Jan.

Course Comments: Can walk anytime at full fee. Yardage books. Burnt Pine usually closed Monday. Only members may use Burnt Pine practice facility without a tee time

Golf Packages: Through resort

Discounts: Twilight. Resort guests

Places to Stay Nearby: DESTIN: Days Inn (904) 837–2599; SANDESTIN: Sandestin Beach Resort (904) 267–0800, (800) 277–0800; FORT WALTON BEACH: Holiday Inn (904) 243–9181, (800) HOLI-DAY; Marina Bay Resort (904) 244–5132

Local Attractions: Beaches, water sports, boating, fishing, camping, hiking, shelling, Destin Fishing Museum, Museum of the Sea and Indian, Eden State Gardens, Seaside Peninsula. Fort Walton Beach. Valparaiso. Niceville. Panama City Beach. Pensacola. Destin Chamber of Commerce (904) 837–6241. Walton County Chamber of Commerce (904) 892–3191

Directions: The resort is 20 miles east of Fort Walton Beach and north of Destin on Hwy. 98

Closest Commercial Airports: Pensacola (70 min.), Fort Walton Beach (35 min.), Panama City (50 min.)

Recommended Golf Courses in Florida

Within 2 Hours of Panama City:

Bluewater Bay, Niceville, (904) 897–3241, (800) 874–2128, Resort. Magnolia/Marsh: 18/6669/72. Bay/Lake: 18/6803/72

Club at Hidden Creek, Navarre, (904) 939–4604, Semiprivate, 18/6878/72

Emerald Bay Golf and Country Club, Destin, (904) 837–5197, Semiprivate, 18/6800/72

Hombre Golf Club, Panama City, (904) 234–3673, Semiprivate, 18/6842/72

Indian Bayou Golf and Country Club, Destin, (904) 837–6191, Semiprivate, 18/6952/72

Killearn Country Club and Inn, Tallahassee, (904) 893–2144, (800) 476–4101(FL) (800) 362–7287 (U.S.), Resort. South: 9/3532/36. East: 9/3493/36. North: 9/3367/36

Marcus Pointe, Pensacola, (904) 484–9770, Public, 18/6730/72

The Moors Golf Club, Milton, (904) 995–4653, (800) 727–1010, Public, 18/6956/72

Perdido Bay Golf Club, Pensacola, (904) 492–1223, (800) 874–5355, Public, 18/7154/72

Santa Rosa Golf and Beach Club, Santa Rosa Beach,(904) 267–2229, Public, 18/6608/72

Seascape Resort, Destin, (904) 654–7888, (800) 874–9106, Resort, 18/6762/72

Shalimar Pointe Golf and Country Club, Shalimar, (904) 651–1416, (800) 964–2833, Semiprivate, 18/6760/72

Tiger Pointe Golf and Country Club, Gulf Breeze, (904) 932–1333, Semiprivate. West: 18/6744/71. East: 18/7033/72

Tampa/St. Petersburg Area

Course Name: INNISBROOK Copperhead, Island, Sandpiper Golf Courses

Course Type: Resort

Resort: Innisbrook Hilton Resort

Address: U.S. Highway 19
P. O. Drawer 1088
Tarpon Springs, FL 34688–1088

Phone: (813) 942–2000,
(800) 456–2000 (U.S.,

Canada) (Golf Course)
(813) 942–2000 (Resort)
Fax: (813) 942–5577 (Resort)

GOLF COURSE

Head Professional: Jay Overton
Course Length/Par (All Tees): Copperhead: Back 7087/71, Blue 6536/71, White 6149/71, Forward 5506/71. Island: Back 6999/72, Middle 6557/72, Forward 5943/72. Sandpiper One/Two: Back 5969/70, Middle 5524/70, Forward 4733/70. Sandpiper Two/Three: Back 6210/70, Middle 5726/70, Forward 4926/70. Sandpiper Three/One: Back 6245/70, Middle 5788/70, Forward 5001/70
Course Slope/Rating (All Tees): Copperhead: Back 140/74.4, Blue 132/71.9, White 125/70.41, Ladies' Forward 128/72. Island: Back 133/73.2, Middle 129/71.3, Ladies' Forward 130/74.1. Sandpiper One/Two: Back 122/68.7, Middle 116/66.4, Ladies' Forward 115/66.9. Sandpiper Two/Three: Back 125/69.8, Middle 119/67.4, Ladies' Forward 116/68.1. Sandpiper Three/One: Back 119/69.8, Middle 115/67.6, Ladies' Forward 115/68.4
Course Architects: Copperhead: Edward Lawrence Packard (1972). Island: Edward Lawrence Packard (1970). Sandpiper: Sandpiper One/Two/Three: Edward Lawrence Packard (1971)
Golf Facilities: Full Pro Shop X, Snack Bar X, Lounge X, Restaurant X, Locker Room X, Showers X, Club Rental X, Club Repair X, Cart Rental X, Instruction X, Practice Green X, Driving Range X, Practice Bunker X, Club Storage X
Tee-Time Reservation Policy: After registration, 48 hrs. in advance of desired tee time. Reciprocity for members of country clubs 1 time per yr.
Ranger: Yes
Tee-off-Interval Time: 8 min. and 9 min.
Time to Play 18 Holes: 4½ hrs.
Course Hours/Earliest Tee-off: 7:30 a.m.
Green and Cart Fees: Peak Season: Island: $110 for 18 holes with cart. Sandpiper: $95 for 18 holes with cart.

Copperhead: $130 for 18 holes with cart. Lowest rates end of May to Nov.
Credit Cards: All major cards
Season: Year round. Busiest season Jan. to March, Oct. to early Nov.
Course Comments: Cart mandatory. Yardage books available for all courses. Must be a resort guest, member, or guest of member or have reciprocal play privileges to play golf course. Golf institute on site
Golf Packages: Available year round through resort. Lowest rates end of May to Nov..
Discounts: Seasonal (end of May to early Sept.). Lower rates for repeat rounds
Places to Stay Nearby: TARPON SPRINGS: Quality Inn (813) 934–5781, (800) 228–5151. TAMPA: Courtyard by Marriott (813) 874–0555, (800) 321–2211; Crown Sterling Suites Hotel—Tampa Airport (813) 873–8675, (800) 433–4600; Holiday Inn Busch Gardens (813) 971–4710, (800) HOLIDAY; Hyatt Regency Tampa (813) 225–1234, (800) 233–1234; Radisson Bay Harbor Inn (813) 281–8900, (800) 333–3333; Sheraton Grand Hotel Tampa—Westshore (813) 286–4400, (800) 325–3535; Wyndham Harbour Island Hotel (813) 229–5000, (800) WYNDHAM. ST. PETERSBURG: Best Western—North (813) 522–3191, (800) 528–1234. ST. PETERSBURG BEACH: Don Cesar (813) 360–1881, (800) 247–9810; St. Petersburg Beach Hilton Inn (813) 360–1811, (800) 445–8667; Stouffer Renaissance (813) 894–1000, (800) HOTELS-1; Tradewinds Resort (813) 367–6461, (800) 237–0707. WESLEY CHAPEL: Saddlebrook Resort (813) 973–1111, (800) 729–8383
Local Attractions: TAMPA: Lowry Park Zoological Garden, Museum of Science and Industry, Tampa Museum of Art, University of South Florida, fishing, boating, jai alai, Tampa Stadium and professional football, Tampa Bay Performing Arts Center, theater, concerts, restaurants. ST. PETERSBURG: Bayfront Center Theater/Arena, Boyd Hill Nature Park, the Pier, St. Petersburg Historical Museum, Salvador Dali Museum,

Sunken Gardens; water sports including swimming, skin diving, water-skiing, fishing, boating; professional baseball spring training, greyhound racing, concerts and other events at Bayfront Center, St. Petersburg Coliseum, Florida Suncoast Dome, restaurants. St. Petersburg Area Chamber of Commerce (813) 821–4069. Tampa/Hillsborough Convention and Visitors Association, (813) 223–1111, (800) 826–8358. Greater Tarpon Springs Chamber of Commerce (813) ·937–6109

Directions: From Tampa International Airport (35 mi.): Hwy. 275 south to Hwy. 60 west to Clearwater to Hwy. 19 north, 10 mi. north between Alderman and Klosterman (left side) is main gate

Closest Commercial Airports: Tampa International (35 min.), Orlando International (2½ hrs.)

RESORT

Date Built: 1973

No. of Rooms: 1000 1-bedroom, 2-bedroom and deluxe suites in 28 low-rise lodges

Meeting/Exhibit Rooms: 27. Capacity of Largest: 2400 persons banquet style. Meeting Space: 65,000 sq. ft.

Room Price Range: $192 per night for 2 persons to $368 for deluxe peak season (Jan. to early May). Lowest rates May, mid-Sept. to mid-Oct., mid-Dec. to early Jan.

Lounges: Grappa, Copperhead Lounge

Restaurants: Copperhead Clubhouse: Copperhead Grille, Clubhouse Snack Bar, Copperhead Lounge. Island Clubhouse: Toscana Restaurant, Hacker's Pub. Sandpiper Clubhouse: Sandpiper Dining Room, Sandpiper Lounge, Clubhouse Snack Bar

Entertainment: Music, dancing at Copperhead, Island, Sandpiper clubhouses

Credit Cards: All major cards

General Amenities: Babysitting available, children's programs for ages 4–12 and teenagers year round, wildlife preserve; 3 conference centers with 65,000 sq. ft. of space and audiovisual, banquet and secretarial-support services; Island Clubhouse beauty salon

Recreational Amenities: Exercise and Fitness Center and exercise programs, 6 swimming pools, bicycling, fishing, nature walks; Nick Bollettieri Tennis Academy with 11 clay, 4 Laykold courts (8 lighted) with instruction, pro shop; 4 racquetball courts, 9-station par course; Island Clubhouse salon for men and women including saunas, massages and more; basketball, volleyball, boating, horseshoes

Reservation and Cancellation Policy: 1 night's deposit required for each person. Deposits are required through credit card or check to hold reservations and may vary based on plan and accommodation type selected. 14-day cancellation policy to avoid penalties

Comments and Restrictions: No pets allowed, but nearby kennels can be recommended. Innisbrook has a no-tipping policy. A service charge is included in all rates to cover services except food and beverage. Each food and beverage check carries an individual service charge. Additional tipping optional. American and European plans available. Taxes additional to base rates

INNISBROOK

The Innisbrook Resort and Country Club is located 30 minutes north of Tampa just west of Hwy. 19. The Copperhead Course at Innisbrook is the flagship course among its 63 holes of golf. The course is rated one of America's 100 Greatest Golf Courses by *Golf Digest* and has been rated the number one course in Florida by *Golfweek* magazine. It is the site of the JCPenney Classic and hosted the 1990 NCAA Division I Men's Championship.

The Copperhead was designed by Edward Lawrence Packard and opened in 1972. Packard, who designed all the courses here, was born in Northampton, Massachusetts in 1912, received a degree in landscape architecture from Massachusetts State College in 1935 and with Brent Wadsworth formed the golf course design firm of Packard and Wadsworth in 1954.

Packard handled the design end and Wadsworth the construction side. Packard's son Roger joined the firm in the early seventies, and the senior Packard retired to Innisbrook in 1986. Packard is credited with reflecting environmental concern in his golf-course designs and was among the earliest advocates of the use of waste water for golf-course irrigation. He was also considered very adept at integrating golf-course and real-estate development in a harmonious design. Among Packard's several golf courses are the Boots Randolph Golf Course in Cadiz, Kentucky; the Silver Lake Country Club in Akron, Ohio, with Brent Wadsworth; the Lick Creek Golf Club in Pekin, Illinois, with Roger Packard; and the Eagle Creek Golf and Tennis Club in Naples, Florida.

The Copperhead Course plays 7087 yards from the back tees, with a robust 140 slope rating and a 74.4 USGA rating from that distance. The course is well treed, as the rolling fairways snake their way through 172 acres of beautiful, pine-covered terrain reminiscent of the Carolinas. There are 73 sand traps and 10 water hazards on Copperhead, and the Tifdwarf hybrid Bermuda greens are varied in size, moderately fast and undulating.

The 576-yard par-5 fifth is the number-1-handicap hole on the course. The tee shot has to avoid bunkers on both sides of the landing area on this long, uphill hole. The approach shot is onto a left-to-right-angled, skull-shaped green with a large trap to the left and a series of traps beginning on the right from approximately 50 yards out to the green. This is the most photographed hole at Innisbrook due to the elevation changes and signature shrubbery. A difficult par 4 on this side is the 456-yard sixth, a downhill dogleg right. The second shot is to an elevated green from a likely sidehill lie on the sloping fairway. The 235-yard par-3 eighth is the longest par 3 on the course. It plays to a narrow, deep green protected by trees and bunkers on both sides.

The three finishing holes at Copperhead are fine tests of golf. The 458-yard par-4 sixteenth is considered the most intimidat-ing par 4 on the course. The tee shot on this dogleg right is to a landing area bordered by a large lake. The long second shot is to a deep green straddled by bunkers and protected by overhanging trees. The 211-yard par-3 seventeenth requires a long iron or wood to reach a large green flanked by bunkers to the left, right and rear. The finishing hole is a long, beautiful 432-yard up-hill par 4. The tee shot landing area is well protected by traps on the left, and the approach shot has to negotiate a series of traps on the right and a large trap to the left of the deep, undulating green. Copperhead requires distance and accuracy because of the well-guarded fairways, uphill holes and elevated greens, water hazards, trees and omnipresent bunkers. When you reach the greens, they will be undulating and difficult. The blue tees measure 6536 yards and the whites are 6149 yards. It is probably best to start from one of these positions. The forward tees are sloped at 128 with a 72 USGA rating from 5506 yards.

The Island Course, a 6999-yard par-72 layout, is also an excellent test of golf. Its forward tees are a difficult 5943 yards with a slope of 130 and a USGA rating of 74.1 for the ladies. *Golf Digest* rates this one of the best resort courses in the United States. The course opened in 1970 and has 74 sand traps, with water hazards on more than half its holes. The most challenging hole on the Island Course is the 561-yard par-5 seventh, which is a slight dogleg left flanked by a lake on the right and a swamp on the left. The green is well guarded by traps left, rear and right. A difficult par 4 on this course is the 456-yard sixteenth, an unforgiving 435 yards from the middle tees and 391 yards from the forward tee. The first shot is to a landing area straddled by fairway bunkers. The approach shot must avoid water on the left and an oak tree on the right to reach a large green protected by a trap on the left.

The Sandpiper Course is a user-friendly combination of three nine-hole courses that vary in length from 6245 yards to 5969 yards from the back tees. The most difficult combination is probably the One/Two courses because of the 53 sand bunkers and

12 holes with water hazards on these combined nines. Although the distances aren't great at the Sandpiper, shot placement is essential, and the well-trapped, undulating greens tend to provide somewhat smaller targets than the other courses.

Each golf course at Innisbrook has its own clubhouse with complete pro shop, restaurants, snack bar, lounges, locker room and showers, as well as practice greens, bunkers and driving ranges. Each club has its own staff, and instruction can be provided to individuals and groups by the PGA professionals and their assistants. Year-round golf packages are available, with the lowest rates usually available from May to November. There are 1000 guest suites housed in 28 lodges on the 1000 acres of rolling forests and lakes. These lodges are named for famous golf courses around the world and are nestled around the resort's three golf courses. The suites feature separate bedrooms, living areas and fully equipped kitchens.

The complex also includes a centrally located conference center with 27 meeting rooms and 65,000 square feet of space. The complex consists of three complete centers—Harstan, Tamarron and Carnelian—each with full theatrical and audiovisual capabilities. Groups of up to 2400 persons can be accommodated for special dining and social events in- and outdoors. Additional meeting space is available in the exccutive wing at the Tamarron Center and within the 2-bedroom deluxe suites. Innisbrook has won recognition by *Meetings and Conventions*, *Corporate and Incentive Travel*, and *Successful Meetings* magazines as one of the best meeting facilities in the United States. The resort has an American Automobile Association Four-Diamond rating and a Four-Star rating from the *Mobil Travel Guide*.

Innisbrook has a full range of recreational activities in addition to golf. These include the 15-court Tennis Academy, 6 swimming pools, 4 racquetball courts, a 9-station par course, a fitness center with complete exercise programs, bicycling, basketball, volleyball, fishing, boating and numerous other activities. The Tennis Institute offers a series of year-round intensive instructional clinics for all levels of play. A special juniors program is offered during the summer months.

The Recreation Center is for young people and their families. This facility includes a children's play area, putt-putt golf, video-game room, fishing rod and bicycle rental desk and snack bar. Innisbrook's children's activity program, "Zoo Crew," welcomes young people ages 4 to 12 to participate in daily activities such as field excursions, golf and tennis instructional clinics, arts and crafts, and luncheons. There are special activities for teenagers, including dances and swimming parties. These programs are offered year-round and are administered by a full-time recreation director and qualified counselors.

With all of these excellent golf, meeting and conference, recreational and other facilities, it is easy to see why *Golf* magazine has awarded Innisbrook its silver medal for golf-resort excellence. In addition to its quality golf courses, varied golf packages and day-to-day instruction programs, Innisbrook has a Golf Institute that was founded by host professional Jay Overton almost 20 years ago. The Golf Institute offers a variety of instructional programs. There are also Junior Golf Institute programs offering instruction for all skill levels, ages 10 to 17. You must be a registered resort guest or a club member, or have reciprocity privileges to play the Innisbrook golf courses.

Course Name:　WORLD WOODS
　　　　　　　　　Pine Barrens, Rolling
　　　　　　　　　Oaks, Short Courses

Course Type:　Public
Address:　　　17590 Ponce DeLeon Boulevard
　　　　　　　Brooksville, FL 34614
Phone:　　　　(904) 796–5500
Fax:　　　　　(904) 382–5221

GOLF COURSE

Director of Golf: Stan Cooke
Course Length/Par (All Tees): Pine Barrens: Tournament 6902/71, Back 6458/71, Middle 6032/71, Forward 5301/71. Rolling Oaks: Tournament 6985/72, Back 6520/72, Middle

6069/72, Forward 5245/72. Short: Back 1842/29, Middle 1596/29, Forward 1336/29

Course Slope/Rating (All Tees): Pine Barrens: Tournament 140/73.7, Back 134/71.6, Middle 129/69.6, Ladies' Forward 132/70.9. Rolling Oaks: Tournament 136/73.5, Back 131/71.4, Middle 125/69.5, Ladies' Forward 128/70.7. Short: NA/NA

Course Architect: Tom Fazio (1993)

Golf Facilities: Full Pro Shop X, Snack Bar X, Lounge X, Restaurant X, Locker Room X, Showers X, Club Rental X, Club Repair No, Cart Rental X, Instruction X, Practice Green X, Driving Range X, Practice Bunker X, Club Storage X

Tee-Time Reservation Policy: Up to 1 month in advance. Up to 60 days in advance with prepayment by cashiers check or money order

Ranger: Yes

Tee-off-Interval Time: 8 min.

Time to Play 18 Holes: 4½ hrs.

Course Hours/Earliest Tee-off: 8:02 a.m.

Green and Cart Fees: $79.50 for 18 holes Fri., Sat., Sun., holidays; $69 for 18 holes weekdays. Short course $21.30 for unlimited play

Credit Cards: MasterCard, Visa

Season: Year round. Busiest Dec. through May

Course Comments: Carts mandatory

Golf Packages: No

Discounts: Seasonal mid-May through Nov.

Places to Stay Nearby: Holiday Inn (904) 796–9481, (800) HOLIDAY. HERNANDO BEACH: Hernando Beach Motel and Condos (904) 596–2527. HOMOSASSA: Ramada Inn (904) 596–7888, (800) 272–6322; Riverside Inn (904) 628–2474. WEEKI WATCHI: Holiday Inn (904) 596–2007, (800) HOLIDAY; Weeki Watchi Resort Hotel (904) 596–1094. ORLANDO: Disney's Grand Floridian Beach Resort (407) W–DISNEY; The Peabody Orlando (407) 352–4000, (800) PEABODY. TAMPA BAY: Marriot Residence Inn (813) 281–5677, (800) 331–3131; Wyndham Don CeSar Beach Resort (813) 360–1881, (800) 282–1116

Local Attractions: BROOKSVILLE: Hernando Historical Museum. HOMOSASSA: Homosassa Springs State Wildlife Park, Yulee Sugar Mill State Historic Site, boating, fishing, camping, hunting, hiking, horseback riding. Greater Hernando County Chamber of Commerce, Tourist Information Center, 31178 Cortez Blvd., Ridge Manor, FL 34602 (904) 799–7275, (800) 601–4580

Directions: From Orlando (90 min. northwest): Take Hwy. 50 west to Brooksville and Hwy. 98. Take Hwy. 98 west approximately 11 miles to World Woods. From Tampa (90 min. northeast): Take Hwy. 19 north to Hwy. 98. Turn right (east) on Hwy. 98 and drive approximately 5 miles to World Woods

Closest Commercial Airports: Tampa International (1 hr. 20 min.); Orlando International (2 hrs.)

WORLD WOODS GOLF CLUB

World Woods, situated 90 minutes northeast of Tampa and 90 minutes northwest of Orlando, is one of the best public golf facilities anywhere. This obscure site not only features two of the best golf courses built in the 1990s—Pine Barrens and Rolling Oaks—it also has an excellent 27-acre, four-sided practice range with multiple stations on each side, a 2-acre putting course, par 3, 4, and 5 practice holes, and a 9-hole short course. This is all owned by Japanese businessman and golf aficionado Yukihisa Inoue. Both courses and the entire practice area were designed by Tom Fazio, creator of Wild Dunes in South Carolina, Jupiter Hills and Black Diamond Ranch in Florida, and many other fine courses.

The Rolling Oaks layout offers a choice of four tee distances. The course has large oaks and rolling, sandy-soiled terrain that give it a North Carolina flavor. The toughest hole on the front side is the 458-yard par-4 ninth whose tee shot must carry a large pond and avoid a bunker to the right of the landing area. The approach is uphill to a deep green guarded by a bunker to its left and another to its right. Just about every hole on this course seems outstanding and memorable. A favorite of mine on the back side is the demanding and scenic 234-yard par-3 sixteenth which plays from an elevated tee to a green framed by trees and guarded to the front left by a bunker.

On virtually all of the holes at World Woods you will be hitting from an elevated tee and you will have a full view of the work cut out for you. The task presented by the Pine Barrens course, reminiscent in some minor respects of Pine Valley, can be quite intimidating, especially if bunker play isn't your favorite pastime. Pine Barrens is a lightly treed but heavily bunkered layout with oceans of waste areas. The back nine has some excellent hole sequences beginning with the 429-yard par-4 thirteenth which plays from an elevated tee over a waste bunker. The approach is to a large green with another huge waste bunker to its left. Next a 527-yard par 5 swings left and uphill through a gauntlet of waste bunkers to a tiered, forward-sloping green with a severe dropoff to its left. The 330-yard par-4 fifteenth offers two routes to a green set in an amphitheatre-like hillside. A shot to the left enables you to play your approach from an elevated ridge down to the green, or you can play to a target landing area to the right and more directly in front of the green. Positioning, club selection, and management of one's temper are important at Pine Barrens.

As of yet there are no homes or commercial enterprises within World Wood's 2100 acres. It's just you, the rolling hills, and a series of inspiring golf holes.

Recommended Golf Courses in Florida

Within 1 Hour of Tampa:

Bardmoor North Golf Club, Largo, (813) 397–0483, Public, 18/6950/72

Bloomingdale Golfers Club, Valrico, (813) 685–4105, Semiprivate, 18/7165/72

Citrus Hill Golf Club, Hernando, (904) 746–4425, Semiprivate. Oaks: 18/6323/70. Meadows: 18/5885/70

Dunedin Country Club, Dunedin, (813) 733–7836, Semiprivate, 18/6565/72

Eagles Golf Club, Odessa, (813) 920–6681, Public. Lakes: 9/3630/36. Oaks: 9/3564/36. Forest: 9/3504/36

Fox Hollow Golf Club, New Port Richey, (813) 376–6333, (800) 943–1902, Public, 18/7138/72

The Golf Club at Cypress Creek, Ruskin, (813) 634–8888, Semiprivate, 18/6839/72

Huntington Hills Golf and Country Club, Lakeland, (813) 859–3689, Semiprivate, 18/6631/72

Imperial Lakes Golf Club, Palmetto, (813) 747–4653, Semiprivate, 18/6658/72

Lansbrook Golf Club, Palm Harbor, (813) 784–7333, Semiprivate, 18/6719/72

Mangrove Bay Golf Course, St. Petersburg, (813) 893–7800, Public, 18/6700/72

Oak Hills Golf Club, Spring Hill, (904) 683–6830, Public, 18/6774/72

Rainbow Springs Golf and Country Club, Dunnellon, (904) 489–3566, Semiprivate, 18/6721/72

The River Club, Bradenton, (813) 751–4211, Public, 18/7004/72

River Hills Country Club, Valrico, (813) 653–3323, Semiprivate, 18/7004/72

Rosedale Golf and Country Club, Bradenton, (813) 756–0004, Semiprivate,

Saddlebrook, Wesley Chapel, (813) 973–1111, (800) 729–8383, Resort. Saddlebrook: 18/6603/70. Palmer: 18/6469/71

Seven Hills Golfer's Club, Spring Hill, (904) 688–8888, Semiprivate, 18/6715/72

Seven Springs Golf and Country Club, Newport Richey, (813) 376–0035, Semiprivate, 18/6566/72

Seville Golf and Country Club, Weeki Wachi, (904) 596–7888, (800) 232–1363, Public, 18/7140/72

Summerfield Golf Club, Riverview, (813) 671–3311, Semiprivate, 18/6883/71

Tournament Players of Tampa Bay, Lutz, (813) 949–0091, Semiprivate, 18/6898/72

University Park Country Club, University Park, (813) 359–9999, Semiprivate, 18/6951/72

Walden Lakes Golf and Country Club, Plant City, (813) 754–8575, Semiprivate. Hills/Lakes: 18/6797/72. Oaks/Pines: 18/6479/72

Westchase Golf Club, Tampa, (813) 854–2331, Public, 18/6710/72

Within 1 Hour of Sarasota:

Calusa Lakes, Nokomis, (813) 484–8995, Semiprivate, 18/6800/72

The Club at Oak Ford, Sarasota, (813) 371–3680, Semiprivate. Live Oak: 9/3300/36. Myrtle: 9/3404/36. Palm: 9/3349/36

The Country Club at Jacaranda West, Venice, (813) 493–2664, Semiprivate, 18/6602/72

Long Boat Key Club, Longboat Key, (813) 383–0781, (800) 282–0113 (FL), (800) 237–8821 (outside FL), Resort. Islandside: 18/6792/72. Blue: 9/3386/36. Red: 9/3323/36. White: 9/3426/36

Plantation Golf and Country Club, Venice, (813) 493–2000, Semiprivate. Bobcat: 18/6880/72. Panther: 18/6311/72

Riverwood Golf Club, Port Charlotte, (813) 764–6661, Semiprivate, 18/6938/72

Tatum Ridge Golf Links, Sarasota, (813) 378–4211, Public, 18/6757/72

Waterford Golf Club, Venice, (813) 484–6621, Public, 18/6601/72

Southwestern

Course Name: EASTWOOD GOLF COURSE

Course Type: Public
Address: 4600 Bruce Herd Lane
                Fort Myers, FL 33905
Phone: (941) 275–4848

GOLF COURSE

Director of Golf: Richard Lamb
Course Length/Par (All Tees): Back 6772/72, White 6226/72, Gold 5568/72, Ladies' Forward 5116/72

Course Slope/Rating (All Tees): Back 130/73.3, White 125/70.7, Gold 109/66.0, Ladies' Forward 120/68.9
Course Architects: Bruce Devlin and Robert von Hagge (1977)
Golf Facilities: Full Pro Shop X, Snack Bar X, Lounge No, Restaurant No, Locker Room No, Showers No, Club Rental X, Club Repair Minimal, Cart Rental X, Instruction X, Practice Green X, Driving Range X, Practice Bunker X, Club Storage No
Tee-Time Reservation Policy: 1 day in advance from 8 a.m.
Ranger: Yes
Tee-off-Interval Time: 7 to 8 min.
Time to Play 18 Holes: 4 hrs., 15 min.
Course Hours/Earliest Tee-off: 7 a.m.
Green Fees: $32 for 18 holes peak season mid-Dec. to mid-Apr.
Cart Fees: $20 for 18 holes per cart, $15 for 9 holes per cart
Credit Cards: MasterCard, Visa
Season: Year round. Busiest season mid-Dec. to mid-April
Course Comments: Walking permitted after 3 p.m. mid-Dec. to mid-Apr. After 1 p.m. otherwise. Yardage book available. 8 a.m. and 1 p.m. shotgun start on Sat. Resident memberships
Golf Packages: None
Discounts: Seasonal (mid-Apr. to mid-Dec.). Annual fee/residents only. Juniors. Twilight
Places to Stay Nearby: Seawatch-on-the-Beach (813) 463–4469, (800) 237–8906; Courtyard by Marriott (813) 275–8600, (800) 443–6000; Best Western Robert E. Lee Motor Inn (813) 997–5511, (800) 274–5511; Sanibel Harbor Resort (813) 466–4000; Sundial Beach Resort (941) 472–4151, (800) 237–3102; Sheraton Harbor Place (813) 337–0300, (800) 325–3535
Local Attractions: Thomas Edison's winter home, Fort Myers Historical Museum, Babcock Wilderness Adventures' swamp buggy excursions, J. N. "Ding" Darling National Wildlife Refuge (Sanibel Island), Collier Automotive Museum (Naples), Naples Dinner Theatre, Nature Center and Planetarium

of Lee County, Ringling Museum of Art (Sarasota), Corkscrew Swamp Sanctuary, Cabbage Key, beaches, boating, fishing, Eden Vineyards Winery, scuba diving, tennis, spring training baseball exhibitions. Lee County Visitor and Convention Bureau (941) 335–2631, (800) 237–6444. Naples Area Chamber of Commerce (941) 262–6141. Sanibel–Captiva Chamber of Commerce (941) 472–1080. Sarasota Convention and Visitors Bureau (941) 957–1877, (800) 522–9799

Directions: From Fort Myers/Southwest Regional airport (10 min.): I–75 north, to exit 22 (Colonial), left turn to Ortiz Ave., right turn on Ortiz north 1/4 mi. to course

Closest Commercial Airports: Fort Myers/Southwest Regional (10 min.), Miami International (2 hrs.)

EASTWOOD GOLF COURSE

The Eastwood Golf Course, designed by Bruce Devlin and Robert von Hagge, opened in 1977 and has long been ranked by *Golf Digest* as one of the best public golf courses in America. Devlin and von Hagge have designed a variety of golf courses in Florida and elsewhere after they first teamed up in 1966 to redesign the Lakes Golf Club in Devlin's native New South Wales, Australia. Some of their later collaborations in Florida include Bay Point (Lagoon Legend Course), Panama City; Colony West Golf Club (Course no. 2), Tamarac; Doral Country Club (Gold), Miami; Key Biscayne Golf Club; and Marco Shores Country Club, Marco Island. Like many southern Florida courses, Eastwood is relatively flat, with water coming into play on more than half the holes. There are no parallel fairways to speak of, and this course is not ensconced in an obtrusive real-estate development.

The number-1-handicap hole at Eastwood is the 399-yard par-4 third hole, which has a large lake on the left that runs from behind the tee almost up to the green. The fairway is a relatively narrow 35 yards wide, with pine trees on the right and a north wind coming into the face of the golfer. After a straight tee shot, the second shot is often a long iron or wood onto a large, pear-shaped, undulating green, with two traps to the left and to the right rear, and one to the left front. The 414-yard par-4 tenth hole is the number-2-handicap hole, a dogleg left over lake water. A tee shot of 150 yards is required to reach the fairway, and a total distance of at least 200 yards is needed to set up a reasonable second shot to reach a large, well-protected green with traps left, right and back and water on the left.

The front nine is generally tight and tree-lined, with many bunkers and undulating greens that are difficult to approach because of the numerous traps protecting them in front. It is difficult to bump and run on this course; you usually have to hit the green on the fly. The 233-yard par-3 fourth hole is an example of how difficult and challenging the par-3 holes at Eastwood are. Trees protect the fairway on the right, and the large green is protected front and back by sizeable traps. The 177-yard par-3 sixth hole starts from an elevated tee and stretches across a lake to a large green protected on the right by a trap. This hole is considered to be one of the prettiest on the course.

The back nine has 39 bunkers, large greens and plays long and tight, especially during the winter, when the wind can be more of a factor. The fourteenth hole, a 573-yard par 5, has a large lake running up the left fairway and around the green. Approximately 275 yards from the tee, the fairway narrows severely and has water and two bunkers left and right. The second shot comes into a fairway that narrows again, with a trap to the right approximately 100 yards from the green. Two large traps protect a large green front and right back. You have to fly onto the green, over the front trap, with water awaiting behind the green.

In recent years Fort Myers has spent $4.4 million to improve the Fort Myers Country Club, Eastwood's sister course, and Eastwood. Eastwood, which hosts 70,000 rounds per year, is a self-sustaining enterprise, supported by green fees, cart rentals and memberships. Both the Men's and Women's Southwest Florida Amateur is held here annually.

Course Name: GATEWAY GOLF AND COUNTRY CLUB

Course Type: Semiprivate
Address: 11360 Championship Drive
Fort Myers, FL 33913
Phone: (813) 561–2621
Fax: (813) 561–2621

GOLF COURSE

Director of Golf: Greg Wetzel
Course Length/Par (All Tees): Back 6974/72, Blue 6606/72, White 6204/72 Forward 5323/72
Course Slope/Rating (All Tees): Back 130/73.7, Blue 127/71.9, White 122/69.9, Ladies' Forward 120/70.6
Course Architect: Tom Fazio (1989)
Golf Facilities: Full Pro Shop X, Snack Bar X, Lounge X, Restaurant X, Locker Room No, Showers No, Club Rental X, Club Repair X, Cart Rental X, Instruction X, Practice Green X, Driving Range X, Practice Bunker X, Club Storage X
Tee-Time Reservation Policy: Public: 2 days
Ranger: Yes
Tee-off-Interval Time: 8 min.
Time to Play 18 Holes: 4 hrs.
Course Hours/Earliest Tee-off: 7:22 a.m.
Green and Cart Fees: Peak Season: $106 for 18 holes with cart (mid-Jan. to mid.-Mar.)
Credit Cards: American Express, Master-Card, Visa
Season: Year round. Busiest season Jan. through April 1
Course Comments: Cart mandatory for public. Members can walk after 2 p.m.
Golf Packages: None
Discounts: Seasonal. Reduced rates after 11 a.m.
Places to Stay Nearby: Seawatch-on-the-Beach (813) 463–4469, (800) 237–8906; Boathouse Beach Resort (813) 481–3636, (800) 237–8906; Courtyard by Marriott (813) 275–8600, (800) 443–6000; Best Western Robert E. Lee Mo-tor Inn (813) 997–5511, (800) 274–5511; Sanibel Harbor Resort (813) 466–4000; Sheraton Harbor Place (813) 337–0300, (800) 335–3535; Sundial Beach Resort (941) 472–4151, (800) 237–3102

Local Attractions: Thomas Edison's winter home, Fort Myers Historical Museum, Babcock Wilderness Adventures' swamp buggy excursions, J. N. "Ding" Darling National Wildlife Refuge (Sanibel Island), Collier Automotive Museum (Naples), Naples Dinner Theatre, Nature Center and Planetarium of Lee County, Ringling Museum of Art (Sarasota), Corkscrew Swamp Sanctuary, Cabbage Key, beaches, boating, fishing, Eden Vineyards Winery, scuba diving, tennis, spring training baseball exhibitions. Lee County Visitor and Convention Bureau (813) 335–2631, (800) 237–6444. Naples Area Chamber of Commerce (813) 262–6141. Sanibel–Captiva Chamber of Commerce (813) 472–1080. Sarasota Convention and Visitors Bureau (813) 957–1877, (800) 522–9799
Directions: From I–75, exit 21 onto Daniels Rd., east 5 mi. to golf course
Closest Commercial Airports: Southwest Florida International, Fort Myers (5 min.); Miami International (2 hrs.)

GATEWAY GOLF AND COUNTRY CLUB

Gateway Golf and Country Club is a 6974-Scottish links-like layout designed by Tom Fazio and situated 5 miles east of Interstate 75 in Fort Myers. This beautifully sculpted layout features a variety of mounds, more than 90 bunkers and water on more than half the holes. The Tifdwarf Bermuda-grass greens are large, undulating, fast and well protected by mounds, sand and water. Variable winds can also be a factor on Gateway. Fazio has adopted Cape Cod-style mounded traps to this golf course, which hosted the 1990 and 1991 Ben Hogan Gateway Open, a stop on the professional satellite tour.

The front nine concludes with a tough par 5, a 568-yard challenge whose tee shot is over the edge of a lake on the right to a landing area guarded by a large bunker on the left and water to the right. The second shot is toward a tiered, deep green that is well protected by huge bunkers to the left and right and another large trap to the left-front. This used to be the finishing hole on the golf course until the nines were recently reversed. This better enables you to ease into the tough and memorable nine ahead.

The back nine starts out with a 394-yard par 4 paralleled by a lake on the right. The approach shot is to a large, three-tiered green protected by a large bunker to the front-left and water to the right. The 146-yard par-3 eleventh plays to a medium-sized green situated on a peninsula and fronted by a large trap. The next hole is one of the most difficult holes at Gateway. A straight, 464-yard par 4, this hole is bordered by a lake on the left and Cape Cod fairway bunkers and trees on the right. Two accurate, long shots are required to reach the deep, kidney-shaped green in regulation. The twelfth measures 450, 428 and 341 yards from the other tee distances.

A memorable par 3 on this side is the 181-yard fourteenth, the signature hole on the course. The tee shot is to a medium-sized green beautifully framed by cypress trees and guarded by a large bunker to the right. The finishing hole is a lengthy 580-yard par 5 that is bordered by a large lake from tee to green. The tee shot is to a generous landing area, but the second shot must avoid two large bunkers to the right. The huge, 10,500-square-foot, three-tiered green is well protected by a large waste bunker and water to its left and a series of mounds and Cape Cod bunkers to its right-front, right and rear. Few golfers reach this green in two shots.

Tom Fazio has designed many quality golf courses, including the Pelican's Nest Golf Club in nearby Bonita Springs; Wild Dunes in Charleston, South Carolina; and many others. The Gateway Golf and Country Club has a spacious, modern clubhouse with complete amenities. Within walking distance is an ample practice area and in-struction is available from the staff of PGA professionals.

Course Name: THE GOLF CLUB AT MARCO

Course Type: Resort
Resort: Marriott's Marco Island Resort and Golf Club
Address: 400 S. Collier Boulevard Marco Island, FL 33937
Phone: (813) 394–2511, (800) 438–4373
Fax: (813) 394–4645

GOLF COURSE

Director of Golf: Pat Brannigan
Course Length/Par (All Tees): Back 6898/72, Middle 6471/72, Forward 5416/72
Course Slope/Rating (All Tees): Back 137/73.4, Middle 126/71.4, Forward 122/70.9
Course Architect: Joe Lee (1991)
Golf Facilities: Full Pro Shop X, Snack Bar X, Lounge X, Restaurant X, Locker Room X, Showers X, Club Rental X, Club Repair X, Cart Rental X, Instruction X, Practice Green X, Driving Range X, Practice Bunker X, Club Storage X
Tee-Time Reservation Policy: Guest: 30 days in advance. Outside play: 48 hrs.
Ranger: Yes
Tee-off-Interval Time: 8 min.
Time to Play 18 Holes: 4½ hrs.
Course Hours/Earliest Tee-off: 7:32 a.m.
Green and Cart Fees: Peak Season: $120 for 18 holes with cart, $60 for 9 holes with cart
Credit Cards: All major cards
Season: Year round. Busiest season Jan. through March
Course Comments: Cart mandatory. 9-hole rates only available during peak season
Golf Packages: Available through resort
Discounts: Seasonal (early June to Sept.)
Places to Stay Nearby: Radisson Suite Beach Resort (813) 394–4100, (800) 333–3333; Eagle's Nest Beach Resort (813) 394–5167, (800) 237–8906; Marco Bay Resort (813) 394–8881.

NAPLES: Edgewater Beach Hotel (813) 262–6511, (800) 821–0196; Registry Resort (813) 597–3232, (800) 247–9810; Ritz–Carlton Hotel (813) 598–3300; La Playa Beach and Racquet Inn (813) 597–3123; Comfort Inn (813) 649–5800, (800) 228–5150; Naples Beach Hotel and Golf Club (813) 261–2222; World Tennis Center and Resort (813) 263–1900, (800) 292–6663

Local Attractions: Everglades National Park, major league baseball spring training, Briggs Nature Center, Edison winter home, Jungle Larry's Zoological Park, Collier Automotive Museum, Corkscrew Swamp sanctuary, greyhound dog racing

Directions: From Naples (15 mi.): U.S. 41 to State Road 951 south to Marco Island Bridge, resort on the right 3 mi. from bridge

Closest Commercial Airports: Naples (30 min.); Southwest Florida International, Fort Myers (1 hr.); Miami International (2 hrs.)

RESORT

Date Built: 1971, with additions and improvements since then

No. of Rooms: 735 guest rooms, suites, villas and lanais

Meeting/Exhibit Rooms: 29. Capacity of Largest: 2000 persons reception style. Meeting Space: 48,000 sq. ft.

Room Price Range: $269 to $374 peak season (end Dec. to early June) with buffet breakfast. $129 to $214 off season (early June to early Sept.). Other packages and seasonal rates available

Lounges: Quinn's on the Beach, Voyager Lounge, Tiki Bar and Grill, lobby lounge

Restaurants: Tuscany Dining Room and Grille, Voyager Restaurant, Cafe del Sol, Pizzeria and Groceria, Quinn's on the Beach

Entertainment: Live music in Quinn's and Voyager Restaurant

Credit Cards: All major cards

General Amenities: "Kids stuff" children's program for ages 5 to 13, babysitting, barber and beauty salon, shelling and sightseeing cruises, boutique and souvenir shops, meeting and conference facilities for small groups to banquets for 1500 with audiovisual, food service and secretarial support

Recreational Amenities: 16 tennis courts (4 lighted), tennis shop and instruction, 3 swimming pools, beach volleyball, bicycling, sailing, water-skiing, fishing; health club with Universal work-out system including stair steppers, rowing machines, life cycles and weights; scuba diving and snorkeling; aquaslimnastics, aerobics, yoga and other fitness activities; game room with table tennis

Reservation and Cancellation Policy: 3-day cancellation policy to avoid penalties

Comments and Restrictions: No pets allowed. Taxes and gratuities additional

THE GOLF CLUB AT MARCO

The Golf Club at Marco Island is a 6898-yard layout designed by Joe Lee. This relatively flat layout was cut out of forests of Australian pine and palm and wends its way through marshes, cypress swamps and tropical thickets. There are 74 traps on the golf course, and water comes into play on 15 holes. The landing areas are well protected by water and sand. The Bermuda-grass greens are moderately fast, medium sized and well trapped. Winds from the northeast and the nearby Gulf of Mexico can also be a factor at Marco Island.

The first hole, a 405-yard par 4 from the back tees, often plays into the wind, making it more difficult to reach the green in regulation. The tee-shot landing area on this dogleg left is guarded by two traps on the right and one on the left. The deep green is straddled by two large traps. The finishing hole on the front nine is a 547-yard par-5 dogleg-left bordered by water to the right on the tee shot. The temptation is to cut as much of the right corner as possible to have a chance to reach the green in two. To the left of the tee-shot landing area is a pair of large bunkers. The second shot is toward a deep green that is bordered by a trap on the right and protected by water to the left. Approach shots that are short of the green can be caught by traps to the right or water guarding the left side of the fairway.

The number-1-handicap hole is the 451-yard par-4 thirteenth. The tee-shot landing area is guarded by water on the left, and the approach is to a large green guarded by a trap on the left and framed by trees. One of the most memorable holes at the Golf Club at Marco is the 165-yard par-3 sixteenth. The tee shot is all carry over water to a deep, right-to-left-angled bulkheaded green that is protected by three traps to the left and a huge bunker to the right.

The finishing hole at Marco Island emphasizes the need for golf-course management and strategic shot making on this layout. The tee shot on this 398-yard par 4 is to a landing area guarded by water on the right and a large bunker to the left. The approach is over a small lake to a shallow green fronted by a waterway and guarded by a large trap to the rear. Two accurate shots are required to reach this green in regulation. A heavily faded drive, or a tee shot that is too long, will reach the water. A weak or hooked approach shot will also be in the drink.

After your round of golf, the complete amenities of an 8000-square-foot old Florida-style clubhouse await you. A complete pro shop, locker rooms and dining facilities are available, as well as an outside 14-acre practice facility that includes golf instruction from PGA club professionals and staff at the John Jacobs' Practical Golf School. Golf and other packages are available through the on-site 735-room Marriott year round. A "golf tour package" offered in late 1992 included a Gulf-view guest room, breakfast for 2, unlimited golf with cart for 2 and other amenities for $155 during the summer months and $225 after August.

The Marco Island Resort and Golf Club, situated on 3½ miles of beach on the Gulf of Mexico, just 30 minutes from Naples, has won a variety of golf, convention and hospitality awards from *Golf Digest*, *Meetings and Conventions*, *Condé Nast Traveler* and *Successful Meetings* magazines. Activities including fishing, tennis, boating, health club and others are conveniently available at Marco Island. There are 8 boutique and specialty shops on-site, and there are 6 restaurants with everything from fresh seafood to pizza. There is also 48,000 square feet of meeting and conference space, including ballrooms, meeting rooms, executive board rooms, outdoor reception areas and an array of professional support services from the meeting planning staff at the Marriott. Easily reachable from Marco Island are many excellent golf courses, as well as the sites of Naples, the Everglades National Park, Fort Myers and other Gulf islands such as Sanibel and Captiva.

Southwestern Florida has become a major golf destination, and Marriott's Marco Island resort is one of the largest on Florida's west coast. Rated one of America's best new golf courses by *Golf Digest* magazine, the Golf Club at Marco is worth a visit.

Course Name: LELY FLAMINGO ISLAND CLUB

Course Type: Resort
Address: 8004 Lely Resort Boulevard
               Naples, FL 33963
Phone: (813) 793–2223
Fax: (813) 774–4980

GOLF COURSE

Director of Golf: Dan Mullaly
Course Length/Par (All Tees): Back 7171/72, White 6527/72, Gold 6018/72, Forward 5377/72
Course Slope/Rating (All Tees): Back 135/73.9, White 129/70.9, Gold 125/68.6, Ladies' Gold 134/74.2, Forward 126/70.6
Course Architect: Robert Trent Jones, Sr. (1990)
Golf Facilities: Full Pro Shop X, Snack Bar X, Lounge X, Restaurant X, Locker Room X, Showers X, Club Rental X, Club Repair X, Cart Rental X, Instruction X, Practice Green X, Driving Range X, Practice Bunker X, Club Storage No
Tee-Time Reservation Policy: 3 days in advance
Ranger: Yes

Tee-off-Interval Time: 8 min.

Time to Play 18 Holes: 4½ hrs.

Course Hours/Earliest Tee-off: 7:30 a.m.

Green and Cart Fees: Peak Season: $110 for 18 holes with cart

Credit Cards: Discover, MasterCard, Visa

Season: Year round. Busiest season early Jan. to mid-April

Course Comments: Yardage book available

Golf Packages: Available through travel agencies and local hotels

Discounts: Twilight, seasonal

Places to Stay Nearby: FORT MYERS: Sanibel Harbour Resort (813) 466–4000; Sheraton Harbor Place (813) 337–0300, (800) 325–3535; Best Western Robert E. Lee Manor Inn (813) 997–5511, (800) 528–1234. NAPLES: Edgewater Beach Hotel (813) 262–6511, (800) 821–0196; Registry Resort (813) 597–3232, (800) 247–9810; Ritz–Carlton Hotel (813) 598–3300, (800) 241–3333; La Playa Beach and Racquet Inn (813) 597–3123; Comfort Inn (813) 649–5800, (800) 228–5150. SANIBEL/CAPTIVA: Casa Ybel Resort (813) 472–3145, (800) 448–2736; South Seas Plantation Resort and Yacht Harbour (813) 472–5111, (800) 237–1260; Sundial Beach and Tennis Resort (813) 472–4151, (800) 237–4184

Local Attractions: FORT MYERS: Eden Vineyards Winery and Park, Thomas A. Edison's winter home, Henry Ford's winter home, Fort Myers Historical Museum, major league baseball spring training. NAPLES: Collier Automotive Museum, Collier County Museum, Naples Nature Center, Briggs Nature Center, Corkscrew Swamp Sanctuary, Jungle Larry's Zoological Park, restaurants, shopping, beaches, boating, fishing. SANIBEL ISLAND: J. N. Darling National Wildlife Refuge. Captiva Island

Directions: From I–75 to exit 15, County Rd. 951 south to resort (on right 5 or 6 mi.)

Closest Commercial Airports: Naples (10 min.); Southwest Florida International, Fort Myers (1 hr.); Miami International (2 hrs.)

LELY FLAMINGO ISLAND CLUB

The Lely Flamingo Island Club is a challenging 7171-yard, Robert Trent Jones, Sr.-designed golf course that serves as a centerpiece for Lely resort, a planned community that also has a private golf club, the Classics, designed by Gary Player. Future plans include a third golf course designed by Lee Trevino with resort-style amenities such as a tennis ranch, European health spa, hotel and shopping amenities.

Water can come into play on thirteen holes at Lely Flamingo, and the course is especially demanding from the back tees. The par-3 second hole, for example, plays 204 yards from the back tees and 150 yards from the regular tees. The tee shot is to a deep, two-tiered green well protected by traps and guarded by water. The greens at Lely Flamingo are large, moderately undulating and well protected by traps. The rolling fairways are protected by palmettos and cypress trees.

The number eight hole is a tough dogleg-left par 4 that plays 422 yards from the back tees and 390 yards from the regular tees. The tee shot is to a landing area guarded by a cluster of bunkers on the right. The approach is over water to a green that is shallow on the left and right sides but approximately 40 yards deep in the center. As with most holes at Lely Flamingo, the angle of approach to each green is extremely important.

A challenging par 5 on the front side is the number-1-handicap seventh, a 596-yard dogleg-left whose tee-shot landing area is straddled by large bunkers. The second shot is down a narrowing fairway that is guarded by a series of bunkers from approximately 150 yards into the green. The 501-yard par-5 eleventh is more moderate in length, but a wall of bunkers in front of the green provides a formidable obstacle to anyone trying to reach this gambler's hole in two. The 213-yard fourteenth is probably the most challenging par 3 on the course. The tee shot is all carry over water to a green well protected by traps in front and to the right. Tricky winds from the Gulf of Mexico increase the difficulty of this hole.

Lely Flamingo has a 300-yard-deep driving range, putting and chipping greens, and a teaching area with instruction at all levels. The clubhouse is now a temporary facility but includes locker rooms, showers and a short-order restaurant.

Course Name: PELICAN'S NEST
              GOLF CLUB
              Panther/Hurricane,
              Seminole/Gator Courses

Course Type: Resort
Address: 4450 Bay Creek Drive SW
              Bonita Springs, FL 33923
Phone: (813) 947–4600, (800) 952–
              NEST
Fax: (813) 947–6809

GOLF COURSE

Director of Golf: Mark Iwinski
Course Length/Par (All Tees): Panther/
Hurricane: Back 6919/72, Blue 6475/72,
White 5831/72, Forward 5079/72. Semi-
nole/Gator: Back 7072/72, Blue
6632/72, White 6128/72, Forward
5303/72
Course Slope/Rating (All Tees): Pan-
ther/Hurricane: Back 136/74.1, Blue
129/72.8, White 121/68.9, Ladies' For-
ward 130/72.9. Seminole/Gator: Back
137/74.7, Blue 130/72.4, White
124/70.7, Ladies' Forward 121/69.7
Course Architect: Tom Fazio (Huricane,
Gator, 1985; Seminole, 1988; Panther,
1993)
Golf Facilities: Full Pro Shop X, Snack
Bar X, Lounge X, Restaurant X,
Locker Room X, Showers X, Club
Rental X, Club Repair X, Cart Rental
X, Instruction X, Practice Green X,
Driving Range X, Practice Bunker X,
Club Storage X
Tee-Time Reservation Policy: Up to 2
days in advance
Ranger: Yes
Tee-off-Interval Time: 8 to 9 min.
Time to Play 18 Holes: 4½ hrs.
Course Hours/Earliest Tee-off: 7:22 a.m.
Green and Cart Fees: Peak season (mid-
Jan. through March): $125 for 18 holes
with cart

Credit Cards: American Express, Master-
Card, Visa
Season: Year round. Busiest season Jan. to
April
Course Comments: Cart mandatory. Yard-
age book available
Golf Packages: None
Discounts: Seasonal. Lowest rates mid-
April to Jan.
Places to Stay Nearby: FORT MYERS:
Sanibel Harbour Resort (813) 466–4000;
Sheraton Harbor Place (813) 337–0300,
(800) 325–3535; Best Western Robert E.
Lee Manor Inn (813) 997–5511, (800)
528–1234 NAPLES: Edgewater Beach Ho-
tel (813) 262–6511, (800) 821–0196;
Registry Resort (813) 597–3232, (800)
247–9810; Ritz–Carlton Hotel (813)
598–3300, (800) 241–3333; La Playa
Beach and Racquet Inn (813) 597–3123;
Comfort Inn (813) 649–5800, (800) 228–
5150. SANIBEL/CAPTIVA: Casa Ybel Re-
sort (813) 472–3145, (800) 448–2736;
South Seas Plantation Resort and Yacht
Harbour (813) 472–5111, (800) 237–
1260; Sundial Beach and Tennis Resort
(813) 472–4151, (800) 237–4184
Local Attractions: FORT MYERS: Eden
Vineyards Winery and Park, Thomas
A. Edison's winter home, Henry Ford's
winter home, Fort Myers Historical Mu-
seum, major league baseball spring train-
ing. NAPLES: Collier Automotive
Museum, Collier County Museum,
Naples Nature Center, Briggs Nature
Center, Corkscrew Swamp Sanctuary,
Jungle Larry's Zoological Park, restau-
rants, shopping, beaches, boating, fish-
ing. SANIBEL ISLAND: J. N. Darling
National Wildlife Refuge. Captiva Island
Directions: From Southwest Florida Inter-
national Airport (25 min.): I–75 south to
exit 19, west to Hwy. 41, Hwy. 41 south
3 mi. to golf course
Closest Commercial Airports: Southwest
Florida Regional, Fort Myers (25min.);
Miami International (2 hrs.)

PELICAN'S NEST GOLF CLUB

Pelican's Nest Golf Club is rated one of
the best public golf courses in the United
States by *Golf Digest* magazine and is one

of the many fine golf courses in southwestern Florida. Designed by Tom Fazio, Pelican's Nest features four nine-hole layouts that can be played in any combination. The original eighteen holes opened at Pelican's Nest in 1985 and was ranked among the top 3 new public courses in the United States. A third nine was completed in 1988, and the final nine was opened in 1993.

Each hole at Pelican's Nest, which is set in a real-estate development called Pelican Landing, is cut out of oaks, pines and palmettos. The Bermuda fairways are well protected by trees and a variety of mounds and bunkers. The Tifdwarf Bermuda greens are moderately fast and vary in depth from 24 to 43 yards. Winds from the north can be a factor during the winter months. Shot placement and golf-course management are essential in order to score at Pelican's Nest.

The 3461-yard Panther nine has water on all of its holes including the tough par-3 seventh, "Eagle Trace," a 212-yard challenge that plays over the edge of wetlands to a green guarded by three traps to the left and front-left. "Moonscape" provides a difficult and memorable finishing hole. The tee shot on this 452-yard par-4 dogleg right must avoid water to the right and three bunkers and more water to the left. The approach is to a deep green backed by mounds and guarded to its left-front by a bunker.

An outstanding par 4 on the 3458-yard Hurricane nine is the 370-yard eighth, called "Spring Creek," which is bordered by water on the left from tee to green and is intermittently treed on the right. An accurate tee shot is required to hit the narrow fairway, and many golfers hit a long iron or fairway wood off the tee. The 33-yard deep, skull-shaped green is guarded by railroad ties and Estero Bay on the left and a large trap on the right. All of the holes at Hurricane are paralleled by water.

The 3491-yard Gator nine finishes with a tough 434-yard par 4 called "Black Rush." The other tee distances are 416, 401 and 335 yards. The drive must avoid a cluster of bunkers on the right, beginning 170 yards from the green. The best strategy is to keep the ball center or left of center in order to have a clear shot at a deep, two-tiered green straddled by two large traps. Farther right of the green is a stream that can catch approach shots that fade right. Water can come into play on six holes on Gator.

Seminole also has an excellent par-4 finishing hole called "Valley of Sin" that measures 440 yards from the back tees. The tee-shot landing area is bracketed by water, a large bunker and trees on the left and a series of mounds and trees and palmettos on the right. The approach shot is usually a long iron to a deep, two-tiered green guarded by a large trap to the right-front and another trap to the rear.

Pelican's Nest is a very difficult test of golf from the back tees where many forced carries are required to reach landing areas. The four tee distances enable any golfer to find a reasonable challenge on this beautiful golf course.

Recommended Golf Courses in Florida

Within 1 Hour of Fort Myers:

Coral Oaks Golf Course, Cape Coral, (813) 283–4100, Public, 18/6623/72

Golden Gate Country Club, Naples, (813) 455–9498, Semiprivate, 18/6570/72

Lochmor Country Club, North Fort Myers, (813) 995–0501, Semiprivate, 18/7000/72

Marco Shores Country Club, Naples, (813) 394–2581, Public, 18/6879/72

Naples Beach Hotel and Golf Club, Naples, (813) 261–2222, Resort, 18/6462/72

Oxbow Country Club at Port La Belle, La Belle, (813) 675–4411, Semiprivate, 18/6882/72

Port Charlotte Golf Club, Port Charlotte, (813) 625–4109, Semiprivate, 18/6681/72

South Seas Plantation, Captiva Island, (813) 992–5100, Resort, 18/6900/72

Spanish Wells Country Club, Bonita Springs, (813) 992–5100, Private (access through golf packages), 18/6900/72

Vines Country Club, Fort Myers, (813) 267–7003, Private (limited access through local hotels), 18/7029/72

Worthington Country Club, Bonita Springs, (813) 495–1750, Semiprivate, 18/6851/72

Florida: Useful Information

Florida Division of Tourism, 126 Van Buren St., Tallahassee, FL 32399, (904) 487–1462, (904) 487–1462

Department of Natural Resources, Division of Recreation and Parks, Marjory Stoneman Douglas Bldg., 3900 Commonwealth Blvd., Mail Station 535, Tallahassee, FL 32399–3000, (904) 488–9872 (recreation information)

Department of Natural Resources, Marjory Stoneman Douglas Bldg., 3900 Commonwealth Blvd., Tallahassee, FL 32399, (904) 488–7910 (saltwater fishing regulations, information)

Florida Trail Association, P. O. Box 13708, Gainesville, FL 32604, (904) 378–8823 (recreation information)

Game and Water Fish Commission, 620 S. Meridian St., Tallahassee, FL 32399–1100, (904) 488–4676 (fresh-water fishing and hunting information)

Supervisor's Office, 227 N. Bronough St., Ste. 4061, Tallahassee, FL 32301, (904) 942–9300, (800) 200–CAMP (national forest information and reservation)

Atlanta Area

Course Name: **CALLAWAY GARDENS Mountain View, Garden View, Lake View, Sky View Courses**

Course Type: Resort
Resort: Callaway Gardens
Address: Highway 27
Pine Mountain, GA 31822–2000
Phone: (800) CALLAWAY
(Golf Course)
(706) 663–2281
(800) CALLAWAY (Resort)

GOLF COURSE

Director of Golf: Don Ferrone
Course Length/Par (All Tees): Mountain View: Back 7057/72, Middle 6630/72, Ladies' Forward 5848/74. Garden View: Back 6392/72, Middle 6108/72, Forward 5848/72. Lake View: Back 6006/70, Ladies' Forward 5452/71. Sky View: Back 2096/31, Middle 1961/31, Forward 1822/31
Course Slope/Rating (All Tees): Mountain View: Back 138/74.1, Middle 129/72.3, Ladies' Forward 122/73.2. Garden View: Back 121/70.7, Middle 117/69.2, Ladies' Forward 123/72.7. Lake View: Back 115/69.4, Ladies' Forward 122/70.3. Sky View: NA/NA
Course Architects: Mountain View: Dick Wilson (1963), Joe Lee (remodeled, 1991). Garden View: Joe Lee (1968). Lake View: Dick Wilson and Joe Lee (9 holes, 1949, 9 holes, 1963). Sky View: Joe Lee (1969)
Golf Facilities: Full Pro Shop X, Snack Bar X, Lounge X, Restaurant X, Locker Room No, Showers X, Club Rental X, Club Repair Minor, Cart Rental X, Instruction X, Practice Green X, Driving Range X, Practice Bunker X, Club Storage X
Tee-Time Reservation Policy: Guests or groups with guaranteed reservation: anytime. Public: 24 hrs. in advance
Ranger: Yes
Tee-off-Interval Time: 8 min.
Time to Play 18 Holes: 4½ hrs.

Course Hours/Earliest Tee-off: 8 a.m.
Green and Cart Fees: Mountain View: $80 for 18 holes. Garden View: $65 for 18 holes. Lake View: $65 for 18 holes. Sky View: $28 for 9 holes
Pull Carts: $3 for 18 holes
Credit Cards: American Express, MasterCard, Visa
Season: Year round. Busiest months March and April
Course Comments: Mountain View: No walking. Can walk Garden View, Lake View after 5 p.m. Can walk Sky View anytime
Golf Packages: Available through resort. Highest rates March 1 to end of Nov. Lowest rates Dec. 1 to Feb.
Discounts: Twilight rates
Places to Stay Nearby: Davis Inn (706) 346–2668; King's Gap Inn (706) 628–5929; White Columns Motel (706) 663–2312; Mountain Top Inn and Resort (800) 533–6376; BED AND BREAKFAST: Wedgewood Bed and Breakfast (706) 628–5659
Local Attractions: Village of Pine Mountain, Roosevelt Riding Stables, Chipley Historical Center, Franklin D. Roosevelt State Park, Innsbrook Little Theatre, Pine Mountain Trail, Pine Mountain Wild Animal Park. Warm Springs. Atlanta. Pine Mountain Tourist Bureau (706) 663–4000, (800) 441–5502. Pine Mountain Chamber of Commerce (706) 663–8850
Directions: From Atlanta (70 mi.): I–85 south to I–185, I–185 south to exit 14, take exit 14. Turn left on Hwy. 27, 11 mi. to resort. From Columbus (30 miles): I–85 north, take exit 1. Turn right on Hwy. 18, go 17 mi. to 354, take 354 to Hwy. 27, follow signs to resort
Closest Commercial Airports: Columbus Metro (45 min.), Hartsfield Atlanta International (1 hr., 15 min.)

RESORT

Date Built: 1952
No. of Rooms: 350 guest rooms and suites as well as 155 1- to 4-bedroom cottages and 49 1- to 4-bedroom villas

Meeting/Exhibit Rooms: 11. Capacity of Largest: 900 persons. Meeting Space: 36,000 sq. ft.

Room Price Range: $89 single to $675 for 4-bedroom villa. Golf, summer family recreation plans, and other packages available

Lounge: Vineyard Green

Restaurants: Georgia Room, Plantation Room, Gardens Restaurant, Veranda Restaurant, Country Kitchen, Flower Mill Restaurant, Champions (at the Mountain View golf course)

Entertainment: Live entertainment, dancing in Vineyard Green

Credit Cards: All major cards except Diners Club

General Amenities: Gardens and the John A. Sibley Horticultural Center, Cecil B. Day Butterfly Center, Pioneer Log Cabin; Conference Center with audiovisual, banquet, secretarial services; picnic grounds, Mr. Cason's Vegetable Garden, country store, seasonal celebrations

Recreational Amenities: 17 tennis courts, Discovery Bicycle Trail, fishing, beach, miniature golf, water-skiing, racquetball, sailing, canoeing, paddleboats, steeplechase (Nov.), swimming pools, DP "Fit For Life" Fitness Center with state-of-the-art equipment and sauna

Reservation and Cancellation Policy: 1 day's room rate deposit. 7-day cancellation notification required to receive full refund

Comments and Restrictions: When more than 2 adults per room, $15 additional charge for each extra adult (18 or older). Rollaway beds available in Inn only. Taxes additional to base rates

CALLAWAY GARDENS

Callaway Gardens is a 14,000-acre resort situated among woodlands, lakes, gardens and wildlife less than 70 miles southwest of Atlanta and 30 miles north of Columbus. Cason J. Callaway conceived the idea of Callaway Gardens in 1935, when he planned to preserve the natural surroundings, protect wildlife and endangered species of plant life, and provide the public with a beautiful garden setting for education, inspiration and recreation. He and his wife, Virginia Hand Callaway, eventually realized their dream. Since the Gardens opened in 1952, more than 20 million people have visited, enjoying the many species of butterflies, birds and other wildlife to be found here. The Callaways' legacy is a marvelous gift to all who visit here.

Callaway Gardens has 63 holes of golf available highlighted by the 7057-yard Dick Wilson–designed and Joe Lee–remodeled Mountain View Course, which is the home of the PGA Tour's Buick Challenge. *Golf* magazine has awarded Callaway Gardens a Silver Medal Award as one of the best golf resorts in America, and *Golf Reporter* magazine rates Callaway Gardens' courses among the best in Georgia. Mountain View is rated one of the best resort courses by *Golf Digest*. Several lakes are on the property, and Mountain View, Garden View, Lake View and Sky View all have magnificent views of these waters, azaleas, dogwoods, pine, hollies, chrysanthemums and many other splendid plants and animals.

The Mountain View Course has a hefty 138 slope rating and a 74.1 USGA rating. This is a tight, tree-lined course, with more than 60 sand bunkers, most of them guarding the large, fast, undulating and elevated Bermuda-grass greens. There are four water holes on the course, and two lateral water hazards. The fifteenth hole, a 530-yard par 5, is one of the most challenging. This was the sixth hole until Mountain View was redesigned by Joe Lee in preparation for the Buick Challenge. Water runs along the right side of this fairway from the tee to the green, where it cuts in front. The fairway slopes from left to right toward the water, and trees line the fairway on both sides. The classic advice here is to keep the ball in play and avoid the hazards. A big hitter will be tempted to reach the green in two. This requires coming onto the green over water on the approach shot with a long iron or a wood.

The par-3 holes at Mountain View are somewhat long and challenging. A favorite is the 212-yard fifth, which plays over a valley from plateau to plateau to a deep green that slopes from right to left and is guarded by two traps on the right. If you miss the target, the ball is likely to kick down the hill from this elevated green. The finishing hole at Mountain View is a 432-yard par 4, which plays straight to a green trapped to the left rear and front right. Two right-fairway bunkers guard the landing area approximately halfway to the green. The fairway dips, then rolls up to a plateaued landing area approximately 152 yards from the green, which slopes forward and slightly to the left.

The Garden View is a 6392-yard par-72 Joe Lee–designed layout that runs along a trail of beautiful orchards and vineyards. The fairways are wider and more forgiving than those on Mountain View, and most of the holes are straight with relatively few bunkers (mostly around the greens) and only one water hole. The number-1-handicap hole on this user-friendly golf course is the 531-yard par-5 third, which plays straight to a large green guarded by two traps flanking the narrow entranceway to the green.

Lake View is a beautifully situated 6006-yard par-70 layout designed by Dick Wilson and Joe Lee. This was the original course at Callaway Gardens, and it is beautifully landscaped with azaleas and other flowers, and dogwoods. It sits right on Mountain View Lake, and its signature hole is the 152-yard par-3 fifth, which plays from an island tee over water to a well-trapped green in front of the Gardens Restaurant. Water comes into play on nine holes on this scenic layout.

Sky View is a Joe Lee–designed par-31 nine-hole executive course that plays 2096 yards from the back tees and includes four par-4 holes ranging from 280 to 338 yards.

Sky View, Garden View and Mountain View are served by the Mountain View Fairway Shop, which includes golf merchandise, shower facilities and food services. Instruction is available from the staff of PGA professionals and assistants. Practice facilities include a driving range with target greens, practice sand bunkers and a putting green. The Lake View course has its own separate pro shop and food-service, instructional and practice facilities. You can walk all of the courses except Mountain View. The public can play any of the courses but can reserve tee times only 24 hours in advance. A variety of golf packages are available at Callaway Gardens, with the lowest rates usually offered from December through February.

Across Route 27 is the 350-room Callaway Gardens Inn, with meeting and conference facilities that can accommodate up to 900 persons (banquet style), 17 tennis courts, and racquetball courts. Restaurants at Callaway include the elegant Georgia Room, Plantation Room, the Gardens, Veranda, Country Kitchen and Flower Mill restaurants. Accommodations include guest rooms and suites at the inn as well as luxurious Mountain Creek Villas or casual country cottages.

There is no end to the recreational opportunities at Callaway Gardens, which has a variety of buildings and activities spread throughout the property. The lakes are available for sailing, fishing, boating and swimming. There are gardens and floral displays at the John A. Sibley Horticultural Center. The Cecil B. Day Butterfly Center, which encompasses 4½ acres, houses a tropical conservatory with 50 species of butterflies in free flight. There is a pioneer log cabin and the Ida Cason Callaway Memorial Chapel. Mr. Cason's 7½-acre vegetable garden has a wonderful medley of approximately 400 varieties of fruits, vegetables and exotic herbs and spices. This is the southern filming site for the PBS series "The Victory Garden." Mountain Creek Lake also offers some of the South's finest bass and bream fishing.

The "Fit for Life" Fitness Center provides state-of-the-art equipment and professional counseling on exercise and nutrition. And there are 23 miles of roads and paths for joggers and bicyclists. Some major events at Callaway Gardens include Spring Celebration, Masters Water Ski Championships, The Steeplechase at Callaway, Fantasy in Lights, and organ concerts at the Ida Cason Callaway Memorial Chapel. The trails of Callaway Gardens include azalea trails, with over 700 varieties of cultivated azaleas blooming from late March to May, and several other walks through Meadowlark Gardens; Mr. Cason's Vegetable Garden; and Robin Lake Walk, Laurel Springs Trail, Chapel Trail and Mountain Creek Lake Trail, a 3-hour adventure with mallard ducks, green herons, turtles, squirrels, azaleas, rhododendra and wildflowers.

Callaway Gardens has won numerous hospitality awards including the *Mobil Travel Guide*'s Four-Star rating. Today, Callaway Gardens is a public educational, horticultural and charitable organization operated by the nonprofit Ida Cason Callaway Foundation. Callaway Gardens Resort, Inc., is a wholly owned subsidiary that operates the recreational lodging and retail facilities here. Aftertax proceeds go to the foundation to support its efforts.

Course Name: LAKE LANIER ISLANDS GOLF CLUB

Course Type: Resort
Resort: Lake Lanier Islands Hilton Resort
Address: 7000 Holiday Road Lake Lanier Islands, GA 30518
Phone: (770) 945–8787 (Golf Course), (770) 945–8787, (800) 768–LAKE (Resort)
Fax: (770) 932–5471 (Resort)

GOLF COURSE

Director of Golf: Scott Sayen

Course Length/Par (All Tees): Back 6341/72, Blue 6104/72, White 5659/72, Forward 4935/72

Course Slope/Rating (All Tees): Back 124/70.1, Blue 120/68.8, White 116/67.2, Ladies' Forward 117/68.3

Course Architect: Joe Lee (1988)

Golf Facilities: Full Pro Shop X, Snack Bar X, Lounge X, Restaurant No, Locker Room No, Showers X, Club Rental X, Club Repair No, Cart Rental X, Instruction X, Practice Green X, Driving Range X, Practice Bunker X, Club Storage Guests Only

Tee-Time Reservation Policy: Guests: At time of guaranteed or confirmed reservation. Public: Up to 1 wk. in advance

Ranger: Yes

Tee-off-Interval Time: 8 min. weekends, 10 min. weekdays

Time to Play 18 Holes: 4 hrs., 15 min.

Course Hours/Earliest Tee-off: 7:30 a.m. weekends, holidays; 8 a.m. weekdays

Green and Cart Fees: Peak season (Mar.-Oct.): $55 for 18 holes plus tax Fri., Sat. Sun., holidays; $50 for 18 holes plus tax Mon.-Thurs. Nov. – Feb. $39 plus tax

Credit Cards: All major cards

Season: Year round. Busiest season April to July

Course Comments: Cart mandatory. Cart path only

Golf Packages: Available through resort

Discounts: None

Places to Stay Nearby: Stouffer Renaissance Pine Isle Resort (770) 945–8921, (800) 468–3571

Local Attractions: Lake Lanier Islands Beach and Water Park, Chateau Elan/local winery, Lanierland Music Park. Helen, GA (German Alpine village). ATLANTA: Underground Atlanta, professional sports, Woodruff Arts Center, High Museum of Art, Emory University, Botanical Gardens, 700 Atlanta, Carter Presidential Center, Martin Luther King's birthplace. Atlanta Convention and Visitors Bureau (404) 521–6600

Directions: From Atlanta (65 mi.): I–85 north to I–985 to either exit 1 or 2. Or take Hwy. 400 to Hwy. 20, then follow signs

Closest Commercial Airport: Hartsfield Atlanta International (1 hr.)

RESORT

Date Built: 1989

No. of Rooms: 224 hotel rooms, including 12 suites

Meeting/Exhibit Rooms: 13. Capacity of Largest: 350 persons. Meeting Space: 11,000 sq. ft.

Room Price Range: $115 for single to $250 for suites peak season (Apr.-Oct.). Golf and other packages available

Lounge: Emerald Pub

Restaurants: Sylvan's on Lanier, Emerald Pub

Entertainment: Live music on holidays, special occasions

Credit Cards: All major cards

General Amenities: Babysitting, children's activities (May to Aug.); meeting and conference facilities with audiovisual, food-service and secretarial-support services

Recreational Amenities: Fitness center with weight room, sauna, whirlpool; swimming pool, beach, boating, bicycling, horseback riding, fishing, water skiing, houseboats, jogging paths, nature trails, boat rentals, RV campgrounds, miniature golf, beach and water park with water rides, camping, tennis

Reservation and Cancellation Policy: Credit card guarantee required. 48 hrs. cancellation notice for full refund

Comments and Restrictions: No pets allowed. Taxes in addition to base rates

LAKE LANIER ISLANDS GOLF CLUB

Lake Lanier Islands Hotel and Golf Club was opened in 1989 and is situated on Lake Sidney Lanier, a 38,000-acre manmade lake located 1 hour north of Atlanta. The resort was funded with a loan from the state of Georgia and now operates under the Lake Lanier Islands Authority, a not-for-profit entity. The resort has 224 rooms, including 12 suites, 11,000 square feet of meeting and conference facilities, and recreational facilities including a fitness center, beach, boating, fishing, swimming, bicycling, waterskiing, horseback riding, camping and jogging. A large proportion of the resort's business comes from company groups.

Also situated on this 1200-acre island is the 6341-yard par-72 golf course designed by Joe Lee and named one of the best new resort golf courses in the nation by *Golf Digest* in 1989. The bentgrass greens are large, moderately fast and undulating. Thirteen holes border Lake Lanier, and 75 sand bunkers strategically protect landing areas and greens. The landing areas are narrow from the back tees and more open from the shorter tee positions. The fairways are rolling, and there are some significant elevation changes from tee to fairway. The course was cut out from the woods, and if the ball strays you will be in the water or beneath the pines.

The number-1-handicap hole at Lake Lanier is the 436-yard par-4 fifth, which is completely bordered by the lake on the right. The tee shot has to carry water to a landing area, and the approach shot has to carry water again to a deep green protected by a trap and water on the right and a pair of traps to the left and rear. If the tee shot is kept to the left, you can come in over land to the deep, forward-sloping green. The sixth hole is a picturesque par 3 that plays 185 yards to a wide, shallow green with traps to the left and front and water to the right and front. The finishing hole is a tough par 4 that plays 415 yards to a wide, shallow, two-tiered green with a trap to the front and left and two traps to the rear. The tee-shot landing area has two large bunkers on the right.

The clubhouse at Lake Lanier Islands has a limited-menu restaurant, pro shop, and minimal locker and shower facilities. Golf instruction is available from the PGA professionals and assistants. A driving range, practice green and practice bunker are close to the clubhouse. Golf packages are available through the resort. Walking is not allowed, and it takes a little over 4 hours to play the course on an average day.

Within a short driving distance from the resort are campgrounds, Lake Lanier Islands Beach and Water Park, various boat-launch facilities, Lanier Sailing Academy, stables and other amenities. Houseboats with a maximum capacity of 10 persons and group boats that hold up to 45 passengers, as well as ski boats, pontoon boats, sport boats and island skimmers, can be rented. The Stouffer Renaissance Pine Isle Golf Course is within 15 minutes of the Lake Lanier Islands Resort, and Atlanta is only an hour south, should you care to pursue the cultural offerings, spectator sports and night life there.

Course Name: STONE MOUNTAIN
PARK GOLF COURSE
Stonemont, Lakemont,
Woodmont Courses

Course Type: Public
Address: Highway 78/P.O. Box 778
Stone Mountain, GA 30086
Phone: (404) 498–5716 (Tee Times)
(404) 498–5714 (State Park)
(404) 879–9900, (800) 879–
9900 (Evergreen Conference
Center and Resort)

GOLF COURSE

Head Professional: Duane Laricey
Course Length/Par (All Tees):
Stonemont: Back 6683/72, Middle
6094/72 Forward 5020/72.
Lakemont/Woodmont: Back 6598/72,
Middle 6098/72, Forward 5231/72
Course Slope/Rating (All Tees):
Stonemont: Back 133/72.6, Middle
128/71.2, Forward 121/69.1.
Lakemont/Woodmont: Back 130/71.6,
Middle 119/69.0, Ladies' Forward
120/69.4
Course Architects: Stonemont: Robert
Trent Jones, Sr. (front 9, 1971), John La
Foy (back 9, 1992). Lakemont: John La
Foy (9 holes, 1989). Woodmont: Robert
Trent Jones, Sr. (9 holes, 1971)
Golf Facilities: Full Pro Shop X, Snack
Bar X, Lounge X, Restaurant X,
Locker Room No, Showers No, Club
Rental X, Club Repair Minor, Cart
Rental X, Instruction X, Practice
Green X, Driving Range X, Practice
Bunker X, Club Storage At Resort
Tee-Time Reservation Policy: Tuesday
7 a.m. prior to weekend for Sat., Sun.,
holidays. Weekday tee times up to 1
week in advance
Ranger: Yes
Tee-off-Interval Time: 10 min.
Time to Play 18 Holes: 4½ hrs.
Course Hours/Earliest Tee-off: 8 a.m.
Green and Cart Fees: $40 for 18 holes,
$20 for 9 holes with cart
Credit Cards: American Express, Master-
Card, Visa
Season: Year round
Course Comments: Cart mandatory

Golf Packages: Available through Evergreen Hotel (404) 879–9900, (800) 722–
1000, on site
Discounts: None
Places to Stay Nearby: Evergreen Conference Center and Resort (404) 879–9900,
(800) 722–1000; Stone Mountain Park
Inn (404) 469–3311; Holiday Inn Atlanta—Decator Conference Plaza (404)
371–0204, (800) HOLIDAY
Local Attractions: Dekalb Farmer's
Market, Dekalb Historical Society,
Emory University, Fernbank Science
Center, Stone Mountain State Park
(3200 acres). ATLANTA: Atlanta Botanical Garden, Atlanta History Center,
Carter Presidential Center, Museum of
the Jimmy Carter Library, Georgia
state capitol, Antebellum Plantation,
Atlanta Zoo; Martin Luther King, Jr.,
national historic site; Six Flags over
Georgia, World of Coca-Cola™;
Scitrek, Science and Technology
Museum of Atlanta; High Museum
of Art, restaurants, shopping, horse
racing, auto racing; professional base-
ball, football, basketball; theater and
concerts in Civic Center Auditorium,
Robert W. Woodruff Memorial Arts
Center, Alliance Theatre. Atlanta
Convention and Visitors Bureau,
(404) 521–6600. Atlanta Chamber of
Commerce (404) 586–8430
Directions: From Hartsfield Atlanta Inter-
national Airport (30 mi.): I–285 north
and east to exit 30B to Hwy. 78 east to
Stone Mountain Park and golf courses.
From Atlanta (16 mi.): Hwy. 20 east to
I–285, then same directions as above
Closest Commercial Airport: Hartsfield
Atlanta International (45 min.)

STONE MOUNTAIN PARK GOLF COURSE

Stone Mountain State Park is on 3200
acres and has the largest granite outcropping on earth. The Confederate Memorial
on the north face of this 825-foot-high
outcropping is the world's largest sculpture.
There are two eighteen-hole golf courses
at Stone Mountain, including the Stonemont, which includes nine holes designed

by Robert Trent Jones, Sr., and nine by John La Foy. The Lakemont/Woodmont eighteen includes the Lakemont nine, designed by La Foy, and the Woodmont nine, designed by Jones. The courses, which have been cut through tall, mature forests, are rolling, tight, well bunkered, and, in the case of Lakemont, guarded by water. There are magnificent views of forests, granite mountains, and Stone Mountain Lake here.

The Stonemont eighteen plays 6683 yards from the back tees. On the front nine you start out with a 451-yard par 4 that plays straight down a tree-lined fairway to a wide, shallow green protected by a trap on the left. A tough par 3 at Stonemont is the fifteenth, which plays 230 yards to a large green protected by traps both left and right. The par 5s on the Stonemont course are relatively short. The 518-yard third is a dogleg left around a tree-lined corner to a medium-sized green protected by a trap on the right. The 496-yard sixteenth is straight down a tree-lined fairway to a deep green with traps both left and right.

The original Stonemont holes, designed by Jones, are holes one through five and fifteen through eighteen. New holes designed by La Foy to extend Stonemont to eighteen holes make up the balance of the course. The new Stonemont eighteen opened in May 1992.

A tough hole on the 6595-yard Lakemont/Woodmont eighteen is the 418-yard par-4 eleventh, which plays straight to a large green guarded by a creek in front and surrounded left, right and rear by four traps. Depending on your tee shot and ability to hit long irons from the fairway, you might have to lay up on this one. A difficult par 3 on this side is the 188-yard sixteenth, which affords you a view of the magnificent Stone Mountain sculpture of Robert E. Lee and his colleagues. The green on this hole is wide, shallow and protected by large traps front and rear. The finishing hole is a 513-yard par-5 dogleg left to a large, deep green trapped left and right. Fairway bunkers guard the tee-shot landing area on the left. Another large bunker is in the fair-

way 120 yards from the green. Typically all the bentgrass greens on this eighteen are somewhat large.

The front-side Lakemont nine, which is somewhat shorter than the back nine at 3154 yards from the back tees, features the 274-yard par-4 sixth, a dogleg left with water to the left and a rock quarry to the right. A difficult par 3 on this side is the 222-yard second hole, which plays away from Stone Mountain Lake to a large green with a large bunker to the right.

Within the Stone Mountain complex is the Evergreen Conference Center and Resort, which opened in 1989. This facility has easy access to the golf courses and offers a variety of reasonably priced tennis, fitness, family, golf and other packages. The hotel has 250 guest rooms, including 29 suites; a 192-seat restaurant; veranda dining area with a panoramic view of the lake; and cocktail lounges. The 40,000-square-foot conference center includes 11 meeting rooms, 3 executive board rooms, a 126-seat amphitheater, a ballroom and an exhibit hall. Full audiovisual, food-service and secretarial-support services are available.

Other recreational facilities include indoor and outdoor swimming pools, a fully equipped fitness center, tennis courts, jogging trails, bicycling and the recreational amenities of the 363-acre lake with its 3200 surrounding acres. All of this is conveniently located 16 miles from Atlanta and 30 miles from Hartsfield International Airport.

Stone Mountain will be the site of five events in the 1996 Summer Olympics: rowing, canoeing, archery, tennis and indoor cycling (velodrome) all will be staged in the park. Permanent rowing and canoeing courses will be constructed on the lake, and the Olympic tennis facility will be a permanent addition.

Course Name: STOUFFER RENAISSANCE PINE ISLE RESORT

Course Type: Resort
Resort: Stouffer Renaissance Pine Isle Resort

Address: 9000 Holiday Road
                Lake Lanier Islands, GA
                30518
Phone: (770) 945–8921 (Golf Course)
                (770) 945–8921,
                (800) 468–3571 (Resort)
Fax: (770) 468–3571 (Resort)

GOLF COURSE

Director of Golf: Larry Thomas
Head Professional: John Combs
Course Length/Par (All Tees): Back
  6527/72, White 6154/72, Gold 6025/72,
  Forward 5297/72
Course Slope/Rating (All Tees): Back
  122/71.4, White 117/69.4, Gold 117/69,
  Forward 116/65.9. Ladies' Back
  122/NA, Ladies' White 117/74.8, La-
  dies' Gold 117/74.3, Ladies' Forward
  116/70.5
Course Architects: Gary Player, Ron
  Kirby and Arthur Davis (1973)
Golf Facilities: Full Pro Shop X, Snack
  Bar X, Lounge X, Restaurant X,
  Locker Room X, Showers X, Club
  Rental X, Club Repair Limited, Cart
  Rental X, Instruction X, Practice
  Green X, Driving Range X, Practice
  Bunker X, Club Storage X
Tee-Time Reservation Policy: Guests:
  Reserve at time of reservation. Public: 5
  days in advance for weekends and holi-
  days, 1 week in advance for weekdays.
  Credit card deposit required
Ranger: Yes
Tee-off-Interval Time: 8 min.
Time to Play 18 Holes: 4½ hrs.
Course Hours/Earliest Tee-off: 7:30 a.m.
Green and Cart Fees: $59 for 18 holes
  Fri., Sat., Sun., holidays; $54 for 18
  holes Mon. to Thurs., with cart
Credit Cards: All major cards
Season: Year round. Busiest season March
  to Oct.
Course Comments: Can walk after 5 p.m.
  Yardage book available. Annual member-
  ships available
Golf Packages: Available through resort
Discounts: Twilight rates. Seasonal dis-
  counts (lowest rates late Nov. to mid-
  Mar.)

Places to Stay Nearby: Lake Lanier
  Islands Hilton Resort (770) 945–8787,
  (800) 768–LAKE
Local Attractions: Lake Lanier Islands
  Beach and Water Park, Chateau Elan/
  local winery, Lanierland Music Park.
  Helen, GA (German Alpine village).
  ATLANTA: Underground Atlanta, profes-
  sional sports, Woodruff Arts Center,
  High Museum of Art, Emory University,
  Botanical Gardens, 700 Atlanta, Carter
  Presidential Center, Martin Luther
  King's Birthplace. Atlanta Convention
  and Visitors Bureau (404) 521–6600
Directions: From Hartsfield Atlanta Inter-
  national Airport (65 mi.): I–85 north to
  I–985 to Gainesville, GA. To exit
  2/Friendship Rd., exit and take left at
  exit ramp, 1 mi. to Rte. 13, take left and
  first right on Holiday Rd. Follow to
  Lake Lanier Islands and Resort. From
  Tennessee and I–75 south: I–75 south to
  I–285 north/east, then I–85 north, follow
  directions above. From the Carolinas:
  I–85 south to junction of Rte. 20/exit 46.
  At end of exit ramp take right. Go 2 mi.
  to I–985, take I–985 and follow direc-
  tions above
Closest Commercial Airport: Hartsfield
  Atlanta International (1 hr.)

RESORT

Date Built: 1973
No. of Rooms: 250 guest rooms, suites and
  spa rooms
Meeting/Exhibit Rooms: 25. Capacity of
  Largest: 400 persons. Meeting Space:
  30,000 sq. ft.
Room Price Range: $145 1-bedroom to
  $245 2-bedroom peak season (late Mar.
  to late Dec.). Golf and other packages
  available
Lounge: Champions Lounge
Restaurants: Breezes, Clubhouse, Grille
  Room, Marina Grill
Entertainment: Live music
Credit Cards: All major cards
General Amenities: Business-meeting and
  conference facilities with audiovisual,
  banquet, secretarial-support services;
  shuttle services to Atlanta Hartsfield International Airport, children's programs,

babysitting, organized games, loaner cameras, video games, theme parties, party boats

Recreational Amenities: Sailing (38,000-acre Lake Lanier), volleyball, water sports, aerobics classes, horseback riding, massage therapy, basketball, horseshoes, table tennis, saunas, shuffleboard, boat rentals, fishing, water-skiing, pontoon boats, house boats, bicycle rentals, hiking and jogging trails, indoor/outdoor swimming pool, 7 indoor/outdoor lighted tennis courts, fitness center with Nautilus, Lifecycle, StairMaster machines

Reservation and Cancellation Policy: 1 night's deposit required. Changes or cancellations should be made 14 days prior to scheduled arrival to avoid penalties

Comments and Restrictions: Children under 18 yrs. of age are complimentary when sharing the same room with adults. Add $20 for each additional person (adult) per room. Taxes additional to base rates

STOUFFER RENAISSANCE PINE ISLE RESORT

The Stouffer Renaissance Pine Isle Resort is 1 hour north of Atlanta on Lake Sidney Lanier, a 38,000-acre man-made lake named for Sidney Clapton Lanier, a nineteenth-century poet laureate of Georgia, because of the tribute he gave the area in his "Song of the Cattahoochee." The resort borders Lake Lanier, and its land is leased from the Army Corps of Engineers. Its 6527-yard par-72 golf course is beautifully situated on the lake and is considered by *Golf Digest* to be one of the best resort golf courses in America. Stouffer Pine Isle was designed in the early 1970s by Gary Player, Ron Kirby and Arthur Davis. At that time it was called the Pine Isle Country Club. The greens are bentgrass and are large, and moderate to fast depending on the season. The course is rolling and well treed with beautiful pine, dogwood and many other hardwoods. The azaleas are beautiful in spring if the deer don't get them first. It is not easy to get a flat lie on this course, and it is likely that you will use every club in your bag. A good short game is handy because of the tricky greens and the many traps protecting them.

The par-5 fifth hole is the signature hole and the first of eight water holes on the course. A 489-yard dogleg left with water on the left all the way to, and in back of, the green, this hole tempts the golfer to try to cut off distance over the water on the left to reach the green in two. The second shot is also likely to be over water to the deep, two-tiered green if you're a big hitter. Or the second shot can be a layup to a narrowing fairway with water on the left and three bunkers to the right from 50 yards into the putting surface. During the winter, the wind can be in your face on this hole, making it play much tougher.

The back nine has four memorable finishing holes. The 248-yard par-3 fifteenth is a beautiful hole, playing over water to a very narrow, deep green with two huge traps on the left and one on the right. Beyond this peninsula green is Lake Lanier. The fifteenth plays a less daunting 161 yards from the white tees. The 405-yard par-4 sixteenth plays over water to a landing area protected by a fairway bunker on the left. The next shot is slightly uphill to a recently enlarged green with a bunker to the right and in front. Previously, the bunker was completely in front of a smaller green, making the second shot very nasty. The tee distance for the blue, white, and gold tees are identical on this difficult hole.

The seventeenth is a 195-yard par 3 and is the number-8-handicap hole on the course. The tee is beautifully situated at one of the highest points on the course and plays to a deep, two-tiered green approximately 20 feet below. There are large traps left and right of this forward-sloping green, making the tee shot especially difficult if the pin is on the back shelf. The 365-yard par-4 eighteenth is not long, but it is tricky. A dogleg left, with water on the left all the way to and around a peninsula holding the green, the tee shot is over water to a landing area straddled by two fairway bunkers. The second shot is over water that cuts sharply into the fairway. Because of the angle, it is not easy to judge distance, so you might have to hit a ball or two into the water to find out. The green is narrow and deep and slopes somewhat toward the water. Three traps, including a large one paralleling the right side of the green, provide something more to think about.

The clubhouse has locker rooms, showers, a snack bar and a pro shop. Individual and group instruction are available from the staff of professionals. The 250-room hotel with additional restaurants including the Champions Lounge is within walking distance of the first tee, driving range and putting green. A variety of golf packages are available through the hotel. Other package plans for families, tennis aficionados and honeymooners are also offered. It is possible to play the course if you are not a guest of the resort, but hotel guests and annual members have preference for tee times.

The resort itself has a variety of facilities and activities on its 1200-acre site. These include the recreational benefits of Lake Lanier, which provides fishing, boating and excursion opportunities. A variety of organized games and activities, including tennis (7 courts), horseback riding, bicycling, hiking, jogging, basketball, swimming and volleyball, are available. There is over 30,000 square feet of meeting space in numerous configurations (25 meeting rooms) with full audiovisual, food service and secretarial support available. There are four restaurants, with live entertainment and dancing in the Champions Lounge. The resort has won various hospitality awards, including the American Automobile Association's Four-Diamond and *Mobil Travel Guide*'s Four-Star designations.

Course Name: WHITE COLUMNS GOLF CLUB

Course Type: Public
Address: 300 White Columns Drive
              Alpharetta, GA 30201
Phone: (770) 343-9025

Fax: (770) 772-0686

GOLF COURSE

Head Professional: Scott Mahr
Course Length/Par (All Tees): Back 7053/72, Blue 6517/72, White 6015/72, Forward 5087/72
Course Slope/Rating (All Tees): Back 137/73.6, Blue 123/71.1, White 114/67.4, Ladies' Forward 116/69.0
Course Architect: Tom Fazio (1994)
Golf Facilities: Full Pro Shop X, Snack Bar X, Lounge No, Restaurant X, Locker Room X, Showers X, Club Rental X, Club Repair X, Cart Rental X, Instruction X, Practice Green X, Driving Range X, Practice Bunker X, Club Storage No
Tee-Time Reservation Policy: Up to 5 days in advance
Ranger: Yes
Tee-off-Interval Time: 8 min.
Time to Play 18 Holes: 4½ hrs.
Course Hours/Earliest Tee-off: 7:58 a.m.
Green and Cart Fees: $80 for 18 holes Sat., Sun., holidays; $70 for 18 holes weekdays
Credit Cards: American Express, MasterCard, Visa
Season: Year round. Busiest Apr. through Sept.
Course Comments: Walking allowed at full golf fee rate. Yardage book available
Golf Packages: No
Discounts: No
Places to Stay Nearby: Residence Inn by Marriott (770) 664–0664, (800) 331–3131. ATLANTA: Nikko Atlanta Hotel (404) 881–9898, (800) 952–0702. BUCKHEAD: Embassy Suites of Buckhead (404) 261–7733, (800) 362–2779; Ritz-Carlton Buckhead (404) 237–2700, (800) 241–3333. ROSWELL: Courtyard by Marriott (770) 992–7200, (800) 443–6600
Local Attractions: ALPHARETTA: Greater North Fulton County Chamber of Commerce, 1025 Old Roswell Rd., Roswell, GA 30076 (770) 993–8806. ATLANTA: See page 00
Directions: From Atlanta (40 min. north): Take GA 400 north to Exit 9 (Haynes Bridge Rd.) and turn left. At Academy

St. turn left and cross Hwy. 9. Academy St. becomes Milton Ave. and then Mid-Broadwell Rd. From Mid-Broadwell Rd. turn right onto Mayfield Rd., then left on Freemanville Rd. The entrance to White Columns is approximately 5 min. on your left

Closest Commercial Airport: Hartsfield Atlanta International (1 hr.)

WHITE COLUMNS GOLF CLUB

Rated among "The Top 10 You Can Play" for 1994 by *Golf* magazine, White Columns is emblematic of the growth of quality golf courses in the Atlanta area. This Tom Fazio–designed layout is nestled in the scenic rolling hills called the crab-apple area, just north of the city. When you step into the handsomely appointed club-house with its large, well-stocked pro shop, comfortable grill room, locker rooms and showers, patio, and spacious tournament function areas, there is an air of quality and competence about the place. The nearby practice area features an expansive teeing area with six target greens, two putting and chipping greens, practice bunkers, and a private instruction practice area set back from the madding crowd.

The golf course covers 250 rolling, treelined acres and features pronounced elevation changes, sizeable bunkers, forced carries over lakes, creeks and marshland ponds, and a variety of interesting angles of attack to the large, well-guarded, Cren-shaw bentgrass greens. One of the most difficult holes on the front side is the 421-yard par-4 fourth which plays from ele-vated tees to a landing area protected by bunkers and trees. The approach is uphill to a deep, forward-sloping green with swales and dropoffs to its right and a bank with swales to its left. An incoming wind often adds to the difficulty of this hole. The back nine concludes with two great holes, a 208-yard par 3 that dramatically drops at least 100 feet to a large, tree-framed green protected by bunkers, and next a 413-yard par 4—a blind dogleg left that starts from an elevated tee and then swings uphill to a sizeable green with water and traps to its right and a steep bank on the left.

The White Columns is owned by Fuji Development which also owns the nearby Golf Club of Georgia, one of the best private clubs in the state. White Columns is part of an unobtrusive 550-acre residential community featuring homes starting in the low $300,000 range. The plan is to keep White Columns a quality daily fee golf course with country club amenities.

Recommended Golf Courses in Georgia

Within 1 Hour of Atlanta:

Barrington Hall Golf Club, Macon, (912) 757–8358, Semiprivate, 18/7062/72

The Boulders Course, Acworth, (404) 917–5151, Public, 18/6759/71

Centennial Golf Club, Acworth, (404) 975–1000, Public, 18/6849/72

Chateau Elan Golf Club, Braselton, (770) 867–0417, Public, 18/7030/71

The Champions Club of Atlanta, Al-pharetta, (404) 343–9700, Semiprivate, 18/6725/72

Chattahoochee Golf Club, Gainesville, (404) 532–0066, Public, 18/6700/72

Chicopee Woods Golf Course, Gainesville, (404) 534–7322, Public, 18/7040/72

Eagle Watch Golf Club, Woodstock, (404) 591–1000, Public, 18/6896/72

Fields Ferry Golf Club, Calhoun, (706) 625–5666, Public, 18/6824/72

Georgia National Golf Club, McDonough, (404) 914–9994, Public, 18/6874/72

Hamilton Mill Golf Club, Dacula, (404) 945–4653, 18/6810/72

Harbor Club, Greensboro, (706) 453–4414, (800) 505–4653, Semiprivate, 18/6988/72

Hard Labor Creek Golf Course, Rutledge, (706) 557–2143, Public, 18/6437/72

Lake Arrowhead Country Club, Waleska, (404) 681–2230, Semiprivate, 18/6400/72

Lakeside Country Club, Atlanta, (404) 344–3629, Public, 18/6522/71

Lane Creek Golf Club, Bishop, (706) 769–6699, (800) 842–6699, Public, 18/6725/72

Metropolitan Golf Club, Lithonia, (404) 981–7696, Semiprivate, 18/6030/72

The Oaks Golf Course, Covington, (404) 221–0200, Public, 18/6420/70

Olde Atlanta Golf Club, Suwanee, (404) 497–0097, Semiprivate, 18/6800/71

Orchard Hills Golf Club, Newman, (404) 251–5683, Public, 18/7100/72

Plantation Golf Course, Stockbridge, (404) 830–8616, Semiprivate, 18/6612/72

Riverpines Golf Club, Alpharetta, (404) 422–5960, Public, 18/6511/70

River's Edge Golf Course, Fayetteville, (404) 460–1098, Semiprivate, 18/6810/71

Royal Lakes Golf and Country Club, Flowery Branch, (404) 535–8800, Semiprivate, 18/6851/72

St. Marlo Golf Club, Duluth, (404) 495–7725, Public, 18/6900/72

Sconti Golf Club, Big Canoe, (706) 268–3323, Resort. Choctaw/Cherokee: 18/6371/72. Cherokee/Creek: 18/6276/72. Choctaw/Creek: 18/6247/72

Southerness Golf Course, Stockbridge, (404) 808–6000, Semiprivate, 18/6766/72

Towne Lake Hills Golf Club, Woodstock, (404) 592–9969, Public, 18/6757/72

University of Georgia Golf Course, Athens, (404) 369–5739, Semiprivate, 18/6939

Whitewater Creek Country Club, Fayetteville, (404) 461–6545, Semiprivate, 18/6739/72

Augusta Area

Course Name: JONES CREEK GOLF CLUB

Course Type: Public
Address: 4101 Hammond's Ferry Evans, GA 30809
Phone: (706) 860–4228

GOLF COURSE

Head Professional: Greg Hemann
Course Length/Par (All Tees): Back 7008/72, Blue 6557/72, White 6126/72, Forward 5430/72
Course Slope/Rating (All Tees): Back 137/73.8, Blue 131/71.9, White 124/70.0, Ladies' Forward 130/72.4
Course Architect: Rees Jones (1986)
Golf Facilities: Full Pro Shop X, Snack Bar X, Lounge X, Restaurant X, Locker Room X, Showers X, Club Rental X, Club Repair Minor, Cart Rental X, Instruction X, Practice Green X, Driving Range X, Practice Bunker X, Club Storage X
Tee-Time Reservation Policy: Members have priority for tee times. From Fri. 8 p.m. public can book up to 6 days in advance
Ranger: Yes
Tee-off-Interval Time: 8 min.
Time to Play 18 Holes: 4½ hrs.
Course Hours/Earliest Tee-off: 7:30 a.m. peak season
Green and Cart Fees: $42 for 18 holes Sat., Sun., holidays with cart or walking (limited); $39 for 18 holes Fri. with cart or walking (limited); $32 for 18 holes Mon.-Thurs. with cart or walking (limited)
Credit Cards: American Express, MasterCard, Visa
Season: Year round. Closed Christmas Day only
Course Comments: Can walk anytime weekdays, after 1 p.m. weekends and holidays. Yardage book available. Limited memberships available
Golf Packages: Available
Discounts: None
Places to Stay Nearby: Holiday Inn West (706) 738–8811, (800) HOLIDAY; Sheraton Augusta Hotel (706) 855–8100, (800) 325–3535; Radisson Inn (404) 868–1800, (800) 333–3333; Landmark Hotel of Augusta (706) 722–5541
Local Attractions: Augusta Ballet, Maxwell Performing Arts Theatre, Augusta Players Playhouse, Augusta Symphony, Augusta National Golf Course, fishing, boating, swimming, tennis, Olde Towne Historic District, Augusta Richmond County Museum, Augusta riverboat cruises, Gertrude Herbert Institute of Art, Meadow Garden, Sacred Heart Cultural Center, St. Paul's Episcopal Church.

Chamber of Commerce (706) 821–1300.
Tourist Bureau (706) 721–3276

Directions: From Atlanta (130 mi.): I–20
south, Bellaire/exit 63, to stop sign and
turn left over interstate, go through all
stop lights to stop sign, Evans Two
Locks Rd., right, 2 mi. to Jones Creek
on left, follow main road to clubhouse

Closest Commercial Airports: Augusta/
Bush Field (20 min.), Savannah Interna-
tional (2 hrs.), Hartsfield Atlanta
International (2½ hrs.)

JONES CREEK GOLF CLUB

The Jones Creek Golf Club is situated
in a 520-acre planned community 20 minutes from downtown Augusta, Georgia,
and 5 minutes from the Augusta National
Golf Course. The 7008-yard layout is a
Rees Jones design with woodlands, winding creeks and rolling terrain. Water
comes into play on eight holes, and the
large bentgrass greens tend to be undulating and quick, and are well protected by
traps. The course is ranked by *Golf Digest* as one of the top 75 public golf
courses in the United States. With its impressive clubhouse, modeled after the
Shinnecock Hills Golf Club on Long
Island, New York (built in 1892),
and surrounding upscale community,
Jones Creek has the feel of a private
resort course but has reasonable fees,
especially considering the quality of the
facility.

Jones Creek should be a challenge to
golfers of all levels. The course is
sloped at 137 with a USGA rating of
73.8 from the back tees, but there are
four tee distances, the shortest being
5430 yards. One of the toughest holes
on the course is the 456-yard par-4
seventh, a dogleg left playing down a
tight, tree-lined fairway to a deep green
with two traps to the left and one on
the right. The second shot is a severe
70- to 80-foot drop to the putting surface. This hole plays 432 yards from
the blue tees and 401 yards from the
whites, so it should be a challenge to
anyone. A beautiful but tough hole on
the front side is the 220-yard par-3

second, which plays over water to a large
green with two traps in front and one to the
right.

The back nine at Jones Creek has
more water but is about the same distance as the front side. The two finishing
holes are long, difficult par 4s, both
doglegs. The 460-yard seventeenth is
well treed and bends to the left to a deep
green that is somewhat elevated. Four
fairway bunkers protect the tee-shot landing area, and the green is guarded left,
right and rear by a total of four traps.
The 452-yard eighteenth is a dogleg to
the right from an elevated tee with a
severe drop to the landing area, which is
protected by a trap to the left. The shot to
the green is back uphill, making the hole
play extremely long. The green is wide,
shallow and protected by a trap on the
right.

After your trip around the golf course,
a well-appointed clubhouse awaits you. Its
classic architecture features Palladian windows, Doric columns, and French doors.
Knickers, the clubhouse restaurant, provides everything from light meals to more
formal dinners, and the pro shop, which
has been recognized by *Golf Shop Operations* magazine as one of the best in the
country, offers a complete line of golf
apparel and equipment. Individual and
group instruction is available at the complete practice facilities. And the clubhouse has complete locker-room and
shower facilities for men and women.

Jones Creek has been recognized by the
Golf Reporter as the best pay-per-play
course in Georgia. It draws golfers from
all over the state and, especially at the
time of the Masters Tournament, which is
held only 4½ miles away, from all over
the world.

The combination of a beautifully maintained, well-designed golf course; excellent amenities; reasonable rates; and
scenic pines, maples, oaks, dogwoods
and a variety of other beautiful flora and
fauna on these rolling hills makes golf a
great experience at Jones Creek.

Course Name: PORT ARMOR

Course Type: Resort
Address: 1 Port Armor Parkway
                (off Highway 44)
                Greensboro, GA 30642
Phone: (706) 453–4564,
                (800) 804–7678 (Resort)
                (706) 804–7678 (Resort)
Fax: (706) 453–2802 (Resort)

GOLF COURSE

Head Professional: Jeff Maynor
Course Length/Par (All Tees): Back
  6926/72, Blue 6285/72, White
  5860/72, Forward 5177/72
Course Slope/Rating (All Tees): Back
  140/74.0, Blue 132/71.2, White
  128/70.5, Ladies' Forward 131/72.8
Course Architect: Robert Cupp (1986)
Golf Facilities: Full Pro Shop X, Snack
  Bar X, Lounge X, Restaurant X,
  Locker Room X, Showers X, Club
  Rental X, Club Repair Minor, Cart
  Rental X, Instruction X, Practice
  Green X, Driving Range X, Practice
  Bunker X, Club Storage X
Tee-Time Reservation Policy: Up to 1 yr.
  in advance with credit card guarantee
Ranger: Yes
Tee-off-Interval Time: 8 min.
Time to Play 18 Holes: 4½ hrs.
Course Hours/Earliest Tee-off: 8 a.m.
Green and Cart Fees: $53 for 18 holes
  with cart
Credit Cards: American Express, Master-
  Card, Visa
Season: Year round. Busiest season April
  to Sept.
Course Comments: Carts mandatory.
  Yardage book available
Golf Packages: Available through resort
Discounts: None
Places to Stay Nearby: Inn on the Green
  (adjacent to golf course) (706) 453–
  7366; Jameson Inn (706) 453–9135.
  BED AND BREAKFAST: Early Hill Bed
  and Breakfast (706) 453–7876
Local Attractions: Tennis, Lake Oconee
  with boating, fishing, waterskiing,
  swimming; Georgia College; Oconee
  National Forest with hunting, fishing,
  camping, hiking, picnicking. Athens.

Macon. Augusta. Atlanta. Greensboro
Chamber of Commerce (706) 453–7592
Directions: From Atlanta (65 mi.): I–20
  east to exit 53, south (right) on Hwy.
  44 for 6 mi., course on the right. From
  Augusta (65 mi.): I–20 west toward
  Atlanta, take exit 53/Greensboro, left on
  Hwy. 44, 6 mi. to Port Armor on the
  right
Closest Commercial Airports: Athens
  (45 min.); Lewis B. Wilson, Macon
  (1 hr., 15 min.); Augusta/Bush Field
  (1½ hrs.); Hartsfield Atlanta International (1½ hrs.)

PORT ARMOR

The 6926-yard par-72 Port Armor
Course is the cornerstone of a 600-acre
real-estate development on Lake Oconee
approximately 65 miles east of Atlanta and
65 miles west of Augusta. The Port Armor
course was designed by Robert Cupp, formerly a golf-course designer with Jack
Nicklaus. In 1985 Cupp established his
own firm in southern Florida. Cupp collaborated with Nicklaus on the Grand Traverse
(the Bear Course) in Acme, Michigan; the
Park Meadows Golf Course in Park City,
Utah (also with Jay Morrish); and many
other quality layouts. He has a home near
the Port Armor course and justifiably takes
great pride in what is now one of the top-
ranked courses in the state of Georgia.

The number-1-handicap hole at Port
Armor is the 457-yard par-4 fourth, which
is a slight dogleg left bordered by Lake
Oconee on the left from tee to green. To
quote directly from the yardage book and
from Robert Cupp, the architect:

Number 4 is a perfect example of chal-
lenge and reward, or strategic golf. The
fairway is expansive and can bail you out
to the right as far as you like. However,
your approach to the green is much more
difficult from the right side of the fairway.
Hit your driver. You need to carry the
swale across the fairway, and it is a much
more difficult shot to the green from down
in the swale.

Once you have reached position "A,"
as it is known, the view is spectacular. The

backdrop of the green is 2 miles of Lake Oconee, so you don't want to be long.

From the gold (back) tees it is a different hole than from the member's tees. It's a long carry to the fairway and it is deceiving because the intended line of flight appears to be farther to the left than it really should be. Aim the ball towards the first spot of open fairway that you see and draw the ball. (If you can't play this shot you are on the wrong tee.) From the member's tee the carry is much easier and almost 100 yards shorter.

You will notice from the landing area that there is a roll across the putting surface. If you look closely, you will be able to see whether the pin is in front or in back of this roll. If it is in back, it is at least one more club. The roll will test your ability to gauge the speed of your putts.

The golf course is clearly laid out in front of you at Port Armor, and the fairways tend to roll as they wind their way through the development. The Bermudagrass greens tend to be small to medium-sized, undulating, and moderate in speed. Water comes into play on half the holes. The elevation on the course can change 30 to 40 feet on a given hole. Bunkers, mounds or water guard every green.

The finishing holes on both the front and back side are excellent. The 442-yard par-4 ninth is a slight dogleg to the right, with water coming into play on the second shot into the hole. Cupp's comments from the yardage book:

This is one of the most demanding drives on the golf course because there is a severe contour on both sides of the fairway (but no bunkers). It will be possible to advance the ball, but the chances of getting it close will be much less from the rough. The approach is a middle to long iron to an extremely large putting surface guarded by a pond on the right side. The green is completely open on the left, and again, there are no bunkers.

The putting surface has two levels, and the change of elevation features a "muffin" in the right front corner of the putting surface. In contrast, Cupp elected to close out the eighteen with a much shorter hole. The 351-yard eighteenth is a dogleg left requiring a second shot over water to the smallest green on the course. Cupp's thoughts, again from the yardage book:

This tee shot is deceiving. In truth, you have a 75-yard-wide target. Literally, you can hit the ball almost anywhere. Don't be taken with the vista of the green in front of the clubhouse. Please notice the bunkers on the left side of the fairway along the lake. From most of the tees, particularly from the gold tees, the one small section of fairway that you can see is the best approach angle to the green. That is the left side of the fairway, very close to the bunkers that lie along the lake.

The approach is purely heroic. You have no option but to play the ball over the lake with the short iron. Again, club selection is extremely important. The green is deeper than it appears. There is a high back-right pin placement guarded by bunkers that makes the final approach very exciting. Again, like #16, the toughest birdie, and maybe the toughest birdie on the entire golf course, is the pin directly above the bunker in the front of the green.

Given Cupp's comments, it would help to have him come along for us to fully appreciate his golf course. As an interim measure, the helpful yardage book at Port Armor can serve as a surrogate architect.

At the nineteenth hole is a 20,000-square-foot clubhouse with pro shop, bar, restaurant, club rentals, locker rooms and showers. The staff of professionals provides individual and group instruction. Tee times can be made a year in advance with a credit card guarantee. April through September is the peak season, and Port Armor is especially busy around the time of the Masters Tournament in nearby Augusta.

The Inn on the Green is within walking distance of the golf course and has 28 guest rooms beginning from around $90 a night for single occupancy. Golf packages can be obtained through the inn, which has tennis courts, conference meeting-room facilities for up to 65 persons, and complete audiovisual and banquet-service capabilities. There is also a private dining area, billiard room, library, croquet, tennis courts, a health spa with exercise equipment, swimming pool, boating, fishing, volleyball, horseshoes, sauna and hydro shower available at the inn. A veranda affords you a view of Lake Oconee.

Lake Oconee is the second-largest lake in the state of Georgia, with 19,050 acres of water and 374 miles of wooded shoreline. Sport fish in the lake include largemouth, white, striped and hybrid bass; black crappie; bream and catfish. There are four marinas on the lake, and area residential and golf communities include Port Armor, Reynolds Plantation, and Harbor Club.

Course Name: REYNOLDS PLANTATION GOLF CLUB Plantation, Great Waters Courses

Course Type: Resort
Address: 100 Linger Longer Road
              Greensboro, GA 30642
Phone: (800) 733–LAKE

GOLF COURSE

Head Professionals: Plantation: Tom Fowler. Great Waters: Rick Dodd
Course Length/Par (All Tees): Plantation: Back 6656/71, White 6017/71, Ladies' Forward 5162/72. Great Waters: Back 7048/72, Blue 6545/72, White 6022/72, Forward 5057/72
Course Slope/Rating (All Tees): Plantation: Back 125/71.2, White 119/68.5, Ladies' Forward 117/69.1. Great Waters: Back 140/74.7, Blue 135/72.4, White 130/70.1, Forward 118/68.0
Course Architects: Plantation: Robert Cupp with Fuzzy Zoeller, Hubert Green (1988). Great Waters: Jack Nicklaus (1993)
Golf Facilities: Full Pro Shop X, Snack Bar X, Lounge X, Restaurant X, Locker Room X, Showers X, Club Rental X, Club Repair X, Cart Rental X, Instruction X, Practice Green X, Driving Range X, Practice Bunker No, Club Storage X
Tee-Time Reservation Policy: Up to 3 days in advance for non-members
Ranger: Yes

Tee-off-Interval Time: 8 min.
Time to Play 18 Holes: 4½ hrs.
Course Hours/Earliest Tee-off: 8 a.m.
Green and Cart Fees: Plantation: $75.26 for 18 holes. Great Waters: $95 for 18 holes with $25 for mandatory caddie before 2 p.m.
Credit Cards: American Express, MasterCard, Visa
Season: Year round. Mar. through May busiest months
Course Comments: Walking allowed on Plantation after 4 p.m. Caddies required on Great Waters until 2 p.m.
Golf Packages: Can be arranged through marketing dept.
Discounts: Inquire at pro shop
Places to Stay Nearby: See page 00
Local Attractions: See page 00
Directions: From I–20 take Exit 53 (South). Proceed south onto Hwy. 44 and continue 7 miles to the Reynolds Plantation entrance at Linger Longer Rd.
Closest Commercial Airports: Athens (45 min.); Lewis B. Wilson/Macon (1 hr. 15 min.); Hartsfield Atlanta International (1½ hrs.); Bush Field/Augusta (1½ hrs.)

REYNOLDS PLANTATION GOLF CLUB

Reynolds Plantation is situated within a 4000-acre residential resort community on 19,000-acre Lake Oconee midway between Atlanta and Augusta. Within the property is a 680-acre peninsula that juts into the lake providing a perfect site for Jack Nicklaus's highly acclaimed 7048-yard Great Waters course. Nine holes on Great Waters are directly along the lake. The front nine is routed through rolling hills and dense forests of pine and hardwoods. It is only at the ninth that Lake Oconee becomes visible and remains so until you reach the finishing hole. The 472-yard par-4 fifth hole, a dogleg left that twice plays over a stream cutting and bordering the fairway, is reminiscent of the par-5 thirteenth at Augusta's Amen Corner. Bobby Jones, a cofounder of Augusta National, didn't like par 5s, so perhaps Nicklaus has here bowed to the wishes of his childhood hero. The ninth, a 392-yard par 4, has a tee shot to a landing area framed by trees and guarded by a bunker to the left. The approach is to a side-angled green backed by bunkers and bordered on its right and front by Lake Oconee.

Many of the holes on the back side are spectacular as they work their way out and back on the fingers of the land reaching into the lake. The 349-yard par-4 eleventh plays from an elevated tee straight out toward the lake which also borders the fairway on the left. The approach is to a shallow 75-yard-wide monster green guarded by water and four sand bunkers. The 540-yard par-5 finishing hole is bordered on the left by the lake and provides the classic question of whether to go for the green—buttressed by a winding stone wall and guarded front and left by the lake—on the second shot.

Nicklaus, who owns a cottage and a home site at Reynolds Plantation, now has more than thirty years of golf course design experience and many of his courses, including Valhalla in Kentucky, English Turn in Louisiana, and Muirfield in Ohio, are rated among the best in the country. As opposed to some of Jack's earlier efforts, Great Waters with its four tee distances is eminently playable by all levels of golfer.

Another quality course on this property is the tight but less punishing Reynolds National Club Plantation course, designed by Robert Cupp with help from Hubert Green and Fuzzy Zoeller, Rated one of the best new resort courses when it opened in 1988, the Plantation course is cut through woods and has fewer holes on the lake. Each course has its own clubhouse, practice facilities, and staff of professionals. With 374 miles of shoreline, Lake Oconee provides excellent fishing and boating opportunities. Other amenities on site include tennis, a fitness center, swimming pools, bicycling, and jogging. You may opt to stay at one of the one-, two- or three-bedroom golf cottages convenient to the golf courses. A third 18-hole course is likely to open at Reynolds Plantation before the year 2000.

Columbus

Course Name: BULL CREEK East, West Courses

Course Type: Public
Address: 7333 Lynch Road
Columbus, GA 31820
Phone: (706) 561-1614

GOLF COURSE

Director of Golf: Jeff Baggott
Course Length/Par (All Tees): East: Back 6705/72, Middle 6420/72, Ladies' Forward 5430/74. West: Back 6921/72, Middle 6480/72, Ladies' Forward 5385/74
Course Slope/Rating (All Tees): East: Back 124/71.2, Middle 120/69.4, Ladies' Forward 125/74.7. West: Back 130/72.5, Middle 126/70.8, Ladies' Forward 121/69.9
Course Architects: Joe Lee and Ward Northrop (18 holes, 1972). Ward Northrup (additional 9 holes, 1988; additional 9 holes, 1992)
Golf Facilities: Full Pro Shop X, Snack Bar X, Lounge No, Restaurant X, Locker Room X, Showers X, Club Rental X, Club Repair Minor, Cart Rental X, Instruction X, Practice Green X, Driving Range X, Practice Bunker X, Club Storage X
Tee-Time Reservation Policy: Noon on Wednesdays for weekends (Sat., Sun., holidays), open tee times weekdays
Ranger: Yes
Tee-off-Interval Time: 10 min.
Time to Play 18 Holes: 4 hrs.
Course Hours/Earliest Tee-off: 7:30 a.m. peak season/open to dark
Green and Cart Fees: $28 for 18 holes Sat., Sun., holidays with cart; $26 weekdays. Walking allowed anytime for $10.60 less
Credit Cards: MasterCard, Visa
Season: Year round. Busiest Mar.-July
Course Comments: Can walk anytime. Yardage book available. Nine hole rates during the week. Teaching center on site
Golf Packages: None

Discounts: Weekend twilight; under 23; student; county resident or attending school in county

Places to Stay Nearby: La Quinta Motor Inn (706) 568–1740, (800) 531–9100; Ramada Inn (706) 322–2522, (800) 228–2828; Econo Lodge (706) 682–3803, (800) 446–5900; Holiday Inn Airport (706) 324–0231, (800) HOLIDAY; Columbus Hilton (706) 324–1800, (800) HILTONS; Sheraton Columbus Airport Hotel (706) 327–6868, (800) 325–3535; Mountaintop Inn and Resort (404) 323–7331.

Local Attractions: Columbus Museum, Confederate Naval Museum, National Infantry Museum, historic district, Patterson Planetarium, Springer Opera House, Columbus College Fine Arts Auditorium, various Warm Springs tours, Callaway Gardens, Pine Mountain. Columbus Convention and Visitors Bureau (706) 322–1613

Directions: From Atlanta (1½ hrs.): I–185 south, US 80 east to Lynch Rd. (exit 7). From Macon (1 hr.): US 80 to Lynch Rd., make right (just past Pratt and Whitney)

Closest Commercial Airports: Columbus Metropolitan (10 min.), Atlanta (1½ hrs.)

BULL CREEK

Bull Creek Golf Course has 36 holes of golf with the West course ranked by *Golf Digest* as among the best public golf courses in America. Bull Creek, which is situated on the Alabama border southwest of Atlanta and southwest of Macon, opened in 1972 with the original Joe Lee–designed course. Another 18, added in stages of 9 holes each, were designed by Ward Northrop and completed in 1988 and 1992. The golf facility began as a joint effort between the City of Columbus and Muscogee County. The county furnished the land, cleared, graded and shaped it, while the city provided the necessary funds for the construction of the layout. Today the course is a municipal golf course, but it is self-sustaining. Revenues from golf activities are reinvested in the course. Green fees

for unlimited golf are less than $20. You have to go a long way to look for a better bargain than that.

The West course was developed out of forest land adjacent to Bull Creek and watershed lakes, including a 650-acre lake nearby. The course is moderately hilly with elevation changes. The fairways are well treed, and there are over 70 bunkers on the course. The greens are medium sized, moderately fast and somewhat undulating. Water comes into play on 6 holes on this layout. Most of the tees are elevated, providing a clear view of the work to be done.

An example of a hole that puts a premium on accuracy, as many holes on this course do, is the 555-yard par-5 opening hole which plays straight down a corridor of trees to an amoeba-shaped green protected by traps all around. Another good hole on this side is the 385-yard par-4 dogleg-right fourth whose tee shot must carry a ravine to set up an approach to a deep green guarded left, rear and right by and arc of bunkers. The ideal approach angle is from the left side of the fairway. But as one approaches the optimum tee-shot landing area, the fairway narrows and cedar trees to its left and right can come into play.

The back nine has some interesting water holes. The 180-yard par-3 fourteenth is over water to a wide, shallow green fronted by a bunker and guarded by traps to the left and right with stands of trees to the right and rear of this beautifully framed hole. Next is the 400-yard par-4 fifteenth, Bull Creek's signature hole, which is a dogleg right bordered by Bull Creek Lake on the right all the way to the green. Trees line the left side all the way, and the tee shot has to avoid a fairway bunker and water on the right and the trees on the left. The second shot is over the water's edge to a right-to-left-angled deep green protected by a trap to the left and right. This is a picturesque but potentially dangerous hole.

Possibly the most difficult par on the back nine is the 420-yard par-4 sixteenth, which is a slight dogleg left, well treed from tee to green. Three left fairway traps protect the landing area on the tee shot. A long tee shot, however, is likely to leave you with a downhill or sidehill lie. The second shot is then up to an elevated green that is protected in front by two traps and in back by another one. An incoming wind can sometimes make this hole play even longer.

Joe Lee, the designer of the original eighteen at Bull Creek, was born in Florida and has designed many excellent golf courses in the southern part of the United States and elsewhere. Lee was an excellent athlete and eventually became a professional golfer. He became close friends and a partner of Dick Wilson, the noted golf architect, honing his skills under Wilson's guidance. In 1965, after Wilson's death, he started his own practice and designed the Island Club in St. Simon Island with Rocky Roquemore, the Jekyll Island Golf Club's Pine Lakes Course, the Callaway Gardens Golf Club Skyview Course in Pine Mountain, and numerous other golf courses in Georgia. Ward Northrop, who designed the second eighteen at Bull Creek, was an assistant of Joe Lee and formed his own Florida-based design firm in 1972. He has designed the Ansley Golf Course in Atlanta; the Lands West Golf Course in Douglasville; and the Summit Chase Golf and Country Club golf course in Snellville, Georgia.

Savannah/St. Simons Island Areas

Course Name: OSPREY COVE

Course Type: Public
Address: 123 Osprey Drive
                    P.O. Box 878
                    St. Marys, GA 31558–0878
Phone: (912) 882–5575,
                    (800) 352–5575

GOLF COURSE

Head Professional: Daryl Jack
Course Length/Par (All Tees): Back 6791/72, Blue 6269/72, Gray 5812/72, Forward 5263/72
Course Slope/Rating (All Tees): Back 130/73.0, Blue 125/71.5, Gray 119/70.0, Ladies' Forward 120/71.1
Course Architect: Mark McCumber (1990)
Golf Facilities: Full Pro Shop X, Snack Bar X, Lounge X, Restaurant X,

Locker Room X, Showers X, Club Rental X, Club Repair X, Cart Rental X, Instruction X, Practice Green X, Driving Range X, Practice Bunker X, Club Storage X
Tee-Time Reservation Policy: 1 wk. in advance for outside play. Tee times available after 9:00 a.m. on weekends. Closed Mondays
Ranger: Yes
Tee-off-Interval Time: 7 and 8 min.
Time to Play 18 Holes: 4½ hrs.
Course Hours/Earliest Tee-off: 8 a.m.
Green Fees: $43 for 18 holes weekends, holidays; $35 for 18 holes Mon. to Fri. $21 for 9 holes weekends, holidays; $16 for 9 holes Mon. to Fri.
Cart Fees: $15 for 18 holes per person; $8 for 9 holes
Credit Cards: American Express, Master-Card, Visa
Season: Year round. Busiest season March through May, Sept., Oct.
Course Comments: Walking allowed on a limited basis, usually weekday afternoons
Golf Packages: Inquire at pro shop
Discounts: Replays. Member and property owner, local county, seniors on weekdays
Places to Stay Nearby: Comfort Inn (912) 729–6979, (800) 228–5150; Charter-house (912) 882–6250, (800) 768–6250; Holiday Inn (912) 729–3000, (800) HOLIDAY; Riverview Hotel (912) 882–3242; Chart House (800) 768–6250. BED AND BREAKFAST: Goodbread House Bed and Breakfast (912) 882–7490. CUMBER-LAND ISLAND: Greyfield Inn (904) 261–6408
Local Attractions: St. Marys historic district, Cumberland Island National Seashore, Okefenokee Swamp, boating, fishing, camping, National Park Service for Cumberland Island National Seashore (912) 882–4335. St. Marys Tourism Council (912) 882–4000
Directions: I–95, to exit 1, 2 mi. east on St. Marys Rd. (35 mi. north of Jacksonville, FL)
Closest Commercial Airports: Bruns-wick (45 min.), Jacksonville Interna-

tional, FL (45 min.), Savannah International (1½ hrs.)

OSPREY COVE

Osprey Cove is a Mark McCumber–designed 6791-yard 72-hole layout just east of I–95 on the Florida–Georgia border. The course is part of a 900-acre real-estate development with more than 3 miles of marsh-front property on the St. Marys River. McCumber has won the Doral Open, Western Open, and Tournament Players Championship, among other PGA events. He was born in Jacksonville, Florida, just down the road from St. Marys, and became involved in the golf course construction business with his brothers in the 1970s. He has designed numerous courses in Florida, among them Cutter Sound Country Club, Stuart; Deep Creek Golf Club, Port Charlotte; Dunes Country Club, Sanibel Island; Magnolia Point Golf and Country Club, Green Cove Springs; and Ravines Golf Club, Middleburg.

This golf course is in a picturesque natural setting composed of rolling fairways and greens, natural salt marshes, and mature woodlands. The layout wends its way through this wonderful natural habitat with long, scenic intervals from green to the next tee. The greens are large, fast and undulating, especially when the weather heats up. The tee-shot landing areas are generous, and water comes seriously into play on only three holes. One of those is the 184-yard par-3 fourth, which is the signature hole at Osprey Cove. On this hole, the tee shot is often into the wind and is over a marsh to a large, flat green protected by traps on the left and right front. There is some bailout to the right, but water is to the front and left of the green.

Most of the greens are well trapped like that on the sixth hole, a par 5 that plays 526 yards from the back tees. The tee shot is to an open fairway with two bunkers on the left. But the second shot has to negotiate a narrowing fairway with water on the right and bunkers on the left. The left-to-right-sloping green is surrounded by four traps. The finishing hole on the front side is a 371-yard par 4 that is a dogleg right to a huge double green shared with the eighteenth hole. The first shot is to a wide landing area, but the second shot has to avoid three traps to the right front of the long, narrow green and a huge waste bunker on the left. The finishing hole is a 500-yard dogleg-right par 5. The tee-shot landing area is guarded by a series of bunkers on the left, and the shot coming into the deep double green must avoid three traps on the left and the waste bunker on the right.

The clubhouse at Osprey Cove offers a large pro shop, men's and women's locker rooms, and an excellent restaurant. Individual and group lessons are available from the PGA professional staff in the practice area, which includes an nine-hole putting green, chipping green and driving range with five target-practice greens at various distances. Golf packages are available through local motels, and tee times can be made 1 week in advance. The busiest months are March through May, September and October.

Osprey Cove and St. Marys are within easy access of Savannah, Sea Island, St. Simons Island, Jekyll Island, Cumberland Island National Seashore and Jacksonville, Florida. St. Marys itself has several buildings on the National Register of Historic Places and has a ferry service to the Cumberland Island National Seashore, which features backpacking, camping, beaches, saltwater fishing and other recreational opportunities. Boats for deep-sea fishing and dinner and pleasure cruises are also available from St. Marys.

Course Name: **THE SEA ISLAND GOLF CLUB**
The Nines of Sea Island: Plantation, Seaside, Retreat, Marshside; St. Simons Island Club

Course Type: Resort
Resort: The Cloister
Address: 100 Retreat Boulevard
                        St. Simons Island, GA 31522
Phone: (912) 638–5118 (Golf Course)
                        (912) 638–5119 (Golf
                        Learning Center)

(912) 638–3611,
(800) 732–4752 (Resort)
Fax: (912) 638–5153 (Resort)

GOLF COURSE

Director of Golf: John Gerring
Head Professional: Tommy Cason (Island Club). Karen Delehanty (Sea Island)
Course Length/Par (All Tees): Plantation/Seaside: Back 6900/72, Green 6445/72, Blue 5841/72, Forward 5174/72. Seaside/Retreat: Back 6710/72, Green 6322/72, Ladies' Red 5582/72, Forward 5186/72. Retreat/Marshside: Back 6518/72, Green 6107/72, Blue 5309/72, Forward 5056/72. Marshside/Seaside: Back 6576/72, Green 6155/72, Blue 5371/72, Forward 5008/72. Retreat/Plantation: Back 6842/72, Green 6397/72, Blue 5779/72, Forward 5222/72. Plantation/Marshside: Back 6708/72, Green 6230/72, Blue 5568/72, Forward 5048/72. St. Simons Island Club: Back 6470/72, Middle 6114/72, Forward 5361/72
Course Slope/Rating (All Tees): Plantation/Seaside: Back 134/73.4, Green 128/71.3, Blue 120/69.5, Forward 115/69.1. Seaside/Retreat: Back 133/72.6, Green 130/70.9, Blue 121/68.6, Ladies' Forward 110/70.1. Retreat/Marshside: Back 130/71.2, Green 127/69.5, Blue 115/66.5, Forward 111/69.5. Marshside/Seaside: Back 130/71.3, Green 126/69.4, Blue 113/66.4, Forward 108/69.4. Retreat/Plantation: Back 135/72.8, Green 129/71.1, Blue 123/69.5, Forward 117/69.3. Plantation/Marshside: Back 132/71.9, Green 126/69.8, Blue 118/68.0, Forward 113/68.5. St. Simons Island Club: Back 133/71.0, Middle 129/69.4, Ladies' Forward 124/70.9
Course Architects: Plantation: Walter Travis (1927), Harry S. Colt and Charles Hugh Alison (renovation, 1929). Seaside: Harry S. Colt and Charles Hugh Alison (1929), Rees Jones (renovation, 1992). Retreat: Dick Wilson (1960). Marshside: Joe Lee (1973). St. Simons Island Club: Joe Lee (1975)

Golf Facilities: Full Pro Shop X, Snack Bar X, Lounge X, Restaurant X, Locker Room X, Showers X, Club Rental X, Club Repair X, Cart Rental X, Instruction X, Practice Green X, Driving Range X, Practice Bunker X, Club Storage X
Tee-Time Reservation Policy: Anytime. Limit of 3 tee-time reservations in advance at the Cloister. No public play at the Sea Island Golf Club during March, April
Ranger: Yes
Tee-off-Interval Time: 9 min.
Time to Play 18 Holes: 4½ hrs.
Course Hours/Earliest Tee-off: 8:30 a.m.
Green Fees: Resort guests and members: $50 daily fee at Sea Island Golf Club. Public: $90 daily fee at Sea Island Golf Club. Daily rate at St. Simons Island Club $45
Cart Fees: Cloisters: $30 for 18 holes and $22 for 9 holes per cart at Sea Island Golf Club. $15 for 18 holes per person at St. Simons Island Club
Credit Cards: MasterCard, Visa
Season: Year round. Busiest season March to May
Course Comments: Cart and/or caddies required for play started before 4:00 p.m. Can walk St. Simons Island Club after 3:30 p.m. Yardage book available. Caddies available. Pull carts not allowed
Golf Packages: Available through the Cloister
Discounts: Golf packages
Places to Stay Nearby: King and Prince Hotel and Villas (912) 638–3631; Sea Palms Golf and Tennis Resort (912) 638–3511; Queen's Court (912) 638–8459. LITTLE ST. SIMONS ISLAND: River Lodge and Cedar House (912) 638–7472
Local Attractions: Island Art Center, St. Simons Lighthouse, Museum of Coastal History, Ft. Frederica National Monument, St. Simons Village, Bloody Marsh Memorial, Jekyll Island. Jekyll Island Convention and Visitors Bureau (912) 635–3636, (800) 841–6586 (U.S. and Canada). St.

Simons Island Chamber of Commerce (912)638–9014

Directions: From Savannah (82 mi.): I–95 south, Hwy. 17 exit, Hwy. 17 east to St. Simons Island. From Jacksonville, FL (2 hrs.): I–95 north, Hwy. 17 exit, Hwy. 17 east to St. Simons Island

Closest Commercial Airports: Jacksonville International, FL (1½ hrs.); Savannah International (2 hrs.) (Cloister private shuttle service available from Brunswick/Glynco; Hartsfield Atlanta; Jacksonville International; McKinnon, St. Simons Island)

RESORT

Date Built: 1928

No. of Rooms: 264, including main building, River House, guest houses, Beach House

Meeting/Exhibit Rooms: 14. Capacity of Largest: 900 persons. Meeting Space: 7000 sq. ft.

Room Price Range: From $160 for single, $105 for double off season to $346 for single; from $198 for double peak season (mid-March to end of Nov. and Christmas). Golf and other packages such as tennis, honeymoon, sports, spa and others available year round

Lounges: Loggia Bar, Club Room Bar, Sea Island Golf Club, Island Club Lounge

Restaurants: Main dining room, Ocean Room at Beach Club, St. Simons Island Club, Sea Island Golf Club

Entertainment: Live music, dancing

Credit Cards: None. Checks accepted. Billing after departure available

General Amenities: Programs for children including manners instruction, dancing instruction, shopping, painting classes, summer music festival, movies, jeep tours, gardens, nature walks, duplicate bridge, birding expeditions, local tours, bingo games, beauty shops, post office, flower shop, meeting and conference facilities in Plantation Center

Recreational Amenities: Beach sailing, cabanas, 2 swimming pools, steam room, boat cruises, fishing charters, riding stables, skeet shooting, 18 tennis courts, swimming lessons, scuba, snorkeling, lawn games, shuffleboard, table tennis, bicycling, marshmallow roasts and other organized activities for young people; Beach Club Spa with fitness classes, individualized training, massage therapy

Reservation and Cancellation Policy: Reservations require deposit. Early reservations suggested. Cancellation notice must be received in writing 7 days prior to arrival to avoid penalties

Comments and Restrictions: No pets. 17% service charge added to all rates and packages. Subject to Georgia and local tax. No room charge for children under 19 in room with parents. Discounts for stays 30 days and longer. Coats and ties are required for men and young men over 12 in the dining room and clubroom

THE SEA ISLAND GOLF CLUB

The Cloister is a five-star resort located on the grounds of Retreat Plantation, a former cotton plantation on Sea Island, a 5-mile-long strip of land along the southern coast of Georgia, equidistant between Jacksonville, Florida and Savannah, Georgia. The island was relatively uninhabited until 1924, when the causeway from the mainland town of Brunswick to St. Simons Island was completed. The Cloister, which was originally a 46-room hotel, was opened in 1928, and President Calvin Coolidge showed up to help open it. The original main hotel and River House are Spanish Mediterranean style architecture, and subsequent buildings are reminiscent of the Caribbean. Since its inception, the resort has always been under one management, the Sea Island Company, owned by the Alfred W. Jones family.

Tradition and modern recreational conveniences are blended in grand style at the Cloister, which has ballroom dance lessons and manners classes for children, as well as modern physical fitness, tennis, swimming and a variety of other facilities. Both the St. Simons Island Golf Club and the Sea Island Golf Club are accessible to resort guests. These include the Plantation and Seaside courses at the Sea Island Golf

Club, which were designed by the renowned Walter Travis, Henry S. Colt and Charles Hugh Alison in the late 1920s.

Travis was born in Maldon, Australia, in 1862 and won the U.S. Amateur and British Amateur even though he didn't take up golf until he was 35. He was founder and editor of *American Golfer* magazine and author of *The Art of Putting* and *Practical Golf*. He learned golf-course design as an apprentice to John Duncan Dunn, who collaborated with Travis on the Ewanok Country Club Course in Travis's beloved Manchester, Vermont, where he is buried. Travis also designed the Oceanside nine at nearby Jekyll Island, Georgia, in 1926.

The Plantation Course has recently had its greens redesigned and some drainage areas improved under the guidance of Rees Jones. Jones will also do some remodeling on the other courses at Sea Island, but their basic design and character will not change. The Plantation Course nine plays 3516 yards from the back tees, and has elevated Bermuda-grass greens that are small and often well trapped. Water comes into play on five of the holes, and the mature large oaks and pine trees can come into play if your ball strays.

The number-1-handicap hole on Plantation is the 534-yard par-5 fourth, hole which is aptly called "Alligator." Water on the left, as well as two bunkers straddling the fairway landing area on the tee shot. The second shot is toward a small green surrounded by trees and protected by traps right, left and front-right. There is water to the left from 200 to 100 yards into the green and trees on the right. A pretty hole on this side is the 155-yard par-3 seventh, which plays over water to a green protected left, front and right by water. Plantation is situated on the site of an old cotton plantation, whose famous Sea Island cotton once filled these sweeping fairways.

The 3384-yard Seaside Course was designed by Harry S. Colt and Charles Hugh Alison in 1929. At the same time they redesigned Travis's Plantation nine to form a coherent eighteen that *Golf Digest* ranks as one of the best resort golf courses in America. Colt was born in St. Amands, England,

in 1869 and studied law at Cambridge University, where he became captain of the golf team. An excellent amateur golfer, he became a full-time golf architect in the early 1900s. He is believed to be the first designer not to have been a professional golfer, the first to consistently use a drawing board in preparing golf course designs and the first to prepare tree-planting plans for his layouts. He trained a number of designers, including Alister MacKenzie, his partner for a short time, who became excellent golf-course architects. One of them, Charles Hughes Alison, born in 1882 in Preston, Lancashire, England, became his partner. Alison was also an outstanding golfer, having played at Malvern and Oxford University and later in various amateur competitions. During their 20-year partnership, Colt handled most of the design work in Europe and Alison worked extensively in the Far East and North America. Colt designed Pine Valley in Clementon, New Jersey, with George Crump in 1919. Many consider Pine Valley the best golf course in the world. Colt and Alison designed the Burning Tree Country Club in Bethesda, Maryland, in 1924; the Old Oaks Country Club in Purchase, New York, in 1927; and many other fine courses.

The Seaside nine, like Plantation, is rather flat and has large traps and small, relatively flat Bermuda-grass greens that are elevated and protected by bunkers. Lowland marshes run adjacent to most of the holes, and the wind is variable, making some shots very unpredictable. Georgian Bobby Jones considered Seaside a great nine, and the great Mickey Wright spoke kindly of the course, even after hitting some shots into the marshes on the 424-yard par-4 seventh in an LPGA tournament. This is the number-1-handicap hole and plays more than 220 yards over marshes if you want to reach the left fairway for an ideal second shot. The small, elevated green has a large trap to the front right. The right side of the fairway is pinched by a large trap 240 yards from the tee. Another difficult hole on Seaside is the 377-yard par-4 fourth, which has marshlands in front of the tee and all the way up the left fairway to the green. The right fairway is guarded by three bunkers near the tee-shot landing area and two to the right and in front of the small elevated green. The temptation is to cut off as much of the fairway distance as possible by going over the marsh on the left.

Also well worth playing at Sea Island are the Retreat and Marshside nines. Retreat, a 3326-yard layout, was designed by Dick Wilson and opened in 1960. The wind makes play changeable on this course, which averages over five bunkers per hole. The greens are somewhat large compared to the older Seaside and Plantation layouts, but they are well trapped. For example, the number-1-handicap 424-yard par-4 fourth plays straight to a medium-sized green with three traps left and right front, and one to the rear. Water and trees line the fairway all the way to this well-guarded target. The 472-yard par-4 ninth is protected by trees on the right and water on the left on the tee shot. The second shot is onto a green with two left-fairway traps 70 yards to 35 yards from the small green, which is surrounded by three traps. Wind, water, trees, sand and elevated greens make the Retreat a challenging test of golf.

Joe Lee designed the Marshside nine, which opened in 1973. At 3192 yards, this is considered the most difficult nine at Sea Island, because errant drives are heavily penalized by the marshes, which fringe seven holes. The elevated greens are medium sized and well trapped. Large oak and pine trees can also provide formidable obstacles. The 487-yard par-5 second hole is a scenic and interesting double dogleg with marshes on the left all the way to the green. Water is on the right from 165 yards into the medium-sized putting surface protected by traps both left and right. On the first shot the golfer is tempted to cut as much of the left corner as possible, but the fairway narrows with water on the right in the landing area 225 to 275 yards from the tee. If you succeed, you have less than 200 yards to the green, but it's always possible to hit the ball into the water. The number-1-

handicap hole is the 525-yard par-5 dogleg-right seventh, which is well treed and narrow. Its medium-sized green is protected by five traps to the left and right from 90 yards in. The finishing hole is a tough, straight 434-yard par 4, with three traps guarding the fairway landing area and two traps guarding a kidney-shaped green on the left. To the left, on your second shot, is the old plantation burying ground.

Golfers at Sea Island have access to the nearby eighteen-hole St. Simons Island Club, which was also designed by Joe Lee. The most difficult hole on this layout is the 536-yard par-5 eighth, which plays straight to a small green protected by three traps and water farther left. The tee shot is to a landing area guarded by one fairway bunker to the left. The second shot is up a narrowing fairway with water on the left all the way to the green. The 353-yard par-4 eighteenth is a beautiful finishing hole and is the signature hole at the St. Simons Island Club. The left side of the fairway is bordered by water from tee to green. The putting surface is protected by water to the left, a large trap to the left, and another large trap in front. The St. Simons Island Club course is well-protected by tall pines, sand bunkers and water hazards. The small hand-mown greens are fast, well trapped and slightly undulating. Strategic shot placement is rewarded on this scenic layout.

The St. Simons Club is also owned by the Cloister and has its own restaurant, banquet facilities, locker rooms and showers, as well as a pro shop with golf instruction available from the staff. Practice facilities include a driving range, practice green and chipping area. Memberships are available on an annual-fee basis, and Cloister guests (as well as the general public) can play the course. Caddies are available, and you can walk after 3:30 p.m. Packages are available through the Cloister.

One clubhouse serves the four nine-hole golf courses at the Sea Island Golf Club. Men's and women's locker rooms, a restaurant and a full service pro shop are housed here. Individual and group lessons are available at the new Golf Learning Center, which is a joint venture between *Golf Digest* and the Sea Island Company. The learning center is a 4-part facility including both indoor and outdoor practice and instructional areas. These features full-swing and short-game practice areas, which include two greens, four bunkers, mounds, rough and fairway areas as well as a driving area with five target greens ranging from 50 to 200 yards out. The indoor areas include swing-training studios featuring driving nets, and putting and chipping areas with video and other instructional analysis capabilities. There is a video and book library with conference-room and review areas. Daily, weekly, monthly and even yearly instructional programs are available from the PGA professionals and apprentices on staff. Also available at the Sea Island Golf Club is a custom club shop that manufactures custom clubs, provides custom fitting analysis and makes repairs.

The resort is situated on 5 miles of beach, and its rooms are contained in low-lying buildings: the Beach House, guest houses, the River House and the original main building. The Cloister has won many hospitality awards, including a Five-Diamond rating from the American Automobile Association, a Five-Star rating from the *Mobil Travel Guide* and a Silver Medal Award as one of America's finest golf resorts from *Golf* magazine. There are four restaurants at the resort, including the main dining room, which includes formal jacket-and-tie dining with music in the background. The Cloister operates under a full three-meal American plan, and meals can be taken at four locations, including the golf clubs.

Numerous activities are available at the Cloister resort, including tennis, skeet shooting, water sports, bicycling, swimming, spa amenities, horseback riding, nature tours, and organized programs for children and adults. There are also many shops on site, including beauty shops and barbershops, a package store and flower shop, surf shop, tennis shops, golf shops and post office. Rooms are available on the ocean or farther back and a variety of golf, tennis, honeymoon, and seasonal Thanksgiving and Christmas packages are available.

The Cloister has excellent meeting and conference capabilities. In 1983, the Plantation Center, which includes classroom, theater, conference, reception and banquet areas for as many as 900 persons, was completed. Other more intimate meeting areas are located in the Plantation House and the Fountain Room. The Gazebo is available for larger outdoor gatherings. In addition to its various hospitality and golf and tennis awards, the Cloister has received recognition as a premier meeting and convention destination from *Meetings and Conventions*, *Diversion*, and other magazines.

The resort is also noted for its immaculate and beautifully landscaped grounds, which are rich with azaleas, oleander, crepe myrtle, oak, pine and other lush vegetation that beautifully complements the Spanish Mediterranean and Caribbean architecture. In recognition of its outstanding landscaping, the Cloister has received the Professional Grounds Management Society Grand Award, and the *Washington Post* has rated the golf courses among America's seven most scenic golf courses.

St. Simons and Sea Island have a long and rich history. In 1568 the Spanish Franciscans established a mission here, the Retreat Plantation later became a world class cotton supplier, and many a dignitary has stayed here, including George and Barbara Bush, who honeymooned here in 1945. If it's golf and recreation that you're interested in, this is one of the best places to be.

Course Name: SAVANNAH INN AND COUNTRY CLUB

Course Type: Public
Address: 612 Wilmington Island Road
Savannah, GA 31410
Phone: (912) 897–1615 (Golf Course)

GOLF COURSE

Director of Golf: Charlie Dubbertin
Course Length/Par (All Tees): Back 6876/72, Middle 6528/72, Forward 5328/72

Course Slope/Rating (All Tees): Back 137/73.5, Middle 132/71.2, Ladies' Forward 128/70.6

Course Architects: Donald Ross (1927), Willard Byrd (renovation, 1966)

Golf Facilities: Full Pro Shop X, Snack Bar X, Lounge X, Restaurant X, Locker Room X, Showers X, Club Rental X, Club Repair Minor, Cart Rental X, Instruction X, Practice Green X, Driving Range X, Practice Bunker X, Club Storage X

Tee-Time Reservation Policy: Up to 1 year in advance

Ranger: Yes

Tee-off-Interval Time: 8 min.

Time to Play 18 Holes: 4 hrs.

Course Hours/Earliest Tee-off: 8 a.m.

Green and Cart Fees: $48.10 Fri., Sat., Sun., holidays for 18 holes; $32.20 weekdays for 18 holes with cart

Credit Cards: American Express, Master-Card, Visa

Season: Year round

Course Comments: Cart mandatory. Yardage book available. Memberships available.

Golf Packages: Inquire at pro shop

Discounts: Twilight rates after 12 p.m.

Places to Stay Nearby: Desoto Hilton (912) 238–1234, (800) 228–9000; Ballastone Inn (912) 236–1484; Eliza Thompson House (912) 236–3620, (800) 348–9378; Hyatt Regency Savannah (912) 238–1234, (800) 233–1234; Sheraton Savannah Resort and Country Club (912) 897–1612, (800) 533–6707; Best Western Savannah Riverfront Inn (912) 233–1011; Quality Inn Airport (912) 964–1421; Howard Johnson's Historic District (912) 232–9371. BED AND BREAKFAST: R.S.V.P. Savannah Bed and Breakfast Service (912) 232–RSVP, (800) 729–7787

Local Attractions: Historic district, Ships of the Sea Museum, Telfair Mansion and Art Museum, Cotton Exchange, Colonial Park Cemetery, Riverfront Plaza, Central of Georgia Railroad Roundhouse Complex, Savannah History Museum, Savannah Science Museum, churches, City Market; forts, including Fort Jackson, Fort Pulaski National Monument; squares; tours, including Negro Heritage Tour, Historic Savannah, Savannah River Cruise Lines. Savannah Chamber of Commerce and Convention Visitors Bureau (912) 944–0456, (800) 444–2427

Directions: From I–95 north and south (30 min.): I–16 east to Lynes Pkwy., exit right onto Lynes Pkwy. to Hwy. 80 east exit, turn left on Hwy. 80 east. Follow Hwy. 80 east approximately 10 mi., bear right on Hwy. 367 (Johnny Mercer Dr.), follow to Wilmington Island and make first right onto Wilmington Island Rd. to golf course. From Savannah Airport (30 min.): Turn right on Hwy. 307, follow Hwy. 307 south to I–16 east, then pick up directions from above

Closest Commercial Airports: Savannah International (30 min.); Jacksonville International, FL (2½ hrs.)

SAVANNAH INN AND COUNTRY CLUB

The Savannah Inn and Country Club is located on Wilmington Island overlooking the Wilmington River. This classic Donald Ross–designed rolling layout has medium-sized Bermuda-grass greens in excellent condition with subtle breaks and undulations. Most of the greens are well protected by large bunkers, and bunkers are strategically placed near the fairway landing areas. There are water hazards on ten holes. These hazards include four man-made lakes and a winding stream. Live oaks draped in Spanish moss, and pine and palm trees add to the charm of this golf course.

The number-1-handicap hole at the Country Club is the 420-yard par-4 fifth, which plays straight to a green protected by bunkers to the left and right. The narrow fairway is lined by trees on the left and a stream on the right. A fairway bunker on the left further narrows the tee-shot landing area.

The *Atlanta Constitution* newspaper has rated the fifteenth hole at the Country Club one of the most difficult and best holes in Georgia. The tee shot on this 385-yard par 4 has to negotiate a stream on the left and a series of fairway traps and a stream farther right. The approach shot is to a deep green with a trap on the left and another on the right.

Wind can be a factor on the Country Club course. This is especially true of the 516-yard par-5 finishing hole, which is a dogleg right. The wind is usually into the golfer's face. The first shot is generally played to the left of a large lake that borders the fairway. Big hitters will try to carry this hazard, which requires a 250-yard drive. If you succeed, the green is very reachable in two. If you take the safer route, the second shot is a layup to the right of a series of three bunkers running up the left side of the fairway. The approach shot is to an undulating green well protected by large bunkers.

The clubhouse at the Country Club includes a grill, cocktail lounge and bar, men's and ladies' locker rooms and sauna. The pro shop carries a full line of equipment, golfing apparel and accessories. And instruction is available from the staff of professionals. Practice facilities include a driving range, practice bunker and practice green. The historic downtown Savannah district is only 8 miles from the resort. Many sites, including the Ships of the Sea Museum, Cotton Exchange, City Market, Telfair Mansion and Art Museum, Colonial Park Cemetery and other interesting attractions, are easily accessible. There are many excellent restaurants in Savannah, and the many squares in the city are beautiful.

Course Name: SOUTHBRIDGE GOLF CLUB

Course Type: Semiprivate
Address: 415 Southbridge Boulevard
Savannah, GA 31405
Phone: (912) 651–5455,
(800) 852–4255 (outside GA)

GOLF COURSE

Director of Golf: Phil Wagoner
Course Length/Par (All Tees): Back 6990/72, Blue 6458/72, White 6002/72, Ladies' Forward 5181/72

Course Slope/Rating (All Tees): Back 133/73.3, Blue 129/71.3, White 125/69.3, Ladies' Forward 121/69.9
Course Architect: Rees Jones (1988)
Golf Facilities: Full Pro Shop X, Snack Bar X, Lounge X, Restaurant X, Locker Room No, Showers No, Club Rental X, Club Repair X, Cart Rental X, Instruction X, Practice Green X, Driving Range X, Practice Bunker X, Club Storage Limited
Tee-Time Reservation Policy: Members: 2 wks. in advance. Public: 1 wk. in advance. Outings for groups 1 mo. in advance; larger outings longer
Ranger: Yes
Tee-off-Interval Time: 7 and 8 min.
Time to Play 18 Holes: 4 hrs., 15 min.
Course Hours/Earliest Tee-off: 7 a.m.
Green and Cart Fees: $36 for 18 holes with cart Fri., Sat., Sun., holidays, 29.50 for 18 holes with cart weekdays
Credit Cards: Discover, American Express, MasterCard, Visa
Season: Year round. Busiest season March to May, Sept. to early Nov.
Course Comments: Can walk during week, weekends after 1 p.m. Must carry bag
Golf Packages: Available through local motels and hotels. Inquire at golf course or any motel or hotel in Savannah
Discounts: Various. Tues. mornings peak season, women, seniors off-season. Junior rates all the time
Places to Stay Nearby: Desoto Hilton (912) 238–1234, (800) 228–9000; Ballastone Inn (912) 236–1484; Eliza Thompson House (912) 236–3620, (800) 348–9378; Hyatt Regency Savannah (912) 238–1234, (800) 233–1234; Sheraton Savannah Resort and Country Club (912) 897–1612, (800) 533–6707; Best Western Savannah Riverfront Inn (912) 233–1011; Quality Inn Airport (912) 964–1421; Howard Johnson's Historic District (912) 232–9371. BED AND BREAKFAST: R.S.V.P. Savannah Bed and Breakfast Service (912) 232–RSVP, (800) 729–7787
Local Attractions: Historic district, Ships of the Sea Museum, Telfair Mansion and

Art Museum, Cotton Exchange, Colonial Park Cemetery, Riverfront Plaza, Central of Georgia Railroad Roundhouse Complex, Savannah History Museum, Savannah Science Museum, churches, City Market; forts, including Fort Jackson, Fort Pulaski National Monument; squares; tours, including Negro Heritage Tour, Historic Savannah, Savannah River Cruise Lines. Savannah Chamber of Commerce and Convention Visitors Bureau (912) 944–0456, (800) 444–2427

Directions: From I–95 to I–16 toward Savannah, take airport exit, course can be seen from exit (6 mi. west of Savannah off I–16)

Closest Commercial Airports: Savannah International (10 min.), Jacksonville International, FL (2 hrs.), Hartsfield Atlanta International (4 hrs.)

SOUTHBRIDGE GOLF CLUB

The Southbridge Golf Club is part of a real-estate development in a growing suburb just west of downtown Savannah. It was designed by Rees Jones and opened in 1988. Located just off I–16, the course was carved out of oak, pine and dogwood forests, providing eighteen separate tee-to-green experiences as you work your way back to the clubhouse. The fairways are rolling, with typical Rees Jones mounds bordering them and funneling the ball back into the fairway. You can, however, also get uneven lies here, or the ball can kick off these humps in a manner that you hadn't contemplated.

The Bermuda greens at Southbridge tend to be large, moderately fast, undulating and elevated. Most are well trapped, and bunkers often come into play near tee-shot landing areas. Water is directly in play or lurking on more than half the holes. The course is straightforward in that you can see most of the holes from tee to green, but there is a mixture of left and right doglegs. There tend to be mounds and gentle fall-offs around the greens, and tee distances range from 6990 yards from the back tees to 5181 yards from the forward tees. Any golfer should be able to

find a comfortable tee distance among the four total yardage options offered.

The par-3 holes at Southbridge tend to be difficult. The number-four hole, the signature hole, plays 194 yards over water to a wide, shallow, three-tiered green with mounds surrounding it. The 209-yard second hole plays to another wide, shallow green, with a huge trap directly in front of it and another to the right. The 172-yard twelfth plays over water to a wide, shallow green trapped in back, and the 216-yard fourteenth plays to a deep green with traps left and right.

The par-5 finishing holes on both sides are excellent golf challenges. The ninth is a dogleg right with large bunkers on the right at the knee of the dogleg. The approach shot is to a large green with a huge trap in front and smaller traps to the rear. Farther right of the green, which slopes forward from right to left, is water. The 577-yard eighteenth is also a dogleg, bending left from a well-bunkered corner to a large, narrow, deep green with several traps guarding it from 100 yards in. The green is severely elevated from the fairway and slopes back to front, and the right third of the putting surface drops sharply downward.

The clubhouse, beautifully situated in the middle of a stand of tall trees, does not have locker-room and shower facilities available to the public but does have a complete pro shop and restaurant with bar and grill. Nearby are practice facilities including a practice bunker, chipping area, 10,000-square-foot practice green and a 325-by-100-yard-wide practice range. Instruction is available in individual and small-group lessons from the PGA professionals and assistants at Southbridge. You can walk this course during the week and after 1 p.m. on weekends and holidays. Golf packages are available through local hotels and motels, which personnel in the Southbridge golf pro shop can direct you to. And, if you elect to stay in downtown Savannah, Southbridge is easily reachable from there.

Recommended Golf Courses in Georgia

Within 1 1/2 Hours of Savannah:

Forest Hills Golf Club, Augusta, (706) 733–0001, 18/6780/72

Foxfire Golf Club, Vidalia, (912) 538–8670, Semiprivate, 18/6118/72

Hampton Golf Club, St. Simons Island, (912) 634–0255, Semiprivate, 18/6465/72

Henderson Golf Club, Savannah, (912) 920–4653, Public, 18/6650/71

Jekyll Island Golf Resort, Jekyll Island, (912) 635–2368, Public. Oleander: 18/6679/72. Pine Lakes: 18/6802/72. Indian Mound: 18/6596/72. Oceanside: 9/3298/36

Little Ocmulgee, McRae, (912) 868–6651, Public, 18/6625/72

Oak Grove Island Golf Club, Brunswick, (912) 262–9575, Semiprivate, 18/6910/72

St. Simons Island Club, St. Simons Island, (912) 638–5130, Public, 18/6490/72

Sea Palms Resort, St. Simons Island, (912) 638–3351, Resort. Tall Pines/Great Oaks: 18/6658/72. Sea Palms 9/3000/36

Wallace Adams Golf Course, McRae, (912) 868–6651, Public, 18/6625/71

Albany Area:

Francis Lake Golf Course, Lake Park, (912) 559–7961, Public, 18/6458/72

Georgia Veteran's State Park Course, Cordele, (912) 276–2377, Public, 18/7088/72 (1 hr. from Albany)

Columbus:

Maple Ridge Golf Club, Columbus, (706) 656–0966, Public, 18/6652/71

Fields of Rosemont Hills Plantation, LaGrange, (706) 845–7425, Public, 18/6569/72

Northeast Mountains:

Innsbruck Golf Club of Helen, Helen, (706) 878–2100, Resort, 18/6748/72

Northwest Mountains:

Brasstown Valley Crowne Plaza Resort, Young Harris, (706) 379–9900, (800) 227–6963, Resort, 18/7100/72

Nob North Golf Course, Cohutta, (706) 694–8505, Public, 18/6573/72

Scanti Golf Club at Big Canoe, (706) 268–5703 (Golf Course), (706) 268–3333 (Resort), Resort, 18/6276/72

Stonebridge Golf Club, Rome, (404) 498–5714, Public, 18/6816/72

Windstone Golf Club, Ringgold, (615) 894–1231, Semiprivate, 18/6616/72

Georgia: Useful Information

Georgia Department of Industry, Trade and Tourism, P.O. Box 1776, Atlanta, GA 30301, (404) 656–3590, (800) 847–4842

Department of Natural Resources Communications Office, 205 Butler St., SE, Ste. 1352, Atlanta, GA 30334, (404) 656–3530 (recreation information)

Game and Fish Division, Department of Natural Resources, 205 Butler St., SE, Ste. 1258, Atlanta, GA 30334, (404) 493–5770 (fishing and hunting regulations)

U.S. Forest Service, 1720 Peachtree Rd., NW, Atlanta, GA 30367, (404) 347–2384

HAWAII

The Island of Hawaii

Course Name: HAPUNA GOLF
                           COURSE

Course Type: Resort
Resort: Hapuna Beach Prince Hotel
Address: 62–100 Kaunaoa Drive
                          Mauela, HI 96743–9706
Phone: (808) 8800–3000 (Golf Course)
                          (800) 882–6060 (Resort)
Fax: (808) 880–3010 (Golf Course)
                          (808) 88–3200 (Resort)

GOLF COURSE

Director of Golf: Joe Root
Head Professional: Ron Castillo
Course Length/Par (All Tees): Back
   6875/72, Blue 6534/72, Orange
   6029/72, Forward 5067/72
Course Slope/Rating (All Tees): Back
   134/72.1, Blue 130/69.9, Orange
   122/66.8, Forward 117/64.4. Ladies'
   Orange 129/74.7, Forward 117/68.9
Course Architects: Arnold Palmer and Ed
   Seay (1992)
Golf Facilities: Full Pro Shop X, Snack Bar
   X, Lounge X, Restaurant X, Locker
   Room X, Showers X, Club Rental X,
   Club Repair X, Cart Rental X, Instruc-
   tion X, Practice Green X, Driving Range
   X, Practice Bunker X, Club Storage X
Tee-Time Reservation Policy: Up to 2
   days in advance for public. At time of
   confirmed reservation for resort guests
Ranger: Yes
Tee-off-Interval Time: 8 min.
Time to Play 18 Holes: 4½ hrs.
Course Hours/Earliest Tee-off: 7 a.m.
Green and Cart Fees: $130 for 18 holes
   for outside play; $80 for 18 holes for re-
   sort guests
Credit Cards: American Express, Master-
   Card, Visa, JCB
Season: Year round. Busiest Dec. through
   Mar.
Course Comments: Cart mandatory.
   Yardage book available
Golf Packages: Through resort
Discounts: Twilight rate from 3 p.m.
   Resort guests
Places to Stay Nearby: See Mauna Kea
   page 241

Local Attractions: See Mauna Kea page 241
Directions: From Kona Airport (40 min.):
   Hwy. 19 north to resort on the right
Closest Commercial Airports: Kona (40
   min.); Hilo International (1½hrs.)

RESORT

Date Built: 1994
No. of Rooms: 350 rooms including 36
   suites
Meeting Rooms: 8. Capacity of Largest:
   900 persons. Meeting Space: 14,200 sq.
   ft. inside, over 60,000 sq. ft. outside
Room Price Range: Rooms from $325 to
   $460, suites from $800 to $5,500. Modi-
   fied American plan, packages available
Lounges: Beach Bar, Reef Lounge
Restaurants: Arnie's, Bistro, Coast Grille,
   Hakone, Ocean Terrace
Entertainment: Live music
Credit Cards: All major cards
General Amenities: Retail shops; meeting
   and conference amenities including
   audiovisual, banquet, secretarial, and
   other services
Recreational Amenities: Outdoor swim-
   ming pool, fitness center, spa with
   massage, sauna, steamrooms; 13 tennis
   courts, horseback riding at Mauna Kea
Reservation and Cancellation Policy:
   One night deposit required to hold a
   reservation. 14 day cancellation policy
   to receive refund
Comments and Restrictions: No pets.
   Amenities at Mauna Kea, 3 min. away,
   available to guests of the Hapuna Beach
   Prince

HAPUNA GOLF COURSE

The Hapuna Golf Course is a new Arnold
Palmer and Ed Seay layout that is part of the
new Hapuna Beach Prince Hotel, a sister to
the recently renovated Mauna Kea, situated
on 1839 acres on the Kohala coast. The
course is a chain of green islands set in the
natural lava terrain from the shoreline of the
Pacific to elevations above 700 feet as you
work your way up the slopes toward the
Kohala Mountains in the distance. Variable
winds can affect play at Hapuna. It is possible to face 20 miles per hour headwinds on
the 366-yard par-4 first hole, for example. If

you miss the fairways at Hapuna, you are dead because your ball will be nestled in a lava crevice or enveloped by native vegetation. There are only 75 acres of playable tees, fairways, greens, and rough at Hapuna, thus accuracy is essential.

The front nine works its way upland away from the ocean. A good hole on this side, considered the more difficult of the two nines, is the 441-yard par-4 sixth which often plays into the wind. The drive is to a hidden landing area framed by two small bunkers and the approach is to a narrow green with a sharp dropoff to its left. The putting surface is bordered by a long bunker on the left. Another strong par 4 on this course is the 419-yard seventeenth, a dogleg right that plays to a narrow landing area on the tee shot. The approach is to a small green with no bunkers but penal native terrain all around it. There are no more than four sand bunkers on any hole at Hapuna. The bunkers are large and sculpted, but the greens tend to be small or medium-sized. Water comes into play only on the 545-yard par-5 third, the 435-yard par-4 ninth, and the scenic 159-yard par-3 thirteenth. Reading the quick, subtle, Bermuda Tifdwarf greens is tricky because of the ocean and mountain setting.

The Hapuna clubhouse has a fitness center with massage, aerobics, and other amenities. Arnie's restaurant, one of seven restaurants and lounges within the resort, overlooks the golf course. Nearby is a practice range, putting and chipping greens and a practice bunker. The golf course was rated among "The Top 10 New Courses in the United States" by *Golf* magazine in 1994. The Hapuna Beach Prince Hotel is within walking distance of the golf course and has a full range of modern resort amenities.

Course Name: MAUNA LANI RESORT GOLF COURSES North, South Courses

Course Type: Resort
Resort: Mauna Lani Resort
Address: 68–1310 Mauna Lani Drive Kohala Coast, HI 96743–9704

Phone: (808) 885–6655 (Golf Course)
               (808) 885–6622,
               (800) 367–2323 (Resort)
Fax: (808) 885–9612 (Golf Course)

GOLF COURSE

Head Professional: Scott Bridges

Course Length/Par (All Tees): North: Back 6968/72, Middle 6335/72, Ladies' Forward 5398/72. South: Back 7015/72, Middle 6370/72, Ladies' Forward 5331/72

Course Slope/Rating (All Tees): North: Back 136/70.3, Middle 130/70.2, Ladies' Forward 124/71.4. South: Back 133/73.2, Middle 127/70.3, Ladies' Forward 122/70.3

Course Architects: North: Homer Flint and Raymond Cain (9 holes, 1981). Robin Nelson/Rodney Wright/Homer Flint (remodel and additional 9, 1991). South: Homer Flint and Raymond Cain (9 holes, 1981). Robin Nelson/Rodney Wright/Homer Flint (remodel and additional 9, 1991)

Golf Facilities: Full Pro Shop X, Snack Bar X, Lounge X, Restaurant X, Locker Room No, Showers X, Club Rental X, Club Repair X, Cart Rental X, Instruction X, Practice Green X, Driving Range X, Practice Bunker X, Club Storage X

Tee-Time Reservation Policy: Resort guests: 14 days in advance. Condominium guests: 14 days in advance. Public: 3 days in advance from 7 a.m.

Ranger: Yes

Tee-off-Interval Time: 8 min.

Time to Play 18 Holes: 4 hrs., 15 min.

Course Hours/Earliest Tee-off: 7:08 a.m.

Green and Cart Fees: Resort guests: $80 for 18 holes with cart. Public: $150 for 18 holes with cart

Credit Cards: American Express, MasterCard, Visa, JCB

Season: Year round. Busiest season Jan. to May

Course Comments: Cart mandatory

Golf Packages: Available through resort April to Nov.

Discounts: Mauna Lani Resort guests. Hawaii residents

Places to Stay Nearby: Mauna Lani Point Condominiums (808) 885–5022, (800) 642–6284; Ritz Carlton Mauna Lani (808) 885–2000, (800) 845–9905; The Bay Club (808) 885–7979, (800) 426–6367. BED AND BREAKFASTS: Hawaii's Best Bed and Breakfasts (808) 885–4550, (800) BNB-9921; Go Native Hawaii (808) 935–4178, (800) 662–8483; My Island B&B (808) 967–7216, (808) 967–7110; Holualoa Inn (808) 324–1121

Local Attractions: Puukohala Heiau, Samuel M. Spencer Beach Park, Kamuela Museum, Hale Kea shopping complex, Parker Ranch Visitor Center and Museum, Kohala Ranch, Ackerman Gallery, Kahua Ranch, Mookini Heiau, Lapakahi State Historical Park, garden tours, whale watching, plantation and factory tours. Hawaii Visitors Bureau (808) 961–5797. Kohala Coast Resort Association (808) 885–4915. Keauhou Visitors Association (808) 322–3866. Big Island Group (808) 885–5900

Directions: From Keahole Airport (30 min.): Hwy. 19 north to resort, follow signs

Closest Commercial Airports: Keahole (30 min.), Hilo International (2 hrs.)

MAUNA LANI RESORT

Date Built: 1972

No. of Rooms: 354 rooms, suites, bungalows, villas

Meeting Rooms: 7. Capacity of Largest: 600 persons reception style. Meeting Space: 9544 sq. ft.

Room Price Range: $260 to $520 for single or double, $795 for suites, $3015 to $3850 for bungalows, $395 per day for 1-bedroom ocean villas, $925 for 2-bedroom ocean villas per day, European plan. Golf, tennis, honeymoon and other packages available

Lounge: Bar

Restaurants: Canoe House, Bay Terrace, Ocean Grill, Knickers, Beach Club, Gallery

Entertainment: Dinner music, hula dancing

Credit Cards: All major cards

General Amenities: Beauty salon, flower shop, other shops on site; historic tours, supervised children's program (seasonal), babysitting, meeting and conference facilities with audiovisual and banquet services, Hawaiian quilting, hula lessons, lei making, weaving, shopping tours, helicopter and plane tours

Recreational Amenities: 10 Plexi-pave tennis courts with pro shop, instruction; health spa with free weights, Universal equipment, rowing machines, treadmills, massage, Jacuzzi, wet and dry sauna; swimming pool; ocean activities including scuba diving, sailing, snorkeling, windsurfing, boogie boarding, deep-sea fishing, catamaran cruises, glass-bottom boat tours, surfing; aerobic exercise programs, aquatoning, hunting, horseback riding, jogging trails

Reservation and Cancellation Policy: 2 nights' deposit required to guarantee reservation. Guests may specify either European plan or modified American plan. Refund will be made if cancellation notice is received at least 2 wks. prior to arrival date

Comments and Restrictions: No charge for 3rd person using existing bedding; no charge for crib. Charge for rollaway $20 per day. Minimum of 3-night stay required in ocean villas. Modified American plan $65 per person additional per day for adults. Rates and gratuities additional to base rates

MAUNA LANI RESORT

The Mauna Lani Resort is beautifully situated on 29 ocean-front acres on the Kohala coast of Hawaii. Until 1972, the land was owned by Francis Hyde I'i Brown, a descendant of Papa I'i, who served as a general under Kamehameha I, a noted Hawaiian warrior who consolidated the Hawaiian Islands after defeating a group of independent chieftains in the late 1700s. During Brown's 40-year ownership, numerous improvements were made to the property, and when he sold the site to Mauna Lani Resort, its first golf course was named after him. Recently, the original Francis H. I'i Brown Course, which was designed by Homer Flint and Raymond Cain and opened in 1981, was divided in two, and an additional eighteen holes were designed by Robin Nelson, Rodney Wright and Homer Flint, to form two eighteen-hole layouts, the North Course and the South Course, which opened in 1991. The original Francis H. I'i Brown Course was always ranked among the best resort courses in the country, and the resort itself, which covers 3200 acres, has been rated by *Golf* magazine as one of the twelve best golf resorts in the United States.

This entire site is located on the prehistoric Kaniku lava flow and is dotted with ancient, spring-fed Hawaiian fish ponds. Historic parks and preserves with petroglyphs, shelter caves, trails and man-made ponds can be found above coves and sheltered beaches below. The "Big Island," Hawaii, is just over 4000 square miles and is the second largest volcanic island in the world, after Iceland. The backdrop for Mauna Lani are the "mountains reaching heaven" which include Mauna Kea (13,796 ft.), Mauna Loa (13,967 ft.), and Huala Lai (8,271 ft.). Winds come from these mountains as well as the ocean to add to the difficulty of the beautiful golf courses. Vegetation such as fountain grass, mesquite trees, prickly poppy, coconuts, Milo trees and a variety of succulents flourish here.

The North Course plays 6968 yards from the back tees and is characterized by rolling terrain and mesquite (Kiawe) forests that often come into play. A 230-acre protected archaeological district lies on the northern boundary of the course, and feral goats, whose ancestors were originally brought to the island in the late 1700s, roam the entire golf course. The North Course's fourth through twelfth holes are the back nine from the Francis H. I'i Brown Course.

The number-1-handicap hole on the North Course is the par-4 ninth, which plays 459 yards from the back tees. The tee shot is to a wide fairway heading straight toward the ocean. The second shot is to a green guarded by a tidal pond and sand on the right, and more sand on the left. Below is the blue ocean in contrast with the storm-tossed salt-and-pepper rock beach. If a kona wind is blowing, the approach shot to the narrow green can be very difficult.

The 140-yard par-3 seventeenth is another signature hole from the original golf course. The tee shot is from an elevated tee to a grassy target surrounded by lava. Sand is behind and in front of the green. The elevated tee on the 412-yard finishing hole offers a panoramic view of the ocean and a dogleg-left fairway guarded by traps both left and right. The wind can either help or hinder you on this hole. The approach shot is to a deep green with traps left, rear and right. A right-to-left wind can sometimes carry your ball over the edge of the lava flow into the historic nature preserve below.

The South Course, which plays 7015 yards from the back tees, is built on the prehistoric Kanika lava flow. It includes the front nine from the Francis H. I'i Brown Course. This layout winds through stark, rugged lava, and it is said that the volcano goddess Pele watches over the course. Accuracy and distance are at a premium on these rolling, lava-protected fairways. From the middle tees, which play 6370 yards, the course is much more forgiving.

The number-1-handicap hole is the 601-yard par-5 fourth. The tee shot is bordered by water on the left and lava and sand on the right. The fairway narrows and funnels into a long, narrow green that is heavily guarded by water on the left and more sand and lava on the right. The green slopes back to front with mounds to the rear. Sometimes a tail wind from the trade winds can help you get to the green more easily.

The 202-yard par-3 fifteenth used to be one of the signature holes on the original Francis H. I'i Brown course. Tee shots from the back and middle tees must carry the ocean to a large, two-tiered green protected by sand all around. Crosswinds can complicate play on this hole, as can whale watching, which golfers often do in winter when the large creatures swim by in the ocean below.

The Senior Skins Game is held on the South Course at Mauna Lani Bay in January.

In 1990 Arnold Palmer was the big winner, taking home $240,000. He was also the winner in 1992. Palmer, Lee Trevino, Gary Player, Chi Chi Rodriguez and Jack Nicklaus went head to head in 1991. Nicklaus won $310,000 in 1 day, the biggest 1-day prize of his career, by sinking a 40-foot eagle putt on the par-5 tenth hole against Gary Player. This putt alone was worth $285,000.

There is a full pro shop with restaurant and snack bar facilities at the Mauna Lani clubhouse. Individual and group instruction are available from the staff of professionals. The practice facility includes a driving range, practice bunker and putting green. Golf packages are available most of the year. The price goes up depending on accommodations and dining arrangements. Packages do not apply to bungalow accommodations.

The Mauna Lani Bay Hotel overlooks the ocean and the Kohala Coast. The main structure faces the ocean and is in the atrium style, with waterfalls, fish-filled ponds, and beautiful trees and plants. Most rooms have ocean views, and some have views of the Mauna Kea and Mauna Loa mountains.

The 5 restaurants range from the the alfresco Bay Terrace and informal Ocean Grill to the newest restaurant, the Canoe House, which features Pacific Rim cuisine in an ocean-front setting. Guests also have charge privileges at the Beach Club and the Gallery restaurants of the surrounding Mauna Lani Resort.

Shops on the grounds include the sundry shop, collections by Liberty House, Lahaina Gallery, Jewelry by Hildgund, HFM Oriental Antiques, and golf and tennis shops. There is no shortage of recreational activities here, including the 10-court tennis garden (rated five stars by *World Tennis* magazine), jogging trails, a health club, swimming pool, and the beach fronting the main building. There are 3 miles of secluded shoreline with alternating inlets of sand and lava on Mauna Lani Bay. Water activities including scuba diving, snorkeling, sailing, windsurfing and boat cruises are available. There is also nearby hunting, horseback riding, helicopter and plane rides, plus a wide range of scenic and historic tours.

More than 50 acres of palm-fringed, prehistoric ponds sprawl throughout the property, maintained still with the makaha, sluice gates, used in traditional Hawaiian aquatic settings. In remote fringes of the property, isolated springs and pools abound, filled with glistening water filtered by the lava. The resort's 3200 acres also include a rich collection of restored archaeological sites, ranging from ancient fish ponds and foot paths to a fascinating complex of cave dwellings complete with petroglyphs.

Mauna Lani has won numerous hospitality awards, including the American Automobile Association's Five-Diamond Award, which is awarded to fewer than 60 of nearly 20,000 North American hotels and resorts considered for the honor. Whether you decide to stay at the bungalows on a $20,000 "indulgent weekend," at the regular hotel or to play either of the golf courses, it's hard to go wrong by visiting this island paradise.

Course Name: MAUNA KEA GOLF COURSE

Course Type: Resort
Resort: Mauna Kea Beach Hotel
Address: 62–100 Mauna Kea Beach Drive
                Kohala Coast, HI 96743–9706
Phone: (808) 880—3480 (Golf Course)
                (808) 822–7222 (Resort),
                (800) 882–6060 (Resort
                Reservations)
Fax: (808) 880—3112 (Resort
                Reservations)
                (808) 882–7552 (Golf Shop)
Telex: (808) 882–7007 (Hotel)

GOLF COURSE

Director of Golf: Joe Root

Course Length/Par (All Tees): Back 7114/72, Blue 6737/72, Orange 6365/72, Forward 5277/72

Course Slope/Rating (All Tees): Back 143/73.6, Blue 138/71.9, Orange 134/70.1, Forward 125/65.2, Ladies' Orange 137/75.7, Ladies' Forward 124/70.0

Course Architects: Robert Trent Jones, Sr. (1965), Robert Trent Jones, Jr. (green redesign, 1975)

Golf Facilities: Full Pro Shop X, Snack Bar X, Lounge X, Restaurant X, Locker Room X, Showers X, Club Rental X, Club Repair X, Cart Rental X, Instruction X, Practice Green X, Driving Range X, Practice Bunker No, Club Storage X

Tee-Time Reservation Policy: First day of arrival, then 1 day in advance

Ranger: Yes

Tee-off-Interval Time: 8 min.

Time to Play 18 Holes: 4 hrs., 15 min.

Course Hours/Earliest Tee-off: 7 a.m. Latest for 18 holes 2 p.m., for 9 holes 4 p.m.

Green and Cart Fees: Resort guests: $85 for 18 holes with cart. Public: $135 for 18 holes with cart

Credit Cards: All major cards

Season: Year round. Busiest seasons Feb. to March, Christmas, Easter

Course Comments: Cart mandatory. Yardage book available

Golf Packages: Available through resort. Not available during Annual Golf Pro-Am or Annual Golf Invitational. Minimum stay of 3 nights for golf packages. Reservations must be made in advance

Discounts: None

Places to Stay Nearby: Mauna Lani Point Condominiums (808) 885–5022, (800) 642–6284; Aston Kona by the Sea (808) 329–0200, (800) 367–5124; Hapuna Beach Prince Hotel (808) 882–1111; Hilton Waikoloa Village (808) 885–1234; Kona Coast Resort (808) 324–1721, (800) 367–8047; Kanaloa at Kona (808) 322–2272, (800) 777–1700; Aston Shores at Waikoloa (808) 885–5001, (800) 922–7866. BED AND BREAKFASTS: Hawaii's Best Bed and Breakfasts (808) 885–4550, (800) BNB-9921; My Island B&B (808) 967–7216, (808) 967–7110

Local Attractions: Pu'uhonua O Honaunau National Historical Park, Pu ukohoa Heiau (restored temple), Lapa Kahi State Historical Park, Hawaii Volcanoes National Park, Waipi 'o Valley, seasonal festivals such as the Macadamia Nut Augustfest, coffee and macadamia nut factories, Hulihee Palace, Ku'ula Fishing Shrine, Turtle Rock, Akaka Falls State Park, Chain of Craters Road, Devastation Trail, Halemaumau Fire Pit in Kilauea Crater, Lava Tree National Park, Lyman Museum and House, Mokuai Kaua Church, Parker Ranch Visitor Center and Museum, Suisan Fish Market, Thurston Lava Tube. Hawaii Visitors Bureau (808) 923–1811. Kohala Coast Resort Association (808) 885–4915. Keauhou Visitors Association (808) 332–3866. Big Island Group (808) 885–5900

Directions: From Keahole Airport (19 mi.): Hwy. 19 south to resort

Closest Commercial Airports: Keahole (30 min.), Hilo International (1½ hrs.)

RESORT

Date Built: 1965

No. of Rooms: 310 rooms and suites

Meeting Rooms: 4. Capacity of Largest: 400 persons banquet style. Meeting Space: 7000 sq. ft.

Room Price Range: $250 to $420 per day, single or double occupancy. Golf, tennis, wedding, honeymoon, anniversary and other packages available. Modified American plan available. Private residences available for rent, European plan, $450 to $1250 per day

Lounges: Copper Bar, Batik Bar

Restaurants: Pavilion, Terrace, Batik, Garden, 19th Hole, Hau Tree

Entertainment: Cocktail music at the Terrace's Copper Bar, Batik Bar; dancing at the Terrace, Pavilion

Credit Cards: All major cards

General Amenities: Children's programs, Mauna Kea art collection with more than 1600 Asian and Pacific treasures, driving tours of the island, clambakes and luaus, helicopter sightseeing, walking tours, Hawaiian crafts classes, meeting and conference facilities with audiovisual and food services

Recreational Amenities: 13 outdoor tennis courts with pro shop, instruction, swimming, snorkeling, skin diving, sailing, windsurfing, scuba diving, fishing, cruising, sailing, swimming pool, para-course exercise trail, jogging course, horseback-riding stables; fitness center with 10 Nautilus machines, 4 Lifecycles, 2 Lifesteps, computerized stationary bicycles with instruction; hunting, massage, sauna, volleyball, shuffleboard, croquet

Reservation and Cancellation Policy: 1 night's deposit must be received by resort within 14 days from date of confirmation. For modified American plan, $65 per person per night deposit. Deposit refundable if room canceled 14 days prior to arrival date. Seasonal packages must be reserved with 3 nights' deposit. No refund on unused portions of packages

Comments and Restrictions: Room taxes and gratuities additional. Maximum of 3 persons per room. $25 for additional person. Lower additional rates for modified American plan for children ages 5 to 12

MAUNA KEA GOLF COURSE

Mauna Kea Golf Course is a 7114-yard Robert Trent Jones, Sr., gem situated on the Kohala Coast on the island of Hawaii. Jones, who has built or remodeled more than 450 courses throughout the world, considers the Mauna Kea one of the best five he has ever built. In 1962 Laurance Rockefeller invited him to inspect what was then a barren lava field. Jones had built a course on sand at Dorado Beach, Puerto Rico, for Rockefeller, and Rockefeller wanted to build a resort hotel with a golf course at Mauna Kea. Jones developed a method of growing grass on the barren site, and by 1964 the golf course was opened. Greens and fairways had painstakingly been carved out of lava rock, and innovative procedures were developed to enable the desertlike surface to support plant life. This included building an elaborate underground automatic watering system that, controlled by timing devices, pumps more than a million gallons of water per day onto the 150-acre layout. The volcanic lava rock was crushed by heavy equipment, as was coral dredged from nearby Kawaihae Harbor. Seven inches of

this material was laid over the surface of the course, which was then planted with a new variety of hybrid Bermuda grass that had similar qualities to bentgrass but was more suited to Hawaii's tropical climate.

The fairways on this rolling course rise from sea level to 300 feet. The greens are large, undulating and well protected by many of Mauna Kea's 120 strategically placed sand bunkers. Robert Trent Jones, Jr., redesigned the course in 1975 to accommodate higher-handicap golfers as well as PGA tour players. More refinements were made in 1983 to offer more tee distances for different levels of play. Currently there are a minimum of four tee distances from each hole, and the total eighteen-hole yardage ranges from 7114 to 5277 yards. Some holes have six positions, including the famous number three.

The par-3 third hole plays over water from tee distances here of 182, 179, 172, 158, 151, and 116 yards to the front of the green, so an average player should be able to avoid the abyss and the ocean below. But a pin placement to the rear could require a shot of almost 230 yards from the rear tees. The green is 52 yards deep at its longest spot, with three traps on its left, one left and in front, two right and in front, and another to the rear. The ocean is immediately in front of the golfer and to the right. The wind, of course, can always be a factor on this beautiful and infamous oceanside hole. This was the first golf hole in Hawaii to be selected among the top 100 golf holes in the world by *Golf* magazine.

Another dramatic par 3 at Mauna Kea is the 247-yard eleventh, which plays to a deep green with a narrow entrance protected by two traps to the right and one to the left. The other tee distances to the middle of the green are 208, 181 and 166 yards. This is considered by many to be one of the most difficult par 3s anywhere not over water. When Jack Nicklaus shot a record 275 in four rounds here in 1964, he never hit this green on a tee shot and never parred the hole.

The number-1-handicap hole on the course is the 413-yard par-4 fourth, which plays uphill to a dramatically elevated green. This makes the approach shot a considerable challenge. The first shot has to avoid two bunkers on the left that begin 210 yards from the back tee. The second shot is up to a deep, heart-shaped green with a narrow opening squeezed by two traps in front. Next is a difficult 593-yard par-5 fifth hole with a tee shot to a somewhat open landing area with two bunkers to the right. The second shot is to a tightening fairway, and the approach shot is up to a deep, elevated green with a narrow entrance way protected by two traps on the right and another on the left.

By the time you reach the 428-yard par-4 finishing hole, you are standing on a tee at a 200-foot elevation looking at the Pacific Ocean, the Mauna Kea Hotel, a beautiful array of coconut palms, rainbow shower, monkey pod, Chinese banyon, wili-wili and other foliage dotting the golf course. Beyond, you might see the snow-capped Mauna Kea, or "White Mountain." By now you've noticed that you've hit to seven significantly elevated greens and that the course plays even longer than the scorecard indicates. The eighteenth is a slight dogleg to the right, and fairway bunkers flank the tee-shot landing area. The approach shot is to a large green protected by three traps on the right and front and another left and somewhat in front.

Mauna Kea opened in 1964 with the "Big Three of Golf" —Nicklaus, Palmer and Player—baptizing the course with 72-hole scores of 275, 275 and 278, respectively. Since then, other quality golf resorts have sprung from the lava of the beautiful Kona Coast. Mauna Kea has been rated by *Golf Digest* as one of the top 100 golf courses in the United States, and *Golf* ranks it one of the 100 greatest courses in America. *Golf* also rates Mauna Kea one of the 12 best golf resorts in America. The 72-hole 275 scores by Palmer and Nicklaus are still the record at Mauna Kea.

Mauna Kea provides excellent individual and group instruction at its practice facilities, which include a driving range, a practice bunker, a chipping green and a putting green. The 150-acre golf facility is both beautiful and challenging, with views of the ocean from every hole. The rolling fairways and elevation changes demand that you get into position to hit from a reasonably flat lie and approach the greens from the proper angle. Long hitters have to contend with narrow landing areas, and the average player is challenged by the numerous bunkers and difficult greens. It is important to get the ball to the proper quadrant of the green when coming in on approach shots. Position is everything at Mauna Kea.

A variety of golf and other packages is available at this resort. The minimum stay is 3 nights for 2 people. Golf packages with meals are additional to the base rates, which begin at approximately $1155 per couple for a 4-day and 3-night stay. Additional nights are available on request. Nonguests are allowed to play the course, and carts are mandatory. Mauna Kea regularly offers a variety of resort packages, including honeymoon and anniversary, tennis, scuba diving, family and friends, and others.

The Mauna Kea Beach Hotel is beautifully situated overlooking the Pacific Ocean. It has won numerous hospitality awards including being ranked among America's top ten resorts by the ZAGAT United States Hotel Survey. The hotel has 310 mountain-, beach-, and ocean-view rooms, and you have the option to rent a private residence. There are 6 fine restaurants and island clambakes and luaus are offered. There is a choice of European plan (rooms only) or modified American plan throughout the year, and you can dine on a wide range of local and international specialties such as mahi mahi, macadamia waffles, lomilomi salmon, hulihuli pig or baked bananas and taro. Another specialty is sashimi lamb chops with garlic, black sesame seed crust, red wine and coriander root butter sauce, and seven-vegetable tart. These are only a few examples of the culinary tour de force here. At the other extreme, you can get a world-class hot dog or a specially prepared "healthful meal."

Mauna Kea prides itself on its environmental preservation efforts and its efforts to serve only the best fresh fruits, vegetables, meat, poultry and fish of Hawaii. The resort has developed relationships with small, independent truck farmers and fishermen to ensure that there is a rich and diverse range of foods to choose from. The Mauna Kea even provides marketing and other business advice to many of its suppliers, including ranchers, a sugar company, a smokehouse operation and others. It has also won recognition for its historic preservation efforts on behalf of Mo'okini Heiau, a 1500-year-old Hawaiian temple near the Mauna Kea. And it has won the Heritage Award from the Historic Hawaii Foundation for developing multimedia educational programs pertaining to points of historic and cultural interest around the island.

A broad range of recreational activities is available at Mauna Kea and the surrounding area. *Tennis* magazine has rated Mauna Kea one of the 50 greatest U.S. tennis resorts. The oceanside tennis park at Mauna Kea features 13 Plexi-pave courts, a video training facility, professional instruction, clinics, exhibition matches and tournaments. *World Tennis* consistently rates Mauna Kea a five-star tennis resort.

Water activities are varied and exciting at the nearby natural white-sand Kauna'oa Beach. Snorkeling, surfing, kayaking, windsurfing, scuba diving, fishing, cruises, or just relaxing by the fresh-water pool is an option. A fitness center includes a variety of Nautilus machines and other equipment. Activities such as horseback riding, croquet, volleyball, aerobics classes, and supervised fitness training are provided by the resort.

Mauna Kea Resort has a full range of children's activities from mid-June through Labor Day and during Christmas and Easter vacations. Trained counselors supervise crafts, games, nature walks, piñata parties and other events for children ages 6 to 11. *Family Circle* named it among the top 125 U.S. family resorts in 1991, and *Condé Nast Traveler* has also spoken highly of the resort's family amenities.

A unique feature of the Mauna Kea Beach Hotel is its acclaimed collection of 1600 pieces of Pacific and Asian art. When Laurance Rockefeller conceived of Mauna Kea, he envisioned "a private estate offering a cross-cultural resort experience" on what was then a desolate, remote, Pacific coastline. The firm Skidmore, Owings and Merrill was hired to provide an architectural "frame" (the hotel) for the art collection that includes objects like a 1300-year-old Indian Buddha, regal Hawaiian quilts, and New Guinea ritual masks and drums. Guided tours of the collection are conducted weekly by Don Aanov, professor of art history at the University of Hawaii-Hilo, who describes this extensive collections of Asian and Pacific art.

The Hawaiian Islands, extending 1500 miles across the Pacific, are merely the summits of an immense volcanic mountain range that stretches 3500 miles along the ocean's floor to Kamchatka, Russia. Mauna Kea rises 13,796 feet above Hawaii's surface and over 30,000 feet from its base on the ocean floor. Hawaiians believed the summit region was the abode of the gods. The Mauna Kea volcano last erupted approximately 3600 years ago.

This is a perfect place to see what Hawaii's golf gods have in store for you.

Course Name: WAIKOLOA GOLF CLUB
Kings', Beach Courses

Course Type:	Resort
Resort:	Hyatt Regency Waikoloa
Address:	Off Highway 19/HCO2 Waikoloa, HI 96743
Phone:	(808) 885–4647 (Kings' Course) (808) 885–6060 (Beach Course), (808) 885–1234, (800) 233–1234 (Hyatt Regency) (808) 885–6789, (800) 537–9800 (Royal Waikoloan Hotel) (808) 885–5001, (800) 992–7866 (Shores at Waikoloa)
Fax:	(808) 885–0038 (Kings' Course) (808) 885–6546 (Beach Course), (808) 885–7474 (Hyatt Regency)

GOLF COURSE

Director of Golf: Dennis Rose, Jr.
Head Professional: Dave Wunder
Course Length/Par (All Tees): Kings':
Back 7074/72, Championship 6584/72,
Resort 6010/72, Forward 5459/72.
Beach: Back 6507/70, Middle 5920/70,
Forward 5144/70
Course Slope/Rating (All Tees): Kings':
Back 133/75, Championship 127/73,
Resort 124/71, Ladies' Forward 119/72.
Beach: Back 133/71, Middle 126/68,
Ladies' Forward 118/69
Course Architects: Kings': Tom Weiskopf
and Jay Morrish (1990). Beach: Robert
Trent Jones, Jr. (1981)
Golf Facilities: Full Pro Shop X, Snack
Bar X, Lounge X, Restaurant X,
Locker Room No, Showers X, Club
Rental X, Club Repair X, Cart Rental
X, Instruction X, Practice Green X,
Driving Range X, Practice Bunker X,
Club Storage X
Tee-Time Reservation Policy: Anytime in
advance
Ranger: Yes
Tee-off-Interval Time: 8 min.
Time to Play 18 Holes: 4 hrs. 15 min.
Course Hours/Earliest Tee-off: 7 a.m.
Green and Cart Fees: Kings': Resort
guests: $82 for 18 holes, $50 for 9
holes. Public: $98 for 18 holes, $60
for 9 holes. Beach: Resort guests: $70
for 18 holes, $45 for 9 holes. Public:
$90 for 18 holes, $55 for 9 holes. All
fees include golf carts, unlimited use
of practice facilities with range balls
Credit Cards: All major cards
Season: Year round. Busiest season
mid-Dec. to May
Course Comments: Cart mandatory
Golf Packages: Available through resort
hotels
Discounts: Twilight rates. Seasonal promotional programs through golf shop
Places to Stay Nearby: Shores of
Waikoloa (condominiums) (808) 885–
5001, (800) 992–7866; Waikoloa Villas at Waikoloa Resort (condominiums) (808) 883–9144, (800)
657–7887; Hyatt Regency Waikoloa
(808) 885–1234, (800) 233–1234;
Royal Waikoloan (808) 885–6789, (800)
537–9800; Mauna Lani Point Condominiums (808) 885–5022, (800) 642–
6284. BED AND BREAKFAST: Hawaii's
Best Bed and Breakfasts (808) 885–
4550, (800) BNB-9921
Local Attractions: KAILUA-KONA: Hulihee
Palace, Kailua Pier, Ahuena Heiau,
Mokuaikaua Church, shopping. KO-
HALA: Mt. Hualalai, Puukohola Heiau,
Samuel M. Spencer Beach Park, Kamuela Museum, Hale Kea shopping
complex, Parker Ranch Visitor Center
and Museum, Kawaihae Harbor, Kohala
Ranch, Kahua Ranch, Lapakahi State
Historical Park. Hawaii Visitors Bureau
(808) 329–7787. Kohala Coast Resort
Association (808) 885–4915. Big Island
Group (808) 885–5900
Directions: From Keahole Airport (17
mi.): North on Hwy. 19 to golf courses
Closest Commercial Airports: Keahole
(30 min.), Hilo International (1½ hrs.)

WAIKOLOA GOLF CLUB

The Waikoloa Golf Club has two superb
golf courses: the Kings' Course, designed
by Tom Weiskopf and Jay Morrish, and the
Beach Course, designed by Robert Trent
Jones, Jr.

The Kings' Course opened in 1990 and
was runner-up in *Golf Digest*'s annual
best new resort course rankings. This
7074-yard course has large, firm, moderately fast, undulating, greens. They are
hand mown and in excellent condition.
Several well-placed bunkers guard the
greens, and there are six water hazards
on this layout. Tom Weiskopf has described this as a "second-shot course
like Augusta," and Jay Morrish comments, "The variety expressed in the
green design, the sophisticated bunker
strategy, and the multiple tee placements all work together to create a golf
course that can challenge the great players of the world, or be a fun experience
for those less skilled."

An interesting hole on the front side is
the 327-yard par-4 fifth, which you might
be able to drive with a wind behind you. It
plays 293, 277 and 256 yards from the

other tee positions. The green curls to the left behind a huge left-side waste bunker, however, so recovery can be difficult if you miss. This is a typical second-shot hole requiring a well-positioned drive that avoids the large lava-dotted waste area on the left and the traps on the right. The green is elevated and has drop-off areas that penalize a poorly hit approach shot.

The 442-yard sixteenth is a difficult par 4. This hole is indicative of how the course becomes more challenging as you get farther into your round of golf. The tee shot has to avoid black lava to the left and a huge right-side bunker 250 yards from the back tee. The approach shot is to a deep, left-to-right-angled, two-tiered green protected by a lake on the left and a large trap on the right. A crosswind can make this hole very difficult to play.

The Beach Course, a 6507-yard golfer-friendly layout, was opened in 1981. It winds through solid lava flows and historic sites, including the King's Trail, ancient Hawaiian petroglyphs and burial caves. The greens on the Beach Course are large, moderately fast and undulating. They are well protected by large sand traps and water hazards. There are some severe elevation changes on this course, and positioning and accuracy, especially on approach shots to quadrants of the green, are most important.

The number-1-handicap hole on the Beach Course is the 390-yard par-4 second hole, which plays into the wind. A lake is in front of the deep green, but you can't see it from the tee and it is likely to be a long carry over this water on your approach shot. A large trap guards the left side of the putting surface, and a smaller trap and more water protect the right.

A strong par 3 on the front side is the 205-yard seventh, which plays all the way over water to a large green flanked by two huge bunkers. A beautiful par 5 is the 502-yard twelfth, which is a sharp dogleg left to a narrow, deep green protected by two traps on the left and one on the right. The

dogleg is guarded by bunkers both left and right, and the fairway tightens considerably from 250 yards into the green.

The 416-yard par-4 finishing hole is a challenging dogleg left whose tee shot plays over lava to a narrowing fairway protected by a huge bunker on the right, 250 yards from the back tees. The approach shot is to an extremely narrow, deep green bordered by large traps on both sides. The front nine at the Beach Course plays toward magnificent Mauna Kea Mountain, and the back nine plays toward the Pacific Ocean.

Each golf course has a clubhouse with full-service golf shop, restaurant and grill, but minimal locker-room facilities because of the courses' proximity to resort hotels. Driving ranges, practice greens and chipping and practice bunkers are available at both courses, and individual instruction is easily arranged from the staff of professionals and assistants. Golf packages can be obtained through the on-site Shores luxury condominiums and the local resort hotels.

The Waikoloa and other resort hotels offer tennis, horseback riding, deep-sea fishing and a variety of other ocean sports, including swimming, snorkeling, skin diving, windsurfing, sailing and catamaran cruises. The resort area overlooks beautiful white-sand beaches at Anachoomala Bay. Several restaurants at the hotels serve a variety of specialties ranging from seafood to ethnic cuisine. Dancing and the best of Hawaiian entertainment is offered.

Golf and other packages are available through the local hotels. Meeting and conference facilities in theater, banquet, boardroom, classroom and outdoor settings are available. Another golf course you'll want to play while visiting here is the Waikoloa Village Golf Club, a 6687-yard Robert Trent Jones, Jr. layout beautifully situated in the Mauna Kea Mountain foothills, approximately 10 minutes from the Kings' and Beach golf courses.

Kauai

Course Name: KAUAI LAGOONS RESORT
Kiele, Lagoons Courses

Course Type: Resort
Resort: Kauai Marriott Resort and Beach Club
Address: Rice Street
Kalapaki Beach
Lihue, HI 96766
Phone: (808) 246–5061,
(800) 634–6400 (Golf Course) (808) 245–5050,
(800) 220–2925 (Resort)
Fax: (808) 246–5097 (Resort)
Telex: 7431211

GOLF COURSE

Director of Golf: Ron Rawls
Course Length/Par (All Tees): Kiele: Back 7070/72, Blue 6637/72, White 6164/72, Forward 5417/72. Lagoons: Back 6942/72, Blue 6545/72, White 6108/72, Forward 5607/72
Course Slope/Rating (All Tees): Kiele: Back 137/73.7, Blue 131/71.4, White 125/69.1, Ladies' Forward 117/66.5. Lagoons: Back 135/72.8, Blue 129/70.6, White 121/68, Ladies' Forward 121/67
Course Architect: Kiele: Jack Nicklaus (1988), Lagoons: Jack Nicklaus (1989)
Golf Facilities: Full Pro Shop X, Snack Bar X, Lounge X, Restaurant X, Locker Room X, Showers X, Club Rental X, Club Repair X, Cart Rental X, Instruction X, Practice Green X, Driving Range X, Practice Bunker X, Club Storage X
Tee-Time Reservation Policy: Up to 30 days in advance
Ranger: Yes
Tee-off-Interval Time: Kiele: 10 min. Lagoons: 8 min.
Time to Play 18 Holes: 4½ hrs.
Course Hours/Earliest Tee-off: 7:30 a.m.
Green and Cart Fees: Resort guests: Kiele: $110 for 18 holes with cart. Lagoons: $70 for 18 holes with cart. Lagoons fee includes spa admission, same-day practice facility. Public: Kiele: $145 for 18 holes with cart. Lagoons: $110 for 18 holes with cart
Credit Cards: All major cards
Season: Year round. Busiest season Nov. to March
Course Comments: Cart mandatory. $10 charge for practice facility use if not playing golf that day
Golf Packages: Available through resort
Discounts: Hawaii residents
Places to Stay Nearby: Hale Lihue Motel (808) 245–3151; Kauai Resort (808) 245–3931, (800) 367–5004; Hyatt Regency Kauai (808) 742–1234, (800) 228–9000; Outrigger Kauai Beach Hotel (808) 245–1955. BED AND BREAKFAST: Bed and Breakfast Hawaii (808) 822–7771, (800) 773–1632
Local Attractions: NORTHEAST: Wailua Falls, Opaekaa Falls, Fern Grotto, Kamakila, Kilauea Lighthouse, Ke'e Beach State Park. LIHUE AND SOUTH: Kauai Museum, Kilohana, Spouting Horn. WEST AND KOKEE: Fort Elizabeth, Kalalau Lookout, Waimea Canyon, National Tropical Botanical Gardens, Kokee State Park, Niihau, plantation tours, shopping, horseback riding, hiking, camping; water sports including beaches, surfing, snorkeling, scuba diving, boating, fishing, hunting. Hawaii Visitors Bureau (808) 245–3971. County Department of Parks and Recreation (808) 245–8821; Kauai Visitor Center (808) 822–0987, (808) 822–5113
Directions: From Lihue Airport (1 mi.): To main intersection Hwy. 56, left (south) at Rice St., follow signs to resort
Closest Commercial Airport: Lihue (5 min.)

RESORT

Date Built: 1987
No. of Rooms: 846, including 41 suites, 46 Royal Beach Club rooms
Meeting Rooms: 14. Capacity of Largest: 1450 persons banquet style. Meeting Space: 41,000 sq. ft.
Room Price Range: $195 for standard room to $1700 for suites. Golf, tennis, spa and other packages available. Seasonal specials
Lounges: Paddling Club Disco, Kalapaki Grill, Colonnade Lounge

Restaurants: Terrace, Kalapaki Grill, Colonnade, Prince Bill's, Duke's Canoe Club, Cook's at the Beach, Tempura Garden, Inn on the Cliffs, Sharky's Fish Market, Sirena Del Lago, Masters

Entertainment: Disco dancing at Paddling Club, Hawaiian entertainment, jazz at Inn on the Cliffs

Credit Cards: All major cards except Discover

General Amenities: Wildlife tours, horse and carriage rides, shopping, wedding chapel by the sea, 40 shops, meeting and conference facilities with audio-visual and food services; child care, including Camp Kalapaki for children ages 6 to 12

Recreational Amenities: 8 Plexi-pave tennis courts with instruction, pro shop; European Spa and Wellness Center with Turkish steam room, Finnish sauna, whirlpool and exercise equipment; 26,000-sq.-ft. swimming pool; water sports including sailing, canoe tours, cruises, snorkeling, surfing; Kalapaki Beach, horseback riding

Reservation and Cancellation Policy: 2 nights' deposit or credit card guarantee due 15 days from date of booking.

Comments and Restrictions: No pets allowed. Taxes additional to base rates

KAUAI LAGOONS RESORT

The Kauai Marriott Resort and Beach Club, formerly The Westin Kauai at Kauai Lagoons, is rated among the top twelve golf resorts in America by *Golf* magazine. This is because the Kiele and Lagoons courses designed by Jack Nicklaus grace the 800-acre premises, beautifully situated on Kalapaki Beach on Nawiliwili Bay. The resort property is bordered by the Lihue Airport and includes over 1 mile of choice ocean coastline.

Kauai Lagoons offers 36 spectacular holes of challenging golf in a beautiful setting overlooking the ocean. The Kiele Course, perched above the pounding surf of the Pacific, was named America's best new resort golf course for 1989 by *Golf Digest* magazine. The 7070-yard Kiele layout has three other tee-distance options at 6637, 6164 and 5417 yards. This course features fast, undulating, hand-mown

Bermuda-grass greens; tricky trade winds; numerous bunkers; and water hazards on eight holes. The course has been integrated well with the natural landscape, which features rolling hills, deep ravines, lagoons and rich tropical vegetation such as mango and guava trees. Exotic birds, including Australian black swans, East African crowned cranes, Indian hill mynas, and Chilean flamingos may well be inspecting your swing tempo.

Kiele, sloped at 137 from the back tees, is one of the most difficult courses in the state. It has some especially demanding par 3s, including the 207-yard thirteenth, which plays over a huge gulch to a large, two-tiered green protected by traps left and right. In the ravine is an ocean inlet and heavy tropical vegetation. The tee is perched on a high bluff overlooking beautiful Nawiliwili Bay, and the green is somewhat below and across the abyss. A tail wind and the drop to the green make club selection crucial. If you miss to the right, you'll be chipping toward a narrow green from a downhill lie. Don't be short or you'll have to reload.

The most difficult hole on the Kiele Course is the 436-yard par-4 third, which plays directly into the wind. A huge fairway trap that begins within tee-shot range and runs up to the green is a major obstacle. The approach shot is to a deep, left-to-right-angled green with several traps protecting it.

The 431-yard par-4 eighteenth is a great finishing hole, with a green that sits out on a small peninsula surrounded by a beautiful lagoon. The right fairway is bordered by water all the way to the green, and out-of-bounds is on the left. The approach shot has to carry water to a wide, shallow target fronted by water and a bunker. Sand traps protect the rear. This hole plays more like a par 5, and it is an extremely difficult target to reach in regulation.

The clubhouse at Kauai Lagoons has a full pro shop, restaurant, bar, and ladies' and men's locker rooms and showers. It is accessible to a spa, with whirlpool, Jacuzzi, massage and other amenities. Golf instruction is available from PGA professionals and assistants. Personal instruction, clinics and nine-hole playing lessons are easily arranged. Generous driving-range, pitching and putting areas are convenient to the clubhouse, which serves both golf courses.

The 6942-yard Lagoons Course is a gently rolling links-style course with few water hazards and small, moderately fast, undulating greens. This course is flatter than the Kiele layout and has generous tee-shot landing areas, but a premium is placed on positioning, accuracy and approach shots to the tricky putting surfaces. Wind is a factor also, as Jack Nicklaus illustrated when he needed a driver and a 3-wood to reach the 414-yard par-4 during a practice round here. The wind also tends to knock down shots on the 426-yard par-4 second, the number-1-handicap hole on the course. This slight dogleg left has an approach shot to a shallow green protected by several bunkers. If the pin is placed to the left, the approach shot has to carry two bunkers in front of the green.

The 458-yard par-4 finishing hole is a good way to end the round. The tee shot on this dogleg right has to avoid a huge bunker near the landing area on the right. Grass and sand bunkers line the right and left sides of the fairway on the approach shot. The target is a large, two-tiered green, with bunkers both left and right. Pin placement can make a big difference on this hole. It should be added that there is no shortage of grass and sand bunkers on the Lagoons Course, making it a challenging and varied layout. *Golf* magazine rated Lagoons one of the ten best new golf resorts of 1989.

The Lagoons Course is considered the easier of the two layouts at Kauai Lagoons, but you'll enjoy them both. Golf and other packages are available through the Marriott Resort, which, as the Westin, won numerous hospitality awards, including the American Automobile Association's Four-Diamond Award. *Successful Meetings* and *Meetings and Conventions* magazines have recognized the resort as an ideal meeting resort. There is a total of more than 41,000 square feet of modern banquet and conference facilities here, with state-of-the-art audiovisual equipment and banquet facilities for more than 1450 people.

Recreational facilities at Kauai Lagoons include 8 Plexi-pave tennis courts at the Racquet Club, which also has a 612-seat lighted stadium court for exhibitions, a pro shop and a variety of instructional clinics and individual lesson options. *World Tennis* gives these programs and facilities a five-star rating. Other resort activities include horseback riding for all levels of riders and water sports at the 26,000-square-foot swimming pool and nearby Kalapaki Beach. The 40 acres of lagoons and waterways immediately behind the hotel complex on a 500-acre plateau can be toured by outrigger canoes and launches. Wildlife tours through the lagoons provide glimpses of kangaroos, wallabies, llamas, and exotic birds. Coastal sailing on a state-of-the-art, high-speed racing catamaran is another popular activity, as are snorkeling, scuba diving, fishing and surfing. Views from the resort include memorable vistas of the Pacific Ocean, Ha'upu Mountain and the beautiful Kauai Lagoons.

The Spa and Health Club within the Kauai Lagoons Golf Club is a complete European spa with separate facilities for men and women. Services include classes in aerobics, tai chi, aquacize and yoga, as well as access to exercise and weight facilities. The Wellness Center provides a full range of health and wellness counseling, nutritional analysis, body composition and lifestyle appraisal. And there are massages, facials, herbal wrap, steam baths and saunas.

Within easy reach of Kauai Lagoons is a stunning and wildly varied landscape such as the lush Hanalei valley to the north, where a narrow road takes you to the rugged Na Pali coast and road's end. The southern coast features white sands and emerald waters. The center of the island is dominated by 5000-foot Mount Waialene, whose summit, often shrouded in clouds, produces a variety of spectacular waterfalls and rushing rivers that wind their way to the sea.

If you'd like to play world-class golf on an island paradise, Kauai Lagoons is the place to be.

**Course Name: POIPU BAY RESORT
GOLF COURSE**

Course Type: Resort
Resort: Hyatt Regency Kauai
1571 Poipu Road
Kaloa, Kauai, HI 96756
Golf Course: 2250 Ainako Street
Kaloa, Kauai, HI 96756
Phone: (808) 742–8711, (800) 858–6300
(Golf Course), (808) 742–1234,
(800) 233–1234 (Resort)
Fax: (808) 742–7155 (Golf Course),
(808) 742–1557 (Resort)

GOLF COURSE

Director of Golf: Ron Kaiaana, Jr.
Head Professional: Michael Castillo
Course Length/Par (All Tees): Back
6959/72, Blue 6499/72, White 6023/72,
Forward 5241/72
Course Slope/Rating (All Tees): Back
132/73.4, Blue 129/71.3, White
125/69.0, Ladies' Forward 121/70.9
Course Architect: Robert Trent Jones, Jr.
(1991)
Golf Facilities: Full Pro Shop X, Snack
Bar X, Lounge X, Restaurant X, Locker
Room X, Showers X, Club Rental X,
Club Repair X, Cart Rental X, Instruc-
tion X, Practice Green X, Driving Range
X, Practice Bunker X, Club Storage X
Tee-Time Reservation Policy: At time of
confirmed resort reservation. Up to 1
month in advance for the public
Ranger: Yes
Tee-off-Interval Time: 8 min.
Time to Play 18 Holes: 4 hrs. 15 min.
Course Hours/Earliest Tee-off: 7:00 a.m.
Green and Cart Fees: $125 for 18 holes
for outside play; $85 for 18 holes for
resort guests
Credit Cards: All major cards
Season: Year round
Course Comments: Cart mandatory. Yard-
age book available
Golf Packages: Through resort
Discounts: Twilight rates. Resort guests
Places to Stay Nearby: Kuhio Shores
(808) 742–7555, (800) 367–8022; Gar-
den Isle Cottages (808) 742–1470;
Sheraton Kauai Hotel (808) 742–1661,

(800) 325–3535; Stouffer Poipu Beach
Resort (808) 742–1681, (800) 426–4122
Local Attractions: Fern Grotto, Fort Eliza-
beth, Kalalau Lookout, Kamokila, Kauai
Museum, Kilauea Lighthouse, Kilohana,
Opaekoa Falls, Spouting Horn, Waimea
Canyon, water sports, fishing, boating,
hiking, bicycling, horseback riding,
restaurants, shopping
Directions: From Lihue Airport (25 min.):
Go west on Rte. 50 then south on Rte.
52 to Poipu Rd. Proceed 3 mi. down
Poipu Rd. to resort and golf course
Closest Commercial Airport: Lihue
Airport (25 min.)

RESORT

Date Built: 1990
No. of Rooms: 600 rooms including 41
1- and 2-bedroom suites
Meeting Rooms: 19. Capacity of Largest:
1500 persons theater style. Meeting
Space: 65,000 sq. ft.
Room Price Range: From $295 to $465.
Packages available year round
Lounges: Stevenson's Library, Seaview
Lounge, Kuhio's, Tidepool Lounge,
Captain's Bar
Restaurants: Tidepools, Donderos, Ilima
Terrace, Poipu Bay Grill and Bar, The
Dock, Kupono Cafe, Seaview Terrace
Entertainment: Dancing and live entertain-
ment at Kuhio's
Credit Cards: All major cards
General Amenities: Clothing stores, art
gallery, jewelry store; Camp Hyatt chil-
dren's program; meeting and conference
facilities with audiovisual, food, secretarial, and other support services
Recreational Amenities: Snorkeling, scuba
diving, fishing, boating, Anara Spa and
fitness center with steam, sauna, whirlpool, lava rock shower; 2 swimming
pools, 3 jacuzzis, 4 tennis courts, action
swimming pool with waterfalls and
slides, volleyball, stables and horseback
riding, 5 acres of beach-rimmed lagoon
Reservation and Cancellation Policy: Advance deposit required. Up to 14 day cancellation policy. Deposit requirements and
cancellation policy vary by season
Comments and Restrictions: No pets

POIPU BAY RESORT GOLF COURSE

Situated 95 miles northwest of Honolulu, Kauai, a 350,000-acre lushly green island, offers quiet hospitality and excellent golf. The Poipu Bay Resort is located on the south side of the island, a spot noted for sunny beaches and clear skies. The Robert Trent Jones, Jr. designed Poipu Bay Resort Golf Course overlooks the beach and the ocean cliffs and features rolling fairways sometimes bordered by ancient Hawaiian archeological sites. Poipu Bay's links-style course covers 210 acres, including 35 acres of tropical plants, has four lakes, more than 80 stategically placed bunkers, and tricky winds. Should a ball land in the sacred archeological sites (called Heiaus), the ball is considered irretrievable, and the player receives a stroke penalty. Water can come into play on eleven holes and once you reach the large, undulating Bermuda grass greens, your putting skills will be tested.

The four finishing holes along the ocean provide a memorable conclusion to a scenic round at Poipu Bay. The 427-yard par-4 fifteenth plays from an elevated tee to a landing area framed by bunkers to the right and the Pacific to the left. The approach shot must negotiate the two bunkers straddling the entanceway to a deep, rolling green. The 501-yard par-5 sixteenth tilts toward the ocean to the left making it advisable to play to the right-center of the fairway. The approach is to a very deep green with a question mark of bunkers running from its rear to its lower right. The 201-yard par-3 seventeenth runs downhill and downwind to a green bracketed by two large bunkers. The finishing hole, a 550-yard par 5, requires a long and accurate tee shot that avoids a large bunker to the right of the landing area to provide an opportunity to reach the green in two. The deep putting surface is guarded by a lake to the left and large bunkers to its rear and right.

A short walk from the 18th green is the 21,000 square foot golf clubhouse and restaurant which features the Poipu Bay Grill and Bar. This oasis offers everything from spicy mai tais to Poipu Bay pork ribs. At different times you will see humpback whales, monk seals, green sea turtles, and other creatures in the nearby ocean. Adjacent to the golf course is the 50-acre Hyatt Regency Kauai oceanfront resort, a *Golf* magazine Silver Medal winner. The Hyatt Regency and Poipu Bay host the PGA Grand Slam of Golf in early November. The golf course is rated among the best in Hawaii by *Golf Digest*. Practice facilities include a generous 10-acre driving range, 12,000 square feet of putting greens, practice bunkers, and a teaching area.

Course Name: PRINCE COURSE Makai (Ocean, Lakes, Woods), Prince Courses

Course Type: Resort
Resort: Princeville Resort
Address: Off Highway 56
                P.O. Box 3040 Princeville, HI 96722–3040
Phone: (808) 826–5000 (Golf Course)
                (808) 826–3040 (Resort),
                (800) 826–4400 (U.S.) (Resort)
Fax: (808) 826–4653 (Resort)

GOLF COURSE

Director of Golf: Bob Higgins
Head Professionals: Makai: Greg Anderson. Prince: Bob Caldwell
Course Length/Par (All Tees): Makai Ocean/Woods: Back 6912/72, Middle 6455/72, Ladies' Forward 5631/73. Makai Ocean/Lakes: Back 6900/72, Middle 6206/72, Forward 5519/72. Makai Woods/Lakes: Back 6878/72, Middle 6447/72, Ladies' Forward 5543/73. Prince: Back 7309/72, Blue 6960/72, White 6521/72, Gold 6005/72, Ladies' Forward 5338/72
Course Slope/Rating (All Tees): Makai Ocean/Woods: Back 133/72.7, Middle 123/69.3, Ladies' Forward 115/70.6. Makai Ocean/Lakes: Back 134/72.7 Middle 127/69.7, Ladies' Forward 114/70.0. Makai Woods/Lakes: Back 129/72.3, Middle 125/69.3, Ladies' Forward 114/69.8. Prince: Back 144/75.6, Blue 137/73.7, White 135/71.7, Gold 131/69.4, Ladies' Forward 127/72

Course Architect: Makai: Robert Trent Jones, Jr. (1972). Prince: Robert Trent Jones, Jr. (1990)

Golf Facilities: Full Pro Shop X, Snack Bar X, Lounge X, Restaurant X, Locker Room X, Showers X, Club Rental X, Club Repair X, Cart Rental X, Instruction X, Practice Green X, Driving Range X, Practice Bunker X, Club Storage X

Tee-Time Reservation Policy: Up to 30 days in advance

Ranger: Yes

Tee-off-Interval Time: Makai: 8 min. Prince: 10 min.

Time to Play 18 Holes: Makai: 4 hrs. Prince: 4 hrs., 45 min.

Course Hours/Earliest Tee-off: 7:30 a.m.

Green and Cart Fees: Makai: Resort guests: $95 for 18 holes with cart. Public: $115 for 18 holes with cart. Prince: Resort guests: $120 for 18 holes with cart. Public: $150 for 18 holes with cart

Credit Cards: All major cards

Season: Year round. Busiest season mid-Dec. to March, Aug.

Course Comments: Cart mandatory. Yardage book available. Golfers without a registered handicap are asked to play the Prince course after 10:30 a.m.

Golf Packages: Available through resort

Discounts: Hawaii residents

Places to Stay Nearby: Hanalei Bay Resort (808) 826–6522, (800) 657–7922; Sandpiper Village (808) 826–9613, (800) 367–5205. BED AND BREAKFASTS: Bed and Breakfast Hawaii (808) 822–7771, (800) 733–1632; Kay Barker's Bed and Breakfast (808) 822–3073

Local Attractions: Native Hawaiian Museum, Kokee State Park, beaches, camping, hiking, fishing, water sports, Waimea Canyon, Fern Grotto, Port Elizabeth, Kalalau Lookout, Kamokila, Kauni Museum, Kilauea Lighthouse, Kilohana, Opaekaa Falls, Spouting Horn, shopping, restaurants, plantations and gardens, hunting, "The End of the Road" at Ke'e Beach. Hanalei. Hawaii Visitors Bureau (808) 245–3971. Kauai Visitor Center (808) 822–0987, (808) 822–5113. Kauai

Department of Public Works, Department of Parks and Recreation (808) 245–8821. State Department of Land and Natural Resources (808) 245–4444

Directions: From Lihue Airport (28 mi.): Hwy. 56 north to resort

Closest Commercial Airports: Princeville (commuter) (10 min.), Lihue (1 hr.)

RESORT

Date Built: 1985

No. of Rooms: 252 rooms and suites

Meeting Rooms: 6. Capacity of Largest: 540 persons banquet style. Meeting Space: 16,226 sq. ft.

Room Price Range: $295 for garden-view room to $3000 for royal suite. Golf and other packages available year round

Lounges: Pool Bar, Living Room

Restaurants: La Cascata, Cafe Hanalei and Terrace, Beach Restaurant

Entertainment: Live music, dancing

Credit Cards: All major cards

General Amenities: Helicopter tours, handicapped-adapted rooms, private movie cinema, shopping in Princeville Center, beauty salon, educational activities, complimentary supervised children's program (ages 5 to 12), indoor and outdoor meeting and conference facilities with audiovisual and banquet services

Recreational Amenities: 6 tennis courts, horseback riding, water sports including snorkeling, wind surfing, scuba diving, sailing; swimming pool, fitness center, jogging paths, bicycling; Prince Rejuvenation Spa with fitness, wellness, beauty treatments, massage and other amenities

Reservation and Cancellation Policy: 1 night's credit card or check deposit per room required within 10 days of confirmation. Refund of deposit will be made if cancellation received at hotel at least 72 hrs. prior to planned date of arrival

Comments and Restrictions: Taxes additional to base rates. No charge for children under 18 when occupying same room as adult, using existing bedding. Cribs available at no charge

PRINCE COURSE

Kauai is the oldest of the Hawaiian Islands and encompasses 350,000 acres of land, most of it rich, green and untamed. The Princeville Resort is situated on 11,000 acres on the north shore of Kauai, overlooking Hanalei Bay near the village of Hanalei. Not far from here is the Shrine of Laka, the goddess of the hula, which is loyally visited by island dancers. The Princeville Hotel, which has just gone through a $100-million renovation, majestically overlooks Pacific waters from tiered plateaus on the side of a cliff. The hotel has 252 guest rooms and suites with niceties such as hand-carved furniture from Italy, Chinese porcelain, spa bathtubs and panoramic views of the ocean. There is even a staff of butlers here to keep everyone suitably pampered 24 hours a day.

Also a bit out of this world are the 45 holes of Robert Trent Jones, Jr.-designed golf awaiting you at the 27-hole Makai Course and the 18-hole Prince Course. The Makai Course, opened in 1972, comprises three nines that fan out from the clubhouse toward the ocean and the inland woods. The Lakes nine works inland, then back toward the ocean and its cliffs. This course was named for the lakes situated on three holes on the layout. The Woods nine is inland and features beautiful mountains and towering waterfalls as well as heavily treed fairways with stately Norfolk pine and rock-garden-style bunkers. The Ocean nine works its way to the seaside and cliffs, then comes back to the clubhouse, which features a full-service pro shop, a snack bar and restaurant, and adjoining tennis courts and tennis pro shop. The Makai nines weave through a recently completed multimillion-dollar resort renovation. These courses were Robert Trent Jones, Jr's., first solo design effort in Hawaii and have been ranked among the top 100 golf courses in America, best courses in each state and America's 75 best resort courses by *Golf Digest* magazine. While the Ocean and Lake Courses tend to be the most popular combination, any of these nines is well worth playing.

The Ocean Course measures 3467 yards from the back tees and has some challenging and spectacular par 3s. The 178-yard third plays from an elevated tee to a large green protected by traps and a beautiful lake in front. The view from the tee is of the Pacific Ocean, Hanalei Bay and Bali Hai beyond. Club selection is critical here because of tail winds and the spectacular 100-foot drop to the target below. The 204-yard seventh requires a long, accurate tee shot that can carry a 160-foot deep ravine with the ocean and black lava rock below.

The Lakes Course plays 3433 yards and has a strong finishing hole. This 544-yard par 5 requires the golfer to clear two lakes to reach a large green flanked by traps. The first shot is over a lake, forcing the golfer to decide whether to go for the green on the second shot or to lay up to the lake that fronts the green. This hole has often determined the winner of the many tournaments that have been held here, including the LPGA Kemper Open. In a recent LPGA World Match Play Championship, Betsy King defeated Deb Richard on the ninth hole in the final round. The ninth plays 440 yards from the ladies' tees.

The most difficult hole at Makai is the 447-yard par-4 sixth on the Woods Course. This long dogleg right usually plays into the trade winds, which can randomly affect play on all the layouts at this resort. The tee shot has to avoid a right-side fairway bunker. The approach shot is to a green well protected by three traps. The bunker fronting the green requires you to carry a strong, accurate long iron or wood all the way to the target.

Besides supervising the extensive renovations at Makai, Robert Trent Jones, Jr., also designed the new Prince Course, which opened to wide acclaim in 1990. It was promptly named the best new resort course of 1990 by *Golf Digest*, which now rates it the number 1 golf course in Hawaii's very competitive golf market. This magnificent 7309-yard layout has five sets of tees and covers 390 acres, including deep ravines, tropical jungles, streams and waterfalls. Construction crews moved 385,000 cubic yards of dirt while building the course, and the practice facility alone covers 13 acres of valuable Hawaiian real estate.

Before you step onto the first tee at the Prince Course, you can savor the panoramic views from Mt. Namalakoma on your left to the Pacific and Bali Hai in the distance. The golf course has one of the highest slope ratings (144) in Hawaii from the back tees. Variation in elevation and hillside lies; water hazards; fast, undulating greens; tricky winds and formidable grass and sand bunkering make this a challenging venue. Fortunately, the variety of distances enables you to select the degree of difficulty that suits you. If you don't have a registered handicap, however, you are requested to play after 10:30 a.m. on the Prince.

The Prince is one of those courses that could have any one of several signature holes. The 390-yard par-4 twelfth, "Eagle's Nest," is often a leading candidate for most memorable hole here. The tee shot is from an elevated tee to a narrow fairway bordered by dense jungle. The green is surrounded by ferns and tropical foliage, with the Anini Stream a hazard on both sides. Shot placement is at a premium on this spectacular hole.

Or you might consider the 588-yard par-5 "Burma Road" hole, the dramatic dogleg-left tenth. A large ravine filled with tropical vegetation borders the entire hole on the left and fronts the green on the approach. The right side of the fairway features a series of bunkers that begin 225 yards from the back tees. The approach shot on this hole is generally into the wind to a wide, shallow green with four bunkers to the left front and another toward the rear. This is a daunting hole.

A scenic and difficult par 3 on the Prince is the 205-yard seventh, "Da Pali," with the Pacific Ocean and Anini Beach on the left. From the back tees, the shot has to carry 180 yards of ocean crevasse to a deep green with traps left, rear and right and ocean all around. There are nine tee distances, ranging from 98 to 205 yards, to

choose from. The drop from the tee to the beach is approximately 450 feet.

The spectacular new 60,000-square-foot clubhouse at the Prince has a full-service pro shop, men's and ladies' locker rooms, a health and beauty spa, function and seminar rooms, restaurant and lounge. Golf instruction is available at both the Makai and the Prince from the staff of PGA professionals and assistants. Each course has a driving range, practice bunkers and putting green. Golf packages are offered by the resort year round.

The Princeville Resort offers more than 16,000 square feet of meeting space and can accommodate banquet groups of up to 540 persons. A variety of restaurants at the resort serve everything from simple meals to more elaborate cuisine such as Mediterranean Italian, pancakes with macadamia nuts and guava syrup, spiced chicken paillard with pommelo and scallion salad and a sweet curry sauce, and grilled opakapaka with black bean batter and crispy leeks.

Recreational activities at the Princeville Resort include tennis, horseback riding, and water sports such as surfing, swimming, snorkeling, scuba diving, fishing and boating. There is also a fitness center and new health club and spa on site, as well as jogging trails and a swimming pool. Seasonal special events include the Hanalei Music Festival, the King-Kong Triathlon, Hanalei Stampede, polo and the Hanalei Taro Festival. The Princeville Hotel hosts a variety of activities for guests ranging from wine tastings to Hawaiiana classes. The resort's complimentary supervised children's program, Keiki Aloha, for young guests ages 5 to 12 years, includes special excursions, craft lessons, and much more. There is also an in-house movie theater, which presents feature-length films.

The international artwork gracing the Princeville Hotel, the state-of-the-art electronic windows in each room and the native water birds in the reclaimed Puu Poa Marsh all provide the distinct impression that Princeville Resort's golf and resort amenities are world class in every way.

**Course Name: WAILUA MUNICIPAL
                GOLF COURSE**

Course Type: Public
Address: Highway 56
              Lihue, HI 96766
Phone: (808) 241–6666

GOLF COURSE

Head Professional: Larry Lee, Sr.

Course Length/Par (All Tees): Back
6981/72, Middle 6585/72, Ladies'
Forward 5974/73

Course Slope/Rating (All Tees): Back
136/73.8, Middle 134/71.9, Ladies'
Forward 122/73.1

Course Architect: Toyo Shirai (back 9,
1920; front 9, 1962)

Golf Facilities: Full Pro Shop X, Snack
Bar X, Lounge X, Restaurant X,
Locker Room X, Showers X, Club
Rental X, Club Repair X, Cart Rental
X, Instruction X, Practice Green X,
Driving Range X, Practice Bunker X,
Club Storage No

Tee-Time Reservation Policy: 7 days in
advance for 2 or more players

Ranger: Yes

Tee-off-Interval Time: 6 min.

Time to Play 18 Holes: 4 hrs.

Course Hours/Earliest Tee-off: 7 a.m.

Green Fees: Nonresidents: $35 for 18
holes weekends, holidays; $25 for 18
holes Mon. to Fri.

Cart Fees: $14 for 18 holes

Credit Cards: None—cash or traveler's
check

Season: Year round. Busiest season Dec.
to April

Course Comments: Can walk anytime.
Driving range open until 10 p.m.
Mon.-Sat.

Golf Packages: None

Discounts: Hawaii residents

Places to Stay Nearby: Hale Lihue Motel
(808) 245–3151; Kauai Marriott Resort
(808) 245–5050, (800) 220—2925;
Kauai Resort (808) 245–3931, (800)
922–7866; Outrigger Kauai Beach Hotel
(808) 245–1955, (800) 462–6262. BED
AND BREAKFAST: Bed and Breakfast
Hawaii (808) 822–7771, (800) 773–1632

Local Attractions: NORTHEAST: Wilua
Falls, Opaekaa Falls, Fern Grotto,
Kamakila, Kilauea Lighthouse, Ke'e
Beach State Park. LIHUE AND SOUTH:
Kauai Museum, Kilohano, Spouting
Horn. WEST AND KOKEE: Fort Elizabeth,
Kalalau Lookout, Waimea Canyon,
National Tropical Botanical Gardens,
Kokee State Park, Niihau, plantation
tours, shopping, horseback riding, hik-
ing, camping; water sports including
beaches, surfing, snorkeling, scuba
diving, boating, fishing, hunting. Hawaii
Visitors Bureau (808) 245–3971. Kauai
Department of Public Works, Depart-
ment of Parks and Recreation (808) 245–
8821. Kauai Visitor Center (808) 822–
0987, (808) 822–5113

Directions: From Lihue Airport (2 mi.):
North on Hwy. 56, follow signs to golf
course

Closest Commercial Airport: Lihue (5 min.)

WAILUA MUNICIPAL GOLF COURSE

Just north of the Lihue Airport in Kauai
is the Wailua Municipal Golf Course, the
best municipal golf course in the state of
Hawaii. This 6981-yard layout was designed by Toyo Shirai, who served as green
superintendent at Wailua.

Shirai added 200 yards to a par-35 layout he inherited after World War II, then
designed what is now the current front
nine, which was carved out of sand dunes
and ironwood trees and opened on January
13, 1962. Wailua had become a quality
eighteen-hole layout and was honored in
1975 as the site of the 50th Annual USGA
Amateur Public Links Championship. The
Public Links was also held here in 1985
and 1996. *Golf Digest* has regularly ranked
Wailua among America's 75 best public
golf courses. Not many golf courses that
have been designed without the benefit of
a professional architect that received this
kind of national recognition.

Wailua covers 215 acres of scenic seaside
land and extends over a mile from end to end
along beautiful Wai'lua Beach. The course
features large, fast, undulating greens with a
variety of shapes. A variety of doglegs appear
on this somewhat flat course, and there is a

direct water hazard on only one hole. Mature trees such as coconuts and pines line some of the fairways, and they can be a problem if the ball strays. Most of the sand bunkers are strategically placed around the greens. The ever present trade winds are always a factor at Wailua.

The most difficult hole on the course is the 456-yard par-4 second hole, a dogleg left, which is bordered on the left by the Pacific and crossed by ocean winds. Keep the tee shot left of center but avoid hooking the ball onto Wai'lua Beach. The second shot is to a large green protected by traps both left and right. The next hole is a difficult 245-yard par 3 that plays to a deep green flanked by two huge bunkers.

The back nine starts out with a challenging par 5 that plays 541 yards to a large green protected by traps to the left and right. A right-side fairway trap can catch your tee shot if you are not careful. The 173-yard par-3 seventeenth is a beautiful hole, probably the most memorable one on the course. The tee shot is from an elevated plateau looking down at a deep right-to-left-angled green backed by the Pacific Ocean. The tee shot is often into the wind, and a series of traps protect the front of the green.

Though extremely busy, Wailua Municipal expedites play by using marshals on the course, which is open every day except Christmas and New Year's. Its peak season is from mid-December through April. The clubhouse has a locker room and showers, short-order restaurant, bar and pro shop, and a lighted practice range stays open until 10 p.m. six days a week. You can walk the golf course anytime, and the green fees are reasonable considering the quality of the course and its high maintenance standards. Singles cannot reserve tee times but can get on the course fairly easily.

The hurricane that swept Kauai in September of 1992 caused extensive damage to the golf clubhouse at Wailua, forcing it to close. It is now back in good shape and remains one of the best golf bargains in Hawaii.

Lanai

Course Name:　THE CHALLENGE AT MANELE

Course Type:　Resort
Resort:　　　The Manele Bay Hotel
Address:　　P.O. Box 774
　　　　　　Lanai City, HI 96763
Phone:　　　(800) 321–4666, (808) 565–7700
　　　　　　(Golf Course, Resort)
Fax:　　　　(808) 565–2483 (Resort)

GOLF COURSE

Director of Golf: Gary Campbell
Course Length/Par (All Tees): Back 7039/72, Gold 6684/72, Blue 6310/72, White 5841/72, Forward 5024/72
Course Slope/Rating (All Tees): Back 132/73.3, Gold 129/71.6, Blue 125/69.8, White 122/67.8, Forward 114/64.0, Ladies' White 129/73.2, Forward 119/68.8
Course Architect: Jack Nicklaus (1993)
Golf Facilities: Full Pro Shop X, Snack Bar X, Lounge X, Restaurant X, Locker Room X, Showers X, Club Rental X, Club Repair X, Cart Rental X, Instruction X, Practice Green X, Driving Range X, Practice Bunker X, Club Storage X
Tee-Time Reservation Policy: At time of confirmed resort reservation. Up to 30 days in advance for outside play
Ranger: Yes
Tee-off-Interval Time: 10 min.
Time to Play 18 Holes: 4 hrs. 45 min.
Course Hours/Earliest Tee-off: 7:30 a.m.
Green Fees: $150 for 18 holes for outside play; $100 for 18 holes for resort guests
Cart Fees: $22 for 18 holes per person
Credit Cards: All major cards
Season: Year round. Busiest Nov. through May
Course Comments: Cart mandatory. Yardage book available
Golf Packages: Through resort
Discounts: Resort guests, residents
Places to Stay Nearby: See page 258
Local Attractions: See page 258
Directions: Lanai is 25 minutes by air from Honolulu. More than 100 flights arrive at Lanai airport per week. The resort provides regular transportation

between the airport, the resort, and destinations such as Lanai City and the Manele Boat Harbor

Closest Commercial Airport: Lanai Airport (20 min.)

RESORT

Date Built: 1991

No. of Rooms: 250 rooms including 28 suites. All accomodations have lanais

Meeting Rooms: 4 rooms, 2 terraces. Capacity of Largest: 299 persons. Meeting Space: 12,000 sq. ft.

Room Price Range: $250 for a terrace room to $495 for an ocean deluxe room. Suites are from $700 to $2,000 per night. Modified American, American and European plans available

Lounges: Hale Aheahe (House of Gentle Breezes)

Restaurants: Ihilani Dining Room, Hulopo'e Court, The Clubhouse, The Pool Grille

Entertainment: Live music

Credit Cards: All major cards

General Amenities: Shops, library, children's activities program including art, hiking, tennis, golf, pool parties and more; Lanai Conference Center with audiovisual, food, secretarial, and other services available; 4-wheel drive vehicle rental

Recreational Amenities: Jeep tours, archaelogical walks, garden tours, whale watching, boat day trips; Spa at Manele Bay, fitness center, 6 plexi-paved tennis courts, swimming, fishing, scuba diving, snorkeling, aerobics, horseback riding, hunting, fishing

Reservation and Cancellation Policy: To guarantee reservations, a deposit of 2 nights room rate is required within 14 days of the reservation request. Deposits will be returned in full when cancellations are received at least 14 days prior to arrival.

Comments and Restrictions: No additional charge for children 15 years or younger sharing room with adult(s). Guests at The Manele Bay Hotel have access to amenities at The Lodge at Koele 10 min. away

THE CHALLENGE AT MANELE

The Challenge at Manele is a links-style Jack Nicklaus design that complements upcountry Experience at Koele ten minutes to the north. This seaside golf course is adjacent to The Manele Bay Hotel which sits high above the white sand beach of Hulopoe Bay. In the distance you can see the island of Kahoolawe.

This target-style course is built around acres of natural lava outcropping. Of the 350 acres devoted to The Challenge, only 85 acres are grassed. Three holes cut across steep ravines high above the sea. The large, Bermuda grass greens are moderately undulating. There are five tee distances to chose from at The Challenge and some holes offer additional tee boxes should the golfer wish to avoid forced carries. There are an excellent variety of holes with elevation changes, sea breezes, vegetation such as stands of kiawe and ilima trees, and other factors adding to the diversity of the round. The par 4s, for example, play anywhere from 345 yards (No. 13) to 462 yards (No. 5) from the back tees. If you miss the landing areas on this course, your ball will likely be in a ravine or gully, native underbrush, a large bunker, huge waste areas, or the ocean.

One of the five holes that run close to the ocean at The Challenge is the 202-yard par-3 twelfth that plays out over the water to your left to a large green with a bunker to its right. Another ocean hole is the 444-yard par-4 seventeenth, a dogleg right bordering the ocean to the right, which defies you to cut off as much of the corner as you dare in order to have a good approach opportunity. Your second shot is downhill to a cliffside, kidney-shaped green defended by a large mound and a bunker in front. Like many holes on this course, you will be inclined to reach for your camera before addressing the ball. Whales and dolphins cavorting in the ocean are another natural distraction at The Challenge.

The 250-room Manele Bay Hotel is a *Golf* magazine Gold Medal Resort. It has won many hospitality awards including a top-10 ranking among *Condé Nast Traveler* magazine's "Top 100 World's Best" resorts.

The Manele Bay Hotel has beautiful court-yard gardens, a conference center, a carefully preserved archeological site, spa, and numerous recreational activities. Among its various dining experiences is the Ihilani (heavenly splendor), a French Mediterranean gourmet restaurant serving seared ahi sashimi, fricasse of squab breast, and other delicacies. Guests at the hotel may also use the facilities at The Lodge at Koele. Because there is relatively little rainfall in this region, golf is a sunny year round option.

Course Name: THE EXPERIENCE AT
               KOELE

Course Type: Resort
Resort: The Lodge at Koele
Address: P.O. Box L
               Lanai City, Lanai, HI 96763
Phone: (808) 565–4653 (Golf Course),
               (808) 567–7300 (Resort),
               (800) 321–4666 (Central
               Reservations)
Fax: (808) 565–3868 (Resort)

GOLF COURSE

Director of Golf: Gary Campbell
Head Professional: Marc Orlowski
Course Length/Par (All Tees): Back 7014/72, Championship 134/71.5, Resort 6217/72, Forward 5425/72
Course Slope/Rating (All Tees): Back 141/73.3, Championship 134/71.5, Resort 130/69.7, Forward 123/66.6
Course Architects: Greg Norman and Ted Robinson (1991)
Golf Facilities: Full Pro Shop X, Snack Bar X, Lounge X, Restaurant X, Locker Room X, Showers X, Club Rental X, Club Repair X, Cart Rental X, Instruction X, Practice Green X, Driving Range X, Practice Bunker X, Club Storage X
Tee-Time Reservation Policy: At time of confirmed reservation. Up to 30 days in advance for the public
Ranger: Yes
Tee-off-Interval Time: 10 min.
Time to Play 18 Holes: 4½ hrs.
Course Hours/Earliest Tee-off: 8:00 a.m.

Green and Cart Fees: $150 for 18 holes for outside play; $100 for 18 holes for resort guests
Credit Cards: All major cards
Season: Year round. Busiest Nov. through Jan., Apr. through July
Course Comments: Cart mandatory
Golf Packages: Through resort
Discounts: For resort guests
Places to Stay Nearby: Hotel Lanai (808) 565–7211, (800) 624–8849; The Manele Bay Hotel (800) 321–4666
Local Attractions: Garden of the Gods, Hulope Beach, Keomuku, Lanaihale, Manele Bay, Shipwreck Beach, hiking, snorkeling, boating, fishing. Maui Visitors Bureau (also handles Lanai) (808) 871–8691
Directions: Lanai is easily reached by air from Honolulu, 25 min. away. More than 100 flights per week serve the island. The resort provides regular transportation to and from the airport and other sites
Closest Commercial Airport: Lanai Airport (10 min.)

RESORT

Date Built: 1990
No. of Rooms: 102 rooms and suites. All accomodations have lanais
Meeting Rooms: 6. Capacity of Largest: 299 persons. Meeting Space: 12,000 sq. ft.
Room Price Range: From $295 to $495 for a room. Suites from $600 to $1,100
Lounges: The Tea, The Music Room (for tea)
Restaurants: Formal Dining Room, The Terrace, The Clubhouse Grill
Entertainment: Music room with live music and sound system
Credit Cards: All major cards
General Amenities: The Lanai Conference Center with audiovisual, food, secretarial, and other support services; retail shop, 4-wheel drive vehicle rental, gardens, library
Recreational Amenities: Jeep rides, 3 tennis courts, heated swimming pool, game room, whirlpool, horseback riding, hunting, croquet, lawn bowling, 18-hole

executive putting course, beach and boating activities, hiking, archaelogical tours

Reservation and Cancellation Policy: To guarantee reservations, a deposit in the amount of 2 nights room rate is required within 14 days of the reservation request. Deposits will be refunded in full when cancellations are received at least 14 days prior to scheduled arrival

Comments and Restrictions: Guests of The Lodge at Koele have full access to amentities at The Manele Bay Hotel 10 min. away

THE EXPERIENCE AT KOELE

Lanai, 13 miles wide and 18 miles long, is called the Pineapple Island largely as a result of the efforts of Jim Dole who bought the island in 1922 for $1.1 million and developed the Dole Plantation and the harbor at Kaumalapau from which to ship his produce. Castle and Cook, the current parent company of Dole and 98 percent owner of the island, has moved into the tourism business by developing the 102-room Lodge at Koele and the 248-room luxury Manele Bay Hotel. The Lodge is reminiscent of a fine country estate. It is tucked in an upcountry setting and features an extensive collection of Pacific art, Japanese hillside gardens, and Hawaiian fruit gardens.

At The Lodge is The Experience at Koele, 7014-yard Ted Robinson, and Greg Norman-designed gem that sits at 2000 feet, with panoramic views of the islands of Maui and Molokai across the deep blue Pacific. The course is lush with Norfolk pine and indigenous island plants, has seven lakes and flowing streams, cascading waterfalls, fast bentgrass greens and an assortment of elevation changes and strategically placed bunkers. The first seven holes meander across a high country plateau before you reach the eye-popping eighth. This 444-yard par 4 looks out over a mile-long valley 250 feet down through the mist to a green guarded on the right by a 70-foot-tall sentinel eucalyptus. A good drive is required to avoid a large lake that will catch errant balls to the right. Fortunately the four tee distances on the course provide playable options for most golfers, although the forward tees at 5425 yards will be no picnic for the ladies.

The back nine begins with four holes that generally have favorable tailwinds. The final five usually play into stiff tradewinds. This makes the 435-yard par-4 fifteenth especially tough. Players tee off across a bevy of waterfalls leaving a long shot to the green. The waterfalls are just another scenic distraction on a memorable course that has no forced carries. The greens have openings in front that enable you to run the ball into the putting surface.

Golf magazine rated The Experience among the "Top Ten New Resort Courses" in 1991 and the resort has won several hospitality awards including *Meeting and Conventions* magazine's Gold Tee Award and *Condé Nast Traveler*'s "Readers Choice Award" for being among the best resorts in the world. The 35-foot-high beamed ceilings and natural stone fireplaces, local art, and cuisine such as wild rice waffles with spiced apple and Vermont maple syrup or roasted Lanai venison loin provide an added dimension to your golf experience at Lanai.

Maui

Course Name: KAPALUA GOLF CLUB Bay, Village, Plantation Courses

Course Type: Resort
Resort: Kapalua Bay Hotel and Villas
Address: 1 Bay Drive
Lahaina, HI 96761
Phone: (808) 669–8044 (Golf Course)
(808) 669–5656,
(800) 367–8000 (Resort)
Fax: (808) 669–4694 (Resort)
Telex: 7432249+

GOLF COURSE

Director of Golf: Marty Keiter
Head Professional: Bruce Glasco
Course Length/Par (All Tees): Bay: Back 6600/72, Middle 6051/72, Ladies' Forward 5124/72. Village: Back 6632/71, Middle 6001/71, Ladies' Forward 5134/71. Plantation: Back 7263/73, Middle 6547/73, Ladies' Forward 5627/75

Course Slope/Rating (All Tees): Bay: Back 138/71.7, Middle 133/69.2 Ladies' Forward 121/69.2. Village: Back 139/73.3, Middle 130/70.4, Ladies' Forward 122/70.9. Plantation: Back 142/75.2, Middle 135/71.9, Ladies' Forward 129/73.2

Course Architects: Bay: Arnold Palmer (1975). Village: Arnold Palmer (1980). Plantation: Bill Coore and Ben Crenshaw (1991)

Golf Facilities: Full Pro Shop X, Snack Bar X, Lounge X, Restaurant X, Locker Room X, Showers X, Club Rental X, Club Repair X, Cart Rental X, Instruction X, Practice Green X, Driving Range X, Practice Bunker X, Club Storage X

Tee-Time Reservation Policy: 7 days in advance. Groups can reserve further in advance

Ranger: Yes

Tee-off-Interval Time: 10 min.

Time to Play 18 Holes: 4 hrs.

Course Hours/Earliest Tee-off: 6:40 a.m.

Green Fees: Resort guests: Plantation: $80 for 18 holes. Public: $125 for 18 holes. Resort Guests: Bay, Village: $75 for 18 holes. Public: $115 for 18 holes

Cart Fees: $15 for 18 holes per person

Credit Cards: All major cards except Discover

Season: Year round. Busiest season Nov. to Dec., April

Course Comments: Cart mandatory. Yardage book available. Caddies available. Complete practice facilities at Bay, Plantation. Village has putting green. Complete locker-room facilities at Plantation only. Ritz-Carlton Hotel also on site

Golf Packages: Available through resort mid-April to mid-Dec.

Discounts: Resort guests. Twilight rate. Hawaii residents

Places to Stay Nearby: Ritz-Carlton Kaplua (808) 669–6200, (800) 241–3333 (On site); Napali Kai Beach Club (808) 669–6271, (800) 367–5030; Coconut Inn (808) 669–5712, (800) 367–8006; Embassy Suites (808) 661–2000, (800) 462–6284; Maui Marriott (808) 667–1200, (800) 228–9290; Pioneer Inn (808) 661–3636. BED AND BREAKFASTS: Bed and Breakfast Hawaii (808) 822–7771, (800) 733–1632; Bed and Breakfast Maui-Style (808) 879–7865, (800) 848–5567

Local Attractions: WEST MAUI: Lahaina Town, Kahakuloa, Baldwin Home, Brig Carthaginian. CENTRAL MAUI: Iao Valley, Hale Hoikeike. HALEAKALA AND UP-COUNTRY: Tedeschi Vineyards and Winery. HALEAKALA HANA AREA: Hana, Helani Gardens, Hookipa Beach, Paia, hunting, fishing, beaches, shopping, camping, hiking, water sports, land tours, air tours, Lahaina-Kaanapali and Pacific Railroad, Maui Tropical Plantation, whale watching. Maui Visitors Bureau (808) 871–8691. Maui Chamber of Commerce (808) 871–7711

Directions: From Lahaina: Hwy. 30 to Office Rd., turn left onto Office Rd. at Kapalua exit. Follow signs to resort

Closest Commercial Airports: Kapalua-West Maui (10 min.), Kahului (1 hr.), Hana (4½ hrs.)

RESORT

Date Built: 1978

No. of Rooms: 194 guest rooms, including 1- and 2-bedroom suites, parlor suites, 125 1- and 2-bedroom villas

Meeting Rooms: 4. Capacity of Largest: 250 persons banquet style. Meeting Space: 70,000 sq. ft.

Room Price Range: $215 for a garden-view guest room to $1250 for a 2-bedroom suite. Golf, tennis, ocean adventure and other packages available year round

Lounge: Bay Lounge

Restaurants: Garden, Bay Club, Pool Terrace, Plantation House, Market Cafe. Additional restaurants at nearby Ritz-Carlton

Entertainment: Piano soloist in Bay Club, piano soloist in Bay Lounge

Credit Cards: All major cards

General Amenities: Kapalua shops, supervised children's programs, lectures, rooms for guests with disabilities, babysitting, garden tours, full-service beauty salon, meeting and conference facilities with audiovisual and food services

Recreational Amenities: Tennis Garden with 10 lighted Plexi-pave courts, tennis camps with instruction; scuba diving, windsurfing, boating, snorkeling, surfing, 3 beaches, 2 hotel swimming pools; exercise facility with stair climber, treadmill, multicisor, ergometers; aerobics, aquacise classes; 9 swimming pools in villa complexes, fishing, jogging trails, horseback riding. Additional facilities at the on site Ritz-Carlton

Reservation and Cancellation Policy: 3 night's deposit due 14 days from time of booking. Full refund if cancellation received at least 14 days prior to arrival. For Christmas holiday (Dec. 20 to Jan. 1) cancellations must be received by Nov. 1

Comments and Restrictions: Taxes and gratuities additional to base rates. No additional charge for children 14 years or younger sharing room with parent. 4 persons maximum to a 1 bedroom, 6 persons maximum to a 2 bedroom

KAPALUA GOLF CLUB

The ancient Hawaiian name Kapalua means –arms embracing the sea, referring to the lava-flow peninsulas characterizing Kapalua's dramatic coastline. The Kapalua Bay Hotel and Villas is situated on 1500 acres of land surrounded by a 23,000-acre pineapple plantation overlooking the white sand beaches of Kapalua Bay. This resort is ranked among the best golf resorts in America by *Golf* magazine.

There are three excellent golf courses at Kapalua Bay, and each has its own practice facilities and staff. Arnold Palmer designed both the Bay Course and the Village Course, and each have been ranked among America's 75 best resort courses by *Golf Digest* magazine. The 6600-yard par-72 Bay Course borders the beautiful Oneloa Bay on the Pacific. Palm trees, ironwoods, stately cook pines and other varieties line the rolling fairways. The medium-sized greens are moderately fast and undulating, and are well protected by sand traps. The greens are tricky and always break toward

the ocean. The front nine wends its way up and down hills and through stands of mature trees. The back nine plays on somewhat higher ground with no holes directly on the ocean.

The beautiful and challenging par-3 fifth hole on the Bay Course plays 205 yards over the ocean to a large green guarded by traps right, rear and to the left. The wind is generally behind the golfer, but many balls seem to find the water or land in the sand surrounding the green.

The most difficult holes on the course are both fairly short par 4s. The 372-yard second hole plays straight to a wide, extremely shallow green with two traps to the rear and a large trap to the left and front. The fairway has a low valley to the right on the tee shot, and there is a shelf on the left. The approach shot is exceedingly difficult, especially if the pin is tucked between the two bunkers on the left. The 371-yard sixteenth plays over a stream in front of the tee to a fairway split vertically by another stream and guarded on the right by two fairway bunkers. The second shot is onto a deep, narrow-throated green squeezed by two large bunkers on the left and right.

The 6632-yard par-71 Village Course was opened in 1980, 5 years after the Bay Course. There are many elevation changes and beautiful ocean vistas from this layout, which winds its way through cook pines, pineapple fields, coconut trees and other high native vegetation such as breadfruit, lychee and mango trees, and ginger and tileaf plants. There is every possibility that you will not get a flat lie in many situations on this layout, and there are a variety of sand bunkers and water hazards to further confound you. The number-1-handicap hole is the 514-yard dogleg-right par-5 fifth, which plays uphill to a large green surrounded by three large sand bunkers. The first shot is to a relatively open fairway, but the second shot can catch a series of bunkers beginning approximately 125 yards from the green. And of course the hole plays longer because of its upward climb. It is in this area of the course that there is a beautiful man-made lake with fish, ducks and geese to add another delightful surprise and element of magic to the Kapalua golf experience.

The 465-yard par-4 eighteenth is a beautiful finishing hole. It plays down a corridor of trees to a narrow, very deep green with a large pond on the right. The approach shot is difficult on this hole because of the narrowness of the green, the trees on the left and the water on the immediate right.

The newest golf course at Kapalua Bay is the formidable 7263-yard Plantation Course, designed by Bill Coore and Ben Crenshaw. Opened in 1991, the Plantation Course was named runner-up as the best new resort course by *Golf Digest*. This is the site of the Kapalua International, a combined professional and amateur event benefiting more than 20 Maui charities. This 240-acre layout was formerly part of the pineapple plantation and has fewer trees and wider landing areas than the other courses. The course plays 6547 yards from the middle tees and 5627 yards from the front. Many locals say that this course doesn't play as long as it seems, but that is up to you to decide.

The greens on the Plantation Course tend to be large, moderately fast, undulating and well protected by large traps. Some holes have as many as thirteen sand bunkers, but there are no water hazards on the course. There are some dramatic elevation changes and magnificent ocean and mountain vistas as you work your way around the Plantation. Ravines also add to the challenge and beauty of the golf course. The 203-yard par-3 eighth, for example, plays over a huge ravine to a deep left-to-right-angled, sloping green surrounded by six sand traps. You'll be very happy with a par on this one.

The next hole, the 521-yard par-5 ninth, is the number-1-handicap hole on the course. The tee shot is to a landing area bordered by a huge valleylike ravine on the right. The question is whether to go over the valley to the elevated green on the second shot or to lay up to a narrow area bordered by three traps on the left and five traps on the right. There is a huge drop-off into a gorge on the right should you miss the green.

The dramatic 663-yard par-5 finishing hole is downhill all the way, and a tail wind actually enables some golfers to reach it in two! The approach to the huge, deep green is bordered by sand bunkers on the left from 100 yards in. This hole is considered to be the signature hole at the Plantation.

The golf shop at the Bay Club at Kapalua is regularly rated one of America's 100 best by *Golf Shop Operations* magazine. The Plantation Course has a new 33,000-square-foot clubhouse with luxurious locker rooms, a 200-seat dining room, a casual grill and fully stocked pro shop. Instruction is available from the staff of professionals and assistants at the Bay and Plantation golf courses. Golf packages, 1-day golf schools, playing lessons, private lessons and lessons with video analysis are among the rich array of golf options available here.

The Kapalua Bay Hotel and Villas has 191 guest rooms and 3 suites located in 7 separate structures ranging from three to six stories in height. There are also 125 luxuriously appointed 1- and 2-bedroom villas. Three excellent ocean-view restaurants serve a variety of delicacies ranging from fresh island fish to international cuisine. The Kapalua Bay Hotel and Villas' dining facilities offer a selection of over 400 California and European wines.

In addition to 54 holes of world-class golf, Kapalua has a full range of recreational activities including swimming pools; exercise and fitness-training facilities; aerobics; aquacise; ocean activities including deep sea fishing, scuba diving, surfing and boating; and other diversions. The Tennis Garden has 10 plexipave courts, 4 lighted for night play, a pro shop and instruction from U.S. Professional Tennis Association certified tennis professionals. A variety of tennis programs, camps and special events such as the Kapalua Junior/Veteran Senior Championships are offered. *Tennis* magazine ranks Kapalua one of the 50 greatest U.S. tennis resorts. Kapalua's touring professional is Betsy Nagelsen. A variety of tennis packages are available through the resort. Additional recreation, meeting and restaurant facilities are available at the 550-room on site Ritz-Carlton, opened in 1992.

Kapalua is an excellent meeting and conference site. It features a variety of conference rooms, and banquet, theater and outdoor meeting areas ranging from a 3000-square-foot ballroom to the Cliff House, a rustic meeting place perched above Namala Bay. Among its awards for quality meeting and conference facilities, Kapalua Bay has received the Golden Tee Award as an excellent golf and conference center from *Meetings and Conventions* magazine.

**Course Name: MAKENA RESORT
                         North, South Courses**

Course Type: Resort
Resort: Maui Prince Hotel
Address: 5400 Makena Alanui
                       Kihei, HI 96753–9986
Phone: (808) 879–3344 (Golf Course),
                       (808) 874–1111,
                       (800) 321–MAUI (Resort)
Fax: (808) 879–8530 (Golf Course),
                       (808) 879–8763 (Resort)

GOLF COURSE

Director of Golf: Howard Kihune, Jr.
Course Length/Par (All Tees): North: Back 6914/72, Blue 6567/72, Orange 6151/72, Forward 5303/72. South: Back 7017/72, Blue 6629/72, Orange 6168/72, Forward 5529/72
Course Slope/Rating (All Tees): North: Back 139/72.1, Blue 136/70.4, Orange 132/68.4, Ladies' Forward 128/70.9. South: Back 138/72.6, Blue 134/70.7, Orange 129/68.5, Ladies' Forward 130/70.1
Architect: Robert Trent Jones, Jr. (1993)
Golf Facilities: Full Pro Shop X, Snack Bar X, Lounge X, Restaurant X, Locker Room X, Showers X, Club Rental X, Club Repair X, Cart Rental X, Instruction X, Practice Green X, Driving Range X, Practice Bunker No, Club Storage X
Tee-Time Reservation Policy: At time of confirmed reservations. Up to 3 days in advance with credit card guarantee

Ranger: Yes
Tee-off-Interval Time: 10 min.
Time to Play 18 Holes: 4½ hrs.
Course Hours/Earliest Tee-off: 6:30 a.m.
Green and Cart Fees: $110 for 18 holes for outside play, $80 for 18 holes for resort guests
Credit Cards: All major cards
Season: Year round. Busiest Nov. through May
Course Comments: Carts mandatory. Yardage book available
Golf Packages: Through resort
Discounts: Twilight, resort guests
Places to Stay Nearby: WEST MAUI: Kapalua Bay Hotel and Villas (808) 669–5656, (800) 367–8000; Maui Marriott (808) 667–1200, (800) 228–9290; Napili Kai Beach Club (808) 661–3611, (800) 733–7777; Plantation Inn (808) 667–9225, (800) 433–6815; Pioneer Inn (808) 661–3636
Local Attractions: Alexander and Baldwin Sugar Museum, Baldwin Home, Brig Carthaginian, Hale Hoikeike, Halea Kala, Lahaina, Paia, Tedeschi Vineyards and Winery, whale watching, shopping, art galleries, restaurants, beaches, bicycling, camping, hiking, fishing, boating, scuba diving, snorkeling
Directions: From Kahuli Airport (1 hr.): Take Hwy. 380 south to Hwy. 350 to resort 1½ mi. past Paia on the Hana Hwy.
Closest Commercial Airport: Kahuli (1 hr.)

RESORT

Date Built: 1986
No. of Rooms: 310 rooms including 20 suites
Meeting Rooms: 15. Capacity of Largest: 750 persons. Meeting Space: 81,000 sq. ft. of indoor and outdoor
Room Price Range: $220 for standard room to $820 for oceanfront 1-bedroom
Lounges: Molokini Lounge
Restaurants: Cafe Kiowai, Hakone, Makena Clubhouse, Prince Court
Entertainment: Live music, dance
Credit Cards: All major cards
General Amenities: Executive center for business travellers, meeting and

conference audiovisual, banquet, secretarial and other services; library, Prince Kids Club program, retail shops

Recreational Amenities: 6 tennis courts with pro shop, aerobics, lei making, exercise room, massage therapy, ocean sports including snorkeling, scuba, and others; boating, fishing, whale watching cruises; ping pong, volleyball, croquet, shuffle board, badminton, horseback riding, wine tasting, and more

Reservation and Cancellation Policy: Deposit and cancellation requirements vary by season

Comments and Restrictions: No pets

MAKENA RESORT

Maui has approximately 80,000 residents, comprises 729 square miles, and entertains over two million tourists a year. The depression between its two volcanoes, West Maui's 5788-foot Puu Kukui and 10,023-foot Haleakala, led to the name "Valley Isle" to characterize Maui. Toward the southern tip of the island along the ocean road south of Kihei is the AAA Five Diamond 1800-acre Makena Resort featuring two Robert Trent Jones, Jr.–designed golf courses and the 310-room Maui Prince Hotel.

The Makena Resort courses are expanded versions of Robert Trent Jones, Jr.'s 18-hole layout completed in 1981. The North Course has mountain views of the Holeakala crater and provides dramatic elevation changes and vistas of the island and the Pacific. Holes from the old course have been successfully blended into the North as holes No. 1 through No. 5 and No. 15 through No. 18. The 620-yard par-5 fourteenth, the longest hole on the course, begins from a tee set at 800 feet and drops downhill toward the ocean. The 433-yard par-4 finishing hole, a dogleg left, plays to a tee shot landing area guarded by bunkers on both sides. The approach must carry a cluster of bunkers guarding the front of the green. There are several well-placed bunkers at Makena, and the Bermuda greens tend to be fast and true. The North Course's native rock walls, natural gullies and stream beds, indigenous Kiawe trees,

and scenic elevation changes add to the beauty and difficulty of the golf course.

The South Course has natural, rolling fairways, mountain and ocean views, and two signature holes that run near the ocean. The 188-yard par-3 fifteenth plays straight toward the Pacific. If you hit long or left, your ball will be in the ocean. The 390-yard par-4 sixteenth plays to a landing area bordered by the ocean to the left. The second shot is to a green framed by traps with breathtaking views of the ocean beyond.

Both of these golf courses are tough driving courses, especially from the back tees. Errant tee shots will find a bunker, rough, or native vegetation. Wind is usually not a significant factor at Makena although it can kick up in the afternoon. The Makena Resort has won *Meetings and Conventions* magazine's Golden Tee Award as a highly desirable golf meeting place. And it is rated among the best golf courses in Hawaii by *Golf Digest*. The Maui Prince offers full resort and meeting amenities ranging from supervised children's programs to award-winning Hawaiian regional cuisine with delicacies including Kona lobster cake and Hawaiian snapper. Within easy reach of Makena are the resort areas of Wailea, Kaanapali, and Kapalua.

Course Name: WAILEA GOLF CLUB
　　　　　　　Blue, Emerald, Gold Courses

Course Type: Resort
Address: 　　120 Kaukuhi Street
　　　　　　　(Blue Course)
　　　　　　　100 Golf Club Drive
　　　　　　　(Emerald, Gold Courses)
　　　　　　　Maui, HI 96753
Phone: 　　　(808) 875–5155 (Blue Course)
　　　　　　　(808) 875–5111 (Emerald,
　　　　　　　Gold Courses)
Fax: 　　　　(808) 874–3038 (Golf Courses)

GOLF COURSE

Senior Head Professional: Rick Castillo
Head Professional: Rusty Hathaway (Blue Course)
Course Length/Par (All Tees): Blue: Back 6758/72, Middle 6152/72, Forward 5291/72. Emerald: Back 6825/72, Blue 6395/72, White 5871/72, Forward

5401/72. Gold: Back 7070/72, Blue 6653/72, White 6152/72, Forward 5442/72

Course Slope/Rating (All Tees): Blue: Back 130/71.6, Middle 125/68.9, Ladies' Forward 117/72.0. Emerald: Back 134/72.0, Blue 132/70.0, White 127/60.2, Ladies' Forward 119/69.5. Gold: Back 139/73.0, Blue 136/71.4, White 131/69.0, Ladies' Forward 124/71.0

Course Architect: Blue: Arthur Jack Snyder (1972). Emerald: Robert Trent Jones, Jr. (1994). Gold: Robert Trent Jones, Jr. (1994)

Golf Facilities: Full Pro Shop X, Snack Bar X, Lounge X, Restaurant X, Locker Room X, Showers X, Club Rental X, Club Repair X, Cart Rental X, Instruction X, Practice Green X, Driving Range X, Practice Bunker X, Club Storage X

Tee-Time Reservation Policy: Blue, Emerald: Resort guests: Up to 5 days in advance. Public: 3 days in advance. Gold: Resort Guests: Up to 30 days in advance. Public: 7 days in advance

Ranger: Yes

Tee-off-Interval Time: 8 min.

Time to Play 18 Holes: 4½ hrs.

Course Hours/Earliest Tee-off: 6:36 a.m.

Green and Cart Fees: Resort guests: Blue, Emerald: $85 for 18 holes with cart, Gold: $90 for 18 holes with cart. Public: Blue, Emerald: $125 for 18 holes with cart, Gold: $135 for 18 holes with cart

Credit Cards: All major cards

Season: Year round. Busiest season Dec. to May

Course Comments: Cart mandatory

Golf Packages: Available through resort

Discounts: Resort guests. Hawaii residents

Places to Stay Nearby: Maui Intercontinental Wailea Resorts and Condominiums (808) 879–1922, (800) 367–2960; Stouffer Renaissance Wailea (808) 879–4900, (800) 992–4532; Four Seasons Resort Wailea (808) 874–8000, (800) 334–6284; Destination Resorts' Villas at Wailea (808) 879–1595, (800) 367–5246; Grand Wailea Resort and Spa (808) 875–1234, (800) 888–6100; Kea

Lani Hotel (808) 875–4100, (800) 882–4100. CENTRAL INFORMATION: Wailea Destination Association (800) 78–ALOHA. BED AND BREAKFASTS: Bed and Breakfast Hawaii (808) 822–7771, (800) 733–1632; Bed and Breakfast Maui-Style (808) 879–7865, (800) 848–5567; Bed and Breakfast Honolulu (808) 595–7533, (800) 288–4666

Local Attractions: Kihei, Mt. Haleakala, Haleakala National Park, Kula Botanical Gardens, Tedeschi Vineyards and Winery. WEST MAUI: Baldwin Home, Brig Carthaginian, Io Valley Tour. CENTRAL MAUI: Alexander and Baldwin Sugar Museum, Hale Hoikeike, Iao Valley. NORTHEAST SHORE/HANA: Hana, Helani Gardens, Hookipa Beach, Paia, whale watching, restaurants, beaches, camping, arts and crafts. Maui Visitors Bureau (808) 871–8691. Maui Chamber of Commerce (808) 871–7711

Directions: From Kahului Airport (17 mi.): Hwy. 350 to Hwy. 31, south (left) to Wailea exit, follow signs to resort hotels, golf courses

Closest Commercial Airport: Kahului (5 min.)

WAILEA GOLF CLUB

The Blue course at the Wailea Golf Club, designed by Arthur Jack Snyder is ranked among the best resort golf courses in America by *Golf Digest* magazine. The 6758-yard Blue Course was opened in 1972, before there were any hotels or condominiums here. Now there is a 1500-acre residential resort with 6 hotels, 6 condominium developments and 4 residential entities. The master plan is for 3500 hotel rooms, 3000 condominium units, 800 to 1000 single-family homesites. This community lies on the southwest coast of Maui and at the foot of Mt. Haleakala, a 10,023-foot dormant volcano. This mountain shelters the golf courses from wind and rain, but you still have magnificent views of the Pacific Ocean and the surrounding mountains.

The Orange Course, also designed by Arthur Jack Snyder and opened in 1978, was leveled to make room for the new Emerald and Gold courses designed by

Robert Trent Jones, Jr. and opened to wide acclaim in 1994. The Blue Course, site of the LPGA Women's Kemper Open, is on rolling terrain with more than 70 sand bunkers, most of them clustered around medium-sized, heavily undulating Bermudagrass greens. There are four man-made lakes on the course, two of them on the 206-yard par-3 second hole. Both of these lakes have to be carried to reach the two-tiered putting surface well guarded by two bunkers on the right.

The most difficult hole on the Blue Course is the 562-yard par-5 fourth, which starts out with an uphill tee shot. The second shot is from a level plateau that then runs downhill toward a very tightly trapped green with two large sand bunkers on the right and another on the left.

As you work your way through the foothills of Mt. Haleakala, the breathtaking beauty of the ocean and natural lava formations, hibiscus, plumeria, bougainvillea and hundreds of other flowering plants and trees awaits you. The run of three finishing holes, beginning with the difficult 542-yard par-5 sixteenth, begins from the highest point on the course, where you can see the Wailea community; the neighboring islands of Lanai, Kahoolawe, Molokai; and the islet of Molokini.

The first two shots on sixteen should be down the left side of the fairway to put you in position to come onto a green protected by a huge bunker on the left and three traps on the right. Intermittent trees and the sand make this a very tight green to approach. The 420-yard par-4 seventeenth plays straight to a deep green protected by large sand traps back, left and to the front right. The tee shot is through a narrow chute of trees and must avoid a fairway bunker on the right. The 178-yard finishing hole is a beautiful par 3 that plays over a pond to a deep green with four huge traps seemingly everywhere. The combination of tight fairways, well-trapped greens and tricky tiered, undulating putting surfaces makes this a beautiful and challenging test of golf.

The designer of this course, Arthur Jack Snyder, was born in Rosedale, Pennsylvania, in 1917. He graduated with a degree in land-scape architecture from Pennsylvania State University and entered private practice as a golf architect in 1958, after owning land-scape-architectural firms and working as a golf-course superintendent at the Oakmont Country Club in Pennsylvania and at White Mountain Country Club in Pinetop, Arizona. He has designed and remodeled numerous golf courses in Arizona, the western states and Hawaii, including Arroyo de Oso Golf Course, Albuquerque, New Mexico; the Royal Kaanapali Golf Course (redesigned the South Course) and Camelback (Indian Bend) Golf Course, Scottsdale, Arizona.

Awaiting you at the clubhouse is the Fairway Restaurant, bar, and a well-stocked pro shop. The practice area includes a driving range, practice bunker and two putting greens. Individual and group instruction is available from the staff of professionals and assistants. Golf packages for all three of these courses are available through the Maui Intercontinental Resort and the other on-site properties. Reduced green fees are available to those staying at these accommodations even if not on a golf package.

Oahu

Course Name: KOOLAU GOLF COURSE

Course Type: Public
Address: 45–550 Kionaole Road
Kaneohe, Oahu, HI 96744
Phone: (808) 236–4653
Fax: (808) 235–7737

GOLF COURSE

Head Professional: Parris Ernst
Course Length/Par (All Tees): Back 7310/72, Blue 6857/72, White 6455/72, Silver 6191/72, Forward 5119/72
Course Slope/Rating (All Tees): Back 162/76.4, Blue 158/74.4, White 154/72.5, Silver 132/71.0, Ladies' Forward 134/72.9
Course Architects: Dick Nugent and Jack Tuthill (1992)
Golf Facilities: Full Pro Shop X, Snack Bar X, Lounge X, Restaurant No, Locker Room No, Showers No, Club Rental X, Club Repair X, Cart Rental

X, Instruction X, Practice Green X, Driving Range X, Practice Bunker X, Club Storage No

Tee-Time Reservation Policy: Up to 2 months in advance

Ranger: Yes

Tee-off-Interval Time: 8 min.

Time to Play 18 Holes: 4½ hrs.

Course Hours/Earliest Tee-off: 7:00 a.m.

Green and Cart Fees: $100 for 18 holes Sat., Sun., holidays; $90 for 18 holes weekdays

Credit Cards: American Express, Master-Card, Visa

Season: Year round. Busiest March and April

Course Comments: Can walk but must pay full fee. Difficult to walk

Golf Packages: Inquire at pro shop

Discounts: Twilight after 1:30 p.m. Residents

Places to Stay Nearby: HONOLULU: Ala Moana Hotel (808) 955–4811, (800) 367–6025; Aston Waikiki Beach Tower (808) 926–6400, (800) 92–ASTON; Hawaiian Regent (808) 922–6611, (800) 367–5700; Hawaiian Waikiki Beach Hotel (808) 922–2511, (800) 877–7666; Ilikai Hotel Nikko Waikiki (808) 949–3811, (800) 367–8434; New Otani Kaimana Beach (808) 923–1555, (800) 356–8264; Sheraton Waikiki (808) 922–4422, (800) 325–3535

Local Attractions: See page 268

Directions: From Honolulu (20 min.): Take Hwy. 61 (Pali Hwy.) north then go left (west) on Rte. 83. Drive past Pali Golf Club and under H-3 overpass then take first left and follow signs to golf course

Closest Commercial Airport: Honolulu International (20 min.)

KOOLAU GOLF COURSE

"Bring as many balls as your handicap is." Thus spoke assistant golf professional Rock Young when trying to explain the difficulty of Koolau, rated the most difficult golf course anywhere. Even from the 6455 yard "regular tees," this course has a slope of 154, approximately that of Pine Valley, and a rating of 72.5.

Koolau, designed by Dick Nugent and Jack Tuthill, was deliberately conceived as a difficult private course where club members would pay a $250,000 initiation fee to be beaten up on the links. Situated on the north side of Oahu twenty minutes northwest of Honolulu, Koolau is bordered by the Koolau Mountain Range, gets heavy rainfall and has deep ravines crossing most holes on the golf course. Seven holes have forced carries and teeming, deep tropical vegetation that swallows up strayed golf balls in short order. Koolau is target golf at its extreme. If you hit one of the 80 bunkers, it will probably be with a sigh of relief.

The signature hole on the golf course is the spectacular 476-yard par-4 finishing hole, billed "the most difficult par 4 in the world." The tee shot is over a tropical forest ravine and requires a minimum carry of 170 yards. A 260-yard drive is needed from the back tees in order to have an iron shot at the large green which is well guarded by bunkers to its left, right and rear. The greens at Koolau are undulating and quick, adding to the difficulty of the course.

Serving the golf course is a 260,000-square-foot marble-floored unfinished clubhouse, a vestige of big golf dreams gone bad. The Japanese owners of this development have financial problems and ownership will soon transfer. Koolau is now open to any golfer who can afford enough golf balls to complete a round.

Course Name: KO OLINA GOLF CLUB

Course Type: Resort
Address: 92–1220 Aliinui Drive
Ewa Beach, HI 96707
Phone: (808) 676–5300 (Reservations/Starter), (800) 626–4447
Fax: (808) 676–5100 (Golf Course)

GOLF COURSE

Director of Golf: Craig Williamson

Head Professional: Brad Weaver

Touring Professional: Robert Gamez

Course Length/Par (All Tees): Back 6867/72, Middle 6324/72, Forward 5358/72

Course Slope/Rating (All Tees): Back 137/72.8, Middle 133/71.0, Ladies' Forward 125/71.3

Course Architect: Ted Robinson (1990)

Golf Facilities: Full Pro Shop X, Snack Bar X, Lounge X, Restaurant X, Locker Room X, Showers X, Club Rental X, Club Repair X, Cart Rental X, Instruction X, Practice Green X, Driving Range X, Practice Bunker X, Club Storage X

Tee-Time Reservation Policy: Up to 1 wk. Large groups well in advance

Ranger: Yes

Tee-off-Interval Time: 8 min.

Time to Play 18 Holes: 4½ hrs.

Course Hours/Earliest Tee-off: 7 a.m.

Green and Cart Fees: Nonresidents: $45 for 18 holes with cart

Credit Cards: All major cards

Season: Year round

Course Comments: Cart mandatory. Yardage book available

Golf Packages: Available through resort

Discounts: Residents. Twilight rates after 2:30 p.m. ($65 with cart); after 4 p.m. ($35 with cart)

Places to Stay Nearby: HONOLULU: Kahala Hilton (808) 734–2211, (800) 367–2525. WAIKIKI: Royal Hawaiian Hotel (808) 923–7311, (800) 325–3535; Hyatt Regency Waikiki (808) 923–1234, (800) 233–1234; Colony Surf Hotel (808) 923–5751, (800) 252–7873; Waikikian on the Beach (808) 949–5331, (800) 922–7866 (USA), (800) 445–6633 (Canada). BED AND BREAKFAST: Pacific Hawaii Bed and Breakfast (808) 262–6026, (800) 254–5030; Bed and Breakfast Honolulu (808) 595–7533, (800) 288–4666; Bed and Breakfast Hawaii (808) 822–7771, (800) 733–1632

Local Attractions: Arizona Memorial, Bishop Museum, Diamond Head Center, Honolulu Zoo, Iolani Palace, Pali Lookout, Polynesian Cultural Center, Sea Life Park, Waikiki Aquarium, Waimea Falls Park, beaches, plantations, botanical gardens, Hawaii Children's Museum, shopping, restaurants, night clubs, horseback riding, University of Hawaii. Waikiki. Honolulu. Eastern Oahu. Hawaii Visitors Bureau (808) 923–1811

Directions: From Honolulu: Hwy. 1 west to the Ko Olina exit, follow signs to resort

Closest Commercial Airport: Honolulu International (20 min.)

KO OLINA GOLF CLUB

The Ko Olina Golf Club, situated 200 yards from the Pacific Ocean in Oahu, was designed by Ted Robinson and opened in 1990. This 6867-yard par-72 layout has rolling fairways; medium-sized, moderately fast, undulating greens; and a variety of sand bunkers protecting the fairway landing areas and putting surfaces. Water hazards appear on half the holes, and the trade winds and kona winds can greatly affect the way the golf course plays. Although the landing areas are generous at Ko Olina, the Bermuda grass rough is long and difficult, so you want to keep away from it if you expect to have a chance of reaching the green in regulation. Many of the greens are tiered, making the calculation of distance and shot positioning of tee shots essential. Pin position can play a major role in determining the difficulty of these tricky greens.

Ko Olina starts out with a par 5 that seems reasonably short at 518 yards, except that you are hitting into the east-to-west trade winds, making this a true three-shot par 5. The tee shot is to a landing area protected by a large sand bunker on the right. The second shot should be kept toward the left because of the large sand bunker on the right 100 yards from a deep, right-to-left-angled green protected front and right by a large sand trap. Another large bunker guards the rear.

The second hole, a 412-yard par 4, is considered to be the most difficult hole on the course because it plays into the wind. The tee-shot landing area is severely squeezed by traps on the left and water on the right. The second shot is to a deep, left-to-right-angled green protected by two pot bunkers on the left and one to the right and rear. The combination of an incoming wind and an elevated green make accurate club selection essential on this hole.

The 444-yard par-4 seventh hole has a tricky tee shot from an elevated tee over a deep swale that can be a nightmare if the ball doesn't carry over 200 yards to the fairway. The second shot is to a medium-sized green protected by a small bunker on the right and another to the rear.

A beautiful and tricky par 3 is the eighth. Depending on wind conditions, you might use anything from a wood or a 1-iron to a 7-iron on this 195-yard golf challenge. A large pond and waterfalls are on the left and toward the front of a two-tiered green backed by trees and mounded banks. To the right is a large bunker that is easy to find on the tee shot.

The eighteenth hole (which is also the signature hole) at Ko Olina provides a memorable way to complete an excellent golf experience. The tee shot on this 428-yard par 4 should be kept as far to the left (but in the fairway) as possible. The wind will be behind you, so distance should not be a concern. The second shot is over a large pond that runs all the way to a two-tiered green backed by a large bunker and protected by waterfalls on the left. Club selection and accuracy are obviously of the essence on this approach shot because there is little bail-out room.

The 35,000-square-foot modern clubhouse at Ko Olina is characterized by its trilevel design and Hawaiian pitched roofs. There are locker rooms and showers, a complete pro shop and 2 restaurants in the clubhouse, which has spectacular views of the golf course and surrounding area. On site are 2 practice greens, a practice bunker and driving range. Instruction is available from the staff of PGA professionals.

The entire real-estate development, including the 170-acre Ko Olina Golf Club, is 642 acres and features the Hotel Ihilani Resort and Spa. The Ihilani (which means "heavenly splendor" in Hawaiian) has 390 guest rooms, 4 restaurants, swimming pools, tennis club, health spa and many other amenities. Many golf packages and other programs are available through the Ihilani.

Ko Olina means "fulfillment of joy," and as far as the golf course is concerned, this is likely to be true, especially if you are playing well. The course was given honorable mention as the best new resort course in 1990 by *Golf Digest*. The Ko Olina Senior Invitational, a 54-hole Senior PGA Tour event with a purse of $500,000 was held here in 1992. The beauty of the course, located just 30 minutes from downtown Honolulu, is accentuated by thousands of coconut palms, banyans, monkeypots, silver buttonwoods, flowering bougainvillea, firecracker plants and fragrant plumeria. Ponds and lakes that flow through rock gardens and waterfalls that cascade down hillsides add a soothing element to this first-rate layout. You should add Ko Olina to your list of Hawaiian golf courses to play.

Course Name: SHERATON MAKAHA GOLF CLUB

Course Type: Semiprivate
Address: 84–626 Makaha Valley Road, Box 896 Makaha, HI 96792
Phone: (808) 695–9544 (Golf Course)
(808) 695–9511,
(800) 334–8484
Fax: (808) 695–8496

GOLF COURSE

Director of Golf: Calvin Nelson

Course Length/Par (All Tees): Back 7091/72, Middle 6398/72, Forward 6002/72

Course Slope/Rating (All Tees): Back 139/74.3, Middle 138/71.7, Ladies' Forward 125/73.3

Course Architect: William P. Bell (1969)

Golf Facilities: Full Pro Shop X, Snack Bar X, Lounge X, Restaurant X, Locker Room No, Showers No, Club Rental X, Club Repair X, Cart Rental X, Instruction X, Practice Green X, Driving Range X, Practice Bunker X, Club Storage X

Tee-Time Reservation Policy: Sheraton Waikiki guests: At time of reservation. Public: Up to 2 wks. in advance

Ranger: Yes

Tee-off-Interval Time: 8 min.

Time to Play 18 Holes: 4 hrs., 15 min.

Course Hours/Earliest Tee-off: 6:30 a.m.

Green and Cart Fees: Sheraton Waikiki guests: $70 for 18 holes with shared cart, $35 for 9 holes with shared cart.

Public: $135 for 18 holes with shared cart, $67.50 for 9 holes with shared cart

Credit Cards: All major cards

Season: Year round. Busiest season Dec. to March

Course Comments: Cart mandatory. Yardage book available

Golf Packages: Inquire at pro shop

Discounts: Hawaii residents April 1 to late Dec.

Places to Stay Nearby: HONOLULU: Kahala Hilton (808) 734–2211, (800) 367–2525; WAIKIKI: Alana Royal Hawaiian Hotel (808) 923–7311, (800) 325–3535; Hyatt Regency Waikiki (808) 923–1234, (800) 233–1234; Colony Surf Hotel (808) 923–5751, (800) 252–7873; Waikikian on the Beach (808) 949–5331, (800) 922–7866 (USA), (800) 445–6633 (Canada). BED AND BREAKFAST: Pacific Hawaii Bed and Breakfast (808) 262–6026, (800) 254–5030; Bed and Breakfast Honolulu (808) 595–7533, (800) 288–4666; Bed and Breakfast Hawaii (808) 822–7771, (800) 733–1632

Local Attractions: Ala Moana Shopping Center, Pearl Harbor, Makaha Beach, Yokohama Beach, Kaneaki Heiau, Waianae Shopping Mall, Waimea Falls Park, Polynesian Cultural Center, Aloha Stadium, Sea Life Park, Arizona Memorial, Bishop Museum, Diamond Head Center, Honolulu Zoo, Iolani Palace, Pali Lookout, Waikiki Aquarium, beaches, plantations, botanical gardens, Hawaii Children's Museum, shopping, restaurants, night clubs, horseback riding, University of Hawaii. Waikiki. Honolulu. Eastern Oahu. Hawaii Visitors Bureau (808) 923–1811

Directions: From Honolulu International Airport (26 mi.): Hwy. 1 west (Waianae), Hwy. 1 becomes Farrington Hwy. to Makaha Valley Rd. and resort

Closest Commercial Airport: Honolulu International (45 min.)

SHERATON MAKAHA GOLF CLUB

The Hawaiian island of Oahu is 608 square miles in land area and has 80 percent of Hawaii's 1.1 million population.

It is also a tourist mecca. The number of its hotels and tourist attractions have increased exponentially since World War II. Much of the action is centered in Honolulu and Waikiki, but on the western side of the island, below the Waianae Mountains, which rise to over 4000 feet, is a quiet golf oasis. In the Makaha Valley is the Sheraton Makaha Golf Club, which overlooks the Pacific. At the beginning of the valley is the first tee of the William P. Bell-designed Makaha golf course, a 7091-yard par-72 layout that is rated one of the best in Hawaii.

The Bermuda-grass greens at Makaha are large, fast and heavily undulating. They are in excellent condition and are well guarded by a variety of sand bunkers. There are ten water hazards on this layout, and the wind is a major factor as it sweeps down the valley toward the ocean. The golf course begins at the base of the valley, and you work your way up into the mountain foothills and back to the clubhouse on each nine. From the back tees the course is long and requires excellent shot making, especially on approaches coming into the well-protected, undulating greens. Putts on these tricky putting surfaces tend to break toward the ocean.

The number-1-handicap hole at Makaha is the 460-yard par-4 fifth, one of many long, challenging par 4s on the course. The tee-shot landing area on this dogleg right is bordered on the right side by two large sand bunkers. The approach shot is to a large green with sizeable sand traps to the left and right. The tee shot should be long and slightly left of center to have a good chance of reaching this green in regulation. This hole, along with the next three, usually plays into the prevailing trade winds, which sweep down the valley toward the ocean. If a kona wind is going the opposite way, the holes are generally easier to play. Wind watching is a constant preoccupation when golfing at Makaha.

Two lengthy par 3s at Makaha are excellent tests of golf. The 242-yard sixth has trees and out of bounds on the left until you reach an opening to the left of the deep, two-tiered green. Traps to the left, right and right front guard the putting surface, which is flanked by palm trees on the right. Left-to-right winds often push the tee shot to the right on this hole, but it is difficult to gauge the wind because of the protecting trees. The 220-yard seventeenth plays to a medium-sized green guarded by bunkers both left and right. The wind can either be with you or against you on this hole. The green is difficult to hold, and tee shots tend to run with the grain toward the back of the green.

The 422-yard par-4 eighteenth is a scenic finishing hole as you come back toward the clubhouse and the ocean. The tee shot should be kept right-of-center on this dogleg left, which has fairway bunkers on the left side of the landing area. The approach is to a tightly guarded green with several sand traps and water to the left and right as you come into the target. The wind is generally behind the golfer on this hole, whose green is difficult to hold because the ball tends to run away from the green.

There is a full pro shop, restaurant, bar and snack bar at the Makaha but no locker rooms or showers because most people who play here are resort guests, or they return to their hotels or homes nearby. A driving range, practice bunkers and practice putting greens are provided, and instruction is available. The course is very rarely closed because of rain, but it gets enough to keep it and its beautiful foliage in excellent condition.

The Makaha Valley has had a variety of owners dating back to thirteenth-century Polynesian explorers. European settlers developed cattle ranches; coffee, sugar and rice plantations; and other enterprises. In 1946, the financier Chinn Ho developed a plan to make the valley a destination resort. The golf course has been ranked among America's 75 best resort courses by *Golf Digest*. The 6369-yard Makaha Valley Country Club, also designed by William P. Bell and opened in 1969, is accessible to resort guests and open to the public. This is an excellent course in and of itself, and it provides good preparation for the more difficult 7091-yard layout.

Recommended Golf Courses in Hawaii

Within 45 Minutes of Honolulu:

Barbers Point Golf Course (active, retired military personnel and guests), Barbers Point, (808) 682–3088, 18/6394/72

Hawaii Country Club, Wahiawa, (808) 621–5654, Semiprivate, 18/5861/72

Mid-Pacific Country Club, Kailua, (808) 261–9765, Semiprivate, 18/6848/72

Olamana Golf Links, Waimanalo, (808) 259–7926, Public, 18/6081/72

Pali Golf Course, Kaneohe, (808) 296–7254 (Starting Time), (808) 261–9784 (Clubhouse), Public, 18/6494/72

Pearl Country Club, Aiea, (808) 487–3802, Public, 18/6750/72

Oahu:

Ewa Beach International Golf Club, Ewa Beach, (808) 689–8317, Semiprivate, 18/6777/72

Makaha Valley Country Club, Waianae, (808) 695–7111, Public, 18/6369/71

Ted Makalema Golf Course, Waipahu, (808) 296–8888, Public, 18/5946/71

Turtle Bay Country Club, Kahuku, (808) 293–8574, Resort, 18/7036/72

Waikele Golf Club, Waipahu, (808) 676–9000, Semiprivate, 18/6663/72

West Loch Golf Course, Ewa Beach, (808) 671–2291, Public, 18/6479/72

Maui:

Pukalani Country Club, Maui, (808) 572–1314, Public, 18/6945/72

Royal Kaanapali Golf Course, Kaanapali Beach at Lahaina, (808) 661–3691, Resort. North: 18/6305/72. South: 18/6250/72

Sandalwood Wailuka, (808) 242–7090, Public, 18/6537/72

Silversword Golf Club, Kihei, (808) 874–0777, Public, 18/6801/71

Waiehu Municipal Golf Course, Waiehu (near Kahului), (808) 243–7400 (Starting

Time), (808) 244–5934 (Pro Shop), Public, 18/6330/72

Kauai:

Kiahuna Golf Club, Koloa, (808) 742–9595, Resort, 18/6353/70

Kukuiolono Golf Course, Kalaheo, (808) 332–9151, Semiprivate, 9/2981/36

Island of Hawaii:

Hilo Municipal Golf Course, Hilo, (808) 959–9601, (808) 959–7711, Public, 18/6325/71

Kona Country Club, Kailua Kona, (808) 322–2595, Resort. Ocean: 18/6589/72. Mauka: 9/3210/36

Makulei Hawaii Country Club, Kailua-Kona, (808) 325–6625, Public, 18/7091/72

Sea Mountain Golf Course, Pahala, (808) 928–6222, Resort, 18/6492/72

Volcano Golf and Country Club, Volcano National Park (near main entrance), (808) 967–7331, Semiprivate, 18/6270/72

Waikoloa Village Golf Club, Waikoloa Village, (808) 883–9621, Semiprivate, 18/6687/72

Waimea Country Club, Kamuela, (808) 885–8777, Semiprivate, 18/6661/72

Molokai:

Kaluakoi Hotel and Golf Club, Maunaloa, (808) 552–2739, Resort, 18/6600/72

Hawaii: Useful Information

Hawaii Visitors Bureau, Waikiki Business Plaza, 2270 Kalakaua Ave., Ste. 801, Honolulu, HI 96815, (808) 923–1811

Regional Tourist Offices:

350 Fifth Ave., Ste. 827, (800) 353–5846, New York, NY 10118, (212) 947–0717, (800) 353–5846

National Park Service, 300 Ala Moana Blvd., Ste. 6305, Box 50165, Honolulu, HI 96850, (808) 541–2693 (park information)

District Office of the Hawaii Department of Land and National Resources, Division of State Parks, 1151 Punchbowl St., Rm. 310, Honolulu, HI 96813, (808) 548–7455 (state parks and historic areas)

Bed and Breakfasts Centralized Booking Services:

Bed and Breakfast Hawaii, Box 449, Kapaa, HI 96746, (800) 733–1632

Bed and Breakfast Pacific Hawaii, 970 N. Kalaheo Ave., A 218, Kailua, HI 96734, (808) 262–6026

Bed and Breakfast Honolulu, 3242 Kaohinani Dr., Honolulu, HI 96817, (800) 288–4666

Boise Area

Course Name: QUAIL HOLLOW
GOLF CLUB

Course Type: Public
Address: 4520 N. 36th Street
Boise, ID 83703
Phone: (208) 344–7807

GOLF COURSE

Head Professional: Todd Bindner
Course Length/Par (All Tees): Back
6394/70, White 5751/70, Forward
4557/70
Course Slope/Rating (All Tees): Back
129/70.7, White 121/66.0, Forward
123/66.8
Course Architects: Robert von Hagge and
Bruce Devlin (1982)
Golf Facilities: Full Pro Shop X, Snack
Bar X, Lounge No, Restaurant No,
Locker Room X, Showers X, Club
Rental X, Club Repair X, Cart Rental
X, Instruction X, Practice Green X,
Driving Range X, Practice Bunker X,
Club Storage No
Tee-Time Reservation Policy: 1 wk. in
advance
Ranger: Weekends
Tee-off-Interval Time: 10 min.
Time to Play 18 Holes: 4½ hrs.
Course Hours/Earliest Tee-off: Dawn to
dark
Green and Cart Fees: $28 for 18 holes
with cart Sat., Sun., holidays. $25 for
18 holes with cart weekdays. $15 for
9 holes with cart
Credit Cards: MasterCard, Visa
Season: Year round. Busiest season March
to Nov.
Course Comments: Memberships available
Golf Packages: None
Discounts: Seniors, juniors
Places to Stay Nearby: Red Lion Downtowner (208) 344–7691, (800) 547–
8010; Best Western Airport Motor Inn
(208) 384–5000, (800) 528–1234; Holiday Inn Airport (208) 344–8365, (800)
HOLIDAY; Danha Hotel (208) 342–
3611; Ramada Inn (208) 344–7971,
(800) 727–5010; Doubletree Club Hotel
at Park Center (208) 345–2002, (800)

222–8733. BED AND BREAKFAST: Idaho
Heritage Inn (208) 342–8066
Local Attractions: Boise Art Museum,
Idaho State Historical Museum, Boise
State University, Boise Zoo, Boise tour
trains, horse racing, Les Bois Park, bo-
tanical gardens, Snake River, Discovery
Center of Idaho, Boise Tour Train, Old
Idaho Penitentiary, state capitol, World
Center for Birds of Prey. Boise Conven-
tion and Visitors Bureau (208) 344–
7777, (800) 635–5240 (outside ID)
Directions: From Route 44 (State St.) turn
north on 36th St., proceed 1.7 mi. to
course
Closest Commercial Airport: Boise
Municipal (15 min.)

QUAIL HOLLOW GOLF CLUB

The Quail Hollow Golf Club, nestled in
the foothills above Boise, "The City of
Trees" was designed by Robert von Hagge
and Bruce Devlin. The course has been
ranked among the best layouts in the state
of Idaho by *Golf Digest* and has hosted the
Rocky Mountain section of the PGA Championship and the Idaho State Ladies' Amateur.

The 6394-yard par-70 layout is hilly,
with some dramatically elevated tees,
bentgrass greens and bluegrass tees and
fairways. The front nine in particular is a
target golf layout. The course is well
bunkered, and water comes into play on
eleven holes.

The number-1-handicap hole at Quail
Hollow is the 400-yard par-4 sixth, which
plays downhill, then uphill to an undulating
green. In the majority of cases, shots have
to be flown onto the green at Quail Hollow,
because most of them are well protected
by traps. Another difficult par 4 at Quail
Hollow is the tenth, a dogleg left that plays
399 yards to an undulating green with a
water hazard in front, left and behind.

A signature hole is the beautiful 207-
yard par-3 second, which plays from plateau to plateau over a gully to an undulating green with four bunkers surrounding
it. The 428-yard par-4 eighteenth is a good
finishing hole. This dogleg right plays from
an elevated tee to a landing area with a
water hazard on the right. The second shot

is to a huge, undulating double green shared with the fifth hole.

Devlin and von Hagge, Quail Hollow's architects, began their partnership in Devlin's native Australia in 1966, when he was asked by the members of the Lakes Golf Club in New South Wales to recommend an architect to redesign their course. Devlin suggested von Hagge, a trainee of Dick Wilson, and after collaborating on the Lakes Golf Club project they designed and remodeled many quality golf courses, including remodeling the Doral Country Club courses in Miami, Florida; and designing the original Chase Oaks Golf Course in Plano, Texas; the Colony West Golf Club, Tamarac, Florida; and the Tournament Players Club in Woodlands, Texas. Quail Hollow was originally called the Shamanah Golf Club and was completed in 1982.

Recommended Golf Courses in Idaho

Within 1 Hour of Boise:

Eagle Hills Golf Course, Eagle, (208) 939–0402, Public, 18/6485/72

Kimberland Meadows Resort, New Meadows, (208) 347–2163, Resort, 18/6966/72

McCall Municipal Golf Course, McCall, (208) 634–7200, Public, 18/6399/71

Purple Sage Golf Course, Caldwell, (208) 459–2223, Public, 18/6564/71

Shadow Valley Golf Club, Boise, (208) 939–6699, Public, 18/6433/72

Lewiston Area

Course Name: COEUR D'ALENE

Course Type: Resort
Resort: The Coeur d'Alene
Address: On the Lake
               Coeur d'Alene, ID 83814–
               1941
Phone: (208) 765–4000 (Golf Course)
               (208) 765–4000, (800) 841–
               5868 (ID), (800) 688–5253
               (U.S. and Canada) (Resort)
Fax: (208) 667–2707 (Resort)

GOLF COURSE
Director of Golf: Mike Delong
Course Length/Par (All Tees): Back 6309/71, Tan 5899/71, Mauve 5490/71, Forward 4446/71
Course Slope/Rating (All Tees): Back 121/69.6, Tan 117/68.2, Ladies' Mauve 121/71.2, Ladies' Forward 105/64.5
Course Architect: Scott Miller (1991)
Golf Facilities: Full Pro Shop X, Snack Bar X, Lounge X, Restaurant No, Locker Room X, Showers X, Club Rental X, Club Repair Minor, Cart Rental X, Instruction X, Practice Green X, Driving Range X, Practice Bunker X, Club Storage X
Tee-Time Reservation Policy: Resort and Holiday Inn guests: At time of hotel reservation. Public: Up to 3 days in advance of play date
Ranger: Yes
Tee-off-Interval Time: 10 min.
Time to Play 18 Holes: 4½ hrs.
Course Hours/Earliest Tee-off: 7 a.m. to 4 p.m.
Green and Cart Fees: Resort or Holiday Inn guests: $95 for 18 holes. Public: $150 for 18 holes. All fees include cart, range balls, forecaddy
Credit Cards: All major cards
Season: April 1 to Nov. 1. Busiest season July to Sept.
Course Comments: Can walk, but caddy $35 additional. Forecaddies included with fees. Nongolfers are charged $21 to accompany golfers. 16 or more players for a tournament
Golf Packages: Available through resort or Holiday Inn (208) 765–3200. Lower rates April to May, Oct. 1 to closing
Discounts: Resort guests. Seasonal (lowest Apr., Oct.). Golf packages
Places to Stay Nearby: Econo Lodge (208) 765–3011, (800) 446–6900; Coeur d'Alene Holiday Inn (208) 765–3200, (800) HOLIDAY; Comfort Inn (208) 765–5500, (800) 221–2222. BED AND BREAKFASTS: Greenbriar Bed and Breakfast Inn (208) 667–9660; McFarland House Bed and Breakfast (208) 667–1232; Warwick Inn Bed and Breakfast (208) 765–6565

Local Attractions: Farragut State Park, Priest Lake, Post Falls, factory outlets, North Idaho College, Museum of North Idaho, fishing, Coeur d'Alene Greyhound Park, Silverwood Theme Park, seasonal festivals, Cataldo Mission of the Sacred Heart, Wallace, Coeur d'Alene District Mining Museum, Sierra Silver Mine Tour. Coeur d'Alene Convention and Visitors Bureau (208) 664–0587, (800) 232–4968 (outside ID), (800) 544–9855 (Canada). Coeur d'Alene Chamber of Commerce (208) 664–3194. Coeur d'Alene Tribal Council (208) 274–3101

Directions: From Spokane, WA (40 mi.): I–90 to exit 11, right, follow sign to City Center, Coeur d'Alene on the lake

Closest Commercial Airports: Spokane International, WA (1 hr.); Seattle–Tacoma International (5 hrs.); Calgary International, Canada (6 hrs.); Boise Municipal (8 hrs.)

RESORT

Date Built: 1986

No. of Rooms: 338 rooms and suites, 1- to 3-bedroom condominiums

Meeting Rooms: 22. Capacity of Largest: 2200 persons. Meeting Space: 23,000 sq. ft.

Room Price Range: $129 to $289 for regular rooms; $2500 for penthouse suite. Golf, ski, other packages available. Highest golf season rates July to Sept., lowest rates Oct. - Nov. and Mar - June

Lounges: Beverly's Lounge, Whisper Bar, Shore Lounge

Restaurants: Beverly's, Dockside, Beach House, Lobby Cafe, seasonal eating areas

Entertainment: Live music, dancing in Shore Lounge

Credit Cards: All major cards

General Amenities: Marine convenience store, floating boardwalk, marina, Coeur d'Alene Plaza shopping center and hotel with 32 shops; meeting and conference facilities with audiovisual and food services

Recreational Amenities: 4 tennis courts, water-skiing, fishing, boating, horseback riding, excursion boats, ice skating, skiing, sleigh riding, indoor swimming pool and wading pool, 2 exercise studios, Jacuzzis, sauna, steam room, indoor golf, bowling, racquetball, outdoor swimming pool, canoeing, hiking, biking, hunting

Reservation and Cancellation Policy: Credit-card guarantee required to hold reservation. 24-hour cancellation notice required for full refund

Restrictions: No pets allowed. Kennels can be arranged. No additional room charge for children in rooms with parents. Hotel tax additional

COEUR D'ALENE

The Coeur d'Alene Resort is a $60-million hotel and recreation complex located on beautiful Lake Coeur d'Alene in northern Idaho. The resort is the realized dream of Duane Hagadone and Jerry Jaeger, two local boys who made good.

Coeur d'Alene has 338 guest rooms and suites, including the opulent 3300-square-foot penthouse Hagadone suite with glass-bottomed swimming pools and Jacuzzis suspended over a patio balcony. Beverly's, one of its two main restaurants, received a Travel Holiday Fine Dining Award. The resort also has a waterfront conference center that can accommodate up to 2200 persons, and there are 3 lounges, the world's longest floating boardwalk, 4 tennis courts, and an indoor recreation center with swimming pool, bowling alley, racquetball court, and computerized golf. The readers of *Condé Nast Traveler* have rated Coeur d'Alene the best mainland resort in America.

The golf course was designed by Scott Miller, who formerly worked with Jack Nicklaus's design firm, and now works out of Scottsdale, Arizona. Miller was born in Wichita, Kansas, and worked two summers on the construction crew at Shoal Creek in Alabama, a Nicklaus design. After graduating from Colorado State with a landscape architecture degree in 1978, he worked briefly for a course contractor in Florida and then co-designed the LaPaloma Golf Club in Tucson, Arizona, with Nicklaus; Rancho Mirage Country Club in Rancho Mirage, California, with Nicklaus, Jay Moorish and Robert Cupp; and various other excellent courses. The Coeur d'Alene course received honorable mention as best new resort course in 1991 from *Golf Digest* magazine. It has also been ranked one of the best courses in the state of Idaho.

The Coeur d'Alene Resort Golf Course was designed to evolve from the predominant natural features of the site: an expansive lakeshore, a forested ridge, gently rolling interior woodland and Fernan Creek. These features have been melded with forest, rock, lake and creek to create a four-teed layout that can fit the game of any golfer. Distances range from 4446 yards on the forward tees to 6309 yards on the back tees. The course is entirely bentgrass, and bunkers are primarily used to guard the greens.

The number-1-handicap hole at Coeur d'Alene is the 566-yard par-5 ninth, which plays straight to a small green guarded by three traps on the right and four on the left, beginning approximately 75 yards from the hole. The par-4 holes are probably the most difficult, including the 451-yard eighteenth, a slight dogleg left. The tee shot is over a pair of sand bunkers on the right. The approach shot is to a multitiered green with a huge trap on the right beginning 50 yards in front of the green.

Then there is the famous floating green, whose tee distance changes everyday because it sits on adjustable flotation devices. The contour of the green is formed by foam components ranging from 6 to 68 inches high. The contours are covered by a vinyl liner, which in turn is covered by 12 to 18 inches of soil. The green is designed to move, providing a playable length ranging from 100 to 175 yards (measured from the center of the back tee to the center of the green). The movement is controlled by a computer, and the length of the hole is displayed each day at the tee. Legend has it that the idea for the floating green came to Duane Hagadone as he watched a tugboat pull a boom of logs across the lake. When you're the boss you can do anything.

The 15,546-square-foot clubhouse at the Coeur d'Alene has a pro shop that was recently nominated by *Golf Shop Operations* magazine as one of the best in the country.

The clubhouse structure was designed by R. G. Nelson, the designer of the main buildings at the resort. The clubhouse features a snack bar with a magnificent view of the lake, which has 135 miles of shoreline.

Golf carts are mandatory at Coeur d'Alene, unless you opt to hire a walking caddy. Included in the green fees is the price of a forecaddy who will spot balls, rake traps, read greens, tend flags, and clean clubs and balls for each golf group. Golf packages are available through the resort and the nearby Holiday Inn for up to 128 golfers at a time.

These and other special offers, including ski packages, are available at the resort. The Coeur d'Alene becomes a first-class ski resort in the winter with the nearby Hagadone Hospitality–owned Silver Mountain providing a 3.1-mile gondola ride and a 3400-foot vertical drop. Or skiers can select the varied terrain of the Schweitzer Mountain Resort. During the summer months, the surrounding countryside provides resort guests with a variety of recreational opportunities such as fishing, hunting, hiking, horseback riding, rafting, canoeing, water-skiing, sailing and riding on one of the resort's 3 excursion boats. The Coeur d'Alene area is estimated to have 111 lakes with more than 200,000 acres of fresh-water scenery and recreation. Other attractions in the region include Priest Lake, with its 70 miles of shoreline and 150-foot-tall cedars; the Cataldo Mission of the Sacred Heart, which was constructed by the Coeur d'Alene Indians; Wallace, one of the few towns listed in its entirety on the National Register of Historic Places; the Sierra Silver Mine Tour; the Coeur d'Alene Greyhound Park and more. During the summer months Coeur d'Alene's northern latitude gives you 15 hours of daylight to explore the area or to hit golf balls.

Coeur d'Alene began as Fort Sherman, named after the Civil War general, in the 1870s. Area gold and silver discoveries added to its growth, and it went on to become a logging and recreational area, with fishing, boating, hunting and skiing at the forefront. Visiting this part of the world is an experience you shouldn't miss.

Recommended Golf Courses in Idaho

Within 2 Hours of Lewiston:

Avondale Golf and Tennis Club, Hayden Lake, (208) 772–5963, Semiprivate, 18/6525/72

Hidden Lakes Golf Resort, Sandpoint, (208) 263–1642, Public, 18/6668/71

The Highlands Golf and Country Club, Post Falls, (208) 773–3673, 18/6369/72

Stoneridge Golf Course, Blanchard, (208) 437–4682, Public, 18/6522/72

Twin Lakes Village, Rathdrum, (208) 687–1311, Semiprivate, 18/6158/71

University of Idaho Golf Course, Moscow, (208) 885–6171, Public, 18/6637/72

Pocatello Area

Course Name: ELKHORN RESORT

Course Type: Resort
Resort: Elkhorn Resort and Golf Club
Address: Elkhorn Road/P.O. Box 6005
Sun Valley, ID 83354
Phone: (208) 622–3309 (Golf Course)
(208) 622–4511, (800) 355–4676 (Resort)
Fax: (208) 622–3261 (Resort)

GOLF COURSE

Director of Golf: Jeff Steury
Course Length/Par (All Tees): Back 7101/72, Middle 6524/72, Forward 5701/72
Course Slope/Rating (All Tees): Back 133/72.4, Middle 128/70.3, Ladies' Forward 126/73.0
Course Architects: Robert Trent Jones, Sr., and Robert Trent Jones, Jr. (1975)
Golf Facilities: Full Pro Shop X, Snack Bar X, Lounge X, Restaurant X, Locker Room X, Showers X, Club Rental X, Club Repair Limited, Cart Rental X, Instruction X, Practice Green X, Driving Range X, Practice Bunker No, Club Storage X

Tee-Time Reservation Policy: Resort guests: Anytime from time of reservation. Public: Up to 30 days in advance with credit card guarantee
Ranger: Yes
Tee-off-Interval Time: 10 min.
Time to Play 18 Holes: 4 hrs., 15 min.
Course Hours/Earliest Tee-off: 7:30 a.m.
Green and Cart Fees: Resort guests: $75 for 18 holes with cart, $45 for 9 holes with cart. Public: $86 for 18 holes with cart, $54 for 9 holes with cart
Credit Cards: American Express, Discover, MasterCard, Visa
Season: May to Oct. Busiest season mid-June to mid-Sept.
Course Comments: Cart mandatory peak season. Peak season: 9-hole rates apply after 4 p.m., before 9 a.m.
Golf Packages: Available through resort. Lowest rates mid-April to mid-June and mid-Sept. to closing
Discounts: Resort guests. Seasonal mid-Apr.-mid-June, after mid-Sept.
Places to Stay Nearby: Sun Valley Inn (208) 622–4111; Sun Valley Lodge and Apartments (208) 622–4111; Bitterroot Property Management (208) 726–5394, (800) 635–4408; Base Mountain Properties (208) 726–5601, (800) 521–2515; Resort Reservations (208) 726–3374, (800) 635–8242. KETCHUM: Idaho Country Inn (208) 726–1019; River Street Inn (208) 726–3611; Best Western Christiana Lodge (208) 726–3351, (800) 535–3241; Christophe Condominiums and Hotel (208) 726–7525, (800) 521–2515; Heidelberg Inn (208) 726–5361. Sun Valley Centralized Reservation Service (800) 786–8259. Sun Valley–Ketchum Chamber of Commerce (208) 726–3423, (800) 634–3347. Fax (208) 726–4533
Local Attractions: Challis National Forest, Salmon National Forest, Sawtooth National Recreation Area, art and music festivals, ballooning, glider flights, fishing, boating, hiking, camping, skiing, white-water rafting, horseback riding, bicycling, swimming, hunting, ghost towns, rock climbing, Hemingway tour, gold mine tours, art galleries, antiques. Ketchum. Sawtooth National Recreation

Area Headquarters (208) 726–7672. Sun Valley–Ketchum Chamber of Commerce (208) 726–3423, (800) 634–3347

Directions: I–84 to Hwy. 75 in Twin Falls, north on Hwy. 75 to Sun Valley, right on Elkhorn Rd. to resort

Closest Commercial Airports: Haily Sun Valley Airport (20 min.); Boise Municipal (3 hrs.); Idaho Falls (3 hrs.); Salt Lake City International, UT (5½ hrs.)

RESORT

Date Built: 1973

No. of Rooms: 132 hotel rooms, 90 condominiums

Meeting Rooms: 12. Capacity of Largest: 350 persons banquet style. Meeting Space: 3500 sq. ft.

Room Price Range: $78 value season (Nov., Dec., April, May) to $598 for penthouses per night. Recreation, golf, ski and other special offers available year round

Lounges: Atrium Lounge, Showcase Saloon

Restaurants: Plaza Grill, Tequila Joe's, Jesse's, Clubhouse, Treat Haus

Entertainment: Live music in Atrium Lounge, Horizon Ballroom, Showcase Saloon

Credit Cards: All major cards

General Amenities: Children's center for ages 1 to 12, babysitting, seasonal events including concerts, Elkhorn Village, shops, year-round festivals, events and entertainment such as Sun Valley Repertory Theatre, jazz, art auctions, dance performances and others; meeting and conference facilities with audio-visual, food, and other services

Recreational Amenities: Horseback riding, skiing, children's ski programs, 18 tennis courts, indoor health center with exercise equipment, saunas, Jacuzzis, 2 outdoor Olympic–sized pools, additional 1 pool per condo, bicycling, hiking, jogging paths

Reservation and Cancellation Policy: Deposit by credit card or check in the amount of 50% of total amount due within 14 days of reservation. Cancellation notice must be received 14 days prior to arrival to avoid penalties. Full forfeiture of deposit without proper cancellation notification

Comments and Restrictions: No pets. Lodge rates are single or double occupancy with additional guests $10 each with a maximum of 4 occupants. Children under 12 years of age may stay free when sharing the room with an adult. Christmas season reservation policies more stringent. Taxes additional to base rates

ELKHORN RESORT

The Elkhorn Resort Course is a 7101-yard par-72 Robert Trent Jones, Sr., and Robert Trent Jones, Jr., layout within walking distance of this Sun Valley year-round hotel and recreation center. Elkhorn is ranked among the best publicly accessible golf courses in America by *Golf Digest* and as one of the top courses of any kind in the state of Idaho. The resort itself is a 3000-acre self-contained pedestrian community.

The front nine at Elkhorn is hilly, and the back nine flatter. The latter is the more difficult side, with seven holes affected by water. There are more than 85 bunkers on the golf course. The bentgrass greens are elevated, large and undulating, and well trapped in the Robert Trent Jones tradition.

The front nine, which plays 400 yards longer, has two long par 5s. The first, the 644-yard fifth hole, plays downhill from an elevated tee with magnificent views of the Sawtooth Mountains. This hole is straight and open, with fairway bunkers guarding the landing areas on the first two shots. The green is large and guarded by traps to the left and right. The 592-yard par-5 ninth is the number-1-handicap hole, a dogleg right to a deep green with a trap to the right and another trap and a stream to the left.

Water comes into play on the back nine, which requires more demanding accuracy and club selection than the front. Two challenging par 4s on this side are the 423-yard twelfth and the 434-yard seventeenth. The twelfth is a sharp dogleg left to a landing area with a cluster of fairway bunkers to the left and right. The tee shot has to carry a stream, and the golfer must decide how much of the left corner can be cut without hitting the bunkers on that side of the fairway. The second shot is to a green guarded by a trap to the front and left and a stream to the right and rear.

The seventeenth hole is another sharp dogleg left, with a stream bordering the right fairway and a group of fairway bunkers protecting the left side of the tee-shot landing area. The approach to the green requires considerable accuracy because of the trap directly in front of the green, another trap to the left and a stream to the right.

The most difficult hole on the Elkhorn course is probably the 224-yard par-3 third, rated the number-5-handicap hole on the course. The tee shot is to a deep green fronted by a trap, requiring you to bring it in by air to have a chance for a par or better.

Accommodations at Elkhorn include suites in the lodge and studio to 4-bedroom condominiums. Amenities such as shops, restaurants, a general store, tennis, swimming, and an exercise center are within walking distance. The surrounding area features a variety of outdoor recreational activities including bicycle touring, white-water rafting, gliding, fly fishing, hot-air ballooning, and skiing in wintertime. Silver Creek and Big Wood River are ideal for fly fishing, and the Sawtooth National Recreation Area has over 300 alpine lakes noted for trout fishing, boating and sailing. The nearby Salmon River remains one of the few undammed waterways in America and is ideal for white-water rafting. Guides can take you into this wilderness teeming with deer, elk, black bear, mountain lion and other magnificent species. This is Ernest Hemingway country.

The Elkhorn has a variety of meeting and conference options, and Sun Valley has more than 60 restaurants to choose from. Many seasonal and recreational packages are offered by the Elkhorn and art, music and other festivals in Sun Valley are scheduled year round. The Elkhorn has earned the prestigious Four-Diamond Award from the American Automobile Association.

Course Name: SUN VALLEY

Course Type: Resort
Resort: Sun Valley
Address: Sun Valley Road
Sun Valley, ID 83353
Phone: (208) 622–2251
(Golf Course)
(800) 786–8259 (Resort)
Fax: (208) 622–3700 (Resort)

GOLF COURSE

Head Professional: Rick Hickman
Course Length/Par (All Tees): Back 6565/72, Middle 6057/72, Ladies' Forward 5241/73
Course Slope/Rating (All Tees): Back 128/71.1, Middle 122/68.6, Ladies' Forward 125/70.4
Course Architects: William P. Bell (9 holes, 1938), George Von Elm (9 holes, 1962), Robert Trent Jones, Jr., and Don Knott (additional 2 holes, 1979; renovation, 1980)
Golf Facilities: Full Pro Shop X, Snack Bar X, Lounge No, Restaurant No, Locker Room X, Showers X, Club Rental X, Club Repair X, Cart Rental X, Instruction X, Practice Green X, Driving Range X, Practice Bunker X, Club Storage X
Tee-Time Reservation Policy: Resort guests: At time of reservation. Public: 2 days in advance
Ranger: Yes
Tee-off-Interval Time: 10 min.
Time to Play 18 Holes: 4½ hrs.
Course Hours/Earliest Tee-off: 7 a.m.
Green Fees: Resort guests: $64 for 18 holes. Public: $74 for 18 holes
Cart Fees: $15 for 18 holes per person
Credit Cards: All major cards
Season: End of April to end of Oct. Busiest season July, Aug.
Course Comments: Cart mandatory during busiest season mid-June to mid-Sept. Golf Digest Golf School on site (800) 243–6121
Golf Packages: Available through resort. Lowest rates generally spring and fall
Discounts: Juniors, seniors, season passes, seasonal discounts

Places to Stay Nearby: Bitterroot Property Management (208) 726–5394, (800) 635–4408; Elkhorn (208) 622–4511, (800) 355–4676; Base Mountain Properties (208) 726–5601, (800) 521–2515; Resort Reservations (208) 726–3374, (800) 635–8242. KETCHUM: Idaho Country Inn (208) 726–1019; River Street Inn (208) 726–3611; Best Western Christiana Lodge (208) 726–3351, (800) 535–3241; Christophe Condominiums and Hotel (208) 726–7525, (800) 521–2515; Heidelberg Inn (208) 726–5361. Sun Valley Centralized Reservation Service (800) 786–8259. Sun Valley–Ketchum Chamber of Commerce (208) 726–3423, (800) 634–3347. Fax (208) 726–4533

Local Attractions: Challis National Forest, Salmon National Forest, Sawtooth National Recreation Area, art and music festivals, ballooning, glider flights, fishing, boating, hiking, camping, skiing, white-water rafting, horseback riding, bicycling, swimming, hunting, ghost towns, rock climbing, Hemingway tour, gold mine tours, art galleries, antiques. Ketchum. Sawtooth National Recreation Area Headquarters (208) 726–7672. Sun Valley–Ketchum Chamber of Commerce (208) 726–3423, (800) 634–3347

Directions: Hwy. 75 to Ketchum, turn right at Sun Valley Rd. (first light), 1 mi. to golf course

Closest Commercial Airports: Haily Sun Valley Airport (25 min.); Twin Falls Regional (1½ hrs.); Boise Municipal (2½ hrs.); Idaho Falls (2½ hrs.); Salt Lake City International, UT (5 hrs.)

RESORT

Date Built: 1938

No. of Rooms: 600 hotel rooms, 1- to 4-bedroom condominiums, cottages

Meeting Rooms: Lodge: 7. Inn: 11. Capacity of Largest: Lodge: 170 persons banquet style; Inn: 900 persons banquet style. Meeting Space: Lodge: 12,318 sq. ft. Inn: 15,541 sq. ft.

Room Price Range: $74 for standard single, off season (early April to June, Oct. to mid-Dec.) to $330 for inn apartment suite peak season (mid-Dec. to March,

June to Sept.). Golf and other packages available

Lounges: Lodge: Duchin Bar

Restaurants: Lodge: Dining Room, Gretchen's Coffee Shop. Inn: Ram Restaurant, Continental Cafeteria, several village restaurants

Entertainment: Live music nightly in Duchin Bar

Credit Cards: All major cards

General Amenities: Beauty salon, barber shop, shops, hospital and medical clinic, opera house (movies), playschool children's program for ages 6 mos. to 6 yrs., summer youth programs for ages 6 to 16, ice shows; meeting and conference facilities in reception, banquet, convention, theater and classroom styles with audiovisual and food services

Recreational Amenities: Whirlpool, massage, swimming pools, sports center (arranges all sports ticket purchases), volleyball, trap and skeet shooting, 18 outdoor tennis courts with pro shop, instruction, glider rides, bicycling, horseback riding, fishing, archery, bowling, hunting, ice skating (indoor and outdoor rinks), camping, hiking

Reservation and Cancellation Policy: 1 night's room and tax deposit required within 14 days after booking reservations. All condominiums rented on weekly basis require deposit of one-half of the total weekly amount. Cancellations must be received 14 days prior to scheduled arrival to avoid forfeiting deposit. All cancellations subject to a cancellation charge

Comments and Restrictions: No pets allowed. Children 17 and under stay free when in the same unit as their parents. Taxes additional to base rates

SUN VALLEY

In 1935 Averell Harriman, then chairman of the board of the Union Pacific Railroad and a longtime skier, came up with an idea to attract railway passenger traffic to the West. He decided to build a destination ski resort and hired an Austrian count, Felix Schaffgotsch, to find an ideal location. Schaffgotsch chose Ketchum, Idaho, in the northern Rocky Mountains. Harriman purchased the 4300-acre Brass Ranch and hired publicity genius Steve Hannagan, who transformed sand dunes into Miami Beach, and by 1938 Sun Valley was born. In 1964, Union Pacific sold Sun Valley to the Januss Corp., and it was further developed into a vacation village for young families. Some popular recreational activities here include skiing, ice skating, tennis, horseback riding, fishing, bicycling, hunting, hiking, camping, trap and skeet shooting, boating, white-water rafting, gliding, and swimming.

The original golf course at Sun Valley was a William P. Bell nine-hole layout that opened in 1938. George Von Elm was in the process of building a second nine when he died in 1962. Robert Trent Jones, Jr., was hired to complete and remodel the course, which he did with Don Knott. Today the hilly, well-treed, well-bunkered layout is one of the best public or private golf courses in Idaho and one of the top 75 resort courses in America by *Golf Digest*. There is water on thirteen of the holes here, and Trail Creek, an excellent trout stream, winds through the course. The bentgrass greens are large, moderately fast, undulating and well guarded by water and sand. There are well placed hazards near landing areas. You should try for accuracy rather than distance on this 6565-yard par-72 layout. Course management and club selection are essential, because you will be penalized if you err too far.

Sun Valley starts out with a 360-yard golfer-friendly par 4, but then you run into the dogleg-left 428-yard par-4 second, the number-1-handicap hole. Trees line the left side of the fairway, and the first shot from an elevated tee must carry Trail Creek. The tee shot has to get to the corner of the dogleg for you to see the green, but a shot that goes through the dogleg will be under the trees on the right. The approach is over the creek again to a green well guarded by a bunker to the left front.

Sun Valley has some interesting and challenging par-3 holes, including the 244-yard fifteenth, which is rated the number-4-handicap hole on the course. From the back tees, the tee shot is through a narrow chute of trees and over the creek to a green protected both left and right by sand traps. The green has a creek to its right rear and trees to the rear. The tee distances of 180 and 135 yards from the other tee positions are more forgiving on this difficult par 3.

The most difficult par 5 at Sun Valley is the 545-yard ninth, a dogleg left down a well-protected fairway to a green bordered by water on the left. Trees are to the rear and right and bunkers to the right. The first shot has to reach a fairway guarded by bunkers, with water on the left and water and trees on the right. If the second strays, it will be in the trees on the right or perhaps in the water on the left. Most golfers try to be within pitching-wedge range after the second shot.

The golf clubhouse at Sun Valley is modest, but the pro shop is excellent, as are the practice facilities; these include a practice range that is 600 yards deep and 125 yards wide and has practice bunkers and two practice greens. Individual and group golf instruction are provided by a staff of teaching professionals.

Sun Valley is a self-contained resort community with many accommodations, restaurants, shops and recreational amenities.

Meeting and conference facilities are available at the Sun Valley Lodge and the Sun Valley Inn. The lodge has 12,300 square feet of space and 7 meeting rooms, including the opera house, which seats 344 persons. The inn has 15,500 square feet of space and 11 meeting areas, including a convention center that accommodates 900 people banquet style.

In addition to the shops, restaurants and recreational amenities of Sun Valley, there is much to see and do in nearby Ketchum's art galleries, shops, restaurants and other attractions. There are also many outdoor recreation areas in the vicinity, including Challis National Forest, with 250 lakes, 1000 miles of fishing streams, 1600 miles of trails, campgrounds and white-water rafting. Other area attractions include Craters of the Moon National Monument, Salmon National Forest, and Sawtooth National

Recreation Area. Seasonal festivals, including antique fairs, music festivals, Sun Valley Octoberfest, Sun Valley Christmas Eve and Torchlight Parade and many others take place year round.

Sun Valley offers a variety of golf, skiing and other packages and seasonal discounts. Inquire through the central reservations office or the Sun Valley–Ketchum Chamber of Commerce (208) 726–3423, (800) 634–3347. And don't miss the Sun Valley Ice Show. Skating greats including Dick Button, Peggy Fleming, Brian Boitano, Dorothy Hamill, Scott Hamilton, Sonja Henie, Victor Petrenko, Katarina Witt, Kristi Yamaguchi and many others have all skated here.

Recommended Golf Courses in Idaho

Within 1 Hour of Pocatello:

Blackfoot Municipal Golf Course, Blackfoot, (208) 785–9960, Public, 18/6899/72

Highland Golf Course, Pocatello, (208) 237–9922, Public, 18/6612/72

Pinecrest Municipal Golf Course, Idaho Falls, (208) 529–1485, Public, 18/6430/70

Idaho: Useful Information

Idaho Travel Council, 700 W. State St., 2nd Floor, Boise, ID 83720, (800) 635–7820

Idaho Parks and Recreation Department, State House Mall, Boise, ID 83720–8000, (208) 327–7444, (800) 635–7820 (recreation information)

Idaho Fish and Game Department, Box 25, 600 S. Walnut, Boise, ID 83707, (208) 334–3700 (fishing and hunting regulations)

U.S. Forest Service, Northern Region (Northern Idaho), Federal Building, P.O. Box 7669, Missoula, MT 59807, (406) 329–3511

U.S. Forest Service, Intermountain Region (Southern Idaho), 2501 Wall Ave., Ogden, UT 84401, (801) 629–8600

Bloomington/ Normal/Peoria Area

Course Name: LICK CREEK GOLF COURSE

Course Type: Public
Address: 2210 North Parkway Drive
            Pekin, IL 61555
Phone: (309) 346–0077

GOLF COURSE

Head Professional: None
Course Length/Par (All Tees): Back 6957/72, Middle 6583/72, Ladies' Forward 5729/73
Course Slope/Rating (All Tees): Back 128/72.8, Middle 126/70.7, Forward 125/72.9
Course Architects: Edward Lawrence Packard and Roger Packard (1976)
Golf Facilities: Full Pro Shop Limited, Snack Bar X, Lounge No, Restaurant No, Locker Room X, Showers X, Club Rental X, Club Repair No, Cart Rental X, Instruction X, Practice Green X, Driving Range X, Practice Bunker No, Club Storage X
Tee-Time Reservation Policy: Up to 1 wk. in advance, only 3 tee times can be reserved by 1 person
Ranger: Yes
Tee-off-Interval Time: 8 min.
Time to Play 18 Holes: 4½ hrs. to 5 hrs.
Course Hours/Earliest Tee-off: 5:30 a.m. to dark
Green Fees: $16 for 18 holes Sat., Sun., holidays; $13 for 18 holes weekdays
Cart Fees: $14 for 18 holes, $8 for 9 holes
Credit Cards: MasterCard, Visa
Season: End of March to late Oct.
Course Comments: Can walk anytime
Golf Packages: None
Discounts: Residents, seniors, juniors
Places to Stay Nearby: PEKIN: Best Western (309) 347–5533, (800) 528–1234; Mineral Springs Motel (309) 346–2147. PEORIA: Courtyard by Marriott (309) 686–1900, (800) 321–2211; Hotel Pere Marguette (309) 637–6500, (800) 322–3561 (IL); Holiday Inn Brandywine (309) 686–8000, (800) HOLIDAY. BLOOMINGTON–NORMAL: Best Western

(309) 662–0000, (800) 528–1234; Holiday Inn–Normal (309) 452–8300, (800) HOLIDAY; Days Inn East (309) 663–1361, (800) 325–2525
Local Attractions: PEKIN: Dirksen Congressional Center, Tazewell County Courthouse and historic area. PEORIA: Belle Reynolds Museum, Bradley University, Cornstock Theatre, Illinois Antique Center, Illinois Historical Water Museum, Lakeview Museum of Arts and Sciences, Peoria Historical Society, St. Mary's Cathedral and Museum tours, Weaver's Angus Farm/Peoria Polo Club, Wildlife Prairie Park, Paradise Riverboat Gambling. Springfield. Peoria Convention and Visitors Bureau (309) 676–0303, (800) 747–0302. Pekin Chamber of Commerce (309) 346–2106
Directions: Rte. 9 to Parkway Dr., north on Parkway (4½ mi.), course on right
Closest Commercial Airports: Greater Peoria (30 min.), Springfield/Capital (1 hr.), Chicago O'Hare International (4 hrs.)

LICK CREEK GOLF COURSE

Pekin, Illinois, is the birthplace and burial place of former senator Everett McKinley Dirksen, who left these flat farmlands to become one of the most powerful senators in Washington. Pekin is also the home of Lick Creek Golf Course, a 6957-yard par-72 layout designed by Edward Lawrence Packard with his son Roger.

Lick Creek was carved out of woodlands situated on rolling terrain on one of the highest points in Pekin. This challenging layout features large, moderately fast, rolling bentgrass greens that are invariably well protected by large sand bunkers. There are well-placed traps in many strategic fairway landing areas, and water comes into play on three holes. Because of the relatively high elevation for these parts, wind can affect strategy and shot making on this tight layout. The rolling terrain tends to leave you with uneven lies, which add to the difficulty of the course. It is very important to play position golf at Lick Creek.

The fifth, sixth and seventh holes at Lick Creek are ruefully called the "Bermuda Triangle" because they are tightly treed, tough golf challenges. The fifth hole is a 410-yard par-4 dogleg right. The tee shot is down a tree-lined fairway that starts to bend to the right approximately 150 yards from a deep green protected by a large trap on the right.

The 586-yard par-5 sixth is not for the squeamish. The tee shot is over a gully to a fairway 210 yards from the back tees. The second shot is down a narrowing fairway lined with trees. The approach shot is to a small, fast, forward-sloping, crowned green protected by two traps to its front left and right. If your first two shots don't set up properly you may be in trouble; it is not easy to hold this green when coming in from a distance.

The 385-yard par-4 seventh is a tightly treed dogleg right. The approach shot is downhill to a medium-sized, right-to-left-sloping green tightly squeezed in front by two traps.

Another tough par 4 at Lick Creek is the 406-yard par-4 fourteenth, a dogleg left. The fairway is tightly treed and slopes to the left. If your tee shot is short and left, it is likely to kick into the trees down the slope. The approach shot is to a medium-sized forward- and left-sloping green that is protected by traps left, rear and right with a drop-off to the rear.

The eighteenth hole at Lick Creek is an excellent finishing hole. A 527-yard par 5, it provides you with a choice of two routes to a large green almost completely surrounded by five traps. Should you elect to go left, the hole plays 527 yards and requires you to lay up to the right of a lake on your second shot. Should you elect to go right, your tee shot should be as close to the pond, 276 yards from the back tees, as possible. The second shot then has to carry approximately 125 yards of lake to reach a landing area or the green. The center of the green is 188 yards from the front edge of the pond.

Amenities are minimal at Lick Creek, but the green fees are quite low, and you can walk the course anytime. The pro shop has a snack bar but no head professional. There are minimal locker-room, pro-shop

and shower facilities. Practice facilities include a driving range and putting green. *Golf Digest* has included Lick Creek on its America's 75 best public golf courses list.

Recommended Golf Courses in Illinois

Within 1 Hour of Peoria:

Hawthorne Ridge Golf Club, Aledo, (309) 582–5641, Public, 18/NA/72

Gibson Woods Golf Club, Monmouth, (309) 734–9968, Public, 18/6362/72

Illinois State University Golf Course, Normal, (309) 438–8065, Public, 18/6400/71

Ironwood Golf Course, Normal, (309) 454–9620, Public, 18/6960/72

Newman Golf Course, Peoria, (309) 674–1663, Public, 18/6838/71

Prairie Vista Golf Course, Bloomington, (309) 823–4217, Public, 18/6748/72

Chicago Area

Course Name: **CANTIGNY GOLF COURSE**
Hillside, Lakeside, Woodside Courses

Course Type: Public
Address: 27 W. 270 Mack Road
Wheaton, IL 60187
Phone: (708) 668–3323 (Golf Course)
(708) 668–8463 (Tee Times)
(708) 260–8194 (Fairways Restaurant) (708) 668–5161 (Concert and Museum Information)

GOLF COURSE

Head Professional: Danny Mulhearn
Course Length/Par (All Tees): Woodside/Lakeside: Back 6709/72, Middle 6267/72, Forward 5421/72. Lakeside/Hillside: Back 6625/72, Middle 6201/72, Forward 5167/72. Hillside/Woodside: Back 6760/72, Middle 6268/72, Forward 5214/72
Course Slope/Rating (All Tees): Woodside/Lakeside: 130/72.4, Middle 127/70.3, Forward 114/65.7, Ladies' Forward 123/71.6. Lakeside/Hillside:

Back 126/71.1, Middle 122/69.2, Forward 108/64.3, Ladies' Forward 117/69.4. Hillside/Woodside: Back 125/72.2, Middle 119/70.2, Front 105/64.9, Ladies' Forward 115/69.5

Course Architect: Roger Packard (1989)

Golf Facilities: Full Pro Shop X, Snack Bar X, Lounge X, Restaurant X, Locker Room X, Showers X, Club Rental X, Club Repair X, Cart Rental X, Instruction X, Practice Green X, Driving Range X, Practice Bunker X, Club Storage No

Tee-Time Reservation Policy: Can be made from 7 a.m. to 3 p.m. Mon. and 7 a.m. to 5 p.m. Tues. through Sun. Reservations may be made up to 7 days in advance. All reservations require a confirming credit card number. 24-hr. cancellation required to avoid penalties

Ranger: Yes

Tee-off-Interval Time: 10 min.

Time to Play 18 Holes: 4½ hrs.

Course Hours/Earliest Tee-off: 7 a.m.

Green Fees: $60 for 18 holes, $22 for 9 holes

Cart Fees: $15 for 18 holes per cart, $8 for 9 holes per person

Pull Carts: $5

Credit Cards: American Express, Discover, MasterCard, Visa

Season: Mid-April to late Oct.

Course Comments: Can walk anytime. Course closed Mon. except Memorial Day, Labor Day

Golf Packages: None

Discounts: Seniors, juniors for 9-hole play only ($14)

Places to Stay Nearby: NAPERVILLE: Courtyard by Marriott (708) 505–0550, (800) 321–22111; Sheraton Inn (708) 505–4900, (800) 325–3535. AURORA: Travelodge Hotel (708) 896–0801, (800) 255–3050. SCHAUMBURG–CHICAGO O'HARE AIRPORT AREA: Embassy Suites—Woodfield (708) 397–1313; Holiday Inn—Woodfield (708) 310–0500, (800) 465–4329; Hyatt Regence O'Hare (708) 696–1234, (800) 233–1234; La Quinta Motor Inn (708) 517–8484, (800) 531–5900; Schaumberg Marriott (708) 240–0100, (800) 228–9290. OAK BROOK:

Hyatt Regency Oak Brook (708) 573–1234, (800) 233–1234; Stouffer Oak Brook (708) 573–2800, (800) HOTELS–1

Local Attractions: Wheaton College, Billy Graham Center Museum, Cosley Animal Farm and Museum, Robert R. McCormick Museum, First Division Museum at Cantigny. NAPERVILLE: Naper Settlement Museum Village, Naperville Riverwalk. AURORA: Aurora Fire Museum, Aurora Historical Museum, Aurora Transportation Center, Blackberry Farm and Historic Village, Near Eastside Historic District, Paramount Arts Centre, Scitech, Glen Ellyn/Du Page County Forest Preserve. See also Chicago listing on pages 297. Du Page Convention and Visitors Bureau (708) 241–0002, (800) 232–0502. Chicago Tourism Council (312) 280–5740, (800) ITS–CHGO

Directions: From Chicago O'Hare International Airport (45 min.): Rte. 294 to Rte. 88, west on Rte. 88 to Winfield, north on Winfield to Mack Rd., east on Mack Rd. (1½ mi.) to golf course

Closest Commercial Airport: Chicago O'Hare International (45 min.)

CANTIGNY GOLF COURSE

The Cantigny (pronounced Canteeny) Golf Course is situated on what is the estate of Colonel Robert R. McCormick, former publisher and editor of the *Chicago Tribune*. The original estate was 1500 acres but now encompasses 500 acres of open and wooded land and, as requested by Col. McCormick in his will, is maintained as a source of recreation and education for the public. Today Cantigny is composed of 4 areas: 2 museums, 10 acres of gardens, and 27 holes of golf. The eighteen-hole Woodside/Lakeside championship golf course, designed by Roger Packard, was named the best new public course in 1989 by *Golf Digest* magazine. The name Cantigny comes from the French village that was the site of the U.S. Army's first offensive battle in Europe during World War I. Mr. McCormick served as an artillery battalion commander in the First Division, which successfully fought in that battle.

The golf courses encompass approximately one-half of this rustic 500-acre parcel in Wheaton, just west of Chicago. More than $11 million was invested in the courses and the magnificent clubhouse, which is four stories tall and has 22,000 square feet of space. Inside are administrative offices, locker rooms and showers, a full-service bar and restaurant, pro shop and meeting rooms including a penthouse-like boardroom that overlooks the former estate and the golf courses. This facility and others are administered by the Robert R. McCormick Trusts and Foundation, based in Chicago.

The 6709-yard par-72 Woodside nine and Lakeside nine is a beautiful adventure in the woods. Trees including alder, Douglas fir, birch, ash, dogwood, maple, linden and other varieties adorn the property. Plants such as chrysanthemums, coreopsis, phlox, oriental poppies, iris, day lilies and hundreds of others brighten the landscape. The golf-course playing area is bentgrass from tee to green and is kept in excellent condition. The facility is closed on Mondays to keep the high standards of course conditioning adhered to at Cantigny.

The fairways are well treed but not oppressively narrow. The greens are small to medium sized, moderately fast, undulating and strategically but not excessively trapped. Water hazards in the form of streams and ponds appear on twelve holes. Shot placement and strategy are important at Cantigny; the course is a fair test of golf. If the ball strays too far, it is likely to find sand or water. Minimally, you will probably end up behind one of the mature trees on the property.

There are a number of memorable and challenging holes at Cantigny, starting with Woodside and the 539-yard par-5 second hole, the number-1-handicap hole on this side. The tee shot is down a rolling fairway bordered by a stream on the right. The second shot is to a peninsulalike landing area almost completely bordered by the stream. The approach shot is over a stream to a small green with a trap on the left. A scenic and challenging par 3 on Woodside is the 165-yard eighth, which plays over a large pond to a large, forward-sloping dual green

shared with the sixth hole on the Hillside nine.

A beautiful and difficult par 3 on the Lakeside nine is the 191-yard fourth, which plays over a corner of a large pond that begins to the left of the fairway approximately 70 yards onto a right-to-left-sloping green protected on the right by a huge sand trap.

The finishing hole is a tricky 365-yard par-4 dogleg left. The tee shot is to a narrow landing area bordered by Swan Lake on the right and trees and water on the left. Also to the right is a large bunker in the profile of Dick Tracy, whose syndicated cartoon detective dramas helped the McCormick family generate the revenue that made Cantigny possible. The approach shot is to a large green with bunkers front and rear and water framing the left, right and back. There is very little margin for error on this approach.

Because Cantigny has become so popular and well recognized by leading golf publications, Hillside, the former nine-hole course, has been added to the rotation with the front nine of the eighteen-hole championship course (now called Woodside) and the back nine (now Lakeside). All three nines are used for morning tee-offs, and golfers can select which combination of nines, all designed by Roger Packard, they wish to play. Two nines are used in the afternoon for eighteen-hole play, and one nine is held, on a rotating basis, for nine-hole play.

The Hillside Course plays 3340 yards from the back tees, and five bunkers have been added to this layout, which is also bentgrass from tee to green; has small to medium-sized, moderately undulating putting surfaces; and features water on three holes. An excellent golf hole on this nine is the par-4 sixth. The tee shot is to a landing area on a peninsula with water right, left and ahead of you. The approach is over water to a large, double, two-tiered green shared with the eighth hole on the Woodside nine. The combination of three quality nines now adds to the variety and accessibility of golf at Cantigny.

The practice facilities at Cantigny include an ample driving range, practice bunkers, chipping green and 2 putting greens. You can walk the course anytime. The Cantigny philosophy is to provide a daily-fee facility but to treat people like they are at a country club. And that is the feeling that you get, both on and off the course. Some outings are held at Cantigny, but there are no leagues and no memberships. Reservations can be made in foursomes up to 1 week in advance. The reservation system is computerized. Those golfers with less than a foursome can reserve a tee time on the same day they wish to golf if space is available.

Instruction is available at Cantigny, which has adult weekday golf clinics, an adult weekend golf academy and a junior golf school, as well as individual and group lessons. A USTA tennis professional is based here, as are adult and junior tennis academies. Cantigny has 6 tennis courts.

The rest of the McCormick Estate includes a greenhouse; 10 acres of gardens; picnic areas; the Robert R. McCormick Museum, which was the mansion of Colonel McCormick; and the First Division Museum, which is a repository for the division's historical papers and artifacts and contains McCormick's extensive military history library. Today it is recognized by the U.S. Army as the official museum of the First Division. Indoor concerts are held in the mansion library, and outdoor concerts are held every Sunday from May through September. The weekly concerts attract more than 300,000 people a year, and over 100,000 people visit the McCormick mansion annually.

Cantigny is now recognized as one of America's top 75 public courses in America by *Golf Digest* magazine. With the McCormick legacy and resources, Cantigny is an example of what can be done in the public interest to create a beautiful and well-managed recreational facility. Be sure to put Cantigny on your travel list.

Course Name: COG HILL
No. 1, No. 2, No. 3,
No. 4/Dubsdread

Course Type: Public
Address: 12294 Archer Avenue at
119th Street
Lemont, IL 60439
Phone: (708) 257–5872
Fax: (708) 257–3665
(Administrative Offices)

GOLF COURSE

Head Professional: Jeff Rimsnider
Course Length/Par (All Tees): No. 1: Back 6294/72, Middle 6006/71, Ladies' Forward 5621/72. No. 2: Back 6295/72, Middle 5978/72, Forward 5755/72. No. 3: Back 6437/72, Middle 6193/72, Forward 5321/71. No. 4/Dubsdread: Back 6997/72, Middle 6366/72, Forward 5874/72

Course Slope/Rating (All Tees): No. 1: Back 117/69.9, Middle 114/68.3, Ladies' Forward 118/71.3. No. 2: Back 120/69.4, Middle 118/68.4, Ladies' Forward 120/72.3. No. 3: Back 117/70.1, Middle 114/69.1, Ladies' Forward 114/69.9. No. 4/Dubsdread: Back 142/75.6, Middle 138/71.8, Ladies' Forward 134/76.7

Course Architects: No. 1: Bert F. Coghill (NA), Dick Wilson and Joe Lee (renovation, 1963). No. 2: Dick Wilson and Joe Lee (renovation, 1963). No. 3: Dick Wilson and Joe Lee (1964). No. 4/Dubsdread: Dick Wilson and Joe Lee (1964), Joe Lee (renovation, 1977)

Golf Facilities: Full Pro Shop X, Snack Bar X, Lounge X, Restaurant X, Locker Room X, Showers X, Club Rental X, Club Repair X, Cart Rental X, Instruction X, Practice Green X, Driving Range X, Practice Bunker X, Club Storage No

Tee-Time Reservation Policy: No. 1, No. 2, No. 3: Up to 6 days in advance. No. 4/Dubsdread: 90 days in advance with credit card guarantee/purchase

Ranger: Yes
Tee-off-Interval Time: No. 1, No. 2, No. 3: 7 and 8 min. No. 4/Dubsdread: 9 and 10 min.
Time to Play 18 Holes: 4½ hrs.

Course Hours/Earliest Tee-off: Sunrise to sunset

Green Fees: No. 1, No. 3: $31 for 18 holes weekends, $27 Mon. to Fri. No. 2: $38 for 18 holes weekends, $35 for 18 holes Mon. to Fri. No. 4/ Dubsdread: $90 for 18 holes with cart. No. 4 fee includes 1/2 cart fee. Lower rates after 3 p.m.

Cart Fees: $26 for 18 holes. Lower rates after 3 p.m.

Pull Carts: $2.50 for 18 holes. $1.50 after 3 p.m.

Credit Cards: Discover, MasterCard, Visa

Season: No. 1, No. 2, No. 3 open year round, weather permitting. No. 4/ Dubsdread: April to Oct. 31

Course Comments: Can walk anytime but must pay $85 fee on No. 4/ Dubsdread. Yardage book available. Caddies available for $14 plus tip for 18 holes per day. Golf Learning Center on site

Golf Packages: None

Discounts: Twilight rate after 3 p.m. on courses 1, 2 and 3. Juniors, parent/child rate, clergy

Places to Stay Nearby: WILLOWBROOK: Holiday Inn (708) 325–6400, (800) HOLIDAY; Budgetel (800) 4–BUDGET; Red Roof Inn (708) 323–8811, (800) 843–7663; Days Inn (708) 325–2900, (800) 329–7466 ; Fairfield Inn (708) 789–6300, (800) 228–2800. DOWNTOWN CHICAGO: See Places to Stay in Chicago on page 297

Local Attractions: CHICAGO: See Local Attractions in Chicago on page 297. Chicago Tourism Council, 163 E. Pearson St., Chicago, IL 60611, (312) 280–5740, (800) ITS–CHGO. Illinois Office of Tourism, 310 S. Michigan Ave., Suite 108, Chicago, IL 60604, (312) 793–2094

Directions: From Chicago (32 mi.): Hwy. 55 south, to Hwy. 83 south, to Hwy. 171 south, course on the right (119th St./Parker Rd.), 6 mi. from the intersection of I–55 and Hwy. 83

Closest Commercial Airport: Chicago O'Hare International (45 min.)

COG HILL

Joe Jemsek and his son, Frank, are the owners of seven eighteen-hole golf courses in the suburban Chicago area—two at St. Andrews in West Chicago, one at Pine Meadow in Mundelein, and four at Cog Hill. The Dubsdread (Cog Hill No. 4), designed by Dick Wilson and Joe Lee, is ranked among the first 25 courses on *Golf Digest*'s America's 75 best public golf courses list. Dubsdread is the home of the Motorola Western Open. It was here that Robert Gamez shot a record 64 during the 1989 USGA Public Links Championship.

Jemsek is a golf legend considered by many to be the Patron Saint of public golf. Now in his late 70s, Jemsek started his career as a caddy for 65 cents a round. At age 17, he turned professional and toured but returned to Chicago to learn golf from the ground up; that is, he mastered all phases of golf-course operations, including the food-service and merchandising end. In 1939, he bought the St. Andrews Golf Club. Then he purchased Cog Hill (1951) and restored Pine Meadow (1985). It is Joe and Frank Jemsek's goal to bring quality public golf to the community.

Joe Jemsek is founder of the National Association of Public Golf Courses; pioneered the first television golf series, "Pars, Birdies and Eagles" (1949); and has won numerous awards, including the Herb Graffis Award from the National Golf Foundation and the Western Golf Association Gold Medal of Appreciation. He was the first PGA member and public-course owner to be elected to the USGA Executive Committee. Jemsek was one of 100 heroes of golf selected by *Golf* magazine in 1989, and he recently received the Junior Development Award of *Golf Digest* magazine for his program for 500 boys and girls, co-sponsored by the Lemont Park District, and for his many junior tournaments.

Dubsdread is the most noteworthy of Cog Hill's four quality courses and plays 6997 yards from the back tees with a slope rating of 142 and PGA rating of 75.6. This rolling layout is populated with many mature trees; has large, moderately fast, undulating bentgrass greens; and has several large sand bunkers protecting the putting surfaces and strategic landing areas on the fairways. The 446-yard par-4 first hole, for example, is a dogleg left with five bunkers guarding the tee-shot landing area at the knee of the dogleg. The approach is to a large, two-tiered green protected by large traps to the left and right front of the green. Another two traps flank the green behind. The number-1-handicap hole on the course is the 575-yard par-5 ninth, which plays straight down a well-treed fairway to a large green guarded by two huge traps that severely narrow the entrance way to the putting surface. The tee-shot landing area is protected by a bunker on the right. The next shot has to avoid a large bunker that cuts into the fairway 50 yards from the green.

The finishing holes at Dubsdread are beautiful and challenging. The 397-yard par-4 sixteenth is a dogleg left with a narrow tee-shot landing area guarded by trees and water on the left and trees and a bunker on the right. The approach shot is to a deep, elevated green protected by three bunkers on the right from 80 yards in and another to the left front. The 401-yard par-4 seventeenth is a dogleg right with a somewhat open tee-shot landing area. The second shot is uphill to a deep green protected in front by two large sand traps straddling the entrance way.

The 448-yard par-4 eighteenth plays to a large green with two traps to the right, water to the left, and the clubhouse beyond. The tee shot must avoid three traps to the right of the landing area and another to the left. The combination of distance, strategically placed fairway bunkers, mature trees, a variety of doglegs, and large, challenging greens well protected by bunkers makes Dubsdread a memorable and difficult test of golf.

The large clubhouse at Cog Hill has a full-service restaurant open from 7:30 a.m. to dusk weekdays, from 5:30 a.m. to dusk weekends; banquet and meeting rooms; locker rooms and showers. A full-service pro shop is located in a separate building. The main clubhouse serves courses No. 1 and No. 3. Another building serves courses No. 2 and No. 4/Dubsdread and has a snack-bar restaurant and a limited line of merchandise. There is a caddy program at Cog Hill and the courses can be walked any time.

There is an excellent golf learning center at Cog Hill, with individual, group instruction and playing lessons available. The practice area includes a grass hitting area, putting greens, target greens, sand traps and a covered lesson area. Video swing analysis is available. Several teaching professionals are on hand to help you with your golf game.

The three other golf courses at Cog Hill are well worth playing. They cover terrain similar to Dubsdread and have comparable design and maintenance quality. The No. 1 course, originally built by Bert F. Coghill and redesigned by Dick Wilson and Joe Lee in 1963, plays 6294 yards from the back tees. Course No. 2 was also remodeled by Wilson and Lee in 1963 and plays 6295 yards from the back tees. The No. 3 course is an original Wilson and Lee design and plays a bit longer, at 6437 yards from the back tees. These courses are a bit easier and less expensive to play than Dubsdread, but they provide a challenging and enjoyable round of golf.

Course Name: HERITAGE BLUFFS PUBLIC GOLF CLUB

Course Type: Public
Address: 24355 W. Bluff Road
                    Channahon, IL 60410
Phone: (815) 467–7888
Fax: (815) 467–3932

GOLF COURSE

Head Professional: Mark Fehrenbacher
Course Length/Par (All Tees): Back 7106/72, Blue 6586/72, White 6002/72, Forward 4967/72
Course Slope/Rating (All Tees): Back 132/73.9, Blue 128/71.3, White 118/68.9, Ladies' White 128/74.1, Forward 104/64.1, Ladies' Forward 112/68.4
Course Architect: Dick Nugent (1993)
Golf Facilities: Full Pro Shop X, Snack Bar X, Lounge X, Restaurant X, Locker Room No, Showers No, Club Rental X, Club Repair X, Cart Rental X,

Instruction X, Practice Green X,
Driving Range X, Practice Bunker X,
Club Storage No

Tee-Time Reservation Policy: Up to 7
days in advance. Credit card guarantee
required

Ranger: Yes

Tee-off-Interval Time: 10 min.

Time to Play 18 Holes: 4½ hrs.

Course Hours/Earliest Tee-off: Sunrise

Green Fees: $31 for 18 holes, $20 for 9
holes Fri., Sat., Sun., holidays, $24 for
18 holes, $12 for 9 holes weekdays.

Credit Cards: MasterCard, Visa

Season: Apr. through Nov., weather permitting. Busiest June through Labor Day

Course Comments: Long but walkable.
Yardage book available

Golf Packages: No

Discounts: Residents

Places to Stay Nearby: JOLIET: Holiday
Inn (815) 729–2000, (800) HOLIDAY.
MORRIS: Holiday Inn (815) 942–6600,
(800) HOLIDAY. NAPIERVILLE: Red
Roof Inn (708) 369–2500, (800) 843–
7663; Travelodge (708) 505–0200, (800)
578–7878. CHICAGO O'HARE INTERNA-
TIONAL: Hyatt Regency O'Hare (708)
696–1234, (800) 233–1234

Local Attractions: See page 297

Directions: From downtown Chicago (42
mi. southwest): Take Hwy. 57 to I–80
west to I–55 to Exit 247 (Bluff Rd.).
Make a right onto Bluff Rd. and proceed 2 blocks to the golf course

Closest Commercial Airport: Chicago
O'Hare International (1 hr. 15 min.)

HERITAGE BLUFFS GOLF CLUB

Heritage Bluffs is a scenic and challenging Dick Nugent–designed public golf club
situated on 166 acres of rolling terrain
graced by oak, pine and wetlands southwest
of Chicago. Brent Wadsworth, owner of
Wadsworth Construction, a noted golf course
construction company, lives in this area, and
his construction superintendent lives near the
golf course. As a result, the combined skills
of Nugent and Wadsworth have given the
town of Channahon one of the finest new
public golf courses in the region.

The first hole at Heritage Bluffs is a 437-
yard Scottish links-style par 4 with a variety
of mounds, moguls and bunkers. The tee shot
is to an area framed by two fairway bunkers
and the approach is to a deep green. The golf
course is bentgrass from tee to green and
weaves through land featuring ridges, bluffs,
and remnants of an old strip mine. The 422-
yard par-4 second hole drops 50 feet to a fairway with out-of-bounds to the left and
wetlands to the right. Heritage Bluffs, at this
point, has served notice that you must be accurate off the tee, especially if you play from
the back tees. Local golfers suggest that the
average player tee it up from the whites, a
distance of 6002 yards, to avoid some of the
nastier obstacles this course can offer. The approach shot on the second hole is to a deep
green framed by bunkers and backed by a
grass hollow.

The greens at Heritage Bluffs come in a
variety of shapes and sizes ranging from
the wide but shallow 26-yard-deep putting
surface on No. 13, a 167-yard par 3, to the
narrow 50-yard-deep green on No. 9, a 557-
yard par 5. The greens are well protected
by moguls, sand bunkers, water hazards,
and grass bunkers that demand positioning
and an ability to hit delicate recovery shots
when approaches stray.

The 402-yard par-4 finishing hole, a
dogleg left, requires a 200-yard drive over
wetlands to a narrow landing area framed
by trees. The approach must then negotiate
an alley of trees and ridges to reach a deep
green protected by a bunker on each side.
The nearby practice area with target greens,
practice bunker, and putting green is rated
among the best in the Chicago area. The
clubhouse is modest, the staff is friendly,
and the fees afford you one of the best
quality golf bargains anywhere.

Course Name: KEMPER LAKES

Course Type: Public
Address: Old McHenry Road
               Long Grove, IL 60049
Phone: (708) 320–3450
Fax: (708) 320–4315

GOLF COURSE

Head Professional: Emil Esposito

Course Length/Par (All Tees): Back 7217/72, Blue 6680/72, White 6265/72, Forward 5638/72

Course Slope/Rating (All Tees): Gold 143/76.2, Blue 141/73.8, White 135/71.7, Ladies' Forward NA/73.5

Course Architects: Ken Killian and Dick Nugent (1979)

Golf Facilities: Full Pro Shop X, Snack Bar X, Lounge X, Restaurant X, Locker Room X, Showers X, Club Rental X, Club Repair X, Cart Rental X, Instruction X, Practice Green X, Driving Range X, Practice Bunker X, Club Storage X

Tee-Time Reservation Policy: From 6 a.m., up to 2 wks. in advance of playing date

Ranger: Yes

Tee-off-Interval Time: 10 min.

Time to Play 18 Holes: 4½ hrs.

Course Hours/Earliest Tee-off: 7 a.m.

Green and Cart Fees: $100 for 18 holes with cart

Credit Cards: MasterCard, Visa

Season: April 1 to mid-Nov., weather permitting

Course Comments: Walking permitted at full golf fee. Yardage book available

Golf Packages: Available through clubhouse manager

Discounts: None

Places to Stay Nearby: LINCOLNSHIRE: Marriott's Lincolnshire Resort (708) 634–0100, (800) 228–9290; Courtyard by Marriott, (708) 634–9555, (800) 321–2211; Hawthorn Suites Hotel (708) 945–9300. NORTHBROOK: Ramada Inn (708) 298–2525, (800) 2RAMADA; Sheraton North Shore Inn (708) 498–6500, (800) 535–9131. ARLINGTON HEIGHTS: Radisson (708) 364–7600, (800) 333–3333. See also Chicago listing on page 297

Local Attractions: Historic Village of Long Grove. LINCOLNSHIRE: Marriott's Lincolnshire Theater. ARLINGTON HEIGHTS: Arlington International Race Course. EVANSTON: Evanston Art Center, Evanston Historical Society, Mitchell Indian Museum, Northlight Theatre, Northwestern University. See also Chicago listing on page 297. Lake County Convention and Visitors Bureau (708) 662–2700, (800) LAKE–NOW

Directions: 8 mi. west of Rte. 294/94 on Rte. 22 west to Old McHenry Rd., north on Old McHenry Rd. (1 mi.)

Closest Commercial Airport: Chicago O'Hare International (45 min.)

KEMPER LAKES

In 1989, when the PGA Championship was played at the 7217-yard par-72 Kemper Lakes layout, it was only the third time a public course hosted the tournament. The other two courses so honored were the Pebble Beach Golf Links in California and the Tanglewood Golf Club in North Carolina. Kemper Lakes is not your average public golf course. Designed by Ken Killian and Dick Nugent, with additional input from Jack Tuthill, former tournament director of the PGA Tour, Kemper Lakes is ranked among the 100 best courses of any kind in America by *Golf Digest*.

Kemper Lakes started to become a reality when the Kemper Group decided to move its operations from Chicago to southwestern Lake County, 40 miles northwest of the Loop. They purchased 540 acres of land largely composed of wetlands and prairie farmland. To maintain the openness and rural ambience of the area, the company decided to construct a golf course with the following objectives:

- Kemper Lakes would be a daily-fee course open to anyone.
- It would be operated as a recreation business, to make a profit.
- *Golf Digest* would recognize the quality and conditioning of Kemper Lakes and rank it among the top 100 U.S. golf facilities within 5 years.
- The design and conditioning of Kemper Lakes would be of such high caliber that a major tournament would select the site for its championship within 10 years.

By 1989, 10 years after the course opened, all of these objectives were met.

The original wetlands have now become 125 acres of lakes. Water comes into play on ten holes at Kemper Lakes. The rolling layout features large, fast, moderately undulating bentgrass greens well guarded by large, deep traps and well-placed water hazards. There are slightly over 60 bunkers on this open layout, and the overwhelming bulk of them are around the greens.

The course starts out at a gradual pace, beginning with two short par 4s, a reasonable par 3, and a short par 5. The 442-yard par-4 fifth is a bit more of a challenge. The tee shot on this slight dogleg right has to avoid pine trees on the right side of the fairway and out of bounds on the left. The approach shot is to a deep, undulating green protected by a huge bunker on the left and two traps to the right. An incoming wind and a pin placement to the right back of the green can make this a nasty hole.

The number-1-handicap hole at Kemper Lakes is the 448-yard par-4 ninth, which plays uphill to a narrow, deep, hourglass-shaped green protected by two bunkers on the left and another on the right. The front of the green slopes left to right, and the back is relatively flat. The tee shot has to negotiate two large fairway bunkers on the left and another on the right. The combination of distance and well-placed bunkers make this a challenging golf hole.

The eleventh hole is a beautiful dogleg-right par 5 that plays 534 yards from the back tees. The tee shot must avoid mature oak trees to the left and right of the landing area. Big hitters are able to reach the large, wide green on the second shot by carrying the pond immediately in front of it. The average golfer will lay up and hit a pitching wedge to the target, which is backed by two large bunkers and framed by trees.

The finishing holes at Kemper Lakes are well known for their beauty and difficulty. The 578-yard par-5 fifteenth is the longest hole on the course and a true three-shot par 5. The driving area is protected by three traps on the right and another on the left. The second shot is slightly uphill to a landing area to the left of a large bunker where the fairway, bordered by trees on the left, turns left toward a deep green guarded by large bunkers left, right and rear.

The 469-yard par-4 sixteenth is the longest par 4 on the course. A lake runs along the right side from tee to green, and the tee-shot landing area is bracketed on the right by this water and on the left by two large bunkers. The approach shot should be from the left side of the fairway to a narrow, deep green protected by water to the right and a large bunker to the left. The green's edge slopes toward the water, so it is not advisable to be short coming in.

The 203-yard par-3 seventeenth is all carry over water to a deep green protected on three sides by a lake and flanked by two deep bunkers to the right. If you bail out to the right, it's no fun hitting from a tricky bunker toward a narrowing, undulating target and the water beyond. Fortunately, there are other tee distances on this hole— 172, 142, and 82 yards. Even so, you still have to cope with the wind and a possible difficult pin placement.

The 433-yard dogleg-left par-4 eighteenth isn't for the faint of heart. The left side of the fairway is bordered by a lake from tee to green, and the tee-shot landing area is protected further by two large bunkers on the right. The tee shot has to be in position to set up a reasonable approach from less than 200 yards to a medium-sized green guarded by a pond on the right, a trap to the rear, another trap to the left and the water further left, which cuts in to narrow the entrance way to the green. This hole will test your nerves and your golf game.

The clubhouse at Kemper Lakes has excellent facilities, including locker rooms, showers, full-service restaurant and bar, banquet and meeting facilities, and a quality pro shop that has traditionally been recognized by *Golf Shop Operations* magazine as one of the best in the country. Practice facilities include an ample driving range, practice bunkers and putting greens. Individual and group instruction are available from the staff of PGA professionals.

This beautifully landscaped facility is replete with fruit trees, elms, oaks, pines and other varieties. And, of course, there is water, water, everywhere. If you want to play a public golf course that maintains championship standards, this is your spot.

The 92nd U.S. Women's Amateur was held here in 1992.

Course Name: PINE MEADOW GOLF CLUB

Course Type: Public
Address: 1 Pine Meadow Lane/
P.O. Box 387
Mundelein, IL 60060
Phone: (708) 566–4653
Fax: (708) 566–9320

GOLF COURSE

Head Professional: Joe Jemsek
Course Length/Par (All Tees): Back 7129/72, Blue 6614/72, White 6161/72, Forward 5412/72
Course Slope/Rating (All Tees): Back 135/74.3, Blue 129/71.7, White 119/69.5, Forward 112/64.5, Ladies' Back 141/79.9, Ladies' Blue 136/78.6, Ladies' White 130/74.7, Ladies' Forward 121/70.3
Course Architects: Joe Lee and Rocky Roquemore (1985)
Golf Facilities: Full Pro Shop X, Snack Bar X, Lounge X, Restaurant No, Locker Room No, Showers No, Club Rental X, Club Repair X, Cart Rental X, Instruction X, Practice Green X, Driving Range X, Practice Bunker X, Club Storage No
Tee-Time Reservation Policy: Anytime in advance, Visa or MasterCard to purchase tee time. Refunds for more than 48-hr. cancellation notice. Rain refunds
Ranger: Yes
Tee-off-Interval Time: 7½ min.
Time to Play 18 Holes: 4 hrs.
Course Hours/Earliest Tee-off: Sunrise to sunset
Green Fees: $56 for 18 holes, $30 for 18 holes twilight rate
Cart Fees: $26 for 18 holes, $18 for 18 holes per person
Pull Carts: $2 for 18 holes
Credit Cards: MasterCard, Visa
Season: 3rd week in March to Thanksgiving
Course Comments: Can walk anytime. Yardage book available. Caddies available. Lighted practice facility/learning center open year round
Golf Packages: None
Discounts: Juniors, clergy, parent/child
Places to Stay Nearby: MUNDELEIN: Super 8—Mundelein (708) 949–8842, (800) 800–8000; Holiday Inn (708) 949–5100, (800) HOLIDAY. LINCOLNSHIRE: Marriott's Lincolnshire Resort (708) 634–0100, (800) 228–9290; Hawthorn Suites Hotel (708) 945–9300. NORTHBROOK: Ramada Inn (708) 298–2525, (800) 2RAMADA; Sheraton North Shore Inn (708) 498–6500, (800) 535–9131. CHICAGO O'HARE AIRPORT AREA: O'Hare Hilton (312) 686–8000, (800) HILTONS; O'Hare Marriott (312) 693–4444, (800) 228–9290. See also Chicago listing on pages297
Local Attractions: Historic Village of Long Grove. LINCOLNSHIRE: Marriott's Lincolnshire Theater. ARLINGTON HEIGHTS: Arlington International Race Course. EVANSTON: Evanston Art Center, Evanston Historical Society, Mitchell Indian Museum, Northlight Theatre, Northwestern University. See also Chicago listing on page 297. Lake County Convention and Visitor Bureau (708) 662–2700, (800) LAKE–NOW
Directions: I–94 to Hwy. 176, west on Hwy. 176 (4 mi.) to Butterfield Rd., north 3/4 mi. on Butterfield to golf course
Closest Commercial Airport: Chicago O'Hare International (45 min.)

PINE MEADOW GOLF CLUB

Pine Meadow Golf Club is one of the excellent Chicago area public golf courses owned by Joe Jemsek and his son Frank. Joe has long been one of the strongest supporters of quality public golf in America. Pine Meadow is a 7129-yard par-72 layout in Mundelein, Illinois, less than 1 hour northwest of Chicago. Mundelein is named for Cardinal Mundelein, an avid golfer who originally had an eighteen-hole layout built on the land, a beautiful arboretum, where Pine Meadow now stands. The Jemseks leased the land from the Chicago Archdiocese and commissioned Joe Lee and Rocky

Roquemore to remodel the old course into an excellent golf course that all golfers could enjoy. By all accounts they succeeded, because Pine Meadow was voted America's best new public course in 1986 by *Golf Digest,* and it has subsequently been ranked among the top 25 within *Golf Digest*'s America's 75 best public golf courses list. Within 1 hour's drive of Pine Meadow are four other public golf courses in the top 75—Kemper Lakes, Cantigny, Forest Preserve National, and the Jemsek-owned Cog Hill No. 4.

One of the first things that strikes you when you step up to the first tee at Pine Meadow are the rolling hills and tree-lined beauty of this former arboretum surrounding St. Mary's of the Lake Seminary. As you wend your way through the 240-acre property you will be struck by the beauty and challenge of each hole covered with bentgrass from tee to green. The putting surfaces are large, fast, undulating, and well guarded by large sand traps. Lakes and ponds come into play on six holes. Each hole is a separate, self-contained, memorable golf experience.

A challenging par 4 on the front nine is the 472-yard third hole, a dogleg left to a deep, two-tiered green guarded by a large bunker to the left and another to the right. The tee shot is to a landing area flanked by a lake and trees on the left and another lake on the right. This hole plays a demanding 442, 418, and 401 yards from the other tee distances. Total yardage at Pine Meadow ranges from 7129 to 5335 yards, enabling most golfers to find a comfortable distance to play from.

There are many memorable holes on the back nine, beginning with the 195-yard par-3 twelfth, which plays to a deep, two-tiered green protected by large bunkers front-left, back-left and right. This hole is beautifully framed by pine and apple trees. The 541-yard par-5 thirteenth has a tee shot to a landing area in front of a water hazard that cuts the fairway. The second shot is over the water and is most likely to a landing area bracketed by two large bunkers and trees to the right and trees and a large bunker to the left. The approach is to a deep, tree-framed, two-tiered

green with large traps to the right and left. Should you land in the rough on any of these holes, the 2-inch deep grass could be a major deterrent. And, of course, the many mature trees at Pine Meadow often always seem to be in your way.

Fourteen is a beautiful, 393-yard par-4 dogleg right. The tee shot must carry a water hazard from an elevated tee to reach the fairway, which begins 210 yards from the back tees. To the left of the fairway, as you approach a deep, two-tiered green, is a series of three large bunkers and trees. To the right is a water hazard all the way from the beginning of the fairway to the right front of the green. The 563-yard par-5 fifteenth is a well-treed dogleg left. The tee shot has to carry part of Lake Schroeder to a landing area guarded by trees. If you are playing from the blue or white tees, you have to carry less water, but three large bunkers to the left, beginning approximately 250 yards from the green, come into play. The second shot is down a tree-lined fairway, then uphill toward a deep, two-tiered green with three large traps on the right beginning 95 yards from the putting surface. To the left and front of the green is a huge trap over 40 yards long, and another large trap is directly to the left of the putting surface. The combination of trees, bunkers, water and elevated green make this a challenging hole.

The finishing hole at Pine Meadow is a 440-yard par-4 dogleg right. The first shot is from an elevated tee to a tree-lined landing area with one large bunker to the right. The approach is to a somewhat small, two-tiered green guarded by a pond, which begins 100 yards from the green on the right. Three traps protect the left, back and right of the green. An accurate and delicate touch on this approach shot is required to reach this green in regulation.

The clubhouse at Pine Meadow is modest, with no locker rooms or showers, but it has a full-service pro shop. There is a snack bar, and bar. Nearby is one of the best practice facilities you will see anywhere. The lighted driving range has five target greens with bunkers, practice bunkers and practice greens. Individual and group instruction is available. There is also a caddy training program here, something you'll rarely see on a public golf course any more. You can walk Pine Meadow anytime.

Course Name: PRAIRIE LANDING GOLF CLUB

Course Type: Public
Address: 2325 Longest Drive
            P.O. Box 256
            West Chicago, IL 60186–0256
Phone: (708) 208–7602
Fax: (708) 208–7630

GOLF COURSE

Head Professional: Renie Calkin
Course Length/Par (All Tees): Back 6862/72, Gold 6346/72, White 5584/72, Ladies' Forward 117/67.1
Course Slope/Rating (All Tees): Back 131/73.8, Gold 126/71.1, White 119/68.7, Forward 114/64.8, Ladies' Forward 119/69.3
Course Architect: Robert Trent Jones, Jr. (1994)
Golf Facilities: Full Pro Shop X, Snack Bar X, Lounge X, Restaurant X, Locker Room X, Showers X, Club Rental X, Club Repair X, Cart Rental X, Instruction X, Practice Green X, Driving Range X, Practice Bunker X, Club Storage No
Tee-Time Reservation Policy: Up to 7 days in advance with credit card guarantee for foursomes. Up to 2 days in advance for less than 4 players
Ranger: Yes
Tee-off-Interval Time: 10 min.
Time to Play 18 Holes: 4½ hrs.
Course Hours/Earliest Tee-off: 6:30 a.m.
Green and Cart Fees: $69 for 18 holes with or without cart
Credit Cards: All major cards
Season: Apr. to mid-Nov. Busiest May through Oct.
Course Comments: Can walk anytime. Yardage book available
Golf Packages: Inquire at pro shop
Discounts: Twilight, replay, junior
Places to Stay Nearby: GENEVA: The Harrington (708) 208–7433. NAPERVILLE: Courtyard by Marriott (708) 505–0200, (800) 321–2211; Wyndham Garden Hotel-Naperville (708) 505–3353, (800) WYNDHAM. WHEATON: BED AND BREAKFAST: The Wheaton Inn (708) 690–2600
Local Attractions: WHEATON: Wheaton College, Cantigny, Robert R. McCormick Museum, DuPage County Historical Museum. Greater Wheaton Chamber of Commerce, 331 W. Wesley, Wheaton, IL 60187 (708) 668–2739. CHICAGO area: See page 297
Directions: From downtown Chicago (35 miles): Take Hwy. 290 west to Hwy. 88 west to Rte. 59 north to Rte. 38 west. Proceed 3 mi. east to Kautz Rd. Turn right on Kautz and proceed 500 yds. to golf course on the right
Closest Commercial Airports: Chicago O'Hare International (1 hr.); Midway Chicago (1 hr.)

PRAIRIE LANDING GOLF CLUB

Prairie Landing is another impressive addition to golf-rich Chicago's treasure trove of quality, publicly accessible golf courses. Designed by Robert Trent Jones, Jr., this treeless, links-style layout is part of the Du Page County Airport and was developed as a catalyst for regional economic development. The year-round clubhouse incorporates the McChesney House, an 1868 landmark building, and offers amenities such as spacious locker rooms, fine dining, meeting and banquet facilities, and a fully stocked pro shop. Adjacent to the clubhouse is a 10-acre full length practice range with 8 target greens, greenside bunkers, two separate huge putting greens and a chipping area. A unique feature of Prairie Landing is its three hole practice course which includes two par-4 holes and a par 3.

The golf course has rolling hills and undulating fairways. It is completely bentgrass from tee to green with 56 acres of wetlands, marshes and streams, variable winds, and fescue rough. Over 130 sand bunkers guard the ample fairways and large, undulating greens. A memorable hole on the front side is the 406-yard par-4 fifth whose fairway is split by water from tee to green. A tee shot to the left fairway must avoid the stream and a huge bunker that can catch 225-yard drives from the back tees. A tee shot to the right fairway is to a landing area guarded by water and a long bunker on the left. The approach is over the stream, wetlands, and a bunker guarding the tightly angled green. The approach from the left side, which requires a more difficult drive, offers a deeper target angle with the stream and bunker to the right.

Prairie Landing provides sizeable landing areas and the opportunity to run the ball up onto the greens. But if you miss, you are likely to be in snarly rough, a bunker or a water hazard. The round concludes with a 569-yard par-5 dogleg left whose tee shot landing area is guarded by bunkers to the left. Two heroic shots—the second over water cutting into the left side of the fairway—are required to have a chance for a birdie or an eagle on this hole. The deep green is guarded by bunkers to its right front and rear. Water is on the left and edges slightly in front of the green. The other tee distances on this great finishing hole are 543, 504, and 459 yards. An infinite variety of shot angles and strategies can be played from any of Prairie Landing's tee distances making it a course you'll want to revisit.

Course Name: RUFFLED FEATHERS GOLF CLUB

Course Type: Semiprivate
Address: 1 Pete Dye Drive
Lemont, IL 60439
Phone: (708) 257–1000
Fax: (708) 257–1067

GOLF COURSE

Head Professional: Terry Lowe
Course Length/Par (All Tees): Back 6878/72, Blue 6369/72, White 5919/72, Gold 5273/72, Forward 4455/72
Course Slope/Rating (All Tees): Back 134/73.1, Blue 127/70.9, White 120/68.7, Gold 110/65.7, Forward 101/62.3, Ladies' White 131/74.1, Ladies' Gold 123/70.7, Ladies' Forward 105/66.1
Course Architects: Pete and P. B. Dye (1991)

Golf Facilities: Full Pro Shop X, Snack Bar X, Lounge X, Restaurant X, Locker Room X, Showers X, Club Rental X, Club Repair X, Cart Rental X, Instruction X, Practice Green X, Driving Range X, Practice Bunker X, Club Storage X
Tee-Time Reservation Policy: Up to 7 days in advance for non-members
Ranger: Yes
Tee-off-Interval Time: 10 min.
Time to Play 18 Holes: 4½ hrs.
Course Hours/Earliest Tee-off: 6 a.m.
Green and Cart Fees: $85 for 18 holes with or without cart
Credit Cards: All major cards
Season: Apr. through Nov. Busiest June through Labor Day
Course Comments: Can walk anytime but must pay full golf fee. Yardage book available
Golf Packages: Group outings. Inquire at pro shop
Discounts: Twilight rates after 4 p.m.
Places to Stay Nearby: See page 297
Local Attractions: See page 297
Directions: From downtown Chicago (1 hr. southwest): Take Rte. 55 south to Rte. 83 south to Rte. 171 south. Exit left (east) on Derby Rd. to golf course
Closest Commercial Airport: Chicago O'Hare International (45 min.)

RUFFLED FEATHERS GOLF CLUB

Ruffled Feathers, home of the Illinois PGA, is a Pete and P. B. Dye–designed course in the rolling hills southwest of Chicago. There are over one hundred sand bunkers on Ruffled Feathers. There are also mounds, swales, grass bunkers, and water hazards that can come into play on seventeen holes. The course, with five tee distances, offers a variety of shot angles and strategies that will challenge any golfer. As with all Dye courses, you might be chagrined, but you'll never be bored.

The par 3s at Ruffled Feathers are scenic, difficult, and memorable. The 193-yard third plays over water along the right edge to a deep, narrow green that slopes severely to the right toward the water. A tee shot that misses to the left demands a delicate bunker or chip shot that can easily slide off the green into the hazard. The back nine features a peninsula par 3, the tenth, that can be played from distances of 68 to 155 yards. There is no margin for error on this target hole.

Water lines the entire left side of the 442-yard par-4 finishing hole which plays straight to a huge green guarded by two bunkers to its right, another to its rear, and water to its left. The tee shot landing area is bracketed by water and two huge bunkers. A drive pulled to the left is gone and a tee shot pushed right can easily set the stage for a water-bound flier out of a bunker or the rough. By this time it is evident that you have played a shotmaker's course that requires strategic planning and careful execution.

There are numerous doglegs on this layout and bewildering green configurations such as the 19-yard wide and 64-yard deep target on the 578-yard, par-5 fourth or the small, oval green on the 328-yard par-4 fourteenth. The former has two bunkers to its left and the latter has two bunkers to its right, another to its front left, and is almost surrounded by water.

A short walk from the 18th green is the clubhouse restaurant which provides a panoramic view of the oaks, pines, and wetlands of this scenic parkland golf course. Or you can regroup at the ample practice range and orchestrate your next attack on one of the Dye family's more recent challenges.

Places to Stay in Chicago

WILLOWBROOK: Holiday Inn (708) 325–6400, (800) HOLIDAY; Budgetel (800) 4–BUDGET; Red Roof Inn (708) 323–8811, (800) 843–7663; Days Inn Bull Ridge (708) 325–2900, (800) 329–7466; Fairfield Inn (708) 789–6300, (800) 228–2800. CHICAGO DOWNTOWN: Chicago Hilton and Towers (312) 922–4400, (800) HILTONS; Chicago Marriott (312) 836–0100, (800) 228–9290; Drake (312) 787–2200, (800) 55DRAKE; Forum Hotel (312) 944–0055; Four Seasons Hotel (312) 288–8800, (800) 332–3442; McCormick Center Hotel (312) 791–1900, (800) 621–6909; Ritz Carlton (312) 787–3580, (800) 621–6906; Westin Hotel (312) 943–7200, (800) 879–5444; Sutton Place Hotel (312) 266–2100, (800) 543–4300; Lenox House Suites (312) 337–1000, (800) 44–LENOX; The Whitehall Hotel (312) 944–6300, (800) 948–4255; Nikko Chicago (312) 744–1900, (800) NIKKOUS; Stouffer Renaissance Chicago (312) 372–7200, (800) HOTELS–1; Swissotel (312) 565–0565, (800) 63SWISS

Local Attractions in Chicago

Adler Planetarium, Art Institute of Chicago, Board of Trade, Brookfield Zoo, Chicago Botanic Garden, Chicago Children's Museum, Chicago Historical Society, Field Museum of Natural History, Grant Park, multimedia "Here's Chicago" presentation (Water Tower Pumping Station), John G. Shedd Aquarium, Lincoln Park, Lincoln Park Zoo, Merchandise Mart, Museum of Broadcast Communications, Museum of Science and Industry, University of Chicago, Sears Tower, University of Illinois at Chicago, restaurants, theater, concerts, shopping; spectator sports including the Chicago Bears, Cubs, Bulls, Blackhawks, White Sox; music clubs featuring jazz and blues; recreation including boating, fishing, other activities; Arlington International Race Course (horse racing). Chicago Tourism Council, 163 E. Pearson St., Chicago, IL 60611, (312) 280–5740. Illinois Office of Tourism, 310 S. Michigan Ave., Ste. 108, Chicago, IL 60604, (312) 793–2094

Recommended Golf Courses in Illinois

Within 1 1/2 Hours of Chicago:

Balmoral Woods Country Club, Crete, (708) 672–7448, Public, 18/6683/72

Big Run Golf Club, Lockport, (815) 838–1057 or (312) 972–1652, Public, 18/6654/72

Blackberry Oaks Golf Course, Bristol, (708) 553–7170, Public, 18/6258/72

Bonnie Brook Golf Club, Waukegan, (708) 360–4730, Public, 18/6701/72

Bon Vivant Country Club, Bourbonnais, (815) 935–0403, (800) 248–7775, Public, 18/7498/72

Carillon Golf Club, Plainfield, (815) 886–2132, Public, 18/6607/72

Cinder Ridge Golf Links, Wilmington, (815) 476–4000, Public, 18/6803/72

George W. Dunne National Golf Course, Oak Forest, (708) 535–3377, Public, 18/7170/72

Edgebrook Country Club, Sandwich, (815) 786–3058, Semiprivate, 18/6100/72

Fox Bend Golf Course, Oswego, (708) 554–3939, Public, 18/6800/72

Glenwoodie Country Club, Glenwood, (708) 758–1212, Public, 18/6715/72

Golf Club of Illinois, Algonquin, (708) 658–4400, Public, 18/7011/71

Klein Creek Golf Club, Winfield, (708) 690–0101, Public, 18/6673/72

Lakewood Golf Club, Lakewood, (815) 477–0055, Public, 18/6891/72

Marengo Ridge Golf Club, Marengo, (815) 923–2332, Public, 18/6636/72

The Meadows Club of Blue Island, Blue Island, (708) 385–1994, Public, 18/6550/71

Midlane Country Club, Wadsworth, (708) 244–1990, Public, 18/7073/72

Naperbrook Golf Course, Plainfield, (708) 378–4215, Public,18/6755/72

The Oak Club, Genoa, (815) 784–5678, Public, 18/7032/72

The Odyssey Golf Course, Tinley Park, (708) 429–7400, Public, 18/7095/72

Old Orchard Country Club, Mt. Prospect, (708) 255–2025, Public, 18/6022/70

Orchard Valley Golf Club, Aurora, (708) 907–0500, Public, 18/6745/72

Pheasant Run Resort, St. Charles, (708) 584–6300, Resort, 18/6315/71

Plum Tree National Golf Club, Harvard, (815) 945–7474, (800) 851–3578, Public, 18/6448/72

Schaumberg, (708) 885–9000, Public, 18/6552/71

Seven Bridges Golf Club, Woodridge, (708) 964–GOLF, Public, 18/7118/72

Springbrook Golf Course, Naperville, (708) 420–4215, Public, 18/6896/72

Steeplechase Golf Club, Mundelein, (708) 949–8900, Public, 18/6827/72

Timber Trails Country Club, LaGrange, (708) 246–0275, Public, 18/6197/71

Village Links of Glen Ellyn, (708) 469–8180, Public, 18/6933/72

Wedgewood Golf Course, Joliet, (815) 741–7270, 18/6519/72

Northern Illinois (West Of Chicago)

Course Name: **EAGLE RIDGE**
North, South, East, General Courses

Course Type: Resort
Resort: Eagle Ridge Inn and Resort
Address: U.S. Route 20/Box 777
              Galena, IL 61036
Phone: (815) 777–2500 (Golf Course)
              (815) 777–2444,
              (800) 892–2269 (Resort)
Fax: (815) 777–0445 (Resort),
              (815) 777–4522

GOLF COURSE

Director of Golf: John J. Schlaman
Course Length/Par (All Tees): North: Back 6836/72, Middle 6386/72, Ladies' Forward 5578/72. South: Back 6762/72, Middle 6361/72, Ladies' Forward 5609/72. General: Back 7000/72, Middle 6600/72, Forward 5800/72. East: Back 2648/34, Middle 2461/34, Forward 2255/34
Course Slope/Rating (All Tees): North: Back 134/73.4, Middle 129/70.9, Ladies' Forward 127/72.3. South: Back 133/72.9, Middle 128/71.1, Ladies' Forward 128/72.4. General: Back NA/NA, Middle NA/NA, Forward NA/NA. East: Back NA/33.1, Middle NA/32.3, Forward NA/33.2
Course Architect: North: Roger B. Packard (1977). South: Roger B. Packard (1984). General: Roger B. Packard and Andy

North (1996). East: Roger B. Packard (1991)

Golf Facilities: Full Pro Shop X, Snack Bar X, Lounge X, Restaurant X, Locker Room X, Showers X, Club Rental X, Club Repair Minor, Cart Rental X, Instruction X, Practice Green X, Driving Range X, Practice Bunker X, Club Storage X

Tee-Time Reservation Policy: All tee times must be reserved in advance. Guests: From time of reservation. Public: 1 wk. in advance from 8 a.m.

Ranger: Yes

Tee-off-Interval Time: 9 min.

Time to Play 18 Holes: 4½ hrs.

Course Hours/Earliest Tee-off: 8 a.m. to dark

Green Fees: North, South: $77 for 18 holes. General: NA. Inquire at pro shop. East: $32 for 9 holes

Cart Fees: North, South: $28 for 18 holes. General: Inquire at pro shop. East: $7.50 for 9 holes

Credit Cards: All major cards

Season: April 1 to Dec. 1

Comments: Can walk after 4 p.m.

Golf Packages: Available through resort

Discounts: Seasonal. Twilight after 3 p.m.

Places to Stay Nearby: Best Western Quiet House Suites (815) 777–257, (800) 343–6562; Desoto House Hotel (815) 777–0090, (800) 528–1234; Grant Hills Motel (815) 777–2116; Palace Motel (815) 777–2043

Local Attractions: Belvedere Mansion and Gardens, Grant Hills Antique Auto Museum, Ulysses S. Grant Home State Historic Site, Galena/Jo Daviess County History Museum, art galleries, antiquing, museums, mansions, riverboat gambling, arts festivals, fairs, concerts, walking tours of historic Galena. Galena/Jo Daviess County Convention and Visitors Bureau (800) 747–9377

Directions: From Chicago (150 mi.): I–90 to Rte. 20, Rte. 20 west to Galena territory, follow signs to inn

Closest Commercial Airports: Municipal, Dubuque, IA (45 min.); Chicago O'Hare International (3 hrs.); General Mitchell International, Milwaukee, WI (3½ hrs.)

RESORT

Date Built: 1979

No. of Rooms: 430, including 80 inn rooms, 320 rooms in resort rental homes

Meeting Rooms: 16. Capacity of Largest: 400 persons. Meeting Space: 10,000 sq. ft.

Room Price Range: $125 to $450 per person. Golf and other packages available

Lounge: Woodlands

Restaurants: Dining Room, Ranch at the Ridge and Scoops Ice Cream Parlour. General Store on site

Entertainment: Music in Woodlands Lounge and The Ranch at the Ridge

Credit Cards: All major cards

General Amenities: Youth programs, babysitting, meeting and conference facilities with audiovisual and food sevices

Recreational Amenities: Beach, boating, fishing, fitness center, indoor golf, bicycling, horseback riding, jogging track, indoor pool, outdoor pool, sauna, windsurfing, cross-country skiing, outdoor tennis, Jacuzzi, nature trails

Reservation and Cancellation Policy: Credit card guarantee or deposit required to hold reservation. 72-hr. cancellation notice for inn, 7-day cancellation notice for homes

Comments and Restrictions: No pets. Taxes additional to base rates

EAGLE RIDGE

Approximately 150 miles northwest of Chicago lie 6800 acres of glacier-carved, rolling valleys, ridges and hills that include the Eagle Ridge Inn and Resort. Developed in the 1970s from farmland purchased by the Branninger Organization, Eagle Ridge is a winner of *Golf Digest*'s coveted Silver Medal Award as one of the best golf resorts in the United States.

There are 4 clubhouses at Eagle Ridge and 63 holes of golf. The North Course, designed by Roger B. Packard and opened in 1977, is a 6836-yard layout from the back tees. Water runs through the rolling hills and flatlands of the course, coming into play on seven holes on the back nine.

The number-1-handicap par-4 third hole plays 446 yards from the back tees. Relatively straight, the first shot is hit from a slightly elevated tee to a narrow fairway with trees to the left and a long fairway bunker to the right, approximately 240 yards away. The ideal tee shot is to the left center, with the second shot coming onto a large, 45-yard-deep, elongated green that has a shelf in the back and is protected by a bunker on the right.

The number-2-handicap par-4 seventeenth hole is a slight dogleg right playing 439 yards from the back tees. Trees are strategically placed on the left and right of the fairway, and two fairway bunkers begin approximately 210 yards from the tee. The second shot is onto a deep green angled slightly right and sloping forward. An oak tree on the right can come into play on this approach shot. The golfer should keep this approach below the hole on this tricky green.

One of the more spectacular holes at Eagle Ridge North Course is the par-3 eighth hole, which plays over water on the left from an 80-foot high elevated tee to a small, two-tiered green. It is the only hole that crosses any part of 220-acre Lake Galena, the centerpiece of the resort complex.

The 6762-yard South Course is also an excellent Packard layout opened in 1984.

This course was named among America's Best New Resort Courses of the Year by *Golf Digest* in 1985. It has since been rated among the best golf courses in Illinois by *Golf Digest* and *GolfWeek*. And there is a 2648-yard 9-hole course, also designed by Packard.

The addition of the General Course in 1996 puts Eagle Ridge in the top echelon of midwest golf facilities. The General, named for local hero Ulysses S. Grant, has pronounced elevation changes, rock outcroppings, water hazards featuring many creeks, treelined fairways and bentgrass tees, fairways and greens. A memorable hole on this course is likely to be the 405-yard par-4 fourteenth whose tee shot plays from an elevated tee with dramatic views of Illinois, Iowa and Wisconsin. Behind the tee are limestone outcroppings and 250 feet below, somewhere in the distance, is the green.

Prior to the opening of the General Course, Eagle Ridge was rated a *Golf* magazine Silver Medal Winner as one of the top golf resorts in America. Accommodations are available at the Eagle Ridge Inn, or you can stay at one of the 333 fully equipped 1- to 4-bedroom resort homes. A variety of activities including tennis, fishing, horseback riding, sailing and swimming is offered. Also available are a full fitness center and award-winning conference facilities, which can accommodate groups of up to 400 persons.

Golf packages and other specials are available at Eagle Ridge. The on site Golf Academy offers alumni, two-day, playing lesson, three-day, and women's programs. Individual lessons are also available from the staff of professionals. Restaurants include the Dining Room, which has spectacular views of Lake Galena, and The Ranch at the Ridge, a more casual spot.

Southern

Course Name: **SPENCER T. OLIN COMMUNITY GOLF COURSE**

Course Type: Public
Address: 4701 College Avenue
                and Illinois Highway 140
                Alton, IL 62002
Phone: (618) 465–3111
                (314) 355–8128 (in MO)
Fax: (618) 465–3119

GOLF COURSE

Director of Golf: Rob Dillinger
Course Length/Par (All Tees): Back 6941/72, Middle 6414/72, Forward 5049/72
Course Slope/Rating (All Tees): Back 132/72.8, Middle 126/70.7, Ladies' Forward 117/68.5
Course Architect: Arnold Palmer (1989)
Golf Facilities: Full Pro Shop X, Snack Bar X, Lounge X, Restaurant X, Locker Room No, Showers No, Club Rental X, Club Repair X, Cart Rental X, Instruction X, Practice Green X,

Driving Range X, Practice Bunker X, Club Storage No

Tee-Time Reservation Policy: Up to 1 wk. in advance. Reservations restricted only to foursomes prior to 12 noon (April to Oct.) on Sat., Sun., holidays

Ranger: Yes

Tee-off-Interval Time: 9 min.

Time to Play 18 Holes: 4 hrs., 20 min.

Course Hours/Earliest Tee-off: 6:30 a.m.

Green and Cart Fees: $50 for 18 holes with cart Sat., Sun., holidays, $42 Fri., $38 Mon.-Thurs.

Credit Cards: American Express, Master-Card, Visa

Season: Year round, weather permitting

Course Comments: Cart mandatory

Golf Packages: Inquire at pro shop

Discounts: Seasonal. Residents.

Places to Stay Nearby: ALTON: Holiday Inn, Alton Parkway (618) 462–1220, (800) HOLIDAY; Ramada Inn (618) 463–0800, (800) 272–6232; Super 8 Motel (618) 465–8885, (800) 800–8000. ST. LOUIS: Courtyard by Marriott Downtown (314) 241–9111, (800) 321–2211; Doubletree Hotel and Conference Center (314) 532–5000, (800) 221–8733; Drury Inn at Union Station (314) 231–3900, (800) 325–8300; Holiday Inn Airport West (314) 291–5100, (800) HOLIDAY; Hyatt Regency—St. Louis (314) 231–1234, (800) 233–1234; St. Louis Airport Marriott (314) 423–9700, (800) 228–9290; Ritz Carlton St. Louis (314) 863–6300, (800) 241–3333. BED AND BREAKFAST: Geandough House (314) 771–5447

Local Attractions: Antique district, Confederate Monument, Lincoln/Douglas Square, Museum of History and Art. ST. LOUIS: St. Louis Zoological Park, Missouri Botanical Garden, St. Louis Science Center, St. Louis Union Station, Center of Contemporary Arts, Washington University, St. Louis Art Museum, St. Louis Symphony, theater, art galleries, concerts, National Museum of Transport, Antique Toy Museum, History Museum of the Missouri Historical Society, St. Louis Cathedral, August A. Busch Memorial Wildlife area; professional baseball, hockey, and soccer; Anheuser–Busch Brewery, river boat cruises, Goldenrod Showboat, National Bowling Hall of Fame, Gateway Arch. St. Louis Convention and Visitors Commission (314) 421–1023, (800) 247–9791. Greater Alton/Twin Rivers Convention and Visitors Bureau (618) 465–6676, (800) 258–6645

Directions: From St. Louis: From Rte. 270, east over Chain of Rocks Bridge, Illinois 3 north (9 mi.), right onto Adams Pkwy., first right exit, Illinois 140 (14 mi.), to Gordon F. Moore Park, follow signs to golf course

Closest Commercial Airport: Lambert–St. Louis International, MO (20 min.)

SPENCER T. OLIN COMMUNITY GOLF COURSE

The Spencer T. Olin course is an Arnold Palmer–designed 6941-yard par-72 layout located 35 minutes from downtown St. Louis on rolling, well-treed terrain with well-placed bunkers and water in the form of streams and ponds coming into play on half the holes. All the greens are very large, moderately fast and undulating. The course was designed to challenge the low-handicap golfer but not to create unnecessary nightmares for the average player. A wide variety of plants and trees is found on the well-groomed course, including sycamore, pin oak, cedar, birch, blue spruce and others.

The 406-yard par-4 eighth hole is considered by many to be one of the best holes on the course. The number-1-handicap hole, it is a dogleg left that plays downwind around a large pond guarding the left fairway from halfway to the hole all the way into the green. A ravine guards the right side of the fairway, so you have to get your tee shot to the landing area to have a second shot onto the green, which is backed by two traps. The wind is usually behind the golfer, but if there is no wind it is difficult to reach the green in regulation.

The fourth hole is another challenging par 4. This dogleg right plays 425 yards, generally into the wind. The first shot is to a plateaued fairway, and the second shot is to a relatively narrow but long cathedral green. This green slopes from back to front toward the water immediately in front of it. Distance, accuracy and club selection on the second shot are keys to this hole. The large green can easily require three putts.

The number-2-handicap hole is the 439-yard twelfth, a dogleg left whose tee shot has to negotiate two fairway bunkers on the left and right to reach a broad landing area. The second shot is over a large pond that edges into the fairway on the left approximately 50 yards from the green. The putting surface is long but angled left to right, so the target area is somewhat shallow. Five traps guard the green in the back. Probably a tougher par 4 is the 472-yard sixteenth, which plays over a ravine to a long dogleg left requiring two long, accurate shots to a green that has no bunkers but is well banked. The finishing hole is a 503-yard par 5 that is relatively straight. This hole embodies Palmer's philosophy that good golf courses have good par 5s. On this one, you can try to reach the green in two, but fairway bunkers to the left and right can penalize you, and eight bunkers protect the green left front and back. As with all the holes on this course, it is possible to run the ball onto the green by hitting the fairway first.

The birth of the Spencer T. Olin Community Golf Course was in 1955, when Spencer T. Olin, an amateur golfer and successful businessman from Walton, Illinois, was paired with first-year touring professional Arnold Palmer for the Pro–Am tournament at the Greenbrier, in West Virginia. The two won the event and formed a friendship that many years later would be the foundation for developing Alton's first and only Palmer-designed golf course. The city of Alton provided the land, the Spencer T. Olin Foundation contributed $5.5 million for development and construction, and the Arnold Palmer Golf Management Company has a 20-year lease to manage the course, which provides country-club-quality facilities and playing conditions to the public golfer.

The 1996 Ladies National Public Links Championship was played at the Spencer T. Olin course.

Recommended Golf Courses in Southern Illinois

Belk Park Golf Club, Wood River, (618) 251–3115, Public, 18/6761/72

Fox Creek Golf Club, Edwardsville, (618) 692–9400, (800) 692–9401, Public, 18/7027/72

The Orchards Golf Club, Belleville, (618) 233–8921, (800) 452–0358, Public, 18/6405/71

Rend Lake Golf Course, Benton, (618) 6291962353, Public, Three nines: 18/6861/72, 18/6812/72, 18/6835/72

Springfield Area

Course Name: EAGLE CREEK

Course Type: Resort
Resort: Inn at Eagle Creek Resort and Conference Center
Address: Eagle Creek State Park Road Findlay, IL 62534
Phone: (217) 756–3456 (Golf Course) (800) 876–3245 (Resort)
Fax: (217) 756–3411 (Resort)

GOLF COURSE

Director of Golf: Jerry Groark
Head Professional: Steven Nickerson
Course Length/Par (All Tees): Back 6908/72, Blue 6559/72, White 5901/72, Forward 4978/72
Course Slope/Rating (All Tees): Back 132/73.5, Blue 127/71.6, White 121/68.6, Ladies' Forward 115/69.1
Course Architect: Ken Killian (1990)
Golf Facilities: Full Pro Shop X, Snack Bar X, Lounge X, Restaurant X, Locker Room X, Showers X, Club Rental X, Club Repair Minor, Cart Rental X, Instruction X, Practice Green X, Driving Range X, Practice Bunker X, Club Storage X
Tee-Time Reservation Policy: Guests on golf packages: At time of resort reservation. Public/guests not on golf packages:

Anytime with credit card guarantee of tee time

Ranger: Yes

Tee-off-Interval Time: 8 min.

Time to Play 18 Holes: 5 hrs.

Course Hours/Earliest Tee-off: 7 a.m.

Green and Cart Fees: Peak season May-Oct. $45 for 18 holes with cart Fri., Sat., Sun., holidays; $40 for 18 holes with cart Mon. to Thurs.

Credit Cards: All major cards

Season: Year round. Busiest season May to Aug.

Course Comments: Carts mandatory

Golf Packages: Available through resort

Discounts: Seasonal rates. Low season Nov.-Apr.

Places to Stay Nearby: Shelby Historic House and Inn (217) 774–3991, (800) 342–9978; Lithia Resort (217) 774–2882; Spillway Motel (217) 774–9591. BED AND BREAKFAST: Williams' House Bed and Breakfast (217) 774–2807

Local Attractions: SHELBYVILLE AREA: Eagle Creek State Park, camping, boating, hiking, tennis, Winter Festival of Lights and other seasonal events, Amish settlements in Arcola and Arthur. SPRINGFIELD: Oliver P. Parks Telephone Museum, Illinois State Historical Library, Illinois State Museum, Knight's Action Park, Lincoln Depot, Lincoln's family pew at First Presbyterian Church, Lincoln home, Lincoln Memorial Garden and Nature Center, Lincoln tomb, old state capital. DECATUR: Governor Oglesby Mansion, Scovill Zoo, Birks Museum, Kirkland Fine Arts Center, Lincoln log-cabin, courthouse, Lincoln Trail Homestead State Park, Macon County Historical Museum complex, James Millikin homestead, Rock Spring Center for Environmental Discovery. Lake Shelbyville Visitors Association (217) 774–2244. Springfield Convention and Visitors Bureau (217) 789–2360, (800) 545–7300. Decatur Area Convention and Visitors Bureau (217) 423–7000, (800) 252–3376

Directions: From Decatur (30 min.): Rte. 121 southeast to Rte. 128 south, 11 mi., left to Findlay, cross railroad tracks, signs to Eagle Creek Resort. From Springfield (70 mi.): Rte. 29 to Taylorville, take Assumption Black Top Rd., east to Findlay across railroad tracks, follow signs south to Eagle Creek Resort

Closest Commercial Airports: Mattoon (30 min.); Decatur (30 min.); Greater Peoria (1½ hrs.); Terre Haute, IN (1½ hrs.); Lambert–St. Louis International, MO (2 hrs.); Chicago O'Hare International (4½ hrs.)

RESORT

Date Built: 1989

No. of Rooms: 138 guest rooms, 10 additional executive suites with fireplaces

Meeting Rooms: 7. Capacity of Largest: 400 persons banquet style. Meeting Space: 6788 sq. ft.

Room Price Range: From $100 in season (April to Oct.). Golf, Little Theatre, honeymoon, holiday and other packages available year round

Lounge: Rumors

Restaurants: Wild Flowers Dining Room, Rumors

Entertainment: Live music Fri., Sat. April through Oct.

Credit Cards: All major cards

General Amenities: Supervised children's programs from ages 2 to teens, local tours; meeting and conference facilities in classroom, board-room, theater, banquet and reception configurations with audiovisual and food services; separate conference retreat building with kitchen, bath, conference room, 10 bedrooms

Recreational Amenities: Marina and boat launch, 4 tennis courts, hiking trails, indoor swimming pool, private sand beach, boating; exercise room with exercise bicycles, equipment, sauna, whirlpool; archery, bicycling, cross-country skiing, fishing, hunting, basketball, volleyball, horseshoes, badminton

Reservation and Cancellation Policy: 1 night's deposit and tax required to hold reservation. Must cancel up to 24 hrs. in advance to avoid penalties

Comments and Restrictions: No pets allowed. Taxes additional to base rates

EAGLE CREEK

Eagle Creek is a Ken Killian–designed 6908-yard par-72 layout set on the 400-acre Eagle Creek Resort and Conference Center site in Eagle Creek State Park, which is on the shore of Lake Shelbyville in Findlay, Illinois. Lake Shelbyville is an 11,100-acre, 20-mile-long creation of the Army Corps of Engineers, which dammed the Kaskaskia River in 1970 to create this recreational wonder. The Lake Shelbyville area supposedly is now among the top 3 tourist attractions in Illinois, behind Chicago's Lincoln Park Zoo and Museum of Science and Industry.

Killian designed Kemper Lakes, Forest Preserve National and many other excellent golf courses in Illinois and elsewhere. Eagle Creek rated an honorable mention in the resort category for best new courses of 1990 by *Golf Digest*. The course, which is bentgrass from tee to green, features a variety of doglegs, large greens, bunkers, and tree-lined fairways. Ravines, valleys and fingers of water from the adjacent lake add to the challenge and beauty of Eagle Creek. This is a shot-maker's golf course, requiring accuracy, careful club selection and course management. If you miss a landing area, it is highly possible that you will be in the woods, a bunker, the water or a ravine, or you will have an uneven lie of some sort.

The four sets of tees at Eagle Creek enable you to choose a distance suitable to your game. The shortest distance is 4978 yards. Originally, much of the underbrush bordering the fairways was kept in place, but many lost balls and long rounds later it was trimmed back a bit so you can finish in less than 5 hours. After starting at 20,500 rounds in its first full season, the course has become better known and is getting busier. Approximately 25 percent of play comes from the local area, the rest being from resort guests and vacationers.

The back nine at Eagle Creek is somewhat tighter than the front nine. This includes the 573-yard par-5 twelfth, which is the signature hole on the golf course. The first two shots are down a narrow, tree-lined fairway to a plateau that overlooks a large green protected front and rear by bunkers. Beyond is a beautiful view of Lake Shelbyville. The greens at Eagle Creek tend to be moderately fast and very undulating.

Another excellent hole on the back nine is the 395-yard par-4 fourteenth, a dogleg left to a deep green framed by two large traps, one to the left and another to the right. Farther left is a water hazard. The tee shot is to a landing area to the right of a water hazard. The approach is to the right-to-left and forward-sloping green. One of the pleasures of playing Eagle Creek is the isolation of each hole from all others as you work your way over rolling fairways framed by ash, birch, maple, and other varieties of trees.

A challenging and picturesque par 3 at Eagle Creek is the 170-yard eighth, which is all carry from a beautiful tree-framed tee over a ravine to an ample green with bunkers protecting it in front. It is not wise to be long on this hole because you'll be chipping back toward the slick, downward-sloping putting surface.

The finishing hole is a 535-yard double-dogleg par 5. The tee shot should be hit just over a rise before the well-treed landing area. The second shot is to another landing area bordered by trees to the right and a water-filled ravine to the left. The approach is to a narrow, deep, elevated green well protected by bunkers to the right and left.

The clubhouse at Eagle Creek has a pro shop, locker rooms and showers, restaurant and bar. Practice facilities include a driving range, practice bunker, chipping green and putting green. Individual and group instruction is available from the professionals on staff.

Accommodations at Eagle Creek include 138 guest rooms, featuring 10 additional executive suites with fireplaces; and a separate building, the Eagle's Nest Conference Retreat, oriented toward small meetings and conferences. Eagle Creek has won *Meetings and Conventions* magazine's Gold Tee Award for having outstanding golf and conference facilities. The Inn at Eagle Creek can handle meetings for groups of up to 600 persons in theater, banquet, reception, and classroom settings.

The hotel has two restaurants and a separate cocktail lounge. The decor features paintings, quilts and furnishings crafted in local Amish communities.

Recreational facilities include tennis courts, hiking trails, fishing, boating, an exercise room, sauna, whirlpool, bicycling, and a variety of other activities. The facilities in Eagle Creek Park are available, and tours can be made to Amish communities nearby, and in Decatur and Springfield, the home of many Abraham Lincoln historic sites. Golf packages are available through the Inn at Eagle Creek. The combination of quality golf and a beautiful recreational setting makes a visit here worthwhile.

Course Name: THE RAIL GOLF COURSE

Course Type: Public
Address: Route 124 North/R.R. 5
Springfield, IL 62707
Phone: (217) 525–0365
Fax: (217) 525–6510

GOLF COURSE

Head Professional: Vince Alfonso, Jr.
Course Length/Par (All Tees): Back 6583/72, White 5975/72, Forward 5406/72
Course Slope/Rating (All Tees): Back 120/71.1, White 114/68.7, Ladies' Forward 116/70.6
Course Architect: Robert Trent Jones, Sr. (9, 1970, 9, 1975)
Golf Facilities: Full Pro Shop X, Snack Bar X, Lounge X, Restaurant X, Locker Room X, Showers X, Club Rental X, Club Repair X, Cart Rental X, Instruction X, Practice Green X, Driving Range X, Practice Bunker X, Club Storage No
Tee-Time Reservation Policy: Up to 5 days in advance
Ranger: Yes
Tee-off-Interval Time: 8 min.
Time to Play 18 Holes: 4 hrs. 20 min.
Course Hours/Earliest Tee-off: Sunrise
Green Fees: $28 for 18 holes, $14 for 9 holes
Cart Fees: $24 for 18 holes, $12 for 9 holes per cart

Credit Cards: All major cards
Season: Mar. to mid-Dec. Busiest June through Labor Day
Course Comments: Can walk anytime. Yardage book available
Golf Packages: No
Discounts: Junior, senior, value added modified twilight program
Places to Stay Nearby: Holiday Inn East (217) 529–7171, (800) HOLIDAY; Red Roof Inn (217) 759–4302, (800) THE-ROOF; Renaissance Springfield (217) 544–8800, (800) 228–9898; Springfield Hilton (217) 789–1530, (800) 445–8667
Local Attractions: Lincoln Home, Lincoln–Herndon law offices, Old State Capitol, Lincoln tomb, Lincoln Depot, Executive Mansion, Dana–Thomas House, State Museum, State Capitol, Lincoln's New Salem, Oliver Parks Telephone Museum, Washington Park Botanical Gardens, Edwards Place, Lawrence Memorial Library, Grand Army of the Public Memorial Museum, Henson Robinson Zoo, Adams Wildlife Sanctuary, Camp Butler National Cemetery, Lincoln Memorial Gardens, Vachel Lindsay Home, seasonal events and festivals. Springfield Convention and Visitors Bureau, 109 N. 7th St., Springfield, IL 62701 (217) 789–2360, (800) 545–7300
Directions: From Springfield (20 min.): Take I–55 north to Sherman Exit and proceed south on Rte. 124 to the golf course on the right
Closest Commercial Airports: Capitol City Springfield (5 min.); Lambert–St. Louis International (1½ hrs.)

THE RAIL GOLF COURSE

When you discuss The Rail Golf Course with Vince Alfonso, Jr., its Head Professional and general manager, you can't help but be favorably influenced by his enthusiasm for golf. Vince believes that golf should be fun. He claims, for example, that his clubhouse's "Birdie" mixed fruit drink is the best drink east of the Pecos. He uses golf guides, not rangers, to monitor speed of play. And on hot days he gives away iced tea and other drinks to customers navigating his mature, Robert Trent Jones, Sr. layout, a stop on the LPGA Tour.

The Rail is a rolling, open layout with very large, undulating bentgrass greens. Sizeable bunkers guard the putting surfaces and landing areas. Water can come into play on six of the holes. The most difficult hole on the course is the 165-yard par-3 sixteenth which plays to a shallow, two-tiered forward sloping green with a lake in front and to the right of the putting surface. Bunkers also protect this hole, and variable winds can add to its difficulty.

The Rail practice area features target pins with yardages clearly marked, practice bunkers, and a practice green. This course has been rated among the most "woman friendly" courses by *Golf for Women* magazine and it is a favorite among public golfers. In this region are many Land of Lincoln sites including Abraham Lincoln's burial place. And don't forget to try Vince Alfonso's pork barbecue.

Recommended Golf Courses in Illinois

Within 1 Hour of Springfield:

Hickory Point Golf Club, Decatur, (217) 421–7444, Public, 18/6855/72

Lake Shore Golf Club, Taylorville, (217) 824–5521, Public, 18/6813/72

Illinois: Useful Information

Illinois Tourist Information Center, 310 S. Michigan Ave., Chicago, IL 60604, (312) 793–2094

Illinois Office of Tourism, 620 E. Adams St., Springfield, IL 62706, (217) 782–7139

Illinois Office of Tourism, 2209 W. Main St., Marion, IL 62959, (618) 997–4371, (800) 223–0121

Chicago Tourism Council, Pumping Station, 163 E. Pearson St., Chicago, IL 60611, (312) 280–5754

Springfield Convention and Visitors Bureau, 109 N. 7th St., Springfield, IL, (217) 789–2360, (800) 545–7300

Illinois Gaming Board, (217) 524–0226 (Mississippi river boat gambling locations)

U.S. Forest Service, Eastern Region, 310 W. Wisconsin Ave., Ste. 500, Milwaukee, WI 53203, (414) 297–3693 (regional national forest information)

Illinois Department of Conservation, Division of Fisheries, 524 S. Second St., Springfield, IL 62706, (217) 782–6302 (fishing and hunting regulations)

Indianapolis Area

Course Name: BRICKYARD CROSSING

Course Type: Public
Address: 4400 West Sixteenth Street
Indianapolis, IN 46222
Phone: (317) 484–6572
Fax: (317) 484–6571

GOLF COURSE

Head Professional: Rollie Schroeder
Course Length/Par (All Tees): Back
6994/72, Blue 6621/72, White 6028/72,
Forward 5038/72
Course Slope/Rating (All Tees): Back
137/74.5, Blue 130/71.7, White
122/68.4, Forward 116/68.3
Course Architect: Pete Dye (1993)
Golf Facilities: Full Pro Shop X, Snack
Bar X, Lounge X, Restaurant X,
Locker Room X, Showers X, Club
Rental X, Club Repair X, Cart Rental
X, Instruction X, Practice Green X,
Driving Range X, Practice Bunker X,
Club Storage No
Tee-Time Reservation Policy: Up to 2
weeks in advance
Ranger: Yes
Tee-off-Interval Time: 10 min.
Time to Play 18 Holes: 5 hrs.
Course Hours/Earliest Tee-off: 8 a.m.
Green and Cart Fees: $70 for 18 holes
with or without cart
Credit Cards: All major cards
Season: Apr. through Oct. Busiest May
through Labor Day
Course Comments: Can walk but must
pay full golf fee. Yardage book available
Golf Packages: Inquire at pro shop
Discounts: No
Places to Stay Nearby: Canterbury Hotel
(317) 634–3000, (800) 538–8186; Court-
yard by Marriott (317) 635–4443, (800)
321–2211; Holiday Inn Crowne Plaza
Union Station (317) 631–2221, (800) 465–
4329; Radisson Plaza and Suites (317)
846–2700, (800) 333–3333; Residence
Inn by Marriott (317) 872–0462, (800)
331–3131; Speedway Motor Inn (on site)
(317) 241–2500; Westin Hotel Indianapolis (317) 262–8100, (800) 228–3000

Local Attractions: Benjamin Harris Home,
The Children's Museum of Indianapolis,
Conner Prairie, Eagle Creek Park and
Nature Preserve, Eiteljorg Museum of
American Indian and Western Art, Home
of James Whitcomb Riley, Indianapolis
Motor Speedway, Indianapolis Zoo, Indi-
ana World War Memorial, State Capitol,
Union Station, The Natorium, Indiana
State Library, NFL Indianapolis Colts,
NBA Indiana Pacers, AAA professional
baseball. The Indianapolis City Center,
201 S. Capitol Ave., Indianapolis, IN
46225 (317) 237–5200, (800) 323–INDY
Directions: From Indianapolis International
Airport (15 min.): Take Rte. 465 north
to Speedway/Claremont Exit. Take
Crawfordsville Rd. (Sixteenth St.) east
to golf course adjacent Motor Speedway
Closest Commercial Airport: Indianapolis
International (15 min.)

BRICKYARD CROSSING GOLF COURSE

Brickyard Crossing is a complete remake
of The Speedway Golf Course designed by
William H. Diddel, a native of Indianapolis,
in 1929. A PGA event, the 500 Festival Open
Invitational Tournament, was played on The
Speedway which had nine holes within the
oval track of the Indianapolis Motor Speedway, a National Historic Landmark. The last
500 Festival was held in 1968 and was won
by Billy Casper, Jr. The golf course faded
into near oblivion until Tony George, president of the Speedway, retained Pete Dye, a
former insurance salesman in Indianapolis
and tournament chair for the first two years
of the 500 Festival, to build a new course
that would attract a PGA event. The new
6994-yard par-72 layout was opened in 1993
and is host to a Senior PGA Tour event in
September.

Pete Dye moved more than 1.5 million
cubic yards of earth and sculpted rolling
terrain, knolls, dramatic viewing mounds,
lush bentgrass fairways, and large undulating bentgrass greens. Little Eagle Creek
runs through the golf course, weaving and
winding its way through eight holes. Three
lakes can come into play on three other
holes. Some holes such as the 190-yard

par-3 seventh or the 445-yard par-4 eleventh have only one sand bunker. The 382-yard par-4 ninth, on the other hand, has more than twenty bunkers. Rechristened Brickyard Crossing, one enters the oval of the Speedway to play holes numbers seven through ten, then the golfer returns through a tunnel to finish the round. The trip into the Speedway is worth the green fee.

The final four holes at Brickyard Crossing underline the challenge of this Dye design. The 545-yard par-5 fifteenth requires a heroic second shot to clear the creek that cuts in front of and along the left side of the green. A layup shot leaves approximately 150 yards to a 40-yard-deep putting surface. The 435-yard par-4 sixteenth is bordered from tee to green by the creek on the left side. The 52-yard-deep green can be reached in two, but it is then easy to three putt on this undulating monster. The 203-yard par-3 seventeenth plays to a deep green bordered by three bunkers to its left and the creek to the right. Another bunker guards the right front of the green. The 457-yard par-4 finishing hole requires a long, accurate tee shot that will set up a controlled, well-lofted approach to a large green protected by the creek to the right, a bunker in front, and other bunkers left and rear. These last four holes are especially difficult because they usually play into a prevailing south wind. Fortunately there are three other tee distances to chose from.

Within walking distance of the eighteenth is an excellent practice facility with a double-ended driving range, practice putting greens, and practice bunkers. Pete Dye has made a silk purse out of what formerly was a golf sow's ear.

Course Name: EAGLE CREEK GOLF COURSE
Eagle Creek, West Nine

Course Type: Public
Address: 8802 West 56th Street
Indianapolis, IN 46234
Phone: (317) 297–3366

GOLF COURSE

Head Professional: Jerry Hayslett

Course Length/Par (All Tees): Eagle Creek: Back 7154/72, Blue 6771/72, White 6200/72, Ladies' Forward 5005/72. West Nine: Back 3205/36, Forward 2955/36

Course Slope/Rating (All Tees): Eagle Creek: Back 139/74.6, Blue 134/72.1, White 123/69.2, Forward 116/68.2. West Nine: Back 107/33.7, Forward 101/33.3

Course Architects: Pete Dye and David Pfaff (1975)

Golf Facilities: Full Pro Shop X, Snack Bar X, Lounge No, Restaurant No, Locker Room X, Showers X, Club Rental No, Club Repair X, Cart Rental X, Instruction X, Practice Green X, Driving Range X, Practice Bunker X, Club Storage No

Tee-Time Reservation Policy: Call (317) 297–3366 to reserve tee time

Ranger: Yes

Tee-off-Interval Time: 8 min.

Time to Play 18 Holes: 5 hrs., 20 min.

Course Hours/Earliest Tee-off: Sunrise to sunset. Tee times available Sat., Sun., holidays from 6 a.m. to 3 p.m. No tee times required on West Course

Green Fees: Eagle Creek: $20 Fri., Sat., Sun., holidays for 18 holes, $18 weekdays. West Nine: $9.50 for 9 holes

Cart Fees: $13 for 18 holes per player, $13 for 9 holes per cart

Pull carts: $2.50 for 18 holes

Credit Cards: MasterCard, Visa

Season: March 1 to Dec. 23

Course Comments: Can walk anytime during week and after 3 p.m. weekends. West Nine Course does not require tee times in advance. City passes available

Golf Packages: None

Discounts: City passes, daily specials

Places to Stay Nearby: See page 307

Local Attractions: See page 307. Indianapolis Convention and Visitors Association (317) 639–4282

Directions: I–465 north, to 2nd exit at 56th St., left at light, drive 2½ mi., course on right at flashing yellow light

Closest Commercial Airports: Indianapolis International (20 min.); Hulman Field, Terre Haute (1 hr., 45 min.); Standiford

Field, Louisville, KY (2 hrs.); Chicago O'Hare International, IL (3 hrs.)

EAGLE CREEK

Eagle Creek was constructed by the City of Indianapolis and designed by Pete Dye, a former resident of Indianapolis, and David Pfaff. The rolling, 7154-yard layout was formerly a farm, and part of the clubhouse was built from the original farmhouse. The entire golf complex at Eagle Creek, which includes a 3205-yard nine-hole course, the West Nine, covers 500 acres. Eagle Creek crosses three ravines and runs through a forest. The front side is a bit more open than the back. There are water hazards on thirteen holes, and the greens tend to be medium sized, moderately fast, undulating, and well protected by large bunkers.

There is a choice of four tee distances at Eagle Creek covering 7154, 6771, 6200, and 5005 yards. Target golf is required here, as the topography of the course suggests, and you can be heavily penalized by sand, trees, water and uneven lies if you don't hit the right landing areas.

The number-1-handicap hole is the 566-yard par-5 ninth, which plays from an elevated tee straight to a wide, shallow green with no sand bunkers in the area. The most difficult hole on the back nine is the 427-yard par-4 sixteenth, which is a blind dogleg left. The approach shot is over a ravine to a wide, shallow, elevated green guarded by traps front-left and rear. The average golfer seldom reaches this green in regulation.

The 508-yard par-5 fourteenth is the signature hole at Eagle Creek. This hole is sometimes adjusted and played as a par 4 in tournament situations. The approach shot is to an elevated green fronted by a ravine, making it difficult to reach in two. The green is fairly narrow, deep and guarded by large sand traps to the left and right. The most difficult par 3 at Eagle Creek is the 208-yard fifteenth, which plays to a wide, shallow green protected by two traps to the rear and another trap in front and to the left.

Eagle Creek was the site of the 1982 National Public Links Championship and

has been rated among America's 75 best public courses by *Golf Digest*. You can walk the course anytime during the week and after 3 p.m. on weekends and holidays. The length and terrain makes it a difficult course to walk, however. Eagle Creek has adopted a computerized reservation system that requires you to register to get into the system and be eligible to reserve times up to 7 days in advance. Or you can call the pro shop to discuss walk-on possibilities.

Eagle Creek's architect, Pete Dye, was born in Urbana, Ohio, in 1925 and was employed as a life insurance salesman in Indianapolis. He was an excellent amateur golfer, winning the Indiana Amateur in 1958, and he served as chairman of the Green Committee at the Country Club of Indianapolis. In 1959 Dye left the insurance business after considerable success and with his wife Alice, a native of Indianapolis and a superb golfer, designed his first golf course the same year. Alice has won 7 Indiana Women's Amateur titles, 3 Florida State Women's Amateur titles, 2 USGA Women's Senior titles and numerous other titles during her career. Among her many strong and valid golf-architecture opinions is her belief that there should be more than one set of tees for women.

Pete Dye, influenced by a trip he and Alice took to Scotland's great golf courses in the early 1960s, began to incorporate Scottish-style architectural features into his course design, including small greens, undulating fairways, pot bunkers, railroad-tie bulkheads and deep native rough. Among Pete Dye's Indiana courses are Crooked Stick Golf Club, Carmel; El Dorado Country Club (9 holes), Greenwood, with Alice Dye; Harbour Trees Golf Club, Noblesville, with David Pfaff; Heather Hills Country Club, Indianapolis, with Alice Dye; Monticello Country Club, Monticello, with Alice Dye; and William S. Sahn Municipal, Indianapolis, with Alice Dye.

Now, of course, the Dye family, including Pete and Alice's sons Perry and Paul, and Pete's brother Ray, are well known in the world of golf architecture.

Course Name: GOLF CLUB OF INDIANA

Course Type: Public
Address: 6905 S. 525 East Lebanon
              Lebanon, IN 46052
Phone: (317) 769–6388

GOLF COURSE

Head Professional: Mickey Powell
Course Length/Par (All Tees): Back
  7084/72, Middle 6438/72, Forward
  5498/72
Course Slope/Rating (All Tees): Back
  140/73.2, Middle 130/72.3, Ladies'
  Forward 122/72.7
Course Architects: Charles Maddox and
  Mickey Powell (1974)
Golf Facilities: Full Pro Shop X, Snack
  Bar X, Lounge X, Restaurant No,
  Locker Room X, Showers X, Club
  Rental X, Club Repair X, Cart Rental
  X, Instruction X, Practice Green X,
  Driving Range X, Practice Bunker X,
  Club Storage No
Tee-Time Reservation Policy: Call anytime
  in advance, 2 foursomes must guarantee
  tee time with credit card, 12 players or
  more with a group deposit
Ranger: Yes
Tee-off-Interval Time: 8 min.
Time to Play 18 Holes: 4½ hrs.
Course Hours/Earliest Tee-off: 6:30 a.m.
  weekends, holidays, 7:30 a.m. weekdays
  to dusk
Green Fees: $35 for 18 holes, $15 for 9
  holes (after 3 p.m.)
Cart Fees: $10 per person per cart, $6 for
  9 holes
Credit Cards: MasterCard, Visa
Season: March 1 to Nov. 30. Busiest June-
  Sept.
Course Comments: Can walk anytime.
  Yardage book available. Memberships
  available
Golf Packages: None
Discounts: Twilight rates
Places to Stay Nearby: See page 307.
Local Attractions: See page 307. Indian-
  apolis Convention and Visitors Associa-
  tion (317) 639–4282
Directions: From Indianapolis (30 min.):
  I–465 west, I–65 north, Zionsville exit

(130), left on Hwy. 334, 1½ mi. to golf
course (follow signs)
Closest Commercial Airports: Indianapolis
  International (30 min.); Chicago O'Hare
  International, IL (3 hrs.)

GOLF CLUB OF INDIANA

  The Golf Club of Indiana is a 7084-yard
layout situated on what used to be farmland, 20 minutes northwest of Indianapolis.
The golf course is owned by Mickey Powell, a former president of the Indiana PGA,
who designed the course with Charles
Maddox in the mid-1970s.

  Maddox was born in Centralia, Illinois,
and worked for the family construction
business, which became involved in golf-
course development in the Chicago area in
the early 1900s. After World War I, Maddox teamed up with Frank MacDonald and
built a number of golf courses, several of
which Maddox owned. They also constructed golf courses for other architects
such as Robert Bruce Harris and C. D.
Wagstaff. After losing most of his golf-
course holdings during the Depression,
Maddox got out of the golf-course construction business but returned to it after World
War II and began designing golf courses in
the 1950s. He built courses for prominent
architects including Edward Lawrence
Packard and designed many courses including the Isle of Dauphine Country Club, Isle
of Dauphine, Alabama; Majestic Oaks
Country Club, Blaine, Minnesota; and the
Turkey Creek Country Club, Gary, Indiana,
with Frank MacDonald.

  The Golf Club of Indiana is an open,
rolling course with more than 75 sand
bunkers and water hazards on 15 holes.
The bentgrass greens are moderately fast,
large and very undulating. The greens are
well guarded by sand and water, making
tee-shot positioning, club selection and
approach shots onto the greens extremely
important. Trees have been planted on the
golf course over the years, and as they
mature they are becoming more of a factor.

  The Golf Club of Indiana starts out with
moderate par 4 and par 5 holes, then hits
you with a 226-yard par 3 from the back
tees. The combination of distance and sand

traps protecting the large target makes this a challenging hole. Two substantial bunkers squeeze the front of the green, leaving an alleyway 14 yards wide as an entrance way. There is another large trap to the rear and right of the putting surface.

The 406-yard par-4 fourth hole is a major challenge because of bunkers, water hazards and the wind blowing into the golfer's face. A good tee shot is required on this slight dogleg right, as a pond on the right side is potential trouble. The approach shot is down a severely narrowing fairway to a deep green guarded by a large pond and trap on the left and another large trap on the right. This hole has been labeled one of the most difficult par 4s in Indiana.

The number-1-handicap hole is the 472-yard par-4 fifth, a slight dogleg right to a deep green protected by large traps to the left front and right front of the green and a large pond to the left beginning 90 yards from the putting surface. Again, a strong tee shot is required to have any chance of reaching this green in regulation, but a large pond to the left of the landing area is something to worry about. Because of the size of the greens, your work is cut out for you once you get there. Three putts are not unusual at the Golf Club of Indiana.

The 410-yard par-4 sixteenth is rated the most difficult hole on the back side. Sand bunkers guard the right side of the tee-shot landing area beginning approximately 250 yards from the back tees and 210 yards from the middle tees. The approach shot is down a narrowing fairway to a narrow, deep green with a tight entrance way straddled by two large sand traps. A pond to the left of the fairway should not come into play, but wind can make judging direction, distance and club selection on this hole difficult.

The clubhouse at the Golf Club of Indiana includes an excellent pro shop that has been selected by *Golf Shop Operations* magazine as one of the best in the United States. The Golf Club of Indiana has been rated one of the top 75 public golf courses in America by *Golf Digest*. A PGA tour qualifier for men is held here every

autumn, and this course has been a regular site for the Indiana Intercollegiate Golf Tournament. Low handicappers will be challenged by the 7084-yard back-tee distances, and the other two tee positions provide a fine test for mere mortals.

Course Name: THE LEGENDS OF INDIANA GOLF COURSE

Course Type: Public
Address: 2100 Hurricane Road
P.O. Box 39
Franklin, IN 46131
Phone: (317) 736–8186
Fax: (317) 736–8608

GOLF COURSE

Director of Golf: Ted Bishop
Head Professional: Alex Brickley
Course Length/Par (All Tees): Back 7007/72, Blue 6698/72, White 6118/72, Forward 5245/72
Course Slope/Rating (All Tees): Back 132/74, Blue 130/72.4, White 123/70.2, Ladies' Forward 121/71.1
Course Architect: Jim Fazio (1992)
Golf Facilities: Full Pro Shop X, Snack Bar X, Lounge X, Restaurant No, Locker Room No, Showers No, Club Rental X, Club Repair X, Cart Rental X, Instruction X, Practice Green X, Driving Range X, Practice Bunker X, Club Storage No
Tee-Time Reservation Policy: Up to 7 days in advance. Groups of 20 or more and out-of-state golfers may call farther in advance
Ranger: Yes
Tee-off-Interval Time: 7 to 9 min.
Time to Play 18 Holes: 4½ hrs.
Course Hours/Earliest Tee-off: 6:30 a.m.
Green and Cart Fees: $39 for 18 holes with cart, $29 for 18 holes walking
Credit Cards: MasterCard, Visa
Season: Mar. through Dec. Busiest June through Labor Day
Course Comments: Can walk anytime
Golf Packages: No
Discounts: Twilight
Places to Stay Nearby: FRANKLIN: Days Inn (317) 736–8000, (800) 329–7466. INDIANAPOLIS: See page 307

Local Attractions: FRANKLIN: Johnson County Museum of History. INDIANAPOLIS: See page 307

Directions: From downtown Indianapolis (30 min.): Take I–65 south to Exit 90. Turn right at exit ramp and drive 1 mile to East View Rd. Turn right and proceed to 4-way stop sign (Hurricane Rd.) Turn right on Hurricane to golf course

Closest Commercial Airport: Indianapolis International Airport (30 min.)

THE LEGENDS OF INDIANA GOLF CLUB

The Legends of Indiana is a venture of Sam Carmichael, golf coach at Indiana University, Bobby Knight, its legendary basketball coach, and a few other select golf enthusiasts who wanted a convenient, quality public golf course. There are few trees on this links-style Jim Fazio-designed layout on 350 acres just south of Indianapolis. But there are 95 sand bunkers, 8 lakes, 2 creeks, and tricky winds. Well-positioned shots are required to avoid deep rough, the omnipresent bunkers, and the many water hazards.

One of the most difficult holes on the course is the 428-yard par-4 fourth. The approach shot is to an elevated green guarded by water that cuts in front of it from the right. The front right of the green is protected by a bunker and two more are behind the green. A missed shot to the right or short is likely to find the water, and anything long or left leaves a dangerous wedge or chip shot towards trouble. Another tough par 4 at The Legends is the 455-yard dogleg left twelfth. The tee shot must avoid a series of bunkers bordering each side of the landing area. The approach is to a deep green guarded by bunkers to its left.

The Legends is the site of the 1996 Indiana State Amateur and is rated among the best golf courses in the state by *Golf Digest*. The course has an excellent practice facility and has recently added nine holes of golf and an 18-hole par-3 course to meet local golfing demand.

Course Name: **OTTER CREEK GOLF COURSE**
North, West, East Courses

Course Type: Public
Address: 11522 East 50 North
Columbus, IN 47203
Phone: (812) 579–5227
Fax: (812) 579–9051

GOLF COURSE

Director of Golf: Greg Bishop
Head Professional: Keith Clark
Course Length/Par (All Tees): North/West: Back 7258/72, Blue 6897/72, White 6537/72, Forward 5690/72. North/East: Back 7224/72, Gold 6858/72, Blue 6418/72, Forward 5581/72. West/East: Back 7126/72, Gold 6785/72, Blue 6315/72, Forward 5403/72

Course Slope/Rating (All Tees): North/West Back 138/75.6, Blue 135/74.0, Gold 131/72.2, Forward 119/69.1, Ladies' Forward 128/73.5. North/East: Back 137/75.6, Gold 133/73.9, Blue 127/71.6, Forward 116/69.8, Ladies'Forward 125/73.0. West/East Back 137/75.0, Gold 133/73.4, Blue 128/71.2, Forward 114/68.0, Ladies' Forward 123/71.9

Course Architect: North/West: Robert Trent Jones, Sr. (1964). East: Rees Jones (1995)

Golf Facilities: Full Pro Shop X, Snack Bar X, Lounge X, Restaurant X, Locker Room X, Showers X, Club Rental X, Club Repair X, Cart Rental X, Instruction X, Practice Green X, Driving Range X, Practice Bunker X, Club Storage X

Tee-Time Reservation Policy: Anytime in advance. Credit card guarantee required

Ranger: Yes

Tee-off-Interval Time: 10 min.

Time to Play 18 Holes: 4½ hrs.

Course Hours/Earliest Tee-off: 7 a.m. to dusk

Green and Cart Fees: $70 for 18 holes with cart Fri., Sat., Sun., holidays; $60 for 18 holes with cart Mon. to Thurs.

Credit Cards: American Express, MasterCard, Visa

Season: Mid-April to mid-Oct.

Course Comments: Can walk anytime. Yardage book available

Golf Packages: Available

Discounts: Unlimited golf plans daily (price varies), twilight rates, season passes, players card, juniors. Lower seasonal rates before May, from early Oct.

Places to Stay Nearby: Holiday Inn (812) 372–1541, (800) HOLIDAY; Ramada Inn (812) 376–3051, (800) 272–6232; Days Inn (812) 376–9951, (800) 325–2525; Columbus Inn (812) 378–4289, (800) 228–2828

Local Attractions: Historic homes tours, music festivals, antique shopping, bicycling, canoeing, camping, 15 city-operated parks, 26 outdoor tennis courts, Indianapolis Museum of Art (Columbus Gallery). Hope (Moravian community). Nashville, IN. Indianapolis. Louisville, KY. Cincinnati, OH. Columbus Chamber of Commerce (812) 372–1954, (800) 486–6564

Directions: From Indianapolis: I–65 south, State Rd. 31 south (first Columbus exit), follow signs to Otter Creek (20 min.). When you get to Columbus, take left on 50 North to golf course. From Columbus: Hwy. 46 east out of Columbus 6 mi., through Petersville, look for a sign on the right, take Hwy. 650 east to golf course on the right

Closest Commercial Airports: Indianapolis International (1 hr.); Standiford Field, Louisville, KY (1 hr., 15 min.); Greater Cincinnati International, OH (1½ hrs.)

OTTER CREEK GOLF COURSE

Columbus, Indiana, is the site of one of the best golf courses in the state, and it is open to the public. Otter Creek is situated in the southern Indiana countryside on 218 acres of well-treed, rolling land, with the Clifty and Otter creeks wandering through. The North/West course playing area is completely bentgrass, with 169 acres of bluegrass rough and four tee distances ranging from 7258 yards from the back tees to 5690 yards from the forward tees—4 acres of tee boxes alone. There are over 90 North Carolina white-sand-filled bunkers on this excellent layout designed by Robert Trent Jones, Sr. Water comes into play on five holes, including "Alcatraz," the course's signature hole.

Alcatraz is the 191-yard par-3 thirteenth, which plays over Clifty Creek to a deep, forward-sloping green with traps to the left and right. Streams run to the left and right of the green, and the tree direction does not line up directly with the green, instead following the creek bed. As a result, the tendency is to hit the ball to the right and toward a bridge if an adjustment isn't made. A shot to the left will be in an area heavy with undergrowth and sycamores.

The number-1-handicap hole at Otter Creek is the formidable 616-yard par-5 fifth, which provides unlimited shot-making opportunities with trees, sand, out of bounds, an undulating fairway and a tiered green coming into play. On the tee shot, the fairway rolls uphill 200 yards and bends right 30 yards to a bunker. Most second shots are hit from an undulating fairway down a tree-lined alleyway toward a two-tiered, forward-sloping green with traps on the left and right. There is a very small opening to this green, with trees on the right and two fairway bunkers on the left that must be avoided before you get to the putting surface.

The toughest par 4 on the course is the 472-yard fourth, which is a slight dogleg right. The fairway narrows, slopes downward and begins its undulation 200 yards from the tee. Left and right fairway bunkers guard this area. The second shot is likely to be a downhill lie to a slightly elevated green that is wide, shallow, undulating and crowned. A small trap is to the left of the green, and a large trap is to the right and forward. For most golfers, this hole seems like a par 5.

In 1995 a third nine, the East, was added to Otter Creek, designed by Rees Jones, the son of the original architect. The East nine compatibly fits with either of the original nines to make this the best 27 holes of golf in Indiana. Water can come into play on four of these new holes including the hefty 465-yard par-4 seventh. A dogleg left bordered by water from tee to green, the drive from the back tee can cut as much of the water as the golfer would dare. The approach is to an ample green framed by a large bunker to the right and the water to the left. There is a choice of four tee distances at Otter Creek but the combination of bunkers, mature trees, length and water hazards make this a formidable test of golf.

The award-winning clubhouse at Otter Creek was designed by noted architect Harry Weese and has magnificent views of the golf course. Housed here are the Legends restaurant and banquet facilities, a pro shop, locker rooms and a separate snack bar. Banquet facilities can accommodate 300 guests, and many tournaments, outings and other social gatherings are held here. Otter Creek offers a variety of golf packages in cooperation with local hotels and motels. Other services such as celebrity referral services, motivational and entertaining after-dinner speakers, and music and entertainment at pro challenges and other events can be provided.

Group and individual instruction is available from the staff of professionals at Otter Creek. The course has 7 acres of practice range, a practice chipping green and a 15,000-square-foot putting green. Championship events have been held here, including the 1991 U.S. Amateur Public Links Championship, the American Junior Golf Association Championship, and the Indiana Men's State Amateur Championship. Since it opened in 1964, the course has been listed among the top 25 public golf courses in America by *Golf Digest*.

Columbus, Indiana, a town of 31,000, has an inordinate number of buildings designed by excellent architects such as I. M. Pei and Eliel Saarinen. While you're here, an architectural tour is worth your time.

South Bend Area

Course Name: **BLACKTHORN GOLF CLUB**

Course Type: Public
Address: 6100 Nimtz Parkway
              South Bend, IN 46628
Phone: (219) 232–4653
Fax: (219) 234–2640

GOLF COURSE

Head Professional: Brian D. Godfrey
Course Length/Par (All Tees): Back 7069/72, Green 6473/72, White 5825/72, Foward 5036/72
Course Slope/Rating (All Tees): Back 135/75.2, Green 129/72.7, White 121/69.9, Ladies' Forward 120/70.1
Course Architect: Michael Hurdzan (1994)
Golf Facilities: Full Pro Shop X, Snack Bar X, Lounge X, Restaurant X, Locker Room X, Showers No, Club Rental X, Club Repair X, Cart Rental X, Instruction X, Practice Green X, Driving Range X, Practice Bunker X, Club Storage No
Tee-Time Reservation Policy: Up to 7 days in advance
Ranger: Yes
Tee-off-Interval Time: 9 min.
Time to Play 18 Holes: 4½ hrs.
Course Hours/Earliest Tee-off: 6 a.m.
Green Fees: $45 for 18 holes Fri., Sat., Sun., holidays, $40 for 18 holes weekdays
Cart Fees: $11 for 18 holes per person
Credit Cards: All major cards
Season: Year round, weather permitting. Busiest June through Labor Day
Course Comments: Can walk anytime. Yardage book available. Memberships available
Golf Packages: Inquire at golf shop
Discounts: Twilight, seasonal specials, reduced rates for St. Joseph County residents
Places to Stay Nearby: Days Inn (219) 277–0510, (800) 325–2525; Holiday Inn-Downtown (219) 232–3941, (800) HOLIDAY; South Bend Marriott (219) 234–2000, (800) 228–9290
Local Attractions: The Oliver Mansion (Copshalom), Potawatomi Zoo, Studebaker Museum, University of Notre Dame, Stanley Coveleski Stadium (minor league baseball), seasonal festivals. Chamber of Commerce of St. Joseph County, 401 E. Colfax Ave., P.O. Box 1677, South Bend, IN 46634 (219) 234–0051, (800) 828–7881
Directions: From South Bend (10 min.): Take Hwy. 20 west past the airport to

Olive Rd. Proceed north on Olive 1 mile to a stop sign (Nimtz Rd.). Turn right to golf course

Closest Commercial Airports: Michiana Regional (5 min.); Chicago O'Hare International (2 hrs.); Indianapolis International (2½ hrs.)

BLACKTHORN GOLF CLUB

Just west of downtown South Bend near the Michiana Regional Airport is the Blackthorn Golf Club, designed by Mike Hurdzan and situated on 220 rolling acres. Part of a regional development project that includes plans for a hotel conference center, a business center featuring fiber optics and other new age industrial amenities, Blackthorn has been rated among the best new golf courses of 1994 by *Golf Digest*. The course is on former farmland, features bentgrass throughout and has an excellent practice facility with two putting greens, a full driving range, and an extra practice hole, "The Blarney." Affectionately called "The Ultimate Mulligan," The Blarney plays 266 yards from the back tees and can serve as a prelude to selecting one of four tee distances on the opening hole at Blackthorn.

The first three holes ease you into the course, then you reach the 554-yard par-5 fourth, which plays up a gauntlet of sand bunkers, pine, oak, and other trees to a wide, shallow target protected by a cluster of bunkers to its front left and another to its rear. Bunkers border the right side of the fairway from 150 to 90 yards in to the green. The next hole, the 465-yard par-4 fifth, is the most difficult hole on the front side. It plays straight to a green protected by bunkers to its right and left. One hundred seventy yards from the green is a huge oak set in the center of the fairway. Another difficult par 4 is the 454-yard seventeenth which plays straight to a deep, narrow target bordered by a bunker to its right. The round concludes with a winding, downhill 534-yard par 5. The second shot must avoid water to the left and bunkers guarding both sides of the fairway. The approach from 50 yards in to the green becomes very narrow as bunkers frame the

entranceway. To the left front of the green is water.

Playing Blackthorn is like taking a walk in the park. The trees, mounds, grass bunkers, occasional water hazards, sand bunkers, slopes, swales, and intermittent winds add definition, variety, and subtlety to this shotmakers course.

Southern Indiana

Course Name: COVERED BRIDGE GOLF CLUB

Course Type: Public
Address: 12510 Covered Bridge Road Sellersburg, IN 47172
Phone: (812) 246–8880
Fax: (812) 246–8881

GOLF COURSE

Head Professional: Lenny Hartlage
Course Length/Par (All Tees): Fuzzy 6832/72, Back 6372/72, Middle 5943/72, Forward 4957/72
Course Slope/Rating (All Tees): Fuzzy 128/73, Back 124/70.8, Middle 119/69, Forward 108/64, Ladies' Middle 126/74.7, Ladies' Forward 114/68.8
Course Architects: Fuzzy Zoeller and Clyde B. Johnson (1994)
Golf Facilities: Full Pro Shop X, Snack Bar X, Lounge X, Restaurant X, Locker Room X, Showers X, Club Rental X, Club Repair X, Cart Rental X, Instruction X, Practice Green X, Driving Range X, Practice Bunker X, Club Storage X
Tee-Time Reservation Policy: Up to 4 days in advance for non-members. Minimum of 2 players required to reserve a tee time. Credit card required to guarantee a tee time. 24 hr. in advance cancellation policy
Ranger: Yes
Tee-off-Interval Time: 10 min.
Time to Play 18 Holes: 4½ hrs.
Course Hours/Earliest Tee-off: 8 a.m.
Green and Cart Fees: $60 for 18 holes Fri., Sat., Sun., holidays; $50 for 18 holes weekdays
Credit Cards: All major cards
Season: Mid-Feb. through mid-Jan. Busiest May through Labor Day

Course Comments: Carts required. Walking allowed after 4:30 p.m.

Golf Packages: Contact pro shop

Discounts: Seasonal

Places to Stay Nearby: SELLERSBURG: Days Inn (812) 246–4451, (800) 392–7466. JEFFERSONVILLE: Ramada Inn (812) 284–6711, (800) 272–6232. LOUISVILLE: The Brown Hotel (502) 583–1234, (800) 866–7666; Hyatt Regency (502) 587–3434, (800) 523–1234; Seelbach Hotel (502) 585–3200, (800) 333–3399

Local Attractions: JEFFERSONVILLE: Hillerich and Bradsby Co., Inc., Howard Steamboat Museum. NEW ALBANY: Culbertson Mansion State Historic Site. LOUISVILLE: Cave Hill Cemetery, Churchill Downs, Colonel Harland Sanders Museum, Farmington, J.B. Speed Art Museum, Kentucky Art and Craft Center, Kentucky Center for the Arts, Kentucky Fair and Exposition Center, Locust Grove, Louisville Science Center, Louisville Zoo, Rauch National Planetarium, Zachary Taylor National Cemetery, boat tours, fishing, University of Louisville, Fairgrounds Stadium home of AAA professional baseball. The Louisville Visitors Bureau, 400 S. 1st St., Louisville, KY 40202 (502) 582–3732 or (502) 584–2121

Directions: From downtown Louisville (25 min.): Take Hwy. 65 north to Exit 7/U.S. 60. Take Hwy. 60 west 5 miles, follow signs to golf course

Closest Commercial Airport: Louisville Standiford Field Airport (30 min.)

COVERED BRIDGE GOLF CLUB

Frank Urban "Fuzzy" Zoeller, winner of the 1977 Masters, the 1984 U.S. Open, and several other tournaments, was born in Albany, Indiana and is designer and part owner of Covered Bridges in nearby Sellersburg. Covered Bridge, which pays homage to the covered bridges occasionally found in this region of Indiana just north of Louisville, is the centerpiece of a golf course real estate development. Members have tee time priority on this open, golfer-friendly layout on former farmland.

More than half of Covered Bridge's holes can be seen from the clubhouse which overlooks the double green of Nos. 9 and 18, both par 5s. These holes are separated by a long lake which borders both fairways up to the wide green that is backed by an array of bunkers. The course offers some challenging par 3s including the 195-yard eighth which plays over a lake to a two-tiered green guarded by a big bunker in front and bunkers to its rear. The 192-yard twelfth plays to a deep green surrounded by bunkers with a stream to its right.

Almost one thousand trees have been planted on this course that will become more difficult as they mature.

Course Name: SULTAN'S RUN GOLF COURSE

Course Type: Public
Address: 1490 Meridian Road
              Jasper, IN 47546
Phone: (812) 482–1009
Fax: (812) 482–3798

GOLF COURSE

Director of Golf: Tom Jones

Head Professional: Rusty Mason

Course Length/Par (All Tees): Back 6894/72, Gold 6498/72, Silver 6034/72, Forward 5043/72

Course Slope/Rating (All Tees): Back 132/72.8, Gold 127/70.5, Silver 123/68.7, Ladies' Forward 120/68.1

Course Architects: Tom Jones and Allen Sternberg (1992)

Golf Facilities: Full Pro Shop X, Snack Bar X, Lounge X, Restaurant No, Locker Room X, Showers X, Club Rental X, Club Repair X, Cart Rental X, Instruction X, Practice Green X, Driving Range X, Practice Bunker X, Club Storage X

Tee-Time Reservation Policy: Anytime in advance for out of town players

Ranger: Yes

Tee-off-Interval Time: 9 min.

Time to Play 18 Holes: 4½ hrs.

Course Hours/Earliest Tee-off: 6:30 a.m.

Green and Cart Fees: $40 for 18 holes Sat., Sun., holidays with cart, $29 for 18

holes walking; $35 for 18 holes weekdays with cart, $24 for 18 holes walking

Credit Cards: All major cards

Season: Year round weather permitting. Busiest Memorial Day through Labor Day

Course Comments: Difficult walking course but you can walk after 1 p.m. weekends and holidays, noon weekdays

Golf Packages: Inquire at pro shop

Discounts: Twilight rate after 3 p.m.

Places to Stay Nearby: Days Inn (812) 482–6000, (800) 742–7482; Holiday Inn Holodome (812) 482–5555, (800) 872–3176. BED AND BREAKFAST: Powers Inn (812) 482–3018

Local Attractions: JASPER: Indiana Baseball Hall of Fame, Jasper Civic Auditorium/Krempp Gallery, Holy Family Church, St. Joseph Church, seasonal festivals, antiques, camping. Jasper Chamber of Commerce (812) 482–6866. HUNTINGBURG: Huntingburg League Stadium, Old Town Hall. Huntingburg Chamber of Commerce (812) 683–5699. SANTA CLAUS: Santa Claus Post Office. Santa Claus Chamber of Commerce (812) 937–2848

Directions: From Louisville (1 hr.): Take I–64 west to Hwy. 162. Take Hwy. 162 into Jasper, then take Hwy. 164 east to Meridian Rd. Take right 1 mile to golf course. From Evansville (1 hr.). Take I–64 east to Hwy. 231 and proceed north into Jasper. Turn right on Fifteenth St. and drive 1½ miles to the golf course

Closest Commercial Airports: Evansville (1 hr.); Indianapolis International (1½ hrs.); Standiford Field, Louisville, KY (1 hr.)

SULTAN'S RUN GOLF COURSE

Sultan's Run, one hour's drive northwest of Louisville, is named for Supreme Sultan, a champion horse who roamed the region and sired many other winners. This well-treed, rolling layout opens with "Sultan's Great Day," a tough 430-yard par 4 lined with trees on the right and bordered by trees and a wildlife refuge on the left. The wide green is backed by grass mounds and protected by two bunkers to its left. The par 3s at Sultan's Run are both beautiful and difficult, especially from the back tees. The 218-yard fifth, "Barbados Exit," plays from any of six tee distances over Fancy Miniken Lake to a wide, shallow green backed by bunkers and bordered by another bunker to its left.

A run of three good golf holes begins with the 192-yard par-3 sixteenth, "Talent Contest," which plays downhill to a large green set against the backdrop of Lake Lili O' Lee. No. 17, the 436-yard par-4 "King of Siam," requires a tee shot to the right center to have a clear view to the deep green bordered by two sand bunkers to its left. The 429-yard par-4 finishing hole, "Supreme Sultan," is a beautiful and dramatic dogleg right that defies you to cut the trees bordering the right turn. The approach is to a deep green with rock outcroppings to its left, waterfalls to its rear, two moon crater bunkers to its right front, a hidden lake to the right and another on the left.

You are advised to select the proper tee distance for your game at Sultan's Run. Horse farms surround this scenic and challenging layout. The greens are bentgrass, have subtle breaks, and are medium sized. Sultan's Run has a majestic clubhouse overlooking the 18th, full banquet and restaurant facilities, and a quality practice facility with target greens, practice bunkers, and a putting green.

Terre Haute Area

Course Name: HULMAN LINKS GOLF COURSE

Course Type: Public
Address: Chamberlain Road off Route 40 Terre Haute, IN 47803
Phone: (812) 877–2096

GOLF COURSE

Head Professional: C. James Peo

Course Length/Par (All Tees): Back 7225/72, Blue 6740/72, White 6440/71, Ladies' Forward 5775/72

Course Slope/Rating (All Tees): Back 144/74.9, Blue 141/72.7, White 138/71.4, Ladies' Forward 134/73.4

Course Architects: David Gill and Garrett Gill (1978)

Golf Facilities: Full Pro Shop X, Snack Bar X, Lounge X, Restaurant X, Locker Room X, Showers X, Club Rental X, Club Repair X, Cart Rental X, Instruction X, Practice Green X, Driving Range X, Practice Bunker X, Club Storage No

Tee-Time Reservation Policy: You can call Wednesday 8 a.m. for Sat., Sun., holiday tee times. Weekday tee times can be reserved in advance. Season-pass holders have priority

Ranger: Yes

Tee-off-Interval Time: 10 min.

Time to Play 18 Holes: 4 hrs., 15 min.

Course Hours/Earliest Tee-off: 7 a.m. to dark

Green Fees: $22 plus tax for 18 holes Sat., Sun., holidays; $18.50 plus tax for 18 holes Mon. to Fri.; $11 plus tax for 9 holes Sat., Sun., holidays; and $9.25 plus tax for 9 holes Mon. to Fri.

Cart Fees: $10.50 plus tax for 18 holes, $5.25 plus tax for 9 holes per person

Credit Cards: MasterCard, Visa

Season: March to mid-Dec.

Course Comments: Can walk anytime. Yardage book available

Golf Packages: None

Discounts: Season-pass rates; seasonal discounts

Places to Stay Nearby: Larry Bird's Boston Connection (812) 235–3333; Drury Inn (800) 325–8300; Holiday Inn/Holidome (812) 232–6081, (800) HOLIDAY; Best Western (812) 234–7781, (800) 528–1234; Park Inn International (812) 238–2424; Super 8 Lodge (812) 232–4890, (800) 800–8000; Mid–Town Motel (812) 232–0383. BED AND BREAKFAST: Deer Run Bed and Breakfast (812) 466–3390

Local Attractions: Historic district, crafts, covered bridges, Terre Haute Ethnic Festival, Indiana State University, Saint Mary-of-the-Woods College, Eugene V. Debs home, Historical Museum of the Wabash Valley, Rose–Hulman Institute of Technology Gallery, Sheldon Swope Art Gallery, Turman Art Gallery, Dobbs Park Memorial Grove. Terre Haute Park and Recreation (812) 232–2727. Terre Haute Convention and Visitors Bureau of Vigo County (812) 234–5555

Directions: From center of Terre Haute: 6 mi. east on Rte. 40, right on Chamberlain Rd. to golf course

Closest Commercial Airports: Hulman Field, Terre Haute (5 min.), Indianapolis International (1 hr., 45 min.)

HULMAN LINKS GOLF COURSE

Hulman Links has perennially been rated one of America's best 75 public golf courses in America by *Golf Digest*. This is a beautiful facility located on 230 acres of rolling hills in western Indiana. The Hulman Links clubhouse was built in 1984 and stands on a knoll overlooking the 7225-yard layout, which was designed by David Gill and Garrett Gill and opened in 1978. The clubhouse encompasses more than 8000 square feet and includes a pro shop, locker room and showers, restaurant, bar and banquet facility. There are beautiful views of the golf course from wicker chairs on the covered veranda outside this facility.

Doglegs and significant elevation changes are abundant at Hulman Links. Often you can't see the green from the tee. Fortunately, you have four tee positions to choose from. There are water hazards on five holes on the more open front side and one hole with a water hazard on the tighter, well-treed back side. The bentgrass greens are large, fast and undulating, with an array of well-placed sand traps protecting them. Virtually all the landing areas are protected by a combination of trees, bunkers and water hazards. And it's always possible to have an uneven lie and a blind shot on this long, difficult course.

The number-1-handicap hole on Hulman Links is the 580-yard par-5 sixth, a long, narrow dogleg right that has a lateral water hazard on the left, all the way to the green. There is also water on the right. The first two shots have to be long and straight, and the second shot has to avoid two fairway bunkers situated on the right, 100 yards from the slightly elevated green. As you come onto the large green, there are five traps on the left, beginning from the 80-yard mark, and two large traps just to the right and in front of the putting surface.

The two finishing holes at Hulman Links are long and difficult. The 455-yard par-4 seventeenth plays down a tree-lined fairway straight to a deep green guarded by three traps on the right and two on the left. The tee-shot landing area is guarded on the right by three large sand bunkers, and it is always possible to be stymied by the trees. The eighteenth is a beautiful 460-yard par-4 double dogleg with two water hazards to negotiate. The first is a small lake on the left, 215 yards from the back tee, and the second is another lake, on the right and 310 yards from the back tee. Depending on the tees you are playing from and how strong you are off the tee, it is possible to reach either of these lakes because of a tail wind and the firmness of the fairways. Beginning 240 yards from the back tee, three bunkers guard the right side of the fairway, and if your tee shot is to the right you will have to carry the second lake to reach the green, which has two traps to the right and one to the left. This is as fine a finishing hole as you'll want to play.

The Anton Hulman family donated land and funds to the city of Terre Haute for the development of this golf facility and the parklands around it. Herman Hulman started a wholesale distribution company in Terre Haute in the nineteenth century, and his grandson, Anton "Tony" Hulman, went on to diversify the family business, after having been an outstanding athlete in prep school and at Yale. In 1945, Tony Hulman saved the Indianapolis Motor Speedway from extinction by buying the track from Eddie Rickenbacker for $700,000. Tony died in 1977, but the family still owns and runs the Speedway, among other things. The Hulman Links is also part of the Hulman family legacy.

David Gill, the designer of Hulman Links, was born in Iowa and started his own golf-architecture firm in the early 1950s, after working as a design and construction assistant for architect Robert Bruce Harris. He has designed Bunker Hills Municipal in Coon Rapids, Minne-sota; Meadowbrook Golf Club in Rapid City, South Dakota, with Garrett Gill; and other fine public and private courses, mostly in the Midwest.

Recommended Golf Courses in Indiana

Within 1 Hour of Indianapolis:

Bear Slide Golf Club, Cicero, (317) 984–3837, (800) 252–8337, Semiprivate, 18/7041/71

Fox Prairie Golf Club, Noblesville, (317) 776–6357, Public, 18/6946/72

Hanging Tree Golf Club, Westfield, (317) 896–2474, Semiprivate, 18/6519/71

The Links Golf Club, New Palestine, (317) 861–4466, Public, 18/7054/72

Royal Highlands Golf Club, Knightstown, (317) 345–2123, Public, 18/6452/71

Bloomington Area:

Indiana University Golf Club, Bloomington, (812) 855–7543, Public, 18/6891/71

Otis Park Golf Club, Bedford, (812) 279–9092, Public, 18/6308/72

Salt Creek Golf Club, Nashville, (812) 988–7888, Public, 18/6407/72

Within 1 Hour of Evansville:

Christmas Lake, Santa Claus, (812) 544–2271, Resort, 18/6660/72

French Lick Springs Golf and Tennis Resort, French Lick, (812) 936–9300, Resort. Country Club: 18/6291/70. Valley: 18/6003/70

Oak Meadow Golf Club, Evansville, (812) 867–6489, Resort, 18/6406/72

Within 1 Hour of Fort Wayne:

Autumn Ridge Golf Club, Ft. Wayne, (219) 637–8727, Semiprivate, 18/7103/72

Brookwood Golf Club, Ft. Wayne, (219) 637–8727, Semiprivate, 18/7103/72

Wabash Valley Golf Club, Geneva, (219) 368–7388, Public, 18/6375/71

Zollner Golf Course at Tri-State University, Angola, (219) 665–4269, Public, 18/6628/72

Within 1 Hour of Kokomo:

Green Acres Golf Club, Kokomo, (317) 883–5771, Public, 18/6782/72

Honeywell Golf Course, Wabash, (219) 563–8663, Public, 18/6550/72

Purdue University Golf Course, West Lafayette, (317) 494–3139, Public. North: 18/6852/72. South: 18/6428/71

Rock Hollow Golf Club, Peru, (317) 473–6100, Public, 18/6944/72

Walnut Creek Golf Course, Marion, (317) 998–7651, Public, 18/6880/72

Muncie Area:

Valley View Golf Course, Middletown, (317) 354–2698, Semiprivate, 18/6421/72

Winchester Golf Club, Winchester, (317) 584–5151, Public, 18/6540/72

Within 1 Hour of New Albany:

Grand Oak Golf Club, West Harrison, (812) 637–3945, Semiprivate, 18/6365/71

Hidden Creek Golf Club, Sellersburg, (812) 246–2556, Public, 18/6756/71

Valley View Golf Club, Floyd Knobs, (812) 923–7291, Public, 18/6523/71

Within 1 Hour of South Bend:

Elbel Park Golf Course, South Bend, (219) 271–9180, Public, 18/6700/72

Erskine Park Golf Club, South Bend, (219) 291–3216, Public, 18/6100/70

Jaday Creek Golf Course, Granger, (219) 277–4653, Public, 18/6940/72

Pheasant Valley Golf Club, Crown's Point, (219) 663–5000, Semiprivate, 18/6869/72

Swan Lake Golf Club, Plymouth, (219) 936–9798, Public. East: 18/6345/72. West: 18/6507/72

Within 1 Hour of Terre Haute:

Geneva Hills Golf Club, Clinton, (317) 832–8384, Public, 18/6303/72

Indiana: Useful Information

Tourism Development Division, 1 N. Capitol, Ste. 700, Indianapolis, IN 46204–2288, (317) 232–8860, (800) 289–6646

Hoosier National Forest, 811 Constitution Ave, Bedford, IN 47421, (812) 275–5987 (national forest information)

Indiana Department of Natural Resources, 402 W. Washington St., Rm. 298, Indianapolis, IN 46204, (317) 232–4200 (fishing and hunting regulations)

Course Name: AMANA COLONIES GOLF COURSE

Course Type: Public
Address: Rural Route 1/Box 8500
              County Road W 22
              Amana, IA 52203
Phone: (319) 622–6222,
              (800) 383–3636
Fax: (319) 277–7605

GOLF COURSE

Director of Golf: Gary Gabrielson
Course Length/Par (All Tees): Back
  6824/72, Blue 6468/72, White 6194/72,
  Gold 5804/72, Forward 5228/72
Course Slope/Rating (All Tees): Back
  136/73.3, Blue 129/71.1, White 126/70,
  Gold 118/68, Ladies' Forward 119/70
Course Architect: William J. Speare (1991)
Golf Facilities: Full Pro Shop X, Snack
  Bar X, Lounge X, Restaurant X,
  Locker Room X, Showers X, Club
  Rental X, Club Repair X, Cart Rental
  X, Instruction X, Practice Green X,
  Driving Range X, Practice Bunker No,
  Club Storage X
Tee-Time Reservation Policy: 30 days in
  advance. Over 30 days up to 1 yr. in ad-
  vance with credit card guarantee
Ranger: Yes
Tee-off-Interval Time: 9 min.
Time to Play 18 Holes: 4½ hrs.
Course Hours/Earliest Tee-off: 6:30 a.m.
Green Fees: $54.50 for 18 holes Fri., Sat.,
  Sun., holidays; $49.50 for 18 holes
  Mon.-Thurs.
Cart Fees: $29.50 for 18 holes Fri., Sat.,
  Sun., holidays; $27.50 for 18 holes
  Mon.-Thurs.
Credit Cards: American Express, Master-
  Card, Visa
Season: April to mid-Nov. Busiest season
  June to Aug.
Course Comments: Carts mandatory.
  Limited private membership
Golf Packages: None
Discounts: Twilight, seasonal
Places to Stay Nearby: Holiday Inn (319)
  668–1175, (800) HOLIDAY; Ox Yoke
  Inn (319) 622–3441, (800) 233–3441;
Guest House Motor Inn (319) 622–3599.
BED AND BREAKFASTS: Babi's Bed and
  Breakfast (319) 662–4381; Die Heimat
  Country Inn (319) 622–3937; Dusk to
  Dawn Bed and Breakfast (319) 622–
  3029
Local Attractions: Amana Arts Guild,
  Amana Society's General Store, lantern
  makers, basket makers, bakery, Lily
  Lake and Indian Dam, factory outlets,
  antiques, nature trail, Mill Stream Brew-
  ing Co., Museum of Amana History,
  furniture industry shops and tours, spe-
  cialty foods, shopping, Amana Woolen
  Mill, wineries, bicycling, seasonal festi-
  vals, camping, Barn Museum, Old
  Creamery Theatre, Amana Refrigeration,
  Amana Meat Shop and Smoke House.
  Cedar Rapids. West Branch. Iowa City.
  Kalona. Amana Travel Council (319)
  622–3828, (800) 245–5465
Directions: I–80, to exit 225 (Hwy. 151
  N), take Hwy. 151 N into Amana, take
  left on Hwy. 220 west, 2 mi. to nursing
  home, take right to golf course
Closest Commercial Airports: Cedar
  Rapids Municipal (15 min.); Des
  Moines International (2 hrs.)

AMANA COLONIES GOLF COURSE

The story of Amana begins in Germany
in 1714, when the Community of True
Inspiration was formed by Eberhard Ludwig Gruber and John Friedrich Rock.
Because of religious persecution from the
government and difficult economic times,
the community emigrated to America in
1843. By 1845, over 800 Inspirationists
had settled near Buffalo, New York, and
called their new community Ebenezer.

A communal system was established
and remained essentially unchanged for 89
years. All land and buildings were owned
by the community. Families were assigned
living quarters, and each individual over
school age worked at assigned tasks in the
kitchens, fields, factories or shops.

Because of the need for more land, the
community moved westward in 1854, and
the village of Amana was established along
the Iowa River in Iowa. The word Amana
comes from the Song of Solomon:

*"Behold, thou art fair, my love . . .
thou has doves' eyes within thy locks . . . thy
lips are like a thread of scarlet, and thy
speech is comely. . . . Thou art all fair, my
love. . . . Come with me from Lebanon, my
spouse with me from Lebanon: look from the
top of Amana. . . ."*

Eventually, a total of 26,000 acres of land
was purchased and 6 more villages settled. In
1932 the people voted to abandon the communal system and incorporated their holdings, issuing stock in the profit-sharing
Amana society. The Amana Church Society
continues as the religious foundation of the
Amanas. The Amana villages are now registered national historic landmarks and have
been placed on the Hiawatha Pioneer Trail.
The Amana Society is a corporation through
which people own and operate their 26,000
acres of land, the Amana Woolen Mill,
Amana Furniture Shop, the Amana Homestead Meat Shops and other businesses. The
Amana Society does not have an ownership
interest in Amana Refrigeration, Inc., however, which is a subsidiary of the Raytheon
Company.

The Amana Colonies Golf Course is
located just 25 miles south of Cedar Rapids
and 1/4 mile north of Middle Amana. This
excellent 6824-yard and William J. Speare–
designed layout is ranked among the top five
public and private courses in Iowa and was
rated one of the best new courses to open in
1990 by *Golf* magazine. This beautiful layout
is cut out of dense hardwood forests, has rolling fairways with a variety of elevation
changes, has water hazards on five holes and
features large, undulating bentgrass greens that
are well protected by sand traps. The bentgrass
fairways are tightly treed, and there is a strong
likelihood that you will not be hitting from a
flat lie. There are five tee distances to choose
from on this layout.

Because Amana Colonies covers 300
acres of land, each hole is isolated and a
unique golf experience. This land has been
leased for 100 years from the Amana Society.
The 191-yard par-3 eighth is one of the more
memorable holes on the course. It plays from
an elevated tee completely over water to a
large green with sand bunkers left and right.
If the pin placement is back, the green is hard

to hold because it slopes from the middle
of the green toward the rear. There are
seven tee positions to choose from on this
challenging hole.

The 432-yard par-4 twelfth is one of the
best golf holes on the course. The tee shot is
down a corridor of trees to a well-protected
landing area. The approach shot is uphill to a
large, narrow, deep green that is elevated and
protected by large sand bunkers on the left
and right. A creek runs down the left side of
the fairway from tee to green. In aggregate,
the par 4s tend to be the most difficult holes
at Amana.

The most difficult par 5 is the 522-yard
second hole, a double dogleg that is tightly
treed and strategically bunkered from tee to
green. The tee shot plays downhill toward a
right-to-left-bending corner with large bunkers
protecting the right side. The second shot is
down a fairway and over a gully that bends
back to the right and has more bunkers to the
right of the landing area. The third shot is severely uphill to a large green that is guarded
by traps to the left, rear and right. On this hole,
as with most holes at Amana, course management and shot placement are more important
than length.

The majestic clubhouse at Amana Colonies has a full pro shop, locker rooms and
showers, full lunch and dinner service, and a
snack bar. Groups and outings of up to 150
golfers can be handled here, and individual
or group instruction is available from the professional and his staff. There is a magnificent
view of the scenic middle pond and the eighteenth green from the dining room and car-
peted clubhouse deck.

Practice facilities at Amana include a driving range and putting green. Condominiums
are available for rent on the property, or you
can stay at any of the motels or bed and
breakfasts in the historic Amana Colonies,
which you should take time to see. Amana
Colonies has a fascinating mix of museums,
wineries, a brewery, restaurants, inns, furniture factories, and arts-and-crafts shops that
are a testimony to the history, dedication,
skill and adaptability of the residents. Almost
2 million people visit the Amana Colonies
each year—it is the biggest tourist attraction
in the State of Iowa.

Recommended Golf Courses in Iowa

Within 1 Hour of Cedar Rapids:

Finkbine Golf Course, Iowa City, (319) 335–9556, Public, 18/6850/72

Glynn's Creek, Davenport, (319) 285–6444, Public, 18/7036/72

Muscatine Golf Course, Muscatine, (319) 263–4735, Public, 18/6471/72

Pheasant Ridge Golf Course, Cedar Falls, (319) 273–8647, Public, 18/6472/72

Squaw Creek Golf Course, Marion, (319) 398–5182, Public, 18/6629/72

Twin Pines Golf Course, Cedar Rapids, (319) 398–5183, Public, 18/5909/72

Within 1 Hour of Des Moines:

Bos Landen Golf Club, Pella, (515) 628–4625, (800) 916–7888, Public, 18/6632/72

Jester Park, Granger, (515) 999–2903, Public, 18/6801/72

Lake Panorama National Golf Course, Panora, (515) 755–2024, (800) 766–RESORT, 18/7001/72

Venker Memorial Golf Course, Ames, (515) 294–6727, Public, 18/6543/72

Waveland Golf Course, Des Moines, (515) 242–2911, Public, 18/6419/72

Burlington Area:

Sheaffer Golf Course, Fort Madison, (319) 528–6214, 18/6303/72

Carter Lake:

Shoreline Golf Course, Carter Lake, (712) 347–5173, Public, 18/6657/72

Clinton:

Valley Oaks Golf Club, Clinton, (319) 242–7221, Semiprivate, 18/6855/72

Iowa City

Pleasant Valley Golf Club, Iowa City, (319) 337–7209, Public, 18/6472/72

Within 1½ Hours of Sioux City:

Emerald Hills Golf Club, Arnolds Park, (712) 332–5672, Semiprivate, 18/6600/72

Green Valley Golf Club, Sioux City, (712) 252–2025, Public, 18/7190/72

Spencer:

Spencer Golf and Country Club, Spencer, (712) 262–2028, Semiprivate, 18/6888/72

Spirit Lake Area:

Brooks Golf Club, Okoboji, (712) 332–5011, Public, 18/6228/72

Okoboji Vu Golf Course, Spirit Lake, (712) 337–3372, Public, 18/6051/70

Waterloo:

Gates Park Golf Course, Waterloo, (319) 291–4485, Public, 18/6833/72

Iowa: Useful Information

Iowa Department of Economic Development, 200 E. Grand Ave., Des Moines, IA 50309, (515) 242–4705, (800) 345–IOWA

Department of Natural Resources, Wallace State Office Bldg., East 9th St. and Grand Ave., Des Moines, IA 50319–0034, (515) 281–5145 (recreation information)

Department of Natural Resources, Wallace State Office Bldg., East 9th St. and Grand Ave., Des Moines, IA 50319–0034, (515) 281–5145 (fishing and hunting regulations)

Course Name: ALVAMAR GOLF CLUB

Course Type: Public
Address: 1800 Crossgate Drive
Lawrence, KS 66047
Phone: (913) 842–1907

GOLF COURSE

Head Professional: Brad Demo
Course Length/Par (All Tees): Back 7096/72, Middle 6398/72, Forward 5489/72
Course Slope/Rating (All Tees): Back 135/74.7, Middle 133/71.4, Forward 111/67.0
Course Architect: Bob Dunning (1968)
Golf Facilities: Full Pro Shop X, Snack Bar X, Lounge Beer, Restaurant No, Locker Room No, Showers No, Club Rental X, Club Repair X, Cart Rental X, Instruction X, Practice Green X, Driving Range X, Practice Bunker X, Club Storage No
Tee-Time Reservation Policy: Up to 7 days in advance
Ranger: Yes
Tee-off-Interval Time: 8 min.
Time to Play 18 Holes: 4½ hrs.
Course Hours/Earliest Tee-off: 7 a.m. Sat., Sun., holidays; 8 a.m. Mon. to Fri.
Green Fees: $32 for 18 holes Sat., Sun., holidays; $21 for 18 holes Mon. to Fri.; $14 for 9 holes Sat., Sun., holidays; $10 for 9 holes Mon. to Fri.
Cart Fees: $12.50 for 18 holes, $6.50 for 9 holes per person
Pull Carts: $3 for 18 holes, $2 for 9 holes
Credit Cards: Discover, MasterCard, Visa
Season: Year round
Course Comments: Can walk anytime
Golf Packages: None
Discounts: Twilight rates
Places to Stay Nearby: Days Inn (913) 843–9100, (800) 325–2525; Holiday Inn (913) 841–7077, (800) HOLIDAY; Best Western (913) 841–6500, (800) 528–1234; Quality Inn University (913) 842–7030; Bismark Inn (913) 749–4040. BED AND BREAKFAST: Halcyon House Bed and Breakfast (913) 841–0314

Local Attractions: University of Kansas, Lawrence Community Theater, Riverfront Plaza, Victorian architecture, Clinton Lake, Lawrence Arts Center, seasonal arts festivals, Elizabeth M. Watkins Community Museum, Dyche Museum of Natural History, Spencer Museum of Art. Information Center (open 24 hrs.) (913) 864–3506. Convention and Visitors Bureau (913) 865–4411
Directions: From Kansas City (40 mi.): I–70 west, 2nd Lawrence exit, head south on Iowa St. to Clinton Pkwy., turn right on Clinton Pkwy., 2 mi. on right, sign for golf course on Crossgate Dr.
Closest Commercial Airport: Kansas City International (1 hr.)

ALVAMAR GOLF CLUB

The Alvamar Golf Club is, according to Golf Digest, one of the top 75 public golf courses in the nation. This 7096-yard par-72 layout was designed by Bob Dunning and is located in the Alvamar section of Lawrence, Kansas, home of the University of Kansas. Bob attended the university and became a professional golfer in the 1920s. He became interested in golf-course architecture after serving as a greenkeeper and eventually assisted Ralph Plummer in establishing several veterans hospital courses after World War II. He was considered a turfgrass expert and was highly regarded as a greens consultant. He designed golf courses full-time beginning in 1960. Dunning remodeled and designed several courses in his native Kansas, including Dubs Dread in Piper, Leawood South in Leawood, and Pawnee Prairie in Wichita. Dunning died in 1979 at the age of 78.

Alvamar is a rolling course with very large, fast, slightly undulating bentgrass greens. The front nine is a bit more open than the back nine. Water comes into play on five holes. The number-1-handicap hole is the 419-yard par-4 sixth, an uphill dogleg right with trees on both sides of the fairway. Another difficult hole is the 411-yard par-4 fourteenth, a tight dogleg left and right with a lateral hazard and out of bounds on the left hand side.

The two finishing holes at Alvamar are a good test of your game. The 564-yard par-5 seventeenth is a dogleg right up a tightly treed fairway to a green guarded by a pond in front. The 402-yard par-4 eighteenth is straight to a large green with a huge pond in front and three bunkers guarding the putting surface.

The Kansas Open, a mini tour event, is held at Alvamar every year, and the University of Kansas golf team practices on this course. The clubhouse has a pro shop and snack bar but no locker room or showers. Group and individual instruction is available at the on-site driving range, practice green and practice bunker. Within walking distance of Alvamar is the eighteen-hole private Alvamar Golf Course. The Alvamar public course is open year round, weather permitting, and you can walk anytime.

Course Name: **BUFFALO DUNES GOLF COURSE**

Course Type: Public
Address: Route 83
Garden City, KS 67846
Phone: (316) 276-1210

GOLF COURSE

Head Professional: Paul Parker
Course Length/Par (All Tees): Back 6767/72, Middle 6443/72, Forward 5598/72
Course Slope/Rating (All Tees): Back 126/73.2, Middle 123/71.8, Forward 112/71.2
Course Architect: Frank Hummel (1976)
Golf Facilities: Full Pro Shop X, Snack Bar X, Lounge Beer, Restaurant No, Locker Room No, Showers No, Club Rental X, Club Repair X, Cart Rental X, Instruction X, Practice Green X, Driving Range X, Practice Bunker X, Club Storage No
Tee-Time Reservation Policy: Up to 1 week in advance from 5 p.m.
Ranger: Yes
Tee-off-Interval Time: 8 min.
Time to Play 18 Holes: 4 hrs. 15 min.
Course Hours/Earliest Tee-off: 7 a.m.
Green Fees: $12 daily fee Sat., Sun., holidays; $10 daily fee weekdays

Cart Fees: $17 for 18 holes, $9.50 for 9 holes per cart. Pull carts $2 for 18 holes
Credit Cards: No. Cash or check
Season: Year round, weather permitting. Busiest May through Labor Day
Course Comments: You can walk anytime. Private carts allowed at $6.25 plus tax trail fee
Golf Packages: No
Discounts: Juniors, seniors, twilight (2 hrs. before dark)
Places to Stay Nearby: Best Western Wheatlands (316) 276–2387, (800) 528–1234; Red Baron Best Western (316) 275–4164, (800) 528–1234; Super 8 Motel (316) 275–9625, (800) 800–8000
Local Attractions: Finnup Park and Lee Richardson Zoo, seasonal festivals including Beef Empire Days held in early June. Garden City Area Chamber of Commerce, 1511 E. Fulton Terrace, Garden City, KS 67846–6165 (316) 276–3264
Directions: From Garden City go south (15 min.) on Rte. 83 to golf course
Closest Commercial Airports: Garden City Municipal (20 min.); Amarillo, TX (3½ hrs.); Pueblo, CO (3½ hrs.); Wichita (3½ hrs.)

BUFFALO DUNES GOLF COURSE

"We're not at the edge of the world, but you can see it from here." That's how Paul Parker, Head Professional at Buffalo Dunes, characterizes Garden City, a major wheat, alfalfa, corn, and cattle center in Western Kansas. South of Garden City is Buffalo Dunes, a Frank Hummel design and one of golf's best bargains.

Wind and rough are major factors to consider at this open links-style course set out on the Great Plains. The most difficult hole on the course is the 564-yard par-5 sixteenth which plays straight into the wind. It is easy to find the notoriously difficult Buffalo Dunes rough on this hole. Typically the bluegrass fairways at Buffalo Dunes are 30 to 35 yards wide. Light rough is ten to fifteen feet wide, then you reach the native tall grass that can be two to three feet high. This high rough can eat your golf balls and cause you endless frustration if you stray the ball too far at Buffalo Dunes. The second shot on the sixteenth is a lay up to avoid a pond that cuts from the right and alongside the right of an undulating green with bunkers to its left. A mound blocks your view of the water until after you hit your second shot and march toward the green. Another difficult hole immediately follows. The 189-yard par-3 seventeenth plays uphill and into the wind. The green is not visible from the tee.

Frank Hummel, a native of LaJunia, Colorado, started his own design firm in 1968 after working as an engineer in Pueblo. He has designed many courses in Colorado, Kansas, Montana, Nebraska, and Wyoming. Buffalo Dunes allows walking anytime and has a daily green fee of less than $15.

Garden City is named Garden City because of the beautiful gardens of Mrs. William D. Fulton, wife of a founder of this town. If you come here in June, you can participate in Beef Empire Days, a 10-day festival that includes cattle shows, western art exhibits, rodeo, and cookouts.

Course Name: **DEER CREEK GOLF CLUB**

Course Type: Semiprivate
Address: 700 West 133rd Street
              Overland Park, KS 66209
Phone: (913) 681–3100

GOLF COURSE

Head Professional: David J. Richardson
Course Length/Par (All Tees): Back 6870/72, White Long 6368/72, White Short 5948/72, Forward 5120/72
Course Slope/Rating (All Tees): Back 137/74.5, White Long 128/72.5, White Short 124/64.5, Ladies' Forward 113/68.5
Course Architect: Robert Trent Jones, Jr. (1989)
Golf Facilities: Full Pro Shop X, Snack Bar X, Lounge X, Restaurant X, Locker Room X, Showers X, Club Rental X, Club Repair X, Cart Rental X, Instruction X, Practice Green X, Driving Range X, Practice Bunker X, Club Storage X

Tee-Time Reservation Policy: Members: 2 wks. in advance. Public: 1 day in advance
Ranger: Yes
Tee-off-Interval Time: 10 min.
Time to Play 18 Holes: 4½ hrs.
Course Hours/Earliest Tee-off: Dawn to dusk
Green and Cart Fees: $50 for 18 holes with cart weekends and holidays, $42 for 18 holes with cart weekdays
Credit Cards: Discover, MasterCard, Visa
Season: Year round
Course Comments: Can walk anytime. Lighted driving range. Memberships available. Use of banquet facilities, conferences, tournaments and outings are mostly Mon., Tues.; outings anytime. Golf schools
Golf Packages: Available through local hotels. Inquire at clubhouse
Discounts: Twilight rates, replays
Places to Stay Nearby: OVERLAND PARK: Doubletree Hotel (913) 451–6100, (800) 325–2525; Marriott Overland Park (913) 451–8000, (800) 228–9290; Club House Inn—Overland Park (913) 648–5555, (800) CLUB INN; Hampton Inn (913) 341–1551, (800) 426–7866; Ramada Inn and Suites Overland Park (913) 888–8440, (800) 228–2828; Courtyard by Marriott (913) 339–9900, (800) 321–2211. KANSAS CITY: Adam's Motel (816) 737–0200, (800) 231–5838; Hallmark Inn Midtown/Med Center (913) 236–6880; Kansas City Marriott Suite Country Club (816) 931–4400, (800) 228–9290; Holiday Inn Sports Complex (816) 353–5300, (800) 621–6258; Ritz Carlton Kansas City (816) 756–1500, (800) 241–3333
Local Attractions: OVERLAND PARK: Deanne Rose Children's Farmstead, National Collegiate Athletic Association/Visitors Center, arboretum, Metcalf South shopping center. KANSAS CITY: Grinter Place Museum, Hallmark Visitors Center, Lyric Theater; jazz, blues, night clubs; professional hockey, baseball, football; rodeo, theater, concerts, restaurants, Kansas City Museum, Kansas City Zoo, Crown Center shopping,

Nelson–Atkins Museum of Art, seasonal festivals, Toy and Miniature Museum, Woodlands Racetrack (horse racing and dog racing), Worlds of Fun/Oceans of Fun entertainment complex, horseback riding, parks, tennis, other recreational activities. INDEPENDENCE, MO: Harry S. Truman Library, Old Shawnee Town. SHAWNEE: Johnson Country Historical Museum. LIBERTY, MO: Jesse James Bank Museum. Kansas City Convention and Visitors Bureau (816) 221–5242, (800) 767–7700

Directions: From I–435: Hwy. 69 south, Olathe exit, left on Hwy. 150 east, 2 traffic lights to Metcalf Ave., left onto Metcalf, right on 133rd St., course in view

Closest Commercial Airport: Kansas City International (45 min.)

DEER CREEK GOLF CLUB

Deer Creek is located in Overland Park, Kansas, a suburb 20 min. southwest of Kansas City. Deer Creek is part of a real-estate development in the Tomahawk Creek Valley with homes starting from approximately $300,000. The course, which winds its way through the development, was designed by Robert Trent Jones, Jr., and opened in 1989. It immediately became part of the Ben Hogan Tour, and *Golf Digest* lists it among the top five courses, public or private, in Kansas. Deer Creek is public, with resident members, corporate members and the general public among those who play 35,000 rounds of golf a year here. Tournaments may be scheduled for charity, fund raising, corporate meetings or company outings on Monday or Tuesday.

The 6870-yard layout has a hefty slope rating of 137 and a USGA rating of 74.5 from the back tees. This is due to the well-treed fairways, with beautiful oak, maple, ash, hickory, sycamore and other varieties, 85 bunkers, 13 water holes, and up-and-down terrain. The bentgrass greens are medium sized and fast, with subtle undulation. They are in excellent condition, as are the bluegrass fescue rough and bunker areas and the zoysia tees and fairways. You can walk the course anytime, and in the process

you are likely to see deer, quail, fox, geese and other animal friends.

The rich variety of holes at Deer Creek require good course management, accurate club selection and strategic thinking. Often a variety of strategic options are available to the golfer as sand, water, trees and the interesting mix of green shapes, sizes and pin placements come into play. Each hole has a name, and the number-1-handicap hole is number three, aptly called "Great One." This 422-yard par 4 is a slight dogleg left to a wide but shallow green with a stream and a large trap in front, and two traps to the rear. The tee shot is downhill, over a stream, to an undulating fairway with a stream running up the left side to the green. There is no room for the ball to stray on any of your shots here.

The fifteenth hole, "Devastation," is a 227-yard par 3 and has been voted one of the most difficult holes in the Kansas City area. The tee is slightly elevated, and the green is deep and narrow, with a trap on each side and a stream in front. An embankment in back and to the sides of the green provides an amphitheater effect. The tee shot is often into the wind. Those who regularly play Deer Creek call this the shortest par 5 in town.

The finishing hole, "Gambler," is another potentially treacherous beauty. A 527-yard par 5, this hole plays straight to a narrow, deep green with two traps to the left and a long trap to the right from 65 yards into the putting surface. A stream runs up the left side, cuts the fairway 300 yards from the tee, then runs up the right side before turning away from the trap. Long hitters will have to decide whether to go for the green in two or lay up. To be considered is the narrow entrance to the target guarded by trees and traps.

The modern clubhouse sits above a valley and features a panoramic view of the golf course. It provides the ambience of a private club and includes a restaurant and grill that is open seven days a week and serves breakfast, lunch, dinner and Sunday brunch. A special dining room, full-service catering and banquet services are available. The clubhouse also has a complete pro shop, locker rooms and showers, club rental, club repair and club storage. Individual and group instruction is available, and the on-site driving range and practice area is lighted at night.

Course Name: TERRADYNE RESORT HOTEL AND COUNTRY CLUB

Course Type: Resort
Address: 1400 Terradyne Road
                       Andover, KS 67002
Phone: (316) 733–5851 (Golf Course),
                       (316) 733–2582 (Resort)

GOLF COURSE

Head Professional: Doug Atherly
Course Length/Par (All Tees): Back 6843/72, Middle 6215/72, Forward 5048/72
Course Slope/Rating (All Tees): Back 139/74.3, Middle 135/71.5, Forward 121/70.2
Course Architect: Don Sechrest (1987)
Golf Facilities: Full Pro Shop X, Snack Bar X, Lounge X, Restaurant X, Locker Room X, Showers X, Club Rental X, Club Repair X, Cart Rental X, Instruction X, Practice Green X, Driving Range X, Practice Bunker X, Club Storage X
Tee-Time Reservation Policy: Up to 7 days in advance
Ranger: Yes
Tee-off-Interval Time: 7 min.
Time to Play 18 Holes: 4 hrs. 15 min.
Course Hours/Earliest Tee-off: 7 a.m.
Green Fees: $25 for Terradyne Resort Hotel guests. You must be a guest, member, or guest of a member to play the course
Cart Fees: $10 per person for 18 holes
Credit Cards: American Express, Master-Card, Visa
Season: Year round. Busiest June through Labor Day
Course Comments: Walking allowed anytime
Golf Packages: Through hotel. Inquire at hotel or pro shop
Discounts: Resort guests

Places to Stay Nearby: You must be a guest of the Teradyne Resort Hotel, a member, or the guest of a member to play the course. WICHITA: Bed and Breakfast at Willowbend (316) 636–4032; Inn at the Park (316) 652–0500, (800) 258–1951; Max Paul...An Inn (316) 689–8101; Wichita Marriott (316) 651–0333, (800) 228–9290
Local Attractions: WICHITA: Botanica, Children's Museum, Indian Center Museum, Lake Afton Public Observatory, Old Cow Town Museum, Omnisphere and Science Center, Sedgewick County Zoo, Wichita Art Museum, Wichita Center for the Arts, Wichita State University, minor league professional baseball, Wichita Greyhound Park, seasonal festivals. Wichita Convention and Visitor's Bureau, 100 S. Main, Wichita, KS 67202 (316) 265–2800
Directions: Terradyne is 10 mi. east of Wichita. Take Central Ave. east to 159th St. Turn left and proceed 1/4 mi. to golf course
Closest Commercial Airport: Wichita (30 min.)

TERRADYNE GOLF CLUB

The Terradyne Resort Hotel and Country Club golf course is a Don Sechrest–designed, open, links-style layout ten miles east of Wichita. In order to succeed at Terradyne, you have to cope with the wind that can blow up to 40 miles per hour. You also have to keep that ball on the short grass or you will likely be in sand, water, or thick rough. Water can come into play on half the holes here including the 465-yard par-4 opening hole, a dogleg right whose approach shot is to a huge double green squeezed by bunkers in front and water to its right. Two difficult and memorable holes on the back side are the 594-yard par-5 eleventh and the 225-yard par-3 twelfth. The eleventh, whose tee shot landing area is narrowed by a bunker on the right, is difficult to reach in two because of a pond cutting in front of the green from the right. The picturesque twelfth plays over water to a deep green protected by a bunker to its left.

Terradyne's designer, Don Sechrest, was born in St. Joseph, Missouri, played on the golf team at Oklahoma State where he received a B.S. degree in business, briefly played on the PGA Tour, then went into practice as a golf course architect in the late 1960s. Among his designs are the Ames Golf and Country Club in Iowa, Page Belcher's Stone Creek Course in Oklahoma, and the Southwind Country Club in Kansas.

You must be a member of Terradyne, a guest of a member or a resort guest to play the course. Terradyne is rated among the top five golf courses in Kansas by *GolfWeek*. A variety of golf packages are available through the resort whose rates generally range from $75 for a standard room to $250 for an executive suite.

Recommended Golf Courses in Kansas

Dodge City:

Mariah Hills Golf Course, Dodge City, (316) 225–8182, Public, 18/6868/71

Within 1 1/2 Hours of Kansas City:

Dubs Dread Golf Club, Kansas City, (913) 721–1333, Public, 18/6987/72

Heritage Park Golf Course, Olathe, (913) 829–4653, Public, 18/6909/71

Lake Shawnee Golf Course, Topeka, (913) 267–2295, Public, 18/6013/69

Rolling Meadows Golf Course, Junction City, (913) 238 4303, Public, 18/6900/72

Sunflower Hills, Bonner Springs, (913) 721–2727, Public, 18/7001/72

Manhattan Area:

Custer Hill Golf Club, Fort Riley, (913) 239–5412, Semiprivate, 18/6750/72

Salina:

Salina Municipal Golf Club, Salina, (913) 826–7450, Public, 18/6650/70

Within 1 Hour of Wichita:

Hesston Municipal Golf Park, Hesston, (316) 327–2331, Public, 18/6526/71

MacDonald Golf Course, Wichita, (316) 688–9391, Public, 18/6750/72

Quail Ridge Golf Course, Winfield, (316) 221–5645, Public, 18/6826/72

Turkey Creek Golf Course, McPherson, (316) 241–8530, Public, 18/6241/70

Willow Bend Golf Club, Wichita, (316) 636–4653, Semiprivate, 18/6700/72

Kansas: Useful Information

Kansas Department of Commerce, Travel and Tourism Development Division, 400 S.W. 8th St., 5th Fl., Topeka, KS 66614 (800) 252–6727 (KS), (913) 296–2009 (outside KS)

Kansas Wildlife and Parks, 3300 S.W. 29th St., Topeka, KS 66614, (913) 273–6740 (recreation information)

Kansas Wildlife and Parks, 3300 S.W. 29th St., Topeka, KS 66614, (913) 273–6740 (fishing and hunting regulations)

Course Name: GRIFFIN GATE GOLF COURSE

Course Type: Resort
Resort: Marriott's Griffin Gate
Address: 1800 Newtown Pike
(Route 922)
Lexington, KY 40511
Phone: (606) 254–4101 (Golf Course)
(606) 231–5100,
(800) 228–9290 (U.S. and
Canada) (Resort)
Fax: (606) 255–9944 (Resort)

GOLF COURSE

Director of Golf: John Faulk
Course Length/Par (All Tees): Back
6801/72, Blue 6296/72, White 5948/72,
Forward 4970/72
Course Slope/Rating (All Tees): Back
132/73.1, Blue 128/71.5, White
124/69.5, Forward 119/69.0
Course Architect: Rees Jones (1981)
Golf Facilities: Full Pro Shop X, Snack
Bar X, Lounge X, Restaurant X,
Locker Room X, Showers X, Club
Rental X, Club Repair X, Cart Rental
X, Instruction X, Practice Green X,
Driving Range No, Practice Bunker
No, Club Storage X
Tee-Time Reservation Policy: Resort
guests: 2 months in advance, groups 1
yr. Members: 1 wk. in advance. Public:
7 days in advance, call from 7:30 a.m.
Ranger: Yes
Tee-off-Interval Time: 10 min.
Time to Play 18 Holes: 4½ hrs.
Course Hours/Earliest Tee-off: Sunrise
Green and Cart Fees: Peak season rates:
$59 for 18 holes with cart Sat., Sun.,
holidays; $49 for 18 holes with cart
Mon. to Thurs.
Credit Cards: All major cards
Season: Year round. Busiest seasons April,
Aug. to Oct.
Course Comments: Cart mandatory.
Yardage book available
Golf Packages: Available through Marriott.
Value seasons mid-Nov. to late Feb.
Discounts: Off-season mid-Nov. to mid-
March, twilight

Places to Stay Nearby: See page 332
Local Attractions: See page 332
Lexington Visitors and Convention
Bureau (606) 233–1221, (800) 848–1224
Directions: From Bluegrass Field Airport,
Lexington (15 min.): Rte. 60 east to
New Circle Rd. (Circle 4) north, to New-
town Pike north (Rte. 922), 1½ mi. on
the right
Closest Commercial Airports: Bluegrass
Field, Lexington (15 min.); Standiford
Field, Louisville (1 hr., 15 min.);
Greater Cincinnati International (1½
hrs.); Yeager, Charleston (2 hrs.)

RESORT

Date Built: 1981
No. of Rooms: 388 guest rooms plus 24
junior suites, hospitality suites,
presidential-level suites
Meeting Rooms: 15. Capacity of Largest:
1370 persons banquet style. Meeting
Space: 19,000 sq. ft.
Room Price Range: $125 double weekday
to $850 for best suite peak season (late
Feb. to mid-Nov.). Golf, honeymoon
and other packages available. Special
weekend rates
Lounges: Pegasus Lounge
Restaurants: Mansion, J.W.'S Steakhouse,
Griffin Gate Gardens
Entertainment: Music and dancing in
Pegasus Lounge
Credit Cards: All major cards
General Amenities: Hair salon, gift shop,
outside babysitting services; meeting
and conference facilities in theater, conference, banquet, reception configurations with audiovisual and food services
Recreational Amenities: 3 lighted outdoor
tennis courts, indoor and outdoor swimming pools, health club, sand volleyball,
croquet, sauna, game room, whirlpool,
horseshoes
Reservation and Cancellation Policy:
Credit card guarantee or prepayment.
Must cancel by 6 p.m. of scheduled
arrival date. Reservations must be
guaranteed for package plans with
complete payment in advance or credit
card guarantee. Packages not available
in groups

Comments and Restrictions: Maximum number of people in a room is 5. Packages are for 2 people. Taxes additional to base rates. $20 one-time pet fee

GRIFFIN GATE GOLF COURSE

Griffin Gate is a 6801-yard par-72 Rees Jones layout situated on 250 acres of rolling hills just north of downtown Lexington. Marriott owns the golf course and the on-site seven-story, 388-room hotel with 2 swimming pools, 3 outdoor tennis courts, physical fitness facilities, meeting rooms, and 2 restaurants. Another restaurant, the Mansion, is in an elegant restored nineteenth-century mansion adjacent to the resort.

The golf course has been selected by *Golf Digest* as one of the best resort golf courses in America. It is open year round to hotel guests, golf-club members and the general public. The layout has water hazards on twelve of its eighteen holes, more than 65 sand bunkers, and medium to large greens that are well protected by sand and water. Although there are a variety of trees on this course, including pine, dogwood and locust, they don't normally come into play except on the seventh, eleventh and fifteenth holes. Most of the greens are level relative to the fairway, but traps often make it difficult to reach the green on the roll.

The first tee, an easy walk from the hotel and clubhouse, looks out on a 470-yard par 5 with a medium-sized, forward-sloping green protected by three large traps on the right and right front and one trap on the left. The tee shot is to a landing area guarded on the left by two fairway bunkers. The second shot is slightly downhill toward a reachable green, but watch out for the stream crossing the fairway 120 yards from the putting surface. Water is also on the left, and traps surround the green. Nevertheless, this is a potential birdie opportunity.

The course quickly starts to get more difficult and more interesting, often in subtle ways. The 169-yard par-3 second is short, but the green is wide, very shallow and protected by huge traps on the left and right. The 497-yard par-5 dogleg-left third is the signature hole here. It is short, but bunkers guard the tee-shot landing area,

and the fairway is fairly narrow. The second shot is toward a medium-sized, right-to-left-angled green with traps to the left and rear and a wide stream guarding the front. Club selection and knowing when to lay up are important here. After a short, straight, 150-yard par 3, you have the number-1-handicap 457-yard par-4 fifth. There is a huge 135-yard distance between the back tees and the blue tees on this hole, which is a dogleg left to a deep green protected by huge traps left and back. If you try to cut the corner on the dogleg, four huge bunkers are waiting for you on the left, from 190 to 125 yards into the green. The tee shot from the back tees is over a wide stream.

The finishing hole on the front nine is a long 568-yard par 5 to a tiered green with two huge traps left and left front and two more to the right and right front. The tee-shot landing area is squeezed by two fairway bunkers, and the second shot has to avoid a large bunker 130 yards from the green on the right. Because of all the sand, it is difficult to run the ball onto the green. The front nine has three par 5s and three par 3s. The toughest par 3 is the 238-yard eighth, which plays to a narrow, forward-sloping, two-tiered green guarded by two large traps to the right and one to the left. This is a very intimidating hole, especially if the pin is on the back shelf.

The back nine starts out with one of the toughest holes on the course, a 495-yard dogleg-left par 5 with water crossing in front of the tees and running up the left fairway to the green. Your first shot can bite off as much of the dogleg as you'd like, but the fairway is narrow and it is easy to hit the water on the left. On the second shot, you're looking at four large bunkers from 140 yards into a deep, forward-sloping, two-tiered green. Because of the bends in the fairway, distances are not easy to calculate on this hole. The finishing hole is a 406-yard par 4 from the back tees. The drive is slightly uphill and must split two fairway bunkers. The second shot is to a deep green with four traps left, right and rear.

Griffin Gate is an interesting blend of long par 3s, longish par 4s, short par 5s with hazards on the second shot and long par 5s with bunkers to keep you honest. You get an occasional breather, but the combination of well-placed bunkers, water, strategic doglegs and sloping and undulating, cleverly angled greens and traps requires all of your clubs and most of your wits.

The clubhouse at Griffin Gate has women's and men's locker rooms, a bar and grill, and a pro shop that was recently recognized by *Golf Shop Operations* magazine as one of the best in the country. The staff of professionals provides group and individual lessons, including playing lessons. At present the practice area is limited because a former driving range has become part of the residential housing that borders the course. Griffin Gate is the former site of the Bank One Classic and now holds a variety of professional minitour and sectional events. Approximately 50 percent of the play at Griffin Gate is from on-site Marriott guests, 30 percent is from members and the balance from the public. A variety of golf packages are available, as are seasonal discounts. Tournament groups, hotel guests and members have tee-time reservation priority.

Course Name: KEARNEY HILL GOLF LINKS

Course Type: Public
Address: 3403 Kearney Road
                    Lexington, KY 40511
Phone: (606) 253–1918

GOLF COURSE

Head Professional: Larry Smith
Course Length/Par (All Tees): Back 6987/72, Middle 6501/72, Forward 5362/72
Course Slope/Rating (All Tees): Back 128/73.5, Middle 122/70.5, Forward 118/70.1
Course Architects: Pete Dye and P.B. Dye (1989)
Golf Facilities: Full Pro Shop X, Snack Bar X, Lounge No, Restaurant No, Locker Room X, Showers X, Club Rental X, Club Repair Minor, Cart Rental X, Instruction X, Practice

Green X, Driving Range X, Practice Bunker X, Club Storage No
Tee-Time Reservation Policy: Threesomes or foursomes up to 7 days in advance
Ranger: Yes
Tee-off-Interval Time: 10 min.
Time to Play 18 Holes: 4 hrs., 45 min.
Course Hours/Earliest Tee-off: 8:30 a.m.
Green Fees: $20 for 18 holes
Cart Fees: $8 for 18 holes per person
Pull Carts: $3 for 18 holes
Credit Cards: MasterCard, Visa
Season: Year round
Course Comments: Can walk anytime. Yardage book available
Golf Packages: None
Discounts: County civil servants, seniors, juniors, Ladies' Day (Tues.), golf discount card, twilight rate
Places to Stay Nearby: Holiday Inn North (606) 233–0512, (800) HOLIDAY; La Quinta Motor Inn (606) 231–7551, (800) 531–5900; Courtyard by Marriott (606) 253–4646, (800) 321–2211; Campbell House Inn, Suites and Golf Club (606) 255–4281, (800) 432–9254 (KY), (800) 354–9235 (outside KY); Best Western Regency/Lexington Inn (606) 293–2202, (800) 528–1234; Radisson Plaza Hotel Lexington (606) 231–9000, (800) 333–3333
Local Attractions: University of Kentucky, American Saddle Horse Museum, Hunt–Morgan house, Lexington Cemetery, Red Mile Harness Track, Henry Clay's Estate (Ashland), Keenland Race Course, Kentucky Guild Gallery, Kentucky Horse Park, Headley–Whitney Museum, Lexington Children's Museum, Mary Todd Lincoln house, Waveland state historic site, Raven Run Nature Sanctuary, Spendthrift Farm. Lexington Visitors and Convention Bureau (606) 233–1221, (800) 848–1224
Directions: From New Circle Rd.; exit Rte. 25/Georgetown Rd., 3½ mi., Kearney Rd. left, ½ mile
Closest Commercial Airport: Bluegrass Field, Lexington (20 min.)

KEARNEY HILL GOLF LINKS

Kearney Hill is a new Dye-designed golf course owned and operated by the city of Lexington. Ranked one of the best golf courses in the state of Kentucky by *Golf Digest*, Kearney Hill is a 6987-yard par-72 bentgrass layout situated on 200 acres of land in northwestern Lexington. The high maintenance standards, as exemplified by its hand-mown greens, 10-minute tee-off-time interval and relatively late, 8:30 a.m. earliest tee-off time, are hallmarks of the Kearney Hill operation. Since Kearney Hill opened, the Bank One Senior PGA Tour Classic, formerly held at Griffin Gate in Lexington, has been held on this layout.

The abundance of difficult bunkers and the tricky winds at Kearney add to its challenge. Fairway position relative to pin position on the large, fast, undulating, well-protected greens is critical. The number-1-handicap par-5 seventh hole is 574 yards starting from an elevated tee whose first shot is to a fairway protected to the left and right by bunkers approximately 250 yards distant. The second shot is to an open area unless you get to the green, which has several traps to the front and left.

There are four long and tough par 4s on Kearney Hill. The 453-yard fourth hole is straight but has a huge trap on the left running up to the green from 100 yards out. A large bunker protects the back of the green. The 469-yard ninth hole is a boomerang-shaped dogleg to the right, with a large trap to the right and in front of the green. The 468-yard thirteenth is a dogleg right with a large right-fairway trap beginning approximately 190 yards from the green, which is protected on the left and right by two huge, elongated traps. The 433-yard seventeenth is a slight dogleg right with water immediately to the left of the tee and water beginning on the right approximately 225 yards from the green and continuing beyond it. The green is protected on the left front and right front by traps. Another fairway bunker, to the left and approximately 220 yards from the tee, makes the tee-shot landing area very tight.

The number-2-handicap 539-yard par-5 fourteenth is relatively straight from an elevated tee that comes down to a fairway swale, then gradually up to the green. From 120 yards into this horseshoe-shaped green bunkers can cause problems. One is to the left at 120 yards, and three stretch from 100 yards into the green on the right side. An additional two traps, including a huge craterlike trap in front, protect the green itself. The 531-yard par-5 eighteenth is a strong finishing hole that plays straight to an elevated green surrounded by amphi-theater-style banking typical of this course. To the left of the green is a huge, elongated trap that runs into the green from 130 yards out. Two other traps are to the right front of the green.

Kearney Hills has an excellent 10-acre practice facility with two large bentgrass practice tees and a 300-yard-long driving area. There are two practice putting greens and one practice chipping green. The clubhouse has a snack bar, men's and women's locker rooms and showers, and a complete pro shop, with individual and group instruction available.

Course Name: **LASSING POINTE GOLF CLUB**

Course Type: Public
Address: 2266 Double Eagle Drive
              Union, KY 41091
Phone: (606) 384–2266
Fax: (606) 384–2983

GOLF COURSE

Director of Golf: Jeff Kruempelman

Course Length/Par (All Tees): Back 6724/71, Black 6256/71, White 5784/71, Forward 5153/71

Course Slope/Rating (All Tees): Back 132/72.2, Black 128/70.1, White 123/67.9, Forward 118/65.1, Ladies' White 129/73.0, Ladies' Forward 122/69.5

Course Architect: Michael Hurdzan (1994)

Golf Facilities: Full Pro Shop X, Snack Bar X, Lounge Beer only, Restaurant No, Locker Room No, Showers No, Club Rental X, Club Repair X, Cart Rental X, Instruction X, Practice Green X, Driving Range X, Practice Bunker X, Club Storage No

Tee-Time Reservation Policy: Up to 7 days in advance

Ranger: Yes

Tee-off-Interval Time: 11 min. weekdays, 14 min. weekends

Time to Play 18 Holes: 4½ hrs.

Course Hours/Earliest Tee-off: 7:45 a.m.

Green and Cart Fees: $32.50 for 18 holes Fri., Sat., Sun., holidays with cart, $22.50 for 18 holes without cart; $31.50 for 18 holes weekdays with cart, $21.50 for 18 holes without cart

Credit Cards: MasterCard, Visa

Season: Late Apr. through Oct. Open weekends in Nov.

Course Comments: Can walk anytime. Closed Mondays. Yardage book available

Golf Packages: No

Discounts: Juniors, seniors

Places to Stay Nearby: COVINGTON: Embassy Suites (606) 261–8400, (800) 362–2779. FLORENCE: Commonwealth Hilton (606) 371–4400, (800) 445–8667; Fairfield Inn by Marriott (606) 371–4800, (800) 228–2800; Holiday Inn Florence (606) 371–2700, (800) HOLIDAY; Ramada (606) 371–4700, (800) 272–6232. CINCINNATI: The Cincinnatian Hotel (513) 381–3000, (800) 942–9000; Omni Netherland Plaza (513) 421–9100, (800) THE–OMNI; Westin Hotel Cincinnati (513) 621–7700, (800) 228–3000

Local Attractions: COVINGTON: Riverboats, Big Bone Lick State Park, Oldenberg Brewery and Entertainment Complex. FLORENCE: Turfway Park Race Track. CINCINNATI: Cincinnati Art Museum, Cincinnati Zoo and Botanical Garden, Harriet Beecher Stowe House, Mount Airy Forest, The Museum Center at Union Terminal, Cincinnati Historical Society Museum, Cincinnati Museum of Natural History, Paramount's Kings Island, Surf Cincinnati Waterpark, Taft Museum, horseracing at River Downs in Kentucky, Riverfront Stadium and NFL football, major league baseball, University of Cincinnati, Xavier University, restaurants, shopping, nightlife. Cincinnati Convention and Visitors Bureau, 300 W. 6th St., Cincinnati, OH 45202 (513) 621–2142, (800) 344–3445

Directions: From Greater Cincinnati Airport (30 min. southwest): Take I–75 south to Exit 180 (Union/Florence). Take right onto Rte. 42 and proceed 5 miles to Double Eagle Dr. and the golf course

Closest Commercial Airport: Greater Cincinnati International (30 min.)

LASSING POINTE GOLF COURSE

Lassing Pointe is a lush Mike Hurdzan-designed course on rolling former farmland and woodlands at the highest point in Boone County. Operated by the County of Boone, Lassing Pointe was purchased from the school board and a fee of 25 cents per round will be paid to the board for the next twenty years to cover the purchase price. The maintenance of this bentgrass layout is impeccable, partly due to the limited number of rounds allowed and the carts on paths only rule. The course is closed one day a week for maintenance and tee off interval times range from a generous 11 to 14 minutes. Lassing Pointe is noted for its ample fairways, sizeable greens, mature trees, and interesting design challenges that offer a variety of strategic options on most holes. Variable winds can add to the difficulty of this layout.

A tough par 5 at Lassing Pointe is the 521-yard eighth which requires two heroic shots to reach a wide, shallow green backed by bunkers and fronted by a lake and a huge bunker. Most golfers will lay up and hit a lofted club to the target on the third shot. A favorite par 3 is the 187-yard fourteenth which plays over water to a wide, shallow target backed by three bunkers. Brush guards the left rear of the green making a pin position to the left extremely difficult. The 441-yard par-4 finishing hole culminates at one of the biggest single greens you'll ever see. This 101-yard-deep monster juts out onto a peninsula and can easily leave you with a four putt opportunity.

Lassing Pointe is a well-managed, challenging layout with touches such as cart path yardage designations at twenty-five yard intervals from 250 yards in to the green to expedite play. The golf course, which is a pleasure to walk, has won recognition as one of the best in Kentucky by *Golf Digest*.

Recommended Golf Courses in Kentucky

Bowling Green Area:

Barren River State Park Golf Course, Lucas, (502) 646–4653, Public, 18/6440/72

Covington Area:

The Golf Courses at Kenton County, Independence, (606) 371–3200, Public. Fox Run: 18/7005/72. Pioneer: 18/6059/70. The Willows: 18/6791/72

Within 1 Hour of Frankfort:

Juniper Hills Golf Course, Frankfort, (502) 875–8559, Public, 18/6147/70

Lincoln Homestead, Springfield, (606) 336–7461, Public, 18/6359/71

Lexington Area:

Gibson Bay Golf Course, Richmond, (606) 623–0225, Public, 18/7113/72

Old Bridge Golf Club, Danville, (606) 236–6051, (800) 783–7153, Public, 18/6472/72

Players Club of Lexington, Lexington, (606) 255–1011, Semiprivate. Island: 9/3360/36. Lake: 9/3458/36. Creek: 9/3529/36

London:

Crooked Creek Golf Club, London, (606) 877–1933, Semiprivate, 18/7007/72

Louisville Area:

Cabin Brook, Versailles, (606) 873–8404, Public, 18/7027/72

Doe Valley Golf Club, Brandenburg, (502) 422–3397, Semiprivate, 18/6471/71

Maywood Golf Course, Bardstown, (502) 348–6600, Public, 18/6965/72

Nevel Meade Golf Course, Prospect, (502) 228–9522, Public, 18/6956/72

Quail Chase Golf Course, Louisville, (502) 239–2110, Semiprivate. South/West: 18/6728/72. South/East: 18/6715/72. West/East: 18/6493/72

Owensboro:

Ben Hawes Park Golf Course, Owensboro, (502) 685–2011, Public, 18/6591/71

Within 1 Hour of Paducah:

Boots Randolph Golf Course, Cadiz (Lake Barkley State Park), (502) 924–9076, Public, 18/6625/72

Kentucky Dam Village Golf Course, Gilbertsville, (502) 362–4271, Public, 18/6622/72

Miller Memorial Golf Course, Murray, (502) 762–2238, Public, 18/6229/71

Western Hills Golf Course, Hopkinsville, (502) 885–6023, Public, 18/6907/72

Kentucky: Useful Information

Kentucky Department of Travel Development, Capital Plaza Tower, Frankfort, KY 40601, (800) 225–TRIP

U.S. Forest Service, Daniel Boone National Forest, 100 Vaught Rd., Winchester, KY 40391, (606) 745–3100 (national forest information)

Department of Parks, Capital Plaza Tower, Frankfort, KY 40601, (800) 255–PARK (recreation information)

Department of Fish and Wildlife Resources, 1 Game Farm Rd., Frankfort, KY 40601, (502) 564–3400

Course Name: THE BLUFFS ON THOMPSON CREEK

Course Type: Resort
Address: Freeland Road at
Highway 965
P.O. Box 1220
St. Francisville, LA 70775
Phone: (504) 634–5551 (Golf Course)
(504) 634–3410 (Lodge)
Fax: (504) 634–3528 (Golf Course
Administrative Office)

GOLF COURSE

Head Professional: Ronnie Melancon
Course Length/Par (All Tees): Back
7151/72, Blue 6533/72, Green 5980/72,
Forward 44781/72
Course Slope/Rating (All Tees): Back
143/74.6, Blue 135/71.1, Green 130/69.9,
Ladies' Green 139/75, Forward 123/69.0
Course Architects: Arnold Palmer, Ed
Seay and Harrison Minchew (1988)
Golf Facilities: Full Pro Shop X, Snack
Bar X, Lounge X, Restaurant X,
Locker Room X, Showers X, Club
Rental X, Club Repair X, Cart Rental
X, Instruction X, Practice Green X,
Driving Range X, Practice Bunker X,
Club Storage X
Tee-Time Reservation Policy: At time of
confirmed reservation at the Lodge on
site
Ranger: Yes
Tee-off-Interval Time: 10 min.
Time to Play 18 Holes: 4½ hrs.
Course Hours/Earliest Tee-off: 8 a.m.
Green and Cart Fees: $67 plus tax for 18
holes with cart Fri., Sat., Sun., holidays;
$57 plus tax for 18 holes with cart Mon.
to Thurs.
Credit Cards: All major cards
Season: Year round
Course Comments: Carts mandatory.
Memberships available. You must be a
member, guest of a member, or guest at
the Lodge to play the course
Golf Packages: Available through the
Lodge
Discounts: Seasonal mid-summer and mid-
winter packages. Inquire at the Lodge

Places to Stay Nearby: ST. FRANCISVILLE:
St. Francis Hotel on the Lake (504) 635–
3821, (800) 826–9931 (LA), (800) 523–
6118 (outside LA); Milbank Historic Inn
(504) 634–5901; Propinquity (504) 635–
6540; Asphodel Inn (504) 654–6868,
(800) 424–6869; St. Francisville Inn
(504) 635–6502; Ramada Hotel St.
Francisville (504) 635–3821, (800) 826–
9931 (LA). BATON ROUGE: Hilton (504)
924–4000; Courtyard by Marriott (504)
924–6400, (800) 321–2211; Sheraton
Baton Rouge (504) 925–2244; Holiday
Inn East (504) 293–6880, (800) HOLI-
DAY; Bellemont Hotel and Convention
Center (800) 272–8300 (LA), (800) 535–
8486 (outside LA)
Local Attractions: ST. FRANCISVILLE AREA:
Audubon State Commemorative Area,
Greenwood Plantation, Rosedown
Plantation, Afta Villa Gardens, Oakley
Plantation. BATON ROUGE: State Capitol,
L.S.U. Rural Life Museum, restaurants,
Louisiana Arts and Science Center com-
plex, USS *Kidd*, Governor's Mansion,
old arsenal, Pentagon barracks, Baton
Rouge Zoo, river boat tours, Louisiana
State University, West Baton Rouge
Museum. Baton Rouge Area Convention
and Visitors Bureau (504) 383–1825,
(800) LAROUGE. St. Francisville West
Feliciana Parish Tourist Commission
(504) 635–6330
Directions: From Hwy. 61, just south of
St. Francisville, exit and turn east onto
Hwy. 965. Proceed 6 miles to Freeland
Rd., follow signs to The Lodge at The
Bluffs
Closest Commercial Airports: Baton
Rouge Metropolitan–Ryan Field (25
min.), New Orleans International (2 hrs.)

THE BLUFFS ON THOMPSON CREEK

The Bluffs on Thompson Creek is a
7151-yard par-72 layout designed by
Arnold Palmer, Ed Seay and Harrison
Minchew and beautifully situated amidst
bluffs and woodlands where John James
Audubon painted 80 of his famous "Birds
of America" series. St. Francisville, home
of this golf course, is just outside Baton
Rouge in plantation country, a fertile

region along the Mississippi River where white-columned mansions flourished near fields of cotton and sugar cane after people of English descent settled here in the late 1700s. Many historic buildings, Civil War monuments and battlefields, and spectacular plantations and lush gardens make this area of special interest.

Harold Leone, Managing Partner of The Bluffs, is originally from Texas and is a longtime golf enthusiast. He first saw Arnold Palmer in a tournament in 1965 when Leone was 15 years old. Later Leone had the distinct pleasure of meeting with and persuading Palmer to design a world-class golf course in this special setting that John James Audubon would approve of. Palmer was active in the design, visiting the site many times during the construction, and Leone joined him for a round in the fall of 1991. Leone shot 73 and Palmer carded a 69 on that day.

The Bluffs on Thompson Creek meanders through a 674-acre real-estate development, but the golf course was laid out before the rest of the land was committed for specific home sites. Unusual for Louisiana, there are severe contour and dramatic elevation changes at The Bluffs, following the natural flow of the terrain. Although the entire golf course was carved through thick forests of mature pines and hardwoods, fairway landing areas are generous and level. However, a stray tee shot will most likely wind up in a water hazard, fairway bunker or the woods. The Tifdwarf Bermuda-grass greens at the Bluffs tend to be large, quick and very undulating. Many of these greens are multitiered, demanding accuracy on approach shots to avoid three putts. There are 71 sand bunkers on the course, and water hazards are in play on 17 holes. At 143 from the championship tees, the Bluffs has the highest slope rating in the state of Louisiana.

Many of the holes at The Bluffs on Thompson Creek are memorable. The first hole, a 422-yard par 4, is a dogleg left playing along the edge of the bluffs to approximately 60 feet above Thompson Creek. To the right are fairway traps and trees protecting the tee-shot landing area. The approach is to a large green at the bluff's edge protected by bunkers.

The 525-yard par-5 twelfth hole is routed through Sweetwood Hollow, which is sometimes called the "Amen Corner" at The Bluffs. The tee shot on the twelfth is over a ravine to a plateaued landing area protected by bunkers. The second shot is to a landing area guarded by water on the right and a series of bunkers on the left. The approach is to a deep green with a trap to the rear.

The most memorable hole on the course is the 228-yard par-3 seventeenth, which plays from a dramatically placed bluff-top tee down to a large peninsula green guarded by traps on the left and front and water to the right and behind the green. The elevation drop is 50 feet from tee to green, making proper club selection essential. The par 3s at the Bluffs run in four different directions on the course layout, increasing the variety of wind fluctuations you have to consider before hitting your tee shot.

The finishing hole at the Bluffs runs back along the bluff which is on the left from tee to green. The tee shot on this challenging uphill 535-yard par 5 plays along Thompson Creek to a landing area guarded by a bunker and a lake on the right. The uphill second shot is to a small landing area guarded by bunkers. The large, deep, severely undulating green is protected by bunkers front and rear, and is located at the edge of the highest point above the creek.

The clubhouse at the Bluffs has a restaurant, lounge, meeting rooms, locker rooms and showers. The full-service restaurant features Louisiana and European cuisine and is open for breakfast, lunch and dinner daily. The practice facilities include a driving range, practice green and practice bunker. Professional instruction is available. Tennis, swimming, croquet and nature trails are within walking distance of the lodge.

The Lodge at The Bluffs includes 39 guest suites consisting of a living room, bedroom, bath, stocked honor bar and veranda. Other suite amenities include refrigerator, coffee maker, telephone, color television and a game table. The veranda offers views across the golf practice area toward the high bluffs along Thompson Creek.

Executive conference facilities at The Bluffs comfortably accommodate groups of up to 75 attendees but are most popular with smaller groups of 15 to 40 executives.

Golf Digest and other golf publications rate The Bluffs on Thompson Creek one of the best courses of any kind in the state of Louisiana. The Bluffs has already hosted the Louisiana State Amateur, the Southeastern Conference Golf Championship amd numerous other quality events.

After you play here, perhaps you will share the sentiments of John James Audubon as quoted on The Bluffs scorecard:

To leave these 'sweet woods' was painful, for in them we always enjoyed Peace and the sweetest pleasures of admiring the greatest of the Creator in all His unrivalled works.

Within easy reach of The Bluffs on Thompson Creek is Natchez, New Orleans and Baton Rouge. Attractions such as the Audubon State Commemorative Area at the Oakley Plantation, Rosedown Plantation and Gardens, Civil War battlefields and cemetaries, antique shops, restuarants and many other historic homes and gardens are in the immediate area.

Recommended Golf Courses in Louisiana

Within 1 Hour of Baton Rouge:

Belle Terre, La Place, (504) 652–5000, Semiprivate, 18/6840/72

Santa Maria Golf Course, Baton Rouge, (504) 752–9667, Public, 18/7051/72

Florien:

Toro Hills Resort, Florien, (318) 586–4661, Resort, 18/6548/72

Within 1 Hour of Lafayette:

Le Vieux Chenes Golf Club, Youngsville, (318) 837–1159, Public, 18/6824/72

Squirrel Run Golf Club, New Iberia, (318) 367–0863, Resort, 18/6773/72

Lake Charles:

Mallard Cove Golf Course, Lake Charles, (318) 491–1204, Public, 18/6803/72

Monroe:

Chennault Park Golf Course, Monroe, (318) 329–2454, Public, 18/7044/72

Within 1 Hour of New Orleans:

Bayou Oaks Golf Courses, New Orleans, (504) 483–9396, Public. Championship: 18/7061/72. Lakeside: 18/6054/70. Wisher: 18/6465/72

Eastover Country Club, New Orleans, (504) 245–7347, Semiprivate, 18/6710/72

Oak Harbor Golf Club, Slidell, (504) 646–0110, Public, 18/6890/72

Shreveport:

Huntington Park Golf Course, Shreveport, (318) 673–7765, Public, 18/7294/72

Louisiana: Useful Information

Louisiana Office of Tourism, P.O. Box 94291, Baton Rouge, LA 70804, (800) 33–GUMBO

Greater New Orleans Tourist and Convention Commission, 1520 Sugar Bowl Dr., New Orleans, LA 70112, (504) 566–5031

Kisatchie National Forest, 2600 Shreveport Hwy., Pineville, LA 71360, (318) 473–7160 (national forest information)

Louisiana Office of State Parks, Department of Culture, Recreation and Tourism, P.O. Drawer 1111, Baton Rouge, LA 70821, (504) 342–8111 (recreation information)

Louisiana Department of Wildlife and Fisheries, P.O. Box 15570, Baton Rouge, LA 70895, (504) 765–2918 (fishing and hunting regulations)

Course Name: **SABLE OAKS GOLF CLUB**

Course Type: Public
Address: 505 Country Club Drive
South Portland, ME 04106
Phone: (207) 775–6257

GOLF COURSE

Head Professional: Jim Furlong
Course Length/Par (All Tees): Back 6359/72, Middle 6056/72, Forward 4786/72
Course Slope/Rating (All Tees): Back 138/71.8, Middle 134/70.4, Forward 118/68.0, Ladies' Forward 123/71.4
Course Architects: Geoffrey Cornish and Brian Silva (1989)
Golf Facilities: Full Pro Shop X, Snack Bar X, Lounge No, Restaurant No, Locker Room No, Showers No, Club Rental X, Club Repair X, Cart Rental X, Instruction X, Practice Green X, Driving Range No, Practice Bunker No, Club Storage No
Tee-Time Reservation Policy: From 7 days in advance. Up to 12 months in advance for outings
Ranger: Yes
Tee-off-Interval Time: 8 min.
Time to Play 18 Holes: 4 hrs., 15 min.
Course Hours/Earliest Tee-off: 6 a.m. weekends, 6:30 a.m. weekdays
Green Fees: $29 for 18 holes Sat., Sun., holidays; $23 for 18 holes weekdays. $12 for 9 holes weekdays only
Cart Fees: $22 for 18 holes, $14 for 9 holes
Credit Cards: MasterCard, Visa
Season: Mid-April to mid-Nov.
Course Comments: Can walk anytime. Yardage book available
Golf Packages: None
Discounts: Twilight rate, after 3 p.m.
Places to Stay Nearby: Portland Marriott (207) 871–8000, (800) 752–8810; Portland Regency (207) 744–4200, (800) 727–3436; Sheraton Tara (207) 775–6161, (800) 325–3535; Holiday Inn, West (207) 774–5601, (800) HOLIDAY; Quality Suites (near airport) (207) 775–2200, (800) 7–JETPORT; Ramada Inn and Conference Center (207) 774–5611
Local Attractions: Sprint Point Museum, restaurants, historic tours, boat cruises, L. L. Bean (Freeport), Scarborough Downs Racetrack, beaches, Joan Whitney Payson Gallery of Art, Portland Museum of Art, Victoria Mansion, Historic Old Port, Portland Head Light, Henry Wadsworth Longfellow home, Portland Observatory, factory outlets, Maine Mall, Sebago Lake, downtown waterfront, Portland Repertory Ballet, Portland Symphony Orchestra, theater, antiques, art galleries, Children's Museum of Maine, seasonal festivals, camping, fishing, boating. Portland Convention and Visitors Bureau (207) 772–4994. Maine State Parks Reservations (207) 289–3824, (800) 442–6305. Portland Chamber of Commerce (207) 772–2811
Directions: From exit 7 of Maine Turnpike (I–95): Maine Mall Rd. north past the Mall to Running Hill Rd., turn left, then take 2nd right onto Country Club Dr. to the Sable Oaks Golf Club
Closest Commercial Airports: Portland International (5 min.); State Airport, Augusta (1 hr., 15 min.); Logan International, Boston (2 hrs.); Bangor International (2½ hrs.)

SABLE OAKS GOLF CLUB

Designed by Geoffrey Cornish and Brian Silva and completed in 1989, Sable Oaks was first conceived as a residential and office-building development. The decision has been made not to build residences, but there remains a golf course that is ranked as one of the best in Maine and has received the National Golf Foundation Public Achievement Award.

The course is a gently rolling, tightly treed layout with a creek running through six fairways. White birches and pines make the course a particular challenge, as do the winds coming off the ocean 3 miles to the east. A premium is put on accuracy rather than distance on this 6359-yard layout. The landing areas are usually generous, but the greens, which are large, moderately fast, and undulating, are generally well protected by traps. Water hazards in the form of ponds and streams are found on more than half the holes.

There are a number of difficult par 4s at Sable Oaks, beginning with the 431-yard third, the number-2-handicap hole on the course. The tee shot is down a tree-lined fairway to a landing area just before a brook that crosses the fairway. The second shot is to a deep, elevated green well protected on the right and rear by four traps and left and front by three more. There is a narrow neck of fairway into the green, making it easy to catch the traps on either side on the approach shot.

A nice run of holes on the back nine begins with the 462-yard par-4 twelfth, the number-1-handicap hole. This is a sharp dogleg left with a tee shot to a plateau bordered by a stream that cuts across the fairway. The next shot is to a deep green with a large bunker right and in front. The 182-yard par-3 thirteenth has a tee shot over a ravine that is directly below a shallow green protected by three traps to the rear and a drop-off to the ravine in front. It is not advisable to be short on this hole.

The 480-yard par-5 fourteenth is the signature hole on the course. Jackson Brook, which wends its way through the entire golf course, crosses the fairway just after the tee-shot landing area. The second shot is generally a mid-iron to a landing area just before the stream, which runs back across the fairway just below the green. A big hitter will go for the green in two, but it is guarded by banks that slope down to the brook in front and has four bunkers on the left and to the rear.

The finishing hole is a tough 422-yard dogleg-right par 4 that plays over a small pond to an open landing area. The second shot is a difficult approach to a wide, shallow green tightly guarded in front by two traps on the right and one on the left.

Sable Oaks has a full pro shop and instruction available on a group or individual basis. The practice facilities do not include a full driving range or a practice bunker, however. A nearby 227-room Marriott offers golf packages at Sable Oaks and has many meeting-room, restaurant, tennis and other facilities. Group rates for 12 or more golfers are available.

Course Name: **THE SAMOSET RESORT GOLF CLUB**

Course Type: Resort
Resort: Samoset Resort
Address: 220 Warrenton Street
              Rockport, ME 04856
Phone: (207) 594–1431 (Golf Course),
              (207) 594–2511,
              (800) 341–1650 (Resort)
Fax: (207) 594–0722 (Resort)

GOLF COURSE

Head Professional: Bob O'Brian

Course Length/Par (All Tees): Back 6415/70, White 6021/70, Forward 5411/70

Course Slope/Rating (All Tees): Back 128/70.3, White 122/68.4, Ladies' Forward 120/70.1

Course Architects: NA (9 holes, 1902), Bob Elder (remodeled 9, added 9, 1978), Bob Elder with Geoffrey Cornish (remodeled, 1995)

Golf Facilities: Full Pro Shop X, Snack Bar X, Lounge X, Restaurant X, Locker Room No, Showers No, Club Rental X, Club Repair X, Cart Rental X, Instruction X, Practice Green X, Driving Range X, Practice Bunker X, Club Storage X

Tee-Time Reservation Policy: At time of confirmed reservations at resort. Public may reserve up to 2 days in advance

Ranger: Yes

Tee-off-Interval Time: 7 and 8 min.

Time to Play 18 Holes: 4½ hrs.

Course Hours/Earliest Tee-off: 7 a.m.

Green Fees: $48 for 18 holes, $27 for 9 holes

Cart Fees: $28 for 18 holes, $18 for 9 holes per cart

Credit Cards: All major cards

Season: Apr. through Nov. Busiest months mid-June through Labor Day

Course Comments: Can walk anytime. Yardage book available

Golf Packages: Through the resort

Discounts: Seasonal. Lowest rates before mid-May and after mid-Oct.

Places to Stay Nearby: ROCKPORT: Bread and Roses Inn & Bakery (207) 236–6116; Glen Cove Motel (207) 594–4062. BELFAST: The Jeweled Turret Inn (207) 338–2304, Londonberry Inn (207) 338–3988. CAMDEN: High Tide Inn on the Ocean (207) 236–3724; Lord Camden Inn (207) 236–4325, (800) 336–4325; Norumbega Inn (207) 236–4646; Whitehall Inn (207) 236–4325, (800) 789–6565

Local Attractions: Old Conway House, Owls Head Transportation Museum, Farnsworth Art Museum and Library, Shore Village Museum, Mathews Museum of Maine Heritage, Mid-Coast Children's Museum, bicycle tours, boating, fishing, hiking, antiquing, restaurants, seasonal festivals, camping. Rockport-Camden-Lincolnville Chamber of Commerce, P.O. Box 919, Camden, ME 04843 (207) 236–4404

Directions: From the south take Maine Turnpike to Exit 9, Rte. 95 to Exit 22, Rte. 1 north through Rockland. Turn right on Waldo Ave. to the resort. From the north take Rte. 1 south to Rockland. Turn left on Waldo Ave. to the resort

Closest Commercial Airports: Knox County Airport (10 min.); Bangor International (1½ hrs.); Portland Jetport (2 hrs.); Boston Logan International, MA (4 hrs.)

RESORT

Date Built: 1889

No. of Rooms: 150 guest rooms and suites, 72 time-share condominiums, 31 town-houses

Meeting Rooms: 10. Capacity of Largest: 650 persons. Meeting Space: 22,500 sq. ft.

Room Price Range: $105 for non-ocean-view room off season to $375 for 2-bedroom condominium peak season (July 4 through Labor Day). Packages available year round

Lounges: Golf Clubhouse, Breakwater Lounge, Pool

Restaurants: Breakwater Lounge and Patio, Golf Clubhouse, Poolhouse and Indoor Golf and Ski Touring Center snackbars, Marcelis

Entertainment: Live entertainment including music and comedy

Credit Cards: All major cards

General Amenities: Meeting and conference facilities with audiovisual, food-service, and secretarial support capabilities; retail shops, children's programs, nearby antiquing

Recreational Amenities: Indoor and outdoor swimming pools, 2 outdoor tennis courts, Samoset Fitness Center with Nautilus and other equipment, massage, sauna, hot tubs, video arcade, racquetball, aerobics, volleyball, basketball, lawn games, bicycling, shuffleboard, nearby boating and fishing, winter skiing

Reservation and Cancellation Policy: A deposit equal to one night's stay or package charge is required. Credit card charged at the time reservation is made. Advance cancellation requirements (vary by season) must be met to ensure a full refund. If no rollaway bed required, children 16 years of age and under stay free when sharing a room with parents

Comments and Restrictions: No pets. Local kennels available

THE SAMOSET RESORT GOLF CLUB

The Samoset Resort Golf Club, sometimes called "The Pebble Beach of the East," borders the Atlantic Ocean on Penobscot Bay. The resort, which sits on 230 acres, evolved from the Bay Pines Hotel which was built in 1887. In 1902 it was purchased and renovated by the Riccar family of Poland Spring. The resort was renamed The Samoset for the Indian chief who welcomed the Europeans to New England. A nine hole golf course was built in 1902 to meet the demand for the increasingly popular game. In the 1990s the resort went through a $1.2 million renovation. The golf course had four holes remodeled; a new irrigation system and mounding were added.

Most of the holes at Samoset are parallel to the ocean, and six holes border it. The signature hole is the 485-yard par-5 fifth, a slight dogleg right that usually has a right to left wind coming off the bay. A perfect drive will leave about 175 yards to a huge green that is well guarded by bunkers to its front left, front center, and behind. Crosswinds are prevalent on most holes at Samoset and, if you have a tendency to hit the ball from right to left, at least four holes, including the 239-yard par-3 third which plays over the water from the back tees, could be problematic. The ability to position the ball on the fairway and overcome the elements to approach with accuracy are necessary to score at Samoset.

The linksland-style golf course is easy to walk. It is rated among the best golf courses in Maine by *Golf Digest,* and the resort, which has guest rooms, suites, and condominiums, has received the AAA Four Diamond Award. The signature restaurant, Marcel's, has received several *Wine Spectator* Awards for its fine wine selections and the resort offers numerous activities including meeting and conference amenities. Within a short distance are quaint seaside tourist towns such as Camden, and the lower regions of Acadia National Park. Rockland, the largest town on Penobscot Bay, is Maine's major lobster distribution center and the point of departure to several bay islands.

Course Name: SUGARLOAF GOLF CLUB

Course Type: Resort
Resort: The Sugarloaf Inn
Address: Route 27
Carrabassett Valley, ME 04947
Phone: (207) 237–2000, x6812 (Golf Course)
(800) THE–LOAF (Resort)

GOLF COURSE

Head Professional: Scott Hoisington
Course Length/Par (All Tees): Back 6922/72, Middle 6400/72, Ladies' Forward 5324/72
Course Slope/Rating (All Tees): Back NA/NA, Middle 137/70.8, Ladies' Forward 136/73.7

Course Architect: Robert Trent Jones, Jr. (1984)
Golf Facilities: Full Pro Shop X, Snack Bar X, Lounge X, Restaurant X, Locker Room No, Showers No, Club Rental X, Club Repair No, Cart Rental X, Instruction X, Practice Green X, Driving Range X, Practice Bunker X, Club Storage X
Tee-Time Reservation Policy: Resort guests: At time of reservation. Outside play: From 5 days in advance
Ranger: Yes
Tee-off-Interval Time: 10 min.
Time to Play 18 Holes: 4 hrs., 45 min.
Course Hours/Earliest Tee-off: Dawn to dusk
Green Fees: $61 for 18 holes; $37 for 9 holes
Cart Fees: $14 for 18 holes per person, $8 for 9 holes per person
Credit Cards: All major cards
Season: Mid-May to mid-Oct. Busiest season Aug.- Sept.
Course Comments: Cart mandatory. Yardage book available. Locker-room and shower facilities through nearby Sugartree Health Club
Golf Packages: Available through Sugarloaf Inn and Sugarloaf Mountain Condominiums. Lowest rates up to July 3, and Oct.
Discounts: Inquire
Places to Stay Nearby: Central reservation and information service for accommodations (800) THE–LOAF (U.S.), (800) 343–3915 (Canada). CARRABASSETT: Sugarloaf Mountain Hotel (207) 237–2222, (800) 527–9879; Lumberjack Lodge (207) 237–2141; Judson's Motel (207) 235–2641; Valley Motel (207) 235–2730. STRATTON: Stratton Plaza Hotel, (207) 246–2000. KINGFIELD: Herbert (207) 265–2000; Inn on Winter's Hill (207) 265–5421
Local Attractions: CARRABASSETT: Western Maine Children's Museum; hiking, bicycling, hunting, skiing, fishing, boating, antiques, crafts, camping, Poplar Stream Falls, Bigelow Range, Crocker Mountain Cirque, Rangeley Lake State Park, Small's Falls, Mt. Blue State Park,

Dead River Area Historical Society, Stanley Museum. Sugarloaf Chamber of Commerce (800) THE–AREA, (207) 235–2100

Directions: From the west: Rte. 2 to Farmington, north (36 mi.) on Hwy. 27 to Carrabassett Valley. From the south: I–95 to Rte. 4, west to Farmington, north (36 mi.) to Carrabassett Valley on Hwy. 27

Closest Commercial Airports: State Airport, Augusta (1½ hrs.); Bangor International (2 hrs.); Portland International (2½ hrs.); Quebec City, Canada (3½ hrs.); Dorval International, Montreal, Canada (3¾ hrs.)

SUGARLOAF GOLF CLUB

Carrabassett Valley is in the heart of ski country in western Maine. The Sugarloaf Golf Club was designed by Robert Trent Jones, Jr., and was runner-up in 1986 for *Golf Digest*'s best new resort course. *Golf Digest* now rates this 6922-yard layout the best golf course of any kind in Maine.

This spectacular layout was carved out of the Maine woods and has magnificent mountain and forest views from its eighteen tree-lined, demanding, self-contained holes. The Carrabassett River winds its way through the layout, which has some dramatic elevation changes. The tight fairways are beautifully framed by white birch, and the generous, undulating greens are well guarded by bunkers and water, which comes into play on eight holes. The combination of well-placed bunkers, tight fairways, challenging greens, tricky doglegs and uneven lies on this rolling terrain make Sugarloaf an excellent test of golf.

The 355-yard tenth is an example of a scenic hole that requires a well-placed tee shot and an extremely accurate pitching wedge or 9-iron onto a difficult green. The first shot is to a landing area that squeezes into a narrow fairway protected by two large traps. The second shot is to a shallow green guarded by bunkers in front. There is an abrupt fall-off from the back of the green to the chilly waters of the Carrabassett River. As with most holes at Sugarloaf,

club selection and the gauging of distance and direction are very essential.

The 222-yard par-3 eleventh is one of the most beautiful holes on the course. The tee shot is from an elevated tee over the river and down 125 feet to a large green backed by sand bunkers. The elevation drop and likely wind complicate distance calculations and choice of club on this hole. After your first swing you will be on the green, in sand, in the woods or in the river.

The most difficult par 5 at Sugarloaf is the 554-yard twelfth, whose tee shot is to an open landing area bordered by trees and the river on the left. The second shot has to carry a series of bunkers that cut the fairway approximately 175 yards from the green. The approach shot is to a large green flanked by bunkers both left and right. The river runs below the left side of the green, making a miss to the left a potential disaster.

The Sugarloaf Golf Club has a fully stocked pro shop, driving range, putting green, and food and beverage service. A variety of golf schools and packages are offered, with accommodations available through the Sugarloaf Inn or Sugarloaf Mountain Condominiums. This includes use of the Sugartree Health Club facilities, with an indoor pool, sauna, Jacuzzis, racquetball, weight room and tanning salon. And you have the use of the Sugarloaf Inn outdoor pool and tennis courts.

Packages are available for 2, 3, and 5 days and typically include deluxe accommodations at the Sugarloaf Inn, green and cart fees, breakfast each morning at the inn and use of the aforementioned facilities. Golf-school packages include accommodations, breakfast and lunch, use of the facilities, 5 hours of daily instruction, unlimited use of the practice facilities and videotaped analysis of your game. Golf schools are available without prearranged lodging, and you can play the course anytime. Call in advance to reserve a tee time.

Golf carts are not required but they are necessary on this arduous up-and-down course. While Sugarloaf is a well-known ski resort in the winter, there are many recreational opportunities in this scenic New England area during the warmer months. These include fishing, boating, biking, camping, bicycling, and general touring of local towns, parks and historic sites.

In addition to golf packages, the Sugarloaf Inn offers mountain biking, white water-rafting, hiking and other packages. Meanwhile, the Sugarloaf Golf Club provides you with an opportunity to play the best golf course in the state.

Course Name: WATERVILLE
                        COUNTRY CLUB

Course Type: Semiprivate
Address: Country Club Road
                     P.O. Box 459
                     Waterville, ME 04901
Phone: (207) 564–9861

GOLF COURSE

Head Professional: Steve Pembroke
Course Length/Par (All Tees): Back 6412/73, White 6108/73, Ladies' White 5781/73, Ladies' Forward 5466/73
Course Slope/Rating (All Tees): Back 124/69.6, White 121/68.2, Ladies' White 118/72.4, Ladies' Forward 114/70.6
Course Architects: NA (9 holes, 1916), Orrin Smith (renovation, 1938), Geoffrey Cornish and William Robinson (added 9 holes, 1966)
Golf Facilities: Full Pro Shop X, Snack Bar X, Lounge X, Restaurant X, Locker Room X, Showers X, Club Rental X, Club Repair X, Cart Rental X, Instruction X, Practice Green X, Driving Range X, Practice Bunker X, Club Storage X
Tee-Time Reservation Policy: Members: From 1 wk. in advance. Public: Same day
Ranger: Yes
Tee-off-Interval Time: 8 min.
Time to Play 18 Holes: 4 hrs.
Course Hours/Earliest Tee-off: 7 a.m.
Green Fees: $38 for 18 holes June, July, Aug.
Cart Fees: $18 for 18 holes
Pull Carts: $2 for 18 holes
Credit Cards: None—cash or check only
Season: April 1 to Nov. 1

Course Comments: Can walk anytime. Busiest season June to Aug.
Golf Packages: None
Discounts: Seasonal discounts
Places to Stay Nearby: Anchorage Inn (207) 872–5577; Holiday Inn (207) 873–0111, (800) HOLIDAY; Inn at Silver Grove (207) 873–7724; Howard Johnson's Motor Lodge (207) 873–3335, (800) 446–4656; Budget Host Airport Inn (207) 873–3366
Local Attractions: Reddington Museum, Belgrade Lakes, camping, fishing, boating, hiking, Colby College, hunting. AUGUSTA: Arboretum, Maine State Museum, University of Maine, Fort Western, Blaine House, Winthrop Lakes, Cumston Hall. Mid-Maine Chamber of Commerce (207) 873–3315. Kennebec Valley Chamber of Commerce (207) 623–4559
Directions: I–95 from the south: 1st Waterville exit, after off-ramp take left under underpass, Kennedy Memorial Dr. to Country Club Rd. (3/4 mi.) on left. I–95 from the north: 2nd Waterville exit, turn right. Follow above directions
Closest Commercial Airports: State Airport, Augusta (30 min.); Bangor International (1 hr.); Portland International (1½ hrs.)

WATERVILLE COUNTRY CLUB

Waterville is situated on the west bank of the Kennebec River 19 miles north of Augusta, the state capital. Within 5 miles is the resort area of the 7 Belgrade Lakes, and the China Lake region is only 9 miles away. Waterville is called "Elm City" because these trees are abundant in the area, including the Waterville Country Club, which is beautifully situated on an elevated piece of rolling, wooded land that commands a view of Mt. Washington to the west and the Camden Range to the east. *Golf Digest* rates Waterville one of the best golf courses in the state of Maine.

This 6412-yard layout is difficult because it is hilly and well treed with mature elm, oak, maple, pine and other varieties. The course started out as a nine-hole course in 1916. It was remodeled in 1938, and another nine was added in the early

1960s. The greens are large, fast and have little undulation. Most are guarded by two or three sand bunkers. The number-1-handicap hole is the 430-yard fifth, a dogleg left. The tee shot is down a tree-lined fairway, and the approach is to an elevated green protected by traps on both sides.

The back nine begins with its two most difficult holes, both par 4s. The first is a 435-yard dogleg right that plays downhill to a large, fast, forward-sloping green that can be extremely difficult if you are above the hole. The tee shot has to avoid a right-fairway trap. The eleventh is another downhill hole; it plays 430 yards and has magnificent views of the trees and mountains, especially in the fall.

The par 3s on the back nine tend to be long and challenging. The 235-yard thirteenth has a tight, downhill tee shot to a large undulating green 50 feet below. The putting surface is well-guarded by traps both left and right. This hole and the 215-yard sixteenth are considered to be among the best par 3s in the state. The sixteenth also has a large green that is extremely well protected by traps to the right front, left, and rear. If the pin is placed to the right of the green, the front trap has to be carried on the tee shot, making the target very hard to reach indeed.

The Waterville Country Club has full clubhouse facilities including a restaurant, snack bar, full pro shop, locker room and showers. Instruction is available at the nearby driving range, sand bunker and practice green. You can walk the course anytime. Limited tee times are available for nonmembers and can only be made on the day you'd like to play. The green fees are modest, considering the quality of the course.

Recommended Golf Courses in Maine

Augusta Area:

Kennebec Heights Golf Club, Farmingdale, (207) 623–9831, Public, 18/6650/72

Natanis Golf Club, Vassalboro, (207) 622–3561, Public.

Arrowhead: 9/2953/35. Indian Territory: 9/3347/72. Tomahawk: 9/3280/36

Within 1 1/2 Hours of Bangor:

Bangor Municipal, Bangor, (207) 945–9226, Public, 18/6430/71, 9/3215/36

Kebo Valley Golf Club, Bar Harbor, (207) 288–3000, Public, 18/6102/70

Penobscott Valley Country Club, Orono, (207) 866–2423, Semiprivate, 18/6350/72

Va Jo Wa Golf Course, Island Falls, (207) 463–2128, Resort, 18/6223/72

Within 1 1/2 Hours of Portland:

Bethel Inn Golf Club, Bethel, (207) 824–2475, Resort, 18/6663/72

Biddleford and Saco Country Club, Saco, (207) 282–5883, Public, 18/6192/71

Brunswick Golf Club, Brunswick, (207) 725–8224, Semiprivate, 18/6609/72

Poland Spring Golf Club, Poland Spring, (207) 998–6002, Resort, 18/6196/71

Val Halla Golf Course, Cumberland, (207) 829–2225, Public, 18/6574/72

Presque Isle Area:

Aroostook Valley Country Club, Fort Fairfield, (207) 476–8083, Semiprivate, 18/6304/72

Rangeley:

Mingo Springs, Rangeley, (207) 864–5021, Public, 18/5923/70

Maine: Useful Information

Maine Publicity Bureau, 209 Main St., Farmingdale, ME 04344, (207) 582–9300, (800) 533–9595 (recreation information, general tourist information)

Department of Inland Fisheries and Wildlife, 284 State St., Augusta, ME 04333, (207) 289–2871 (fishing and hunting regulations)

Maine Innkeepers Association, 305 Commercial St., Portland, ME 04101, (207) 773–7670 (publishes statewide lodging and dining guide)

Course Name: HOG NECK GOLF COURSE

Course Type: Public
Address: Old Cordova Road
Easton, MD 21601
Phone: (410) 822–6079

GOLF COURSE

Head Professional: Mark Herrmann
Course Length/Par (All Tees): Back 7089/72, Blue 6514/72, White 5976/72, Forward 5464/72. Executive Course: Back 2184/32, Blue 2041/32, White 1845/32, Forward 1676/32
Course Slope/Rating (All Tees): Back 125/73.8, Blue 120/71.2, White 115/68.7, Forward 118/71.1. Executive Course: Back 90/28.98, Blue 88/28.92, White 86/28.3, Ladies' Forward 88/29.30
Course Architects: Lindsay Ervin and Charles Maddox (1976)
Golf Facilities: Full Pro Shop X, Snack Bar X, Lounge No, Restaurant No, Locker Room X, Showers X, Club Rental X, Club Repair X, Cart Rental X, Instruction X, Practice Green X, Driving Range X, Practice Bunker X, Club Storage No
Tee-Time Reservation Policy: Call previous Saturday 7 a.m. for following Mon. through Sun.
Ranger: Yes
Tee-off-Interval Time: 8 to 10 min.
Time to Play 18 Holes: 4½ hrs.
Course Hours/Earliest Tee-off: 7 a.m. to sunset Sat., Sun., holidays; 8 a.m. to sunset weekdays
Green Fees: $30 for 18 holes, $10 for 9 holes (after 4 p.m.). Executive Course: $10
Cart Fees: $24 for 18 holes, $12 for 9 holes per cart
Pull Carts: $2 for 18 holes
Credit Cards: MasterCard, Visa
Season: Feb. 1 to Dec. 31
Course Comments: Can walk anytime
Golf Packages: None
Discounts: Residents, twilight
Places to Stay Nearby: EASTON: Comfort Inn (410) 820–8333, (800) 228–5150; Tidewater Inn (410) 822–1300. ST. MICHAELS: Inn at Perry Cabin (410) 745–5178; Harbourtowne Golf Resort and Conference Center (410) 745–9066, (800) 446–9066
Local Attractions: EASTON: Historical district, shopping. ST. MICHAELS: Museum of Costume, Chesapeake Bay boat cruises, charter fishing, Chesapeake Bay Maritime Museum, seafood restaurants, boating, shopping. Talbot County Chamber of Commerce (410) 822–4606. Historical Society of Talbot County (410) 822–0773
Directions: From Chesapeake Bay Bridge: Rte. 50 south toward Easton (59 mi.) to 59 mi. marker. Take a left on Rabbit Hill Rd., to Old Cordova Rd., right to golf course (1½ mi.). From Easton: Rte. 50 north to Rte. 309, take right to Old Cordova Rd., take left to golf course (1½ mi.)
Closest Commercial Airports: Baltimore–Washington International (1 hr., 15 min.); Washington National, D.C. (1½ hrs.)

HOG NECK GOLF COURSE

One day in the early 1970s Bill Corkran, then the Easton town engineer, got a telephone call from Mrs. W. Alton Jones. Mrs. Jones owned Hog Neck Farm and wanted to give it to the town for recreational purposes. Mrs. Jones played golf, and her husband had been very active at the Augusta National Golf Club. Eventually the land was transferred to Talbot County, and plans were made to build a golf course. Charles Maddox and Lindsay Ervin were brought in to design and build the course. In 1976, the 7089-yard par-72 layout was completed, and today it is ranked one of the best public golf courses in the United States.

The course has four tee distances to choose from, and there is a 2184-yard par-32 Executive Course for beginners and those who want to sharpen their short game. All of the distances on the score cards are in meters, which is a bit disconcerting at first. This is because there was a strong metric movement in the United States in the 1970s. The United States is still a stubborn island of inches and yards in a world that uses the metric system. Hog Neck however, is idiosyncratically at the vanguard of our once and future golf metric applications. We'll use yards here, however.

Hog Neck's front nine is somewhat different from the back nine. The front nine comes out of the trees and is open and windy, with strategically placed sand traps, fairway bunkers and water hazards. The back nine is tightly treed, and the greens are well protected by traps. Holes twelve through seventeen are considered to be among the most difficult holes on the course.

The 473-yard par-4 twelfth plays down a corridor of trees to a skull-shaped green guarded by traps to the left and right. A stream crosses the fairway 70 yards in front of the green. The thirteenth is a 218-yard par 3 to a large green with traps to the left, right and rear. This is the longest par 3 on the course. The fourteenth is a marathon 603-yard par 5 with trees lining the fairway all the way to a green well protected by five traps. The 436-yard par-4 fifteenth is also tree-lined, with a bunker on the right approximately 250 yards from the back tees. The second shot is to a deep green with a pond to the left and in front and two traps on each side of the putting surface.

Like all the holes on the back nine, driving accuracy and distance are at a premium on the 438-yard par-4 sixteenth. This hole plays straight down an alley of trees to a small, elevated green protected by traps on the left, right and to the rear. A stream cuts the fairway 100 yards from the green. One of the most beautiful holes at Hog Neck is the 200-yard seventeenth, a par 3, which plays 200 yards from an elevated tee to a large green surrounded by four traps. A stream with a beautiful orchid bridge crosses the fairway in front of the green.

The finishing hole at Hog Neck is a 522-yard par 5. The fairway is narrow and tree-lined. Traps guard the right side on the tee shot, and another large right-side bunker is 100 yards from the green. The putting surface is completely surrounded by five

traps, making it almost impossible to reach the green in two. The combination of trees, 114 sand traps, wind, well-placed water hazards and medium-sized to large, undulating greens make Hog Neck a challenging golf course. You can walk the course anytime, and that is truly be an enjoyable experience.

Practice facilities at Hog Neck include a generous driving range, a large practice putting green, a chipping area and a green with sand traps. The clubhouse includes a pro shop, locker room, showers and snack bar. Instruction is available from the staff of professionals on site.

Hog Neck can easily accomodate outings and tournaments but focuses on play for the public golfer. The course has long been recognized its service and quality at a reasonable price.

Course Name: QUEENSTOWN HARBOR GOLF LINKS **Lakes, River Courses**

Course Type: Public
Address: 310 Links Lane
              Queenstown, MD 21658
Phone: (410) 827–6611,
              (800) 827–5257
Fax: (410) 827–5258

GOLF COURSE

Head Professional: Trent Wright

Course Length/Par (All Tees): Lakes: Back 6537/71, White 6001/71, Gold 5216/71, Forward 4576/71. River: Back 7110/72, White 6599/72, Gold 5894/72, Forward 5026/72

Course Slope/Rating (All Tees): Lakes: Back 124/71, White 118/68.4, Gold 105/65, Forward NA/NA. River: Back 138/74.2, White 132/71.8, Gold 124/68.6, Ladies' Forward 123/69

Course Architect: Lindsay Ervin. River: (1991), Lakes: (9, 1991, 9, 1994)

Golf Facilities: Full Pro Shop X, Snack Bar X, Lounge Beer, Restaurant No, Locker Room No, Showers No, Club Rental X, Club Repair No, Cart Rental X, Instruction X, Practice Green X, Driving Range X, Practice Bunker X, Club Storage No

Tee-Time Reservation Policy: Up to 7 days in advance from 12 p.m. Credit card required to hold reservation

Ranger: Yes

Tee-off-Interval Time: 10 min.

Time to Play 18 Holes: 4½ hrs.

Course Hours/Earliest Tee-off: 6:30 a.m.

Green and Cart Fees: $60 for 18 holes Fri., Sat., Sun., holidays with cart, $50 for 18 holes with cart weekdays; $40 for 18 holes Mon.-Thurs. walking

Credit Cards: MasterCard, Visa

Season: Year round. Busiest Apr. through Oct.

Course Comments: Can walk Mon.-Thurs. Yardage book available. No pull carts

Golf Packages: Inquire at pro shop

Discounts: Twilight

Places to Stay Nearby: ANNAPOLIS: Annapolis Holiday Inn and Conference Center (410) 224–3150, (800) HOLI-DAY; Annapolis Marriott Waterfront Hotel (410) 268–7555, (800) 336–0072; Governor Calvert House (410) 263–2641; Loew's Annapolis Hotel (410) 263–7777, (800) 23–LOEWS; Residence Inn by Marriott (410) 573–0300, (800) 331–3131. BED AND BREAKFASTS: Maryland Inn (410) 263–2641, (800) 847–8882; Reynolds Tavern (410) 263–2641; State House Inn (410) 263–2641; William Page Bed and Breakfast Inn (410) 626–1506

Local Attractions: ANNAPOLIS area: Antietam National Battle Field, William Paca House and Garden, Maritime Museum, Hammond–Harwood House, Banneker–Douglas Museum of Afro–American Life and History, Government House, Helen Avalynne Tawes Garden, Maryland State House, Old Treasury House, U.S. Naval Academy, historic tours, antiquing, restaurants, fishing, boating, seasonal festivals. Baltimore. Annapolis Public Information and Tourism Office, 160 Duke of Gloucester St., Annapolis, MD 21401 (410) 263–7940. Baltimore Area Visitors Center, 300 W. Pratt St., Baltimore, MD 21201 (410) 837–4636, (800) 282–6632

Directions: From Baltimore–Washington International Airport (45 min.): Take Hwy. 50 east towards Annapolis. Cross Chesapeake Bay Bridge then take 301 north to golf course

Closest Commercial Airports: Baltimore-Washington International (45 min.); Washington National (1½ hrs.)

QUEENSTOWN HARBOR GOLF LINKS

The Queenstown Harbor Golf Links is a bentgrass Lindsay Ervin design that wends its way through wetlands and lakes along the Chesapeake Bay near Annapolis. Winds sweep from east to west off the bay, generally providing headwinds or tailwinds that must be calibrated throughout your round. The preponderance of wetlands often requires you to play target golf that will force you to seek safe landing areas from which to approach the large, well-bunkered greens. The 585-yard par-5 finishing hole on The River Course, for example, has a tee shot landing area surrounded by wetlands. The next shot is to a landing area with wetlands to the left and bunkers to the right.

The toughest hole on The River is the 538-yard par-5 seventh, a true three shot par 5 that requires a controlled drive to avoid wetlands cutting the fairway. The second shot is either a heroic effort over wetlands to the target, or a layup. Strong tailwinds often come into play here.

Water can come into play on a dozen holes on The Lakes course which is a shorter and easier test than The River. A great par 3 on The Lakes is the 210-yard seventeenth which often plays with the aid of a tailwind to a large, two-tiered green framed by bunkers. Because of the wetlands and bentgrass fairways, a cart-paths-only rule is enforced at Queenstown. However, you can walk this course and enjoy the special ambiance of the Chesapeake.

Recommended Golf Courses in Maryland

Within 1 Hour of Baltimore:

Enterprise Golf Course, Mitchellville, (301) 249–2040, Public, 18/6587/72

Mount Pleasant Golf Course, Baltimore, (410) 254–5100, Public, 18/6757/71

Northwest Park Golf Course, Wheaton, (301) 598–6100, Public, 18/7185/72, 9/2687/34

Pine Ridge Golf Course, Lutherville, (410) 252–1408, Public, 18/6820/72

Poolesville Golf Course, Poolesville, (301) 428–8143, Public, 18/6757/71

Redgate Municipal Golf Course, Rockville, (301) 340–2404, Public, 18/6486/72

Turf Valley Country Club, Ellicott City, (410) 465–1504, Resort, 18/6825/70

Wakefield Valley Golf and Conference Center, Westminster, (410) 876–6662, Semiprivate. Gold: 9/3369/36. Green: 9/3559/36. White: 9/3415/36

Eastern Shore Area:

Bay Club, Berlin, (410) 641–4081, (800) 229–2582, Public, 18/6956/72

The Beach Club Golf Links, Berlin, (410) 641–4653, (800) 435–9223, Semiprivate, 18/7020/72

Eagle's Landing Golf Club, Berlin, (410) 213–7277, Public, 18/7003/72

Nutters Crossing, Salisbury, (410) 860–4653, Semiprivate, 18/6033/70

Ocean City Golf and Yacht Club, Berlin, (301) 641–1778, (800) 442–3570, Public. Bayside: 18/6526/72. Seaside: 18/6520/73

Ocean Pines Golf and Country Club, Berlin, (301) 641–8653, Semiprivate, 18/6927/72

River Run Golf Club, Berlin, (301) 641–7200, Resort, 18/6705/71

Within 1/2 Hour of Easton:

Harbourtowne Resort and Country Club, St. Michaels, (301) 745–5183 (Pro Shop), (301) 745–9066, (800) 446–9066 (Resort), Resort, 18/6271/70

Southwestern:

Breton Bay Golf and Country Club, Leonardtown, (301) 475–2300, Semiprivate, 18/6933/72

Swan Point, Issue, (301) 259–2074, (800) 242–SWAN, Semiprivate, 18/6762/72

Western:

Black Rock Golf Course, Hagerstown, (301) 791–3040, Public, 18/6646/72

Golf Club at Wisp, McHenry, (301) 387–4911, Semiprivate, 18/7122/72

Maryland: Useful Information

Maryland Office of Tourism Development, Redwood Tower, 9th Fl., 217 E. Redwood St., Baltimore, MD 21202, (800) 543–1036

Tidewater Administration, Department of Natural Resources, Tawes State Office Bldg., Annapolis, MD 21401, (301) 974–3211 (fishing regulations), (301) 974–3195 (hunting regulations)

Forest, Park and Wildlife Service, Tawes State Office Bldg., Annapolis, MD 21401, (301) 269–3195 (recreation information), (301) 768–0895 (campsite information)

Baltimore Visitors Information Center, 300 W. Pratt St., Baltimore, MD 21201, (800) 282–6632; International Visitors Center (301) 837–7150

Course Name: THE CAPTAIN'S GOLF COURSE

Course Type: Public
Address: 1000 Freeman's Way
Brewster, MA 02631
Phone: (508) 896–5100

GOLF COURSE

Head Professional: Mike Robichaud

Course Length/Par (All Tees): Back 6794/72, Middle 6176/72, Forward 5388/72

Course Slope/Rating (All Tees): Back 130/72, Middle 126/69.4, Ladies' Forward 117/70.5

Course Architects: Geoffrey Cornish and Brian Silva (1985)

Golf Facilities: Full Pro Shop X, Snack Bar X, Lounge Bar/Beer and Wine, Restaurant No, Locker Room No, Showers No, Club Rental X, Club Repair Outside, Cart Rental X, Instruction X, Practice Green X, Driving Range X, Practice Bunker X, Club Storage No

Tee-Time Reservation Policy: 2 days in advance from 6 p.m. by telephone; 2 weeks in advance if prepaid by check. Members have tee-time priority on weekends

Ranger: Yes

Tee-off-Interval Time: 7½ min.

Time to Play 18 Holes: 4½ hrs.

Course Hours/Earliest Tee-off: 8 a.m. Sat., Sun., holidays; 7 a.m. weekdays

Green Fees: $40 for 18 holes peak season July 4-Labor Day

Cart Fees: $22 for 18 holes, $9 for 9 holes per person

Credit Cards: Cash for green fees, carts. American Express, MasterCard, Visa for merchandise

Season: March to Dec. Busiest season April to Oct.

Course Comments: Can walk anytime. Yardage book available. Memberships available to residents. Weekend rate applies only to June, July, Aug.; daily rate applies otherwise

Golf Packages: None

Discounts: Twilight rate after 3 p.m. Seasonal discounts

Places to Stay Nearby: BREWSTER: Old Sea Pines Inn, (508) 896–6114; Ocean Edge Resort and Conference Center (508) 896–9000; Skyline Motel (617) 385–3707. BED AND BREAKFAST: Isaiah Clark House (508) 896–2223. EAST ORLEANS: Nauset Knoll Motor Lodge (508) 255–2364. CHATHAM: Chatham Bars Inn (508) 945–0096, (800) 527–4884

Local Attractions: Cape Cod Museum of Natural History, Nauset Beach, Nickerson State Park, fishing, whale watching, boating, beaches, camping, Cape Cod League summer baseball. Provincetown. Hyannis Port. Cape Cod Chamber of Commerce (508) 362–3225

Directions: Rte. 6 (Mid Cape Hwy.) to exit 11, turn right, 1½ mi., right onto Freeman's Way, 2 mi. to golf course on right

Closest Commercial Airports: Barnstable Municipal, Hyannis (30 min.); Logan International, Boston, (2 hrs.)

THE CAPTAIN'S GOLF COURSE

The Captain's Golf Course is a 6794-yard Geoffrey Cornish and Brian Silva layout on Cape Cod, Massachusetts, the site of many quality resort, private and public golf courses. The Captain's was rated the best new public course in 1985 by *Golf Digest*. The State Amateur Qualifier has been held here, and it is a very popular golf course among local players and those who vacation on the Cape.

The holes on this flat, tree-lined layout are all named after sea captains, including Captain Soloman Freeman, who lived from 1800 to 1887 and was the master of the good ship *Malabar*. The name Freeman permeates this area, including the Freeman Inn and Freeman's Way, where the golf course is located. The Yankee mariners honored at the Captain's come from an earlier time, when maritime peril and adventures were interwoven with the everyday lives of New Englanders and Cape Cod. Elijah Cobb (1768–1849), for example, was an orphan at age 6 and became a mariner at age 14 for wages of $3.50 a month. Cobb, by then a ship's captain, was at the Place de la Concorde in Paris in 1794 when Robespierre was beheaded during the Reign of Terror. Captain Cobb was in the capital to get his ship, *Crescent*, released from the port of Brest, where it had been impounded by the French. Cobb got his ship out of France and, through skill and cunning, lived a long life as a shipmaster, sometime smuggler, and traveler to the ends of the earth. He retired after 49 years of sailing and spent his last days in Brewster. His hole at the Captain's Golf Course is a tricky 353-yard par-4 dogleg left with a large trap to the right front of the green.

The bentgrass greens at the Captain's tend to be fast and are medium sized with subtle undulations. Large, strategically placed sand bunkers are near the fairways and greens on every hole, and trees tend to make strategy and accuracy more important than distance on most holes. Wind too can be a major factor on some holes. There is, however, only one water hazard on the course.

The most difficult hole on the front side is the 398-yard par-4 second, named after Captain Elisha Bangs (1805–66). Two large right-fairway bunkers come into play from 190 to 125 yards into a deep green guarded by two large traps on the right and to the rear. A difficult par 3 on this side is the 217-yard eighth, named after Captain Freeman Foster, who lived from 1782 to 1870. The tee shot is to a large green flanked by two large traps. Pin placement can often make this hole difficult.

Some of the more challenging holes on the Captain's are on the back nine, beginning with the 406-yard par-4 dogleg-left "Captain Charles Lincoln" (1804–77). The recommended tee shot is a draw to the right side because the landing area slopes left toward the trees lining the fairway. The second shot is onto a deep, narrow green protected by two large bunkers on the right. The 448-yard par-4 thirteenth, the "Captain Jeremiah Mayo" (1786–1867), is the number-1-handicap hole on the course. This is the most difficult driving hole at the Captain's because of the narrow landing area, the left-sloping fairway and trees that catch many tee shots, especially on the left. The

approach shot is to a medium-sized, left-to-right-angled green with a large bunker left and slightly in front of the green.

The par-5 fourteenth, the "Captain Charles Myrick" (1841–1905), is the only water hole on the course. The fairway on this 573-yard challenge splits left and right around a pond that runs 150 yards into the green. The tee shot is to a fairway guarded by a large bunker on the left. The second shot should be a layup to the right side of the fairway parallel to the edge of the pond, leaving approximately 110 to 130 yards to a narrow, deep green on the left side of the water hazard. It is almost impossible to reach this green in two, and if you try you have to contend with the fairway to the left, which is severely squeezed by water on the right and trees on the left.

Geoffrey Cornish has been an extremely capable and prolific golf architect in New England and the rest of North America. A native of Winnipeg, Manitoba, Canada, Cornish earned degrees in agronomy from the University of British Columbia (B.A.) and the University of Massachusetts (M.S.) and began his golf-architecture career under the great golf architect Stanley Thompson in the 1930s.

After a stint as a greenskeeper at the St. Charles Country Club in Winnipeg and a tour of duty with the Canadian Army in World War II, he briefly rejoined Thompson's firm, worked with pioneer turfgrass scientist Lawrence S. Dickson at the University of Massachusetts, then began his own golf-architecture practice in 1952. One of his earlier partners was William G. Robinson who moved to the Northwest in 1977. In 1983 Cornish collaborated with Brian Silva on the Captain's. He redesigned the Wethersfield Country Club in Connecticut; the Interlachen Country Club in Edina, Minnesota; Preakness Hills Country Club in Paterson, New Jersey; and has collaborated on a number of other redesigns and original golf courses.

By 1980 Geoffrey Cornish had designed more courses in New England than any other architect in history. Cornish has authored numerous articles on course design and turfgrass as well as *The Golf*

Course (Rutledge Press, New York), an excellent book on golf-course design and golf-course-architects biographies, and including names, locations and origins of golf courses by leading architects. This book, and its revised edition, *The Architects of Golf* (HarperCollins, New York) was written with Ronald E. Whitten, a leading editor and writer of articles on golf architecture for *Golf Digest*. It has been a primary source for biographical material and historical research on golf courses and architects for this book.

Returning to the Captain's, the course is well worth playing. The clubhouse facilities are modest but there is a practice range, practice green and practice bunker with instruction available from the professional and his staff. There is a full pro shop, and you can walk the golf course anytime. The pantheon of eighteen captains will be waiting for you.

Course Name: COUNTRY CLUB OF NEW SEABURY Blue, Green Courses

Course Type: Resort
Resort: New Seabury Cape Cod Resort and Conference Center
Address: Shore Drive West P.O. Box 549 New Seabury, MA 02649
Phone: (508) 477–9110 (Golf Course) (508) 477–9111, (800) 999–9033 (Resort)
Fax: (508) 477–2402 (Resort)

GOLF COURSE

Director of Golf: Danny Coon
Head Professional: Mike Pry
Course Length/Par (All Tees): Blue: Back 7200/72, Blue 6909/72, White 6508/72, Forward 5764/72, Green: Back 5939/70, Forward 5105/68
Course Slope/Rating (All Tees): Blue: Back 138/74, Blue 130/72.7, White 128/70.8, Forward 128/72.1. Green: Back 110/68.2, Forward 106/67.2
Course Architects: Blue: William Mitchell (1964), Rees Jones (redesign, 1987), Green: William Mitchell (1964)

Golf Facilities: Full Pro Shop X, Snack Bar X, Lounge X, Restaurant X, Locker Room X, Showers X, Club Rental X, Club Repair X, Cart Rental X, Instruction X, Practice Green X, Driving Range X, Practice Bunker X, Club Storage X
Tee-Time Reservation Policy: 24 hrs. in advance to reserve tee times. Members have priority. Outside play not allowed mid-June to mid-Oct.
Ranger: Yes
Tee-off-Interval Time: 7 and 8 min.
Time to Play 18 Holes: 4½ hrs.
Course Hours/Earliest Tee-off: 6 a.m. to dark Sat., Sun., holidays; 7 a.m. to dark Mon. to Fri.
Green Fees: Blue: $60 for 18 holes. Green Course: $40 for 18 holes. Peak-season rates June, July, Aug. Lower rates at other times
Cart Fees: $13 for 18 holes per person
Credit Cards: American Express, Master-Card, Visa
Season: Year round. Busiest season July, Aug.
Course Comments: Can walk Blue Course anytime before May 1, after mid-Oct., after 3 p.m. May to early Oct. Can walk Green Course anytime. Must be a member or guest of member to play during summer months
Golf Packages: Available through resort
Discounts: Seasonal. Lowest rates mid-Oct. to April
Places to Stay Nearby: FALMOUTH: Best Western Falmouth Marina (508) 548–4300, (800) 528–1234; Holiday Inn (508) 540–2500, (800) HOLIDAY; Sheraton Inn (617) 540–2000, (800) 325–3535; Captain Tom Lawrence House (508) 540–1445; Peacock's Inn on the Sound (508) 457–9666; Mostly Hall (508) 548–3786. HYANNIS: Tara Hyannis Hotel and Resort (508) 775–7775, (800) 843–8272
Local Attractions: Horseback riding, bicycling, fishing, beaches, boating, swimming, whale watching, Cape Cod League summer baseball, camping, Shawme Crowell State Forest. Woods Hole. Falmouth. Nantucket. Hyannis.

Martha's Vineyard. Cape Cod Chamber of Commerce (508) 362–3225

Directions: From Boston (70 mi.): Southeast Expressway (Rte. 3 or Rte. 93 south) and follow signs to Cape Cod. Cross the Sagamore Bridge onto Rte. 6. Take exit 2 off Rte. 6. Bear right off the exit ramp onto Rte. 130 toward Mashpee. In Mashpee follow signs to New Seabury to Mashpee traffic circle. Follow signs to resort. From New York City (6 hrs.): I–90 north to Providence, RI. Rte. 195 to Cape Cod, to Rte. 28 at Bourne Bridge. Take Rte. 28 south to Rte. 151 exit. Bear right on Rte. 151 to Mashpee traffic circle. Follow signs to resort

Closest Commercial Airports: Barnstable Municipal, Hyannis (30 min.); Providence, RI (1½ hrs.); Logan International, Boston (2 hrs.)

RESORT

Date Built: 1962

No. of Rooms: 165 1- and 2-bedroom villas with kitchen, bath

Meeting Rooms: 12. Capacity of Largest: 250 persons banquet style. Meeting Space: 8412 sq. ft.

Room Price Range: $210 for studio to $380 for 2 bedroom per night peak season (July 10 to Sept. 6). Off season Jan. to Feb. Packages from approximately $40 per person per day

Lounges: Various bars in restaurants throughout resort

Restaurants: Beach and Cabana Club, Raw Bar, Marketplace Cafe, New Seabury Restaurant, Popponesset Inn, Players Club

Entertainment: Outdoor concerts in summer, live music at Popponesset Inn, summer weekends

Credit Cards: All major cards except Diners Club

General Amenities: Cruises and sightseeing, antiquing; meeting and conference facilities in classroom, conference, theater and banquet formats with audiovisual, food service, secretarial support; Popponesset Marketplace with 26 shops

Recreational Amenities: 16 all-weather tennis courts with pro shop, instruction, 3½ miles of beach, swimming, fishing, clamming, boating, Nautilus center with private fitness instruction available, basketball, volleyball, croquet, bocce, horseshoes, soccer, softball, swimming pool

Reservation and Cancellation Policy: 50% of full amount must be paid by check or credit card 2 wks. from date reservation made. 15-day cancellation notice prior to scheduled arrival date required for full refund. All cancellations subject to $20 per unit handling fee. If length of stay shortened, deposit forfeited for unused nights

Comments and Restrictions: No pets. Taxes and gratuities additional to base rates

COUNTRY CLUB OF NEW SEABURY

The Country Club of New Seabury is part of a residential real-estate development and conference center on the southwest shore of Cape Cod between Falmouth and Hyannis. The Blue Course at New Seabury has been ranked as one of the best resort golf courses in the United States by *Golf Digest*. This 7200-yard par-72 layout is beautifully situated along the water. This adds to the difficulty of New Seabury's rolling venue because the winds are often strong and unpredictable. Water hazards appear on half the holes, and well-placed sand traps protect every green. The bentgrass greens tend to be large, fast and undulating. The general strategic advice here is to pretend you are in the British Open and keep the ball low to take some of the wind out of play, especially on the front nine.

The 425-yard par-4 third hole is the number-1-handicap hole on the course and is also its signature hole. The first shot is to a landing area guarded by a fairway bunker on the right. The approach shot is onto a large, forward-sloping green with traps left and right. The wind tends to swirl on this hole, making it more unpredictable and difficult. As you work your way down the fairway, Nantucket Sound is on your left and Martha's Vineyard is in the distance.

Another tough par 4 on this side is the 435-yard seventh, which plays straight to a green well protected by large traps to the left and right. On the tee shot, the fairway narrows and is squeezed by bunkers on the left and right. Depending on the wind, you are hitting anything from a 3-iron to a pitching wedge on your second shot. The par 3s at New Seabury are long and difficult from the back tees—all of them are over 200 yards in length. The fourteenth hole, for example, plays 220 yards to a deep green flanked by two large traps.

The most difficult hole on the back nine is the double-dogleg 540-yard par-5 fifteenth. The tee shot has to avoid ponds to the left. The second shot is down a narrow opening between a pond on the right and a bunker on the left, as the dogleg cuts back to the right. The approach shot is to a deep green with traps to the left and right.

Overall, the par 3s and par 4s are the most difficult at New Seabury, with the par 5s averaging a bit over 500 yards from the back tees. However, the wind can change all the rules of direction and distance on any given day. There are four tee distances to choose from, ranging from 5764 to 7200 yards. Another course, the Green Course, is located here. It plays 5939 yards and is par 70 from the back tees and plays 5105 yards and is par 68 from the forward tees. Both layouts were originally designed by William Mitchell and opened in 1964. Rees Jones has redesigned some of the holes since then.

Mitchell was born in Salem, Massachusetts, and became involved in golf-course maintenance and design at an early age. His father, Robert A. Mitchell, was a respected golf-course superintendent and taught at the Essex County (Massachusetts) Agricultural School in the 1920s. William Mitchell became greenskeeper at Lake Sunapee Golf Club in North Sutton, New Hampshire, and established a turf farm specializing in velvet bentgrass for greens. After gaining experience in golf-course construction, he became a golf-course designer after serving in World War II. Among the over 150 layouts that he has designed are McCann Memorial Golf

Course, Poughkeepsie, New York; Mactaquac Provincial Park Golf Course, New Brunswick, Canada; and the Longboat Key Club (Islandside Course), Sarasota, Florida. Mitchell was an advocate of separate courses specifically designed for women golfers, and he is credited with having coined the title "executive course" to describe shorter courses with only par-3 and par-4 holes. Mitchell died in West Palm Beach, Florida, in 1974.

New Seabury has a full pro shop, locker room and showers, restaurant facilities and a practice area that includes a driving range, practice bunker and practice green. Individual and group lessons are available from the staff of professionals. A daily resort clinic for a maximum of 12 people is held during the summer months. Outside play is generally not allowed during the resort's peak season from mid-June to mid-October but is allowed at other times. Play is usually 50 percent from club members, 25 percent from resort guests, and the balance from conferences and groups. You can walk the Blue Course anytime from mid-October to May, and walking is always allowed on the Green Course. The courses are open year round and the green fees are daily fees. Golf packages are available but usually confined to spring and late fall. A variety of other packages are available year round. All golf packages offer 1 round of golf per person, per night stay, carts not included.

Accommodations at New Seabury include over 160 1- and 2-bedroom villas with kitchens. Villas are available within 4 of the 13 "villages" in this 3000-acre resort. A variety of recreational amenities are available, including tennis, swimming, boating, beaches, fishing, bicycling, a Nautilus fitness center and other activities. Lessons and tournaments can be arranged at the tennis club. Many restaurants are located within the development, and Cape Cod, Martha's Vineyard, and Nantucket can easily be reached from here.

New Seabury also has more than 8400 square feet of adjustable conference and meeting space with audiovisual and banquet capabilities for groups of up to approximately 250 persons. A staff of meeting and service specialists is available to assist in meeting and conference planning and activities.

Whether you come to New Seabury just for golf, or for a meeting, a family vacation, a second honeymoon, recreation, or for any combination of the above, it's a fine thing to be in olde Cape Cod.

Recommended Golf Courses in Massachusetts

Cape Cod Area:

Ballymeade Country Club, North Falmouth, (508) 540–4005, Semiprivate, 18/6928/72

Bayberry Hills Golf Course, Yarmouth, (508) 394–5597, Public, 18/7172/72

Cape Cod Country Club, Hatchville, (508) 563–9842, Public, 18/6300/71

Cranberry Valley Golf Course, Harwich, (508) 430–7560, Public, 18/6745/72

Dennis Highlands Golf Course, East Dennis, (508) 385–8347, Public, 18/6076/71

Dennis Pines Golf Course, Dennis, (508) 385–8698, Public, 18/6525/72

Falmouth Country Club, East Falmouth, (508) 548–3211, Public, 18/6535/72

Farm Neck Golf Club, Oak Bluffs, (508) 693–3057, Semiprivate, 18/6806/72

Ocean Edge Golf Club, Brewster, (508) 896–5911, Resort, 18/6665/72

Old Barnstable Fairgrounds Golf Course, Marston Mills, (508) 420–1141, Public, 18/6503/72

Quashnet Valley Country Club, Mashpee, (508) 477–4412, Semiprivate, 18/6410/72

Springfield Area

Course Name: CRUMPIN–FOX CLUB

Course Type: Public
Address: Parmeater Road
              Bernardston, MA 01337
Phone: (413) 648–9109

GOLF COURSE

Head Professional: Ronald D. Beck

Course Length/Par (All Tees): Back 7007/72, Blue 6508/72, Gold 6095/72, Forward 5432/72

Course Slope/Rating (All Tees): Back 141/73.8, Blue 138/71.3, Gold 133/70.1, Ladies' Forward 122/72.1

Course Architects: Roger Rulewich and Robert Trent Jones, Sr. (9 holes, 1978; 9 holes, 1990)

Golf Facilities: Full Pro Shop X, Snack Bar X, Lounge X, Restaurant X, Locker Room X, Showers X, Club Rental X, Club Repair X, Cart Rental X, Instruction X, Practice Green X, Driving Range X, Practice Bunker X, Club Storage X

Tee-Time Reservation Policy: Up to 48 hrs. in advance. Package guests may reserve tee times earlier

Ranger: Yes

Tee-off-Interval Time: 10 min.

Time to Play 18 Holes: 4½ hrs.

Course Hours/Earliest Tee-off: 7 a.m. to dark

Green Fees: $55 for 18 holes, $28 for 9 holes

Cart Fees: $14 for 18 holes per person, $9 for 9 holes per person

Credit Cards: MasterCard, Visa

Season: April 1 to Nov. 15

Course Comments: Can walk anytime. Golf clinics, junior camps, memberships available

Golf Packages: Golf and dinner package ($75) includes $15 dinner credit

Discounts: Replays on same day if tee times available

Places to Stay Nearby: GREENFIELD: Howard Johnson's (800) 654–2000; Super 8 Motel (413) 774–5578. BED AND BREAKFASTS: Brandt House Bed and Breakfast (413) 774–3329; Old Dearfield Inn (413) 774–5587

Local Attractions: Old Deerfield, Memorial Hall Museum. Deerfield. Amherst. Northampton. Holyoke. Franklin County Chamber of Commerce (413) 773–5463

Directions: I–91, exit 28 to Rte. 10 north, 1 mi. to Parmeater Rd., left to golf course

Closest Commercial Airports: Bradley International, Hartford, CT (1 hr., 20

min.); Logan International, Boston (2 hrs.); County Airport, Albany, NY (2½ hrs.); La Guardia, NY (4½ hrs.); John F. Kennedy International, NY (4½ hrs.)

CRUMPIN–FOX CLUB

The Crumpin–Fox Club is a beautiful golf course cut out of the hills and woods of north central Massachusetts. The first nine, designed by Roger Rulewich and Robert Trent Jones, Sr., was built in 1978, and the second nine in 1990. The bentgrass greens are large, fast, slightly elevated and undulating. There are more than 60 sand bunkers on the course, most of them around the greens. Water hazards appear on half the holes.

The number-1-handicap hole at Crumpin–Fox is the 592-yard par-5 eighth, which is a beautiful signature hole bordered by a lake on the left and woods on the right all the way to a wide, shallow green fronted by water and backed by traps on a sloped hillside. The tee shot has to stay in play between the lake and the trees. The distance and position on the second shot are critical to have a level lie for an approach shot over the lake to the green. This is a true three-shot par-5 hole with formidable distances from all four tee positions—592, 568, 529 and 472 yards.

A tough and beautiful par 4 on the back side is the 424-yard tenth, which plays straight up a corridor of trees to a wide, elevated, kidney-shaped green guarded by a large trap in front and another on the right. A brook borders the left side on the tee shot and fronts the green on the approach shot. The tee shot will be stymied by a stand of trees on the right if it strays too far in that direction.

Another breathtaking par 5 is the 527-yard fourteenth, which plays from an elevated tee with a view to a large green fronted by a lake and flanked by two large bunkers. On the tee shot, a brook on the right can be a problem, as can a huge fairway bunker on the left. The second shot is typically a layup in front of the lake, but this approach should not be too close to a large tree on the right. Then it's a matter of

pin position and your ability to hit a lofted club.

The finishing hole at Crumpin–Fox is a challenging 413-yard par-4 whose tee shot is down a tree-lined fairway. The second shot is to a deep, elevated, skull-shaped green protected by a large pond on the left, a trap between the pond and the green on the left and a huge bunker on the right. It is a formidable task to hold the green on the approach shot.

The Crumpin–Fox has a relaxing clubhouse with an excellent pro shop, locker rooms and showers, and a restaurant. A deck overlooks the eighteenth green, and a patio overlooks the first tee in this wooded setting. A variety of instructional programs are available at the club, including private lessons, group lessons, specialized clinics, golf institutes, junior camps and custom programs. The 3-day Crumpin–Fox Golf Institute, for example, features 15 hours of instruction with video analysis, a student/instructor ratio of no more than 4 to 1 and a total institute of no more than 12 students.

The Crumpin–Fox Club was conceived in 1969 as the dream of David Berelson. He hired Roger Rulewich and Robert Trent Jones to locate a site and design a championship golf course. The first construction phase included Phases Restaurant, situated high atop a hill with a panoramic view of the Pioneer Valley. This restaurant is on the property and is a short drive from the clubhouse, which has its own food-service facilities including a barbecue area for groups. Phases Restaurant is part of a popular golf and dinner package at the Crumpin–Fox.

During the construction of the golf course in 1977, Andy St. Hilaire of Bernardston bought the project from Berelson and completed what is now the back nine holes. In 1987, the property was sold to William A. Sandri and, under the direction of Rulewich, construction was begun on what is now the front nine. The eighteen-hole 7007-yard layout opened in 1990 and was named one of the top ten new golf courses you can play by *Golf* magazine in 1991. *Golf Digest* now lists it as one of the best public golf courses in America, and it is the only public golf course in Massachusetts on that publication's best courses in each state list. Crumpin–Fox was the site of the U.S. Open Qualifier in 1991 and 1994, further attesting to its rapid recognition as a quality golf facility. The pro shop has received recognition from *Golf Shop Operations* magazine as the best small golf shop in America, and it is ranked among the top 100 overall.

This is a difficult walk through the rows of pine, oak, maple, birch and other scenic varieties, but walking is allowed anytime. There are moose, bear, deer and other creatures in the area, and including, yes, fox.

The name of the course was derived from the Bernardston-based Crump Soda Co., which was sold in June 1953 to Eli Fox, thus becoming the Crump & Fox Soda Co.

You'll like it here.

Western Area

Course Name: TACONIC GOLF CLUB

Course Type: Semiprivate
Address: 19 Meacham St.
                Williamstown, MA 01267
Phone: (413) 458–3977
Fax: (413) 458–2654

GOLF COURSE

Head Professional: Rick Pohle
Course Length/Par (All Tees): Back 6640/71, Blue 6230/71, White 6002/71, Forward 5202/71
Course Slope/Rating (All Tees): Back 127/71 7, Blue 124/69.0, White 121/68.9, Ladies' Forward 123/69.9
Course Architect: NA (1896), John Van Kleek and Wayne Stiles (remodel, 1927)
Golf Facilities: Full Pro Shop X, Snack Bar X, Lounge X, Restaurant X, Locker Room X, Showers X, Club Rental X, Club Repair X, Cart Rental X, Instruction X, Practice Green X, Driving Range X, Practice Bunker X, Club Storage X
Tee-Time Reservation Policy: Up to 7 days in advance for public play. Open to the public Sat., Sun., holidays after 1

p.m.; weekdays from 8 to 11 and after 1:30 p.m.
Ranger: Yes
Tee-off-Interval Time: 8 min.
Time to Play 18 Holes: 4½ hrs.
Course Hours/Earliest Tee-off: 7 a.m.
Green and Cart Fees: $80 for 18 holes with cart
Credit Cards: MasterCard, Visa
Season: Mid-Apr. through mid.-Nov.
Course Comments: Walking allowed but full golf fee must be paid
Golf Packages: No
Discounts: Williams students, alumni
Places to Stay Nearby: The 1896 Motel (413) 458–8125; The Maple Terrace Motel (413) 458–9677; The Orchards (413) 458–9611; The Williams Inn (413) 458–9371; The Willows Motel (413) 458–5768
Local Attractions: WILLIAMSTOWN: Williams College, Williamstown Theatre, Clark Art Institute, Williams College Museum of Art, music, theater, seasonal festivals, antiquing, historic tours, hiking, camping, fishing, Hopkins Memorial Forest. LENOX: Tanglewood Summer Music Festival, The Mount (Edith Wharton Restoration). PITTSFIELD: Hancock Shaker Village, Berkshire Ballet, Berkshire Public Theatre, Berkshire Museum, The Mohawk Trail, covered bridges. Williamstown Board of Trade, P.O. Box 357, Williamstown, MA 01267 (413) 458–9077. Berkshire Visitor's Bureau (413) 443–9186
Directions: From center of town take Rte. 43 south to Meacham St. and the golf course
Closest Commercial Airports: Albany County, NY (1½ hrs.); Greater Hartford International, CT (1 hr.)

TACONIC GOLF CLUB

The Taconic Golf Club was designed by Wayne Stiles and John Van Kleek who formed a design partnership in 1924 and had offices in Boston, New York City, and St. Petersburg until the firm dissolved just before the Depression. The firm remodeled and developed several courses in New England including the Rutland Country Club in

Vermont and the Nashua Country Club in New Hampshire. The Taconic Golf Club is on the Williams College campus and was the site of the ninth U.S. Junior Championship in 1956. It was here that Jack Nicklaus, who never won a Junior Amateur, was defeated by Jack D. Rule, Jr., 1 up in the semifinals. The Taconic also has been the site of the Men's NCAA Championship (1958, 1972) and the U.S. Women's Amateur (1963). The Taconic is the site of the 1996 U.S. Senior Amateur in honor of the club's 100th anniversary.

The Taconic is a rolling, well-treed, traditionally designed golf course that plays longer than its 6575 yards would indicate because of elevation changes and incoming wind. The three finishing holes, beginning with the 420-yard par-4 sixteenth, are a fine way to end the round. The tee shot on No. 16 is often into the wind and the approach, usually a long-iron or wood, is to a firm, forward-sloping, elevated green guarded by bunkers on both sides. The 220-yard par-3 seventeenth is all carry to a green bracketed by bunkers. An upslope to the putting surface will stop any short tee shot dead. The finishing hole, a 510-yard par 5, can be played as a conservative, well-positioned three-shot par 5 or two heroic shots can be attempted to reach the green in two. Bunkers guard each side of the green and out of bounds is to the left of the fairway.

To score well at The Taconic, you have to play well on the first six holes because the course becomes increasingly difficult thereafter. A strayed shot can usually be found and advanced, but you are likely to be stymied by a tree or impeded by heavy rough. Position and the ability to properly approach the fast, true, subtle bentgrass greens on this course is exceedingly important. If you miss on the pin side of the greens at The Taconic, it is virtually impossible to get up and down in two shots.

Recommended Golf Courses in Massachusetts

Within 1¹/₂ Hours of Boston:

Atlantic Country Club, Plymouth, (508) 888–6644, Public, 18/6728/72

Bradford Country Club, Bradford, (508) 372–8357, Public, 18/6660/71

Crystal Springs Country Club, Haverhill, (508) 374–9621, Public, 18/6706/72

Far Corner Golf Course, West Boxford, (508) 352–8300, Public, 18/6189/72

Gamon Municipal Golf Course, Lynn, (617) 592–8232, Public, 18/6100/70

Gardner Municipal Golf Course, Gardner, (508) 632–9703, Public, 18/6106/71

George Wright Golf Course, Hyde Park, (617) 364–8997, Public, 18/6166/70

Juniper Hill Golf Club, Northborough, (508) 393–2444, Public. Lakeside: 18/6216/71. Riverside: 18/6306/71

Maplegate Country Club, Bellingham, (508) 966–4040, Public, 18/6815/72

New England Country Club, Bellingham, (508) 883–2300, Public, 18/6641/71

Norton Country Club, Norton, (508) 285–2400, Semiprivate, 18/6505/71

Pembroke Country Club, Pembroke, (617) 826–3983, Semiprivate, 18/6532/72

Poquoy Brook Country Club, Lakeville, (508) 947–5261, Public, 18/6175/72

Rehoboth Country Club, Rehoboth, (508) 252–6259, Public, 18/6365/72

Shaker Hills, Harvard, (508) 772–9900, Public, 18/6850/71

Sheraton Tara Ferncroft Country Club, Danvers, (508) 777–5614, Resort, 18/6536/72, 9/1500/27

South Shore Country Club, Hingham, (617) 749–8479, Public, 18/6444/72

Sterling Country Club, Sterling, (508) 422–3335, Semiprivate, 18/6662/71

Stow Acres Country Club, Stow, (508) 568–8690 (Pro Shop), (508) 568–1100 (Tee Times), Public. South: 18/6520/72. North: 18/6909/72

Trull Brook Golf Club, Tewksbury, (508) 851–6731, Public, 18/6350/72

Wachusett Country Club, West Boylston, (508) 835–4453, Semiprivate, 18/6608/72

Within 1¹/₂ Hours of Springfield:

Chicopee Country Club, Chicopee, (413) 592–4156, Public, 18/7010/72

Cranwell Resort and Conference Center, Lenox, (413) 637–1364, Resort, 18/6324/71

Hickory Ridge Country Club, Amherst, (413) 253–9320, Semiprivate, 18/6794/72

Oak Ridge Golf Club, Gill, (413) 786–9693, Semiprivate, 18/6819/70

Western:

Wahconah Country Club, Dalton, (413) 684–1333, Semiprivate, 18/6541/71

Waubeeka Golf Links, South Williamston, (413) 458–8355, Public, 18/6296/72

Massachusetts: Useful Information

Massachusetts Office of Travel and Tourism, 100 Cambridge St., 13th Fl., Boston, MA 02202, (617) 727–3201, (800) 447–MASS

Division of Fisheries and Wildlife, Department of Environmental Management, 100 Cambridge St., Boston, MA 02202, (617) 727–3151 (fishing and hunting regulations)

Bureau of Recreation, Division of Parks and Forests, Department of Environmental Management, 100 Cambridge St., Boston, MA 02202, (617) 727–3180

Course Name: THE ORCHARDS
GOLF CLUB

Course Type: Public
Address: 62900 Campground Road
Washington, MI 48094
Phone: (810) 786–7200
Fax: (810) 786–7205

GOLF COURSE

Director of Golf: Doug Grove
Head Professional: Jeff Stalcup
Course Length/Par (All Tees): Back
7026/72, Blue 6457/72, White 5868/72,
Forward 5158/72
Course Slope/Rating (All Tees): Back
133/73.9, Blue 125/71.0, White
120/68.5, Ladies' Forward 122/70.1
Course Architect: Robert Trent Jones, Jr.
(1993)
Golf Facilities: Full Pro Shop X, Snack Bar
X, Lounge X, Restaurant X, Locker
Room X, Showers X, Club Rental X,
Club Repair X, Cart Rental X, Instruc-
tion X, Practice Green X, Driving Range
X, Practice Bunker X, Club Storage X
Tee-Time Reservation Policy: Up to 30
days in advance
Ranger: Yes
Tee-off-Interval Time: 9 min.
Time to Play 18 Holes: 4½ hrs.
Course Hours/Earliest Tee-off: 7 a.m.
Green and Cart Fees: $60 for 18 holes
Fri., Sat., Sun., holidays; $50 for 18
holes weekdays
Credit Cards: All major cards
Season: Mid-Mar. through late Fall,
weather permitting
Course Comments: Can walk anytime at
full golf fee. Yardage book available.
Golf schools and junior camps on site
Golf Packages: No
Discounts: Twilight rates. Lower seasonal
rates until mid-May, from mid-Oct. until
end of season
Places to Stay Nearby: DETROIT: Marriott
Detroit Metro Airport (313) 941–9400,
(800) 228–9290; Westin Hotel Renaissance Center (313) 568–8000, (800)
228–3000. TROY: Courtyard by Marriott
(810) 528–2800, (800) 321–2211. WAR-
REN: Residence Inn by Marriott (810)
558–8050, (800) 331–3131; Van Dyke
Park Hotel and Conference Center (810)
939–2860.

Local Attractions: DEARBORN: Dearborn
Historical Museum, Henry Ford Mu-
seum and Greenfield Village. DETROIT:
Belle Isle, Children's Museum, Detroit
Civic Center, Detroit Historical Mu-
seum, Detroit Institute of Fine Arts,
Detroit Zoological Park, Motown His-
torical Museum, Detroit Tigers major
league baseball at Tiger Stadium, NFL
Detroit Lions at Pontiac Silverdome,
Detroit Pistons NBA basketball at The
Palace, NHL Detroit Redwings hockey
at Joe Louis Arena, boat tours, restau-
rants, shopping. Detroit Visitor Informa-
tion, Hart Plaza, 2 East Jefferson Ave.,
Detroit, MI 48226 (313) 567–1170
Directions: The Orchards is 30 mi. north
of downtown Detroit. From M–53 (Van
Dyke Expressway) turn west on 28 Mile
Rd. Proceed to Campground Rd. (4-way
stop) and turn right (north) to golf course
Closest Commercial Airport: Detroit
Metropolitan (1 hr.)

THE ORCHARDS GOLF CLUB

The Robert Trent Jones, Jr.-designed
Orchards Golf Club is on rolling woodlands 30 miles north of Detroit whose
skyline can be seen from the first tee. The
course, which weaves its way through old
apple orchards, wooded uplands, and prairie grasses, has the feel of a traditional
1920s golf course. The front nine is tighter
than the back nine, which must be reached
through a tunnel that runs under Campground Road across from the clubhouse.
The wind can be a factor at The Orchards,
especially on high points of the golf
course, and uneven lies can add difficulty
to your round. However, the greens tend to
have open areas in front allowing you to
run the ball up onto the large, bentgrass
putting surfaces. The tall fescue rough
provides aesthetically pleasing sightlines,
but can be difficult to escape if you stray
the ball.

The 441-yard par-4 ninth is one of the
most difficult holes at The Orchards. The

hole climbs uphill toward the clubhouse with the wind coming into you from the left. The drive must avoid a bunker to the left of the landing area and big hitters might catch one of a series of three bunkers to the right. Houses line the right side of the fairway which tends to slope severely left. The large green, built into a hill approximately 45 feet above the tee, has a collection of seven bunkers that run from below the green up to its left. The front nine has well-treed fairways, almost fifty sand bunkers, scenic but treacherous wetlands, and a beautiful variety of doglegs and dramatic holes such as the 193-yard par-3 second that plays over wetlands to a medium-sized green squeezed by two bunkers. Depending on the time of year, an incoming wind can make this hole even tougher.

The back nine, a more open and windswept collection of holes, ends with a beautiful downhill 413-yard par 4 whose approach must avoid a pond to the right of the deep, undulating green. A favorite hole of mine on this side is the 382-yard par-4 thirteenth, a treelined, blind dogleg right from the back tees. A well-positioned tee shot is required to have a high percentage approach on this scenic bunkerless hole.

The Orchards is on the site of a former early 19th century land grant farm that is now a 525-acre residential real estate development. The octagonal domed modern clubhouse has a quality pro shop and its restaurant provides views of the first tee and practice putting green. The Orchards is a welcome addition to publicly accessible golf in the Detroit area.

Course Name: RATTLE RUN

Course Type: Public
Address: 7163 St. Clair Highway
St. Clair, MI 48079
Phone: (810) 329–2070

GOLF COURSE

Head Professional: Rick Budzinski
Course Length/Par (All Tees): Back 6891/72, Blue 6498/72, Green 5946/72, Forward 5197/75

Course Slope/Rating (All Tees): Back 139/75.1, Blue 135/73.4, Ladies' Green 134/75.6, Forward 124/70.4
Course Architect: Lou Powers (1978)
Golf Facilities: Full Pro Shop X, Snack Bar X, Lounge X, Restaurant No, Locker Room No, Showers No, Club Rental X, Club Repair X, Cart Rental X, Instruction X, Practice Green X, Driving Range X, Practice Bunker X, Club Storage X
Tee-Time Reservation Policy: Up to 1 wk. in advance
Ranger: Yes
Tee-off-Interval Time: 8 min.
Time to Play 18 Holes: 4½ hrs.
Course Hours/Earliest Tee-off: Dawn
Green Fees: $39 for 18 holes Sat., Sun., holidays; $29 for 18 holes weekdays
Cart Fees: $22 for 18 holes per cart, $14 for 9 holes per cart
Pull Carts: $2 for 18 holes
Credit Cards: MasterCard, Visa
Season: April through Nov. Busiest season Aug., Sept.
Course Comments: Can walk anytime
Golf Packages: Inquire at pro shop
Discounts: Seniors, juniors, replays, twilight
Places to Stay Nearby: PORT HURON: Thomas Edison Inn (810) 984–8000, (800) 451–7991; Victorian Inn (810) 984–1437; Econo Lodge (810) 984–2661, (800) 446–6900; Knight's Inn (810) 982–1022. ST. CLAIR: St. Clair Inn (810) 329–2222. SARNIA AREA: Best Western Guildwood Inn (519) 337–7577, (800) 528–1234; Days Inn (519) 383–6767, (800) 329–7466; Holiday Inn (519) 332–3326, (800) HOLIDAY
Local Attractions: PORT HURON: Antiques, fishing, hunting, boating, Fort Gratiot Lighthouse, Knowlton Ice Museum, Museum of Arts and History. Blue Water Convention and Travel Bureau (810) 987–8687, (800) 852–4242. Greater Port Huron–Marysville Chamber of Commerce (810) 982–0891
Directions: From Port Huron: I–94 west, exit 257, take right at off ramp, 2 mi. to 4-way stop, take left, 1.1 mi. to 4-way stop, take left, .7 mi. to golf course

Closest Commercial Airports: Bishop International, Flint (1 hr.); Detroit Metropolitan (1 ½ hrs.)

RATTLE RUN

Rattle Run, with a slope rating of 139 from the back tees and a USGA rating of 75.1, is one of the more difficult publicly accessible golf courses in Michigan. The 6891-yard layout was designed by the original owner, the late Lou Powers, who is past president of the Michigan PGA. It has been listed among America's best 75 public courses by *Golf Digest,* but recently the maintenance has been a bit erratic. If you are in this area, however, approximately 40 miles northeast of Detroit, you should give Rattle Run a try, if only because it is a challenging test of golf.

There are lateral or direct water hazards on almost every hole at Rattle Run, which has medium-sized to large greens that are well protected by bunkers. Also, there are more than 90 sand bunkers here. There are several memorable and excellent holes on the course, which is rolling and open, with strategically placed mature trees and some dramatic elevation changes. The most difficult hole on the course is the 448-yard par-4 sixth, a dogleg right, which plays uphill to a large green protected by traps on the left and right. The tee-shot landing area narrows and is protected by bunkers and water on either side of the fairway. It is advisable to keep the tee shot left of center on this hole.

Another difficult par 4 on this side is the 431-yard seventh, which plays downhill to a small green protected by a trap to the left and two others to the right. Trees border the fairway on the left, and a stream parallels the fairway on the right. A stray tee shot on this hole will quickly add strokes to your score. The 409-yard dogleg-left par-4 fourth is considered one of the best in Michigan. The slightly elevated tee shot is to a relatively open area, but the approach shot is down a tree-protected, narrowing fairway to a green fronted by two traps and guarded by a stream directly to the rear. There is very little margin for error on this approach shot, which has to be flown in to the green.

The back nine starts out with another excellent par 4, a 407-yard slight dogleg right bordered by a stream on the right that cuts back in front of the green. Two bunkers flank the tee-shot landing area, and three traps guard the green, one to the left front and two to the front. The approach shot is uphill. The next hole, a 507-yard straightaway par 5 is well treed from tee to green. A bunker guards the right fairway on the first shot, and two bunkers protect the fairway on the approach. For those who attempt to reach the green in two, there is water directly in front of the green, which is also trapped to the left and right. A difficult par 3 on the back nine is the 238-yard fourteenth, which requires a long, straight shot to a small green guarded by a trap on the right. This hole is well treed and is difficult from all tee distances, which are 220 yards from the blue, 208 yards from the green, and 208 yards (par 4) from the ladies' forward tees. This is the number-6-handicap hole on the course.

After you play Rattle Run, you realize that you have played a golf course with an interesting variety of excellent golf holes, especially the par 4s. The variety of water hazards; sand bunker placements; doglegs; green contours, shapes and sizes; mature, strategically placed trees; and elevation changes make you think strategically as you work your way around this layout. If you like to play golf and aren't too concerned about country-club-style amenities or brand-name golf-course designers, this course is worth a visit.

Course Name: TIMBER RIDGE GOLF CLUB

Course Type: Public
Address: 16339 Park Lake Road
              East Lansing, MI 48823–9401
Phone: (517) 339–8000,
            (800) 874–3432 (MI)

GOLF COURSE

Head Professional: Paul M. Hughes
Course Length/Par (All Tees): Back 6497/72, Middle 6061/72, Forward 5048/72

Course Slope/Rating (All Tees): Back 137/72.7, Middle 133/71.9, Ladies' Forward 128/70.7

Course Architect: Jerry Mathews (1989)

Golf Facilities: Full Pro Shop X, Snack Bar X, Lounge X, Restaurant X, Locker Room X, Showers X, Club Rental X, Club Repair X, Cart Rental X, Instruction X, Practice Green X, Driving Range X, Practice Bunker X, Club Storage X

Tee-Time Reservation Policy: Up to 1 wk. in advance

Ranger: Yes

Tee-off-Interval Time: 8½ min.

Time to Play 18 Holes: 4½ hrs.

Course Hours/Earliest Tee-off: 6:45 a.m.

Green Fees: $40 for 18 holes Fri., Sat., Sun., holidays; $35 for 18 holes weekdays. $20 for 9 holes Fri., Sat., Sun. holidays; $18 for 9 holes weekdays

Cart Fees: $20 for 18 holes, $10 for 9 holes

Pull Carts: $4 for 18 holes, $2 for 9 holes

Credit Cards: Discover, MasterCard, Visa

Season: Mar. through Nov. Busiest season June through Aug.

Course Comments: Walking and 9-hole play permitted anytime weekdays. Cart and 18-hole play required before 2 p.m. Sat., Sun., holidays. Memberships available

Golf Packages: Available through local hotels

Discounts: None

Places to Stay Nearby: Best Western Midway Motor Lodge (517) 627–8471, (800) 528–1234; Comfort Inn (517) 349–8700, (800) 221–2222; Park Inn International (517) 351–3300; Radisson (517) 323–4963, (800) 333–3333; Sheraton Inn (517) 323–7100, (800) 325–3535; Holiday Inn University Place (517) 337–4440, (800) 878–8444; University Inn (517) 351–5500, (800) 221–8466; Motel 6 (517) 484–8722, (800) 437–7486; South Lansing Super 8 Motel (517) 393–8008, (800) 800–8000

Local Attractions: Michigan State University, Carl G. Fenner Arboretum, state capitol, Michigan Historical Museum, Impression 5 Science Museum, R. E. Olds Museum, Potter Park Zoo, Kresge Art Museum, Abrams Planetarium, Michigan State Museum, Wharton Center for the Performing Arts, Boarshead Michigan Public Theater, Michigan State University Performing Arts Company, Greater Lansing Symphony Orchestra. Convention and Visitors Bureau of Greater Lansing (517) 487–6800, (800) 648–6630. Fax: (517) 487–5151

Directions: From Detroit (85 mi.): I–96 west to Lansing, exit 110, Okemus Rd., turn right on Okemus until dead end, left on Lake Lansing Rd. (cross divided highway) to first stop sign. Turn right on Park Lake Rd., golf course 1½ mi. on right. From Grand Rapids (60 mi.): I–96 east to Lansing, Hwy. 127 north, I–69 east, exit 92 (Webster Rd.), left on Webster, left on Park Lake, 1½ mi. on left

Closest Commercial Airports: Capitol City, Lansing (30 min.); Grand Rapids (1 hr., 15 min.); Detroit Metropolitan (1 hr., 45 min.)

TIMBER RIDGE GOLF CLUB

The Timber Ridge Golf Course is beautifully situated near Michigan State University on forested land that was formerly a tree nursery. The golf course is the centerpiece of a real-estate development but is open to the public anytime. As you might expect, this is a tightly treed golf course that puts a premium on shot making and accuracy. Once you get onto the golf course, you are in a world all your own among mature pine, maple, oak, wild cherry, elm and other varieties of trees. Timber Ridge has been rated among America's 75 best public courses by *Golf Digest.*

The bentgrass greens at Timber Ridge are large, moderately fast and undulating. They are usually protected by at least two sizeable sand traps and possibly water, which comes directly into play on seven holes. The number-1-handicap hole is the 437-yard par-4 dogleg-right fifth, which plays from an elevated tee down a tree-lined fairway to a deep green protected by traps left and right. Two bunkers guard the tee-shot landing area on the left. One of my favorite holes on the front nine is the 358-yard par-4 dogleg-right seventh. The tee shot is blind, down a tree-lined fairway to a plateau that looks down to a large green well protected by traps left and right with water farther in front of it.

The three finishing holes at Timber Ridge provide an excellent way to end the round. The 169-yard par-3 sixteenth plays downhill to a large green guarded by water on the right and a large bunker to the front and left. There is also a large trap to the rear of the large putting surface. The 504-yard par-5 seventeenth plays over water on the blind tee shot, which must clear a rise beyond the water so you can see the green. The second shot is downhill toward a green protected by traps left and right. Trees line both fairways from tee to green.

The 455-yard par-4 eighteenth is rated the most difficult hole on the back nine. The tee shot is down a tree-lined corridor to a landing area in front of a large pond that cuts into the fairway from left to right and fronts the green, which is well protected by traps. The medium sized, forward-sloping, undulating green is surrounded by a beautiful cathedral of trees. The tee shot should be to the right to take the water out of play as much as possible on the approach shot.

The combination of mature trees, scenic water hazards, rolling hills and dramatic elevation changes, large greens and sand traps, and generous distances between greens and succeeding tees makes Timber Ridge a demanding and aesthetically pleasing golf experience. The clubhouse has a modern, country-club feel, and it includes a full pro shop, banquet room, snack bar restaurant with views of the first tee, and locker rooms and showers. Banquet services are available for up to 200 persons. Golf packages are available through many local hotels and motels. Inquire at these establishments or at Timber Ridge.

Lessons are available from the staff of professionals at Timber Ridge, which is generally open from April to November, weather permitting. A driving range, practice bunker and putting green are on the premises.

Recommended Golf Courses in Michigan

Within 1 Hour of Detroit:

Cascades, Jackson, (517) 788–4323, Public, 18/6614/72

Devil's Ridge Golf Club, Oxford, (810) 969–0100, Public, 18/6772/72

Dunham Hills Golf and Country Club, Hartland, (810) 887–9170, Public, 18/6763/72

Faulkwood Shores, Howell, (517) 546–4180, Public, 18/6828/72

Fox Hills Country Club, Plymouth, (313) 453–7272, Public. Golden Fox: 18/6783/72. Three nines: 9/3064/36, 9/3334/36, 9/3450/36

Glacier Club, Washington, (810) 781–2288, Semiprivate, 18/7018/72

Greystone Golf Club, Romeo, (810) 752–7030, Public, 18/6861/72

Heather Highlands Golf Club, Holly, (810) 634–6800, Public, 18/6845/72

Huron Golf Club, Ypsilanti, (313) 487–2441, Public, 18/6755/72

Indian Springs Metro Park Golf Course, White Lake, (313) 625–7870, Public, 18/6688/71

Kensington Metro Park Golf Club, Milford, (313) 685–9332, Public, 18/6381/71

The Majestic at Lake Walden, Hartland, (810) 632–5235, (800) 762–3280, Public. First/Second: 18/7035/72. Second/Third: 18/6757/72. First/Third: 18/6612/72

Pine Knob Golf Club, Clarkston, (810) 625–4430, Public, 18/6647/72

Pine Trace Golf Club, Rochester Hills, (810) 852–7100, Public, 18/6610/72

Pohlcat Golf Course, Mt. Pleasant, (517) 773–4221, (800) 292–8891, Resort, 18/6810/72

Rouge Park Golf Club, Detroit, (313) 837–5900, Public, 18/6314/72

Salem Hills Golf Club, Northville, (810) 437–2152, Public, 18/6966/72

Springfield Oaks Golf Course, Davisburg, (810) 625–2540, Public, 18/6235/71

Stonebridge Golf Club, Ann Arbor, (313) 429–8383, 18/6932/72

Sycamore Hills Golf Club, Mt. Clemens, (810) 598–9500, Public. South: 9/3150/36. West: 9/3155/36. North: 9/3085/36

Tanglewood Golf Club, South Lyon, (810) 486–3355, Public. North/South: 18/7077/72. South/West: 18/6922/72. North/West: 18/7117/72

Taylor Meadows Golf Club, Taylor, (313) 295–0506, Public, 18/6075/71

Northeast/Bay City And North

Course Name: ELK RIDGE GOLF COURSE

Course Type: Public
Address: Highway 33 at Rouse Road
               Route 1, Box 28A
               Atlanta, MI 49709
Phone: (517) 785–2275,
               (800) 626–4355
Fax: (517) 785–3484

GOLF COURSE

Club Manager: Scott Landane
Course Length/Par (All Tees): Back 7033/72, Blue 6615/72, White 6103/72, Forward 5261/72
Course Slope/Rating (All Tees): Back 144/75, Blue 141/73.5, White 134/70.8, Forward 135/70.1
Course Architect: Jerry Mathews (1991)
Golf Facilities: Full Pro Shop X, Snack Bar X, Lounge X, Restaurant X, Locker Room X, Showers X, Club Rental X, Club Repair No, Cart Rental X, Instruction X, Practice Green X, Driving Range X, Practice Bunker No, Club Storage No
Tee-Time Reservation Policy: Anytime in advance
Ranger: Yes
Tee-off-Interval Time: 10 min.
Time to Play 18 Holes: 4½ hrs.
Course Hours/Earliest Tee-off: 6:30 a.m.

Green and Cart Fees: $60 for 18 holes with cart, $30 for 9 holes with cart
Credit Cards: Discover, MasterCard, Visa
Season: May through Oct. Busiest season May to Aug.
Course Comments: Cart mandatory
Golf Packages: None
Discounts: Twilight, seniors (Mon. to Wed.)
Places to Stay Nearby: GAYLORD: Best Western (517) 732–7541, (800) 678–7541; Days Inn (517) 732–2200, (800) 325–2525. ALPENA: Best Western (517) 356–9087, (800) 528–1234
Local Attractions: GAYLORD: Bavarian Falls Park, Call of the Wild Museum, hunting, fishing, camping, boating, skiing. ALPENA: Sportsmen's Island Wildlife Sanctuary, Besser Natural Area, Jesse Besser Museum and Planetarium, Thunder Bay Underwater Preserve. Gaylord Convention and Tourist Bureau (517) 732–4000, (800) 342–9657. Convention and Visitors Bureau of Thunder Bay Region (517) 354–4181, (800) 582–1906
Directions: Hwy. 32 to Hwy. 33. Take Hwy. 33 5 mi. north to Rouse Rd. Go west 1 mi. on Rouse Rd. to golf course
Closest Commercial Airports: Cherry Capital, Traverse City (2 hrs.); Tri–City International, Saginaw (2½ hrs.); Detroit Metropolitan (3½ hrs.)

ELK RIDGE GOLF COURSE

Elk Ridge Golf Course is located in northern Michigan, 3½ hours from Detroit. This Jerry Mathews–designed 7033-yard layout was named runner-up as best new public course in 1991 by *Golf Digest*. The course, a former hunting preserve, is owned by Lou Schmidt, who owns the Honey Baked Ham Co. headquartered in Detroit.

Elk Ridge covers more than 425 acres of scenic woodlands and wetlands. The golf course is tightly treed, with large, moderately fast, undulating bentgrass greens that are well bunkered. Most of the greens on this course are elevated slightly above the fairway. There are many good holes at Elk Ridge, including the 203-yard par-3 fourth, which is all carry over a pond to a large, two-tiered green fronted by water and protected by traps to the left, rear and right. The 203-yard par-3 sixth is all carry over wetlands to a deep, tiered green backed by traps and guarded by two small traps on the left and right.

The back nine starts with a 184-yard par 3 that plays from an elevated tee to a wide, shallow green 120 feet below. Traps guard the left rear and left front of the target. A pig shaped bunker, in honor of the meat business that helped create this course, guards the right front of the green.

The 381-yard par-4 dogleg-left sixteenth is the signature hole at Elk Ridge. The tee shot is to a landing area just before a large sand bunker guarding the right corner of the dogleg. To the left of the fairway are wetlands that can be carried should you try to cut the corner. The fairway narrows severely, however, as you move from right to left toward a landing area closer to the green. The approach shot is to a large green guarded to the left, right and rear by three traps.

The finishing hole at Elk Ridge is a formidable 600-yard par 5 that is a double dogleg left then right to a large green fronted by wetlands and guarded by traps left and right. Two good shots are required to put you in a position to carry 170 yards of wetlands that front the green.

Each hole at Elk Ridge is a separate and arresting golf experience. As you work your way through the woods of red and white pine and hardwoods, you might come across elk, deer, wild turkey, blue herons, bald eagles and other animal species. The variety of elevation changes; subtle, undulating greens; doglegs; tree-lined fairways; bunkers and hazards make Elk Ridge one of the most challenging golf courses in Michigan with a slope rating of 144 and a USGA rating of 75 from the back tees.

**Course Name: LAKEWOOD SHORES RESORT
          The Gailes,
          Resort Courses**

Course Type: Resort
Resort: Lakewood Shores Resort

Address: 7751 Cedar Lake Road
              Oscoda, MI 48750
Phone: (517) 739–2075 (Golf Course),
              (800) 882–2493 (Resort)
Fax: (517) 739–1351 (Golf Course)

GOLF COURSE

Head Professional: Craig Peters
Course Length/Par (All Tees): The Gailes: Championship 6954/72, Back 6393/72, Middle 6073/72, Forward 5246/73. Resort Course: Back: 6806/72, Middle 6511/72, Ladies' Forward 5295/74
Course Slope/Rating (All Tees): The Gailes: Championship 137/74.6, Back 132/72.7, Middle 129/71.1, Ladies' Forward 132/72.0. Resort Course: Back 120/72.9, Middle 117/71.5, Forward 115/70.9
Course Architects: The Gailes: Kevin Aldridge (1992). Resort Course: Bruce Mathews and Gerry Mathews (1969)
Golf Facilities: Full Pro Shop X, Snack Bar X, Lounge X, Restaurant X, Locker Room No, Showers No, Club Rental X, Club Repair X, Cart Rental X, Instruction X, Practice Green X, Driving Range X, Practice Bunker X, Club Storage X
Tee-Time Reservation Policy: At time of confirmed reservations in on-site condominiums or call anytime
Ranger: Yes
Tee-off-Interval Time: The Gailes: 10 min. Resort: 8 min.
Time to Play 18 Holes: 4½ hrs.
Course Hours/Earliest Tee-off: 7 a.m.
Green Fees: Gailes: $50 for 18 holes Fri., Sat., Sun., holidays, $45 for 18 holes weekdays.
Resort Course: $30 for 18 holes Fri., Sat., Sun., holidays, $23 for 18 holes weekdays
Cart Fees: $12.50 per person for 18 holes
Credit Cards: All major cards
Season: Apr. thorugh Oct. Busiest mid-June through late Aug.
Course Comments: Walking allowed anytime. Yardage book available. On-site accomodations
Golf Packages: Through resort

Discounts: Twilight. Seasonal (lowest rates Apr. to mid-May, mid-Sept. through Oct.)

Places to Stay Nearby: OSCODA: Redwood Motor Lodge (517) 739–2021; Rest All Inn (517) 739–8822. BED AND BREAKFAST: Huron House (517) 739–9255. TAWAS CITY: Smith's Pine Haven Resort (517) 362–2321

Local Attractions: Fishing, hunting, camping, hiking, boating, beaches, Huron National Forest, seasonal festival, Paul Bunyan statue, lumberman's monument. Oscoda–Au Sable Chamber of Commerce, 4440 N. U.S. 23, Oscoda, MI 48750 (517) 739–7322

Directions: From Detroit, Flint, Saginaw, and Bay City take I–75 north to Exit 188 at Standish. Turn north on U.S. 23 to Oscoda. In Oscoda turn left on Hwy. F–41 then right at the first traffic light onto Cedar Lake Rd. Proceed 4½ miles to the golf course on the left

Closest Commercial Airports: Tri-City International, Saginaw (1½ hrs.); Detroit Metropolitan (3½ hrs.)

LAKEWOOD SHORES GOLF CLUB

The Lakewood Shores Resort is situated in logging country along Lake Huron three hours north of Detroit. Lakewood Shores opened in the late 1960s with a golfer-friendly Bruce and Jerry Mathew-6806 yard par 72 layout, a fine resort course. Owner Stan Aldridge, who also is the owner of Indianwood in Lake Orion, Michigan, site of the 1994 U.S. Women's Open, decided that a Scottish links-style course should be added to the venue. Kevin Aldridge, his son, after much research in the British Isles, completed the stunning new Gailes course in 1992 and it was immediately recognized as one of the best new resort courses in America.

The Gailes is swept with variable Huron winds, has 130 stacked sod faced bunkers, is framed by a variety of mounds and has hidden fairway bunkers, a winding creek that can eat golf balls, and deep grass that will make strayed shots vanish forever. If you do not properly position fairway shots, the green will be hidden by mounds. If you land on these mounds you will have a tedi-

ous uneven lie that is likely to cost you at least one stroke. The course is bentgrass from tee to green and some of the greens are huge, most notable the double greens accomodating No. 2 and No. 17, and No. 11 and No. 14.

A good run of holes at The Gailes begins with the 553-yard par-5 eleventh, "Wall's Edge," a dogleg left that lures you into cutting the corner only to have your view on the second shot obscured by a large fairway mound. A shot over the green is a disaster because of a ten foot drop to a bunker. The 140-yard par-3 twelfth, "Wee Burn," is much like Troon's "Postage Stamp" hole with its minuscule target, a grassy mound to the left, and dropoffs from the other sides of the putting surface. The 489-yard par-4 thirteenth, "XX," requires a long, well-placed drive that provides a clear view to a deep green guarded by small bunkers to its left and right front. The golfer must avoid the burn running up the left side and cutting the fairway 170 yards from the green.

Course management skills, course knowledge, an ability to bump and run shots under the wind, and the patience to adapt to variable wind conditions are needed to score at the Gailes. The variety of holes and the subtle suprises on this course will make you want to play it again and again.

Course Name: TREETOPS SYLVAN RESORT
Fazio, Jones, Smith, Threetops Courses

Course Type: Resort
Resort: Treetops Sylvan Resort
Address: 3962 Wilkinson Road Gaylord, MI 49735
Phone: (517) 732–6711, (800) 444–6711 (Golf Course and Resort)
Fax: (517) 732–6595 (Golf Course and Resort)

GOLF COURSE

Head Professional: Rick Smith
Course Length/Par (All Tees): Fazio: Back 6832/72, Blue 6302/72, White

5886/72, Forward 5039/72. Jones: Back 7060/71, Blue 6399/71, White 5817/71, Forward 4972/71. Smith: Back 6653/72, Blue 6285/72, White 5863/72, Gold 5413/72, Forward 4604/72. Threetops: Back 9/1182/27, Forward 9/940/27

Course Slope/Rating (All Tees): Fazio Back 135/73.2, Blue 125/70.7, White 121/68.6, Ladies' Forward 123/70.1. Jones: Back 146/75.8, Blue 137/72.6, White 127/69.7, Ladies' Forward 124/70.2. Smith: Back 137/72.7, Blue 130/70.7, White 126/68.6, Gold 121/66.7, Forward 118/66.8

Course Architects: Fazio: Tom Fazio (1992). Jones: Robert Trent Jones, Sr. (1987). Smith: Rick Smith (1993). Threetops: Rick Smith (1992)

Golf Facilities: Full Pro Shop X, Snack Bar X, Lounge X, Restaurant X, Locker Room X, Showers X, Club Rental X, Club Repair X, Cart Rental X, Instruction X, Practice Green X, Driving Range X, Practice Bunker X, Club Storage X

Tee-Time Reservation Policy: Anytime in advance

Ranger: Yes

Tee-off-Interval Time: 10 min.

Time to Play 18 Holes: 5 hrs.

Course Hours/Earliest Tee-off: Dawn to dusk

Green and Cart Fees: Fazio: Resort guests: $64 for 18 holes with cart, $45 for 9 holes with cart. Outside play: $80 for 18 holes with cart, $45 for 9 holes with cart. Jones: Resort guests: $58 for 18 holes with cart, $40 for 9 holes with cart. Outside play: $72 for 18 holes with cart, $40 for 9 holes with cart. Smith: Resort Guests: $54 for 18 holes with cart, $40 for 9 holes with cart. Outside play: $64 for 18 holes with cart, $40 for 9 holes with cart. Threetops: Resort guests: $15. Outside play: $20

Credit Cards: American Express, Master-Card, Visa

Season: May to Oct. Busiest season mid-May through Sept.

Course Comments: Cart mandatory. Tree-top Golf Academy on site

Golf Packages: Available through resort

Discounts: Resort guests, seasonal rates, replays. Twilight rate after 3 p.m. or later depending on season. Replay after 2 p.m.

Places to Stay Nearby: Best Western Gaylord (517) 732–7541, (800) 678–7541; Days Inn (517) 732–2200, (800) 325–2525; El Rancho Stevens (dude ranch) (517) 732–5090; Holiday Inn (517) 732–2431, (800) HOLIDAY; Quality Inn (517) 732–5193, (800) 228–5151

Local Attractions: Fishing, hunting, camping, boating, hiking, Bavarian Falls Park, Call of the Wild Museum, seasonal festivals, Otsego Lake State Park, skiing. Gaylord Area Tourist Bureau (517) 732–6333, (800) 342–9567

Directions: From I–75: Gaylord exit 282, east on M32 (Main St.) through Gaylord to Wilkinson Rd., left on Wilkinson Rd. to golf course and resort

Closest Commercial Airports: Cherry Capital, Traverse City (45 min.); Grand Rapids (3½ hrs.); Capitol City, Lansing (3½ hrs.); Detroit Metropolitan (5½ hrs.)

RESORT

Date Built: 1954

No. of Rooms: 233 standard, queen, standard deluxe, efficiency, queen deluxe, king deluxe, president, hospitality, 2- and 3-bedroom units, chalets

Meeting Rooms: 15. Capacity of Largest: 830 persons banquet style. Meeting Space: 21,189 sq. ft.

Room Price Range: $77 for standard room to $264 for 3-room suite, peak season (late May to late Sept.). Off-season rates, golf packages, ski packages and other special rates available

Lounges: Sports Bar, Fairways Grille

Restaurants: Fairways Grille, Horizon Room

Entertainment: Live entertainment in Fairways Grille

Credit Cards: American Express, Master-Card, Visa

General Amenities: Day-care services for ages 1 through 12, Edelweiss Shop, meeting and conference facilities with audiovisual and banquet services

Recreational Amenities: 2 outdoor swimming pools, sauna, weight room, whirlpool, 2 indoor swimming pools, volleyball, skiing, 2 tennis courts, hiking trails

Reservation and Cancellation Policy: Credit card or deposit for 1 night to guarantee reservation. Cancellations must be made at least 14 days in advance of the day of arrival to avoid penalties.

Comments and Restrictions: No pets allowed. Taxes additional to base rates. Children 17 and under sleep free in parents' rooms

TREETOPS SYLVAN RESORT

The Robert Trent Jones, Sr., course at Treetops is carved out of woods in Gaylord, Michigan, approximately a 5½-hour drive northwest of Detroit. This course was runner-up in *Golf Digest*'s best new resort course ratings for 1987. Because of the trees, hilliness, severe elevation changes and 7060-yard length of Treetops, it has one of the highest slope ratings (146) in the state of Michigan. The bentgrass greens on this layout are moderately fast, undulating and well protected by large sand traps. There are water hazards on six holes and strategically placed fairway bunkers on eight holes.

The yardage is a bit shorter on the front nine than the back nine on the Jones layout, which has a distance of 6399 yards from the blue tees (slope 137/USGA rating 72.6). After a 524-yard par 5 and a 201-yard par 3 (from the back tees), you reach the 419-yard par-4 third, the number-1-handicap hole. The tee shot is over a large, intimidating ravine to a fairway that begins approximately 160 yards away. From 175 yards into the green, there is another large ravine on the left. Also, bunkers are to the right of the tee-shot landing area, approximately 165 yards from the green. The approach shot is to a narrow, deep, forward-sloping green with a large bunker to the left front and a grass bunker and large sand bunker to the right. A beautiful cathedral of trees is in the background as you come into this target. There are severe drop-offs on all sides of the green.

The signature hole on the Jones course is the 180-yard par-3 sixth hole, which plays from an elevated tee to a narrow, deep, left-to-right-sloping green 120 feet below. Two large traps guard the right of the green, and another two are on the left. Depending on the wind and pin position, you will need less club than the yardage indicates. The view from the tee provides you with a spectacular panorama of trees for miles around. This originally prompted Robert Trent Jones, Sr., to name the course Treetops.

The finishing hole on the Jones course is a long, 579-yard uphill par 5 that starts out with a tee shot to a landing area guarded by a left-fairway bunker. The second shot is up a corridor of trees toward a small, crowned green. Two large traps and a grass bunker protect the front of the green.

The Treetops Jones golf course has no easy holes. Many are beautiful and memorable, but you will be penalized if you make mistakes on just about any shot. In addition to elevation changes, trees, and variations in slope on the greens and fairways, the size, shape and positioning of the greens and their protecting bunkers add another challenging element to this layout. The green on the 363-yard par-4 fifteenth, for example, is over 40 yards deep but only 12 yards wide, and is almost completely surrounded by five sand traps. The green itself also has three small, flat tiers. The thirteenth hole, a 208-yard par 3 fronted by water, has an extremely wide (37 yards) green that is only 21 yards deep. A trap protects the front center of the green and another large trap is on the right. All of these sizes, shapes and angles provide much food for thought when developing your shot-making strategy on the Jones layout.

The chalet-style clubhouse at the Jones course has an excellent pro shop, bar and snack bar, locker rooms and showers. An outside wraparound balcony with umbrella tables provides scenic views of the golf course and surrounding forest. A practice green, driving range and practice bunker are offered at Treetops, and individual and group lessons are available from the staff of professionals. Instruction includes video analysis and clinics focusing on specific aspects of the game. A series of extensive golf instructional programs is offered May through September at the on-site Treetops Golf Academy.

A few miles away at Treetops North is the Fazio course, Fazio's first course in the state of Michigan. The Fazio covers 240 wooded acres, has over 70 bunkers and one water hazard. The course is bentgrass from tee to green with bluegrass and fescue bent rough. This course is less severe than the Jones but offers a fine test of golf. It was selected among the "Top 10 New Courses You Can Play" by *Golf* magazine in 1993 and was rated among the best new resort courses by *Golf Digest* that same year.

Also at Treetops North is the Rick Smith Signature course, a 6653-yard par-70 layout designed by Treetop's head professional. Smith is not only an internationally recognized golf instructor, he is also a good golf course designer. The Smith features 135 bunkers and has a variety of elevation changes as it winds through hardwoods and pine. At times you will be pleasantly distracted by panoramic views of the Michigan north country as you work your way around this course. It was named the "Best New Course of the Year" by *GolfWeek* in 1994. Within less than six years, beginning with the opening of the Jones course, Treetops Sylvan has evolved from a regional ski destination to a nationally recognized golf attraction.

An extra bonus at Treetops is the Treetops par-3 course which is also located at Treetops North. Also designed by Rick Smith, this 1182-yard par-27 course course has 30 bunkers and covers 40 acres. This challenging short course, which some have called the best par-3 layout in the country, plays from hilltop to hilltop with dramatic vertical drops in between.

Golf packages for the courses can be arranged through the Treetops Sylvan Resort, a year-round resort featuring standard deluxe rooms and suites at the inn, as well as a variety of 2- and 3-room units with efficiency kitchenettes. Meeting and conference facilities are available for groups of up to 830 persons and recreational amenities include indoor and outdoor swimming pools, tennis courts, sauna, Jacuzzi, hiking trails, weight rooms, and nearby skiing facilities. The Horizon Room restaurant offers fine or casual dining, and the Fairways Grille serves light meals and has live entertainment Thursday through Saturday evenings for your dancing and listening pleasure. There is also the Sports Bar, which features a pool table, dart boards, a basketball hoop and over 500 domestic and imported beers.

Course Name: WILDERNESS VALLEY GOLF RESORT Black Forest, Valley Courses

Course Type: Semiprivate
Address: 7519 Mancelona Road
Gaylord, MI 49735
Phone: (616) 585–7090
Fax: (616) 585–7010

GOLF COURSE

Director of Golf: Gerry Schmidt

Head Professional: Jeff Luczak

Course Length/Par (All Tees): Black Forest: Back: 7044/73, Blue 6496/73, White 6129/73, Ladies' Forward 5282/74. Valley: Back 6519/71, Middle 6098/71, Forward 4889/71

Course Slope/Rating (All Tees): Black Forest: Back 140/74.5, Blue 133/72.0, White 126/70.0, Ladies' Forward 127/71.4. Valley: Back 126/NA, Middle 121/NA, Forward 115/NA

Course Architects: Black Forest: Tom Doak (1989). Valley: Al Watrous (1972)

Golf Facilities: Full Pro Shop X, Snack Bar X, Lounge X, Restaurant X, Locker Room No, Showers No, Club Rental X, Club Repair X, Cart Rental X, Instruction X, Practice Green X, Driving Range X, Practice Bunker X, Club Storage X

Tee-Time Reservation Policy: Call anytime. 48-hr. cancellation policy

Ranger: Yes

Tee-off-Interval Time: Black Forest: 8 min. Valley: 7 min.

Time to Play 18 Holes: Black Forest: 4½ hrs. Valley: 4 hrs.

Course Hours/Earliest Tee-off: 6 a.m.

Green and Cart Fees: Black Forest: $70 for 18 holes Sat., Sun., holidays; $60 for 18 holes weekends. Valley: $38 for 18 holes Sat., Sun., holidays; $35 weekends

Credit Cards: Ameican Express, Discover, MasterCard, Visa

Season: Apr. through Oct. Busiest Jun. through Aug.

Course Comments: You can walk anytime at full golf fee. Black Forest very difficult to walk

Golf Packages: Contact pro shop

Discounts: Twilight

Places to Stay Nearby: GAYLORD: Best Western Royal Crest (517) 732–6451, (800) 528–1234; Comfort Inn (517) 732–7541, (800) 4–CHOICE; Hidden Valley Resort and Golf Club (517) 732–5181, (800) 752–5510; Holiday Inn (517) 732–2431, (800) HOLIDAY; Treetops Sylvan Resort (517) 732–6711, (800) 444–6711

Local Attractions: Call of the Wild Museum, hunting, fishing, hiking, camping, seasonal festivals, Otsego Lake County Park, beaches, boating, horseback riding, antiquing, winter skiing. Gaylord Area Convention and Tourism Bureau, 101 W. Main St., P.O. Box 3069, Gaylord, MI 49735 (517) 732–6333, (800) 345–8621

Directions: From Gaylord take I–75 south to Mancelona Rd. Exit. Proceed west on Mancelona to golf course

Closest Commercial Airports: Cherry Capitol, Traverse City (1½ hrs.); Detroit Metropolitan (3 hrs.)

WILDERNESS VALLEY

The Jewel of Wilderness Valley's golf course real estate development 30 minutes southwest of Gaylord features the Black Forest course, a Tom Doak design cut through the rolling woodlands. After taking a long cart ride or walk to the first tee, you become enveloped in your own golf woodland world. Each hole is a separate entity and there is often a considerable distance from the green to the next tee. The 443-yard par-4 second hole is representative of the challenges you'll face at Black Forest. This treelined dogleg right requires you to keep your tee shot to the left or else the ball will likely kick down the left-to-right sloping fairway into the trees. The approach is to a two-tiered green with a bunker to its left and trees to the right. The fairway rolls like a convulsive carpet as swales on mounds define the fairway from 200 yards in to the target. One of my favorite holes on the front side is the 238-yard par-3 fifth which takes many golfers a driver to reach. The tee shot is from an elevated tee over a swale to a two-tiered green with a cluster of bunkers to its left. A short tee shot to the left makes it difficult to hit a solid recovery shot up to the green.

An excellent par 5 on the back nine is the 504-yard sixteenth, a dogleg right with water on the right. This hole often plays downwind, but in October the wind was coming into the golfer's face, making the hole play considerably longer. The large pond to the right runs up along the right side of the green, the smallest on the course. The fairway squeezes in as you approach the target and a bunker 50 yards in front of the green often catches approach shots. There are 86 bunkers on this course. Water comes into play only on Nos. 16 and 17. There are few radical elevation changes, but there are often uphill, downhill, and sidehill slopes to contend with. The undulating bentgrass greens are usually large and quick.

Another good test of golf at Wilderness Valley is the Valley Course, designed by Al Watrous in the early 1970s. This will serve as a good tune-up course before you attack Black Forest. Wilderness Valley has a modest clubhouse and a practice area with driving range, practice green, and practice bunker. The Black Forest course has been rated among the best in Michigan by *Golf Digest*.

Recommended Golf Courses in Michigan

Northeast/Bay City and North:

Alpena Golf Club, Alpena, (517) 354–5052, Public, 18/6319/70

Bay Valley Inn Hotel and Resort, Bay City, (517) 686–5400, (800) 292–5028, Resort, 18/6610/71

Eagle Glen Golf Course, Farwell, (517) 588–9357, Public, 18/6602/72

The Forests, Frankenmuth, (517) 652–9229, Resort, 18/6825/72

Garland Resort, Lewiston, (517) 786–2211, (800) 968–0042 (Resort), Resort. Monarch: 18/7188/72. Reflections: 18/6434/72. Swampfire: 18/6868/72

Gaylord Country Club, Gaylord, (616) 546–3376, Semiprivate, 18/6852/72

Hidden Valley Resort and Club, Gaylord, (517) 732–4653, Resort, 18/6305/71

Huron Breeze, Au Gres, (517) 876–6868, Public, 18/6806/72

Indian River Golf Club, Indian River, (616) 238–7011, Semiprivate, 18/6718/72

The Lake Golf Club, Gaylord, (517) 731–1406, (800) 525–3719, Public, 18/6312/71

The Natural at Beaver Creek Resort, Gaylord, (517) 732–1785, Resort, 18/6350/72

Marsh Ridge Resort, Gaylord, (517) 731–1563, (800) 968–2633, 18/6100/71

Michaywe Hills Resort, Gaylord, (517) 939–8911, (800) 322–6636 (MI), Resort, The Pines: 18/6835/72

Pine River Golf Club, Standish, (517) 846–6819, Public, 18/6250/71

Pleasant Hills Golf Club, Mt. Pleasant, (517) 772–0487, Public, 18/6012/72

Rock at Woodmoor, Drummond Island, (906) 493–1006, (800) 999–6343, Resort, 18/6837/72

Thunder Bay Golf Resort, Hillman, (517) 742–4875, (800) SAY–YESS, Resort, 18/6466/73

Vassar Golf and Country Club, Vassar, (517) 823–7221, Semiprivate, 18/6493/72

White Pine National Golf Club, Spruce, (517) 736–3279, Public, 18/6987/72

Northwestern

Course Name: **BOYNE HIGHLANDS RESORT**
Donald Ross Memorial, Heather, Moor Courses

Course Type: Resort
Resort: Boyne Highlands
Address: Michigan Highway 119 Harbor Springs, MI 49740
Phone: (616) 526–2171 (Golf Course) (616) 549–2441, (800) GO BOYNE, (Resort)
Fax: (616) 526–5636 (Resort)

GOLF COURSE

Director of Golf: Bernie Friedrich

Head Professionals: Moor: Jason Deweerd. Heather: Brian O'Neill. Ross: Dan Turcott

Course Length/Par (All Tees): Moor: Back 7179/72, Gold 6521/72, White 6032/72, Forward 5459/72. Heather: Back 7218/72, Gold 6554/72, White 6090/72, Forward 5263/72. Donald Ross Memorial: Back 6840/72, Middle 6308/72, Forward 4977/72

Course Slope/Rating (All Tees): Moor: Back 131/74, Gold 127/71.3, White 122/69.1, Ladies' Forward 118/70. Heather: Back 131/73.2, Gold 126/71.2, White 119/68.1, Ladies' Forward 111/67.8. Donald Ross Memorial: Back 131/73.2, Middle 126/70.7, Ladies' Forward 117/68.3

Course Architects: Moor: Robert Trent Jones, Sr. (9 holes, 1968), William Newcomb (9 holes, 1975). Heather: Robert Trent Jones, Sr. (9 holes, 1968), William Newcomb (9 holes, 1975). Donald Ross Memorial: William Newcomb, Jim Flick, and Everett Kircher (1989)

Golf Facilities: Full Pro Shop X, Snack Bar X, Lounge X, Restaurant X, Locker Room X, Showers X, Club Rental X, Club Repair X, Cart Rental X, Instruction X, Practice Green X, Driving Range X, Practice Bunker X, Club Storage X

Tee-Time Reservation Policy: Resort guests: At time of reservation. Outside play: Moor: Anytime. Heather, Ross: Up to 30 days in advance

Ranger: Yes

Tee-off-Interval Time: 9 min.

Time to Play 18 Holes: 4½ hrs.

Course Hours/Earliest Tee-off: 6:30 a.m.

Green and Cart Fees: Resort guests: Moor: $55 for 18 holes with cart. Heather: $76 for 18 holes with cart. Ross: $68 for 18 holes with cart. Outside play: Moor: $69 for 18 holes with cart. Heather: $98 for 18 holes with cart. Ross: $89 for 18 holes with cart

Credit Cards: American Express, Discover, MasterCard, Visa

Season: Late April to mid-Oct.

Course Comments: Cart mandatory. Yardage book available. Memberships available

Golf Packages: Avalable through resort

Discounts: Resort guests. Midweek and seasonal (May to mid-June, late Aug. through Oct. excluding Labor Day weekend, Fri., Sat. in Sept.) Twilight rate (Heather, Moor). Replays on space-available basis

Places to Stay Nearby: Birchwood Inn (616) 526–2151, (800) 530–9955; Best Western of Harbor Springs (616) 347–9050, (800) 528–1234; Harborside Inn (616) 526–6238; Harbor Springs Cottage Inn (616) 526–5431

Local Attractions: Antiquing, boating, fishing, hunting, hiking, camping, bicycling, skiing, skating. Charlevoix. Harbor Springs. PETOSKEY: Little Traverse Historic Museum. Boyne Country Convention and Visitors Bureau (616) 348–2755, (800) 456–0197 (outside MI)

Directions: Off Hwy. 119 between Petoskey and Harbor Springs

Closest Commercial Airports: Cherry Capital, Traverse City (1½ hrs.); Grand Rapids (4 hrs.); Detroit Metropolitan (5 hrs.); Chicago O'Hare International, IL (7 hrs.)

RESORT

Date Built: 1964

No. of Rooms: Bartley House: 68 rooms. Pleasantview: 70 condominium units. Inverness: 54 units

Meeting Rooms: 15. Capacity of Largest: 500 persons banquet style. Meeting Space: 22,000 sq. ft.

Room Price Range: $90 for hotel room to $280 for 4-bedroom loft-unit condo per night. Golf packages including weekend and weekday as well as other packages available year round

Lounges: Slopeside Bar, Country Club Grill

Restaurants: Main Lodge Dining Room, Country Club of Boyne (resort guests only)

Entertainment: Young American's Dinner Theater

Credit Cards: All major cards

General Amenities: Meeting and conference facilities with audiovisual and food services

Recreational Amenities: 4 outdoor tennis courts, 3 heated swimming pools, saunas, whirlpools, hiking, bicycling, fishing on Lake Michigan, Little Traverse Bay, streams, boating, cross-country and downhill skiing with instruction, ice skating

Reservation and Cancellation Policy: 1 night's deposit required to hold reservation. 10-day cancellation notice required to avoid penalties

Comments and Restrictions: No pets allowed. Taxes additional to basic rates

BOYNE HIGHLANDS RESORT

Boyne Highlands Resort is on the eastern shore of Lake Michigan in northern Michigan, approximately 360 miles northeast of Chicago. The resort includes three excellent eighteen-hole championship golf courses, ample practice facilities and other recreational activities including tennis, swimming, hiking and boating and fishing nearby. In the winter, this year-round resort features downhill and cross-country skiing as well as other winter sports. Accommodations include regular hotel rooms and suites at the main lodge or condominium units at the nearby Heather Highlands Inn, which includes Pleasantview and Inverness, or Bartley House. There are dining facilities at the main lodge and the Country Club of Boyne, a private club open to resort guests.

Short-order food is also served at the golf courses themselves.

The Moor Course at Boyne Highlands plays 7179 yards from the back tees and is a combination of nine holes designed by Jones and nine compatible holes designed by Newcomb. Jones had designed the first eighteen-hole course at Boyne Highlands in the late 1960s, and Newcomb added an additional eighteen in the mid-1970s. The courses were then integrated to form the current Moor and Heather layouts. The Moor is more of a target course, with strategically placed bunkers and smaller bentgrass greens that are flatter and seemingly faster than Heather's. Water comes into play on eleven holes. The front nine is more rolling than the back nine which is more level, with an abundance of water hazards.

The front nine features some long par 3s. The 218-yard fourth plays to a wide, shallow forward-sloping green guarded by a trap to the left front and another to the right. The 222-yard sixth is to another wide, shallow green backed by trees and fronted by a large bunker. Additional trees guard the right side of the green.

The 555-yard par-5 eighth hole is a severe dogleg left with a well-placed water hazard to the left of the landing area. The challenge is to carry this hazard should you wish to reach the deep, forward-sloping green in two. The second shot is toward a target guarded by marsh on the left and a series of five bunkers to the front right, front and right from 100 yards into the green.

The finishing hole is a 580-yard double dogleg called the "zigzag" hole. The tee shot is to a landing area to the right of a pond. You can try to carry the pond, a distance of over 225 yards from the back tee, but a twin-trunk maple awaits you on the other side of the water hazard. The second shot, if you are too far right, has to contend with a large tree 100 yards from the green and a pond to the right and in front of the green. The green is large and forward sloping and is guarded by two traps to the left and one to the rear.

The Heather Course is a 7218-yard par-72 layout. Nine holes were designed by

Robert Trent Jones, Sr., and another nine by William Newcomb. The Heather has generous, rolling fairways and large, fast, undulating bentgrass greens strategically protected by sizeable bunkers. Water comes into play on eight holes. The Heather is a challenging golf course requiring strategic play. Most of the obstacles are in the form of sand, water, and tricky greens.

The 563-yard par-5 dogleg-left fifth is the number-1-handicap hole on the course, and one of its most memorable holes. You are tempted to try to cut the left corner of the dogleg on the tee shot, but a large pond to the left that runs all the way to the green tends to give one second thoughts. The second shot is toward a large green that slopes forward and to the left. A trap guards the right front of the green.

The par-3s on the Heather Course are excellent. The 173-yard sixth plays over a marsh to a small, forward-sloping green protected by marshland in front and traps on either side. The 200-yard sixteenth has a tee shot to a narrow, deep green that slopes left to right and is guarded by two traps to the left and a larger one to the right.

The finishing hole on the Heather Course provides an excellent way to end the round. The tee shot on this 468-yard par 4 is to a landing area in front of a large pond. The approach shot must carry approximately 160 yards of water to reach a wide, shallow, forward-sloping green backed by two bunkers. If you are long, you will have a tricky sand-wedge or chip shot toward a putting surface sloping back and toward the water.

The newest course at Boyne Highlands is the Donald Ross Memorial, a 6840-yard par-72 layout designed by Newcomb, Jim Flick and the resort's owner, Everett Kircher. *Golf Digest* awarded this course an honorable mention in its best new resort course category for 1990. There are many memorable and outstanding holes on the Ross course because each hole is a replica of Ross-designed holes on courses throughout the United States and Scotland. The number four hole, for example, is a replica of the 441-yard par-4 hole no. fourteen at Ross's Pinehurst Course No. 2 at the Pinehurst Country Club in North Carolina. The tee shot is to a landing area well protected by trees and bunkers on both sides. The approach is to a small, narrow, forward-sloping green with traps left-front, right-front and right-rear.

The holes at Ross Memorial are as follows: Yardage—

Hole No.	Par	Back Tees
1	4	390

Seminole Golf Club, no. 6,
North Palm Beach, Florida

2	4	331

Plainfield Country Club, no. 4,
Plainfield, New Jersey

3	3	201

Oakland Hills South Course, no. 17,
Birmingham, Michigan

5	5	596

Oak Hill East Course, no. 13,
Rochester, New York

6	4	419

Scioto Country Club, no. 2,
Columbus, Ohio

7	4	354

Inverness Club, no. 18,
Toledo, Ohio

8	3	183

Charlotte Country Club, no. 11,
Charlotte, North Carolina

9	5	496

Bob O'Link Golf Club, no. 11,
Highland Park, Illinois

10	4	463

Royal Dornoch Golf Club, no. 14,
Dornoch, Scotland

11	4	343

Salem Country Club, no. 13,
Peabody, Massachusetts

12	3	153

Detroit Golf Club, no. 3,
Detroit, Michigan

13	5	498

Seminole Golf Club, no. 15,
North Palm Beach, Florida

14	4	441

Pinehurst No. 2 Course, no. 2,
Pinehurst, North Carolina

15	4	377

Aronimink Golf Club, no. 11,
Newtown Square, Pennsylvania

16	5	578

Pinehurst No. 2 Course, no. 16,
Pinehurst, North Carolina

11	73	176

Wannanoiset, no. 8,
Rumford, Rhode Island

18	4	405

Oakland Hills South Course, no. 16,
Birmingham, Michigan

The holes are not exact duplicates but are close facsimiles. Yardages of most of the duplicated holes are identical to the originals, however, as are the elevations between tees and greens. Tee-shot landing zones, bunkers and ponds have been carefully sized and positioned to match their models. And extreme care has been taken to capture and reproduce the size, shape and subtleties of the greens.

Boyne Highlands has two pro shops. One shares the Moor and Ross courses and has its own practice range, putting greens and practice bunker. The Heather course is served by the second pro shop, which also has a nearby practice range, putting greens and practice bunker. Short-order food such as sandwiches is available at these facilities as are individual and group instruction. The new Boyne Country Club clubhouse and its restaurant, locker rooms, showers and other amenities are accessible to resort guests only. Nonguests can play these courses but can make tee times only up to 30 days in advance on the Heather and Ross coursesand pay slightly higher green fees on all the courses.

Many golf package options are available through the resort. A variety of weekend and midweek seasonal discounts is offered in the spring, generally up to mid-June, and from late August through October, with some weekends such as Labor Day and Memorial Day excluded.

Golf magazine has awarded a silver medal to Boyne Highlands as one of the best golf resorts in America. A visit here provides you with outstanding golf by some of the best golf-course designers.

Course Name: BOYNE MOUNTAIN
RESORT
Alpine, Monument,
Hemlock Executive
Courses

Course Type: Resort
Resort: Boyne Mountain Resort
Address: Boyne Mountain Road
off Michigan Highway 131
Boyne Falls, MI 49713
Phone: (616) 549–2441 (Golf Course)
(800) GO BOYNE (Resort)
Fax: (616) 549–2912 (Resort)

GOLF COURSE

Director of Golf: Bernie Friedrich
Head Professional: Brian Sanderson
Course Length/Par (All Tees): Alpine:
Back 7017/72, Gold 6546/72, White
6014/72, Forward 4986/72. Monument:
Back 7086/72, Gold 6377/72, White
5744/72, Forward 4904/72. Hemlock
Executive: 1869/30
Course Slope/Rating (All Tees): Alpine:
Back 129/73.6, Gold 123/71.4, White
118/68.7, Ladies' Forward 114/68.4.
Monument: Back 139/75.0, Gold
132/71.6, White 126/68.6, Ladies'
Forward 122/68.9. Hemlock Executive:
NA/NA
Course Architects: Alpine: William New-
comb (1971). Monument: William New-
comb and Stephen Kay (1986). Hemlock
Executive: Everett Kircher (1952), Steve
Kircher (renovation 1991)
Golf Facilities: Full Pro Shop X, Snack
Bar X, Lounge X, Restaurant X,
Locker Room X, Showers X, Club
Rental X, Club Repair No, Cart Rental
X, Instruction X, Practice Green X,
Driving Range X, Practice Bunker X,
Club Storage X
Tee-Time Reservation Policy: Resort
guests: From time of reservation. Out-
side play: Up to 1 mo. in advance with
credit card guarantee
Ranger: Yes
Tee-off-Interval Time: 9 min.
Time to Play 18 Holes: 4 hrs.
Course Hours/Earliest Tee-off: 6:30 a.m.
Green and Cart Fees: Resort guests: Alpine:
$60 for 18 holes with cart. Monument:

$60 for 18 holes with cart. Executive
Course at reduced rates. Outside play:
Alpine: $70 for 18 holes with cart.
Monument: $80 for 18 holes with cart.
Executive: $15 for 18 holes, $10 for 9
holes
Credit Cards: All major cards
Season: April to mid-Oct. Busiest season
June through Aug.
Course Comments: Cart mandatory.
Yardage book available
Golf Packages: Available through resort
Discounts: Seasonal (April to mid-May,
Sept. through Oct.). Twilight rate Sun.
to Thurs. after 3 p.m.
Places to Stay Nearby: Birchwood Inn
(616) 526–2151, (800) 530–9955; Best
Western of Harbor Springs (616) 347–
9050, (800) 528–1234; Harborside Inn
(616) 526–6238; Harbor Springs Cot-
tage Inn (616) 526–5431
Local Attractions: Antiquing, boating, fish-
ing, hunting, hiking, camping, bicycling,
skiing, skating. Charlevoix. Harbor
Springs. PETOSKEY: Little Traverse
Historic Museum. Boyne Country Con-
vention and Visitors Bureau (616) 348–
2755, (800) 456–0197 (outside MI)
Directions: On U.S. 131 between Traverse
City and Petoskey
Closest Commercial Airports: Cherry
Capital, Traverse City (1 hr.), Grand
Rapids (4 hrs.), Detroit Metropolitan
(5 hrs.)

RESORT

Date Built: 1947
No. of Rooms: 204 hotel rooms, suites,
minisuites, villas, condominiums in the
Main Lodge, Boynehof Lodge, Edel-
weiss Lodge, Mountain Villa Deer Lake
Meeting Rooms: 13. Capacity of Largest:
800 persons banquet style. Meeting
Space: 15,000 sq. ft.
Room Price Range: $72 for hotel room to
$315 for 2-bedroom condominium.
Golf, ski and other packages are avail-
able year round
Lounge: Snow Flake Lounge
Restaurants: Beach House Restaurant,
Eriksen's Restaurant

Entertainment: Piano music at Beach House Restaurant

Credit Cards: All major cards

General Amenities: Babysitters can be recommended, supervised children's activities; meeting and conference space in theater, classroom, dining and reception formats, with audiovisual and food services

Recreational Amenities: 14 tennis courts with instruction, pro shop; 3 heated outdoor swimming pools, whirlpool, sauna, skeet shooting, boating on Deer Lake, hiking, fishing, downhill and cross-country skiing with ski schools, bicycling

Reservation and Cancellation Policy: 1 night's deposit required to hold regular room reservations or $75 per person deposit for packages. 10-day cancellation notice required to avoid penalties

Comments and Restrictions: No pets allowed. Taxes additional to base rates. American and European plans available

BOYNE MOUNTAIN RESORT

Boyne Mountain, a year-round resort near Lake Michigan, approximately 5 hours northwest of Detroit, features 45 holes of golf designed by William Newcomb. Born in Logansport, Indiana in 1946, Newcomb, who won the Indiana Open as an amateur in 1961, attended the University of Michigan, earned degrees in architecture and landscape architecture, and worked for Pete Dye as a golf course architect while finding time to win the Michigan Amateur in 1967. In 1968, he formed his own golf-course-design firm. He has lectured at Michigan State and the University of Michigan, where he also has coached the golf team. Newcomb has designed, remodeled and added to several courses in Michigan including the Heather and Moor courses of the Boyne Highlands Resort; the Grand Traverse Golf Club (Spruce Run Course), Acme; and the Travis Pointe Country Club in Ann Arbor, with Jim Lipe.

The Alpine Course, a 7017-yard par-72 layout, meanders through valleys, orchards and hardwood forests. The course works its way down Boyne Mountain and provides scenic views of the surrounding valley.

This course has ample strategically placed fairway bunkers and sand traps protecting its small to medium-sized, moderately fast bentgrass greens. Because of elevation changes on this hilly terrain, you are likely to have a sidehill, downhill or uphill lie to contend with. There are also some well-placed trees and seven water hazards to challenge your game.

The number-1-handicap hole on the Alpine is probably the most difficult hole on the course. This 447-yard par-4 dogleg left has a tee shot to a narrow fairway guarded by trees and three fairway bunkers on the left, and trees on the right. A well-placed tee shot is required to avoid being blocked by the trees or stymied by a trap on the second shot. The approach is to a small, elevated green protected by two bunkers to the right front and trees to the left.

The two finishing holes on the Alpine conclude a round of golf that should require every club in your bag. The 180-yard par-3 seventeenth plays to a wide, shallow, forward-sloping green surrounded by five traps. This green is usually extremely fast, so you especially do not want to be above the hole or behind the green. The 539-yard par-5 eighteenth has a tee shot to a landing area guarded by trees and a pond on the left. The second shot will most likely be a layup to a landing area protected by a stream that cuts across the fairway 50 yards from the green. The approach shot is over the stream to a wide, shallow, forward-sloping green guarded by a trap to the right.

Practice facilities at Boyne Mountain include a large driving range, a large putting green, chipping greens and practice bunkers. The clubhouse includes a restaurant, locker rooms, showers and a pro shop. Individual and group instruction is available from the staff of professionals. Boyne Mountain offers a number of midweek and weekend golf packages. There are also seasonal discounts in the spring and fall, with selected weekends such as Memorial Day and Labor Day excluded. Nonguests can play the golf courses but pay higher fees and cannot reserve tee times earlier than up to one month in advance.

The Boyne Mountain Monument Course was designed by Newcomb with Stephen Kay and opened in 1986. It was named the best new resort course by *Golf Digest* in 1987. Some holes at Monument have been named for golfing greats. Honored thus far are Walter Hagen, Paul Runyan, Kathy Whitworth, Gene Sarazan, Bobby Jones, Chuck Kocsis and Sam Snead. Gene Sarazan chose the par-5, 519-yard fifth hole for the late, great Walter Hagen, who won 2 U.S. Open, 4 British Open and 5 PGA Championships. The tee shot on this dogleg left is to a landing area guarded by trees. The second shot is to a landing area guarded on the right by five bunkers that run from 100 yards out to the right side of a two-tiered green backed by another bunker. Trees line the left side of the fairway.

The Monument is a shot maker's course. The front nine is tighter than the back nine. The fairways are strategically protected by trees, traps and an occasional pond. The small to medium-sized greens are well protected by traps and water hazards. The 537-yard par-5 tenth, the Kathy Whitworth hole, for example, has a tee shot to a landing area surrounded by rough and guarded by a series of bunkers on the right. The second shot is to another fairway island surrounded by rough and a series of five traps on the right. The approach shot is to a wide, shallow, forward-sloping green fronted by a creek. Most putts on these fast bentgrass greens run away from the mountain and toward water.

The finishing hole at Monument, the Sam Snead, is both beautiful and memorable. The tee shot on this 446-yard par-4 dogleg right is to a landing area guarded by three bunkers and trees on the right. The approach shot is all carry over water to a forward-sloping, island green with a bunker on the right. Bring enough balls to complete this hole, especially if the wind is kicking up off the water.

An excellent nine-hole executive course, Hemlock, can also be played at Boyne Mountain. This course was the first golf facility at Boyne Mountain and was remodeled in 1991. Boyne Mountain provides a full range of golf amenities and challenges for family golf or the serious, low handicapper.

Accommodations at the 5000-acre Boyne Mountain Resort include hotel rooms, suites, minisuites, villas and complete 1-, 2-, and 3-bedroom condominium facilities. Buildings include the Main Lodge, Boynehof Lodge, Edelweiss Lodge, and Mountain Villa condominiums. Two miles away is the secluded Deer Lake "retreat," which consists of executive villas located at the foot of the Monument and Alpine golf courses and on Deer Lake. Breakfast, lunch and dinner are available at the Deer Lake Beach House, or you can eat at the main lodge. There is also food service at the golf courses, and banquets, cookouts and other plan packages are available at Boyne Mountain.

Boyne Mountain has more than 15,000 square feet of meeting and exhibit space, with several classroom, banquet, theater, and reception-room configurations. The resort has audiovisual and food services and meeting-planning support as well as a paved, 4200-foot jet strip to accommodate private aircraft.

Recreation facilities include 14 tennis courts at a tennis center ranked as one of the 50 best in the United States by *World Tennis* magazine. Tournaments and instruction can be arranged on 3 different court surfaces. Hiking, swimming, whirlpools, sauna, skeet shooting, boating, fishing, bicycling and other recreational amenities are available. In the winter, Boyne Mountain becomes one of the most popular downhill and cross-country skiing areas in northern Michigan. Ski lessons and a variety of ski packages are available through the resort.

Boyne Mountain is located in a popular and beautiful recreational center of Michigan. There are many excellent public and resort golf courses in this area. You will not be disappointed when you play golf at Boyne Mountain.

Course Name: **DUNMAGLAS GOLF COURSE**

Course Type: Public
Address: 06800 Burgess Road
Charlevoix, MI 49720
Phone: (616) 547–1022
Fax: (616) 547–0190

GOLF COURSE

Head Professional: Steve Braun
Course Length/Par (All Tees): Back 6897/72, Grey 6427/72, White 6105/72, Ladies' Forward 5334/74
Course Slope/Rating (All Tees): Back 142/74, Grey 134/71.7, White 192/70.2, Ladies' Forward 127/70.9
Course Architects: Larry Mancour, Chuck MacGillivray, Dean Refrim (1991)
Golf Facilities: Full Pro Shop X, Snack Bar X, Lounge X, Restaurant X, Locker Room No, Showers No, Club Rental X, Club Repair No, Cart Rental X, Instruction X, Practice Green X, Driving Range X, Practice Bunker X, Club Storage X
Tee-Time Reservation Policy: Anytime. 24-hr. cancellation policy
Ranger: Yes
Tee-off-Interval Time: 10 min.
Time to Play 18 Holes: 4 hrs. 40 min.
Course Hours/Earliest Tee-off: 7 a.m.
Green and Cart Fees: $79 for 18 holes Fri., Sat., Sun., holidays; $75 for 18 holes weekdays
Credit Cards: Discover, MasterCard, Visa
Season: May through mid-Oct. Busiest Memorial Day through Labor Day
Course Comments: Can walk anytime but difficult. Yardage book available
Golf Packages: Inquire at pro shop
Discounts: Group discounts for 12 or more golfers. Twilight rates. Seasonal (peak season rates Memorial Day weekend through Labor Day)
Places to Stay Nearby: CHARLEVOIX: Weathervane Terrace Hotel (616) 547–9955, (800) 552–0021. HARBOR SPRINGS: Best Western of Harbor Springs (616) 347–9050, (800) 528–1234; Boyne Highlands Resort (616) 549–2441, (800) GO–BOYNE. BOYNE FALLS: Boyne Mountain Resort (616) 549–2441, (800) GO–BOYNE. PE-
TOSKEY: Bay Winds Inn (616) 347–4193, (800) 204–1748; Best Western (616) 347–3925, (800) 528–1234. TRAVERSE CITY: Grand Traverse Resort (616) 938–1620, (800) 748–0303; Sugar Beach Resort Hotel (616) 938–0100, (800) 509–1995
Local Attractions: CHARLEVOIX: Lake Charlevoix, boating, fishing, camping, hiking, antiquing, seasonal festivals, winter skiing. Charlevoix Area Chamber of Commerce, 408 Bridge St., Charlevoix, MI 49720 (616) 547–2100. Petoskey-Harbor Springs–Boyne Country Visitors Bureau, 401 E. Mitchell St., P.O. Box 694, Petoskey, MI (616) 348–5584, (800) 845–2828
Directions: From Petoskey take Rte. 31 south to Burgess Rd. Turn left and proceed 10 min. to golf course. From Charlevoix take 31 north to Burgess Rd. Turn right and proceed 10 min. to golf course
Closest Commercial Airports: Cherry Capitol, Traverse City (1 hr. 10 min.); Grand Rapids (2½ hrs.); Capitol City, Lansing (3½ hrs.); Detroit Metropolitan (5 hrs.)

DUNMAGLAS GOLF COURSE

Dunmaglas is a challenging new golf course woven through hilly woodlands and meadows in Charlevoix within view of Lake Michigan. Rated among the best courses in this golf-rich state by *Golfweek* and *Golf Digest*, Dunmaglas requires you to hit good shots all the time. The front nine features the 436 yard par-4 fourth, the most difficult on the course. An accurate tee shot of 225 yards is needed to have a view to the green on this demanding dogleg left. The approach is across wetlands to a well-bunkered green backed by a pine forest. The bentgrass greens at Dunmaglas tend to be built into the hillsides, are medium speed, and are small to moderate in size.

The back nine on this course opens up into meadowlands that provide the atmosphere of Scottish links. A good par 5 on this side is the 532-yard eleventh whose tee shot is from a wooded tee area into meadowlands. The second shot is toward an undulating green guarded by grass bunkers. An excellent par 3 on the back nine is the 198-yard thirteenth which plays from an elevated tee, sometimes into a severe westerly wind off the lake. Thirty-five feet below the tee is a well-bunkered, large green surrounded by wildflowers, fescue grass, and meadows. Some golfers become frustrated by the demands of Dunmaglas, which has a slope of 142 from the back tees. But most golfers will find this a scenic and memorable golf experience.

Course Name: **GRAND TRAVERSE RESORT**
The Bear, Spruce Run Courses

Course Type: Resort
Resort: Grand Traverse Resort
Address: 100 Grand Traverse Village Blvd./P.O. Box 404 Grand Traverse Village (Acme), MI 49610–0404
Phone: (616) 938–1620 (Golf Course) (800) 748–0303 (Resort)
Fax: (616) 938–5495 (Resort)

GOLF COURSE

Director of Golf: Ken Hornyak
Course Length/Par (All Tees): The Bear: Back 7065/72, Middle 6176/72, Forward 5281/72. Spruce Run: Back 6741/72, Middle 6049/72, Ladies' Forward 5139/73
Course Slope/Rating (All Tees): The Bear: Back 145/75.8, Middle 138/71.9, Ladies' Forward 131/72. Spruce Run: Back 125/72.4, Middle 117/69.0, Ladies' Forward 116/69.2
Course Architects: The Bear: Jack Nicklaus (1985). Spruce Run: William Newcomb and Stephen Kay (1979)
Golf Facilities: Full Pro Shop X, Snack Bar X, Lounge X, Restaurant X, Locker Room X, Showers X, Club Rental X, Club Repair X, Cart Rental X, Instruction X, Practice Green X, Driving Range X, Practice Bunker X, Club Storage X
Tee-Time Reservation Policy: Resort guests: Up to 3 mos. in advance. Outside play: Up to 2 wks. in advance

Ranger: Yes
Tee-off-Interval Time: 10 min.
Time to Play 18 Holes: The Bear: 4½ hrs. Spruce Run: 4 hrs.
Course Hours/Earliest Tee-off: 7 a.m. to dark in summer, 8 a.m. to dark in spring, fall
Green and Cart Fees: Resort guests: The Bear: $91 for 18 holes with cart Fri., Sat., Sun., holidays; $81 for 18 holes with cart weekdays. Spruce Run: $61 for 18 holes with cart Fri., Sat., Sun.; $51 for 18 holes with cart weekdays. Outside play: The Bear: $99 for 18 holes with cart Fri., Sat., Sun., holidays; $91 for 18 holes with cart weekdays. Spruce Run: $71 for 18 holes with cart Fri., Sat., Sun., holidays; $61 for 18 holes with cart weekdays. Highest rates June through Labor Day
Credit Cards: American Express, Diners Club, MasterCard, Visa
Season: Mid-April to Oct. Busiest season and highest rates June through Labor Day
Course Comments: Cart mandatory. Full and midweek golf memberships available
Golf Packages: Available through resort
Discounts: Twilight. Seasonal rates spring, fall
Places to Stay Nearby: Pointes North Inn (616) 938–9191, (800) 678–1267; Best Western Four Seasons (616) 946–8424, (800) 528–1234; Waterfront Park Inn Resort (616) 938–1100, (800) 678–4011; Heritage Inn (616) 947–9520; Hampton Inn (616) 946–8900, (800) 426–7866; Park Place Hotel (616) 946–5000, (800) 748–0133; Stonewall Inn (616) 223–7800; Neahtawanta Inn (616) 223–7315
Local Attractions: Interlochen Center for the Arts, Grand Traverse Bay with boating, fishing, Clinch Park, The Music House, Con Foster Museum, Sleeping Bear Dunes National Lakeshore, Dennos Museum, Amon's Orchard tours, Chateau Grand Traverse, Leelanau Wine Cellars. Grand Traverse Convention and Visitors Bureau (616) 947–1120, (800) 872–8377
Directions: From Traverse City (6 mi. northeast): U.S. 31 to Hwy. M–72

Closest Commercial Airport: Cherry Capital, Traverse City (15 min.)

RESORT

Date Built: 1980

No. of Rooms: 750 luxury rooms and condominium suites

Meeting Rooms: 34. Capacity of Largest: 2000 persons banquet style. Meeting Space: 85,000 sq. ft.

Room Price Range: $85 for studio condominium off season (mid-Oct. to May 30) to $305 for golfside 3-bedroom condominium peak season (May 31 to mid-Oct.). Golf, getaway, romantic, and other packages available year round

Lounges: Trillium Nightclub, Club Deli, Sandtrap Bar, Beach Club, Afterdeck

Restaurants: Club Deli, Trillium, Paparazzi, Orchard Room, Sandtrap, Beach Club

Entertainment: Live music in Trillium Nightclub

Credit Cards: All major cards

General Amenities: Children's Center, supervised children's programs, babysitting service, Tower Gallery of specialty shops; resort spa and salon with massage including Swedish and shiatsu, health and beauty services; meeting and conference facilities with audiovisual and food services

Recreational Amenities: Health and racquet club with 9 indoor and outdoor Deco Turf II tennis courts, pro shop, instruction, 4 racquetball courts; whirlpools, saunas, aerobics, weight training, indoor and outdoor swimming pools, skiing, fishing, beaches nearby, boating and water sports, video-game room

Reservation and Cancellation Policy: Reservations may be made up to 1 yr. in advance. Credit card, check or money order for 1 night's lodging required to hold reservation. 72-hour cancellation notice in advance of booked arrival date required to avoid penalties

Comments and Restrictions: No pets allowed. AARP rates available. Taxes additional to basic rates. Packages must be booked at least 24 hrs. in advance of arrival. No refunds on unused portions of packages

GRAND TRAVERSE RESORT

The Grand Traverse Resort is a 1400-acre vacation and conference destination located along the shores of Lake Michigan's Grand Traverse Bay in central northern Michigan. The golf centerpiece of this resort is The Bear, a 7065-yard Scottish-style golf course designed by Jack Nicklaus. There is also an excellent 6741-yard Bill Newcomb–designed layout at Grand Traverse. The Bear was rated the fifth best golf course in the state of Michigan by *Golf Digest* in 1991, which also rates it among the top 75 resort courses in America.

The Bear features seemingly generous landing areas on tee shots but demands more accuracy as you approach the large, fast, tiered, undulating bentgrass greens that are protected by bunkers, mounds and water hazards which come directly into play on twelve holes. Nicklaus uses a variety of sizes and shapes of greens to make the course more interesting and challenging. The 194-yard par-3 fourth, for example, plays over a marsh to a very shallow (13 yards) but wide, forward-sloping green backed by grass mounds and a bunker and fronted by wetlands. Out of bounds is to the left. Because of the water, most golfers will be long on this hole, but that is likely to leave a difficult downhill recovery from the mounds or the bunker. Or you are likely to be above the hole with a tricky downhill putt toward the water. Variable winds can be a factor on this hole and on the entire golf course, which rolls through open expanses.

The number-1-handicap hole on the Bear is the 451-yard par-4 second hole. The tee shot is blind and uphill until you are approximately halfway to the green. To the left is a treed fairway with a large bunker protecting the landing area. To the right is mounded rough that drops off severely away from the fairway. The approach shot is to a deep but narrow left-to-right-sloping green protected by five traps. Again, Nicklaus requires you to hit a good tee shot to have a chance of executing a demanding approach shot.

One of my favorite holes on the back nine is the 413-yard par-4 twelfth, which plays slightly uphill then gradually downhill and over a pond to a narrow, deep, forward-sloping green. The green is guarded by trees and a trap on the left, two traps on the right, and a large pond farther right, which curls left around the front of the green. There is little margin for error on the approach shot here.

The finishing hole on the Bear is a long, beautiful par 4 that plays 467 yards from the back tees. The tee shot on this dogleg right should be kept to the left to avoid mounded rough and a drop-off to the right. The second shot must clear a large pond to reach a narrow, deep green bordered by mounds and grass bunkers to the rear.

The 6741-yard par-72 Spruce Run Course, formerly called the Grand Traverse Resort Course, is a more traditional layout featuring large, moderately fast, undulating well-trapped greens and strategically bunkered fairways. Water hazards appear on more than half the holes. A challenging par 4 on this layout is the 452-yard third whose tee shot is to a landing area guarded by a trap on the left. The approach must carry a small pond in front of a green guarded by traps front, left and rear. A tough par 3 on the front side is the 215-yard eighth, which is bordered by a stream to the left from tee to green. Four bunkers protect the right side of the green from 50 yards in.

The finishing hole at Spruce Run is a 508-yard par 5. If the ball is kept too far to the right, the approach to the green is over a pond that guards the right front. This is a scenic ending to a fine test of golf overlooking East Grand Traverse Bay.

Both golf courses at Grand Traverse are served by a clubhouse with pro shop, locker rooms, showers, a bar and a full-service restaurant. The practice area includes 2 driving ranges, practice greens and chipping greens. Golf packages are available through the resort. The resort offers its own academy and golf school.

Group and individual lessons are available from the resort's staff of professionals.

Other recreational facilities at Grand Traverse include an indoor/outdoor health and racquet club, 9 tennis courts, 4 racquetball courts, aerobics studio, indoor and outdoor swimming pools and whirlpools, weight room, saunas, pro shop, and a children's activity center. The resort features a full-service health spa and salon that offers massage, body wraps and other amenities. There are also skiing facilities on site and nearby at this year-round retreat. *Golf* magazine has recognized Grand Traverse as one of the best golf resorts in America, and *Family Circle* magazine has rated it one of the best family resorts in America.

Accommodations are available in a seventeen-story glass tower; six-story resort hotel; and studio, 1-, 2- and 3-bedroom condominiums. The Shores condominium complex features a beach club on East Grand Traverse Bay.

Grand Traverse Resort also has over 85,000 square feet of meeting space, including Governors' Hall, which features state-of-the-art conference equipment with audiovisual, food-service and other support systems. *Successful Meetings* and *Meetings and Conventions* magazines have recognized Grand Traverse as being among the best resorts for its meeting, golf and other facilities.

Course Name: HIGH POINTE GOLF CLUB

Course Type: Public
Address: 5555 Arnold Road
                       Williamsburg, MI 49690
Phone: (616) 267–9900

GOLF COURSE

Head Professional: Dave Dolengowski

Course Length/Par (All Tees): Back 6849/71, Middle 6153/71, Forward 5101/71

Course Slope/Rating (All Tees): Back 135/72.9, Middle 122/69.4, Ladies' Forward 121/69.6

Course Architect: Tom Doak (1989)

Golf Facilities: Full Pro Shop X, Snack Bar X, Lounge X, Restaurant X,

Locker Room No, Showers No, Club Rental X, Club Repair Minor, Cart Rental X, Instruction X, Practice Green X, Driving Range X, Practice Bunker X, Club Storage X

Tee-Time Reservation Policy: Anytime. 48-hr. cancellation policy

Ranger: Yes

Tee-off-Interval Time: 7 and 8 min.

Time to Play 18 Holes: 4½ hrs.

Course Hours/Earliest Tee-off: 7 a.m. to dark

Green and Cart Fees: $55 for 18 holes with cart Fri., Sat., holidays; $45 for 18 holes with cart Sun. to Thurs. $30 for 9 holes with cart

Credit Cards: Discover, MasterCard, Visa

Season: April to Oct. Busiest season June through Aug.

Course Comments: Walking allowed depending on course traffic

Golf Packages: Available through hotels. Inquire at golf course

Discounts: Season passes, twilight rates, spring and fall rates

Places to Stay Nearby: Pointes North Inn (616) 938–9191, (800) 678–1267; Best Western Four Seasons (616) 946–8424, (800) 528–1234; Waterfront Park Inn Resort (616) 938–1100, (800) 678–4011; Heritage Inn (616) 947–9520; Hampton Inn (616) 946–8900, (800) 426–7866; Park Place Hotel (616) 946–5000, (800) 748–0133; Grand Traverse Resort (616) 938–2100, (800) 748–0303; Stonewall Inn (616) 223–7800; Neahtawanta Inn (616) 223–7315

Local Attractions: Interlochen Center for the Arts, Grand Traverse Bay with boating, fishing, Clinch Park, Con Foster Museum, Sleeping Bear Dunes National Lakeshore, Amon's Orchard tours, Chateau Grand Traverse, Lee Lancer Wine Cellars. Grand Traverse Convention and Visitors Bureau (616) 947–1120, (800) 872–8377

Directions: U.S. 31 to M–72 west (3 mi.) to Arnold Rd., right on Arnold Rd. to golf course

Closest Commercial Airports: Cherry Capital, Traverse City (10 min.); Grand Rapids (2½ hrs.); Capitol City, Lansing (3 hrs.); Detroit Metropolitan (4½ hrs.)

HIGH POINTE GOLF CLUB

High Pointe, a par-71 course, plays 6849 yards from the back tees and was built on the site of an old cherry orchard a few miles east of the Jack Nicklaus–designed "Bear" resort course at Grand Traverse. The front nine works its way through open, rolling fields, while the back nine is hillier and more forested, and is reminiscent of a British heathland course.

High Pointe provides an interesting and memorable mix of deep pot bunkers, hidden sand traps, natural elevation changes, a combination of vast, treeless fairways and narrow tree-lined fairways, and a variety of hole designs and strategies. Strategic shot making, careful club selection, and innovative course management are part of High Pointe's challenge. The wind coming off nearby Lake Michigan adds another dimension of uncertainty on this course.

Architect Tom Doak borrows from Scotland's North Berwick's Redan hole to create the excellent 199-yard par-3 fourth at High Pointe. The tee shot plays to an elevated green fronted by a large sand bunker. The tendency is to use too much club to avoid this obstacle, but the green runs away from the golfer toward two deep, hidden pot bunkers to the rear. There is also a scenic old barn on this memorable hole.

The 451-yard par-4 eighth is another demanding hole. The tee shot has to avoid bunkers on the left. The approach shot is to a large, two-tiered green fronted on the left by a trap. On the right, approximately 50 yards from the green, is another large bunker. Should you reach the green in regulation, three putts are not uncommon on this hole.

As you play the back nine, hopefully you have become more adept at reading the terrain and targeting your shots to safe landing areas. No doubt you have used just about every club in your bag. The 512-yard finishing hole is a beautiful double dogleg left then right, the only water hole on the course and the only par 5 on the back nine. The tee shot is over water to a landing area on the right. On the next shot you can lay up to the left or try to carry a large pond to a large, two-tiered green with traps left and rear. This is an appropriately memorable way to end your round at High Pointe.

Doak, the designer of High Pointe, one of America's top 75 public golf courses, is not your ordinary golf-course architect. After a brief stint at M.I.T., Doak graduated from Cornell University's landscape architecture program. He also earned a special grant to study the great golf courses of Great Britain and has since published a highly regarded, 40-copy limited-edition book titled *The Confidential Guide to Golf Courses*, which rates 200 of the world's best courses. Since 1988, Doak has been an administrator of *Golf* magazine's biennial rankings of the 100 greatest courses in the world and has written a variety of articles on golf. Doak worked as a golf-course architect for Pete Dye, assisting him with the completion of the Long Cove Club and the Stadium Course at PGA West. He assisted Perry Dye in the design of the TPC at Riverdale Dunes and has worked on courses in the Myrtle Beach area. At this writing, Doak is only 31 years old.

The modern clubhouse at High Pointe has a full pro shop, snack bar, bar and restaurant but no locker room and showers. An outdoor deck overlooks the beautiful rolling fairways of the golf course. A driving range, practice bunker and practice green are available at High Pointe, as are individual lessons, playing lessons, group lessons and video swing analysis.

High Pointe is situated in one of the best golf regions in the United States. Northwestern Michigan has excellent publicly accessible golf courses designed by Jack Nicklaus, Arnold Palmer, Robert Trent Jones, Sr., William Newcomb and others, all within a few hours' drive of High Pointe and the Traverse City area. Put this golf course on your travel schedule and keep your eye on Mr. Doak.

Course Name: SHANTY CREEK RESORT
Legend, Shanty Creek, Schuss Mountain Courses

Course Type: Resort
Resort: Shanty Creek
Address: One Shanty Creek Rd.
Bellaire, MI 49615
Phone: (616) 533–8621,
(800) 678–4111 (Resort)
Fax: (616) 533–7001 (Resort, Sales Marketing) (616) 533–7050 (Resort, Front Desk)

GOLF COURSE

Director of Golf and Head Professional: Rodger Jabara

Professionals: Schuss Mountain: Roger Gieseck. Legend: Roger Bliss

Course Length/Par (All Tees): Legend: Back 6764/72, Blue 6269/72, White 5801/72, Forward 4953/72. Shanty Creek: Back 6276/71, Middle 6019/71, Forward 4770/71. Schuss Mountain: Back 6922/72, Middle 6394/72, Forward 5383/72

Course Slope/Rating (All Tees): Legend: Back 137/73.6, Blue 130/71.4, White 121/69.4, Ladies' White 124/69.6, Ladies' Forward 129/75.0. Shanty Creek: Back 120/71.7, Middle 117/70.4, Ladies' Forward 116/70.7. Schuss Mountain: Back 127/73.4, Middle 122/70.9, Ladies' Forward 126/71.2

Course Architects: Legend: Arnold Palmer and Ed Seay (1985). Shanty Creek: William Diddle (1965). Schuss Mountain: Warner Bowen and William Newcomb (9 holes, 1972; 9 holes, 1977)

Golf Facilities: Full Pro Shop X, Snack Bar X, Lounge X, Restaurant X, Locker Room X, Showers X, Club Rental X, Club Repair X, Cart Rental X, Instruction X, Practice Green X, Driving Range X, Practice Bunker X, Club Storage X

Tee-Time Reservation Policy: Resort guest: At time of reservation. Outside play: Up to 14 days in advance for Fri., Sat., Sun., holidays. Up to 30 days in advance for Mon.-Thurs.

Ranger: Yes

Tee-off-Interval Time: Legend: 10 min. Shanty Creek, Schuss Mountain: 8 min.

Time to Play 18 Holes: 4½ hrs.

Course Hours/Earliest Tee-off: 7 a.m.

Green and Cart Fees: Resort guests: Legend: $85 for 18 holes with shared cart. Shanty Creek: $45, Schuss Mountain: $55 for 18 holes with shared cart. Outside play: Legend: $95 for 18 holes with shared cart. Shanty Creek: $50, Schuss Mountain: $65 for 18 holes with shared cart.

Credit Cards: American Express, MasterCard, Visa

Season: Mid-April to late Oct. Busiest season Aug.

Course Comments: Cart mandatory. Yardage book available for Legend

Golf Packages: Available through resort. Lower rates weekends mid-April to mid-May, mid-Sept. to end of season

Discounts: Resort guests. Replays same day. Twilight rate on Shanty Creek, Schuss Mountain courses

Places to Stay Nearby: CHARLEVOIX: Foster Boat Works Inn (616) 547–0025; Pointes North Inn (616) 547–0055, (800) 678–2422. PETOSKEY: Best Western Inn (616) 347–3925, (800) 528–1234; Apple Tree Inn (616) 348–2900. BED AND BREAKFAST: Bear and the Bay Bed and Breakfast (616) 347–6077. TRAVERSE CITY: Best Western Four Seasons (616) 946–8424; Waterfront Park Inn Resort (616) 938–1100; Stonewall Inn (616) 223–7800; Neahtawanta Inn (616) 223–7315

Local Attractions: Fishing, hunting, camping, mountain biking, antiquing, hiking, boating, skiing. TRAVERSE CITY: National Cherry Festival, Dennos Museum, Interlochen Center for the Arts, Con Foster Museum, Sleeping Bear Dunes National Lakeshore. Charlevoix. Petoskey. Bellaire Michigan Chamber of Commerce (616) 533–6023. Grand Traverse Convention and Visitors Bureau (616) 947–1120, (800) 872–8377

Directions: From Traverse City (45 min.): U.S. 31 north and east to Michigan 72 east to U.S. 131 to Michigan 88 west to resort. From Mancelona and Michigan 88: Michigan 88 west to resort

Closest Commercial Airports: Cherry Capital, Traverse City (45 min.); Grand Rapids (3 hrs.); Capitol City, Lansing (3½ hrs.); Detroit Metropolitan (4½ hrs.)

RESORT

Date Built: 1963

No. of Rooms: 600 rooms, suites, 1- to 3-bedroom condominiums and villas

Meeting Rooms: 22. Capacity of Largest: 700 persons banquet style. Meeting Space: 28,000 sq. ft.

Room Price Range: $84 for 1 room, double occupancy (March to May) to $475 for 3- or 4-bedroom chalet home for 11 to 12 persons. Golf, ski, holiday, midweek and other packages available year round. Peak season late Dec. to mid-March, mid-June to Sept.

Lounges: Lakeview Lounge, Ivanhof Lounge

Restaurants: Lakeview Dining Room, Ivanhof, Arnie's Golf Club Deck

Entertainment: Live entertainment 5 nights per week

Credit Cards: All major cards

General Amenities: Supervised children's programs from infant to 12, babysitting, meeting and conference facilities with audiovisual and banquet services

Recreational Amenities: 6 outdoor tennis courts, instruction available; fitness center with Nautilus equipment, steam room, hot-tub sauna, massage, 2 racquetball courts, fishing, biking, winter sports such as skiing and skating, 2 indoor swimming pools, outdoor swimming pools, boating, jogging, hunting, Lake Bellaire

Reservation and Cancellation Policy: $75 deposit required on rooms, $150 deposit on condominiums. Advance deposit by credit card, check or money order. Reservations may be canceled without penalty by calling 5 days prior to arrival date

Comments and Restrictions: No pets allowed. Taxes additional to base rates. Children 17 and under sleep free when in same room with parents. No refunds on partial use of packages

SHANTY CREEK

The Shanty Creek Resort is located in northern Michigan approximately 45 minutes northeast of Traverse City. The resort has 54 challenging holes of golf, featuring the Legend, a 6764-yard par-72 Arnold Palmer and Ed Seay layout, which opened in 1985. This course is ranked among America's 75 best resort courses by *Golf Digest* magazine.

The Legend has large, fast, undulating bentgrass greens that are well protected by large bunkers. The fairways are rolling and well treed, with strategically placed bunkers in the landing areas. There are water hazards on six holes at the Legend. From some vantage points on this beautiful golf course you can see Lake Michigan, the nearby town of Bellaire, and Torch Lake. The oak, pine, maple, birch, spruce and other varieties of trees create a beautiful and challenging backdrop for golf.

One of the most memorable holes at the Legend is the 433-yard par-4 third, a dogleg right, which has magnificent views of the surrounding countryside from an elevated tee. The first shot should be kept to the left center to avoid a huge trap to the right of the landing area. The approach is to a deep green protected on the left by two large bunkers and guarded by another on the right. A cathedral of trees frames this challenging golf hole.

The number-1-handicap hole on the course is the 501-yard par-5 seventh, also a dogleg right, with a lake to the right at the bend of the dogleg. The tee shot is to the left center but has to avoid a small trap to the left approximately 250 yards from the tee. The second shot will most likely be a layup to avoid Shanty Creek, which cuts in front of a shallow, elevated green surrounded by four sand traps.

A pretty par 3 on the back nine is the 173-yard twelfth, which plays to a large, deep green flanked by a huge bunker to the right front and a smaller bunker to the left. Farther left is a lake. A more difficult par 3 is the 190-yard fifteenth, which has a deep green with a huge sand bunker to the left and directly in front of the green. To the right is another large trap. Next is an excellent 442-yard par 4 that doglegs right to a deep green guarded by three traps to the left and another large trap to the right. A series of bunkers guards the left side of the fairway 225 yards from the back tees. This hole is tree-lined from tee to green.

The combination of elevation changes; well-treed fairways; doglegs; bunkers and water hazards; and sizeable, quick greens provides a challenging golf experience for all levels of play. Shot strategy, club selection and course management are important here. Tee distances range from 6764 from the back tees to 4953 yards from the forward tees.

The other golf courses at Shanty Creek are worth playing. The 6276-yard par-71 Shanty Creek Course, formerly called the Deskin Course, was designed by William Diddle and opened in 1965. This layout is wide open and more forgiving than the Legend, but more trees have recently been planted, so this course will become more difficult as time goes on. Shanty Creek features two long par 3s on the back nine. The 216-yard eleventh plays to a large green backed by a sizeable sand trap. The 232-yard seventeenth has a deep green squeezed in front by large traps on each side of the putting surface.

The 6922-yard par-72 Schuss Mountain Golf Course was designed by Warner Bowen and William Newcomb, covers 160 acres and has medium-sized to large, fast, undulating bentgrass greens. This course is longer and tighter than the Shanty Creek layout but does not have the dramatic elevation changes characteristic of the Legend. The back nine does have some interesting changes in terrain, however. There are nine water hazards on this layout, whose first nine opened in 1972 and whose second nine was completed in 1977. The 397-yard par-4 dogleg-right eighteenth caps off four strong finishing holes at Schuss Mountain. The tee shot is to a landing area bracketed by ponds on each side of the fairway. The second shot is to a well-bunkered green with another pond to the right. Schuss Mountain is the home of the Allied Signal Michigan Golf Classic and is one of the more popular golf courses in Michigan.

The golf courses at Shanty Creek are part of a real-estate and recreational development. Accommodations include individual lodge rooms, villas, condos, and suites throughout the property.

A variety of golf packages are offered at Shanty Creek. The lowest weekend rates are generally found April to mid-May, and late September to closing. There are mid-week specials from mid-May to mid-June and after Labor Day.

Shanty Creek has two clubhouses, one serving the Legend and Shanty, the other serving the Schuss Mountain Course. A complete pro shop, locker rooms and showers, and restaurant facilities are available. Practice facilities include a driving range, practice bunker and putting green. Individual and group instruction is available from the staff of professionals. The golf courses are open to the public at slightly higher rates than resort guests. Carts are generally mandatory, but walking is allowed on the Schuss Mountain and Shanty Creek courses at selected times.

Besides the quality golf at this resort, there are excellent publicly accessible golf courses in the region. Also available in this popular tourist area is a variety of seasonal festivals, antique shows, restaurants and recreational activities.

Recommended Golf Courses in North-western Michigan

North of Cadillac:

A-Ga-Ming Golf Course, Kewadin, (616) 264–5081, (800) 678–0122, Public, 18/6663/72

Antrim Dells Golf Course, Atwood, (616) 599–2679, (800) 872–8561, Public, 18/6606/72

Belvedere Golf Club, Charlevoix, (616) 547–2611, Semiprivate, 18/6715/72

Crystal Mountain Resort, Thompsonville, (616) 378–2000, (800) 968–7686, Resort, 18/6414/72

Fox Run Country Club, Grayling, (517) 348–4343, Public, 18/6268/72

Gull Lake View Golf Club, Augusta, (616) 731–4148, Public. East: 18/6002/70. West: 18/6300/71

Kincheloe Memorial Public Golf Course, Kincheloe, (906) 495–5706, Public, 18/7100/72

Little Traverse Bay Golf Club, Harbor Springs, (616) 526–6200, Resort, 18/6865/72

Matheson Greens Golf Course, Northport, (616) 386–5171, (800) 443–6883, 18/6609/72

Mistwood Golf Course, Lake Ann, (616) 275–5500, Public, 18/6715/72

Pinecroft Golf Club, Beulah, (616) 882–9100, Public, 18/6447/72

Sugarloaf Resort, Cedar, (616) 228–1880, (800) 968–0576, Resort, 18/6813/72

Southwestern/Middle Western

Course Name: GRAND HAVEN GOLF CLUB

Course Type: Public
Address: 17000 Lincoln Road
               Grand Haven, MI 49417
Phone: (616) 842–4040

GOLF COURSE

Head Professional: David Cornelius
Course Length/Par (All Tees): Back 6789/72, Middle 6179/72, Forward 5536/72
Course Slope/Rating (All Tees): Back 124/71.9, Middle 119/69.2, Ladies' Forward 119/71.4
Course Architect: Bruce Mathews (1965)
Golf Facilities: Full Pro Shop X, Snack Bar X, Lounge X, Restaurant X, Locker Room X, Showers X, Club Rental X, Club Repair X, Cart Rental X, Instruction X, Practice Green X, Driving Range X, Practice Bunker No, Club Storage X
Tee-Time Reservation Policy: 1 wk. in advance from 7 a.m. for Sat., Sun., holidays (May to Sept.). Call anytime for other dates. 18-hole fee required before

2 p.m. on weekends. Members can secure weekend tee times in advance

Ranger: Yes

Tee-off-Interval Time: 7 min.

Time to Play 18 Holes: 4½ hrs.

Course Hours/Earliest Tee-off: Sunrise to sunset

Green Fees: $34 for 18 holes Sat., Sun., holidays; $32 for 18 holes weekdays. $17 for 9 holes Sat., Sun., holidays; $16 for 9 holes weekdays

Cart Fees: $22 for 18 holes per cart, $11 for 9 holes per cart

Pull Carts: $2.25 for 18 holes, $1.50 for 9 holes

Credit Cards: MasterCard, Visa

Season: March to Nov.

Course Comments: Can walk anytime. Memberships available

Golf Packages: None

Discounts: Seasonal

Places to Stay Nearby: Days Inn (616) 842–1999, (800) 329–7466; Harbor House Inn (616) 846–0610; Highland Park Hotel (616) 842–6483; Best Western (616) 842–4720, (800) 528–1234; Khardomah Lodge (616) 842–2990; Holiday Inn (616) 846–1000, (800) HOLIDAY

Local Attractions: Grand Haven State Park, Hoff Master State Park, beaches, water sports, charter-boat fishing, Harbor Steamer, Tri-Cities Historical Museum, World's Largest Musical Fountain, boardwalk, Gillette Nature Center, Muskegon Race Course. Grand Haven–Spring Lake Area Convention and Visitors Bureau (616) 842–4499. Chamber of Commerce (616) 842–4910

Directions: From Grand Rapids (35 mi.): 96 west to exit 9/Spring Lake Grand Haven, Hwy. 104 to U.S. 31 south, through Grand Haven, to Lincoln St., turn right to golf course

Closest Commercial Airports: Muskegon County (30 min.); Kent County International, Grand Rapids (50 min.); Chicago O'Hare International (3½ hrs.)

GRAND HAVEN GOLF CLUB

The Grand Haven Golf Club is a privately owned public golf course located near Lake Michigan's eastern shore in a popular vacation area approximately 165 miles northeast of Chicago. The course is located on timbered duneland and has been on *Golf Digest*'s list of the top 75 public courses since 1984. Grand Haven was designed by Bruce Mathews, who was born in Hastings, Michigan, received a landscape architecture degree from Michigan State, and was once owner and operator of his self-designed Grand Haven Country Club. Mathews formed a partnership with his son Jerry in 1960, and they collaborated on the design of many courses in the Midwest and especially Michigan. Some of their projects in Michigan include Forest Akers (West Course), East Lansing; Antrim Dells Golf Club (9 holes), Atwood; Wilderness Valley Golf Club, Gaylord; and the Salem Hills Golf Club, Northville.

Grand Haven is a 6789-yard par-72 layout with large, well-trapped greens and fairways lined with pine, maple, oak and other varieties of trees. Accurate drives and good iron play are required on this course, with its tight, rolling fairways. The number-1-handicap hole is the 493-yard ninth, a par-5 dogleg to the right that plays into a large, elevated, undulating green protected by traps front-right and front-left. The tee shot should be faded around the corner, leaving a straight second shot down a tree-protected fairway with out of bounds on the left. It is difficult to reach this green in two, mainly because of the traps, which severely narrow the entrance to the target.

The 462-yard par-4 fourteenth hole could well be the most difficult hole on the course. This is a gorgeous hole during autumn leaf season, but with woods on the left and right you can't let the ball stray. The second shot comes onto a large, undulating kidney-shaped green with a large trap at the right front.

A challenging par 3 on the Grand Haven course is the 207-yard tenth, which plays to a large, undulating green with a trap to the left front. The fairway is tree-lined, and the green can easily be three-putted like all the other large, undulating, bentgrass greens that are typical on this course. Most of the greens are protected by only one or two bunkers, and there are no fairway bunkers at Grand Haven. Because of the tightly treed fairways, shot placement, club selection and sound course management are necessary to score on this golf course.

You can walk Grand Haven any time, and reduced seasonal rates usually apply in the spring and fall. Individual lessons are available from the staff at Grand Haven, which has a driving range and putting green, but no practice bunker. The clubhouse has a full pro shop, locker rooms, showers, restaurant and bar.

Grand Haven is in a summer vacation area and is especially noted for its beaches, boardwalk, and Lake Michigan charter fishing fleet, which pursues king salmon, coho salmon, lake trout, brown trout, and steelhead. Numerous parks and camping areas are in the region. Seasonal events include flower shows, sailing regattas, antique shows, art shows, farmers' markets, bicycle races, music festivals and other activities.

Course Name: THOROUGHBRED GOLF CLUB

Course Type: Resort
Resort: Double JJ
Address: Water Road/P.O. Box 94
Rothbury, MI 49452
Phone: (616) 893–GOLF (Golf Course), (616) 894–4444 (Resort)
Fax: (616) 893–5355 (Golf Course, Resort)

GOLF COURSE

Head Professional: Jeff Howland
Course Length/Par (All Tees): Back 6900/72, Blue 6463/72, White 6063/72, Forward 4851/72
Course Slope/Rating (All Tees): Back 147/74.4, Blue 141/72.5, White 135/70.0, Forward 126/69.5
Course Architect: Arthur Hills (1993)
Golf Facilities: Full Pro Shop X, Snack Bar X, Lounge X, Restaurant X, Locker Room X, Showers X, Club Rental X, Club Repair X, Cart Rental X, Instruction X, Practice Green X, Driving Range X, Practice Bunker X, Club Storage X

Tee-Time Reservation Policy: At time of confirmed reservation at the resort. Up to 2 weeks in advance for the public. In season (mid-May through mid-Sept.) tee times more than 1 week in advance require a non-refundable deposit transferable only with 48-hr. prior notification
Ranger: Yes
Tee-off-Interval Time: 9 min.
Time to Play 18 Holes: 4½ hrs.
Course Hours/Earliest Tee-off: 7 a.m.
Green and Cart Fees: $59 for 18 holes with or without cart
Credit Cards: All major cards
Season: Apr. through Nov. Busiest July through Labor Day
Course Comments: Can walk anytime at full golf fee. Difficult course to walk
Golf Packages: Through resort
Discounts: Twilight. Lower seasonal rates prior to mid-May, after mid-Sept. Replays. Resort guests. Group discounts
Places to Stay Nearby: MUSKEGON: Best Western Park Plaza Hotel (616) 733–2651, (800) 528–1234; Holiday Inn Muskegon Harbor (616) 722–0100, (800) GO–LAKE. WHITEHALL: Ramada Inn (616) 893–3030, (800) 272–6232; Super 8 Motel (616) 894–4848; Michillinda Beach Lodge (616) 893–1895
Local Attractions: WHITEHALL: Blue Lake Fine Arts Camp, Montague City Museum, White River Light Station Museum. White Lake Area Chamber of Commerce, 124 W. Hanson St., Whitehall, MI 49461 (616) 893–4585. Muskegon: Fire Barn Museum, Michigan's Adventure Amusement Park, Heritage Village, Muskegan County Museum, Muskegon Museum of Art, Pleasure Island Water Fun Park, USS *Silversides*, boating, fishing, camping, hiking, seasonal festivals, hunting. Muskegon Area Convention and Visitors Bureau, 349 W. Webster Ave., P.O. Box 1087, Muskegon, MI 49443–1087 (616) 722–3751
Directions: Thoroughbred is located 20 mi. north of Muskegon. Exit U.S. 31 at Winston Rd./Rothburg Exit. Turn east on Winston Rd. then north on Water Rd. The resort and golf course are on the right

Closest Commercial Airports: Muskegon County (30 min.); Kent County International, Grand Rapids (1 hr.); Detroit Metropolitan (3½ hrs.); Chicago O'Hare International, IL (3½ hrs.)

RESORT

Date Built: 1937

No. of Rooms: 58 hotel and condo rooms, 70 ranch rooms

Meeting Rooms: 14. Capacity of Largest: 300 persons banquet style. Meeting Space: 15,000 sq. ft.

Room Price Range: $69 for a single to $279 for a 3-bedroom condominium. All inclusive American plan and other packages offered

Lounges: Chuckwagon, Wagon Wheel, Watering Hole, Conference Center

Restaurants: Chuck Wagon, Watering Hole, Silver Dollar, Golf Course Snack Bar, Sundance Saloon and Steakhouse

Entertainment: Live music, disc jockey, stage shows, rodeo

Credit Cards: Discover, MasterCard, Visa

General Amenities: Meeting and conference facilities with audiovisual and food service; country western dance instruction, mechanical bull riding, rodeos, hayrides, simulated holdups, cookouts, and other activities

Recreational Amenities: Horseback riding, private lake, boating, heated swimming pool, hot tubs, archery and rifle ranges, volleyball, mini-golf, shuffleboard, baseball, horeshoes, tennis, winter cross-country skiiing, snowmobiling

Reservation and Cancellation Policy: A $50 per person deposit is required to make a reservation. Deposits made before mid-Feb. are refundable with 14-day cancellation notice. Deposits made thereafter are not refundable

Comments and Restrictions: No children under 18 years of age except for family weekends at dude ranch part of resort. Hotel and condominiums are unrestricted. No pets. Guest horses can be boarded

THOROUGHBRED GOLF CLUB

The Thoroughbred Golf Club is an Arthur Hills-designed gem situated on 350 acres within the largest adult dude ranch in the United States. The ranch, which is on rolling woodlands north of Muskegon five miles from Lake Michigan, has been open since 1937 and has long been a Mecca for lady horseback riders in particular. The resort, under new ownership since the 1980s, added the golf course and opened part of the resort to families in order to attract a more diverse clientele. The golf course features hardwood trees, fruit trees, pine, cranberry bogs, scenic Carpenter Lake, ponds, and a variety of elevation changes. The fairways are generous, but if you miss the target areas it will cost you strokes. The variety of doglegs on the course require you to carefully calibrate distance and club selection in order to avoid penalties. The winds sweeping off Lake Michigan can be a factor in rare instances when the trees do not block the breezes.

The most difficult hole to par at Thoroughbred is the 446-yard second, a dogleg left that plays from an elevated tee and wraps around wetlands to the left and is bordered by trees on the right. There are six tee box choices here, but you must reach an elevated landing area to the left on the fairway in order to have a clear view of the small green. Positioning and local knowledge help one's score at Throughbred, which has a hefty slope of 147 from the tips and still has a slope of 130 from the Whites at just over 6000 yards. Each hole on the course is a self-enclosed golf experience. The course is bentgrass from tee to green and the greens vary in size and shape depending on the strategy of the hole. The longer holes tend to allow runup shots that can reach the green, but the shorter par 4s, such as the 358-yard sixteenth, must be reached in the air because bunkers guard the front of its shallow green.

The 580-yard dogleg left par 5 finishing hole provides a scenic and daunting conclusion to a golf course you will not likely tire of playing. To the left is Carpenter Lake from tee to green. Along the right side are rows of mature trees. If the wind is behind you, you can try a heroic drive over water to a crest twenty feet above the lake. That leaves a makeable approach to a green protected by bunkers. Or you can methodically plot three shots to reach the putting surface. Near the 18th is a clubhouse sporting a western-style wagon wheel design motif.

The Thoroughbred dude ranch has spartan accomodations with no telephone or television. Or you may opt to stay in more modern accommodations near the golf course which is a few minutes up the road from the main resort restaurant. A new conference facility and other new amenities have recently come on line at The Thoroughbred. Golf packages are available through the resort. The golf course is one of those unique surprises like Shattuck Inn in New Hampshire, McCormick Woods in Washington, and World Woods in Florida. You drive down a country road and all of a sudden you come upon a golf wonderland.

Recommended Golf Courses in Southwest and Middle Michigan

Within 2 Hours of Grand Rapids:

Bedford Valley Golf Course, Battle Creek, (616) 965–3384, Public, 18/6876/72

Binder Park Golf Course, Battle Creek, (616) 966–3459, Public, 18/6328/72

Candlestone Inn and Golf Resort, Belding, (616) 794–1580, Resort, 18/6692/72

Clearbrook Golf Club, Saugatuck, (616) 857–2000, Semiprivate, 18/6453/72

Grand View Golf Course, New Era, (616) 861–6616, Public, 18/6258/72

Hampshire Country Club, Dowagiac, (616) 782–7476, Public, 18/7030/72

Kutke Golf Course, Big Rapids, (616) 592–2213, Public, 18/6729/72

L.E. Kaufman Golf Course, Wyoming, (616) 538–5050, Public, 18/6812/72

Lake Doster Golf Club, Plainwell, (616) 685–5308, Semiprivate, 18/6570/72

Lake Michigan Hills Golf Club, Benton Harbor, (616) 849–2722, Public, 18/6911/72

Marywood Golf Club, Battle Creek, (616) 968–1168, Public, 18/6729/72

The Meadows Golf Club, Allendale, (616) 895–1000, Public, 18/7034/71

Milham Park Municipal Golf Course, Kalamazoo, (616) 344–7639, Public, 18/6578/72

Pines Golf Course of Lake Isabella, Weidman, (517) 644–2300, Public, 18/6800/72

Saskatoon Golf Club, Alto, (616) 891–9929, Public. Blue/White: 18/6750/72. Red/Gold: 18/6300/71

Scott Lake Country Club, Comstock Park, (616) 784–1355, Semiprivate, 18/6333/72

Stonehedge Golf Course, Augusta, (616) 731–2300, Semiprivate, 18/6656/72

Thornapple Creek Golf Club, Kalamazoo, (616) 344–0040, Public, 18/6960/72

Wallinwood Springs Golf Club, Jenison, (616) 457–9920, Semiprivate, 18/6751/72

Michigan: Useful Information

Travel Bureau, Michigan Department of Commerce, P.O. Box 30226, Lansing, MI 48909, (800) 5432–YES

Department of Natural Resources, Information Services Center, P.O. Box 30028, Lansing, MI 48909, (517) 373–1220 (recreation, fishing, hunting information)

U.S. Forest Service, Eastern Region, 310 W. Wisconsin Ave., Ste. 500, Milwaukee, WI 53203, (414) 297–3693, (800) 280–CAMP (national forest information)

Detroit Visitor Information Center, Hart Plaza at 2 E. Jefferson Ave., Detroit, MI 48226, (313) 567–1170

Course Name: BUNKER HILLS GOLF COURSE
East, West, North, Executive Courses

Course Type: Public
Address: 1313 Coon Rapids Boulevard
Coon Rapids, MN 55433–5397
Phone: (612) 755–4141
Fax: (612) 754–0891

GOLF COURSE

Head Professional: Dick Tollette, Jr.
Course Length/Par (All Tees): East/West: Back 6946/72, Middle 6574/72, Ladies' Forward 5863/73. West/North: Back 6893/72, Middle 6534/72, Ladies' Forward 5725/73. North/East: Back 6799/72, Middle 6424/72, Forward 5618/72. Executive Course: 9/2800/32
Course Slope/Rating (All Tees): East/West: Back 133/73.4, Middle 129/71.7, Ladies' Forward 128/74.2. West/North: Back 135/73.1, Middle 131/71.5, Ladies' Forward 130/73.6. North/East: Back 130/72.7, Middle 126/71.0, Ladies' Forward 126/72.6. Executive Course: NA/NA
Course Architects: East, North, West: David Gill (1968), remodeled by Joel Goldstrand (1990). Executive Course: Joel Goldstrand (1971)
Golf Facilities: Full Pro Shop X, Snack Bar X, Lounge X, Restaurant X, Locker Room X, Showers X, Club Rental X, Club Repair X, Cart Rental X, Instruction X, Practice Green X, Driving Range X, Practice Bunker X, Club Storage No
Tee-Time Reservation Policy: Up to 3 days in advance from after 2 p.m.
Ranger: Yes
Tee-off-Interval Time: 8 and 9 min.
Time to Play 18 Holes: 4½ hrs.
Course Hours/Earliest Tee-off: 6:20 a.m.
Green Fees: $30 for 18 holes Fri., Sat., Sun., holidays; $29 for 18 holes weekdays; Executive Course: $7
Cart Fees: $24 for 18 holes per cart
Credit Cards: Cash or check for golf fees. All major cards for merchandise

Season: Apr. through Oct. Busiest July through Labor Day
Course Comments: You can walk anytime
Golf Packages: No
Discounts: Patron card, junior, senior
Places to Stay Nearby: COON RAPIDS: Country Inn and Suites by Carlson (612) 780–3797, (800) 456–4000. MINNEAPOLIS NORTH: BLOOMINGTON: Best Western Bradbury Suites Hotel (612) 893–9999, (800) 528–1234; Days Inn Airport at Mall of America (612) 854–8400, (800) DAYS–INN; Holiday Inn International Airport (612) 854–9000, (800) HOLIDAY; Mall of America Grand Hotel (612) 854–2244, (800) 222–8733; Wyndham Hotel (612) 831–3131, (800) WYNDHAM. BROOKLYN CENTER: Inn on the Farm (612) 569–6330. BROOKLYN PARK: The Northland Inn and Executive Conference Center (612) 536–8300. MINNEAPOLIS: See page 395
Local Attractions: See page 395. Greater Minneapolis Convention and Visitors Association, 4000 Multifoods Tower, 33 S. 6th St., Minneapolis, MN 55402 (900) 860–0092, (612) 661–4700
Directions: From Minneapolis (35 min. northwest): Take Rte. 35W north to Hwy. 10 west to Hwy. 65 north. Take Hwy. 65 north to Hwy. 242. Proceed west on Hwy. 242 to golf course at Bunker Hill Dr. intersection
Closest Commercial Airport: Minneapolis–St. Paul International (45 min.)

BUNKER HILLS GOLF COURSE

Bunker Hills, site of the PGA Burnet Senior Classic, is a short drive north of Minneapolis. This rolling layout has three nines lined with pine, oak, and other varieties. The large bentgrass greens are guarded by sizeable bunkers and any tee shot strayed from the fairway is likely to be stymied by a tree or nestled in deep rough. Water can come into play on nine holes and out-of-bounds is a possibility on some others.

The most difficult holes at Bunker Hills tend to be the long par 4s. The 450-yard sixth on the East Course plays down a treelined corridor with out-of-bounds to the left. The approach is to a large green bracketed by bunkers. The 440-yard sixth on the West Course also has out-of-bounds to its left. Two long, accurate shots are required to reach a deep forward-sloping green in regulation. The 450-yard fifth hole on the North Course is a dogleg left that flows around a corner of trees to a deep, undulating green with no bunkers. There are no wide open holes at Bunker Hills. Well-positioned shots and distance are required to score, especially from the back tees. The course is an easy walk through the woods although the distance from a few greens to the next tee are lengthy.

This is a solid, well-managed public golf facility. More than 100,000 rounds are played here annually. Bunker Hills has hosted the U.S.G.A. Public Links (1976), the Minnesota State Open (1970, 1980) and many other championships.

Course Name: EDINBURGH USA

Course Type: Public
Address: 8700 Edinbrook Crossing
Brooklyn Park, MN 55443
Phone: (612) 424–7060

GOLF COURSE

Head Professional: Craig Waryan
Course Length/Par (All Tees): Back 6701/72, Club 6335/72, Intermediate 5799/72, Forward 5255/72
Course Slope/Rating (All Tees): Back 132/73, Club 127/71.3, Intermediate 122/68.7, Ladies' Intermediate 122/73.7, Ladies' Forward 128/70.7
Course Architect: Robert Trent Jones, Jr. (1987)
Golf Facilities: Full Pro Shop X, Snack Bar X, Lounge X, Restaurant X, Locker Room X, Showers X, Club Rental X, Club Repair X, Cart Rental X, Instruction X, Practice Green X, Driving Range X, Practice Bunker X, Club Storage X
Tee-Time Reservation Policy: Up to 4 days in advance beginning at 2 p.m. Reservations may be made for threesomes or foursomes
Ranger: Yes
Tee-off-Interval Time: 9 min.

Time to Play 18 Holes: 4 hrs., 45 min.
Course Hours/Earliest Tee-off: 7 a.m.
Green Fees: $33 for 18 holes, $16 for 9 holes (after 4 p.m.)
Cart Fees: $24 for 18 holes, $12 for 9 holes
Pull Carts: $3 for 18 holes
Credit Cards: American Express, MasterCard, Visa
Season: Mid-April to Oct. Busiest season May through Aug.
Course Comments: Can walk anytime. Yardage book available
Golf Packages: None
Discounts: Residents, patrons, juniors, seniors. Twilight rate. Group package rates
Places to Stay Nearby: COON RAPIDS: Mall of America Grand Hotel (612) 854–2244, (800) 662–3232; Country Suites (612) 780–3797. BLOOMINGTON: Embassy Suites Airport (612) 884–4811; Day's Inn Minneapolis Airport (612) 854–8400, (800) 326–7466; Marriott Hotel Bloomington (612) 854–7441, (800) 228–9290. MINNEAPOLIS NORTH: See page 395. MINNEAPOLIS: See page 395
Local Attractions:
See page 395. Minnesota Office of Tourism (612) 296–5029, (800) 657–3700
Directions: From downtown Minneapolis (15 min.): I–94 west to Hwy. 252, Hwy. 252 north to 85th Ave., left on 85th (1 mi.), golf course on the right
Closest Commercial Airport: Minneapolis–St. Paul International (25 min.)

EDINBURGH USA

Edinburgh USA golf course is located 15 minutes northwest of Minneapolis. The 6701-yard layout was designed by Robert Trent Jones, Jr., and opened in 1987. It was promptly selected as runner-up for best new public course of 1987 by *Golf Digest* and is now considered one of the top 50 public golf courses in America by that publication. Edinburgh was the site of the National Public Links Championship in 1992.

The land for this golf course was a private gift to the town, and Edinburgh's philosophy statement notes:

The golf course shall . . . provide a wholesome leisure time activity for as many residents as possible and to encourage non-residents to utilize the course to its maximum potential. The philosophy encompasses that residents of all ages and golfing skills will find the course a pleasurable experience.

According to a National Golf Foundation survey, Minnesota leads all states in percentage of residents (17.6) who play golf. Edinburgh has already become a very popular place to play.

The course was built on 158 acres of woodland, and the tees, greens and rolling fairways are bentgrass. The greens are moderately fast and undulating and vary in size from 25 yards deep to a sizeable 41 yards. The largest green is the eighteenth, which is shared with the ninth hole and the practice putting green. The greens are well protected by many of the 73 large sand bunkers on the course, and many of the fairway landing areas are protected by trees, water and sand. There are four tee distances to choose from at Edinburgh USA. Shot placement, careful club selection and course management are required to score on this layout.

The golf course starts out with the most difficult par 5 on the front side, a 520-yard dogleg left from the back tees. Huge bunkers on the left and right await you, beginning approximately 200 yards from the tee. The second shot is down a narrowing fairway with trees on the left and intermittent trees on the right. Two traps guard the left and front left of the medium-sized green.

The number-1-handicap hole at Edinburgh is the 424-yard par-4 seventh, a dogleg left that plays to a deep green with two large bunkers flanking a narrow entrance way. Two large traps are on the right at the corner of the dogleg, beginning approximately 190 yards from the back tees.

If you can successfully manage the last four holes of the course, you probably will have had a good round at Edinburgh. The 532-yard par-5 fifteenth is a narrow, well-treed dogleg right with a huge fairway trap on the right beginning 190 yards from the back tees. The second shot is down a narrow fairway that begins to turn right 150 yards from the green. A large bunker runs

for approximately 30 yards along the left side of this turn. The small green is well guarded by a huge trap in front and to the right. Another trap is on the left. The 149-yard par-3 sixteenth plays to a deep green blockaded by three traps left-front, front, and right-front.

The signature hole at Edinburgh is the 387-yard par-4 seventeenth, which plays to a fairway almost completely surrounded by water and bordered on the left and top by a waste bunker. The second shot is all carry over water to a deep peninsular green protected by traps and water to the left, front and right. The water, sand and limited bail-out room make this a daunting hole for many golfers.

The 397-yard par-4 finishing hole is a dogleg left with a huge 80-yard-long bunker on the right corner of the dogleg. The approach shot is to a triple green guarded to the right and front by a huge trap. There are other small traps both left and right and a huge bunker far to the rear.

Awaiting you at the nineteenth hole is a huge Scottish-manor-style clubhouse with three restaurants, private and public locker rooms for men and women, and an excellent pro shop. Individual and group instruction is available at Edinburgh. There is a generous driving range, sand bunker and chipping green, and a putting green. You can walk the golf course anytime at Edinburgh. This is an exceptional public golf facility.

Course Name: **MAJESTIC OAKS GOLF CLUB Platinum, Gold, Executive Courses**

Course Type: Public
Address: 701 Bunker Lake Boulevard Ham Lake, MN 55304
Phone: (612) 755–2142 (Pro Shop, Tee Times) (612) 755–2140 (Clubhouse)

GOLF COURSE

Director of Golf: Bill Folkes
Course Length/Par (All Tees): Platinum: Back 7013/72, White 6561/72, Gold 6112/72, Ladies Forward 5268/72. Gold:

Back 6366/72, Middle 5879/72, Forward 4848/72. Executive: Back 1795/29, Forward 1750/30

Course Slope/Rating (All Tees): Platinum: Back 129/73.9, White 125/71.4, Gold 121/69.8, Ladies' Forward 126/71.6. Gold: Back 123/71.2, Middle 118/68.6, Ladies' Forward 120/68.4. Executive: Back 73/28.1, Ladies' Forward 81/29.5

Course Architects: Platinum: Charles Maddox (1972). Gold: Garrett Gill (1991). Executive Nine: Charles Maddox (1972)

Golf Facilities: Full Pro Shop X, Snack Bar X, Lounge X, Restaurant X, Locker Room X, Showers X, Club Rental X, Club Repair X, Cart Rental X, Instruction X, Practice Green X, Driving Range X, Practice Bunker X, Club Storage No

Tee-Time Reservation Policy: Up to 4 days in advance

Ranger: Yes

Tee-off-Interval Time: 8 min.

Time to Play 18 Holes: 4½ hrs.

Course Hours/Earliest Tee-off: 6:40 a.m.

Green Fees: Platinum: $24 for 18 holes Sat., Sun., holidays; $19 for 18 holes Mon. to Fri. Gold: $22 for 18 holes Sat., Sun., holidays; $17 for 18 holes Mon. to Fri. Executive: $8 for 9 holes Sat., Sun., holidays; $7 for 9 holes Mon. to Fri.

Cart Fees: $22 for 18 holes, $11 for 9 holes

Pull Carts: $3 for 18 holes

Credit Cards: Discover, MasterCard, Visa

Season: Mid-April to end of Oct.

Course Comments: Can walk anytime

Golf Packages: Available for corporate tournament functions. Contact pro shop

Discounts: Juniors, seniors, patron card, junior season tickets. Twilight after 6 p.m.

Places to Stay Nearby: HAM LAKE: AmericInn (612) 755–2100. COON RAPIDS: Country Suites (612) 780–3797. BLOOMINGTON: Embassy Suites Airport (612) 884–4811, (800) 362–2779; Day's Inn Minneapolis Airport (612) 854–8400, (800) 329–7466; Marriott Hotel Bloomington (612) 854–7441, (800) 228–9290; Mall of America Grand Hotel (612) 854–2244, (800) 222–8733,

Sofitel Bloomington (612) 835–1900, (800) 876–6303. MINNEAPOLIS NORTH: Holiday Inn (612) 566–8000, (800) HOLIDAY; Northland Inn and Executive Conference Center (612) 536–8300, (800) 441–6422; Day's Inn Minneapolis North (612) 566–4140, (800) 325–2525; Inn on the Farm (612) 566–5903. MINNEAPOLIS: Embassy Suites (612) 333–3111, (800) 362–2779; Holiday Inn Metrodome (612) 333–4646, (800) 448–DOME; Hyatt Regency (612) 370–1234, (800) 233–1234; Minneapolis Marriott City Center (612) 349–4000, (800) 228–9290; Omni North Star (612) 338–2288, (800) THE–OMNI; Whitney Hotel (612) 339–9300, (800) 248–1879

Local Attractions: BLOOMINGTON: Mall of America. MINNEAPOLIS NORTH: Brooklyn Park Historical Farm, Anoka County Parks and Recreation. MINNEAPOLIS: Guthrie Theater, Walker Art Center, Hennepin Center for the Arts; Metrodome—professional football, baseball, basketball, other events; convention center, Minneapolis Institute of Arts, Orchestra Hall/Minnesota Orchestra, historic Orpheum Theater, University of Minnesota, historic Saint Anthony Main Shopping and Entertainment Center, historic State Theater, Mississippi Mile, Riverplace, Mystic Lake Casino, Grand Casino-Hinckley, dining, night clubs, shopping. ST. PAUL: Ordway Music Theatre, Science Museum of Minnesota, Minnesota Museum of Art, Jemne Building, World Theater, Stroh Brewery, Stillwater and St. Paul Railroad river tours. EDEN PRAIRIE: Air Museum Planes of Fame, Lake Minnetonka, St. Croix River Valley. Minnesota Office of Tourism (612) 296–5029, (800) 657–3700; Greater Minneapolis Convention and Visitors Bureau (612) 296–5029, (800) 860–0092

Directions: From Minneapolis (30 min.): Rte. 35W north to Hwy. 118. Take Hwy. 118 west to Hwy. 65 north (6 mi.) to Bunker Lake Blvd. Golf course on right (1/4 mi.)

Closest Commercial Airport: Minneapolis–St. Paul International (45 min.)

MAJESTIC OAKS COUNTRY CLUB

Majestic Oaks' eighteen-hole Platinum Course is listed as one of the top 75 public courses in the United States by *Golf Digest*. As its name suggests, giant oak trees dominate the course which is located in a real-estate development 25 miles northwest of downtown Minneapolis. From the back tees, Majestic Oaks is a 7013-yard challenge. One-third of the course is tree-lined. Additional trees, recently planted, will make the course even tighter. The bluegrass rough is cut at 3 inches, and water comes into play on thirteen holes. The tees, fairways and greens are bentgrass and the greens are large, fast, undulating and well trapped. The bunkers surrounding these greens are deep, making a good short game essential. Most of the holes on this gently rolling golf course are slight doglegs, and many of the greens are elevated.

A tough par 4 on the Platinum Course is the 422-yard par-4 dogleg-right seventh, which plays to a deep green guarded by bunkers to the left and right. A fairway bunker is to the right side of the landing area. The approach to the green is guarded by bunkers on the left side of the fairway approximately 75 yards from the green.

Another tough par 4 is the 415-yard tenth hole, which is a dogleg to the right to a heavily contoured, fast green protected by sand traps both left and right. If you can get your tee shot to the corner of the dogleg, you will have 150 yards to the green.

A tough par 5 at Majestic Oaks is the 550-yard sixteenth, which is straight and well guarded by a stream and a series of fairway bunkers on the left. A water hazard on the right comes into play on the second shot and the approach shot is to a green well protected by three bunkers.

The combination of length, water hazards, abundant sand traps, and large, undulating, elevated greens makes the Majestic Oaks Platinum Course a good golf challenge. Charles Maddox, the Platinum Course's designer, was born in Illinois and designed several other midwestern golf courses, including the Brookview Country Club in Minneapolis; the Olympic Hills Golf Club in Eden Prairie, Minnesota; and the Raisin River Country Club in Monroe, Michigan. Maddox also designed the 1795-yard par-29 Executive nine at Majestic Oaks.

The Gold Course, designed by Garrett Gill, opened in 1991. Gill is a native of Illinois and designed the excellent Hulman Links in Terre Haute, Indiana, with his father David Gill, also a noted golf architect. The Gold Course plays 6366 yards from the back tees and adds another option to this busy golf course. Although shorter in length than the Platinum Course, the Gold is equally difficult because of its narrow landing areas guarded by water, trees, and thick rough. A challenging par 4 on the front side is the 433-yard second, a slight dogleg left with trees bordering the tee shot landing area. The approach is to a narrow green bracketed by water on both sides. A bunker to the front and left guards the entranceway to the target.

A difficult and memorable hole on the back side is the 516-yard par-5 twelfth, a double-dogleg that requires an accurate tee shot to avoid bunkers and water to the right. Large oak trees guard the left side of the fairway on the drive and more oaks protect the right side on the second shot. An accurate approach to the green is required in order to avoid a bunker to its left or heavy rough to the right. A shot over the green will be under the trees.

Majestic Oaks also has a short nine hole course whose tee distances range from 90 to 325 yards from the back tees. Any of the courses can be walked anytime.

Course Name: **THE PINES**
                   Lake, Woods,
                   Marsh Courses

Course Type: Resort
Resort: Grand View Lodge
Address: South 134 Nokomis
               Nisswa, MN 56468
Phone: (218) 963–3146 (Golf Course)
               (218) 963–2234, (800) 432–
               3788 (MN), (800) 345–9625
               (outside MN) (Resort)
Fax: (218) 963–2269 (Resort)

GOLF COURSE

Director of Golf: Mark Neva

Course Length/Par (All Tees): Lakes/Woods: Back 6837/72, Blue 6452/72, White 6139/72, Forward 5112/72. Woods/Marsh: Back 6874/72, Blue 6471/72, White 6152/72, Forward 5134/72. Marsh/Lakes: Back 6883/72, Blue 6479/72, White 6159/72, Forward 5210/72

Course Slope/Rating (All Tees): Lakes/Woods: Back 137/74.2, Blue 134/72.4, White 131/71.0, Forward 121/66.4, Ladies' White 140/76.3, Ladies' Forward 128/70.76. Woods/Marsh: Back 139/73.9, Blue 136/72.1, White 133/70.1, Forward 117/65.8, Ladies' White 136/76.6, Ladies' Forward 129/71.3. Marsh/Lakes: Back 141/74.3, Blue 138/72.7, White 135/71.3, Forward 119/66.0, Ladies' White 144/76.5, Ladies' Forward 132/70.2

Course Architect: Lake, Woods: Joel Goldstrand (1990). Marsh: Joel Goldstrand (1994)

Golf Facilities: Full Pro Shop X, Snack Bar X, Lounge X, Restaurant X, Locker Room X, Showers X, Club Rental X, Club Repair X, Cart Rental X, Instruction X, Practice Green X, Driving Range X, Practice Bunker X, Club Storage X

Tee-Time Reservation Policy: Resort guests: At time of registration. Outside play: 24 hrs. in advance

Ranger: Yes

Tee-off-Interval Time: 8 min.

Time to Play 18 Holes: 4 hrs., 20 min.

Course Hours/Earliest Tee-off: 6:52 a.m.

Green Fees: Public: Resort guests on meal plan: $33.50 for 18 holes, $17.50 for 9 holes. Resort guests in cabin: $39.50 for 18 holes, $24.50 for 9 holes. Outside play: $49.50 for 18 holes Fri., Sat., Sun., holidays; $43.50 for 18 holes weekdays. $25.50 for 9 holes

Cart Fees: $14.50 for 18 holes per person per cart, $10.50 for 9 holes per person per cart

Pull Carts: $4.50 for 18 holes

Credit Cards: All major cards

Season: April 25 to Oct. 20. Busiest season mid-June to early Sept.

Course Comments: Can walk anytime. Yardage book available. Golf discount cards allowed only Mon. to Thurs.

Golf Packages: Available through resort

Discounts: Twilight rate after 4:30 p.m.

Places to Stay Nearby: NISSWA: Days Inn of Nisswa (218) 963–3500, (800) 329–7466; Lazy Brook Resort (218) 963–2503. BRAINERD: Cragun's Pine Beach Lodge and Conference Center (218) 829–3591, (800) 272–4867; Holiday Inn (218) 829–1441, (800) HOLIDAY; Madden's on Gull Lake (218) 829–2811; Best Western Paul Bunyan Inn (218) 829–3571, (800) 528–1234

Local Attractions: Brainerd Raceway, Paul Bunyan Amusement Center, shopping area, Paul Bunyan Arboretum, Crow Wing County Museum, Heartland Symphony Orchestra, Minnesota Resort Museum, Crow Wing State Park, hunting, fishing, boating, swimming, hiking, camping. Minnesota Travel Information (612) 296–5024, (800) 657–3700. Brainerd Area Chamber of Commerce (218) 829–2838

Directions: From Twin Cities (142 mi.): I–94 west to exit 178 (Clearwater/Annadole), turn right through Clearwater and Clear Lake. Hwy. 10 north past St. Cloud to Hwy. 371, through Brainerd, 14 mi. north of Brainerd left at stoplights onto Hwy. 77, follow signs 1 mile to resort

Closest Commercial Airports: Brainerd (30 min.); Minneapolis–St. Paul International (3 hrs.)

RESORT

Date Built: 1919

No. of Rooms: 12 rooms in main lodge, 60 cottages and town homes

Meeting Rooms: 9. Capacity of Largest: 425 persons banquet style. Meeting Space: 7500 sq. ft.

Room Price Range: $85 to $200, modified American plan, depending on season, occupancy. Spring and fall, special holiday weekend and other packages available

Lounge: Totem Pole Lounge

Restaurants: Historic Lodge, Pine Room

Entertainment: Movies, dancing, square dancing, card tournaments, backgammon tournaments, flower shows, Las Vegas night, water olympics, lawn game olympics

Credit Cards: Discover, MasterCard, Visa

General Amenities: Sightseeing by bus, boat, children's programs for ages 3 to 12, recreation center, social director, babysitting, painting lessons, conference-room facilities with audiovisual and banquet services

Recreational Amenities: Marina, boating, sailing, fishing, indoor swimming pool, saunas, whirlpool, water-skiing, bicycling, shuffleboard, table tennis, croquet, board games, horseshoes, volleyball, 11 tennis courts, nature trail, exercise room

Reservation and Cancellation Policy: Advance deposit of $150 or more required and applied to the last night of your stay. Deposits refunded (less a $25 handling fee) if notice received 30 days prior to arrival or less than 30 days if your space can be rerented

Comments and Restrictions: Resort open May 1 to Oct. 15. Pets not allowed. Area kennels available. Accommodations offered on modified American plan, which includes lodging, 2 meals daily, unlimited tennis, unlimited 9-hole golf, discounted golf at the Pines and other benefits. State tax and 15% service charge added to room rates

THE PINES

Grand View Lodge is located 142 miles northwest of Minneapolis and 120 miles west of Duluth. Listed on the National Register of Historic Places, the 1919 lodge at Grand View features 12 rooms. Close by are over 60 lake town homes and cottages, many of which border Gull Lake and Roy Lake, and a 1500-foot natural sand beach. Grand View Lodge was established as a resort in 1937, after being purchased by Reginald Frederick Brown Lee "Brownie" Cote from M. V. Baker, who in 1919 had built the log main lodge to house prospective clients interested in buying lake-shore property on Gull Lake. In 1990, Grand View opened the 6832-yard

par-72 Pines golf course (now the Lakes/Woods), a fully bentgrass course designed by Joel Goldstrand that winds its way through beautiful central Minnesota woodlands. Another nine, the Marsh Course, was built in 1994 to add to the quality and quantity of golf at the Grand Lodge resort.

Because of the well-treed fairways and water that comes into play on many holes, the Pines courses require accurate, strategic shot making. The Pines offer a choice of four tee-distance positions. The resort also has a par-35 nine-hole Gardens Course, which features some of the 15,000 flowers on the property.

Some notable holes on the Lakes/Woods layout include the 152-yard par-3 seventh, which plays over a large pond that extends from the front of the tee to the left side of the long, narrow green protected on the right by two traps. The par-3 ninth hole provides two separate greens connected by a narrow bentgrass strip with distances of 212 and 182 yards to either target. The shorter distance is to a well-banked smaller green protected by four traps to the front and to the right. The longer distance is to a deep green that will likely leave a difficult putt if you reach the target in regulation. The eighteenth hole, the ninth hole on the Woods, is a testing 541-yard par-5 hole with a dogleg left down a tree-lined fairway to a green protected left and left-front by a pond. Two bunkers are located on the right and right front. A long drive to the right center of the fairway leaves you over 200 yards to the green, which is very large and undulating.

The most difficult holes on this course are two long par 4s. The number-1-handicap 433-yard second hole on the Lakes is a slight dogleg right through a corridor of trees to a deep green elongated left to right, sloped toward the front, and protected in front by two bunkers. The first shot should be right center and the next shot has to negotiate a swale in front of the green. Another difficult hole is the 454-yard par-4 eleventh, the second hole on the Lakes. This dogleg left plays from an elevated tee down a tree-lined fairway to a large, roundish green protected on the left by a small bunker. The tee shot should be kept right center leaving a clear but long second shot onto the green.

The Marsh nine compatibly fits with the other two venues. Built around a marsh that can come into play on four holes, this layout offers some interesting par 4s that require shotmaking and accuracy. The 351-yard par-4 fourth requires a tee shot that safely clears the edge of the wetlands to set up a short approach to a wide, shallow green fronted by two bunkers and guarded to its rear by another. The round concludes with a run of three long par 4s highlighted by the 451-yard seventh, a dogleg right whose approach is to a deep green guarded by a phalanx of bunkers to its left, another to its right and one more to its rear. The par 4s tend to be the most difficult holes on these courses with some relief provided by the par 5s which measure in the 475 to 547 yard range from the back tees.

The rest of the amenities at Grand View are first class. The tennis facilities including 11 Laykold courts has prompted *Tennis* magazine to name Grand View one of the 50 best tennis resorts in the United States. Grand View has a variety of banquet, reception and conference-room facilities with the capacity for up to 500 guests. The rooms in the historic main lodge have been newly remodeled, and the cottages and town homes range from honeymoon style to 8-bedroom cabins accommodating from 2 to 20 people. All guests are on a modified American plan, and numerous social activities, games, and sports are available.

The resort offers weekday golf packages from Sunday through Thursday that include accommodations, one round of golf on the Pines courses, and use of the facilities, including the 9-hole executive course. Those staying at the resort get reduced rates on the Pines courses.

The area around the Pines resort has several hundred lakes and rivers. It has long been a popular recreation and resort area for fishing, hunting, boating, camping and hiking in Minnesota. This is an excellent area for family vacations, conferences or a place to get away from it all and play on golf courses that received honorable mention for best new golf course of 1991 from *Golf Digest* magazine. Since then, the Pines nines have consistently been rated the best public golf courses in Minnesota by that publication. *Golf* magazine has named Grand View Lodge one of the best golf resorts in the United States.

Recommended Golf Courses in Minnesota

Central Minnesota Within 1½ Hours of Brainerd:

Albion Ridges Golf Club, Annandale, (612) 963–5500, Public, 18/6502/72

Alexandria Golf Club, Alexandria, (612) 763–3605, Semiprivate, 18/6310/72

Balmoral Golf Course, Battle Lake, (218) 864–5414, Public, 18/6132/72

Breezy Point Resort, Breezy Point, (218) 562–7177, Resort. Championship: 18/6601/72. Traditional: 18/5192/68

Cuyuna Country Club, Deerwood, (218) 534–3489, Semiprivate, 18/6273/71

Headwaters Country Club, Park Rapids, (218) 732–4832, Semiprivate, 18/6455/72

Izaty's Golf and Yacht Club, Onamia, (612) 532–4575, (800) 533–1728, Resort, 18/6481/72

Little Crow Country Club, Spicer, (612) 354–2296, Semiprivate, 18/6765/72

Madden's on Gull Lake, Brainerd, (218) 829–7118, Resort. East: 18/5920/72. West: 18/5086/67. Social 9: 9/1760/28

Tianna Country Club, Walker, (218) 547–1712, Semiprivate, 18/6550/72

Wendigo Golf Course, Grand Rapids, (218) 327–2211, Public, 18/6756/72

Duluth:

Enger Park Golf Course, Duluth, (218) 723–3451, Public, 18/6434/72, 9/3405/36

Lester Park, Duluth, (218) 525–1400, Public. Front/Back: 18/6371/72. Back/Lake: 18/6606/72. Front/Lake: 18/6599/72

Superior National Golf Course, Lutsen, (218) 663–7195, Public, 18/6323/72

Mankato:

North Links Golf Course, North Mankato, (507) 947–3355, Public, 18/6073/72

Within 1 Hour of Minneapolis–St. Paul:

Baker National Golf Course, Medina, (612) 473–0800, Public, 18/6762/72

Braemar Golf Course, Edina, (612) 941–2072, Public. Red/White: 18/6739/71. Red/Blue: 18/6377/71. Blue/White: 18/6692. Executive: 9/1408/29

Brooktree Municipal Golf Course, Owatonna, (507) 451–0370, Public, 18/6648/71

Cannon Golf Club, Cannon Falls, (507) 263–3126, Semiprivate, 18/6200/71

Elk River Country Club, Elk River, (612) 441–4111, Semiprivate, 18/6480/72

Fox Hollow Golf Club, Rogers, (612) 428–4468, Semiprivate, 18/6726/72

Gross Golf Course, Minneapolis, (612) 789–2542, Public, 18/6575/71

Inverwood Golf Course, Inver Grove Heights, (612) 457–3667, Public, 18/6724/72

Island View Country Club, Waconia, (612) 442–5666, Semiprivate, 18/6540/72

Keller Golf Course, St. Paul, (612) 484–3011, Public, 18/6566/72

Les Bolstad Golf Club (University of Minnesota), St. Paul, (612) 627–4000, Public, 18/6123/71

The Links at Northfork, Ramsey, (612) 241–0506, Public, 18/6989/72

Mississippi National Golf Links, Red Wing, (612) 388–1874, Public. Lowlands/Midlands: 18/6035/70. Midlands/Highlands: 18/6488/71. Lowlands/Highlands: 18/6215/71

Monticello Country Club, Monticello, (612) 295–4653, Public, 18/6390

New Prague Golf Club, New Prague, (612) 758–3126, Public, 18/6335/72

Wedgewood Valley Golf Club, Woodbury, (612) 731–4779, Public, 18/6790/72

Willinger's Golf Club, Northfield, (612) 440–7000, Public, 18/6711/72

Northwest of Minneapolis–St. Paul:

Bemidji Town and Country Club, Bemidji, (218) 751–9215, Semiprivate, 18/6535/72

Detroit Country Club, Detroit Lakes, (218) 847–5790, Resort, 18/5941/71

Marshall Golf Club, Marshall, (507) 537–1622, Semiprivate, 18/6565/72

Wildflower at Fair Hills, Detroit Lakes, (218) 439–3357, (800) 323–2849, Public, 18/6965/72

Rochester Area:

Cedar River Country Club, Adams, (507) 582–3595, Public, 18/6211/72

Maple Valley Golf and Country Club, Rochester, (507) 285–9100, Semiprivate, 18/6270/71

Northern Hills Golf Course, Rochester, (507) 281–6170, Public, 18/6315/72

Willow Creek Golf Club, Rochester, (507) 285–0305, Semiprivate, 18/6053/70

Minnesota: Useful Information

Minnesota Travel Information Center, 375 Jackson St., 250 Skyway Level, St. Paul, MN 55101, (612) 296–5029, (800) 657–3700

Greater Minneapolis Convention and Visitors Association, 1219 Marquette Ave., Ste. 300, Minneapolis, MN 55403, (612) 348–4313, (900) 860–0092 (Minneapolis tourist information)

St. Paul Chamber of Commerce, 600 North Central Tower, 101 N.W. Center, 55 E. 5th St., St. Paul, MN 55101, (612) 297–6985, (800) 627–6101 (St. Paul information)

Minnesota Department of Natural Resources Information Center, 500 Lafayette Rd., Box 40, St. Paul, MN 55146, (612) 296–6157 (recreation information), (612) 296–4506 (fishing and hunting regulations)

Chippewa National Forest, Supervisor's Office, Cass Lake, MN 56633, (218) 335–8600 (National forest information)

Superior National Forest, Box 338, Duluth, MN 55804, (218) 720–5324 (National forest information)

Course Name: KIRKWOOD NATIONAL GOLF CLUB

Course Type: Semiprivate
Address: Highway 4/P.O. Box 747
        Holly Springs, MS 38635
Telephone: (601) 252–4888

GOLF COURSE

Head Professional: Tim Corrigan
Course Length/Par (All Tees): Back 7129/72, Gold 6639/72, Blue 6234/72, White 5700/72, Forward 4898/72
Course Slope/Rating (All Tees): Back 135/73.6, Gold 131/72.5, Blue 128/70.6, White 124/69.3, Forward 116/68.2
Course Architects: Ed Connor, Tracey May, Harris Gholson II (1994)
Golf Facilities: Full Pro Shop X, Snack Bar X, Lounge X, Restaurant X, Locker Room X, Showers X, Club Rental No, Club Repair X, Cart Rental X, Instruction X, Practice Green X, Driving Range X, Practice Bunker X, Club Storage X
Tee-Time Reservation Policy: Up to 7 days in advance
Ranger: Yes
Tee-off-Interval Time: 10 min.
Time to Play 18 Holes: 4½ hrs.
Course Hours/Earliest Tee-off: 7:30 a.m.
Green and Cart Fees: $42 for 18 holes Sat., Sun., holidays; $32 for 18 holes weekdays
Credit Cards: MasterCard, Visa
Season: Year round
Course Comments: Walking allowed anytime
Golf Packages: No
Discounts: Juniors, seniors
Places to Stay Nearby: HOLLY SPRINGS: Heritage Inn (601) 252–1120. MEMPHIS: Peabody Memphis Hotel (901) 529–4000, (800) PEABODY; Memphis Marriott (901) 362–6200, (800) 228–9290; Holiday Inn Crowne Plaza (901) 527–7300, (800) HOLIDAY
Local Attractions: HOLLY SPRINGS: 19th century homes, Kate Freeman Clark Art Gallery, Marshall County Historical Museum, Holly Springs National Forest, hiking, camping, hunting, fishing, boating, seasonal festivals. Memphis. Holly Springs Chamber of Commerce, 154 S. Memphis St., Holly Springs, MS 38635 (601) 252–2943
Directions: Kirkwood National is 40 miles southeast of Memphis, TN. Take Hwy. 78 to Holly Springs Exit. Take Hwy. 4 through Holly Springs. Golf course 3 mi. outside of town
Closest Commercial Airport: Memphis International (45 min.)

KIRKWOOD NATIONAL GOLF COURSE

Kirkwood National is a new course built on former farmland and cotton fields just outside of Holly Springs, 40 miles southeast of Memphis. This hilly, treelined layout has water hazards on half its holes including the 132-yard par-3 fifteenth. This hole, patterned after the No. 12 hole at Augusta National, is guarded by a pond in front and bunkers to its rear. The shallow green is a difficult target, especially when the pin is to the right.

The fairways at Kirkwood National provide sizeable landing areas. But if you stray the ball, you will be penalized by the water hazards, difficult rough, bunkers, or perhaps you will be stymied by trees. Wind can also be a factor on some holes including the 476-yard par-4 fourteenth which often plays directly into the wind. The longest hole on the course is the 614-yard par-5 fifth, a dogleg requiring three shots to reach its two-tiered green protected by a bunker to its left and another to its rear. The fairway takes a sharp ninety degree turn when you get to within 150 yards of this green.

The Kirkwood National course is bentgrass from tee to green. The practice area includes driving range, putting and chipping greens, and practice bunkers. A new clubhouse with pro shop, restaurant, and full locker room facilities will open in 1996. In 1995, Kirkwood was rated one of the best new public golf courses by *Golf Digest*.

Course Name: TIMBERTON GOLF CLUB

Course Type: Semi-private
Address: 22 Clubhouse Drive
3900 Highway 11 South
Hattiesburg, MS 39401
Phone: (601) 584–4653
Fax: (601) 543–0622

GOLF COURSE

Director of Golf: James Ray Carpenter
Head Professional: Ron Hickman
Course Length/Par (All Tees): Back 7028/72, Green 6463/72, White 6153/72, Forward 5439/72
Course Slope/Rating (All Tees): Back 131/73.1, Green 128/70.5, White 127/69.7, Ladies' Forward 128/71.4
Course Architect: Mark McCumber (1991)
Golf Facilities: Full Pro Shop X, Snack Bar X, Lounge X, Restaurant X, Locker Room X, Showers X, Club Rental X, Club Repair X, Cart Rental X, Instruction X, Practice Green X, Driving Range X, Practice Bunker X, Club Storage Limited
Tee-Time Reservation Policy: Up to 13 days in advance. Members have preferred tee times
Ranger: Yes
Tee-off-Interval Time: 7 min.
Time to Play 18 Holes: 4 hrs. 15 min.
Course Hours/Earliest Tee-off: 8 a.m.
Green and Cart Fees: $45 for 18 holes Sat., Sun., holidays; $35 for 18 holes weekdays
Credit Cards: MasterCard, Visa
Season: Year round. Busiest Apr. through Sept.
Course Comments: Cart mandatory. 18-hole lighted putting course on site
Golf Packages: Through Cabot Lodge (601) 264–1881
Discounts: Inquire at pro shop
Places to Stay Nearby: Cabot Lodge (601) 264–1881; Comfort Inn (601) 268–2170, (800) 228–5150; Econo Lodge (601) 264–0010, 446–6900; Hampton Inn (601) 264–8080, (800) 426–7866; Holiday Inn (601) 268–2850, (800) HOLIDAY; Quality Inn (601) 544–4530, (800) 228–5151

Local Attractions: HATTIESBURG: University of Southern Mississippi, William Carey College, Hattiesburg Civic Arts Council Saenger Gallery, DeSoto National Forest, fishing, hunting, camping, hiking. Natchez. Vicksburg. Jackson. Gulf Coast. New Orleans. Hattiesburg Convention and Visitors Bureau, 6443 U.S. 49, P.O. Box 16122, Hattiesburg, MS 39404–6122 (601) 268–3220, (800) 63–TOURS
Directions: From downtown Hattiesburg (10 min. south). Take Hwy. 11 south to the golf course
Closest Commercial Airports: Pine Belt Regional, Hattiesburg (15 min.); Jackson (1½ hrs.), New Orleans International, LA (2½ hrs.)

TIMBERTON GOLF CLUB

The Timberton Golf Club is located two hours northeast of New Orleans and one hour from the Gulf of Mexico. Pine trees, dogwood, and other varieties border this Mark McCumber-designed layout. Timberton's landing areas are generous, but accurate approach shots to the Bermuda grass targets are required to score. Among the most difficult holes at Timberton are the par 4s including the 440-yard fifth, modeled after the thirteenth at Augusta National. This hole has a left-to-right sloping fairway and an uphill approach that must avoid a stream that cuts the fairway and runs to the left side of the target. There is water in the form of streams, small ponds, and lakes at Timberton, but most of these hazards do not come directly into play. The par 5s at Timberton require shotmaking rather than strength. The 540-yard dogleg right fifteenth, for example, takes two well-placed shots and a wedge to reach a deep green guarded by a stream in front and a bunker on each side. A heroic second shot is required to reach the target in two. Difficult par 3s on the course include the 219-yard fourteenth which plays to a deep green bracketed by bunkers. The finishing hole at Timberton is a 394-yard par-4 dogleg right whose ample tee shot landing area is bordered by a lake to the far right. The approach must carry a pond to reach a three-tiered green framed by two deep bunkers.

Timberton offers four tee distances to accomodate any golfer. Practice facilities include two putting and chipping greens, a driving range, a huge putting green, and an 18-hole lighted putting course. A bed and breakfast is scheduled to be built near the ninth hole to accomodate guest golfers. Timberton, built on the former site of a lumber mill, is rated among the best golf courses in Mississippi by *GolfWeek* and *Golf Digest*.

Recommended Golf Courses in Mississippi

Within 1 Hour of Biloxi:

Broadwater Beach Golf Club, Biloxi, (800) 221–2816 (MS), (800) 647–3964 (outside MS), Resort. Sun: 18/7168/72. Sea: 18/6214/71

Diamondhead Country Club, Diamondhead, (601) 255–3910, (800) 346–8741, Resort. Cardinal: 18/6831/72. Pine: 18/6817/72

Mississippi National Golf Club, Gautier, (601) 497–2372, (800) 477–4044, Public, 18/7003/72

Pass Christian Isles Golf Club, Pass Christian, (601) 452–3830, Semiprivate, 18/6438/72

Rainbow Bay Golf Club, Biloxi, (601) 388–9670, (800) 638–4902, Resort, 18/6196/71

Royal Gulf Hills, Ocean Springs, (800) 638–4902, Resort, 18/6294/72

St. Andrews Country Club, Ocean Springs, (601) 875–7730, Semiprivate, 18/6460/72

Southwind Country Club, Biloxi, (601) 392–0400, Semiprivate, 18/6202/72

Sunkist Country Club, Biloxi, (601) 388–3961, Semiprivate, 18/6276/72

Tramark Golf Course, Gulfport, (601) 863–7808, Public, 18/6350/72

Windance Country Club, Gulfport, (601) 832–4871, Semiprivate, 18/6678/72

Olive Branch:

Plantation Golf Course, Olive Branch, (601) 895–3530, Semiprivate, 18/6773/72

Wedgewood Golf Course, Olive Branch, (601) 895–7490, Semiprivate, 18/6863/72

Oxford:

Ole Miss Golf Club, Oxford, (601) 234–4816, Public, 18/6682/72

Starkville:

Mississippi State University Golf Course, Starkville, (601) 325–3028, Public, 18/6926/72

Mississippi Beach Region:

The Mississippi Beach region has numerous hotels with a variety of golf packages available.

Highest rates tend to be during the February through May season. Detailed information is available from Harrison County Tourism Commission, P.O. Box 6128, Gulfport, MS 39506–6128, (601) 896–6699, (800) 237–9493 (mainland U.S. and Canada)

Mississippi: Useful Information

Division of Tourism Development, Mississippi Department of Economic and Community Development, P.O. Box 22825, Jackson, MS 39205, (601) 359–3297, (800) 647–2290

Mississippi Department of Wildlife, Fisheries and Parks, P.O. Box 451, Jackson, MS 39205, (601) 362–9212 (fishing and hunting regulations; state park recreational information)

Mississippi Gulf Coast Convention and Visitors Bureau, P.O. Box 6128, Gulfport, MS 39506, (601) 896–6699, (800) 237–9493 (deep-sea fishing and general tourist information)

U.S. Dept. of Agriculture and Forest Service, 100 West Capitol St., Ste. 1141, Jackson, MS 39269, (601) 965–4391, (800) 280–CAMP (national forest information and reservations)

Mississippi Arts Commission, 239 North Lamar St., Ste. 207, Jackson, MS 39215, (601) 359–6030 (information on the arts in Mississippi)

Course Name: LODGE OF THE
FOUR SEASONS
Robert Trent Jones
Championship,
Seasons Ridge,
Executive Courses

Course Type: Resort
Resort: The Lodge of Four Seasons
Address: Lake Road HH
P.O. Box 215
Lake Ozark, MO 65049
Phone: (573) 365–8532
(Championship) (573) 365–
8544 (Seasons Ridge)
(573) 365–1440 (Executive)
(573) 365–3001,
(800) THE–LAKE (Resort)
Fax: (573) 365–8525 (Resort)

GOLF COURSE

Director of Golf: Chris Clark
Head Professional: Seasons Ridge: Bob
Neiberbing
Course Length/Par (All Tees): Champion-
ship: Back 6406/72, Middle 5947/72,
Forward 5241/72. Seasons Ridge: Back
6416/72, White 6020/72, Yellow
5461/72, Forward 4657/72. Executive:
1700/30
Course Slope/Rating (All Tees): Champi-
onship: Back 133/71.0, Middle
124/69.6, Forward 124/70.8. Seasons
Ridge: Back 130/71.4, White 124/69.3,
Yellow 120/66.6, Ladies' Yellow
126/72.4, Ladies' Forward 118/71.0.
Executive: NA/NA
Course Architects: Championship: Robert
Trent Jones, Sr. and Roger Rulewich
(1974). Seasons Ridge: Ken Kavanaugh
(1991). Executive: NA (1966)
Golf Facilities: Full Pro Shop X, Snack
Bar X, Lounge X, Restaurant X,
Locker Room X, Showers X, Club
Rental X, Club Repair X, Cart Rental
X, Instruction X, Practice Green X,
Driving Range X, Practice Bunker X,
Club Storage X
Tee-Time Reservation Policy: After reser-
vation at resort, up to 90 days in advance
Ranger: Yes

Tee-off-Interval Time: 8 and 10 min.
Time to Play 18 Holes: Championship:
4½ hrs. Seasons Ridge: 4 hrs., 15 min.
Course Hours/Earliest Tee-off: 7 a.m.
Green and Cart Fees: Championship: $69
for 18 holes with cart Fri., Sat., Sun.,
holidays; $59 for 18 holes with cart
weekdays. Seasons Ridge: $59 for 18
holes with cart Fri., Sat., Sun.,holidays;
$49 for 18 holes with cart weekdays.
Executive Nine: $20 for 18 holes with
cart Fri., Sat., Sun., holidays; $13 for 18
holes weekdays. $15 for 9 holes, cart $8
for 9 holes
Credit Cards: All major cards
Season: Year round. Busiest season June,
July
Course Comments: Cart mandatory. Walking on Executive Course only. Must be
a resort guest, member or guest of member to play the Championship course
Golf Packages: Available through resort
Discounts: Seasonal rates. Property owners
Places to Stay Nearby: Must be a resort
guest, member or guest of member to
play the Championship course. Marri-
ott's Tan-Tar-A (573) 348–3131, (800)
826–8272; Best Western Dogwood Hills
Resort and Golf Club (573) 348–1735,
(800) 528–1234; Inn at Grand Glaize
(573) 348–4731
Local Attractions: See page 406. Missouri
Division of Tourism (314) 751–4133,
(800) 877–1234
Directions: I–70 to Hwy. 54, south on
Hwy. 54 to Business 54/Bagnell Down
exit, Business 54 to Lake Rd. HH west,
follow signs to resort
Closest Commercial Airports: Springfield
Regional (1 hr., 45 min.), Kansas City
International (3 hrs.), Lambert–
St. Louis International (3 hrs.)

RESORT

Date Built: 1966
No. of Rooms: 311 standard, superior in
Lakeside building; deluxe in Main Lodge;
premier Marina Bay and Lancido section.
Choices of single room to 3-bedroom villa
Meeting Rooms: 30. Capacity of Largest:
1200 persons banquet style. Meeting
Space: 30,000 sq. ft.

Room Price Range: $139 for single or double weekdays to $320 for 3-bedroom villa peak season. Golf and other packages available

Lounges: The Fifth Season, Sandtrap at HK's, Lobby Bar

Restaurants: Sea Chase Restaurant, Atrium Sidewalk Cafe, Old Country Deli, Toledo Room, HK's Restaurant

Entertainment: Dancing in the Toledo Room

Credit Cards: All major cards

General Amenities: Movie theater, shopping, Japanese gardens, babysitting services, meeting and conference facilities with audiovisual and food services, supervised youth programs, retail shops, hair salon

Recreational Amenities: 14 outdoor swimming pools, 1 Olympic indoor pool, heated indoor/outdoor pool, private beach; fitness center with cardiovascular and strength equipment, aerobics room, racquetball; spa with whirlpools, sauna, steam, massage, facials, hair care, herbal wraps; fishing, horseback riding, bicycling, hiking, trap shooting, bowling, billiards, boating, water-skiing, racquet and country club with 19 courts including clay, tournament stadium, instruction; cross-country skiing, cruises, 200-slip marina, table tennis

Reservation and Cancellation Policy: 1 night's deposit required to hold reservation. 3-day advance cancellation notice prior to scheduled date of arrival required to avoid penalties

Comments and Restrictions: Taxes additional to base rates

LODGE OF THE FOUR SEASONS

The Lodge of the Four Seasons Resort covers 3200 rolling acres and 72 miles of shoreline on the Lake of the Ozarks, one of Missouri's premier recreation and vacation spots. Many activities offered here revolve around the lake which features boating, water-skiing, swimming, fishing and other water activities. The resort also has 45 holes of golf, including the 6406-yard Robert Trent Jones Championship Course, which has been ranked among the best in the state by *Golf Digest*.

This is a hilly, tight layout carved out of trees bordering the Lake of the Ozarks. The course has over 80 strategically placed sand traps guarding medium-sized to large bentgrass greens and most fairway landing areas. A variety of water hazards is found on this layout, including the 214-yard par-3 thirteenth, which plays over a lake to a wide green fronted by six bunkers.

An excellent par 5 on the Robert Trent Jones Course is the 531-yard twelfth, a slight dogleg right. The first shot is to a landing area guarded by bunkers on the right and trees on the left. The second shot is down a narrowing fairway protected by trees on both sides. The green is fronted by two bunkers, with another to the right side and a fourth to the rear. This hole is a typical example of how a premium is put on positioning and accuracy rather than distance on the Championship Course. Poorly played shots are likely to be in the sand, woods or water.

The 6577-yard par-72 Seasons Ridge Course is the newest addition to the golf venue at the Lodge of Four Seasons. Designed by Ken Kavanaugh, Seasons Ridge is a demanding course with a variety of elevation changes, beautiful vistas of the lake, well-guarded fairways and greens, and a choice of four tee positions to hit from.

The Lodge of the Four Seasons Resort has a Golf University that offers a curriculum developed by Ken Blanchard, author of *The One-Minute Manager*. Video swing analysis and instruction at the complete practice facilities that include indoor and outdoor driving ranges are available at the resort. A variety of golf packages starting from less than $100 per person including room, green fees, cart and other amenities, are offered.

The resort has a complete range of recreational options for the entire family, including supervised children's programs, fishing, boating, horseback riding, tennis with instruction available, trap shooting, racquetball, billiards and table tennis, water-skiing and other water sports. The conditioning center includes cardiovascular and strength equipment, a lap pool, aerobics room, sauna, and whirlpool. Fitness assessment and supervised conditioning programs are available, and other activities such as wilderness hiking and bicycling are easily accessible. *Tennis* magazine has rated the 19 court tennis complex and its Dennis Van der Meer Tennis University among the 50 greatest tennis resorts in the country.

Room accommodations range from single or double rooms to 2010-square foot 3-bedroom villas with 2 bathrooms, kitchens, courtyards, wood burning fireplaces, patios and wet bars. For a relaxing golf vacation, the Lodge of the Four Seasons is one of Missouri's best resorts.

Course Name:	**MARRIOTT'S TAN-TAR-A GOLF CLUB Oaks, Hidden Lakes Courses**
Course Type:	Resort
Resort:	Marriott's Tan-Tar-A Resort, Golf Club and Spa
Address:	State Road KK Osage Beach, MO 65065–0188
Phone:	(573) 348–8521 (Golf Course) (573) 348–3131, (800) 826–8272 (Resort reservations and information)
Fax:	(573) 348–3206 (Resort)

GOLF COURSE

Director of Golf: Tom Gray

Course Length/Par (All Tees): Oaks: Back 6442/71, White 6002/71, Yellow 5329/71, Forward 3943/70. Hidden Lakes: Back 3015/35, Middle 2705/35, Ladies' Forward 2232/36

Course Slope/Rating (All Tees): Oaks: Back 143/72.1, White 137/70.1, Yellow 126/65.9, Forward 103/62.5. Hidden Lakes: Back 134/35.2, Middle 131/34.3, Ladies' Forward 123/33.4

Course Architects: Oaks: Bruce Devlin and Robert von Hagge (1980). Hidden Lakes: Jim Lewis (1970)

Golf Facilities: Full Pro Shop X, Snack Bar X, Lounge X, Restaurant X, Locker Room X, Showers X, Club Rental X, Club Repair X, Cart Rental X, Instruction X, Practice Green X, Driving Range X, Practice Bunker X, Club Storage X

Tee-Time Reservation Policy: Resort guests: Up to 30 days in advance. Public: Up to 14 days in advance

Ranger: Yes

Tee-off-Interval Time: 9 min.

Time to Play 18 Holes: 4½ hrs.

Course Hours/Earliest Tee-off: 6:30 a.m.

Green and Cart Fees: $60 Fri., Sat. Sun. holidays for 18 holes with cart. $50 Mon.-Thurs. for 18 holes with cart. $34 for 9 holes with cart

Credit Cards: All major cards

Season: Year round. Busiest season May to Sept.

Course Comments: Cart mandatory. Yardage book available

Golf Packages: Available through resort

Discounts: Twilight. Seasonal rates

Places to Stay Nearby: Best Western Dogwood Hills Resort and Golf Club (573) 348–1735, (800) 528–1234; Inn at Grand Glaize (573) 348–4731

Local Attractions: Country music, Ozark Caverns, Ozark national scenic riverways, boating, fishing, camping, beach and water sports such as water-skiing, hiking. BRANSON: Shepherd of the Hills Homestead, Shepherd of the Hills Outdoor Theatre, Silver Dollar City, historic district, country music, Table Rock Dam. COLUMBIA: University of Missouri—Columbia, including George Caleb Bingham Gallery, botany greenhouses and herbarium, and other sites; State Historical Society of Missouri. JEFFERSON CITY: State capitol, Missouri Veterinary Museum. SPRINGFIELD: Buena Vista's Exotic Animal Paradise, Fantastic Caverns, Museum of Ozarks' History, Springfield Nature Center. Missouri Division of Tourism (314) 751–4133, (800) 877–1234

Directions: 2½ mi. southwest of Grand Glaize Bridge on Hwy. 54, 2 mi. west on State Rd. KK

Closest Commercial Airports: Springfield Regional (1½ hrs.), Kansas City

International (3 hrs.), Lambert–St. Louis International (3 hrs.)

RESORT

Date Built: 1962

No. of Rooms: 930 guest rooms, suites, housekeeping cottages

Meeting Rooms: 26. Capacity of Largest: 2200 persons banquet style. Meeting Space: 65,000 sq. ft.

Room Price Range: $139 for standard room, single or double occupancy, to $799 for 6-bedroom suite. Mid-May to mid-Sept. rates. Lower seasonal rates available. Golf and other packages available

Lounges: Night Winds, Jetty Bar, Landing, Tradewinds, Mr. D's, Duffers

Restaurants: Wind Rose, Black Bear Lounge, The Oaks, Burger King, Sbarro Pizza

Entertainment: Music in Night Winds Lounge

Credit Cards: All major cards

General Amenities: Babysitting services, meeting and conference facilities with audiovisual and food services, social programs, supervised children's programs, playground, camera rentals

Recreational Amenities: 5 swimming pools, 4 wading pools, rental boats and motors, marina and ramp, fishing; water sports such as water-skiing, wave runners; 6 tennis courts (4 lighted, 2 indoor), horseback riding, sporting clays, health club, saunas, whirlpool, massage, jogging trails, ice skating, bowling, mopeds, excursion boat, miniature golf, 4 racquetball courts, fishing guides, billiards, table tennis, shuffleboard

Reservation and Cancellation Policy: Deposit required to hold reservation. Cancellation notice required at least 2 days before scheduled arrival date to avoid penalties

Comments and Restrictions: No pets allowed. Taxes additional to base rates

TAN-TAR-A GOLF CLUB

The Missouri Ozarks encompass approximately 33,000 square miles of rugged hills, plateaus and deep valleys. The Osage River is a primary tributary of the Missouri, and on the Osage, Bagnell Dam creates the 95-square-mile Lake of the Ozarks. Marriott's Tan-Tar-A Resort, Golf Club and Spa is in this popular recreation area, which features boating, fishing, hunting, camping, hiking, bicycling and many other activities.

The 6442-yard par-71 Oaks layout at Tan-Tar-A (a Blackfeet Indian phrase loosely meaning "one who moves swiftly") was designed by Bruce Devlin and Robert von Hagge, who have many quality golf courses to their credit. Though short, this well-treed, strategically bunkered, rolling layout will challenge any golfer, as evidenced by its slope rating of 140. As you might imagine, the course is hilly and tight, placing a premium on strategy, accuracy and golf-course management. There are water hazards on nine holes at the Oaks course.

One of the more memorable and challenging holes on the front nine is the ninth, a 528-yard par-5 dogleg right. The first shot is from an elevated tee downhill and the second shot is a long iron to a plateaued area at the corner of the dogleg. This gives you a view downhill to a deep green guarded by large ponds in front and to the left. There is also a large trap to the front right. Most players lay up to an area approximately 100 yards from the green, leaving a downhill-lie third shot to the green.

A challenging par 4 on the back nine is the 414-yard thirteenth, which plays from an elevated tee to a tight landing area with a creek paralleling the right fairway. The approach is to a deep green with traps on the left and right. A shot that strays slightly to the right will kick into the creek. As you approach the green there is a beautiful view of the Lake of the Ozarks.

A scenic par 3 at Tan-Tar-A is the 163-yard eighth, which is all carry over a lake to a wide, shallow green fronted by three traps and backed by another. Club selection and accuracy are obviously critical here. Many of the bentgrass greens at Tan-Tar-A are medium sized or small and undulating, and they are always well guarded.

The Oaks Course has a restaurant, bar, locker rooms, showers, and pro shop.

Nearby are complete practice facilities and lessons are available from the staff of PGA professionals at Tan-Tar-A. A variety of golf packages are available from the resort. Tan-Tara's Oak Course was the host site for the 1994 PGA Club Pro Championship.

The Marriott Tan-Tar-A Resort has a variety of recreational facilities including a marina, boating, fishing, sporting clays, tennis, racquetball, health spa, horseback riding, bowling, ice skating and many others. Babysitting services and supervised children's programs are offered. And there are a variety of banquet, boardroom, class-room and other meeting facilities, including a 30,000 square-foot meeting hall.

Meetings and Conventions magazine has presented the resort with its Gold Tee Award for golf and conference-facility excellence. Tan-Tar-A has an American Automobile Association 4-Diamond rating. *Golf Shop Operations* magazine has rated the Oaks course pro shop one of the best in America.

**Course Name: MISSOURI BLUFFS
                 GOLF CLUB**

Course Type: Public
Address: 18 Research Park Circle
               St. Charles, MO 63304
Phone: (314) 939–6494

GOLF COURSE

Head Professional: Dick Shaiper
Course Length/Par (All Tees): Back 7047/71, Gold 6610/71, Blue 6205/71, White 5801/71, Forward 5197/71
Course Slope/Rating (All Tees): Back 140/74.4, Gold 136/72.4, Blue 132/70.5, White 125/68.5, Ladies' White 120/72.7, Ladies' Forward 115/69.2
Course Architect: Tom Fazio (1994)
Golf Facilities: Full Pro Shop X, Snack Bar X, Lounge X, Restaurant X, Locker Room X, Showers X, Club Rental X, Club Repair Off Site, Cart Rental X, Instruction X, Practice Green X, Driving Range X, Practice Bunker X, Club Storage X
Tee-Time Reservation Policy: Up to 4 days in advance. 24-hr. cancellation policy
Ranger: Yes

Tee-off-Interval Time: 10 min.
Time to Play 18 Holes: 4 hrs. 15 min.
Course Hours/Earliest Tee-off: 6:30 a.m.
Green and Cart Fees: $100 plus tax for 18 holes Fri., Sat., Sun., holidays; $75 plus tax for 18 holes weekdays
Credit Cards: American Express, Master-Card, Visa
Season: Year round. Busiest mid-May to mid-Oct.
Course Comments: Can walk anytime at full golf fee
Golf Packages: Inquire at pro shop
Discounts: Twilight, frequent player
Places to Stay Nearby: ST. CHARLES: Best Western (314) 946–1000, (800) 528–1234; Boone's Lick Trail Inn Bed & Breakfast (314) 947–7000; Comfort Inn St. Charles/St. Louis Airport (314) 949–8700, (800) 228–5150; Econo Lodge (314) 946–9992, (800) 446–6900. ST. LOUIS: Doubletree Hotel and Conference Center (314) 532–5000, (800) 222–8733; Drury Inn at Union Station (314) 231–3900, (800) 325–8300; Ritz-Carlton (314) 241–9500, (800) 325–7353
Local Attractions: ST. CHARLES: First State Capitol Historic Site, Goldenrod Show-boat, The Lewis and Clark Center. DEFI-ANCE: Daniel Boone Home. St. Louis. St. Charles Convention and Visitors Bureau (314) 946–7776, (800) 366–2427. St. Louis Convention and Visitors Bureau (314) 421–1023, (800) 247–9791
Directions: Missouri Bluffs is 20 miles west of St. Louis. Take Hwy. 40 west-bound to Hwy. 94 Exit. Proceed back over Hwy. 40 on Hwy. 94 and make a left on the service road. Go 1 mi. to Research Park Circle and make a left to the golf course
Closest Commercial Airport: Lambert International St. Louis (30 min.)

MISSOURI BLUFFS GOLF CLUB

St. Charles was founded by French Canadians in 1769 and the area was called Les Petites Cotes—"the little hills"—for the low bluffs along the Missouri River. Now set in these hills 20 miles west of St. Louis is a new Tom Fazio-designed golf course featuring treelined fairways, a variety of elevation changes, and well-bunkered bentgrass greens.

The par 3s at Missouri Bluffs are long and strong, especially the 221-yard seventh which plays from an elevated tee to a plateaued green with a bunker to its front left. The most memorable hole on this layout is the 529-yard par-5 fifteenth whose first shot is from an elevated tee down to an ample landing area 100 feet below. The next shot is uphill toward a well-bunkered, large, undulating green. Adjustments to elevation changes and uneven lies are required to succeed at Missouri Bluffs whose terrain makes this course demanding from all tee distances.

The folks at Missouri Bluffs like to claim that they are renting you a private club for a day when you come to this privately owned public golf course. The modern clubhouse has a dining area, locker rooms and showers, a good pro shop, and banquet facilities for 150. The driving range has a three-tiered teeing area, and there are putting and chipping greens and practice bunkers. *Golf Digest* rates this course among the best new public courses of 1995. It is a welcome addition to a region in need of good public golf facilities.

Recommended Golf Courses in Missouri

Cape Giradeau:

Bent Creek Golf Course, Jackson, (314) 243–6060, Semiprivate, 18/6958/72

Within 1/2 Hour of Kansas City:

Excelsior Springs Golf Club, Lake St. Louis, (816) 630–3731, Public, 18/6650/72

Longview Lake Golf Course, Kansas City, (816) 761–9445, Public, 18/6835/72

Paradise Golf Club, Smithville, (816) 532–4100, Public. Outlaw: 18/6988/72. Posse: 18/6663/72

Shamrock Hills Golf Club, Lee's Summit, (816) 537–6556, Public, 18/6301/71

Shirkey Golf Club, Richmond, (816) 776–9965, Semiprivate, 18/6907/71

Swope Memorial Golf Course, Kansas City, (816) 523–9081, 18/6274/72

Lake of the Ozarks Region:

Lake Valley Golf and Country Club, Camdenton, (573) 346–7218, Semiprivate, 18/6430/72

North Port National Golf Club, Lake Ozark, (573) 365–1100, Resort, 18/7150/72

Within 1 Hour of St. Louis:

Cherry Hills Golf Club, Grover, (314) 450–4113, Public, 18/6450/72

Crystal Highlands Golf Club, Crystal City, (314) 933–3880, Public, 18/6551/72

Eagle Lake Golf Course, Farmington, (314) 756–6660, Semiprivate, 18/7093/72 (1½ hrs. south of St. Louis)

Hawk Ridge Golf Club, Lake St. Louis, (314) 516–2828, Public, 18/6619/72

Innisbrook Estates Golf Club, Wright City, (314) 745–3000, Resort, 18/6465/70

Quail Creek Golf Club, St. Louis, (314) 487–1988, Public, 18/6984/72

Tapawango National Golf Club, St. Louis, (314) 349–3100, Public, 18/7151/72

Springfield:

Deer Lake Golf Club, Springfield, (417) 865–8888, Public, 18/7001/72

Hidden Valley Golf Links, Clever, (417) 743–2860, Public, 18/6611/73

Honey Creek Golf Club, Aurora, (417) 678–3353, Public, 18/6732/71

Pointe Royale Golf Club, Branson, (417) 334–4477, Semiprivate, 18/6300/70

Missouri: Useful Information

Missouri Division of Tourism, P.O. Box 1055, Jefferson City, MO 65102, (314) 751–4133, (800) 877–1234

Missouri Department of Natural Resources, Division of Parks, Recreation and Historic Preservation, P.O. Box 176, Jefferson City,

MO 65102, (314) 751–3443, (800) 334–6946 (recreation information)

Missouri Department of Conservation, P.O. Box 180, Jefferson City, MO 65102, (314) 751–4115 (fishing and hunting regulations)

National Forests in Missouri, 401 Fairgrounds Rd., Rolla, MO 65401, (314) 364–4621, (800) 280–CAMP (national forest information and reservations)

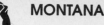

Course Name: **BUFFALO HILL GOLF CLUB Championship, Cameron Courses**

Course Type: Public
Address: North Main Street
P.O. Box 1116
Kalispell, MT 59901
Phone: (406) 756–4545

GOLF COURSE

Head Professional: Dave Broeder
Course Length/Par (All Tees): Championship: Back 6525/72, Middle 6247/72, Ladies' Forward 5258/74. Cameron: Back 3001/35, Ladies' Forward 2950/35
Course Slope/Rating (All Tees): Championship: Back 131/71.4, Middle 128/70.2, Ladies' Forward 125/70.3. Cameron: Back 122/68.0, Ladies' Forward 132/73.7
Course Architect: Championship: Robert Muir Graves (1977). Cameron: Unknown (1930s)
Golf Facilities: Full Pro Shop X, Snack Bar X, Lounge X, Restaurant X, Locker Room X, Showers No, Club Rental X, Club Repair X, Cart Rental X, Instruction X, Practice Green X, Driving Range X, Practice Bunker X, Club Storage X
Tee-Time Reservation Policy: 48 hrs. in advance from 7 a.m.
Ranger: Yes
Tee-off-Interval Time: 7 and 8 min.
Time to Play 18 Holes: 4½ hrs.
Course Hours/Earliest Tee-off: Dawn to dusk
Green Fees: Championship: $28 for 18 holes. Cameron: $13 for 9 holes
Cart Fees: $20 for 18 holes per cart, $10 for 9 holes per cart
Pull Carts: $3 for 18 holes, $1.50 for 9 holes
Credit Cards: Discover, MasterCard, Visa
Season: April to Nov. Busiest season June to mid-Sept.
Course Comments: Can walk anytime. Memberships available

Golf Packages: Available through local motels. Contact Flathead Valley Golf Association (406) 892–2111, (800) 543–3105
Discounts: March, April, Oct., Nov. package discounts. Contact Flathead Valley Golf Association or inquire at clubhouse
Places to Stay Nearby: Best Western Outlaw Inn (406) 755–6100, (800) 528–1234; Cavanaugh's (406) 752–6660, (800) THE–INNS; Motel 6 (406) 752–6355; Red Lion Motel (406) 755–6700, (800) 547–8010; Historical Kalispell Hotel (406) 752–5145. BED AND BREAKFAST: Brick Farmhouse Bed and Breakfast (406) 756–6230. Contact Flathead Valley Golf Association (406) 892–2111
Local Attractions: KALISPELL: Hungry Horse Dam, Conrad Mansion, Lone Pine State Park, Hockaday Center for the Arts. WHITEFISH: Big Mountain chairlift ride, Whitefish Lake State Recreation Area, Flathead National Forest, Glacier National Park. POLSON: Flathead Lake, Big Arm State Recreation Area, Elmo State Recreation area, Miracle of America Museum, Polson–Flathead Historical Museum, Polson Feed Mill, fishing, hunting, boating, camping, hiking, skiing. DAYTON: Mission Mountain Winery. PABLO: Flathead Indian Reservation. BROWNING: Museum of the Plains Indian. Kalispell Tourist Information (406) 756–7128. Glacier National Park (406) 888–5441
Directions: Intersection of Hwys. 2 and 93, follow signs, 6 blocks north from the intersection
Closest Commercial Airports: Glacier International (10 min.); Johnson Bell, Missoula (2½ hrs.)

BUFFALO HILL GOLF CLUB

The Buffalo Hill Golf Club course is located in the Flathead Valley in northwest Montana's "Glacier Country," which features Glacier National Park; magnificent wildlife such as mountain goats, bighorn sheep and bear; and rivers and wilderness lakes. This is a major resort area with guest ranches; abundant outdoor recreation including fishing, hunting, skiing, boating, camping, hiking and other activities; and tourist attractions such as restaurants, galleries, shops and museums. There are also many excellent public golf courses in this region, and Buffalo Hill is one of the best. In fact, it is ranked among the top 75 public golf courses in America by *Golf Digest* and is rated one of the best public or private courses in Montana by the same publication.

This beautiful, tight, tree-lined course is situated near Flathead Lake, the largest natural fresh-water lake in the western United States. Well known for its fishing, the lake is bordered by 6 state parks, as well as Wild Horse Island State Park, which is accessible only by boat. An original nine-hole course, the Cameron, was developed during the 1930s, and the clubhouse, a log structure with a magnificent stone fireplace, was built as part of a W.P.A. project during the Depression. Robert Muir Graves designed the 6525-yard 18-hole Championship Course, which opened in 1977.

An abundance of pine, willow, poplar, mountain ash, birch and other varieties of trees guards this target golf course, which has the Stillwater River running through it. The bentgrass greens are small, undulating, moderately fast, and strategically guarded by traps and mounds. There are many elevation changes at Buffalo Hill, which starts out on a plateau and then drops to a floodplain area beyond the fifth hole. Some of the most challenging holes are at the beginning of the course, which starts out with a 429-yard par-4 dogleg left playing down a tree-lined fairway to a green guarded by traps both left and right.

The second hole, a formidable 598-yard par 5, is the number-1-handicap hole on the course. The wind is often in the golfer's face, making it nearly impossible to reach the green in two. The tee shot is uphill to a plateaued landing area, then the fairway rolls down and back up to an undulating, elevated green. Few eagles have been made on this challenging hole in recent years.

A beautiful, long par 3 on the front side is the 225-yard fifth, which plays from an elevated tee to a well-trapped green 50 feet below. The sixth is a dogleg left with the river running along the left side of the fairway. The knee of the dogleg is approximately 190 yards from the tee and the corner can be cut on the left. The second shot is onto a well-trapped green with a large tree capable of obstructing shots coming in from the left.

An excellent hole on the back nine is the 412-yard par-4 seventeenth, a dogleg left. The fairway is severely sloped right to left, making it likely that you will have a sidehill and downhill lie on your approach shot to a green approximately 40 feet below. Unless you hit the ball 265 yards off the tee, this green will not be visible on the second shot. Should you play the ball too far to the left on the tee shot, the ball will kick out of bounds toward the river.

Although Buffalo Hill is not a long course, the combination of elevation changes; uneven lies; small, tricky, undulating greens; doglegs; tightly treed fairways; water hazards and strategically placed traps make this a fine test of golf. The Montana State Amateur has recently been held at Buffalo Hill, and the winning score for the tournament was over par. Be prepared to manage your golf game when you play Buffalo Hill.

Course Name: EAGLE BEND GOLF CLUB
Lake, Ridge Courses

Course Type: Semiprivate
Address: 279 Eagle Bend Drive
               P.O. Box 960
               Bigfork, MT 59911
Phone: (406) 837–7300,
               (800) 255–5641
Fax: (406) 837–7348

GOLF COURSE

Head Professional: Lon Hinkle
Course Length/Par (All Tees): Lake: Back 3497/36, Middle 3125/36, Forward 2574/36. Ridge: Back 6724/72, Middle 6189/72, Forward 5352/72
Course Slope/Rating (All Tees): Lake: Back 124/71.0, Middle 119/69.3, Ladies' Forward 121/70.6. Ridge: Back

121/71.2, Middle 117/69.1, Forward
118/69.7

Course Architect: Lake: Bill Hull (1988).
Ridge: Bill Hull (front 9, 1984) Jack
Nicklaus II (back 9, 1995)

Golf Facilities: Full Pro Shop X, Snack
Bar X, Lounge X, Restaurant X,
Locker Room X, Showers X, Club
Rental X, Club Repair X, Cart Rental
X, Instruction X, Practice Green X,
Driving Range X, Practice Bunker X,
Club Storage X

Tee-Time Reservation Policy: Up to 3
days in advance, or anytime for $3 ad-
vance booking fee

Ranger: Yes

Tee-off-Interval Time: 7 and 8 min.

Time to Play 18 Holes: 4 hrs. 15 min.

Course Hours/Earliest Tee-off: 7:30 a.m.

Green Fees: Ridge: $45 for 18 holes.
Lake: $35 for 18 holes. Lake: $19 for 9
holes

Cart Fees: $12 for 18 holes per person,
$8 for 9 holes per person

Pull Carts: $4 for 18 holes, $2 for 9 holes

Credit Cards: All major cards

Season: April through Oct. Busiest season
mid-June to mid-Sept.

Course Comments: Can walk anytime

Golf Packages: Available through hotels.
Contact Flathead Valley Golf Association (800) 934–5864

Discounts: Seasonal. Group packages

Places to Stay Nearby: Averill's Flathead
Lake Lodge (406) 837–4391; Timbers
Motel (406) 837–6200; Bayview Resort
(406) 837–4843; Marina Cay Resort
(406) 837–5861, (800) 433–7836 (MT),
(800) 433–6516 (outside MT). BED AND
BREAKFASTS: Burgraf's Country Lane
Bed and Breakfast (406) 837–4608;
O'Duachain Country Inn Bed and Break-
fast (406) 837–6851. HOUSEBOAT RENT-
ALS: Polson (406) 883–3700

Local Attractions: Hunting, fishing, hik-
ing, camping, boating, skiing, gambling,
horseback riding, Glacier National Park,
Flathead Lake, Wild Horse Island State
Park, National Bison Range, Bob Mar-
shall Wilderness, Flathead National
Wild and Scenic River, Museum of the
Plains Indian. Bigfork Summer Play-

house, Jewel Basin Hiking Area, Way-
farers State Recreation Area, Bigfork
Art and Cultural Center. POLSON: Big
Arm State Recreation Area, Elmo State
Recreation Area, Miracle of America
Museum, Polson–Flathead Historical
Museum, Polson Feed Mill. Bigfork
Tourist Information (406) 756–7128.
Glacier National Park (406) 888–5441

Directions: Hwy. 35 to Bigfork, to Holt
Dr. (just north of Bigfork), west on Holt
Dr. to golf course

Closest Commercial Airports: Kalis-
pel/Glacier International (25 min.);
Johnson Bell Missoula (1 hr., 45 min.)

EAGLE BEND GOLF CLUB

Eagle Bend Golf Club is one of the
newer courses in Montana's Flathead River
Valley. Its original 18, the Ridge and the
Lake, was selected runner-up as the best
new public golf course in 1989 by *Golf
Digest.* More recently it has been rated
among the best public golf courses in
America and the best public or private golf
course in Montana by the same publication.
In 1995, a new nine designed by Jack Nicklaus II, now the back nine of the Ridge,
was added to the golf venue here.

Eagle Bend is the centerpiece of a golf-
ing community real-estate development on
the northeastern shore of Flathead Lake in
Bigfork, Montana, home of the Bigfork
Summer Playhouse, the Jewel Basin Hiking
Area, Wayfarers State Recreation Area, Big
Fork Art and Cultural Center and other at-
tractions. In the surrounding area is Glacier
National Park and Big Mountain, one of
Montana's best ski resorts.

The golf courses wend their way
through a planned golf real estate community. There are water hazards on several
holes, and the moderately undulating
greens are medium to large in size, medium fast and well protected by bunkers
and water. A difficult hole on the front side
of the Ridge course is the par-4 sixth, that
plays a hefty 461 yards to a sizeable green
guarded left, front-right and rear by large
sand traps. The tee shot is up onto a hill
that often cannot be cleared by high handicappers. If you do clear the hill, it is likely

that you will have a tricky downhill lie on your approach shot. A scenic par 3 on this side is the 181-yard third hole, which affords beautiful views of Flathead Lake and the Mission Mountains from its elevated tee. The green, approximately 25 feet below, is well guarded by many bunkers. A variable wind coming off the lake and the nearby Flathead River can make club selection tricky on this hole.

The new back nine on the Ridges has rolling hills and several elevation changes with views of the river and lake from four of its holes. One of the more memorable and challenging holes on this side is the 211-yard par-3 sixteenth which plays to a wide, shallow green fronted by a bunker and almost surrounded by water. There is no bail out room on this scenic hole.

The Lake nine, which borders Eagle Bend's Yacht Harbor, works its way toward Flathead Lake and the river and has water on seven of its holes. This side features an "Amen Corner"—holes five, six and seven. The fifth is a 434-yard par 4 that plays straight to a green well guarded by traps to the rear and right. A lateral hazard, trees on the left and more trees on the right, make length and accuracy essential on this hole.

The 200-yard par-3 sixth has a lateral water hazard and plays to a narrow, deep green guarded by bunkers on the left and right. Pin placement to the back left and tucked behind the sand traps can make this hole especially difficult. The 412-yard par-4 seventh is a dogleg left, with water on the left from tee to green. The green has sand and water on the left and more sand bunkers on the right. An oncoming wind off Flathead Lake adds to the difficulty of this hole.

Eagle Bend has a clubhouse with locker rooms, showers, pro shop and a quality restaurant that serves lunch and dinner year round and breakfast from Memorial Day through Labor Day. Locker-room facilities are accessible only to members. On site is the Bigfork Athletic club with racquetball, squash and handball courts; a headed lap pool, tennis courts, weight room, exercise equipment and more.

A variety of annual green fees, nonresident memberships, range passes, junior plans, corporate passes, and other options is available. Also, you can consult the Flathead Valley Golf Association for information about local area golf packages.

The practice facility at Eagle Bend is an impressive 8 acres, with driving range, practice bunker and 2 practice greens. Individual and group instructional programs are available, including video instruction and swing analysis. The real-estate sales office is always open.

For a combination of the natural beauty of northwestern Montana and excellent golf, Eagle Bend provides a quality golf experience. The addition of the new Ridge nine will only add to the award-winning golf amenities at Eagle Bend.

Course Name: **WHITEFISH LAKE GOLF CLUB North, South Courses**

Course Type: Public
Address: Highway 93 North/Box 666
                Whitefish, MT 59937
Phone: (406) 862–4000 (Tee-Times only)
                (406) 862–5960 (Golf Shop)

GOLF COURSE

Head Professional: Mike Dowaliby

Course Length/Par (All Tees): North: Back 6556/72, Middle 6297/72, Forward 5556/72. South: Back: 6563/71, Middle 6144/71, Ladies' Forward 5358/72

Course Slope/Rating (All Tees): North: Back 118/69.8, Middle 116/68.7, Ladies' Forward 113/70.1. South: Back 122/70.5, Middle 120/69.0, Ladies' Forward 120/70.3

Course Architect: Original 9: NA (1936). Second 9: NA (1964). Third 9: Keith Helstrom (1980). Woods, Lake, Mountain: John Steidel (remodel, 1993). Fourth 9: John Steidel (remodel and addition, 1992)

Golf Facilities: Full Pro Shop X, Snack Bar X, Lounge X, Restaurant X, Locker Room X, Showers X, Club Rental X, Club Repair X, Cart Rental X, Instruction X, Practice Green X,

Driving Range X, Practice Bunker X, Club Storage X

Tee-Time Reservation Policy: Up to 2 days in advance from 7 a.m. Limit of 2 tee times per call

Ranger: Yes

Tee-off-Interval Time: 8 min.

Time to Play 18 Holes: 4 hrs.

Course Hours/Earliest Tee-off: 7 a.m.

Green Fees: $28 for 18 holes, $15 for 9 holes

Cart Fees: $24 for 18 holes, $15 for 9 holes per cart

Pull Carts: $3 for 18 holes, $2 for 9 holes

Credit Cards: MasterCard, Visa

Season: April 15 to Oct. 15. Busiest season July and Aug.

Course Comments: Can walk anytime. Memberships available

Golf Packages: Available through local motels. Inquire at pro shop. Contact Flatland Valley Golf Association (800) 392–9795

Discounts: Seasonal passes

Places to Stay Nearby: Bay Point Estates (406) 862–2331, (800) 327–2108; Alpinglow Inn at Big Mountain Ski and Summer Resort (406) 862–6966; (406) 862–3511, (800) 858–5439 (U.S.), (800) 637–7547 (Canada) for other lodging; Grouse Mountain Lodge (406) 862–3000, (800) 321–8822; Chalet Motel (406) 862–5581; Kandahar Lodge (406) 862–6098; Wildwood Condominiums (406) 862–2282, Pine Lodge Quality Inn (406) 862–7600, (800) 228–5151

Local Attractions: KALISPELL: Hungry Horse Dam, Conrad Mansion, Lone Pine State Park, Hockaday Center for the Arts. WHITEFISH: Big Mountain chairlift ride, Whitefish Lake State Recreation Area, Flathead National Forest, Glacier National Park. POLSON: Flathead Lake, Big Arm State Recreation Area, Elmo State Recreation area, Miracle of America Museum, Polson–Flathead Historical Museum, Polson Feed Mill, fishing, hunting, boating, camping, hiking, skiing. DAYTON: Mission Mountain Winery. PABLO: Flathead Indian Reservation. BROWNING: Museum of the Plains Indian. Whitefish Tourist Information

(406) 756–7128. Glacier National Park (406) 888–5441

Directions: From the east: Hwy. 2 west to Hwy. 40, west on Hwy. 40 to Hwy. 93 through Whiteface to golf course. From the west take I–90 north to Hwy. 93. Follow signs, course on Hwy. 93

Closest Commercial Airports: Kalispel/Glacier International (15 min.); Johnson Bell, Missoula (2½ hrs.)

WHITEFISH LAKE GOLF CLUB

The Whitefish Lake Golf Club is located in northwestern Montana, next to the Big Mountain Ski and Summer Resort and 30 miles west of Glacier National Park. Whitefish Lake has 36 holes of golf. The original nine was built in 1936 as a W.P.A. project during the Depression. The most recent nine was added in 1992 after various renovations and improvements over the years. *Golf Digest* currently ranks Whitefish Lake among the top five golf courses in the state of Montana.

The fairways at Whitefish Lake are well protected by pine, tamarack, birch and other varieties of trees. The bentgrass greens are large and fast, with subtle breaks and undulations on both the North and South courses. Bunkers are strategically placed, and there are water hazards on 9 of the 36 holes. From various spots on the golf course there are beautiful views of the Big Mountain ski runs and Whitefish Lake.

The signature hole at Whitefish Lake is the 194-yard par-3 fourth on the North Course (formerly the Woods nine). From the tee there is a splendid view of Big Mountain. The tee shot is over a small lake to a wide green bordered on three sides by water and backed by bunkers. A difficult hole on this side is the 435-yard par-4 third, which plays straight to a deep green guarded by a bunker on the right. The left is out of bounds, and to the right trees guard the fairway. Should you miss the green on your approach shot, you are likely to be in the trees or will have a tricky lob shot to reach the putting surface.

The back nine of the North, formerly the Lake Course, features the tough 396-

yard par-4 twelfth, a dogleg left that plays to a deep green guarded by two traps on the left. The hole is tree-lined from tee to green, with out of bounds on the right. As with most holes at Whitefish, length is not as important here as accuracy and club selection.

The South Course is another outstanding golf venue. A challenging hole here is the 486-yard par-5 third. The tee shot is over a stream that cuts the fairway. The next shot is toward a deep green guarded by a bunker on the left. Another good hole on this layout is the 200-yard par-3 seventh which plays to a green protected by wetlands and bunkers.

Looking back from the green to the tee you will get a breathtaking view of Big Mountain.

Practice facilities at Whitefish Lake include a driving range, practice bunker, chipping green and two practice putting greens. Individual and group instruction is available from the PGA teaching professionals on the staff.

The golf shop has been selected among the "Best 100 Golf Shops in America" by *Golf Shop Operations* magazine. You can walk the course anytime, and golf packages are available through the Flathead Valley Golf Association, or you can inquire at the pro shop. Over 70,000 rounds of golf are played here annually, but with two golf courses tee times are easy to schedule.

John Steidel, the designer and redesigner of the North and South courses was born in Nyack, New York, in 1950. He graduated from the University of California at Berkeley with a degree in landscape architecture and worked as a golf architect for Robert Muir Graves. After further graduate studies he worked in golf architecture and designed the Pacific Hills Country Club nine in Maltaz, Montana; and Canyon Lakes Golf and Country Club in Kennewick, Washington, with Peter Thomson, Michael Wolveridge, and Ronald Fream.

Recommended Golf Courses in Montana

Big Sky Golf Club, Big Sky, (406) 995–4706, Resort, 18/6750/72

Larchmont Golf Course, Missoula, (406) 721–4416, Public, 18/7114/72

Meadow Lake Golf Resort, Columbia Falls, (406) 892–2111, (800) 321–4653, Resort, 18/6714/72

Mission Mountain Country Club, Ronan, (406) 676–4653, Semiprivate, 18/6478/72

Polson Country Club, Polson, (406) 883–2440, Public, 18/6756/72

Red Lodge Mountain Resort and Golf Club, Red Lodge, (406) 446–3344, Resort, 18/6779/72

Montana: Useful Information

Montana Travel Promotion Division, Department of Commerce, 1424 9th Ave., Helena, MT 59620, (406) 444–2654, (800) 548–3390 (outside MT)

Montana Department of Fish, Wildlife and Parks, 1420 E. 6th Ave., Helena, MT 59620, (406) 444–2535, (800) 444–1200 (fishing and hunting regulations)

U.S. Forest Service, Northern Region, Federal Bldg., Missoula, MT 59801, (406) 329–3750, (800) 280–CAMP (national forest information and reservations)

Course Name: SHADOW RIDGE GOLF COURSE

Course Type: Semiprivate
Address: 1501 South 188th Plaza
Omaha, NE 68130
Phone: (402) 333–0500
Fax: (402) 333–8393

GOLF COURSE

Director of Golf: Steve Shanahan

Course Length/Par (All Tees): Back 7013/72, Diamond 6416/72, Blue 5872/72, Forward 5176/72

Course Slope/Rating (All Tees): Back 137/74.6, Diamond 132/71.9, Blue 127/69.4, Forward 120/66.3, Ladies' Blue 126/73.6, Ladies' Forward 116/69.8

Course Architects: Tom Sieckmann with Golf Research (1994)

Golf Facilities: Full Pro Shop X, Snack Bar X, Lounge X, Restaurant X, Locker Room No, Showers No, Club Rental X, Club Repair X, Cart Rental X, Instruction X, Practice Green X, Driving Range X, Practice Bunker X, Club Storage No

Tee-Time Reservation Policy: Up to 1 week in advance for the public

Ranger: Yes

Tee-off-Interval Time: 10 min.

Time to Play 18 Holes: 4 hrs. 15 min.

Course Hours/Earliest Tee-off: 7 a.m.

Green Fees: $45 for 18 holes Fri., Sat., Sun., holidays; $35 for 18 holes weekdays. $25 for 9 holes Fri., Sat., Sun., holidays; $20 for 9 holes weekdays

Cart Fees: $12 for 18 holes, $7.50 for 9 holes per rider

Credit Cards: MasterCard, Visa

Season: Apr. through Oct. Busiest June through Labor Day

Course Comments: You can walk anytime. No pull carts

Golf Packages: No

Discounts: Twilight

Places to Stay Nearby: Best Western Central Executive Center (402) 397–3700, (800) 528–1234; Embassy Suites Hotel (402) 397–5141, (800) 362–2779; The Offutt House (404) 553–0951; Omaha Marriott (402) 399–9000, (800) 228–9290; Ramada Inn-Airport (402) 342–5100, (800) 272–6232

Local Attractions: Aksarben Coliseum, Boys Town, The General Clock House Museum, Fontenelle Forest Nature Center, Joslyn Art Museum, The Omaha Children's Museum, Omaha's Henry Doorly Zoo, Strategic Air Command Museum, Western Heritage Museum, Great Plains Black Cowboy Museum, University of Nebraska, Standing Bear Lake, Glenn Cunningham Lake, seasonal festivals. Omaha Convention and Visitors Bureau, 6800 Maryland Rd., Suite 202, Omaha, NE 68106–2627 (402) 444–4660

Directions: From downtown Omaha (20 min.): Take I–80 west to Hwy. 680 north to Pacific St. Exit. Proceed west on Pacific St. approx. 4 mi. to golf course on the left at 187th St.

Closest Commercial Airport: Omaha Eppley Air Field (45 min.)

SHADOW RIDGE GOLF COURSE

Shadow Ridge is a new semiprivate course ensconced in an upscale real estate development on the west side of Omaha. This Tom Sieckman-designed layout is bentgrass from tee to its sizeable, well-bunkered greens. The course is rolling and open with variable winds a consideration on many holes. Newly planted trees will add to the difficulty of this layout. Water can come into play on ten holes. The club suggests that men with a handicap below 8 play the back tees, a 7013-yard journey sloped at a hefty 137 with a rating of 74.6. There are three other tee distances to chose from.

A difficult hole on the front side is the 414-yard par-4 ninth whose tee shot should be positioned to the left-center of the fairway to provide a clear approach to a deep, two-tiered green protected by bunkers to the rear, right, and front left. A lake guards the right side. The longest hole on the course is the 593-yard par-5 eleventh which drops 200 feet to a three-tiered green guarded by a lake to its right, a fescue mound in front, and a bunker to its rear. A scenic par 3 on the course is the 170-yard twelfth which plays over a small lake to a green edged by water and guarded by bunkers front and rear.

Across from the temporary clubhouse at Shadow Ridge is an excellent practice facility with two practice bunkers, a pitching green, a putting green, and two fairways with nine target greens. Shadow Ridge is rated among the best golf courses in Nebraska by *GolfWeek* and *Golf Digest*.

Course Name: WOODLAND HILLS

Course Type: Public
Address: 6000 Woodland Hills Drive
              Eagle, NE 68347
Phone: (402) 475–4653
Fax: (402) 780–5507

GOLF COURSE

Head Professional: Todd Peterson
Course Length/Par (All Tees): Back 6592/71, Gray 6245/71, White 5885/71, Forward 4955/71
Course Slope/Rating (All Tees): Back 125/71.3, Gray 121/69.7, White 121/71.7, Ladies' Forward 121/69.8
Course Architect: Jeffrey D. Brauer (1990)
Golf Facilities: Full Pro Shop X, Snack Bar X, Lounge X, Restaurant No, Locker Room No, Showers No, Club Rental X, Club Repair X, Cart Rental X, Instruction X, Practice Green X, Driving Range X, Practice Bunker No, Club Storage X
Tee-Time Reservation Policy: Up to 30 days with credit card guarantee. Up to 7 days without credit card
Ranger: Yes
Tee-off-Interval Time: 7 and 8 min.
Time to Play 18 Holes: 4½ hrs.
Course Hours/Earliest Tee-off: Sunrise
Green Fees: $21 for 18 holes
Cart Fees: $10.50 for 18 holes per person
Credit Cards: Discover, MasterCard, Visa
Season: Year round
Course Comments: You can walk anytime. Yardage book available
Golf Packages: Inquire at pro shop
Discounts: Special coupon offers

Places to Stay Nearby: LINCOLN: Best Western Airport Inn (402) 475–9541, (800) 528–1234; Comfort Suites (402) 464–8811; The Cornhusker (402) 474–7474, (800) 793–7474; Holiday Inn Airport (402) 475–4971, (800) HOLIDAY; Residence Inn by Marriott (402) 483–4900, (800) 331–3131; The Rogers House (402) 476–6961
Local Attractions: University of Nebraska, Salt Creek Lakes, Nebraska State Fair and other seasonal events, Antelope Park, Elder Art Gallery, Folsom's Children's Zoo and Botanical Gardens, Lincoln Children's Museum, Museum of Nebraska History, National Museum of Roller Skating, Pioneers Park and Nature Center, Sheldon Memorial Art Gallery and Sculpture Garden, State Capitol, Thomas P. Kennard House, University of Nebraska State Museum, fishing, water sports. The Lincoln Convention and Visitors Bureau, 1221 N St. 320, P.O. Box 83737, Lincoln, NE 68501 (402) 434–5337, (800) 423–8212
Directions: From Omaha (35 min. southeast): Take I–80 southeast to Exit 420 (Greenwood). Take Hwy. 63 south to Hwy. 34. Take Hwy. 34 west to Eagle. Then take Hwy. 43 south (4 mi.) to the golf course
Closest Commercial Airports: Lincoln (30 min.); Omaha Eppley Air Field (40 min.)

Recommended Golf Courses in Nebraska

Columbus:

Quail Run Golf Course, Columbus, (402) 564–1313, Public, 18/7042/72

Grand Island:

Grand Island Golf Course, Grand Island, (308) 385–5340, Public, 18/6752/72

Kearney:

Meadowlark Hills Golf Course, Kearney, (308) 233–3265, Semiprivate, 18/6485/71

Lincoln:

Highland Hills Golf Course, Lincoln, (402) 441–6081, Public, 18/7021/71

Himark Golf Course, Lincoln, (402) 488–7888, Public, 18/6700/72

Holmes Park Golf Course, Lincoln, (402) 441–8960, Public, 18/6752/72

Mahoney Golf Course, Lincoln, (402) 441–8969, 18/6459/70

Pioneers Golf Course, Lincoln, (402) 474–8966, Public, 18/6478/71

McCook:

Heritage Hills Golf Course, McCook, (308) 345–5032, Semiprivate, 18/6715/72

Omaha:

Applewood Golf Course, Omaha, (402) 444–4656, Public, 18/6916/72

Benson Golf Course, Omaha, (402) 444–4626, Public, 18/6814/72

Indian Creek Golf Course, Elkhorn, (402) 289–0900, Public, 18/7236/72

Tiburon Golf Club, Omaha, (402) 895–2688, Semiprivate. Three nines: 18/6887/72, 18/6932/72, 18/7005/72

Valley:

Pines Country Club, Valley, (402) 359–4311, Semiprivate, 18/6650/72

Nebraska: Useful Information

Nebraska Travel and Tourism Division, P.O. Box 9466, Lincoln, NE 68509, (800) 742–7595 (NE), (800) 228–4307 (outside NE)

Nebraska Game and Parks Commission, P.O. Box 30370, Lincoln, NE 68503, (402) 471–0641 (recreation information)

U.S. Forest Service, Rocky Mountain Region, 11177 W. 8th St., Lakewood, CO 80225, (303) 234–4185, (800) 280–CAMP (national forest information and reservations)

NEVADA

Las Vegas Area

**Course Name: DESERT INN
COUNTRY CLUB**

Course Type: Resort
Resort: Sheraton Desert Inn Resort
and Casino
Address: 3145 Las Vegas Blvd. South
Las Vegas, NV 89109
Phone: (702) 733–4290
(Golf Course)
(702) 733–4444,
(800) 634–4678 (Resort)
Fax: (702) 733–4790 (Resort)

GOLF COURSE

Director of Golf: Dave Johnson
Head Professional: Kevin Paulsen
Course Length/Par (All Tees): Back
7066/72, Blue 6685/72, White 6270/72,
Forward 5791/72
Course Slope/Rating (All Tees): Back
124/73.9, Blue 121/72.1, White
118/69.8, Ladies' Forward 121/72.7
Course Architect: Lawrence Hughes
(1951)
Golf Facilities: Full Pro Shop X, Snack
Bar X, Lounge X, Restaurant X,
Locker Room X, Showers X, Club
Rental X, Club Repair X, Cart Rental
X, Instruction X, Practice Green X,
Driving Range X, Practice Bunker X,
Club Storage X
Tee-Time Reservation Policy: Resort
guests: 1 yr. in advance or at time of
registration. Outside play: 2 days in
advance
Ranger: Yes
Tee-off-Interval Time: 8 min.
Time to Play 18 Holes: 4½ hrs.
Course Hours/Earliest Tee-off: 6 a.m. to
8 a.m. according to season
Green and Cart Fees: Resort guests: $135
for 18 holes with cart Fri., Sat., Sun.
holidays; $115 for 18 holes with cart
Mon. to Thurs. Outside play: $165 for
18 holes with cart
Credit Cards: All major cards
Season: Year round. Busiest season March
to May
Course Comments: Cart mandatory.
Yardage book available

Golf Packages: Year round. Available
through resort
Discounts: None
Places to Stay Nearby: Bally's Casino
Resort Las Vegas (702) 739-4111, (800)
634–3434; Best Western Main Street Inn
(702) 382–3455, (800) 528–1234; Caesar's Palace (702) 731–7110, (800) 834–
6661; Treasure Island (702) 894–7111,
(800) 944–7444; MGM Grand (702)
891–1111, (800) 929–1111; Luxor Las
Vegas (702) 262–4444, (800) 288–1000;
Harrah's Las Vegas (702) 369–5500,
(800) HARRAHS; Rio Suite Hotel and
Casino (702) 252–7600, (800) 634–
3101; Flamingo HiltonLas Vegas (702)
733–3111, (800) 732–2111; Golden Nugget Hotel (702) 385–7111, (800) 634–
3403; Mirage (702) 791–7111, (800)
456–7111; Residence Inn by Marriott
(702) 796–9300, (800) 331–3131; Sands
Hotel (702) 733–5000, (800) 446–4678;
Alexis Park (702) 796–3300, (800) 223–
0888; Aladdin Hotel and Casino (702)
736–0111, (800) 634–3424; Courtyard
by Marriott (702) 791–3600, (800) 321–
2211; Riviera Hotel and Casino (702)
734–5110, (800) 634–6753; Ramada
SuiteSt. Tropez Hotel (702) 369–5400,
(800) 666–5400; Dunes Hotel (702) 737–
4110, (800) 777–7777; Holiday Ca-
sino/Holiday Inn (702) 369–5000, (800)
634–6765. Las Vegas Convention and
Visitors Authority Room Reservations
(702) 383–9100, (800) 332–5333
Local Attractions: Circus Circus, Imperial
Palace Hotel Auto Collection, Las Vegas
Museum of Natural History, Binion's
Hotel, Liberace Museum, Lied Discovery Children's Museum, Nevada State
Museum and Historical Society, Old
Mormon Fort, Red Rock Canyon Recreation Lands, Ripley's Believe It or Not,
University of Nevada–Las Vegas, Valley
of Fire State Park, Wet 'N Wild, hunt-
ing, mountain climbing, swimming, boat-
ing, activities in area parks such as
Toiyabe National Forest and on Lake
Mead, Spring Mountain Ranch, Las
Vegas Stars AAA professional baseball,
theater, concerts, restaurants, night
clubs, gambling, shopping, Grand

Canyon and other air tours, Lake Mead/Hoover Dam, Great Basin National Park, horseback riding, ghost towns. Las Vegas Chamber of Commerce (702) 457–4664. Las Vegas Convention and Visitors Authority (702) 733–2323

Directions: From McCarran International, Las Vegas (15 min.): Swenson Rd. to Tropicana, left at Tropicana to Las Vegas Blvd., right turn onto Las Vegas Blvd., resort approximately 1/2 mile on the right

Closest Commercial Airports: McCarran International, Las Vegas (15 min.); Los Angeles International (6 hrs.)

RESORT

Date Built: 1950

No. of Rooms: 821 rooms, including singles, doubles, minisuites, 1- to 4-bedroom suites

Meeting Rooms: 9. Capacity of Largest: 775 persons banquet style. Meeting Space: 41,000 sq. ft.

Room Price Range: $95 for regular rooms, double occupancy, to over $1500 for 4-bedroom suite. Golf, spa, tennis, gourmet and other packages available year round

Lounge: Winners

Restaurants: Tara's Point, Monte Carlo, Portafino, Ho Wan

Entertainment: Crystal Room, Winners, 24-hour casino

Credit Cards: All major cards

General Amenities: Casino gambling with race and sports book, slot machines; meeting and conference facilities in banquet, theater, conference-room and other configurations with audiovisual and food services; shopping arcade

Recreational Amenities: 10 outdoor tennis courts (5 lighted) with instruction available; spa with weight training, jogging track, massage, whirlpools, steam, sauna, therapy pools and other amenities; swimming pool, 10 outdoor hydrowhirl pools

Reservation and Cancellation Policy: Credit card or 1 night's deposit to guarantee reservation. 48-hr. cancellation to avoid penalties

Comments and Restrictions: No pets. No rollaway beds. Children under 12 free of charge if staying with parents. Room tax and gratuities additional to base rates

DESERT INN COUNTRY CLUB

The Desert Inn's 7066-yard 18-hole championship golf course is an oasis amidst the glitter and glitz of sunny downtown Las Vegas. This Lawrence Hughes–designed layout is beautifully situated on 136 parklike acres with rolling fairways and large, undulating Bermuda-grass greens protected by sizeable sand bunkers. Mature trees, including palm, fig, pine, oleander, olive and other varieties, can easily come into play, and there are water hazards in the form of four lakes on seven holes. The Desert Inn is perennially listed as one of the best resort golf courses in America by *Golf Digest* and is the only resort course in the United States to host annually three professional tour eventsthe PGA's Las Vegas Invitational, the PGA Senior Tour's Las Vegas Senior Classic and the LPGA's Desert Inn Invitational.

One of the most famous holes at Desert Inn is the 214-yard par-3 seventh, which has been rated one of the most difficult golf holes on the PGA tour. A precise shot to the green is required because it is protected by a lake and by an intimidating stone wall in front and sand traps front and rear. The green is three-tiered and elevated, making it possible to hit the target and roll the ball back down into the water. This is the number-3-handicap hole on the course.

The number-1-handicap hole is the 431-yard par-4 ninth, a long and narrow hole that plays to a large green with traps to the left, right and to the rear. Water, which borders the left side of the fairway cuts very close to the green as you approach the target. The longest hole on the course is the 578-yard par-5 fifth, which has a large, well-guarded green protected by four large traps. The tee-shot landing area is guarded by two large bunkers and out-of-bounds on the right.

The back nine features a range of strategically trapped holes, including three strong finishing holes. The 178-yard par-3 sixteenth plays over water to a large green encricled by bunkers. The 418-yard par-4 seventeenth is a dogleg right to a deep green flanked by two traps on the left and a huge bunker on the right. The tee shot has to avoid water and a huge bunker on the right and a pair of bunkers on the left. The approach is over water cutting across the fairway approximately 100 yards from the target. The 436-yard par-4 finishing hole is a slight dogleg right with a long lake protecting the right side of the fairway. The approach shot is onto a large green with traps to the left and rear. Out-of-bounds and bunkers guard the left of the tee shot landing area and the approach is made difficult by water that cuts in front of the green from the right.

The clubhouse facility at Desert Inn is a modern, two-story structure overlooking the eighteenth green. The golf shop, locker rooms, Champions Deli and 2 meeting rooms are located on the main floor. On the second level is the Terrace Room, a banquet facility, and outside is an ample practice area, including a large practice driving range, sand bunker, one practice putting green and a practice chipping green. A staff of PGA teaching professionals are at the course daily. Golf packages are available year round.

There is a variety of recreational amenities at the Desert Inn resort in addition to golf, including an Olympic-sized swimming pool; shuffleboard courts, tennis courts (5 lighted) with instructional programs; exercise track; a complete 16,000-square-foot dual-facility (e.g. men's and women's) health spa with programs in hydrotherapy, thermotherapy, massage, skin care, toning and fitness, and 10 outdoor hydrowhirl spas. There are also excellent restaurants and the Crystal Room, featuring regular "showstopper" entertainment extravaganzas. The Desert Inn Hotel and Casino is rated a Four-Diamond establishment by the American Automobile Association.

The Desert Inn has a long tradition of attracting and entertaining celebrities from all walks of life. Presidents Lyndon Johnson, John F. Kennedy and Gerald Ford have been here, as have Charles Schulz, Joe DiMaggio, Frank Sinatra and many others. There is also a rich tradition of golf at the Desert Inn. The winners of the PGA Tournament of Champions, held here from 1953 through 1966, include Sam Snead, Jack Nicklaus and Arnold Palmer. That was when the prize money, $10,000 in silver dollars, was delivered to the champion in a wheelbarrow. Other PGA, PGA Seniors and LPGA event winners at the resort include Chi Chi Rodriguez, Nancy Lopez, Al Geiberger, and Pat Bradley. Jack Nicklaus and Al Geiberger share the course record with scores of 62.

Whether you are coming here just for the golf or for the entertainment excitement of the Desert Inn and Las Vegas, there is little possibility of boredom at this resort.

Course Name: THE LEGACY GOLF CLUB AT GREEN VALLEY

Course Type: Resort
Address: 130 Par Excellence Drive
Henderson, NV 89014
Phone: (702) 897–2187
Fax: (702) 897–2282

GOLF COURSE

Director of Golf: Ed Francese
Head Professional: Dave Barnhart
Course Length/Par (All Tees): Back 7233/72, Blue 6744/72, White 6211/72, Forward 5340/72
Course Slope/Rating (All Tees): Back 136/74.9, Blue 128/72.1, White 118/69.1, Ladies' Forward 120/70.1
Course Architect: Arthur Hills (1989)
Golf Facilities: Full Pro Shop X, Snack Bar X, Lounge X, Restaurant X, Locker Room X, Showers X, Club Rental X, Club Repair X, Cart Rental X, Instruction X, Practice Green X, Driving Range X, Practice Bunker X, Club Storage X
Tee-Time Reservation Policy: Public may reserve a tee time during the current month and the following month
Ranger: Yes

Tee-off-Interval Time: 8 min.

Time to Play 18 Holes: 4 hrs. 45 min.

Course Hours/Earliest Tee-off: 6 a.m.

Green and Cart Fees: $60 for 18 holes Fri., Sat., Sun., holidays; $50 for 18 holes weekdays

Credit Cards: American Express, Master-Card, Visa

Season: Year round. Busiest Oct.-Nov., Mar. through May

Course Comments: Cart required. Junior golf programs. Yardage book available

Golf Packages: No

Discounts: Annual discount program. Twilight rates 4 hrs. before sunset. Lower seasonal rates mid-June to mid-Sept.

Places to Stay Nearby: HENDERSON: Best Western Lake Mead Motel (702) 564–1712. LAS VEGAS: Alexis Park (702) 796–3300, (800) 582–2228; Caesar's Palace (702) 731–7110, (800) 634–6661; Golden Nugget (702) 385–7111; (800) 634–3454, Harrah's (702) 369–5500, (800) HARRAHS; MGM Grand (702) 891–1111, (800) 929–1111; The Mirage (702) 791–7111, (800) 627–6667; Rio Suite Hotel and Casino (702) 252–7600, (800) 777–1400; Sheraton Desert Inn (702) 733–4444, (800) 634–6909

Local Attractions: Lake Meade, Grand Canyon, Casino gambling, shows, restaurants, Circus Circus, Guiness World of Records Museum, Imperial Palace Antique and Classic Auto Collection, King Tut's Tomb and Museum, Las Vegas Natural History Museum, The Liberace Museum, Discovery Children's Museum, University of Nevada–Las Vegas, Red Rock Canyon National Conservation Area, Wet N' Wild, The Zoological–Botanical Park, hunting, fishing, boating, hiking, camping, Las Vegas Stars professional baseball, Valley of Fire State Park. Las Vegas Convention and Visitors Authority, 3150 S. Paradise Rd., Las Vegas, NV 89109 (702) 892–0711

Directions: From downtown Las Vegas (25 min.): Take Las Vegas Blvd. to Sunset Rd. Make left turn on Sunset to Green Valley Parkway. Take right turn on Green Valley to Wigwam and golf course

Closest Commercial Airport: Las Vegas McCarren International (10 min.)

THE LEGACY GOLF CLUB

The Legacy is an Arthur Hills–designed golf course set within a residential real estate development 9 miles from downtown Las Vegas. This rolling layout has few trees, but strategically placed bunkers and devilish mounds accentuated by lava grass and lava rock can add strokes to your score if your shots wander. Variable winds can also affect play at The Legacy.

The 473-yard par-4 third hole offers all you can handle on this golf course. The tee shot must avoid the 100-yard-long fairway bunker to the right and the approach to the two-tiered green must skirt the bunker guarding the left of the putting surface. The large, hand-mowed Penncross bentgrass greens at The Legacy require accurate approach shots in order to avoid multiple putts. An incoming wind on this long hole can make it play like a par 5.

The tee box at the 193-yard par-3 tenth has four tee distances, each signifying a card suit—spades, hearts, diamonds, and clubs. The tee shot on this hole is to a three-tiered green with a large bunker and some native desert to the right. A scenic par 5 on the back nine is the 515-yard seventeenth whose tee shot landing area is bordered by bunkers to the left and right. The second shot is toward a 40-yard-deep target with water to its left and bunkers to its right.

Within an easy walk of the modern Legacy clubhouse is a 30-station driving range, a short game practice area, and a 12,000 square foot putting green. The golf course caters to outings and the local tourist trade. The Legacy is rated one of the best golf courses in Nevada by *Golf Digest*.

Recommended Golf Courses in Nevada

Within 1 Hour of Las Vegas:

Angel Park Golf Course, Las Vegas, (702) 254–4653, Public. Mountain: 18/6722/71. Palm: 18/6743/71

Calvada Valley Golf and Country Club, Pahrump, (702) 727–4653, Semiprivate, 18/7036/71

Las Vegas Golf Club, Las Vegas, (702) 646–3003, Public, 18/6631/72

Las Vegas Hilton Country Club, Las Vegas, (702) 796–0013, (800) 884–1818, Resort, 18/6815/71

Las Vegas Indian Wells Country Club, Henderson, (702) 451–2106; Public, 18/6713/71

Las Vegas Pointe Resort, Las Vegas, (702) 658–1400, Public, 18/7158/72

Mirage Golf Club, Las Vegas, (702) 369–7111, 18/7078/72

Painted Desert Golf Course, Las Vegas, (702) 645–2568, Public, 18/6840/72

Royal Kenfield Country Club, Henderson, (702) 434–9000, Public, 18/7053/72

Sahara Country Club, Las Vegas, (702) 796–0013, Public, 18/6815/72

Sun City Las Vegas Golf Club, Las Vegas, (702) 254–7010, Semiprivate. Highland Falls: 18/6512/72. Palm Valley: 18/6849/72

Reno/Tahoe Area

Course Name: **DAYTON VALLEY COUNTRY CLUB**

Course Type: Semiprivate
Address: 51 Palmer Drive
               Dayton, NV 89403
Phone: (702) 246–7888
Fax: (702) 246–7894

GOLF COURSE

Director of Golf: Tom Duncan
Head Professional: Jim Kepler
Course Length/Par (All Tees): Back 7218/72, Championship 6637/72, Regular 5897/72, Forward 5161/72
Course Slope/Rating (All Tees): Back 136/72.9, Championship 130/70.1, Regular 124/67.2, Forward 118/64.2. Ladies': Back 140/79.1, Championship 133/75.7, Regular 129/72.1, Forward 121/68.4
Course Architects: Arnold Palmer and Ed Seay (1991)

Golf Facilities: Full Pro Shop X, Snack Bar X, Lounge X, Restaurant X, Locker Room X, Shower No, Club Rental X, Club Repair X, Cart Rental X, Instruction X, Practice Green X, Driving Range X, Practice Bunker X, Club Storage X
Tee-Time Reservation Policy: Up to 2 weeks in advance. Up to 1 year for groups of 20 or more
Ranger: Yes
Tee-off-Interval Time: 10 min.
Time to Play 18 Holes: 4½ hrs.
Course Hours/Earliest Tee-off: 7 a.m.
Green and Cart Fees: $70 for 18 holes
Credit Cards: MasterCard, Visa
Season: Year round. Busiest Dec.-Jan., July through Oct.
Course Comments: You can walk anytime at full golf fee
Golf Packages: Inquire at pro shop
Discounts: Seasonal. Lower rates from mid-Oct. through mid-May
Places to Stay Nearby: DAYTON: Days Inn (702) 883–3343, (800) 329–7466. CARSON CITY: Best Western Trailside Inn (702) 883–7300, (800) 528–1234. RENO: See page 430
Local Attractions: CARSON CITY: Seasonal festivals, Bowers Mansion Park, Nevada State Railroad Museum, Stewart Indian Museum. Carson City Convention and Visitors Bureau, 1900 S. Carson St., Suite 200, Carson City, NV 89701 (800) 638–2321. VIRGINIA CITY: The Castle, Piper's Opera House, Virginia and Truckee Railroad. Virginia City Visitors Bureau (702) 847 0177. Virginia City Chamber of Commerce (702) 847–0311. RENO: See page 431
Directions: From Reno–Cannon International Airport (1 hr.): Take Hwy. 395 south to Carson City. Turn east and proceed 10 mi. on Hwy. 50 to Dayton. Turn right at traffic signal in Dayton (Dayton Valley Rd.) and drive 3 mi. to golf course on the right
Closest Commercial Airport: Reno-Cannon International (1 hr.)

DAYTON VALLEY COUNTRY CLUB

The Dayton Valley Country Club is an Arnold Palmer and Ed Seay gem that is the centerpiece of a multimillion-dollar real estate development in the high desert one hour southeast of Reno. The course, which plays a formidable 7218 yards from the back tees, has 36 acres of lakes that can come into play on a majority of the holes. The course starts amicably with two friendly par 4s, a short par 5, a reasonable par 3, a moderate par 4, and then grabs you with a 179-yard par 3 over water to a green guarded by a huge bunker to its left. Next is a 426-yard par 4 whose tee shot has to avoid water on the left and whose approach shot must stay out of water to its right and left, and sand to the left. The eighth hole is a 529-yard par 5 lined with water down the right side and a deep green bracketed by water and backed by sand. The finishing hole on the front side is a tough 450-yard par 4 with water to the left of the tee shot landing area and water to the left and in front of a small, slightly elevated green protected by bunkers to its left.

The back nine concludes with a 537-yard par 5 whose first two shots must avoid sand and water to reach a deep green sandwiched between water to the left and sand to the right. If strayed shots don't find sand or water at Dayton Valley, your ball is likely to have an uneven lie among mounded areas along the fairways and around the greens. Over 2 million acres of earth were moved to ensure that you would find a golf challenge here.

Annual memberships are available at Dayton Valley. Plans for a new clubhouse and a hotel are in progress. The ample practice area includes a three-tiered range teeing area with six target greens, a chipping green, and a putting green. Dayton Valley is rated among the best golf courses in Nevada by *Golf Digest*.

Course Name: EDGEWOOD TAHOE

Course Type: Public
Address: Lake Parkway and Highway 50/P.O. Box 5400 Stateline, NV 89449

Phone: (702) 588–3566 (Pro Shop)
(702) 588–2787 (Clubhouse)

GOLF COURSE

Head Professional: Lou Eiguren

Course Length/Par (All Tees): Back 7491/72, Blue 6960/72, White 6544/72, Forward 5749/72

Course Slope/Rating (All Tees): Back 139/75.8, Blue 133/72.8, White 128/70.9, Ladies' Forward 130/72.5

Course Architect: George Fazio (1968)

Golf Facilities: Full Pro Shop X, Snack Bar X, Lounge X, Restaurant X, Locker Room X , Showers X, Club Rental X, Club Repair Limited, Cart Rental X, Instruction X, Practice Green X, Driving Range X, Practice Bunker X, Club Storage X

Tee-Time Reservation Policy: 2 wks. in advance from 6:30 a.m. (summer)

Ranger: Yes

Tee-off-Interval Time: 12 min.

Time to Play 18 Holes: 4½ hrs.

Course Hours/Earliest Tee-off: 7 a.m. (June to August), 8 a.m. otherwise

Green and Cart Fees: $125 for 18 holes with cart. Cart fees charged even if walking

Credit Cards: American Express, Master-Card, Visa

Season: First wk. in May to first wk. in Oct.

Course Comments: Can walk anytime but must pay cart fee. Yardage book available. Course closed 1 wk. in July for celebrity golf championship

Golf Packages: None

Discounts: None

Places to Stay Nearby: See Reno/Lake Tahoe area listing on page 430

Local Attractions: See Reno/Lake Tahoe area listing on page 431

Directions: From Lake Tahoe Airport (20 min.): Hwy. 50, right at South Lake Tahoe exit, right on Lake Pkwy. to course

Closest Commercial Airport: Lake Tahoe (20 min.)

EDGEWOOD TAHOE

According to *Golf Digest,* and most golfers who have been fortunate enough to play here, Edgewood Tahoe is one of America's best public golf courses. Situated on a 250-acre site at an elevation of 6200 feet and adjacent to Lake Tahoe, the course has a magnificent setting on what used to be a cattle ranch. The land was first purchased by the Park family in 1860, after they arrived in Tahoe by covered wagon from Missouri. The present owners are descendants of the original owners, and a Park family home, built in the 1860s and serving as an inn and a Pony Express station, still stands near the golf course.

Designed by George Fazio and completed in 1968, Edgewood Tahoe is kept in immaculate condition. Only up to 160 golfers per day play the course. Edgewood Tahoe has approximately 80 sand bunkers and many of them protect the large, undulating and terraced bentgrass greens that are usually fast. It is a considerable distance to reach most holes from the back tees. Then you have to cope with sand traps and huge greens that can yield three putts or more.

Many strategically placed tall trees come into play on the layout, which plays 7491 yards from the back tees. Water is a factor on eleven holes. The course plays shorter than the scorecard would indicate because of the high altitude, and there are four playing distances to choose from. Magnificent views of Lake Tahoe and the surrounding mountains make Edgewood Tahoe a memorable golf experience.

The longest hole at Edgewood Tahoe is the daunting 602-yard par-5 third hole, which is a slight dogleg to the right with a stream crossing the fairway about 100 yards in front of the tee and water bordering the left fairway almost to the green. Two fairway traps begin 175 yards from the tee, and another large trap is on the left, 230 yards out. The first shot is in between these traps, and the second shot should be hit slightly left down the tree-lined fairway. The green, which is slightly elevated, is large and is protected in front and to the left by large traps. It is not easy to reach this green in regulation.

A beautiful and challenging hole on the front nine is the 441-yard par-4 sixth, which is downhill to a deep green protected by three traps in front and one large trap in back. Water begins on the right side of the fairway from 100 yards in front of the putting surface and runs past the green to the right. The landing area on the tee shot is relatively narrow and protected by three fairway bunkers, two left and one right. The green has two levels with a swale through its center.

The 462-yard par-4 ninth hole is the number-1-handicap hole from the back tees. It has a narrow first shot through trees to a dogleg-right fairway. Two bunkers on the left protect the turn of the dogleg. The second shot opens up to a large, deep, two-tiered green protected by one large trap on the left and three on the right.

Water comes into play on six of the last nine holes, beginning with the number-2-handicap 431-yard par-4 tenth hole, whose green is protected on the front left by a large pond almost 100 yards long. The tee shot should be hit to the right of the pond, leaving 130 to 150 yards to a large green surrounded by four traps, with the front protected by water. The front part of the green slopes toward the water.

The 558-yard par-5 sixteenth is a spectacular hole with a tee shot from an elevated tee straight between two fairway bunkers that begin approximately 230 yards away. The next shot is down the narrow, tree-protected fairway to a landing area. Large pines squeeze in at this point, including two on the edge of traps on the right. The green is a hefty 48 yards deep and is protected by long traps bordering its left and right sides. Reaching this green in less than regulation is almost impossible because the prevailing winds are from green to tee.

Awaiting you at the nineteenth hole is the Terrace Lakeside Restaurant and Cocktail Lounge, which overlooks Lake Tahoe and the mountains beyond. Fazio, who also designed Jupiter Hills in Florida and many other golf courses, created a great course at Edgewood Tahoe. Jodie Mudd won the 1980 USGA Public Links Championship here, and Miller Barber won the USGA Senior Open here in 1985. The course is ranked among the best golf courses, public and private, in the state of Nevada by *Golf Digest,* and it is always ranked among the best public golf courses in the United States by leading golf publications.

Lake Tahoe is the largest Alpine lake in North America. It is 22 miles long, 12 miles wide and contains enough water to cover the state of California to a depth of 14 inches. Stateline is on the lower southeast corner of the lake at the California border and only 10 miles from the Lake Tahoe airport. Because of the mountains, lakes and rivers in the area, an abundance of year-round recreational activities is available, ranging from fishing, camping, boating and hunting, to skiing, ice-skating, sleighing and sledding. In the area are also many other quality golf courses accessible to the public. Approximately one hour from Stateline are the bright lights of Reno, which features several hotels, night clubs and gambling casinos as well as such attractions as the Nevada Museum of Art, the excellent William F. Harrah Foundation National Automobile Museum, and the Fleischman Planetarium.

The Incline Village/Crystal Bay Visitor and Convention Bureau can provide you with complete information and brochures, (702) 832–1606, (800) GO-TAHOE, and room reservations can be obtained through the Reno-Sparks Convention and Visitors Authority (702) 827–7366, (800) 367–7366.

Course Name: THE GOLF CLUB OF GENOA LAKES

Course Type: Semiprivate
Address: 1 Genoa Lakes Drive
               P.O. Box 350
               Genoa, NV 89411
Phone: (702) 782–4653
               (702) 588–GOLF
Fax: (702) 782–5899

GOLF COURSE

Director of Golf: Randy Fox
Course Length/Par (All Tees): Back 7263/72, Blue 6738/72, White 6057/72, Forward 5008/72

Course Slope/Rating (All Tees): Back 134/73.5, Blue 127/71.2, White 120/68.2, Forward 117/67.6
Course Architects: Peter Jacobsen and John Harbottle III (1993)
Golf Facilities: Full Pro Shop X, Snack Bar X, Lounge X, Restaurant X, Locker Room X, Showers X, Club Rental X, Club Repair X, Cart Rental X, Instruction X, Practice Green X, Driving Range X, Practice Bunker X, Club Storage X
Tee-Time Reservation Policy: Up to 30 days in advance
Ranger: Yes
Tee-off-Interval Time: 8 and 9 min.
Time to Play 18 Holes: 4½ hrs.
Course Hours/Earliest Tee-off: 6 a.m.
Green and Cart Fees: $75 for 18 holes Fri., Sat., Sun., holidays; $60 for 18 holes weekdays
Credit Cards: All major cards
Season: Year round. Busiest June through Labor Day
Course Comments: Can walk but you must pay full golf fee. Memberships available
Golf Packages: Inquire at pro shop
Discounts: Seasonal mid-Oct. through Apr.
Places to Stay Nearby: CARSON CITY: Days Inn (702) 883–3343, (800) 329–7466. CARSON VALLEY: Carson Valley Inn (702) 782–9711. SOUTH LAKE TAHOE: Embassy Suites Resort (916) 544–5400, (800) 362–2779; Forest Inn Suites (916) 541–6655, (800) 822–5950. STATELINE: Caesar's Tahoe (702) 588–3515, (800) 648–3353; Harrahs Hotel and Casino (702) 588–6611, (800) HAR-RAHS; The Ridge Tahoe (702) 588–3553, (800) 334–6000
Local Attractions: GENOA: Genoa Courthouse Museum, Morman Station Historic State Park, Great Basin National Park. LAKE TAHOE: Gatekeeper's Log Cabin Museum, boat cruises, fishing, hiking, camping, hunting, Ponderosa Ranch, D. L. Bliss State Park, Ehrman Mansion, Heavenly Valley Tram, The Ms. Dixie II Talac Historic Site, gambling, restaurants, nightclubs, winter skiing

Directions: From Stateline (18 miles east): Take Hwy. 50 south to Hwy. 207 east to Hwy. 206 north to golf course

Closest Commercial Airports: Lake Tahoe (45 min.); Reno–Cannon International (1 hr.)

THE GOLF CLUB AT GENOA LAKES

Within twenty miles and 1800 feet lower than Lake Tahoe is Carson Valley, home of the Golf Club at Genoa Lakes. This Peter Jacobsen and John Harbottle design anchors a 630-acre planned, gated residential community. The 7263-yard par-72 golf course has numerous wetland areas, including the Carson River, and the Sierra Mountains loom in the distance. This links-style course has water on 14 holes, but provides ample landing areas and large greens. The toughest hole on the course, aptly called "Long" in the droll Scottish tradition, is the 474-yard par-4 seventh, a slight dogleg left that plays uphill and often into the wind. The tee shot must skirt a large bunker guarding the right side of the right-to-left sloping fairway. A pond and heavy rough are on the left. The approach is to an elevated, deep, forward-sloping green protected by a bunker on the left. The greens at Genoa Lakes tend to be quick, grainy, and tricky because of the mountain setting.

A challenging par 3 on the back nine is the 232-yard fourteenth, "Cottonwood," a scenic hole that plays out of the cottonwoods by the river to a large, forward-sloping green with grass bunkers to its right. The most daunting par 5 on the course is the 652-yard thirteenth, "Plateau," that presents a dogleg left tee shot from the back tees. Bunkers and trees guard the left side. The second shot must avoid a pond on the right and the approach is to a green guarded by bunkers to its left front and right. The green slopes away toward the rear from its center. This hole plays 589, 564, and 517 yards from the other tee positions.

Genoa Lakes rewards distance, accuracy, and well-conceived approach shots that will leave one and two putt opportunities on the large greens. You will use all your clubs as you think your way around this superb layout, rated one of the best in Nevada by *Golf Digest*. A new clubhouse is scheduled to open in 1996 and a second course, designed by John Harbottle, is planned for 1997.

Course Name: INCLINE VILLAGE GOLF RESORT Championship, Executive Courses

Course Type: Public
Address: 955 Fairway Boulevard (Championship Course) 690 Wilson Way/P.O. Box 7590 (Executive Course) Incline Village, NV 89450
Phone: (702) 832–1144 (Championship Course) (702) 832–1150 (Executive Course)

GOLF COURSE

Head Professional: John Hughes

Course Length/Par (All Tees): Championship: Back 6910/72, Middle 6446/72, Forward 5350/72. Executive: Back 3513/58, Forward 3002/58.

Course Slope/Rating (All Tees): Championship: Back 129/72.6, Middle 124/70.5, Forward 123/70.5. Executive: Back 94/56.6, Forward 85/57.3.

Course Architects: Championship: Robert Trent Jones, Sr. (1964). Executive: Robert Trent Jones, Jr. (1969)

Golf Facilities: Full Pro Shop X, Snack Bar X, Lounge No, Restaurant X, Locker Room X, Showers X, Club Rental X, Club Repair X, Cart Rental X, Instruction X, Practice Green X, Driving Range X, Practice Bunker No, Club Storage No

Tee-Time Reservation Policy: Anytime from May 1 forward, up to 14 days in advance with credit card guarantee required

Ranger: Yes

Tee-off-Interval Time: 8 min.

Time to Play 18 Holes: 4 hrs., 15 min. (peak season)

Course Hours/Earliest Tee-off: 6 a.m.

Green and Cart Fees: Championship: $80 for 18 holes with cart from May through mid-June, $100 for 18 holes with cart afterward. Twilight rate 5 p.m. $50 for 18 holes with cart. Executive: $45 for 18 holes with cart, twilight rate $25 for 18 holes with cart

Credit Cards: MasterCard, Visa

Season: May 1 to Oct. 31

Course Comments: Can walk anytime, but must pay cart fees

Golf Packages: Residents

Discounts: Seniors, juniors

Places to Stay Nearby: See Reno/Lake Tahoe area listing on page 430

Local Attractions: See Reno/Lake Tahoe area listing on page 431

Directions: From San Francisco (4 hrs.): I–80 to CA Hwy. 267 to NV Hwy. 28, to Incline Village. From Reno-Cannon International Airport (45 min.): I–395 south to Hwy. 431, 18 miles on Hwy. 431 to Incline Village, take left on Country Club, right on Fairway

Closest Commercial Airport: Reno-Cannon International (45 min.)

INCLINE VILLAGE GOLF RESORT

The Incline Village Championship Course is rated one of the best public or private courses in the state of Nevada and one of the best public golf courses in the United States by *Golf Digest* magazine. Designed by Robert Trent Jones, Sr., and opened in 1964, the Championship Course plays 6910 yards from the back tees and is situated at 6500 feet above sea level in a spectacular mountain setting at the less developed northern end of Lake Tahoe.

Robert Trent Jones, Sr., one of the most accomplished golf architects of all time, was born in England in 1906, moved to the United States with his parents in 1911, became a scratch golfer while still a teenager and attended Cornell University, where he devised his own golf-course architecture curriculum from the existing curriculum. While still at Cornell he designed several greens at the Sodus Bay Golf Course in New York. After graduating from Cornell in 1930, Jones became a partner with the renowned Canadian golf architect Stanley Thomson. These architects were strong advocates of the strategic-design theory of golf-course architecture.

Today Jones is widely accepted as the most influential golf-course architect in history. He designed well over 400 courses in the United States and in more than 20 countries, ranging from Japan to Martinique. Many of his golf courses are in this book; a few of them include the Peachtree Golf Club in Atlanta, Georgia, with Robert Tyre "Bobby" Jones; Lakeridge Country Club in Reno, Nevada, with his son, Robert Trent Jones, Jr.; Spyglass Hill Golf Links, Pebble Beach, California; Cornell University Golf Course (9 holes), Ithaca, New York; Lower Cascades Golf Course, Hot Springs, Virginia; the Ferncroft Country Club in Danvers, Massachusetts, with his son Rees Jones; and many others. As part of his legacy, Robert Trent Jones also left his sons Robert Trent Jones, Jr., and Rees Jones, both excellent golf-course architects.

Incline Village's Championship Course has tightly cut, rolling fairways bordered by towering pines. This layout demands accuracy as well as distance. On approach shots, golfers are faced with heavily bunkered greens and lateral water hazards on almost every hole. Water comes into play on twelve holes, including every hole except the fourth on the front nine. The course record of 64, held by touring professional Julius Boros, still stands.

The number-1-handicap hole is the 619-yard par-5 fourth, which is tightly treed with out of bounds on the right on the first two shots. It is a relatively straight hole; and there are two bunkers on the right approximately 200 yards from the tee. On the second shot is a bunker to the left and one in the center of the fairway about 100 yards from a large green protected on the left by three traps and on the right by another one. The 428-yard par-4 twelfth hole is the number-2-handicap hole and is a slight dogleg right that is likely to leave you with a sidehill approach shot to a green protected in front by traps both left and right.

Among the local favorites on the Championship Course is the 221-yard par-3 fifth hole, which usually has a tee shot into the wind. There is no room for error on the left due to a stream running from tee to green and a large pond sitting in front of the kidney-shaped putting surface. The green is also protected in front by a fairway bunker to the right of the pond and about 25 yards from the green. A trap also protects the back of the green.

The 406-yard par-4 sixteenth hole has a dramatic view of the fairway, with Lake Tahoe in the distance. This hole is a sharp dogleg right with a stream running up the right side of the fairway. The stream cuts across the fairway approximately 125 yards in front of the green, which is trapped to the left, front and rear. The first shot should be laid up in front of the stream, but you have to avoid three fairway bunkers along the left at the turn of the dogleg. If you are feeling ambitious and want to cut the dogleg by going over the top on your tee shot, you have to clear 80-foot-tall pine trees.

There is also the Executive Golf Course at Incline Village, which measures 3513 yards and is a par 58. The course was designed by Robert Trent Jones, Jr., and is one of the best of its kind in the United States. This course is also carved out of the pines, with no harsh transition areas and no artificial landscaping. The Executive Golf Course features fourteen par 3s averaging over 170 yards in length and has hosted the National Championship of Executive Courses.

Incline Village holds a number of corporate and group outings each year. Refreshments and services ranging from brunch to rental clubs, cocktail parties, dinners, tournament awards and other amenities are available. Nearby are the bright lights of Reno and Lake Tahoe in this year-round resort area. You can walk the course anytime, but the full cart and green fee must be paid. The season at Incline Village is generally a comparatively short May through October, but tee times are taken with a credit-card guarantee anytime during the season. Don't

miss this wonderful golf opportunity if you are in the area.

There are many indoor and outdoor recreational activities and attractions in the Reno/Lake Tahoe area. Reno is less than an hour from Incline Village, and there are a number of day trips one can make to Virginia City, Carson City, Truckee, Gerlach, Pyramid Lake, and Fallon. The Incline Village/Crystal Bay area has elaborate hotel complexes such as the 458-room Hyatt Regency Lake Tahoe and the 200-room Cal-Neva Lodge Resort Hotel, which have a casino as well a health club, dining, swimming and other facilities.

Places to Stay in the Reno/Lake Tahoe Area

Caesar's Tahoe (702) 588–3515, (800) 648–3353; Clarion Hotel Casino (702) 825–4700, (800) 762–5190; Ridge Tahoe (702) 588–3131, (800) 334–1600; Flamingo Hilton Reno (702) 322–1111, (800) 648–4882; Harrah's Casino/Hotel Reno (702) 786–3232, (800) 648–3773; Harrah's Lake Tahoe (702) 588–6611, (800) HARRAH'S; Holiday Inn Convention Center (702) 825–2940, (800) 722–7366; Incline Village and Hotel Cal–Neva Lodge Resort Hotel and Casino, Hyatt Regency Lake Tahoe Resort/Casino (702) 832–1234, (800) 233–1234; Best WesternDaniel's Motor Lodge (702) 329–1351, (800) 528–1234; La Quinta Inn (702) 348–6100, (800) 531–5900; Motel 6 Reno Central (702) 786–9852, (800) 437–7486; Incline Village/Crystal Bay Condominiums Club Tahoe Resort (702) 831–5750, (800) 527–5154; Incline Village Sales Company (702) 831–3349; Vacation Station (702) 831–3664, (800) 841–7443. For additional information on camp-grounds, parks, picnic areas and beaches, contact: Reno City Parks and Recreation (702) 785–2262; Sparks Leisure Services Department (702) 356–2376; Washoe County Parks and Recreation (702) 785–6133; Incline Village General Improvement District (702) 832–1225; United States Forest Service (702) 331–6444

Local Attractions in the Reno/Lake Tahoe Area

Ballooning, bicycle rentals, boating, fishing, hiking, mountain biking, horseback riding, hunting, rafting, soaring, tennis, windsurfing, camping, night clubs, music and dance, restaurants, Nevada Museum of Art/ E. L. Weigand Gallery, Wilbur D. May Museum and Arboretum/Botanical Gardens, William F. Harrah Foundation, National Automobile Museum, Wilk Island Fun Resort Adventure Park, Fleischmann Planetarium, Mineral Museum, Nevada Museum, factory outlet shopping, gambling, lake cruises, Virginia City.

Information on Reno/Lake Tahoe area hiking, mountain biking and trails: U.S. Forest Service, Carson Division, (702) 882–2766. Hunting information can be obtained from the Nevada Department of Wildlife, 1100 Valley Rd., Reno, NV 89512, (702) 789–0500. Skiing and other snow recreation information can be obtained from the Sierra Ski Marketing Council, P.O. Box 9137, Incline Village, NV 89450. See the "Places to Stay" section of this listing for campground and park information sources.

General visitor information can be obtained from Incline Village/Crystal Bay Chamber of Commerce (702) 831–4440; Incline Village/Crystal Bay Visitors and Convention Bureau (702) 832–1606, (800) GO-TAHOE; Reno Chamber of Commerce (702) 786–3030; Reno-Sparks Convention and Visitors Authority (702) 827–7366, (800) 367–7366; Reno Downtown Visitors Center (702) 329–3558; Sparks Downtown Visitors Center (702) 358–1976; Stateline Chamber of Commerce (702) 588–4591. Be sure to obtain a copy of the Reno-Tahoe Visitor Guide

Recommended Golf Courses in Nevada

Within 1 Hour of Reno/Tahoe:

Eagle Valley Golf Club, Carson City, (702) 887–2380, Public. East: 18/6658/72. West: 18/6851/72

Lake Ridge Golf Course, Reno, (702) 825–2200, Public, 18/6703/71

Northgate Golf Club, Reno, (702) 747–7577, Public, 18/6966/72

Rosewood Lakes Golf Course, Reno, (702) 857–2892, Public, 18/6693/72

Elko

Ruby View Golf Course, Elko, (702) 738–6212, Public, 18/6928/72

Spring Creek Golf Course, Elko, (702) 753–6331, Semiprivate, 18/6230/71

Laughlin:

Emerald River Golf Course, Laughlin, (702) 298–0061, Resort, 18/6809/72

Mesquite:

Oasis Resort Hotel Casino, Mesquite, (702) 346–7820 (Oasis), (702) 346–5232 (Palms), (800) 621–0187, Resort. Oasis: 18/6982/72. Palms: 18/7008/72

Nevada: Useful Information

Commission on Tourism, Capitol Complex, Carson City, NV 89710, (800) 638–2328

Nevada Division of State Parks, Capitol Complex, Carson City, NV 89710, (702) 687–4387, (800) 237–0774 (state park recreation information)

Nevada Department of Wildlife, State Headquarters, 1100 Valley Rd., Reno, NV 89512, (702) 688–1500 (fishing and hunting regulations)

U.S. Forest Service, Intermountain Region, 324 25th St., Ogden, UT 84401, (801) 625–5306, (800) 280–CAMP

Northern

Course Name: **THE BALSAMS RESORT Panorama, Coashaukee Courses**

Course Type: Resort
Resort: The Balsams Grand Resort Hotel
Address: Route 26 Dixville Notch, NH 03576
Phone: (603) 255–4961 (Golf Course) (603) 255–3400, (800) 255–0800 (NH), (800) 255–0600 (U.S. and Canada) (Resort)
Fax: (603) 255–4221 (Resort)

GOLF COURSE

Director of Golf: Bill Hamblen
Course Length/Par (All Tees): Panorama: Back 6804/72, Middle 6097/72, Forward 5069/72. Coashaukee: Back 1917/32
Course Slope/Rating (All Tees): Panorama: Back 136/73.9, Middle 130/70.5, Forward 115/67.8. Coashaukee: Back 78/57.6
Course Architect: Panorama: Donald Ross (1912). Coashaukee: N/A
Golf Facilities: Full Pro Shop X, Snack Bar X, Lounge X, Restaurant X, Locker Room X, Showers X, Club Rental X, Club Repair X, Cart Rental X, Instruction X, Practice Green X, Driving Range X, Practice Bunker No, Club Storage X
Tee-Time Reservation Policy: Resort guests and visitors from 3 days in advance
Ranger: Yes
Tee-off-Interval Time: 10 min.
Time to Play 18 Holes: 4 hrs.
Course Hours/Earliest Tee-off: 7 a.m.
Green Fees: Resort guests: Included in base hotel American plan rates at all times. Public: $50 daily fee
Cart Fees: $32 for 18 holes per cart
Credit Cards: American Express, Discover, MasterCard, Visa
Season: Mid-May to mid-Oct.
Course Comments: Can walk anytime. Yardage book for Panorama Course available

Golf Packages: Available through resort. Resort packages offered late May through June, early Sept. to late Oct.
Discounts: None
Places to Stay Nearby: BED AND BREAKFASTS: New Hampshire Bed and Breakfast (603) 279–8348; Hearth and Hillsides Inn Association/Reservations and Information (800) 356–3596, (603) 356–2044; Appalachian Mountain Club Huts and Lodges (603) 466–2727. NORTH CONWAY: White Mountain Hotel (603) 356–7100, (800) 533–6301; Cranmore Inn (603) 356–5502. JACKSON: Christmas Farm Inn (603) 383–4313, (800) 443–5837; Inn at Thorn Hill (603) 383–4242; Dana Place Inn (603) 383–6822, (800) 537–9276. BRETTON WOODS: Mount Washington Hotel (603) 278–1000, (800) 258–0330
Local Attractions: Dixville Notch State Park, skiing, hiking, camping, Lost River Gorge, Mt. Washington, factory outlets, fishing, boating, horseback riding, hunting, White Mountain National Forest, antiques, covered bridges. GLEN: Heritage New Hampshire, Storyland. BRETTON WOODS: Mt. Washington Cog Railway. FRANCONIA: Franconia Notch State Park. Berlin. Sugar Hill. Lincoln. Woodstock. North Conway. Waterville Valley. Mount Washington Valley Visitors Bureau (603) 745–8720, (800) FINDMTS. Dixville Notch State Park (603) 788–3155. State Park Hrs. and General Information (603) 224–4666
Directions: From New York City (390 mi.) and Connecticut: I–95 to New Haven; north on I–91 to St. Johnsburg, VT; Rte. 2 east to Lancaster, NH; Rte. 3 to Colebrook, NH; east on Rte. 26 to Dixville Notch. From Boston (219 mi.): I–93 north to exit 35 past Francona Notch, NH; Rte. 3 to Colebrook, NH; east on Rte. 26 to Dixville Notch. From Montreal (152 mi.): East on Auto Rte. 10 to Magog; Rte. 55 south 8 mi. to Rte. 141 to Coaticook; Rte. 147 south to Norton, VT; east on Rte. 114 to Rte. 3; south to Colebrook; east on Rte. 26 to Dixville Notch

Closest Commercial Airports: Portland International, ME (2½ hrs.); Dorval International, Montreal, Canada (3 hrs.); Burlington International, VT (3 hrs.); Manchester Municipal (3 hrs.)

RESORT

Date Built: 1866

No. of Rooms: 232 rooms in the Dixville House, Balsams Inn, the Hampshire House

Meeting Rooms: 19. Capacity of Largest: 600 persons. Meeting Space: 4900 sq. ft.

Room Price Range: $149 for standard double room to $189 Balsams deluxe double room per person, per night, American plan. $189 for single room standard. Tower Suite (couples only) $575. Parlor suites $150 additional to double-room rates. Golf, Indian Summer, social season and other packages available

Lounges: Dining Room, Ballroom, Wilderness Lounge

Restaurants: Main dining room, Panorama; Golf Club House, Coffee Shop

Entertainment: Dancing, theater, night club, movies, chamber music, lectures, craft and culinary demonstrations

Credit Cards: American Express, Discover, MasterCard, Visa

General Amenities: Shops, supervised children's programs, library, hayrides, natural history program, teen entertainment, wine tastings, meeting and conference facilities with audiovisual and food service

Recreational Amenities: Aerobics, badminton, basketball, bicycling, billiards, board games; boating and canoeing, bocce, croquet, fishing, game room, hiking, climbing and walking trails; horseshoes, ice-skating, table tennis, shuffleboard, skiing, swimming in heated outdoor pool or lake, 6 tennis courts, volleyball

Reservation and Cancellation Policy: 1 night's deposit equal to the total rate for accommodation of your party required on all reservations and will be credited only to the last night of your reservation. For deposit refund, 14-day cancellation notice required prior to your scheduled arrival. A $25 service charge is deducted from deposit refunds. Telephone reservations will be held only 10 days without deposit

Comments and Restrictions: No pets. Taxes and gratuities additional to base rates. Summer season late May to mid-Oct., winter season mid-Dec. to early April. 15% service charge added to standard rate May, June, Sept. and Oct. Advance reservations for specific rooms cannot be assured on stays of less than 7 nights. From early July through late Aug., stays of less than 4 nights involving either Fri. or Sat. may not be reserved earlier than 10 days prior to arrival

THE BALSAMS RESORT

The Panorama Golf Course, as its name suggests, is one of the most magnificent of all golf-course layouts designed by the Scottish master Donald Ross. Built high up on the western side of Keyser Mountain, golfers are treated to spectacular views of the Connecticut river valley of northern New Hampshire, impressive Mount Monadnock in Vermont, and the rolling hills of the Province of Quebec in Canada to the north.

Nearly every shot on the course requires that the mountainside setting be considered. This is particularly true of putting. First-time players swear their ball breaks uphill until they learn to orient themselves to the mountain's slope. Small to medium-sized greens are hard to hit and hold, but the signature grass-walled sand bunkers that border most greens only on the right and left have been placed by Ross to serve as definition and perspective aids rather than as difficult hazards. In many cases the bunkers are larger than the greens themselves.

The Panorama course is relatively wide and forgiving, but generally it is best to approach the green so that you are hitting your approach into the slope of the mountain. The key is to correctly position your ball for a proper approach shot to the green because the greens are small, crowned and not that easy to hold. The approach shot is often a blind shot, because the greens are almost always elevated. Generally you should approach the green from the right. When you get to the putting surface, remember that putts tend to roll away from the mountain from east to west.

The first holes at the Panorama start from a high point, roll down over well-treed terrain, then work their way back up to the clubhouse. The third hole, for example, is a challenging par-4 dogleg left. The tee shot is reasonably straightforward to a landing area around the 150-yard marker. The second shot, however, is to an elevated green that is wide but only 22 yards deep. If your drive is not in proper position, a shot that is not lofted high and aimed properly is unlikely to hold this green, which has out of bounds behind it.

The 545-yard par-5 sixth, the number-1-handicap hole, is a slight dogleg-left uphill hole. The tee shot is over a small pond in front of the tee and should be kept to the right, as should the next shot. The approach is to another small, elevated green bordered by an exposed boulder on the left and a trap on the right.

By now you are aware that Donald Ross has masterfully used natural knolls, dunes and the natural contours of the land to create a wonderful golf challenge. Ross's original course was intended to play at approximately 6000 yards, but the tees have been adjusted for today's longer shots to make the course play as the architect originally intended. The combination of elevation change; likely uneven lies; blind approach shots; small, crowned greens; wind; fifteen holes with water hazards; and tricky putting surfaces makes this a great test of golf. Ross resided at the Balsams and personally supervised the construction of the course. Originally resort guests played on a six-hole layout designed by Charles Thom in 1897.

The back nine on the Panorama Golf Course begins with a level tenth hole, goes downhill on holes eleven through thirteen, uphill the next three holes, and then is flat on seventeen before you try the dramatic finishing hole. This 560-yard par 5 rises 145 feet from the tee to a narrow green.

The approach from 150 yards rises approximately 85 feet to the green, making the eighteenth the most difficult hole in the state.

There is also a nine hole par-32 executive course, the Coashaukee, which plays 1917 yards with holes ranging from 110 to 313 yards in length. This is an excellent place to practice or to begin learning the game.

This Ross course and the resort itself might have become extinct if one of the current owners, Steve Barba, had not taken over the management of the place in the early 1970s. Barba had been a caddy at the Panorama even after golf carts began to replace caddies who learned their craft at the hotel's caddy camp. In 1971, while Barba was teaching at Michigan State, he came back to the hotel and became involved in managing it. Eventually he formed an operating company for the resort with some partners and they have successfully brought it back to its former glory.

You are truly in another world when you first feast your eyes on The Balsams' 15,000 Shangri-La–like acres high in the mountains of northern New Hampshire. The Balsams heritage started in 1866 when the Dix House was opened to accommodate vacationers and travelers through Dixville Notch. Today the resort is a world-class destination resort with award-winning cuisine, rich cultural programs, a wide range of recreational activities, meeting and convention facilities, family-oriented children's programs and on-site shops such as a craft shop and silversmith shop. The Balsams is the only resort in New England rated both Four Stars by the *Mobil Travel Guide* and Four Diamonds by the American Automobile Association.

The Balsams has a "social season" that extends from the Fourth of July holiday week through Labor Day holiday week. During this part of summer, the hotel operation is entirely dedicated to the entertainment and accommodation of private guests and their personal vacations. "Convention season" takes place during the periods immediately preceding and following social season. The hotel does accept social guests during convention season based on availability, but the entertainment and activity schedule is curtailed. You can play golf anytime during this period, however, and special packages are available, starting from approximately $150 per person, per night, double occupancy, including the best-available accommodations, breakfast and dinner, unlimited golf, one golf cart per room per night for one round of eighteen holes, and a program of activities for nongolfers.

The Balsams has over 400 labels of both domestic and imported wine to enhance its excellent dining facilty. American plan meals feature such delicacies as roast-stuffed breast of duck, poached fillet of Boothbay Harbor haddock, and Ducktrap River smoked trout. Vegetarian meals are served, as is a wide variety of breakfast foods ranging from Scottish kippers to shredded wheat.

Recreational activities are varied and wide-ranging at this beautiful resort, which features 6 tennis courts with a pro shop and instructors, boating, fishing, hiking, bicycling, swimming, billiards and a variety of other activities. The resort closes from mid-October until mid-December, when it becomes a winter wonderland for skating, snowmobiling, cross-country skiing, alpine skiing and snow shoeing. A brief break is then taken from early April until late May, when the resort opens again until October. During the winter this area has approximately 250 inches of snow.

The golf course has two fully equipped pro shops and a mountain-top clubhouse with locker room, shower, dining and lounge facilities along with a staff of PGA teaching professionals who provide individual or group instruction. A practice green is available, but there is no driving range. All recreational amenities, including green fees, are included in the resort's base American plan prices which include 3 meals a day. *Golf* magazine rates The Balsams among the best golf resorts in America.

If you are looking for a classic Donald Ross golf experience at one of the best resorts and recreation areas in the United

States, visit the Balsams. You'll never forget it.

Recommended Golf Courses in New Hampshire

North of Hanover

Jack O'Lantern Resort, Woodstock, (603) 745–8121 (Office), (603) 745–3636 (Pro Shop), Resort, 18/5829/70

Mountain View Golf Course, Whitefield, (603) 837–2511, Resort, 9/2873/35

Mount Washington Hotel and Golf Club, Bretton Woods, (603) 278–1000, Resort, 18/6638/71

North Conway Country Club, North Conway, (603) 356–9391, Public, 18/6659/71

White Mountain Country Club, Ashland, (603) 536–2227, Public, 18/6408/71

Southern

Course Name: BRETWOOD GOLF COURSE
North, South Courses

Course Type: Public
Address: East Surrey Road
                Keene, NH 03431
Phone: (603) 352–7626

GOLF COURSE

Head Professional: Matt Barrett
Course Length/Par (All Tees): North: Back 6974/72, Blue 6434/72, White 5822/72, Forward 5140/72. South: Back NA/72, Blue NA/72, White NA/72, Ladies' Forward NA/72
Course Slope/Rating (All Tees): North: Back 134/73.9, Blue 128/71, White 128/68.4, Ladies' Forward 120/70.1. South: Back 129/72.1, Blue 126/70.8, White 123/69.5, Ladies' Forward 120/70.1
Course Architects: Geoffrey Cornish and William G. Robinson (18 holes, 1968), Geoffrey Cornish (9 holes, 1995), Hugh Barrett (9 holes, 1995)
Golf Facilities: Full Pro Shop X, Snack Bar X, Lounge Beer, Wine, Restaurant No, Locker Room No, Showers X, Club Rental X, Club Repair X, Cart

Rental X, Instruction X, Practice Green X, Driving Range X, Practice Bunker X, Club Storage No

Tee-Time Reservation Policy: Members: Call Tues. for following Sat. or Sun. tee times. Outside play: Call Wed. for following Sat. or Sun. tee times. First come, first served weekdays

Ranger: Yes

Tee-off-Interval Time: 8 min.

Time to Play 18 Holes: 4½ hrs.

Course Hours/Earliest Tee-off: Dawn to dusk

Green Fees: $28 for 18 holes weekends, holidays; $24 for 18 holes Mon. to Fri. $14 for 9 holes weekends, holidays; $13 for 9 holes Mon. to Fri.

Cart Fees: $20 for 18 holes, $10 for 9 holes

Pull Carts: $2 for 18 holes, $1 for 9 holes

Credit Cards: Discover, MasterCard, Visa

Season: Mid-April to mid-Nov. Busiest season June to Aug.

Course Comments: Can walk anytime

Golf Packages: None

Discounts: All-day green fees

Places to Stay Nearby: Carriage Barn Guest House (603) 357–3812; Chesterfield Inn (800) 365–5515; Days Inn (603) 352–7616, (800) 325–2525; Ramada Inn (603) 357–3038; Valley Green Motel (603) 352–7350. BED AND BREAKFAST: Monadnock Bed and Breakfast Association (603) 585–6540

Local Attractions: KEENE: Monadnock Children's Museum, Colonial Theater, Horatio Colony House Museum, Wyman Tavern Museum, Colony Mill Marketplace. MONADNOCK REGION: Friendly Farm, Cathedral of Pines, bicycle touring, Monadnock State Park. Peterborough. Hancock. Fitzwilliam. Monadnock Travel Council (603) 532–6637. Keene Chamber of Commerce (603) 352–1303

Directions: From I–91, exit 3, east on Rte. 9, follow Blue "H" hospital signs to Court St., take East Surrey Rd. left 2 mi. to golf course. From New Hampshire Rte. 3, exit 7, Rte. 101A west to 101 west, onto Main St. At second set of lights make right, follow hospital signs,

1 mi. past hospital make right on East Surrey Rd., 2½ mi. to golf course

Closest Commercial Airport: Manchester Municipal (1½ hrs.)

BRETWOOD GOLF COURSE

The Bretwood Golf Course is an excellent, privately owned public golf course situated on former farmland in the southwestern corner of New Hampshire. Bretwood's eighteen-hole North Course was designed by Geoffrey Cornish and William G. Robinson and is rated one of the best golf courses in New Hampshire by *Golf Digest*. Bretwood has large, moderately fast bentgrass greens that are mowed daily. Pin placements are also rotated daily to withstand wear and tear on this popular layout. The ample tee areas with four tee positions are also well maintained. Tee distances range from 6974 to 5140 yards.

Landing areas are generous on these rolling fairways, but mature oak, maple, pine, spruce, hemlock, apple and other tree varieties can come into play if the ball strays too far. The Ashuelot River winds through the course, and there are direct or lateral water hazards on almost every hole. The combination of water and large sand traps can make it a challenge to reach the large, undulating putting surfaces. And when you get there, it might take a few putts to get down.

The number-1-handicap hole on Bretwood's North Course is the 612-yard second hole, whose tee shot is down a row of intermittent maples, spruces, pines and hemlocks toward a deep, two-tiered green guarded by a large bunker on the right. The second shot is flanked by the river on the left and must avoid a pond on the right as you work your way down the fairway. As you approach the green, the river is only 15 yards from the left-front edge. Most golfers are very happy with a par on this endurance test.

A memorable par-3 hole at Bretwood is the 145-yard thirteenth, which has an island green that is huge but has little margin for error. The 434-yard tenth hole is a difficult par 4. On the tee shot it plays down a corridor of trees. The approach is to a tiered green protected by a pond on its left front. To the rear is the omnipresent river, which is only 20 yards from the green. Another tough par 4 is the 450-yard ninth, a slight dogleg right to a deep green flanked by a pond on the right and a trap to the left and toward the front. The second shot is likely to be a long iron or a wood, which can easily find these hazards.

The finishing hole would seem to be a very manageable 378-yard par 4, except that the deep green is very sharply angled right to left, making it a shallow target if your tee shot is too far right. A fairway bunker can catch a tee shot hit for position down the left side, and a trap to the left front of the green can easily block approach shots coming in from that angle. Farther right of the green is a pond, which can also catch errant approach shots.

The South Course at Bretwood is a nine-hole Cornish-designed course that the Barrett family, which owns and manages Bretwood, has recently turned into an eighteen-hole layout by adding another nine holes designed by Hugh Barrett. In their way was the dwarf wedge mussel, an endangered species that resides in the Ashuelot River. The Barretts have successfully negotiated with the Environmental Protection Agency, Army Corps of Engineers and other parties to gain permission to expand the golf course. Running a quality golf facility is more complicated than the game itself sometimes.

The clubhouse facility is modest but functional. The two-story, 5600-square-foot structure has rest rooms and showers, a snack bar restaurant, a pro shop, and a beer and wine bar. A balcony overlooks the golf course and practice area, which includes a generous, 300-yard-long practice range, chipping green and putting green. Individual and group lessons are available from Matt Barrett, a member of the founding family, and his staff. You can walk the course anytime, and tee times are only taken for weekend play. Members can make these tee times 2 days earlier than nonmembers.

Keene, New Hampshire, and the Bretwood Golf Course are located in the Monadnock region, where Grand Monadnock Mountain, at 3165 feet, dominates the landscape. This region has a countryside of gently rolling farmland, town meeting houses on village greens and winding roads that command a leisurely pace. The area's natural beauty, 39 towns and villages, outdoor recreational amenities and cultural events should be made part of your golf outing.

Bretwood itself is a beautifully maintained golf course and a challenging golf experience.

Course Name: THE COUNTRY CLUB OF NEW HAMPSHIRE

Course Type: Public
Address: Kearsarge Valley Road
                   P.O. Box 142
                   North Sutton, NH 03260
Phone: (603) 927–4246

GOLF COURSE

Head Professional: Kevin Gibson
Course Length/Par (All Tees): Back 6727/72, Middle 6226/72, Forward 5396/72
Course Slope/Rating (All Tees): Back 125/71.6, Middle 122/69.6, Ladies' Forward 127/71.7
Course Architects: Wayne Stiles and John Van Kleck (9 holes, 1930), William Mitchell (9 holes, 1963)
Golf Facilities: Full Pro Shop X, Snack Bar X, Lounge X, Restaurant X, Locker Room X, Showers X, Club Rental X, Club Repair X, Cart Rental X, Instruction X, Practice Green X, Driving Range X, Practice Bunker X, Club Storage X
Tee-Time Reservation Policy: Up to 1 wk. in advance
Ranger: Yes
Tee-off-Interval Time: 8 min.
Time to Play 18 Holes: 4½ hrs.
Course Hours/Earliest Tee-off: Dawn to dusk
Green Fees: $30 daily fee Sat., Sun., holidays; $25 for 18 holes weekdays
Cart Fees: $22 for 18 holes
Credit Cards: Discover, MasterCard, Visa

Season: April 1 to Nov. 1. Busiest June–Sept.

Course Comments: Can walk anytime

Golf Packages: Available through motel on premises. Inquire at pro shop

Discounts: Twilight rates

Places to Stay Nearby: Motel on premises (603) 927–4246. NEWPORT: Inn at Coit Mountain (603) 863–3583, (800) 367–2364. SUNAPEE: Dexter's Inn (603) 763–5571, (800) 232–5571; Seven Hearths Inn (603) 878–3285. HANOVER: Hanover Inn (603) 643–4300, (800) 443–7024. NEW LONDON: New London Inn (603) 526–2791. Lodging Reservation Service, Sunapee Region (603) 763–2495, (800) 258–3530

Local Attractions: Covered bridges, boating, camping, hiking, antiquing, bicycling, Mount Sunapee State Park. ENFIELD: Lower Shaker Village. GRAFTON: Ruggles Mine. HANOVER: Dartmouth College, Hood Museum of Art, Hopkins Center for Creative and Performing Arts, crafts. SUNAPEE: Lake Sunapee. CANAAN: Canaan historic tours. CLAREMONT: Historic tours, Saint Gandius National Historic site. Hanover Chamber of Commerce (603) 643–3115. Lake Sunapee Business Association (603) 763–2495, (800) 258–3530 (in New England)

Directions: I–89 to exit 10, on northeast side of highway take a right at T, go 1/2 mi. to first left, turn left and go 1½ mi. to course

Closest Commercial Airport: Manchester Municipal (45 min.)

THE COUNTRY CLUB OF NEW HAMPSHIRE

The Country Club of New Hampshire is just west of Interstate 89 in the wooded foothills of Mount Kearsarge. Wayne Stiles and John Van Kleck designed an original nine in 1930, then in 1963 William Mitchell remodeled the entire course, which now totals eighteen excellent holes. The Country Club of New Hampshire is ranked among the best courses in the state of New Hampshire by *Golf Digest.*

Water comes into play on seven holes, and most of the large, concave greens are guarded by well-placed traps. There are several doglegs on the course. The front nine tends to be level, whereas the back nine is hilly, longer and more difficult. The 440-yard tenth hole is a tough dogleg right that plays over a stream on the tee shot. The first shot has to reach a landing area over 200 yards away for the golfer to have any chance of reaching the green in regulation. The fairway slopes from left to right, however, and you will most likely be playing a difficult sidehill lie on your second shot. The green is a deep target that slopes left to right and back to front. A trap protects the front right of the putting surface. Too much club will carry the ball over the back of the green and down a hill.

A challenging par 3 on the back side is the 217-yard fifteenth, which plays to a very deep green with three formidable bunkers left, right and directly in front of the green. The 144-yard par-3 eleventh is all carry over water to a large green with a huge trap between the right front of the target and the water.

The number-1-handicap hole on the course is the beautiful 445-yard par-4 sixteenth, which heads straight toward Mount Kearsarge. This dogleg right plays to an open landing area, but the long approach shot has to get by a large bunker to the left and front of the green. Another trap on the right and approximately 50 yards from the putting surface can also be a nemesis.

The finishing hole is a 510-yard par 5 that plays straight to a large green squeezed in front by two large bunkers. The tee shot is over water, which should not come into play as it is directly in front of the tee. There are, however, a group of bunkers in the center and right fairway that can easily catch your tee shot. The approach, especially if you're trying to reach the green in two, is a real challenge on this hole.

When you hole your last putt, the clubhouse is only a few feet away. Facilities include a restaurant, bar and full pro shop, and a 28-room motel is just across the road should you opt to stay here. Practice facilities include a driving range and putting green.

The Country Club of New Hampshire is in a beautiful, rustic region of west central New Hampshire that includes Lake Sunapee; Lake Sunapee State Park; Hanover, the home of Dartmouth College; and a wide range of inns, bed and breakfasts, historic sites and recreational amenities ranging from golf to water sports on Lake Sunapee, which is 10 miles long and 3 miles wide. The Country Club of New Hampshire is a good way to discover this area.

Course Name: EASTMAN GOLF LINKS

Course Type: Semiprivate
Address: Clubhouse Lane
Star Route 3, Box 1
Grantham, NH 03753
Phone: (603) 863–4500

GOLF COURSE

Head Professional: Dick Tuxbury
Course Length/Par (All Tees): Back 6731/71, Middle 6338/71, Ladies' Forward 5369/73
Course Slope/Rating (All Tees): Back 137/73.5, Middle 133/71.7, Ladies' Forward 128/71.9
Course Architects: Geoffrey Cornish and Bill Robinson (1972)
Golf Facilities: Full Pro Shop X, Snack Bar X, Lounge X, Restaurant X, Locker Room X, Showers X, Club Rental X, Club Repair X, Cart Rental X, Instruction X, Practice Green X, Driving Range X, Practice Bunker X, Club Storage For Club Members
Tee-Time Reservation Policy: Up to 2 days in advance
Ranger: Yes
Tee-off-Interval Time: 8 min.
Time to Play 18 Holes: 4½ hrs.
Course Hours/Earliest Tee-off: 8 a.m. weekdays, 7:30 a.m. weekends
Green Fees: $37 for 18 holes
Cart Fees: $15.50 for 18 holes per person
Credit Cards: MasterCard, Visa
Season: Late Apr. to early Nov. Busiest June through Labor Day

Course Comments: Can walk during the week. Yardage book available. Condominium rentals on site (603) 863–4444
Golf Packages: No
Discounts: No
Places to Stay Nearby: GRANTHAM: Gray Ledges (603) 863–1002. HANOVER: The Hanover Inn (800) 443–7024. NEW LONDON: New London Inn (603) 526–2791. LEBANON: Days Inn (603) 448–5070, (800) 329-7466
Local Attractions: HANOVER: Dartmouth College, Hood Museum of Art, Hopkins Center, crafts. CLAREMONT: Claremont Historical Society Museum, Claremont Opera House and Atrium, Saint–Gaudens National Historic Site, camping, hiking, fishing, boating, antiquing, historic homes and museums, winter skiing. Claremont Chamber of Commerce (603) 543–1296. Hanover Chamber of Commerce (603) 643–3115. Lebanon Chamber of Commerce (603) 448–1203
Directions: Take Rte. 89 to Exit 13/Rte. 10. Take Rte. 10 southwest to golf course 500 yds. from Rte. 89
Closest Commercial Airports: Concord (40 min.); Manchester Municipal (1 hr.); Logan International, Boston, MA (2 hrs.)

EASTMAN GOLF LINKS

Eastman Golf Links is part of a real estate recreational development featuring tennis, skiing, boating, swimming, hiking, and other activities. Designed by Geoffrey Cornish and Bill Robinson, the course is wooded, on rolling hills, and has no parallel fairways. Sidehill, uphill, and downhill lies are common at Eastman which demands accuracy from tee to green.

The number one handicap hole on the course is the 421-yard par-4 ninth, a dogleg right that bends uphill to a medium-sized green protected on both sides by small bunkers. The greens on this layout are Penncross bentgrass, subtly undulating and moderately fast. A beautiful hole, especially during the leaf season, is the 466-yard par-4 twelfth whose tee shot provides a scenic view of wooded mountains. The fairway is treelined all the way to a moderately sized green. Another difficult hole at

Eastman is the 14th, a 417-yard par-4 dogleg left that climbs uphill to a green protected in front by a large pond. This is one of four holes at Eastman where water can come into play.

Eastman provides a quality resort-style golf experience. The golf course is rated among the best in New Hampshire by *Golf Digest* and hosts a variety of local tournaments.

Course Name: **PORTSMOUTH COUNTRY CLUB**

Course Type: Semiprivate
Address: Portsmouth Avenue
Greenland, NH 03840
Phone: (603) 436–9719

GOLF COURSE

Head Professional: Joel St. Laurent
Course Length/Par (All Tees): Back 7068/72, Middle 6609/72, Ladies' Forward 6202/78
Course Slope/Rating (All Tees): Back 125/73.6, Middle 122/71.5, Ladies' Middle 140/79.4, Ladies' Forward 135/77.1
Course Architects: Robert Trent Jones, Sr., and Frank Dunne (1957)
Golf Facilities: Full Pro Shop X, Snack Bar X, Lounge X, Restaurant No, Locker Room X, Showers X, Club Rental X, Club Repair X, Cart Rental X, Instruction X, Practice Green X, Driving Range X, Practice Bunker No, Club Storage X
Tee-Time Reservation Policy: Up to 24 hrs. in advance
Ranger: Yes
Tee-off-Interval Time: 8 min.
Time to Play 18 Holes: 4½ hrs.
Course Hours/Earliest Tee-off: 6 a.m.
Green Fees: $50 for 18 holes
Cart Fees: $20 for 18 holes per cart
Pull Carts: $3 for 18 holes
Credit Cards: Discover, MasterCard, Visa
Season: Mid-April to mid-Nov.
Course Comments: Can walk anytime. Memberships available
Golf Packages: None
Discounts: None

Places to Stay Nearby: PORTSMOUTH: Sise Inn (603) 433–1200, (800) 267–0525; Howard Johnson's (603) 436–7600, (800) 446–4656; Holiday Inn (603) 431–8000, (800) HOLIDAY; Sheraton Portsmouth Hotel and Conference Center (603) 431–2300, (800) 325–3535. HAMPTON BEACH: Ashworth by the Sea (603) 926–6762, (800) 345–6736 (outside NH)
Local Attractions: Portsmouth Trail historic walking tour, deep-sea fishing, Portsmouth harbor cruises, Children's Museum of Portsmouth, Water Country Water Park, Port of Portsmouth Maritime Museum, Rye Beach, Odiorne Point State Park, island tours, factory outlets, boating, camping, hiking. Seacoast Council on Tourism (603) 436–7678, (800) 221–5623 (outside NH). Portsmouth Chamber of Commerce (603) 436–1118
Directions: From I–95 north: Exit 3, left and west on Rte. 101, follow signs (1/2 mile), course on right. From I–95 south: Exit 3A, right and west on Rte. 101, follow signs (1/2 mile), course on right
Closest Commercial Airports: Portland International, ME (1 hr.); Manchester Municipal Airport (1 hr.); Logan International, Boston, MA (1 hr. 10 min.)

PORTSMOUTH COUNTRY CLUB

The Portsmouth Country Club was originally a private club but is now owned by the club members and is open to the public. In 1957 Robert Trent Jones, Sr., with the assistance of Frank Dunne, completed this 7068-yard layout, which is the longest in the state of New Hampshire. It is also the only Robert Trent Jones, Sr., course in the Granite State. Portsmouth Country Club is bordered by Great Bay, and approximately half the course is situated on a peninsula that protrudes into the bay. As you might guess, wind is a major variable when considering how to play this demanding golf course.

The bluegrass greens here are medium sized to large, moderately fast, undulating and protected by a few large sand traps. There are few fairway bunkers on this open layout, which has water hazards on four holes. There is no out of bounds here, and the marshlands are played as lateral water hazards.

The number-1-handicap hole on the golf course is the 514-yard par-5 fourth, which is a dogleg left to a large green tightly protected in front by sand traps to the left and right. On the left is the Great Bay, which you can try to cross to the elevated green on your second shot, or you can lay up and try to reach the right-to-left-sloping green in three. You'll find that most of the greens at the Portsmouth Country Club are slightly elevated and well protected in front. This generally forces you to fly the ball into the target.

From the back tees, there are eight par-4 holes that measure over 400 yards, including the 472-yard twelfth, which is the longest par 4 in New Hampshire. This hole bends slightly right to a small green that juts out into the Great Bay on a peninsula called Pierce's Point. The combination of distance, the small target (which is guarded by a trap on the left) and wind, which is usually oncoming, makes this a tough golf hole.

A tricky par 3 at Portsmouth is the 175-yard fifth, which has water on the left as you come onto a green protected by two traps, one to the right and the other front-right. The water comes very close to the green at high tide, and the wind coming off the bay is always a factor. A pin placement tucked behind the front trap makes this hole a challenging test of golf.

Usually ranked among the top five golf courses in New Hampshire by *Golf Digest*, Portsmouth Country Club has hosted many tournaments, including the New Hampshire Open, the New Hampshire Amateur, and the New England Amateur. The facilities include a clubhouse with restaurant, bar, banquet room, locker rooms and showers. A small pro shop is in a separate building. A driving range and practice green are available, as is instruction. You can walk the course anytime, and getting on it is fairly easy, but it is busier during the summer season.

Course Name: SHATTUCK INN GOLF COURSE

Course Type: Public
Address: 28 Dublin Road
                     Jaffrey, NH 03452
Phone: (603) 532–4300

GOLF COURSE

Head Professional: Lyman J. Doane II
Course Length/Par (All Tees): Back 6701/71, White 6077/71, Gold 5412/71, Forward 4632/71
Course Slope/Rating (All Tees): Back 145/74.1, White 140/70.1, Ladies' Gold 142/74.7, Ladies' Forward 139/73.1
Course Architect: Brian Silva (1991)
Golf Facilities: Full Pro Shop X, Snack Bar X, Lounge No, Restaurant No, Locker Room No, Showers No, Club Rental No, Club Repair X, Cart Rental X, Instruction X, Practice Green X, Driving Range X, Practice Bunker X, Club Storage No
Tee-Time Reservation Policy: Up to 30 days in advance weekdays, Wed. before weekends
Ranger: Yes
Tee-off-Interval Time: 10 min.
Time to Play 18 Holes: 4½ hrs.
Course Hours/Earliest Tee-off: 7 a.m. till dark
Green Fees: $35 for 18 holes, $20 for 9 holes
Cart Fees: $22 for 18 holes, $11 for 9 holes
Credit Cards: American Express, Master-Card, Visa
Season: May 1 to Nov. 1
Course Comments: Can walk anytime
Golf Packages: Available through some hotels
Discounts: None
Places to Stay Nearby: Monadnock Inn (603) 532–7001; Benjamin Prescott Inn (603) 532–6637; Woodbound Inn (603) 532–8341
Local Attractions: MONADNOCK REGION: Friendly Farm, Cathedral of Pines, camping, hiking, boating, fishing, other outdoor recreational activities at nearby Mount Monadnock, skiing. MANCHESTER: Currier Museum of Art, Manches-

ter Historic Association, Manchester Institute of Arts and Sciences. KEENE: Monadnock Children's Museum, Colonial Theater, Horatio Colony House Museum, Wyman Tavern Museum, Colony Mill Marketplace. Peterborough. Hancock. Fitzwilliam. Monadnock Travel Council (603) 532–6637

Directions: From Hartford 91 north: To Rte. 10 exit (Bernardston), Rte. 10 east to Rte. 119 East to Rte. 202, north on Rte. 202 to Jaffrey Center, Rte. 124 left, west 2.3 mi.

Closest Commercial Airports: Manchester Municipal (1½ hrs.); Logan International, Boston, MA (2 hrs.)

SHATTUCK INN GOLF COURSE

When you drive down country road 124 and come upon the Shattuck Inn Golf Course, you'll think it has been there since the Pilgrims arrived in New England. Actually, it was opened in 1991 and was designed by Brian Silva. At 145 from the back tees, the course has one of the highest slope ratings in New England, and many claim it is too difficult because of its sixteen holes with wetlands or water.

The Shattuck Inn Golf Course is one of the most beautiful and challenging anywhere. Crossed by 33 bridges and alive with fox, deer, blue heron, beaver and many other varieties of wildlife and foliage, playing Shattuck Inn is like playing a wetlands nature preserve.

Many of the holes are beautiful and challenging. Number ten, a 426-yard par 4, is a downhill dogleg left sloping into a tightly protected large green with bunkers to the right and left front. In the background is Mount Monadnock. The number-1-handicap hole is the 612-yard par-5 fifth hole, which is relatively straight but well protected by a corridor of trees and rock that requires accuracy as you work your way down the fairway to the well-bunkered green. Because of the wetlands, rocks, trees and well-placed traps, accuracy and shot placement strategy are extremely important at Shattuck Inn.

Shattuck Inn provides you with an interesting array of distances and hole configurations to choose from. The par 5s range from 544 yards to 612 yards from the back tees; the par 4s, 315 yards to 432 yards; and the par 3s, 160 to 200 yards. One of my favorite holes is the first, because your initial impression as you get out of your car and see the old, yet-to-be-restored inn is that you must have come to the wrong place. After you leave the pro shop and walk around the corner to the first tee, the panorama of a nature preserve awaits you as you look from the slightly elevated tee to the target, 357 yards away. The hole is a dogleg left par 4, and the first shot has to hit a landing area approximately 210 yards away to avoid wetlands on the left and water that cuts the fairway. The approach is to a mildly undulating green protected by bunkers on the left and right.

As you work your way around the Shattuck Inn layout, you become oblivious to everything except the beautiful course at hand. There are no highways abutting the holes, no real-estate development, and very few distractions except for wildlife, your fellow golfers and the search for an occasional lost ball.

At this writing *Golf Digest* rates Shattuck Inn the best golf course in the state of New Hampshire.

**Course Name:　SKY MEADOW
　　　　　　　　COUNTRY CLUB**

Course Type:　Semiprivate
Address:　　　2 Sky Meadow Drive
　　　　　　　Nashua, NH 03062
Phone:　　　　(603) 888–9000

GOLF COURSE

Head Professional: Richard Ingraham
Course Length/Par (All Tees): Back 6590/72, Middle 6036/72, Forward 5127/72
Course Slope/Rating (All Tees): Back 133/73.3, Middle 128/70.8, Ladies' Forward 131/71.2
Course Architect: William Amick (9 holes, 1986; 9 holes, 1988)
Golf Facilities: Full Pro Shop X, Snack Bar X, Lounge X, Restaurant X, Locker Room X, Showers X, Club Rental X, Club Repair X, Cart Rental

X, Instruction X, Practice Green X, Driving Range X, Practice Bunker No, Club Storage X

Tee-Time Reservation Policy: Members: Up to 7 days in advance from 7 a.m. Outside play: 48 hrs. in advance

Ranger: Yes

Tee-off-Interval Time: 9 min.

Time to Play 18 Holes: 4½ hrs.

Course Hours/Earliest Tee-off: 6:30 a.m.

Green and Cart Fees: $72.50 for 18 holes with cart Sat., Sun., holidays; $62.50 for 18 holes with cart Fri., $52.50 for 18 holes with cart Mon. to Thurs.

Credit Cards: American Express, Master-Card, Visa

Season: Mid-April to mid-Nov.

Course Comments: Cart mandatory, though members can walk in afternoon

Golf Packages: None

Discounts: None

Places to Stay Nearby: Sheraton Tara Hotel (603) 888–9970, (800) 325–3535; Holiday Inn of Nashua (603) 888–1551, (800) HOLIDAY; Nashua Marriott Hotel (603) 880–9100, (800) 228–1234; Clarion Somerset Hotel (603) 595–4100, (800) 252–7466; Best Western Haymark Motor Inn (603) 888–1200, (800) 528–1234

Local Attractions: WITHIN 2 HRS.: The New Hampshire coast, Hampton Beach, Odiorne Point State Park, Portsmouth, Great Island, Isle of Shoals, factory outlets, fishing, boating, camping, hiking. LAKES REGION: Lake Winnipesaukee, Center Harbor Children's Museum, Wakefield Corner, Meredith–Laconia League of New Hampshire, Lake Sunapee, Dartmouth College, Monadnock State Park, Cathedral of Pines, camping, boating, fishing, hiking, rafting. Boston. Cornish. Keene. Hancock. Peterborough. Seacoast Council on Tourism (603) 436–7678, (800) 221–5623 (outside NH). Lakes Region Chamber of Commerce (western NH) (603) 352–1303. Lake Sunapee Business Association (603) 763–2495, (800) 248–3530 (in New England). Hanover Chamber of Commerce (603) 643–3115. Monadnock Travel Council (603) 352–1303. Peterborough Chamber of Commerce (603)

924–7234. Nashua Chamber of Commerce (603) 891–2471

Directions: From Boston (35 mi.): I–95 to Rte. 3 north, take exit 1, turn left onto Spit Brook Rd. (1½ mi.), golf course on your left. From Manchester (25 mi.): Rte. 3 south to exit 1, right on Spit Brook Rd. (1½ mi.) to golf course on your left

Closest Commercial Airports: Manchester Municipal (45 min.); Logan International, Boston, MA (1 hr., 15 min.)

SKY MEADOW COUNTRY CLUB

Sky Meadow, a 6590-yard par-72 layout ensconced in a 257-acre real-estate development in Nashua, is rated among the top 5 golf courses in New Hampshire by *Golf Digest*. William Amick designed this modern strategic layout, which features contoured fairways, sizeable bentgrass greens and a variety of sand bunkers and water hazards. Amick played on the Ohio Wesleyan University golf team and formed his own golf-course design business in 1959. He has remodeled and designed numerous golf courses including the Sawgrass Golf Club Oakbridge Course in Ponte Vedra Beach, Florida; Green Meadows Country Club in Augusta, Georgia; the Three Pines Country Club in Woodruff, South Carolina; and the Vineyards Golf Club in Naples, Florida. He has helped establish higher standards for integrating real-estate development with golf-course design, has helped popularize shorter courses, and has advocated the use of shorter-distance golf balls to reduce course length. The Eagle Landing Country Club in Hanahan, South Carolina, designed by Amick, is the first course designed to use modified golf balls.

There are many memorable and challenging holes at Sky Meadow including the tough 231-yard par-3 third which plays from a dramatic elevated tee to a wide, shallow target more than 150 feet below. The green is protected by bunkers left-front and right. Another good hole on this side is the 409-yard par-4 dogleg-left ninth. The tee shot must be hit to an elevated plateau guarded by a fairway bunker on the left.

The second shot is also uphill to a broad, shallow target cut into the side of an amphitheaterlike hill. A large bunker guards the back of the green.

The back nine begins with the number-1-handicap hole. A 506-yard downhill par 5, it is a dogleg right to a green well protected by water front, left and right. The first shot has to avoid a right–hand bunker at the midpoint of a narrowing fairway. The second shot can either be a layup to a landing area just in front of the water hazard before the green, or a heroic attempt can be made to reach the medium-sized target in two. This is a good example of how doglegs, water hazards, and well-protected greens make Sky Meadow a beautiful and challenging layout.

The 188-yard par-3 eleventh is one of the most beautiful and memorable holes on the course. The tee shot is to a small island green protected by a trap on the right. A mid- or long iron is required from the back tees, and there is no place to bail out on this hole. The par 3s at Sky Meadow are among the best holes on the course.

The combination of elevation changes, well-protected fairways, sidehill lies, water hazards and strategically bunkered greens makes Sky Meadow play longer and more difficultly than it would first seem.

Sky Meadow offers country club quality amenities including a new 30,000 square foot clubhouse with full pro shop, restaurant, locker rooms and showers, banquet facilities and a function hall.

Paying a visit to this well-maintained golf course, which is only 35 miles north of Boston, is well worth your time.

Recommended Golf Courses in New Hampshire

Within 2 Hours of Concord:

Campbell's Scottish Highlands Golf Course, Salem, (603) 894–4653, Public, 18/6249/71

John H. Cain Golf Club, Newport, (603) 863–7787, Semiprivate, 18/6415/71

Concord Country Club, Concord, (603) 228–8936, Semiprivate, 18/6539/70

Hanover Country Club, Hanover, (603) 646–2000, Public, 18/5876/69

Keene Country Club, Keene, (603) 352–9722, Semiprivate, 18/6200/72

Laconia Country Club, Laconia, (603) 524–1273, Semiprivate, 18/6483/72

Lake Sunapee Country Club and Inn (open to guests of inn and Fairway Motel), New London, (603) 526–6440, Semiprivate, 18/6770/70

Overlook Country Club, Hollis, (603) 465–2909, Public, 18/6290/71

Passaconaway Country Club, Litchfield, (603) 424–4653, Public, 18/6855/71

Southegan Woods Golf Club, Amherst, (603) 673–0200, Public, 18/6487/72

Windham Golf and Country Club, Windham, (603) 434–2093 Public, 18/6442/72

Wentworth-by-the-Sea, Rye, (603) 433–5010, Semiprivate, 18/6179/70

New Hampshire: Useful Information

Office of Vacation Travel, 172 Pembroke Rd., P.O. Box 856, Concord, NH 03301, (603) 271–2343, (800) 678–5040

Fish and Game Department, 2 Hazen Dr., Concord, NH 03301, (603) 271–3421 (fishing and hunting regulations)

U.S. Forest Service, U.S. Department of Agriculture, P.O. Box 638, Laconia, NH 03246, (603) 524–6450 (national forest information)

New Hampshire Council on the Arts, 40 Main St., Concord, NH 03301, (603) 271–2789

White Mountain National Forest, Box 638, Laconia, NH 03246 (603) 524–6450

Course Name: GREAT GORGE
COUNTRY CLUB
Lake, Quarry,
Rail Courses

Course Type: Public
Resort: The Seasons Resort and
Conference Center
Address: Route 517/P.O. Box 637
McAfee, NJ 07428
Phone: (201) 827–5757 (Golf Course)
(201) 827–6000, (800) 835–
2555 (Resort)
Fax: (201) 827–2955 (Resort),
(201) 827–1864 (Golf
Course)

GOLF COURSE

Head Professional: Thomas Manziano
Course Length/Par (All Tees):
Lake/Quarry: Back 6819/71, Green
6412/71, White 5988/71, Ladies'
Forward 5390/72. Quarry/Rail: Back
6826/71, Green 6419/72, White
5973/71, Forward 5439/71. Rail/Lake:
Back 6921/72, Green 6487/72, White
6047/72, Ladies' Forward 5555/73
Course Slope/Rating (All Tees):
Lake/Quarry: Back 131/73.3, Green
127/71.3, White 123/69.5, Forward
118/66.8, Ladies' White 131/74.8,
Forward 124/71.5. Quarry/Rail: Back
126/72.7, Green 122/70.8, White
118/68.8, Forward 114/66.9, Ladies'
White 126/74.1, Forward 121/71.7.
Rail/Lake: Back 128/73.4, Green
124/71.4, White 120/69.4, Forward
116/67.2, Ladies' White 128/74.7,
Forward 123/72.0
Course Architects: George Fazio and Tom
Fazio (1971)
Golf Facilities: Full Pro Shop X, Snack
Bar X, Lounge X, Restaurant X,
Locker Room X, Showers X, Club
Rental X, Club Repair Minor, Cart
Rental X, Instruction X, Practice
Green X, Driving Range X, Practice
Bunker No, Club Storage X
Tee-Time Reservation Policy: Resort
guests: At time of reservation. Open
play: Up to 30 days in advance

Ranger: Yes
Tee-off-Interval Time: 9 min.
Time to Play 18 Holes: 4½ hrs.
Course Hours/Earliest Tee-off: 7 a.m.
Green and Cart Fees: $72 for 18 holes
with cart Sat., Sun., holidays; $49 for 18
holes with cart weekdays
Credit Cards: All major cards
Season: Mid-March to mid-Nov.
Course Comments: Cart mandatory.
Yardage book available
Golf Packages: Available through resort
Discounts: Seasonal rates (to May 1, late
fall)
Places to Stay Nearby: Appalachian Motel
(201) 764–6070
Local Attractions: Vernon Valley Action
Park, Stokes State Forest, High Point
State Park, hiking, camping, fishing,
boating. New Jersey Division of Travel
and Tourism (800) JERSEY–7
Directions: From New York City (57 mi.):
Lincoln Tunnel to Rte. 3 west, to Rte.
46 west, to Rte. 23 north to Hamburg
Turnpike, right on Rte. 94 north for 2.7
mi. and straight ahead on Rte. 517.
George Washington Bridge to I–80 west
to Rte. 23 north (follow directions above
from Rte. 23). From N.J. Turnpike exit
15W, Garden State Pkwy. exit 145, to
Rte. 280 west, to Rte. 80 west, to Rte.
15 north to Rte. 94, right on Rte. 94, 11
mi. to Rte. 517 to resort. From Tappan
Zee Bridge, N.Y. Thruway to Suffern,
Rte. 17 north to Rte. 17A, west on Rte.
17A to Warwick, NY. Left on Rte. 94 to
McAfee, NJ, right turn onto Rte. 517
and to resort
Closest Commercial Airports: Newark
International (1 hr.); La Guardia, NY
(2 hrs.); John F. Kennedy International,
NY (2 hrs.)

RESORT

Date Built: 1970
No. of Rooms: 567 standard, deluxe, 1-bed-
room suites, executive suites, French
suites, presidential suites
Meeting Rooms: 33. Capacity of Largest:
1000 persons banquet style. Meeting
Space: 65,000 sq. ft.

Room Price Range: $108 weekdays standard to $520 for 2-bedroom presidential suite peak season (May to Aug. Off season Nov. to Dec., Mar. to April.) Packages and specials available year round

Lounge: Bar at the Seasons Grille

Restaurants: Deli, Seasons Grille, Cafe in Park

Entertainment: Club Olana—Cabaret theater with dancing, shows and live music

Credit Cards: All major cards

General Amenities: Billiards room, children's playground, playhouse activity center for children available on weekends, game room with video arcade games, meeting and conference facilities with audiovisual and food services

Recreational Amenities: Horseback riding, skiing, hiking, 75-ride water park, 3 indoor and 4 lighted outdoor tennis courts, swimming pools; health and fitness center with Universal weight system, treadmills, stationary bicycles, step machines, rowing machines, steam and sauna, indoor pool; Jacuzzi, jogging trails, basketball, volleyball

Reservation and Cancellation Policy: Credit card or deposit for 1 night's fees to guarantee reservation. 48-hr. cancellation policy

Comments and Restrictions: No pets. Taxes and gratuities additional to base rates

GREAT GORGE COUNTRY CLUB

The Great Gorge Country Club is a 27-hole layout designed by George and Tom Fazio and carved out of the forests, hills and rock of northwestern New Jersey approximately one hour from the George Washington Bridge. This course used to be part of the original Playboy Club at Great Gorge but now it and the golf course are separately owned and operated.

There are three nine-hole courses—Lake, Quarry, and Rail—at Great Gorge that can be played in any combination. The Lake/Quarry combination is rated the most difficult, but many golfers favor the Rail/Lake layout. The Lake nine is also tight and, unlike Quarry and Rail, has no parallel holes. The toughest hole on this

layout is the 450-yard par-4 second hole, which is uphill to a crowned green flanked by traps. A water hazard lies behind this green, which is not easy to hold with a long iron or a wood. The finishing hole on Lake is a 422-yard par 4 whose tee shot is over a gully to a landing area with a large bunker on the right. The approach shot is to a long, narrow green well guarded by a large trap to its front and left. There is a severe drop-off if you miss on the left side of this green.

The Fazio design team left some "natural elements" on the golf course when it was constructed including a silo that stands on the difficult 592-yard par-5 second hole on Quarry. This sharp dogleg left plays downhill to the dogleg, about halfway to the hole, then flattens out to a forward-sloping green protected by a huge trap on the right. The silo is to your left on the approach shot, and it is out of bounds on either side of the fairway and behind the green.

Two difficult par 4s on Quarry include the 443-yard fifth hole, which plays to a landing area framed by two fairway bunkers and giant mountains of granite. The approach shot is to a deep green protected by a trap on the left. The 449-yard seventh is the number-1-handicap hole on this nine and plays down a tight fairway with water on the left and right. The green is narrow and deep, with a large trap to the right.

The Rail nine is a more open layout but has its share of interesting holes. The 182-yard par-3 third hole plays to a large green flanked by two large traps with cement railroad pillars in them—these used to hold a railroad trestle, and they are in play. A tough hole on the Rail is the 575-yard par-5 sixth, a dogleg right with out-of-bounds on the right and a stream cutting the fairway approximately 175 yards from the green.

The combination of trees, water hazards, hilly lies and well-placed bunkers, in addition to some long par 4s, makes Great Gorge a solid golf challenge. Practice facilities here include a driving range, practice bunker and putting green. Individual and group instruction is available from the professionals on staff. The clubhouse has a snack bar, restaurant, full pro shop, locker room and showers.

There is a variety of additional recreational amenities at the Seasons Resort, including horseback riding, tennis, swimming and a health and fitness center among others. In winter, this is a major regional skiing area. There are 3 restaurants at the resort, live entertainment, and a range of standard and suite accommodations that have recently been completely remodeled.

The Seasons Resort also has a state-of-the-art conference center with audiovisual and banquet facilities. It has over 30 meeting room options ranging from small conference rooms to theater- and banquet-style setups. As many as 1000 persons can be accommodated for banquet functions. Complete secretarial services are also available.

A variety of reduced rate packages is available at this 43-acre resort with magnificent views of the surrounding 4000-acre Great Gorge ski area and the golf courses.

Recommended Golf Courses in Northern New Jersey

Within 1 Hour of New York City:

Bowling Green Golf Club, Milton, (201) 697–8688, Semiprivate, 18/6689/72

Crystal Springs Golf and Country Club, Hamburg, (201) 827–1444, Public, 18/6885/72

Farmstead Golf and Country Club, Lafayette, (201) 383–1666. Clubview/Lakeview 18/6680/71. Lakeview/Valleyview 18/6221/69. Clubview/Valleyview: 18/6161/68

Flanders Valley Golf Course, Flanders, (201) 584–5382, Public. White/Blue: 18/6765/72. Red/Gold: 18/6770/72

High Point Country Club, Montague, (201) 293–3282, Semiprivate, 18/6783/73

River Vale Country Club, River Vale, (201) 391–2300, Public, 18/6470/72

Sunset Valley Golf Course, Pompton Plains, (201) 835–1515, Public, 18/6483/70

Central

Course Name: HOMINY HILL GOLF COURSE

Course Type: Public
Address: Mercer Road/off Route 537
                Colts Neck, NJ 07722
Phone: (908) 462–9222

GOLF COURSE

Head Professional: Alan Roberts
Course Length/Par (All Tees): Back 7059/72, Middle 6470/72, Ladies' Forward 5794/72
Course Slope/Rating (All Tees): Back 132/74.4, Middle 127/71.7, Ladies' Forward 128/73.9
Course Architect: Robert Trent Jones, Sr. (1964)
Golf Facilities: Full Pro Shop X, Snack Bar X, Lounge No, Restaurant No, Locker Room X, Showers X, Club Rental X, Club Repair No, Cart Rental X, Instruction No, Practice Green X, Driving Range X, Practice Bunker No, Club Storage No
Tee-Time Reservation Policy: Must buy nonresident reservation card (in person) to get into computerized reservation system. Walk-on times day of play, first come, first served
Ranger: Yes
Tee-off-Interval Time: 9 min.
Time to Play 18 Holes: 4½ hrs.
Course Hours/Earliest Tee-off: 6 a.m. Sat., Sun., holidays; 7 a.m. weekdays
Green Fees: $36 for 18 holes Sat., Sun., holidays; $33 for 18 holes weekdays. Twilight rate $27 for 18 holes Sat., Sun., holidays; $25 for 18 holes weekdays
Cart Fees: $25 plus tax for 18 holes
Pull Carts: Available
Credit Cards: Cash for golf fees. American Express, MasterCard, Visa for merchandise
Season: Mid-March to Dec. 23
Course Comments: Can walk anytime
Golf Packages: None
Discounts: Residents (I.D. card), seniors, students (high school), twilight
Places to Stay Nearby: Colts Neck Inn (908) 409–1200; Sheraton Eatontown Hotel and Conference Center (908) 542–

6500, (800) 325–3535. FREEHOLD: Sheraton Gardens (908) 462–9616. NEW BRUNSWICK: Hyatt Regency (908) 873–1234, (800) 233–1234. PRINCETON: Nassau Inn (609) 921–7500, (800) 862–7728; Scanticon Princeton Conference Center Hotel (609) 452–7800, (800) 222–1131. RED BANK: Courtyard by Marriott (908) 530–5552, (800) 228–9290; Oyster Pointe Hotel, Marina and Conference Center (908) 530–8200, (800) 345–3484

Local Attractions: Freehold Raceway, Monmouth Battlefield State Park, Battleground Arts Center, New Jersey shore, Englishtown Flea Market, Garden State Arts Center. Atlantic City. New York City. Princeton. Monmouth County Department of Public Information and Tourism (908) 431–7476. Western Monmouth Chamber of Commerce (908) 462–3030

Directions: From New York (1½ hrs.): Garden State Pkwy. south, exit 123/Rte. 9 south to Rte. 18 south, Rte. 537 east, club entrance 1 mi. on right

Closest Commercial Airports: Newark International (45 min.); Philadelphia International, PA (1 hr., 15 min.); La Guardia, NY (2 hrs.); John F. Kennedy International, NY (2 hrs.)

HOMINY HILL GOLF COURSE

The Hominy Hill Golf Course is part of the Monmouth County Park System and is approximately equidistant between New York and Philadelphia, in Colts Neck, New Jersey, just west of the Garden State Parkway. The golf course was formerly a private club built by industrialist Henry Mercer in 1964. Robert Trent Jones designed the course, and it has been rated by *Golf Digest* as one of the top 75 public golf courses in America ever since the county acquired the club in 1977. In 1986 Hominy Hill received the New Jersey Turfgrass Association and New Jersey Golf Course Superintendents Association Annual Recognition Award for outstanding turf grass management. Nearby Howell Park, also in the Monmouth County system, is also one of the top-rated public courses in the country.

Hominy Hill is an open course with large, fast, undulating greens; more than 110 sand bunkers; water on four holes; and high and difficult rough. This 7059-yard layout has rolling fairways flowing over land that was formerly a dairy farm. The par 3s at Hominy are fairly long and difficult. The toughest one is the 209-yard sixteenth, which plays straight to a large, undulating green with traps to the left and right. The 207-yard eleventh is difficult because the golfer is usually hitting into the wind to a large green with water and bunkers to the left. If you miss to the right, you are faced with a nasty chip shot to a green that slopes away from you toward the water.

Two of the most difficult par 4s on the course are the 435-yard eighth and the 458-yard tenth. The eighth plays straight to a narrow, deep green protected by a bunker on the right-front side. The approach shot is extremely difficult because the green rises abruptly from the fairway from 60 yards in, and the narrow green makes a small target for a long iron or a fairway wood. The tenth is a long dogleg right whose second shot is onto a narrow, deep, elevated green that is difficult to reach in two. Typically at Hominy Hill if you try to cut a dogleg, you just might find one of the ubiquitous sand bunkers or the rough, which is very difficult. The wind on this course, which is set on a hill, can also complicate shot making.

The 537-yard seventeenth is an excellent par 5 that is difficult to reach in two. The first shot is straightforward, but the second might have to contend with large, mature trees that protect the entrance way from 80 yards in. There is also a group of fairway bunkers on both sides of the narrowing fairway in this area. Many players use a driver, long iron, and wedge to avoid trouble on this hole.

Facilities in the clubhouse include a snack bar restaurant, dining room, locker rooms and showers, and a pro shop. The practice area has a limited driving range, or warmup area, and a practice green. To get a tee time as a nonresident of the county, you have to reserve on the same day on a first-come, first-served basis, or you have to pay a fee (in person) for a nonresident access card to a computerized tee-time reservation system. Because of the high population density and limited access to quality public golf facilities in the region, this is an attempt to give local residents tee-time priority and to rationalize the reservation system. At some golf courses in this area, people still wait in cars overnight to get a tee time on a first-come, first-served basis, return home to sleep a few hours, then come back to play. What one won't do to play golf.

You can walk the Hominy Hill Golf Course anytime. Although the practice facilities at Hominy Hill are limited, the Monmouth Park System runs a number of instructional clinics as well as tournaments for all age groups. Hominy Hill has hosted the 1983 USGA Public Links, the 1990 Jersey State Amateur, and the 1995 U.S. Ladies Public Links.

Course Name: **HOWELL PARK GOLF COURSE**

Course Type: Public
Address: Preventorium Road
Farmingdale, NJ 07727
Phone: (908) 938–4771

GOLF COURSE

Head Professional: Dave Laudien
Course Length/Par (All Tees): Back 6916/72, Middle 6302/72, Forward 5725/72
Course Slope/Rating (All Tees): Back 126/72.3, Middle 120/70.2, Ladies' Forward 125/72.5
Course Architects: Frank Duane (1972), Geoffrey Cornish and Brian Silva (renovation, 1985)
Golf Facilities: Full Pro Shop X, Snack Bar X, Lounge No, Restaurant No, Locker Room No, Showers No, Club Rental X, Club Repair No, Cart Rental X, Instruction X, Practice Green X, Driving Range X, Practice Bunker X, Club Storage No

Tee-Time Reservation Policy: Must buy nonresident reservation card (in person) to get into computerized reservation system. Walk-on times day of play, first come, first served
Ranger: Yes
Tee-off-Interval Time: 9 min.
Time to Play 18 Holes: 4½ hrs.
Course Hours/Earliest Tee-off: 6 a.m. Sat., Sun., holidays; 7 a.m. weekdays
Green Fees: $36 for 18 holes Sat., Sun., holidays; $33 for 18 holes weekdays
Cart Fees: $26 for 18 holes
Pull Carts: $2.75
Credit Cards: Cash for golf fees. Master-Card, Visa for merchandise
Season: March 15 to Dec. 23
Course Comments: Can walk anytime. No power carts Mondays, ranges and practice green closed. Nonresident reservation card can be purchased on premises
Golf Packages: None
Discounts: Resident senior citizens, juniors, twilight
Places to Stay Nearby: FREEHOLD: Sheraton Gardens (908) 462–9616. RED BANK: Courtyard by Marriott (908) 530–5552, (800) 228–9290; Oyster Point Hotel, Marina and Conference Center (908) 530–8200, (800) 345–3484. PRINCETON: Nassau Inn (609) 921–7500, (800) 862–7728; Scanticon Princeton Conference Center Hotel (609) 452–7800, (800) 222–1131. NEW BRUNSWICK: Hyatt Regency (908) 873–1234, (800) 233–1234. SPRING LAKE: The Breakers (908) 449–7700
Local Attractions: Freehold Raceway, Monmouth Battlefield State Park, Battleground Arts Center, Englishtown Flea Market, Allaire State Park, Garden State Arts Center, horseback riding, New Jersey shore, Atlantic City. Princeton. Monmouth County Department of Public Information and Tourism (908) 431–7476
Directions: Garden State Pkwy. south, exit 98, follow signs. From New Jersey Turnpike: Exit 31B, follow signs to Howell Park and golf course
Closest Commercial Airports: Newark International (1 hr.); Philadelphia Inter-

national, PA (1½ hrs.); La Guardia, NY (2 hrs.); John F. Kennedy International, NY (2 hrs.)

HOWELL PARK GOLF COURSE

Howell Park is the first public course owned by Monmouth County, New Jersey and is consistently rated among the best public golf courses in the United States by *Golf Digest*. The course was designed by Frank Duane and opened in 1972. Formerly a gently rolling dairy farm along a mile and a half of the Manasquan River, the eighteen-hole par-72 course plays 6916 yards from the back tees and is known for its manicured bentgrass fairways and fast, sloping greens. Playing this course demands exacting tee and approach shots to score well.

Water, mostly from a stream from the Manasquan River, comes into play on about half the holes at Howell Park. The course can play somewhat tight because of the many mature pine, oak and maple trees that populate the course. The number-2-handicap hole at Howell Park is the 517-yard par-5 eleventh hole, which is a dogleg to the right with two fairway traps guarding the corner, about 250 yards from the back tees. Some players can cut the dogleg by going over the trees on the right, leaving 150 to 175 yards to the hole. The green is protected by traps to the right and left front.

The number-1-handicap hole is the 557-yard par-5 second hole, which plays over a stream on the first shot to a slight dogleg right protected by a trap on the right approximately 225 yards from the tee. It is difficult to reach the green in two because the wind is usually in the golfer's face. Another difficult hole is the 391-yard par-4 twelfth, which has a stream in front of the elevated tee and doglegs slightly to the right. A fairway trap is at the left corner of the dogleg approximately 220 to 240 yards from the tee, and trees are on the right side of the fairway. From 150 yards into the hole the fairway runs uphill to an elevated green protected by two traps left and right front. Some of the par 3s, especially the longer ones, can provide an interesting challenge at Howell Park. The 157-yard seven-teenth plays over a stream to a large green protected by a sizeable bunker in the back. And the 222-yard thirteenth plays to a green that is well protected by traps to the left and right.

Approximately 40,000 to 50,000 rounds of golf are played at Howell Park during its 9-month season. Outings and groups are not encouraged, but various local, club and county tournaments are held here, and Pee Wee programs benefit local resident youngsters. A computerized reservation system is open to residents and nonresidents, although it is possible to walk on. There are a full-service pro shop and modest snack bar in the clubhouse, with a driving range and putting area nearby. Another quality course within the Monmouth County park system is the Hominy Hill Golf Course, a short distance away.

Duane, the designer of the Howell Park Golf Course, was born in the Bronx, New York, in 1921, studied landscape architecture in the State University of New York system and worked for Robert Trent Jones, Sr., until 1963 when he went out on his own. Shortly thereafter, he was stricken with myelitis but continued to work though confined to a wheelchair. He worked in a partnership with Arnold Palmer in the 1970s and designed and co-designed numerous courses, including the Stumpy Lake Golf Club in Norfolk, Virginia, with Robert Trent Jones, Sr.; the Landings (Magnolia) of Skidaway Island, Georgia, with Arnold Palmer; the Duke University Golf Course in Durham, North Carolina, with Robert Trent Jones, Sr.; and many others. The Howell Park Golf Coursewas opened in 1972. Geoffrey Cornish remodeled it in 1985 with Brian Silva.

Golf House

Golf House is the museum and library of the United States Golf Association in Far Hills, New Jersey. The United States Golf Association was founded in 1894 and provides a number of useful functions that help maintain the quality and standards of golf. It conducts national championships, selects international teams, sets policy on amateur status and equipment standards, raises funds, writes the official rules of golf, oversees the handicapping and course-rating systems, promotes the development of new and better turfgrasses, preserves the game's history and encourages fair play. The USGA Executive Committee oversees a variety of activities and committees such as handicapping, equipment standards, public golf, rules of golf and other important facets of golf.

The USGA conducts the following championships: the U.S. Amateur, the U.S. Open, the U.S. Women's Amateur, the U.S. Amateur Public Links, the U.S. Women's Amateur Public Links, the U.S. Junior Amateur, the U.S. Girl's Junior Amateur, the U.S. Women's Open, the U.S. Senior Amateur, the U.S. Senior Women's Amateur, the U.S. Senior Open, the U.S. Mid-Amateur, and the U.S. Women's Mid-Amateur. More than 6100 golf clubs and courses in the United States and abroad are USGA member clubs, and approximately 250,000 golfers belong to the USGA's Associates Program.

Golf House, built in 1919 and the former home of Thomas H. Frothingham, is a shrine for those in the pantheon of golf. Portraits, photos, equipment, exhibits and other memorabilia pertaining to Bobby Jones, Ben Hogan, Glenna Collett Vare, Arnold Palmer, Mickey Wright, Francis Ouimet, Babe Zaharias, Byron Nelson and many other great golfers are housed here. A variety of exhibits has appeared at Golf House, including "Women in Golf," clubs and equipment with significant historical value and other interesting topics. There is also an excellent library and photo archive at Golf House.

Museum memorabilia, books and prints are available for purchase. Contact Golf House, United States Golf Association, Far Hills, NJ 07931, (908) 234–2300.

Recommended Golf Courses in Central New Jersey

Within 1 Hour of Newark:

Beaver Brook Country Club, Clinton, (908) 735–4022, (800) 433–8567, Semiprivate, 18/6546/72

Quail Brook Golf Course, Somerset, (908) 560–9528, Public, 18/6591/71

Shark River Golf Course, Neptune, (908) 422–4111, Public, 18/6176/71

Woodlake Golf and Country Club, Lakewood, (908) 367–4500, Semiprivate, 18/6766/72

Atlantic City Area

Course Name: MARRIOTT'S SEAVIEW GOLF RESORT
Pines, Bay Courses

Course Type: Resort
Resort: Marriott's Seaview Golf Resort
Address: U.S. Route 9/Shore Road
Absecon, NJ 08201
Phone: (609) 652–1800 (Golf Course)
(609) 652–1800,
(800) 228–9290 (Resort)
Fax: (609) 652–2307 (Resort)

GOLF COURSE

Director of Golf: Pat Bartley
Head Professional: Matt Gillogly
Course Length/Par (All Tees): Pines: Back 6885/71, Middle 6394/71, Ladies' Forward 5837/75. Bay: Back 6263/71, Middle 5981/71, Ladies' Forward 5586/74
Course Slope/Rating (All Tees): Pines: Back 132/73, Middle 128/70.7, Ladies' Forward 128/73.2. Bay: Back 113/69, Middle 111/67.7, Ladies' Forward 115/70.7
Course Architects: Pines: William Flynn and Howard Toomey (9 holes, 1930), William Gordon (9 holes, 1957). Bay: Donald Ross (1915), William Gordon and David Gordon (renovation, 1957)
Golf Facilities: Full Pro Shop X, Snack Bar X, Lounge X, Restaurant X, Locker Room X, Showers X, Club Rental X, Club Repair X, Cart Rental X, Instruction X, Practice Green X, Driving Range X, Practice Bunker X, Club Storage X
Tee-Time Reservation Policy: Resort guests: 30 days in advance. Outside play: 1 day in advance Fri., Sat., Sun. holidays; 7 days in advance weekdays

Ranger: Yes

Tee-off-Interval Time: 10 min.

Time to to Play 18 Holes: 4½ hrs.

Course Hours/Earliest Tee-off: 7 a.m.

Green and Cart Fees: Peak season: $89 for 18 holes with cart, $45 for 9 holes with cart

Credit Cards: All major cards

Season: Year round. Busiest season mid-April to Oct.

Course Comments: Cart mandatory. Yardage book available. Members have tee-time priority. John Jacobs' Practical Golf School on site (602) 991–8587

Golf Packages: Available through resort. (Nov. through Feb. lowest discount packages)

Discounts: Seasonal (Nov. to end of April). Twilight

Places to Stay Nearby: ABSECON: Comfort Inn (609) 641–7272, (800) 228–5150. SOMERS POINTE: Sands Country Club (609) 927–1007; Marriott's Residence Inn (609) 927–6400, (800) 331–3131. ATLANTIC CITY: Trump Plaza Hotel and Casino (609) 441–6000, (800) 677–7378; Best Western Golf and Tennis Inn (609) 641–3546, (800) 528–1234; Ramada Boardwalk Plaza Suite Hotel (609) 344–1200, (800) 228–9898; Claridge Casino Hotel (609) 340–3400, (800) 257–8585; The Grand (609) 347–7111, (800) 257–8677; Caesar's Atlantic City (609) 348–4411, (800) CAESARS; Harrah's Casino Hotel (609) 441–5000, (800) 2HARRAH

Local Attractions: Atlantic City boardwalk and casinos, deep-sea fishing, Brigantine National Wildlife Preserve, The Pine Barrens, Atlantic City Race Course, beaches, historic Towne of Smithville. Atlantic City Convention and Visitors Bureau (609) 348–7100

Directions: From Baltimore, MD/ Washington, DC (3 hrs.): I–95 north to N.J. Turnpike, to Atlantic City Expressway, to exit 12. Take exit 12, left on Pomona Rd. (north), right on Jimmie Leeds Rd. (east) to end, right on Rte. 9 to resort. From New York City (3 hrs.): I–87 west to Garden State Pkwy. south, exit 48 (one way) to Rte. 9 south, 7.4 mi. south

on Rte. 9, resort on right. From Philadelphia (45 min.): Rte. 765 to Atlantic City Expressway east. Refer to Baltimore/DC directions above

Closest Commercial Airports: Atlantic City International (30 min.); Philadelphia International, PA (1 hr.); Newark International, NJ (2 hrs.); La Guardia, NY (3 hrs.); John F. Kennedy International, NY (3 hrs.)

RESORT

Date Built: 1913

No. of Rooms: 299 guest rooms, 19 suites, 18 executive bedrooms, 2 vice–presidential suites

Meeting Rooms: 16. Capacity of Largest: 500 persons banquet style. Meeting Space: 14,000 sq. ft.

Room Price Range: $79 to $695 per room depending on season. Peak season early May to mid-Nov. Golf and other packages as well as seasonal discounts available

Lounge: Lobby Bar, Grill Bar

Restaurants: Main Dining Room, Grill Room, Oval Room

Entertainment: Live music in Main Dining Room, Lobby Bar (weekends)

Credit Cards: American Express, Diners Club, MasterCard, Visa

General Amenities: Babysitting, gift shop; meeting and conference facilities including theater, classroom, conference, reception and banquet rooms with audio-visual, banquet, and secretarial service

Recreational Amenities: Indoor and outdoor swimming pools, 8 tennis courts (4 lighted), exercise room, whirlpool, steam room, saunas, pocket billiards, table tennis, card tables, video games, basketball court, 2 paddle tennis courts, jogging and walking trail, volleyball, indoor tennis and racquetball nearby

Reservation and Cancellation Policy: Credit card guarantee or deposit required to hold room reservation. 3-day cancellation notice requested for full refund

Comments and Restrictions: No pets. Kennels nearby. Maximum of 5 people to a room. Taxes and gratuities additional to base rates

MARRIOTT'S SEAVIEW GOLF RESORT

Seaview is a 670-acre golf resort overlooking Reeds Bay just west of Atlantic City, New Jersey. Built in 1913 by Clarence J. Geist, the Seaview Country Club began as a private course when the noted golf architect Donald Ross was brought in to design the Bay Course, which was completed in 1915. At that time, Ross was living in Pinehurst, North Carolina, where he remained until his death in 1948. The Bay Course was among his earlier courses, which also include Pinehurst, North Carolina, Country Club Courses No. 2 (nine holes) and No. 3; the Country Club of Havana in Cuba; the Crestmont Country Club in West Orange, New Jersey, and the Echo Lake Country Club in Westfield, New Jersey, both with George Low, Sr.; the Beverly Country Club in Chicago; and the Wellesley Country Club in Massachusetts. Ross got around, and eventually, during the 1920s, he had more than 3000 workers employed annually in the construction of his golf courses.

In 1930, the original nine holes of the Pines Course, which was designed by the firm of William Flynn and Howard Toomey, was opened. Flynn and Toomey also designed the James River course at the Country Club of Virginia in Richmond; nine holes at the Country Club in Brookline, Massachusetts; and Shinnecock Hills in Southampton, Long Island. Today's first, second and twelfth through eighteen holes are Flynn and Toomey's original nine at the Pines Course. They also remodeled Ross's original Bay Course of that time. In 1957 William Gordon, who had worked with Flynn and Toomey, completed the final nine holes of the Pines with the assistance of his son, David Gordon.

When Marriott purchased Seaview in 1985, a learning center was designed by Al Janis and built on acreage formerly occupied by holes seven, eight, and nine of the Pines Course. Janis replaced those holes with three new holes. The learning center is now used by the John Jacobs' Practical Golf Schools, which offer a range of individual and group instruction at Seaview. The center comprises two 30,000-square-foot bentgrass tees; 4 chipping, putting and bunker areas; and target greens on the driving range.

The 6263-yard Bay Course retains much of its original Donald Ross charm. The greens are small and undulating in the tradition of old-style courses, with well-placed bunkers guarding the greens and fairway landing areas. More than 100 bunkers appear on this relatively open, flat layout that can be affected considerably by wind coming off the bay.

The number-1-handicap hole on the Bay Course is the 432-yard par-4 fourth, which plays straight to a small green. The tee-shot landing area is bracketed by five bunkers on the right and two large bunkers on the left. The second shot is all carry due to a mound in front of the green. The 194-yard par-3 seventh is the only hole requiring a carry over water. The tee shot is to a roundish, forward-sloping, undulating green with a large trap to the left front and another large one to the right front, with two smaller traps behind it. The finishing hole on this side is a 492-yard par 5 that plays straight to a small green with a large trap to its right. The tee-shot landing area has two large traps to the left and trees to the right. The second shot has to carry three huge bunkers that cut the fairway 145 to 100 yards into the hole. Or you have to play up and hit a mid-iron to the elevated green that slopes severely from right to left.

The toughest par 4 on the back nine on the Bay Course is the 416-yard fourteenth, which plays directly to a small green flanked on the left and right by huge bunkers. The tee shot has to clear three bunkers at the beginning of the fairway 195 yards from the back tee. The second shot can be rolled onto the flat green, but the entranceway between the traps seems small from a distance. A tough par 3 is the 219-yard sixteenth, which plays straight to a medium-sized green with a large trap to the left and a waste area to the right. Club selection is the key here. Miss to the left if you have to.

My favorite hole on this side is the 357-yard par-4 tenth, a dogleg left with three fairway bunkers on the right affecting the tee shot, which has to be played right-of-center to avoid being blocked by trees to the left on the second shot. The narrow green slopes severely from back to front, with a huge bunker to the left and front. If your drive is long and left, it will catch another bunker 260 yards from the back tee.

The Pines Course is longer and tighter than the Bay Course. It has tree-lined fairways, less wind, more doglegs, slightly larger greens and over 70 bunkers. The number-1-handicap hole is the 434-yard par-4 fourth, which is a heavily treed dogleg right with a huge bunker on the right at the corner of the turn. It is almost impossible to carry this 60-yard-long bunker. To the left is a narrow landing area and trees. If you go into the woods you have to keep batting the ball to get out because it's not out of bounds. The second shot, usually a wood or a long iron, is slightly downhill to a medium-sized green with a large trap on the right front and trees to the left. The 555-yard par-5 ninth is a classic three-shot par 5 with water cutting the middle of the wooded fairway 250 yards from the tee. The second shot is uphill toward a very small green with two huge traps in the fairway 80 yards from the green and two more to the right and left in front of the putting surface.

A tough par 3 is the 241-yard fifteenth, which plays to a large, two-tiered green. Two huge bunkers are in front and on the left of the green from 100 yards in. Behind the green is an amphitheater bank with another large trap. The eighteenth hole is a 551-yard par 5 through a gauntlet of trees and bunkers that protect both the narrow tee-shot landing area and the landing area for the second shot. The green is elevated, with two large traps left and right extending well in front of the green.

At the clubhouse is a fully stocked pro shop, and men's and women's locker rooms and showers. There are also complete practice facilities at Seaview. Individual and group instruction is available from the on-site professionals and at the John Jacobs' Practical Golf Schools that gener-

ally run from mid-May through mid-October. The four-story colonial-style hotel has facilities for small and large conference groups of up to 500 persons, and the Main Dining Room and Grill Room provide a variety of fare ranging from elegant cuisine to sandwiches and basic breakfasts. Recreational facilities include a Universal weight room, indoor and outdoor swimming pools, 8 tennis courts, a hydrotherapy pool, sauna and steam baths. Seaview has earned a Four-Star rating from the *Mobil Travel Guide*.

Recommended Golf Courses in Southern New Jersey

Within 1 Hour of Atlantic City:

Blue Heron Pines Golf Club, Galloway, (609) 965–4653, Public, 18/6777/72

Buena Vista Country Club, Buena, (609) 697–3733, Public, 18/6869/72

Cape May National Golf Club, Cape May, (609) 884–1563, Semiprivate, 18/6857/71

Greate Bay Resort and Country Club, Somers Point, (609) 927–0066, Resort, 18/6750/71

Ocean County Golf Course at Atlantis, Little Egg Harbor, (609) 296–2444, Public, 18/6845/72

Pennsauken Country Club, Pennsauken, (609) 662–4961, Public, 18/6006/70

Rancocas Golf Club, Willingboro, (609) 877–5344, Public, 18/6634/71

New Jersey: Useful Information

New Jersey Department of Commerce and Economic Development, Division of Travel and Tourism, CN 826, Trenton, NJ 08625, (800) JERSEY–7

Division of Parks and Forestry, State Park Service, 501 E. State St., CN 404, Trenton, NJ 08625, (609) 292–2797, (800) 843–6420

Department of Environmental Protection, Division of Fish, Game and Wildlife, 501 E. State St., CN 400, Trenton, NJ 08625, (609) 292–2965 (fishing and hunting regulations)

Course Name: COCHITI LAKE GOLF COURSE

Course Type: Public
Address: Highway 22/P.O. Box 125
Cochiti Lake, NM 87041
Phone: (505) 465-2239

GOLF COURSE

Head Professional: None
Course Length/Par (All Tees): Back 6451/72, Middle 5996/72, Forward 5292/72
Course Slope/Rating (All Tees): Back 119/70.0 Middle 115/68.3, Ladies' Forward 117/71
Course Architect: Robert Trent Jones, Jr. (1989)
Golf Facilities: Full Pro Shop X, Snack Bar X, Lounge No, Restaurant No, Locker Room X, Showers X, Club Rental X, Club Repair X, Cart Rental X, Instruction X, Practice Green X, Driving Range X, Practice Bunker X, Club Storage No
Tee-Time Reservation Policy: From 7 days in advance. Groups (3 or more foursomes) can be booked 1 yr. in advance
Ranger: Yes
Tee-off-Interval Time: 10 min.
Time to Play 18 Holes: 4½ hrs.
Course Hours/Earliest Tee-off: Sunrise to sunset
Green Fees: $23 for 18 holes Sat., Sun., holidays; $19 for 18 holes Mon. to Fri., $15 for 9 holes Sat., Sun., holidays; $13 for 9 holes Mon. to Fri.
Cart Fees: $20 for 18 holes for 2 riders, $14 for 9 holes for 2 riders
Pull Carts: $4.50 for 18 holes, $3.50 for 9 holes
Credit Cards: Discover, MasterCard, Visa
Season: Year round
Course Comments: Can walk, but difficult
Golf Packages: None
Discounts: None
Places to Stay Nearby: SANTA FE: Santa Fe Hotel (505) 982-1000, (800) 825-9876; Bishop's Lodge (505) 983-6377, (800) 732-2240; Inn of the Anasazi (505) 988-3030, (800) 688-8100; La Fonda Hotel (505) 982-5511, (800) 523-5002; Hilton Inn (505) 988-2811, (800) 445-8667; La Posada de Santa Fe (505) 983-6351; Rancho Encantado (505) 982-3537, (800) 722-9339; La Quinta Motor Inn (505) 471-1142, (800) 531-5100. ALBUQUERQUE (45 min.): Hyatt Regency (505) 842-1234, (800) 233-1234; Albuquerqe Doubletree (505) 247-3344, (800) 528-0444; Sheraton Old Town (505) 843-6300, (800) 325-3535; Holiday Inn (505) 345-3511, (800) 465-4329; Albuquerque Marriott (505) 881-6800, (800) 228-9290
Local Attractions: SANTA FE: Dining, The Palace of the Governors Museum, Museum of International Folk Art, Mission of San Miguel of Santa Fe, Museum of Fine Arts, Institute of American Indian Arts Museum, music, architecture, Pecos National Monument, Bandelier National Monument, Chaco Culture National Historic Park (pueblo ruins), state capitol, Santa Fe Opera, theater, concerts, camping, hunting, fishing, hiking, bicycling, rafting. ALBUQUERQUE: Dining, Old Town, Pueblo Indian Cultural Center, Dav Vietnam Veterans National Memorial, Albuquerque Museum, New Mexico Museum of Natural History, Sandia Peak tramway and ski area, University of New Mexico, shopping, crafts, festivals. Albuquerque Convention and Visitors Bureau (505) 243-3696, (800) 284-2282. Santa Fe Convention and Visitors Bureau (505) 984-6760, (800) 777-2489
Directions: From Albuquerque: I-25 north, exit 259, west on Hwy. 22 (16 mi.), through Pena Blanca, over the Rio Grande, 2 mi. other side of Cochiti Lake
Closest Commercial Airport: Albuquerque International (45 min.)

COCHITI LAKE GOLF COURSE

The land where the Cochiti Lake Golf Course is now situated was originally leased by a Texas-based real-estate-development company. It is now owned and operated by the Pueblo Indians, who occupied the original land. The 6451-yard par-72 course, 40 miles southwest of Santa Fe, was designed by Robert Trent Jones, Jr., and opened in 1989.

Pueblo means "village dweller," which is what these descendants of the Anasazi and Mogollan peoples were when the early Spanish explorers in this region noted their distinct architecture: permanent, compact, multi-chambered houses made of stone and adobe. The Cochiti pueblos date back to at least the thirteenth century. The Pueblo Indians did not constitute a tribe; each Pueblo culture was a village that functioned as an autonomous political entity. The Pueblo peoples speak many different languages and currently there are approximately 30 pueblo villages. Economically all Pueblos are primarily agriculturists, but today many are wage earners in large nearby cities such as Albuquerque and Santa Fe. All return home for important ceremonies. All aspects of Pueblo life are integrated or interwoven into a worldview based on the simple tenet that people must live in harmony with nature.

Nestled in the desert near Cochiti Lake, which abuts the Santa Ana Indian Reservation, Cochiti Lake Golf Course is rated by *Golf Digest* as one of the best in the state of New Mexico and one of the best public golf courses in the United States. A rolling layout with water coming into play on four holes, Cochiti has large, fast, undulating greens. Large bunkers strategically protect every green and occasional spots on the fairways. The course is dotted with pine and cedar trees but is relatively open. If you stray, however, rocks, rough, sand, high milk grass, scrubgrass and other nasty natural elements can quickly add strokes to your score. For this reason, many golfers use long irons and 3-woods off the tee at Cochiti.

The number-1-handicap, 440-yard par-4 fourteenth hole bends slightly left. A large fairway bunker is located on the left edge approximately halfway to the green, which is protected by three traps to the right, left and back. The thirteenth hole, a 530-yard par 5, is considered one of the most difficult holes on the course. It is a winding, narrow, double dogleg that requires a relatively straight tee shot to the first corner. If

you reach it and then try to cut the right dogleg by going directly to the green, you are looking at three long traps surrounding the front and sides of the undulating putting surface. Two additional bunkers protect the left fairway beginning 100 yards from the green.

Another difficult hole is the 415-yard par-4 ninth, a dogleg left with the knee of the dogleg a bit more than halfway to the green and well protected by three bunkers as the landing area narrows. The tee shot is from a magnificent elevated tee that overlooks the golf course and the fairway more than 100 feet below. The second shot is uphill to a green that has a large trap to the left rear. The twelfth hole, another tough par 4, also has a dramatic elevated tee and plays 415 yards to a green protected by two traps left and right toward the back of the green.

The greens at Cochiti are bentgrass, and the fairways and tees are Kentucky bluegrass. With a green fee of under $25, this has to be one of the most beautiful bargains in golf.

Course Name: THE INN OF THE MOUNTAIN GODS

Course Type: Resort
Resort: The Inn of the Mountain Gods
Address: P.O. Box 269
              Mescalero, NM 88340
Phone: (505) 257–7444,
              (800) 446–2963 (Golf Course)
              (800) 545–9011 (Resort)
Fax: (505) 257–6173 (Resort)

GOLF COURSE

Head Professional: Daniel Nunez
Course Length/Par (All Tees): Back 6819/72, Middle 6416/72, Forward 5459/72
Course Slope/Rating (All Tees): Back 132/72.1, Middle 128/70.1, Forward 116/65.5, Ladies' Forward 128/NA
Course Architect: Ted Robinson (1976)
Golf Facilities: Full Pro Shop X, Snack Bar X, Lounge X, Restaurant X, Locker Room X, Showers X, Club

Rental X, Club Repair X, Cart Rental X, Instruction X, Practice Green X, Driving Range No, Practice Bunker No, Club Storage X

Tee-Time Reservation Policy: Resort guests: At time of hotel reservation. Outside play: From 2 wks. in advance

Ranger: Yes

Tee-off-Interval Time: 8 min.

Time to Play 18 Holes: 4 hrs. 15 min.

Course Hours/Earliest Tee-off: 7 a.m.

Green Fees: Resort guests: $35 for 18 holes. Outside play: $50 for 18 holes

Cart Fees: $20 for 18 holes per cart, $14 for 9 holes per cart

Credit Cards: All major cards

Season: March to Dec. Busiest season June to Aug. Course open except for Jan., Feb. depending on weather

Course Comments: Cart mandatory

Golf Packages: Available through resort. Packages offered April to Sept.

Discounts: Seasonal (Oct. 1 to May 1). Golf course closed Jan., Feb.

Places to Stay Nearby: RUIDOSO AREA: High Country Lodge (505) 336–4321, (800) 845–7265; West Winds Lodge and Condos (505) 257–4031; Monjeau Shadows Country Inn (505) 336–4191; Village Lodge at Innsbrook Resort (505) 258–5442, (800) 722–8779; Dan Dee Cabins—Resort (505) 257–2165

Local Attractions: Ruidoso Downs horse racing, St. Joseph's Mission, camping, fishing, hunting, skiing, shopping, hiking; seasonal festivals, including an arts and crafts show and Mescalero Apache ceremony and rodeo. Ruidoso Chamber of Commerce (505) 257–7395. Mescalero Tourism (505) 257–7395

Directions: From El Paso (124 mi.): I–10 north to Hwy. 70, take Hwy. 70 east to Mescalero, 19 mi. west toward Ruidoso, follow signs to Inn of the Mountain Gods. From Albuquerque (191 mi.): I–25 south to Hwy. 380, take Hwy. 380 east to Hwy. 54, take Hwy. 54 south to Hwy. 70, take Hwy. 70 east to Mescalero, follow signs to resort

Closest Commercial Airports: El Paso International, TX (2½ hrs.); Albuquerque International (3½ hrs.)

RESORT

Date Built: 1975

No. of Rooms: 250

Meeting Rooms: 10. Capacity of Largest: 650 persons. Meeting Space: 16,269 sq. ft.

Room Price Range: $80 to $125 per person, European plan. Highest rates June to Sept., lowest rates Nov. to March

Lounges: Inada Lounge, Goskan Bar, Nanstane Bar, Apache Tee

Restaurants: Dom Li Ka Dining Room, Top of the Inn, Hot Dog Stand, Apache Stand

Entertainment: Live music

Credit Cards: All major cards

General Amenities: Meeting facilities with audiovisual and food services, babysitting services

Recreational Amenities: Skiing, horse racing, tennis (6 outdoor, 2 indoor courts), archery, horseback riding, trap and skeet shooting, basketball, volleyball, fishing, bicycling

Reservation and Cancellation Policy: 1 night's deposit required. Refundable if notice of cancellation received 10 days prior to arrival time

Comments and Restrictions: No pets allowed. No extra charge for children under 12 sharing a room with adults. Food/beverage tax, 16% food/beverage service charge, sales tax, room tax additional to base rates

THE INN OF THE MOUNTAIN GODS

The Inn of the Mountain Gods is a beautifully situated mountain resort set at 7200 feet in the Sacramento Mountains of south central New Mexico. The resort is located in the heart of the beautiful, rugged, heavily forested 460,000-acre Apache Indian Reservation and is owned and operated by the Mescalero Apache Tribe. The Mescalero Apache Indian Reservation was established by executive order of President Ulysses S. Grant on May 27, 1873. The Mescaleros numbered about 400 persons when the reservation was established, but other Apaches, including the Lipan and Chiricahua bands, subsequently joined the Mescalero tribe.

The reservation is mountainous, with the east-slope streams draining into the Pecos River and the west-slope waters flowing into the Tularosa Basin. The highest point within the reservation is the summit of Ski Apache, which is 12,003 feet above sea level. The winter months are not severe, with the lowest temperature at 19° December through February. The highest temperatures are in the 80s in July, and the rainy season is in July and August. The reservation spans 27 miles from north to south, is 36 miles wide and is covered with pine, fir, spruce, aspen, white oak, piñon and juniper. The reservation Apache population is approximately 3200 people.

The Apaches produced many great leaders, including the legendary chiefs Geronimo and Cochise. The Mescaleros today are governed by a tribal council of eight members, with an elected president and vice president rather than a chief. The principal source of income for the tribe is from timber sales, but the tribe operates various other enterprises such as cattle farms, the Ski Apache Resort, and the Inn of the Mountain Gods. The resort, situated on a 150-acre lake, has 250 guest rooms and a variety of meeting, dining and recreational facilities including archery, horseback riding, indoor and outdoor tennis, trap and skeet shooting, basketball, volleyball, bicycling, fishing and camping.

The golf course is a 6819-yard Ted Robinson–designed layout with dramatic elevation changes; wind; well-treed fairways; and medium-sized to large, slightly undulating bentgrass greens. Accuracy is much more important than distance at the Inn of the Mountain Gods.

There are some beautiful and difficult par 3s on this rolling golf course. The 227-yard eighth plays from an elevated tee down to a deep green protected by traps on the left, right and to the rear. The 212-yard twelfth is over water to a green with a large trap and more water on the left. The finishing hole is another long par 3, measuring 229 yards, which is almost all carry over a corner of Lake Mescalero to a green guarded by a trap and water on the left and another trap on the right.

One of the more difficult par 4s on this course is the 440-yard second hole, a dogleg left that requires two long, accurate shots to reach the green in regulation. It should be noted that deer, elk, bear and mountain lion have the right of way on this golf course.

Within one hour of Mescalero are 25 museums, 68 annual events such as native American festivals, 2 national monuments, 5 state monuments, 112 restaurants, 2 ski areas, 3 fishing areas and many camping grounds within 1.1 million acres of national forest containing what is called the Apache Trails. In recounting the centuries-long traditions and rich history of this people, Wendell Chino, president of the Mescalero Apache Tribal Council, noted that the traditional Apache religion was based on the belief in the supernatural and the power of nature. In particular, within this homeland are the Four Sacred Mountains that include Sierra Blanca, Guadalupe, Three Sisters Mountain and Obscura Mountain Peak that represent the four directions of the universe. The Inn of the Mountain Gods resort is situated in this special ancestral place.

A major entertainment attraction in this area is the quarter horse and thoroughbred racing held from early May to early December at Ruidoso Downs. The Inn of the Mountain Gods offers golf packages from April through December. Other packages, such as ski, "great escape" and tennis packages, are available.

This is a unique experience because of the awesome natural setting of the golf course; the quality of the layout; and the rich native American, Spanish and frontier cultural traditions of the area. The Inn of the Mountain Gods course has been rated among the top 25 resort courses in America by *Golf Digest* and is ranked second of all golf courses in the state of New Mexico.

Course Name: PIÑON HILLS GOLF COURSE

Course Type: Public
Address: 2101 Sunrise Parkway
Farmington, NM 87401
Phone: (505) 326–6066

GOLF COURSE

Pro Shop Manager: Shawn Holmes
Course Length/Par (All Tees): Back 7249/72, Blue 6736/72, White 6239/72, Forward 5522/72
Course Slope/Rating (All Tees): Back 140/74.3, Blue 131/71.5, White 128/69.2, Ladies' Forward 126/71.1
Course Architect: Ken Dye (1990)
Golf Facilities: Full Pro Shop X, Snack Bar X, Lounge No, Restaurant No, Locker Room No, Showers No, Club Rental X, Club Repair X, Cart Rental X, Instruction X, Practice Green X, Driving Range X, Practice Bunker X, Club Storage No
Tee-Time Reservation Policy: 1 wk. in advance from 7 a.m.
Ranger: Yes
Tee-off-Interval Time: 10 min.
Time to Play 18 Holes: 4½ hrs.
Course Hours/Earliest Tee-off: 6:30 a.m. summer months
Green Fees: $13 for 18 holes Sat., Sun., holidays; $11 for 18 holes weekdays. $9 for 9 holes Sat., Sun., holidays; $7.50 for 9 holes weekdays
Cart Fees: $14 for 18 holes, $9 for 9 holes
Credit Cards: All major cards except American Express
Season: Year round, weather permitting. Busiest season mid-Feb. to mid-Sept.
Course Comments: Can walk anytime. Closed Tuesdays Nov. to May.; open 7 days per week May to Oct. Annual passes available. Tournament services. Can get walk-on tee time day of play
Golf Packages: None. Tournaments welcome
Discounts: Annual pass
Places to Stay Nearby: Best Western Inn (505) 327–5221, (800) 528–1234; Comfort Inn (505) 325–2626, (800) 221–2222; La Quinta Inn (505) 327–4706, (800) 531–5900; Holiday Inn (505) 327–9811, (800) HOLIDAY; Farmington Lodge (505) 325–0233
Local Attractions: Angel Peak Recreation Area, Bisti Wilderness, Farmington Museum, Aztec Museum, Chaco Culture National Historical Park, Aztec Ruins National Monument, Salmon Ruin, Four Corners Monument, Navajo Lake State Park, Shiprock Pinnacle, Navajo Reservation. Farmington Convention and Visitors Bureau (505) 326–7602, (800) 448–1240. New Mexico Economic Development and Tourism Department (505) 827–0291, (800) 525–2040. Navajo Land Tourist Office (602) 871–6659
Directions: Hwy. 64 to Farmington, look for Broadway (Hwy. 64) and Butler intersection (stop light), go north on Butler to Sunrise Pkwy. (on right), follow Sunrise Pkwy. to golf course
Closest Commercial Airports: Four Corners Regional/Farmington (5 min.), Albuquerque International (3½ hrs.)

PIÑON HILLS GOLF COURSE

Piñon Hills is situated in Farmington, approximately 5900 feet above sea level on the Western Colorado Plateau. Rich with American Indian culture, Farmington is also in the Upper Sonoran life zone of New Mexico with cedar, piñon, juniper and oak, and in the upper reaches, ponderosa pine as characteristic tree species. It is a hub of the Four Corners area, where Arizona, Colorado, Utah and New Mexico meet. Durango, Colorado, is only 45 minutes northeast, and Albuquerque is 3½ hours to the southeast. The Anasazi, a highly religious group of early Rio Grande farmers and potters, thrived in this region from A.D. 800 to 1300, then disappeared. Today's Acoma, Zuñi, Saudi, Jemez and other Pueblo tribes are likely to be descendants of that great Anasazi culture. The Four Corners area itself features Navajo, Ute and Hopi civilizations.

From the early sixteenth century the Spaniards sent expeditions to New Mexico, and in 1821 newly liberated Mexico, a former Spanish colony, claimed the area. Santa Fe became the capital of New Mexico and trade as well as conflict with the native Indian tribes thrived. By 1848, after the Mexican–American War, northern New Mexico became the property of the United States, and in 1868, after a series of infamous Indian wars, the Navajos signed a treaty granting them the land they now occupy in the Four Corners area. Their 25,000-square-mile reservation is approximately the size of the state of West Virginia. New Mexico was admitted to the Union on January 6, 1912, and with its rich Indian, Mexican and Spanish heritage, English is, to this day, the second language of many of those in the state.

Opened in 1990, Piñon Hills has been ranked by *Golf Digest* as the best golf course in the state of New Mexico. The 7249-yard par-72 layout is the first eighteen-hole public golf course in Farmington, and it was built on leased land at a cost of $3.1 million. It is well managed by the Farmington Parks and Recreation Department, having been profitable the first year it opened. Proceeds are put directly back into the golf course for maintenance and capital improvements. The course is sculpted into the beautiful northwestern New Mexico high desert terrain. Water comes into play on three holes, and there are many elevation changes on the course.

A minimum of four tee positions can be played on the Piñon Hills course, providing any golfer with a wide variety of distances and playing angles. The high elevation gives the ball more carry. You have to be able to properly select clubs and calibrate distances accordingly on this layout. The 548-yard par-5 eighth hole, a double dogleg left, then right, is the number-1-handicap hole on the course and is its toughest hole. The tee shot is uphill to a landing area guarded by a large bunker on the left. The second shot is to a deep green that slopes right to left and forward, and has a huge trap in back and another to the right.

The signature hole at Piñon Hills is the 228-yard par-3 fifteenth, which plays from an elevated tee over an arroyo to a medium-sized, three-tiered green trapped to the left, right and back. Another dramatic par-3 is the 235-yard third hole, which also plays over an arroyo down to a green that seems wedged into a valley, with high banks on the left and right and a drop-off to the rear.

The two finishing holes at Piñon Hills are both par 5s, beginning with the 563-yard seventeenth, a dogleg left to a deep left-to-right-angled green with two huge traps on the left and left front. The final hole, measuring 597 yards, plays over two small arroyos. The tee shot is to a landing area just in front of the first arroyo, and the second is toward a narrow, deep three-tiered green trapped both left and right, with an amphitheaterlike bank to the rear. The second shot has to clear two arroyos. It is almost impossible to reach the green in two, and club selection is crucial on the third shot, depending on pin position.

Piñon Hills is open year round, weather permitting. From November to May it is closed Tuesdays. Annual passes are available, and tournaments are welcome. The peak season is from mid-February to mid-September. To build a local following for the game and course, golf instruction is emphasized at Piñon Hills. In addition to the driving range, there are two practice greens and a chipping green. Piñon Hills has hosted the state high school championship and no doubt will eventually be a national tournament site.

The Navajos consider the country around Four Corners sacred land. The miles of barren plains marked by dramatic mesas, and red-rock and sandstone cliffs are beautifully counterposed by the juniper- and piñon pine-covered hills that meet the deep blue sky. Ken Dye, a principal of Finger, Dye and Spann in Texas, survived a rigorous architectural competition to create a beautiful and challenging golf venue in a magnificent natural setting.

Course Name: **SANTA ANA GOLF COURSE (Formerly Valle Grande) Tamaya, Rio Grande, Coronado Courses**

Course Type: Public
Address: 288 Prairie Star Road
Bernalillo, NM 87004
Phone: (505) 867–9464

GOLF COURSE

Head Professional: Roger Martinez
Course Length/Par (All Tees):
Tamaya/Rio Grande: Back 7082/71;
Blue 6482/71, White 5870/71, Forward

5044/71. Tamaya/Coronado: Back 7077/72, Blue 6469/72, White 5922/72, Forward 4922/72. Rio Grande/Coronado: Back 7001/71, Blue 6517/71, White 5894/71, Forward 5056/71

Course Slope/Rating (All Tees): Tamaya/Rio Grande: Back 119/72.1, Blue 114/69.5, White 108/66.7, Ladies' Forward 122/68.2. Tamaya/Coronado: Back 116/71.3, Blue 113/69.3, White 108/66.8, Ladies' Forward 120/67.3. Rio Grande/Coronado: Back 117/71.7, Blue 112/69.3, White 106/66.4, Ladies' Forward 118/68.4

Course Architect: Ken Killian (1991)

Golf Facilities: Full Pro Shop X, Snack Bar X, Lounge X, Restaurant X, Locker Room No, Showers No, Club Rental X, Club Repair X, Cart Rental X, Instruction X, Practice Green X, Driving Range X, Practice Bunker X, Club Storage No

Tee-Time Reservation Policy: 3 days in advance from 7:30 a.m. for Sat., Sun. 7 days in advance for weekdays

Ranger: Yes

Tee-off-Interval Time: 10 min.

Time to Play 18 Holes: 4 hrs.

Course Hours/Earliest Tee-off: Sunrise

Green Fees: $23 for 18 holes Sat., Sun., holidays; $18 for 18 holes weekdays

Cart Fees: $10 for 18 holes per person

Pull Carts: $3.75 for 18 holes peak season

Credit Cards: MasterCard, Visa

Season: Year round. Busiest season April to Oct.

Course Comments: Can walk anytime

Golf Packages: None

Discounts: Seasonal, twilight

Places to Stay Nearby: ALBUQUERQUE: See Albuquerque, Santa Fe page 455

Local Attractions: See Albuquerque, Santa Fe on page 455. Albuquerque Convention and Visitors Bureau (505) 243–3696, (800) 284–2282. Santa Fe Convention and Visitors Bureau (505) 984–6760, (800) 777–2489

Directions: From Albuquerque: 20 min. north on I–25, Placitas exit 242, left to Jemez Canyon Dam Rd., right to golf course. From Santa Fe: 35 min. south on I–25, Placitas exit 242, right to Jemez Canyon Dam Rd. and golf course

Closest Commercial Airport: Albuquerque International (45 min.)

SANTA ANA GOLF COURSE

The Santa Ana Golf Course, opened in 1991 as Valle Grande, is set in the farmlands of the Santa Ana Pueblo on the west bank of the Rio Grande, with magnificent views of the Sandia Mountains. The 27-hole course has three separate nines on 270 acres. They were designed by Ken Killian, the architect of Kemper Lakes Golf Course, Hawthorn Woods, Illinois; and Forest Preserve National Golf Course, Oak Forest, Illinois, both with Dick Nugent. Valle Grande is on a 50-year lease from the Santa Ana Pueblo Indians, who will eventually manage the course.

New Mexicans Michael Irene and Kit Walker spearheaded this project and had the patience and vision to spend 2½ years negotiating the lease and another 2½ years lining up investors in the property, which in effect is owned by a sovereign nation, the Pueblos. During construction, four archaeological sites were found on the land, one from the time of Coronado and the others containing important Indian artifacts. At critical stages of the construction, archaeologists monitored excavation work and flagged off areas that might have endangered significant relics. Today most of the excavating is being done with irons and woods.

The course itself is an open, links-style layout with eight crystal-blue lakes intermingled with the three nines that can be played in any combination. The Tamaya nine is 3534 yards from the back tees and starts off with a relatively straightforward 405-yard par 4 to a medium-sized green with subtle undulations and protected by grass pot bunkers. The number-1-handicap dogleg-right par-4 seventh plays 460 yards to an elongated green protected by two traps to the left and three grass bunkers to the right. The tee shot has to negotiate four bunkers edging the right fairway near the landing area. The second shot is difficult to hold because the wind blows from left to right and the narrow green slopes in the same direction. The ninth hole is a short but tricky par 4. It is 335 yards long and doglegs right around a lake beginning halfway to the hole and running behind a green protected by three large traps. The question is how much of the water you can carry without washing your ball.

The Rio Grande nine plays 3548 yards from the back and features the 633-yard par-5 eighth as its number-1-handicap hole. Long and straight, this hole starts from an elevated tee that drops 50 to 60 feet to a rolling fairway lined on the left by a cottonwood forest, which is out of bounds. The green is elevated and protected by several grass pot bunkers.

The Coronado nine is 3543 yards in length, with a 594-yard par-5 sixth as its number-1-handicap hole. The first two shots are straight down a narrow fairway. Two large traps guard the left side of a deep green from 100 yards in. The signature hole on this layout is the 167-yard par-3 eighth hole, called "Our Lady of the Sorrows" because distant church spires can be seen from the tee. The green is split, with a lake in front and the larger side on the left with sand and grass pot bunkers to the rear. The finishing hole on Coronado is a 538-yard par 5 that requires a straight drive and second shot. The third shot is onto an elevated green protected by a small lake on the right and a huge bunker left. If you try to reach the hole in two, you have to play the right side on the tee shot and try to come onto the green over the lake. Most players lay up on this hole.

The clubhouse at Santa Ana is a spacious, modern facility designed in the southwestern style. A full-service restaurant, complete pro shop, locker room and showers are available. The driving range is the largest practice facility in the area, with three tiers of teeing ground, practice bunkers, mounds and target greens that simulate course conditions. Located within 45 minutes of Santa Fe and Albuquerque, Santa Ana is a rising star in the desert.

Course Name: TAOS COUNTRY CLUB

Course Type: Semiprivate
Address: Route 68/P.O. Box 254
                  Rancho de Taos, NM 87557
Phone: (505) 758–7300
Fax: (505) 758–4678

GOLF COURSE

Director of Golf: James "Tad" Bourg
Head Professional: Glen McCargar
Course Length/Par (All Tees): Back 7302/72, Blue 6817/72, White 6103/72, Forward 5310/72
Course Slope/Rating (All Tees): Back 129/73.6, Blue 122/73.1, White 118/68.2, Ladies' Forward 125/69
Course Architect: Jep Wille (1992)
Golf Facilities: Full Pro Shop X, Snack Bar X, Lounge X, Restaurant X, Locker Room X, Showers X, Club Rental X, Club Repair X, Cart Rental X, Instruction X, Practice Green X, Driving Range X, Practice Bunker X, Club Storage X
Tee-Time Reservation Policy: Up to 1 week in advance
Ranger: Yes
Tee-off-Interval Time: 8 min.
Time to Play 18 Holes: 4½ hrs.
Course Hours/Earliest Tee-off: 7 a.m.
Green Fees: $30 for 18 holes Sat., Sun., holidays; $25 for 18 holes weekdays plus tax
Cart Fees: $20 for 18 holes per cart
Credit Cards: All major cards
Season: Mar. through Nov. weather permitting. Busiest June and July
Course Comments: You can walk anytime
Golf Packages: Inquire at pro shop
Discounts: Twilight
Places to Stay Nearby: TAOS: Casa Benevidas (505) 758–1772; Historic Taos Inn (505) 758–2233, (800) TAOS–INN; Hotel St. Francis (505) 983–5700, (800) 529–5700; Quail Ridge Inn (505) 776–2211, (800) 624–4448; Residence Inn by Marriott (505) 988–7300, (800) 331–3131. SANTA FE: The Bishop's Lodge (505) 983–6377; (800) 732–2240; El Dorado Hotel (505) 988–4455, (800) 955–4455; Hotel Santa Fe (505) 982–1200, (800) 529–5700; Inn of the

Anasazi (505) 988–3030, (800) 688–8100.
BED AND BREAKFASTS: Adobe Adobe
(505) 983–3133; Alexander's Inn (505)
986–1431; Four Kachinas Inn (505) 982–
2550; Spencer House (505) 988–3024; A
Starry Night Bed and Breakfast (505) 758–
3873, (800) 732–8267. Santa Fe Accomodations, 320 Arnst Rd., Santa Fe, NM
87501 (505) 984–8682, (800) 745–9910

Local Attractions: TAOS: The Fechin
House and Studio, Harwood Foundation,
Kit Carson Home and Museum, Kit
Carson State Park, Martinez Hacienda,
Millicent Rogers Museum, Taos School
of Music. SANTA FE: Cathedral of St.
Francis Assisi, Center for Contemporary
Arts of Santa Fe, Mission of San Miguel
of Santa Fe, Museum of International
Folk Art, Palace of the Governors, Insti-
tute of American Indian Arts Museum,
Museum of New Mexico, El Rancho De
Las Golondrinas, Santa Fe Opera, Santa
Fe Children's Museum, State Capitol,
Wheelwright Museum of the American
Indian, horseback riding, rafting, hiking,
camping, art galleries, missions,
churches, restaurants, seasonal festivals,
Santa Fe Forest's Pecos Wilderness.
Santa Fe Convention and Visitors
Bureau, P.O. Box 909, Santa FE, NM
87504–0909 (505) 984–6760, (800) 777–
2489. Taos County Chamber of Com-
merce, 1139 Paseo del Pueblo Sur, P.O.
Drawer 1, Taos, NM 87571

Directions: From Santa Fe (1 hr. northwest): Drive north on Rte. 68 to golf
course on the left

Closest Commercial Airport: Albuquerque
International (2 hrs.)

TAOS COUNTRY CLUB

The Taos Country Club is the realized
dream of James "Tad" Bourg, a native
Texan who played college golf in the Lone
Star State, moved west, formed a real estate development partnership, then retained
his friend and pro mini-tour colleague, Jep
Wille, to design and thread a championship
golf course through the native brush near
Taos. Set at 7000 feet where the high desert meets the southern Rockies, the Taos
Country Club course can be played from

any of four tee distances. Taos becomes
especially difficult from the two back tee distances because a strayed shot is more likely
to find the native desert brush surrounding
the fairways. It is unlikely that you'll find
your ball in this brush and if you do, it will
probably be an unplayable lie.

Taos starts out with two reasonable par
4s and then you reach the 456-yard par-4
third, the most difficult hole on the course.
The tee shot is to a narrow landing area
and the approach is to a well-bunkered
bentgrass green. The greens at Taos are fast
and large with some undulation. The fairways are Kentucky bluegrass. A challenging par 3 on this layout is the 215-yard
sixteenth which often plays into the wind
during the winter months. The target is
large with a sizeable pot bunker to the left,
one front right, and another back right. A
difficult par 5 on the back nine is the 535-
yard fourteenth which requires an accurate
tee shot to the right of a bunker to the left
of the landing area. The second shot is usually a layup to the right of a cluster of fairway bunkers or you can try to reach the
shallow, wide green in two.

The Taos Country Club has a large
practice facility with driving range, practice
bunkers, and chipping and putting greens.
The golf course accounts for 156 acres of
the 400-acre development which will have
65 homes with prices averaging in the high
six figures. Nearby are the towns of Taos
and Santa Fe, major tourist attractions
noted for Spanish and Native American art,
architecture and artifacts as well as museums, restaurants, artist communities, and
recreational activities ranging from winter
skiing and white water rafting to concerts.

Course Name: **UNIVERSITY OF NEW
MEXICO
South, North Courses**

Course Type: Public
Address: 3601 University Blvd. SE
Albuquerque, NM 87131–
3046
Phone: (505) 277–4546
(South Course)
(505) 277–4140
(North Course)

GOLF COURSE

Director of Golf: Henry D. Sandles

Managers: South: Andy Boyd. North: Barbara Berry

Course Length/Par (All Tees): South: Back 7253/72, Blue 6882/72, White 6480/72, Forward 6167/72. North: Back 3333/36, Forward 2936/36

Course Slope/Rating (All Tees): South: Back 128/73.8, Blue 125/72.1, White 121/70.3, Forward 120/69.4, Ladies' Forward 131/75.1. North: Back 114/69.2, Ladies' Forward 115/71.6

Course Architects: South: Robert (Red) Lawrence (1966). North: William H. Tucker, Sr. (originally 18 holes, 1951)

Golf Facilities: Full Pro Shop X, Snack Bar X, Lounge No, Restaurant No, Locker Room X, Showers X, Club Rental X, Club Repair X, Cart Rental X, Instruction X, Practice Green X, Driving Range X, Practice Bunker X, Club Storage No

Tee-Time Reservation Policy: South: From Thursday 7:30 a.m. for the following weekend. Weekend reservations only for 3 or more golfers. After 7 a.m. reservations can be made for weekday tee times up to 1 wk. in advance. North: Reservations required on 9-hole North Course mid-March to Oct. for Sat., Sun., holidays only

Ranger: Yes

Tee-off-Interval Time: 8 min.

Time to Play 18 Holes: 4 hrs.

Course Hours/Earliest Tee-off: 6:20 a.m. summer

Green Fees: South: $50 for 18 holes weekends, holidays; $42 for 18 holes Mon. to Fri. North: $10 for 9 holes

Cart Fees: South: $22 for 18 holes per cart. North: $6 for 9 holes

Pull Carts: $4 for 18 holes, $2 for 9 holes

Credit Cards: MasterCard, Visa

Season: Year round. Busiest season May to July

Course Comments: Can walk anytime. Yardage book availble. 3-hole beginner course on site

Golf Packages: None

Discounts: Twilight, faculty memberships, seniors, students

Places to Stay Nearby: See Albuquerque, Santa Fe page 455

Local Attractions: See Albuquerque, Santa Fe page 455. Albuquerque Convention and Visitors Bureau (505) 243–3696, (800) 284–2282. Santa Fe Convention and Visitors Bureau (505) 984–6760, (800) 777–2489

Directions: I–25 south, exit Rio Bravo (go to stop sign), make left under I–25, 2nd complex on left

Closest Commercial Airport: Albuquerque International (10 min.)

UNIVERSITY OF NEW MEXICO

The University of New Mexico South Golf Course is ranked as one of the best public golf courses in the United States by *Golf Digest*. It is also one of the top public or private golf courses in New Mexico. It has been the site of several major tournaments, including PGA and LPGA qualifying events, men's and women's intercollegiate invitationals, NCAA championships and numerous regional and state tournaments.

The UNM South Course is a unique 21-hole challenge designed by Robert "Red" Lawrence of Tucson. Lawrence was born in White Plains, New York, and started in golf design by working for Walter Travis. In the 1920s he constructed several Toomey and Flynn designs in Florida, including 36 holes at the Boca Raton Hotel. During the Depression Lawrence became course superintendent at Boca Raton but left after World War II to pursue golf architecture full-time in Florida, then later in Arizona. Some of his work includes the Camelback Golf Club (Padre Course), Scottsdale, Arizona; Desert Forest Country Club, Carefree, Arizona; and several other courses in Arizona, Florida, and New Mexico. He was a charter member of the American Association of Golf Course Architects, and president in 1956 and 1964.

The extra three holes on the South Course are regular-length practice holes near the driving range. The course itself is a 7253-yard par-72 bentgrass challenge with many traps, five water hazards, and elevated tees and greens. This layout also provides the golfer with the opportunity to shoot across arroyos and gullies, and up, down, around and between hills, ridges and valleys. The course itself is a high desert layout and is relatively open. The length, wind and hazards make the course difficult.

The South Course starts out with five reasonable holes to warm you up. The first is a 551-yard par 5 with a slight dogleg to the left, water on the left and a green protected by three traps to the left, back and right. The second hole is a 435-yard par 4, relatively straight to a large, deep green with traps to the right front and to the left. The next hole is a 160-yard par 3 to a kidney-shaped green surrounded by four traps with an opening in front of the green. The par-4 fourth hole plays 383 yards, with a slight dogleg right to a roundish green protected by two traps to the left and one large trap to the right. The par-4 fifth hole plays 449 yards from the back tees straight to a large green protected by traps to the left front, right and left rear.

The final four holes of the front nine are more difficult, with numbers eight and nine being the toughest. The 248-yard par-3 eighth hole plays from an elevated tee to a large elevated green that is protected to the left and rear by four traps. The 604-yard par-5 number nine is the number-1-handicap hole on the course. A dogleg to the right with an uphill tee shot, this hole requires three strong shots for an average golfer to reach the green in regulation. The putting surface is huge and protected by five traps on either side. The second shot is downhill and high desert wasteland is to the left and right all the way to the hole.

The back nine greets you with the 457-yard par-4 tenth, a severe dogleg right that curls back to the green, which is 39 yards in depth and protected by traps left, back and right. You can't cut the corner on this hole, and a driver and a long iron are usually required to reach the green. The number-2-handicap hole on the course is the 554-yard par-5 fourteenth, which plays straight to a green protected by five traps left, front and right. Typically, the green is large, medium fast and undulating.

The South Course is home to the University of New Mexico golf team, and there are seven certified PGA and LPGA professionals available for instruction at the ample practice facilities. The 3333-yard par-36 nine-hole North Course is also available for play. Reservations are required on this course on weekends and holidays from mid-March to October. A variety of membership packages are available for both courses.

The North Course was originally eighteen holes and was the first course in America to measure longer than 7000 yards when it was designed by William H. Tucker, Sr., and opened in 1951. Tucker was born in England, where he learned the art of turf management from his father, who was an employee of Wimbledon Commons. He became a golf professional and worked on golf-course construction crews. He later emigrated to the United States and became the successful designer of more than 120 golf courses before retiring to Albuquerque after World War II. Tucker died in 1954, and shortly thereafter the William H. Tucker Invitational for College Men and Women was played on his original North Course, which measured 7300 yards from the championship tees. When the South Course was built in the 1960s, the North Course was reduced to a nine-hole course to accommodate the University's growing need for land to construct new buildings. Today the Tucker tournament is played on the South Course and is called the McGuire Intercollegiate Invitational. The nine-hole North Course is approximately 5 miles from the South Course and is a popular walking course.

Recommended Golf Courses in New Mexico:

Albuquerque:

Arroyo del Oso Golf Course, Albuquerque, (505) 884–7505, Public, 18/6892/72

Double Eagle Country Club and Lodge, Albuquerque, (505) 898–7001, Resort, 18/6895/72

Ladera Golf Course, Albuquerque, (505) 836–4449, Public, 18/7060/72

Paradise Hills Golf Club, Albuquerque, (505) 898–7001, Public, 18/6895/72

Las Cruces:

New Mexico State University, Las Cruces, (505) 646–3219, Public, 18/7040/72

Ruidoso:

Links at Sierra Blanca, Ruidoso, (505) 258–5330, (800) 854–6571, Public, 18/7003/72

Within 1/2 Hour of Santa Fe:

Angel Fire Resort, Angel Fire, (505) 377–3055 (Golf Course), (505) 377–2301 (Resort), Resort, 18/6624/72

Socorro:

New Mexico Tech Golf Course, Socorro, (505) 835–5335, Public, 18/6688/72

New Mexico: Useful Information

New Mexico Dept. of Tourism, Lamy Bldg., Rm. 106, 491 Old Santa Fe Trail, Santa Fe, NM 87503, (505) 827–4000, (800) 545–2040 (outside NM)

State Park and Recreation Division, 141 E. De Vargas, Santa Fe, NM 87503, (505) 827–7465 (recreation information)

Department of Game and Fish, Villagra Bldg., Santa Fe, NM 87503, (505) 827–7882 (fishing and hunting regulations)

National Forest Service, Southwest Region, 517 Gold Ave. SW, Albuquerque, NM 87102, (505) 842–3292, (800) 280–CAMP (national forest information and reservations)

New York City and Long Island

Course Name: BETHPAGE
Black, Blue, Red, Yellow, Green Courses

Course Type: Public
Address: Round Swamp Road
Farmingdale, NY 11735
Phone: (516) 249–0701 (Golf Course)
(516) 249–0700 (Park Administration, Information)

GOLF COURSE

Head Professional: Chuck Workman

Course Length/Par (All Tees): Black: Back 7065/71, Forward 6556/71. Blue: 6513/72. Red: 6537/70. Green: 6267/71. Yellow: 6171/71

Course Slope/Rating (All Tees): Black: Back 139/73.6, Forward 131/70.5, Ladies' Forward 138/75.7. Blue: Back 123/72.2, Ladies' Back 128/75.6. Red: Back 126/72.7, Ladies' Back 129/75.6. Green: Back 117/70.1, Ladies' Back 123/73.7. Yellow: Back 113/69.4, Ladies' Back 123/72.9

Course Architects: Black: A. W. Tillinghast (1936). Blue: A. W. Tillinghast (1935), Frank Duane (renovation, 1962). Red: A. W. Tillinghast (1935), Frank Duane (renovation, NA). Green: Frank Duane (NA). Yellow: Alfred H. Tull (1958)

Golf Facilities: Full Pro Shop X, Snack Bar X, Lounge X, Restaurant X, Locker Room X, Showers X, Club Rental X, Club Repair X, Cart Rental X, Instruction X, Practice Green X, Driving Range X, Practice Bunker X, Club Storage X

Tee-Time Reservation Policy: First come, first served

Ranger: Yes

Tee-off-Interval Time: 7½ and 8½ min.

Time to Play 18 Holes: 4½ hrs.

Course Hours/Earliest Tee-off: Sunrise to sunset weekends, 6 a.m. weekdays

Green Fees: $18 for 18 holes Sat., Sun., holidays; $14 for 18 holes weekdays

Cart Fees: $24 for 18 holes, $16 for 9 holes

Pull Carts: $2.50 for 18 holes

Credit Cards: Cash for golf fees. All major cards for merchandise

Season: Bethpage Black, March to end of Nov.; Blue, Red, Green, Yellow courses year round

Course Comments: Walking only on Black and Green courses. Carts allowed on others

Golf Packages: None

Discounts: Seniors (Mon. to Fri.), New York State residents, twilight, seasonal

Places to Stay Nearby: MELVILLE: Radisson Plaza Hotel (516) 755–4000, (800) 333–3333; Huntington Hilton (516) 845–1000, (800) 445–8667. PLAINVIEW: Marriott Residence Inn and Conference Center (516) 433–6200, (800) 331–3131; Holiday Inn (516) 349–7400, (800) HOLIDAY. UNIONDALE: Long Island Marriott Hotel and Conference Center (516) 794–3800, (800) 288–9290. GARDEN CITY: Garden City Hotel (516) 747–3000, (800) 547–0400. WESTBURY: Island Inn (516) 228–9500, (800) FOR–ROOM

Local Attractions: BETHPAGE: Meadowbrook Polo Club, Plaza Playhouse, Plain Edge Playhouse. WITHIN 1 HOUR: Jones Beach State Park, Shea Stadium, Fire Island National Seashore, Nassau Coliseum, Oyster Bay, Old Westbury Gardens, Planting Fields Arboretum, Nassau County Museum of Art, Sagamore Hill National Historic Site, Hofstra University, Vanderbilt Museum, Belmont Park Race Track, Westbury Music Fair, C. W. Post College, concerts, theater, camping, boating, fishing. New York City. Long Island Tourism and Convention Commission (800) 441–4601

Directions: From New York City (36 mi.): Long Island Expressway (I–495), to Seaford exit, take Oyster Bay (Hwy. 135) Expressway south to exit 8, take Powell Ave., left, signs into park

Closest Commercial Airports: John F. Kennedy International (45 min.); La Guardia (45 min.); Long Island/ MacArthur, Ronkonkoma (45 min.)

BETHPAGE

The Bethpage Black Course has long been considered one of the finest golf courses of any kind in America. *Golf Digest* regularly ranks it in its list of top public golf courses, and the course is also included in that publication's list of the best courses in New York State, public or private. *Golf* magazine lists Bethpage Black in its 100 greatest courses in America public or private, and at the same time has included it in its "50 Best Buys for a Buck in Public Golf" list.

Bethpage Black is one of five courses located in Bethpage State Park on Long Island, which is approximately one hour east of New York City. The park contains 1475 acres of fields and beautiful rolling woodland devoted to recreation. Picnic areas, playing fields, tennis and horseback-riding trails are among the other amenities available in the park. Bethpage Black and two of the other nearby courses were designed by A. W. Tillinghast during the Depression, when over 1800 people were employed at the park as part of a W.P.A. project. The Black Course, a 7065-yard par-71 layout, was the last course that Tillinghast designed, and the course can only be walked, which is a real pleasure.

Tillinghast was a member of a wealthy Philadelphia family and was known as an aristocratic raconteur. After a visit to St. Andrews, Scotland, while in his 20s, Tillinghast took up golf and became an excellent amateur player. He laid out a golf course in 1906 at the request of Charles Worthington, the pump-manufacturing millionaire, at what is now known as Shawnee-on-Delaware. He eventually formed his own golf-architecture firm and designed Baltusrol Golf Course (Upper and Lower courses), Springfield, New Jersey; Winged Foot Golf Course (East and West courses), Mamaroneck, New York; Brook Hollow Golf Course, Dallas, Texas; and many others. Tillinghast became a millionaire but during the Depression lost his money. In 1942, he died at the age of 67, nearly a pauper at his daughter's home in Toledo, Ohio. His legacy of well-designed golf courses remains, however.

The Bethpage Black Course is hilly, with well-groomed fairways and small to medium-sized, undulating bentgrass greens that are well-protected by traps. Tillinghast's tendency was to have two sets of tee markers usually only about 20 yards apart. He usually used fairway bunkers only on one side of the fairway, and his green-side bunkers tend to flank the putting surface or pinch the front. His greens are likely to be narrow in front and wider in back with no traps. Instead, behind them are drop-offs.

Bethpage Black is beautifully treed but relatively open, and water comes into play on only one hole, the 195-yard par-3 eighth, which has two ponds to the left front of the green and a considerable amount of sand in back. The tee shot is downhill, but you can't see the second pond from the tee. The Black Course, as you will learn, requires position golf. Placement is required both off the tee and from the fairway, especially to avoid well-placed bunkers.

The front nine has five holes with significant doglegs including the first hole, another tough par 4, which plays 430 yards, bends to the right and has a small, well-guarded green with a trap on the left and two to the right. Eleven of these greens are elevated and tend to favor soft, high, arching approach shots. This type of approach is especially necessary on holes two, four, fifteen and seventeen.

The number-1-handicap hole at Bethpage is the 446-yard par-4 fifth, which plays from an elevated tee to an elevated green protected by bunkers to the left front, right and rear. The tee shot has to carry a huge right-fairway bunker that ends approximately 200 yards from the tee. The next hole is a rough, 404-yard par-4 dogleg left whose landing area at the knee of the dogleg is protected by bunkers on the left and right, providing little margin for error. The second shot is onto a green trapped on the left and right.

The back nine begins with three consecutive doglegs left, including the 480-yard par-4 twelfth hole, which has a huge fairway bunker to carry, approximately 210 yards from the tee. The second shot is to a green with a narrow opening through two traps, one left and the other right. The number-2-handicap 438-yard par-4 fifteenth has a tough uphill second shot to a green well trapped in front. If you miss to the right you can roll the ball downhill and out of bounds. The sixteenth is a long, 466-yard par 4 whose green has large traps on the left and right. Next is a 200-yard par 3 that has three traps front and left and two right and back. The finishing hole, a par 4, is straight and measures 378 yards, but it is extremely narrow midway home, with fairway traps left and right. Again, the green is well-trapped to the right and in back.

The other four courses in this 90-hole golf complex are the Blue, 6513 yards, par 72; Red, 6537 yards, par 70; Green, 6267 yards, par 71 and Yellow, 6171 yards, par 71. The Blue and Red Courses were also designed by Tillinghast. An attractive clubhouse of Long Island colonial design serves all five courses and contains locker rooms and showers for men and women, a pro shop, cocktail lounge, dining porch and grill. A private dining room is available for group luncheons. Picnic catering is also available.

Four courses are open year round, but the Black Course is given a rest from December through February. Playing Bethpage Black is a pilgrimage any golfer should make. This is one of the few chances for the public to play a well-maintained, accessible Tillinghast course.

Course Name: MONTAUK DOWNS STATE PARK

Course Type: Public
Address: South Fairview Avenue
Montauk, NY 11954
Phone: (516) 668–1100 (Pro shop),
(516) 668–1234 (Tee times),
(516) 668–5000
(Park Information)

GOLF COURSE

Head Professional: Kevin Smith
Course Length/Par (All Tees): Back 6762/72, Middle 6289/72, Forward 5797/72

Course Slope/Rating (All Tees): Back 133/73.3, Middle 128/70.5, Ladies' Forward 135/75.9
Course Architects: Robert Trent Jones, Sr., and Rees Jones (1968)
Golf Facilities: Full Pro Shop X, Snack Bar X, Lounge X, Restaurant X, Locker Room X, Showers X, Club Rental X, Club Repair Minor/Send Out, Cart Rental X, Instruction X, Practice Green X, Driving Range X, Practice Bunker X, Club Storage X
Tee-Time Reservation Policy: Up to 7 days in advance. Reservation system: (516) 668–1234
Ranger: Yes
Tee-off-Interval Time: 8 to 10 min.
Time to Play 18 Holes: 4 hrs. 45 min.
Course Hours/Earliest Tee-off: 5:30 a.m. Sat., Sun., holidays; 6 a.m. weekdays peak season (summer)
Green Fees: $25 for 18 holes Sat., Sun., holidays; $20 for 18 holes Mon. to Fri.
Cart Fees: $24 for 18 holes per cart, or $12 per rider
Credit Cards: Cash for golf fees. All major cards for merchandise
Season: Late March to Dec. 1
Course Comments: Can walk anytime. Yardage book available
Golf Packages: Available through golf shop
Discounts: Seniors (state residents), twilight
Places to Stay Nearby: MONTAUK: Beachcomber Resort (516) 668–2894; Driftwood on the Ocean (516) 668–5744; Sting Ray (516) 668–3344; Montauk Yacht Club Resort and Marina (516) 668–3100; Gurney's Inn (516) 668–2345. SAG HARBOR: Baron's Cove (516) 725–2100; Sag Harbor Inn (516) 725–2944. EAST HAMPTON: East Hampton House (516) 324–4300; Maidstone Arms (516) 324–5006; Bassett House Inn (516) 324–6127; 1770 House–Philip Taylor (516) 324–1770. SOUTHAMPTON: Southampton Resort at Cold Spring Bay (516) 283–7600; Village Latch Inn (516) 283–2160. CONDOMINIUMS: Dune Resorts (516) 668–3800, (800) LAST WAV
Local Attractions: Boating, swimming at Long Island beaches, fishing, antiquing, shopping, restaurants, whale watching,

horseback riding, wineries, camping, hiking, bicycling, Montauk Point Lighthouse Museum, Shelter Island. EAST HAMPTON: Guild Hall Museum, restaurants, shopping. SAG HARBOR: Whaling and Historical Museum, restaurants, antiques, shopping, historic buildings. SOUTHAMPTON: Historical Museum, Morton National Wildlife Refuge, beaches, restaurants, shopping, Parrish Art Museum. Long Island Tourism and Convention Commission (800) 441–4601. Montauk Chamber of Commerce (516) 668–2428

Directions: From New York City (130 mi.): I–495 east (Long Island Expressway) to exit 70, Manorville Rd. south to Rte. 27, Rte. 27 east to Montauk, 1 mi. east of village, left on County Rd. 77, 1/2 mi. to South Fairview, left on South Fairview to golf course

Closest Commercial Airports: Long Island/MacArthur, Ronkonkoma (1 hr.); La Guardia (2 hrs.); John F. Kennedy (2 hrs.)

MONTAUK DOWNS STATE PARK

Montauk Downs was originally built in 1926 by H.C.C. Tippetts and C. H. Anderson. In 1968 it was redesigned by Robert Trent Jones, Sr., and Rees Jones. This 6762-yard par-72 layout, situated near the easternmost tip of Long Island, in Montauk Downs State Park, is approximately a 2½ hour drive from New York City. This is a major vacation and second-home area, making Montauk Downs a rather busy place. You can walk the course anytime and green fees are very reasonable considering the quality and condition of the golf course. Montauk Downs is rated among the top 75 public courses in America by *Golf Digest.*

This rolling and open golf course features small, moderately fast, well-bunkered, undulating bentgrass greens. The greens are usually elevated, requiring the golfer to fly the ball into the target. Fairway bunkers, trees and water hazards are minimal, but they are well-placed near strategic fairway landing areas. The greens are an interesting variety of shapes and sizes, with bunkers and other obstacles nearby. This course, which has total yardage distances of 6762, 6289, and 5797 from three tee positions, is an excellent test for any level of play.

The number-1-handicap hole at Montauk is the 452-yard par-4 ninth, a slight dogleg right. The tee shot is to a landing area guarded by two bunkers on the left and one on the right. The approach is to a slightly elevated, shallow green protected by traps to the left, front and right.

An interesting par 5 on the front side is the 508-yard seventh, a dogleg left. The tee shot is to a landing area with trees to the right. You can elect to lay up on the second shot or go for the two-tiered green that is well-protected by a large trap to the left, a trap to the right front and a pond to the left front. A tricky par 3 on this side is the 152-yard second, which plays to a wide, shallow green fronted by two bunkers and protected on the right side by another. The swirling winds from nearby Lake Montauk further complicate this hole.

The signature hole at Montauk is the 213-yard par-3 twelfth, the most difficult par 3 on the course. The wide, shallow, elevated green is fronted by two traps on a downward-sloping bank. Another bunker guards the back of the green. The 441-yard par-4 finishing hole plays straight to a medium-sized green squeezed on both sides by large bunkers. Another trap is to the rear of the green. The tee shot has to avoid a cluster of traps to the left, beginning 225 yards from the back tees.

Montauk provides a varied and memorable golf experience with a range of distances, greens, bunker placements, and water-hazard positions. The par 4s, for example, measure from the 347-yard sixth to the 452-yard ninth. Wind conditions and the demand for precision on approach shots make this an excellent test of golf.

Within walking distance of the clubhouse is a putting green, practice range, 6 tennis courts and a swimming pool. The clubhouse has a restaurant, pro shop, locker rooms, showers, 2 bars and a grill room. Montauk is well worth the visit.

Recommended Golf Courses in New York

New York City and Long Island:

Bergen Point Golf Club, West Babylon, (516) 661–8282, Public, 18/6630/71

Crab Meadow golf Club, Northport, (516) 757–8800, Public, 18/6575/70

Island's End Golf and Country Club, Greenport, (516) 477–0777, Semiprivate, 18/6600/72

La Tourette Golf Course, Staten Island, (718) 351–1889, Public, 18/6692/72

Marriott's Wind Watch Hotel and Golf Club, Hauppauge, (516) 232–9850, Resort, 18/6405/71

Oyster Bay Golf Course, Woodbury, (516) 364–3977, Public, 18/6351/70

Pine Hills Country Club, Manorville, (516) 878–4343, Public, 18/7050/71

Rock Hill Country Club, Manorville, (516) 878–2250, Public, 18/7050/71

Spring Lake Golf Club, Middle Island, (516) 924–5115, Public. Thunderbird: 18/7048/72. Sandpiper: 9/3053/36

Smithtown Landing Golf Club, Smithtown, (516) 360–7618, Public, 18/6114/72

Swan Lake Golf Club, Manorville, (516) 369–1818, Public, 18/7011/72

Hudson River Valley

Course Name: SPOOK ROCK

Course Type: Public
Address: 199 Spook Rock Road
                       Ramapo, NY 10901
Phone: (914) 357–6466

GOLF COURSE

Head Professional: Martin Bohen
Course Length/Par (All Tees): Back 6894/72, White 6366/72, Gold 5741/72, Forward 4853/72
Course Slope/Rating (All Tees): Back 129/73.3, White 125/70.9, Gold 122/73.3, Forward 111/70.9
Course Architect: Frank Duane (1970)
Golf Facilities: Full Pro Shop X, Snack Bar X, Lounge X, Restaurant No, Locker Room X, Showers X, Club Rental X, Club Repair X, Cart Rental X, Instruction X, Practice Green X, Driving Range X, Practice Bunker X, Club Storage No
Tee-Time Reservation Policy: Sun. at 6 p.m. for Mon. to Thurs. tee times. Thurs. 7 a.m. for Fri., Sat., Sun., holiday tee times
Ranger: Yes (summer)
Tee-off-Interval Time: 7 to 9 min.
Time to Play 18 Holes: 5 hrs.
Course Hours/Earliest Tee-off: 6 a.m. Fri., Sat., Sun., holidays; 7 a.m. Mon. to Thurs.
Green Fees: $40 for 18 holes Sat., Sun., holidays; $30 for 18 holes Mon. to Fri.
Cart Fees: $24 for 18 holes per cart; $13 for 9 holes per cart except weekends in July, Aug.
Credit Cards: Cash or local check for golf fees. MasterCard, Visa for merchandise
Season: Mid-March to mid-Dec. Busiest season June to Sept.
Course Comments: Can walk anytime. Yardage book available. Local residents have tee-time reservation preference. Golf school on site
Golf Packages: None
Discounts: Resident ID cards, juniors, seniors, twilight rate from 3 p.m. or 4 p.m. depending on season ($16 weekdays, $21.50 weekends and holidays)
Places to Stay Nearby: Holiday Inn (914) 357–4800, (800) HOLIDAY. MAHWAH, NJ: Sheraton Crossroads (201) 529–1660, (800) 325–3535. TARRYTOWN: Courtyard by Marriott (914) 631–1122, (800) 321–2121; Tarrytown Hilton Inn (914) 591–8200, (800) 445–8667; Westchester Marriott (914) 631–2200, (800) 228–9290
Local Attractions: NYACK: Art galleries, antiques, restaurants, historic district. TARRYTOWN: Headless Horseman Bridge, Philipsburg Manor, Sleepy Hollow Cemetery, Lyndhurst, Sunnyside, Washington Irving Memorial. STONY POINT: Stony Point Battlefield historic site, Bear Mountain State Park. Piermont. West Point. New York City. Orange County Chamber of Commerce

(914) 342–2522. Rockland County Chamber of Commerce (914) 353–2221

Directions: New York State Thruway exit 14B, Airmont Rd., bear right (left from south), 1 mi. to light, left on Spook Rock, follow signs to course (1/4 mi. on left)

Closest Commercial Airports: Newark International, NJ (1 hr.); Stewart International, Newburgh (1 hr.); La Guardia (1½ hrs.)

SPOOK ROCK

Spook Rock is a 6894-yard par-72 Frank Duane–designed layout located approximately 30 miles northwest of New York City's George Washington Bridge. This excellent facility is operated by the Town of Ramapo Department of Parks and Recreation. Spook Rock is consistently highly rated on *Golf Digest*'s America's 75 best public courses list. Now in the midst of a capital improvement program, the course is in better condition than ever.

A walk along Spook Rock's rolling, tree-lined fairways is like a walk through a beautiful park. Many interesting dogleg holes are to be found, hazards such as fairway bunkers and ponds are well placed, and the large greens tend to be moderately fast and well guarded by two or three traps and an occasional water hazard. Shot placement and course management are important at Spook Rock. If the ball strays, you will add considerable distance to the course, and you will likely end up under a tree, in a bunker or in a water hazard. The tee distance options of 6894, 6366, 5741 and 4853 yards provide a comfortable choice of course length for any golfer.

The first hole is a nice introduction to Spook Rock. The left side of the fairway on this 428-yard par-4 dogleg left is tree-lined from tee to green. The right is a bit more open. Ideally the tee shot should be hit just to the right of the bunkers guarding the left turn of the dogleg. That leaves an approach of 150 to 175 yards to a large green guarded by two large bunkers to the left and right.

One of the more challenging holes on the front nine is the 392-yard par-4 fifth.

This is a sharp dogleg left uphill to a large green protected by two bunkers to the right front. On the tee shot you have to decide how much of the dogleg you want to try to cut. Two bunkers to the left beginning approximately 200 yards from the back tees, force you to clear them, go left and risk being stymied by trees and rough, or go right and be in the fairway but 200 yards from the target. The second shot is uphill, forcing you to use at least one additional club to reach the putting surface.

A difficult hole on the back nine is the 548-yard par-5 fifteenth. Both sides of the fairway are tree-lined from tee to green. The tee shot is to a landing area flanked by a bunker on the right and two bunkers on the left. The second shot must avoid a series of bunkers to the right and approximately 125 yards from the green. The approach is to a sizeable green with a bunker to the left and two more to the right. The entranceway to the green is squeezed in front by the bunkers.

A memorable and beautiful par 3 on the back nine is the 202-yard thirteenth, which plays over the corner of a large pond to the left to a large green guarded by a bunker to the left and another to the right. Farther right is another large pond that has been known to catch a few golf balls.

The clubhouse at Spook Rock includes a snack bar restaurant, small pro shop, locker rooms and showers. There is also a separate banquet facility for group outings and other occasions. A putting green and a sizeable lighted driving range are located in front of the clubhouse and just to the left of the first tee. Individual and group instruction is available from the staff of PGA professionals.

Recommended Golf Courses in New York

The Hudson River Valley (South of Albany):

Blue Hill Golf Club, Pearl River, (914) 735–2094, Semiprivate, 18/6471/72

Central Valley Golf Club, Central Valley, (914) 928–6924, Semiprivate, 18/5639/71

Garrison Golf Club, Garrison, (914) 424–3604, Semiprivate, 18/6470/72

IBM Mid Hudson Valley Golf Course, Poughkeepsie, (914) 433–2222, Semiprivate, 18/6691/72

McCann Memorial Golf Course, Poughkeepsie, (914) 471–3917, Public, 18/6524/72

Mohansic Golf Club, Yorktown Heights, (914) 962–4049, Public, 18/6500/70

Otterkill Golf and Country Club, Campbell, (914) 427–2301, Public, 18/6761/72

Rockland Lake State Park Golf Club, Congers, (914) 268–6250, Public. Championship: 18/6864/72. Executive: 18/5560/54

Segalla Country Club, Amenia, (914) 373–9200, Public, 18/6617/72

Thomas Carvell Country Club, Pine Plains, (518) 398–7101, Public, 18/7025/73

Wallkill Golf Club, Middletown, (914) 361–1022, Public, 18/6437/72

West Point Golf Course (military personnel and guests), West Point, (914) 938–2435, 18/6007/70

Catskills

Course Name: **THE CONCORD CHAMPIONSHIP GOLF CLUB Monster, International, Challenger Courses**

Course Type: Resort
Resort: The Concord
Address: Highway 42
    Kiamesha Lake, NY 12751
Phone: (914) 794–4000 (Golf Course)
    (914) 794–4000 (Resort)
    (800) 431–3850 (Reservations only, U.S., Toronto, Montreal)
Fax: (914) 794–7471 (Resort)

GOLF COURSE

Director of Golf: Steve Downey
Course Length/Par (All Tees): Monster: Back 7966/72, Blue 7471/72, White 6989/72, Forward 6548/72. International: Back 6619/71, Middle 5968/71, Forward 5554/71. Challenger: 2200/3 (9 holes)
Course Slope/Rating (All Tees): Monster: Back NA/NA, Blue 142/76.4, White 137/74.1, Forward 129/72.2, Ladies' Forward 142/80.7 and 144/78.5. International: Back NA/NA, Middle 124/71.8, Forward 125/73.6. Challenger: NA/NA
Course Architects: Monster: Joe Finger, Jimmy Demaret, Ray Parker and Jack Burke, Jr. (1963). International: A. H. Tull (1951). Challenger: A. H. Tull (1951)
Golf Facilities: Full Pro Shop X, Snack Bar X, Lounge X, Restaurant X, Locker Room X, Showers X, Club Rental X, Club Repair X, Cart Rental X, Instruction X, Practice Green X, Driving Range X, Practice Bunker X, Club Storage X
Tee-Time Reservation Policy: Resort Guests: At time of reservation. Public: Up to 7 months in advance
Ranger: Yes
Tee-off-Interval Time: 8 min.
Time to Play 18 Holes: Championship, Challenger: 5 hrs.; International: 4 hrs.
Course Hours/Earliest Tee-off: 7 a.m.
Green and Cart Fees: Resort guests: Monster: $60 for 18 holes with cart. International: $40 for 18 holes with cart, $25 walking. Challenger: $5 for 9 holes. Outside play: Monster: $90 for 18 holes with cart weekends, $80 Mon. to Fri. International: $55 for 18 holes with cart. Challenger: $5 for 9 holes
Credit Cards: All major cards
Season: April to Nov. Busiest July and Aug.
Course Comments: Can walk International, Challenger
Golf Packages: Available through resort
Discounts: Periodic seasonal and midweek specials
Places to Stay Nearby: MONTICELLO: Best Western Monticello (914) 796–4000, (800) 528–1234; Kutsher's Country Club (914) 794–6000, (800) 431–1273. ELLENVILLE: Nevele Country Club (914) 647–6000, (800) 647–6000; Lodge (914) 796–3000. GROSSINGER: Grossinger's Hotel (914) 292–1450. LIBERTY: Holiday Inn Express (914) 292–7171, (800) HOLI-

DAY. CALLICOON: Villa Roma Country Club (914) 887–4880, (800) 533–6767 (NY), (800) 621–5656 (outside NY)

Local Attractions: MONTICELLO: Antique shops, Monticello Raceway. LIVINGSTON MANOR: Catskill Fly Fishing Center, Catskill Park, hunting, fishing, camping, boating, hiking, skiing, other outdoor recreation. Sullivan County Office of Public Information (800) 882–CATS (in NY), (800) 342–5826 (outside NY)

Directions: From New York City (2 hrs.): George Washington Bridge to Palisades Parkway (NJ) to New York Thruway north to exit 16 (Rte. 17 west). Rte. 17 west to exit 105B (Rte. 42), north on Rte. 42, follow signs to resort. From Scranton, PA: Rte. 84 east to Rte. 17 west to exit 105B, north on Rte. 42, follow signs to resort. From Boston (4½ hrs.) and New England states: Massachusetts Turnpike to Sturbridge exit/Rte. 86, south to Rte. 84, west to exit 4W in New York to Rte. 17, west to exit 105B, north on Rte. 42, follow signs to resort

Closest Commercial Airports: Stewart International, Newburgh (1 hr.); La Guardia (2 hrs.); John F. Kennedy International (2 hrs.); Newark International, NJ (2 hrs.)

RESORT

Date Built: 1938

No. of Rooms: 1250. Towers: Large rooms, some with 1½ baths. Superior: Large room with 1 full bath. Standard: Standard-sized room with 1 full bath. Private bath: Smaller-sized room with 1 full bath. Clubhouse: 42 rms.

Meeting Rooms: 35. Capacity of Largest: 3000 persons banquet style. Meeting Space: 170,000 sq. ft.

Room Price Range: $168 to $193 per person per room, double occupancy, full American plan (3 meals). Golf, tennis and holiday packages available

Lounge: Club Bar

Restaurants: 6 dining rooms, Little Club coffee shop, deli, golf clubhouse, outdoor pool/patio

Entertainment: Night club acts and shows in 2900-seat Imperial Room. Entertainment in Night Owl Lounge, Disco, Cordillion Room, Little Club

Credit Cards: All major cards

General Amenities: Babysitting services, day camps year round for youngsters over 3 years old, bird watching, meeting and conference facilities with audio-visual and food services, shops and boutiques

Recreational Amenities: Atrium fitness center with Universals, StairMasters, aerobics, free weights, trainers; indoor and outdoor swimming pools, 24 outdoor and 19 indoor tennis courts, 18-hole miniature golf course, basketball, men's and ladies' steam rooms, saunas, health club, cold plunge pools; volleyball, table tennis, swimming, boating, fishing, horseback riding, skiing, skating, handball, paddleball, bocce ball, bowling, jogging, aquaslimnastics

Reservation and Cancellation Policy: $50 deposit per person required to hold reservations. Cancellation notice or change in reservation dates must be received 1 wk. prior to arrival date to avoid penalties

Comments and Restrictions: Pets not allowed, but kennels available nearby. Taxes additional to base rates

THE CONCORD GOLF CLUB

The Concord Resort is the home of "the Monster," voted by *Golf* and *Golf Digest* magazines one of the top 100 golf courses, public or private, in the United States. The course is called "the Monster" largely because of its length and difficulty. The scorecard lists the back tees at 7966 yards, but usually the blue tees, at 7471 yards, are used for tournament play. The other distances are 6989 and 6548 yards, making this one of the most difficult golf courses for women anywhere. The course was designed and built by the team of Joe Finger, Jimmy Demaret, Jack Burke, Jr., and Ray Parker, the resort's owner. The Parker family still owns and manages the Concord Resort, which is set on 2000 acres of beautiful rolling land in the foothills of the Catskill Mountains.

In addition to length, "the Monster" has very large, moderately fast, undulating greens with large, strategically placed bunkers. The fairways are beautifully framed by mature trees, but there is generous landing room on most tee shots. Water hazards in the form of streams, ponds and lakes appear on ten holes. Because of the length of this golf course, many golfers tend to press and overswing to cover more territory. This usually leads to trouble. When you do reach these ample greens at the Concord, it is very easy to three-putt. A chart designating the day's pin position is handed out by the starter. It is very important to come onto the greens from the proper angle and distance, depending on pin position. Club selection and placement are also critical because of strategically placed fairway bunkers, mature trees, water hazards and greens that are often over 35 yards deep.

A formidable par 5 on "the Monster" is the 610-yard fourth hole. The tree-lined fairway offers a reasonably generous landing area on the first shot. On the second shot, depending on the length and direction of your tee shot, you will try to carry a long water hazard that runs up the middle of the fairway, or you will have to play to the right, leaving a longer shot to the large green protected by traps to the front, left and right.

An excellent and challenging par 3 on this side is the 231-yard seventh, which plays to a large green with a large bunker in front, another to the right and a third to the rear. An errant shot to the left will run down a slope toward the woods and rocks.

The two finishing holes on "the Monster" are both memorable and difficult. The 420-yard par-4 seventeenth forces you to choose between trying to carry a lake on the left to reach a small landing area approximately 250 yards away or playing to a safer landing area that lies between the lake on the left and another on the right. The second choice leaves you with a longer, more difficult approach to an extremely deep green, well guarded by six traps. As with many holes on "the Monster," seventeen provides you with a choice, but you are likely to have a more difficult shot when you choose the lesser of two evils.

The 476-yard par-4 eighteenth is straight and long from any of the tee positions. Two quality shots are required to reach a green that is almost 50 yards deep and well guarded by sand traps. A large bunker to the right guards the tee-shot landing area. It is a bit disconcerting to realize that even if you reach this green in regulation, it is possible to have a 100-foot putt.

There are two separate clubhouses at the Concord. One serves the Championship Course, and the other serves the 6619-yard par-71 International Course and the Challenger, a 2200-yard, nine-hole executive course. Full amenities including locker rooms, showers, pro shop, bar and restaurant are offered at these facilities. A driving range, putting greens and practice bunkers are also available. A variety of golf school programs is offered at the Concord. Golf packages are available through the resort. The clubhouse of "the Monster" offers 42 luxurious rooms should you elect not to stay at the main hotel, which has more than 1200 rooms. And you can take clinics or individual golf instruction from the Class A PGA professionals on staff at any time.

Many other recreational amenities are offered at the Concord, including 43 tennis courts with instruction available; indoor and outdoor swimming pools; jogging trails; horseback riding; a 33,247-square foot health and fitness center with Universals, StairMasters, free weights, heated indoor pool, massage therapists, and other amenities; boating on Kiamesha Lake; miniature golf and other activities. The Concord is a year-round resort with downhill and cross-country skiing, ice skating, tobogganing and other activities in the winter.

For years the Concord has featured some of the best-known names in entertainment. Recently, stars including the late Peter Allen, Willie Nelson, Joan Rivers, Wayne Newton, Ann-Margret, Yakov Smirnoff, James Brown and Andrew Dice Clay have appeared here. The resort offers a variety of American plan (3 meals) packages year round, including tennis, holiday, singles and others. A typical golf weekend package for 3 nights and 4 days in a standard room based on double occupancy and with unlimited golf on all courses (cart fees not included), accommodations and three meals a day begins from approximately $400.

The Concord also has one of the largest meeting and convention facilities in New York State. There is a total of more than 170,000 square feet of space in the 122,640-square-foot main exhibition center and other locations. There is also a variety of theater, banquet, classroom, and small meeting options to choose from at the Concord. In aggregate, the Concord has more meeting and exhibit space than any hotel in North America.

The Concord is only 90 miles northwest of New York City and is easily reachable from metropolitan area airports. It's well worth the trip to play one of the best golf courses in the United States. *Golf Digest* has rated "the Monster" one of America's 75 best resort courses.

South Central New York

Course Name: EN-JOIE GOLF CLUB

Course Type: Public
Address: 722 West Main Street
              Endicott, NY 13760
Phone: (607) 785–1661
Fax: (607) 754–2781

GOLF COURSE

General Manager and Head Professional: Bill Dennis

Length/Par (All Tees): Back 7016/72, Blue 6521/72, White 6088/72, Ladies' Forward 5205/74

Course Slope/Rating (All Tees): Back NA/NA, Blue 123/70.4, White 120/68.5, Ladies' Red 118/69.8

Course Architects: Ernest Smith (1927). Pete Dye (remodeled, 1984)

Golf Facilities: Full Pro Shop X, Snack Bar X, Lounge X, Restaurant X, Locker Room X, Showers X, Club Rental X, Club Repair X, Cart Rental X, Instruction X, Practice Green X, Driving Range X, Practice Bunker X, Club Storage X

Tee-Time Reservation Policy: First come first served. Members have tee time priority 7 a.m. to 12 p.m. weekends

Ranger: Yes

Tee-off-Interval Time: 7 and 8 min.

Time to Play 18 Holes: 4 hrs. 15 min.

Course Hours/Earliest Tee-off: 6 a.m. Fri., Sat., Sun., holidays; 7 a.m. weekdays

Green Fees: $20 for 18 holes Fri., Sat., Sun., holidays; $18 for 18 holes weekdays

Cart Fees: $20 per cart for 18 holes

Credit Cards: All major cards except American Express

Season: Apr. through Nov. Busiest June through Labor Day

Course Comments: Can walk anytime. Yardage book available. Seasonal memberships

Golf Packages: Inquire at pro shop

Discounts: Seniors, juniors

Places to Stay Nearby: BINGHAMTON: Best Western Binghamton Regency (607) 722–7575, (800) 528–1234; Holiday Inn–Arena (607) 722–1212, (800) HOLIDAY; Hotel DeVille (607) 722–0000. ENDICOTT: Best Western Homestead Inn (607) 754–1533, (800) 528–1234; Kings Inn (607) 754–8020, (800) 531–4667. VESTAL: Marriott Residence Inn (607) 770–8500, (800) 331–3131

Local Attractions: BINGHAMTON: Roberson Museum and Science Center, Ross Park Zoo, SUNY Binghamton, minor league professional baseball. ELMIRA: Arnot Art Museum, Chemung County Historical Society Museum, Mark Twain Burial Place, Mark Twain Musical Drama, Elmira College, National Soaring Museum. Broome County Chamber of Commerce, Metrocenter, 49 Court St., P.O. Box 995, Binghamton, NY 13902 (607) 772–8860

Directions: From Binghamton (12 miles): Take Rte. 17 west to Exit 69. Take Rte. 17C west to golf course. From Elmira (15 miles): Take Rte. 17 east to 2nd Owego exit. Follow 17C 12 miles to golf course

Closest Commercial Airports: Broome County Binghamton (30 min.); Hancock Syracuse International (2 hrs.)

EN-JOIE GOLF CLUB

The En-Joie Golf Club is a traditional layout on rolling, wooded hills on the southern tier of upstate New York near Binghamton. The course is owned by the village of Endicott who bought it from the Endicott Johnson company. The "En" in the course's name stands for Endicott and the "Joie" is short for Johnson, George F. Johnson. Mr. Johnson owned the local shoe company, Endicott Johnson, and had the course built for his employees in the 1920s. The course was sold to the village in 1963 and has been the site of the PGA Tour's B.C. (Broome County) Open since 1971. Winners of this event include such notables as John Daly, Fred Couples, Calvin Peete, and native son Joey Sindelar who still resides in nearby Horseheads, New York.

En-Joie is lined with mature trees and features moderate sized, bentgrass greens typically guarded by a few bunkers and an occasional water hazard. Water can come into play on eight holes and variable winds add to the challenge of this course. The 485-yard sixth, which plays as a par 5 for normal play and as a par 4 during the PGA event, is traditionally rated one of the most difficult holes on the tour. The tee shot must avoid water that cuts into the left landing area which is guarded by huge trees to the right. The approach is uphill to a forward-sloping green whose narrow entrance is squeezed by a trap on each side. En-Joie is a thinking golfer's strategic course. Elevation changes, uneven lies, and natural obstacles such as trees and the wind require constant adjustments during a round.

There are five par 5s and five par 3s at En-Joie. Two tough par 3s, the 185-yard seventh and the 185-yard eighth, add to the challenge of the front nine. The seventh plays to a 30-yard-deep green with a bunker to its front right and another to its rear. The eighth has a similarly-shaped green guarded by bunkers to its left and another to its right. Another scenic and difficult par 3 is the 204-yard sixteenth which plays over water to a small green guarded by a bunker short left, another to the rear and water to the right.

En-Joie has reasonable green fees, allows you to walk anytime, and is one of the few older public golf courses that hosts a PGA Tour event. More than 40,000 rounds of golf are played here annually. Golfers from many states and Canada make their pilgrimage to En-Joie.

Recommended Golf Courses in New York

Catskill Area:

Grossinger Golf Club, Liberty, (914) 292–9000, Public, Lake/Valley: 18/6791/71. Valley/Vista 18/6702/71. Lake/Vista 18/6625/72

Hanah Country Inn and Golf Resort, Margaretville, (914) 586–4849, (800) 752–6494, Public, 18/7033/72

Kutsher's Hotel and Country Club, Monticello, (914) 794–6000, Resort, 18/7001/71

Lochmor Golf Club, South Fallsburg, (914) 434–9079, Semiprivate, 18/6286/72

Nevele Hotel and Country Club, Ellenville, (914) 647–6000, (800) 647–6000, Resort, 18/6600/70

Swan Lake Golf and Country Club, Swan Lake, (914) 292–8000, Semiprivate, 18/6820/71

Tarry Brae Golf Course, South Fallsburg, (914) 434–2620, Public, 18/6888/72

Tennanah Lake Golf and Tennis Club, Roscoe, (607) 498–5502, Resort, 18/6769/72

Villa Roma Golf Course, Callicoon, (914) 887–5097, (800) 727–8455, Resort, 18/6231/71

Recommended Golf Courses in New York

South Central:

Conklin Players Club, Conklin, (607) 775–3042, Public, 18/6772/72

Cornell University Golf Club, Ithaca, (607) 257–3661, Semiprivate, 18/6823/72

Endwell Greens Golf Club, Endwell, (607) 785–4653, Public, 18/7053/72

Mark Twain Golf Club, Elmira, (607) 737–5770, Public, 18/6829/72

Soaring Eagles Golf Club, Horseheads, (607) 796–9350, Public, 18/6625/72

Central New York

Course Name: COLGATE UNIVERSITY SEVEN OAKS GOLF CLUB

Course Type: Semiprivate
Address: East Lake Road and Payne Street Hamilton, NY 11346
Phone: (315) 824–1432

GOLF COURSE

Head Professional: Marian Burke Blain
Course Length/Par (All Tees): Back 6915/72, White 6423/72, Ladies' Forward 5849/74
Course Slope/Rating (All Tees): Back 128/73.4, White 124/71.4, Ladies' Forward 125/NA
Course Architect: Robert Trent Jones, Sr. (front 9, 1957; back 9, 1964)
Golf Facilities: Full Pro Shop X, Snack Bar X, Lounge X, Restaurant X, Locker Room X, Showers X, Club Rental X, Club Repair X, Cart Rental X, Instruction X, Practice Green X, Driving Range X, Practice Bunker No, Club Storage X
Tee-Time Reservation Policy: Up to 2 wks. in advance on weekends, holidays. Outside play allowed after 1 p.m. Sat., Sun., holidays
Ranger: As needed
Tee-off-Interval Time: 10 min.
Time to Play 18 Holes: 4 hrs.
Course Hours/Earliest Tee-off: 7 a.m.
Green Fees: $45 for 18 holes Sat., Sun., holidays, $22.50 for 9 holes. $35 for 18 holes weekdays, $17.50 for 9 holes.
Cart Fees: $22 for 18 holes, $12.50 for 9 holes
Pull Carts: $2.14 for 18 holes

Credit Cards: MasterCard, Visa
Season: Mid-April to end of Nov.
Course Comments: Can walk anytime. Yardage book available. Season passes and memberships available. General public cannot play until after 1 p.m. on Sat., Sun., holidays
Golf Packages: Available through Colgate Inn (315) 824–2300
Discounts: Juniors, Colgate affiliates such as alumni
Places to Stay Nearby: HAMILTON: Colgate Inn (315) 824–2300. CAZENOVIA: Braeloch Inn (315) 655–3431; Linclaen House (315) 655–3461. COOPERSTOWN: Otesaga Hotel (607) 547–9931; Cooper Motor Inn (607) 547–2567
Local Attractions: Colgate University, antiques. COOPERSTOWN: National Baseball Hall of Fame and Museum, Farmers' Museum, Fenimore house; Glimmerglass Opera Theatre, Lake Otsego, Glimmerglass State Park, boating, fishing, hunting, camping, hiking. SYRACUSE: Syracuse University, Carrier Dome, Burnet Park Zoo, Erie Canal Museum, Everson Museum of Art, Landmark Theater, New York State Fairgrounds, Syracuse Chiefs baseball, Salt City Center for the Performing Arts. UTICA: Utica Blue Sox baseball, Munson–Williams Proctor Institute; Children's Museum of History, Natural History, and Sciences; historic Erie Canal cruises, Oneida County Historical Society Museum, Utica Zoo
Directions: Rte. 20 to Rte. 12B, south on 12B to Hamilton, left on Payne St. at Colgate Inn to golf course
Closest Commercial Airports: Hancock International, Syracuse (1 hr.); Oneida County/Utica (1 hr.); Albany County (2 hrs.); Buffalo International (3½ hrs.); La Guardia (4½ hrs.); John F. Kennedy International (4½ hrs.)

SEVEN OAKS GOLF CLUB

Seven Oaks Golf Course is a Robert Trent Jones, Sr., designed 6915-yard layout located in Hamilton, New York, home of Colgate University, a small liberal arts college. The head professional here is Marian

Burke Blain, noticeably and regrettably one of the few female head professionals at any of the golf courses in this book. Marian grew up in Hamilton, a village of approximately 2000, and is a Class A PGA professional.

Robert Trent Jones, Sr. was retained to design Seven Oaks in 1934, just after he graduated from nearby Cornell. Jones laid out the course in 2 days after walking the land with his friend Gene Sarazen. Because the Depression and other problems delayed the project, the first nine was not opened until 1957. The eighteen-hole course was completed in 1964, much as Robert Trent Jones originally designed it. He was invited back to Seven Oaks in 1977 when Colgate hosted the 1977 Division I NCAA Championship. Scott Simpson finished first in that tournament.

The Seven Oaks Golf Course has rolling fairways; mature trees; and large, moderately fast, slightly undulating bentgrass greens strategically guarded by sizeable bunkers. Water comes into play on twelve holes, all of which are dedicated to a Colgate class, faculty member or friend who helped make this golf course possible. The combination of distance, well-placed trees and hazards, bunkers and large, subtle greens makes this a fine test of golf.

The first hole, a 433-yard par-4 entitled "the Pioneer," is a slight dogleg left with strategically placed pine trees guarding the fairway. From the tee you can see the Colgate University campus with many of its dormitories and classroom buildings clustered in the hills beyond. The approach shot must carry a stream that crosses in front of a large green guarded by bunkers to the left and right. Your tee shot can't stray too far left or you will be out of bounds. Going too far right leaves a very long distance to the dance floor.

The number-1-handicap hole at Seven Oaks is the 441-yard par-4 sixth, which requires two long, accurate shots to reach a slightly elevated green guarded by traps to the left and right. The 183-yard par-3 eighth plays to a large, forward-sloping two-tiered green guarded by traps on the left and right and toward the front. This is rated the most difficult par 3 at Seven Oaks. The combination of wind, a narrow opening to the green, and pin placement makes this a very difficult hole.

The back nine starts with the 380-yard par-4 tenth, which is a slight dogleg left. Water cuts the fairway approximately 250 yards from the tee and a pond guards the green in front. The green is guarded by two traps to the right and another to the left. The 528-yard dogleg right twelfth is a tricky par 5 with a tee shot that must clear a stream cutting the fairway approximately 160 yards from the back tees. The second shot is over another stream toward a large green protected left, right and rear by large bunkers.

A difficult par 3 on this side is the 221-yard eleventh, which plays over a stream to a large green guarded by traps to the left, right and rear. If the pin is tucked behind the trap to the left, this hole becomes even more difficult.

Seven Oaks is the home of the Colgate University Golf Team and is a challenging and tranquil place to play golf in a rustic, beautiful part of central New York State.

Course Name: LEATHERSTOCKING GOLF CLUB

Course Type: Resort
Address: Highway 80
Cooperstown, NY 13326
Phone: (607) 547–9853 (Golf Course)
(607) 547–9931 (Resort)
Fax: (607) 547–9675
(Otesaga Hotel)

GOLF COURSE

Head Professional: Rick Woolcott
Course Length/Par (All Tees): Back 6388/72, Middle 6006/72, Forward 5175/72
Course Slope/Rating (All Tees): Back 124/71, Middle 120/69.3, Ladies' Forward 116/69.2
Course Architect: Devereaux Emmett (1927)
Golf Facilities: Full Pro Shop X, Snack Bar X, Lounge X, Restaurant X, Locker Room X, Showers X, Club Rental X, Club Repair X, Cart Rental X, Instruction X, Practice Green X,

Driving Range No, Practice Bunker X, Club Storage X

Tee-Time Reservation Policy: Call anytime

Ranger: Yes

Tee-off-Interval Time: 8 min.

Time to Play 18 Holes: 4½ hrs.

Course Hours/Earliest Tee-off: 6:30 a.m.

Green Fees: $61 daily fee Sat., Sun., holidays; $45 daily fee weekdays

Cart Fees: $15 plus tax for 18 holes per person

Pull Carts: $3 for 18 holes

Credit Cards: All major cards

Season: Mid-April to Oct. 31

Course Comments: Can walk weekdays

Golf Packages: None

Discounts: None

Places to Stay Nearby: Otesaga Hotel (607) 547–9931; Cooper Motor Inn (607) 547–2567; Hickory Grove Inn and Restaurant (607) 547–8100; Deer Run Motel (607) 547–8600; Lake View Motel (607) 547–9740. ONEONTA: Holiday Inn (607) 433–2250, (800) HOLIDAY; Master Hosts Inn (607) 432–1280, (800) 251–1962

Local Attractions: National Baseball Hall of Fame and Museum, Fenimore house, Farmers' Museum, camping, swimming, boating, fishing, Lake Otsego boat tours, hunting, Glimmerglass Opera Theater, antiques and auctions, New York State Historical Association, Glimmerglass State Park. ONEONTA: Minor league baseball, Hartwick College, Soccer Hall of Fame, Yager Museum, Science Discovery Center, Catskill Symphony Orchestra. Cooperstown Chamber of Commerce (607) 547–9983. Otsego County Tourism (800) 843–3394

Directions: Rte. 20 to Hwy. 80, south on Hwy. 80 to Cooperstown and golf course

Closest Commercial Airports: Oneida County/Utica (45 min.); Hancock International, Syracuse (2 hrs.); Albany County (2 hrs.)

LEATHERSTOCKING GOLF CLUB

Lake Otsego in Cooperstown, New York, is known as the "Glimmerglass," from the *Leatherstocking Tales* of James Fenimore Cooper. Set along this beautiful lake is the 6388-yard par-72 Leatherstocking Golf Course, a Devereaux Emmett design in the old style. Emmett, a native of New York City, designed and remodeled many golf courses in New York State, including the Garden City Golf Club; the McGregor Golf Club in Saratoga; and the Glen Head Country Club (formerly Women's National Golf and Country Club). Before his passing in 1934, Emmett also designed many courses in partnership with his son and Alfred H. Tull.

Leatherstocking is within walking distance of the grand old Otesaga Hotel, which overlooks the lake just to the right of the eighteenth green. Also nearby is the Farmer's Museum, the National Baseball Hall of Fame and Museum and the rest of Cooperstown, one of the most beautiful towns in New York State. It is on this golf course that many a Hall of Fame inductee has hit golf balls. The Otesaga has a brochure listing all the Hall of Famers, including many avid golfers like Ty Cobb, Babe Ruth, Mickey Mantle and Johnny Bench.

The Leatherstocking is a placement course with medium-sized, fast, undulating greens well guarded by many of the more than 100 sand bunkers on the course. Water comes into play on four holes, and the wind coming off the lake is often a factor. The two finishing holes provide a memorable way to end a round at Leatherstocking. The 169-yard par-3 seventeenth is all carry over the edge of Black Bird Bay to a large green guarded by traps to the right and rear. This green is now actually farther—190 yards—than it measures on the scorecard. The tee shot on eighteen is from an island tee over as much of Black Bird Bay as you want to try to carry. The next shot is down a fairway lined by the bay on the left all the way to a two-tiered green that has one bunker to its right and water to its rear.

The combination of bunkers; tricky, elevated greens that require all carry on approach shots; and the likelihood of various uneven lies on this rolling terrain makes Leatherstocking an excellent golf challenge. Although Leatherstocking is short, misplaced shots can quickly add strokes to your score. There is always the potential for daydreaming as you look out across the Glimmerglass while touring this scenic, rolling layout. Green fees at Leatherstocking are daily rates, and you can walk the course during the week. Just down the road at the other end of the lake is the nine-hole Otsego Golf Club, ([607] 547–9290), one of the oldest golf courses in America. You can stay at the Otesaga Hotel or the many inns, bed and breakfasts or motels in the area.

Recommended Golf Courses in Central New York

Within 1 Hour of Syracuse:

Arrowhead Golf Course, East Syracuse, (315) 656–7563, Public, 18/6700/72

Barker Brook Golf Course, Oriskany Falls, (315) 821–9992, Public, 18/6257/72

Dutch Hollow Country Club, Owasco, (315) 784–5052, Semiprivate, 18/6460/71

Foxfire Golf Club, Baldwinsville, (315) 638–2930, Public, 18/6887/72

Green Lakes State Park Golf Club, Fayetteville, (315) 637–0258, Public, 18/6212/71

Radisson Greens Golf Club, Baldwinsville, (315) 638–0092, Semiprivate, 18/7010/72

Western New York

Course Name: GLEN OAK GOLF
COURSE
Course Type: Public
Address: 711 Smith Road
P.O. Box 179
East Amherst, NY 14051
Phone: (716) 688–5454

GOLF COURSE

Head Professional: Mike Clawson
Course Length/Par (All Tees): Back 6730/72, Middle 6232/72, Forward 5561/72
Course Slope/Rating (All Tees): Back 129/72.4, Middle 122/70.8, Ladies' Forward 118/71.9
Course Architect: Robert Trent Jones, Sr. (1972)

Golf Facilities: Full Pro Shop X, Snack Bar X, Lounge X, Restaurant X, Locker Room X, Showers X, Club Rental X, Club Repair X, Cart Rental X, Instruction X, Practice Green X, Driving Range X, Practice Bunker No, Club Storage X
Tee-Time Reservation Policy: Up to 3 days in advance
Ranger: Yes
Tee-off-Interval Time: 6 to 10 min. (variable)
Time to Play 18 Holes: 4½ hrs.
Course Hours/Earliest Tee-off: Sunrise to sunset
Green and Cart Fees: $40 for 18 holes with cart Sat., Sun., holidays before noon; $28 for 18 holes with cart Mon. to Fri.
Credit Cards: MasterCard, Visa
Season: March 15 to Nov. 15, weather permitting
Course Comments: Cart mandatory. Yardage book available
Golf Packages: None
Discounts: None
Places to Stay Nearby: BUFFALO: Sheraton Inn Buffalo Airport (716) 681–2400, (800) 323–3331; Buffalo Airport Days Inn (716) 631–0800, (800) 329–7466; Hyatt Regency Buffalo (716) 856–1234, (800) 233–1234. GRAND ISLAND: Holiday Inn (800) HOLIDAY. AMHERST: Marriott (716) 689–6900, (800) 228–9290; Holiday Inn Buffalo–Amherst (716) 691–8181, (800) HOLIDAY; Lord Amherst Motor Hotel (716) 839–2200
Local Attractions: Niagara Falls. BUFFALO: Professional baseball, hockey, football, Albright Knox Art Gallery, Miss Buffalo Charter Cruises on Lake Erie, Buffalo Philharmonic Orchestra, Studio Arena Theater, harness racing at Buffalo Raceway (Hamburg, NY), Buffalo Museum of Science, Buffalo and Erie County Historical Society, Buffalo Zoological Society, Theodore Roosevelt Inaugural National Historic site, State University of New York at Buffalo, boating, fishing, skiing at nearby Kissing Bridge and Holiday Valley. Greater Buffalo Convention and Visitors

Bureau (716) 852–0511, (800) BUF-
FALO. Buffalo Parks Department (716)
851–5806

Directions: Hwy. 290 to Hwy. 990 (end),
make left, and first right on Smith Rd.

Closest Commercial Airports: Buffalo
International (15 min.); Hancock
International, Syracuse (2 hrs.); Lester
B. Pearson International, Toronto,
Canada (2½ hrs.)

GLEN OAK GOLF COURSE

Glen Oak Golf Course is a 6730-yard
Robert Trent Jones, Sr., layout located in
East Amherst, a suburb of Buffalo. Glen
Oak was originally intended as a private
country club but is now a privately owned
facility open to the public. The course was
rated one of the top 75 public golf courses
in America in 1988 by *Golf Digest*.

This flat, well-manicured layout features
large, moderately fast, undulating bentgrass
greens. Most of the greens are well protected by large Robert Trent Jones, Sr.–
signature bunkers, and water hazards
appear on thirteen holes. Mature trees and
strategically placed fairway bunkers add to
the beauty and challenge of Glen Oak.

One of the more memorable holes on
the course is the 534-yard par-5 finishing
hole. This double dogleg has a tricky tee
shot over water twice to a landing area
bordered by a stream on the left and a fairway bunker on the right. Woods guard both
sides of the fairway. The second shot is
over the stream to a landing area guarded
by a series of bunkers on the left from 100
yards in and a large pond to the right. The
approach is to a narrow, deep, elevated
green with water to the right and a bunker
to the left and forward. The green is beautifully framed by trees.

Glen Oak offers a rich variety of holes
with water hazards, traps, trees, creative
green configurations and numerous
doglegs. Club selection, course management, and positioning, especially as you
come onto the greens are very important to
score at Glen Oak.

Glen Oak has hosted the Dunlap Open,
Buffalo District Championship, and the
Western New York PGA Championship.

Fewer than 40,000 rounds a year are
played here, enabling you to play a quality
golf course in an uncrowded setting.

Recommended Golf Courses in New York

West of Syracuse:

Bristol Harbour Golf Club, Canandaigua,
(716) 396–2460, (800) 288–8248, Resort,
18/6668/72

Centerpointe Country Club, Canandaigua,
(716) 924–5346, Semiprivate, 18/6717/71

Chautauqua Golf Club, Chatauqua, (716)
357–6211, Resort. Hill: 18/6412/72. Lake:
18/6462/72

Deerfield Country Club, Brockport,
(716) 392–8080, Semiprivate. North/South:
18/7083/72. East: 9/3005/35

Deerwood Golf Course, North Tonawanda,
(716) 695–8525, Public, 18/6948/72

Durand Eastman Golf Course, Rochester,
(716) 342–9810, Public, 18/6089/72

Peek'N Peak Resort Golf Club, Clymer,
(716) 355–4141, Resort, 18/6260/72

River Oaks Golf Club, Grand Island,
(716) 773–3336, Semiprivate, 18/7389/72

Shadow Pines Golf Club, Penfield,
(716) 385–8550, Public, 18/6763/72

Sheridan Park Golf Club, Tonawanda,
(716) 875–1811, Public, 18/6534/71

Terry Hills Golf Course, Batavia,
(716) 343–0860, (800) 825–8633, Public,
18/6072/72

Tri-County Country Club, Forestville,
(716) 965–9723, Semiprivate, 18/6639/71

Wayne Hills Country Club, Lyons,
(315) 946–6944, Public, 18/6854/72

Willowbrook Country Club, Lockport,
(716) 434–0111, Public, 18/6018/71

Northern

**Course Name: THE SAGAMORE
GOLF CLUB**

Course Type: Resort
Resort: The Sagamore

Address:	110 Sagamore Road
	Bolton Landing, NY 12814
Phone:	(518) 644–9400 (Golf Course)
	(518) 644–9400,
	(800) 358–3585, (Resort)
Fax:	(518) 944–2851
	(Conference Sales)

GOLF COURSE

Head Professional: Tom Smack

Course Length/Par (All Tees): Back 6706/70, Middle 6410/70, Forward 5265/71

Course Slope/Rating (All Tees): Back 130/72.9, Middle 128/71.5, Ladies' Forward 122/73

Course Architect: Donald Ross (1928)

Golf Facilities: Full Pro Shop X, Snack Bar X, Lounge X, Restaurant X, Locker Room X, Showers X, Club Rental X, Club Repair Minor, Cart Rental X, Instruction X, Practice Green X, Driving Range X, Practice Bunker No, Club Storage X

Tee-Time Reservation Policy: Resort guests: At time of reservation. Outside play: Up to 1 day in advance

Ranger: Yes

Tee-off-Interval Time: 8 min.

Time to Play 18 Holes: 4 hrs. 15 min.

Course Hours/Earliest Tee-off: 7:30 a.m.

Green Fees: Resort guests: $52 daily fee. Outside play: $65 daily fee

Cart Fees: $16 for 18 holes per person, $10 for 9 holes per person

Credit Cards: American Express, Diners Club, MasterCard, Visa

Season: Mid-April to mid-Nov. Busiest season June to Sept.

Course Comments: Cart mandatory. Seasonal memberships available

Golf Packages: Available through Sagamore resort

Discounts: None

Places to Stay Nearby: Melody Manor Resort (518) 644–9750; Victorian Village Resort Motel (518) 644–9400. LAKE GEORGE: Holiday Inn Turf (518) 668–5781, (800) HOLIDAY; Georgian (518) 668–2096; Ramada Inn of Lake George (518) 668–3131, (800) 272–6232; Howard Johnson's Tiki Resort Hotel (518) 668–5744, (800) 446–4656; Roaring Brook Ranch and Tennis Resort (518) 668–5767, (800) 882–7665

Local Attractions: Bolton Historical Society Museum, antiques, shopping tours at outlet and retail malls, Blue Mountain Lake, Adirondack Museum, Fort Ticonderoga, boating, fishing, camping, bicycling, ballooning, Glens Falls minor league baseball, white-water rafting. Saratoga Springs. Manchester, VT. Lake George Village. Bolton Landing Chamber of Commerce (518) 644–3831

Directions: From Albany (70 mi.): Northway (Rte. 87N) north to exit 22, Rte. 9 north into Bolton Landing, make left at light on Federal Hill Rd. to golf course

Closest Commercial Airports: Albany County (2 hrs.); Dorval International, Montreal, Canada (4 hrs.)

RESORT

Date Built: 1883

No. of Rooms: Main hotel: 100 rooms, including 46 suites. Lodges: 240 rooms, including 120 suites. Executive retreat: 10 bilevel suites

Meeting Rooms: 14. Capacity of Largest: 720 persons banquet style. Meeting Space: 15,760 sq. ft.

Room Price Range: $79 per person, low season (mid-May, Nov.-Apr.) to $390 peak season. Golf, holiday, spa, skiing and other packages offered year round. American and European plans available

Lounges: Van Winkles, Veranda Lobby Lounge

Restaurants: Trillium, Club Grill, Mister Brown's Cafe, Pool Terrace, Sagamore

Entertainment: Dancing, music, craft programs, fashion shows, culinary demonstrations, bingo, stress-management seminars, wine tasting, casino nights, rodeo

Credit Cards: All major cards

General Amenities: Playground, hairdresser; supervised children's programs for ages 6 to 12, teens; dinner cruises, spa boutique, movies, surrey rides, art shop, spouse programs, meeting and conference facilities with audiovisual and banquet services

Recreational Amenities: Downhill, cross–country skiing, Lake George and beach, boating, swimming, 6 indoor and outdoor tennis courts with instruction available, racquetball court; health spa with Keiser strength training circuit, Lifecycles, StairMasters, treadmills, rowing machines; indoor swimming pool, volleyball, game room, boat rentals and fishing charters, miniature golf, croquet, luxury yacht cruises, jogging trails, horseback riding, exercise classes

Reservation and Cancellation Policy: 1 night's room rate required as a deposit to secure each reservation. Deposits applied to the designated length of stay. Any changes of arrival or departure dates and cancellations must be made at least 14 days prior to arrival date or will result in forfeiture of the deposit

Comments and Restrictions: Daily rate does not include tax or service charge. Rates are modified American plan or European plan. Pets $50 extra charge

THE SAGAMORE GOLF CLUB

The Sagamore is an American Automobile Association Four-Diamond resort and national historic landmark resort set on 70 acres of land overlooking Lake George in the southeast region of the Adirondack Mountains. The resort began operating over 100 years ago, when Myron O. Brown and a group of investors bought Green Island and opened the Sagamore in 1883. Since then various owners and renovations have come and gone. In the 1980s, builder and real-estate developer Norman Wolgin purchased the hotel and after investing more than $70 million, returned it to its former grandeur. It is now rated among the best golf resorts in America by *Golf* magazine. This is a very short list containing fewer than 60 of the best resorts in the United States, and the Sagamore is the only one in New York State on the list.

Within a few miles drive of the resort is the Sagamore Golf Club, which features a 6706-yard par-70 Donald Ross-designed golf course that sits on a mountain ridge overlooking Lake George. This scenic, tightly treed, up-and-down layout features old Scottish-style greens that are small, often crowned, usually elevated and guarded by deep bunkers. Shot making and course management are required to score on this layout, which, after an investment of more than $3 million, has been restored to excellent condition. Each hole is a unique and self-contained experience as you work your way through avenues of pine and birch.

The first hole at Sagamore, a 430-yard par 4, provides a beautiful and challenging foreshadowing of what your round has to offer. Your view is from an elevated tee within walking distance of an elegant stone clubhouse with a quality restaurant and outdoor patio set in the woods. Down the tree-lined fairway is a green protected by traps to the left and right. Beyond the green is a backdrop of Lake George and miles of rolling mountains and forests beyond. The approach shot to the green is severely uphill which makes the hole much more difficult than it would at first appear.

The number-1-handicap hole at Sagamore is the 417-yard par-4 seventh, which is an uphill dogleg left. The tee shot is blind, and it takes a drive of approximately 225 yards to reach the corner of the tree-lined dogleg, whose fairway slopes to the right. Anyone who slices the ball is likely to have trouble negotiating this turn. The approach is to a small, elevated green with a bunker on the right. By now you have begun to notice that it is very possible to get a downhill or sidehill lie at Sagamore and that the approaches to the greens are not easy to hold, especially if you are hitting a long iron or fairway wood to a small, crowned, elevated target from an uneven lie.

Another tough and memorable hole at Sagamore is the 437-yard par-4 thirteenth, which plays down a tree-lined fairway from an elevated tee. The tee shot is to a landing area 150 to 200 yards from an elevated green guarded by a pond to the left and approximately 50 yards in front of the green. There are no bunkers on this hole, but the combination of distance, trees, water and elevation change to the green makes it a great test of golf.

A picturesque but difficult par 3 at Sagamore is the 225-yard fourteenth, which plays from an elevated tee to a green 150 feet below. Bunkers protect the left and right sides of the green, which, like most of the greens at Sagamore, has open areas in front to reach the putting surface on the roll. At twilight on a July evening, my gallery here was a group of foxes who watched from the left fairway but did not applaud.

There is a pro shop within walking distance of the clubhouse and the first tee. The clubhouse has a restaurant, meeting rooms, bar, locker rooms and showers. Many golfers who stay at the Sagamore take their meals at this scenic locale. Practice facilities include a driving range and putting green but no practice bunker. Lessons are available, and golf packages can be obtained through the resort. Outside play is allowed, but tee times, when available, can be arranged only up to 1 day in advance.

The resort itself is on a 70-acre island with magnificent views of Lake George and the mountains beyond. Accommodations are available in the main hotel, lodges or executive retreat. More than 15,000 square feet of meeting and conference space are available, including banquet, theater, boardroom, classroom, and outside reception areas of all shapes and sizes. A nineteenth-century wooden cruise ship, the *Morgan,* is available for parties and cruises, and a full range of audiovisual, conference-planning and food services are also available. The Sagamore earned the Gold Tee Award from *Meetings and Conventions* magazine for its excellent golf and conference facilities, the only facility in New York State to be so honored.

Recreational amenities at the Sagamore include indoor and outdoor lighted tennis courts in the Court Complex, which also includes a racquetball court, pro shop, courtside lounge, and game room. The pool building includes a spa with separate men's and women's clubs with exercise rooms, saunas, whirlpools, hot and cold plunge pools, massage, and other amenities. Boating and swimming are easily accessible on Lake George, which includes a marina and private beach. Other activities such as wine tasting, croquet, tours, fishing, craft programs, casino nights, horseback riding, seminars, culinary demonstrations and more make up the busy and varied recreational venue at the Sagamore. Within one hour are Saratoga Springs; Fort Ticonderoga; Manchester, VT; and other places of interest. In the winter Sagamore turns into a center for cross-country and downhill skiing, skating and other activities.

The Sagamore offers supervised children's programs for ages 6 to 12 and a variety of activities for teenagers. The resort has an American plan that includes breakfast and dinner. There are several restaurants at the resort ranging from formal dining requiring jacket and tie and alfresco dining near the lake to light snacks and other fare. The Club Grill at the Country Club is part of the modified American plan and serves lunch and dinner. Dinner cruises are also available on the *Morgan.*

The Sagamore provides the ambience of a landmark nineteenth-century grand hotel with all the modern amenities in a beautiful setting. The golf course is also in the grand style of Donald Ross, master architect.

Course Name: SARANAC INN GOLF AND COUNTRY CLUB

Course Type: Public
Address: Route 30 (between Saranac Lake and Tupper Lake)
                    Saranac Inn, NY 12982
Phone: (518) 891–1402

GOLF COURSE

Owner: Walter Smachlo

Course Length/Par (All Tees): Back 6631/72, Middle 6453/72, Forward 5263/71

Course Slope/Rating (All Tees): Back 124/71.5, Middle 122/70.6, Ladies' Forward 128/NA

Course Architect: Unknown (original course, estimated 6 holes, circa 1900). Seymour C. Dunn (Renovation, design of modern course 1917)

Golf Facilities: Full Pro Shop X, Snack Bar X, Lounge X, Restaurant X,

Locker Room No, Showers No, Club Rental X, Club Repair X, Cart Rental X, Instruction No, Practice Green X, Driving Range X, Practice Bunker No, Club Storage X

Tee-Time Reservation Policy: Anytime
Ranger: No
Tee-off-Interval Time: 8 min.
Time to Play 18 Holes: 4 hrs.
Course Hours/Earliest Tee-off: 7:15 a.m. to 4:30 p.m.
Green and Cart Fees: $50 for 18 holes with cart for a single, $45 for 18 holes with a shared cart
Credit Cards: MasterCard, Visa
Season: Memorial Day to Columbus Day
Course Comments: Cart mandatory
Golf Packages: Through 10-room on-site motel. Inquire at pro shop
Discounts: None
Places to Stay Nearby: TUPPER LAKE: Wawbeek (518) 359–2656. SARANAC LAKE: Comfort Inn (518) 891–1970; The Pointe (518) 891–5674, (800) 255–3530; Hotel Saranac (518) 891–2200, (800) 937–0211; Cranberry Meadows Town Houses (518) 891–2010. LAKE PLACID: Best Western Golden Arrow (518) 523–3353, (800) 528–1234; Lake Placid Lodge (518) 523–2700; Mirror Lake Inn (518) 523–2544; Blackberry Inn Bed and Breakfast (518) 523–3419; Lake Placid Hilton (518) 523–4411, (800) 445–8667; Whiteface Inn Resort and Club (518) 523–2551; Holiday Inn Grandview (518) 523–2556, (800) HOLIDAY. BOLTON LANDING: Sagamore (518) 644–9400, (800) 228–2121. INDIAN LAKE: Timberlock (518) 648–5494, (800) 457–1621. BIG MOOSE: Big Moose Inn (315) 357–2042
Local Attractions: Fishing, boating, hunting, hiking, camping, skiing, skating, white-water rafting, rock climbing, antiques, crafts. BLUE MOUNTAIN LAKE: Adirondack Museum, Adirondack Lakes Center for the Arts. LAKE PLACID: Winter Olympic training facilities, Adirondack North Country Crafts Center, High Falls Gorge, Ausable Chasm, Paul Smiths, Lake George, Fort Ticonderoga, Mount Marcy, Whiteface Mountain ski

area. RAQUETTE LAKE: Sagamore Great Estates Tours (315) 354–5311, Sagamore Lodge national historic site. For the Adirondack Guide, published yearly by the Sagamore Conference Center: Sagamore Rd., Raquette Lake, NY 13436, (315) 354–5303. Directories of accommodations and campgrounds: New York State Department of Commerce, Adirondack Region, 90 Main St., Lake Placid, NY 12946, (518) 523–2412, (800) 225–5697. Adirondack Mountain Club Lodgings and Programs (518) 523–3441. Adirondack Mountain Club Trail Guides and Field Guides, 172 Ridge St., Glen Falls, NY 12801, (518) 793–7737. Chambers of Commerce: Tupper Lake (518) 359–3328, Saranac Lake (518) 891–1990, Lake Placid (518) 523–2445. Adirondack Park Visitor Information (518) 327–3000, (800) 462–6236 (NY), (800) 255–5515 (Northeast states)
Directions: From Saranac Lake (20 min.): Rte. 86 to Rte. 30, turn left on Rte. 30 toward airport, continue 6 mi. past airport, golf course on the left. From Tupper Lake (25 min.): Rte. 30 south (16 mi.), golf course on the right
Closest Commercial Airports: Adirondack Regional, Saranac (10 min.); Burlington International, VT (2½ hrs.); Dorval International, Montreal, Canada (2½ hrs.); Albany County (3 hrs.); Hancock International, Syracuse (4½ hrs.)

SARANAC INN GOLF AND COUNTRY CLUB

The Adirondack State Park, located in northern New York State, has nearly 6 million acres of land and is the largest park in the continental United States. Approximately 42 percent of this territory, which is almost the size of the state of Vermont, is state-owned forest preserve designated forever wild. The park has 31,000 miles of rivers and streams, 2759 lakes and ponds, and almost 50 peaks with altitudes higher than 4000 feet. There are 130,000 year-round residents in 105 communities within the park, and there are about 250,000 seasonal residents.

For many years families have come to the Adirondacks to vacation, fish, hunt, camp, hike, climb rocks, ski, skate and enjoy the great outdoors. Some of the early vacationers were wealthy individuals such as J. P. Morgan, Marjorie Merriweather Post and William West Durant. When the nouveau riche invaded socially desirable spas such as Saratoga, the old rich retreated to large and isolated hotels along the northern lakes including Saranac, the eventual home of the Saranac Inn. Many of these families built "camps" of their own, some of them opulent retreats made from local materials, primarily stone and wooden logs. Marjorie Merriweather Post's Topridge, created in the 1920s, became a complex of 68 buildings on Upper St. Regis Lake, accessible only by water. When fully occupied, Topridge had a staff of 85.

Upper Saranac Lake, which had relatively little camp development for a variety of reasons, did have the Saranac Inn, a grand log hotel set on a peninsula jutting out into Upper Saranac Lake, with a magnificent view of Whiteface Mountain.

According to Saranac Inn's owner, Walter Smachlo, 85 acres of land were cleared at the turn of the century to make room for the original golf course commissioned by the Saranac Inn Association. By 1901, the Inn was promoting its new golf amenities. Later, in 1917, Seymour Dunn was retained by Harrington Mills, president of Saranac Inn, to finalize the design of the current golf course. Dunn, who was born in Prestwick, Scotland, and died in 1959 in Lake Placid, New York, at the age of 77, considered Saranac Inn to be one of the best of the many courses he designed in Europe and America.

After falling on hard times the Saranac Inn burned in 1978. The golf course is now owned by Walter Smachlo who was a caddy at the Inn. Smachlo has put considerable time and money into upgrading this 6631-yard layout which is open, with rolling fairways and large, moderately fast, undulating greens well guarded by bunkers. There are many excellent and memorable holes on this layout, which one never gets tired of playing.

The first hole is a straight 415-yard par 4 with trees lining the right side of an ample fairway. If the ball strays to the left on your tee shot, you might be in heavy rough or a fairway bunker, making it almost impossible to reach the green in regulation. Most players keep the drive right of center to get more distance and to take a large bunker in front of the large, forward-sloping green out of play. This green is protected to the left by a bunker and has another to its right.

The second hole seems like an endless par 5, even though it is only 532 yards from the back tees. The tee shot is to an open expanse, but if you don't hit the fairway you will be in the rough on the left or far enough right to lose considerable yardage. The second shot is straight toward a flat green with no bunkers. If you hit to the left you will be in thick rough; to the right is a downhill slope and more trouble. The approach is tricky because there are few immediate points of reference such as bunkers and trees to gauge distance from.

The 230-yard par-3 seventh is possibly the most difficult hole to par on the course. The tee shot has to clear a large mound directly in front of the green. You have to hit a lofted wood or long iron over the mound and hold the green, which is backed by woods. Or you can run the ball through an opening on either side of the mound and hope to be around the green.

Probably the most difficult par 4 on the back nine is the 407-yard eleventh, which plays straight to an elevated green that has a slippery slope from back to front. It is usually difficult to hold this green on the approach shot, and if you are above the hole when you get there, it is very easy to three-putt.

The three finishing holes at Saranac are a fine way to end the round. The 200-yard par-3 sixteenth has a tee shot over a pond and swale up to an elevated green flanked by large traps. You have to reach the green in the air, because a bank in front of the green tends to stop short shots cold. If you miss too far to the left or right, the ball will be in a bunker or the woods.

The 423-yard par-4 dogleg-right seventeenth entices you to cut the dogleg, but if you miss, the ball will kick down a slope and possibly be out of bounds in the trees. If your tee shot is too far left, you have lost distance and face a shot out of difficult rough. The approach is to a deep green well guarded by traps on both sides.

The finishing hole is a beautiful 532-yard par 5 with trees on the right from tee to green. Bordering the left is a less formidable row of trees separating eighteen from the first fairway. The tee shot should be hit to the center or right-center to roll down a hill. Regrettably, the golfer is usually left with some sort of downhill lie or is on level ground but short. The second shot is to a flat area in a valley, and the approach is uphill to a beautiful, well-trapped green backed by a banked amphitheater. If you are short, you are likely to be in traps to the left or right. If you are behind the green, you are likely to have a delicate chip shot off a bank or out of a trap toward a slippery green sloping toward the fairway.

The clubhouse at the Saranac Inn Golf Course is modest, with a restaurant, small pro shop, and no locker room or shower facilities. A driving range is situated to the right of the first tee. There is a putting green nearby but no practice bunker. No pro or instruction is available at this golf course. A small 10-room motel is on the property. Golf packages are available through this facility. Inquire at the pro shop.

The halcyon days of the great camps and grandiose inns in the Adirondacks are gone. This region is the burial ground for many golf courses built to entertain the "flatlanders" who came from crowded metropolitan areas to rediscover natural beauty and, perhaps, themselves. As J. Peter Martin, also a former caddy at Saranac Inn, notes in his excellent book, *Adirondack Golf Courses Past and Present* (Adirondack Golf, Box 492, Lake Placid, NY 12946), the Antlers Golf Course, Raquette Lake (1925); Hurricane Lodge Golf Course, Keene (1914); Ampersand Hotel Golf Course, Saranac Lake (1897); Sagamore Hotel Golf Course, Long Lake (1920); and St. Regis River Golf Course,

Paul Smiths (1896) are among the many that have not survived. The Saranac Inn Golf and Country Club is a living legacy of that bygone era and an excellent place to tee it up.

Course Name:　SARATOGA SPA STATE PARK Championship, Executive Courses

Course Type:　Public

Address:　Route 9
Saratoga Springs, NY 12866

Phone:　(518) 587–8804 (Tee-Time Reservations)
(518) 584–2008 (Championship Course)
(518) 584–2007 (Executive Course)
(518) 584–2535 (Spa Park Office)
(518) 584–3000 (Gideon Putnam Hotel)

GOLF COURSE

Head Professionals: John Taylor, Jack Polanski

Course Length/Par (All Tees): Championship: Back 7025/72, Middle 6344/72, Forward 5663/72. Executive: Back 1635/29, Forward 1605/29

Course Slope/Rating (All Tees): Championship: Back 130/73.7, Middle 125/70.6, Ladies' Forward 122/72.5. Executive: NA/NA

Course Architect: William Mitchell (1966)

Golf Facilities: Full Pro Shop X, Snack Bar X, Lounge X, Restaurant X, Locker Room X, Showers X, Club Rental X, Club Repair X, Cart Rental X, Instruction X, Practice Green X, Driving Range X, Practice Bunker No, Club Storage X

Tee-Time Reservation Policy: From 9 a.m. Thurs. for Sat., Sun., holidays. Call Fri. for Sun., holidays. First come, first served on weekdays. Hourly tee times allocated for walk-ons

Ranger: Yes

Tee-off-Interval Time: 7 and 8 min.

Time to Play 18 Holes: 4½ hrs.

Course Hours/Earliest Tee-off: Championship: 6 a.m. Executive: 7 a.m.

Green Fees: Championship: $17 for 18 holes Sat., Sun., holidays; $14 for 18 holes weekdays. Executive: $13 for 18 holes Sat., Sun., holidays; $11 for 18 holes weekdays. $8 for 9 holes Sat., Sun., holidays; $7 for 9 holes weekdays

Cart Fees: $19 for 18 holes for 2 persons

Pull Carts: $2 for 18 holes

Credit Cards: Cash for green fees. MasterCard, Visa for merchandise

Season: Mid-April to mid-Nov. Busiest season June, July, Aug.

Course Comments: Can walk anytime

Golf Packages: None

Discounts: Juniors, seniors (Mon. to Fri.)

Places to Stay Nearby: Gideon Putnam Hotel and Conference Center (518) 584–3000, (800) 732–1560. SARATOGA: Sheraton Renaissance Inn (518) 584–4000, (800) 325–3535; Holiday Inn (518) 584–4550, (800) HOLIDAY; Old Bryan Inn (518) 587–2990; Best Western Playmore Farms (518) 584–2350, (800) 528–1234; Roosevelt Suites and Motel (518) 584–0980; Adelphi Hotel (518) 587–4688; Inn at Saratoga (518) 583–1890, (800) 252–7466. BED AND BREAKFASTS: Six Sisters Bed and Breakfast (518) 583–1173; Chestnut Tree Inn Bed and Breakfast (518) 587–8681; Westchester House Bed and Breakfast (518) 587–7613

Local Attractions: Saratoga Performing Arts Center, Roosevelt Bath House, Lincoln Bath House, Saratoga's Home-Made Theater, 3 outdoor swimming pools, hard-surface and clay tennis courts, hiking and jogging trails, speed-skating track, cross-country skiing trails and ski shop, National Museum of Dance, Spa Little Theater. SARATOGA: Yaddo Rose Gardens, Petrified Sea Gardens, Saratoga Lake, antiques, Skidmore College, National Museum of Thoroughbred Racing, Casino and Congress Park, Saratoga Historical Museum, Saratoga Race Course, restaurants, seasonal festivals, Saratoga Harness Hall of Fame, Saratoga National Historic Park. Saratoga Springs Chamber of Commerce (518) 584–3255

Directions: From I–87 Northway, exit 13N, Rte. 9 north (3 mi.), park and golf course on the left

Closest Commercial Airport: Albany County (45 min.)

SARATOGA SPA STATE PARK

Saratoga Springs is one of the premier resort towns in New York State and features Saratoga Spa and its naturally carbonated waters, which began to draw the rich and famous beginning in the early nineteenth century. By the early twentieth century the springs were threatened with depletion, so in 1909 a state reservation was formed to preserve this valuable natural resource. Later, the state reservation evolved into a state park with over 2000 acres of land. It now includes the Saratoga Performing Arts Center; bath houses, including the Roosevelt Bath and Lincoln Bath houses; 3 outdoor swimming pools; running courses; picnic areas; walking trails, hard-surface and clay tennis courts; cross-country skiing and skating areas; the National Museum of Dance, the Gideon Putnam Hotel; and other facilities. A centerpiece of this park is an excellent eighteen-hole golf course and a nine-hole par-29 course.

The 7025-yard par-72 Saratoga Spa State Park Championship golf course was designed by William Mitchell and opened in 1966. Mitchell, a native of Salem, Massachusetts, designed more than 150 original courses and remodeled more than 200 before he died in 1974 at age 62. Golf courses of his design in New York State include the McCann Memorial Golf Course in Poughkeepsie; Otterkill Golf and Country Club in Newburgh; Glenn Cove Municipal; Kutshers Hotel Golf Club in Monticello; and the Putnam Country Club in Lake Mahopac.

Saratoga Spa is a well-treed, relatively flat layout with large, fairly slow, moderately undulating greens. Bunkers are strategically placed in key fairway landing areas and around the greens. The most formidable aspect of the course is its length from the back tees and the tightness of some of the holes. However, the course plays a more manageable 6344 yards from the middle tees and 5663 yards from the forward tees.

The Saratoga Spa starts out with the number-1-handicap hole on the course. This dogleg-right par 4 plays 465 yards from the back tees to a large green well guarded by two bunkers to the left and right front of the green. The tee shot is to a landing area guarded on the left by a large bunker. Most golfers will have a wood or a long iron to the green on the second shot. This is not an easy way to begin a round of golf.

The second hole is the toughest par 3 on the course. The tee shot is to a large green protected by a trap to the right front and a pond also to the right. The distance is a hefty 220 yards from the back tees. The 460-yard par-5 third is another difficult hole. The tee shot is to a landing area guarded by a trap on the right. On the second shot, you have to decide whether to try to clear a large pond approximately 50 yards in front of an elevated green or whether you want to lay up. Many golfers can be seen placing balls in the drop area in front of this pond after hitting into the hazard. If you've survived these three holes, you will probably score well at Saratoga. The combination of a par-3 second hole and a difficult third hole with a water hazard does tend to slow up play. The pace of play usually picks up after this point.

The finishing hole at Saratoga is a challenging 445-yard par 4 that is a slight dogleg left. The first shot is to a tree-lined fairway, and the long approach is to the large green flanked by two sizeable traps. If you have been playing from the back tees, it's the long par 3s and par 4s that tend to make this a difficult course to score on.

The clubhouse at Saratoga Spa has a restaurant, locker rooms and showers. The pro shop is in a separate building a short walk away. Golf instruction is available at the practice facilities, which include a driving range and putting green but no practice bunker. A few hundred feet away is the Gideon Putnam Hotel and Conference Center. This excellent facility has over 20 private function rooms for meetings and conferences.

Its Grand Ballroom holds up to 500 guests for banquets. The original Gideon Putnam was built in 1803 to accommodate the growing surge of tourism in Saratoga. Should you have the time and inclination, take the time to explore the rest of the park and its recreational and cultural facilities.

Saratoga and the surrounding area have many tourist attractions including shops, restaurants, Skidmore College, factory outlet stores, antiques, boating, fishing, the Yaddo Artist Retreat and Gardens, the Saratoga Race Course, the National Museum of Thoroughbred Racing and other sites.

Recommended Golf Courses in New York

Northern (including the Adirondacks):

Adirondack Golf and Country Club, Peru, (518) 643–8403, (800) 346–1761, Public, 18/6851/72

Amsterdam Municipal Golf Course, Amsterdam, (518) 842–4263, Public, 18/6370/71

Ballston Spa Country Club, Ballston Spa, (518) 885–7935, Semiprivate, 18/6215/71

Bluff Point Golf and Country Club, Plattsburgh, (518) 563–3420, (800) 438–0985, Semiprivate, 18/6309/72

Hiland Golf Club, Queensbury, (518) 761–4653, Public, 18/6848/72

Malone Golf Club, Malone, (518) 483–2926, Public. East: 18/6545/72. West: 18/6592/71

The New Course at Albany, Albany, (518) 489–3526, Public, 18/6300/71

Thendara Golf Club, Old Forge, (315) 369–3136, Public, 18/6435/72

Thousand Islands Resort, Alexandria Bay, (315) 482–9454, Resort, 18/6219/72

Watertown Golf Club, Watertown, (315) 782–4040, Semiprivate, 18/6309/72

Westport Country Club, Westport, (518) 962–4470, Public, 18/6544/72

Windham Country Club, Windham, (518) 734–9910, Public, 18/6088/71

Whiteface Inn Resort and Country Club, Lake Placid, (518) 523–2551, Resort, 18/6293/72

New York: Useful Information

Department of Economic Development, Division of Tourism, 1 Commerce Plaza, Albany, NY 12245, (518) 474–4116, (800) 225–5697 (U.S.)

New York Convention and Visitors Bureau, 2 Columbus Circle, New York, NY 10019–1823, (212) 397–8222

Forest Supervisor, Finger Lakes National Forest, P.O. Box W, Montour Falls, NY 14865, (607) 594–2750, (800) 280–CAMP (information and reservations)

New York State Office of Parks, Recreation and Historic Preservation, Agency Bldg. #1, Empire State Plaza, Albany, NY 12238, (518) 474–0456 (recreation information)

Division of Fish and Wildlife, State Environmental Conservation Department, 50 Wolf Rd., Albany, NY 12233, (518) 457–3521 (fishing and hunting regulations)

New York Department of Transportation, Waterways Division, 1220 Washington Ave., Albany, NY 12232, (518) 457–6376 (recreational map and guide to New York State canals)

Course Name: **BRYAN PARK AND GOLF CLUB Champions, Players Courses**

Course Type: Public
Address: 6275 Bryan Park Road
(off Highway 29)
Brown Summit, NC 27214
Phone: (910) 375–2200

GOLF COURSE

Director of Golf: Chris Leclerc
Course Length/Par (All Tees): Champions: Back 7135/72, White 6622/72, Gold 5977/72, Forward 5395/72. Players: Back 7076/72, White 6499/72, Gold 5925/72, Forward 5260/72
Course Slope/Rating (All Tees): Champions: Back 130/74.4, White 125/71.6, Gold 120/68.7, Ladies' Forward 122/71.0. Players: Back 128/73.7, White 124/70.4, Gold 116/67.7, Ladies' Forward 122/69.5
Course Architects: Champions: Rees Jones (1990). Players: George Cobb (1974), Rees Jones (renovation, 1988)
Golf Facilities: Full Pro Shop X, Snack Bar X, Lounge X, Restaurant X, Locker Room X, Showers X, Club Rental X, Club Repair X, Cart Rental X, Instruction X, Practice Green X, Driving Range X, Practice Bunker X, Club Storage No
Tee-Time Reservation Policy: 2 mos. in advance for weekdays (some limitations). Wed. prior for weekends
Ranger: Yes
Tee-off-Interval Time: 8 min.
Time to Play 18 Holes: 4½ hrs.
Course Hours/Earliest Tee-off: 7 a.m. weekends, 7:30 a.m. weekdays
Green Fees: Champions: $24 for 18 holes Fri., Sat., Sun., holidays, $22 for 18 holes weekdays. Reynolds: $22 for 18 holes Fri., Sat., Sun., holidays, $20 for 18 holes weekdays
Cart Fees: $10 for 18 holes per person
Credit Cards: MasterCard, Visa
Season: Year round
Course Comments: Cart mandatory on Champions peak season (March 1 to Oct. 31). Can walk Players anytime. Yardage book available
Golf Packages: Available
Discounts: Residents of Greensboro, seasonal (Nov. to Feb.), twilight, juniors, seniors
Places to Stay Nearby: Holiday Inn Four Seasons (910) 292–9169, (800) 242–6556; Greensboro–High Point Marriott (910) 852–6450, (800) 228–9290; Ramada Hotel and Conference Center (910) 275–0811, (800) 272–6232; Sheraton Greensboro Hotel and Conference Center (910) 379–8000, (800) 325–3535; Best Western–Greensboro Inn (910) 275–0741, (800) 528–1234
Local Attractions: Greensboro Historical Museum, Greensboro Cultural Center, art galleries, professional sports including Class A baseball, University of North Carolina–Greensboro, Greensboro Arboretum, Blandwood mansion and carriage house, Natural Science Center, Barn Dinner Theatre, Carolina Theatre, Richard Petty Museum, music and dance events, the Bog Garden. Greensboro Area Convention and Visitors Bureau (910) 274–2282, (800) 344–2282
Directions: From Greensboro: U.S. 29 north, 5 mi., to Bryan Park exit, follow signs to golf course. From Winston-Salem: I–40 to U.S. 29 north to Bryan Park exit. From the north: U.S. 29 south to Bryan Park exit, follow signs to golf course
Closest Commercial Airports: Piedmont Triad International, Greensboro (30 min.); Raleigh/Durham (1½ hrs.); Charlotte/ Douglas International (2 hrs.)

BRYAN PARK AND GOLF CLUB

Bryan Park is an excellent 36-hole municipal golf facility operated by the Greensboro Parks and Recreation Department. The eighteen-hole Champions Course is a long and demanding 7135 yards from the back tees. Eleven holes are affected by water, namely, Lake Townsend, which is a centerpiece of the 1000-acre park. The course is also well treed and has rolling, hilly fairways. There are many high banks above the lake, necessitating the use of timber bulkheading to support the soil. The Champions Course is heavily bunkered, and the fairways are often protected by mounds and beautiful stands of oak, pine, cedar, poplar and dogwood. The lips of the bunkers tend to be high, sometimes forcing the golfer just to hit out rather than attempt a longer shot. Most of the bentgrass greens are medium sized, slightly elevated, and undulating.

The most difficult hole on the Champions Course is the 535-yard par-5 sixth hole, whose tee shot is straight toward a deep, two-tiered green. The lake guards the left side of the fairway all the way to the green, and water comes into play on the second shot because the lake cuts in front of the green. The signature hole at Champions is the 457-yard par-4 thirteenth, a long dogleg right with the lake on the right all the way to and behind the green, which juts out on a peninsula. On the tee shot, you have to decide how much of the right fairway you want to cut off. That option is somewhat limited, however, by large right-fairway bunkers approximately halfway to the green. The second shot is to the deep, undulating green protected by four bunkers, a bank on the left, and water beyond.

The Champions Course is also characterized by excellent and difficult par 3s. The 230-yard fourteenth is the most difficult one on the course. Its tee shot is all carry to a slightly elevated green with the lake to the right and rear. A huge bunker guards the front of the green, which is medium sized and undulating, and slopes from back to front.

The finishing hole at Champions is a long, straight 469-yard par 4. Two large traps straddle the fairway landing area on the tee shot, and the second shot is a long iron or a wood to a huge green well protected by traps left and right-front. This hole plays like a par 5.

In 1990 Bryan Park's Champions Course was ranked the second best new public course in America by Golf Digest. Rees Jones, the son of Robert Trent Jones, Sr., designed the course and remodeled the eighteen-hole Players Course, which was originally designed by George Cobb in the 1970s. After graduating from Yale and studying landscape architecture at Harvard University's Graduate School of Design, Jones joined his father's golf-course design firm and was involved in the design or supervision of numerous golf courses. Since 1974, he has had his own golf-architecture firm and has designed more than fifty golf courses including the No. 7 course at Pinehurst with Keith Evans; the Country Club of New Seabury (Blue Course) in South Mashpee, Massachusetts (re-modeled); Jones Creek Golf Club, Augusta, Georgia, with Keith Evans; and the Stoney Creek Golf Course in Wintergreen, Virginia, also with Keith Evans. More recently Rees has designed the acclaimed Sandpines golf course in Florence, Oregon, LPGA International in Daytona, Florida and many others in this book.

The 7076-yard Players Course at Bryan Park is more open than the Champions Course and is well worth playing. The par 3s are a bit more difficult from the back tees than those at the Champions. For example, the 206-yard third hole plays to a green protected by water in front. Traps on the left and right force you to carry the ball at least 185 yards and still hold the green. The most difficult hole on the course is the 449-yard par-4 first hole, which plays straight to a deep slightly elevated green trapped by bunkers left and right. You get some relief from the par 5s, which are relatively short, especially from the regular white tees. And there are fewer traps and less water on this eighteen.

The clubhouse at Bryan Park has men's and women's locker rooms and showers, a full pro shop and a snack bar. Staff PGA teaching professionals provide individual and group instruction. Junior clinics are held at the park, as are sports camps that include golf, tennis, sailing and soccer instruction for young people. Several local college and high school teams play at Bryan Park. A private enterprise fund has recently been set up to rechannel revenue from the park activities, including the golf course, back into improvements to the facility. A long-term planning program is in place to further improve the golf course.

It should also be noted that Bryan Park has a 22,000-square-foot enrichment center with several meeting rooms and a complete kitchen for food service. This was donated by Joseph and Kathleen Bryan, after whom the park was named. The center has a magnificent lobby area and a terrace overlooking the golf course.

Course Name: OAK HOLLOW GOLF COURSE

Course Type: Public
Address: 1400 Oakview Road
                       High Point, NC 27265
Phone: (910) 883–3260

GOLF COURSE

Director of Golf: Steve High
Course Length/Par (All Tees): Back 6483/72, Middle 6022/72, Forward 4796/72
Course Slope/Rating (All Tees): Back 121/70.5, Middle 116/68.2, Ladies' Forward 119/68.5
Course Architect: Pete Dye (1972)
Golf Facilities: Full Pro Shop X, Snack Bar X, Lounge No, Restaurant No, Locker Room X, Showers X, Club Rental X, Club Repair Limited, Cart Rental X, Instruction X, Practice Green X, Driving Range X, Practice Bunker X, Club Storage No
Tee-Time Reservation Policy: 48 hrs. in advance from 7:45 a.m. in person. 8 a.m. Thurs. prior to weekend by phone
Ranger: Yes
Tee-off-Interval Time: 8 min.
Time to Play 18 Holes: 4 hrs., 15 min.
Course Hours/Earliest Tee-off: 8 a.m.
Green Fees: $16 for 18 holes weekends, $13 for 18 holes weekdays. $8 for 9 holes weekdays
Cart Fees: $10 for 18 holes per person. $5 for 9 holes per person
Pull Carts: $2 for 18 holes, $1 for 9 holes
Credit Cards: MasterCard, Visa
Season: Year round
Course Comments: Can walk anytime. Yardage book available. 9-hole play allowed weekdays
Golf Packages: None

Discounts: Residents— juniors, seniors, ladies
Places to Stay Nearby: Radisson Hotel (910) 889–8888, (800) 333–3333; Howard Johnson (910) 886–4141, (800) 446–4656; Holiday Inn Market Square (910) 886–7011, (800) HOLIDAY. Greensboro: Airport Marriott (910) 852–6450, (800) 228–9290; Sheraton Greensboro Hotel and Conference Center (910) 379–8000, (800) 325–3535; Embassy Suites Hotel (910) 668–4535, (800) 362–2779
Local Attractions: High Point Museum/ Historical Park, Angela Peterson Doll and Miniature Museum, Shakespeare Festival, Oktoberfest, Piedmont Environmental Center, Mendenhall Plantation, High Point College, Furniture Library and tours, tennis, boating. High Point Chamber of Commerce (910) 889–8151
Directions: I–40, exit Hwy. 68 airport exit, south to High Point, right on Centennial to dead end and Oak View, right on Oak View to golf course
Closest Commercial Airports: Piedmont Triad International, Greensboro (15 min.); Raleigh/Durham (1½ hrs.); Charlotte/Douglas International (1½ hrs.)

OAK HOLLOW GOLF COURSE

High Point, North Carolina, is approximately 15 minutes from Greensboro and has two public golf courses of note, Blair Park and Oak Hollow. Blair Park, built in the 1930s, is a 6463-yard par-72 layout with a completely equipped clubhouse with pro shop, locker rooms, showers and a grill room. In the past, qualifying rounds for the Greater Greensboro Open were held there. Oak Hollow, designed by Pete Dye and opened in 1972, is rated among America's best public golf courses by *Golf Digest*.

Located in Oak Hollow Park, a large recreational complex built around a 720-acre lake on the northeastern edge of the city, Oak Hollow includes some of Dye's signature design features, such as sand bunkers lined with pilings, an island tee, fairways shored up with railroad ties, grass traps and a green situated on a peninsula. These features, coupled with rolling terrain and medium-sized to small undulating, fast greens, make the 6483-yard par-72 course a challenge for all levels of golfers.

Twelve of the holes on the course are water holes, including holes five and six, two of the most challenging on the front nine. The fifth hole is a 477-yard par 5. It doglegs to the left and requires a 225-yard carry over water from the back tees. The undulating green is set on a peninsula and is protected by traps to the left and back.

The number-1-handicap sixth hole is a 420-yard par 4 featuring a sharp, 90-degree dogleg to the left and an island tee. Water to the left accompanies the fairway all the way to the green. The second shot can be more difficult if the pin placement is at the left back of the green, forcing the golfer to come in over a left-front sand trap. The green also slopes forward toward the trap.

On the back nine, the number-2-handicap hole is the 420-yard par-4 eleventh hole, which is relatively straight but has a large tree on the left side of the fairway approximately 120 yards from the hole. The tee shot should thus be hit to the right side of the fairway. The second shot is onto a large, three-tiered green that is almost 35 yards wide but is also shallow. A lake runs along the left side of the fairway to the green and in front of the putting surface, adding to the difficulty of this hole.

Other facilities in Oak Hollow Park include a boat marina, tennis courts, picnic areas and a family camping area. High Point offers a number of recreational and tourist attractions, including annual events such as the North Carolina Shakespeare Festival and Oktoberfest. The city itself was founded along two principal transportation routes in the heart of a rich hardwood forest region. Around the turn of the century, community leaders invested $2 million in the development of furniture factories, and today High Point is the hub of America's furniture production. It is also the nation's hosiery center and has a wide range of other industries.

Course Name: **TANGLEWOOD PARK Championship, Reynolds Courses**

Course Type: Public
Address: Route 40
Clemmons, NC 27012
Phone: (910) 766–5082
(Golf Course)
(910) 766–0591
(Park Office)

GOLF COURSE

Director of Golf: Brent Jessup
Course Length/Par (All Tees): Championship: Back 7048/72, Middle Back 6538/72, Middle Front 6014/72, Ladies' Forward 5119/74. Reynolds: Back 6469/72, Regular 6061/72, Forward 5432/72 or 5066/72
Course Slope/Rating (All Tees): Championship: Back 140/74.5, Middle Back 135/72.3, Middle Front 130/69.9, Ladies' Forward 130/70.9. Reynolds: Back 125/71, Regular 120/68.5, Ladies' Forward 120/70.2
Course Architect: Robert Trent Jones, Sr. (1957)
Golf Facilities: Full Pro Shop X, Snack Bar X, Lounge Beer/Wine, Restaurant X, Locker Room X, Showers X, Club Rental X, Club Repair Limited, Cart Rental X, Instruction X, Practice Green X, Driving Range X, Practice Bunker X, Club Storage No
Tee-Time Reservation Policy: Up to 7 days in advance. Only foursomes can make reservations on weekends, holidays
Ranger: Yes
Tee-off-Interval Time: 8 min.
Time to Play 18 Holes: 4½ hrs.
Course Hours/Earliest Tee-off: 7:30 a.m.
Green Fees: Championship: $64 for 18 holes. Reynolds: $28 for 18 holes Fri., Sat., Sun., holidays, $22 weekdays
Cart Fees: $14 for 18 holes per person
Credit Cards: All major cards
Season: Year round
Course Comments: Can walk Championship Jan., Feb. Can walk Reynolds anytime. Pull carts not allowed on Championship
Golf Packages: None

Discounts: Seasonal rates, specials, twilight

Places to Stay Nearby: Holiday Inn (910) 766–9121, (800) HOLIDAY; Tanglewood Motel and Manor House and Tanglewood Park Accommodations (910) 766–0591; Winston–Salem Hyatt (910) 725–1234, (800) 233–1234; Brookstown Inn (910) 725–1120. GREENSBORO: Hilton Inn Airport (910) 299–7650, (800) 445–8667. HIGH POINT: Holiday Inn (910) 886–7011, (800) HOLIDAY

Local Attractions: HIGH POINT: Furniture center, Furniture Library. WINSTON-SALEM: Reynolds House, Nature Science Center, old Salem, Bethabara Park, Stroh Brewery, Southeastern Center for Contemporary Art. GREENSBORO: Greensboro Historical Museum, Greensboro Cultural Center, Carolina Theatre. Winston–Salem Convention and Visitors Bureau (910) 725–2361, (800) 331–7018

Directions: From Charlotte: Rte. 77 north to I–40, east on I–40, 25 min. from intersection on I–40. From Winston-Salem (7 mi.): I–40 southwest to Clemmons, follow signs to park

Closest Commercial Airports: Piedmont Triad International, Greensboro (40 min.); Raleigh/Durham (2 hrs.); Charlotte/Douglas International (2 hrs.)

TANGLEWOOD PARK

If you were to imagine a perfect public park, Tanglewood Park in Clemmons, North Carolina, might be a good version of it. The 1152-acre park is bordered on its western boundary by the Yadkin River, a derivation of an Indian word for "big trees." Sauras, Saponos, Tutelos, Keyauwee and Eastern Sioux tribes were here before settlers came to this area in the 1700s. A fort was built on these grounds in 1759, and a cemetery dating back to the original settlers can be seen on the property.

In 1921 some of the parkland was sold to William N. Reynolds, the brother of tobacco magnate R. J. Reynolds. Tanglewood then became a working farm with cattle, horses, chickens and a full staff to maintain the property, which served as one of Reynolds's various homes. Additional purchases of land increased the size of the

farm to almost 1200 acres, and numerous improvements were made, including renovations and additions to the Manor House, which was built in 1848 and now serves as a bed and breakfast inn. The property was willed to the citizens of Forsyth County and was converted into a public park following Reynolds's death in 1951. It has evolved into one of the finest public parks in America. Today it is operated by a not-for-profit corporation, the Forsyth County Park Authority, Inc., which manages the park on behalf of Forsyth County.

The Championship Course at Tanglewood is a 7048-yard par-72 layout designed by Robert Trent Jones, Sr., and was opened in 1957. The course has been ranked among the best public golf courses in the United States by *Golf Digest.* The pro shop has been rated one of the nation's 100 best by *Golf Shop Operations* magazine. During the late 1980s, the R. J. Reynolds Corporation, which continues to be a major benefactor of Tanglewood, contributed almost a million dollars to renovate the clubhouse and the Championship Course, which hosted the 1974 PGA Tournament, which was won by Lee Trevino. The 1986 USGA Public Links was also held here, and more recently Tanglewood has been the site of the Vantage Championship, a PGA Senior Tour event.

The Championship Course is a rolling layout with few radical changes in elevation. Pine, oak, and maple permeate the course, but the layout is reasonably open, with many large traps protecting large, undulating bentgrass greens. Water comes into play on only three holes, but fairway bunkers are well placed to guard landing areas. Many greens have to be reached in the air because traps often prevent an approach shot from being rolled onto the putting surface. The course is sloped at 140 with a USGA rating of 74.5 from the back tees. There is almost a 2000-yard difference in course length between the front and back tees. With four tee distances to choose from, any golfer should enjoy this course.

The number-1-handicap hole on the Championship Course is the fifth, which plays a long 608 yards from the back tees to a wide, shallow green trapped all around. The tee shot has to avoid fairway bunkers on the right, as does the second shot. The approach shot must reach the green on the fly. During the 1974 PGA Championship no one reached this green in two.

The front side finishes with a string of three tough holes. The 243-yard par-3 seventh plays to a narrow, deep green with two huge traps to the right and another to the left. Again, there is a very narrow entrance way to the green, and water is farther left if you heavily hook the ball. This hole plays 208 yards from the middle back tees and 190 from the middle front. The 430-yard par-4 eighth is a slight dogleg left to a comparatively small 6048-square-foot green flanked by huge traps left and right, one front, and another left and farther front. The 425-yard par-4 ninth is straight to a wide, shallow green with two large traps to the front and one at the rear. Two left-fairway bunkers squeeze the landing area halfway to the hole.

The 420-yard par-4 fourteenth has been rated by *Golf Digest* as one of the best 100 holes in America from the championship tees. The tee shot is over a long lake that runs down the left side of the fairway to a landing area protected by two bunkers on the right. The second shot is likely to be from a sidehill lie onto a skull-shaped green completely surrounded by five traps. The finishing hole is a beautiful 425-yard par-4 dogleg right. Tanglewood's old church is on a distant hilltop next to the clubhouse. The old cemetery is out of bounds and to the left of the narrow, deep green, which is protected by three large traps. The tee shot must negotiate two large fairway bunkers on the right at the knee of the dogleg, then the second shot is a long uphill poke to the well-protected green.

The 6469-yard par-72 Reynolds Course, named in honor of William N. Reynolds, is another fine golf course. This is a tighter, hillier layout, with water coming into play on several holes.

Pull carts can be used on the Reynolds Course, which can be walked anytime. Pull carts are not allowed on the Championship Course, though walking is allowed with some restrictions. Both courses are well maintained, and 2 driving ranges, a par-3 course, a miniature golf course and putting facilities are on site. Professional instruction for groups and individuals is available.

The balance of the recreational dining and lodging amenities at Tanglewood Park should be visited. The Manor House Bed and Breakfast Inn has 29 well-appointed rooms in the original nineteenth-century house and adjoining lodge. Three meals a day are served at the Manor House, or you can eat at the clubhouse grill overlooking the park's Championship Course. Available for day or night play are 9 clay and hard-surface tennis courts. Jogging trails include courses of up to 8.1 miles. Fishing can be enjoyed at Mallard or Skillpot Lake, and stables, a legacy of Reynolds's horse-breeding days, provide trail rides, riding lessons, carriage rides and horse-boarding facilities. Tractor-pulled hay rides and sing-alongs are another option. Steeplechase races and polo matches also take place here.

Boat rentals, softball fields, volleyball courts, horseshoe pits, shuffleboard courts, a swimming pool and waterslide, bicycle rental, nature trails, and camping are also offered at Tanglewood Park, which has a magnificent rose garden and arboretum. A variety of housing accommodations including cottages, lodge apartments, guest houses, tent and RV camping sites, a motor lodge, and the Manor House is available. Guests of the Manor House Bed and Breakfast Inn get reduced golf rates. Meeting facilities for outings, seminars, weddings, conferences and other events are also on site. These include a concert shell area, children's center, the Manor House Trophy Room, arboretum, church and barn. Food services are available.

Tanglewood was originally named after Hawthorne's *Tanglewood Tales*, a collection of children's myths. Through the largesse of the Reynolds family and other benefactors, Tanglewood has become a verdant playground for children young and old.

Recommended Golf Courses in North Carolina

Within 1 Hour of Greensboro:

Carolina Lakes Golf Course, Sanford, (910) 499–5421, Public, 18/6248/70

Jamestown Park Golf Club, Jamestown, (910) 454–4912, Public, 18/6665/72

Quarry Hills Country Club, Graham, (910) 578–2602, Semiprivate, 18/6617/70

Stoney Creek Golf Club, Stoney Creek, (910) 449–5688, Public, 18/7063/72

Pinehurst Area

Course Name: PINEHURST
                 Course Numbers 1, 2, 3, 4, 5, 6, 7, 8

Course Type: Resort
Resort: Pinehurst Resort and Country Club
Address: Carolina Vista
              P.O. Box 4000
              Pinehurst, NC 28374
Phone: (910) 295–6811 (Golf Course)
              (910) 295–8141 (Tee Times)
              (910) 295–6811,
              (800) 672–4644 (NC),
              (800) 487–4653 (outside NC) (Resort)

GOLF COURSE

Director of Golf: Don Padgett
Head Professionals: Course Nos. 1-5: Lou Ferguson. No. 6: Danny Ackerman. No. 7: Ling Sriraman. No. 8: Matt Massei
Course Length/Par (All Tees): No. 1: Back 5780/70, Ladies' Forward 5329/73. No. 2: Back 7020/72, Middle 6401/72, Ladies' Forward 5966/74. No. 3: Back 5593/70, Ladies' Forward 5198/72. No. 4: Back 6919/72, Middle 6396/72, Ladies' Forward 5696/73. No. 5: Back 6827/72, Middle 6338/72, Ladies' Forward 5658/73. No. 6: Back 7157/72, Blue 6603/72, White 6168/72, Ladies' Forward 5430/72. No. 7: Back 7114/72, Blue 6719/72, White 6216/72, Ladies' Forward 4924/72. No. 8: Back 7092/72, Blue 6698/72, White 6288/72, Green 5805/72, Forward 5177/72

Course Slope/Rating (All Tees): No. 1: Back 114/67.4, Ladies' Forward 117/70.1. No. 2: Back 131/74.1, Middle 127/71.4, Ladies' Forward 135/74.2. No. 3: Back 112/67.2, Ladies' Forward 114/70.1. No. 4: Back 126/73.3, Middle 117/70.8, Ladies' Forward 119/71.8. No. 5: Back 130/73.4, Middle 123/71.2, Ladies' Forward 131/74.7. No. 6: Back 137/75.6, Blue 132/73.2, White 129/71.3, Ladies' Forward 125/71.2. No. 7: Back 145/75.6, Blue 142/73.7, White 130/70.4, Ladies' Forward 124/69.7. No. 8: Back 135/74.0, Blue 125/71.7, White 121/69.8, Green 114/67.3, Ladies' Green 122/72.5, Forward 112/68.9

Course Architects: No. 1: Donald Ross (1899). No. 2: Donald Ross (9 holes, 1901; 9 holes, 1907). No. 3: Donald Ross (9 holes, 1907; 9 holes, 1910). No. 4: Donald Ross (9 holes, 1914; 9 holes 1919), Robert Trent Jones, Sr. (renovation, 1973), Rees Jones (renovation, 1983). No. 5: Ellis Maples (1961), Robert Trent Jones, Sr. (renovation, 1974). No. 6: George Fazio and Tom Fazio (1979), Tom Fazio (renovation, 1991). No. 7: Rees Jones (1986). No. 8: Tom Fazio (1996)

Golf Facilities: Full Pro Shop X, Snack Bar X, Lounge X, Restaurant Except Course 6, Locker Room X, Showers X, Club Rental X, Club Repair X, Cart Rental X, Instruction X, Practice Green X, Driving Range X, Practice Bunker X, Club Storage X

Tee-Time Reservation Policy: 60 days in advance for all registered golf-package golfers. You must be a member, guest or registered at the resort to play Pinehurst
Ranger: Yes
Tee-off-Interval Time: Nos. 1, 3-8: 8 min. No. 2: 10 min.
Time to Play 18 Holes: 4 hrs., 15 min.
Course Hours/Earliest Tee-off: 6:30 a.m.
Green Fees: Peak season rates are early March to early June, mid-Sept. to mid-Nov. Green fees on the less expensive courses can be under $40. The more expensive courses are Nos. 2, 7 and 8 which have surcharges of $50 additional

on No. 2 course, $25 additional on No. 7, $45 additional on No. 8 for 18 holes. A variety of golf packages are offered year round

Cart Fees: $19 plus tax per person per cart

Credit Cards: All major cards

Season: Year round. Busiest seasons April and May, Sept. through Oct., Nov.

Course Comments: Nos. 1-5: Must take cart or caddy. Yardage book available for No. 2. Advantage Golf School on site. Caddies available on No. 2 and No. 8

Golf Packages: Numerous seasonal, instructional, varying-length golf packages. Cart fees not included in golf packages

Discounts: Seasonal–lowest golf-package rates mid-Nov. to early March; highest golf-package rates early March to early June, mid-Sept. to mid-Nov.

Places to Stay Nearby: See Pinehurst area listing on pages 509.

Local Attractions: See Pinehurst area listing on page 509.

Directions: From Rte. 1 south: To Sanford, take Rtes. 15/501 south from Sanford to Pinehurst, take Hwy. 2 west, 1½ mi. to resort. From Rte. 1 north: To Aberdeen, left at first traffic light in Aberdeen to Hwy. 5, Hwy. 5 to traffic light, make right, resort on left

Closest Commercial Airports: Pinehurst Moore County Airport (10 min.); Raleigh/Durham (1 hr., 15 min.); Piedmont Triad International, Greensboro (1 hr., 20 min.); Charlotte/Douglas International (2 hrs.)

RESORT

Date Built: 1895

No. of Rooms: Pinehurst Hotel: 310 rooms. Manor Inn: 49 rooms. 130 1-, 2-, 3-bedroom condominiums

Meeting/Exhibit Rooms: 18. Capacity of Largest: 1075 persons theater style. Meeting Space: 50,000 sq. ft.

Room Price Range: $144 to $194 for single room peak season early Mar. to early June modified American plan including breakfast and dinner. Lower seasonal rates at other times. Golf and other packages available year round.

Lounges: Ryder Cup Lounge, 91st Hole, Mulligans Manor Inn Sports Bar

Restaurants: Carolina Dining Room, Donald Ross Grill, Ryder Cup Lounge, Mulligans Manor Inn Sports Bar

Entertainment: Music and dancing in Carolina Dining Room, music in Mulligans

Credit Cards: All major cards

General Amenities: Babysitting services, children's playground, tennis shop, resort shops, meeting and conference facilities with audiovisual, food service, conference-planning support services

Recreational Amenities: Lawn bowling, 3 croquet courts, 24 hard-surface and Har-Tru courts (4 lighted), fitness center with Cybex/Eagle resistance-training circuit, Quinton treadmills, Lifesteps, rowers, wind-racer cycles, Life Cycles, Cybex upper-body ergometers; boating and sailing on 200-acre Lake Pinehurst, 5 outdoor swimming pools, carriage rides, fishing, volleyball, bicycling, video computerized golf

Reservation and Cancellation Policy: A per person deposit is required to guarantee reservations. 15-day cancellation notice prior to arrival date required for refund of deposit

Comments and Restrictions: No pets. 15% service charge added to package rate for services. Service charge subject to state sales tax. For all a la carte food and beverage services, 15% added to your check as a service charge. Additional gratuities for exceptional service are at your discretion. Reservations or starting times are required for all recreational activities. Modified American plan. European plan available in condominiums only

PINEHURST

Some places you visit have a certain aura that transcends the individual parts or elements that make up the whole. In golf, Pinehurst is one of those places. As you motor up the tree-lined driveway to the grand old resort hotel, a national historic landmark, or when you stand swatting golf balls on "Maniac Hill" outside the magnificent clubhouse, you might think you died and went to golf heaven.

It all began in 1895 when Boston philanthropist James Walker Tufts purchased 5500 acres of ravaged timberland in North Carolina for about 1 dollar per acre. He was interested in building a luxury health resort, and initially the town was called Tuftstown. It eventually became known as Pinehurst after the area's magnificent trees and "hurst," a wooded plot on rising ground. The firm headed by Frederick Law Olmsted, architect and designer of Central Park in New York City, was hired to design and landscape Pinehurst. The Pinehurst Hotel, originally the Carolina Hotel, opened in 1901, and recreation such as riding, hunting, polo, lawn bowling, bicycling, tennis and archery became part of the social landscape, along with the 222,000 trees and shrubs that Olmsted planted in Pinehurst Village.

In 1898, Dr. D. LeRoy Culver of New York designed the first nine at Pinehurst, and in 1901 Tufts hired Donald Ross, then a young Scottish golf professional, to direct golf operations at Pinehurst. Ross went on to design and remodel more than 400 golf courses in North America prior to his death at Pinehurst in 1948. One of the pleasures of being at Pinehurst is playing Ross's four courses, which he built over a span of twenty years from 1899 to 1919. There are other Ross courses nearby, including Mid Pines Resort, Southern Pines Country Club, and the Pine Needles Country Club; but it is the No. 2 Ross Course at Pinehurst, site of the 1994 U.S. Senior Open and many other significant tournaments, that you'll want to play first. No. 2 is considered to be the best golf course in the state of North Carolina, and that's saying a lot, considering the quality of golf courses in that state. It was also recently ranked seventh among the 100 greatest golf courses in the United States and thirteenth among the 59 greatest golf courses in the world by *Golf* magazine.

The No. 2 Course plays 7020 yards from the back tees and is a rolling layout well guarded by pine trees in particular. It also has more than 115 bunkers. The bentgrass greens are medium sized to large,

moderately fast and mildly undulating. In 1936, when No. 2 was the site of the PGA Championship, Ross commented:

It is obviously the function of the championship course to present competitors with a variety of problems that will test every type of shot which a golfer of championship ability should be qualified to play. Thus it should call for long and accurate tee shots, accurate iron play (and let me say here that I consider the ability to play the longer irons as the supreme test of a great golfer), precise handling of the short game, and finally consistent putting. These abilities should be called for in a proportion that will not permit excellence in any one department of the game to largely offset deficiencies in another.

Over the years, many of the greatest names in golf have played Pinehurst, including Harry Vardon, Bobby Jones, Gene Sarazen, Byron Nelson, Sam Snead, Ben Hogan, Arnold Palmer, Jack Nicklaus, Tom Watson, Glenna Collett Vare, Babe Zaharias, and Patty Berg, to name a few. The main clubhouse and the hotel are replete with fascinating photos and golf memorabilia from Pinehurst's rich golf history.

The number-1-handicap hole on Pinehurst No. 2 is the 445-yard par-4 fifth. This is a dogleg left, bordered by trees and sloping gently downward, then up to a deep green that slopes forward and right to left. From 190 yards to the green there are three traps on the left and another two closer to the putting surface on the right and toward the front. If you place your tee shot too far left while trying to cut some distance off the hole, there is a risk that you will be in the huge fairway bunker. If you are too far right, a long iron or wood is required to reach the green, which might be difficult to hold from that trajectory and angle.

The back nine has a series of outstanding finishing holes. The 436-yard par-4 fourteenth plays from a dramatic, elevated tee to a relatively open fairway with three traps to the right and one to the left of the landing area. The next shot is onto a deep, forward-sloping green guarded by three large traps from approximately 75 yards in.

Trees on the right tend to narrow the fairway. The fifteenth is a 201-yard par 3 that plays to a medium-sized green with two large traps to the right and front, and a larger one to the left and front of the green. Should you happen to hit these bunkers on the tee shot, you are left with 5 to 25 yards out of them to the green.

The par-5 sixteenth is a beautiful 531-yard dogleg left up a well-treed fairway to a deep green protected by seven traps from 90 yards in. Ross comments on the green:

Contours and slopes [at Pinehurst] have been used to break up the greens which are so designed as to always give the player near the cup an opportunity for one putt but have minimized the regulation number for the golfer whose play to the green has been less than accurate. The 16th hole is a fine example of what I have in mind. Here the slope rises gently on the front part of the green and faces slightly away at the rear. Regardless of where a pin may be placed, a player whose approach is either short or strong will be faced with the problem of putting across the ridge formed by this change in slope.

The seventeenth is a 190-yard par 3 that plays from an elevated tee down approximately 20 to 30 feet to a deep green surrounded by five traps. The final hole, a par 4, is a slight dogleg right and plays 432 yards uphill to a medium-sized green with three traps in front. If you try to cut the right side of the corner too much, long, parallel sand traps await you 200 yards from the tee. It is difficult to roll the ball onto the green on the second shot because of the well-trapped entranceway.

The main clubhouse at Pinehurst serves golf courses No. 1 through No. 5, which all begin and end conveniently nearby. The practice area, aptly called "Maniac Hill," provides considerable opportunity to hit balls toward flagged target greens from a deep grass plateau. Nearby is a large putting green. A tall outdoor clock is well situated so you won't miss your tee time. Inside is the Donald Ross Grill, with high, vaulted ceilings, a picture of Ross himself, and an ample range of food and drink. Adjacent is the 91st Hole bar, which looks out onto the golf courses, as does a verandah outside. There is a complete pro shop for clubs and apparel. The halls of the clubhouse have many interesting golf photos and memorabilia reflecting the history of Pinehurst.

The less famous courses served by this clubhouse are well worth playing. The No. 1 Course was the first course built at Pinehurst, in 1899, and plays 5780 yards from the back tees and 5329 yards from the front. The No. 3 Course plays 5593 yards from the back tees and 5198 yards from the front and was completed in 1910. No. 4 was completed by Ross in 1919 and redesigned by Robert Trent Jones, Sr., in 1973 and then his son Rees in 1983. It plays 6919 yards from the back tees. The number-1-handicap hole on the course is the 418-yard par-4 sixteenth, the beginning of three strong finishing holes. The sixteenth is a slight dogleg left and is relatively open, with out of bounds on the left and traps at the dogleg, approximately halfway to the hole. My colleague, Robert Gebhardt, holed a 4-iron for an eagle on this hole and the ball, no doubt, is in a trophy case somewhere in Naples, Florida. There is hope for all of us.

The seventeenth is a 547-yard par 5 that plays straight to a green that slopes forward and right. If you hit your tee shot well, you will catch a downward slope that will also kick the ball right and put you in a position to be around or on the green in two. The final hole is a 446-yard par-4 dogleg left that plays slightly downhill. The left knee of the dogleg is well protected by traps. The green is fairly deep, with a trap on the right.

Course No. 5 at Pinehurst was originally designed by Ellis Maples and opened in 1961. It was renovated by Robert Trent Jones, Sr., in 1974. This course plays 6827 yards from the back tees and winds its way through a real-estate development. The frequent out-of-bounds restrictions, traps, mounds, trees and drop-offs from the greens can make this a difficult golf course. The greens are large, moderately fast and generally well trapped. Water comes into play on five of the holes.

The number-1-handicap hole on No. 5 is the 453-yard par-4 ninth, a dogleg right playing uphill to a plateau, then down and up to a generous green that tilts right to left and forward. One of the most difficult holes on the course is the 410-yard eleventh, a dogleg left par 4 that plays downhill, then slightly uphill to a small green with traps left and right. On the second shot, the fairway narrows considerably as water cuts in on the right from 50 to 100 yards from the hole. A pretty par 3 on the back side is the 200-yard thirteenth, which plays over water from an elevated tee, then uphill to a right-to-left-sloping green with traps left, front and rear.

The No. 6 Course at Pinehurst was designed by George and Tom Fazio and was originally opened in 1979. Tom Fazio redesigned the 7157-yard layout in 1991. This course is served by a separate small clubhouse a few miles from the resort hotel and directly across the road from the main clubhouse. No. 6 does have a driving range and practice putting area, with snack bar food service available at the course. One of the most difficult holes on this course is the 553-yard par-5 tenth, which starts out from a slightly elevated tee, then rolls downward and up to a green protected by a huge trap on the left. The second shot on this hole is extremely difficult because the fairway is severely pinched by water left and right from 200 to 100 yards into the green. The No. 6 Course finishes with three strong holes, beginning with a 232-yard par 3 that drops 75 to 100 feet to a forward-sloping green with a trap in front of it. This hole plays a more reasonable 186 yards from the blue tees and 160 yards from the whites.

The seventeenth is a 419-yard par 4 with magnificent views from an elevated tee. The tee drops severely to a dogleg-left fairway that gradually slopes up toward a forward-sloping green protected by traps left and right. The final hole on the No. 6 Course is a 434-yard straight par 4 slightly uphill to a deep green protected by traps left and right. In addition to distance, well-placed trees, water on five holes, strategically placed traps and out-of-bounds stakes necessitated by real-estate development on some of the holes, the large and fast greens on the No. 6 Course can quickly put strokes on your score. I enjoyed playing this course, and the four tee distances ranging from 5430 yards to 7157 yards should make it possible for anyone to enjoy playing here. *Golfweek* magazine rates No. 6 one of the best courses in North Carolina.

You have to be ready to play golf when you step onto the No. 7 Course at Pinehurst. Designed by Rees Jones and opened in 1986, No. 7 plays 7114 yards and is ranked by *Golf Digest* as one of the best public or private golf courses in North Carolina. No. 7 has a hefty slope rating of 145 from the back tees, 142 from the blues, 130 from the whites and 124 from the forward tees. The USGA ratings are 75.6, 73.7, 70.4 and 69.7, respectively. The course is well treed and well trapped, and has rolling terrain with water coming into play on eight holes. The bentgrass greens are large, fast, undulating and well protected by signature Rees Jones mounds.

After starting out with a reasonable 514-yard par 5, the number-1-handicap hole, the second, appears in the form of a 452-yard par 4 playing straight from an elevated tee down a tree-lined fairway to a right-to-left- and forward-sloping, undulating green protected by mounds and traps. Distance and accuracy on two straight shots are required to have a chance at par on this hole. The ninth hole is a tough 204-yard par 3 uphill and over water to a plateaued green cut into the side of a hill and banked in back. The forward-sloping green has a large trap in front with mounds front and to the right.

I liked several holes in particular on the back nine, which plays about the same distance as the front. The 393-yard par-4 tenth is a dogleg left that drops 75 to 100 feet to the fairway, which then rolls up to a plateaued green with an amphitheater bank in back and several pot bunkers left, right and front. The eleventh is another par-4 dogleg left and plays uphill to a plateaued landing area, then down, then up again to a green with a mounded bank around the green. A very deep bunker in front of the green makes it difficult to avoid trouble on the second shot.

The 203-yard par-3 thirteenth hole plays from plateau to plateau over a huge sand waste area that can be a nightmare if you don't reach the green, which is well banked in front. The finishing hole is a gargantuan 596 yards straight to a green with a very narrow entrance. The green is well protected by pot bunkers, which can make this a long hole indeed.

The No. 7 Course has a clubhouse, pro shop, modest locker room facilities, and snack bar and full restaurant. Outside is an ample driving range with target flags and a putting green just in front of the clubhouse. No. 7 tends to give you more uphill, sidehill and downhill lies than the other Pinehurst courses because of its rolling terrain and mounds. It is also easier to lose balls here, whereas there is relatively little water and the open areas under the pines seem more benign on the other courses. Whatever your golfing preference, you're likely to find it on these courses.

The Centennial Pinehurst No. 8 course, designed by Tom Fazio, is the latest addition to Pinehurst's golf resort. Tom Fazio, who assisted his Uncle George in the design of No. 6 and later renovated it, carved the eminently playable No. 8 out of Pinehurst's old hunting and shooting club acreage. No. 8 plays a healthy 7092 yards from the back tees but offers five tee positions for all levels of golfer. Water can come into play on seven holes on this course which is well bunkered and has a variety of interesting green configurations. The course is well treed and has some pronounced changes in elevation.

There is a challenging range of distances such as the 238-yard par-3 eighth whose tee shot plays from an elevated tee over a marsh to a large green with a bunker to its right. The shortest par 3, from the back tees, is the 149-yard fifth. The longest par 4 is the 464-yard fourth but the 358-yard twelfth, the shortest, provides some relief. There are two true three-shot par 5s on this course, the 604-

yard sixth and the 579-yard eleventh. But Fazio teases you toward the end of the round with a 500-yard par-5 dogleg right on No. 17. Besides the beauty of this course, the variety of doglegs, hole distances, green configurations along with the natural elements of marshes, waste bunkers, pines, rolling terrain and rough will provide an excellent test of golf. The No. 8 course is served by its own clubhouse and caddies are available.

At its Advantage Schools Pinehurst offers a variety of junior and adult instructional programs from March through October. Weekend and week-long programs are available and include lodging, meals, green fees, cart rental, club storage, unlimited range balls, video stroke analysis, personalized club fitting, all Pinehurst amenities, and a "graduation" party and awards ceremony. The junior program is geared for boys and girls ages 11 to 17, and an advanced program for juniors is available. Separate from this program is the option to take individual or group instruction year round from the staff of PGA professionals and assistants on site.

Pinehurst also offers many golf packages, whereby guests can stay at the main hotel, a condominium or the Manor Inn. A modified American plan is offered, and the spring season, which runs from early March to early June, and the fall season, which runs from mid-September to mid-November, tend to have the highest rates. The other seasons are summer (early June to early September) and the evergreen season (mid-November to early March). The evergreen season has the lowest rates for golf packages.

Many other forms of recreation and other packages such as tennis, Thanksgiving, Murder Mystery, and New Year's are available at Pinehurst. There are 28 tennis courts—18 Har-Tru and 10 hard surface (4 lighted), a gun club with nationally rated ranges, 9 trap and 6 skeet fields, 5 swimming pools, a fitness center and a nearby 200-acre lake with sailing, canoeing, swimming and fishing. Children's supervised activity programs and babysitting services are available and games such as badminton, volleyball, croquet and lawn bowling are popular. Carriage rides, hay rides and pony rides are available through the Pinehurst Livery Stables. But golf is the focus of Pinehurst. If you ever get beyond the many activities and facilities at this resort, there are several excellent golf courses within 30 minutes of Pinehurst.

Accommodations at Pinehurst include the 310-room Pinehurst Hotel, the Manor Inn, which has 49 rooms, suites, and parlors; and 140 golf-course and lakeside condominiums, which have 1 to 3 bedrooms with full kitchens. A new $4-million conference and exhibit center provides 50,000 square feet of meeting space. *Meetings and Conventions* magazine has awarded Pinehurst its Gold Tee Award for excellence in golf and meeting facilities, and the American Automobile Association has again awarded Pinehurst its Four Diamond Award.

The resort of course includes ample dining and lounge facilities, including the Carolina Dining Room for more formal meals and the London Grill, Ryder Cup Lounge, Manor Inn Sports Bar (Mulligan's) and the Donald Ross Grill. And it is only a short walk from the resort to Pinehurst Village. Across from the Holly Inn you can observe the stone marker where Tufts drove a stake into the ground in 1895 to mark the center of the village, which was then built to resemble a New England town. Today you can see some of the original cottages that were built on streets called Dogwood, Magnolia and Village Green.

In the old days, Pinehurst ran a rather tight ship, including this restriction:

So select was Pinehurst that the intending visitor to a hotel or cottage must send in advance a certificate from his minister and physician attesting to his religious and moral standing.

You won't have to do that anymore. But you might want to work on your golf swing before you visit this formidable shrine.

Course Name: THE PINE NEEDLES LODGE AND GOLF CLUB

Course Type: Resort
Resort: Pine Needles Lodge and Golf Club
Address: North Carolina Route 2 P.O. Box 88 Southern Pines, NC 28388
Phone: (910) 692–8411 (Golf Course) (910) 692–7111 (Resort)
Fax: (910) 692–5349

GOLF COURSE

Head Professional: Peggy Kirk Bell
Touring Professional: Pat McGowan
Course Length/Par (All Tees): Back 6603/71, Middle 6235/71, Forward 5164/71
Course Slope/Rating (All Tees): Back 128/70.8, Middle 120/68.8, Ladies' Forward 116/68
Course Architect: Donald Ross (1927)
Golf Facilities: Full Pro Shop X, Snack Bar X, Lounge X, Restaurant X, Locker Room X, Showers X, Club Rental X, Club Repair X, Cart Rental X, Instruction X, Practice Green X, Driving Range X, Practice Bunker X, Club Storage X
Tee-Time Reservation Policy: 24 hrs. in advance
Ranger: As required
Tee-off-Interval Time: 7 min.
Time to Play 18 Holes: 3½ hrs.
Course Hours/Earliest Tee-off: 8:00 a.m.
Green Fees: Peak season (mid-March to mid-June, mid-Sept. to late Nov.): $70 daily fee. You must be a guest at the resort to play the course
Cart Fees: $18 plus tax for 18 holes per person
Credit Cards: All major cards except Discover
Season: Year round. Busiest season April, May, June, Sept., Oct.
Course Comments: Can walk Nov. through Feb. Must carry own bag. Yardage book available. Golf schools available. Course open to resort guests only

Golf Packages: Available. Packages generally include unlimited golf at Pine Needles, including green fees and carts

Discounts: Seasonal (late Nov. to mid-March, mid-June to mid-Sept.)

Places to Stay Nearby: See Pinehurst area listing on pages 509

Local Attractions: See Pinehurst area listing on page 509

Directions: From Pinehurst: U.S. Hwy. 1, exit North Carolina Rte. 2, west 1/4 mi. on Hwy. 2, follow signs to resort

Closest Commercial Airports: Pinehurst Moore County Airport (10 min.); Raleigh/Durham (1 hr., 15 min.); Piedmont Triad International, Greensboro (1 hr., 20 min.); Charlotte/Douglas International (2 hrs.)

RESORT

Date Built: 1957

No. of Rooms: 72 guest rooms plus 11 lodges with 5 to 12 individual bedrooms

Meeting/Exhibit Rooms: 12. Capacity of Largest: 300 persons reception style. Meeting Space: 6600 sq. ft.

Room Price Range: $110, single, bed and breakfast, to $185, single, American plan. A variety of bed and breakfast or American plan packages is available in 4 seasonal price structures

Lounge: In The Rough Bar

Restaurant: Main Dining Room

Entertainment: None

Credit Cards: American Express, MasterCard, Visa

General Amenities: Business-conference and meeting capabilities with audio-visual, banquet and secretarial support. A variety of special and seasonal events such as the Pine Needles Invitational, Pine Needles Couples Jamboree and the Pine Needles Turkey Tournament

Recreational Amenities: Heated outdoor pool, 2 lighted grass tennis courts, whirlpool, sauna, pool tables, table tennis, sailing, windsurfing, canoeing

Reservation and Cancellation Policy: Per person deposit required. Deposit refunded if telephone notification of cancellation received 15 days in advance of arrival date. A letter of cancellation must follow to receive deposit refund

Comments and Restrictions: No pets allowed. Excellent kennel nearby. Room, meal and beverage subject to a service charge plus taxes. Jacket required at dinner. Special children's rates when children share accommodations with 2 full-rate adults

PINE NEEDLES GOLF COURSE

The history of Pine Needles begins with the names Donald Ross and Peggy Kirk Bell. Ross designed the 6603-yard par-71 layout, which is just down the road from Pinehurst in the sandhill country of North Carolina. Bell, the teaching professional at Pine Needles, was born in Findlay, Ohio, and bought the golf course in 1953, the year she married Warren E. (Bullet) Bell, her high school sweetheart and former pro basketball player. The Bells bought out their other partners and developed an excellent golf resort featuring the Ross course; 9 lodges; a clubhouse with dining rooms, bar and pro shop; and recreational amenities including a swimming pool and tennis courts. A meeting facility that comfortably accommodates groups of up to 250 is available.

The resort has 72 guest rooms and 10 rustic, Swiss-style lodges with 5 to 12 individual bedrooms. Three lodges, the 19th Hole Lodge, Fairway Lodge and Tee Lodge, have a central living room, bar area, refrigerator and game table. Pine Needles has been host to the 1972 LPGA Titleholders Championship, 1989 USGA Girls' Junior Championship, 1991 USGA Women's Senior Amateur and 1991 LPGA National Teaching Division Championship. *Golf Digest* ranks this resort course among the top 75 in America. Pine Needles will also be the site of the U.S. Women's Open in 1996.

The Ross course at Pine Needles is, as you might expect, a traditional golf course that requires excellent shot making. It is well treed but fairly open, with three water hazards. The bentgrass greens are fast, and relatively small and flat, averaging approximately 5000 square feet. There are 42 traps on this scenic layout, which covers 117 acres. Some tees have been moved back to bring Ross's original design features back into play.

The number-1-handicap hole, and the most difficult on the course, is the 452-yard par-4 second, which plays straight to a plateau, then down to a green protected by three traps. The next hole, a 134-yard par 3, plays over water to another three-trap green. This is a beautiful hole and has been one of the most photographed holes in the country for many years. A tough hole on the back nine is the 426-yard par-4 fifteenth, which requires two straight and accurate shots to a typically small green trapped left and right.

Since her husband passed away in 1984, Peggy Bell has taken more responsibility in managing the resort. Golf instruction, however, is her passion. She is eminently qualified to teach, having graduated from Rollins College with a degree in physical education. She is an original member of the LPGA; was a member of the victorious Curtis Cup team in the 1950s; and has won many amateur and professional golf titles, including the International Four-Ball, which she won with the great Babe Zaharias in 1974. And she was the first winner of the LPGA Senior Championship. She is an LPGA master professional and has won numerous honors for her contributions to golf, including the USGA Bob Jones Award, the National Golf Foundation Joe Graffis Award and the LPGA/Rolex Ellen Griffin Award. *Golf Digest* named her one of the five most influential women in golf and one of the six best women instructors in the United States. She has also developed print and video instructional materials on golf.

The Pine Needles Learning Center offers individual and group instruction, including highly sophisticated video and computer analysis of swing mechanics and techniques. Since 1969, Bell has conducted Golfaris, a trademarked name for either 5 or 7 days of golf immersion, and more than 12,000 golfers have enjoyed this adventure. Daily instruction and nightly group activities are a feature of this in-depth program. According to the Learning Center philoso-

phy, once you are a student you are always a student there. Instructors continually help students via videotapes, photographs or just a refresher phone call. And if you are practicing on your own, Pine Needles has a practice range for 100 golfers including a covered tee area, practice bunkers and putting greens.

During the peak season (mid-March to mid-June and mid-September to late November) the course is reserved exclusively for guests, and no outside play is allowed. You can walk the course from November through February, but you must carry your own bag. It has been a long time since Peggy Kirk Bell and her husband designed and built the first lodge at Pine Needles. The resort keeps getting better every year, while staying on a human scale.

Course Name: THE PIT GOLF LINKS

Course Type: Public
Address: North Carolina Highway 5
                 P.O. Box 5789
                 McIntyre Station
                 Pinehurst, NC 28374
Phone: (910) 944–1600

GOLF COURSE

Director of Golf: Eddie Cox
Course Length/Par (All Tees): Back 6600/71, Spike 6138/72, Half Rail 5690/72, Forward 4759/72
Course Slope/Rating (All Tees): Back 139/72.3, Spike 128/70.2, Half Rail 120/68.9, Ladies' Forward 121/68.4
Course Architect: Dan Maples (1985)
Golf Facilities: Full Pro Shop X, Snack Bar X, Lounge X, Restaurant No, Locker Room X, Showers X, Club Rental X, Club Repair Minor, Cart Rental X, Instruction X, Practice Green X, Driving Range X, Practice Bunker No, Club Storage No
Tee-Time Reservation Policy: Anytime in advance
Ranger: Yes
Tee-off-Interval Time: 8 min.
Time to Play 18 Holes: 4½ hrs.
Course Hours/Earliest Tee-off: 7 a.m.

Green Fees: Peak season (March 1 to mid-June): $64 for 18 holes, $32 for 9 holes

Cart Fees: $17 for 18 holes per person, $8 for 9 holes per person

Credit Cards: MasterCard, Visa

Season: Year round. Busiest season March to May, Oct.

Course Comments: Can walk if not crowded but must pay cart fee

Golf Packages: Available through hotels in area

Discounts: Seasonal (June to Aug., Dec. to Feb.)

Places to Stay Nearby: See Pinehurst area listing on pages 509

Local Attractions: See Pinehurst area listing on page 509

Directions: From U.S. Rte. 1: Exit on N.C. Hwy. 5, take Rte. 5 toward Pinehurst, the Pit is on the right. From Pinehurst (5 min.): N.C. Hwy. 5 south, the Pit is on the left

Closest Commercial Airports: Pinehurst Moore County Airport (10 min.); Raleigh/Durham (1 hr., 15 min.); Piedmont Triad International (1 hr., 20 min.); Charlotte/Douglas International (2 hrs.)

THE PIT GOLF LINKS

Legend has it that in the early 1920s the Aberdeen Sand Co. began work on a 230-acre site near Pinehurst, excavating sand for projects including the Blue Ridge Parkway. Over the years their work, as well as that of others and the forces of nature itself, created a truly unique landscape. In 1984 this piece of land was discovered by Dan Maples, an eminent golf-course architect whose family had been associated with Pinehurst since the nineteenth century.

Maples has designed a number of golf courses including Marsh Harbor Links in Calabash, North Carolina, and many others with his father, Ellis Maples, who died in 1984. The Pit opened in 1985 and has been recognized as one of the best public golf courses in America by *Golf Digest*. *Golfweek* has named it one of the top ten golf courses in North Carolina.

This beautiful layout winds through trees and has numerous bunkers and strategically placed mounds. The par-5 eighth hole, which plays 480 yards from the back tees, is probably one of the most memorable holes on the course. A dogleg left, the first shot plays to a narrow landing area. The second shot has to be long enough to enable you to hit the ball straight up a narrow fairway to an area that begins to open 100 yards from the green. The green is protected by a tree to the left front and a string of traps to the left and rear. There are several mounds and levels on this tricky bentgrass putting surface. The eighth hole is a classic example of why shot placement is essential at the Pit.

The number-1-handicap hole is the par-5 550-yard fifteenth hole, a double dogleg left then right through a narrow, well-treed, mounded fairway. The first shot has to be far enough to the right to enable you to hit the second shot up the tight fairway. The third shot comes onto a small, round green 27 yards deep and protected by a series of mounds.

The second hole is the number-2-handicap hole, a straight but long 579-yard par 5 protected by trees on both sides of the fairway. Three straight, accurate shots are required to reach an egg-shaped green protected by 3 traps to the right front. A series of mounds is to the back left of the green.

Water does not come into play at the Pit until the back nine. The eleventh hole, a 390-yard par-4 dogleg right, has water on the right and the front of the green from 200 yards in; and the 167-yard par-3 twelfth hole has a tee shot to an island green with a huge trap in back and to the right. The 370-yard par-4 thirteenth hole requires a 170-yard carry over water to an open landing area. The second shot is to a 34-yard-deep green protected by two traps front-left and front-right. If you haven't been worn down by the difficulty of this course up until now, these three holes are likely to do you in.

One of my favorite holes at the Pit is the awe-inspiring 232-yard par-3 fourth hole, which plays down a very narrow pine-tree-lined fairway to a medium-sized green surrounded by mounds and more trees. The shot is from an elevated tee, and there is very little room to work the ball, especially from the back tees. The shorter tees at 162, 120 and 103 yards are much more manageable on this track.

The Pit is a wonderful golf experience. Each hole seems unique and a totally separate adventure as you work your way through sand mounds, pines, cedars, sand, water and other real or imagined hazards. It is advisable to play from the spike (6138 yards) or half-rail tees (5690 yards) your first time around this excellently conditioned and memorable layout.

The Pit, which is partly owned by its designer, Dan Maples, is intended to remain a public course with no real-estate development under the current plan. The clubhouse has a good pro shop, snack bar and bar with splendid views of the course. The practice area includes a sizable driving range and practice green. Instruction is available from PGA professionals and assistants. Once you play this course, you'll want to play it again.

Course Name: **TALAMORE GOLF COURSE**

Course Type: Public
Address: 1595 Midland Road
Southern Pines, NC 28387
Phone: (910) 692–5884
Fax: (910) 692–4421

GOLF COURSE

Head Professional: Wink Kinney
Course Length/Par (All Tees): Back 7020/72, Blue 6643/72, White 6053/72, Forward 4945/72
Course Slope/Rating (All Tees): Back 142/72.9, Blue 134/70.8, White 126/67.9, Ladies' Forward 125/69.0
Course Architect: Rees Jones (1991)
Golf Facilities: Full Pro Shop X, Snack Bar X, Lounge X, Restaurant X, Locker Room X, Showers No, Club Rental X, Club Repair X, Cart Rental X, Instruction X, Practice Green X, Driving Range X, Practice Bunker No, Club Storage No
Tee-Time Reservation Policy: Up to 6 months in advance
Ranger: Yes
Tee-off-Interval Time: 8 min.

Time to Play 18 Holes: 4½ hrs.
Course Hours/Earliest Tee-off: 7 a.m.
Green and Cart Fees: $85 for 18 holes with cart
Credit Cards: MasterCard, Visa
Season: Year round. Busiest Mar. through May, Sept. through Nov.
Course Comments: Can walk anytime for full fee. Llama caddies available
Golf Packages: Inquire at pro shop
Discounts: Lower seasonal rates mid-Nov. through mid-Mar., June through Aug.
Places to Stay Nearby: See Pinehurst area listing on page 509
Local Attractions: See Pinehurst area listing on page 509
Directions: From Pinehurst (5 min.): Take Hwy. 2 (Midland) east to golf course
Closest Commercial Airports: Pinehurst Moore County Airport (15 min.); Raleigh/Durham (1 hr. 15 min.); Piedmont Triad International, Greensboro (1 hr. 20 min.); Charlotte/Douglas International (2 hrs.)

TALAMORE GOLF COURSE

When you tee it up on the formidable 607-yard par-5 opening hole at Talamore, you are about to sample many of the nuances and obstacles this course has to offer. The hole swings to the right up a tree-framed slope. Trouble can be found to the right in the form of mounds, bunkers, and dropoffs, and a ball pulled to the left will find bunkers or trees. The approach to the large putting surface is up a ramped ridge with a series of bunkers to the right from 100 yards in to the green. There are an assortment of swales and mounds to the front left of the green, a trap to its left and another farther right. To the rear is a series of mounds. Inaccurate shoots can kick off the mounds, nestle in swales, lodge in bunkers, or burrow in rough. An ability to thrash your way out of these situations with consistency will save you strokes on this difficult layout that provides four tee distances to chose from. The other distances on this hole are 585, 534, and 418 yards.

A challenging par 4 on the front nine at Talamore is the 441-yard dogleg left seventh which requires a 150 to 200 yard carry over vegetation guarding the inside of the turn as the hole swings to the left. The deep, forward-sloping green is slightly up-hill with a bunker to its left and another to its right front. Two solid, well-placed shots are required to reach this green in regula-tion. My favorite par 3 at Talamore is the 233-yard fifteenth that plays from an ele-vated tee down to a medium-sized green with two bunkers to its left, a trap to its rear, and two more traps further right and towards the front. If you miss the target on the tee shot, you have your work cut out for you.

Talamore is one of the newer additions to the Pinehurst area's treasure trove of golf courses. You must hit the ball with distance and keep it on the fairway in order to avoid the subtle penalties exacted by poor hitting positions in rough, on mounds, in swales, under trees, and in sand. Accu-rate approaches to the ample greens are crucial in order to get down in two putts or less. If you miss your approach, your skill with a wedge will be quickly tested.

You can walk Talamore anytime. The Rees Jones-designed course was rated one of the best new courses of 1991 by *Golf Digest*. An exotic option provided at this course is llama caddies that will carry your clubs, but won't second guess your club selection.

Accommodations: Pinehurst Area List

PINEHURST: Condotels of Pinehurst (910) 295–8008, (800) 255–4653; Holly Inn (910) 295–2300, (800) 682–6901 (NC), (800) 533–0041 (outside NC); Magnolia Inn (910) 295–6900, (800) 526–5562; Mid-land Country Club and Knollwood Village (910) 295–5011, (800) 633–8576; Pine Crest Inn (910) 295–6121. ABERDEEN: Best Western/Pinehurst Motor Inn (910) 944–2367, (800) 528–1234; Arborgate Inn (910) 944–5633, (800) 722–7220. SOUTHERN PINES: Days Inn (910) 692–7581, (800) 325–2525; Econo–Lodge (910) 944–2324; Fairway Motel (910) 692–2711; Hampton Inn (910) 692–9266, (800) 333–9266; Holi-day Inn (910) 692–8585, (800) 262–5737; Hotel Belvedere (910) 692–2240; Hyland Hills Resort (910) 692–7615; Mid-Pines

Resort (910) 692–2114, (800) 323–2114. JACKSON SPRINGS: Foxfire Resort and Coun-try Club (910) 295–5555, (800) 736–9347. WEST END: Beacon Ridge Golf and Country Club (910) 673–7700, (800) 762–1107. PIN-EBLUFF: Pine Cone Manor (910) 281–5307; Pines Golf Resort (910) 281–3165, (800) 334–4418. VASS: Woodland Country Club (910) 245–4031, (800) 334–1126. WHISPER-ING PINES: Country Club of Whispering Pines/Villas (910) 949–3777, (800) 334–9536.

All of the above have golf packages of various kinds. Off season tends to be mid-November to mid-March; peak season tends to be mid-March to mid-June and early September to mid-November. For de-tailed information, contact these estab-lishments directly or contact the Pinehurst Area Convention and Visitors Bureau at (910) 692–3330, (800) 346–5362 for its ac-commodations and golfing literature. All of the above are in or within 30 minutes of Pinehurst.

Local Attractions in Pinehurst Area

Bicycling, camping, World Golf Hall of Fame, horseback riding, polo at the Pine-hurst Race Track, tennis, trap and skeet shooting at the Pinehurst Gun Club, North Carolina Zoological Park, shopping, histori-cal and cultural tours including the Na-tional Union Station (Aberdeen), Wey-mouth Woods Nature Preserve, Bethesda Church and Cemetery, Black–Cole house, Boyd Wing of the Southern Pines Library, Cameron Historic District (Southern Pines), Campbell House Galleries, Brilt–Sanders cabin, House in the Horseshoe, Malcolm Blue Farm, McLendon–Bryant place, Sand-hills Horticultural Gardens–Sir Walter Raleigh Gardens, Sandhills Vineyards and Herb Gardens, Sandhills Women's Exchange, Seagrove area potters, Shaw House Tuft Archives at the Given Memo-rial Library, restaurants; seasonal festivals and events such as the Stonebrook Steeple-chase, Tour de Moore bicycle race, the Fine Arts Festival and John Rowe Trap Shooting Championship. Pinehurst Area Convention and Visitors Bureau (910) 692–3330, (800) 346–5362

Recommended Golf Courses in North Carolina

Within 1 Hour of Pinehurst:

Club at Long Leaf, Southern Pines, (910) 692–6100, (800) 889–5323, Semiprivate, 18/6600/71

Deercroft Golf and Country Club, Wagram, (910) 369–3107, Semiprivate, 18/6745/72

Legacy Golf Links, Aberdeen, (910) 944–8825, (800) 344–8825, Public, 18/6989/72

Mid-Pines Resort, Southern Pines, (910) 692–2114, (800) 323–2114, Resort, 18/6515/72

Pinehurst Plantation Golf Club, Pinehurst, (910) 695–3193, (800) 633–2685, Semiprivate, 18/7135/72

Seven Lakes Country Club, West End, (910) 673–1092, Semiprivate, 18/6927/72

Southern Pines Golf Club, Southern Pines, (910) 692–6551, Semiprivate, 18/6426/71

Woodlake Country Club, Vass, (910) 245–4686, (800) 334–1126, Semiprivate, 18/7012/72

Raleigh/Durham Area

Course Name: DUKE GOLF CLUB

Course Type: Semiprivate
Address: Route 751 and Science Drive Durham, NC 27706
Phone: (919) 684–2817 (Golf Course), (919) 490–0999, (800) 443–3853 (Washington Duke Inn, on site)
Fax: (919) 688–0105 (Golf Course), (919) 688–0105 (Washington Duke Inn)

GOLF COURSE

Director of Golf: Rod Myers
Head Professional: Ed Ibarguen
Course Length/Par (All Tees): Back 7005/72, Blue 6729/72, White 6160/72, Ladies' Forward 5388/74
Course Slope/Rating (All Tees): Back 130/73.6, Blue 127/72.8, White 122/70.3, Ladies' Forward 127/73.3
Course Architects: Robert Trent Jones, Sr. (1957), Rees Jones (remodeled, 1994)
Golf Facilities: Full Pro Shop X, Snack Bar X, Lounge X, Restaurant X, Locker Room X, Showers X, Club Rental X, Club Repair X, Cart Rental X, Instruction X, Practice Green X, Driving Range X, Practice Bunker X, Club Storage X
Tee-Time Reservation Policy: Up to 7 days in advance
Ranger: Yes
Tee-off-Interval Time: 10 min.
Time to Play 18 Holes: 4½ hrs.
Course Hours/Earliest Tee-off: 7:30 a.m.
Green Fees: $49 for 18 holes Fri., Sat., Sun., holidays; $34 for 18 holes weekdays
Cart Fees: $16 per person for 18 holes
Credit Cards: American Express, MasterCard, Visa
Season: Year round. Busiest Sept. through Nov., Feb. through Apr.
Course Comments: Can walk anytime except Sat. and Sun. mornings. Yardage book available
Golf Packages: Through the on site Washington Duke Inn (800) 443–3835
Discounts: Twilight rates. Student and university employee discounts
Places to Stay Nearby: On site: Washington Duke Inn (919) 490–0999, (800) 443–3853. DURHAM: Guest Quarters Suite Hotel (919) 361–4660, (800) 424–2900; Holiday Inn Raleigh–Durham Airport (919) 941–6000, (800) HOLIDAY; Marriott (919) 941–6200, (800) 228–9290; Sheraton Inn University (919) 383–8575. BED AND BREAKFASTS: The Inn at Bonnie Brae (919) 471–1639
Raleigh-Durham Attractions: City Market, Executive Mansion, Farmers Market, Hayward Hall, Historic Oakwood, Martin Luther King, Jr. Memorial Gardens, Arts District, North Carolina State University, Duke University, Memorial Auditorium, Durham Bulls minor league baseball, Carolina Mudcats minor league baseball, N.C. Museum of Life and Science, Duke Homestead, Duke Art Museum, Duke Gardens, Royal Center for the Arts, West Point on the

Eno, Research Triangle Park, seasonal festivals, arts, entertainment, restaurants, antiquing, historical tours. Pinehurst. Durham Convention and Visitors Bureau, 101 E. Morgan St., Durham, NC 27701 (919) 687–0288, (800) 446–8604. Greater Raleigh Convention and Visitors Bureau (919) 834–5900, (800) 849–8499

Directions: From I–85 South take Rte. 15–801 Bypass South Exit. Go left on Rte. 751 the take Duke University Exit to golf course. From I–85 North take West Durham Rte. 15–501 Bypass South. Exit left onto Rte. 751 and take Duke University Exit to the golf course

Closest Commercial Airport: Raleigh/Durham (30 min.)

DUKE GOLF CLUB

Just outside the handsome and stately 171-room Washington Duke Inn on the campus of Duke University is the Duke Golf Club, originally designed by Robert Trent Jones, Sr., and recently renovated by his son Rees. This wooded, rolling course features large greens protected by ample bunkers and ponds and streams that come into play on half the holes. Rees Jones, who has renovated many U.S. Open sites including The Country Club, Hazeltine, Baltusrol, and Congressional, did not alter the superb routing of the original course, but added features such as redesigning the greens, fairways, and tee areas and improving the definition of some holes.

The golf course starts with a strong 450-yard dogleg left par 4 that plays from an elevated tee down a treelined fairway with a series of mounded knolls along its left side. The approach is to a deep green that is slightly elevated from the fairway and has a severe drop to a large bunker on its right. Another bunker is to the left of the green. The front side at Duke finishes with three great holes beginning with the 572-yard par-5 seventh which curls to the right to a deep, two-tiered green bordered by a stream in front and arched by six bunkers on its other sides. The tee shot must negotiate a cluster of three bunkers to the right, then the second shot is downhill toward a severely forward-sloping target. The 172-yard par-3 eighth plays uphill to a shallow, wide target set into a hill. A huge bunker protects its front, another bunker is to the left and a third to the right. The 491-yard par-5 ninth, a dogleg left, has a blind tee shot around a treelined corner to the top of a rise. The second shot must clear a swale in front of a deep green with two traps to its right and a huge bunker to its left.

A favorite hole of mine on the back nine is the scenic and challenging 180-yard par-3 twelfth which plays over water to a peninsula green bordered by a huge trap to its left and another to its rear. Another good hole on this side is the 398-yard par-4 sixteenth, a dogleg right that plays from the highest point on the golf course to a landing area framed by trees and four bunkers along the left side. The approach is uphill to a shallow, forward-sloping green protected by a bunker in front and three others to the right.

The Duke Golf Club, home of the university's golf teams, has excellent practice facilities including a range with target greens, two chipping greens, and a putting green. An excellent pro shop is located in the hotel building which houses the Fairview Restaurant, a fine dining establishment, and the Bull Durham bar. The hotel has meeting facilities, a swimming pool, jogging paths, and tennis courts.

Course Name: THE NEUSE GOLF CLUB

Course Type: Semiprivate
Address: 918 Birkdale Drive
                     Clayton, NC 27520
Phone: (919) 550–0550
Fax: (919) 550–0553

GOLF COURSE

Head Professional: David E. Teem
Course Length/Par (All Tees): Back 7010/72, Blue 6626/72, White 6027/72, Forward 5478/72
Course Slope/Rating (All Tees): Back 136/73.5, Blue 129/71.7, White 123/69.1, Ladies' Red 126/72.2
Course Architect: John B. LaFoy (1993)
Golf Facilities: Full Pro Shop X, Snack Bar X, Lounge Beer, Restaurant No, Locker

Room X, Showers X, Club Rental X, Club Repair X, Cart Rental X, Instruction X, Practice Green X, Driving Range X, Practice Bunker X, Club Storage X

Tee-Time Reservation Policy: Up to 7 days in advance. Up to 6 months in advance for groups of 12 or more. Members have tee time priority

Ranger: Yes

Tee-off-Interval Time: 8 min.

Time to Play 18 Holes: 4½ hrs.

Course Hours/Earliest Tee-off: 7:30 a.m.

Green Fees: $22 for 18 holes Fri., Sat., Sun., holidays; $20 for 18 holes weekdays

Cart Fees: $12 per person

Credit Cards: MasterCard, Visa

Season: Year round. Busiest Apr. through Oct.

Course Comments: Can walk after 2 p.m. Fri., Sat., Sun., holidays Apr. through Oct., anytime otherwise. Yardage book available

Golf Packages: No

Discounts: Twilight rates

Places to Stay Nearby: GARNER: Comfort Inn-South Raleigh (919) 779–7888, (800) 228–5150. RALEIGH: Courtyard by Marriott Airport (919) 467–9444, (800) 321–2211; Embassy Suites Hotel (919) 881–0000, (800) 362–2779; Residence Inn by Marriott (919) 878–6100, (800) 331–3131. CHAPEL HILL: The Carolina Inn (919) 933–2001, (800) 962–8519; The Siena Hotel (919) 929–4000, (800) 223–7379. DURHAM: Washington Duke Inn (919) 490–0999. PITTSBORO: Fearington House (919) 542–2121

Local Attractions: See page 510

Directions: From Raleigh (30 min.): Proceed southeast on Hwy. 40 to Rte. 70. Take Rte. 70 southeast to Clayton. Take Hwy. 42 east (left) off Rte. 70 to Glen Laurel Rd. Make a right on Glen Laurel to golf course

Closest Commercial Airport: Raleigh/Durham (45 min.)

THE NEUSE GOLF CLUB

The Neuse Golf Club is the centerpiece of a golf course real estate development cut through wooded hunting ground in the rolling hills southeast of Raleigh. The Neuse River borders the golf course which features Bermuda grass fairways and large, undulating bentgrass greens. There are only thirty-nine sand bunkers on the course and most of them protect the greens which provide an interesting array of shapes and angles to shoot at. A variety of grassy mounds border the fairways and greens leaving tricky recovery shots from these areas. Water from the river and ponds can come into play on eleven holes. There are no parallel holes on the course, so when you get out there, you will be in your own golf world bordered by pine, oak, ash, and maple.

Two of the more memorable holes on the course are Nos. 13 and 14. The 410-yard par-4 thirteenth, a dogleg right, is a target hole whose tee shot must avoid a creek cutting in front of the two back tees and up the left side, and another creek that cuts the fairway beginning 166 yards from the green. The approach is across the creek and uphill to a deep, two-tiered green framed by a deep bunker to its right front and another to the left. Half the holes at the Neuse play uphill adding length and difficulty to this scenic golf course.

The signature hole on the Neuse is the 192-yard par-3 fourteenth that plays to a green guarded by boulders to its right front, a pond to its far right, and a pair of bunkers to its immediate right. A quality par 5 on the course is the 527-yard fifth, a slight dogleg right that is bordered by the Neuse River to the right of the tee shot landing area. The deep green is framed by bunkers with wetlands further to the right.

The Neuse has country club-style amenities at its clubhouse. The practice area has four tiers of teeing area and target flags. There is also a putting green and short game area. The Neuse has hosted Nike and mini-Senior Tour events and is rated one of the best courses in North Carolina by *Golf Digest*. You can walk the course anytime for a very reasonable green fee.

Recommended Courses in North Carolina

Within 1 Hour of the Raleigh/Durham Area:

Country Club of Whispering Pines, Whispering Pines, (910) 949–2311, Semiprivate. East: 18/7138/71. West: 18/6363/71

Devil's Ridge Golf Club, Holly Springs, (919) 557–6100, Semiprivate, 18/7002/72

Foxfire Resort and Country Club, Jackson Springs, (910) 295–4563, Resort. East: 18/6851/72. West: 18/6742/72

Keith Hills Country Club, Buies Creek, (910) 893–5051, (800) 334–4111, Semiprivate, 18/6660/72

Lane Tree Golf Course, Goldsboro, (919) 734–1245, Semiprivate, 18/6963/71

Western North Carolina

Course Name: LINVILLE GOLF CLUB

Course Type: Resort
Resort: Esceola Lodge
Address: P.O. Box 99
Linville, NC 28646
Phone: (704) 733–4363 (Golf Course),
(704) 733–4311,
(800) 742–6717 (Resort)
Fax: (704) 733–9493 (Golf Course),
(704) 733–3227 (Resort)

GOLF COURSE

Head Professional: Tom Dale
Course Length/Par (All Tees): Back 6780/72, White 6279/72, Red 5437/72, Forward 5086/72
Course Slope/Rating (All Tees): Back 135/72.7, White 129/70.4, Red 117/68 5, Ladies' Forward 119/69.3
Course Architect: Donald Ross (1924)
Golf Facilities: Full Pro Shop X, Snack Bar X, Lounge X, Restaurant X, Locker Room X, Showers X, Club Rental X, Club Repair X, Cart Rental X, Instruction X, Practice Green X, Driving Range X, Practice Bunker X, Club Storage X
Tee-Time Reservation Policy: You must be a resort guest to play the course. Up to 4 days in advance
Ranger: Yes
Tee-off-Interval Time: 7 min.

Time to Play 18 Holes: 4 hrs.
Course Hours/Earliest Tee-off: 8 a.m.
Green and Cart Fees: $50 for 18 holes for resort guests
Credit Cards: MasterCard, Visa
Season: May through Oct. Busiest July through Labor Day
Course Comments: Can walk anytime after 5 p.m.
Golf Packages: Through resort
Discounts: Weekly and monthly golf plans. Replay discounts
Places to Stay Nearby: BOONE: Hampton Inn (704) 264–0077, (800) 426–7866; Lovill House Inn (704) 264–4202; Oakwood Inn (704) 262–1047
Local Attractions: LINVILLE: Grandfather Mountain. BOONE: Appalachian Cultural Museum, Blue Ridge Parkway, crafts, boating, fishing, camping, hiking, hunting. Asheville. Mount Mitchell State Park. Boone Chamber of Commerce, 208 W. Howard St., Boone, NC 28607 (704) 264–2225, (800) 852–9506
Directions: Just off Hwy. 221 in Linville
Closest Commercial Airports: Johnson City, TN (1 hr. 10 min.); Asheville (1½ hrs.); Raleigh/Durham (3½ hrs.)

RESORT

Date Built: 1891
No. of Rooms: 31
Meeting Rooms: Space and support for small meetings
Room Price Range: $225 to $350 per couple, modified American plan. Golf and other packages available
Lounges: The Red Fox Tavern
Restaurants: Dining Room, The Partee Room at the golf course
Entertainment: Pianist nightly in Dining Room
Credit Cards: MasterCard, Visa
General Amenities: Children's day camp
Recreational Amenities: Clay tennis courts, croquet, heated swimming pool, hiking trails, children's playground, fishing
Reservation and Cancellation Policy: To guarantee reservation, a deposit of two nights stay is required at time of reservation. To be eligible for a refund, cancellations must be made 21 days in

advance of scheduled arrival. $25 administration fee for cancellations

Comments and Restrictions: Coat and tie for gentlemen, appropriate dress for ladies required in the dining room. Coat and tie required for gentlemen at dinner

LINVILLE GOLF CLUB

The Mobil Four Star Esceola Lodge, first constructed in 1891, is one of the original North Carolina resorts and is listed in the National Register of Historic Places. Tucked within the shadow of Grandfather Mountain at 3860 feet in the heart of the Blue Ridge Mountains west of Asheville, the lodge has been renovated over the years and offers modern amenities such as cable television, but retains its distinctive charm. The Lodge Dining Room features a large native stone fireplace and serves gourmet meals featuring the finest French and New American Cuisine.

Guests of the Esceola Lodge enjoy privileges at Linville Golf Club, a Donald Ross creation completed in 1926. The course is treelined, but provides ample landing area for tee shots. It is surprisingly level for a mountain course and its greens are traditional, small, forward-sloping targets slightly elevated from the fairway and protected by a bunker or two. A stream winds through the golf course and can come into play on several holes including the 449-yard par-4 third, the toughest hole on the course. The tee shot must avoid the stream which cuts the fairway 250 yards from the back tees. The approach is uphill to the forward-sloping, small target.

The par 4s tend to be the most challenging holes at Linville. The 222-yard par-3 twelfth is the most difficult par 3. The 415-yard par-4 finishing hole caps off a great round at Linville. The tee shot on this slight dogleg left is to a landing area with out-of-bounds to the far right. The second shot is to a somewhat forward-sloping green with a bunker to its left. As with all of the holes at Linville,

well-positioned approaches that land below the hole will enable you to score here.

The original impetus for developing the town of Linville came from investors who wanted to develop a mining business from iron ore deposits discovered in nearby Cranberry in the 1880s. The first version of the Esceola provided a summer resort tradition that continues. The Linville replaced an old mining company golf course and became an important recreational attraction in the area. The golf course is open only to members and resort guests. Esceola guests take lunch in the club's Partee restaurant. Nearby is a full practice range, chipping green, and putting green. The resort is a *Golf* magazine silver medal winner. Golf packages are usually available on a limited basis at the beginning and end of the season.

Recommended Golf Courses in North Carolina

Within 2 Hours of Asheville:

Boone Golf Club, Boone, (704) 264–8760, Public, 18/6401/71

Cleghorn Plantation Golf and Country Club, Rutherfordton, (704) 286–9117, Public, 18/6903/72

Etowah Valley Country Club, Etowah, (704) 891–7141, (800) 451–8174, Resort. South/West: 18/7108/72. West/North: 18/7005/73. North/South: 18/6911/73

Fairfield Mountains, Lake Lure, (704) 625–2888, Resort. Apple Valley Golf Club: 18/6726/72. Bald Mountain: 18/6575/72

Glen Cannon Country Club, Brevard, (704) 884–9160, Semiprivate, 18/6548/72

Grove Park Inn, Asheville, (704) 252–2711, (800) 438–5800, Resort, 18/6520/71

Holly Forest Country Club, Sapphire, (704) 743–1174, Resort, 18/6147/70

Hound Ears Club, Blowing Rock, (704) 963–5831, Semiprivate, 18/6165/72

Jefferson Landing Club, Jefferson, (910) 246–5555, Public, 18/7111/72

Maggie Valley Resort Golf Club, Maggie Valley, (704) 926–6013, Resort, 18/6376/72

Mount Glen Golf Club, Newland, (704) 733–5804, Semiprivate, 18/6900/72

Mount Mitchell Golf Club, Burnsville, (704) 675–5454, Public, 18/6475/72

Old Beau Golf Club, Roaring Gap, (910) 363–3044, Semiprivate, 18/6713/72

Reems Creek Golf Club, Weaverville, (704) 645–4393, (800) 762–8379, Semiprivate, 18/6477/71

Springdale Country Club, Canton, (704) 235–8451, Semiprivate, 18/6812/72

Wilmington Area

Course Name: MARSH HARBOR

Course Type: Public
Address: 201 Marsh Harbor Road
              P.O. Box 65
              Calabash, NC 29597
Phone: (910) 579–3161,
              (800) 552–2660

GOLF COURSE

Head Professional: Steve Sovetts
Course Length/Par (All Tees): Back 6690/71, Middle 6000/71, Forward 4795/71
Course Slope/Rating (All Tees): Back 134/73.3, Middle 121/70.0, Ladies' Forward 115/69
Course Architect: Dan Maples (1980)
Golf Facilities: Full Pro Shop X, Snack Bar X, Lounge X, Restaurant No, Locker Room No, Showers X, Club Rental X, Club Repair No, Cart Rental X, Instruction X, Practice Green X, Driving Range X, Practice Bunker No, Club Storage No
Tee-Time Reservation Policy: Reserve 9 months in advance through central booking office. Prepayment required for a tee time made well in advance
Ranger: Yes
Tee-off-Interval Time: 8 min.
Time to Play 18 Holes: 4½ hrs.
Course Hours/Earliest Tee-off: 7 a.m.

Green Fees: Peak season (March 21 to May 15): $70 for 18 holes
Cart Fees: $17 for 18 holes per person
Credit Cards: American Express, Master-Card, Visa
Season: Year round. Busiest season March to May, Sept. 19 to Nov. 13
Course Comments: Cart mandatory. Yardage book available
Golf Packages: Available through hotels in Myrtle Beach area
Discounts: Seasonal
Places to Stay Nearby: SUNSET BEACH: Calabash Motel (910) 579–6576; Carolina Golf and Beach Resorts (800) 222–1524; Odom Co. (cottages) (910) 579–3515. WILMINGTON: Wilmington Hilton Inn (910) 763–5900, (800) 445–8667; Ramada Inn Conference Center (910) 799–1730, (800) 333–3333; Blockade Runner Hotel and Conference Center (910) 256–2251 (Wrightsville Beach). LITTLE RIVER, SC: Harbour Inn (803) 249–3535, (800) 292–0404. NORTH MYRTLE BEACH, SC: Beach Cove Clarion Resort (803) 272–4044, (800) 331–6533; Holiday Inn–North (803) 272–6153, (800) 845–9700; Ocean Creek Resort (803) 272–7724, (800) 845–0353; Sun-A-Bel (villas) (803) 272–2079, (800) 272–2079. See also Myrtle Beach, SC, listing
Local Attractions: Beaches, water sports, fishing, boating, restaurants. Wilmington. Cape Fear coast. Myrtle Beach, SC. NORTH MYRTLE BEACH, SC: Barefoot Landing, Dixie Jubilee, Hurricane Fleet. See also Myrtle Beach, SC, listing. Myrtle Beach, SC, Area Convention and Visitors Bureau (803) 448–1629, (800) 488–8998. Cape Fear Coast Convention and Visitors Bureau (910) 341–4030, (800) 222–4757
Directions: From Myrtle Beach (30 mi.): North on Hwy. 17 to Rte. 179, east toward ocean, follow signs. From Wilmington (1 hr.): South on Hwy. 17 to Rte. 179, east toward ocean, follow signs
Closest Commercial Airports: Myrtle Beach, SC (45 min.); New Hanover International, Wilmington (1 hr.); Charleston International, SC (2 hrs.); Columbia/

Metropolitan, SC (3 hrs.); Charlotte/ Douglas International (3½ hrs.)

MARSH HARBOR

Marsh Harbor is rated one of the best public golf courses in America by *Golf Digest* magazine. It is situated just south of Calabash, North Carolina, near the Intracoastal Waterway and north of Myrtle Beach. Holes one through six and ten through fifteen are tight and well treed on this 6690-yard layout designed by Dan Maples. The Bermuda-grass greens are moderately fast, small- to medium-sized and undulating. This is a shot maker's course, requiring careful club selection and good golf-course management. Water comes into play on half the holes, and well-placed traps protect the greens, which come in interesting shapes, sizes and slope angles.

Marsh Harbor starts you out at a reasonable pace but begins to get a bit testy when you reach the 210-yard par-3 sixth hole, which plays to a narrow, deep, two-tiered green protected by four large traps. The seventh is a 390-yard par-4 dogleg left requiring a tee shot to the center or slightly right to set up a mid-iron second shot to a skull-shaped, two-tiered green protected by traps left-front and right-front. The 210-yard par-3 eighth is bordered on the left by wetlands and salt marsh from tee to green. The deep green is protected by a huge trap on the left. The closing hole on this side is a 540-yard par-5 dogleg left bordered on the left by water from tee to green. The tee shot is to a landing area guarded by a large right-fairway bunker. The corner over the marsh can be cut to the left, leaving you in position to reach the narrow, deep green in two, but the penalties are high if you miss. Also, three traps to the left, front and rear require you to reach the putting surface by air on the approach shot.

The signature and number-1-handicap hole at Marsh Harbor is the aquatic 570-yard par-5 fifteenth. Three well-placed shots are required, beginning with a tee shot to a landing area guarded by four fairway bunkers and wetlands to the right. The second shot is to a landing area with water to the front, right and rear. The third shot is likely to be a mid-iron over a small marsh to a deep green angled right to left and protected by traps left and right. The finishing hole is a short but scenic 330-yard par 4 that plays over wetlands to a landing area guarded by marshlands to the right and a left-fairway bunker 260 yards from the back tees. The next shot is onto a wide, very shallow (17 yards), three-tiered green with a bunker and wetlands in back. Pin position can make this hole more difficult than it first would appear.

At present Marsh Harbor offers minimum food service in the form of a snack bar at the clubhouse. The clubhouse has no locker rooms and showers but does have a pro shop with golf instruction available from 5 PGA professionals and assistants. A driving range and practice putting area are available, but there is no practice bunker. This beautiful and challenging golf course is listed among America's 75 best public golf courses by *Golf Digest*.

Course Name: OYSTER BAY GOLF LINKS

Course Type: Public
Address: Highway 179 and Lake Shore Drive
Sunset Beach, NC 29597
Phone: (910) 579–7391
(800) 337–2315 (Tee Times)

GOLF COURSE

Head Professional: Jeff Hazle

Course Length/Par (All Tees): Back 6685/70, Middle 6305/70, Forward 4665/70

Course Slope/Rating (All Tees): Back 134/71.6, Middle 125/69.2, Ladies' Forward 118/68.0

Course Architect: Dan Maples (1983)

Golf Facilities: Full Pro Shop X, Snack Bar X, Lounge X, Restaurant X, Locker Room No, Showers X, Club Rental X, Club Repair No, Cart Rental X, Instruction X, Practice Green X, Driving Range X, Practice Bunker No, Club Storage No

Tee-Time Reservation Policy: Call in advance. Prepaid check or credit card required to hold tee time. 48-hr. cancellation policy

Ranger: Yes

Tee-off-Interval Time: 8 min.

Time to Play 18 Holes: 5 hrs.

Course Hours/Earliest Tee-off: 7 a.m.

Green and Cart Fees: Peak season (March 21 to May 15): $87 for 18 holes with cart, $43.50 for 9 holes with cart

Credit Cards: American Express, MasterCard, Visa

Season: Year round. Busiest season April, May, Sept., Oct.

Course Comments: Cart mandatory. Yardage book available. Twilight 9-hole play allowed

Golf Packages: Available through hotels. Inquire at clubhouse for golf package locales

Discounts: Seasonal (lower rates June, July, Aug., late Nov., Dec., Jan.). Replays

Places to Stay Nearby: SUNSET BEACH: (condos and cottages): Carolina Golf and Beach Resorts (800) 222–1524; Sunset Properties, Inc. (910) 579–9900; Odom Co. (910) 579–3515. OCEAN ISLE BEACH: Winds Beach and Golf Resort (910) 579–6275, (800) 458–0507 (NC), (800) 334–3581 (outside NC). LITTLE RIVER, SC: Harbour Inn (803) 249–3535, (800) 292–0404. NORTH MYRTLE BEACH, SC: Beach Cove Clarion Resort (803) 272–4044, (800) 331–6533; Holiday Inn North (803)272–6153, (800) 845–9700; Ocean Creek Resort (803) 272–7724, (800) 845–0353; Sun-A-Bel (villas) (803) 272–2079, (800) 272–2079

Local Attractions: Beaches, fishing, boating, restaurants, Bald Head Lighthouse, Bald Head Island, Oak Island beaches, Fort Caswell, historic Southport by the sea, Orton Plantation, Lake Waccamaw State Park, Fort Fisher state historic site, Brunswick Town state historic site. Wilmington. Myrtle Beach, SC, Area Convention and Visitors Bureau (803) 448–1629, (800) 488–8998. Cape Fear, NC Coast Convention and Visitors Bureau (910) 341–4030, (800) 222–4757

Directions: From Myrtle Beach (1 hr.): Rte. 17 north to Rte. 179 (6 mi. to course), take Rte. 179 north toward Calabash to Lake Shore Dr., right (east) to golf course. From Wilmington (1 hr.): Rte. 17 south to Rte. 179, take Rte. 179 north toward Calabash to Lake Shore Dr., right (east) to golf course

Closest Commercial Airports: Hanover International, Wilmington (1 hr.); Myrtle Beach, SC (1 hr.); Columbia Metropolitan, SC (2½ hrs.); Charleston International, SC (3 hrs.);Charlotte/Douglas International (3½ hrs.)

OYSTER BAY GOLF LINKS

When you look at an aerial photo of the Oyster Bay Golf Links, it is a beautiful pattern of lush green grass, trees, several bunkers of white sand, and a startling amount of marshlands and water. The course plays 6685 yards from the back tees, and there is water on all but three holes. Opened in 1983, Oyster Bay was declared the best new resort golf course in America by *Golf Digest*, and it is currently ranked among the best public golf courses in the country. It is also rated among the best public and private golf courses in the state of North Carolina by *Golf Digest*. Because of the water, bunkers and medium-sized to small greens, a premium is placed on accuracy and course management.

Oyster Bay wastes no time in letting you know that you are in for a challenge. The first hole is a 390-yard par-4 dogleg left, with water on the right from 140 yards to a green that is deep but only 19 yards wide and protected by two traps on the left. The next hole is the number-1-handicap hole, a 450-yard par 4 that requires length off the tee over water to a landing area protected by three bunkers on the right. A long second shot is required to reach a narrow, deep green protected by traps to the left and right. The par-4 third hole plays 470 yards, with lots of water in front of a green that is protected on the right by two traps. Your tee shot should be hit straight between two fairway bunkers on the left and another to the right, leaving a mid-iron to the green, which is to your left and over water.

The 550-yard par-5 fifth hole is another exercise in aquatics, with water running completely along the right side of the fairway from the tee to a relatively small green protected by three traps to the left, right and rear. Placement, not distance, is essential to negotiate a narrow fairway with four bunkers on the right and one on the left beginning 250 yards from the green. The finishing hole on the front nine is a tough 560-yard par 5 lined with marsh on the left from tee to green and punctuated with five fairway bunkers left and right. Two accurate shots are required to avoid trouble and reach a small green protected on each side by traps.

The back nine features the beautiful 165-yard par-3 seventeenth, which was built on a mound of oyster shells. You hit to a small island green beautifully banked with oyster shells and protected by two small traps on the right. The most difficult hole on the course is the 470-yard par-4 sixteenth, which has water from tee to green on the right and water on the left up to the fairway. The first shot should be hit down the left side, leaving you a fairway wood or long iron to the green, which is 20 yards wide, 32 yards deep, and protected by traps to the left and the water on the right. Good luck on this one.

The marshes, lagoons, lakes and Intracoastal Waterway at Oyster Bay convey the atmosphere of a wildlife preserve. Birds such as egrets, blue herons, ducks, and swans abound and it can all be enjoyed from the modern, full-service clubhouse after the round.

Recommended Golf Courses in North Carolina

Within 1¹/2 Hours of Wilmington:

Bald Head Island Golf Club, Southport, (910) 457–7310, (800) 234–1666, Resort, 18/6855/72

Brunswick Plantation and Golf Links, Calabash, (910) 287–4533, (800) 848–0290, Public, 18/6779/72

Carolina Shores Golf and Country Club, Calabash, (910) 579–2181, Public, 18/6783/72

The Emerald Golf Club, New Bern, (919) 663–4440, Semiprivate, 18/6924/72

Gauntlet Golf and Country Club, Southport, (910) 253–3008, (800) 247–4806 Semiprivate, 18/7022/72

Lion's Paw Golf Links, Sunset Beach, (910) 579–1801, (800) 828–5035, Public, 18/7003/72

Lockwood Golf Links, Supply, (910) 842–5666, Public, 18/6836/72

North Shore Country Club, Sneads Ferry, (910) 327–2410, Semiprivate, 18/6866/72

Ocean Harbor Golf Links, Calabash, (910) 579–3588, Public, 18/7004/72

Olde Pointe Golf and Country Club, Hampstead, (910) 270–2403, Semiprivate, 18/6913/72

Pearl Golf Links, Calabash, (910) 579–8132, Public. East: 18/6860/72. West: 18/7003/72

Porter's Neck Country Club, Wilmington, (910) 686–1177, Semiprivate, 18/7120/72

Sandpiper Bay Golf and Country Club, Calabash, (910) 579–9120, (800) 356–5827, Public, 18/6503/71

Sea Trail Plantation, Sunset Beach, (910) 579–4350, (800) 546–5748, Public. Maples: 18/6785/72. Rees Jones: 18/6761/72. Willard Byrd: 18/6750/72

Within ¹/2 Hour of Charlotte:

River Bend Golf and Country Club, Shelby, (704) 482–4286, Semiprivate, 18/6509/72

Within 1¹/2 Hours of Elizabeth City (including the Outer Banks):

Albemarle Plantation, Hertford, (919) 426–5555, Public, 18/6504/72

Duck Woods Country Club, Kitty Hawk, (919)261–2609, Private from July-Labor Day, Semiprivate otherwise, 18/6186/72

Nags Head Golf Links, Nags Head, (919) 441–8073, Semiprivate, 18/6100/71

Sea Scape Golf Course, Kitty Hawk, (919) 261–2158, Public, 18/6409/72

Within 1 Hour of Morehead City (Carolina coast):

Carolina Pines Golf and Country Club, New Bern, (919) 447–7121, Semiprivate, 18/6600/72

Fairfield Harbour Golf Course and Harbour Pointe Golf Links, New Bern, (919) 638–8011, (800) 682–8140 (NC), (800) 334–5739 (outside NC), Semiprivate, 18/6654/72, 18/6782/72

Greenbrier Golf Club, New Bern, (919) 633–4440, Semiprivate, 18/6924/72

Morehead City Country Club, Morehead City, (919) 726–4917, Semiprivate, 18/6060/72

Roaring Gap (Northwestern):

High Meadows Golf and Country Club, Roaring Gap, (919) 363–2445, Resort, 18/6487/72

Jefferson Landing, Jefferson, (919) 246–4653, Public, 18/7015/72

North Carolina: Useful Information

Travel and Tourism Division, 430 N. Salisbury St., Raleigh, NC 27611, (919) 733–4171, (800) VISIT–NC (outside Raleigh)

North Carolina Wildlife Resources Commission, 512 N. Salisbury St., Raleigh, NC 27611, (919) 733–3391 (fishing and hunting regulations)

North Carolina Division of Parks and Recreation, P.O. Box 27287, Raleigh, NC 27611, (919) 733–7275 (recreation information)

U.S. Forest Service, P.O. Box 2750, Asheville, NC 28802, (704) 257–4200, (800) 280–CAMP (national forest information and reservations)

Course Name: EDGEWOOD GOLF COURSE

Course Type: Public
Address: 3218 2nd Street North
Fargo, ND 58102
Phone: (701) 232–2824

GOLF COURSE

Head Professional: David Kingsrud
Course Length/Par (All Tees): Back 6330/71, Middle 6045/71, Ladies' Forward 5171/73
Course Slope/Rating (All Tees): Back 122/69.9, Middle 122/68.4, Ladies' Forward 115/68.9
Course Architect: NA (1920s). Robert Bruce Harris (renovation, 1951)
Golf Facilities: Full Pro Shop X, Snack Bar X, Lounge X, Restaurant X, Locker Room X, Showers X, Club Rental X, Club Repair X, Cart Rental X, Instruction X, Practice Green X, Driving Range X, Practice Bunker X, Club Storage No
Tee-Time Reservation Policy: Up to 3 days in advance
Ranger: Yes
Tee-off-Interval Time: 8 min.
Time to Play 18 Holes: 4½ hrs.
Course Hours/Earliest Tee-off: 6:30 a.m.
Green Fees: $16 for 18 holes Fri., Sat., Sun., holidays; $14 for 18 holes weekdays
Cart Fees: $15 for 18 holes, $8 for 9 holes
Pull Carts: $2 for 18 holes
Credit Cards: Cash or check for golf fees. MasterCard, Visa for merchandise
Season: April through Oct.
Course Comments: Can walk anytime
Golf Packages: None
Discounts: Juniors, seniors, twilight
Places to Stay Nearby: FARGO: Best Western Doublewood Inn (701) 235–3333, (800) 528–1234; Comfort Suites (701) 237–5911, (800) 221–2222; Country Inn and Suites (701) 234–0565, (800) 456–4000; Holiday Inn (701) 282–2700, (800) 465–4329; Radisson Hotel (701) 232–7363, (800) 333–3333

Local Attractions: Bonanzaville, U.S.A. Pioneer Village, Regional Museum of the Red River and Northern Plains, casino gambling, Fargo Theater, Roger Maris Baseball Museum, Children's Museum at Yunker Farms, Moorhead State University Regional Science Center, Plains Art Museum, fishing, hunting, camping. WEST FARGO: Bonanzaville, seasonal fairs and festivals. West Fargo Chamber of Commerce (701) 282–4444. Fargo–Moorhead Convention and Visitors Bureau (701) 237–6134. Fargo–Moorhead Indian Center (701) 293–6863
Directions: From downtown Fargo: North on Elm St. to golf course
Closest Commercial Airport: Hector Airport, Fargo (5 min.)

EDGEWOOD GOLF COURSE

The Edgewood Golf Course is a beautiful Robert Bruce Harris–redesigned par-71, 6330-yard layout carved out of a former bird sanctuary in Fargo, North Dakota. Edgewood is rated one of the best golf courses in North Dakota by *Golf Digest* and has been the site of state tournaments, as well as the National Junior Championship.

The course is beautifully maintained with rolling fairways guarded by oaks, elms and other varieties of trees. The medium-sized to large bentgrass greens are fast and undulating, with a few traps guarding each one. Water comes into play on only four holes, including the 426-yard, par-4 tenth, the number-2-handicap hole on the course. This slight dogleg right drops approximately 50 feet from an elevated tee to a medium-sized green protected by water on the right and a trap to the left. The tee shot must avoid a lateral water hazard on the left. A memorable hole on the course, the eleventh, is a 194-yard par 3 featuring waterfalls and beautiful stonework. The tee shot must arc over water to a green guarded by a large trap to the right.

Edgewood is a pleasant journey through a beautiful, wooded layout that requires careful shot placement off the tee and a good short game to score.

NORTH DAKOTA

Course Name: MINOT COUNTRY CLUB

Course Type: Semiprivate
Address: Country Club Road
Box 250, Burlington, ND
58722 (Mailing Address)
Minot, ND 58772
Phone: (701) 839–6169

GOLF COURSE

Head Professional: Chuck Ruppert
Course Length/Par (All Tees): Back 6586/72, Middle 6269/72, Forward 5410/72
Course Slope/Rating (All Tees): Back 124/71.2, Middle 121/69.8, Ladies' Forward 115/70.0
Course Architects: Tom Vardon (Front 9, 1929; Back 9, 1951). John Steidel (renovation, 1985)
Golf Facilities: Full Pro Shop X, Snack Bar X, Lounge X, Restaurant X, Locker Room X, Showers X, Club Rental X, Club Repair X, Cart Rental X, Instruction X, Practice Green X, Driving Range X, Practice Bunker X, Club Storage X
Tee-Time Reservation Policy: Outside play: 24 hrs. in advance
Ranger: No
Tee-off-Interval Time: 8 min.
Time to Play 18 Holes: 4 hrs.
Course Hours/Earliest Tee-off: 7 a.m.
Green Fees: $30 for 18 holes Sat., Sun., holidays; $25 for 18 holes weekdays
Cart Fees: $18 plus tax for 18 holes
Credit Cards: American Express, MasterCard, Visa
Season: April through Nov. Busiest June-Aug.
Course Comments: Can walk anytime. Yardage book available
Golf Packages: None
Discounts: Juniors, replays on the same day
Places to Stay Nearby: MINOT: Holiday Inn (701) 852–4161, (800) HOLIDAY; Best Western International (701) 852–3161, (800) 528–1234; Dakota Inn (701) 838–2700; Fairfield Inn (701) 838–2424; Sheraton–Riverside (701) 852–2504, (800) 468–9968

Local Attractions: Roosevelt Park Zoo, Railroad Museum, hunting, fishing, camping, Dakota Territory Air Museum; gaming including blackjack, bingo and off-track betting; Minot State University, seasonal festivals. Minot Convention and Visitors Bureau (701) 852–6000. Minot Tourist Information Center (701) 839–6613
Directions: From Minot: Take 4th Ave. Northwest for 5 mi., course on left
Closest Commercial Airports: Minot International (10 min.); Mandan Municipal, Bismarck (2 hrs.)

MINOT COUNTRY CLUB

The Minot Country Club is located in Minot, North Dakota, approximately 110 miles north and slightly west of Bismarck, the state capitol. The 6586-yard layout is one of the oldest golf courses in the state and is ranked No. 2 in North Dakota by *Golf Digest*. The front nine was completed in the late 1920s and the back nine in the early 1950s. The Minot Country Club is one of the sites on the North Dakota professional tour and annually hosts the Western North Dakota Charity Pro-Am.

Accuracy is more important than length at the Minot Country Club, which is flat, dotted with evergreens and has very little water. The bentgrass greens are small, fast and undulating. There are very few fairway bunkers, and an average of one or two traps protects each green. The course has five par 5s and five par 3s. The par 5s tend to be short, ranging from 496 to 522 yards in length from the back tees. The par 3s range from 165 to 210 yards from the back tees.

The signature hole at the Minot Country Club is the 206-yard seventh hole, which plays to a deep green guarded by traps to the left and right. Evergreens frame the back of the hole and, coming into the green, there is water to the left.

Minot Country Club was remodeled in 1985 by John Steidel, who served as an assistant to golf-architect Robert Muir Graves in the 1970s before forming his own design firm in 1980.

Course Name: RIVERWOOD GOLF COURSE

Course Type: Public
Address: 725 Riverwood Drive
                Box 2063
                Bismarck, ND 58502
Phone: (701) 223–9915

GOLF COURSE

Head Professional: Dan Waldoch
Course Length/Par (All Tees): Back
6941/72, Middle 6416/72, Forward
5196/72
Course Slope/Rating (All Tees): Back
122/71.9, Middle 120/69.8, Forward
112/68.6
Course Architect: Leo I. Johnson (1969)
Golf Facilities: Full Pro Shop X, Snack
Bar X, Lounge X, Restaurant X,
Locker Room X, Showers No, Club
Rental No, Club Repair X, Cart Rental
X, Instruction X, Practice Green X,
Driving Range X, Practice Bunker X,
Club Storage X
Tee-Time Reservation Policy: 1 day in
advance
Ranger: Yes
Tee-off-Interval Time: 7½ min.
Time to Play 18 Holes: 4½ hrs.
Course Hours/Earliest Tee-off: 7 a.m.
Green Fees: $15 for 18 holes, $12 for
9 holes
Cart Fees: $16 for 18 holes, $8 for 9 holes
Credit Cards: Discover, MasterCard, Visa
Season: April through Nov. Busiest June
through Sept.
Course Comments: Can walk anytime.
Golf shop open year round
Golf Packages: None
Discounts: Seniors, juniors
Places to Stay Nearby: Expressway Inn
(701) 222–2900, (800) 456–6388;
Radisson Inn Bismarck (701) 258–7700,
(800) 333–3333; Best Western Double-
wood Inn (701) 258–7000, (800) 528–
1234; Holiday Inn (701) 223–9600, (800)
HOLIDAY; Sheraton Inn Bismarck Gal-
leria (701) 255–6000, (800) 325–3535
Local Attractions: Camp Hancock histori-
cal site, Dakota Zoo, Lewis and Clark
riverboat cruises, State Historical Soci-
ety and State Historical Museum at
North Dakota Heritage Center, state
capitol, statue of Sacajawea, Fort
Abraham Lincoln State Park, Railroad
Museum, Double Ditch Indian Village.
Bismarck/Mandan Convention and
Visitors Bureau (701) 222–4308. Dakota
Association of Native Americans
(701) 258–0040
Directions: I–94 east to Bismarck Express-
way south. Right on Washington St.,
right on Riverwood Dr. to golf course
Closest Commercial Airport: Mandan
Municipal, Bismarck (5 min.)

RIVERWOOD GOLF COURSE

Riverwood is a 6941-yard, par-72 layout
carved out of cottonwoods and other varieties of trees on a flat river bottom, which is
adjacent to the Missouri River. Although
this golf course is flat with relatively few
traps and waterhazards, the tight, tree-lined
fairways can quickly penalize errant shots.
The bentgrass greens are large, fast, undulating and a bit elevated.

Among the challenging holes at Riverwood is the 450-yard, par-4 dogleg-right
ninth, one of the many doglegs on the
course. A long, accurate tee shot is required
to be in position to reach a forward-sloping, elevated green. Another tough hole is
the 546-yard, par-5 fifteenth, a double
dogleg that also demands length and
accuracy on the first two shots.

Riverwood was designed by Leo I.
Johnson, a native of Homer, Nebraska, who
designed the Emerald Hills Golf Club in
Arnolds Park, Iowa; the Brightwood Hills
Golf Club in New Brighton, Minnesota;
and other layouts in the Midwest. Riverwood has a clubhouse that is open year
round and an ample driving range. The
course has been rated among the top five
courses in the state of North Dakota by
Golf Digest.

Recommended Golf Courses in North Dakota:

Bois De Souix golf Club, Wahpeton,
(701) 642–3673, Public, 18/6675/72

Manvel Golf Course, Manvel, (701) 696–
8268, Public, 18/6357/72 (nine holes
played twice)

Prairie West Golf Course, Mandan, (701) 667–3222, Public, 18/6681/72

Souris Valley Golf Club, Minot, (701) 838–4112, Public, 18/6815/72

North Dakota: Useful Information

North Dakota Tourism Division, Liberty Memorial Bldg., 600 E. Boulevard Ave., Bismarck, ND 58505, (800) 453–5663 (U.S.), (800) 537–8879 (Canada)

North Dakota Parks and Recreation Department, 1424 W. Century Ave., Ste. 202, Bismarck, ND 58502, (701) 221–5357 (recreation information)

North Dakota Game and Fish Department, 100 North Brunswick Expwy., Bismarck, ND 58501, (701) 221–6300

North Dakota Historical Society, Heritage Center, 612 E. Boulevard Ave., Bismarck, ND 58505, (701) 224–2666

Course Name: AVALON LAKES GOLF COURSE

Course Type: Resort
Resort: Avalon Inn
Address: 9519 East Market Street
Warren, OH 44484
Phone: (216) 856–8898 (Golf Course)
(216) 856–1900 (Resort)
Fax: (216) 856–2248 (Resort)

GOLF COURSE

Head Professional: John Diana
Course Length/Par (All Tees): Back 7001/71, White 6453/71, Gold 6097/71 Forward 5324/71
Course Slope/Rating (All Tees): Back 127/74.3, White 122/71.8, Gold 118/70.2, Ladies' Forward 116/70.1
Course Architects: Pete Dye and William Newcomb (1968)
Golf Facilities: Full Pro Shop X, Snack Bar X, Lounge X, Restaurant X, Locker Room X, Showers X, Club Rental X, Club Repair X, Cart Rental X, Instruction X, Practice Green X, Driving Range X, Practice Bunker X, Club Storage X
Tee-Time Reservation Policy: Call anytime
Ranger: Yes
Tee-off-Interval Time: 8 min.
Time to Play 18 Holes: 5 hrs.
Course Hours/Earliest Tee-off: 6 a.m. to dark
Green and Cart Fees: $45 for 18 holes with cart, $27 for 9 holes with cart
Credit Cards: American Express, MasterCard, Visa
Season: March through Nov. Busiest season May to Sept.
Course Comments: Carts required until 4 p.m. Yardage book available. Additional 18-hole golf course (Avalon South) on premises
Golf Packages: Available
Discounts: Seasonal. Twilight
Places to Stay Nearby: Best Western Downtown Motor Inn (216) 392–2515, (800) 528–1234; EconoLodge (216) 544–1301. GIRARD: Holiday Inn Metroplex (216) 759–0606, (800) HOLIDAY

Local Attractions: Packard Music Hall, John Stark Edwards house, Old Warren Public Library, J. W. Packard home, Harriet Taylor Upton house, Henry Perkins home, General Motors assembly plant, Kinsman house, Monument Park, George Kneeland home, Gilmer house. CORTLAND: Historic village, Cortland Opera House. KINSMAN: Clarence Darrow octagon house. Trumbull County Convention and Visitors Bureau (216) 544–3468, (800) 672–9555. Warren Area Chamber of Commerce (216) 393–2565
Directions: From Pittsburgh (70 mi.): Rte. 76/Turnpike to Rte. 680, to I–80. Take I–80 east to Rte. 11, exit at Rte. 11, north on Rte. 11 to second exit, Rte. 82, take Rte. 82 west. Take Howland–Wilson Rd., make right on Howland–Wilson to stop sign. Right on East Market St. to Avalon Inn and golf course. From Cleveland (70 mi.): I–80 east to Rte. 5 bypass to Howland–Wilson exit, make left on Howland–Wilson Rd. to stop sign (East Market St.). Make right on East Market St. to Avalon Inn and golf course
Closest Commercial Airports: Cleveland Hopkins International (1½ hrs.), Greater Pittsburgh International (1½ hrs.)

RESORT

Date Built: 1968
No. of Rooms: 144 rooms and suites
Meeting Rooms: 9. Capacity of Largest: 500 persons banquet style. Meeting Space: 11,000 sq. ft.
Room Price Range: $70 for single to $150 for hospitality suite. Golf, honeymoon, fall, winter and other packages available year round
Lounge: Red Horse Lounge
Restaurants: Tall Oaks, Country Gardens
Entertainment: Piano music
Credit Cards: All major cards
General Amenities: Meeting and banquet rooms with audiovisual and food-service support
Recreational Amenities: Indoor Olympic–sized swimming pool, racquetball, volleyball, 3 indoor/outdoor tennis

courts, fitness center with Nautilus exercise equipment, sauna, Jacuzzi, shuffleboard

Reservation and Cancellation Policy:
1 night's advance deposit for all weekend reservations. Deposit refunded if cancellation made 1 wk. in advance

Comments and Restrictions: No pets. Children under 16 stay free. Swim and tennis club, fitness center memberships available. Taxes additional to base rates

AVALON LAKES GOLF COURSE

Avalon Lakes is a 6825-yard par-71 Pete Dye layout located in Warren, Ohio, midway between Cleveland and Pittsburgh. This course features small to medium-sized greens that are moderately fast, undulating and well protected by large sand traps. Water hazards are located on eleven holes, but the course is flat and open with relatively few fairway bunkers. Avalon Lakes opened in 1968, making it one of Dye's earlier efforts as a full-time architect. He was assisted by William Newcomb, who worked for Dye from 1965 to 1967. Newcomb won the Michigan Amateur in 1967 and started his own golf-course design firm in 1968.

When you first look at Avalon Lakes' scorecard and then play the golf course, you are struck by its difficult par-3 holes. The 184-yard fourth plays to an elevated green almost completely surrounded by four large traps. The 235-yard eighth has a narrow, deep green protected by one huge bunker on each side and trees to the rear. The prevailing westerly winds are generally blowing into your face on this hole, which is rated the number-8-handicap hole on the course. The beautiful 209-yard twelfth plays over a corner of a pond to a deep green fronted by two traps and guarded by another on the right. The 183-yard sixteenth is the shortest hole on the course but has a heavily contoured, forward-sloping green fronted by two traps.

The two finishing holes are challenging par 4s. The 474-yard seventeenth is bordered by water on the right. Any kind of a slice or fade will give you trouble. The green is guarded in front by two traps, and another protects the left rear. The eighteenth is 471 yards long and is rated the number-1-handicap hole on the course. It is a slight dogleg right with trees and a large right-fairway bunker guarding the tee-shot landing area. The large green is fronted by two large bunkers. On this hole it is much better to be long than short on the approach shot.

Avalon Lakes annually hosts the Youngstown-Warren LPGA Classic. In recent years many improvements have been made to the golf course and its amenities. A new pro shop, locker rooms, a restaurant, pavillion and other facilities have been added. Within walking distance of the golf course is the 144-room Avalon Inn, which has 2 restaurants, a lounge, tennis courts, an Olympic-sized swimming pool, a fitness center with Nautilus equipment, racquetball courts, sauna, Jacuzzi and other amenities. There are meeting and conference rooms for banquets, receptions, seminars and other functions. A variety of packages is offered year round, including golf packages. Another eighteen-hole golf course, Avalon South, is also on site.

Avalon Lakes has been ranked one of the best public golf courses in the United States by *Golf Digest*. More recently it has been rated among the top 25 in *Golf Digest*'s America's 75 best resort courses. Avalon Lakes provides an opportunity to play an early Pete Dye course at very reasonable rates.

Course Name: BLUE ASH

Course Type: Public
Address: 4040 Cooper Road
Blue Ash, OH 45241
Phone: (513) 745–8577

GOLF COURSE

Head Professional: Bill Mayer
Course Length/Par (All Tees): Back 6643/72, Middle 6211/72, Forward 5125/72
Course Slope/Rating (All Tees): Back 127/72.6, Middle 122/70.3, Ladies' Forward 124/70.3
Course Architects: Jack Kidwell and Michael Hurdzan (1979)

Golf Facilities: Full Pro Shop X, Snack Bar X, Lounge X, Restaurant No, Locker Room X, Showers X, Club Rental X, Club Repair X, Cart Rental X, Instruction X, Practice Green X, Driving Range No, Practice Bunker X, Club Storage No

Tee-Time Reservation Policy: Reservations required daily from March 21 to Oct. 31; call 5 days in advance. Residents have priority and can reserve tee times up to 7 days in advance

Ranger: Yes

Tee-off-Interval Time: 10 min.

Time to Play 18 Holes: 4½ hrs.

Course Hours/Earliest Tee-off: 7 a.m. to dark

Green Fees: $19 for 18 holes, $10 for 9 holes

Cart Fees: $20 for 18 holes, $10 for 9 holes

Pull Carts: $2.50 for 18 holes

Credit Cards: None—Cash or in-state check only

Season: Year round, weather permitting. Busiest season June to Aug.

Course Comments: Can walk anytime

Golf Packages: None

Discounts: Juniors, seniors (senior rates before 11 a.m. weekdays only), seasonal

Places to Stay Nearby: Holiday Inn— Queensgate (513) 241–8660, (800) HOLIDAY; Garfield House Suite Hotel (513) 421–3555; Omni Netherland Plaza (513) 621–7700, (800) THE–OMNI; Hyatt Regency Cincinnati (513) 579–1234, (800) 233–1234; The Cincinnatian Hotel (513) 381–3000, (800) 942–9000; Westin Hotel Cincinnati (513) 621–7700; Cincinnati Hotel (513) 381–3000; Holiday Inn Northeast (513) 398–8015, (800) 465–4329; Ramada Hotel Blue Ash Hotel and Conference Center (513) 793–4500, (800) 228–2828; Embassy Suites (513) 733–8400, (800) 362–2779; Comfort Suites—Cincinnati Northeast (513) 530–5999, (800) 221–2222; Guest Quarters Suite Hotel (513) 489–3636, (800) 424–2900

Local Attractions: CINCINNATI: Cincinnati Art Museum, Cincinnati Fire Museum, Cincinnati Historical Society Museum, Cincinnati Nature Center, Cincinnati Zoo and Botanical Garden, Contemporary Arts Center, Kings Island (Kings Mills), St. Peter in Chains Cathedral, Surf Cincinnati Water Park, Taft Museum, William Howard Taft national historic site, Ohio River cruises; professional baseball, football at Riverfront Stadium; Sharon Woods Village (Sharonville), restaurants, theater, concerts, University of Cincinnati; recreational activities including hiking, tennis in Cincinnati's parks; boating, fishing. KENTUCKY: Horse racing at Turfway Park Race Track, River Downs Race Track. Cincinnati Convention and Visitors Bureau (513) 621–2142, (800) 344–3445. Clermont County Convention and Visitors Bureau (513) 753–7211. Warren County Convention and Visitors Bureau (800) 433–1072

Directions: From the north: I–71 to Pfeiffer Rd. exit, to Plainfield, right onto Plainfield, Plainfield to Cooper Rd., right onto Cooper Rd. From downtown Cincinnati (25 min.): I–71 north, Pfeiffer Rd. exit, left on Pfeiffer Rd., left on Plainfield, right on Cooper Rd. to golf course

Closest Commercial Airport: Greater Cincinnati International (45 min.)

BLUE ASH

Blue Ash is a rolling, well-treed municipal golf course located in the northeastern suburbs of Cincinnati. This 6643-yard layout was designed by Jack Kidwell and Michael Hurdzan, who also designed the Vineyard, another excellent municipal golf course in the Cincinnati area. Blue Ash has small to medium-sized, fast, undulating bentgrass greens and is well protected by sand bunkers and water, which comes into play on four holes. Because of the mature trees, hills and gullies, and blind holes and doglegs, Blue Ash demands solid course management, position golf, and proper club selection and accuracy rather than extreme distance. The wind here is generally from the west and can affect play on some of the holes. Many of the greens at Blue Ash are crowned and are not easy to hold.

A beautiful and challenging par 4 on the front side is the 419-yard sixth, a dogleg left with a pond that comes into play on the left as you approach a small, crowned green. The number-1-handicap hole on this side is the 514-yard par-5 fifth, a dogleg right that will become more difficult as newly planted trees on both sides of the fairway mature. The second shot is slightly uphill to a medium-sized green protected right and left by bunkers.

As you work your way up- and downhill on this layout, it becomes evident how the natural contours of the land were used to create an excellent test of golf. Fruit trees and ash, maple, pine and other varieties of trees add to the beauty of the course and provide obstacles you have to consider while plotting your course strategy.

The back nine starts out with a beautiful and challenging 528-yard par 5 that plays over a wide gully to a landing area protected by sand bunkers. You have to be long and straight off this tee to avoid trees, the gully and the bunkers. The approach to the undulating green must avoid bunkers to the front left, the right and the rear. Next is an excellent 190-yard par 3 with a narrow entranceway to a green protected by traps to the left, right and rear. From 100 yards into the green are large, mature trees on the right and water on the left.

The finishing hole is a 525-yard par-5 blind dogleg right. The tee shot is over a rise and downhill to a dramatic valley of green fairway protected by trees. The approach shot is uphill to a small green banked in the back and guarded by traps to the right, left and rear.

Blue Ash has a sizeable clubhouse with a good pro shop, locker rooms and showers, and a snack bar restaurant. There are 2 practice greens and a practice bunker but no driving range. Instruction is available from the staff of professionals. You can walk the golf course anytime, although the hilly terrain makes walking a bit strenuous. Nevertheless, when I visited the course on a September day, many golfers were walking.

Michael Hurdzan was born in Wheeling, West Virginia, and graduated from Ohio State University in 1966, earning an M.S. in turfgrass physiology. He later earned a Ph.D. in environmental plant physiology at the University of Vermont. In 1976 he formed a partnership with Jack Kidwell, a golf architect from Columbus, Ohio. Kidwell studied at Utah State University's Agriculture College before purchasing a golf course with his father. He was the professional and superintendent at that club until he became a full-time golf-course architect in 1959. He designed many public layouts before teaming up with Mike Hurdzan. Some of their layouts in Ohio include San Dar Acres Golf Club, Bellville; Shawnee Lookout Golf Club, Cincinnati; and Buttermilk Falls Golf Club in Georgetown.

Blue Ash is ranked among the top 75 public golf courses in America by *Golf Digest* magazine and is an excellent place to test your golf game.

Course Name: COOKS CREEK GOLF CLUB

Course Type: Public
Address: 16405 U.S. Highway 23 South
Ashville, OH 43103
Phone: (614) 983–3636
Fax: (614) 983–4673

GOLF COURSE

Head Professional: Tony Cardinali
Course Length/Par (All Tees): Back 7071/72, Blue 6589/72, White 5972/72, Forward 4995/72
Course Slope/Rating (All Tees): Back 131/73.7, Blue 128/71.3, White 122/68.5, Ladies' White 127/71.5, Ladies' Forward 120/68.2
Course Architect: Michael Hurdzan (9, 1992; 9, 1995)
Golf Facilities: Full Pro Shop X, Snack Bar X, Lounge X, Restaurant No, Locker Room No, Showers X, Club Rental X, Club Repair X, Cart Rental X, Instruction X, Practice Green X, Driving Range X, Practice Bunker X, Club Storage No
Tee-Time Reservation Policy: Up to 7 days in advance
Ranger: Yes
Tee-off-Interval Time: 8 min.
Time to Play 18 Holes: 4 hrs. 20 min.

Course Hours/Earliest Tee-off: 7 a.m.

Green and Cart Fees: $55 for 18 holes Fri., Sat., Sun., holidays; $45 for 18 holes weekdays

Credit Cards: All major cards

Season: Year round weather permitting. Busiest May through Labor Day

Course Comments: Can walk at twilight rate times

Golf Packages: Inquire at pro shop

Discounts: Twilight

Places to Stay Nearby: COLUMBUS: Hyatt on Capitol Square (614) 228–1234, (800) 233–1234; Holiday Inn Crowne Plaza (614) 461–4100, (800) 465–4329; Radisson Airport Hotel and Conference Center (614) 475–7551, (800) 333–3333; The Worthington Inn (614) 885–2600

Local Attractions: COLUMBUS: Columbus Museum of Art, Columbus Zoo, COSI (Center of Science and Industry), Ohio's Center of Science and Industry, Franklin Park Conservatory and Botanical Garden, German Village, Ohio Historical Center, Ohio State University, State Capitol, The Thurber House, Columbus Clippers AAA professional baseball, Columbus Motor Speedway, horse racing, shopping at City Center Mall, The Marketplace at Grandview, arts and entertainment. The Greater Columbus Convention and Visitors Bureau (614) 221–6623, (800) 354–2657

Directions: From Columbus (20 min. south): Take Hwy. 23 south to golf course

Closest Commercial Airport: Columbus (30 min.)

COOKS CREEK GOLF CLUB

Cooks Creek is a 7071-yard par-72 Michael Hurdzan-designed layout on former farmland just south of Columbus. Variable winds can affect play on this open course which has large, subtly undulating, quick bentgrass greens. Water hazards including streams and wetlands can come into play on half the holes at Cooks Creek.

Two of the most difficult holes on the course are on the front nine. The 223-yard par-3 sixth plays over water to a peninsula green with water on three sides, a pair of bunkers to its rear and another to its front right. A sycamore tree guards the left side of the green and an incoming wind often makes this hole extremely tough. A challenging par 4 at Cooks Creek is the 488-yard ninth, a straight hole that requires a 225-yard drive from the back tees to carry a water hazard in front of the landing area. The approach is usually into the wind to a well-bunkered, heavily undulating green with a large waste area to its left.

The practice area at Cooks Creek features a wide two-tiered bentgrass driving range, a practice green, and practice bunkers. When playing this course it is best for most golfers to avoid playing from the difficult back tees in order to enjoy the round. In 1995 *Golf Digest* selected Cooks Creek one of the best new public courses in the United States.

Course Name: EAGLESTICKS GOLF CLUB

Course Type: Public

Address: 2655 Maysville Pike Zanesville, OH 43701

Phone: (614) 454–4900, (800) 782–4493

GOLF COURSE

Head Professional: Michael Durant

Course Length/Par (All Tees): Back 6412/70, Blue 6028/70, White 5397/70, Forward 4137/70

Course Slope/Rating (All Tees): Back 120/70.1, Blue 117/68.3, White 108/65.5, Ladies' Forward 96/63.7

Course Architect: Michael Hurdzan Design Group (1990)

Golf Facilities: Full Pro Shop X, Snack Bar X, Lounge X, Restaurant X, Locker Room No, Showers X, Club Rental X, Club Repair X, Cart Rental X, Instruction X, Practice Green X, Driving Range X, Practice Bunker X, Club Storage X

Tee-Time Reservation Policy: Call anytime

Ranger: Yes

Tee-off-Interval Time: 8 to 10 min.

Time to Play 18 Holes: 4 hrs., 45 min.

Course Hours/Earliest Tee-off: 7 a.m.

Green Fees: $35.50 for 18 holes Sat., Sun. holidays; $30.50 for 18 holes weekdays. $24.50 for 9 holes Sat., Sun., holidays; $21.50 for 9 holes weekdays

Cart Fees: $10.50 for 18 holes per person, $5.50 for 9 holes per person

Credit Cards: American Express, Master-Card, Visa

Season: April to Dec. Busiest season May to Aug.

Course Comments: Can walk anytime except weekends and holidays before 1 p.m. Yardage book available

Golf Packages: Available through local hotels. Contact pro shop

Discounts: Juniors, seniors, twilight rate after 5 p.m.

Places to Stay Nearby: Holiday Inn (614) 453–0771, (800) HOLIDAY; Comfort Inn (614) 454–4144, (800) 4–CHOICE; Fairfield Inn (614) 453–8770, (800) 228–2800; Days Inn (614) 453–3400, (800) 325–2525; Best Western (614) 452–4511, (800) 528–1234

Local Attractions: Putnam historic area, Ohio Ceramic Center, Secrest Auditorium, Zane Grey birthplace, seasonal festivals, Zanesville Art Center, National Road–Zane Grey Museum, Ohio State University (branch), fishing, boating, hiking, other outdoor recreation. Zanesville Chamber of Commerce (614) 452–7571. Zanesville Tourist Information Bureau (614) 453–5004, (800) 743–2303

Directions: From Columbus (1 hr., 15 min.): I–70 east to 7th St. exit in downtown Zanesville. At end of 7th St., make a right turn and cross 6th St. Bridge, follow State Rte. 22. Eaglesticks is located approximately 4 mi. ahead on the right. From Cambridge (1 hr.): I–70 west to State Rte. 146 and Underwood St. exit. Continue straight at bottom of exit ramp. Turn at first left under highway (7th St.). At end of 7th St. follow State Rte. 22 west to signs. Eaglesticks is about 4 mi. on the right, after you cross the 6th St. Bridge

Closest Commercial Airports: Port Columbus International (1 hr., 15 min.)

EAGLESTICKS GOLF CLUB

Eaglesticks Golf Club is a Michael Hurdzan–designed 6412-yard par-70 layout located approximately 60 miles east of Columbus, Ohio, in Zanesville. The course was built on an old horse farm and features medium-sized to large, fast, undulating bentgrass greens protected by a variety of traps. There are over 130 strategically placed sand bunkers on this target golf course, which requires accurate shot-making, especially on approaches to the well-protected greens. You'll also need a putting game to score on the ample, tricky greens. *Golf Digest* rated Eaglesticks second runner-up in the 1992 best new public golf course category.

The number-1-handicap hole at Eaglesticks is the 453-yard par-4 ninth. The tee shot is from an elevated tee to a flat landing area protected by a large bunker on the right. The second shot is down a narrowing fairway to a relatively small green protected by a huge trap on the right, another to the rear and a smaller one to the right front of the green. A row of trees guards the left side of the fairway from tee to green.

Another excellent par 4 on the front side is the 437-yard eighth. The tee shot is to a narrow landing area with a drop-off and a creek on the left, and trees on hilly slopes to the right. It is very possible to have a sidehill lie or be out of bounds after this first shot. The approach is to a large, well bunkered green that slopes severely forward and is banked in back.

The 591-yard par-5 dogleg-left eleventh is considered one of the best holes on the course. This hole plays downhill to a narrow, deep, flat green protected by five traps. The first shot is to an open landing area. The second is over a creek that cuts the fairway approximately 200 yards from the green. The third shot is down a narrowing fairway pinched by two traps in front of the green. Additional bunkers are on the right from 100 yards in.

An excellent par 3 at Eaglesticks is the 180-yard twelfth, which plays from plateau to plateau over a small valley. The large, three-tiered green slopes forward and left to right. It is protected by traps to the left, rear and right. Tricky pin placements can make this a tough par 3.

Facilities at Eaglesticks include a clubhouse with snack bar and pro shop. Next door is the Inn at Eaglesticks, where meals are available from 7 a.m. The driving range has over 1 acre of bentgrass teeing area. A chipping green, putting green and bunker areas are also available. You can walk the course, but golf carts are required until 1 p.m. on weekends and holidays. Individual and group instruction is available.

Eaglesticks is a public golf course privately owned by the J. W. McClelland family. This is a new bright spot for public golf in Ohio. Zanesville was once a leading pottery center, and there are still many pottery works in operation here. This is also the birthplace of author Zane Grey.

Course Name: SHAKER RUN GOLF CLUB

Course Type: Semiprivate
Address: 4361 Pine Tree Rd.
Lebanon, OH 45036
Phone: (513) 727–0007,
(800) 721–0007 (OH)
Fax: (513) 727–4756

GOLF COURSE

Director of Golf: Steve Lambert
Course Length/Par (All Tees): Back 6965/72, Blue 6395/72, White 5794/72, Forward 5075/72
Course Slope/Rating (All Tees): Back 141/75.4, Blue 131/71.8, White 124/69.8, Forward 121/68.8
Course Architect: Arthur Hills (1979)
Golf Facilities: Full Pro Shop X, Snack Bar X, Lounge Beer, Wine, Restaurant No, Locker Room X, Showers X, Club Rental X, Club Repair X, Cart Rental X, Instruction X, Practice Green X, Driving Range X, Practice Bunker X, Club Storage No
Tee-Time Reservation Policy: Up to 7 days in advance
Ranger: Yes
Tee-off-Interval Time: 8 min.
Time to Play 18 Holes: 4½ hrs.
Course Hours/Earliest Tee-off: 7 a.m.

Green Fees: $49 for 18 holes Fri., Sat., Sun., holidays; $39 for 18 holes weekdays
Cart Fees: $11 for 18 holes per person
Credit Cards: American Express, Master-Card, Visa
Season: Mar. through Dec. Busiest June through Labor Day
Course Comments: Walking allowed after 5 p.m. Yardage book
Golf Packages: Inquire at pro shop
Discounts: Twilight, junior
Places to Stay Nearby: LEBANON: Best Western Heritage Inn (513) 932–4111, (800) 528–1234; Golden Lamb Inn (513) 932–5065; Shaker Inn (513) 932–7575. MIDDLETOWN: The Manchester Inn and Conference Center (513) 422–5481; Holiday Inn (513) 424–1201, (800) HOLIDAY
Local Attractions: LEBANON: Warren County Museum, Fort Ancient, Glendower State Memorial, The Golden Lamb Inn-Shaker Museum, seasonal festivals. MIDDLETOWN: Americana Amusement Park. Dayton. Cincinnati. Warren County Convention and Visitors Bureau, 777 Columbus Ave., Lebanon, OH 45036 (513) 933–1138, (800) 433–1072 (OH)
Directions: From Rte. 63 take Hwy. 741 north to Union. Take a left on Union north to Green Tree. Turn left on Green Tree to golf course
Closest Commercial Airports: Dayton (30 min.); Greater Cincinnati International (45 min.)

SHAKER RUN GOLF CLUB

Shaker Run is a shotmaker's course with a variety of elevation changes, moderately sloping bentgrass greens, more than forty sand and waste bunkers, and water in the form of lakes and streams on nine holes. The course begins with a long, open 567-yard par 5 that is dotted with seven bunkers. The approach is to a deep green with a large bunker to its front left, another to its right, and a third to its rear. The course then winds through woodlands and emerges as a more open links-style layout beginning with the eighth hole. The 435-yard par-4 ninth provides a superb finish to the front side. The hole is bordered on the right by water. The tee shot from the back tees plays over water and the approach must carry the stream that cuts back in front of the green from the right side. There is a bunker to the right of this target and more water farther right.

Shaker Run is near the Shaker community of New Lebanon, approximately mid-way between Dayton and Cincinnati. The course was designed by Arthur Hills in the late 1970s when it was owned by the Armco Steel Company. A private partnership recently acquired the club which has private memberships. Shaker Run has a difficult slope of 141 and a rating of 75.4 from the back tees. It is ranked among the best courses in Ohio by *Golf Digest*.

Course Name: THE VINEYARD

Course Type: Public
Address: 600 Nordyke Road
Cincinnati, OH 45230
Phone: (513) 474–3007 (Golf Course)
(513) 521–7275 (Sweetwine Lodge)

GOLF COURSE

Head Professional: Steve Danker
Course Length/Par (All Tees): Back 6789/71, Middle 6254/71, Forward 4747/71
Course Slope/Rating (All Tees): Back 129/73.0, Middle 124/70.6, Forward 113/65.7
Course Architects: Jack Kidwell and Michael Hurdzan (1986)
Golf Facilities: Full Pro Shop X, Snack Bar X, Lounge X, Restaurant X, Locker Room No, Showers No, Club Rental X, Club Repair X, Cart Rental X, Instruction X, Practice Green X, Driving Range No, Practice Bunker No, Club Storage No
Tee-Time Reservation Policy: Up to 5 days in advance (513) 474–3007
Ranger: Yes
Tee-off-Interval Time: 10 min.
Time to Play 18 Holes: 4½ hrs.
Course Hours/Earliest Tee-off: 7:10 a.m. to dark. Last tee-off for 18 holes, 4½

hrs. before sunset; last tee-off for 9 holes 2 hrs. before sunset
Green Fees: $23 for 18 holes, $13.50 for 9 holes
Cart Fees: $10.50 per person
Credit Cards: Cash or check for golf fees. MasterCard, Visa for merchandise
Season: Mid-March to mid-Nov. Busiest season May to Sept.
Course Comments: Can walk anytime. Yardage book available. No outings Sat., Sun. or holidays. Weekend and holiday 18-hole reservations require foursomes
Golf Packages: Available
Discounts: Seniors, juniors
Places to Stay Nearby: Days Inn Cincinnati East (513) 528–3800, (800) 325–2525; Holiday Inn—Queensgate (513) 241–8660, (800) HOLIDAY; Garfield House Suite Hotel (513) 421–3555; Omni Netherland Plaza (513) 621–7700, THE–OMNI; Hyatt Regency Cincinnati (513) 579–1234, (800) 233–1234; Westin Hotel Cincinnati (513) 621–7700 (800) 228–3000; Cincinnatian Hotel (513) 381–3000, (800) 942–9000
Local Attractions: Cincinnati Art Museum, Cincinnati Fire Museum, Cincinnati Historical Society Museum, Cincinnati Nature Center, Cincinnati Zoo and Botanical Garden, Contemporary Arts Center, Kings Island (Kings Mills), St. Peter in Chains Cathedral, Surf Cincinnati Water Park, Taft Museum, William Howard Taft national historic site, Ohio River cruises; professional baseball, football at Riverfront Stadium; Sharon Woods Village (Sharonville), restaurants, theater, concerts, University of Cincinnati; recreational activities including hiking, tennis in Cincinnati's parks; boating, fishing. KENTUCKY: Horse racing at Turfway Park Race Track, River Downs Race Track. Cincinnati Convention and Visitors Bureau (513) 621–2142, (800) 344–3445. Clermont County Convention and Visitors Bureau (513) 753–7211. Warren County Convention and Visitors Bureau (800) 433–1072
Directions: From the north: I–275 to exit 65, Rte. 125, turn right and go west on Rte. 125 (Beechmont Ave.), 4 traffic

lights to Nordyke Rd., left to golf course (1¼ mi.). From downtown Cincinnati: I–471 to I–275 east to Ohio. Take 2nd exit across bridge (exit 71), take Hwy. 52 to New Richmond, exit left at Nine Mile Rd. Go 1 mile, turn left at Nordyke Rd. to golf course

Closest Commercial Airport: Greater Cincinnati International (25 min.)

THE VINEYARD

The Vineyard is a 6789-yard par-71 municipal golf course that is part of the excellent Hamilton County Park District. The district has a network of 6 municipal golf courses, and the Vineyard, which was designed by Jack Kidwell and Michael Hurdzan and opened in 1986, is the newest facility in the parks system. When you drive up to the Sweetwine Lodge clubhouse, you get the impression that you are at a country club. There is a bag drop, and inside the clubhouse is an excellent pro shop that was one of only 20 municipal shops selected for *Golf Shop Operations* magazine's America's 100 best golf shops in a recent poll. There is a restaurant here which serves breakfast and lunch and there are facilities for receptions, parties, business meetings and golf outings.

The golf course itself is in excellent condition, with rolling, well-treed, bentgrass fairways and well-maintained, medium-sized, moderately fast, undulating bentgrass greens. Most of these putting areas are well guarded by sand traps and small lakes. There are 45 white-sand bunkers on the Vineyard course, and three lakes affect play on six holes. The combination of mature trees, rolling fairways, tricky greens, and well-placed bunkers and water hazards make this an interesting and challenging golf course. *Golf Digest* selected the Vineyard as runner-up for the best new public golf course for 1987, and it is now ranked among the top 75 public golf courses in America by that publication.

The golf course is relatively easy at the beginning, but the difficulty builds, especially on the back nine. The most difficult par 4 on the front nine is the 451-yard ninth, which plays from an elevated tee to a landing area with trees and a large bunker to the left. The approach shot is to a large green protected by traps to the left and right. The most difficult par 5 on this side is the 558-yard eighth hole, which is well treed and plays uphill to a green protected by traps on the left and right.

When one talks about the Vineyard with Steve Danker, the head professional, you get a sense that exceptional attention is paid to detail at the golf course, especially those details that meet a golfer's (i.e., customer's) needs. For example, the tee master (i.e., starter) explains the golf course to the golfer before he or she sets out. Courtesy umbrellas are provided to golfers if it rains unexpectedly. Ten-minute intervals are allowed between foursomes to provide a relaxed golfing atmosphere, yet play coordinators (i.e. marshals or rangers) expedite play in a friendly way. Carts are required to stay on paths to ensure quality course maintenance, and the earliest tee-off time is 7:10 a.m., to allow the course to be properly prepared for play. The yardage book at the Vineyard is one of the best I've seen on a municipal course or elsewhere. Numerous distances and points of reference, such as traps and trees, are noted, and pro tips cover hazards, terrain considerations and shot positioning recommendations, including shots to avoid. Education and service are the themes here, creating a very positive golfing ambience.

The back nine starts with a tough, narrow 536-yard par-5 dogleg left that is treed from tee to green. Out of bounds is on the left, and a creek is on the right. After hitting a tee shot to a landing area protected by a trap on the right, the next shot is uphill toward a green that is surrounded by mounds and guarded by a huge bunker on the right. Approximately 50 yards in front of the green the fairway is straddled by two large bunkers in addition to the trees and stream.

Holes twelve through fourteen are excellent holes, including the beautiful and difficult 215-yard par-3 thirteenth, which plays over a small pond to a deep tiered green protected by traps to the left and right. Out of bounds is on the left. The wind generally flows from right to left and can knock down some tee shots. Shots in the traps or to the right side of the green are difficult to recover from.

The 422-yard par-4 eighteenth is a beautiful, dramatic finishing hole. The fairway slopes downhill from left to right off the tee. Out of bounds is on the left, and a creek is on the right. The fairway lie on the second shot will be either downhill or side-hill. The entire hole is well-treed from tee to a green with traps protecting both sides. Recovery shots around the green are very difficult. This is rated the number-1-handicap hole on the course.

Practice facilities at the Vineyard are limited even though the Vineyard is on 145 total acres. This is because the Hamilton County Parks District, whose theme is "space for all species," puts some restrictions on land use. Clinics and individual instruction are given, however. Free junior clinics are given at the 6 county courses and the Inreach Program, which promotes golf among inner-city youngsters, is considered a model program to make golf more economical and accessible. In its literature, Hamilton County clearly states:

If anyone believes he or she has been subjected to discrimination on the basis of race, color, or national origin, he or she may file a complaint alleging discrimination with the Hamilton County Park District or Office of Equal Opportunity, U.S. Department of Interior, Washington, DC.

Recommended Golf Courses in Ohio

Akron Area:

Chippewa Golf Club, Doylestown, (216) 658–6126, (800) 321–1701, Public, 18/6273/71

Fox Den Golf Club, Stow, (216) 673–3443, Public, 18/6468/72

Hawk's Nest Golf Club, Creston, (216) 435–4611, Public, 18/6670/72

J.E. Good Park Golf Club, Akron, (216) 864–0020, Public, 18/6663/71

Raintree County Golf Club, Uniontown, (216) 699–3232, (800) 371–0017, Semiprivate, 18/6881/72

Belpre:

Oxbow Golf Course and Country Club, Belpre, (614) 423–6771, Semiprivate, 18/6733/71

Canton Area:

Skyland Pines Golf Club, Canton, (216) 454–5131, Semiprivate, 18/6467/72:

Tam O'Shanter, Canton, (216) 478–6501, (800) 462–9964, Public. Dales: 18/6569/70. Hills: 18/6385/70

Zoar Village Golf Club, Zoar, (216) 874–4653, Public, 18/6535/72

Within 1 Hour of Cincinnati:

Glenview Golf Course, Cincinnati, (513) 771–1747, Public, 18/6718/72

The Golf Center at Kings Island, (513) 398–7770, Resort. Grizzly: 18/6731/71. Bruin: 18/3428/61

Hueston Woods State Park Golf Course, Oxford, (513) 523–8081, (800) 282–7245, Public, 18/7005/72

Miami Whitewater Forest Golf Course, Harrison, (513) 367–4627, Public, 18/6780/72

Sharon Woods Golf Course, Cincinnati, (513) 769–4325, Public, 18/6652/70

Weatherwax Golf Course, Middleton, (513) 425–7886, Public. Valleyview/Highlands: 18/6756/72. Woodside/Meadows: 18/7174/72

Within 1 Hour of Cleveland:

Chardon Lakes Golf Club, Chardon, (216) 285–4653, Public, 18/6789/71

Fowler's Mill Golf Club, Chesterland, (216) 729–7569, Public. Blue/White: 18/7002/72. White/Red: 18/6385/72. Blue/Red: 18/6595/72

Hemlock Springs Golf Club, Geneva, (216) 466–4044, (800) 436–5625, Public, 18/6812/72

Hilliard Lakes Golf Club, Westlake, (216) 871–9578, Public, 18/6680/72

Hinckley Hills Golf Course, Hinckley, (216) 278–4861, Public, 18/6704/73

Ironwood Golf Course, Hinckley, (216) 278–7171, Semiprivate,18/6360/71

Manakiki Golf Club, Willoughby, (216) 942–2500, Public, 18/6302/72

Orchard Hills Golf and Country Club, Chesterland, (216) 729–1963, Semiprivate, 18/6409/72

Pine Hills Golf Club, Hinckley, (216) 225–4477, Public, 18/6482/72

Punderson State Park Golf Course, Newbury, (216) 546–5465, Public, 18/6600/72

Quail Hollow Resort, Concord, (216) 352–6201, (800) 792–0258, Resort, 18/6712/72

Sleepy Hollow Golf Course, Brecksville, (216) 526–4285, Public, 18/6335/71

Windmill Lakes Golf Club, Ravenna, (216) 297–0440, 18/6936/70

Within 1 Hour of Columbus:

Apple Valley Golf Club, Howard, (614) 397–7664, (800) 359–7664, Public, 18/6946/72

Bent Tree Golf Club, Sunbury, (614) 965–5140, Public, 18/6805/72

Blacklick Woods Golf Course, Reynoldsbury, (614) 861–3193, Public, 18/7069/72

Champions Golf Course, Columbus, (614) 645–7111, Public, 18/6555/70

Darby Creek Golf Course, Marysville, (513) 349–7491, (800) 343–2729, Public, 18/7054/72

Foxfire Golf Club, Lockbourne, (614) 224–3694, Public, 18/6891/72

Granville Golf Course, Granville, (614) 587–4653, Public, 18/6612/71

Indian Springs Golf Club, Mechanicsburg, (513) 834–2111, (800) 752–7846, Public, 18/7138/72

Royal American Links, Galena, (614) 965–1215, Semiprivate, 18/6809/72

Whetstone Golf Club, Caledonia, (614) 389–4343, Public, 18/6600/72

Dayton Area:

Cassel Hills Golf Club, Vandalia, (513) 890–1300, Public, 18/6540/71

Heatherwode Golf Club, Springboro, (513) 748–3222, Public, 18/6730/71

Pipestone Golf Club, Miamisburg, (513) 866–4653, Public, 18/6939/72

The Golf Club at Yankee Trace, Centerville, (513) 438–4653, Public, 18/7139/72

Lima Area:

Bellefontaine Country Club, Bellefontaine, (513) 592–4653, Semiprivate, 18/5824/70

Country Acres Golf Club, Ottawa, (419) 532–3434, Semiprivate, 18/6464/72

Hawthorne Hills Golf Club, Lima, (419) 221–1891, Semiprivate, 18/6710/72

Shelby Oaks Golf Club, Sidney, (513) 492–2883, Public. South/West: 18/6651/72. West/North: 18/6650/72. North/South: 18/6561/72

Mansfield Area:

Pebble Creek Golf Club, Lexington, (419) 884–3434, Public, 18/6554/72

Portsmouth Area:

Shawnee State Park Golf Resort, Friendship, (614) 858–6681, Public, 18/6837/71

Sandusky Area:

Green Hills Golf Club, Clyde, (419) 547–7947, Public, 18/6172/71

Sawmill Creek Golf and Racquet Club, Huron, (419) 433–3789, Resort, 18/6813/71

Thunderbird Hills Golf Club, Huron, (419) 433–4552, Public. North: 18/6464/72. South: 18/6587/72

Toledo Area:

Detwiler Golf Course, Toledo, (419) 726–9353, Public, 18/6756/71

Ironwood Golf Club, Wauseon,
(419) 335–0587, Semiprivate, 18/6965/72

Maumee Bay State Park Golf Course, Oregon, (419) 836–9009, Public, 18/6941/72

Riverby Hills Golf Course, Bowling Green,
(419) 878–5941, Semiprivate, 18/6856/72

Valleywood Golf Club, Swanton,
(419) 826–3991, Semiprivate, 18/6364/71

Warren/Youngstown Area:

Beaver Creek Meadows Golf Course,
Lisbon, (216) 385–3020, Public, 18/6500/71

Hubbard Golf Course, Hubbard,
(216) 534–9026, 18/6122/71

Mill Creek Park Golf Course, Boardman,
(216) 758–7926, Public. North:
18/6412/70. South: 18/6511/70

Salem Hills Golf and Country Club, Salem,
(216) 337–8033, Semiprivate, 18/7146/72

Sugarbush Golf Course, Garretsville,
(216) 527–4202, Public, 18/6854/72

Yankee Run Golf Course, Brookfield,
(216) 448–8096, (800) 446–5346, Public,
18/6501/70

West Lafayette:

River Greens Golf Course, West Lafayette,
(614) 545–7817, Public, 18/6588/72

Wooster Area:

Mohican Hills Golf Club, Jeromesville,
(419) 368–3303, Public, 18/6536/72

Zanesville Area:

Salt Fork State Park Golf Course, Lore
City, (614) 432–7185, (800) 282–7275,
Public, 18/6056/71

Ohio: Useful Information

Ohio Department of Development, Division
of Travel and Tourism, Box 1001, Columbus,
OH 43266–0101, (800) BUCKEYE

Division of Parks and Recreation, Department of Natural Resources, Fountain
Square, Bldg. C, Columbus, OH 43224–
0377, (614) 265–7000 (recreation
information)

Division of Wildlife, Department of Natural
Resources, Fountain Square, Bldg. G, Columbus, OH 43224–0377, (614) 265–6300 (fishing and hunting regulations)

National Forest Information, Eastern
Region Public Affairs Office, 310 W.
Wisconsin Ave., Milwaukee, WI 53203,
(414) 291–3693, (800) 280–CAMP
(information and reservations)

Ohio Campground Owners Association,
3386 Snouffer Rd., Ste. B, Columbus, OH
43235, (614) 764–0279 (privately owned
campgrounds)

Course Name: PAGE BELCHER GOLF COURSE
Stone Creek,
Olde Page Courses

Course Type: Public
Address: 6666 South Union Avenue
Tulsa, OK 74132
Phone: (918) 446–1529

GOLF COURSE

Head Professional: George Glenn
Course Length/Par (All Tees): Stone Creek: Back 6827/71, White 6338/71, Yellow 5905/71, Forward 5532/71. Olde Page: Back 6826/71, White 6338/71, Yellow 5905/71, Forward 5532/71
Course Slope/Rating (All Tees): Stone Creek: Back 121/72, White 116/69.7, Ladies' Yellow 109/73.7, Ladies' Forward 118/71.5. Olde Page: Back 121/72, White 116/69.7, Yellow 109/67.8, Ladies' Yellow 109/73.7, Ladies' Forward 118/71.5
Course Architects: Stone Creek: Don Sechrest (1987). Olde Page: Leon Howard (1977)
Golf Facilities: Full Pro Shop X, Snack Bar X, Lounge No, Restaurant No, Locker Room No, Showers No, Club Rental X, Club Repair X, Cart Rental X, Instruction X, Practice Green X, Driving Range X, Practice Bunker X, Club Storage No
Tee-Time Reservation Policy: 1 wk. in advance through computerized service (918) 582–6000. $2 surcharge for reservations made through computer system
Ranger: Yes
Tee-off-Interval Time: 8 min.
Time to Play 18 Holes: 4½ hrs.
Course Hours/Earliest Tee-off: 6 a.m. to dark
Green Fees: $15 for 18 holes Fri., Sat., Sun., holidays, $13 for 18 holes Mon.-Thurs.
Cart Fees: $9 for 18 holes per person
Pull Carts: $3.82 with $2 refund for 18 holes
Credit Cards: Cash or local check for golf fees. MasterCard, Visa for merchandise

Season: Year round. Busiest season April to Oct.
Course Comments: Can walk anytime. Yardage book available
Golf Packages: None
Discounts: Twilight, juniors, seniors
Places to Stay Nearby: See page 537
Local Attractions: See page538. Metropolitan Tulsa Chamber of Commerce (918) 585–1201
Directions: From I–244 and I–75: I–75 north, exit 61st St., right to Union Ave., left to golf course
Closest Commercial Airport: Tulsa International (10 min.)

PAGE BELCHER GOLF COURSE

The eighteen-hole, 6826-yard Olde Page course was designed and completed by Texas-born Leon Howard in 1977. After graduating from Texas A&M with bachelor's and master's degrees in agronomy, Howard formed a Texas-based landscape architecture firm and concentrated on golf courses. Howard designed and built his first golf course in 1958. Since then he has designed many golf courses in Texas and other parts of the United States, including the Woodhaven Country Club in Fort Worth, Texas; the Trails Golf Club in Moore, Oklahoma; and the Red Apple Inn Golf Course (9 holes) in Heber Springs, Arkansas. The Olde Page golf course hosted the U.S. Women's Public Links in 1988.

The Olde Page Course has large, fast, undulating bentgrass greens with water hazards on half the holes. The course is fairly open, with rolling fairways. The number-1-handicap hole is the 400-yard par-4 fourth hole. The tee shot must be straight to avoid water and trees protecting the tee-shot landing area. A stream cuts the fairway and can be reached on the first shot. The approach shot is to a large green protected by a bunker to the right front. The finishing hole on the course is a 426-yard par-4 dogleg right that is well treed from tee to green. The approach shot is slightly uphill to a large undulating green that usually takes at least one more club than you'd think to get near the pin.

The Stone Creek Course, a tighter layout than Olde Page, was designed by Don Sechrest and opened in 1987. Sechrest is a native of Missouri; a graduate of Oklahoma State, where he played on the golf team; and a former PGA tour player. He started his own golf-course design firm in Tulsa in 1968 and has designed the Shangri-La Country Club (Blue and Gold courses) in Afton, Oklahoma; the Loma Linda Country Club Golf Course in Joplin, Missouri; and the Ames Golf Course and Country Club in Iowa, among others. Stone Creek was runner-up for *Golf Digest*'s best new public golf course in 1988.

The greens at Stone Creek are smaller than Olde Page, and moderately fast and undulating. The course has a variety of long and short par 3s and 4s, and the par 5s average around 500 yards. Accuracy, strategy and club selection are demanded by this layout. A good run of holes begins with the 411-yard par-4 sixth, which is a slight dogleg right. The tee shot must be left-center to avoid being stymied by trees on the approach shot. The second shot is to a narrow, deep green with a trap on the left.

The par-4 seventh is the number-1-handicap hole, and plays 446 yards straight to a deep, heavily undulating green with a bunker on the left and a sharp drop-off to the right. The 215-yard par-3 eighth plays to a large green flanked by bunkers and with a sharp drop-off to the right. The finishing hole is a long par 4 that plays 458 yards to a deep, three-tiered green with three traps to the rear and another to the right front.

Wind can be a factor on both these courses. In summer the prevailing wind is from the south, which provides a tail wind on the final hole but crosswinds and head winds on several others.

A driving range, 4 practice greens, a sand bunker and instruction are available at Page Belcher. You can walk anytime, and green fees are very modest considering the quality of the courses. Several group tournaments are held at this venerable and active municipal facility.

Course Name: FOREST RIDGE GOLF CLUB

Course Type: Public
Address: 7501 E. Kenosha
Broken Arrow, OK 74014
Phone: (918) 357–2282, (918) 357–2443 (Tee times)
Fax: (918) 357–2804

GOLF COURSE

Head Professional: Sam Merideth
Course Length/Par (All Tees): Back 7069/72, Gold 6834/72, Blue 6436/72, White 5914/72, Forward 5341/72
Course Slope/Rating (All Tees): Back 134/74, Gold 132/72.9, Blue 126/71.1, White 119/68.4, Ladies' Forward 112/70.54
Course Architect: Randy Heckenkemper
Golf Facilities: Full Pro Shop X, Snack Bar X, Lounge X, Restaurant X, Locker Room X, Showers X, Club Rental X, Club Repair X, Cart Rental X, Instruction X, Practice Green X, Driving Range X, Practice Bunker No, Club Storage Limited
Tee-Time Reservation Policy: Up to 4 days in advance for public. Up to 1 week in advance for player cardholders
Ranger: Yes
Tee-off-Interval Time: 10 min.
Time to Play 18 Holes: 4 hrs. 15 min.
Course Hours/Earliest Tee-off: 7:30 a.m.
Green and Cart Fees: $60 for 18 holes Fri., Sat., Sun., holidays; $50 for 18 holes weekdays
Credit Cards: All major cards
Season: Year round. June busiest month
Course Comments: Walking allowed at full golf fee
Golf Packages: Inquire at pro shop
Discounts: Frequent golfer players card. Twilight
Places to Stay Nearby: BROKEN ARROW: Econolodge (918) 258–6617, (800) 446–6900; Holiday Inn-South (918) 258–7085, (800) HOLIDAY; Stratford House Inn (918) 258–7556. TULSA: Doubletree Hotel at Warren Place (918) 495–1000, (800) 222–TREE; Radisson Inn Tulsa Airport (918) 835–9911, (800) 333–3333; Residence Inn by Marriott (918)

664–7241, (800) 333–3131; Tulsa Marriott (918) 627–5000, (800) 228–9290

Local Attractions: TULSA: Bell's Amusement Park, Big Splash Water Park, Boston Avenue Methodist Church, Fenster Museum of Jewish Art, Oral Roberts University, Oxley Nature Center, Philbrook Museum of Art, Thomas Gilcrease Museum, Tulsa Historical Society, Tulsa Zoo and Living Museum, fishing, boating, Tulsa Drillers professional baseball, Tulsa Oilers professional hockey, University of Tulsa, restaurants, arts, entertainment, seasonal festivals including the Tulsa State Fair. Tulsa Metro Chamber of Commerce, 616 S. Boston St., Tulsa, OK (918) 585-1201

Directions: From Tulsa (30 min. southeast): Take Hwy. 51 east to Broken Arrow/71st St. Exit. Turn left on 71st and proceed 4½ mi. to golf course at Kenosha

Closest Commercial Airports: Tulsa International (20 min.); Oklahoma City Will Rogers World Airport (2½ hrs.)

FOREST RIDGE GOLF CLUB

Forest Ridge is a links-style golf course with mounds of native vegetation bordering its rolling Bermuda grass fairways. Any ball that is strayed into this local scrub vegetation will be likely unplayable or lost. The bentgrass greens are large, fast, mildly undulating, and are among the best in Oklahoma. Variable winds can greatly affect play at Forest Ridge. For example, the incoming prevailing southerly wind often makes the 402-yard par-4 second play much longer. The course is wooded on holes No. 2 through No. 5 and Nos. 16 through 18, with native grasses and scrub providing a transition zone between the fairway and the trees. The signature hole on this golf course is the 431-yard par-4 sixteenth whose tee shot must carry a ravine, but stop short of a second precipice that winds back across the fairway. The approach is to a severely forward-sloping, deep, two-tiered green with a large bunker to its left with trees and grass swales to its right. Forest Ridge has generous landing areas but requires accuracy to its greens in order to score. This venue is the first effort of Randy Heckenkemper, a graduate of Oklahoma State who worked with Jack Nicklaus, Jay Morrish, and Tom Weiskopf before starting out on his own.

Forest Ridge is the centerpiece of a 750-acre planned residential golf community in the suburbs of Tulsa. It provides a private club atmosphere including excellent practice facilities with a 350-yard driving range with four target greens. Overlooking the course is the clubhouse that includes Cafe Savannah's, a main dining room that seats 80 people, The Glass Veranda meeting and banquet room, The Player's Grill, locker rooms and showers, and modern pro shop. The separate Forest Ridge Swim and Tennis Club has a large swimming pool, four tennis courts, and other amenities. Forest Ridge offers a variety of membership plans or you may pay per play. The course is verdant green year round due to a rye grass overseeding program during the winter months.

Course Name: KARSTEN CREEK GOLF COURSE

Course Type: Semiprivate
Address: Route 5/P.O. 159
               Stillwater, OK 74074
Phone: (405) 743–1658
Fax: (405) 743–8436

GOLF COURSE

Director of Golf: Mike Holder

Head Professional: Tom Jones

Course Length/Par (All Tees): Back 7095/72, Black 6597/72, White 6039/72, Red 5747/72, Forward 4906/72

Course Slope/Rating (All Tees): Back 142/74.8, Black 135/71.9, White 124/69.4, Ladies' White 143/77, Red 140/75.3, Forward 127/70.1

Course Architect: Tom Fazio (1994)

Golf Facilities: Full Pro Shop X, Snack Bar X, Lounge X, Restaurant X, Locker Room No, Showers No, Club Rental X, Club Repair No, Cart Rental X, Instruction X, Practice Green X, Driving Range X, Practice Bunker X, Club Storage No

Tee-Time Reservation Policy: Up to 2 days in advance
Ranger: Yes
Tee-off-Interval Time: 10 min.
Time to Play 18 Holes: 4½ hrs.
Course Hours/Earliest Tee-off: 8 a.m. Fri., Sat., Sun., holidays; 11 a.m. Tues., 9:00 otherwise
Green and Cart Fees: $125 for 18 holes, $60 for 18 holes if guest of member
Credit Cards: All major cards except Discover
Season: Year round. Busiest May through Labor Day
Course Comments: Walking allowed anytime at full golf fee
Golf Packages: Inquire at pro shop
Discounts: No
Places to Stay Nearby: Best Western Stillwater (405) 377–7010, (800) 528–1234; Days Inn (405) 743–2570, (800) 329–7466; Holiday Inn (405) 372–0800, (800) HOLIDAY
Local Attractions: National Wrestling Hall of Fame, Sheerar Cultural and Heritage Center Museum, Gardiner Art Gallery, Oklahoma State University, Oklahoma Museum of Higher Education, seasonal festivals. Oklahoma City. Tulsa. Stillwater Chamber of Commerce (405) 372–5573
Directions: From Stillwater: 6 miles west on Hwy. 51
Closest Commercial Airports: Oklahoma City Will Rogers World Airport (1 hr.); Tulsa International (1 hr.)

KARSTEN CREEK GOLF COURSE

Karsten Creek is a highly acclaimed new Tom Fazio design on 230 acres of treelined terrain within a 1100-acre low density real estate development adjacent to Oklahoma State University in Stillwater. There are only 40 bunkers at Karsten Creek, but strayed balls will cost you strokes should they land in native grass rough or near trees. The wind is another factor to consider. For example, the 428-yard par-4 second, the number-one-handicap hole, plays into the wind as do several other holes at Karsten Creek. The tee shot on No. 2 plays straight down a treelined

fairway and the approach is to an ample bent grass green backed by a bunker with a stunning red rock outcropping. The greens at Karsten Creek are level with the fairway and can be reached with bump and run shots. If you miss the target, it is possible to get up and down because there are no severe bunkers, mounds, or abrupt dropoffs from the putting surface.

The most difficult hole on the back nine is the 464-yard par-4 seventeenth which usually plays into the wind. The tee shot must carry the edge of Lake Louise, a 110-acre beauty that sits below the clubhouse and comes into play on the two finishing holes. The second shot will find the lake if it is pulled too far to the left of No. 17 green, a narrow, deep target.

The practice area at Karsten Creek is exceptional. It covers approximately 40 acres and comprises three sectors: a double-ended practice range with targets; a team range where college golfers and Tour players can hit their own balls; and a short game area with one Bermuda green and a bentgrass green. The clubhouse is a temporary facility with a 1500 square foot pro shop. A permanent clubhouse will go under construction in 1996. Karsten Creek, rated one of the best courses in Oklahoma by *Golf Digest*, should be added to your itinerary.

Recommended Golf Courses in Oklahoma

Ardmore Area:

Falconhead Ranch and Country Club, Burneyville, (405) 276–9824, Semiprivate, 18/6400/72

Lakeview Golf Course, Ardmore, (405) 223–4260, 18/6881/71

Guymon:

Sunset Hills Golf Course, Guymon, (405) 338–7404, Public, 18/6732/71

Within 1 Hour of Oklahoma City:

Cedar Valley Golf Club, Guthrie, (405) 282–4800, Public. Augusta: 18/6602/70. International: 18/6520/70

Cimarron National Golf Club, Guthrie, (405) 282–7888, Public. Aqua Canyon: 18/6515/70. Cimarron: 18/6653/70

Coffee Creek Golf Course, Edmond, (405) 340–4653, Public, 18/6700/70

Earlywine Park Golf Course, Oklahoma City, (405) 691–1727, Public. North: 18/6721/72. South: 18/6728/71

The Golf Course at Cimarron Trails, Perkins, (405) 547–5701, Public, 18/6959/72

John Conrad Regional Golf Course, Midwest City, (405) 732–2209, 18/6854/72

Kicking Bird Golf Course, Edmond, (405) 341–5350, Public, 18/6816/71

Lake Hefner Golf Club, Oklahoma City, (405) 843–1565, Public. North: 18/6970/72. South: 18/6305/70

Silverhorn Golf Club, Oklahoma City, (405) 752–1181, Semiprivate, 18/6758/71

Ponca City:

Lew Wentz Memorial Golf Course, Ponca City, (405) 767–0433, Public, 18/6400/71

Within 1 Hour of Tulsa:

Bailey Golf Ranch, Owasso, (918) 272–9339, Public, 18/6753/72

Heritage Hills Golf Course, Claremore, (918) 341–0055, Public, 18/6760/71

Sapulpa Municipal Golf Course, Sapulpa, (918) 224–0237. Public, 18/6523/70

White Hawk Golf Club, Bixby, (918) 366–4653, Semiprivate, 18/6982/72

Shangri-La Golf Resort, Afton, (918) 257–4204, (800) 331–4060, Resort. Blue: 18/7012/72. Gold: 18/5932/72

South Lakes Golf Course, Jenks, (918) 299–0177, Public, 18/6340/71

Woodward:

Boiling Springs Golf Club, Woodward, (405) 256–1206, Public, 18/6454/71

Oklahoma: Useful Information

Oklahoma Tourism and Recreation Department, 500 Will Rogers Bldg., Oklahoma City, OK 73105, (405) 521–2409, (800) 652–OKLA

Oklahoma Historical Society, 2100 North Lincoln Blvd., Oklahoma City, OK 73105, (405) 521–2491

Department of Wildlife Conservation, 1801 North Lincoln Blvd., Oklahoma City, OK 73105: (405) 521–3851 (hunting and fishing information); tourist reservations for Oklahoma state resorts and cabins; (405) 521–2464, (800) 654–8240

Course Name: SUNRIVER RESORT
GOLF COURSE
Crosswater,
North Woodlands,
South Meadow Courses

Course Type: Resort
Resort: Sunriver Lodge and Resort
Address: Center Drive/P.O. Box 3609
Sunriver, OR 97707
Phone: (503) 593–1221 (Golf Course),
(800) 962–1769 (Tee Times),
(800) 547–3922 (Resort),
(800) 962–1770 (Conference
Sales)
Fax: (503) 593–5458 (Resort)

GOLF COURSE

Director of Golf: Dick Schmidt
Head Professionals: Crosswater: Bradley
Myrick. North Woodlands: Brad
Bedortha. South Meadows: Lyndon
Blackwell
Course Length/Par (All Tees): Crosswater:
Back 7693/72, Silver 7305/72, Blue
6842/72, White 6286/72, Forward
5389/72. North Woodlands: Back
6880/72, Middle 6274/72, Ladies'
Middle 5933/72, Ladies' Forward
5446/72. South Meadows: Back 6960/72,
Middle 6522/72, Ladies' Middle 6386/72,
Ladies' Forward 5847/72
Course Slope/Rating (All Tees): Crosswater:
Back 150/77.0, Silver 144/74.8, Blue
134/72.6, White 128/69.8, Ladies'
Forward 125/70.9, Ladies' Middle
137/75.6. North Woodlands: Back
131/73.0, Middle 125/70.2, Ladies'
Middle 122/73.0, Ladies' Forward
118/70.3. South Meadows: Back
130/72.9, Middle 125/70.8, Ladies'
Middle 123/74.8, Ladies' Forward
116/71.7
Course Architects: Crosswater: Robert
Cupp and John Fought (1995). North:
Robert Trent Jones, Jr., and Don Knott
(1981). South: Fred Federspiel (1968)
Golf Facilities: Full Pro Shop X, Snack
Bar X, Lounge X, Restaurant X,
Locker Room No, Showers No, Club
Rental X, Club Repair X, Cart Rental
X, Instruction X, Practice Green X,
Driving Range X, Practice Bunker X,
Club Storage X
Tee-Time Reservation Policy: Resort
guests: At time of reservation. Outside
play: Up to 30 days in advance with
credit card guarantee
Ranger: Yes
Tee-off-Interval Time: 9 min.
Time to Play 18 Holes: 4½ hrs.
Course Hours/Earliest Tee-off: 6:30 a.m.
Green Fees: Crosswater: $95 for 18 holes
including cart. North Woodlands: Resort
guests: $49 for 18 holes. Outside play:
$59 for 18 holes. South Meadows:
Resort guests: $39 for 18 holes.
Outside play: $49 for 18 holes
Cart Fees: Crosswater: Cart included in
green fee. North Woodlands, South
Meadows $25 for 18 holes per cart
Pull Carts: Available
Credit Cards: All major cards
Season: April through Oct.
Course Comments: Can walk anytime.
Yardage book available for North
Course. Golf Digest golf school on site
Golf Packages: Available through lodge ·
Discounts: Junior with adult before 3 p.m.
on South Course, seniors, resort guests
Places to Stay Nearby: BEND: River
House (800) 452–6878 (OR), (800)
547–3928 (outside OR); Red Lion
Hotel (800) 547–8010; Inn of the Sev-
enth Mountain Resort (503) 382–8711,
(800) 452–6810; Riverhouse Convention
Center (503) 389–3111, (800) 452–
6878; Best Western Entrada Lodge
(503) 382–4080, (800) 528–1234. RED-
MOND: Inn of Eagle Crest (503) 923–
2453, (800) 682–4786
Local Attractions: BEND AREA: Horseback
riding, camping, fishing, hiking, boating, rock climbing, bicycling, white-
water rafting, winter sports, Oregon
High Desert Museum, Lava Cave,
Newberry Crater National Monument,
Smith Rock State Park, Pechutes Brewery and Public House, Mt. Bachelor,
Mt. Hood. Bend Chamber of Commerce (503) 382–3221. Mt. Hood
Information Center (503) 622–4822

Directions: From Bend (15 mi.): Hwy. 97 south, exit Sunriver turnoff, Spring River Rd. (1 mile), follow signs to golf course

Closest Commercial Airports: Redmond Airport, Bend (25 min.); Mahlon Sweet, Eugene (3 hrs.); Portland International (3½ hrs.)

RESORT

Date Built: 1968

No. of Rooms: 211 hotel rooms and over 140 private homes and condominiums, including kitchen suites, fireplace bedrooms

Meeting Rooms: 12. Capacity of Largest: 500 persons reception style. Meeting Space: 19,000 sq. ft.

Room Price Range: $89 for off season (Oct. to mid-Dec., Jan. to mid-May) to $320 per day for a 5-bedroom house peak season (late Dec., late May to Sept.). Golf, ski and other packages available year round

Lounge: Owl's Nest

Restaurants: Meadows Dining Room, Provision Co., Par Patio, McDivot's Café

Entertainment: Live music and dancing at Owl's Nest Lounge

Credit Cards: All major cards

General Amenities: Tours, nature center, hay rides, children's pony rides, supervised children's programs for ages 3 to 14 mid-June to Sept., meeting and conference facilities with audiovisual and food services; 5500-ft. paved airstrip, 80–100 fuel, Jet-a-Fuel available

Recreational Amenities: Fishing, boating, white-water rafting, swimming lessons, 2 swimming pools, bicycling, horseback riding, skiing, ice skating, 28 outdoor Plexi-pave tennis courts, 3 indoor tennis courts, 5 indoor racquetball courts, tennis instruction, hot tubs, massage, horseshoes, board games, volleyball, softball, croquet, basketball, football, Sunriver marina and shop

Reservation and Cancellation Policy: Deposit equal to 1 night's stay must received by Sunriver Lodge within 14 days of booking a reservation to confirm. 21-day cancellation notice to avoid penalties. Package deposit and cancellation policies vary

Comments and Restrictions: No pets allowed. Taxes additional to base rates

SUNRIVER RESORT GOLF COURSE

Sunriver began to emerge centuries ago when volcanic activity formed the rugged Cascade Mountains. Later volcanic eruptions from what is now Lava Butte eventually left a dry lake bed that evolved into a beautiful meadow with surrounding wooded areas and the "Rivière des Chutes," the "river of rapids." Gold prospectors, ranchers, railroad pioneers, cattlemen, wagon trains and sportsmen have since visited these parts, and by 1904 the first hotel was built in what was becoming an outdoor recreation area. The U.S. Army claimed the acreage as a training camp during World War II, but it was abandoned after the war, and by 1965, John D. Gray, founder of Omark Industries and developer of the coastal resort Salishan, and Donald V. McCallum, a Portland attorney, devised Sunriver, a planned resort and residential community.

By 1968 the first homesite was sold. Fred Federspiel designed the 6960-yard par-72 South Meadows Course which was built on the flat and open meadowlands. This golf course served as another recreational attraction for prospective homeowners and vacationers, who also had access to fishing, camping, boating, skiing, bicycling, hiking and other recreational amenities in this beautiful region. Federspiel served as superintendent of several golf courses for many years and designed courses in the Pacific Northwest, including the McNary Golf Course in Salem, Oregon, with Fred Sparks; Salishan in Gleneden Beach, Oregon; and the Santiam Golf Course in Salem.

The South Course is difficult because of its length and the wind that sweeps across the open meadow where it is placed. There are relatively few bunkers on the course, but they are well placed around the medium-sized to large greens. A stream winds its way through the course, and lateral water hazards appear on several holes. The par-3 holes on the South Course are long and difficult—three of them over 200 yards from the back tees. The 221-yard eighth plays straight to a deep green flanked by two large traps to the left and another to the right. The 180-yard fourth plays to a medium-sized green almost completely surrounded by bunkers. The 221-yard thirteenth plays to a deep green guarded by bunkers to the left and right, as is the 214-yard sixteenth.

Robert Trent Jones, Jr., designed the North Woodlands Course, which was opened in 1981. This 6880-yard layout is rated among the top 75 resort courses in the United States by *Golf Digest*. A variety of sand bunkers, lakes, and tree-lined dog-leg fairways makes this course tighter than the South Course. The bentgrass greens are medium-sized, fast and elevated above the relatively flat fairways. The greens are well guarded by a combination of sand bunkers and water hazards. A premium is placed on strategy, accuracy and golf-course management on the North Course.

The signature hole on the course is the 391-yard par-4 seventh, which is pictured on the Sunriver Resort scorecard. The tee shot is from an elevated tee with a direct view of Mount Bachelor and the beautiful panorama of the forests around it. This dog-leg left can be cleared on the left side if you elect to cut the corner, but the penalties are high if your ball strays into the trees. The approach shot is to a green guarded by two traps on the right and another on the left. The fairway bunker on the right side of the tee-shot landing area 160 yards from the green is another obstacle to avoid.

The most difficult par 5 on the North Course is the 530-yard sixth, a dogleg to the left. A left-side fairway bunker guards the landing area on the tee shot. The second shot should be kept to the left to lay up before the bunkers blocking the front of the green. A combination of these obstacles and trees in the approach area make it extremely difficult to reach the green in two. Position on both the tee shot, which has to reach the crest of a hill to the right of the fairway bunker for you to have a view of the green, and the second shot are critical on this hole.

A challenging par 4 on the North Course is the 416-yard finishing hole, a dogleg left to a deep green fronted by a trap and protected by a trap and water farther left and another trap and water farther right. The tee shot has water to its left, and to cut this corner you can risk as much as you care to. The approach shot has to be accurate or you are in sand or water.

The newest addition to Sunriver's golf kingdom is the Crosswater Course, a Robert Cupp and John Fought collaboration that opened in 1995. This 7693-yard par-72 adventure is situated on 274 acres within a low density 605 acre private golf community along the Big Deschutes and Little Deschutes Rivers. Inspired by Scottish heathland courses, this layout demands length, accuracy and strategic shotmaking. There are five tee distances to choose from but, even from the forward tees, the course plays 5389 yards and is sloped at 125 and rated 70.9 for men, and is sloped at 137 and rated 75.6 for women. From the back tees, the par 5s average over 600 yards in length. And even though this is a somewhat level course, most golfers will take at least three shots to reach the green on these holes.

A formidable par 5 on the front nine is the 645-yard par-5 sixth, a double dogleg whose tee shot crosses the Little Deschutes River. On the next shot big hitters might opt to cut the corner as the dogleg swings to the right. But most golfers will hit to a landing area to the right of a fairway bunker approximately 125 yards from a wide green with a bunker to its left. The other tee distances on this hole are 635, 603, 572 and 471 yards.

As its name suggests, water can come into play on several holes at Crosswater, which is surrounded by 120 acres of wetlands. The 456-yard par-4 finishing hole, for example, plays to a landing area guarded by large bunkers to the right. The fairway is cut by the river which must be cleared on the approach shot to a deep green straddled by large bunkers. A short distance from this green are Crosswater's lodge-style clubhouse, a tennis center, and a pool and spa area.

The practice area at Crosswater has a two-tiered expansive grass tee area at the near end of its driving range and another teeing area at the other end. There are five target greens as well as a practice green with bunkers and a separate putting green. All around are scenic views of Mount Bachelor, Broken Top and Tumalo Mountains, the Pulima Peaks and Newberry Crater.

Sunriver offers a variety of golf packages, including air-fare-included packages and specials for senior citizens. Many options are available, but rates tend to be lowest in October through early November, when the courses generally close. Individual and group instruction is available from the staff of professionals at Sunriver. A Golf Digest golf school is on site.

There are a variety of suites as well as private resort homes and condominiums to choose from when staying at Sunriver. There are also extensive meeting and conference facilities, with group recreation packages, audiovisual equipment, organized group activities and tours. Groups of as many as 450 persons can be accommodated.

Year-round recreational amenities at Sunriver are varied and extensive. There are 28 outdoor and 3 indoor tennis courts, with pro shop and professional instruction available, including video analysis, tennis camps and tournament direction. There is a riding stable with horse-drawn wagon rides, children's pony rides, surrey rides, and guided trail rides offered. Bicycling, racquetball, swimming, weight training, white-water rafting and outdoor adventure challenges, along with fly-fishing schools, spin fishing, skiing, boating, hiking and numerous other on- and off-site activities can be found at Sunriver.

Sunriver has won a variety of hospitality awards, including a *Mobil Travel Guide* Four-Star rating and a *Wine Spectator* Award of Excellence. *Golf* magazine has awarded Sunriver its Silver Medal award rating the resort one of the best golf facilities in the United States. Its restaurant, The Meadows Dining Room, is highly regarded and serves such delights as filet mignon

and salmon, venison steak with juniper berry sauce, pasta puttanesca, broiled ahi, and stuffed pheasant breast. Lighter fare is also served at The Meadows and the Provision Company, another restaurant.

Supervised children's programs including special activities for ages 3 to 5, 6 to 10, and 11 to 14 are available during school summer vacation and some other vacation periods, such as Thanksgiving, Christmas, and spring break. Activities range from campfires and dances to white-water rafting and tie-dying. Special area seasonal events for all ages include a street dance, art festival, antique-car rally, chili cookoff, firemen's picnic and other activities. The Sunriver Village also has a shopping area with over 50 shops and restaurants.

In the midst of a national forest at 4000 feet and in close proximity to the Deschutes River and Mt. Bachelor, a world-class ski area, this is one of the West's best recreation areas and a great place to play golf.

Recommended Golf Courses in Oregon

Within 1 Hour of Bend:

Aubrey Glen Golf Club, Bend, (503) 388–8526, Semiprivate, 18/7007/72

Black Butte Ranch Golf Course, Black Butte Ranch, (503) 595–6689, (800) 399–2322, Resort. Big Meadow: 18/6870/72. Glaze Meadow: 18/6560/72

Eagle Crest Golf Club, Redmond, (503) 923–4653, Public. Resort: 18/6693/72. Ridge: 18/6477/72

Meadow Lakes Golf Course, Prineville, (503) 447–7113, (800) 577–2797, Public, 18/6731/72

River's Edge Golf Course, Bend, (503) 389–2828, Public, 18/6647/72

Seventh Mountain Golf Village, Bend, (503) 382–4449, Resort, 18/6694/72

Widgi Creek Golf Club, Bend, (503) 382–4449, Semiprivate, 18/6700/72

Eugene Area

Course Name: TOKATEE

Course Type: Public
Address: 54947 McKenzie Highway
Blue River, OR 97413
Phone: (541) 822–3220,
(800) 452–6371

GOLF COURSE

Head Professional: Don King
Course Length/Par (All Tees): Back 6817/72, Middle 6245/72, Forward 5651/72
Course Slope/Rating (All Tees): Back 126/72, Middle 119/69.7, Ladies' Middle 123/75.1, Ladies' Forward 115/71.5
Course Architect: Ted Robinson (9 holes, 1966; additional 9 holes, 1970)
Golf Facilities: Full Pro Shop X, Snack Bar X, Lounge X, Restaurant X, Locker Room No, Showers No, Club Rental X, Club Repair Minor, Cart Rental X, Instruction X, Practice Green X, Driving Range X, Practice Bunker X, Club Storage X
Tee-Time Reservation Policy: Call anytime in advance
Ranger: Yes
Tee-off-Interval Time: 8 min.
Time to Play 18 Holes: 4 hrs.
Course Hours/Earliest Tee-off: 6 a.m. to dark
Green Fees: $30 for 18 holes, $16 for 9 holes
Cart Fees: $23 for 18 holes per cart
Pull Carts: $3 for 18 holes
Credit Cards: MasterCard, Visa
Season: Mid-Feb. to mid-Nov. Busiest season Aug., Sept.
Course Comments: Can walk anytime.
Golf Packages: Available through local lodges. Inquire at club
Discounts: Juniors, college students during school year only
Places to Stay Nearby: VIDA: Wayfarer Resort (503) 896–3613; Riverside Inn (503) 896–3218. SISTERS: Best Western Ponderosa Lodge (503) 822–3432, (800) 528–1234. BLUE RIVER: Holiday Farm (503) 822–3715; Sleepy Hollow Motel (503) 822–3805; Patio RV Park (505) 822–3596. MCKENZIE BRIDGE: Sportsman's Lodge (503) 822–3243. LEABURG: Marjon Bed and Breakfast (503) 896–3145. CAMPGROUNDS: Williamette National Forest (503) 822–3381

Local Attractions: Fishing, hunting, boating, hiking, camping, Williamette National Forest, waterfalls, mountain lakes, lava formations, Dee Wright Observatory, Koosah Falls, Sahalie Falls, Sawyer's Cave, McKenzie Bridge, Clear Lake. SISTERS: Dick Patterson's Arabian Ranch, Metolius River, Hoodoo Ski Bowl

Directions: From Eugene (48 mi.): Hwy. 126 east, course just east of Blue River, follow the signs

Closest Commercial Airports: Mahlon Sweet, Eugene (1 hr.); Portland International (3½ hrs.)

TOKATEE

"Tokatee," a Chinook Indian word meaning "a place of restful beauty," aptly describes the Tokatee Golf Course. Situated in a wilderness area 1300 feet above sea level in the shadow of the Cascade Range 48 miles east of Eugene, Oregon, Tokatee measures 6817 yards from the back tees and is surrounded by dramatic high mountain peaks. The front nine, completed in 1966, was originally timberland with one large meadow. The back nine, which opened in 1970, was a homestead.

Tokatee has 15 lakes, well-placed sand bunkers, and over 11,000 strategically placed fir trees. The greens are bentgrass, and the bunkers have white sand shipped by rail and truck from Emmett, Idaho. Located on 380 acres of land, it is near the McKenzie River and Cougar Reservoir, an area popular for fishing, hunting, boating, skiing, camping, hiking and sightseeing. The course itself covers approximately 100 acres, and you get the feeling that you are playing golf in the middle of the wilderness.

The first four holes on the front nine are in a meadowlike setting, with the rest meandering among the pine and fir trees. Number seven, a 426-yard par 4, is the number-1-handicap hole. Relatively straight from tee to green, the fairway slopes to the left. A large tree on the right side forces you to hit a perfect tee shot to score. The green is medium-sized and protected by a trap in front. The fairway is lined with intermittent trees and rocks from tee to green. The number-2-handicap hole is the 419-yard par-4 tenth, which is fairly straight down a narrowing fairway that is protected by trees in the tee-shot landing area. The approach shot is to a green angled to the right and well protected on the left by a large trap.

The back nine at Tokatee is a blend of sand, water, rolling greens, doglegs and great scenery. The eleventh is a demanding and picturesque 175-yard par 3, with a lake down the entire right side. A large trap borders the deep, hourglass-shaped green on the left. *Middle Tee* magazine has voted this one of the best par-3 holes in the state. The sixteenth, a 532-yard par 5, provides a beautiful view of Three Sisters Mountain and a relatively wide landing area, with a ditch 165 yards out on the first shot. A lake comes into play 80 yards from the large, two-tiered green.

Tokatee is the realized dream of Nat Giustina, a Eugene lumberman. Giustina took up golf at age 40, bought the land for the course in 1962, started with nine holes, then expanded to eighteen because of popular demand. Giustina, who has since played some of the best courses in the world and is a member of the Eugene Country Club, wanted to build a golf course that would be maintained as well as any course and yet be fair and enjoyable for the middle-handicap golfer. Ray Telfer has been Tokatee's greenskeeper since it opened, and Mickey Sullivan has been the pro since 1973. The course has gained recognition from *Golf Digest*, *Middle Tee*, and *Back Nine* magazines as being one of the best in Oregon. It is also one of the best public golf courses you will find anywhere.

Recommended Golf Courses in Oregon

Within 1 Hour of Eugene:

Emerald Valley Golf Course, Creswell, (503) 895–2174, Public, 18/6873/72

Forest Hills Country Club, Reedsport, (503) 271–2626, Semiprivate, 18/6322/72

Santiam Golf Course, Stayton, (503) 769–3485, Public, 18/6385/72

Trysting Tree, Corvallis, (503) 752–3332, Public, 18/7014/72

Portland Area

Course Name: EASTMORELAND GOLF COURSE

Course Type: Public
Address: 2415 S.E. Bybee Boulevard
                Portland, OR 97202
Phone: (503) 775–2900,
                (503) 292–8570 (Tee Times)

GOLF COURSE

Head Professional: Clark Cumpston
Course Length/Par (All Tees): Back 6508/72, Middle 6142/72, Ladies' Forward 5646/74
Course Slope/Rating (All Tees): Back 123/71.7, Middle 119/71.4, Ladies' Forward 117/71.4
Course Architect: H. Chandler Egan (1917)
Golf Facilities: Full Pro Shop X, Snack Bar X, Lounge X, Restaurant X, Locker Room No, Showers No, Club Rental X, Club Repair X, Cart Rental X, Instruction X, Practice Green X, Driving Range X, Practice Bunker X, Club Storage No
Tee-Time Reservation Policy: 1 wk. in advance in person, 6 days by phone, reservations urged
Ranger: Yes
Tee-off-Interval Time: 7 and 8 min.
Time to Play 18 Holes: 4 hrs., 45 min.
Course Hours/Earliest Tee-off: Sunrise
Green Fees: $19 for 18 holes Sat., Sun., holidays; $17 for 18 holes Mon. to Fri. $10 for 9 holes Sat., Sun., holidays; $9 for 9 holes Mon. to Fri.
Cart Fees: $22 for 18 holes, $11 for 9 holes
Pull Carts: $3 for 18 holes
Credit Cards: Cash or local check for golf fees. MasterCard, Visa for merchandise
Season: Year round

Course Comments: Can walk anytime. Yardage book available

Golf Packages: None

Discounts: Juniors, seniors (time restrictions)

Places to Stay Nearby: River Place Hotel (503) 228–3233, (800) 227–1333; Vintage Plaza Hotel (503) 228–1212, (800) 243–0555; Residence Inn by Marriott—Portland South (503) 684–2603, (800) 331–3131; Holiday Inn Portland Airport and Trade Center (503) 256–5000, (800) HOLIDAY; Marriott Hotel (503) 226–7600; Benson Hotel (503) 228–2000, (800) 426–0670; Riverside Inn (503) 221–0711, (800) 648–6440; Portland Hilton (503) 226–1611; Heathman Hotel (503) 241–4100, (800) 551–0011; Execulodge Portland Airport (503) 255–6511; Mallory Motor Hotel (503) 223–6311, (800) 228–8657. BED AND BREAKFAST: White House Bed and Breakfast (503) 287–7131. LODGING INFORMATION AND RESERVATION SERVICES: Hotel Alternative (apartments, condominiums) (503) 228–0300; New Bed and Breakfast Travel Unlimited (503) 243–7616; Portland Innkeepers Bed and Breakfast Association (P.O. Box 69292, Portland, OR 97201)

Local Attractions: Pioneer Courthouse Square, Portland Center, City Hall, Yamill Marketplace, Skidmore/Old Town historic district, U.S. National Bank building, Tom McCall Waterfront Park, Powell's Books, Galleria, Oregon Art Institute, Oregon Historical Center, Portland Center for the Performing Arts, Salmon St. Plaza and Fountain, Chinatown, Washington Park Zoo, Oregon Museum of Science and Industry, World Forestry Center, International Rose Test Gardens, factory outlets, Japanese Gardens, N.B.A. professional basketball, Pacific Coast league baseball, Portland State University, restaurants. Greater Portland Convention and Visitors Association (503) 222–2223

Directions: From downtown Portland: I–90 east, over Ross Island Bridge on 26, Oregon City exit. Take McLaughlin Blvd. 3/4 mi. to Eastmoreland–Reed exit, take right across overpass, golf-course entrance on left (Bybee Blvd.)

Closest Commercial Airport: Portland International (25 min.)

EASTMORELAND GOLF COURSE

When you sit in the new $1.69-million, 11,000-square-foot clubhouse at Eastmoreland, you wouldn't think you were visiting a municipal golf course. Situated in the heart of Portland, Oregon, and surrounded by Reed College, the Crystal Springs Rhododendron Garden, and a variety of warehouses and residences, Eastmoreland is a verdant oasis for any golfer who wants a walk through beautiful woods.

The 6508-yard layout, designed by H. Chandler Egan in 1917, is relatively flat on the front nine and has more undulation and water on the back nine. The course wends its way through a variety of magnificent, mature coniferous and deciduous trees. These strategically placed trees make the course more difficult than it would first appear.

The number-1-handicap hole is the 410-yard par-4 seventh, which plays flat and straight down a well-protected, tree-lined fairway. The fairway narrows to 35 yards at the 150-yard marker. The generous green measures 30 yards from back to front, slopes slightly forward and is protected by a trap on the right. On the back nine, the number-2-handicap hole is the 462-yard par-5 thirteenth. The tee shot is blind up to the crest of a hill. A 60-foot-deep gully then appears 200 to 220 yards from the green. In front of the green, beginning 60 yards from the front edge, is another deep swale, which then rises to a medium-sized forward-sloping green protected on the right by a trap.

There are several beautiful holes on the course, including the 165-yard par-3 twelfth, which plays over water to a medium-sized, forward-sloping green protected by traps on the left and right, and a huge tree to the right front. The 171-yard par-3 seventeenth is a straight shot across water to a deep, generous green that is almost surrounded by water.

On the back nine Eastmoreland features Crystal Springs Lake, bordered in its entirety by the Crystal Springs Rhododendron Gardens which are spectacular in the spring. The U.S. Amateur Public Links was held at Eastmoreland in 1990, and *Golf Digest* has recognized the layout as one of America's best public courses. Through the original efforts of Superintendent of Parks James O. Conville and T. Morris Dunne of the Multnomah Athletic Club, Eastmoreland was built on 160 acres. The land was granted by the Ladd Estate Co., and with $3000 seed money Portland made a strong commitment to quality public golf, a tradition that continues to this day.

Course Name: **HERON LAKES GOLF COURSE Greenback, Great Blue Courses**

Course Type: Public
Address: 3500 North Victory Boulevard
Portland, OR 97217
Phone: (503) 289–1818

GOLF COURSE

Manager: Barry Kurokawa
Director of Golf: Byron Wood
Course Length/Par (All Tees): Greenback: Back 6579/72, Middle 5938/72, Forward 5224/72. Great Blue: Back 6916/72, Blue 6504/72, White 6056/72, Forward 5285/72
Course Slope/Rating (All Tees): Greenback: Back 124/71.4, Blue 115/68.4, Ladies' Forward 113/69.4. Great Blue: Back 132/73.6, Blue 128/71.3, White 122/69.4, Ladies' White 130/74.2, Ladies' Forward 120/69.8
Course Architect: Greenback: Robert Trent Jones, Jr. (1970). Great Blue: Robert Trent Jones, Jr. (front 9 holes, 1988; back 9 holes, 1992)
Golf Facilities: Full Pro Shop X, Snack Bar X, Lounge X, Restaurant X, Locker Room No, Showers No, Club Rental X, Club Repair X, Cart Rental X, Instruction X, Practice Green X, Driving Range X, Practice Bunker X, Club Storage No

Tee-Time Reservation Policy: Up to 7 days in advance in person. 6 days in advance by telephone
Ranger: Yes
Tee-off-Interval Time: 7 and 8 min.
Time to Play 18 Holes: 4½ hrs.
Course Hours/Earliest Tee-off: 5 a.m.
Green Fees: Greenback: $19 for 18 holes Sat., Sun., holidays, $17 for 18 holes weekdays. $10 for 9 holes Sat., Sun., holidays, $9 for 9 holes weekdays. Great Blue: $22 for 18 holes, $14 for 9 holes
Cart Fees: $11 for 9 holes per person
Pull Carts: $3 for 18 holes, $2 for 9 holes
Credit Cards: Cash or check for golf fees. MasterCard, Visa for merchandise
Season: Year round
Course Comments: Can walk anytime. Yardage book available
Golf Packages: None
Discounts: Seniors, junior passes
Places to Stay Nearby: Residence Inn by Marriott—Portland South (503) 684–2603, (800) 331–3131; Holiday Inn Portland Airport and Trade Center (503) 256–5000, (800) HOLIDAY; Marriott Hotel (503) 226–7600; Benson Hotel (503) 228–2000, (800) 426–0670; Riverside Inn (503) 221–0711, (800) 648–6440; Portland Hilton (503) 226–1611; Heathman Hotel (503) 241–4100, (800) 551–0011; Execulodge Portland Airport (503) 255–6511; Mallory Motor Hotel (503) 223–6311, (800) 228–8657. BED AND BREAKFAST: White House Bed and Breakfast (503) 287–7131. LODGING INFORMATION AND RESERVATION SERVICES: Hotel Alternative (apartments, condominiums) (503) 228–0300; New Bed and Breakfast Travel Unlimited (503) 243–7616; Portland Innkeepers Bed and Breakfast Association (P.O. Box 69292, Portland, OR 97201)
Local Attractions: Pioneer Courthouse Square, Portland Center, City Hall, Yamill Marketplace, Skidmore/Old Town historic district, U.S. National Bank building, Tom McCall Waterfront Park, Powell's Books, Galleria, Oregon Art Institute, Oregon Historical Center, Portland Center for the Performing Arts,

Salmon Street Plaza and Fountain, Chinatown, Washington Park Zoo, Oregon Museum of Science and Industry, World Forestry Center, International Rose Test Gardens, factory outlets, Japanese Gardens, N.B.A. professional basketball, Pacific Coast league baseball, Portland State University, restaurants. Greater Portland Convention and Visitors Association (503) 222–2223

Directions: From I–5: West Delta Park/Expo Center exit (exit 306B), follow the signs to West Delta Park and golf course

Closest Commercial Airport: Portland International (15 min.)

HERON LAKES GOLF COURSE

Located in West Delta Park on the outskirts of Portland, Heron Lakes' Old White and Blue courses, now called Greenback, is ranked among America's top public courses by *Golf Digest*. An additional layout composing the current Red nine and an additional nine completed in 1992 constitutes the Great Blue Course. All of the courses are designed by noted golf architect Robert Trent Jones, Jr., who also designed the Eugene Country Club, with Robert Trent Jones, Sr.; Sunriver Golf Club (North Course, with Don Knott); West Delta Park Golf Club, Portland, with Robert Trent Jones, Sr., and Gary Roger Baird, in Oregon and several other courses in the United States and abroad, including the Sentryworld Golf Club in Stevens Point, Wisconsin, and Cochiti Lake in New Mexico.

Heron Lakes is situated on rolling, open land and is currently served by a temporary clubhouse. The Greenback Course is well bunkered with large, moderately fast, undulating greens. Water comes into play on many holes, and wind can be a major factor. An excellent par 3 on the Greenback Course is the 205-yard fifth hole, which plays to a large, undulating, heart-shaped green with a narrow entrance protected by two traps to the left and to the right front. There is also a trap at the back of the green. A large water hazard is located on the left side, halfway down the fairway to the green.

A challenging hole on the back nine is the 390-yard par-4 eleventh hole, which plays as a slight dogleg left to a large, deep green protected by traps left, right and right-front. The tee shot is to a landing area to the right of a large bunker approximately 235 yards from the back tees.

While the yardage from the back tees on this course is not overly long, the combination of water hazards, wind, well-placed bunkers and tricky, undulating, terraced greens makes this a challenging golf course. If you are not in proper position on tee shots, and if your approach shots are not well placed relative to pin position, your scores can begin to balloon on this challenging layout.

The back nine on the Great Blue, formerly the Red nine, is a rolling layout with hardly any trees. The three toughest holes are the finishing holes. The sixteenth is a 390-yard par 4 playing from an elevated tee down to a green that slopes from back to front toward a water hazard that reaches approximately 100 yards to the fairway from the edge of the green. If your tee shot is to the right, your second shot is over water to the putting surface, which is two-tiered with traps left, right-front, and back. Any shot onto the green from the left center of the fairway will increase the likelihood that the ball will kick into the water.

The seventeenth is a 523-yard par 5 with water on the right side of the fairway and crossing in front of the back tees. Fairway bunkers, which include five on the left side, begin 170 to 250 yards out. There is another bunker 150 yards from the green on the left. The large, two-tiered green slopes left to right and is protected by a large trap to the left and a trap in back.

The 413-yard par-4 eighteenth hole has water running all along the right fairway from tee to green. There are fairway bunkers on the left from 150 yards in. The fairway narrows into the green, which is large, banked in back and heavily trapped. A well-struck, straight tee shot is required on this hole, and an extremely accurate second shot is required to reach the well-protected green.

The clubhouse at Heron Lakes includes a full pro shop and snack bar restaurant. Practice facilities include a putting green, practice bunker and driving range. It is rare that you will find this quality of municipal golf at such reasonable prices anywhere. Portland has a long tradition of maintaining beautiful public parks, and two of its public golf courses, Eastmoreland and Heron Lakes, are ranked among the best in the country. Other public courses in Portland, such as Colwood National, Glendover, Broadmoor, and Rose City, are also highly recommended. You can walk Heron Lakes anytime, and now that there are 36 championship holes, it will be even more pleasurable to play.

Course Name: PUMPKIN RIDGE GHOST CREEK COURSE

Course Type: Semiprivate
Address: 12930 Old Pumpkin Ridge Road Cornelius, OR 97113–6147
Phone: (503) 647–4747
Fax: (503) 647–2002

GOLF COURSE

Director of Golf: Jerry Mowlds
Course Length/Par (All Tees): Back 6839/71, Blue 6490/71, White 6010/71, Forward 5326/71
Course Slope/Rating (All Tees): Back 140/73.8, Blue 136/72.0, White 130/69.2, Ladies' Forward 121/72.1
Course Architect: Robert Cupp (1992)
Golf Facilities: Full Pro Shop X, Snack Bar X, Lounge X, Restaurant X, Locker Room No, Showers No, Club Rental X, Club Repair X, Cart Rental X, Instruction X, Practice Green X, Driving Range X, Practice Bunker X, Club Storage No
Tee-Time Reservation Policy: Up to 6 days in advance by telephone. Up to 7 days in person
Ranger: Yes
Tee-off-Interval Time: 9 min.
Time to Play 18 Holes: 4½ hrs.

Course Hours/Earliest Tee-off: 6:30 a.m. Fri., Sat., Sun., holidays; 7 a.m. weekdays
Green Fees: $75 for 18 holes Fri., Sat., Sun., holidays; $60 for 18 holes weekdays
Cart Fees: $24 for 18 holes per cart
Credit Cards: Discover, MasterCard, Visa
Season: Year round. Busiest July through Labor Day
Course Comments: Can walk anytime. Members have tee time preference. Indoor golf learning center on site. Private course, Witch Hollow, and separate clubhouse
Golf Packages: No
Discounts: Twilight
Places to Stay Nearby: BEAVERTON: Courtyard by Marriott (503) 641–3200, (800) 443–6000. FOREST GROVE: Forest Grove Inn (503) 357–9700. HILLSBORO: Best Western Hallmark Inn (503) 648–3500, (800) 528–1234. PORTLAND: See page 547
Local Attractions: PORTLAND: see page 547
Directions: From downtown Portland (20 min. west): Take Hwy. 26 to North Plains Exit 55. Turn right and proceed 1/4 mi. to Mountaindale Rd. Turn right and go 1/2 mi. to Old Pumpkin Ridge Rd. Turn left to golf course
Closest Commercial Airport: Portland International (45 min.)

GHOST CREEK GOLF COURSE

Ghost Creek Golf Course is a Robert Cupp design on 350 acres twenty minutes west of Portland in the scenic countryside of Washington County. The fairways weave through forests of fir, maple, oak, and ash. Wetlands and creeks add difficulty to the course which has bentgrass tees, fairways, and greens. From Ghost Creek are panoramic views of the Cascades, Coast Range, Tualatin Hills, and the farmland of the Willamette Valley.

Ghost Creek begins with an open, straightaway par 4, then becomes a treelined challenge as it loops its way back toward the open 469-yard par-4 ninth, one of the most difficult holes on the course. This hole, which plays 443, 419, and 368 yards from the other tee distances, requires a long, well-positioned tee shot that enables you to come into a deep green backed by a bunker and bordered by a small lake to its left.

The 454-yard par-4 finishing hole provides a tough conclusion to a scenic round of golf. To the far right is a stream paralleling the fairway. The approach shot is to a bunkerless, two-tiered green with a pond to its right. Just across the pond is Pumpkin Ridge's 350-yard deep practice range which serves the private Witch Hollow course and the public Ghost Creek. Also available are putting and chipping greens and practice bunkers. Each course has its own clubhouse but the Ghost Creek clubhouse has no locker room or shower facilities at present.

Pumpkin Ridge's Ghost Creek Golf Course was rated "Best New Public Course" by *Golf Digest* in 1992. Both Pumpkin Ridge courses are the site of the 1996 U.S. Amateur.

Course Name: SALISHAN GOLF LINKS

Course Type: Resort
Resort: Salishan Lodge
Address: Highway 101
Gleneden Beach, OR 97388
Phone: (503) 764–3632 (Golf Course)
(503) 764–3600, (800) 452–2300 (Resort)
Fax: (503) 764–3697 (Resort)

GOLF COURSE

Head Professional: Grant Rogers
Course Length/Par (All Tees): Back 6439/72, Middle 6246/72, Forward 5693/73
Course Slope/Rating (All Tees): Back 128/72.1, Middle 126/71.1, Ladies' Forward 127/73.6
Course Architects: Fred Federspiel (9 holes, 1965); Robert Muir Graves (remodeled 9 holes, added 9 holes, 1982); William Robinson (renovated 18 holes, 1996)
Golf Facilities: Full Pro Shop X, Snack Bar X, Lounge Beer/Wine, Restaurant No, Locker Room X, Showers No, Club Rental X, Club Repair Outside,

Cart Rental X, Instruction X, Practice Green X, Driving Range X, Practice Bunker No, Club Storage X
Tee-Time Reservation Policy: Resort guests: From time of reservation. Outside play: From 2 wks. in advance
Ranger: Yes
Tee-off-Interval Time: 10 min.
Time to Play 18 Holes: 4 hrs., 15 min.
Course Hours/Earliest Tee-off: 6 a.m. summer
Green Fees: Peak season (Aug. to Oct.): $45 for 18 holes, $30 for 9 holes
Cart Fees: Peak season (Aug. to Oct.): $26 for 18 holes, $15 for 9 holes
Credit Cards: All major cards
Season: Year round. Busiest season June to Oct.
Course Comments: Can walk anytime
Golf Packages: Available through resort
Discounts: Seasonal (Nov. to July). Play cards and memberships available
Places to Stay Nearby: LINCOLN CITY: Inn at Spanish Head (503) 996–2161. NEWPORT: Embarcadero Resort Hotel (503) 265–8521; Shilo Inn (503) 265–7701; Sylvia Beach Hotel (503) 265–5428. DEPOE BAY: Gracie's Landing (503) 765–2322, (800) 228–0448. BED AND BREAKFAST: Palmer House Bed and Breakfast Inn (503) 994–7932; Channel House Country Inn with Bed and Breakfast (503) 765–2140
Local Attractions: Yaquina Bay Lighthouse, fishing charters, whale watching, hunting, antiquing, camping, Oregon State University Marine Science Center Aquarium, seasonal festivals, coastal beaches, boating. Depoe Bay. Newport. Newport Chamber of Commerce (800) 263–7844. Depoe Bay Chamber of Commerce (503) 765–2889. Lincoln City Visitor and Convention Bureau (503) 994–2164
Directions: From Portland (90 mi.): I–5 to Hwy. 99 west to Hwy. 18 west to Hwy. 101, south to Gleneden Beach, follow signs. From Eugene (120 mi.): I–5 north, Hwy. 20 west to Hwy. 101, north to Gleneden Beach, follow signs
Closest Commercial Airport: Portland International (2½ hrs.)

RESORT

Date Built: 1965

No. of Rooms: 205 guest rooms and suites

Meeting Rooms: 14. Capacity of Largest: 500 persons. Meeting Space: 14,000 sq. ft.

Room Price Range: $110, double occupancy off season (Nov. to April) to $250, double occupancy, peak season (July to Oct.). Golf, holiday and other packages available year round

Lounge: Attic Lounge

Restaurants: Cora's, Sun Room, Cedar Tree, Dining Room

Entertainment: Music nightly

Credit Cards: All major cards

General Amenities: Events such as art shows, wine sales, indoor recreation center, nature trails, children's activities, shopping, library, gift shop, art gallery, meeting facilities with audiovisual and food services

Recreational Amenities: Fishing, bicycling, jogging, hiking, indoor swimming pool, fitness equipment, whirlpool, sauna; 1 outdoor and 3 indoor tennis courts with instruction available

Reservation and Cancellation Policy: 1 night's advance deposit by credit card or check. Cancellation required 5 days prior to arrival to avoid penalties

Comments and Restrictions: 2-night minimum required on weekends during summer. Room tax additional. Additional per night charge for pets

SALISHAN GOLF LINKS

The Salishan resort, situated on over 700 acres, commands a breathtaking view of the rugged central Oregon coastline, including Siletz Bay and the dunes, driftwood-strewn sands, and white capped waters of the Pacific beyond. Whale watchers, birders, and beachcombers find the 3 miles of nearby beaches and shoreline irresistible for exploration. The name Salishan itself derives from a Pacific Northwest Indian word meaning "coming together from diverse points to communicate in harmony." That's what the hosts of this five-star resort hope to achieve.

The 6439-yard par-72 golf course is a links-style layout with manicured fairways, Sitka spruce, Douglas fir, hemlock and western red-cedar trees strategically placed on the hillsides. The front nine weaves through forested terrain with water, steep slopes and elevated greens. The back nine is carved out of links land, where millions of years ago the Pacific Ocean covered what is now fairway. With magnificent views of the ocean and Siletz Bay on this side, the golfer faces ocean winds, sand dunes and beach grass. Deer, bobcats, rabbits, squirrels and bald eagles are some of the wildlife that also enjoy the golf course. The bentgrass greens at Salishan tend to be medium-sized, moderately fast, and undulating. They are generally elevated and well trapped.

The number-1-handicap hole is the 426-yard par-4 seventh, a dogleg left that requires the golfer to hit a long, straight tee shot to reach the green in regulation. The first shot should take you beyond the bend of the dogleg, and the second is uphill to a medium-sized green. The putting surface slopes severely forward and left to right, and is protected front-left and front-right by two traps. The number-2-handicap hole is the 433-yard par-4 twelfth, whose green is tucked slightly to the right at the end of a relatively straight fairway. The tee-shot landing area is well guarded by bunkers on the left and right sides. Huge sand dunes wrap around the green totally, beginning to the left of the fairway approximately 175 yards from the pin. The tabletop green slopes from front to back and is difficult to hold. The wind can be a major problem on this hole.

The par-4 seventeenth is the signature hole at Salishan and plays only 271 yards from the back tees over a valley and down a narrow fairway. A conservative tee shot is needed to gain position to reach a tricky green that slopes forward and is protected on the left by a trap and in the back by sand dunes. Although many consider the front nine, a more traditional, treed, Northwest layout, to be more difficult, the back nine, with the prevailing wind off the ocean; narrow, pine-lined fairways; and deep, Scottish-style bunkers, can be just as challenging. This nine was the original nine-hole course designed by Fred Federspiel and opened in 1965. Robert Muir Graves redesigned the original nine and designed the front nine, which opened in the early 1980s.

The golf course has recently been improved thorough a $2 million renovation under the direction of noted golf architect William Robinson. Improvements include a computerized automated irrigation system, more tee area options, and modification to sand bunkers and water hazards. The essential charm and character of the original course remains.

The buildings at Salishan, comprising meeting rooms, dining areas, lodgings, and other facilities, are connected by covered wooden walkways and bridges. The architecture and interior design have an oriental look, and local materials such as flagstone, hemlock, and cedar shakes and siding were used in construction. Handwoven, earth-tone upholstery and original artwork are found in Salishan's villas. The main lodge along with the Longhouse Conference Center provide 14,000 square feet of flexible meeting and conference space. The resort prides itself on a 21,000-bottle, award-winning wine cellar with 875 different selections ranging from regional Pacific Northwest wines to the best European vintages. The Salishan dining room has regularly been rated one of the best restaurants in the state of Oregon.

Recreational activities at Salishan include tennis on the outdoor or 3 indoor Plexi-pave courts; a variety of exercise and fitness options in the indoor recreation center, which has a swimming pool, exercise room, whirlpool, and sauna; jogging and hiking on nature trails through the forest and 3 miles of secluded beach along the Salishan peninsula; and fishing in the nearby Pacific Ocean or coastal rivers. There is also a game room and children's playground, and the Marketplace Mall adjacent to the lodge offers several shops.

The resort offers a number of golf, tennis, holiday and other packages throughout the year. You can walk the course anytime.

Off-season rates are also available November through June. A practice range, putting green and full pro shop are offered at the golf facility. Lessons are available from the capable staff.

The Salishan Golf Links has been rated one of the best resort golf courses in the United States by *Golf Digest*. The combination of a beautiful, challenging golf course perched on the edge of the Pacific and the quality accommodations, cuisine and recreational amenities of the resort make this a memorable place to visit.

Course Name: SANDPINES GOLF COURSE

Course Type: Public
Address: 1201 35th Street
              Florence, OR 97439
Phone: (503) 997–1940,
              (800) 917–4653
Fax: (503) 997–2010

GOLF COURSE

Head Professional: Jim Skaugstad
Course Length/Par (All Tees): Back 6954/72, Blue 6536/72, White 6085/72, Forward 5346/72
Course Slope/Rating (All Tees): Back 129/74, Blue 125/71.7, White 120/69.5, Forward 111/65.8, Ladies' White 129/75.7, Ladies' Forward 123/71.1
Course Architect: Rees Jones (1993)
Golf Facilities: Full Pro Shop X, Snack Bar X, Lounge X, Restaurant No, Locker Room No, Showers No, Club Rental X, Club Repair X, Cart Rental X, Instruction X, Practice Green X, Driving Range X, Practice Bunker X, Club Storage X
Tee-Time Reservation Policy: Up to 2 weeks in advance
Ranger: Yes
Tee-off-Interval Time: 10 min.
Time to Play 18 Holes: 4 hrs. 15 min.
Course Hours/Earliest Tee-off: 6:15 a.m.
Green Fees: $45 for 18 holes
Cart Fees: $26 for 18 holes per cart
Credit Cards: American Express, MasterCard, Visa
Season: Year round. Busiest July through Oct.

Course Comments: Can walk anytime

Golf Packages: Inquire at pro shop

Discounts: Twilight, junior

Places to Stay Nearby: Best Western Pier Point Inn (503) 997–7191, (800) 528–1234; Holiday Inn Express (503) 997–7797, (800) HOLIDAY; Driftwood Shores Resort and Conference Center (503) 997–8263, (800) 422–5091

Local Attractions: FLORENCE: Harbor Vista County Park, Darlingtonia Botanical Wayside, Hecata Lighthouse, Dolly Wares Doll Museum, Sea Lion Caves, Sandland Adventures, Pioneer Museum, boating, fishing, camping, hiking, beaches. Florence Chamber of Commerce, 250 Hwy. 101, Florence, OR 97439, (503) 997–3128

Directions: From Eugene (1 hr. west): Take I–5 to Exit 195–B then take Hwy. 126 west to Florence. Take Hwy. 101 north to 35th St. Proceed west on 35th to golf course

Closest Commercial Airports: Mahlon Sweet, Eugene (1 hr. 15 min.); Portland International (3½ hrs.)

SANDPINES GOLF COURSE

Sandpines is a new Rees Jones-designed layout near the Pacific Ocean one hour west of Eugene. The course was built on rolling sand dunes and quickly became recognized as one of the best new courses of 1993 by *Golf Digest*. Sandpines features trademark Rees Jones turtleback mounding along the fairways and around the large, mildly undulating greens and ample bunker areas. The ocean winds sweep across the golf course, especially during the summer months, but the par 4s and par 5s provide ample space in front of the greens to run the ball under the wind and onto the putting surface. There are over seventy bunkers on this walkable layout that is lined with mature pine and other varieties. Water hazards in the form of small lakes and ponds can come into play on six holes. The bunkers around the moderately fast bentgrass greens are set at a distance from the putting surface, making it difficult to recover quickly from an errant shot.

A memorable hole on the front side is the 426-yard par-4 sixth, a dogleg right with a bunker guarding the right side of the turn. The approach is to a large green with a grass bunker in front and a sand bunker to the right. The signature holes on the course, called "The Crescendo" by the architect, begins with the 348-yard par-4 sixteenth, a slight dogleg right whose landing area is guarded by a large sod-faced bunker. The approach is to a well-bunkered green bordered by a lake to its right. The 203-yard par-3 seventeenth requires a tee shot over the corner of the lake to a deep green protected by water in front and a large bunker to its right. An incoming wind on this hole requires the golfer to add two or three clubs to his normal selection. The 501-yard par-5 finishing hole comes back along the lake which skirts its left side from tee to green. The design of this hole is reminiscent of the 18th at Pebble Beach. A strayed shot to the right might catch one of the fairway bunkers along the right edge. Or a successful heroic tee shot over the corner of the lake might enable you to birdie this fine finishing hole. Tailwinds in the summer improve the chance for a birdie on No. 16 and No. 18.

Sandpines currently has a modest clubhouse, but a complete facility is scheduled for completion in 1996. Nearby, between the first and second fairways, is a state-of-the-art practice facility with a three-tiered teeing area on its driving range, putting greens and practice bunkers. The golf course's treelined holes are reminiscent of Spyglass, its straightforwardness of Pinehurst No. 2, and its links-style dune grass of Ballybunion. The beauty of this layout moves many golfers to buy throwaway cameras to record their scenic Pacific Northwest golf memories at Sandpines.

Recommended Golf Courses in Oregon

Within 1 Hour of Portland:

Forest Hills Golf Course, Cornelius, (503) 357–3347, Semiprivate, 18/6173/72

Langdon Farms Golf Club, Aurora, (503) 678–4653, Public, 18/6930/71

Quail Valley Golf Course, Banks, (503) 324–4444, Public, 18/6603/72

Resort at the Mountain, Welches, (503) 662–3151, (800) 669–4653, Resort. Three nines: 9/3341/36, 9/3053/36, 9/2665/34

Oregon: Useful Information

Oregon Tourism Division, Oregon Dept. of Economic Development, 775 Summer St. NE, Salem, OR 97310, (800) 547–7842

Pacific Northwest National Parks and Forests Association, Pacific Northwest Region, 333 S.W. First Ave., P.O. Box 3623, Portland, OR 97208, (503) 326–2877, (800) 280–CAMP (information and reservations)

Oregon Dept. of Parks and Recreation, 1115 Commercial St. NE, Salem, OR 97310–1001, (503) 378–6305

U.S. Bureau of Land Management, P.O. Box 2965, Portland, OR 97208, (503) 280–7001

U.S. Forest Service, P.O. Box 3623, 319 SW Pine St., Portland, OR 97208, (503) 221–2877 (information and maps)

Oregon Department of Fish and Wildlife, 2501 S.W. 1st St., P.O. Box 59, Portland, OR 97207, (503) 229–5403 (hunting and fishing licenses)

Allentown/Lancaster/Philadelphia Area

Course Name: WYNCOTE GOLF CLUB

Course Type: Semiprivate
Address: 50 Wyncote Drive
Oxford, PA 19363
Phone: (610) 932–8900
Fax: (610) 932–8197

GOLF COURSE

Head Professional: Douglas H. Thompson
Course Length/Par (All Tees): Back 7012/72, Blue 6576/72, White 6074/72, Forward 5454/72
Course Slope/Rating (All Tees): Back 128/73.8, Blue 125/71.8, White 117/69.3, Ladies' Forward 126/71.6
Course Architect: Brian Ault (1993)
Golf Facilities: Full Pro Shop X, Snack Bar X, Lounge No, Restaurant No, Locker Room No, Showers No, Club Rental X, Club Repair X, Cart Rental X, Instruction X, Practice Green X, Driving Range X, Practice Bunker X, Club Storage No
Tee-Time Reservation Policy: Up to 1 week in advance. Credit card to reserve Fri., Sat., Sun., holidays
Ranger: Yes
Tee-off Interval Time: 8 min.
Time to Play 18 Holes: 4½ hrs.
Course Hours/Earliest Tee-off: 7 a.m. Fri., Sat., Sun., holidays; 8 a.m. weekdays
Green and Cart Fees: $65 for 18 holes Fri., Sat., Sun., holidays; $54 for 18 holes weekdays
Credit Cards: All major cards
Season: Mar. through Dec. weather permitting. Busiest May through Oct.
Course Comments: Walking allowed. Yardage book available
Golf Packages: No
Discounts: Twilight, juniors, ladies, seniors
Places to Stay Nearby: KENNETT SQUARE: Longwood Inn (610) 444–3535; Scarlett House (610) 444–9592. LANCASTER: Best Western Eden Resort Inn & Conerence Center (717) 569–6444, (800) 528–1234; The King's Cottage (717) 397–1017; Lancaster Hilton Garden Inn (717) 560–0880; Willow Valley Family Resort and Conference Center (717) 464–2711, (800) 444–1714. STRASBURG: Historic Strasburg Inn (717) 687–7691, (800) 422–2766
Local Attractions: LANCASTER: Seasonal arts and crafts festivals, factory outlet shopping, Amish Country Tours, Dutch Wonderland Family Fun Park, Hands-On House, Children's Museum of Lancaster, Lancaster County Historical Society, Landis Valley Museum, Lancaster County Winery, Wheatland. STRASBURG: The Amish Village, Choo Choo Barn, Traintown U.S.A., Gast Classic Motorcars Exhibit, Railroad Museum of Pennsylvania, Sight and Sound Entertainment Center, Strasbug Country Store and Creamery, Strasburg Rail Road Co., Toy Train Museum, The Village Greens. Swarthmore. Philadelphia. Pennsylvania Dutch Convention and Visitors Bureau, 501 Greenfield Rd., Lancaster, PA 17601 (717) 299–8901, (800) 723–8824
Directions: From Philadelphia (1 hr. southwest): Take Rte. 1 southeast to Rte 10. Proceed north 1/4 mi. on Rte. 10 to the golf course
Closest Commercial Airports: Philadelphia International (1 hr.); Baltimore-Washington International (1½ hrs.)

WYNCOTE GOLF CLUB

Wyncote is a links-style heathland golf course situated on rolling, open farmland one hour southwest of Philadelphia just above the Maryland border. A nickname for "Windy Cottage," Wyncote is part of a golf course real estate development surrounded by farms devoted to raising dairy cows, soybeans, corn, and other agricultural activity.

Wyncote is a shotmaker's course that requires you to conceive strategic paths to the well-bunkered, quick, subtly undulating bentgrass greens. Variable winds can add difficulty to Wyncote where errant shots are likely to have strange lies in thick, mounded rough, or the ball could be nestled in one of the 71 bunkers on the course. These sand bunkers include 15 acres of waste bunkers.

Wyncote begins with a 577-yard par 5 that is mounded along each side and is swept with tricky winds. As you approach the large, double green shared with No. 10, you have to avoid a pond and a cluster of three bunkers to the left, a large bunker to the rear of the green, and a pot bunker to its right. The second hole is an equally difficult 460-yard par 4, a long straight march, usually into the wind, to a deep green with a shelf to its rear, three bunkers guarding its front, and another to its rear. By now it is clear that Wyncote requires target shots to its fairway landing areas and accurate approach shots to its well-guarded greens. A strayed shot is likely to cost you a stroke and once you reach the green a three-putt is always a possibility on these immaculate putting surfaces.

Wyncote provides a marvelous variety of holes and a choice of four tee distances from which to play. The 222-yard par-3 eighth often plays into the wind and sometimes cannot be reached from the back tees. The other tee distances are 180, 147, and 128 yards, but there is always that gigantic bunker to the right of the green to think about. The huge putting surface is surrounded by grass moguls and etched by the bunker. The target actually looks small from the tee, another act of deception on this tricky layout.

The round concludes with a 580-yard par 5 that has a series of mounds to the right and an uphill slope to a fairway plateau on the first shot. It will then take you two shots to reach a deep, two-tiered green guarded by a series of eight bunkers on its right from eighty yards out up to the right of the target. Another bunker protects the rear.

The owner of this golf course, James S. Pepple, a former dairy farmer who carefully researched Scottish heathland golf courses before undertaking this venture, hired Brian Ault to design Wyncote. It was rated one of the best new public golf courses to open in 1993 by *Golf Digest*. And it is now rated among the best in Pennsylvania.

Recommended Golf Courses in Pennsylvania

Within Allentown/Lancaster/Philadelphia Area:

Buck Hill Golf Club, Buck Hill Falls, (717) 595–7730, Semiprivate. White/Blue: 18/6450/72. Blue/Red: 18/6150/70. Red/White: 18/6300/70

Center Valley Golf Club, Center Valley, (610) 791–5580, Public, 18/6904/72

Eagle Lodge Country Club, Lafayette Hill, (610) 825–9198, Resort, 18/6759/71

Five Ponds Golf Club, Warminster, (215) 956–9727, Public, 18/6760/71

Flying Hills Golf Course, Reading, (610) 775–4063, Public, 18/6023/70

Foxchase Golf Club, Stevens, (717) 336–3673, Public, 18/6689/72

Galen Hall Country Club, Wernersville, (610) 678–9535, Semiprivate, 18/6271/72

Hickory Valley Golf Club, Gilbertsville, (610) 754–9862, Public. Red/White: 18/6487/72. White/Blue: 18/6442/72. Red/Blue: 18/6609/72

Locust Valley Golf Club, Coopersburg, (610) 282–4711, Public, 18/6451/72

Mountain Laurel Golf Club, White Haven, (717) 443–7424, (800) 458–5921, Resort, 18/6791/72

Mt. Manor Inn and Golf Club, Marshall's Creek, (717) 223–9062, Resort. Blue/Yellow: 18/6233/71. Orange/Silver: 18/6476/73

Pocono Farms Country Club, Tobyhanna, (717) 894–8943, Resort, 18/6600/72

Paxon Hollow Country Club, Media, (215) 353–0220, Semiprivate, 18/5641/71

Shadowbrook Country Club, Tunkhannock, (717) 836–2151, Resort, 18/6104/71

Shawnee Inn Golf Resort, Shawnee on Delaware, (717) 421–1500, (800) 742–9633, Resort. Red: 9/3362/36. White: 9/3227/36. Blue: 9/3438/36

Upper Perk Golf Course, Pennsburg, (215) 679–5594, Public, 18/6381/71

White Tail Golf Club, Bath,
(610) 837–9626, Public, 18/6432/72

Harrisburg Area

Course Name: **COUNTRY CLUB OF
             HERSHEY
             West, East Courses**

Course Type: Resort
Resort: The Hotel Hershey
Address: 1000 East Derry Rd. (Hershey
              Country Club)
              Hershey, PA 17033
Phone: (717) 533–2464 (Hershey
              Country Club)
              (717) 533–2171 (Resort)
              (800) 437–7439 (Centralized
              Hershey Resort Reservation
              and Information Service)
Fax: (717) 534–3125 (Resort)

GOLF COURSE

Director of Golf: Jay Weitzel
Head Professional: Jim Reed
Course Length/Par (All Tees): West:
   Back 6860/73, Middle 6480/73, Forward
   5908/76. East: Back 7061/71, Middle
   6363/71, Forward 5645/71
Course Slope/Rating (All Tees): West:
   Back 131/73.1, Middle 130/71.3, La-
   dies' Forward 127/74.7. East: Back
   128/73.6, Middle 125/70.5, Ladies'
   Forward 127/71.6
Course Architects: West: Maurice
   McCarthy (1930). East: George Fazio
   (1970)
Golf Facilities: Full Pro Shop X, Snack
   Bar X, Lounge X, Restaurant X,
   Locker Room X, Showers X, Club
   Rental X, Club Repair X, Cart Rental
   X, Instruction X, Practice Green X,
   Driving Range X, Practice Bunker X,
   Club Storage X
Tee-Time Reservation Policy: Hershey
   Lodge or Hershey Country Club guests:
   At time of confirmed reservations
Ranger: Yes
Tee-off-Interval Time: 8 min.
Time to Play 18 Holes: 4 hrs.
Course Hours/Earliest Tee-off: 6:30 a.m.
   seasonal

Green and Cart Fees: West: $89 for 18
   holes weekends, holidays; $84 for 18
   holes Mon. to Fri. East: $69 for 18 holes
   weekends, holidays; $64 for 18 holes
   Mon. to Fri.
Credit Cards: MasterCard, Visa
Season: West: Late March to mid-Nov.
   East: Year round. Busiest season April
   to Oct.
Course Comments: Cart mandatory.
   Caddies available. Yardage book available. Member play and tournaments take
   precedence over all play on both courses
Golf Packages: Available through Hershey
   Hotel or lodge
Discounts: Available
Places to Stay Nearby: Must be a guest of
   the Hotel Hershey or the Hershey Coun-
   try Club to play the courses. Best West-
   ern Inn (717) 533–5665, (800)
   528–1234; Comfort Inn (717) 566–
   2050, (800) 228–5150; Days Inn (717)
   534–2162, (800) 329–7466; Fairway
   Motel (717) 533–5179; Holiday Inn
   (717) 469–0661, (800) HOLIDAY
Local Attractions: Hershey Park, Hershey
   Park Arena and Hershey Park Stadium,
   Zoo America North American Wildlife
   Park, Hershey Gardens, Hershey
   Museum, Hershey Chocolate World,
   Hershey Theater, Milton Hershey
   School, Pennsylvania Patch Country,
   Gettysburg historic battlefields. Harris-
   burg (state capitol). Hershey Information
   and Room Reservations (800) 437–7439
Directions: From Baltimore (100 mi.):
   I–83 north to Rte. 322 at Harrisburg,
   Rte. 322 east to Hershey. From Philadel-
   phia (100 mi.): I–76 west to exit 20,
   Rte. 72 north to Rte. 322, Rte. 322 west
   to Hershey. From Pittsburgh (225 mi.):
   I–76 to exit 19 at Harrisburg, I–263
   north to Rte. 322, Rte. 322 east to Her-
   shey. From New York City (145 mi.):
   George Washington Bridge to I–80 to
   I–287 south to I–78, I–78 west to I–81,
   I–81 south to exit 28, Rte. 743 south to
   Hershey. Follow signs to resort when
   you get to Hershey
Closest Commercial Airports: Harrisburg
   International (15 min.); Philadelphia
   International (2 hrs.); Baltimore–Wash-

ington International (2 hrs.); Washington National, DC (3 hrs.); Pittsburgh International (4 hrs.)

RESORT

Date Built: 1933 (Hotel Hershey), 1967 (Hershey Lodge and Convention Center)

No. of Rooms: Hershey Lodge and Convention Center: 464. Hotel Hershey: 250

Meeting Rooms: Hotel: 12. Country Club: 4. Lodge: 27. Capacity of Largest: Hershey Hotel: 500 persons banquet style. Country Club: 300 persons. Lodge: 1500 persons banquet style. Meeting Space: Hershey Hotel: 16,000 sq. ft. Lodge: 45,000 sq. ft.

Room Price Range: $122 for regular room to $255 for room with Jacuzzi peak season (May to Sept.). A variety of golf, Hershey Park Holiday and other packages available year round. Seasonal discounts also available

Lounges: Forebay Lounge, J. P. Mallard's Lounge, Iberian Lounge

Restaurants: Hotel: Circular Dining Room, Fountain Cafe. Lodge: Zibos, Hearth Restaurant, Tack Room. Country Club: Candlelight Dining Room, Fireside

Entertainment: Music and dancing in J. P. Mallard's Lounge

Credit Cards: All major cards

General Amenities: Game room, shopping at factory outlet stores, seasonal festivals and events; meeting and conference facilities with audiovisual, banquet and secretarial services; carriage rides, babysitting service

Recreational Amenities: Indoor and outdoor swimming pools, 4 lighted tennis courts, platform tennis, exercise room with CAM II weight-lifting equipment and stationary bicycles, chip-and-putt golf course; Hershey Highmeadow Camp with outdoor swimming pools, 260 camp sites; lawn bowling, bicycling, sauna, whirlpool, riding stables

Reservation and Cancellation Policy: Credit card or deposit required to guarantee reservation. Cancellation within 24 hrs. of scheduled arrival date required to avoid penalties

Comments and Restrictions: No pets allowed. Taxes and gratuities additional to base rates

THE COUNTRY CLUB OF HERSHEY

Hershey, "the Sweetest Place on Earth," as the local chamber of commerce would have it, begins with Milton S. Hershey. Hershey was born in 1857 to a rural Pennsylvania German family in Hockersville, now part of the present town of Hershey. He was raised in the Mennonite faith, attended a variety of small schools in the area, and as a teenager was signed on as an apprentice confectioner in the factory of Joseph H. Royer in Lancaster, Pennsylvania. After a few unsuccessful candy ventures of his own, he founded Lancaster Carmel, which he sold to the American Carmel Co. of Philadelphia for $1 million in 1900. He then built the original Hershey factory in Derry Township, where milk, water and land were plentiful. By this time he was married to the former Catharine Sweeney of Jamestown, New York, and had repurchased his family homestead. By 1908 Hershey's business was formally chartered as the Hershey Chocolate Co. and he proceeded to build a town around the factory. This included the Hershey Industrial School (now the Milton Hershey School) for homeless boys, housed in a magnificent building on 486 acres, and numerous other buildings, projects and programs.

Catharine Hershey passed away in 1915, and Milton Hershey continued developing his business and contributing to a wide variety of philanthropic projects. The town prospered during the Great Depression, and to ensure that the local inhabitants were employed, Hershey launched a building campaign. Most of the town's major structures were built between 1932 and 1939. A community building, the Junior–Senior High School of the Milton Hershey School, the sports arena (now Hershey Park Arena) and the Hotel Hershey were among those constructed at that time. The 250-room hotel, which sits on the top of a hill overlooking the Hershey factory, the Milton Hershey School and the rolling hills of central Pennsylvania, was originally going to be patterned after the great Heliopolis Hotel in Cairo. Because of the projected cost, the plans were scaled down, and Hershey had his architect and chief engineer, D. Paul Witmer, derive plans from a picture postcard of a Mediterranean hotel that he admired instead. The Hotel Hershey has a Spanish-influenced fountain lobby, beautiful tiled floors and a magnificent circular dining room overlooking formal gardens that have reflecting pools. Classical music is piped into the gardens to provide a very soothing atmosphere as one contemplates the nine-hole executive golf course below. The construction of this hotel significantly contributed to Hershey's growth as a tourist attraction.

A short distance away is the Country Club of Hershey (formerly the Hershey Country Club), which features two excellent eighteen-hole championship golf courses. The Hershey Country Club West Course was designed by Maurice McCarthy and opened in 1930. McCarthy also designed the nearby Hershey Parkview (renamed the Country Club of Hershey South Course) public golf course. The West Course has been ranked by *Golf Digest* as one of America's 75 best resort courses, and prior to that it was regularly listed in *Golf Digest*'s top 100 golf-course selections. The Country Club of Hershey has been awarded *Golf* magazine's silver medal as a leading American golf-resort facility. The PGA Championship was held here in 1940, and the course is the frequent site of the Pennsylvania Open. The great Ben Hogan was the head professional at the Country Club of Hershey from 1940 to 1950.

The West Course is a rolling, traditional golf course with medium-sized, moderately fast, slightly undulating bentgrass greens. The course is well bunkered, with approximately 120 sand bunkers. Water comes into play on just one hole on this 6860-yard par-73 layout. The first hole on the West Course is the number-1-handicap hole and has been selected as one of the best holes on the LPGA Tour. This 437-yard par-4 dogleg right starts with a tee shot to a flat landing area with a bunker to the right. The second shot is to a partially hidden green with five traps and trees on the left and right. There are more than 175 varieties of trees on this course and the adjacent East Course, which was designed by George Fazio and opened in 1970. These mature oaks, pines, maples and other varieties help make the golf courses beautiful and difficult.

A picturesque par 3 on the West Course is the 176-yard fifth hole, which plays through a narrow chute of trees from an elevated tee situated on a cliff. The tee shot must carry a ravine to a green guarded left and right by large traps 70 feet below. In the background is Hershey's former house, which later served as a clubhouse until the current facility was built. An ardent golf enthusiast, Hershey had a six-hole course before retaining Maurice McCarthy to build the West Course. A difficult par 5 on the back side is the 568-yard thirteenth, which is long, uphill and fairly straight. The first shot is to a tree-protected fairway. On the second shot the fairway dips down in a swale, then up to a plateaued area. This shot must avoid the downward-sloping, tree-protected left side of the fairway. The approach shot is to a green protected by three traps on each side.

The George Fazio–designed East Course plays 7061 yards from the back tees, covers terrain similar to that of the West Course and has water hazards on five holes. The finishing holes on both sides are good golf challenges. The 420-yard par-4 ninth is a slight dogleg left with water on the right and traps on the left off the tee. The second shot is to a sizeable, sharply elevated green protected by three traps on the right and two others to the left and in front. The eighteenth is a 456-yard par 4 cut by a small lake. The second shot is likely to have a downhill lie. The approach over water to a large green guarded by five traps to the left and a large trap to the right. The greens on this course tend to be small to medium sized, moderately fast and undulating.

The Country Club of Hershey, which is approximately 5 minutes from the Hershey Hotel, can be played if you are a member, guest of a member or a guest at the Hershey Lodge or Hotel. It is easier to get tee times at the East Course, and this course is open year round. The West Course usually closes in late November and opens in mid-March, weather permitting. The East Course was once the site of the LPGA Lady Keystone Open. The clubhouse has locker rooms and showers, a full pro shop, meeting rooms, and a few parlor and bedroom rentals. There are lighted tennis courts, an outdoor swimming pool and tennis pro shop nearby. A formal dining room, short-order and snack food services are also offered. A practice range, bunker and putting green as well as instruction are available.

The 6146-yard Country Club of Hershey South Course (formerly the Parkview Golf Course), opened in 1929, is located nearby. This course has hosted both the National Public Links Tournaments and the Pennsylvania Public Links. Also, there are two nine-hole public courses within minutes of the Hotel Hershey: a 2680-yard par-34 course is on the hotel grounds, and the 2316-yard Spring Creek Golf Course is within easy driving distance.

The Hershey Hotel is on the National Register of Historic Places and has a variety of restaurants, meeting and conference facilities, tennis, swimming, bicycling and a variety of other recreational activities and events. The hotel has been designated the family resort of the year by *Family Circle* magazine and has earned a variety of hospitality awards, including the American Automobile Association's Four-Diamond rating. Packages for golf, theme weekends, holidays, Hershey Park and others are available at the Hotel or the nearby 464-room Hershey Lodge, which is situated on a 30-acre site. Another facility is Hershey Highmeadow Camp, which has 260 open and shaded campsites on 55 acres for tent campers and recreational vehicles. Cabins are also available, and there are 2 swimming pools, playgrounds, a game room, a store and a self-service laundry at this year-round site. Golf-package accommodations are available through the Hotel Hershey, the Hershey Lodge and the Hershey Country Club.

The Hershey Lodge has more than 45,000 square feet of meeting, conference and banquet space, and the Hershey Country Club has conference and banquet facilities as well. There is a variety of special events in Hershey ranging from The Great American Chocolate Festival to special exhibits at the 23-acre Hershey Gardens, which feature annuals, tulips, holly, azaleas and more than 850 varieties of roses. In addition to the Hershey Theater, Hershey Park, the Hershey Museum of American Life and numerous other buildings and institutions that Hershey has bequeathed, there are nearby attractions including Gettysburg and Pennsylvania Dutch country.

Milton Hershey died in 1945 at the age of 88 and is buried next to his wife and parents in the Hershey Cemetery. Meanwhile, the nearby Hershey factory, the largest chocolate-manufacturing facility in the world, produces those tasty candies and his philanthropies live on. Not a bad legacy for someone with a fourth-grade education.

Recommended Golf Courses in Pennsylvania

Within 1 Hour of Harrisburg:

Carroll Valley Golf Resort, Fairfield, (717) 642–5848 (Mountain View), (717) 642–8252 (Carroll Valley), Resort. Mountain View: 18/6343/71. Carroll Valley: 18/6633/71

Country Club of Hershey South Course (formerly Hershey Parkview), Hershey, (717) 534–3450, (800) 900–4653, Public, 18/6146/70

Fairview Golf Course, Quentin, (717) 273–3411, Public, 18/6227/71

Hawk Valley Golf Club, Denver, (717) 445–5445, (800) 522–4295, Public, 18/6258/72

Heritage Hills Golf Resort, York, (717) 755–4653, (800) 942–2444, Public, 18/6316/71

Holiday Inn Lancaster Host Resort, Lancaster, (717) 397–7756, (800) HOLIDAY, Resort. Amber: 9/3378/36. Sapphire: 9/3481/36. Emerald: 9/3131/36

Hotel Hershey Golf Course, Hershey, (717) 533–2171, Public, 9/2680/34

Lost Creek Golf Club, Oakland Mills, (717) 463–2450, Public, 18/6579/71

Monroe Valley Golf Club, Jonestown, (717) 865–2375, Public, 18/7015/72

Penn National Golf Club, Fayetteville, (717) 352–3000, (800) 221–7366, Semiprivate, 18/6931/72

Royal Oaks Golf Course, Lebanon, (717) 274–2212, Public, 18/6542/71

South Hills Golf Club, Hanover, (717) 637–7500, Public, 18/6575/71

Spring Creek Golf Club, Hershey, (717) 533–2847, Semiprivate, 9/2316/36

Within 1 Hour of Altoona:

Bedford Springs Hotel and Golf Club, Bedford, (814) 623–8999, 18/7000/74

Downriver Golf Club, Everett, (814) 652–5193, Public, 18/6855/72

Iron Masters Country Club, Roaring Spring, (814) 224–2915, Semiprivate, 18/6644/72

Sinking Valley Country Club, Altoona, (814) 684–0666, Semiprivate, 18/6735/72

Chambersburg Area:

Greencastle Greens Golf Club, Greencastle, (717) 597–1188, Public, 18/6908/72

Majestic Ridge Golf Club, Chambersburg, (717) 267–3444, Public, 18/6538/71

State College

Course Name: TOFTREES RESORT

Course Type: Resort
Resort: Toftrees Resort
Address: 1 Country Club Lane
State College, PA 16803
Phone: (814) 238–7600 (Golf Course)
(814) 234–8000, (800) 252–3551 (PA),
(800) 458–3602 (outside PA) (Resort)
Fax: (814) 238–4404 (Resort)

GOLF COURSE

Head Professional: Darrin Helfrick
Course Length/Par (All Tees): Back 7018/72, Blue 6780/72, White 6427/72, Forward 5567/72
Course Slope/Rating (All Tees): Back 134/74.3, Blue 132/73.3, White 129/71.6, Ladies' White 135/75.3, Ladies' Forward 126/71.8
Course Architect: Edmund Ault (1969)
Golf Facilities: Full Pro Shop X, Snack Bar X, Lounge X, Restaurant X, Locker Room X, Showers X, Club Rental X, Club Repair X, Cart Rental X, Instruction X, Practice Green X, Driving Range X, Practice Bunker X, Club Storage X
Tee-Time Reservation Policy: Resort guests: At time of confirmed reservaton. Outside play: 1 wk. in advance
Ranger: Yes
Tee-off-Interval Time: 8 and 9 min.
Time to Play 18 Holes: 4½ hrs.
Course Hours/Earliest Tee-off: 7 a.m.
Green and Cart Fees: $59 for 18 holes with cart
Credit Cards: All major cards
Season: Mid-April to Oct. Busiest season June, July
Course Comments: Can walk after 3 p.m. any day, before 10 a.m. weekdays
Golf Packages: Available through resort
Discounts: Reduced rate when walking, after 4 p.m., before 10 a.m.
Places to Stay Nearby: Nittany Lion Inn (814) 231–7500, (800) 233–7505; Atherton Hilton (814) 231–2100, (800) 445–8667; Best Western State College (814) 237–8005, (800) 635–1177; Holiday Inn—Penn State (814) 231–3001, (800) HOLIDAY. BED AND BREAKFASTS: Colonel Thomas Hartley Inn (Hartleton) (717) 922–4477; General Potter Farm (Potters Mills) (814) 364–2474; Rest and Repast Central Bed and Breakfast Service for Central PA (814) 238–1484
Local Attractions: Penn State University, hunting, fishing, camping, boating, hiking, wineries, Tussey Mountain Ski Area, horseback riding, Shaver's Creek Environmental Center, ridge soaring, gliderports, Boalsburg Heritage Mu-

seum, Boal Mansion and Museum, Curtin Village and Mansion, Eagle Iron Works, Bald Eagle State Park. Bald Eagle State Park (814) 625–2447. State College Chamber of Commerce (814) 237–7644. State College and Centre County Tourism (814) 231–1400

Directions: Rte. 322, Toftrees exit, follow signs to Toftrees and golf course

Closest Commercial Airports: University Park, State College (10 min.); Harrisburg International (1½ hrs.); Pittsburgh International (3 hrs.); Philadelphia International (3½ hrs.)

RESORT

Date Built: 1976

No. of Rooms: 131, including 109 guest rooms, 22 residence suites

Meeting Rooms: 8. Capacity of Largest: 120 persons banquet style. Meeting Space: 11,650 sq. ft.

Room Price Range: $69 per person per night, single, to $150 per night, double occupancy, for residence suites. Golf, holiday and other packages available

Lounge: Eagle Bar and Grille

Restaurant: Le Papillon

Entertainment: Live music, cabaret theater

Credit Cards: All major cards

General Amenities: Fitness center, organized excursions, horse-drawn carriage rides; meeting and conference facilities with auditorium, classroom, banquet, theater and conference space with audiovisual and food services

Recreational Amenities: 4 lighted tennis courts, pro shop, instruction; heated swimming pool, par-course fitness trail, bicycling, cross-country skiing, volleyball, exercise room

Reservation and Cancellation Policy: 48-hr. cancellation notice required to avoid penalties

Comments and Restrictions: No pets allowed. Taxes additional to base rates

TOFTREES RESORT

The Toftrees Resort golf course has been rated among the top public-access golf courses in the state of Pennsylvania by *Golf Digest*. This 7018-yard Edmund Ault–designed layout is beautifully situated within a 1500-acre wooded real-estate and recreational development 5 minutes away from Pennsylvania State University. The front nine, which plays slightly longer than the back nine, winds its way through well-treed fairways bordered by pine, oak, maple, dogwood, azaleas and laurel. The back nine is bordered by some of Toftrees' unobtrusive condominiums and single-family homes.

The medium-sized, soft, undulating bentgrass greens are well bunkered and often uphill on this up-and-down golf course. Six of the holes are doglegs to the left, so the typical "fader" will not have an easy time negotiating the trees at Toftrees. Often the golfer will be faced with uneven lies, and changes in elevation and sizeable greens. This demands proper club selection and accuracy. Knowledge of pin placement relative to the slope and dimensions of the greens is especially important here. You will find yourself lagging putts quite often.

There are four tee positions to choose from at Toftrees. These distances range from 7018 yards to 5567 yards. The number-1-handicap hole at all distances is the formidable par-5 eighth, which plays 634 yards from the back tees. This hole essentially requires three long, accurate shots down tree-lined fairways to a large green. On the approach, avoid missing to the left, where there is a deep, difficult bunker. The next hole is the signature hole, the par-4 ninth, which plays 380 yards uphill to a large green with a drainage ditch to the left back and a deep bunker to the right. From the back tees, the tee shot has to carry 225 yards over a pond and avoid a bunker on the right in the process. The other tee distances are a more forgiving 363, 293 and 286 yards on this tricky hole.

Another monster par 5 on the course is the 607-yard fourteenth, which plays straight and downhill (eventually) to a large, deep green guarded by traps right and left. The tee shot should be down the center to avoid the out of bounds on the right. The second shot has to be hit to the center or right center to avoid fairway bunkers, and the approach has to be long enough to get safely to the putting surface.

The finishing hole is a challenging 430-yard par-4 dogleg left. The tee-shot strategy is to hit the ball down the left side, leaving you a mid-iron or long iron to a heavily bunkered green. More distance than you would expect is needed to reach the target on this uphill approach shot.

The Marriott organization has recently taken over the management of Toftrees. The entire facility has gone through a $13-million renovation. The pro shop has been expanded and the maintenance level upgraded, as has the quality of individual and group golf-instructional programs. The resort, which has almost 12,000 square feet of meeting space, has been awarded *Meetings and Convention* magazine's Gold Tee Award as one of the 76 best golf conference resorts in North America, Mexico, and the Caribbean. That puts Toftrees in elite company.

Other amenities at Toftrees include 131 rooms and residence suites at very reasonable prices, lighted tennis courts, a heated swimming pool, fitness center, jogging and fitness trails, bicycling, and Le Papillon, an excellent on-site restaurant. The resort has easy access to Pennsylvania State University and the historical, cultural and recreational attractions of the surrounding area. These include wineries, hunting, fishing, boating, Big Ten sporting events, arts festivals and towns such as historic Boalsburg, Bellefonte, Curtin Village and others. The Blue and White golf courses at Pennsylvania State are also worth looking into, as is nearby Spruce Creek, one of America's best trout streams. In winter, this area becomes a haven for downhill and cross-country skiers.

Golf packages, including midweek packages, are available. The practice facilities at Toftrees include driving range, practice bunker and putting green. The clubhouse has ample locker-room and shower facilities.

The population of State College and its five surrounding townships is approximately 80,000. That wouldn't be a sellout at the football stadium. However, the university does enroll more than 38,000 students.

Penn State's football team eats its pre-game meals at Toftrees. If you're here in the fall, you might run into coach Joe Paterno pacing one of the fairways.

Recommended Golf Courses in Pennsyvania

State College Area:

Pennsylvania State University Golf Course, State College, (814) 865–4653, Public. Blue: 18/6525/72. White: 18/6008/72

State College Elks Country Club, Boalsburg, (814) 466–6451, Semiprivate, 18/6358/71

Western/Pittsburgh Area

Course Name: CHAMPION LAKES GOLF CLUB

Course Type: Public
Address: Route 711/Box 285, R.D. 1
              Bolivar, PA 15923
              Phone: (412) 238–5440

GOLF COURSE

Director of Golf: Allison DeStefano
Course Length/Par (All Tees): Back 6608/71, Middle 6205/71, Ladies' Forward 5556/74
Course Slope/Rating (All Tees): Back 133/72.3, Middle 128/69.5, Ladies' Forward 127/72.1
Course Architects: Dick Groat and Jerry Lynch (1966)
Golf Facilities: Full Pro Shop X, Snack Bar X, Lounge X, Restaurant X, Locker Room X, Showers X, Club Rental X, Club Repair No, Cart Rental X, Instruction X, Practice Green X, Driving Range X, Practice Bunker X, Club Storage Limited
Tee-Time Reservation Policy: Anytime in advance
Ranger: Yes
Tee-off-Interval Time: 7 and 8 min.
Time to Play 18 Holes: 4 hrs. 45 min.
Course Hours/Earliest Tee-off: 5:45 a.m. to dark

Green Fees: $25 for 18 holes Sat., Sun., holidays; $20 for 18 holes weekdays. $18 for 9 holes Sat., Sun., holidays; $13 for 9 holes weekdays

Cart Fees: $20 for 18 holes per cart, $10 for 9 holes

Credit Cards: None—cash or check only

Season: Year round, weather permitting. Busiest June -Sept.

Course Comments: Can walk anytime. Bed and breakfast accomodations on site

Golf Packages: Inquire at pro shop

Discounts: Seasonal

Places to Stay Nearby: LIGONIER: Lord Ligonier (412) 238–9545; Ft. Ligonier Motor Lodge (412) 238–6677; Antioch Inn Village (Church Camp, 1½ miles away) (412) 128–3677. INDIANA, PA: Best Western University Inn (412) 349–9620, (800) 528–1234; Holiday Inn (412) 463–3561, (800) HOLIDAY. JOHNSTOWN: Comfort Inn (814) 266–3678, (800) 4–CHOICE; Holiday Inn (412) 254–7777, (800) HOLIDAY. BED AND BREAKFAST: Grant House Bed and Breakfast (412) 238–5135

Local Attractions: LIGONIER: Forbes Rd. Gun Museum, Fort Ligonier, Mister Rogers' Neighborhood of Make-Believe, fishing, hunting, bicycling, camping, boating, hiking, antiquing. Johnstown. Pittsburgh. Ligonier Chamber of Commerce (412) 238–4200

Directions: From Pittsburgh: Pennsylvania Turnpike to Donegal (exit 9), take Rte. 31 to Rte. 711 north to Ligonier, course 7 mi. north of Ligonier. Pennsylvania Turnpike to Irwin (exit 7), Rte. 30 east to Ligonier, course 7 mi. north of Ligonier. Approximately 70 mi. east of Pittsburgh

Closest Commercial Airports: Westmoreland County/Latrobe (30 min.), Pittsburgh International (1½ hrs.)

CHAMPION LAKES GOLF CLUB

Champion Lakes is a tightly treed 6608-yard par-71 layout designed and owned by Dick Groat and Jerry Lynch, two members of the 1960 World Champion Pittsburgh Pirates baseball team. This course has an excellent reputation for its quality of maintenance; fast, true-rolling greens; and difficulty of play. There have been fewer than 10 subpar rounds at Champion Lakes in the last 25 years. You might want to work on your long irons and put away your driver before visiting here.

The rough is generally kept high at Champion Lakes, but there are few fairway bunkers. The trees, rough and water hazards provide enough trouble for any golfer, however. The course has many difficult and memorable holes. The 436-yard par-4 first hole is a slight dogleg right that plays to a deep green well guarded by bunkers to the left, rear and right. Two fairway bunkers have been added to guard the tee-shot landing area. The first hole is rated the number-1-handicap hole on the course. Another tough par 4 on this side is the 411-yard fourth, which plays down a corridor of trees to a deep green guarded by two bunkers to the left and one to the right. The tee shot on this slight dogleg left has to be long enough to avoid a downhill lie on the second shot and far enough right to take the trees on the left out of play on the approach. This is a beautiful golf hole.

The 188-yard eleventh is one of the typically difficult par 3s at Champion Lakes. The tee shot is over a lake to a forward-sloping green fronted by water and guarded by traps left, rear and right-front. A short ball is likely to slide down the slick green into the water below. The 238-yard par-3 sixteenth provides a beautiful view of the golf course as you play to a large green protected by traps to the left and right.

The finishing hole is a 538-yard par-5 dogleg right. The first shot is to the bend in the dogleg, and the second has to clear a pond in the fairway while avoiding a lake to the right. The large green is guarded by sizeable bunkers to the left and right.

Champion Lakes provides you with country-club conditions at very reasonable rates. This golf course is not far from where Arnold Palmer was born and still maintains a residence. He shot a 68 here in 1968. Champion Lakes is considered one of the best-managed, best-maintained and most challenging publicly accessible golf courses in western Pennsylvania.

Course Name: NEMACOLIN
WOODLANDS RESORT
**Links, Mystic Rock
Courses**

Course Type: Resort
Resort: Nemacolin Woodlands Resort
Address: Route 40/P.O. Box 188
Farmington, PA 15437
Phone: (412) 329–6111 (Golf Course),
(412) 329–8555 (Resort),
(800) 422–2736 (Golf
Course, Resort)
Fax: (412) 329–6901 (Golf Course),
(412) 329–6153 (Resort)

GOLF COURSE

Head Professional: Jim Sipes
Course Length/Par (All Tees): Links:
Back 6814/71, White 6532/71, Gold
6267/71, Forward 4835/71. Mystic
Rock: Back 6832/72, White 6300/72,
Gold 5860/72, Forward 4991/72
Course Slope/Rating (All Tees): Links:
Back 128/71.6, White 124/69.7, Gold
121/69.2, Forward 115/67.3. Mystic
Rock: Back 146/75.0, White 141/71.5,
Gold 132/69.7, Forward 125/68.8
Course Architect: Links: NA (1976),
remodeled 1988. Mystic Rock: Pete Dye
(1995)
Golf Facilities: Full Pro Shop X, Snack
Bar X, Lounge X, Restaurant X,
Locker Room No, Showers No, Club
Rental X, Club Repair X, Cart Rental
X, Instruction X, Practice Green X,
Driving Range X, Practice Bunker X,
Club Storage X
Tee-Time Reservation Policy: Up to 45
days in advance for resort guests. Up to
7 days in advance for the public
Ranger: Yes
Tee-off-Interval Time: 10 min.
Time to Play 18 Holes: 4½ hrs.
Course Hours/Earliest Tee-off: 7:30 a.m.
Green and Cart Fees: Links: $62 plus tax
for 18 holes for the public. Mystic
Rock: $90 plus tax for 18 holes for
resort guests
Credit Cards: American Express, Master-
Card, Visa
Season: Apr. through Nov.

Course Comments: Woodland Golf
Academy on site (412) 329-6201
Golf Packages: Through resort
Discounts: Twilight, resort guests, seasonal
rates, early bird discounts
Places to Stay Nearby: FARMINGTON: Sum-
mit Inn Resort (412) 438–8594. UNION-
TOWN: Mt. Vernon Inn (412) 437–2704,
(800) 270–2704. PITTSBURGH: Sheraton
Station Square (412) 261–2000, (800)
255–7488; Pittsburgh Vista (412) 281–
3700, (800) 367–8478
Local Attractions: Hunting, fishing, hik-
ing, camping, boating, winter skiing.
Pittsburgh. Pittsburgh Greater Pittsburgh
Convention and Visitors Bureau, 4 Gateway Center, Pittsburgh (412) 281–9222,
(800) 359–0758
Directions: Nemocolin Woodlands Resort
is 65 miles southeast of Pittsburgh. Take
Rte. 60 south to I–79 south to Rte. 40
east to resort. Or take Pennsylvania
Turnpike to Donegal Exit. Take Rte. 31
east to Rte. 381 south to Rte. 40 east to
resort
Closest Commercial Airport: Pittsburgh
International (1½ hrs.)

RESORT

Date Built: 1970
No. of Rooms: Inn: 98 rooms and suites.
Condominiums: 40 2-bedroom
Meeting Rooms: 23. Capacity of Largest:
350 persons ballroom style. Meeting
Space: 40,000 sq. ft.
Room Price Range: Inn rooms $150 to
$235. Suites $190 to $395. Condomini-
ums $150 to $185. Peak season late
May through Oct. Golf and other
packages available
Lounges: Fables Lounge, Diamond Lil's,
The Tavern
Restaurants: The Golden Trout, Allures,
Caddy Shack, Sun Dial Ski Lodge
Cafeteria
Entertainment: DJs, live music
Credit Cards: All major cards
General Amenities: Meeting and confer-
ence facilities with audiovisual, banquet
and secretarial support; 9 retail shops;
kids' club program for ages 4 through
12, babysitting services

Recreational Amenities: Spa with sauna, whirlpool, steam, weight room, cardiovascular equipment; equestrian center, badminton, basketball, board games, bocce, croquet, horseshoes, ping pong, shuffleboard, 4 swimming pools, volleyball, 4 tennis courts, hiking trails, daily art tour, Woodlands Activity Center with biking, video games, mini golf, children's activities, fishing, pedal boats and more; winter cross-country skiing, sleigh and surrey rides, ski academy

Reservation and Cancellation Policy: $200 deposit per room is required to secure reservations May to Oct. (one night's lodging Nov. through Apr.). 15-day cancellation notice required to receive full refund. Early departure penalties

Comments and Restrictions: Children 12 and under stay free in parents' room (including breakfasts); $20 for each additional adult (including breakfasts)

NEMACOLIN WOODLANDS RESORT

Nemacolin Woodlands Resort is situated on a former private hunting preserve comprising approximately 1000 hilly, wooded acres 65 miles southeast of Pittsburgh. Mr. Joseph Hardy, a Pennsylvanian who made his fortune in the lumber business, purchased the property at auction in 1987 and has since invested over $100 million to turn Nemocolin Woodlands into a fine year-round resort. Mr. Hardy hired Pete Dye, a world class golf architect and entrepreneur, to design Mystic Rock. A few years and $16 million later, in 1995, the course opened and put Nemocolin on the international golf resort map. In 1995 *Golf Digest* rated Mystic Rock one of the best new resort golf courses in the United States.

Mystic Rock is a strategic golf course with trees, streams, wetlands, and a variety of rock outcroppings adding challenge and aesthetic pleasure to the course. There are many tough, memorable holes at Mystic Rock including the 435-yard par-4 dogleg right second which requires a tee shot that carries over 225 yards from the back tee to clear wetlands. A sizeable rock embankment protects the right side at the turn of the dog-

leg. The approach is usually a long-iron to an elevated, kidney-shaped green with a bunker to its left. A pin position tucked to the left rear can bring the bunker into play and make this hole much more difficult. This hole can be played from 391, 373, and 336 yards from the other tee distances. Mystic Rock is bentgrass from tee to green with bluegrass and deeper fescue rough protecting the landing areas. The large, undulating greens provide many pin placement options and demand well-postioned approaches to the target.

A good par 3 on the front side is the 173-yard seventh whose tee shot must carry a sea of high grass and rough to a green protected by bunkers to its left and rear. After passing Mulligan's drive-by snack stand at the turn, you are ready to meet the challenge of the back nine. An outstanding par 5 on this side is the 526-yard sixteenth whose tee shot is from an elevated plateau. The second shot requires you to lay up or attempt to reach a peninsula green in two.

The Links Course at Nemacolin is another solid golf experience. The 6814-yard par-71 layout has a variety of elevation changes that can leave you with tricky, uneven lies and some serious club selection decisions. The most difficult hole on this course is the 441-yard par-4 dogleg right fifteenth which requires a long, accurate tee shot to set up a clear approach to a green backed by a bunker and a lake beyond. There is another bunker to the left of the target. The approach shot is often from a downhill lie, adding to the difficulty of this hole.

Nemacolin Woodlands has a Golf Academy with a full range of instructional aids and options. The practice area has three full size greens, a driving range, target greens and practice bunkers. Nemacolin offers a full range of resort amenitites including a spa, over 40,000 square feet of meeting space, an equestrian center, winter skiing, and much more. Prior to the recent multimilllion dollar renovations at Nemocolin, this resort had a 30-room inn and a fading golf course. Now it is a must visit on your golf itinerary.

Course Name: QUICKSILVER GOLF
CLUB

Course Type: Public
Address: 2000 Quicksilver Road,
Route 980,
Midway, PA 15060
Phone: (412) 796-1811 (Golf Shop)
(412) 796-1594 (Clubhouse)
Fax: (412) 796-1632

GOLF COURSE

Director of Golf: Sean Parees
Head Professional: Rob Murphy
Course Length/Par (All Tees): Back
7085/72, Blue 6755/72, White 6356/72,
Ladies' Forward 5067/73
Course Slope/Rating (All Tees): Back
145/75.7, Blue 139/73.4, White
136/71.5, Ladies' Forward 115/68.6
Course Architect: Don Nagode (1973)
Golf Facilities: Full Pro Shop X, Snack
Bar X, Lounge X, Restaurant X,
Locker Room X, Showers X, Club
Rental X, Club Repair X, Cart Rental
X, Instruction X, Practice Green X,
Driving Range X, Practice Bunker X,
Club Storage X
Tee-Time Reservation Policy: 5 days in
advance with credit card guarantee
Ranger: Yes
Tee-off-Interval Time: 9 min.
Time to Play 18 Holes: 4 hrs., 15 min.
Course Hours/Earliest Tee-off: 6 a.m.
Green Fees: $60 for 18 holes, $32 for 9
holes
Cart Fees: $15 for 18 holes per person,
$8 for 9 holes per person
Pull Carts: $4 for 18 holes, $2 for 9 holes
Credit Cards: American Express, Dis-
cover, MasterCard, Visa
Season: Year round, weather permitting.
Busiest season May to Oct.
Course Comments: Can walk. Carts
required busiest season on weekends
before 2 p.m.
Golf Packages: Available
Discounts: Juniors, seniors, seasonal
reduced rates
Places to Stay Nearby: CARNEGIE:
Howard Johnson's Pittsburgh Airport
(412) 923-2244, (800) 441-4656; Com-
fort Inn Parkway West (412) 787-2600,

(800) 228-5150; Ramada Inn—
Pittsburgh Airport (412) 264-8950,
(800) 272-6232; Pittsburgh Airport Mar-
riott (412) 788-8800, (800) 228-9290.
PITTSBURGH: Pittsburgh Hilton and Tow-
ers (412) 391-4600, (800) 445-8667;
Priory (412) 231-3338; Sheraton Hotel
at Station Square (412) 261-2000, (800)
255-7488
Local Attractions: PITTSBURGH: Pittsburgh
Ballet Theatre, Children's Museum,
opera, Public Theatre, Symphony Society, Carnegie Museum of Art/Natural
History, Carnegie Science Center,
Benedum Center for the Performing
Arts, Station Square, Meadows Racetrack, Fort Pitt Museum, Rodef Shalom
Biblical Botanical Garden, Cathedral of
Learning, Clayton (Henry Clay Frick estate), Frick Art Museum, Duquesne Incline, Pittsburgh Zoo, Point State Park,
Phipps Conservatory, Three Rivers Boat
Cruises, hiking, horseback riding, other
recreational activities; professional football, baseball, hockey, restaurants, shopping, University of Pittsburgh, Carnegie
Mellon University, Duquesne University. Greater Pittsburgh Convention and
Visitors Bureau (412) 281-7711, (800)
366-0093. Pittsburgh Cultural Trust
(800) 288-SHOW for cultural packages
Directions: From Pittsburgh: Rte. 22/30
west, continue on Rte. 22 west to Hwy.
980, south on Hwy. 980 to Midway and
golf course
Closest Commercial Airport: Greater
Pittsburgh International (20 min.)

QUICKSILVER GOLF CLUB

Quicksilver is a Don Nagode–designed
layout located in Midway, just west of
Pittsburgh, Pennsylvania. There are four tee
positions on this challenging layout, which
has a formidable 145 slope rating from the
back tees. The Quicksilver Golf Club is
one of the stops on the Senior PGA Tour.

This challenging golf course is a rolling
layout with few trees that come into play.
The various cuts of rough are kept at ½
in., 1 in., and 4 in., making life difficult if
the ball strays too far from the fairway.
There is a variety of large, strategically

placed fairway bunkers, and most of the large, moderately fast bentgrass greens are well guarded by bunkers. The wind can also be a factor on this open golf course.

One of the more scenic and memorable holes at Quicksilver is the 199-yard par-3 eighth, which plays from an elevated tee to a wide, shallow green fronted by water that curls around the left side and backed by a large bunker. The back nine features one of the toughest par 4s on the course, the 467-yard thirteenth, a dogleg right with trees and a trap at its right corner, beginning approximately 240 yards from the back tee. The second shot is to a wide, deep green guarded by traps to the front and right. One of the most difficult par 5s on the course is the 577-yard fifteenth. The first shot is over a pond to the fairway, which has a trap on the left and water to the right of the landing area. The second shot is toward a deep green guarded on the left and right by traps. Usually three very well struck shots are required to reach this green in regulation.

The modern, three-story clubhouse at Quicksilver has a pro shop, locker rooms and showers, a dining room, a bar and banquet facilities. The practice facilities include a large, grass-teed driving range; sand bunkers and chipping green; and a putting green. Individual and group lessons are available from the staff of PGA professionals.

Quicksilver is one of the best public golf facilities in the Pittsburgh vicinity.

American Golf Hall of Fame

The Foxburg Country Club in Foxburg, Pennsylvania, houses a variety of interesting golf memorabilia, including golf clubs once used by early champions such as J. H. Taylor and Old Tom Morris. There is also a variety of golf balls, including featheries, guttaperchas, and clubs used during the feather ball era. The Foxburg Country Club is 55 miles northeast of Pittsburgh and 4 miles off I–80 at exit 6. American Golf Hall of Fame, Foxburg Country Club, Box 1, Rte. 58, Foxburg, PA 16036, (412) 659–3196.

Recommended Golf Courses in Pennsylvania

Within 1½ Hours of Pittsburgh:

Butler's Golf Course, Elizabeth, (412) 751–9121, Public, 18/6660/72

Cedarbrook Golf Course, Belle Vernon, (412) 929–8300, Public. Gold: 18/6701/72. Red: 18/6100/72

Chestnut Ridge Golf Club, Blairsville, (412) 459–7188, Public. 18/6321/72

Golf Club at Hidden Valley, Hidden Valley, (814) 443–6454, (800) 946–5348, Resort, 18/6579/72

Mayfield Golf Club, Clarion, (814) 226–8888, Public, 18/6990/72

Mohawk Trails Golf Course, New Castle, (412) 667–8570, Public, 18/6324/72

Pine Grove Golf Course, Grove City, (412) 458–9942, Public, 18/6159/72

Saxon Golf Course, Sarver, (412) 353–2130, Public. 18/6678/72. 9/2185/34

Seven Springs Mountain Resort Golf Course, Champion, (814) 352–7777, Resort, 18/6360/71

Stoughton Acres Golf Club, Butler, (412) 285–3633, Public, 18/6059/71

Tam O'Shanter Golf Club, Hermitage, (412) 981–3552, Public, 18/6537/72

Tom's Run Golf Course, Blairsville, (412) 459–7188, Public, 18/6705/72

Bradford Area:

Emporium Country Club, Emporium, (814) 486–7715, Semiprivate, 18/6032/72

DuBois:

Treasure Lake Golf Club, DuBoios, (814) 375–1807, Public, 18/6524/72

Within 1 Hour of Erie:

Bavarian Hills Golf Course, St. Mary's, (814) 834–3602, Public, 18/6290/71

Downing Golf Course, Harbor Creek, (814) 899–5827, Public, 18/7175/72

North Hills Golf Club, Corry,
(814) 664–4477, Public, 18/6800/71

Riverside Golf Course, Cambridge Springs,
(814) 398–4637, Public, 18/6113/70

Scranton-Wilkes Barre Area:

Country Club at Woodloch Springs,
Hawley, (717) 685–2100, Resort,
18/6579/72

Edgewood in the Pines Golf Course,
Drums, (717) 788–1101, Public, 18/6721/72

Mill Race Golf Club, Benton,
(717) 925–2040, Resort, 18/6096/70

Scranton Municipal Golf Course, Lake
Ariel, (717) 689–2686, Public, 18/6650/72

Skytop Lodge Golf Club, Skytop,
(717) 595–8910, Resort, 18/6256/71

Stone Hedge Country Club, Tunkhannock,
(717) 836–5108, Public, 18/6506/71

Sugarloaf Golf Club, Sugarloaf,
(717) 384–4097, Public, 18/6845/72

Tamiment Resort and Conference Center,
Tamiment, (717) 588–6652, (800) 233–
8105, Resort, 18/6858/72

Wilkes-Barre Golf Club, Wilkes-Barre,
(717) 472–3590, Public, 18/6912/72

Williamsport Area:

Bucknell Golf Club, Lewisburg, (717) 523–
8193, Semiprivate, 18/6268/70

Tyoga Country Club, Wellsboro, (717) 724–
1653, Semiprivate, 18/6305/71

White Deer Park and Golf Course,
Montgomery, (717) 547–2186, Public.
Challenge: 18/6605/72. Vintage: 18/6405/72

Pennsylvania: Useful Information

Bureau of Travel Marketing, Pennsylvania
Department of Commerce, 453 Forum
Bldg., Harrisburg, PA 17120, (717) 787–
5453, (800) 847–4872

Forest Supervisor, Allegheny National
Forest, P.O. Box 847, Warren, PA 16365,
(814) 723–5150, (800) 280–CAMP (national forest information and reservations)

Pennsylvania Fish and Boat Commission,
P.O. Box 67000, Harrisburg, PA 17106–
7000, (717) 657–4518 (fishing regulations)

Pennsylvania Game Commission, 2001
Elmerton Ave., Harrisburg, PA 17110–
9797, (717) 787–4250 (hunting regulations)

Pennsylvania Bureau of State Parks, P.O.
Box 8551, Harrisburg, PA 17105–8551,
(717) 787–8800 (state parks information)

Pennsylvania Historical and Museum
Commission, P.O. Box 1026, Harrisburg,
PA 17108–1026, (717) 787–3362

Farm Vacations, Bureau of Marketing,
Department of Agriculture, 2301 N.
Cameron St., Harrisburg, PA 17110,
(717) 787–9948

Recommended Golf Courses in Rhode Island

Exeter Country Club, Exeter, (401) 295–1178, Semiprivate, 18/6919/72

Foster Country Club, Foster, (401) 397–7750, Public, 18/6187/72

Green Valley Country Club, Portsmouth, (401) 849–2162, Semiprivate, 18/6830/71

Montaup Country Club, Portsmouth, (401) 683–9982, Semiprivate, 18/6236/71

North Kingston Municipal Golf Course, North Kingston, (401) 294–4051, Public, 18/6161/70

Richmond Country Club, Richmond, (401) 364–9200, Public, 18/6826/71

Triggs Memorial Golf Course, Providence, (401) 521–8460, Public, 18/6596/72

Rhode Island: Useful Information

Rhode Island Tourism Division, 7 Jackson Walkway, Providence, RI 02903, (401) 277–2601, (800) 556–2484

Department of Environmental Management, 83 Park St., Providence, RI 02903, (401) 277–3075 (fishing and hunting regulations)

Rhode Island Division of Environmental Management, Forest Division Headquarters, 1307 Hartford Pike, North Scituate, RI 02857, (401) 647–3367, (800) 280–CAMP (national forest information and reservations)

Course Name: DUNES WEST GOLF COURSE

Course Type: Public
Address: 3535 Wando Plantation Way
Mount Pleasant, SC 29464
Phone: (803) 856–9000
Fax: (803) 884–7779

GOLF COURSE

Head Professional: Joe Roberts
Course Length/Par (All Tees): Back 6871/72, Middle 6392/72, Forward 5278/72
Course Slope/Rating (All Tees): Back 131/73.4, Middle 125/70.7, Forward 118/69.2
Course Architect: Arthur Hills (1992)
Golf Facilities: Full Pro Shop X, Snack Bar X, Lounge X, Restaurant X, Locker Room X, Showers X, Club Rental X, Club Repair X, Cart Rental X, Instruction X, Practice Green X, Driving Range X, Practice Bunker X, Club Storage X
Tee-Time Reservation Policy: 7 days in advance. Credit card guarantee for any time beyond 7 days. 48-hr. cancellation policy
Ranger: Yes
Tee-off-Interval Time: 8 min.
Time to Play 18 Holes: 4 hrs., 15 min.
Course Hours/Earliest Tee-off: 7 a.m.
Green and Cart Fees: Peak season: $60 for 18 holes with cart weekends, holidays; $50 for 18 holes with cart weekdays (March through May, mid-Sept. through mid-Nov.). Tax additional
Credit Cards: American Express, MasterCard, Visa
Season: Year round
Course Comments: Cart mandatory. Yardage book available
Golf Packages: Available
Discounts: Seasonal (Mid-Nov. to March, June to mid-Sept.)
Places to Stay Nearby: See Charleston area listing on page 579
Local Attractions: See Charleston area listing on pages 579

Directions: Rte. 17 to Rte. 41, west on Rte. 41, 3½ mi., course on right
Closest Commercial Airports: Charleston International (30 min.); Savannah International, GA (2½ hrs.)

DUNES WEST GOLF COURSE

Dunes West is a privately owned public golf course situated on 250 acres of marsh and waterfront land in Mount Pleasant, a suburb of Charleston. This Arthur Hills–designed layout, which plays 6871 yards from the back tees, was named one of the top ten new resort courses in the United States by *Golf* magazine in 1992. Dunes West is a somewhat open golf course with water hazards on six holes; large, moderately fast, undulating Bermuda-grass greens; and rolling fairways.

The five finishing holes at Dunes West are especially strong holes. The 474-yard par-4 fourteenth is a long dogleg right that plays to a large green bordered by a large trap on the right. The fifteenth is a 560-yard par-5 dogleg right. The tee shot has to avoid a series of bunkers on the right. The fairway then splits, with a huge set of bunkers in the center on the approach to the green, which is large and protected by two traps on the right. The 404-yard par-4 sixteenth is a dogleg to the left, with a lake and a series of traps at the right corner of the dogleg. The approach shot is to a green protected by water on the right and traps on the left. The 207-yard par-3 seventeenth plays straight to a deep green with a trap to the rear, water on the right and a small trap to the left. The finishing hole is a dogleg right whose second shot is bordered by an avenue of oaks on the right. These oaks are part of the rows of oaks that line the entranceway of this former plantation site.

The land at Dunes West was once Wando Plantation. Wando is the name given to local Indians by the early European settlers in the area. Dunes West was first part of a land grant to Edmund Bellinger in 1696. A plantation was eventually located here, and the main house and its outbuildings were located in the area where the Dunes West clubhouse now stands. The plantation manufactured bricks and produced rice and cotton. Over the years the plantation was owned by a long line of the local gentry, including Arnoldus Vanderhorst, whose family owned much of Kiawah Island; and later, Henrietta Hartford, who, after her husband's death in the 1930s, was one of America's wealthiest women. Her 32-room plantation house burned in 1942, never to be restored. After World War II the property, then in disrepair, was sold to the Georgia Pacific Co. The current owner, Scratch Golf Co., bought the property in 1991 to develop the Dunes West Golf Club.

A new 12,000-square-foot clubhouse is located on the site of the original plantation house and offers full dining, pro shop and locker-room amenities.

Course Name: **KIAWAH ISLAND RESORT**
The Ocean Course, Turtle Point, Osprey Point, Marsh Point Courses

Course Type: Resort
Resort: Kiawah Island Resort
Address: 12 Kiawah Beach Drive
Kiawah Island, SC 29455
Phone: (803) 768–2121,
(800) 654–2924
(Golf Course)
(803) 768–2121,
(800) 654–2924
(outside SC) (Resort)
Fax: (803) 768–9339 (Resort)

GOLF COURSE

Director of Golf: Tommy Cuthbert
Head Professional: Ocean: Brian Gerard. Turtle Point: Tommy Cuthbert. Osprey Point: Ronnie Miller. Marsh Point: Jim Kelechi
Course Length/Par (All Tees): Ocean: Back 7371/72, Middle 6824/72, Forward 5327/72. Turtle Point: Back 6919/72, Blue 6396/72, White 6014/72, Forward 5205/72. Osprey Point: Back 6678/72, Middle 6015/72, Forward 5122/72. Marsh Point: Back 6203/71, Middle 5841/71, Forward 5055/71
Course Slope/Rating (All Tees): Ocean: Back 139/74.2, Middle 126/70.9,

Ladies' Forward 134/72.1. Turtle Point: Back 132/73.5, Blue 127/71.5, White 122/70.5, Ladies' Forward 122/69.8. Osprey Point: Back 124/71.8, Middle 118/68.8, Ladies' Forward 118/69.4. Marsh Point: Back 126/71.8, Middle 120/69.4, Ladies' Forward 122/69.5
Course Architects: Ocean: Pete Dye (1991). Turtle Point: Jack Nicklaus (1981). Osprey Point: Tom Fazio (1988). Marsh Point: Gary Player (1976)
Golf Facilities: Full Pro Shop X, Snack Bar X, Lounge X, Restaurant X, Locker Room X, Showers X, Club Rental X, Club Repair X, Cart Rental X, Instruction X, Practice Green X, Driving Range X, Practice Bunker X, Club Storage X. (Golf facilities vary by golf course)
Tee-Time Reservation Policy: Resort guests: At time of reservation. Groups 1 yr. in advance. Outside play: 1 day in advance
Ranger: Yes
Tee-off-Interval Time: Ocean: 10 min. Turtle Point, Osprey Point, Marsh Point: 8 min.
Time to Play 18 Holes: Ocean: 4 hrs., 45 min. Turtle Point, Osprey Point, Marsh Point: 4 hrs., 15 min.
Course Hours/Earliest Tee-off: 7 a.m.
Green and Cart Fees: Peak season, outside play: Ocean: $131 for 18 holes with cart, range balls. Turtle Point, Osprey Point: $106 for 18 holes with cart, range balls. Marsh Point: Closed in 1996 for renovation
Credit Cards: American Express, Diners Club, MasterCard, Visa
Season: Year round. Busiest season March to Oct.
Course Comments: Cart mandatory
Golf Packages: Available through the resort year round
Discounts: Seasonal (Nov. 1 to Feb.). Replays (Ocean course excepted)
Places to Stay Nearby: See Charleston area listing on page 579
Local Attractions: See Charleston area listing on pages 579
Directions: From I–95S: I–26 toward Charleston, Mark Clark Expressway

(I–526W) to U.S. 17 south toward Savannah for approximately 5 mi. to Main Rd., turn left and follow signs 17 mi. to Kiawah Island. From I–95N: U.S. 17 north toward Charleston and follow U.S. 17 north for 40 mi. to Main Rd., turn right on Main Rd., follow signs 17 mi. to Kiawah Island

Closest Commercial Airports: Charleston International (45 min.); Savannah International, GA (2 hrs.); Myrtle Beach (2½ hrs.)

RESORT

Date Built: 1974

No. of Rooms: 150 guest rooms, 350 1- to 4-bedroom villas

Meeting/Exhibit Rooms: 23. Capacity of Largest: 600 persons. Meeting Space: 10,600 sq. ft.

Room Price Range: $100 to $225 (peak season March 1 to Oct. 31). Various rates for villas beginning from $195 for 3-bedroom villa. Golf packages, rates and other options available

Lounges: Topsider Lounge, Indigo House

Restaurants: Jasmine Porch, Sundancer's, Indigo House, The Food Court

Entertainment: Live music in Topsider Lounge and for special events

Credit Cards: American Express, Diners Club, MasterCard, Visa

General Amenities: Children's recreational programs, cookouts, guided nature excursions and nature study presentations, market with shopping, marina; complete meeting and conference facilities including audiovisual, food service and secretarial support, bird watching, nature tours

Recreational Amenities: West and East Beach Tennis Clubs with 28 hard-surface or Har-Tru clay tennis courts with two fully staffed pro shops, instructional programs; beach, bicycle tours, nature trails; family, adult, and children's swimming pools; fishing, boating, jogging, volleyball

Reservation and Cancellation Policy: 50% deposit required for 1 wk. stay. 1 night's deposit for less than 1 wk. stay. Can be guaranteed with a credit card or by check

Comments and Restrictions: No pets. Kennel within 5 mi. of resort. Taxes additional to base rates

KIAWAH ISLAND RESORT

Kiawah Island, situated on the Atlantic Ocean 21 miles south of Charleston, South Carolina, was named for the Kiawah Indians, who inhabited the island in the 1600s. Deeded to George Raynor in 1699 by the Lord Proprietor, Kiawah was later sold to Charleston's prominent Vanderhorst family, which owned the island for 180 years. In 1952, Kiawah was sold to C. C. Royal of Aiken, South Carolina, who in 1974 sold it to Kuwaiti investors for development as a resort destination. In 1988 a group consisting chiefly of Charleston businesspeople formed Kiawah Resort Associates and purchased the island, renovated the property, and in 1989 formed an agreement with Landmark Land Co. to assume ownership and management of Kiawah's resort amenities. Virginia Investment Trust now owns the resort amenities, including the golf courses. Kiawah Resort Associates continues to develop its remaining 2000 acres on the island.

The island itself covers 10,000 acres, and is 10 miles long and 1.5 miles across at its widest point. A variety of accommodations is available, including the ocean-front Kiawah Island Inn, as well as 350 1- to 4-bedroom villas. The inn is made up of 4 separate lodges with a total of 150 newly renovated guest rooms. The villas are all privately owned and have a variety of locations throughout the island—ocean front or near the beach, and overlooking beautiful lagoons and fairways.

The resort is ranked among the best golf resorts in America by *Golf* magazine. Kiawah offers four golf courses by world-class designers, and a variety of golf packages and advanced tee times is available for guests of Kiawah Island Inn and the villas. Instructional programs, including private and group lessons, are taught by Kiawah's staff of PGA professionals and assistants. Driving ranges are located at all four golf courses, but the Ocean and

Osprey Point ranges are available only for those playing those courses.

The first course to be built on Kiawah was Marsh Point, designed by Gary Player and opened in 1976. This 6203-yard par-71 layout has thirteen water holes and requires accurate shot placement rather than distance. The Bermuda Tifdwarf greens tend to be small, moderately fast and very undulating. The number-1-handicap hole on this layout is the 405-yard par-4 fourth, which is a slight dogleg right to a deep green with a hump in the middle that makes it difficult to hold. The wind often blows off the marsh and toward the golfer on this hole. Another tough hole is the 345-yard par-4 fifth. The tee shot has to carry a water hazard to a flat fairway, and the second shot is to a small green with no traps but marsh protecting it on the left.

A pretty and interesting hole on the back side is the 520-yard par-5 fifteenth, which plays to a green guarded by bunkers in front. Water runs up the right side of the fairway and cuts into the fairway halfway to the green, forcing you to choose whether to go over the water to the green in two or lay up. The clubhouse at Marsh Point has a pro shop, locker rooms and showers but only vending machines for food and drink. The ninth hole does not come back to the clubhouse, but a facility offering food and drink is located on the tenth hole. The course was closed in 1996 for a complete renovation.

Turtle Point, a 6919-yard par-72 Jack Nicklaus–designed layout, was opened in 1981 and was selected as one of America's top 75 resort courses by *Golf Digest* in 1988. The course is flat and well treed, with medium-sized to large, moderately fast greens well protected by traps. Water comes into play on half the holes. The wind can also come into play, especially on holes fourteen, fifteen and sixteen, which run along the ocean. The 168-yard par-3 fourteenth plays into the wind to a deep green protected by two traps on the left and one trap on the right. The beach dunes are to the right and behind the green beginning from the front tees. The 438-yard par-4 fifteenth has trees to the right and ocean dunes to the left. The green is deep and protected by a large trap on the right. The wind is to your back on this hole, as it is on the sixteenth, a 173-yard par 3. Dunes are to your left on the sixteenth, and a large trap on the right protects the deep green.

The finishing holes move back inland. The 425-yard par-4 eighteenth has water to the left and trees to the right all the way to a shallow but wide green well guarded by traps front and rear. The water is to your left, and the fairway severely narrows as you come onto the green. When you play Turtle Point, shot placement is essential because of the wind, dunes, traps, trees, deep rough, and water hazards. The clubhouse here has locker rooms, a pro shop and snack bar facility.

Osprey Point was designed by Tom Fazio and opened in 1988. This 6678-yard par-72 layout has four natural lakes and water on fifteen different holes. Moguls and mounds surround the Tifdwarf greens, which are medium sized to large, medium speed and undulating. The number-1-handicap hole on this course, which requires accurate shot placement because of water, trees, well-placed traps and wind, is the 453-yard par-4 dogleg-left ninth, which plays over water on the left from the back tees. The fairway is flat on the left with an upper tier on the right. You are usually playing into the wind on this hole, and the question is how much of the corner you want to cut off on the left. The approach shot is to a deep green with water and a bunker on the left.

The signature hole at Osprey Point is the 165-yard par-3 fifteenth, which plays over a huge bunker to a deep green flanked by two traps on the left, one right and water farther left and right. The finishing hole is a dramatic 544-yard par 5, a dogleg left with water on the left from tee to green. The tee shot has to avoid a large fairway bunker on the left and trees on the right. The narrow, deep green can be reached in two with the help of a tail wind, but a large bunker protects the putting surface on the left, and pot bunkers protect the right. The clubhouse at Osprey Point is a newly completed $4 million facility with pro shop, locker rooms and dining facilities.

The Ocean Course is the newest layout at Kiawah and gained considerable attention when it hosted the 1991 Ryder Cup. Designed by Pete Dye and opened in 1991, the Ocean Course is recognized by *Golf* magazine as one of the top 100 golf courses in the world. Dye, whose golf-architect hero is Donald Ross, wanted to create a resort course that people will want to play over and over again. The four tee distances on the par-72 layout range from the 7371-yard back tees to the 5327-yard forward tees, so any golfer can find a comfortable distance. The Atlantic Ocean and some of the resort's 10 miles of beaches are visible from every hole. From an aerial view, it looks as if hole layouts were dropped amidst the dunes.

Dye claims that the fairways are wide in the Ross tradition but that the shots onto the greens are a challenge. For resort play the greens are kept at less than 10 on the stimpmeter, as opposed to faster speeds from 12 and up used for tournament play. The greens vary in size, are undulating and are often guarded by dunes, traps or water. Needless to say, wind is a major factor on the Ocean Course, adding to the many ways that it can be played. Its sophisticated drainage system, which protects the beautiful adjacent wetlands at Kiawah, is considered to be a model for avoiding golf-course chemical runoff.

The number-1-handicap hole on the Ocean Course is the 453-yard par-4 fourth. The tee shot has to carry a marsh, as does the second shot. Depending on the wind, it will take anything from an 8-iron on up to reach the large, round green with dunes back, left and right. Playing against the wind often requires three shots to reach the putting surface.

A beautiful hole on the back nine is the 404-yard par-4 thirteenth, whose tee shot has to carry a canal to reach the fairway. On the second shot the fairway narrows, with water on the right and pot bunkers on the left as you come onto the green. The back of the green and the left side are a combination of dunes, mounds, waste areas and pot bunkers. The par-3 seventeenth, which plays 197 yards from the back tees, is another tough hole that is greatly affected by the wind. The tee shot is over water to a green that slopes toward the water from left to right. There is some landing area to the left of the green, but dunes and waste areas predominate beyond the putting surface. The water runs up almost to the green, making this an extremely difficult par 3.

The Ocean Course has a clubhouse with pro shop, restaurant, bar and locker rooms. All of the courses and facilities are within a short golf-cart ride of each other. The island has a rich assortment of plant and animal life, including white-tailed deer, river otters, bobcats, amphibians, and over 150 species of birds. In 1974 a $1.3-million environmental study was done to ensure that Kiawah's environment would be protected under a master plan for development.

Today the island has two self-contained resort villages, West and East Beach, with hotel accommodations, meeting facilities, dining, shopping and sports in close proximity to the beach. The villages and the rest of the island are interconnected by a 16-mile-long system of bicycling and jogging trails, making it possible to visit the island without an automobile. Kiawah's private residential areas make up the majority of the island and are separated from the more active resort areas.

Recreation at Kiawah includes 2 tennis centers with a total of 28 Har-Tru clay and hard-surface courts, bicycling, hiking, boating, fishing, bird watching, and Kiawah Kollege, a unique hands-on environmental program for young and old. A full-service conference center can handle groups of up to 600.

A variety of dining options is available at any of the 4 restaurants at Kiawah, and theme dinners and cookouts can be arranged. And there are the nearby attractions of Charleston, including restaurants, museums, architecture, seasonal music and art festivals, and historically significant places such as Fort Sumter National Monument and historic houses, which can be viewed during Charleston's Historic Festival of Houses.

The Kiawah Island Inn and Villas resort has won numerous hospitality and other awards. *Tennis* magazine ranks Kiawah Island among the nation's top tennis resorts, and *Family Circle* has named Kiawah one of the best family resorts in America. In addition to golf, a variety of tennis, family holiday and other packages are offered.

Course Name: WILD DUNES Links, Harbor Courses

Course Type: Resort
Resort: Wild Dunes
Address: Palm Boulevard
P.O. Box 5757
Isle of Palms, SC 29451
Phone: (803) 886–6000
(Golf Course)
(800) 845–8880 (Resort)
Fax: (803) 886–2916 (Resort)

GOLF COURSE

Director of Golf: Terry Florence
Head Professional: Links: Clay Cunningham. Harbor: Steve Behr
Course Length/Par (All Tees): Links: Back 6722/72, White 6131/72, Gold 5280/72, Forward 4849/72. Harbor: Back 6446/70, White 5900/50, Forward 4774/70
Course Slope/Rating (All Tees): Links: Back 134/72.9, White 124/69.6, Ladies' Gold 128/71, Ladies' Forward 123/68.7. Harbor: Back 124/70.9, White 117/68.2, Ladies' Forward NA/NA
Course Architect: Links: Tom Fazio (1979). Harbor: Tom Fazio (1985)
Golf Facilities: Full Pro Shop X, Snack Bar X, Lounge X, Restaurant X, Locker Room X, Showers X, Club Rental X, Club Repair X, Cart Rental X, Instruction X, Practice Green X, Driving Range X, Practice Bunker X, Club Storage X
Tee-Time Reservation Policy: At time of confirmed reservation, or up to 6 mos. in advance with credit card. 48-hr. cancellation policy. Members have priority on tee times

Ranger: Yes
Tee-off-Interval Time: 8 min.
Time to Play 18 Holes: 4 hrs., 15 min.
Course Hours/Earliest Tee-off: 7:32 a.m.
Green and Cart Fees: Peak season (mid-March to end of May, Sept., Oct.): Links: $95 plus tax for 18 holes with cart. Harbor: $65 plus tax for 18 holes with cart
Credit Cards: American Express, Discover, MasterCard, Visa
Season: Year round. Busiest season March through May, Sept., Oct.
Course Comments: Cart mandatory on Harbor. Walking allowed on the Links
Golf Packages: Available through resort
Discounts: Seasonal. Peak rates (mid-March to end of May, Sept. to mid-Nov.)
Places to Stay Nearby: See Charleston area listing on page 579
Local Attractions: See Charleston area listings on page 579
Directions: Hwy. 17 north business to Hwy. 703 to resort gate and golf course, follow the signs. From I–95: I–26/Charleston exit, I–26 east to Rte. 17 north, to Hwy. 703, to resort
Closest Commercial Airports: Charleston International (45 min.); Myrtle Beach (2 hrs.); Savannah International, GA (2 hrs.)

RESORT

Date Built: 1978
No. of Rooms: 250 rental villas ranging from studio to 4-bedroom private homes
Meeting/Exhibit Rooms: 16. Capacity of Largest: 350 persons reception style. Meeting Space: 12,400 sq. ft.
Room Price Range: Approximately $125 for a 1-bedroom to $600 for a 6-bedroom daily, peak season (June to Aug.). Various summer family-value, golf, tennis, honeymoon, town and country, holiday packages available
Lounges: Edgar's in Links Clubhouse, Grand Pavilion (beach front, seasonal)
Restaurants: Tradewinds Restaurant, Edgar's Deli, several restaurants on the Isle of Palms and nearby Sullivan's Island, all within a 20-min. drive

Entertainment: Banquet and theme parties can be arranged through catering department

Credit Cards: All major cards

General Amenities: Marina, supervised children's programs; tours to historic Charleston; meeting and conference facilities including theater, classroom, reception, banquet formats with complete audiovisual, food and secretarial support services; babysitting, marina general store

Recreational Amenities: 17 Har-Tru tennis courts (4 with lighting) and instruction; boating and swimming with access to 2½ mi. of Atlantic shoreline, 20 swimming pools, bicycle rentals and bicycling, beach volleyball, jogging, boat cruises to Charleston

Reservation and Cancellation Policy: 1 night's deposit required to reserve accommodations. Deposit forfeited if a cancellation or change is made less than 72 hrs. prior to arrival. Holiday stays and week-long stays require a deposit equal to 50% of rental price for entire stay and will be forfeited if a cancellation or change is made less than 14 days prior to arrival

Comments and Restrictions: Pets not allowed. Kennels located nearby. Rates subject to state and local taxes

WILD DUNES

Wild Dunes, a 1600-acre private oceanfront resort, is situated on a barrier island, with the Intracoastal Waterway on one side and the Atlantic Ocean on the other. The 6722-yard par-72 Links Course is considered to be one of the best golf courses in the United States. *Golf Digest* magazine ranks it among the top 75 resort golf courses in America, and *Golf* magazine has ranked it among the top 100 courses in the world. Hurricane Hugo rearranged this layout a bit a few years ago, but with the help of the Army Corps of Engineers and Tom Fazio, the course designer, the Links Course has been restored.

Wind has a tremendous effect on the degree of difficulty of this course. In general, you should avoid hitting high-risk

clubs such as the driver off the tee, and you should keep the ball low. The rolling fairways can further complicate your game with uneven lies, and the sandy dunes can eat up errant shots. The Bermuda-grass greens tend to be medium sized, moderate to fast, undulating, and well protected by dunes. Often it is difficult to roll the ball onto them because they are so well guarded and because they are slightly elevated.

The number-1-handicap hole on the Wild Dunes Links Course is the 451-yard par-4 ninth, which plays straight to a small green with water to the left and a bunker to the right front. The wind is usually in your face on this hole, leaving a wood or a long iron to the green if you are playing the back tees. The hole plays a more forgiving 375 yards from the middle tees, but the water, dunes and bunker protecting this forward-sloping green can be daunting on the approach shot.

The three finishing holes on the back nine are a challenge to any golfer. The 175-yard par-3 sixteenth is over marsh to a large, forward-sloping green. The next hole, a 405-yard par 4, has ocean and beach dunes to the left and dunes to the right. The second shot is to a left-to-right sloping green well protected by dunes and grass knolls. The 501-yard par-5 eighteenth is a dogleg left with a left-to-right wind on the tee shot. There is likely to be a tail wind on the second shot, which plays to a green guarded by beach and sea oats all around. If you go for the green on your second shot, your ball is likely to find these hazards.

The Harbor Course, another Fazio-designed layout, plays 6446 yards and has water on several of its holes. The two finishing holes on this layout provide an excellent golf challenge. The 464-yard par-4 seventeenth plays over Morgan Creek on the tee shot, leaving a wood or a long iron to a small green protected by marsh on each side. The 434-yard par-4 eighteenth is long, straight and narrow, with a marsh to the left and dunes on the right. Two holes on this side play across Morgan Creek from Sullivan's Island to Wild Dunes, and nine holes are on the scenic Intracoastal Waterway.

Each golf course has its own locker room, restaurant and pro-shop facilities, with professional instruction available under the auspices of two separate head professionals. The golf shop at the Wild Dunes Links Course has been recognized by *Golf Shop Operations* magazine as one of the best in America. One driving range opposite the Links clubhouse serves both courses. The resort has over 12,000 square feet of meeting and conference space with audiovisual, banquet and secretarial support; and recreational facilities include a racquet club with 17 tennis courts. The racquet club has been ranked among the nation's top 50 facilities by both *Tennis* and *Tennis Week* magazines, and has consistently earned *World Tennis* magazine's five-star resort rating. A marina and beach facility provides fishing, boating and swimming activities, including charters. Charleston's shopping and historic sites are only 15 miles away.

A variety of flats, cottages, and villas is available through the resort, and you can play the golf courses even if you are not a resort guest. Tee times should be reserved up to 1 year in advance, however, to guarantee a desirable tee time. The peak season for golf at Wild Dunes is mid-March to the end of May and September through mid-November. The resort itself has its peak season from June through August because of its beach location and family-oriented atmosphere. A variety of golf and other packages is available at Wild Dunes.

The natural setting of Wild Dunes and its easy access to Charleston, one of the most beautiful and well-preserved cities in America, make golfing here a memorable experience. The original property was never cleared and leveled for plantation farming, so it features rolling sand dunes and is wooded with a variety of subtropical trees including palmettos, palms, magnolias, cedars, myrtles and live oaks. The property is home to some 20 species of mammals, including white-tailed deer, opossum, raccoon, grey squirrel, fox squirrel and less charismatic reptiles and amphibians. There are more than 100 species of birds, including pelicans, ducks, gulls, terns, herons, egrets, ibises, and hawks. You will see many of these creatures while you're matching wits with the wind, sand, water and rolling Bermuda-grass terrain on these excellent golf courses.

Places to Stay in the Charleston Area

CHARLESTON: Best Western—King Charles Inn (803) 723–7451, (800) 24–SOUTH; Comfort Inn—Airport (803) 554–6485, (800) 228–5150; Days Inn—Historic District (803) 722–8411, (800) 325–2525; Holiday Inn Riverview (803) 556–7100, (800) HOLIDAY; Meeting St. Inn (803) 723–1882; Mills House Hotel (803) 577–2400, (800) 874–9600; Sheraton Charleston Hotel (803) 723–3000, (800) 325–3535; Omni Hotel at Charleston Place (803) 722–4900, (800) THE–OMNI; Indigo Inn (803) 722–1611, (800) 845–1004; Planters Inn (803) 722–2345, (800) 845–7082; Vendue Inn (803) 577–7970, (800) 845–7900. NORTH CHARLESTON: Charleston Marriott (803) 747–1900, (800) 228–9290; Hampton Inn Charleston Airport (803) 554–7154, (800) HAMPTON; Motel 6 (803) 572–6590; Quality Suites Hotel (803) 747–6324, (800) 228–5151; Ramada Inn—Airport (803) 744–8281, (800) 24–SOUTH; Red Roof Inn (803) 572–9100, (800) THE–ROOF. MOUNT PLEASANT: Shem Creek Inn (803) 881–1000, (800) 24–SOUTH; Middleton Inn and Conference Center (803) 556–0500. SEABROOK ISLAND: Seabrook Island Resort (803) 768–1000, (800) 845–5531

Local Attractions in the Charleston Area

AWENDAW: Cape Romain National Wildlife Refuge. CHARLESTON: Aiken–Rhett house, American Military Museum, Audubon Swamp Garden, Birds I View Gallery, Charles Towne Landing, Charleston Museum, city market, audiovisual presentation "Forever Charleston," College of Charleston, Dock St. Theatre, Drayton Hall, Edmonston–Alston house, Emmanuel African Methodist Church, First Baptist Church, First Scots Presbyterian Church, Fort Sumter tours, French Huguenot

Church, Gibbs Museum of Art, Gray Line water tours, Heyward–Washington house, Joseph Manigatt house, Magnolia Plantation and Gardens, Nathaniel Russell house, Old Exchange and Provost Dungeon, Old St. Andrews Episcopal Church, powder magazine, Second Presbyterian Church, Southern Windjammer, St. John's Lutheran Church, St. Mary's Roman Catholic Church, St. Matthew's Lutheran Church, St. Michael's Episcopal Church, Citadel, Thomas Elfe workshop, restaurants, shopping, antiques, art galleries, beaches, bicycling, fishing, sailing, tennis, minor league professional baseball, theater, dance, concert, festivals including Spoleto Festival USA, Waterfront Park, Confederate Museum, Old Dorchester State Park. MT. PLEASANT: Boone Hall Plantation, Patriot's Point Naval and Maritime Museum, Charleston Naval Base. MCCLELLANVILLE: Hampton Plantation State Park. Charleston Trident Convention and Visitors Bureau, (803) 577–2510. Fax: (803) 723–4853. Charleston Trident Chamber of Commerce Visitor Information Center (803) 722–8338

Recommended Golf Courses in South Carolina

Within 1/2 Hour of Charleston:

Charleston National Country Club, Mount Pleasant, (803) 884–7799, Semiprivate, 18/6928/72

Crowfield Golf and Country Club, Goose Creek, (803) 764–4618, Semiprivate, 18/7003/72

Legend Oaks Plantation, Summerville, (803) 821–4077, Public, 18/6974/72

Links at Stono Ferry, Hollywood, (803) 763–1817, Public, 18/6606/72

Oak Point Golf Course, Johns Island, (803) 768–7431, Public, 18/6759/72

Patriots Point Golf Links, Mount Pleasant, (803) 881–0042, Public, 18/6874/72

Pine Forest Country Club, Summerville, (803) 851–1193, Semiprivate, 18/6905/72

Seabrook Island Resort, Johns Island, (803) 768–2529, Resort. Ocean Winds: 18/6805/72. Crooked Oaks: 18/6832/72

Shadowmoss Plantation Golf Club, Charleston, (803) 556–8251, (800) 338–4971, Semiprivate, 18/6701/72

Hilton Head Area

Course Name: **CALLAWASSIE ISLAND CLUB**
                       Dogwood, Magnolia, Palmetto Courses

Course Type: Semiprivate
Address: 20 Callawassie Drive
                         Okatie, SC 29910
Phone: (803) 785–7888,
                         (800) 221–8431
Fax: (803) 986–2166

GOLF COURSE

Head Professional: Brian Crum
Course Length/Par (All Tees): Palmetto/Magnolia: Back 6956/72, Blue 6462/72, White 6035/72, Orange 5485/72, Forward 5201/72. Palmetto/Dogwood: Back 6930/72, Blue 6416/72, White 5947/72, Orange 5457/72, Forward 5166/72. Dogwood/Magnolia: Back 7064/72, Blue 6514/72, White 6018/72, Orange 5502/72, Forward 5237/72
Course Slope/Rating (All Tees): Palmetto/Magnolia: Back 132/73.2, Blue 130/70.9, White 126/69.0, Orange 120/67.0, Ladies' Forward 120/70.1. Palmetto/Dogwood: Back 131/72.1, Blue 129/71.6, White 127/71.2, Orange 122/68.1, Ladies' Forward 123/70.5. Dogwood/Magnolia: Back 136/73.3, Blue 134/72.4, White 130/72.0, Orange 126/70.0, Ladies' Forward 126/71.0
Course Architect: Tom Fazio: Magnolia, Palmetto (1985), Dogwood (1990)
Golf Facilities: Full Pro Shop X, Snack Bar X, Lounge X, Restaurant X, Locker Room X, Showers X, Club Rental X, Club Repair X, Cart Rental X, Instruction X, Practice Green X, Driving Range X, Practice Bunker X, Club Storage X
Tee-Time Reservation Policy: Up to 14 days in advance

Ranger: Yes

Tee-off-Interval Time: 10 min.

Time to Play 18 Holes: 4 hrs. 15 min.

Course Hours/Earliest Tee-off: 8 a.m.

Green and Cart Fees: $73 for 18 holes. Peak season Mar. 1 to early May, Oct. and Nov.

Credit Cards: American Express, Master-Card, Visa

Season: Year round. Busiest Apr. and May

Course Comments: Carts mandatory for non-member play

Golf Packages: Inquire at pro shop. Through local hotels

Discounts: Seasonal. Lower rates mid-May through Sept., Dec. through Feb.

Places to Stay Nearby: BEAUFORT: Best Western Sea Island Inn (803) 522–2090, (800) 528–1234; Holiday Inn of Beaufort (803) 524–2144, (800) HOLI-DAY; Ramada Limited (803) 524–3322, (800) 272–6232; The Rhett House (803) 524–9030

Local Attractions: BEAUFORT: Beaufort Museum, carriage tours, John Mark Verdier House, St. Helena's Episcopal church, historic tours, antiquing, fishing, boating, hiking, camping, Hunting Island State Park. Greater Beaufort Chamber of Commerce, 1006 Bay St., P.O. Box 910, Beaufort, SC 29901 (803) 5245–3163. For Hilton Head see page 590

Directions: I–95 southbound take Exit 28 to Hilton Head and Hwy. 278 to Rte. 170. Follow Rte. 170 10 mi. to golf course. I–95 northbound take Exit 5 then follow signs to Hilton Head, Rte. 170 and the golf course

Closest Commercial Airports: Hilton Head Municipal (30 min.); Savannah International, GA (1 hr.); Charleston International (2 hrs.)

CALLAWASSIE ISLAND CLUB

Callawassie is an 880-acre private island community midway between Hilton Head and Beaufort. The island, originally inhabited by Yemassee Indians, is bordered by the Checessee and Colleton Rivers which connect to Port Royal Sound and the Atlantic Ocean. Within this real estate development are 27 holes of Tom Fazio–designed golf.

As their names indicate, the Dogwood, Magnolia, and Palmetto nines teem with low country wetland and forest vegetation including thick pine, magnolia, maple, palmetto, hickory, dogwood, and other varieties. Water in the form of streams, ponds and wetlands can come into play on many of these holes which weave between 750 home sites. There is a variety of dog-legs at Callawassie and landing areas are guarded by some combination of large bunkers, water hazards and trees. The greens are large, well-bunkered, moderately fast, and slightly undulating. Winds off the ocean can affect play on many holes, most notably the three finishing holes on the new Dogwood nine.

The Palmetto nine toughens up after the first four holes—two short par 4s, a par 3, and another manageable par 4. The 548-yard par-5 fifth has a pair of bunkers to the right of the tee shot landing area and a pond to the right of its deep green. The 206-yard par-3 sixth requires distance and accuracy to reach a deep green framed by bunkers to its left and right. The 585-yard par-5 seventh has an array of four bunkers to the left of the tee shot landing area. A large bunker to the right front squeezes the entranceway to the large putting surface protected by another bunker to its left.

The Magnolia is considered the most difficult of the nines at Callawassie. The 229-yard par-3 third is the longest par 3 here and the 606-yard dogleg left par-5 eighth is the longest par 5. The eighth is bordered on the left by a water hazard that narrows the tee shot landing area which has a bunker to its right at the turn of the dogleg. The second shot is toward a green with bunkers to its left and front right. The finishing hole on this nine is the scenic 385-yard dogleg right par 4 with wetlands to the right and bunkers to the left on the drive. The approach is to a deep green narrowed in front by a bunker to its left and the wetlands on the right.

The Palmetto and Magnolia formed the front and back nine of the original eighteen built in the mid-1980s. Dogwood was opened in 1992. This nine finishes with four strong holes beginning with a 496-yard par-5 dogleg left that forces you to decide whether to lay up or go for the green on the second shot. The target is guarded by water in front forcing most mortals to play conservatively. The next hole, a formidable 461-yard par 4, begins a series of three holes running along beautiful wetlands. The next hole is a 175-yard par 3 whose tee shot is usually buffeted by winds coming off the water. And the finishing hole, a 423-yard par 4, is a difficult dogleg left whose green is sandwiched by bunkers on both sides.

A great place to review your round of golf is in the $3 million, 26,000 square-foot clubhouse which has formal and informal dining facilities, an excellent pro shop and other amenities. The River Club with swimming and dock facilities, a cookout area and indoor space for meetings and entertaining, and the Tennis Center with four all-weather courts are also on site.

Course Name:　PALMETTO DUNES
RESORT
George Fazio,
Robert Trent Jones,
Arthur Hills Courses
at Palmetto Dunes;
Robert Cupp,
Arthur Hills Courses
at Palmetto Hall

Course Type:　Resort
Resort:　Palmetto Dunes Resort
Address:　Highway 278/P.O. Box 5849
Hilton Head Island, SC
29938
Phone:　(803) 785–1138,
(800) 827–3006 (Tee Times)
(803) 785–1136 (Instructional
Programs)
(803) 785–1161, (803) 785–
1194, (800) 845–6130,
(800) 826–1649 (Resort)
(803) 842–7001 (Fishing,
Cruises and Charters)
(800) 826–1649 (Group Sales
Department)

GOLF COURSE

Director of Golf: Chip Pellerin

Head Professionals: Palmetto Dunes: Fazio: Bobby Downs. Jones: Kenny Conroy. Hills: Clark Sinclair. Palmetto Hall: Bob Faulkner

Course Length/Par (All Tees): Palmetto Dunes: Fazio: Back 6873/70, Blue 6534/72, White 6239/72, Forward 5273/72. Jones: Back: 6710/72, Middle 6148/72, Forward 5425/72. Hills: Back 6651/72, Middle 6122/72, Forward 4999/72. Palmetto Hall: Hills: Back 6918/72, Blue 6582/72, White 6257/72, Forward 4956/72. Cupp: Gold 7079/72, Blue 6522/72, Men's Forward 6042/72, Ladies' Forward 5220/72

Course Slope/Rating (All Tees): Palmetto Dunes: Fazio: Back 132/74.2, Blue 126/72.6, White 123/71.2, Ladies' Forward 117/69.2. Jones: Back 123/72.2, Middle 119/69.3, Ladies' Forward 117/70.7. Hills: Back 127/71.4, Middle 120/65.3, Ladies' Forward 113/68.2. Palmetto Hall: Hills: Back 132/72.2, Blue 123/70.5, White 117/68.9, Ladies' Forward NA/NA. Cupp: Back 141/74.8, Blue 126/70.1, Men's Forward 120/68.4, Ladies' Forward NA/NA

Course Architects: Fazio: George Fazio (1974). Jones: Robert Trent Jones, Sr. (1969). Hills: Arthur Hills (1986). Palmetto Hall: Hill's: Arthur Hills (1991). Cupp: Robert Cupp (1993)

Golf Facilities: Full Pro Shop X, Snack Bar X, Lounge X, Restaurant X, Locker Room X, Showers X, Club Rental X, Club Repair No, Cart Rental X, Instruction X, Practice Green X, Driving Range X, Practice Bunker X, Club Storage X.

Tee-Time Reservation Policy: Resort guests: 60 days in advance. Groups up to 1 yr. in advance. Outside play: 30 days for outside guests. Credit card guarantee required for outside play

Ranger: Yes

Tee-off-Interval Time: 8 min.

Time to Play 18 Holes: 4 hrs., 15 min.

Course Hours/Earliest Tee-off: 7 a.m.

Green and Cart Fees: Outside play peak season (March to May, Oct.): Fazio,

Jones, Hills, Cupp: $71.50 for 18 holes with cart. Hills at Palmetto Dunes: $96 for 18 holes with cart

Credit Cards: American Express, Master-Card, Visa

Season: Year round. Busiest season March to May, Sept. to Oct.

Course Comments: Walking allowed anytime at full golf fee. 9-hole play available at Fazio, Hills and Palmetto Hall after 2 p.m. Yardage book available

Golf Packages: Available through Palmetto Dunes Sand Dollar (800) 845–6130, Hyatt Regency (803) 785–5221, Hilton (803) 842–4695

Discounts: Twilight, seasonal (Nov. to Feb.)

Places to Stay Nearby: See Hilton Head area listing on page 590

Local Attractions: See Hilton Head area listing on page 590

Directions: Southbound on I–95: Exit 28, to Hilton Head and Hwy. 278, to Queens Folly Rd., turn east toward ocean, follow signs to golf courses. Northbound on I–95: Exit 5, follow signs to Hilton Head and Hwy. 278 per the above directions

Closest Commercial Airports: Hilton Head Municipal (5 min.); Savannah International, GA (1 hr.); Charleston International (2 hrs.); Myrtle Beach (5 hrs.); Hartsfield Atlanta International, GA (5 hrs.)

RESORT

Date Built: 1972

No. of Rooms: More than 500 villas and homes

Meeting/Exhibit Rooms: 11. Capacity of Largest: 200 persons. Meeting Space: 11,000 sq. ft.

Room Price Range: $80 for hotel-type room off season (Nov. through Feb.) to over $450 for a 4-bedroom penthouse peak season (March through Aug.). Golf, tennis and other packages are available year round

Lounges: In private restaurants in the resort areas

Restaurants: Hemingway, Cafe, Scott's, Alexander's, Harbour Masters, and various other private restaurants within Palmetto Dunes

Entertainment: At local hotels and restaurants

Credit Cards: All major cards

General Amenities: Seasonal festivals and tournaments, island tours; Shelter Cove Harbour marina with 15½-acre harbor, 170 slips; children's program for ages 5 through 10 including junior golf and tennis programs, shopping, 2 movie theaters, community theater; complete meeting and conference facilities with audiovisual, food service and secretarial support

Recreational Amenities: Boating, fishing, bicycling, swimming (beach and 25 swimming pools), adventure cruises, windsurfing; tennis at Palmetto Dunes Tennis Center with 19 Har-Tru clay, 2 hard-surfaced and 4 Super-Grasse courts (6 lighted) with instruction available, pro shop

Reservation and Cancellation Policy: 50% deposit required for rental homes and villas. 14-day cancellation required for guaranteed refund (60 days for groups)

Comments and Restrictions: Taxes additional to base rates and housekeeping. No refunds will be made for unused package features

PALMETTO DUNES RESORT

Palmetto Dunes on Hilton Head Island is a 2000-acre ocean-front resort and residential community featuring five excellent golf courses designed by George Fazio, Robert Trent Jones, Sr. and Arthur Hills. The resort abounds with recreational opportunities, including tennis at the Palmetto Dunes Tennis Center, with 25 Har-Tru, Super-Grasse, and hard-surface courts, 6 lighted for night play. The center, which includes a pro shop and an instructional staff, is considered one of the best tennis resorts in America. The Shelter Cove Harbour marina includes 170 deep-water berths and a 15½-acre harbor for boating and fishing enthusiasts. And there are miles of beautiful beach nearby.

The harbor complex surrounding the yacht basin is designed like a Mediterranean village, with shops and restaurants to service residents and guests. In addition to boating and deep-sea fishing in the ocean, canoeing and paddleboating can be enjoyed on the resort's lagoons, which run through the golf courses. Both the Hyatt Regency Hilton Head and Hilton (formerly Mariner's Inn) have accommodations and golf packages within Palmetto Dunes, and other golf packages and accommodations are available through Hilton Head Central Reservations (800–845–7018), which represents almost every hotel, motel, and condominium rental agency on the island.

Within the Palmetto Dunes planned community and real-estate development are five championship golf courses within very close proximity of each other. The combination of varying tee distances and degrees of difficulty of these courses provides ample opportunity for any golfer to enjoy the game. PGA-certified professionals are available to provide a wide range of teaching programs, including daily clinics covering putting, chipping and other elements of golf; supervised practice lessons; playing lessons; private instruction; video lessons and a 3-day golf school. Anyone from beginner to professional can benefit from this program as well as from the practice facilities, which include driving ranges, putting greens and chipping bunkers.

The Jones Course was designed by Robert Trent Jones, Sr., and opened in 1969. This course features large, undulating greens and large traps around every green except the 539-yard par-5 fourth. Bunkers come into play around most of the fairway landing areas. Some of the greens are slightly elevated, and water is a factor on eleven of the course's eighteen holes. Wind can add strokes to scores on any of the four Palmetto Dunes courses, but it is usually relatively calm in the summer.

The number-1-handicap hole on the Jones Course is the 510-yard par-5 ninth, which is a dogleg right to a deep green that is well guarded by two traps to the right and one to the left. The wind usually blows from left to right toward water that lines the right fairway from the tee to the back of the green. The 540-yard par-5 tenth hole is a straight shot toward the incoming ocean breeze and a deep green guarded by two traps to the left and another to the right. The left side is out of bounds, and two bunkers guard the landing area on the tee shot.

A good par 3 on this layout is the 198-yard eighth, which plays over water to a wide, very shallow green with traps protecting it left, back and front. The finishing hole is a 390-yard par 4 with a sharp dogleg left. A large fairway bunker protects the right side 170 yards from the green, which is wide, shallow and protected by three traps. Left and right of the fairway is out of bounds. Two accurate shots are required to reach this hole in regulation play. The green itself is wide, shallow, and well protected by a large trap in front and two traps to the rear.

The clubhouse at the Jones Course is a new 9100-square-foot facility with a full-service grill, an outdoor dining patio and decks overlooking the practice green and first tee. A media room for video swing analysis, men's and ladies' locker rooms, and a complete pro shop are available, as are professional instruction and complete practice facilities.

The Fazio Course plays long and narrow, with a variety of trees, including pine, oak, palm, and willow, protecting the fairways. The 6873-yard par-70 layout has only two par 5s but features a series of long par 4s. The wind seems to add 400 yards to the length of the course. The small greens are often well guarded by traps, and water comes into play on half the holes. Some of the holes have huge fairway bunkers, further complicating this picturesque layout.

The number-1-handicap hole on the front side is the long, 431-yard par-4 eighth, which plays straight down a rolling fairway to a deep, elevated, two-tiered green pinched by two traps left-front and right-front. The fairway is guarded by trees and a right-fairway bunker on the tee shot. The ninth hole is a slight dogleg right to a very long green with a huge bunker on the left. The tee shot has to get by two bunkers straddling the fairway, half the distance to the green. Trees on the left and right make it necessary to hit two straight shots to reach the putting surface. The deep, tiered green is guarded by a huge trap to the left and trees to the right and rear.

The four finishing holes on the Fazio Course are very demanding. The 445-yard par-4 fifteenth is straight to a long, elevated green protected left and right by huge bunkers. The first shot has to avoid a large left-side fairway bunker 210 yards from the green, and the second shot always seems to play long. The 425-yard par-4 sixteenth has to negotiate three huge fairway bunkers to reach a deep, multileveled green with a large trap on the left and close to the putting surface. Two traps are to the right rear of the green, and water is to the right of the fairway and green from 100 yards in. Another concern is the lagoon that runs down the entire left side of the fairway.

The seventeenth hole is a great par 3 that plays over water to a long green protected by a trap in front and water front and right. Left is out of bounds and into the trees. Long is your only bailout position. The finishing hole is a long, 462-yard par-4 slight dogleg right that might be the most difficult hole on the course. The tee shot is over a large sandy area to a reasonably wide landing area with some trees both to the left and right. The next shot must carry the edge of a huge left-fairway bunker beginning 125 yards from the narrow, deep green. The green is protected by a trap on the right and well in front of the green, and by two other traps straddling close to the green. Most golfers would settle for a five on this hole.

The Fazio Course has been ranked among *Golf Digest*'s top 100 golf courses. The clubhouse does not have a locker room, but the facilities at one of the other nearby courses can be used. A pro shop and instruction are available, but one of the other driving ranges will have to be used because the Fazio Course doesn't have its own. Light meals are available at the clubhouse.

The 6651-yard Hills Course is heavily wooded, with an interesting mixture of

shapes, sizes and contours of greens, which are protected by sand, water, mounds and trees in a variety of configurations. Water comes into play on half the holes, and the fairways are nicely contoured to coincide with the natural layout of the land. This course is pleasing to the eye and eats up an overly aggressive player. Course management and wise club selection are keys here, especially if the wind is kicking up. Because Hills is built on a series of sand dunes, there are some interesting and dramatic elevation changes on the course.

The front nine has two picturesque par 3s. The 146-yard third is over water to a very deep green protected both right and front by sand and water. The 156-yard eighth is also over water to a wide, shallow green with water and mounds in front. The wind will sometimes knock the ball down and into the water.

The number-1-handicap hole is the 434-yard par-4 seventh, which plays very long into the prevailing wind. Mounds line the fairway on the right, and trees line it on the left. The deep green has two traps to the left and one right, making the second shot more difficult than it would seem. The finishing hole on the front nine is a picturesque 518-yard par 5 down a rolling, tree-lined fairway to a small green protected by water in front and to the left. Depending on how well you hit your tee shot, the second shot could be a very high-risk effort if you are going for the green.

The seventeenth is the signature hole, par 4 that plays 380 yards from tee to green. Water runs on the left from the tee, then across the fairway in front of the deep green, which has to be approached from the fairway on the right on the second shot. If you are short you are in the water, and if you are long you are on an embankment chipping toward the water. Good luck.

The clubhouse at Hills has a pro shop recognized as one of the 100 best in the United States by *Golf Shop Operations* magazine. Complete practice facilities are available, and the clubhouse has food service, locker rooms and showers. Individual and group instruction is available.

The Arthur Hills Golf Course at Palmetto Hall Plantation covers rolling terrain and winds through oak and pine trees. Water and wetlands come into play on eleven holes, and a combination of mounds, bunkers and traps adds to the visual beauty and golfing challenge here. On some holes, such as the beautiful par-5 fifth, there are no traps, but mounds, water, trees and thick Bahia grass provide enough to think about.

On the other hand, huge traps from 130 yards into the green are used to guard the 438-yard par-4 first hole, which is the number-1-handicap hole on the course. This hole plays 420 yards from the blues and 405 yards from the white tees, so no one gets a break here. Mounds on the left line the fairway to a deep, forward-sloping green which is also angled right to left. Ideally, the tee shot should be left-of-center to avoid coming onto the green over the right trap. The 564-yard par-5 ninth looks somewhat like a golf gantlet. The right side has wetlands, bunkers and trees all the way to a long green. The left side has two fairway bunkers, one 200 yards from the green and another 105 yards out. The tee shot has to be left-of-center to avoid the bunkers on the right, then the next shot has to avoid two large bunkers straddling the fairway from 130 yards into the hole. The green itself is surrounded by mounds, with a small bunker to the right.

The finishing hole is a long par-4 dogleg left that plays 439 yards to a very deep green protected by traps right-front, right and right-rear. To the left is water running from in front of the tees to the left of the green, which slopes toward it. The right side of the fairway is lined with dunes. The first shot has to be straight to the fairway, avoiding the water on the left. The second shot has to get by the trap to the right of the green without going into the drink.

The new 14,000-square-foot clubhouse at Palmetto Hall Plantation has locker rooms, showers, a pro shop, pool, tennis, dining and complete golf practice facilities. Group and individual instruction is available. These golf facilities will serve as a centerpiece for a residential community that will border the golf courses. The eighteen-hole golf course designed by Robert Cupp and opened in the spring of 1993 alternates with the Hills Course at Palmetto Hall as a public and private course.

Palmetto Dunes has won numerous hospitality awards, including a Four-Star rating from the *Mobil Travel Guide* and a Four-Diamond Award from the American Automobile Association. A variety of golf packages, golf clinics, golf schools, and individual and group instruction is available at Palmetto Dunes. Outside play is allowed at the resort, and local hotels are convenient should you elect not to stay in the accommodations available directly through Palmetto Dunes.

Within the development is the Hyatt Regency Hilton Head, a 505-room newly renovated hotel situated on the ocean. This resort hotel offers 3 restaurants, 2 lounges, 30,000 square feet of meeting space and recreational facilities, including swimming pools and a health club. Golf packages can be arranged here or through the nearby Hilton, which was formerly the Mariner's Inn. These are the only hotels within the 2000-acre real-estate development and recreational property.

Course Name: **SEA PINES RESORT**
Harbour Town, Ocean, Sea Marsh Courses

Course Type: Resort
Resort: Sea Pines Resort
Address: 32 Greenwood Drive
P.O. Box 7000
Hilton Head Island, SC
29938
Phone: (803) 842–8484
(Harbour Town Course)
(803) 363–4485
(Ocean Course)
(803) 842–1894
(Sea Marsh Course)
(800) SEA–PINES (Reservations and Information)
(803) 785–3333 (Resort)
Fax: (803) 842–1475 (Resort)

GOLF COURSE

Director of Golf: Cary Corbitt

Head Professional: Harbour Town: John Farrell. Ocean Course, Sea Marsh: John Richardson

Course Length/Par (All Tees): Harbour Town: Back 6912/71, Middle 6119/71, Forward 5019/71. Ocean: Back 6614/72, Middle 6213/72, Forward 5284/72. Sea Marsh: Back 6515/72, Middle 6169/72, Forward 5054/72

Course Slope/Rating (All Tees): Harbour Town: Back 136/74, Middle 126/70, Ladies' Forward 117/69. Ocean: Back 133/72.8, Middle 125/69.7, Ladies' Forward NA/NA. Sea Marsh: Back 120/70, Middle 117/69, Ladies' Forward 123/69.9

Course Architects: Harbour Town: Pete Dye and Jack Nicklaus (1969). Ocean: George Cobb (1967). Mark McCumber (Remodeled, 1995). Sea Marsh: George Cobb (1960). Clyde Johnson (Remodeled, 1989). Mark McCumber (Renovations, 1995)

Golf Facilities: Full Pro Shop X, Snack Bar X, Lounge X, Restaurant X, Locker Room X, Showers X, Club Rental X, Club Repair X, Cart Rental X, Instruction X, Practice Green X, Driving Range X, Practice Bunker X, Club Storage X.

Tee-Time Reservation Policy: Resort guests: 90 days in advance. Outside play: 14 days in advance. Credit card guarantee. Members have preferred tee times

Ranger: Yes

Tee-off-Interval Time: 7 min.

Time to Play 18 Holes: 4 hrs.

Course Hours/Earliest Tee-off: 7:30 a.m.

Green and Cart Fees: Peak season (early Mar.-mid-May, Sept.-Nov.): Harbour Town: $169 for 18 holes with cart. Ocean: $85 for 18 holes, $51 for 9 holes with cart. Sea Marsh: $77 for 18 holes, $46 for 9 holes with cart

Credit Cards: American Express, MasterCard, Visa

Season: Year round. Busiest season March to May, Sept. to Nov.

Course Comments: Cart mandatory, but can walk occasionally. Sea Pines Academy of Golf, Sea Pines Academy of Beginner Golf (803) 842-1894

Golf Packages: Available through the Sea Pines Resort

Discounts: Resort guests, twilight, seasonal (Dec. to Feb., June-Aug.). Afternoon specials from 1 p.m. available seasonally. Replays at Ocean and Sea Marsh

Places to Stay Nearby: See Hilton Head area listing on page 590

Local Attractions: See Hilton Head area listing on page 590

Directions: I-95S, exit onto Hwy. 462, follow signs and Hwys. 170 and 278 to Hilton Head, after crossing the bridge to Hilton Head Island, follow U.S. 278 (William Hilton Pkwy.) 12 mi. to first traffic circle, take 2nd right off circle to Greenwood Dr. Welcome Center (Sea Pines) on the right

Closest Commercial Airports: Hilton Head Municipal (10 min.); Savannah International, GA (1 hr.); Charleston International (2 hrs.); Hartsfield Atlanta International, GA (5 hrs.)

RESORT

Date Built: 1960

No. of Rooms: More than 400 condominiums and single-family homes

Meeting/Exhibit Rooms: 11. Capacity of Largest: 200 persons. Meeting Space: 10,000 sq. ft.

Room Price Range: From $114 per day for 1 bedroom low season (Dec. to early Mar., early Sept. through Nov.) to $300 per day for 2 bedroom high season (Mar. through Labor Day). A variety of golf, tennis and other packages available

Lounges: In Sea Pines and Hilton Head

Restaurants: Fairway Pub, Sundeck Cafe, Lakehouse Restaurant, Harbour Town Grill, The Plantation

Entertainment: Live entertainment, dancing at Sea Pines and area restaurants and night clubs

Credit Cards: American Express, Discover, MasterCard, Visa

General Amenities: Babysitting, notary public, seasonal festivals and tournaments, tennis pro shop, supervised children's programs; meeting and conference services including audiovisual, food service and secretarial support

Recreational Amenities: Racquet club with 80 Har-Tru tennis courts, several additional courts on site; horseback riding, bicycling, swimming, boating, forest preserve, guided tours, 26 swimming pools, 15 mi. of leisure trails, marina, beach, fishing, waterskiing, windsurfing, parasailing, fitness center

Reservation and Cancellation Policy: A deposit of 30% of rental for the entire stay required. Balance of stay due and payable on arrival. Cancellation required 14 days prior to arrival for full refund

Comments and Restrictions: No pets allowed. Taxes and maid-service fees additional to base rates. Maximum occupancy for homes and villas is 2 persons per bedroom

SEA PINES RESORT

Sea Pines is a 5,000-acre residential resort community on Hilton Head Island. The resort has three excellent golf courses, including the 6912-yard Harbour Town Golf Links, which was designed by Pete Dye and Jack Nicklaus in the 1960s. Harbour Town is the site of the PGA's MCI Classic and has been ranked as one of the best courses in South Carolina, the United States, and the world by *Golf Digest* and *Golf* magazines. The Harbour Town Golf Links is not only beautiful because of its trees, wildlife and Spanish moss; it is also an extremely demanding course with small greens and tight fairways. Strategy and finesse rather than a power game are required here.

The course was opened in 1969 for the inaugural Heritage Golf Classic. Harbour Town was cut out of 300 acres of oaks, pines and magnolias, and trees are very much a factor when playing this course. The small greens vary from 2000 to 3500 square feet and are not elevated. You will seldom have an extremely long putt, but getting to the green can be a problem because of trees, water (which seriously comes into play on ten holes) and bunkers,

including huge traps on more than half the holes. You will probably have used every club in your bag and tested your ability to recover from many problem situations before retiring to the nineteenth hole, which is in a magnificent clubhouse near Harbour Town's famous lighthouse on the Atlantic Ocean.

Harbour Town is especially noted for its par 3s, which range from 165 to 198 yards from the back tees. The 198-yard fourth is over water to a small green flanked by water to the front and left, and a huge trap to the rear. The 180-yard seventh has water to the right cutting the fairway, water left of the narrow, deep green and sand with pampas grass completely surrounding the putting surface. The 165-yard fourteenth plays over water that runs from the tee to a deep green backed by a pot bunker. The 192-yard seventeenth plays over water to a narrow, deep green with water and sand on the left and a large sand trap on the right. If you hit over the green, which has banks sloping downward and to the left, back and right, the ball can reach the water.

The par 4s at Harbour Town are also excellent. The 378-yard thirteenth was selected for the *World Atlas of Golf Courses* classic survey courses. This hole plays straight to a small green guarded by a huge bunker in front. A well-placed fairway bunker is on the left 220 yards from the back tee, and another is 274 yards away on the right. Two large oak trees, 70 yards from the green, stymie a second shot from the left side, and the bunker in front of the green is banked with cypress planks, which can make getting out of that hazard difficult.

The four finishing holes at Harbour Town are difficult, concluding with the 478-yard par-4 eighteenth. This hole also plays a hefty 458 yards from the middle tees, and the golfer is faced with water on the left all the way to the green. Trees border the right side of the fairway. The approach shot into the small green is difficult because the fairway narrows and is bordered by a long trap on the left as it reaches the putting surface. A bank slopes from the left of the green to water, and traps guard the rear and front of the putting surface.

The Ocean Course, a 6906-yard par-72 layout, was designed by George Cobb, opened in 1967, and was completely redesigned and renovated by Mark McCumber in 1995. Water comes into play on eleven holes, and wind is always a factor. The Bermuda-grass greens are moderately fast and vary in size from medium to large. A variety of new fairway bunkers have been added and the greens are well protected by bunkers and water. The four finishing holes on the Ocean are representative of the extensive remodeling and the new challenges that await you here.

The fifteenth was a 207-yard par 3 that played to a deep, rolling, elevated green surrounded by four traps. The tee box has been raised and now the hole plays 210 yards down to a large green with two bunkers to its right, one front and another toward the rear. The raised tee box now enables you to see the ocean in the distance.

The 374-yard par-4 sixteenth provides a bit of relief before you encounter two long, tough finishing holes. The sixteenth had been a 449-yard par 4. Three bunkers guarding the front of this green and variable winds off the ocean require an accurate tee shot and proper club selection on the approach. The 455-yard par-4 seventeenth, formerly a 536-yard par 5, is bordered by a lagoon on the right up to approximately 40 yards from the green which is guarded by another lagoon on the left. A narrow entrance way leads to the target which has a bunker left-front, two bunkers to the right and another to the rear. An incoming wind makes this hole very difficult.

The round concludes with a 560-yard par 5, redesigned from a 468-yard par 4. A lagoon on the right cuts in and away from the fairway at various intervals and new fairway bunkers in the second shot landing area adds difficulty to the hole. The green, the smallest on the course, is bulkheaded front-right and right with bunkers to the left and another on the right.

The Sea Marsh Course, remodeled by Clyde Johnson in 1989, plays 6515 yards from the back tees and has water as a factor on a majority of its holes. George Cobb, a native of nearby Savannah and designer of many quality golf courses, originally designed this course, which opened in 1960. Cobb attended the University of Georgia, graduating in 1937 with a degree in landscape architecture. He was employed by the National Park Service as a landscape architect until 1941, when he entered the U.S. Marine Corps as an engineering officer. After becoming involved in building various military golf courses, Cobb, a scratch golfer, opened his business as a golf architect and land planner in Greenville, South Carolina, in 1956. Some of his designs in South Carolina include Shipyard Plantation (Clipper and Galleon nines), Hilton Head Island; Port Royal Plantation (Barony Course), Hilton Head Island; and the Fripp Island Ocean Point Golf Links. Cobb died in 1986.

The Sea Marsh Course is an excellent resort course, suitable for all levels of play. The number-1-handicap hole is the 428-yard par-4 eighth, a slight dogleg right to a small green with a trap both on the left. The ninth hole is a dramatic sharp dogleg left. A 505-yard par 5, the first shot is to a landing area just in front of a huge lagoon that borders the fairway on the right. The second shot is over water toward a deep green protected in front, on the left and on the right by four traps.

A variety of golf packages and instructional programs is available at Sea Pines. From March through November instruction is available in the form of package programs at the Sea Pines Academy of Golf, and year-round individual and group instruction is available from the staff of PGA professionals and assistants. A package for beginning golfers is available year round, as is a variety of tennis packages and other offers.

Accommodations are in condominiums and waterfront-area villas that range from 1 to 4 bedrooms and include full kitchens, linens and towels, and cable TV. A limited selection of private homes is also available for rent. The Racquet Club, which has 29 tennis courts, is the home of the Family Circle Magazine Cup Women's Tennis Championships, and a range of tennis activities and instruction, including junior programs, is available. Other recreational activities include horseback riding, fishing, swimming, bicycling and seasonal activities such as concerts, tournaments and food festivals.

Places to Stay in the Hilton Head Area

BEAUFORT: Best Western Sea Island Inn (803) 524–4121, (800) 528–1234; Comfort Inn (803) 525–9366, (800) 228–5150; Holiday Inn (803) 524–1444, (800) HOLIDAY; Howard Johnson Motor Lodge (803) 524–6020, (800) 654–2000. FRIPP ISLAND: Fripp Island Resort (803) 838–2441, (800) 845–4100. HARBOR ISLAND: Harbor Side Rentals (803) 838–4800. HARDEEVILLE: Holiday Inn (803) 784–2151, (800) HOLIDAY; Howard Johnson Motor Lodge (803) 784–2271, (800) 654–2000. HILTON HEAD ISLAND: Hyatt Regency Hilton Head (803) 785–1234, (800) 233–1234; Hilton Head Island Hilton Resort (803) 842–8000, (800) 845–8001; Days Inn Resort and Conference Center (803) 842–6662, (800) 325–2525 (outside SC); Holiday Inn—Oceanfront (803) 785–5126, (800) 465–4329; Crystal Sands Crowne Plaza Resort (803) 842–2000, (800) 334–1881; Red Roof Inn (803) 686–6808, (800) 843–7663; Cottages Conference Center (803) 686–4424, (800) 225–2471; Westin Resort (803) 681–4000, (800) 228–3000

Local Attractions in the Hilton Head Island Area

BEAUFORT: Beaufort Museum, George Parsons Elliott house, John Mark Verdier house, Sheldon Episcopal Church, St. Helena's Episcopal Church. BLUFFTON: Waddell Mariculture Center. DAUFUSKIE ISLAND: Daufuskie Seafari. EDISTO ISLAND: Edisto Beach State Park. HILTON HEAD ISLAND: Adventure cruises, Audubon–Newball Preserve, Harbour Town, Parriss Island, beaches, bicycling, fishing, horseback riding, Rose Hill Plantation polo matches, restaurants, antiques, theater, seasonal festivals, night life, Hunting Island State Park. ST. HELENA ISLAND: Penn

School Historic District and Museum, Savannah National Wildlife Preserve, Victoria Bluff Heritage Preserve, National Cemetery, Pinckney Island National Wildlife Refuge. Hilton Head Island Visitors and Convention Bureau (803) 785–3673. Beaufort County Chamber of Commerce (803) 524–3163

Hilton Head: Useful Information

Golf packages and Hilton Head Central Reservations: Hilton Head Central Reservations, (800) 845–7018 provides excellent assistance and literature regarding golf packages, Hilton Head, and various resorts and properties including hotel, motel and condominium accommodations. It represents almost every property on the island and can assist you in finding golf packages and suitable accommodations. Hilton Head Island Visitors and Convention Bureau, (803) 785–3673

Recommended Golf Courses in South Carolina

Within 1 Hour of Hilton Head:

Country Club of Hilton Head, Hilton Head Island, (803) 681–4653, Semiprivate, 18/6919/72

Fripp Island Ocean Point Golf Links, Fripp Island, (803) 838–2309, (800) 845–4100, Resort, 18/6590/72

Golf Professionals Club, Beaufort, (803) 522–9700, (803) 524–3635, Resort. Players: 18/5929/72. Champions: 18/6811/72

Hilton Head National, Hilton Head Island, (803) 842–5900, Public, 18/6779/72

Indigo Run Golf Club, Hilton Head Island, (803) 689–2200, Semiprivate, 18/7014/72

Island West Golf Course, Hilton Head Island, (803) 689–6660, Public, 18/6830/72

Old South Golf Links, Bluffton, (803) 785–5353, (800) 257–8997, Public, 18/6772/72

Oyster Reef Golf Club, Hilton Head Island, (803) 681–7717, Semiprivate, 18/7027/72

Pleasant Point Plantation, Beaufort, (803) 522–1605, Public, 18/6489/71

Port Royal Resort, Hilton Head Island, (803) 681–3671, Resort. Planter's Row:

18/6642/72. Barony: 18/6530/72. Robber's Row: 18/6642/72

Rose Hill Country Club, Bluffton, (803) 842–3740, Semiprivate. South: 9/3239/36. East: 9/3235/36. West: 9/3583/36

Shipyard Golf Club, Hilton Head Island, (803) 686–8802, Resort. Brigantine: 9/3352/36. Galleon: 9/3364/36. Clipper: 9/3466/36

Myrtle Beach Area

Course Name: ARCADIAN SHORES GOLF CLUB

Course Type: Resort
Resort: Myrtle Beach Hilton
Address: 701 Hilton Road
              Myrtle Beach, SC 29577
Phone: (803) 449–5217 (Golf Course)
              (803) 449–5000,
              (800) Hilton (Resort)

GOLF COURSE

Head Professional: Aubrey Apple, Jr.
Course Length/Par (All Tees): Back 6857/72, Blue 6446/72, White 6028/72, Gold 5636/72, Forward 5113/72
Course Slope/Rating (All Tees): Back 136/73.2, Blue 131/71.1, White 116/68.8, Gold 113/67.7, Ladies' Forward 117/69.9
Course Architect: Rees Jones (1974)
Golf Facilities: Full Pro Shop X, Snack Bar X, Lounge X, Restaurant No, Locker Room X, Showers X, Club Rental X, Club Repair X, Cart Rental X, Instruction X, Practice Green X, Driving Range X, Practice Bunker X, Club Storage No
Tee-Time Reservation Policy: Up to 1 yr. in advance
Ranger: Yes
Tee-off-Interval Time: 8 min.
Time to Play 18 Holes: 4½ hrs.
Course Hours/Earliest Tee-off: 7:30 a.m.
Green and Cart Fees: Peak season (mid-Mar. to late Apr.): $79 for 18 holes with cart
Credit Cards: American Express, Master-Card, Visa

Season: Year round. Busiest seasons: mid-March to mid-May, mid-Sept. to mid-Nov.
Course Comments: Cart mandatory
Golf Packages: Hilton Hotel (800) 248–9228
Discounts: Seasonal
Places to Stay Nearby: See Myrtle Beach area listing on page 604
Local Attractions: See Myrtle Beach area listing on pages 604
Directions: Hwy. 17 to Hilton Rd., turn east on Hilton Rd. toward ocean, clubhouse on the right
Closest Commercial Airports: Myrtle Beach (20 min.); New Hanover International/Wilmington, NC (2 hrs.); Charleston International (2 hrs.); Columbia Metropolitan (3½ hrs.); Charlotte/Douglas International, NC (4 hrs.)

ARCADIAN SHORES GOLF CLUB

The Arcadian Shores Golf Club is located in Myrtle Beach near the Myrtle Beach Hilton. The course was designed in the 1970s by Rees Jones and is well treed and flat, with water on seven holes. There are 64 traps and bunkers on the course, many of which force you to fly your shots onto the heavily medium-sized, fast, undulating bentgrass greens. A golfer whose ball strays on this layout will be heavily penalized, and a good short game, especially out of the traps, is helpful.

Rees Jones, the son of Robert Trent Jones, Sr., has designed, remodeled and added to a number of noteworthy golf courses in the Carolinas. Among his South Carolina golf courses are Bear Creek Golf Course, Hilton Head Island; the Country Club of Hilton Head; Gator Hole Golf Course, North Myrtle Beach; Haig Point Golf Course, Daufuskie Island; Oyster Reef Golf Course, Hilton Head Island; and the Waterway Hills Golf Course at Myrtle Beach. Most of his work has been done east of the Mississippi.

Arcadian starts out with a 527-yard dogleg-left par 5, with two left-side fairway bunkers protecting the knee of the dogleg. The second shot is toward a left-to-right-angled green with traps left, right and right-front, making it difficult to roll the ball onto the green in two. The 201-yard second hole is a beautiful par 3 across water to a deep green with a trap on the left. This hole is considered one of the best par 3s in the Myrtle Beach area. A difficult hole on the front side is the 402-yard dog-leg-left par-4 fifth hole. The fairway is squeezed by two bunkers in the landing area. The green has a huge crown and is trapped front and left. The longer the iron on the second shot, the more difficult it is to hold this well-guarded green.

The thirteenth hole on the back nine is another tough par 4, playing 408 yards to a forward-sloping green guarded by water in front. The tee shot is likely to leave you with a difficult downhill lie coming into this target. The 398-yard par-4 fourteenth has a blind tee shot up a slope that must be cleared to see the green on the second shot. Also, there are traps both to the left and right of the putting surface. The finishing hole at Arcadia is another long par 4, playing 447 yards to a large green trapped left-front and right.

The clubhouse at the golf course includes locker rooms and showers, a full pro shop and a snack bar. Professional instruction for individuals and groups is available from the staff of PGA professionals. Arcadian Shores has been the site of the Carolinas Open, Myrtle Beach Open and the Carolinas PGA Shootout. It is also ranked among America's 75 best resort courses by *Golf Digest* magazine.

The on-site beach-front Hilton has a swimming pool, boating, tennis, business-conference facilities and a variety of other amenities. The Arcadian Shores Golf Course can be played even if you elect not to stay at the hotel.

Course Name: CALEDONIA GOLF AND FISH CLUB

Course Type: Public
Address: 369 Caledonia Drive
                    P.O. Box 1320
                    Pawleys Island, SC 29585
Phone: (803) 237-3675, (800) 483-6800
Fax: (803) 237-4762

GOLF COURSE

Head Professional: Todd Welden
Course Length/Par (All Tees): Back 6503/70, Mallard 6104/70, Wood Duck 5738/70, Forward 4968/70
Course Slope/Rating (All Tees): Back 130/70.8, Mallard 116/69.7, Wood Duck 115/66.9, Ladies' Forward 113/68.2
Course Architect: Mike Strantz (1994)
Golf Facilities: Full Pro Shop X, Snack Bar X, Lounge X, Restaurant X, Locker Room No, Showers X, Club Rental X, Club Repair X, Cart Rental X, Instruction X, Practice Green X, Driving Net X, Practice Bunker X, Club Storage No
Tee-Time Reservation Policy: Up to 1 yr. in advance with deposit. Up to 30 days in advance with credit card guarantee
Ranger: Yes
Tee-off-Interval Time: 8 and 9 min.
Time to Play 18 Holes: 4½ hrs.
Course Hours/Earliest Tee-off: 7:15 a.m.
Green and Cart Fees: $96 for 18 holes peak season (Sept.–mid-Nov., Mar.–mid-May)
Credit Cards: All major cards except Diners
Season: Year round. Busiest peak rate season
Course Comments: Cart mandatory
Golf Packages: Inquire at pro shop. Through local hotels
Discounts: Lowest seasonal mid-Nov. through Feb., mid-May through Aug.
Places to Stay Nearby: PAWLEY'S ISLAND: Pawley's Plantation Golf and Country Club (803) 237-3415, (800) 367-9959; Ramada Inn (803) 237-4261, (800) 272-6232; Litchfield by the Sea Resort and Country Club (803) 237-3000; Seagull Inn (803) 237-4621, (800) 553-7008; Waccamaw House (803) 237-8402, (800) 845-1897
Local Attractions: See Myrtle Beach listings on page 604
Directions: From Myrtle Beach (30 min. south): Take Rte 17 south to Pawley's Island and make a right at light (Waverly). Proceed 3 mi. to 4-way stop (King's River). Go left 1½ mi. to golf course on the right
Closest Commercial Airports: Myrtle Beach (30 min.); New Hanover Interna-

tional/Wilmington, NC (2 hrs.); Savannah International, GA (4½ hrs.)

CALEDONIA GOLF AND FISH CLUB

The Caledonia Golf and Fish Club is situated on the site of an old rice plantation thirty minutes south of Myrtle Beach. This lush golf course features natural lakes, centuries old live oaks, and wetlands. Designed by Mike Strantz, a former assistant to Tom Fazio, Caledonia is now rated among the best golf courses in South Carolina by *Golf Digest* and *GolfWeek*. The name Caledonia comes from the plantation's original founder, Dr. Robert Nesbit, a Scottish immigrant who acquired the property through his marriage to Elizabeth Pawley, after whose family Pawley's Island is named. Just before it became a golf club, this land was used as a fishing and hunting retreat.

There are many good holes at Caledonia, especially the par 4s. The 419-yard fifth, for example, requires an accurate tee shot to avoid two bunkers on the right and a pine tree on the right. The approach is to a crowned green with dropoffs but no bunkers around it. Wind coming off the nearby rice fields often adds distance to this hole.

Water can come into play on six holes on the more difficult back nine. The 167-yard par-3 eleventh plays to a kidney-shaped green guarded by a pond to its left and a creek in front. Two bunkers protect the front right of the target. The most difficult pin placement on the hole is to the rear left of the putting surface requiring the tee shot to come in from right-to-left in order to take the pond out of play. Another good hole on this side is the 417-yard par-4 sixteenth, a dogleg right whose tee shot must avoid a bunker to the left and three more to the right of the landing area. The approach is over a pond fronting the large green. A prevailing incoming wind can make this hole extremely difficult.

Overlooking the golf course is a modern clubhouse desgined after an 18th century plantation house. Many golfers assemble on the wraparound veranda to review their round and contemplate approach shots com-

ing in over water to the green on the 383-yard par-4 finishing hole.

Course Name: HEATHER GLEN GOLF LINKS
One, Two, Three Courses

Course Type: Public
Address: Highway 17 North
P.O. Box 297
North Myrtle Beach, SC
29597
Phone: (803) 249–9000,
(800) 868–4536

GOLF COURSE

Director of Golf: Ben L. Fowler

Course Length/Par (All Tees): One/Two: Back 6769/72, White 6325/72, Gold 5850/72, Forward 5146/72. Three/One: Back 6771/72, White 6310/72, Gold 5706/72, Forward 5053/72. Two/Three: Back 6808/72, White 6391/72, Gold 5838/72, Forward 5127/72.

Course Slope/Rating (All Tees): One/Two: Back 130/72, White 123/70, Gold 118/68.0, Ladies' Forward 117/69.3. Three/One: Back 127/72.4, White 126/70.5, Gold 115/67.1, Ladies' Forward 117/69.3. Two/Three: Back 130/72.4, White 126/70.6, Gold 118/68.8, Ladies' Forward 117/69.3

Course Architect: Willard Byrd and Clyde Johnston (1987)

Golf Facilities: Full Pro Shop X, Snack Bar X, Lounge X, Restaurant X, Locker Room X, Showers X, Club Rental X, Club Repair No, Cart Rental X, Instruction X, Practice Green X, Driving Range X, Practice Bunker X, Club Storage No

Tee-Time Reservation Policy: Call anytime in advance. In season (Sept. to Nov., Feb. to May), payment required 1 mo. in advance. 48-hr. cancellation policy

Ranger: Yes

Tee-off-Interval Time: 8 min.

Time to Play 18 Holes: 4½ hrs.

Course Hours/Earliest Tee-off: 7:16 a.m.

Green and Cart Fees: Peak season (March-May, Sept.-Nov.): $80 for 18 holes with cart

Credit Cards: American Express, Master-
Card, Visa

Season: Year round

Course Comments: Cart mandatory. Yardage book available. Inquire for 9 hole
rates. Any combination of 3 9-hole
courses can be played. Provide your
own toiletries

Golf Packages: Available through hotels in
Myrtle Beach

Discounts: Seasonal

Places to Stay Nearby: See Myrtle Beach
area listing on page 604

Local Attractions: See Myrtle Beach area
listing on pages 604

Directions: From Myrtle Beach (20 min.):
North on U.S. 17, golf course on the left
just south of the North Carolina state
line—Follow the signs

Closest Commercial Airports: New
Hanover International/Wilmington, NC
(45 min.); Myrtle Beach (45 min.);
Charleston International (3 hrs.); Char-
lotte/Douglas International, NC (3½
hrs.); Columbia Metropolitan (3½ hrs.)

HEATHER GLEN GOLF LINKS

Heather Glen was chosen by *Golf
Digest* as America's best new public golf
course in 1987, and the course is currently
listed by that publication as one of the top
75 public golf courses in America. Inspired by the Scottish traditions of Glen
Eagles and St. Andrews, Heather Glen was
built on 200 acres of beautiful land located
in North Myrtle Beach. Featuring numerous elevation changes; 100-year-old pines;
dogwoods, hollies, oaks; and winding
streams and brooks, Heather Glen provides
a combination of three nine-hole golf
courses to choose from. Well-placed water
hazards, unusual bunkers and heather-
laced dunes accentuate the golf challenge
here.

Course One starts you out with a straight
363-yard par 4 uphill to a large, forward-
sloping green protected by traps left and right-
front. The second hole is a picturesque 366-
yard par-4 dogleg left with water on the left
from 180 yards into the green, which is protected by small moundings to the right and
elevated pot bunkers to the left. From this
point the holes get more difficult. The 506-
yard par-5 third has a narrow driving area
from the tee, with a right fairway bunker
midway to the hole. The second shot must
negotiate the rough that runs down the left
side and must avoid the mounds on the
right that partially hide the green. The
deep, elongated, sloping green has a large
trap to the right and smaller pot bunkers
behind and to the left. The number-1-handi-
cap hole on this nine is the 415-yard par-4
fifth, a dogleg left which has a waste bunker down the left side. On the tee shot, the
right side is protected by pot bunkers cut
into high mounding. The second shot is
onto a sizeable green protected by a trap on
the left. You'll be happy to get to the vicinity of the 150-yard marker with your tee
shot so you can come straight in from
there. This opening nine is capped off by
what is quaintly called "the Long Hole," a
447-yard dogleg left, which is the longest
par 4 on the course. A long drive uphill and
generally into the wind is required to be
able to see the green on the second shot. To
further intimidate the golfer the landing
area is bracketed by large fairway bunkers.

Course Two opens with the number-2-
handicap hole on the combined One and
Two eighteen. This 416-yard par-4 dogleg
right plays from an elevated tee over a
stream and an expanse of heavy rough to a
gently rising fairway with a bunker to the
right. The approach shot is to an elevated
green protected by several bunkers beginning 100 yards out. A long waste area also
guards the fairway and green on the right.
"The Spectacle," the 409-yard par-4 eighth,
is a beautiful hole on this side. A dogleg
left, this hole's fairway is cut by a stream. A
pond is on the left. A drive of 175 yards is required to carry the water on the right, and a
200-yard tee shot is needed to negotiate the
left hazard. A huge waste bunker protects the
left fairway beyond the water, and mounds
and bunkers guard the right side. The second
shot is to a large green bunkered to the left
and rear.

Course Three has three strong finishing
holes, beginning with the number-1-handicap
seventh, which is a par-4 slight dogleg right
playing 410 yards from the back tees. The

landing area on the drive is protected by pot bunkers to the left, a small stream crossing the fairway and mounds on the right. The second shot is to a green protected by mounds, but there are no traps. The 525-yard par-5 eighth is a challenging dogleg left with a stream crossing the fairway 190 yards from the green, which is narrow and deep, and protected by a huge pond to the right and rear. There are also several bunkers on the left. This shot can be reached in two by the long hitter, but only at great risk. The finishing hole is a 410-yard par 4, which is a dogleg left sweeping up to an elevated green protected by nine bunkers. A valley effect is created coming into this hole because of the mounding and bunkering on both sides of the fairway.

A nineteenth century British-style clubhouse with full amenities awaits you after playing this challenging course. Privately held by a local partnership, Heather Glen provides resort-quality golf to the public golfer. In that spirit, the yardage book has a brief questionnaire that asks the golfer to evaluate the condition of the greens, fairways, golf carts, snack bar operation, staff service and general ambience at Heather Glen—a good way to improve the golf course and customer service.

Course Name: HERITAGE GOLF CLUB

Course Type: Public
Address: River Road/P.O. Box 1885
               Pawleys Island, SC 29585
Phone: (803) 237–3424,
               (800) 237–2315
               (Starting Time)
               (803) 237–3424
               (Club House)

GOLF COURSE

Director of Golf: Ron Crump
Head Professional: Gene McCaskill
Course Length/Par (All Tees): Back 7075/71, Blue 6575/71, White 6100/71, Forward 5325/71
Course Slope/Rating (All Tees): Back 137/74.2, Blue 128/72.0, White 117/69.6, Ladies' Forward 125/71
Course Architects: Dan Maples and Larry Young (1986)

Golf Facilities: Full Pro Shop X, Snack Bar X, Lounge X, Restaurant X, Locker Room X, Showers X, Club Rental X, Club Repair No, Cart Rental X, Instruction X, Practice Green X, Driving Range X, Practice Bunker No, Club Storage No
Tee-Time Reservation Policy: Up to 1 yr. in advance. Prepayment required for tee times well in advance in season. 48-hr. cancellation policy
Ranger: Yes
Tee-off-Interval Time: 8 min.
Time to Play 18 Holes: 4½ hrs.
Course Hours/Earliest Tee-off: 7 a.m.
Green Fees: Peak season (mid-March to mid-May): $82 for 18 holes with cart
Credit Cards: American Express, Master-Card, Visa
Season: Year round. Busiest season mid-March to mid-May, mid-Sept. to Nov. 31
Course Comments: Cart mandatory. Membership available
Golf Packages: Available through hotels in the area
Discounts: Seasonal
Places to Stay Nearby: See Myrtle Beach area listing on page 604
Local Attractions: See Myrtle Beach area listing on pages 604
Directions: Hwy. 17, follow signs, exit at River Rd., drive west of 17 to golf course
Closest Commercial Airports: Myrtle Beach (45 min.); New Hanover International/Wilmington, NC (1½ hrs.); Charleston International (2½ hrs.); Columbia Metropolitan (3½ hrs.); Charlotte/ Douglas International, NC (3½ hrs.)

HERITAGE GOLF CLUB

The Heritage Golf Club is part of a 600-acre real-estate development that was formerly the site of True Blue and Midway plantations on Pawleys Island, south of Myrtle Beach. Heritage plays 7100 yards from the back tees through a layout featuring giant magnolias, centuries-old oaks, fresh-water lakes and marshes, rice fields, crape myrtle, camellias and azaleas. Water comes into play on eight of the holes, whose Bermuda-grass greens are large, moderately fast and undulating. Dan Maples began as the designer for this course, but Larry Young, the owner of this and several other golf courses in the area, finished it. Heritage is one of the best public golf courses in the country according to *Golf Digest*.

The front side of Heritage is a bit more open than the back side. The course is especially difficult from the back tees, and 69 is the lowest score yet recorded here in competition. The number-1-handicap hole on the course is the 440-yard par-4 fourth, a beautiful, tree-lined slight dogleg left. The tee shot should be right-of-center to have a clear shot onto a deep, right-to-left-sloping green with a trap to its right. A right-side fairway bunker 180 yards from the green has to be avoided on the tee shot.

Another tough hole is the 440-yard par-4 fourteenth, which requires you to go over water twice to a right-to-left-angled green protected by a large trap to the front and water to the left and front. The golfer can decide how much water he or she can carry on the tee shot to reach the fairway, which has two right-side bunkers beginning 210 yards from the green. The second shot has to clear sand or water near the green to reach the putting surface.

The 530-yard par-5 finishing hole is scenic, and fraught with peril as well. Water lines the fairway on the right from tee to green and cuts into the fairway in front of the green. It also cuts into the area between the tees and the fairway. The hourglass-shaped green almost lies on its side perpendicular to the tee. It has several small bunkers behind it and water both right and left. The tee shot has to avoid two right-fairway bunkers in the landing area. Then the decision is whether to go for it in two or lay up. Regardless, the green offers a shallow target, and the water and sand still await you.

Wind can be a factor on this course. For example, the 235-yard par-3 thirteenth often plays longer because of an incoming wind off the nearby Atlantic. The tee shot on this hole is over water to a long, narrow green. A trap protects the green in front, and water guards it left and toward the front.

A 12,000-square-foot clubhouse with restaurant and lounge facilities, locker room, showers and pro shop serves the Heritage Plantation Golf Club and overlooks the Waccamaw River. A rich variety of wildlife ranging from alligators and ospreys to deer and egrets roams the property. Tee times should be reserved as far in advance as possible.

Course Name: THE LEGENDS GOLF CLUB
Heathland, Moorland, Parkland Courses

Course Type: Public
Address: 1500 Legends Drive, Route 501
                   Myrtle Beach, SC 29578
Phone: (803) 236–9318,
                   (800) 552–2660

GOLF COURSE

Director of Golf: Gene McCaskill

Course Length/Par (All Tees): Heathland: Back 6785/71, Middle 6190/71, Forward 5115/71. Moorland: Championship Gold 6832/72, Blue 6405/72, White 5807/72, Forward 4939/72. Parkland: Back 7170/72, Blue 6460/72, Green 6230/72, Forward 5570/72

Course Slope/Rating (All Tees): Heathland: Back 127/72.3, Middle 117/69.0, Ladies' Forward 121/71.0. Moorland: Tournament Gold 130/72.8, Blue 128/73.1, Green 121/69.8, Ladies' Forward 127/71.0. Parkland: Back 131/74.3, Blue 127/71.3, Green 123/70.0, Ladies' Forward 125/71.0

Course Architects: Heathland: Tom Doak (1990). Moorland: Paul Burke Dye (1990). Parkland: Larry Young (1992)

Golf Facilities: Full Pro Shop X, Snack Bar X, Lounge X, Restaurant X, Locker Room X, Showers X, Club Rental X, Club Repair No, Cart Rental X, Instruction X, Practice Green X, Driving Range X, Practice Bunker X, Club Storage No

Tee-Time Reservation Policy: Anytime up to 1 yr. in advance. Advance payment required. 24-hr. cancellation policy

Ranger: Yes

Tee-off-Interval Time: 8 min.

Time to Play 18 Holes: 4½ hrs.

Course Hours/Earliest Tee-off: 7 a.m.

Green and Cart Fees: Peak season (mid-March to mid-May, Sept.-Nov.): $92 for 18 holes with cart

Credit Cards: American Express, Master-Card, Visa

Season: Year round. Busiest season March through May, Oct.

Course Comments: Cart mandatory. Yardage book available. Legends of Golf Academy on site

Golf Packages: Available only through hotels

Discounts: Seasonal

Places to Stay Nearby: See Myrtle Beach area listing on page 604

Local Attractions: See Myrtle Beach area listing on pages 604

Directions: From Myrtle Beach: Rte. 501 north, 4 mi., course on Rte. 501, follow the signs

Closest Commercial Airports: Myrtle Beach (20 min.); New Hanover International/Wilmington, NC (1½ hrs.); Columbia Metropolitan (2½ hrs.); Charleston International (2½ hrs.); Charlotte/Douglas International, NC (3½ hrs.)

THE LEGENDS GOLF CLUB

The Legends Golf Club includes three eighteen-hole courses. The Moorland, a Paul Burke "P. B." Dye design, won an honorable mention in the best new public golf course ratings by *Golf Digest* in 1991. The Heathland is a British-links-style course with few trees, many strategically placed bunkers and some very difficult large greens. The Parkland, which opened in October, 1992, is the latest addition to this excellent golf facility.

The Moorland offers four tee distances ranging from 6832 yards for the back tees to 4939 yards for the forward tees. The Bermuda greens are medium to large in size, moderately fast and undulating. A mixture of sand traps, water hazards and waste areas combined with severely undulating terrain and many bulkheaded areas makes Moorland a difficult test of golf. The Moorland is a target golf course requiring strategic golf-course management and careful club selection.

The number-1-handicap hole on this course is the 465-yard par-4 ninth, which usually plays into the wind. The fairway is heavily banked on the left side and doglegs right to a deep, two-tiered green with a 3-foot drop from back to front. The green is protected on the left front by a bunker, and it has another large trap on the right. Another difficult hole is the 459-yard par-4 twelfth, which plays uphill to a narrow, deep green with a large bunker on the left and a trap to the rear. You have to be good with woods and long irons to have any chance for a par on these holes.

Two thought-provoking holes are the sixteenth and seventeenth. The sixteenth is a 275-yard par 4 that plays from an elevated tee to an elevated green. If you are a big hitter and go for the green on the tee shot, a series of 10 traps and pot bunkers awaits you from 75 yards in. The seventeenth is a 194-yard par 3 that plays completely over sand and natural vegetation to a narrow, deep green. Bring your sand wedge on these holes. The other fourteen holes on the course have more than 50 bunkers and massive sand waste areas as well as numerous well-placed water hazards. That's why the slope is 140 and the USGA rating 76.8 from the back tees.

The Heathland, which was designed by Tom Doak and opened in 1990, has more trees, less undulating greens, and less sand and water than the Moorland course. Each hole has its own name such as "First" (for the first hole, believe it or not), "Short," "Mashie Nibblick" and "Plateau." "Carry" is the 460-yard par-4 number-1-handicap sixth hole and plays from an elevated tee over a sizeable wetlands area to the fairway 200 yards away. The second shot is to a shallow green protected by a bunker on the left and a mound in front. Two long, accurate shots are required to reach this green in regulation. This hole is more forgiving from the 385-yard regulation tees.

Another difficult hole is the 435-yard par-4 tenth, is a dogleg left that is guarded by three severe bunkers on the left. A fade on the drive is probably the safest shot, but this leaves you a long or mid-iron to a large, slightly bowled green with two traps left and to its front. This is considered the most difficult driving hole on the course.

A difficult par 3 is the 210-yard third, called "Port Erroll" that plays uphill to a green 50 yards wide and 31 yards deep. The green is difficult to hold because it slopes from front to back. Pin placement is a major factor on "Port Erroll."

The finishing hole at Heathland is a 430-yard par 4 aptly called "Home" and modeled on the finishing hole at Royal Lytham and St. Annes in England. Seven bunkers from 210 to 120 yards into the green protect the fairway on the tee shot. The second shot is to a narrow, very deep green with three traps to the left and three more to the right. An excellent finishing hole.

A third course, the Parkland, measures a formidable 7170 yards from the back tees. The Parkland was designed by Larry Young, who owns the Legends group of golf courses in South Carolina, which include Heathland, Moorland, Marsh Harbour, Oyster Bay, Heritage Club and Parkland. Parkland features rolling, well-treed fairways, deep sculptured bunkers, and large greens that can easily require three putts. There are many considerable carries off the tee box to reach the fairways, especially from the back tees.

The Clubhouse at the Legends is modeled after clubhouses in Scotland and includes a pub, restaurant, pro shop, and locker and shower facilities. An excellent 30-acre practice facility is located here and includes a 50,000-square-foot putting green. Instruction is available from PGA professionals and assistants.

Course Name: THE LONG BAY CLUB

Course Type: Semiprivate
Address: Highway 9/P.O. Box 330
               Longs, SC 29568
Phone: (803) 399–2222,
               (800) 422–7244

GOLF COURSE

Head Professional: Jerry Cox
Course Length/Par (All Tees): Back 7021/72, Blue 6565/72, White 6139/72, Forward 5598/72
Course Slope/Rating (All Tees): Back 137/74.3, Blue 130/72.1, White 126/70.5, Ladies' Forward 120/72.1
Course Architect: Jack Nicklaus (1988)
Golf Facilities: Full Pro Shop X, Snack Bar X, Lounge X, Restaurant No, Locker Room No, Showers Men, Club Rental X, Club Repair No, Cart Rental X, Instruction X, Practice Green X, Driving Range X, Practice Bunker X, Club Storage No
Tee-Time Reservation Policy: Anytime. Prepay 1 mo. in advance. Check preferred, but credit card acceptable. 7-day cancellation notice required by large groups, 48-hr. for foursomes for full refund
Ranger: Yes
Tee-off-Interval Time: 7 min.
Time to Play 18 Holes: 4 hrs., 45 min.
Course Hours/Earliest Tee-off: 7:30 a.m.
Green and Cart Fees: Peak season (late Sept. to mid-Nov., March 21 to May 15): $95 for 18 holes with cart, $47.50 for 9 holes with cart
Credit Cards: American Express, Master-Card, Visa
Season: Year round. Busiest season mid-March to mid-May, late Sept. to mid-Nov.
Course Comments: Cart mandatory
Golf Packages: Available through local hotels in Myrtle Beach
Discounts: Seasonal (Mid-May to early Sept., mid-Nov. to end of Jan.)
Places to Stay Nearby: See Myrtle Beach area listing on page 604
Local Attractions: See Myrtle Beach area listing on pages 604
Directions: From Myrtle Beach (30 mi.): North on Business 17 to Rte. 9, west on Rte. 9 (9 mi.), golf course on the left just past the Rte. 905 intersection
Closest Commercial Airports: Myrtle Beach (45 min.); New Hanover International/Wilmington, NC (1 hr.); Charleston International (2½ hrs.); Columbia Metro-

politan (3½ hrs.); Charlotte/Douglas International, NC (3½ hrs.)

THE LONG BAY CLUB

Long Bay, designed by Jack Nicklaus and opened in 1988, started out as a 600-member private club. It has since changed ownership and is open to the public, although it has some members. The course is located on former swampland 45 minutes north of Myrtle Beach and slightly west of the Intracoastal Waterway. A considerable amount of land was moved to recontour the course, which is open, flat and mounded in the Scottish-links style. The fairways have generous landing areas, and there is a variety of high-lipped pot bunkers strategically placed near fairway landing areas and around the small Bermuda Tifdwarf greens. Water comes into play on six holes.

The Long Bay course has no doglegs that obscure a clear view to the greens. The fairways usually provide you with relatively flat lies, but if you are off the fairway, you'll be hitting out of a bunker or have an uneven lie of some sort. It is not easy to score pars at Long Bay, because the holes tend to have difficult greens and other impediments such as water and bunkers. The 543-yard par-5 seventh, for example, is a dogleg to the left with water to the left of the fairway. There is also water to the left of the green, and nine bunkers are arrayed around the green from approximately 75 yards in. If you go for it on your second shot, you are likely to be in sand or water. When you reach the putting surface, you'll find a two-tiered green with a huge drop from the higher tier to the lower, which is toward the water on the left. It's on holes like these that you begin to realize that shot strategy and landing the ball on the proper part of the soft greens is essential to score. And if you try to play bogey golf, you will probably be hitting many wedges from mounds and traps around the greens.

The number-1-handicap hole at Long Bay is the 472-yard par-4 fourth, which is long and straight to a narrow, deep, undulating green that slopes back to front. The fairway is generous, but huge waste bunkers

on each side await if the ball strays too far. This hole is difficult primarily because of its length and because it often plays into the wind.

A scenic and tricky par 3 is the 156-yard thirteenth, which plays over water to a flat island green with a trap on the right. The tee is in a treed area, often giving the golfer the illusion that there is no wind. But there usually is, and it can swirl in unpredictable ways. Misses are usually wet on this hole.

Long Bay has three very solid finishing holes. The 433-yard par-4 sixteenth is a dogleg right to an undulating green with three traps to its left. The tee shot has to clear a waste area crossing the fairway approximately 150 to 200 yards from the tee. Waste areas are also situated left and right of the fairway. The 210-yard par-3 seventeenth is straight to an undulating, "7"-shaped green with large bunkers front and back. A large, 15- to 20-foot amphitheaterlike mounded bank surrounds the back of this green. Approach shots can be especially tough if the pin is placed to the rear and left. The 445-yard par-4 eighteenth is a sharp dogleg right from the tee-shot landing area, with water on the right all the way to the green. You can try to cut as much of the dogleg as you think you can manage. The second shot is to a two-tiered green with the low side toward the water. A large bunker protects the front of the green, and if you miss left you have a tough chip to a green sloping toward the water.

The Long Bay Club has a temporary clubhouse with pro shop, snack bar, bar, club rental and club repair. A new, permanent clubhouse with full amenities is a few years away. The golf course is the centerpiece of a real-estate development, but the plan is to keep it open to the public. Four professionals here can provide instruction at the on-site putting green and driving range. A variety of golf-package discounts are available through Myrtle Beach area hotels, and low seasonal rates are generously offered from June to September and from mid-November until the end of January.

In its short life, the Long Bay Club has been ranked among the ten best golf courses in South Carolina, a state with many excellent golf facilities. Some other Nicklaus-designed courses in South Carolina include the Harbour Town Golf Links, Hilton Head Island, with Pete and Alice Dye; the Turtle Point Golf Links, Kiawah Island, with Robert Cupp and Jay Moorish; and the Melrose Golf Course, Daufuskie Island, with Tom Pearson.

Course Name: TIDEWATER GOLF CLUB AND PLANTATION

Course Type: Public
Address: 4901 Little River Neck Road
North Myrtle Beach, SC 29582
Phone: (803) 249–3829 (Golf Shop)
(800) 446–5363 (Tee-Times)

GOLF COURSE

Head Professional: Paul Kline
Course Length/Par (All Tees): Back 7020/72, Blue 6505/72, White 6030/72, Gold 5100/72, Forward 4765/72
Course Slope/Rating (All Tees): Back 140/74.9, Blue 131/70.2, White 126/68.6, Gold 107/65.5, Ladies' Gold 132/70.2, Ladies' Forward 127/67.5.
Course Architect: Ken Tomlinson (1990)
Golf Facilities: Full Pro Shop X, Snack Bar X, Lounge X, Restaurant No, Locker Room X, Showers No, Club Rental X, Club Repair No, Cart Rental X, Instruction X, Practice Green X, Driving Range X, Practice Bunker X, Club Storage No
Tee-Time Reservation Policy: Call anytime in advance up to 12 mos. Deposit required for busiest months (March through May, Sept. through Nov.). Credit card guarantee required. 48-hr. cancellation policy
Ranger: Yes
Tee-off-Interval Time: 9 min.
Time to Play 18 Holes: 4 hrs., 45 min.
Course Hours/Earliest Tee-off: 7 a.m.
Green and Cart Fees: Peak season (early March to mid-May, mid-Oct. to mid-Nov.): $98 for 18 holes with cart
Credit Cards: American Express, MasterCard, Visa

Season: Year round. Busiest months March through May, Sept. through Nov.
Course Comments: Can walk anytime at full golf fee. Yardage book available
Golf Packages: Available through over 70 hotels, local and national
Discounts: Seasonal, replays on availability
Places to Stay Nearby: See Myrtle Beach area listing on page 604
Local Attractions: See Myrtle Beach area listing on pages 604
Directions: From Myrtle Beach (30 min.): Hwy. 17 north, take Cherry Grove exit, stop at end of ramp, turn left. West to Little Neck Rd., turn right onto Little Neck Rd. (at Harbour Gate), 2 mi. to golf course
Closest Commercial Airports: Myrtle Beach (30 min.); New Hanover International/Wilmington, NC (1 hr.); Charleston International (3 hrs.); Columbia Metropolitan (3 hrs.); Charlotte/Douglas International, NC (3½ hrs.)

TIDEWATER GOLF CLUB AND PLANTATION

The Tidewater Golf Club is 15 miles north and slightly west of Myrtle Beach. The 7020-yard par-72 golf course is the first design effort by Ken Tomlinson, a tax and business attorney. Tidewater has 7.3 miles of cart paths wending their way through almost 500 acres of beautiful forest, bluffs, hills, valleys, creeks and lakes midway between the Atlantic Ocean and the Intracoastal Waterway. The course is part of a residential real-estate development that will include homes and townhouses along the Intracoastal Waterway; plantation-style homes in the forest along the inland fairways; and Bermuda/West Indies–styled colonial homes overlooking the ocean and estuarine marshes of Cherry Grove Beach Inlet.

Tomlinson gained considerable golf-course-design experience when he became involved in the development of the Arnold Palmer–designed Musgrove Mill Golf Club in Clinton, South Carolina. The goal was to make this club as excellent and exclusive as Augusta National. After gaining experience from the Musgrove Mill project,

Tomlinson did a considerable amount of additional homework through the USGA, National Golf Foundation and a broad network of golf experts. After the successful development of Tidewater, with a little help from his many friends, Tomlinson will no doubt undertake future projects in the Myrtle Beach area.

Tidewater was named the best new public golf course in America in 1990 by *Golf Digest*, which also lists Tidewater among the ten best golf courses in the state of South Carolina. The course is contoured to the land, with generous landing areas on the long holes and tighter requirements on the shorter holes. The undulating bentgrass greens are large, some more than 50 yards deep. More than 70 well-placed bunkers guard strategic fairway landing areas and greens that vary in depth from 26 to 53 yards. Water comes into play on thirteen holes, and wind can be a factor. There are five tee distances ranging from 4765 yards to the 7020-yard championship tees, so golfers of any level should be able to find a suitable venue. And despite the many obstacles, there is usually a bailout area on most holes.

The number-1-handicap hole on the course is the 465-yard par-4 fifth hole, which plays straight to a deep green protected by traps left and right. Distance makes this hole play tough. A challenging par 3 on this side is the 150-yard third hole, which plays to a large, three-tiered green with seven traps surrounding it and water on the left. The twelfth hole is another beautiful and well protected par 3, with a distance of 180 yards over a marsh to a green with traps and water to the front and to the right. The green slopes severely forward, so if you get above the hole you'll be looking at the huge trap and marsh down below.

Tidewater's signature hole is the 545-yard par-5 thirteenth, which plays straight to a deep green with four traps in front and two on the right. As with holes three, four and twelve, this hole parallels marshland and provides some magnificent views. On the thirteenth, the issue is whether to go for the green on the second shot. The combination of ocean wind and sand traps add to the risk. And when you get to the green, which is tiered on the right and left, three-putting is easy.

The finishing hole at Tidewater is a tough, 440-yard par 4 on the Intracoastal Waterway side of the course. A marsh is on the right from tee to green, and water cuts into the fairway in an area from 85 to 65 yards in front of the green, which is narrow, deep and trapped in back. The green slopes a bit toward the water, and to the left of the green is a bailout area that slopes away from the putting surface. A chip shot from there toward the green and the water can be trouble. An incoming wind usually makes this hole play longer.

There is a temporary clubhouse at Tidewater, with pro shop, snack bar, bar, and club rental. Currently, one pro and three assistants provide instruction at the nearby driving range, which includes a practice bunker. There are plans for a clubhouse in the next few years. The peak season at Tidewater is March through May and October through November. Golf packages are available through several Myrtle Beach area hotels. Lower seasonal rates are available.

Course Name: **WILD WING PLANTATION Avocet, Falcon, Hummingbird, Wood Stork Courses**

Course Type: Public
Address: Highway 501 North
P.O. Box 647
Myrtle Beach, SC 29578
Phone: (803) 347–9464, (800) 736–9464
Fax: (803) 347–5732

GOLF COURSE

Director of Golf: Robert E. Harper
Head Professional: Tim Tilma (Avocet, Falcon)
Course Length/Par (All Tees): Avocet: Back 7127/72, Magenta 6614/72, White 6028/72, Forward 5298/72. Falcon: Back 7082/72, Magenta 6697/72, White 6089/72, Forward 5190/72. Hummingbird: Back 6853/72, Magenta 6310/72, White 5796/72, Forward 5168/72. Wood

Stork: Back 7044/72, Magenta 6598/72, White 6106/72, Forward 5409/72

Course Slope/Rating (All Tees): Avocet: Back 128/74.2, Magenta 119/71.4, White 114/68.5, Forward 118/70.4. Falcon: Back 134/74.4, Magenta 128/72.3, White 117/68.7, Ladies' Forward 118/70.4. Hummingbird: Back 131/73, Magenta 123/70, White 116/72.3, Ladies' Forward 123/69.5. Wood Stork: Back 130/74.1, Magenta 123/71.9, White 118/69.6, Ladies' Forward 121/70.7

Course Architects: Avocet: Larry Nelson, Jeff Brauer (1993). Falcon: Rees Jones (1994). Hummingbird: Willard Byrd (1991). Wood Stork: Willard Byrd (1992)

Golf Facilities: Full Pro Shop X, Snack Bar X, Lounge X, Restaurant X, Locker Room X, Showers No, Club Rental X, Club Repair No, Cart Rental X, Instruction X, Practice Green X, Driving Range X, Practice Bunker X, Club Storage No

Tee-Time Reservation Policy: Call anytime. Credit card required to secure tee time peak season

Ranger: Yes

Tee-off-Interval Time: 9 min.

Time to Play 18 Holes: 5 hrs.

Course Hours/Earliest Tee-off: Sunrise

Green and Cart Fees: Avocet, Falcon: $107 for 18 holes. Hummingbird, Wood Stork: $91 for 18 holes. Peak season rates early Mar. to early May

Credit Cards: All major cards

Season: Year round. Busiest Feb. through May, Sept. to mid-Nov.

Course Comments: Cart mandatory. Yardage book available. Club storage for package golfers only

Golf Packages: Through Wild Wing and Myrtle Beach Hotels

Discounts: Twilight. Lowest seasonal rates in Dec.

Places to Stay Nearby: See Myrtle Beach area listing on page 604

Local Attractions: See Myrtle Beach area listing on page 604

Directions: From Myrtle Beach (15 min. west): Take Rte. 501 west 10 miles to golf course

Closest Commercial Airports: Myrtle Beach (15 min.); New Hanover International/Wilmington, NC (1 hr.); Charleston International (2½ hrs.); Columbia Metropolitan (3½ hrs.); Charlotte/Douglas International, NC (3½ hrs.)

WILD WING PLANTATION GOLF CLUB

Just west of Myrtle Beach's Grand Strand, the heart of a golf region with over one hundred publicly accessible golf courses, is the 1050-acre Wild Wing Plantation with four quality courses. The Avocet course was designed by Larry Nelson, a two-time PGA Champion and 1983 U.S. Open winner, and Jeff Brauer. Avocet features wide fairways, stands of mature Georgia pine, strategically placed bunkers and water hazards on more than half its holes. Earth was moved to shape flatlands into a course with steep mounding, severe contours, huge bunkers, and large Pennlinks bentgrass greens. The finishing hole at Avocet is a picturesque 453-yard par-4 cape hole modeled after C. B. McDonald's famous cape hole at the Mid-Ocean Club in Bermuda. Water borders the left fairway and a cluster of four bunkers guard the tee shot landing area on the right. The gut-wrenching approach is to a deep, two-tiered green bordered by a deep bunker to its left and water farther left. Two excellent shots are required to safely reach this target thus avoiding an unpleasant ending to your round.

The Rees Jones-designed Falcon course starts you out on a challenging golf venture with a short, straight par 4, a manageable dogleg left par 4, and a straightforward par 3 with a huge green. The course then begins to toughen up with a 385-yard par 4 that plays along a lake to a deep green guarded by three pot bunkers to its right and the lake to the left. The next hole is a scenic 525-yard par 5 that bends left around a lake to a small green sandwiched between the water and a huge bunker. The temptation is to cut the water leaving you wet or in a position to reach the green in two. The front nine concludes with a long 469-yard par 4 that plays to a narrow bunker-protected landing area on the tee shot. The approach is to a small green guarded by two bunkers to its left and another to its right.

The back nine begins with a scenic 205-yard par 3 called "Punchbowl" because of the bowl-like slopes that direct slightly errant shots toward the target. The tee shot must carry water in front of the green which is fronted by a bunker and guarded by two more traps to its right and a larger one to its left. The round concludes with another long par 4, a 471-yarder whose tee shot is to a landing area protected by three bunkers to its right. The approach must negotiate a gantlet of twelve bunkers clustered around a small green. At this juncture the golfer has traversed a course with over 100 bunkers, a fascinating variety of hole configurations with greens no deeper than 30 yards, the customary Rees Jones mounding, and six holes with serious water hazards. In addition to Avocet and Falcon, rated among the best in South Carolina by *GolfWeek*, Wild Wing has two more quality layouts designed by Willard Byrd, the Hummingbird and Wood Stork. A modern 33,000 square foot Japanese-style-clubhouse that also has 15,000 square feet of terrace space with outstanding views of the golf courses serves all four venues. Inside is an excellent pro shop, named 1994 Carolinas' PGA Merchandiser of the Year. There is also a restaurant and full locker room amenities.

The multiple tees, bentgrass greens, variable winds, and memorable features such as the 25-acre lake on the Falcon, the double green on Avocet, the wetlands and pine forests of Wood Stork, and the wildlife and links-style wetlands of Hummingbird will provide you with a moveable golf feast at Wild Wing.

Recommended Golf Courses in South Carolina

Within 1 Hour of Myrtle Beach:

Arrowhead Golf Club, Myrtle Beach, (803) 236–3243, Public, 18/6666/72

Azalea Sands Golf Club, North Myrtle Beach, (803) 272–6191, Public, 18/6902/72

Beachwood Golf Club, North Myrtle Beach, (803) 272–6168, Public, 18/6755/72

Belle Terre, Myrtle Beach, (803) 236–8888, (800) 340–0072, Public. Championship: 18/7020/72. Executive: 18/3300/58

Blackmoor Golf Club, Murrells Inlet, (803) 650–5555, Public, 18/6614/72

Burning Ridge Country Club, Conway, (803) 448–3141, Semiprivate. East: 18/6780/72. West: 18/6714/72

Colonial Charters Golf Club, Longs, (803) 249–8809, Public, 18/6901/72

Cypress Bay Golf Club, Little River, (803) 249–1025, Public, 18/6520/72

Dunes Golf and Beach Club, Myrtle Beach, (803) 449–5236, Private (accessible to guests of specific motels), 18/7021/72

Eagle Nest Golf Club, North Myrtle Beach, (803) 249–1449, (800) 543–3113, Semiprivate, 18/6901/72

Gator Hole Golf Course, North Myrtle Beach, (803) 249–3543, (800) 447–2668, 18/6000/70

Glen Dornoch, North Myrtle Beach, (803) 249–2541, (800) 717–8784, Public, 18/6905/72

Litchfield Country Club, Pawleys Island, (803) 237–3411, (800) 922–6348, Semiprivate, 18/6874/72

Man O' War, Myrtle Beach, (803) 347–6600, Public, 18/7027/72

Myrtle Beach National Golf Club, Myrtle Beach, (803) 448–2308, (800) 344–5590, Public. North: 18/6759/72. West: 18/6866/72. South: 18/6464/71

Myrtlewood Golf and Country Club, Myrtle Beach, (803) 449–5134, (800) 283–3633, Semiprivate. Pine Hills: 18/6406/72. Palmetto: 18/6957/72

Pawley's Plantation Golf Club, Pawleys Island, (803) 237–1736, (800) 545–5973, Private (access restricted to guests of specific hotels, members), 18/7026/72

Pine Lakes International Country Club, Myrtle Beach, (803) 449–6459, (800) 446–6817, Semiprivate, 18/6609/71

River Club, Pawleys Island, (803) 237–8755, (800) 344–5590, Resort, 18/6677/72

River Hills Golf and Country Club, Little River, (803) 399–2100, (800) 264–3810, Public, 18/6829/72

Surf Golf and Beach Club, North Myrtle Beach, (803) 249–1524, (800) 765–7873, Semiprivate, 18/6842/72

The Tradition Golf Club, Myrtle Beach, (803) 626–1658, (800) TEEOFFS, Public, 18/6902/72

Willbrook Plantation Golf Club, Myrtle Beach, (803) 237–4900, Semiprivate, 18/6704/72

The Witch, Conway, (803) 448–1300, Public, 18/6702/71

The Wizard, Myrtle Beach, (803) 347–6600, Public, 18/6813/72

Places to Stay in the Myrtle Beach Area

Like Hilton Head, Myrtle Beach has a highly organized tourist industry with various kinds of accommodations for golfers who want "down-and-dirty," low-rent overhead while playing golf at the more than 90 golf courses in the area. Or more elaborate housing for groups, families and large outings can be found. Start with the Myrtle Beach Area Chamber of Commerce, Box 2115, Myrtle Beach, SC 29578, (803) 626–7444, (800) 356–3016, if you are looking for free directories of hotel, motel, condominium and cottage accommodations in the area. Also, ask specifically for golf-package information. Packages are available for special rates at most of the quality golf courses in the vicinity. Or you can contact Myrtle Beach Golf Holiday, P.O. Box 1323, Myrtle Beach, SC 29578, (803) 448–5942, (800) 845–4653. Fax: (803) 626–2039. This service offers accommodations at 93 hotels, motels and condominiums and provides a choice of more than 80 golf courses to play with package rates. A few possible places to stay follow:

CONWAY: Waccamaw Inn (803) 347–7254. GARDEN CITY BEACH: Waters Edge Resort (803) 651–0002, (800) 255–5554. GEORGETOWN: Days Inn (803) 546–2265; Best Western Carolinian (803) 546–5191, (800) 528–1234. LITTLE RIVER: Harbour Inn (803) 249–3535, (800) 292–0404. MYRTLE BEACH: Best Western/the Landmark (803) 448–9441, (800) 528–1234; Breakers Resort Hotel (803) 626–5000, (800) 845–0688; Comfort Inn (803) 626–4444, (800) 228–5150; Cherry Tree Inn (803) 449–6425, (800) 845–2036; Driftwood-on-the-Oceanfront (803) 448–1544, (800) 448–1544; Holiday Inn Downtown (803) 448–4481, (800) 845–0313; Myrtle Beach Hilton and Golf Club (803) 449–5000, (800) 445–8667; Kingston Plantation Radisson Resort Hotel (803) 449–0006, (800) 228–8822; Sheraton Myrtle Beach Martinique (803) 449–4441, (800) 325–3535. NORTH MYRTLE BEACH: Economy Inn (803) 372–6196, (800) 446–6900; Beach Cove Clarion Resort (803) 272–4044, (800) 331–6533 (outside SC); Holiday Inn—North (803) 272–6153, (800) 845–9700; San-A-Bel (villas) (803) 272–2079, (800) 272–2079. PAWLEY'S ISLAND: Litchfield by the Sea Hotel and Resort (803) 237–3000, (800) 845–1897; Litchfield Plantation (803) 237–9121, (800) 869–1410; Quality Inn Seagull (803) 237–4261, (800) 228–5151. SURFSIDE BEACH: Days Inn–Surfside Pier Hotel (803) 238–4444, (800) 433–7599. Myrtle Beach Area Convention Bureau (803) 448–1629, (800) 488–8998. Fax: (803) 448–3010. Georgetown County Chamber of Commerce and Information Center (803) 546–8437, (800) 777–7705

Local Attractions in the Myrtle Beach Area

CONWAY: Horry County Museum. GEORGETOWN: Captain Sandy's Tours, Ghosts of the Coast, Harold Kaminski house, Hopsewee plantation, Island Queen Cruises, Man–Doyle house, Prince George Winyah Episcopal Church, Rice Museum. MURRELLS INLET: Brookgreen Gardens, Captain Dick's Marina, Huntington Beach State Park. MYRTLE BEACH: Myrtle Beach National Wax Museum, Myrtle Beach Pavilion Amusement Park, Outlet Park at Waccamaw, Ripley's Believe It or Not! Museum, South Carolina Hall of Fame, Waccatee Zoo. NORTH MYRTLE BEACH:

Barefoot Landing, Dixie Jubilee, Hurricane Fleet. PAWLEYS ISLAND: Hammock Shops at Pawleys Island. SURFSIDE BEACH: Carolina Opry, seasonal festivals, beaches, water sports, fishing, boating, camping, off-price shopping outlets, restaurants, bicycling. Georgetown County Chamber of Commerce and Information Center, U.S. 17, Georgetown, SC, (803) 546–8436, (800) 777–7705 (USA, Canada). Myrtle Beach Area Convention Bureau, 710 21st Ave. N., Suite J, Myrtle Beach, SC 29577, (803) 448–1629, (800) 488–8998. Fax: (803) 448–3010

Recommended Golf Courses in South Carolina

Within 1 Hour of Aiken:

Cedar Creek Golf club, Aiken, (803) 648–4206, Semiprivate, 18/7206/72

Hickory Knob Golf Club, McCormick, (803) 391–2450, (800) 491–1764, Resort, 18/6560/72

Persimmon Hill Golf Club, Saluda, (803) 275–3522, Public, 18/6925

Pine Ridge Country Club, Edgefield, (803) 637–3570, Semiprivate, 18/6750/72

Within 1 Hour of Columbia:

Crickentree Country Club, Blythewood, (803) 754–8600, Semiprivate, 18/7002/72

Lake Marion Golf Club, Santee, (803) 854–2554, (800) 344–6534, Public, 18/6670/72

Northwoods Golf Club, Columbia, (803) 786–9242, Public, 18/6800/72

Oak Hills Golf Club, Columbia, (803) 786–9242, Public, 18/6894/72

Paw Paw Country Club, Bamberg, (803) 245–4171, Public, 18/6723/72

Santee Cooper Country Club, Santee, (803) 854–2467, Semiprivate, 18/6512/72

Timberlake Plantation Golf Club, Chapin, (803) 345–9909, Semiprivate, 18/6703/72

Within 1 Hour of Florence:

Swamp Fox Golf, Florence, (803) 669–4175. Swamp Fox handles reservations for a variety of quality golf courses within a 1-hr. radius of Florence. Some of the recommended courses closest to Florence are:

Cheraw State Park Golf Course, Cheraw, (803) 537–2215, Public, 18/6900/72

Fox Creek Golf Club, Lydia, (803) 332–0613, Semiprivate, 18/6903/72

The Wellman Club, Johnsonville, (803) 386–2521, (800) 258–2935, Semiprivate, 18/6998/72

Contact Swamp Fox directly for more information

Within 1½ Hours of Greenville:

Keowee Key Country Club, Salem, (803) 944–2222, Resort, 18/6540/72

Links O'Tryon, Campobello, (803) 468–4961, Semiprivate, 18/6728/72

River Falls Plantation, Duncan, (803) 433–9192, Public, 18/6732/72

Stoney Point Golf Club, Greenwood, (803) 942–0900, Semiprivate, 18/6760/72

Verdae Greens Golf Club, Greenville, (803) 676–1500, Resort, 18/6773/72

White Pines Golf Club, Camden, (803) 432–7442, Public, 18/6800/72

Rock Hill Area:

Regent Park Golf Course, Fort Mill, (803) 547–1300, Public, 18/6861/72

South Carolina: Useful Information

Department of Parks, Recreation and Tourism, Inquiry Division, P.O. Box 71, Columbia, SC 29202, (803) 734–0234 or 734–0135 (tourism and recreation information)

South Carolina Wildlife Resource Department, Division of Game and Freshwater Fisheries, P.O. Box 167, Columbia, SC 29202, (803) 734–3886 (fishing and hunting regulations)

U.S. Forest Service, 1835 Assembly St., Room 333, Columbia, SC 29201, (803) 765–5222, (800) 280–CAMP (national forest information and reservations)

Course Name: HILLCREST GOLF AND COUNTRY CLUB

Course Type: Semiprivate
Address: 2206 Mulberry Street Yankton, South Dakota 57078
Phone: (605) 665–4621

GOLF COURSE

Head Professional: None
Course Length/Par (All Tees): Back 6874/72, Middle 6530/72, Ladies' Forward 5726/73
Course Slope/Rating (All Tees): Back 130/72.2, Middle 127/70.6, Ladies' Forward 126/72.2
Course Architects: NA (first 9, 1957), Wally Smith (second 9, 1972)
Golf Facilities: Full Pro Shop X, Snack Bar X, Lounge X, Restaurant X, Locker Room X, Showers X, Club Rental X, Club Repair Minor, Cart Rental X, Instruction X, Practice Green X, Driving Range X, Practice Bunker X, Club Storage X
Tee-Time Reservation Policy: 1 week in advance from 7:30 a.m.
Ranger: No
Tee-Off-Interval Time: 8 min.
Time to Play 18 Holes: 4 hrs.
Course Hours/Earliest Tee Off: 7:30 a.m.
Green Fees: $34 for 18 holes Sat., Sun. holidays; $28 for 18 holes weekdays. $20 for 9 holes Sat., Sun., holidays. $17 for 9 holes weekdays
Cart Fees: $18 for 18 holes per cart, $12 for 9 holes per cart
Pull Carts: $3 for 18 holes, $2 for 9 holes
Credit Cards: MasterCard, Visa
Season: Mid-March to Oct. Busiest season June to Aug.
Course Comments: Can walk anytime. Yardage book available
Golf Packages: None
Discounts: Junior membership rates
Places to Stay Nearby: Yankton Inn and Convention Center (605) 665–2906, (800) 245–9993 (SD), (800) 457–9090 (outside SD); Super 8 Motel (605) 665–6510. BED AND BREAKFAST: Mulberry Inn Bed and Breakfast (605) 665–7116. CAMPING: Lewis and Clark State Recreation Area (605) 668–3435 (information), (605) 668–3600 (reservations)
Local Attractions: Lewis and Clark Playhouse, historic Yankton tours, river boat tours, Dakota Territorial Museum, Fort Randall Casino (gambling), boating, camping, fishing, hunting, Lewis and Clark Lake. Yankton Chamber of Commerce (605) 665–3636
Directions: I–90, exit Hwy. 81 south to Yankton to corner of 23rd, east on 23rd to golf course. From airport (5 min.): 31st St. west to Douglas, left (south) on Douglas to 23rd, left on 23rd to golf course. From I–29 (45 min.): take Hwy. 50 West 33 mi. to Yankton, proceed to Douglas St., then take right to 21st St. (stop sign). Turn right on 21st St. to golf course
Closest Commercial Airports: Chan Gurney Municipal/Yankton (1 mi.), Sioux Falls Regional (1 hr., 15 min.), Pierre Municipal (5 hrs.)

HILLCREST GOLF AND COUNTRY CLUB

Situated on the Missouri River at the Nebraska border, Yankton is just west of Vermillion, in the southeastern corner of South Dakota. The town was named for the Yankton Indians, a major division of Sioux. a confederation of American Indians that once dominated the region. After the arrival of the Dakota Southern Railway in 1877, Yankton became an outfitting point for gold prospectors and eventually a center for agricultural industry. From 1861 to 1883 it was the capital of the Dakota territory. Lewis and Clark Lake is a major fishing, camping and boating area near Yankton, which is also the home of the Hillcrest Golf and Country Club.

The Hillcrest Golf and Country Club is a 6874-yard par-72 layout with rolling, narrow, tree-lined bluegrass fairways. The hilltops afford panoramic vistas of the golf course. The bentgrass greens are small, fast, undulating and generally elevated. Mature trees, including maple, pine and other varieties, often come into play, but there are relatively few sand traps, except around the greens. Accuracy rather than length is important at Hillcrest. If you get into treed areas, the ball usually has to be chipped back into play, although the pines have been trimmed up for more clearance. The rye and bluegrass rough is kept at approximately 2 inches and can be a factor in many situations. The greens tend to slope forward at Hillcrest and it is better to avoid being above the hole. Drop-offs are usually situated behind the elevated greens requiring a lob shot onto a fast downward sloping putting surface if you have to hit a recovery shot.

The most difficult hole on the front nine is the 445-yard par-4 eighth, which plays straight down a tree-lined fairway to a small, elevated green. The tight side is out of bounds all the way, and on the approach shot you have to clear a small pond near the green. This hole generally plays downwind, but that can vary by season. Wind can be a major factor at Hillcrest as can water. There are water hazards on four holes and lateral hazards on six holes.

The number-1-handicap hole on the course is the 580-yard par-5 seventeenth, a narrow dogleg right with out of bounds on both sides of the fairway. The approach shot is to a forward-sloping, undulating green protected by four traps. A tough par 3 on the back side is the 220-yard sixteenth, which plays to a green with a pond to the right that often catches balls. A crosswind usually further complicates play on this hole.

The Hillcrest Golf and Country Club was recently ranked among the top five public and private layouts in the state of South Dakota. Approximately 90 percent of play is by club members, who are given tee time priority. If you are coming to this area from a distance, consideration will be given to accommodate your advance tee time, space permitting.

Course Name: MEADOWBROOK GOLF COURSE

Course Type: Public
Address: 3625 Jackson Boulevard
              Rapid City, South Dakota
              57702
Phone: (605) 394–4191

GOLF COURSE

Head Professional: Mike Goff
Course Length/Par (All Tees): Back 7054/72, Middle 6520/72, Forward 5603/72
Course Slope/Rating (All Tees): Back 138/73, Middle 133/70.7, Ladies' Forward 130/71.7
Course Architect: David Gill (1976)
Golf Facilities: Full Pro Shop X, Snack Bar X, Lounge X, Restaurant X, Locker Room X, Showers No, Club Rental X, Club Repair X, Cart Rental X, Instruction X, Practice Green X, Driving Range X, Practice Bunker X, Club Storage X
Tee-Time Reservation Policy: 1 day in advance
Ranger: Yes
Tee-off-Interval Time: 10 min.
Time to Play 18 Holes: 4½ hrs.
Course Hours/Earliest Tee-off. Dawn to dusk
Green Fees: $18.75 for 18 holes Sat., Sun., holidays; $16.75 for 18 holes Mon. to Fri. $11.50 for 9 holes Sat., Sun., holidays; $9.50 for 9 holes Mon. to Fri
Cart Fees: $18.00 for 18 holes per cart, $10 for 9 holes per cart
Pull Carts: $2 for 9 holes , $3 for 18 holes
Credit Cards: MasterCard, Visa
Season: Year round. Busiest season March through Sept.
Course Comments: Can walk anytime
Golf Packages: Inquire
Discounts: Seniors, juniors, season passes
Places to Stay Nearby: Alex Johnson Hotel (605) 342–1210, (800) 888–2539; Holiday Inn (800) 777–1023, (800) HOLIDAY; Ramada Inn (605) 342–1300, (800) 272–6232; Best Western Town Country (605) 343–5383, (800) 528–1234. BED AND BREAKFASTS: Black Forest Inn Bed and Breakfast Lodge (605) 574–2000, (800) 888–1607; Audrie's Cranbury Corner Bed and Breakfast (605) 342–7788
Local Attractions: Devil's Tower National Monument, Mount Rushmore, recreational lakes, Badlands National Park, Black Hills National Monument, Wind Cave National Park, Jewel Cave Na-

tional Monument, Custer State Park, gambling in Deadwood. Rapid City Convention and Visitors Bureau (605) 343–5744

Directions: From I–90: Exit 57 to downtown, right on Main, left on Jackson Blvd. to golf course

MEADOWBROOK GOLF COURSE

In 1995 *Golf Digest* ranked Meadowbrook the best public golf course in South Dakota. This flat, well-treed 7054-yard par-72 layout is part of the city of Rapid City municipal golf course system. The course was designed by David Gill, a native Iowan, and opened in 1976. Gill earned a degree in landscape architecture from Iowa State University in 1942 and opened his own golf-architecture business in the 1950s, after working for golf architect Robert Bruce Harris. He designed the Hulman Links in Terre Haute, Indiana, with his son, Garrett Gill; Bunker Hills in Coon Rapids, Minnesota; and many other quality golf courses, mostly in the Midwest.

Rapid Creek runs through the golf course, and water comes into play on four holes at Meadowbrook. Officially, the course is in a flood zone, and in 1972 floods did wipe out the golf course, after which Gill rebuilt it into a new eighteen. The many mature poplar, cottonwood, elm, pine and other trees add to the difficulty of the course. There are also more than 100 traps, and they are a major factor around the bentgrass greens, which are large, moderately fast and mildly undulating. There are subtle breaks in many greens and local knowledge is a big asset on this course. If you are playing it for the first time, the course professionals suggest that you play conservative target golf and punch out of trouble or lay up when in doubt.

The number-1-handicap hole at Meadowbrook is the long, 590-yard par-5 sixth hole, which plays like a double dogleg because of the mature trees overhanging the fairway. The tee shot should be hit to the left and in front of a stream that cuts the fairway. The second shot should be hit to a landing area just beyond where the same stream meanders back across the fairway.

The third shot is to a deep green that slopes left and away from you. This green is well protected by two traps on the left and one on the right. The conventional wisdom is that there are no birdie par 5s at Meadowbrook, and a par 5 is seldom if ever reached in two. They measure 551, 590, 560, and 564 yards from the back tees and not much shorter from the middle tees. Also, a swirling wind can further complicate any hole on this golf course.

A difficult par 4 at Meadowbrook is the 447-yard ninth, a long dogleg left to a deep, forward-sloping green protected by traps on the left and right. The 198-yard par-3 twelfth is one of two holes with a significant elevation change on the course. It plays from an elevated tee to a large green trapped both left and right and with a banked drop-off to the rear. Because of the wind, anything from an 8-iron to a 1-iron or a wood can be used on this hole.

The finishing hole is a solid 564-yard par 5 that has Rapid Creek running down the right side from tee to green. Many golfers do not use a driver off the tee because of the need for position rather than distance on the tight fairway. The first shot should be slightly left-of-center. The second is up to a landing area in front of a pond that guards the green which is more than 30 yards deep. This green has traps on the left and right and slopes away from the golfer.

Meadowbrook has one of the best pro shops in western South Dakota. The course is popular with tourists heading for the nearby Black Hills, especially because Meadowbrook is ranked among the best 75 public golf courses in America by *Golf Digest*. However, more than half the rounds here are played by season-pass holders, who get a tremendous bargain for their public golf dollar. The course is open year round, and golf is played from dawn until dusk. The peak season is March through September. And you can walk anytime for less than $20.

Course Name: WILLOW RUN GOLF COURSE

Course Type: Public

Address: East Highway 38 at Hwy. 42
Sioux Falls, South Dakota
57103

Phone: (605) 335–5900

GOLF COURSE

Director of Golf: Dave Hanten

Course Length/Par (All Tees): Back 6500/71, Blue 6090/71, White 5665/71, Forward 4915/71

Course Slope/Rating (All Tees): Back 127/71.1, Blue 123/69.2, White 120/67.4, Ladies' White 127/72.5, Ladies' Forward 119/68.7

Course Architect: Joel Goldstrand (1986)

Golf Facilities: Full Pro Shop X, Snack Bar X, Lounge X, Restaurant No, Locker Room No, Showers X, Club Rental X, Club Repair X, Car[Rental X, Instruction X, Practice Green X, Driving Range X, Practice Bunker No, Club Storage No

Tee-Time Reservation Policy: 1 wk. in advance

Ranger: Yes

Tee-off-Interval Time: 8 min.

Time to Play 18 Holes: 4 hrs., 10 min.

Course Hours/Earliest Tee-off: Sunrise to sunset.

Green Fees: $18.50 for 18 holes weekends, holidays; $15.50 for 18 Mon. to Fri. $11 for 9 holes weekends, holidays, $10 for 9 holes Mon. to Fri .

Cart Fees: $18.50 for 18 holes, $9.50 for 9 holes

Credit Cards: MasterCard, Visa

Season: March 15 to Nov. 1. Busiest season June through Aug.

Course Comments: Can walk anytime. Limited locker facilities. Memberships available

Golf Packages: Inquire at pro shop

Discounts: Juniors, seniors

Places to Stay Nearby: Best Western Rumkota Inn (605) 336–0650, (800) 528–1234; Holiday Inn Airport (605) 336–1020, (800) HOLIDAY, Encore Inn (605) 361–6684, (800) 348–4434 (SD), (800) 962–8881 (outside SD); Howard Johnson Convention Center (605) 336–9000, (800) 654–2000

Local Attractions: Old Courthouse Museum, Mount Rushmore (7 hrs.), Great Plains Zoo and Museum, Civic Fine Arts Center, Sioux Falls College, Augustana College, Shoto-Teien Japanese Gardens, Sioux Falls Teletrack (greyhound racing), falls of the Big Sioux. Sioux Falls Chamber of Commerce (605) 336–1620

Directions: From I–299: To exit 10, take 38 east 3 mi., course on left

Closest Commercial Airport: Sioux Falls Regional (20 min.)

WILLOW RUN GOLF COURSE.

Willow Run is ranked among the top five golf courses in the state of South Dakota by *GolfWeek* magazine. This 6500-yard par-71 layout was designed by Joel Goldstrand, a native of St. Paul, Minnesota, who played on the PGA tour during the 1960s and then served as head professional at the Minneapolis Golf Club. During that time he began to design golf courses, primarily in Iowa and Minnesota, including Double Eagle, a nine-hole reversible layout in Eagle Bend, Minnesota. That course can be started at the first tee or in reverse order from the ninth tee.

A creek runs through Willow Run, and water comes into play on almost every hole. The course is well treed with oak, willow and cottonwood, and the medium-sized bentgrass greens are fast and undulating but not heavily trapped. Willow Run is a target golf course whose landing areas are islands of bentgrass in a sea of blue and rye fairways. Accuracy and course management are more important than distance here.

The number-1-handicap hole at Willow Run is the 525-yard par-5 fifth, which is a sharp dogleg left with tall trees at the corner of the dogleg. A small creek on the right cuts the fairway 275 yards from the back tees, so long hitters have to be careful about going into the water. The green is a large, undulating, three-tiered surface that can yield three putts or more depending on pin placement. Although there are no traps around the green, a creek to the rear of the putting surface can easily come into play.

Another difficult hole is the 410-yard par-4 third, a slight dogleg left from an elevated tee. The tee shot is through a chute of oak trees, and the second shot onto a narrow, deep green. The most memorable hole on the course is the 510-yard par-5 sixteenth, which is a slight dogleg left with a large railroad trestle sitting near the green and parallel to the fairway.

The busiest months at Willow Run are June through August. The course is open from mid-March to November, weather permitting. Group and individual lessons are available on the practice range, putting green or pitching green. The clubhouse is small, with no locker rooms and limited shower facilities, but it does have a restaurant snack bar and pro shop. Willow Run does cater to outings using outside food services. The green fees are very modest and you can walk the course anytime.

South Dakota: Useful Information

Department of Tourism, Capitol Lake Plaza, Pierre, SD 57501, (800) 732–5682

Black Hills, Badlands and Lakes Association, 900 Jackson Blvd., Rapid City, SD 57701, (605) 341–1462

Dakota Heritage and Lakes Association, 818 E. 41st St., Sioux Falls, SD 57105–6028, (605) 336–2602

Great Lakes of South Dakota Association, P.O. Box 786, Pierre, SD 57501, (605) 224–4617

Glacial Lakes Tourism Association, P.O. Box 244, Watertown, SD 57201, (605) 886–7305

Game, Fish and Parks Department 523 E. Capitol, Pierre, SD 57501, (605) 773–3485 (fishing and hunting regulations)

U.S. Forest Service, Black Hills National Forest, Box 792, Custer, SD 57730, (605) 673–4853, (800) 280–CAMP (national forest information and reservations)

Recommended Golf Courses in South Dakota

Aberdeen:

Moccasin Creek Country Club, Aberdeen, (605) 226–0989, Semiprivate, 18/7125/72

Dakota Dunes:

Two Rivers Golf Club, Dakota Dunes, (605) 232–3241, Public, 18/6181/72

Hot Springs:

Southern Hills Golf Course, Hot Springs, (605) 745–6400, Public, NA

Sioux Falls:

Elmwood Golf Course, Sioux Falls, (605) 339–7092, Public, 18/6806/72

Prairie Green Golf Course, Sioux Falls, (605) 339–6076, Public, 18/7179/72

Yankton:

Fox Run Golf Course, Yankton, (605) 665–8456, Public, 18/6696/72

**Course Name: FALL CREEK FALLS
                 STATE PARK GOLF
                 COURSE**

Course Type: Public
Address: Route 3
              Pikeville, TN 37367
Phone: (423) 881–3706 (Golf Course)
              (423) 881–3297 (Park Head-
              quarters) (423) 881–3241
              (Fall Creek Inn)
              (423) 881–3708 (Nature
              Center) (423) 881–3568
              (Camper Check-in Station)

GOLF COURSE

Head Professional: Billy Maxwell
Course Length/Par (All Tees): Back
  6706/72, Middle 6378/72, Forward
  6060/72
Course Slope/Rating (All Tees): Back
  124/72.3, Middle 121/70.8, Ladies'
  Forward 126/74.8
Course Architect: Joe Lee (1972)
Golf Facilities: Full Pro Shop X, Snack
  Bar X, Lounge No, Restaurant No,
  Locker Room X, Showers X, Club
  Rental X, Club Repair No, Cart Rental
  X, Instruction X, Practice Green X,
  Driving Range X, Practice Bunker X,
  Club Storage No
Tee-Time Reservation Policy: Call anytime
Ranger: Yes
Tee-off-Interval Time: 8 min.
Time to Play 18 Holes: 4 hrs., 15 min.
Course Hours/Earliest Tee-off: 7 a.m.
Green Fees: $16 for 18 holes, $8 for 9
  holes
Cart Fees: $18 for 18 holes, $9 for 9 holes
Pull Carts: $2 per day
Credit Cards: American Express, Discover,
  MasterCard, Visa
Season: Year round
Course Comments: Can walk anytime
Golf Packages: None
Discounts: Seniors (Mon., except holi-
  days), juniors
Places to Stay Nearby: Fall Creek Falls
  Inn (423) 881–3241; Dinner Bell Motel
  (423) 447–1414. BED AND BREAKFAST:

Fall Creek Falls Bed and Breakfast
(423) 881–5494
Local Attractions: Cabins, campsites,
  bicycle rentals, boat rentals, fishing,
  horseback riding, hiking, basketball,
  horseshoes, badminton, nature center.
  Fall Creek Falls State Resort Park (423)
  881–3241. Middle East Tennessee Tourism Council (423) 584–8553
Directions From Nashville (2 hrs.): I–40
  east to exit 288 Cookville, south on Hwy.
  111 to the park. Park may also be entered
  from Rte. 30. From Chattanooga (1 hr.):
  Hwy. 27 north to Hwy. 30, take Hwy. 30
  northwest to the Park. From Knoxville
  (1½ hrs.): I–40 west to exit 288 Cookville, south on Hwy. 111 to the Park
Closest Commercial Airports: Lovell,
  Chattanooga (1 hr.); Metropolitan Nashville (2 hrs.); McGhee–Tyson, Knoxville
  (2½ hrs.)

FALL CREEK FALLS STATE PARK GOLF COURSE

Fall Creek Falls State Park is approximately 2 hours southeast of Nashville and
1 hour north of Chattanooga. This beautiful, 16,000-acre park is the second largest
in the Tennessee state park system. It features majestic cascades, deep gorges and
Fall Creek Falls, which, at 256 feet, is one
of the highest waterfalls in America.
Though smaller, the park's other falls
(Piney, Cane Creek, and Cane Creek
Cascades) are also impressive.

The oak and hickory forest that covers
most of the park gives way to tulip poplar
and hemlock forest in the gorges. Mountain
laurel and rhododendron, as well as numerous other plant and animal species, abound
in this pristine setting.

Carved out of the woods is one of the
best public golf courses in America. The
6706-yard par-72 Joe Lee–designed Fall
Creek Falls course has large, moderately
fast Bermuda-grass greens and rolling Bermuda grass fairways. There are few water
hazards here, but the fairways are tightly
treed, and there are more than 65 sand bunkers on the course. Needless to say, shot
placement and positioning are the watchwords at Fall Creek Falls.

One of the tougher holes on this layout is the 393-yard par-4 dogleg-left fourteenth, which plays slightly uphill to a deep green protected by traps on the left. The par-4 fifteenth is the number-1-handicap hole and plays 433 yards to a deep, flat green protected by two traps on the left and one on the right back. The finishing hole is a 550-yard par-5 dogleg right that has several fairway bunkers to the right in addition to the normal, tree-lined venue. The deep, heavily contoured green is well protected by traps front, left and right.

The practice area at Fall Creek Falls is considered to be one of the best facilities in the region. The practice green has 12,000 square feet of well-maintained bentgrass, and there is a special area for chipping and pitching. The practice tee is generous and has two separate driving levels.

The 72-room Fall Creek Falls Inn and Restaurant is situated on nearby Fall Creek Lake. Suites with kitchenettes are available there. There are 3 private meeting and banquet rooms as well as an exercise room and game room, and adult and children's swimming pools. The park also features 2-and 3-bedroom cabins, each completely furnished. All cabins have central heat/air, telephone and color TV and are fully equipped for housekeeping, with linens, and cooking and serving utensils. Ten cabins are on the lake and 10 are on a hill overlooking the lake.

Fall Creek Falls provides 227 campsites at 3 campgrounds. Central bathhouses and showers serve the campgrounds and are provided on a first-come, first-served basis. They cannot be reserved, and the limit of stay is 2 weeks. Fall Creek has 2 group camps, both featuring rustic bunkhouses clustered around central dining halls, bathhouses and recreation buildings. Both camps provide private swimming beaches, playing fields, fire rings and private staff quarters. The park also has 2 group lodges, both completely equipped for housekeeping, food preparation and serving. One lodge serves 104 persons, and the other has 2 buildings, each accommodating 20 people.

The park village green includes the park headquarters, camp store, self-service laundry, craft center, visitor lounge, public pool and bathhouse, recreation center, snack bar and information center. Tennis courts, picnic grounds, ball fields, boating, fishing and hiking are the main recreational amenities in the park. Fishing permits can be obtained here. No privately owned boats are permitted on the lake. Many miles of hiking trails wind through the park and rental bikes are available for the 3 miles of bike trails from the inn to the falls. There is also a nature center at Cane Creek Cascades, and naturalist and recreation programs are presented daily throughout the summer months. As an added attraction, horses can be rented from the park stables and ridden over 4 miles of equestrian trails.

Course Name: THE LEGENDS CLUB OF TENNESSEE North, South Courses

Course Type: Public
Address: 1500 Legends Club Drive
              P.O. Box 680278
              Franklin, TN 37068
Phone: (615) 790–1300
Fax: (615) 791–0166

GOLF COURSE

Head Professional: Dean Goolsby
Course Length/Par (All Tees): North: Back 7190/72, Blue 6574/72, White 6069/72, Forward 5333/72. South: Back 7113/71, Blue 6548/71, White 6001/71, Forward 5290/71
Course Slope/Rating (All Tees): North: Back 132/75, Blue 126/72.4, White 116/69.2, Ladies' Forward 119/70.9. South: Back 129/74.7, Blue 124/72.4, White 119/69.4, Ladies' Forward 121/71.4
Course Architects: Robert Cupp and Tom Kite (1992)
Golf Facilities: Full Pro Shop X, Snack Bar X, Lounge X, Restaurant X, Locker Room X, Showers X, Club Rental X, Club Repair X, Cart Rental X, Instruction X, Practice Green X, Driving Range X, Practice Bunker X, Club Storage X

Tee-Time Reservation Policy: Up to 5 days in advance. Up to 30 days in advance for guests at selected local hotels

Ranger: Yes

Tee-off-Interval Time: 9 min.

Time to Play 18 Holes: 4 hrs.

Course Hours/Earliest Tee-off: 7 a.m.

Green and Cart Fees: $65 for 18 holes Fri., Sat., Sun., holidays; $58 for 18 holes weekdays

Credit Cards: All major cards

Season: Year round. Busiest Sept. and Oct., May and June

Course Comments: Courses alternate daily as public and private. One course open to members, the other to the public

Golf Packages: Inquire at pro shop

Discounts: Twilight

Places to Stay Nearby: FRANKLIN: Holiday Inn Express (615) 794–7591. BRENTWOOD: Hilton Suites Brentwood (615) 370–0111, (800) 445–8667; Residence Inn by Marriott (615) 371–0100, (800) 331–3131. NASHVILLE: See page 614

Local Attractions: See page 614

Directions: From Nashville (20 min.): Take I–65 south to Cool Springs Blvd./Exit 68B. Drive west on Cool Springs Blvd. to the Mack Hatcher Bypass (U.S. 431). Turn right on Mack Hatcher to the first light (Franklin Rd.). Take a right on Franklin to golf course

Closest Commercial Airport: Nashville International (20 min.)

THE LEGENDS CLUB OF TENNESSEE

The Legends Club is located on former farmland just 20 minutes south of downtown Nashville. The club features two Robert Cupp– and Tom Kite–designed courses. The 7190-yard par-72 North Course can be played from any of four tee distances as can the 7113-yard par-72 South Course. Streams and ponds can come into play on twelve holes on these challenging layouts. The open North course features sand-faced bunkers and large bowl-shaped greens whereas the wooded South Course has grass-faced bunkers and smaller greens that seem a natural adjunct to the terrain. The putting surfaces are bentgrass, quick, and have subtle undulations. There are over one hundred bunkers on each course and the rule of thumb is to hit toward fairway bunkers but don't go in them to be in good position for approach shots to the greens.

Among the excellent holes on the South Course is the tough 458-yard par-4 seventh whose first shot is uphill and often into the wind. The second shot is downhill to a forward-sloping green with a bunker to its back right and another to its front left. Another good hole is the 197-yard par-3 thirteenth whose tee shot must carry a creek that cuts in front of a two-tiered green and curls around to its right. One of the most difficult par 5s on the course is the 576-yard seventeenth whose tee shot must lay up short of a creek that cuts the fairway approximately 260 yards from the back tees. The second shot is usually a layup to a landing area in front of the creek which cuts back in front of a two-tiered green. Bunkers guard the putting surface to the right and a large tree rises from the sand making the approach into the sharply sloping target more challenging.

The North Course's longest hole is the 637-yard fourth, a three-shot par 5 that usually requires a controlled tee shot to avoid the creek bordering the right side. The second shot is another wood and the approach is to a three-leveled green with a swale in its center and a shelf to its rear. A difficult par 4 on this side is the 468-yard sixth which plays uphill into the wind. The tee shot must clear a corridor of trees then the approach must find a safe landing area on a bunkerless humpbacked green. The other tee distances on this hole, rated the number one handicap hole on the course, are 419, 389 and 360 yards. A great par 3 on the North is the 225-yard twelfth that plays uphill, often into the wind, to a two-tiered green with bunkers to its right and heavy rough to its left.

The Legends has a variety of membership plans (including non-resident) and outing plans. The 26,000 square-foot clubhouse has a quality pro shop, Legends Club Grille, a stone fireplace, and other country club-style amenities. The 19-acre practice facility includes teeing room for 120 golfers, five target greens, chipping and putting greens, and practice bunkers. *GolfWeek* rates The Legends the best public course in Tennessee.

Course Name: SPRINGHOUSE GOLF
                 CLUB

Course Type: Resort
Resort: Opryland Hotel
Address: 18 Springhouse Lane
             (Golf Course)
             2800 Opryland Dr. (Resort)
             Nashville, TN 37214
Phone: (615) 871–7759 (Golf Course),
             (615) 889–1000 (Resort)
Fax: (615) 871–5906 (Golf Course),
             (615) 871–5728 (Resort
             Reservations)

GOLF COURSE

Director of Golf: Chuck Eade
Course Length/Par (All Tees): Back
  7007/72, Gold 6588/72, Blue 6185/72,
  White 5788/72, Forward 5126/72
Course Slope/Rating (All Tees): Black
  133/74, Gold 128/72, Blue 124/70.1,
  White 118/68.4, Ladies' Forward
  118/70.2
  Course Architect: Larry Nelson (1990)
Golf Facilities: Full Pro Shop X, Snack
  Bar X, Lounge X, Restaurant X,
  Locker Room X, Showers X, Club
  Rental X, Club Repair X, Cart Rental
  X, Instruction X, Practice Green X,
  Driving Range X, Practice Bunker X,
  Club Storage X
Tee-Time Reservation Policy: At time of
  confirmed registration. Up to 7 days in
  advance for public play
Ranger: Yes
Tee-off-Interval Time: 10 min.
Time to Play 18 Holes: 4½ hrs.
Course Hours/Earliest Tee-off: 7 a.m.
Cart and Green Fees: $60 for 18 holes
  with cart, $40 for 18 holes walking
Credit Cards: All major cards
Season: Year round. Busiest May through
  Labor Day
Course Comments: Can walk anytime.
  Yardage book available

Golf Packages: Through the resort
Discounts: Resort guests, Seniors
Places to Stay Nearby: Crowne Plaza
  Nashville (615) 259–2000, (800) 449–
  9825; Loew's Vanderbilt Plaza Hotel
  (615) 320–1700, (800) 336–3335;
  Nashville Marriott (615) 889–9300,
  (800) 228–9290; Sheraton Music City
  (615) 885–2200, (800) 325–3535; Union
  Station Hotel (615) 726–1001, (800)
  331–3123
Local Attractions: Barbara Mandrell
  Country Belle Meade Plantation, Bel-
  mont Mansion, Car Collectors Hall of
  Fame, Checkwood–Tennessee Botanical
  Gardens and Museum of Art, Country
  Music Hall of Fame and Museum,
  Cumberland Science Museum, Nashville
  Toy Museum, Nashville Zoo, Opryland
  USA, Grand Ole Opry, Opryland, State
  Capitol, Tennesse State Museum, Upper
  Room Chapel and Museum, riverboat
  tours, country music, restaurants, Vander-
  bilt University, Nashville Sounds AAA
  minor league baseball, boating, fishing,
  seasonal festivals. Nashville Area Cham-
  ber of Commerce, 161 4th Ave. N.,
  Nashville, TN 37219 (615) 259–4700.
  Tourist Information Center (615) 259–
  4747
Directions: From Nashville International
  Airport (15 min.): Take Rte. 155 (Briley
  Pkwy.) to Exit 12B. Cross Briley to
  light. Turn left to resort.
Closest Commercial Airport: Nashville
  International (15 min.)

RESORT

Date Built: 1977
No. of Rooms: 1891 rooms including 120
  suites
Meeting Rooms: 65. Capacity of Largest:
  4,000 persons.
Meeting Space: 300,000 sq. ft. including
  145,000 sq. ft. of exhibit space
Room Price Range: From $209 to $249.
  Golf packages and other discounts
  available year round
Restaurants and Lounges: 14 hotel restau-
  rants and lounges
Entertainment: General Jackson musical
  showboat, festivals with musical stage

shows, craft fair, antique fair, art shows, storytelling festivals, and other events

Credit Cards: All major cards

General Amenities: 15 shops and boutiques, tropical Victorian Conservatory, meeting and convention support services including audiovisual, secretarial, food service, exhibit and other support, indoor water garden

Recreational Amenities: 5 swimming pools, fitness center with Universal equipment, free weights, Stairmasters, and other

Reservation and Cancellation Policy: One night's deposit required to hold room reservation. 72-hour cancellation notice required for full refund

Comments and Restrictions: No pets

SPRINGHOUSE GOLF CLUB

The Springhouse Golf Club is a Larry Nelson–designed layout on 220 acres at the Opryland Hotel, a 1891-room extravaganza along the banks of the Cumberland River. The Scottish links-style course is named after a picturesque springhouse which dates back to the 1850s and provides a focal point for the signature fourth hole, a 391-yard par 4 that plays from a narrow chute of trees to a landing area bordered by water to its left. The approach is over water to a deep green guarded by a small pond to its right. The springhouse can be seen in the distance to the rear of the green. The most difficult hole on the course is the 449-yard par-4 finishing hole which plays from an elevated tee down a fairway bordered by water from tee to green. The tee shot is to a landing area with a group of bunkers to its left. The approach is to a large green with three bunkers then the water to its lower right.

The Springhouse not only hosts many tourists and golfers attending meetings, it is also a stop on the Senior PGA circuit. Its five tee distances can accomodate all levels of play. But water can come into play on more than half the holes. The greens are large and quick with moderate undulation. Most of the serious bunkers at Springhouse are around the greens.

The 43,000 square foot antebellum clubhouse features The Springhouse Restaurant which provides a view of the Cumberland River and the golf course. This facility can accomodate small board meetings as well as banquets of up to 450 people. The practice area at The Springhouse includes putting greens, chipping greens, a three-tiered teeing area and target flags at the driving range, and a complete golf learning center.

Course Name: STONEHENGE GOLF CLUB

Course Type: Resort
Resort: Fairfield Glade
Address: Fairfield Boulevard off Peavine Road/P.O. Box 1500 Fairfield Glade, TN 38557
Phone: (615) 484–3731 (Golf Course) (615) 484–3778 (Tee-Time Office) (800) 624–8755 (Tee-Time Office) (615) 484–7521 (Resort)

GOLF COURSE

Head Professional: Eddie Moon

Course Length/Par (All Tees): Back 6549/72, Middle 6202/72, Forward 5000/72

Course Slope/Rating (All Tees): Back 131/71.5, Middle 130/70.6, Ladies' Forward 124/70.2

Course Architect: Joe Lee (1984)

Golf Facilities: Full Pro Shop X, Snack Bar X, Lounge X, Restaurant X, Locker Room X, Showers No, Club Rental X, Club Repair X, Cart Rental X, Instruction X, Practice Green X, Driving Range X, Practice Bunker No, Club Storage X

Tee-Time Reservation Policy: Call up to 5 days in advance. Mail or fax up to 30 days in advance

Ranger: Yes

Tee-off-Interval Time: 9 min.

Time to Play 18 Holes: 4½ hrs.

Course Hours/Earliest Tee-off: 7 a.m.

Green and Cart Fees: $50 for 18 holes with cart, $25 for 9 holes with cart

Credit Cards: American Express, MasterCard, Visa

Season: Year round, but sometimes closed Jan. and Feb. Busiest season April, May, Sept., Oct.

Course Comments: Cart mandatory

Golf Packages: Available through resort. Nearby 27-hole Heathhurst Golf Course can be played if resort guest

Discounts: Twilight rate after 2 p.m., resort guests, low season

Places to Stay Nearby: Cumberland Mountain State Rustic Park (615) 484–6138. CROSSVILLE: Cumberland Gardens Resort (615) 484–5285; Ramada Inn (615) 484–7581, (800) 228–2828; Inn at Thunder Hollow (615) 484–9566, (800) 826–4415 (TN), (800) 233–3948 (outside TN); Heritage Inn (615) 484–9505, (800) 762–7065

Local Attractions: Cumberland County Playhouse, Stonehaus Winery, Cumberland general store, Cumberland Mountain State Park, Homestead Tower. Gatlinburg. Nashville. Nashville Chamber of Commerce (615) 259–4700. Gatlinburg Chamber of Commerce (615) 430–4148, (800) 822–1998. Cumberland City/Fairfield Glade Chamber of Commerce (615) 484–8444

Directions: From Knoxville (75 mi.): West on I–40 to Peavine Rd., (exit 322) near Crossville. 6 mi. north on Peavine Rd. to Fairfield Glade entrance. Follow the signs. From Nashville (120 mi.): East on I–40 to Peavine Rd. (exit 322) near Crossville. Follow above instructions. From Chattanooga (1½ hrs.): Hwy. 127 north to Crossville, right at first stoplight in Crossville to Hwy. 70, left toward I–40 to Peavine Rd., north on Peavine, 6 mi. to resort

Closest Commercial Airports: McGhee–Tyson, Knoxville (1 hr.); Metropolitan Nashville (2 hrs.); Lovell, Chattanooga (2 hrs.)

RESORT

Date Built: 1969

No. of Rooms: 98 rooms, including 92 with double bed and 9 king sized (4 persons), 13 villas and villa lofts with kitchens

Meeting Rooms: 6. Capacity of Largest: 300 persons. Meeting Space: NA

Room Price Range: Lodge: $70 off season to $100 peak season (June 1 to Aug. 16, Oct.). Villa suites: $90 off season to $125 prime season (June 1 to Aug. 16, Oct.). Villa loft: $80 off season to $125 peak season (June 1 to Aug. 16, Oct.)

Lounges: Druid Hills, Stonehenge Club, Lounge (at the Lodge)

Restaurants: Sassafras, Druid Hills Country Club, Stonehenge

Entertainment: Disc jockey, dancing

Credit Cards: All major cards

General Amenities: Day-care center with ½-day, daily and weekly rates; meeting and conference center with audiovisual services, banquet services and secretarial support

Recreational Amenities: 4 golf courses (2 private), miniature golf, 2 marinas, horseback riding, 2 indoor and 8 outdoor tennis courts, boat rentals; recreation center with bicycle rentals, basketball courts, video games, tanning beds, small gymnasium with Nautilus; 11 lakes in area, fishing

Reservation and Cancellation Policy: For overnight accommodations requires 24-hr. cancellation notice. 48-hr. cancellation notice on golf packages

Comments and Restrictions: No pets allowed in rental units. Taxes additional to room base rates

STONEHENGE GOLF CLUB

Fairfield Glade is a real-estate development and resort on 12,500 acres of land on the beautiful Cumberland Plateau 65 miles west of Knoxville and 110 miles east of Nashville. The major attraction for golfers is the Joe Lee–designed 6549-yard Stonehenge Golf Course, which was cut out of hardwood forests. *Golf Digest* selected Stonehenge as the best new resort course in America in 1985 and has recognized it as one of the best resort golf courses in the United States. Stonehenge hosts the Tennessee State Open.

Stonehenge is completely bentgrass from tee to green, unusual for this region of the country. As you would expect, the fairways are tightly lined with a variety of trees, including maple, poplar and many other varieties. It is not unusual to see fox

and deer on the golf course. Severe elevation changes on this rolling layout provide
majestic views but also many sidehill lies.
There are slightly over 50 sand bunkers,
with most of them strategically guarding
the medium-sized, moderately fast, undulating greens. Water comes directly into play
on five holes, most notably the 501-yard
par-5 fifteenth, a beautiful dogleg to the
right with water on the left on the tee shot
and a stream running up the right side and
crossing in front of a deep green that has a
trap to the rear left. The tee shot is from a
75-foot cliff and has to be hit over water to
a narrowing landing area bordered by water
to the left and trees on the right. The next
shot has to negotiate the corridor of trees
and clear the stream to reach the green. If
you miss left or right, the ball is likely to
slide into the streams straddling the green
on the left and right.

The number-1-handicap hole at Stonehenge is the very long and well-protected
524-yard par-5 eighth, which plays uphill all
the way to a wide, shallow green with two
traps in front and one in back. No one
reaches this right-to-left, forward-sloping
green in less than three. An excellent par 3
at Stonehenge is the 161-yard fourteenth,
which plays from a cliff down to a narrow,
deep green 100 feet below. A stream parallels
the green on the left, and a trap protects it on
the right. If you miss on the left or to the
rear, there is a severe drop-off from the rock-
walled green. The finishing hole is a 398-
yard par 4 that plays straight down a
tree-lined fairway to a narrow, deep, two-
tiered green protected by traps both left and
right. The approach shot is over a pond that
begins 100 yards from the green and ends
only slightly in front of it.

The clubhouse at Stonehenge has a full
pro shop, bar and restaurant with a locker
room but no showers. Individual and group
instruction is available from the PGA professional and assistants. Group golf clinics
on putting, chipping and other aspects of
the game are offered. The practice area includes a generous 300-yard-long range, a
9000-square-foot putting green and a chipping green. Golf packages are offered year
round through Fairfield Glade, which has 98

rooms as well as accommodations in villas that
include kitchens. Golf-package rates do not
apply to the villas. Peak-season rates are June
1 to mid-August and October. Regardless of
the time of year, both green fees and golf-package rates are very reasonable for this quality
golf course. Those staying at the resort can
also play the Heatherhurst Golf Club, a private
club with three nine-hole layouts that play
from the back tees as follows: Mountain, 3298
yards; Pine, 3074 yards; Creek, 3297 yards.
They can be played in various combinations.

Other recreational activities at Fairfield
Glade include miniature golf, boating, fishing, tennis, bicycling, horseback riding and
a recreation center that includes a fitness
room with Nautilus equipment, basketball
courts and various other amenities. Meeting
and conference facilities include 6 meeting
rooms with audiovisual and food-service
support.

Nearby in Crossville is the Cumberland
Mountain State Rustic Park, 1600 acres of
timberland plateau 2000 feet above sea level,
with a 50-acre lake, swimming, boating, fishing, a recreation lodge, cabins and campsites.

Recommended Golf Courses in Tennessee

Buchanan:

Paris Landing Golf Club, Buchanan,
(901) 644–1332, Public, 18/6612/72

Within 1 Hour of Chattanooga:

Brown Acres Golf Course, Chattanooga,
(615) 855–2680, Public, 18/6923/72

Mocassin Bend Golf Course, Chattanooga,
(615) 267–3585, Public, 18/6409/72

Dyersburg:

Dyersburg Municipal Golf Course, Dyersburg, (901) 286–7620, Public, 18/6592/71

**Within 1 Hour of Kingston–Johnson
City–Bristol Tri-Cities:**

The Crossings Golf Club, Jonesborough,
(615) 348–8844, Semiprivate, 18/6366/72

Graysburg Hills Golf Course, Chuckey,
(615) 234–8061, Public. Knobs/Fodder-
stack: 18/6834/72. Fodderstack/Chimney-
top: 18/6875/72. Chimneytop/Knobs:
18/6743/72

Roan Valley Golf Estates, Mountain City, (615) 727–7931, Semiprivate, 18/6736/72

Within 1 Hour of Knoxville:

Bent Creek Golf Resort, Gatlinburg, (615) 436–3947, (800) 251–9336, Resort, 18/6182/72

Briarwood Golf Course, Crab Orchard, (615) 484–5285, Public, 18/6689/72

Egwami Farms Golf Course, Rockford, (615) 970–7132, Public, 18/6708/72

Gatlinburg Golf Course, Pigeon Forge, (615) 453–3912, Public, 18/6281/72

Graysburg Hills Golf Course, Chuckey, (615) 234–8061, Public, 18/6804/72

Heatherhurst Golf Club, Fairfield Glade, (615) 484–3799, Public. Pine/Creek: 18/6650/72. Creek/Mountain: 18/6700/72. Pine/Mountain: 18/6800/72

River Islands Golf Club, Kodak, (615) 933–0100, (800) 347–4837, Public, 18/7001/72

Three Ridges Golf Course, Knoxville, (615) 687–4797, Public, 18/6825/72

Willow Creek Golf Club, Knoxville, (615) 675–0100, Public, 18/7266/72

Within 1 Hour of Memphis:

Big Creek Golf Course, Memphis, (901) 353–1654, Public, 18/7052/72

Orgill Park Golf Course, Millington, (901) 872–3610 (Golf Shop), (901) 872–7493 (Tee Times), Public, 18/6284/70

Quail Ridge Golf Course, Bartlett, (901) 386–6951, Public, 18/6600/71

Stonebridge Golf Course, Memphis, (901) 382–1886, Public, 18/6788/71

Within 1 Hour of Nashville:

Eastland Green Golf Course, Clarksville, (615) 358–9051, Public, 18/6437/72

Harpeth Hills Golf Course, Nashville, (615) 862–8493, Public, 18/6941/72

Henry Horton State Park, Chapel Hill, (615) 364–2319, Public, 18/7060/72

Hermitage Golf Course, Old Hickory, (615) 847–4001, Public, 18/6795/72

Montgomery Bell Golf Course, Burns, (615) 797–2578, Public, 18/6377/72

Nashboro Village Golf Course, Nashville, (615) 367–2311, Public, 18/6887/72

Rhodes Municipal Golf Course, Nashville, (615) 862–8463, Public, 18/6660/72

Wind Tree Golf Course, Mount Juliet, (615) 754–4653, Public, 18/6557/72

Pickwick Dam:

Marriott's Golf Club at Shiloh Falls, Pickwick Dam, (901) 689–5050, Semiprivate, 18/6713/72

Pickwick Landing State Park Golf Course, Pickwick Dam, (901) 689–3149, Public, 18/6478/72

Tennessee: Useful Information

Tennessee Department of Tourist Development, P.O. Box 23170, Nashville, TN 37202, (615) 741–2158

U.S. Forest Service, 2800 N. Ocoee St., Cleveland, TN 37320, (615) 476–9700, (800) 280–CAMP (national forest information and reservations)

Tennessee Department of Environment and Conservation, Division of State Parks, 401 Church St., 7th Floor of L&C Tower, Nashville, TN 37243, (615) 532–0001, (800) 421–6683 (recreation information)

Tennessee Wildlife Resources Agency, Ellington Agricultural Center, Nashville, TN 37204, (615) 781–6500 (fishing and hunting regulations)

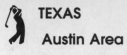
Course Name: BARTON CREEK
Fazio, Crenshaw and
Coore, Lakeside Courses

Course Type: Resort
Resort: Barton Creek Conference
Resort and Country Club
Address: 8212 Barton Club Drive
Austin, TX 78735
Phone: (512) 329–4001 (Golf Course)
(512) 329–4000, (800) 336–
6158 (Resort)
Fax: (512) 329–4597 (Resort)

GOLF COURSE

Head Professionals: Fazio, Crenshaw and
Coore: Greg Smith. Lakeside: Steve
Termeer

Course Length/Par (All Tees): Fazio:
Back 6956/72, Blue 6513/72, White
6231/72, Green 5870/72, Forward
5098/72. Crenshaw and Coore: Back
6678/71, Middle 6066/71, Forward
4843/71. Lakeside: Back 6663/71,
Middle 6046/71, Forward 5063/71

Course Slope/Rating (All Tees): Fazio:
Back 130/72.2, Blue 122/70.5, White
119/69.4, Ladies' Green 126/73.4, La-
dies' Forward 120/69.4. Crenshaw and
Coore: Back 116/70.7, Middle 109/67.7,
Ladies' Forward 110/67.2. Lakeside:
Back 119/70.4, Middle 112/67.7, Ladies'
Forward 110/68.6

Course Architects: Fazio: Tom Fazio
(1986), Crenshaw and Coore: Ben
Crenshaw and Bill Coore (1991).
Lakeside: Arnold Palmer (1987)

Golf Facilities: Full Pro Shop X, Snack
Bar X, Lounge X, Restaurant X,
Locker Room X, Showers X, Club
Rental X, Club Repair X, Cart Rental
X, Instruction X, Practice Green X,
Driving Range X, Practice Bunker X,
Club Storage X

Tee-Time Reservation Policy: Must be a
resort guest, member or guest of member to play courses. Resort guests: Prior
Tues. for weekend tee times, Thurs. for
a weekday tee times

Ranger: Yes
Tee-off-Interval Time: 10 min.

Time to Play 18 Holes: 4½ hrs.
Course Hours/Earliest Tee-off: 7:30 a.m.
weekends, 8 a.m. weekdays
Green Fees: Fazio: $125 for 18 holes Fri.,
Sat., Sun., holidays; $100 for 18 holes
Mon. to Thurs. Crenshaw and Coore:
$95 for 18 holes Fri., Sat., Sun., holi-
days; $85 for 18 holes Mon. to Thurs..
Lakeside: $95 for 18 holes Fri., Sat.,
Sun., holidays; $85 Mon. to Thurs.
Cart Fees: $12 per person
Credit Cards: All major cards except
Discover
Season: Year round. Busiest season mid-
March through July
Course Comments: Can walk anytime
unless the course is unusually busy.
Lakeside closed Mon. Weekend rates
begin Fri. at noon and extend through
Sun.
Golf Packages: Available through resort
Discounts: None
Places to Stay Nearby: Doubletree Hotel
(512) 454–3737, (800) 528–0444; Hyatt
Regency (512) 477–1234, (800) 233–
1234; Marriott Airport North (512)
458–6161, (800) 228–9290; Holiday
Inn Town Lake (512) 472–8211, (800)
HOLIDAY; La Quinta North (512) 452–
9401, (800) 531–5900; Rodeway Inn
University (512) 471–6395, (800) 228–
2000
Local Attractions: Texas state capitol building, University of Texas, National Wild-
flower Research Center, Zilker Park and
other city parks, lake parks west of Austin,
state parks including LBJ Historical Park,
historic sites, Austin Children's Museum,
O. Henry Museum, Texas Memorial Museum, LBJ Library and Museum, Texas
Confederate Museum, country and western music, Austin Museum of Art, seasonal festivals. Austin Convention and
Visitors Bureau (512) 478–0098. Tourist
Information Bureau (512) 463–8586
Directions: From Austin: West to Hwy.
Loop 1 (Mopac), Hwy. Loop 1 south to
Farm Rd. 2244, west on Farm Rd. 2244
under Hwy. 360 (5 mi.), 1½ mi. from
Hwy. 360 to light/Barton Creek Rd. Left
on Barton Creek Rd. to resort

Closest Commercial Airports: Robert C.
Mueller Municipal, Austin (20 min.);
San Antonio International (1½ hrs.)

RESORT

Date Built: 1987

No. of Rooms: 147 guest rooms and suites
in conference center, spa building

Meeting Rooms: 17. Capacity of Largest:
300 persons. Meeting Space: 16,000
sq. ft.

Room Price Range: $130 for single room
to $600 for presidential suite. Golf, spa,
couple's combo and other packages
available

Lounge: Jim Bob's

Restaurants: Palm Court, Tejas Room,
19th Hole, Clubhouse Grille, Terrace
Room (conference building), Dining
Room, Arnie's Bar and Grill (at Lakeside clubhouse)

Entertainment: Arranged with events

Credit Cards: All major cards

General Amenities: Gift shop, tennis shop,
complete meeting and conference facilities with audiovisual and food services,
hair salon, manicure, pedicure, sculptured nail services, babysitting services

Recreational Amenities: Fitness room
with Cybex circuit weight-training
equipment, free weights, abdominal
boards, Lifecycles, treadmills, Stair-
Masters, jogging track; 8 lighted Plexi-
pave tennis courts with instruction
available; indoor swimming pool, whirlpool, sauna, steam room; European-style
spa with massage, herbal wrap, facial,
manicure, pedicure, loofah, body buff

Reservation and Cancellation Policy:
Credit card guarantee required. 1 night's
room and tax penalty if you cancel less
than 15 days prior to scheduled arrival
date

Comments and Restrictions: Service
charges additional for golf packages
and other packages. Taxes additional
to base rates

BARTON CREEK

Barton Creek is one of the premier residential communities, country clubs and conference resorts in the country. It is situated
approximately 20 minutes west of Austin
and has three excellent golf courses on its
4000-acre site. The Fazio Course and the
Crenshaw and Coore Course are within
walking distance of the conference center
and spa. Lakeside, designed by Arnold
Palmer, is approximately 30 minutes to the
west.

The 6956-yard par-72 Fazio Course
opened in 1986 and is rated one of the best
golf courses, public or private, in the state
of Texas. The course has medium-sized to
large, moderately fast Bermuda-grass
greens with some undulations. The Fazio is
not overly bunkered, but it is somewhat
hilly, and water can come into play on
eight holes. To accommodate all levels of
play there are five tee positions ranging
from 5095 to 6956 yards.

The three finishing holes at the Fazio
Course are excellent holes. The 420-yard
par-4 sixteenth is a slight dogleg right
whose tee shot plays to a landing area
guarded by bunkers on the left. A creek
borders the left side of the fairway and
cuts across the fairway, becoming a series
of waterfalls in front of the green. The first
shot has to avoid rolling down the sloping
left side of the fairway and into the traps.
The approach shot has to clear the water.
The next hole is a 203-yard par 3 playing
over a creek in front of the tees to a deep
green protected by a large trap on the left.

The finishing hole has been rated one of
the most beautiful and challenging in the
state of Texas. The view from the tee affords a panoramic scene of the resort and
the golf course. Water is on the left and
trees are on the right on the tee shot of this
546-yard par 5. The second shot is toward
a dramatically elevated small green on a
cliff, with a stone cave beneath it and a
creek and waterfalls in front. Most players
take three shots (at least) to reach this
green, which is trapped in back to the left
and right and has small grass pot bunkers
behind it. The Fazio Course has been rated
as one of the best courses in Texas by *Gulf
Coast Golfer* magazine.

Ben Crenshaw and Bill Coore designed
the 6678-yard Crenshaw and Coore Course,
which opened in 1991. It has a wide vari-

ety of green sizes ranging from 5000 to a huge, 15,000 square feet on the sixteenth hole. The greens are Bermuda Tifdwarf, fast and undulating. Like the adjacent Fazio Course, this course rolls through the Texas Hill Country and has many trees, but little water comes into play.

The number-1-handicap hole is the 464-yard par-4 sixth, which plays long and straight to a large, deep, sunken green that slopes drastically from left to right. The 444-yard par-4 ninth is considered by many to be even more difficult. This slight dog-leg right plays uphill all the way to a deep, relatively flat green. The par-3 eleventh is a beautiful hole, with a waterfall and a deep-faced bunker guarding the green on the right side. The tee shot is 185 yards to a deep, severely forward-sloping green. The beautiful par-4 finishing hole plays 393 yards from the back tees and slightly up-hill. The tee shot is to a landing area guarded by bunkers on the right, and the approach shot is over a creek to a large, forward-sloping green with two large traps on the left and three on the right.

Crenshaw is a native of Austin, and this is his first attempt at an original golf course, after having renovated other lay-outs. Coore grew up in the Pinehurst, North Carolina, area and has designed the Kings Crossing Golf and Country Club in Corpus Christi, and the Rockport Country Club. He helped build the Waterwood National Golf Course in Texas (a Roy Dye design) after graduating from Lake Forest in 1968. The Crenshaw and Coore Course at Barton Creek is the product of their recently formed partnership.

In 1991, the Barton Creek Conference Resort and Country Club acquired the Hidden Hills Country Club, a country club and residential development located on Lake Travis, approximately 30 minutes from the main Barton Creek resort, conference center and spa. The 6663-yard golf course was designed by Arnold Palmer and is now named Barton Creek—Lakeside. The bentgrass greens are medium sized, moderate to fast and undulating. Water comes into play on five of the holes, including the number-1-handicap 536-yard par-5 sixth

hole which plays straight to a wide, shallow green guarded by traps front and rear. If you try to go for the green on the second shot, a large pond directly in front of the green from approximately 75 yards in awaits you. Another difficult hole on Lakeside is the 485-yard par-4 thirteenth, which plays to a large green backed by traps. Two right-fairway bunkers have to be avoided on the tee shot.

The Lakeside site includes a full clubhouse with pro shop, locker rooms and showers, restaurant, bar and grill, and instruction from the PGA professionals and assistants on the premises. A large practice facility includes driving range, practice bunkers and a putting green. There are also 4 lighted tennis courts and an extensive swimming pool area. The overall property incorporates a residential community with lakefront and golf-course homesites as well as "Texas cottages."

The resort has positioned itself as a premier conference center and golf facility, having added 54 holes of golf in less than 10 years. It has won *Meetings and Conventions* magazine's Gold Tee Award as one of the best golf conference destinations in North America. The Fazio and Crenshaw and Coore Courses have their own clubhouse facility, which includes locker room and showers, restaurants, a bar, pro shop and instruction available from a staff of PGA professionals and assistants. Nearby is a driving range with 2 separate tees, practice bunkers and a practice green. *The Dallas Morning News* rated this clubhouse one of the best in Texas.

Adjacent to the clubhouse, in the Executive Fitness Center, is a European-style spa with health and fitness center including Cybex circuit weight-training equipment, free weights, Life Cycles, treadmills, Stairmasters, abdominal boards, a jogging track, swimming pool, whirlpool, sauna and other amenities. There are 17 meeting rooms and a total of more than 16,000 square feet of meeting space at the conference center, which includes a 156-seat tiered amphitheater and full audiovisual, banquet and secretarial-support capabilities. Also in the Conference Center are 147 guest rooms and suites, and 4 restaurants. The *Mobil Travel Guide* has awarded Barton Creek a Four-Star rating.

Barton Creek's Tennis Center offers 8 lighted courts, and group tennis clinics and individual lessons are available from the staff of professionals. The staff will also organize and supervise tournaments for groups of any size. Barton Creek offers a variety of individual golf and spa packages. Peak season dates are March through May and September through November. A Golf Advantage School, offering a variety of golf programs for women, juniors, beginners and seasoned golfers is on site.

Course Name: **HORSESHOE BAY COUNTRY CLUB Ram Rock, Applerock, Slick Rock Courses**

Course Type: Resort
Resort: Horseshoe Bay Country Club Resort and Conference Center
Address: Ranch Road 2147/Box 7766 Horseshoe Bay, TX 98654
Phone: (210) 598–6561 (Ram Rock, Applerock)
               (210) 598–2561 (Slick Rock)
               (210) 598–2511,
               (800) 252–9363 (TX), (800) 531–5105 (outside TX) (Reservations)
Fax: (210) 598–5338 (Resort)

GOLF COURSE

Director of Golf: Scott McDonald
Course Length/Par (All Tees): Ram Rock: Back 6446/71, Regular 6408/71, Executive 5954/71, Forward 5305/71. Applerock: Back 6999/72, Regular 6536/72, Executive 6038/72, Forward 5480/72. Slick Rock: Back 6839/72, Middle 6358/72, Forward 5843/72
Course Slope/Rating (All Tees): Ram Rock: 137/75, Regular 129/72, Executive 117/70.5, Ladies' Forward 121/72. Applerock: Back 134/73.9, Regular 124/71.5, Executive 116/68.7, Ladies' Forward 117/71.6. Slick Rock: Back 125/72.6, Middle 117/70.2, Ladies' Forward 123/73.8

Course Architect: Ram Rock: Robert Trent Jones, Sr. (1979). Applerock: Robert Trent Jones, Sr. (1986). Slick Rock: Robert Trent Jones, Sr. (1974)
Golf Facilities: Full Pro Shop X, Snack Bar X, Lounge X, Restaurant X, Locker Room X, Showers X, Club Rental X, Club Repair X, Cart Rental X, Instruction X, Practice Green X, Driving Range X, Practice Bunker X, Club Storage X
Tee-Time Reservation Policy: 7 days in advance
Ranger: Yes
Tee-off-Interval Time: Ram Rock, Applerock: 10 min. Slick Rock: 8 min.
Time to Play 18 Holes: 4½ hrs.
Course Hours/Earliest Tee-off: 7:30 a.m. in season
Green Fees: Peak season (mid-March to mid-Oct.): $110 for 18 holes
Cart Fees: $10 for 18 holes per person
Credit Cards: All major cards. Cash not taken in pro shop, all charge
Season: Year round. Busiest seasons March through June, late Aug. through Oct.
Course Comments: Cart mandatory
Golf Packages: Available through resort
Discounts: Members and guests of members. Lower rates Nov.-Mar.
Places to Stay Nearby: MARBLE FALLS: Hill Country Motel (210) 693–3637; Comfort Inn (210) 693–7531. Must be a resort guest, member or guest of member to play the courses
Local Attractions: FREDERICKSBURG: Longhorn Caverns, LBJ Ranch, winery tour, Bald Eagle nature tours. AUSTIN: Austin Children's Museum, Discovery Hall, Elisabeth Ney Museum, governor's mansion, Laguna Gloria Art Museum, O. Henry Museum, state capitol, Texas Memorial Museum, University of Texas—Austin, LBJ Library and Museum, Zilker Park, restaurants, theater, country and western music, galleries, seasonal festivals. San Antonio. Austin Visitor Center (800) 888–8287
Directions: From north Austin (50 mi.): Hwy. 183 to Capital of Texas Hwy. (Loop 360), south to Bee Caves Rd., west on Bee Caves to Hwy. 71, west

on Hwy. 71, then proceed to Ranch Rd. 2147 and the resort. From south Austin (55 mi.): Take Hwy. 71 through Oak Hill, then west approximately 50 mi. to Horseshoe Bay turnoff on Ranch Rd. 2147. From Dallas/Ft. Worth (180 mi.): I–35 south to Georgetown, west on Hwy. 29 to Burnet, south on Hwy. 281 through Marble Falls to Ranch Rd. 2147, turn west and proceed 5 mi. to the resort. From Houston (215 mi.): I–10 west to Columbus, west on Hwy. 71 through Austin (see directions for Austin). From San Antonio (80 mi.): I–281 north through Blanco and Johnson City, west on Ranch Rd. 2147 to resort

Closest Commercial Airports: Robert C. Mueller Municipal, Austin (1 hr.); San Antonio International (1½ hrs.); Houston International (5 hrs.); Dallas/Fort Worth International Regional (3½ hrs.)

RESORT

Date Built: 1971

No. of Rooms: 200 to 300 units and 3-bedroom waterfront, golf-course townhouses and other properties

Meeting Rooms: 10. Capacity of Largest: 250 persons banquet style. Meeting Space: 10,000 sq. ft.

Room Price Range: $155 for 1-bedroom unit at the inn to $395 for 3-bedroom unit in season (mid-March through Nov.). Golf, other packages and lower seasonal rates available

Lounge: Anchor Lounge

Restaurants: Yacht Club, Captain's Table, Fairwood Dining Room; Slip Rock Grill and Putter Lounge, Appleheader Grill and Lounge

Entertainment: For group and special occasions, summer live music

Credit Cards: All major cards except American Express

General Amenities: Tennis pro shop, oriental gardens, 6000-foot airstrip on premises, meeting and conference facilities including audiovisual and banquet services

Recreational Amenities: Basketball, volleyball, badminton, paddleball, action tennis, swimming pool, horseback riding, marina, water-skiing, excursion boats, fishing, 14 Lay Kold surface courts (6 lighted outdoor and 4 covered) with locker room, sauna, whirlpool, beach, jogging trails

Reservation and Cancellation Policy: Credit card or check deposit required to guarantee reservation. Cancellation by 4 p.m. the date of arrival required to avoid penalties

Comments and Restrictions: No pets allowed in rooms. In season weekends require a minimum of 2 nights' lodging. No extra charge for 1 child under 12 years of age. Taxes additional to base rates. Extra charge per person per night for each adult. No more than 4 golfers permitted in a match on Fri., Sat., Sun. or holidays. Club amenities operate under a no-cash basis. Various restrictions on children

HORSESHOE BAY COUNTRY CLUB

Horseshoe Bay is a 4000-acre resort on the shoreline of Lake Lyndon B. Johnson in the hill country of Texas, 50 miles west of Austin and 85 miles north of San Antonio. Formerly the home of the Comanche Indians, this territory now features three Robert Trent Jones, Sr., golf courses that have been woven among granite outcroppings, spring-fed creeks, oak trees and lakes. A private country club, guests become temporary members when they stay at the resort, which has a variety of 1-, 2- and 3-bedroom units at the inn, beach houses, golf course hideaways and waterfront properties. Peak season is from mid-March through November.

The Applerock Course was named the best new resort course in America by *Golf Digest* in 1986. This 6999-yard layout is situated on high, rocky, rolling terrain with ravines and streams, and oak, cedar, elm, persimmon, and mesquite trees. The bentgrass greens are medium sized to large, fast and undulating. No more than four traps appear around the greens, there is an average of two fairway bunkers per hole, and water comes into play on six holes. The front nine at Applerock is hilly, and you might have trouble finding a flat lie from time to time.

The number-1-handicap hole on the course is the 451-yard par-4 sixth, a dogleg left to a deep green protected on each side by long traps. The back nine is a bit more interesting than the front, beginning with two straight par-5 holes leading up to the beautiful par-3 twelfth, which plays 179 yards over a lake to a two-tiered green protected by traps both left and right, with oak trees and an old 1-room schoolhouse in the background. The finishing hole is a par-4 dogleg left playing 359 yards to a green with a large trap in front. The tee shot has to negotiate the corner of the dogleg and two large bunkers 200 yards away from the back tees.

The Applerock Course and the 6999-yard Ram Rock Courses are both served by a magnificent clubhouse situated atop a 4-million-year-old rock formation with spectacular views of the lake, Texas hills, greens and fairways. In addition to a fully stocked pro shop, locker rooms and showers, lounge and restaurant, a swimming pool with cascading waterfalls, cabana and bathhouse are located nearby.

The Ram Rock has been rated among the best resort course in Texas by *The Dallas Morning News*. Ram Rock opened in 1979 and features sloped fairways with small, undulating bentgrass greens that are well protected by traps and water. There are over 60 traps on Ram Rock, hazards appear on ten holes and dry creek beds are found on six. The number-1-handicap hole is the 488-yard par-4 second, a dogleg right that plays to a large, deep green guarded by a huge trap on the left and two on the right. Texas professionals surveyed by *Gulf Coast Golfer* magazine have rated Ram Rock the toughest course in the state. Length; wind and water; difficult, elevated greens; sand, narrow fairways, and blind shots make Ram Rock a memorable golf challenge.

A challenging par 3 on the front nine is the 191-yard fourth hole, which plays over water to an island green with traps both front and back. The twelfth is also an excellent par 3 playing 169 yards to a deep green protected by a huge trap on the left

and two traps on the right. Water cuts the fairway approximately 75 yards from the green, but that shouldn't come into play. The eleventh is an excellent par 4, a 399-yard dogleg left that has a stream running along the left fairway and then in front of a green with traps to the left and right and a cluster of trees to the right and front. Water comes into play on half the holes at Ram Rock.

Slick Rock was opened in 1974 and receives the heaviest play from members and resort guests. Slick Rock's scorecard has one picture of golfers driving a golf cart through water which does come into play on thirteen holes of this 6839-yard layout. The number-1-handicap hole, the 575-yard par-5 third, has water on the right 250 yards from the back tees and water to the left of the green, which is guarded by two large traps, one left and front and the other toward the rear. The most famous hole at Slick Rock is the 366-yard fourteenth, which requires you to hit a drive over a $1-million, 100-foot-high waterfall to the fairway. Incidentally, *Golf* magazine voted this the "best waterfall" in its best bets travel section in 1991.

The finishing hole at Slick Rock is an excellent 420-yard par-4 dogleg right to a green protected by traps to the front and left. Water lines the fairway on the tee shot, and three fairway bunkers are clustered 230 to 250 yards from the middle tees. Slick Rock's front nine is routed through colorful granite outcroppings and stands of native oak, cedar, willow and persimmon trees. The back nine is more open, but water comes into play on six of those holes. Slick Rock has its own clubhouse with full-service locker room facilities with saunas, a fully stocked pro shop, lounge and restaurant. At either clubhouse, golf instruction is available from the capable staff of PGA professionals and assistants. Separate full practice facilities are available within a short walk of each clubhouse. Golf packages are available.

The Horseshoe Bay Country Club Resort is the dream of Norman Hurd, who was raised near the Highland Lakes of the Texas hill country. After succeeding as a real-estate developer in Houston, he teamed up in 1970 with his cousin Wayne Hurd, who developed the successful Las Colinas resort in Irving, Texas. Property owners at Horseshoe Bay have come from 48 of the 50 states and several foreign countries. It is ranked as one of the best golf course resorts in America by *Golf* magazine.

A variety of other recreational facilities is offered at Horseshoe Bay, including a yacht club on the shoreline of Lake Lyndon B. Johnson; the Tennis Gardens, which includes 4 covered courts and 10 outdoor courts; a marina to handle boating, fishing and water-skiing; and a swimming pool. There are also stables and a network of horseback-riding trails on the premises, and 3 dining facilities are offered, including the Captain's Quarters, a leading restaurant in the region.

Many leading companies and other organizations have taken advantage of Horseshoe Bay's extensive meeting and conference facilities, which include 10 meeting rooms and 10,000 square feet of space with full audiovisual, banquet and secretarial-support capabilities. A 6000-foot runway at the on-site private airport can accommodate jets, turbo props, multiengine and single-engine aircraft.

Horseshoe Bay is an excellent golf resort destination, and Austin and San Antonio are within easy reach should you want to see two of Texas's most outstanding cities.

Recommended Golf Courses In Texas

Within 1 Hour of Austin:

Circle C Golf Club, Austin, (512) 288–4297, Public, 18/6859/72

Delaware Springs Golf Course, Burnet, (512) 756–8951, Public, 18/6819/72

Forest Creek Golf Club, Round Rock, (512) 388–2874, Public, 18/7084/72

J.F. Sammons Park Golf Course, Temple, (817) 778–8282, Public, 18/6100/70

Jimmy Clay Golf Course, Austin, (512) 444–0999, Public, 18/6857/72

Lady Bird Johnson Municipal Golf Course, Fredericksburg, (210) 997–4010, (800) 950–8147, Public, 18/6432/72

Lakeway Resort, Austin, (512) 261–6600, (800) LAKEWAY, Resort. Yaupon: 18/6595/72. Live Oak: 18/6643/72. Hills of Lakeway: 18/6813/72

Lions Municipal Golf Course, Austin, (512) 477–6963, Public, 18/6001/70

Mill Creek Golf and Country Club, Salado, (817) 947–5698, (800) 736–3441, Resort, 18/6486/71

River Place Golf Club, Austin, (512) 346–6784, Semiprivate, 18/6611/71

Dallas/Fort Worth Area

Course Name:	FOUR SEASONS RESORT AND CLUB Tournament Players Course at Las Colinas
Course Type:	Resort
Resort:	Four Seasons Resort and Club
Address:	4150 North MacArthur Blvd. Irving, TX 75038
Phone:	(214) 717–2530 (Golf Course) (214) 717–0700, (800) 332–3442, (Resort)
Fax:	(214) 717–2477 (Resort)

GOLF COURSE

Director of Golf: Michael Abbot
Head Professional: Doug McNeil
Course Length/Par (All Tees): Back 6826/70, Tournament 6451/70, Member 5961/70, Forward 5337/70
Course Slope/Rating (All Tees): Back 135/73.65 Tournament 129/74.4, Member 122/66.9, Ladies' Forward 116/70.6
Course Architects: Jay Morrish, Byron Nelson and Ben Crenshaw (1986)
Golf Facilities: Full Pro Shop X, Snack Bar X, Lounge X, Restaurant X, Locker Room X, Showers X, Club Rental X, Club Repair X, Cart Rental X, Instruction X, Practice Green X, Driving Range X, Practice Bunker X, Club Storage X
Tee-Time Reservation Policy: Resort guests: 45 days in advance. Outside play: 1 day in advance
Ranger: Yes
Tee-off-Interval Time: 9 min. in a.m., 8 min. in p.m.

Time to Play 18 Holes: 4½ hrs.

Course Hours/Earliest Tee-off: 7:30 a.m.

Green and Cart Fees: Peak season (Apr.-June, Sept.-Nov.): Resort guests: $120 for 18 holes with cart

Credit Cards: All major cards except Discover

Season: Year round. Busiest seasons mid-March through June, Sept. through Oct.

Course Comments: Cart mandatory. Must be a resort guest, member or guest of member to play the course. Byron Nelson Golf School on site

Golf Packages: Available through resort year round

Discounts: Twilight rate 2 to 3 hrs. before sunset

Places to Stay Nearby: Courtyard by Marriott—Las Colinas (214) 550–8100, (800) 321–2211; Dallas Marriott Mandalay at Las Colinas (214) 556–0800, (800) 228–9290; Hyatt Regency—Dallas Fort Worth Airport (214) 453–1234, (800) 233–1234

Local Attractions: DALLAS: Spectator sports at Texas Stadium, the Cotton Bowl, Arlington Stadium, Reunion Arena and others; Galleria, Dallas Zoo, Dallas Arboretum and Botanical Society, Old City Park, John F. Kennedy Memorial Plaza, Dallas Museum of Art, Union Station, Dallas Museum of Natural History, Science Place One and Two, Neiman–Marcus, Age of Steam Railroad Museum, music and art programs at the Dallas Opera, Dallas Repertory Theater and other theatrical groups. FORT WORTH: Amon Carter Museum, Fort Worth Art Museum, Kimbell Art Museum, Fort Worth Museum of Science and History, Fort Worth Stockyards, Log Cabin Historical Complex, Fort Worth Zoological Park, Fort Worth Japanese Garden, various music and art programs, lakes, camping, state parks, ranches. Dallas Chamber of Commerce (214) 746–6677. Fort Worth Convention and Visitors Bureau (817) 336–8791. Arlington Convention and Visitors Bureau (817) 265–7721. Grand Prairie Convention and Visitors Bureau (214) 264–1558

Directions: Rte. 635 LBJ Freeway to MacArthur, south 4 mi. to resort. Rte. 114 to MacArthur, south 2 mi. to resort. Rte. 183 to MacArthur, north 2 mi. to resort

Closest Commercial Airport: Dallas/Fort Worth International Regional (15 min.)

RESORT

Date Built: 1983

No. of Rooms: 365 superior, deluxe rooms, suites and villa rooms

Meeting Rooms: 26. Capacity of Largest: 250 persons. Meeting Space: 20,000 sq. ft.

Room Price Range: $140 for single or double superior room to over $1000 for Nelson Suite. Golf, tennis, fitness, spa and romance packages available. Lower rates Fri., Sat. and low seasonal rates

Lounges: Game Bar, Terrace Lounge

Restaurants: Cafe on the Green, Byrons, Racquets

Entertainment: Lobby piano music

Credit Cards: All major cards except Discover

General Amenities: Child-care center, babysitting, various child amenities; meeting and conference facilities with conference-planning staff, audiovisual, banquet and secretarial services

Recreational Amenities: 176,000-sq.-ft. sports club with fitness center, nutritional counseling, lap pool, 2 outdoor pools, 8 outdoor and 4 indoor tennis courts, 6 racquetball courts, 3 squash courts, 1/8-mile indoor jogging track, half-court basketball area; fitness equipment includes stationary exercise bicycles, treadmills, stair-step machines, sauna, steam, whirlpools, cold plunges, 2 handball courts, free-weight room, exercise classes; spa with Swedish, shiatsu, aromatherapy massages; loofah, herbal wrap and other amenities

Reservation and Cancellation Policy: Reservations must be made in advance and accompanied by a deposit or a credit card guarantee. Package prices include gratuities but not tax. A complete refund provided if reservations canceled

24 hrs. in advance of arrival (48 hrs. for spa programs)

Comments and Restrictions: Taxes additional to base rates

FOUR SEASONS TPC RESORT AND CLUB

The Four Seasons Resort and Club is located in Irving, a suburb of Dallas convenient to the city and the Dallas/Fort Worth International Regional Airport. The 365-guest-room resort features a 176,000-square-foot sports club, with a full-service luxury spa, pool, indoor and outdoor tennis courts, state-of-the-art exercise equipment, racquetball and squash courts, indoor and outdoor jogging tracks, indoor and outdoor swimming pools, and a variety of studio fitness classes such as aerobics, advanced equipment workouts, water exercise, sports stretch, ballet and karate. There are two eighteen-hole championship golf courses at the Four Seasons, including the 6826-yard Tournament Players Course (TPC), which is open to resort guests, club members and their guests only, and the private Cottonwood Valley Course, designed by Robert Trent Jones, Jr.

Jay Morrish designed the TPC Course with the consulting assistance of Byron Nelson and Ben Crenshaw. This is the annual site of the PGA GTE Byron Nelson Classic, named in honor of one of the greatest golfers of all time. Nelson is a native of Texas and still holds the astounding record of winning 11 straight professional tournaments in 1945. He also won 5 major championships, including the 1937 Masters, when he made up 6 shots on fellow Texan Ralph Gudahl in the space of two holes on the final nine holes to go on to win that event.

The TPC Course is a rolling layout with medium-sized, fast, undulating bentgrass greens well protected by traps and water. The course and its practice range, practice bunkers and putting greens are a short walk from the Four Seasons Resort and Club. The first hole is a relatively short dogleg-right 385-yard par 4 from the back tees, with a narrowing fairway beginning 200 yards from the tee. The second shot is to

a left-to-right-angled, skull-shaped green with two traps to the left and forward and one trap to the right. Pin placement on this and most other holes at the TPC greatly affects scores because of the angle and undulation of the greens relative to traps, wind and water in particular.

The number-1-handicap hole is the 474-yard par-4 third, which pro Craig Stadler comments on in a recent Byron Nelson Classic tournament guide:

No. 3 is without a doubt the toughest hole on the golf course. The drive must be long and straight, avoiding the lake to the right. Any drive to the left creates a long iron second shot from an uneven lie, to a two-tiered green. Fortunately this hole is almost always downwind.

Another difficult par 4 on the front side is the long, straight 451-yard eighth, which pro Scott Verplank describes this way:

The 8th hole is easily one of the most challenging holes on the TPC Course. Playing into the prevailing south wind, the eighth demands an accurate tee shot. With the sand trap on the right and the collection bunker on the left, the second shot must be well placed in both direction and distance.

The deep green on this hole is very undulating, which could lead to three putts or more.

The back nine on the TPC also has a collection of difficult par 4s, beginning with the 447-yard dogleg-right tenth, which has water on the left all the way to a wide, shallow green backed by a huge trap. The three finishing holes have often been the scene of dramatic tournament endings, beginning with the 554-yard par-5 sixteenth. From a professional's perspective, Bob Tway has these comments:

No. 16 is a very difficult hole. It requires a long straight drive because the second shot is to a very shallow green so you would like to be hitting a short iron. Playing a long iron or out of the rough would be a very difficult shot to this small green.

A large bunker with islands of grass is located in the center of the fairway approximately 100 yards from the target, well guarded by a large bunker to its right.

The 217-yard par-3 seventeenth is probably the toughest par 3 on the course. It plays to a four-corner green with two traps squeezing one of the corners that protrudes toward the fairway. Peter Jacobson comments:

The 17th hole always plays a major role in the outcome of the championship because you face a very unpredictable shot to the green. Any wind here causes problems with club selection and a firm green makes any pitch shot difficult.

The finishing hole is a 415-yard par-4 slight dogleg left to a deep green protected by two large traps left and right. The wind and pin position can greatly affect the approach shot here.

The Four Seasons Resort and Club prides itself on its meeting and conference facilities, which include 20,000 square feet of space and 26 meeting rooms. These facilities are designed to house small to mid-sized meetings of 5 to 200 people and offer state-of-the-art audiovisual equipment, excellent food-service capabilities and full secretarial support. Golf packages for groups and individuals are offered year round as is a variety of other tennis, spa, fitness and romantic packages.

The TPC pro shop offers a full selection of golf supplies, and instruction is available from the PGA professionals and assistants including videotaped swing analysis. The resort has won numerous awards including *Golf* magazine's Silver Medal Award for being one of America's top golf resorts. *Meetings and Conventions* magazine named the resort one of its first Gold Tee Award recipients, and the Four Seasons has also consistently won numerous hospitality awards such as the *Mobil Travel Guide* Four-Star Award and the American Automobile Association Four-Diamond Award.

Whether you are looking for excellent golf, physical fitness or meeting and convention facilities, a relaxed spa experience or the bright lights of Dallas/Fort Worth, or some combination thereof, the Four Seasons Resort and Club is your spot.

Course Name: **HYATT BEAR CREEK GOLF AND RACQUET CLUB**
East, West Courses

Course Type: Resort
Resort: Hyatt Bear Creek Golf and Racquet Club
Address: 3000 Bear Creek Court (off West Air Field Drive) Dallas-Fort Worth Airport, TX 75261
Phone: (214) 615–6800 (Golf Course) (214) 453–1234, (800) 233–1234 (Resort)
Fax: (214) 456–8668 (Resort)

GOLF COURSE

Head Professional: Larry Box
Course Length/Par (All Tees): East: Back 6670/72, Middle 6282/72, Forward 5620/72. West: Back 6677/72, Middle 6261/72, Forward 5597/72
Course Slope/Rating (All Tees): East: Back 127/72.5, Middle 121/72.3, Ladies' Forward 124/72.4. West: Back 130/72.7, Middle 125/70.5, Ladies' Forward 122/72.5
Course Architect: East: Ted Robinson (1980–81). West: Ted Robinson (1980–81)
Golf Facilities: Full Pro Shop X, Snack Bar X, Lounge X, Restaurant X, Locker Room X, Showers X, Club Rental X, Club Repair Limited, Cart Rental X, Instruction X, Practice Green X, Driving Range X, Practice Bunker X, Club Storage Limited
Tee-Time Reservation Policy: Resort guests: At time of confirmed reservation. Outside play: 5 days in advance from 7 a.m.
Ranger: Yes
Tee-off-Interval Time: 8 min.
Time to Play 18 Holes: 4½ hrs.
Course Hours/Earliest Tee-off: 7 a.m.
Green and Cart Fees: $75 for 18 holes with cart Fri., Sat., Sun., holidays; $65 for 18 holes with cart Mon. to Thurs. Same for resort guests and outside play
Credit Cards: All major cards
Season: Year round. Busiest season March to Nov. with some lag in July and Aug.

Course Comments: Can walk anytime at full golf fee. Yardage book available

Golf Packages: Available through the Hyatt hotel (4 mi. from golf course)

Discounts: Dec. through Feb.

Places to Stay Nearby: FORT WORTH: La Quinta—Fort Worth West (817) 246–5511, (800) 531–5900; Holiday Inn Midtown (817) 336–9311, (800) HOLIDAY; Worthington Hotel (817) 870–1000; Green Oaks Inn and Conference Center (817) 738–7311; DFW Airport Marriott (214) 929–8800, (800) 228–9290; Holiday Inn—DFW Airport North (214) 929–8181, (800) HOLIDAY; La Quinta—DFW Airport (214) 252–6546. DALLAS: Adolphus Hotel (214) 742–8200, (800) 221–9083; Loew's Anatole Dallas (214) 748–1200, (800) 223–0888; Mansion on Turtle Creek (214) 559–2100, (800) 442–3408; Ramada Hotel (214) 357–5601, (800) 2–RAMADA; Westin Hotel Galleria (214) 934–9494, (800) 228–3000

Local Attractions: GREATER DALLAS: New Dallas Museum of Art, professional sports, John F. Kennedy Memorial Plaza, Neiman–Marcus, New Arts Theater, Baylor University, Southern Methodist University, State Fair Park with Museum of Natural History, Science Place/Southwest Museum of Science and Technology, Age of Steam Railroad Museum, Dallas Aquarium, Hall of State, Civil Garden Center, Music Hall, Wax Museum of the Southwest, Texas Christian University, Galleria, International Wildlife Park, Wet n' Wild Amusement Park. FORT WORTH: Modern Art Museum of Fort Worth, Amon Carter Museum, Botanical Garden, Cattlemen's Museum, Kimbell Art Museum, Stockyards Log Cabin Village, Fort Worth Nature Center and Refuge, Museum of Science and Technology. Dallas Convention and Visitors Bureau (214) 746–6677. Fort Worth Convention and Visitors Bureau (817) 336–8791. Arlington Convention and Visitors Bureau (817) 265–7721. Grand Prairie Convention and Visitors Bureau (214) 264–1558

Directions: From Dallas (30 min.): Hwy. 114 to 183 to airport grounds, follow signs to golf course and Hyatt, off Airfield Dr. From Fort Worth (30 min.): Hwy. 121 to 183 to airport, follow signs to golf course and Hyatt, off Airfield Dr.

Closest Commercial Airport: Dallas/Fort Worth International Regional (on site)

RESORT

Date Built: 1974

No. of Rooms: 1389 guest rooms, including 49 suites, 108 VIP rooms

Meeting Rooms: 80. Capacity of Largest: 3000 persons. Meeting Space: 130,000 sq. ft.

Room Price Range: From approximately $140 for single, $160 for double, $350 for suites. Golf packages, seasonal and other special rates available

Lounges: Sullivan O'Shaughnessy's, S.O.S. Sports Bar, lobby/piano bar, Brighton Express

Restaurants: Sullivan O'Shaughnessy's, Papayas, Il Nanno's, Mister G's, S.O.S. Sports Bar

Entertainment: Live DJ in Brighton Express, large-screen TV in sports bar

Credit Cards: All major cards

General Amenities: Babysitting services can be provided, hair salon, 2 covered picnic pavilions with catering for up to 1200 people; complete meeting and conference facilities with 80 meeting rooms in banquet, reception, theater, and conference formats with audio-visual, banquet and complete secretarial support

Recreational Amenities: 3 indoor tennis courts, 4 outdoor lighted tennis courts; 24-hr.-a-day health club with outdoor temperature-controlled pool, treadmill, aerobicycles, stairclimber, weight-training equipment, steam showers, sauna; 10 indoor racquetball courts

Reservation and Cancellation Policy: Credit card guarantee or deposit to hold reservation. Must cancel before 6 p.m. of day of arrival to avoid penalties

Comments and Restrictions: No pets. Taxes additional to base rates

HYATT BEAR CREEK GOLF AND RACQUET CLUB

Hyatt Bear Creek is conveniently located on 335 rolling, green acres inside the Dallas/Fort Worth Airport, midway between Dallas and Fort Worth, Texas. There are two Ted Robinson–designed golf courses here, the East and the West. The East Course, which plays 6670 yards from the back tees, has been rated by *Golf Digest* as one of the top 75 resort courses in America. The West Course, served by the same clubhouse, plays 6677 yards from the back tees and is also a quality golf course. Texas professional golfers surveyed by *Gulf Coast Golfer* magazine have rated the West Course and the East Course among their favorite public golf courses in the state of Texas.

The courses at Bear Creek are rolling and well treed, with streams, ponds and small lakes coming into play on many of the holes. The Bermuda-grass greens are small to medium sized and moderately fast. Most of the greens are elevated and trapped with an average of two or three bunkers. The fairway landing areas are tight, with trees, water or bunkers to consider on most tee shots. The West Course is more open than the East, especially its back nine. The West also tends to have more elevation changes than the East Course, which is more of a target golf course.

The signature hole on the East Course is the 385-yard par-4 dogleg-left fifth, which plays to a plateaued landing area off the tee, then down to a deep green fronted by a pond with traps left and rear. Mature oaks dot the edge of a narrowing fairway from 100 yards into the hole making position on the tee shot critical.

The number-1-handicap hole on the East Course is the 416-yard par-4 second, which usually plays longer because of a head wind from the south. The tee shot is toward a narrowing landing area with trees on the left and two bunkers cutting into the fairway on the right beginning 225 yards from the back tees. The second shot is toward a deep, undulating green with a large trap to the left and another to the right. Trees in the background frame this hole, and water is to the right.

Another tough par 4 on this side is the 418-yard eighth, a slight dogleg right to a deep green protected by traps both left and right, with another trap farther to the front on the left and water farther to the right. The tee-shot landing area is narrow, with trees on the right and a stream that cuts back across the fairway beginning 260 yards from the back tee. Because of the narrowness of the fairway, the trees and a fairway bunker on the left, 230 yards from the back tee, the pros often use two long irons to reach this green. If you are playing from the 380-yard middle tees, you might have to adopt the same strategy to avoid the trees, sand and water cutting the fairway.

Another excellent and difficult par 4 is the 423-yard fifteenth, a narrow dogleg right protected by intermittent trees both left and right and a fairway bunker to the right on the tee shot. The approach shot is to a narrow, deep green with traps both left and back. The wind is generally into the golfer's face on this hole.

The most difficult holes on the West Course are also par 4s. Almost every hole on this course is straight, and water comes directly into play on only four holes. Trees and sand traps often squeeze the target areas, putting a premium on accuracy rather than distance, especially on the front nine. The number-1-handicap hole is the 388-yard par-4 seventh, which is uphill all the way and has an extremely narrow landing area lined by trees and punctuated with a bunker on the left 210 yards from the tee. The green is small, with two traps squeezing the front entrance. A pretty par 3 on the back side is the 178-yard seventeenth, which plays over water to a deep green flanked by two traps and backed by trees. The finishing hole is a 403-yard par-4 dogleg left. The tee shot has to avoid moguls and a sand bunker on the left and trees on the right. The second shot is to a narrow, deep green guarded by oak trees at the entrance and a trap to the left.

The Bear Creek courses host a variety of corporate and charity events, and they have been the site of the Texas State Open, Texas State Junior Championship and PGA Tour qualifiers. The full-service pro shop has won recognition from *Golf Shop Operations* magazines as one of the best pro shops in America.

The green fees at the Hyatt Bear Creek courses are the same for resort guests and the general public, but nonguests can reserve tee times only up to 5 days in advance. You can walk the golf course anytime, and discounts are generally available December through February. Golf packages are available through the resort, and individual and group instruction is available from the staff of PGA professionals and assistants. A driving range, practice bunkers and two putting greens serve both golf courses.

On site is a 1389-room Hyatt Regency Hotel with more than 130,000 square feet of meeting and conference space, including 80 meeting rooms. A variety of restaurants and lounges is located in the hotel, as is a health club with swimming pool, weight-training equipment, aerobics equipment, aerobicycles, sauna and steam. There are also indoor racquetball and tennis facilities within walking distance of the golf club-house, and outdoor tennis courts and pic-nic, badminton, volleyball, croquet and horseshoe areas are nearby.

Course Name: **TIMARRON COUNTRY CLUB**

Course Type: Public
Address: 14000 Byron Nelson Parkway
Southlake, TX 76092
Phone: (817) 481–7529
Fax: (817) 421–8485

GOLF COURSE

Director of Golf: Sandra Haynie
Head Professional: Todd Hartley
Course Length/Par (All Tees): Back 7012/72, Copper 6525/72, White 5949/72, Forward 5309/72
Course Slope/Rating (All Tees): Back 137/74.2, Copper 130/71.5, White 126/68.9, Ladies' Forward 128/69.7
Course Architects: Byron Nelson and Baxter Spann (1994)

Golf Facilities: Full Pro Shop X, Snack Bar X, Lounge X, Restaurant X, Locker Room X, Showers X, Club Rental X, Club Repair X, Cart Rental X, Instruction X, Practice Green X, Driving Range X, Practice Bunker X, Club Storage No
Tee-Time Reservation Policy: Up to 3 days in advance
Ranger: Yes
Tee-off-Interval Time: 10 min.
Time to Play 18 Holes: 4½ hrs.
Course Hours/Earliest Tee-off: Fri., Sat., Sun., holidays: 7:30 a.m.; Weekdays: 8:30 a.m.
Green and Cart Fees: $60 for 18 holes Fri., Sat., Sun., holidays; $45 for 18 holes weekdays
Credit Cards: American Express, Master-Card, Visa
Season: Year round
Course Comments: Cart mandatory. Yardage book available
Golf Packages: No
Discounts: Twilight
Places to Stay Nearby: See page 629
Local Attractions: See page 629
Directions: South of Hwy. 114. From Hwy. 114 exit at Southlake Blvd. Drive 2 mi. south to Carroll. Turn left on Carroll 1/2 mi. to Continental. Turn right to golf course
Closest Commercial Airport: Dallas/Fort Worth International (15 min.)

TIMARRON COUNTRY CLUB

The Timarron Country Club was built on 230 acres of rolling, wooded terrain and is part of a planned, upscale residential community developed by Mobil within minutes of the Dallas/Fort Worth Interna-tional Airport. The club offers country-club style amenities, including a modern, full-service clubhouse with banquet, meeting, and outing facilities. The practice area in-cludes a full driving range, practice putting and chipping greens, and practice bunkers. The course is bentgrass from tee to green and has Big Ear Creek winding through it.

The finishing holes on each side are among this course's more memorable and challenging holes. The 394-yard par-4 ninth, a dogleg right, requires a long, accurate tee shot to leave a short, lefted approach to a wide, shallow green fronted by a lake and guarded by a bunker to its right and another to its rear. Most of the greens at Timarron are ample and well protected by trees, bunkers, or water. The greens vary in size and shape depending on the terrain and hole strategy. This green is only 22 yards deep whereas the green on the 185-yard par-3 third is 46 yards deep.

The 540-yard par-5 eighteenth is a dogleg right that offers you a variety of options depending on your ability and your willingness to take risks. The tee shot is to a fairway that begins to narrow as you get beyond 250 yards from the back tees. The next shot is toward an island green that is very deep, but angled slightly right-to-left with a larger bunker on each side. You can lay up over water to a small landing area that begins 110 yards to the left and front of the target, or you can go for the green in two. The other tee distances on this hole are 525, 503, and 444 yards.

Timarron was designed by Baxter Spann and the legendary Byron Nelson. The course was rated among the best new public golf courses in 1995 by *Golf Digest*.

Recommended Golf Courses in Texas

Within 1 Hour of Dallas/Fort Worth:

Buffalo Creek Golf Club, Rockwall, (214) 771–4003, Public, 18/7018/71

Chase Oaks Golf Club, Plano, (214) 517–7777, Public. Blackjack: 18/6762/72. Sawtooth: 18/6496/72

The Cliffs Golf Club, Graford, (817) 779–3926, (800) 621–8534, Resort, 18/6808/71

Cross Timbers Golf Course, Azle, (817) 444–4940, Public, 18/6734/72

Firewheel Golf Park, Garland, (214) 205–2795, Public. Lakes: 18/6625/71. Old: 18/7054/72

Indian Creek Golf Course, Carrollton, (214) 492–3620, (800) 369–4137, Public. Lakes: 18/7060/72. Creeks: 18/7218/72

Iron Horse Golf Course, North Richland Hills, (817) 485–6666, Public, 18/6575/70

Marriott's Golf Club at Fossil Creek, Fort Worth, (817) 847–1900, Public, 18/6865/72

Riverchase Golf Club, Coppell, (214) 462–8281, Public, 18/6563/71

Riverside Golf Club, Grand Prairie, (817) 640–7800, Public, 18/7025/72

Squaw Valley Golf Course, Glen Rose, (817) 897–7956, (800) 831–8259, Public, 18/7062/72

Sugartree Golf Club, Dennis, (817) 441–8643, Semiprivate, 18/6775/72

Tanglewood Resort and Country Club, Pottsboro, (214) 786–4140, (800) 883–6569, Resort, 18/6993/72

Tension Park Golf Course, Dallas, (214) 670–1402, Public. West: 18/6862/71. East: 18/6762/72

Houston Area

Course Name: WATERWOOD NATIONAL COUNTRY CLUB

Course Type: Resort
Resort: Waterwood National Resort and Country Club
Address: 1 Waterwood Parkway Huntsville, TX 77340–9612
Phone: (409) 891–5050 (Golf Course) (409) 891–5211, (800) 441–5211 (Resort)
Fax: (409) 891–5011 (Resort)

GOLF COURSE

Head Professional: Eddie Dey
Course Length/Par (All Tees): Back 6872/71, Blue 6258/71, White 5480/71, Forward 5029/73
Course Slope/Rating (All Tees): Back 142/73.7, Blue 134/70.6, White 117/69.7, Forward 113/68.0
Course Architects: Roy Dye and Bill Coore (1975)
Golf Facilities: Full Pro Shop X, Snack Bar X, Lounge X, Restaurant X, Locker Room X, Showers X, Club Rental X, Club Repair Minor, Cart Rental X, Instruction X, Practice

Green X, Driving Range X, Practice Bunker X, Club Storage X

Tee-Time Reservation Policy: Resort guests: From 3 mos. in advance. Outside play: 48 hrs. in advance. Some reserved tee times for members

Ranger: Yes

Tee-off-Interval Time: 9 min.

Time to Play 18 Holes: 4½ hrs.

Course Hours/Earliest Tee-off: 7 a.m. weekends, 8 a.m. weekdays

Green Fees: $40 for 18 holes Fri., Sat., Sun., holidays; $27.50 for 18 holes Mon. to Thurs. Same for resort guests and outside play

Cart Fees: $10 per person for 18 holes

Credit Cards: American Express, Discover, MasterCard, Visa

Season: Year round. Busiest season May, June, Sept., Oct.

Course Comments: Can walk anytime. Yardage book available

Golf Packages: Available through resort. Lowest rates Dec. and Jan.

Discounts: Twilight rates after 3 p.m.

Places to Stay Nearby: Westwood Shores Country Club and Resort (409) 594–3502; Park Inn (409) 295–6454, (800) 437–PARK; Motel 6 (409) 291–6927, (800) 437–7486; University Hotel (409) 291–2151; Sam Houston Inn (409) 295–9151, (800) 395–9151; EconoLodge (409) 295–6401, (800) 55–ECONO; Huntsville Inn (409) 295–5725, (800) 822–7281. BED AND BREAKFASTS: Blue Bonnet Bed and Breakfast (409) 295–2072; Whistler Bed and Breakfast (409) 295–2834

Local Attractions: Sam Houston Memorial Park, Sam Houston Memorial Museum, Texas Prison Museum, Gibbs–Powell Home Museum, Samuel Walker Houston Cultural Center, historic buildings tour, Oakwood Cemetery, Huntsville State Park, Sam Houston National Forest, Alabama–Coushatta Indian Reservation, Lake Livingston State Park, camping, fishing, boating, hiking, water sports. Huntsville Chamber of Commerce (409) 295–8113, (800) 289–0389. Livingston Chamber of Commerce (409) 327–4929

Directions: From Houston (98 mi.): I–45 north to Hwy. 190, east on Hwy. 190 at Huntsville, 18 mi. to Waterwood Pkwy., turn left, 8 mi. to resort. Or take U.S. 59 north from Houston to Livingston, exit west on Hwy. 190, 21 mi. to Waterwood Pkwy., turn right, 8 mi. to resort

Closest Commercial Airports: Houston Intercontinental (2 hrs.); Scholes Field, Galveston (3 hrs.); Dallas/Fort Worth International Regional (4 hrs.); Robert C. Mueller Municipal, Austin (4 hrs.); Shreveport Regional, LA (5 hrs.)

RESORT

Date Built: 1975

No. of Rooms: 82 cabanas, forest lodges and suites

Meeting Rooms: 7. Capacity of Largest: 200 persons banquet style. Meeting Space: 6655 sq. ft.

Room Price Range: From $65 for cabana, $45 for lodge, $95 for suite, single or double occupancy. Golf packages available. Lowest rates Dec. through Feb.

Lounge: 19th Hole (at clubhouse), Garden Court

Restaurants: Garden Room, Scorecard (at clubhouse)

Entertainment: Live music Fri., Sat. at Garden Room

Credit Cards: All major cards

General Amenities: Babysitting, recreational area, meeting and conference facilities with audiovisual and banquet support

Recreational Amenities: 4 lighted Lay Kold tennis courts, 4 swimming pools, bicycling; health club with hydraulic weight-training equipment, aerobic exercise classes, saunas; basketball, volleyball, croquet, shuffleboard

Reservation and Cancellation Policy: Credit card guarantee or cash deposit. Must cancel by 6 p.m. on scheduled arrival date to avoid penalties

Comments and Restrictions: No pets. Taxes and gratuities additional to base rates

WATERWOOD NATIONAL COUNTRY CLUB

Waterwood National is 98 miles northwest of Houston on 90,000-acre Lake Livingston. The 6872-yard par-71 Roy Dye–designed layout was opened in 1975 and was subsequently modified by Bill Coore, who helped build the original golf course and later became superintendent at Waterwood before starting his own design business. Waterwood is rated one of the best resort courses in Texas by *The Dallas Morning News*. Waterwood National is an up-and-down, heavily bunkered shot maker's course requiring accuracy more than distance. The course was carved out of deep eastern Texas pine woods, which line the fairways.

The Bermuda-grass greens at Waterwood are medium sized, moderately fast, undulating and strategically guarded by sand traps, mounds, trees and water hazards. There is an abundance of difficult par 4s at Waterwood, starting with the 442-yard first hole, which plays straight down a tight, tree-lined fairway to a wide but shallow green backed by a large trap. The tee shot is over a small pond directly in front of the tee and has to avoid a series of bunkers on the right. The 450-yard fourth plays straight to another wide, shallow green, but this one has a huge trap in front, small pot bunkers to the rear, water to the right and in front of the trap and a small pond to the rear. The tee shot must negotiate a lateral water hazard on the left, a small bunker on the right and a lake farther to the right, which eventually cuts into the area 100 yards in front of the green. The next hole is a 425-yard slight dogleg left whose fairway wraps around two huge sand areas beginning from approximately 225 yards into the green on the left. The small, wide, shallow green is tucked behind a sea of sand and water, which borders the entire right side of the fairway.

There are some great par 3s at Waterwood National. The most difficult one, called "the Cliffs," is the 225-yard fourteenth, which plays completely over a corner of Lake Livingston from a bluff to a narrow, deep green bordered by water

front and left and framed by a long bunker on the right and slightly to the front. The other tee distances are a more forgiving 154, 145, and 86 yards on this beautiful golf hole. The second hole is another long, well-protected par 3 and plays 225 yards to a deep green framed by trees and large traps to the left, right and back. Farther left a water hazard lurks in the woods.

The finishing hole is a scenic 536-yard par 5 that plays up a corridor of trees to a deep green situated on a peninsula, with a huge waste bunker, pot bunkers and water protecting it. The tee shot has to negotiate the trees and two large bunkers to the left. The second shot is most likely a layup to a narrowing fairway bordered by a long waste bunker and water on the left and trees on the right. A big hitter can reach this green in two, but the risks are as great as the rewards on the second shot.

At 142 from the back tees, Waterwood has one of the highest slope ratings in the greater Houston area, and it is probably one of the more difficult courses in the country. The names for some of the holes suggest the difficulty: "the Great Divide," "Devil's Domain," "Blind Bogey" and "Winding Sands." Under the new USGA sloping system, factors such as topography, width of fairways and doglegs, rough and recoverability, water and other hazards, trees, contours, firmness of greens and course design as it relates to prevailing winds are given more weight than previously, along with the actual length of a golf course. These factors are what make Waterwood so tough.

The resort has 82 rooms in cabanas, forest lodges and suites. Reasonably priced golf packages are available. The busiest golf months are May, June, September and October. The Waterwood Health Club has weight equipment, saunas and aerobics classes; there are 4 swimming pools and 4 tennis courts, as well as a marina for boating and fishing. A restaurant, entertainment lounge and snack facilities are located in the clubhouse, and meeting and conference facilities are on site. The lowest rates for golf packages are from December through

February. Single- and double-occupancy package prices are offered year round.

The Waterwood National Country Club has 7 meeting and banquet rooms available accommodating up to 350 people for a reception. *Golf Digest* has rated Waterwood National one of America's 75 best resort courses. Whether you come here for a vacation, meeting or recreational retreat, this will be a very memorable golf experience.

Course Name: THE WOODLANDS TPC, North Courses

Course Type: Resort
Resort: Woodlands Executive Conference Center and Resort
Address: 2301 North Millbend Drive The Woodlands, TX 77380
Phone: (713) 367–7285 (TPC Course) (713) 364–6329 (North Course) (713) 367–1100, (800) 433–2624, (800) 533–3052 (Resort)
Fax: (713) 367–2576 (Resort)

GOLF COURSE

Head Professionals: TPC: Garry Rippy. North: Robert Singletary

Touring Professional: John Mahaffey, Jeff Maggert

Course Length/Par (All Tees): TPC: Back 7045/72, Middle 6387/72, Forward 5302/72. North: Back 6881/72, Middle 6339/72, Forward 5765/72

Course Slope/Rating (All Tees): TPC: Back 135/73.6, Middle 127/70.5, Forward 120/70.3. North: Back 126/72.2, Middle 122/69.7, Ladies' Forward 120/72.1

Course Architects: TPC: Robert von Hagge and Bruce Devlin (1978), Carlton Gipson (renovation, 1984). North: Robert von Hagge and Bruce Devlin (9 holes, 1972; 9 holes, 1974).

Golf Facilities: Full Pro Shop X, Snack Bar X, Lounge X, Restaurant X, Locker Room X, Showers X, Club Rental X, Club Repair X, Cart Rental X, Instruction X, Practice Green X, Driving Range X, Practice Bunker No, Club Storage X

Tee-Time Reservation Policy: Resort guests: At time of confirmed reservation. Outside play: Up to 1 week in advance

Ranger: Yes

Tee-off-Interval Time: 8 min.

Time to Play 18 Holes: 4½ hrs.

Course Hours/Earliest Tee-off: 7 a.m. weekends, 8 a.m. weekdays

Green and Cart Fees: TPC: Peak rates: $90 for 18 holes with cart weekends, holidays; $75 for 18 holes with cart Mon. to Fri. North: Peak rates: $45 for 18 holes weekends; $40 for 18 holes weekdays; $25 for 9 holes weekends; $20 for 9 holes weekdays—carts additional

Credit Cards: All major cards

Season: Year round. Busiest seasons March through May, Sept. through Oct.

Course Comments: Can walk TPC Mon. to Thurs. North can be played only by members, resort guests. Palmer, West courses are private 18-hole courses on site

Golf Packages: Available through resort. Lower rates Jan., Feb., June to Aug., Nov. to Dec.

Discounts: Seasonal

Places to Stay Nearby: Westwood Shores Country Club and Resort (409) 594–3502; Park Inn (409) 295–6454, (800) 437–PARK; Motel 6 (409) 291–6927, (800) 437–7480; University Hotel (409) 291–2151; Sam Houston Inn (409) 295–9151, (800) 395–9151; EconoLodge (409) 295–6401, (800) 55–ECONO; Huntsville Inn (409) 295–5725, (800) 822–7281. BED AND BREAKFASTS: Blue Bonnet Bed and Breakfast (409) 295–2072; Whistler Bed and Breakfast (409) 295–2834

Local Attractions: Sam Houston Memorial Park, Sam Houston Memorial Museum, Texas Prison Museum, Gibbs–Powell Home Museum, Samuel Walker Houston Cultural Center, historic buildings tour, Oakwood Cemetery, Huntsville State Park, Sam Houston National Forest, Alabama–Coushatta Indian

Reservation, Lake Livingston State Park, camping, fishing, boating, hiking, water sports. Huntsville Chamber of Commerce (409) 295–8113, (800) 289–0389. Livingston Chamber of Commerce (409) 327–4929

Directions: From Houston (45 min.): I–45 north, take Rayford–Sawdust exit, left at light under highway on Sawdust Rd., bear right onto Grogan's Mill, take right onto South Mill Bend. Follow signs to course

Closest Commercial Airport: Houston Intercontinental (30 min.)

RESORT

Date Built: 1974

No. of Rooms: 268 guest rooms and suites (standard, 1-bedroom, 2-bedroom)

Meeting Rooms: 30. Capacity of Largest: 1600 persons. Meeting Space: 54,000 sq. ft.

Room Price Range: $109 for standard single off season to $250 for 2-bedroom suite peak season (mid-Jan. to mid-June, mid Sept. to mid-Nov.). Tennis, golf and other packages and special rates available

Lounges: Lobby Bar, Woody's Sports Bar

Restaurants: Woodlands Dining Room, Glass Menagerie Knickers (at TPC clubhouse)

Entertainment: Seasonal entertainment in Glass Menagerie

Credit Cards: All major cards

General Amenities: Babysitting services available, meeting and conference capabilities including audiovisual and food services

Recreational Amenities: Racquet club complex and club tennis center with 24 indoor and outdoor lighted tennis courts, 2 swimming pools, 2 full-service health spas (men's and ladies') with sauna, steam room, hydro-jet whirlpools, massage heat treatment, facials, herbal baths, conditioning equipment including free weights and workout stations; volleyball, billiards, backgammon, bowling, skeet and trap shooting, fishing

Reservation and Cancellation Policy: Credit card guarantee or deposit required

Comments and Restrictions: No charge for children under 15 years of age. Taxes additional to base rates

THE WOODLANDS

The Woodlands is a 268-room resort situated in wooded surroundings on Lake Harrison outside of Houston. Both the Tournament Players Course (TPC), Woodlands Course and the North Course are open to the public. You have to be a resort guest, however, to play the North Course. A variety of year round golf packages is available here, with lower rates being available January, February, June, July, August, November and December. The other months are the busiest at the Woodlands golf courses. A third course, the West, is a private club, as is the Arnold Palmer Course. The Woodlands is the home of the Shell Houston Annual PGA Open.

The 7045-yard TPC Course was designed by Robert von Hagge and Bruce Devlin and was opened in 1978. It was later redesigned by Carlton Gipson. The TPC has large, fast, undulating Bermuda-grass greens with water hazards on half the holes. The greens are generally well protected by sand traps and water. The TPC at the Woodlands has been rated the best resort course in Texas by *The Dallas Morning News*, and *Golf Digest* ranks it among the best resort courses in the United States. *Gulf Coast Golfer* has also ranked it as one of the favorite courses of professional golfers in Texas.

The number-1-handicap hole at the TPC is the 577-yard par-5 sixth, a long, relatively flat dogleg left. Usually at least three shots are required to reach the narrow, deep green. This target is protected by a huge trap to the left and a series of bunkers on the left from approximately 125 yards into the putting surface. The left side of the green slopes to the left making it difficult to hold on the approach shot, depending on pin placement. A difficult par 3 on the front side is a 222 yarder from the back tee that plays to a deep green, well protected by traps both left and right. The distance of 174 yards from the middle tee is more forgiving.

The two finishing holes on the TPC often decide tournament outcomes. The

376-yard par-4 seventeenth is a dogleg left that wraps around a small lake beginning halfway to the green. The fairway slopes toward the water and narrows severely in the tee-shot landing area. The approach shot is to a wide, shallow green with water in front and a trap to the rear. The 437-yard par-4 eighteenth plays to a deep green in an amphitheaterlike setting. Water is on the right from approximately 150 yards into the hole, which has six large traps running from the left front of the green around to the back. On the right is a bank that slopes down to the nearby water.

The TPC has a recently renovated clubhouse with locker rooms, showers and a restaurant, Knickers, with a bar. The pro shop is fully stocked, and individual and group lessons are available from the staff of PGA professionals and assistants. Weekly golf clinics are held here, and an extensive driving range, chipping and putting area, and practice bunkers are offered. There is a private driving area for lessons, and local professionals such as John Mahaffey and Carol Mann often practice here.

The 6881-yard par-72 North Course is well worth playing. This Robert von Hagge and Bruce Devlin–designed layout is well bunkered with more than 75 sand traps. Water comes into play on seven holes. The signature hole on the North Course is the 448-yard par-4 fifteenth, a dogleg left that plays over a stream on the approach shot to a large green protected by two traps on the left.

The Woodlands' Executive Conference Center and Resort also offers 24 tennis courts, including indoor and outdoor lighted courts. These facilities have earned the Woodlands recognition as one of the nation's 50 best tennis resorts by *Tennis* magazine. There are also 2 swimming pools; 2 full-service health spas (men's and women's); and 54,000 square feet of meeting space, including 30 rooms, audiovisual services and banquet capabilities. *Corporate Meetings and Incentives* magazine has rated the Woodlands one of the nation's 10 best conference centers. There are 2 restaurants and 2 lounges at the Woodlands. The resort has an American Automobile Association Four-Diamond rating. In addition to golf packages, tennis packages and other special rates are available at the Woodlands.

Recommended Golf Courses in Texas

Houston Area:

Bay Forest Golf Course, La Porte, (713) 471–4653, Public, 18/6756/72

Bear Creek Golf World, Houston, (713) 855–4720, Public. Challenger: 18/5295/72. Masters: 18/7131/72. Presidents: 18/6562/72

Cape Royale Golf Course, Coldspring, (409) 653–2388, Public, 18/6088/70

Clear Creek Golf Course, Houston, (713) 738–8000, Public, 18/6758/72

Cypresswood Golf Club, Spring, (713) 821–6300, Public. Creek: 18/6937/72. Cypress: 18/6906/72

Del Lago Resort, Montgomery, (409) 582–6100, Resort, 18/6907/72

The Falls Country Club, New Ulm, (409) 992–3128, Semiprivate, 18/6757/72

The Golf Club at Cinco Ranch, Katy, (713) 395–4653, Public, 18/7044/72

Greatwood Golf Club, Sugar Land, (713) 343–9999, Public, 18/6836/72

Old Orchard Golf Club, Richmond, (713) 277–3300, Public. Stables: 9/3324/36. Barn: 9/3564/36. Range: 9/3363/36

Southwyck Golf Course, Pearland, (713) 436–9999, Public, 18/7015/72

Tour 18, Humble, (713) 540–1818, Public, 18/6807/72

Wedgewood Golf Course, Conroe, (409) 441–4653, Public, 18/6817/72

San Antonio Area

Course Name: HILL COUNTRY GOLF CLUB

Course Type: Resort
Resort: Hyatt Regency Hill Country Resort
Address: 9800 Hyatt Resort Drive San Antonio, TX 78251

Phone: (210) 647–1234 (Golf Course, Resort), (800) 233–1234 (Resort reservations)

Fax: (210) 681–9681 (Golf Course), (210) 520–4075 (Resort)

GOLF COURSE

Director of Golf: Paul Earnest

Course Length/Par (All Tees): Back 6913/72, Blue 6481/72, White 5747/72, Forward 4781/72

Course Slope/Rating (All Tees): Back 136/73.9, Blue 130/72, White 115/67.9, Ladies' White 130/72.1, Forward 114/67.8

Course Architect: Arthur Hills (1993)

Golf Facilities: Full Pro Shop X, Snack Bar X, Lounge X, Restaurant X, Locker Room X, Showers X, Club Rental X, Club Repair X, Cart Rental X, Instruction X, Practice Green X, Driving Range X, Practice Bunker X, Club Storage X

Tee-Time Reservation Policy: At time of reservation at resort. Up to 1 week in advance for public

Ranger: Yes

Tee-off-Interval Time: 8 min.

Time to Play 18 Holes: 4½ hrs.

Course Hours/Earliest Tee-off: 7:30 a.m. Sat., Sun., holidays; 8 a.m. weekdays

Green and Cart Fees: $90 for 18 holes Sat., Sun., holidays; $80 for 18 holes weekdays

Credit Cards: All major cards

Season: Year round. Busiest mid-Mar. through May, mid-Sept. to late Nov.

Course Comments: Walking allowed at full golf fee. Yardage book available

Golf Packages: Through resort

Discounts: Lowest seasonal rates Dec.– Jan. Twilight

Places to Stay Nearby: See page 643

Local Attractions: See page 643

Directions: From San Antonio International (20 min. northwest): Go west on Loop 410 to Hwy. 151/Sea World. Drive 4 miles west on Hwy. 151 to resort on the right. From downtown San Antonio take Hwy. 90 west to Hwy. 151 under Hwy. 410. Take Hwy. 151 and proceed 4 miles west to the resort

Closest Commercial Airport: San Antonio International (20 min.)

RESORT

Date Built: 1993

No. of Rooms: 500 rooms and suites

Meeting Rooms: 24. Capacity of Largest: 1700 persons theater style. Meeting Space: 27,000 sq. ft.

Room Price Range: $159 to $220 for standard rooms. Suites start at $405. Golf and other packages offered year round

Lounges: Charlie's Long Bar, Aunt Mary's Porch, Cactus Oak Tavern

Restaurants: The Antlers Lodge, Springhouse Cafe, General Store, Papa Ed's

Entertainment: Live music on weekends

Credit Cards: All major cards

General Amenities: Meeting and conference services including audiovisual, banquet, secretarial and other support; gift shop, car rental agency on site; Camp Hyatt and Rock Hyatt children and teens programs

Recreational Amenities: Four-acre water park with man-made river, sand beach, pool house, swimming pools and outdoor spa, tennis courts, water aerobics, health club with jacuzzi, massage, treadmills, free weights and other equipment; bicycling, volleyball, basketball, billiards, game tables, horseback riding

Reservation and Cancellation Policy: First night's room fee plus tax must be guaranteed by credit card to hold reservation. 72-hr. cancellation notice to receive full refund

Comments and Restrictions: No pets

HILL COUNTRY GOLF CLUB

The Hill Country Golf Club is the centerpiece of a new 200-acre $100 million Hyatt resort on the outskirts of San Antonio. The Arthur Hills-designed layout is a strategic course that provides ample room for maneuver, especially from the two forward tee distances. As the golfer moves back, the course becomes tighter and more hazardous.

The well-treed Hill Country course has generous fairway landing areas, open avenues to the greens, 45 bunkers, grassy hollows, wide swales, rock-lined gulches, four water hazards, and scenic views of the Texas Hill country from various tree-shaded plateaus on the golf course. The sequence of holes on this course is well paced with a variety of par 4s including four that play from under 370 yards from the back tees. The 328-yard third, for example, dares the golfer to cope with a 50-yard-long bunker on the right side beginning from 180 yards in, to a green whose front is guarded by two bunkers and two large trees. If you hit a poor tee shot on this hole you are likely to be in the sand or stymied by the mature trees lining the fairway.

The most difficult holes on the course are the long par 4s such as the 452-yard fifth which plays to a tight, treelined landing area. The approach is to a deep, hogbacked green guarded by a pond to its right and a large bunker to its left. The Bermuda greens on this course tend to be moderately fast, mildly undulating, and of various sizes and shapes depending on the strategy of the hole. The 549-yard par-5 finishing hole plays down a treelined fairway to a huge double green shared with No. 9. A large pond protects the target in front. Two large bunkers several yards short of the green and to the right can easily catch errant approach shots.

A short distance from No. 18 is a large, modern clubhouse with all the amenities including the Antlers Lodge restaurant and the less formal Cactus Oak Tavern. Nearby is a spacious double-ended practice range, a practice green, and chipping area. While you are practicing, you can take in the scenic views of cedar- and oak-lined fairways and open meadows with wild bluebonnets, paintbrush, and prickly pear cactus. On site is a 500-room Hyatt that has everything from standard rooms to a stand-alone two-story guest house. The hotel's meeting room amenities include everything from basic banquet services to water hook-ups for laser presentations.

Course Name: LA CANTERA GOLF CLUB

Course Type: Resort
Address: 16401 La Cantera Parkway
San Antonio, TX 78257
Phone: (210) 558–4653, (800) 446–5387
Fax: (210) 558–1529

GOLF COURSE

Head Professional: Carl Bielstein
Course Length/Par (All Tees): Back 6885/72, Gold 6344/72, Blue 5954/72, Silver 5581/72, Forward 4954/72
Course Slope/Rating (All Tees): Back 132/72, Gold 126/69.3, Blue 117/67.9, Silver 113/66.1, Ladies' Forward 108/67.1
Course Architects: Jay Morrish and Tom Weiskopf (1995)
Golf Facilities: Full Pro Shop X, Snack Bar X, Lounge X, Restaurant X, Locker Room No, Showers No, Club Rental X, Club Repair No, Cart Rental X, Instruction X, Practice Green X, Driving Range X, Practice Bunker X, Club Storage X
Tee-Time Reservation Policy: Up to 14 days in advance
Ranger: Yes
Tee-off-Interval Time: 10 min.
Time to Play 18 Holes: 4 hrs. 15 min.
Course Hours/Earliest Tee-off: 7 a.m. Fri., Sat., Sun., holidays; 7:30 a.m. weekdays
Green and Cart Fees: $80 for 18 holes Fri., Sat., Sun., holidays; $65 for 18 holes weekdays
Credit Cards: All major cards
Season: Year round. Busiest Mar. through May
Course Comments: Yardage book available. Inquire at pro shop about walking policy
Golf Packages: Inquire at pro shop
Discounts: Twilight. Multiple play rate
Places to Stay Nearby: Hyatt Regency Hill Country Resort (210) 647–1234, (800) 233–1234; Hampton Inn-Fiesta Park (210) 561–9058, (800) 426–7866. See page 643 for additional accommodations
Local Attractions: See page 643

Directions: From San Antonio (15 min. northwest): Take I–10 (McDermott Freeway) to La Cantera Pkwy. Exit. Turn onto La Cantera and proceed 1.2 miles to golf course on the right

Closest Commercial Airport: San Antonio International (20 min.)

LA CANTERA GOLF CLUB

La Cantera is a new Jay Morrish and Tom Weiskopf creation near the Fiesta Texas Amusement Park northwest of San Antonio. Situated on 200 acres, La Cantera is the cornerstone of a planned 1000-acre retail and residential development that will include a resort hotel. The generous 15-acre practice area at La Cantera, site of the Texas Open, prepares you to match wits with an often visually intimidating golf course. This layout offers 75 bunkers, severe rock outcroppings, mature trees, a stone quarry, dramatic elevation changes, and an occasional water hazard.

Your golf adventure at La Cantera begins with the 665-yard par-5 opening hole which has a stunning elevated view of the San Antonio skyline 15 miles to the south. The 125-foot elevation drop from tee to green takes you down a treelined fairway to a deep, moderately undulating Bermuda grass green framed by bunkers. The other tee distances on No. 1 are 631, 613, 597, and 549 yards. Fortunately the hole is downhill and the wind is usually behind you.

At the other end of the distance spectrum is the 316-yard par-4 seventh, called "Rattler" because it has a view of The Rattler roller coaster at the nearby amusement park. It also has striking views of San Antonio and the surrounding hill country as it drops 80 feet from the tee to a 43-yard-deep green with bunkers to its left and another to its right. A strayed tee shot can find a pond to the right or it might land in a large bunker to the left. But it is difficult for many golfers to restrain themselves from going for the green on the tee shot.

La Cantera provides a fascinating, scenic, and challenging array of golf holes. The par 5s range from 527 to 665 yards, the par 4s from 316 to 448 yards, and the par 3s from 142 to 202 yards from the back tees. With five tee distances to chose from, any golfer should have an enjoyable time playing this course.

Tom Weiskopf and Jay Morrish have designed other fine golf courses such as Troon North in Scottsdale, Arizona. They have built another winner in San Antonio. *GolfWeek* rates it among the best courses in Texas and *Golf Digest* named it the best new public course in 1995.

Course Name: PECAN VALLEY

Course Type: Public
Address: 4700 Pecan Valley
              San Antonio, TX 78223
Phone: (210) 333–9018
              (800) 336–3418 (Tee-Times)

GOLF COURSE

General Manager: Scott Manda

Course Length/Par (All Tees): Back 7116/72, Middle 6621/72, Forward 5621/72

Course Slope/Rating (All Tees): Back 136/73.9, Middle 123/71.0, Ladies' Forward 113/71.3

Course Architect: J. Press Maxwell (1963)

Golf Facilities: Full Pro Shop X, Snack Bar X, Lounge X, Restaurant X, Locker Room No, Showers No, Club Rental X, Club Repair Minor/Outside, Cart Rental X, Instruction X, Practice Green X, Driving Range X, Practice Bunker X, Club Storage No

Tee-Time Reservation Policy: From 2 wks. in advance. Credit card guarantee required for Fri., Sat., Sun., holiday reservations

Ranger: Yes

Tee-off-Interval Time: 7 and 8 min.

Time to Play 18 Holes: 4½ hrs.

Course Hours/Earliest Tee-off: Sunrise to sunset

Green and Cart Fees: $70 for 18 holes with cart

Credit Cards: American Express, Master-Card, Visa

Season: Year round. Busiest season April, Oct., Nov.

Course Comments: Cart mandatory week-ends, holidays. Yardage book available

Golf Packages: Available through hotels

Discounts: Seniors, military
Places to Stay Nearby: See page 643
Local Attractions: See page 643
Directions: I–37S to Pecan Valley Dr.,
  left on Pecan Valley, drive 2 mi.,
  golf course on right side of road
Closest Commercial Airport: San
  Antonio (20 min.)

PECAN VALLEY

Pecan Valley has perennially been named one of the best public golf courses in the United States by *Golf Digest*. The 7116-yard par-72 layout was designed by James Press Maxwell and opened in 1963. Situated on 200 lushly wooded acres along Salado Creek in the Salado Valley, Pecan Valley was the site of the 50th PGA Championship in 1968. Arnold Palmer finished one shot behind Julius Boros in the championship that year. The Texas Open has been held here on many occasions.

Maxwell was born in Ardmore, Oklahoma, in 1916. The son of golf architect Perry Maxwell, he started in the business after high school by working at such sites as Southern Hills and Augusta National. He designed many courses along the Texas Gulf Coast after starting his own practice in 1952. Some of his Texas golf courses include the Riverbend Country Club in Sugar Land, the Sleepy Hollow Golf and Country Club in Dallas, the Brookhaven Country Club (Championship, Masters courses) in Dallas, and the Riverside Golf Club in Austin. He also designed or remodeled other courses in Alabama, California, Colorado, Louisiana, Oklahoma, Tennessee, Texas, Kansas, New York, Utah and Colorado, where he retired to become a full-time rancher in the 1970s.

Pecan Valley is well populated with mature trees, including a magnificent 800-year-old oak tree. Water hazards appear on half the holes, and there are relatively few sand bunkers, which are located mostly around the medium-sized greens. The Bermuda-grass putting surfaces are large, fast and undulating. If the ball strays here it can be found and played, but you are likely to be poking it from under a tree. Several of the greens are elevated and you will probably get a variety of uneven lies on these rolling fairways.

The course leads off with two difficult par 4s. The first, a 450-yard dogleg left, plays to a generous tree-lined fairway on the first shot. The second shot is over a stream to a forward-sloping green backed by trees and protected by a trap on the left. The second hole is the number-1-handicap hole and plays straight to a wide, shallow, two-tiered, kidney-shaped green with a trap on the right. Water is to the left and right from 125 to 75 yards into the putting surface. The next hole is a picturesque 198-yard par 3 that plays to a left-to-right and forward-sloping green backed by one trap and protected on the right front by another. A gargantuan hole on this side is the 607-yard par-5 sixth, a slight dogleg left, that plays down a tree-lined fairway to a medium-sized green with no sand traps. The approach shot to the forward-sloping green has to carry a stream approximately 75 to 65 yards from the center of the putting surface.

A tough par 4 on the back nine is the 460-yard fourteenth, a tree-lined dogleg right to a small, forward-sloping green with no sand traps. Water is on the right on the tee shot, but the approach to the green is open. Distance is the key on this hole. The 483-yard par-5 finishing hole was a par 4 when Arnold Palmer hooked a 1-iron into the trees on the left to miss a chance to catch Julius Boros on the last day of the 1968 PGA Championship. A stream cuts the tree-lined fairway 165 yards from a very narrow green that is protected by traps both left and right.

The clubhouse at Pecan Valley has a restaurant and bar, men's locker room only, banquet facilities for up to 300 persons, and a full-service pro shop. Many group events are held here, including those for convention visitors from downtown San Antonio which is only 10 minutes away. The busiest months are April, October and November. You can walk the course on weekdays. Instruction at the nearby driving range, practice green or bunkers is available from the professionals and assistants.

Course Name: THE QUARRY

Course Type: Public
Address:　　444 E. Basse Road
　　　　　　San Antonio, TX 78209
Phone:　　　(210) 824–4500
Fax:　　　　(210) 824–3068

GOLF COURSE

Director of Golf: Courtney Connell
Head Professional: Craig Campo
Course Length/Par (All Tees): Back
6740/71, Championship 6128/71,
Regular 5576/71, Forward 4897/71
Course Slope/Rating (All Tees): Back
128/72.4, Championship 120/69.2,
Regular 110/66.7, Ladies' Forward
115/67.4
Course Architect: Keith Foster (1993)
Golf Facilities: Full Pro Shop X, Snack
Bar X, Lounge X, Restaurant X,
Locker Room X, Showers X, Club
Rental X, Club Repair No, Cart Rental
X, Instruction X, Practice Green X,
Driving Range X, Practice Bunker X,
Club Storage X
Tee-Time Reservation Policy: Up to 7
days in advance
Ranger: Yes
Tee-off-Interval Time: 10 min.
Time to Play 18 Holes: 4 hrs. 15 min.
Course Hours/Earliest Tee-off: 7 a.m.
Green and Cart Fees: $75 for 18 holes
Fri., Sat., Sun., holidays; $65 for 18
holes weekdays
Credit Cards: All major cards except Diners
Season: Year round. Busiest Mar.–May,
Sept.–Nov.
Course Comments: Can walk anytime at
full golf fee. Yardage book available
Golf Packages: Inquire at pro shop
Discounts: Twilight
Places to Stay Nearby: See page 643
Local Attractions: See page 643
Directions: The Quarry is 10 minutes
north of downtown San Antonio. Take
Hwy. 281 north to E. Basse Rd. Exit.
Take right turn onto E. Basse to golf
course
Closest Commercial Airport: San Antonio
International (5 min.)

THE QUARRY GOLF CLUB

The Quarry Golf Club is the centerpiece
of a 460-acre mixed-use development in
Lincoln Heights, one mile south of the San
Antonio International Airport. The site was
the former home of the Alamo Cement
Company which left a 90-acre 100-foot
deep quarry in its wake. Designer Keith
Foster who assisted Arthur Hills in designing Walking Stick in Colorado, Bighorn
Country Club in California, the Hyatt Hill
Country Resort in San Antonio, and other
quality courses, creatively incorporated the
back nine of this 165-acre golf course into
the quarry.

The front nine of The Quarry plays
through open fields along creeks and lakes.
The back nine is set in the old quarry and
has a lake bordering holes No. 12, 13 and
14. The 205-yard par-3 twelfth is called
"Alcatraz" because it plays over the edge
of the lake to its target. Another ominous-
sounding hole is the 386-yard par-4 seventeenth, called "Reload." The tee shot must
carry 170 yards from an elevated tee over a
canyon. This provides an intimidating view
as you look down into the abyss and contemplate a wall of sheer rock to your right.
The approach shot on this hole is to a wide
green with a bunker to its left and a large
rock wall to its right.

The front nine on The Quarry plays
3167 yards from the tips and the back nine
plays 3573 yards. The tougher holes are on
the back side, partly bacause of the psycho-
logical impact of the quarry. The clubhouse
restaurant at the Quarry affords you a full
panoramic view of the back nine, one of
the most spectacular and unusual settings
in golf.

The Quarry is not a gimmick course,
however. It should be enjoyable for any
golfer because it has four tee distances to
choose from and the slopes and ratings,
even from the back tees, are reasonable.
The Quarry has already been rated one of
the best courses in the tough Texas golf
market by both *GolfWeek* and *Golf Digest*.
Keith Foster's first effort as an independent
designer is a fine one.

Places to Stay in the San Antonio Area:
Marriott River Walk (210) 224–4555, (800) 228–9290; Hyatt Regency Hill Country (210) 647–1234, (800) 233–1234; Fairmont Hotel (210) 224–8800, (800) 642–3363; Plaza San Antonio (210) 229–1000, (800) 421–1172; Wyndham San Antonio (210) 691–8888, (800) 822–4200; Hilton (210) 222–1400, (800) HILTONS; Menger Hotel (210) 223–4361, (800) 345–9285; Hyatt Regency (210) 222–1234, (800) 228–9000; Holiday Inn River Walk (210) 224–2500, (800) HOLIDAY; La Quinta Motor Inn Market Square (210) 271–0001, (800) 531–5900

Local Attractions: Alamo, Witte Museum, Institute of Texan Cultures, Hemis Fair Plaza, La Villita, Market Square, Menger Hotel, San Jose and other missions in San Antonio, Fiesta Texas, Missions National Historical Park, Lone Star Brewery tour, Buckhorn Hall of Horns Museum, Hertzberg Circus Collection and Circus Museum, San Antonio Museum of Art, Marion Koogler McNay Art Museum, Botanical Center, River Walk, fiesta and seasonal events, Natural Bridge Caverns, Natural Bridge Wildlife Ranch, military base tours, theater, dance, restaurants, Sea World of Texas, San Antonio Zoological Gardens and Aquarium, San Antonio Botanical Gardens, King William Historic Area, Spanish Governor's Palace, restaurants, nightlife, concerts, spectator sports–N.B.A., Texas League. San Antonio Convention and Visitors Bureau (210) 270–8700, (800) 447–3372

Recommended Golf Courses in Texas

San Antonio Area:

Cedar Creek Golf Course, San Antonio, (210) 695–5050, Public, 18/7150/72

Flying El Ranch Golf Course, Bandera, (210) 460–3001, (800) 646–5407, Resort, 18/6635/72

Mission Del Lago Golf Course, San Antonio, (210) 627–2522, Public, 18/7004/72

Topatio Springs Resort and Conference Center, Boerne, (210) 537–4197, Resort, 18/6500/72

Other Recommended Golf Courses in Texas

Amarillo Area:

Hidden Hills Public Golf Course, Pampa, (806) 669–5866, Public, 18/6463/71

John Pitman Municipal Golf Course, Hereford, (806) 363–7139, Public, 18/6480/71

Bay City:

Rio Colorado Golf Course, Bay City, (409) 244–2955, Public, 18/6824/72

Brownsville Area:

Rancho Viejo Resort, Brownsville, (512) 350–4000, (800) 292–7263 (TX), (800) 531–7400 (outside TX), Resort. El Angel: 18/6518/70. El Diablo: 18/6847/70

Shary Municipal Golf Course, Mission, (210) 580–8770, Public. One/Two: 18/6025/71. Two/Three: 18/5883/70. One/Three: 18/6528/73

Valley Inn Country Club, Brownsville, (512) 546–5331, Semiprivate, 18/6537/70

El Paso:

Cielo Vista Golf Course, El Paso, (915) 591–4927, Public, 18/6411/72

Painted Dunes Golf Course, El Paso, (915) 821–2122, Public, 18/6925/72

Galveston Area:

Columbia Lakes Golf Course, West Columbia, (409) 345–5455, (800) 231–1030, Resort, 18/6967/72

Galveston Island Municipal Golf Course, Galveston, (409) 744–2366, Public, 18/6969/72

Hilltop Lakes:

Hilltop Lakes Resort, Hilltop Lakes, (409) 855–2100, Resort, 18/6650/72

Nacogdoches:

Woodland Hills Golf Course, Nacogdoches, (409) 564–2762, Resort, 18/6672/72

Odessa:

Andrews County Golf Course, Andrews, (915) 524–1462, Public, 18/6300/70

Ratliff Ranch Golf Links, Odessa, (915) 368–4653, Public, 18/6800/72

Sam Rayburn:

Rayburn Country Club, Sam Rayburn, (409) 698–2958, Public. Blue: 9/3115/36. Gold: 9/3051/36. Green: 9/3085/36

San Augustine:

Fairway Farm Golf and Hunt Resort, San Augustine, (409) 275–5458, Semi-private, 18/7551/71

San Saba:

San Saba Municipal Golf Course, San Saba, (915) 372–3212, Public, 18/6904/72

Tyler Area:

Garden Valley Golf Resort, Lindale, (903) 882–6107, (800) 443–8577, Resort. Dogwood: 18/6754/72. Hummingbird: 18/6446/71

Peach Tree Golf Club, Bullard, (903) 894–7079, Semiprivate. Oakhurst: 18/6813/72. Peach Tree: 18/5556/70

Waco Area:

White Bluff Golf Club, Whitney, (817) 694–3656, Semiprivate, 18/6845/72

Texas: Useful Information

Tourism Division, Texas Department of Commerce, P.O. Box 12728, Austin, TX 78711, (800) 8888TEX

Texas Parks and Wildlife Department, 4200 Smith School Rd., Austin, TX 78744, (512) 389–4800, (800) 792–1112 (TX)

Bed and Breakfast Texas Style, 4224 W. Red Bird Ln., Dallas, TX 75237, (214) 298–8585, (214) 298–5433

U.S. Forest Service, 701 N. First St., Lufkin, TX 75901, (409) 639–8501, (800) 280–CAMP (information and reservations)

Course Name: GREEN SPRING GOLF COURSE

Course Type: Public
Address: 588 North Green Spring Drive
              Washington, UT 84780
Phone: (801) 673–7888

GOLF COURSE

Head Professional: Kent B. Danjanovich
Course Length/Par (All Tees): Back 6717/71, White 6293/71, Gold 5825/71, Forward 5042/71
Course Slope/Rating (All Tees): Back 131/71.4, White 125/69.3, Gold 119/67.3, Ladies' Forward 118/68.8
Course Architect: Gene Bates (1989)
Golf Facilities: Full Pro Shop X, Snack Bar X, Lounge No, Restaurant No, Locker Room No, Showers No, Club Rental X, Club Repair X, Cart Rental X, Instruction X, Practice Green X, Driving Range X, Practice Bunker X, Club Storage No
Tee-Time Reservation Policy: Mon. morning for following Mon. through Sun.
Ranger: Yes
Tee-off-Interval Time: 8 min.
Time to Play 18 Holes: 4 hrs., 45 min.
Course Hours/Earliest Tee-off: Daylight to dusk
Green Fees: $28.50 for 18 holes, $15.50 for 9 holes. Lower rates June 1 to Sept. 15
Cart Fees: $9.50 for 18 holes per person, $5.25 for 9 holes per person
Pull Carts: $2 per 18 holes
Credit Cards: MasterCard, Visa
Season: Year round. Busiest seasons Jan. through April, Oct., Nov.
Course Comments: Can walk anytime, but cart recommended
Golf Packages: 20-round (9 holes) discounted package (peak season $220, off season $150)
Discounts: Juniors (summer)
Places to Stay Nearby: ST. GEORGE: Holiday Inn/Holidome (801) 628–4235, (800) HOLIDAY; Ramada Inn (801) 628–2828, (800) 272–6232; Thunderbird Inn (801) 673–6123; Hilton (801) 628–0463, (800) 445–8667
Local Attractions: Ghost towns, St. George Mormon Temple, St. George historic walking tour, Washington Cotton Mill, bicycle tours, St. George Art Museum; seasonal events such as antique car show, arts festivals, marathon races, rodeo; Dixie College, Brigham Young winter home, Daughters of Pioneers Museum, Gunlock State Beach/Kolob Canyon, Zion National Park, Pine Valley Recreation Area, water-skiing. Mesquite, NV. Lake Mead, NV. St. George Chamber of Commerce (801) 628–1658. Washington County Travel Council (801) 634–5747, (800) 869–6635
Directions: From Las Vegas (2 hrs.): I–15, Washington exit (No. 10), left (west) 500 yards to golf course
Closest Commercial Airports: St. George Municipal (5 min.); McCarran International, Las Vegas (2 hrs.)

GREEN SPRING GOLF COURSE

The Green Spring Golf Course is a 6717-yard par-71 layout situated in the southwest corner of Utah near Zion National Park. It is approximately a 2-hour drive northeast from Las Vegas. Green Spring is currently rated among the best public or private golf courses in the state of Utah by *Golf Digest*. Designed by Gene Bates and opened in 1989, the course is mutually owned by the adjacent cities of Washington, St. George and Santa Clara.

Each hole on this course is unique, with approximately one-half being flat and the other half up and down. A natural spring runs through the course, and there are water hazards on seven holes. The bentgrass greens are medium sized, moderately fast and undulating. The fairways are rolling, with a series of links-style mounds through the course, providing some interesting kicks, rolls and uneven lies. The greens tend to be well protected by mounds, traps and occasionally water. A beautiful water hole is the 171-yard par-3 fifteenth, which plays over water to a forward-sloping, flat green protected by a small trap forward-right. The 391-yard par-4 eleventh has an approach shot over a pond to a wide, shallow green with water immediately in front and wetlands to the rear. There is desert between the fairways, and it is not uncommon to see rabbits, desert tortoises and an occasional rattlesnake.

The number-1-handicap hole is the 449-yard par-4 sixth, which is a sharp dogleg right. The first shot has to be hit to a narrow landing area along a gorge, and the second is over a stunning red-rock gorge to a deep, angled green with grass bunkers on the left. A beautiful par 3 on this side is the 173-yard fifth, which plays over a gorge down to a triangular green with a tier to the rear and protected by a trap to the right front.

The three finishing holes at Green Spring begin with a difficult 407-yard par-4 sharp dogleg right. The approach shot is over a small gorge onto a two-tiered green with a sand trap in front and slightly below. The 172-yard par-3 seventeenth is over a small desert gorge to a green with traps to the right front and right rear. The 502-yard par-5 dogleg-right finishing hole is downhill all the way to a wide, shallow green with a pot bunker in back. A fairway trap lurks at the dogleg, approximately 260 yards from the back tees.

The practice area at Green Spring has a generous five-tiered driving range with three target greens, a putting green, a chipping green and a practice bunker. The 3000-square-foot clubhouse has a fully stocked pro shop, restaurant and snack bar but no locker rooms or showers at present. January through April, October and November are the busiest months here, and reduced rates can be obtained during the slower summer months. Connecting flights come into nearby St. George, Utah, from Las Vegas and Salt Lake City.

The front side of Green Spring is flat, but the back side is up and down. You can walk the course anytime, but very few do because of the long distances from green to tee on this beautiful and challenging layout.

Nearby St. George was settled by the Mormon pioneers in 1861 and now is a growing town of more than 30,000, with many interesting historical buildings including a majestic Mormon Temple and Brigham Young's winter home. The Washington Cotton Mill was recently restored. It represents an earlier effort to make this area a cotton-producing center. A short drive from St. George is Zion National Park, one of the natural wonders of North America. Today the Washington County area is a growing retirement center, and golf is becoming increasingly popular.

Course Name: PARK MEADOWS GOLF CLUB

Course Type: Semiprivate
Address: 2000 Meadows Drive
P.O. Box 680430
Park City, UT 84068
Phone: (801) 649–2460

GOLF COURSE

Head Professional: Michael Kutcher
Course Length/Par (All Tees): Blue 7338/72, White 6666/72, Ladies' Forward 5816/73
Course Slope/Rating (All Tees): Blue 123/73.7, White 118/70.6, Ladies' Forward 118/71.7
Course Architect: Jack Nicklaus (1983)
Golf Facilities: Full Pro Shop X, Snack Bar X, Lounge X, Restaurant No, Locker Room No, Showers No, Club Rental X, Club Repair X, Cart Rental X, Instruction X, Practice Green X, Driving Range X, Practice Bunker X, Club Storage X
Tee-Time Reservation Policy: 7 days in advance. Credit card guarantee required. Up to 30 days in advance with surcharge
Ranger: Yes
Tee-off-Interval Time: 7 and 8 min.
Time to Play 18 Holes: 4½ hrs.
Course Hours/Earliest Tee-off: 7 a.m. weekends, 8 a.m. weekdays
Green and Cart Fees: $67 for 18 holes with cart peak summer season
Credit Cards: American Express, MasterCard, Visa
Season: Mid-April to mid-Nov.

Course Comments: Can walk course after 2 p.m. Group golf programs and outing services, season membership and rates

Golf Packages: Available. Also contact Deer Valley Lodging (801) 649–4040, (800) 453–3833 for golf packages and condos

Discounts: Seniors, replays; lower rates in spring, fall

Places to Stay Nearby: Inn at Prospector Square (801) 649–8356, (800) 453–3812; Radisson (801) 649–5000, (800) 345–5076; Silver King Hotel (801) 649–5500; Shadow Ridge Hotel (801) 649–3700, (800) 453–1302; Washington School Inn (801) 649–3800, (800) 824–1642; The Yarrow (801) 649–7000, (800) 327–2332; Goldener Hirsch Inn (801) 649–7770, (800) 252–3373; Best Western Landmark Inn (801) 649–7300, (800) 528–1234; Olympic Resort Hotel and Conference Center (801) 649–2900; Stein Eriksen Lodge (801) 649–3700: Deer Valley Lodging (801) 649–4040, (800) 453–3833

Local Attractions: Horseback riding, tennis, Utah Symphony, hiking, fishing, skiing, Kimball Art Center, Park City Museum and Territorial Jail, Park City cultural events, Deer Valley events, camping. Park City Chamber of Commerce/Convention and Visitors Bureau (801) 649–6100

Closest Commercial Airport: Salt Lake City International (45 min.)

PARK MEADOWS GOLF CLUB

Both *GolfWeek* and *Golf Digest* magazines rank Park Meadows among the best public or private golf courses in the state of Utah. This 7338-yard Jack Nicklaus–designed layout is part of an exclusive residential real-estate development. At this writing, the bulk of Park Meadows play comes from corporate and group outings. An extensive array of group tournament, catering and accommodations arrangements are provided.

The golf course itself was opened in 1983, is flat and rolling, and features more than 100 sand bunkers, meandering streams, strategically placed lakes, deep rough and a Scottish-links-style treeless layout. The bentgrass greens are large, fast, undulating and well appointed with mounds and traps. Water hazards appear on more than half the holes, with rustic, arching wooden bridges to aid your journey over them.

The number-1-handicap hole at Park Meadows is the second hole, a par 4 that plays 465 yards to a huge double green shared with the eighth hole. The tee-shot landing area on number two is squeezed by bunkers on the right, and the approach shot is to a wide, shallow green with bunkers front, left and back.

The par 3s at Park Meadows are long and tough. The 220-yard fourth plays to a deep green flanked by traps both left and right. The 200-yard seventh is over water to a well-trapped, three-cornered green. The 209-yard twelfth is to a large green flanked by a huge trap to the left and two traps to the right. The 189-yard fourteenth plays over water to a deep, right-to-left-angled green.

The signature hole at Park Meadows is the 541-yard par-5 fifteenth, which is completely bordered by water on the right. You can play your tee shot to the right to an island landing area approximately 240 yards from the back tees, or you can plan to reach the green in three shots by playing to a narrow landing area to the left. The approach shot is to a large, flat green with water in front and a trap to the right and rear. Pin position and shot placement are critical on this hole.

The finishing hole is one of the many long, challenging par 4s at Park Meadows. It plays 479 yards from the back tees and 451 yards from the middle tees. The tee-shot landing area is guarded by a huge parallel bunker on the left and large bunkers on the right. The green is deep and narrow, with three traps to the right and one to the left.

Golf packages can be arranged through Park Meadows, and instruction, including private lessons, miniclinics and playing lessons, is available. The ample driving range is situated in front of the golf shop, with scenic mountain views of Deer Valley,

Park City, and Park West ski resorts, which are only minutes away. Park City is located in the heart of the Wasatch Mountains, part of the Rocky Mountain Range, and averages 143 inches of snow in winter and 300 inches at the nearby ski resorts. Approximately 5200 people reside in greater Park City year round, and the number triples during the winter.

The town itself was incorporated in 1884, and 23 millionaires made their fortunes here from the mining industry. Today Park City has 64 buildings listed on the National Register of Historic Places. More than $400 million worth of silver has been mined from the surrounding hills. When mineral prices began to fall in the 1930s, ending the boom years, recreational development became the trend, and the first ski resort, Snow Park, opened in 1946. Now the area is a major ski destination, and recent golf-course construction has contributed to its becoming a year-round recreational center.

Because of the strong skiing tradition and amenities here, a wide variety of accommodations for golfers is available, including reservation services, condominiums, owner rentals, hotels and inns, bed and breakfasts, and campgrounds. Summer activities include historic district tours, camping, hiking, ballooning, fishing, cultural events such as the Utah Symphony, mountain biking, tennis and tours to nearby Nevada gambling casinos. For complete information contact the Park City Chamber of Commerce/Convention and Visitor Bureaus (801) 649–6100, (800) 453–1360.

Course Name: SUNBROOK GOLF CLUB

Course Type: Public
Address: Dixie Downs Dr. and Sunbrook Dr.
St. George, UT 84770
Phone: (801) 634–5866
Fax: (801) 634–5866

GOLF COURSE

Head Professional: Reed McArthur

Course Length/Par (All Tees): Back 6818/72, Gold 6411/72, Silver 6136/72, Forward 5286/72

Course Slope/Rating (All Tees): Back 129/73, Gold 126/71.3, Silver 122/69.9, Ladies' Forward 121/71.1

Course Architect: Ted G. Robinson (1990)

Golf Facilities: Full Pro Shop X, Snack Bar X, Lounge Beer, Restaurant No, Locker Room No, Showers No, Club Rental X, Club Repair Off site, Cart Rental X, Instruction X, Practice Green X, Driving Range X, Practice Bunker X, Club Storage No

Tee-Time Reservation Policy: Up to 14 days in advance for Mon.–Thurs. tee times. Up to 6 days in advance for Fri., Sat., Sun., holidays

Ranger: Yes

Tee-off-Interval Time: 10 min.

Time to Play 18 Holes: 4½ hrs.

Course Hours/Earliest Tee-off: 7 a.m.

Green Fees: $29 for 18 holes

Cart Fees: $9.50 for 18 holes per rider

Credit Cards: MasterCard, Visa

Season: Year round. Busiest Jan. through May

Course Comments: Can walk but difficult

Golf Packages: Inquire at pro shop

Discounts: Lowest seasonal Jun. through Sept. Replay discounts

Places to Stay Nearby: See Green Spring Golf Course page 645

Local Attractions: See Green Spring Golf Course page 645

Directions: From Las Vegas (2 hrs.): Take I-15 north to Bluff St. Turn left on Bluff St. over overpass to light (Hilton Dr.). Turn left on Hilton past Hilton Hotel to end of Southgate Country Club. Turn right on Dixie Dr. and proceed 3 miles to golf course

Closest Commercial Airports: St. George Municipal (5 min.); McCarran International, Las Vegas, NV (2 hrs.)

SUNBROOK GOLF CLUB

The Sunbrook Golf Club is a Ted Robinson–designed layout that is cut by the Santa Clara River. The river and ponds can come into play on half the holes. The 200-yard par-3 thirteenth, for example, plays from an elevated tee to a green surrounded by water.

Sunbrook is a target golf course with a variety of elevation changes and many sand bunkers including some nettlesome pot bunkers. If you miss the landing areas on this course, you are likely to be in the water, sand, deep rough, or out of bounds. One of the toughest holes on the course is the 447-yard par-4 sixth, a slight dogleg left. The approach shot on this hole is difficult because most golfers are likely to hit a low trajectory second shot that will be kicked to the right and into a bunker or the small lake to its right.

The greens at Sunbrook tend to be large, fast, and multi-tiered. A good short game is required to score on this course, rated the best public or private course in Utah by *Golf Digest* in 1995.

Course Name: VALLEY VIEW GOLF COURSE

Course Type: Public
Address: 2521 East Gentile Road
Layton, UT 84040
Phone: (801) 546–1630

GOLF COURSE

Head Professional: Ken Pettingill
Course Length/Par (All Tees): Back 7143/72, Blue 6661/72, White 6210/72, Ladies' Forward 5705/74
Course Slope/Rating (All Tees): Back 123/73.2, Blue 119/71.2, White 116/69.2, Ladies' Forward 120/72.3
Course Architect: William Hull (1975)
Golf Facilities: Full Pro Shop X, Snack Bar X, Lounge No, Restaurant No, Locker Room No, Showers No, Club Rental X, Club Repair X, Cart Rental X, Instruction X, Practice Green X, Driving Range X, Practice Bunker X, Club Storage No
Tee-Time Reservation Policy: Up to 1 day in advance from 7 a.m. for Mon.–Thurs. tee times. From Thurs. 7 a.m. for Fri., Sat., Sun., holidays
Ranger: Yes
Tee-off-Interval Time: 8 min.
Time to Play 18 Holes: 4½ hrs.
Course Hours/Earliest Tee-off: 5:44 a.m.

Green Fees: $15 for 18 holes, $7.50 for 9 holes
Cart Fees: $16 for 18 holes, $8 for 9 holes per cart
Credit Cards: Cash or check for green fees. MasterCard, Visa for cart fees and merchandise
Season: Mid-Mar. to mid-Nov. weather permitting
Course Comments: Can walk anytime. Pull carts available. Yardage book available
Golf Packages: No
Discounts: Seasonal punch tickets (20 rounds). Seniors, juniors at selected times
Places to Stay Nearby: LAYTON: La Quinta Inn (801) 776–6700, (800) 221–4731. OGDEN: Best Western High Country Inn (801) 394–9474, (800) 528–1234; Radisson Suite Hotel Ogden (801) 627–1900, (800) 333–3333. SALT LAKE CITY: Doubletree Hotel–Salt Lake City (801) 531–7500, (800) 222–TREE; Little America Hotel and Towers (801) 363–6781, (800) 453–9450; Peery Hotel (801) 521–4300; Residence Inn by Marriott (801) 532–5511, (800) 331–3131
Local Attractions: SALT LAKE CITY: Beehive House, Brigham Young's Grave, Cathedral of the Madeleine, The Church Office Building, Family History Library, Hogle Zoological Gardens, Liberty Park, Pioneer Memorial Museum, Salt Lake Art Center, State Capitol, Temple Square, University of Utah, Natural History Museum, Utah Museum of Fine Arts, Utah Historical Society, Utah Jazz NBA professional basketball, International Hockey League professional hockey, Great Salt Lake. Salt Lake City Convention and Visitors Bureau, 180 S. West Temple St., Salt Lake City, UT 84101–1493 (801) 521–2868
Directions: From Salt Lake (20 min.): Take I–15 north to Farmington then take I–89 north to Layton. Turn left onto Gentile Rd. to golf course
Closest Commercial Airport: Salt Lake International (20 min.)

VALLEY VIEW GOLF COURSE

Valley View is a popular, well-groomed, and difficult municipal golf course in the foothills of the Wasatch Mountains thirty minutes north of downtown Salt Lake City. From this scenic golf course, you can see Salt Lake, the valley, and the mountains.

There are many elevation changes at Valley View, which offers fast, undulating bentgrass greens. Among the many fine holes on this layout is the 437-yard par-4 third, aptly called "Reality." A dogleg left, the tee shot must avoid water bordering the left side yet not slide off the left-to-right sloping fairway into the rough. The second shot is to a small, elevated green that slopes severely from its back left to its right front. A bunker guards the target to the left. A challenging par 3 at Valley View is the 250-yard twelfth, "Pin Point," that plays to a green with out-of-bounds to its far left and right, has a bunker to its left and another two to its right. Many golfers hit a low tee shot to the left in an effort to run the ball onto the putting surface rather than risk a likely kick to the right from a short tee shot.

The round at Valley View ends with a difficult 463-yard par 4 that is flat, but has a lake to the left and a canyon to the right. Two good shots are required to reach this green in regulation.

Valley View has been rated among the best golf courses in Utah for a long time. Many golfers walk this golf course. More than 40,000 rounds are played here each season. During the summer months golfers tee off at sunrise and can play until the sun sets at 10 p.m. With green fees at $15 for 18 holes, this is one of golf's beautiful bargains.

Recommended Golf Courses in Utah

Logan:

Logan River Golf Course, Logan, (801) 750–0123, Public, 18/6502/71

Moab:

Moab Golf Club, Moab, (801) 259–6488, Public, 18/6819/72

Provo Area:

Gladstan Golf Club, Payston, (801) 465–2549, (800) 634–3009, Public, 18/6509/72

Hobble Creek Golf Club, Springville, (801) 489–6297, Public, 18/6315/71

Spanish Oaks Golf Club, Spanish Fork, (801) 798–9816, Public, 18/6358/72

Tri-City Golf Course, American Fork, (801) 756–3594, Public, 18/7077/72

Within 1 Hour of Salt Lake City:

Bonneville Golf Course, Salt Lake City, (801) 583–9513, Public, 18/6824/72

Bountiful City Golf Course, Bountiful, (801) 298–6040, Public, 18/6520/71

Davis Park Golf Course, Fruit Heights, (801) 546–4154, Public, 18/6456/71

Eagle Mountain Golf Course, Brigham City, (801) 723–3212, Public, 18/6769/71

Eaglewood Golf Course, North Salt Lake City, (801) 299–0088, Public, 18/6000/71

Homestead Golf Club, Midway, (801) 654–5588, (800) 327–7220, Resort, 18/7000/72

Mountain Dell Golf Club, Salt Lake City, (801) 582–3812, Public. Canyon: 18/6787/72. Lake: 18/6709/71

Park City Golf Course, Park City, (801) 649–8701, Public, 18/6754/72

Riverbend Golf Course, Riverton, (801) 253–3673, Public, 18/6876/72

Schneiter's Bluff at West Point, (801) 773–0731, Public, 18/6833/72

Wasatach Mountain State Park, Heber City, (801) 654–0532, Public. Canyon/Lake: 18/6942/72. Mountain: 9/3289/36

West Ridge Golf Course, West Valley City, (801) 996–4653, Public, 18/6734/71

Wing Pointe Golf Course, Salt Lake City, (801) 575–2345, Public, 18/7101/72

Wolf Creek Resort Golf Course, Eden, (801) 745–3365, Resort, 18/6845/72

Utah: Useful Information

Utah Travel Council, Council Hall/Capitol Hill, Salt Lake City, UT 84114, (801) 538–1030

Division of Wildlife Resources, 1636 W. North Temple, Salt Lake City, UT 84116–3156, (801) 596–8660 (fishing and hunting regulations)

Division of Parks and Recreation, 1636 W. North Temple, Salt Lake City, UT 84116–3156, (801) 538–7221 (recreation information), (800) 322–3770 (camping reservations)

National Forest Information, Intermountain Region, 324 25th St., Ogden, UT 84401, (801) 629–5306, (800) 280–CAMP (information and reservations)

Course Name: GLENEAGLES GOLF
COURSE

Course Type: Resort
Resort: The Equinox
Address: Route 7A
Manchester Village, VT 05254
Phone: (802) 362–3223 (Golf Course),
(802) 362–4700 (Resort)
Fax: (802) 362–1595 (Golf Course,
Resort)

GOLF COURSE

Head Professional: Richard Wood
Course Length/Par (All Tees): Back
6423/71, Middle 6069/71, Forward
5081/71
Course Slope/Rating (All Tees): Back
129/71.3, Middle 125/69.1, Forward
117/65.2
Course Architects: Walter Travis (1927),
Rees Jones (remodeled, 1992)
Golf Facilities: Full Pro Shop X, Snack
Bar X, Lounge X, Restaurant X,
Locker Room X, Showers X, Club
Rental X, Club Repair X, Cart Rental
X, Instruction X, Practice Green X,
Driving Range No, Practice Bunker
No, Club Storage X
Tee-Time Reservation Policy: At time of
confirmed reservation at resort. Up to 2
days in advance for the public
Ranger: Yes
Tee-off-Interval Time: 7 and 8 min.
Time to Play 18 Holes: 4½ hrs.
Course Hours/Earliest Tee-off: 7:30 a.m.
Green Fees: $80 for 18 holes Fri., Sat.,
Sun., holidays; $70 for 18 holes week-
days
Cart Fees: $17.50 for 18 holes per person
Credit Cards: American Express, Master-
Card, Visa
Season: May through Oct. Busiest July
through Labor Day
Course Comments: Can walk Mon.–Fri.
Sat., Sun., holidays after 3 p.m. Yardage
book available
Golf Packages: Through resort
Discounts: Twilight. Seasonal before June,
after mid-Oct.

Places to Stay Nearby: The 1811 House
(802) 362–1811; The Village Country
Inn (802) 362–1792, (800) 370–0300;
Wilburton Inn (802) 362–2500, (800)
648–4944. DORSET: Inn at West View
Farm (802) 867–5715. ARLINGTON: West
Mountain Inn (802) 375–6516
Local Attractions: Factory outlet stores,
antiquing, American Museum of Flyfish-
ing, Hildene, restaurants, seasonal festi-
vals, camping, hiking, fishing, boating,
hunting. Chamber of Commerce, Man-
chester and the Mountains, Adams Park
Green, Box 928, Manchester, VT 05255,
(802) 362–2100
Directions: From Boston (4 hrs.): Take
Rte. 2 west to I–91 North to Exit 2/
Brattelboro. Then take Rte. 30 north to
Historic Rte. 7A in Manchester. Turn
left and go 1 mile to the Equinox. From
Albany Airport (1½ hrs.): Take Rte. 87
north to Rte. 7 East (becomes 9 East at
NY/VT border). Continue to Bennington
and turn left onto Rte. 7 North. Take
Exit 3, turn left onto Rte. 313, then right
onto Rte. 7A North and proceed 12
miles to the Equinox
Closest Commercial Airports: Albany
County, NY (1½ hrs.); Burlington
International (2½ hrs.); Hartford
International, CT (2½ hrs.)

RESORT

Date Built: 1769
No. of Rooms: 163 rooms and suites,
3-bedroom townhouses
Meeting Rooms: 8. Capacity of Largest:
350 persons. Meeting Space: 8,000 sq. ft.
Room Price Range: $130 standard single
to $520 for a triple suite, townhouses.
Golf and other packages available year
round
Lounges: The Marsh Tavern
Restaurants: Marsh Tavern, Colonade,
The Dormy Grill at the golf course
Entertainment: Live music in Marsh
Tavern
Credit Cards: All major cards
General Amenities: Resort retail shops;
babysitting and child care, summer
children's program; meeting facilities

with audiovisual, banquet, secretarial and other support

Recreational Amenities: 3 Har-Tru tennis courts, paddle tennis, fitness spa with Nautilus and other equipment, horseback riding, carriage rides, board games, shooting and hunting, walking and jogging trails, fishing in stocked Equinox Pond, boating and canoeing, bicycle tours, winter sports including skiing and skating

Reservation and Cancellation Policy: One night deposit is required to confirm reservations. Early departures result in forfeiture of this deposit. Cancellations must be made two weeks in advance to receive full refund

Comments and Restrictions: No accommodation charge for children under 12 sharing a room with an adult. No pets

THE GLENEAGLES GOLF COURSE

The Gleneagles Golf Course is framed in a Currier and Ives-like New England setting at the base of 3800-foot Mount Equinox and just down the hill from the imposing white-columned Equinox Hotel, a National Historic Landmark. The hotel, which dates back to the 18th century, is now a blend of six different architectural styles and 17 different structures. The main building houses 136 rooms including the Presidential suites, three Parlor suites, the Mary Todd Lincoln Suite and the Green Mountain Suite. The Equinox's Marsh Tavern serves such delicacies as smoked ham and sausages. Or you might want to try the Vermont pheasant in the more formal Colonade restaurant. The resort offers a variety of other amenities ranging from spa services to professionally organized and supported meeting and conference facilities. Should you want a townhouse accomodation, they are a short walk from the main hotel building.

The hotel and the golf course were renovated in recent years at a cost of over $12 million. More than $4 million was invested in the golf course to install an irrigation system and completely renovate the course which is now bentgrass from tee to green. The Gleneagles is an old-style golf course

originally designed by Walter Travis in the 1920s. Rees Jones remodeled the course and rebuilt large, undulating greens and added bunkers to a course that retains much of its basic design and character. Gleneagles is a rolling 6423-yard course that demands well-positioned drives and accurate approach shots. On some holes, such as the 336-yard fifth, a blind par 4, it is better to hit an iron or 3-wood off the tee to set up a high percentage approach shot. The second shot on No. 5 is to a small, forward-sloping green with three bunkers to its right and abrupt dropoffs down slopes to the rear, left and right.

My favorite hole on the front side is the 398-yard par-4 eighth whose tee shot is from an elevated tee with a view of the hotel and the mountains in the distance. The drive must avoid a cluster of bunkers to the left. The approach is to a shallow, elevated green with a dropoff to a large bunker to the left. Bunkers protect the front and right side of the target. The second shot must reach the green in the air to avoid these obstacles.

Gleneagles concludes with two solid par 4s. The 435-yard dogleg left seventeenth has a tee shot that must stay to the right of a series of six bunkers guarding the left side. The fairway narrows as it flows up a hill to a medium-sized green guarded by large bunkers to its left, right, and rear. The finishing hole, a 417-yarder, swings left and around a large tree 162 yards from the back tees. The second shot is uphill to a green backed by a bunker and guarded by a fairway trap running from 70 yards to the left and below the green up to the putting surface.

The Equinox has earned a *Golf* magazine Silver Medal as one of the best golf resorts in America. The golf clubhouse has locker rooms and showers, a pro shop, and a modest restaurant called The Dormy Grill. Nearby is a putting green, but there is no practice range or bunkers. Magnificent views of the surrounding countryside can be seen from the clubhouse veranda. The region offers fly fishing on the Battenkill River, historical tours, antiquing, inns, and factory outlet stores. Down the road is the cemetery where Walter Travis is buried. When you play the Gleneagles, be sure to walk it. It's a real old-style pleasure.

Course Name: RUTLAND COUNTRY CLUB

Course Type: Semiprivate
Address: North Grove Street
Rutland, VT 05701
Phone: (802) 773–3254 (Pro Shop)
(802) 773–9153 (Clubhouse)

GOLF COURSE

Head Professional: Greg Nelson
Course Length/Par (All Tees): Back 6062/70, Middle 5701/70, Ladies' Forward 5368/71
Course Slope/Rating (All Tees): Back 125/70.6, Middle 122/69.1, Ladies' Forward 119/71.4
Course Architects: George Low, Sr. (9 holes, 1902), Wayne Stiles and John Van Kleek (added 9, remodeled original 9, 1927–28)
Golf Facilities: Full Pro Shop X, Snack Bar X, Lounge X, Restaurant X, Locker Room X, Showers X, Club Rental X, Club Repair X, Cart Rental X, Instruction X, Practice Green X, Driving Range X, Practice Bunker X, Club Storage X
Tee-Time Reservation Policy: Members: 1 day in advance. Outside play: same day
Ranger: Yes
Tee-off-Interval Time: 9 min.
Time to Play 18 Holes: 4 hrs.
Course Hours/Earliest Tee-off: 7 a.m.
Green Fees: $50 for 18 holes
Cart Fees: $13.50 for 18 holes per person
Credit Cards: MasterCard, Visa
Season: April 1 to Nov. 1. Busiest season June to Aug.
Course Comments: Can walk if playing with member. Yardage book available
Golf Packages: None
Discounts: After Oct.
Places to Stay Nearby: FAIR HAVEN: Vermont Marble Inn (802) 265–8333. - RUTLAND: Inn at Rutland (802) 773–0575; Holiday Inn (802) 775–1911, (800) HOLIDAY; Comfort Inn (802) 775–2200, (800) 228–5150; Best West-

ern (802) 773–3200, (800) 528–1234; Country Inns Along the Trail (inn reservation service) (802) 247–3300. BED AND BREAKFASTS: American–Vermont Bed and Breakfast Reservation Service (802) 827–3827
Local Attractions: Biking, canoeing, fishing, skiing, hiking, water sports, Vermont marble exhibit, crafts, New England Maple Museum, Chaffee Art Gallery, Wilson Castle, Plymouth Notch, antiquing, Killington Ski Area, Pico Peak Ski Area, Green Mountain National State Forest, Gifford Woods State Park, Half Moon State Park. MIDDLEBURY: Middlebury College, Johnson Art Gallery, Vermont State Craft Center. WOODSTOCK: Raptor Center, Billings Farm. Rutland Region Chamber of Commerce (802) 773–2747
Directions: Rte. 4 to Rutland, Rte. 7 north (1 mi.), take left onto Field Ave., golf course on right
Closest Commercial Airports: Rutland State (25 min.); Albany County, NY (1½ hrs.); Burlington International (1½ hrs.)

RUTLAND COUNTRY CLUB

The Rutland Country Club has the feel of an old, established, small-town New England country club, which it basically is. It is also rated the fourth best golf course in Vermont by *Golf Digest*. The original nine at Rutland was designed by George Low, Sr., and opened in 1902. Low was born in Carnoustie, Scotland, in 1874. He was runner-up in the 1899 United States Open and worked as a professional at Baltusrol in Springfield, New Jersey; Ekwanok in Manchester, Vermont; and Huntingdon Valley in Abington, Pennsylvania. He served as golf instructor to 2 U.S. presidents, William Howard Taft and Warren G. Harding. Low's first golf course design in the United States was the Rutland Country Club nine. He also designed the Echo Lake Country Club in Westfield, New Jersey, with Donald Ross; the Rodgers Forge Country Club in Baltimore, with Herbert Strong; the Hotel Champlain Golf Club in Lake Bluff, New York; and a few others. Low died in Clearwater, Florida, in 1950.

Wayne Stiles and Jon Van Kleek remodeled Low's original nine and added another nine during the late 1920s. By 1928 Rutland had a short but difficult eighteen-hole golf course. The 6062-yard par-70 layout has medium-sized to small, moderately fast, subtly undulating bentgrass greens that are well protected by sand traps. The front nine on the course is relatively open, but the back side is more tightly treed and hilly. It is always a possibility that you will be hitting off an uneven lie at Rutland. Course knowledge, course management, strategy, club selection and accuracy are essential. If you don't have good approach shots and a strong short game, it is hard to score here.

The run of holes from twelve to sixteen is the most difficult stretch on the course. The 203-yard par-3 twelfth plays to a deep, left-to-right and forward-sloping green protected on the left and right front by large traps. If you are bringing the ball in from left to right or right to left, it is very possible to catch the sand. A drop-off is to the left of the green, and there are very few level spots on or around the putting surface.

The 539-yard par-5 thirteenth, which plays uphill to a small, right-to-left-sloping, two-tiered green, is the longest hole on the course. It is made more difficult by the initial uphill climb and the three traps guarding the target. The small entranceway to the green is guarded by traps left and right. Shots coming onto this green tend to kick to the left.

The 366-yard par-4 fourteenth plays straight to a narrow, deep green with no sand traps but drop-offs all around. The 129-yard par-3 fifteenth has a narrow left-to-right and forward-sloping green guarded by large sand traps left and right. The first shot is from an elevated tee with a drop of 25 feet to the small target, which provides a tricky putting surface, especially if you land above the hole. There is a severe drop from the right side of the green, which will likely leave you a blind chip shot if you miss in that direction.

The sixteenth is often the decisive hole in match-play events held at the Rutland Country Club. From the tee you have beautiful views of the Rutland Mountains as you prepare to match wits with this 365-yard par-4 dogleg left that runs uphill to a medium-sized, left-to-right and forward-sloping green with a trap and drop-offs to the right. The tee shot has to avoid a fairway trap on the right, halfway to the green. Everything kicks to the right and breaks away from the mountains on this tricky test of golf. Anyone who slices off the tee is likely to have trouble on the sixteenth.

The clubhouse at Rutland has locker rooms and showers, complete dining facilities, a banquet room and a bar. There is an outdoor sitting area with beautiful views of this well-maintained golf oasis. A separate building contains the pro shop, and instruction is available. A driving range, practice green and practice bunker are available, so you can test your skills before enjoying a round.

Course Name: **STRATTON MOUNTAIN COUNTRY CLUB Forest, Lake, Mountain Courses**

Course Type: Semiprivate
Resort: Stratton Mountain Resort
Address: Stratton Mountain Access Road Stratton Mountain, VT 05155
Phone: (802) 297–4114, (802) 297–2200 (VT), (800) 843–6867 (outside VT) (Resort)

GOLF COURSE

Head Professional: David Rihm
Course Length/Par (All Tees):
Lake/Mountain: Back 6602/72, Middle 6117/72, Ladies' Forward 5410/74.
Forest/Lake: Back 6526/72, Middle 6044/72, Ladies' Forward 5153/74.
Mountain/Forest: Back 6478/72, Middle 6119/72, Ladies' Forward 5163/74
Course Slope/Rating (All Tees):
Lake/Mountain: Back 125/72, Middle 123/70.3, Ladies' Forward 116/70.7.
Forest/Lake: Back 125/71.2, Middle 122/69.4, Ladies' Forward 125/69.7.

Mountain/Forest: Back 126/71.2, Middle 123/69.3, Ladies' Forward 126/69.8

Course Architect: Lake, Mountain: Geoffrey Cornish (1965). Forest: Geoffrey Cornish (1986)

Golf Facilities: Full Pro Shop X, Snack Bar X, Lounge X, Restaurant X, Locker Room X, Showers X, Club Rental X, Club Repair X, Cart Rental X, Instruction X, Practice Green X, Driving Range X, Practice Bunker X, Club Storage X

Tee-Time Reservation Policy: Up to 2 weeks in advance

Ranger: Yes

Tee-off-Interval Time: 10 min.

Time to Play 18 Holes: 4½ hrs.

Course Hours/Earliest Tee-off: 7:30 a.m. to 6:00 p.m. (last tee-off)

Green Fees: Resort guests: $53 for 18 holes Fri., Sat., Sun., holidays, $35 for 9 holes; $46 for 18 holes Mon.-Thurs., $30 for 9 holes. Outside play: $66 for 18 holes Fri., Sat., Sun., holidays, $40 for 9 holes; $56 for 18 holes Mon.-Thurs., $35 for 9 holes

Cart Fees: $32 for 18 holes, $18 for 9 holes per cart

Pull Carts: $5 for 18 holes, $3 for 9 holes

Credit Cards: All major cards

Season: Mid-May to end of Oct.

Course Comments: Can walk during week. Yardage book available

Golf Packages: Available through lodging reservations system (800) 843–6867

Discounts: Juniors

Places to Stay Nearby: Stratton Area Lodging Service (802) 824–6915, (800) 677–7829. MANCHESTER: Equinox (802) 362–4700, (800) 362–4747. ARLINGTON: Arlington Inn (802) 375–6532. LONDON-DERRY: Londonderry Inn (802) 824–5226. BONDVILLE: Red Fox Inn (802) 297–2488. JAMAICA: Three Mountain Inn (802) 874–4140. DORSET: Inn at West View Farm (802) 867–5715

Local Attractions: Mountain biking, horseback riding, swimming, indoor and outdoor tennis, gondola rides, hiking, camping, boating, fishing, skiing, ice-skating, country fairs and festivals, Emerald Lake State Park, Hapgood

Pond Recreation Area, Jamaica State Park, Lake St. Catherine State Park, Shaftsbury State Park. MANCHESTER: Crafts and antiques, Dorset Theater, Southern Vermont Art Center, American Museum of Fly Fishing, restaurants, factory outlets, shopping

Directions: I–91 to Brattleboro, Rte. 30 west to town of Bondville, Stratton Access Rd.

Closest Commercial Airports: Rutland State (45 min.); Albany County, NY (2 hrs.); Burlington International (2½ hrs.); Bradley International, Hartford, CT (3 hrs.)

RESORT

Date Built: 1962

No. of Rooms: Stratton Mountain Inn: 125. Stratton Mountain Resort: 120. Stratton Mountain Lodge: 91. 1- to 4-bedroom villas, single and double rooms. Also a choice of other accommodations handled by central booking service

Meeting Rooms: 16. Capacity of Largest: 300 persons banquet style. Meeting Space: 30,000 sq. ft.

Room Price Range: $100 for 1-bedroom villa off season (May to June) to approximately $275 for a 4-bedroom villa peak golf season (July 5 to mid-Oct.). Tennis, golf, ski and other packages available

Lounges: At inns and restaurants nearby

Restaurants: Tenderloins at Stratton Mountain Country Club, Mulligan's Restaurant, Birkenhaus, La Pizzeria at Stratton Mountain Inn

Entertainment: At some local hotels and restaurants

Credit Cards: All major cards

General Amenities: Shopping in Stratton Village Square, Stratton Performing Arts Pavilion music programs, day-care center for children 6 wks. to 5 yrs. of age, day camp for children 6 to 12 yrs. of age (July–Aug.), meeting and conference facilities with audiovisual and food services

Recreational Amenities: 4 indoor and 15 outdoor clay, Har-Tru, Deco Turf II tennis courts, instruction; gondola rides, horseback riding, mountain biking, boating on Stratton Lake, racquetball; exercise room with Nautilus equipment and bicycles, StairMasters, rowing machines and other equipment

Reservation and Cancellation Policy: Deposit of 50% required to hold a reservation. More than 2-day cancellation notice prior to arrival date required to avoid major penalties. Minimum $50 fee per villa reservation assessed for any cancellation

Comments and Restrictions: 2 nights' minimum for all advance reservations. Children under 12 stay free with parents in same villa. Taxes and service charges additional

STRATTON MOUNTAIN COUNTRY CLUB

Stratton Mountain, 81 miles northeast of Albany, New York, is a year-round resort community featuring skiing and other activities in the winter and golf, tennis and a variety of other outdoor recreational activities at other times of the year. There are 27 holes of golf at Stratton, all designed by Geoffrey Cornish. As one might expect, this is a well-treed, hilly course that works its way through rugged Vermont terrain. The bentgrass greens at Stratton are large, moderately fast, and flat. Water in the form of streams and ponds comes into play on more than half the holes. The greens are well trapped, often in front, but there are relatively few fairway bunkers. These courses require strategy and accuracy rather than distance to score effectively.

The second hole on the Lake nine is one of the more challenging par 4s at Stratton. This 418-yard dogleg left plays to a large, oval green protected by a large bunker to the left front and a stream that runs across in front of the green. The tee shot should be to the right of a bunker guarding the left corner of the dogleg so that the approach shot can be flown into the green from approximately 175 yards away. Another good par 4 on this side is the 435-yard eighth, whose tee shot must carry a stream that cuts the fairway approximately 200 yards from the back tees. The approach shot is to a medium-sized, elevated green

well protected by two bunkers to the right and another to the left front. Trees protect the green to the rear, and Stratton Lake is farther to the left.

One of the more memorable holes on the Mountain nine is the 621-yard par-5 fifth, the longest par 5 in Vermont. The tee is slightly elevated, and a stream guards the right fairway most of the way to the green. Two other streams cut the fairway approximately 200 yards and 100 yards from the green. Two straight shots that avoid these hazards and the surrounding trees will leave you with a short- to medium-iron approach to a narrow, elevated, deep green guarded by two bunkers to the right and another to the left. Most golfers are very happy with a par on this test of endurance.

The finishing hole on the Forest nine is another one of the many quality par 4s at Stratton. The tee shot should be kept to the right because the fairway slopes downward to the left. The approach is to a medium-sized green with two bunkers guarding the front and another to the rear. Position off the tee and an accurate approach shot are required to reach this green in regulation.

The clubhouse at Stratton provides locker rooms, showers, a restaurant, bar and pro shop. Instruction is available for groups or individuals. Nearby is the home of the excellent Stratton Golf School, whose facilities, situated on 22 acres, were designed expressly for golf instruction by Arnold Palmer and Geoffrey Cornish. There are 2 large target greens, wide fairway areas, traps and an expansive putting green for chipping and putting practice. Classroom facilities and shelters for practice in rainy weather are located here. A variety of weekend and 2- and 5-day midweek teaching sessions are held at the Stratton Golf School from May through September. Video and photo swing analysis are included in this program, which has a low student-to-instructor ratio and affords access to the 27-hole Stratton Mountain Country Club Course. Accommodations are available at on-site villas, or golfers can arrange for their own housing.

For those golfers playing the Stratton Mountain courses, accommodations are available in 1- to 4-bedroom villas within the real-estate development. These can be rented through a central rental office (800) 843–6867, or accommodations can be arranged at inns or hotels in the area. A variety of restaurants is located within walking distance of the villas. Stratton Village has numerous retail shops, and the nearby towns of Manchester, Manchester Village, Arlington, Weston, South Londonderry and others offer many restaurants, antique stores, historic buildings and other attractions.

Stratton has an excellent 19-court tennis facility with instruction available, and there is a fitness center with Nautilus and other exercise equipment. Other recreational activities such as horseback riding, racquetball, swimming, boating, bicycling, hiking, camping and fishing are available. There is also a variety of meeting facilities at different sites within the development. The Stratton Mountain Resort has been given a Four-Star rating by the *Mobil Travel Guide*.

The Stratton Mountain Country Club is the annual site of the Stratton Mountain LPGA Classic, held here in August every year. Recently, more than $500,000 was spent to improve the golf course for this event. For ticket information contact (802) 297–2200, (800) 843–6867.

Course Name: SUGARBUSH GOLF COURSE

Course Type: Resort
Resort: Sugarbush Inn
Address: Sugarbush Access Road
P.O. Box 307
Warren, VT 05674
Phone: (802) 583–2722 (Golf Course)
(802) 583–2301,
(800) 451–4320 (Resort)
Fax: (802) 583–6303

GOLF COURSE

Head Professional: Michael Aldridge
Course Length/Par (All Tees): Back 6524/72, Middle 5886/70, Ladies' Forward 5187/72

Course Slope/Rating (All Tees): Back 128/71.7, Middle 122/69, Ladies' Forward NA/NA
Course Architect: Robert Trent Jones, Sr. (1963)
Golf Facilities: Full Pro Shop X, Snack Bar X, Lounge X, Restaurant X, Locker Room X, Showers X, Club Rental X, Club Repair X, Cart Rental X, Instruction X, Practice Green X, Driving Range X, Practice Bunker X, Club Storage X
Tee-Time Reservation Policy: Resort guests: At time of reservation. Outside play: 1 day in advance
Ranger: Yes
Tee-off-Interval Time: 10 min.
Time to Play 18 Holes: 4 hrs., 15 min.
Course Hours/Earliest Tee-off: 6:30 a.m. to dusk
Green Fees: Peak season (mid-June to closing): $49 for 18 holes Fri., Sat., Sun., holidays; $40 for 18 holes weekdays
Cart Fees: $15 for 18 holes per person
Pull Carts: $5 for 18 holes, $2.50 for 9 holes
Credit Cards: All major cards
Season: Mid-May to late Oct.
Course Comments: Can walk anytime
Golf Packages: Available through Sugarbush Inn
Discounts: Monthly green pass, juniors (ages 7–17), seasonal (opening to mid-June). Twilight rates after 4 p.m.
Places to Stay Nearby: WARREN: Beaver Pond Farm Inn (802) 583–2861; Seasons Condominium (802) 496–SNOW; Golden Lion Riverside Inn (802) 496–3084; Christmas Tree Inn and Condominiums (802) 583–2211; Pitcher Inn (802) 496–3831. WATERBURY: Holiday Inn at Waterbury–Stowe (802) 244–7822, (800) HOLIDAY; Inn at Thatcher Brook Falls (802) 244–5911, (800) 292–5911. WAITSFIELD: Mad River Inn (802) 496–7900; Waitsfield Inn (802) 496–3979; Inn at Round Barn Farm (802) 496–2276
Local Attractions: Crafts, antiques, restaurants, hiking, boating, fishing, camping, skiing and other sports, soaring, horse-

back riding, Green Mountain National Forest, tennis, covered bridges. Sugarbush Area Chamber of Commerce (802) 496–3409, (800) 828–4748

Directions: Rte. 100 to Sugarbush Access Rd. (north of Warren), west on Sugarbush Access Rd. to Inn and golf course. Follow the signs

Closest Commercial Airports: Burlington International (1 hr.); Albany County, NY (3 hrs.); Dorval International, Montreal, Canada (3 hrs.); Logan International, Boston, MA (4 hrs.)

RESORT

Date Built: 1961

No. of Rooms: 46 rooms and suites. Country Townhome: 1-, 2-, and 3-bedroom townhouses

Meeting Rooms: 7. Capacity of Largest: 200 persons banquet style. Meeting Space: 5664 sq. ft.

Room Price Range: Approximately $95 for standard inn room value season (April 15 to mid-June) to over $485 for 3-bedroom Townhome, 2 nights, peak season (July 1 to Oct. 20). Golf, tennis, skiing and other packages available

Lounges: Grille Down Under, Tap Room, Knickers

Restaurants: Terrace Restaurant, Grille Down Under, Knickers Cafe (at golf course)

Entertainment: Live music periodically at Knickers Cafe, peak season. Night clubs in area

Credit Cards: American Express, MasterCard, Visa

General Amenities: Day-care facilities, outdoor recreation, education and adventure camps for ages 6 to 17 in summer, babysitting referral service, meeting and conference facilities with audiovisual and food services

Recreational Amenities: Sports Pavilion with 11 Har-Tru and clay tennis courts; Sugarbush Sports Center with racquetball, squash, aerobics; Club Sugarbush with indoor pool, weight room, Jacuzzi, sauna; horseback riding, hiking, fishing, boating, bicycling

Reservation and Cancellation Policy: 50% deposit due within 10 days from the date reservation is made. Deposit refunded, less $25 cancellation fee, provided cancellation received 14 days prior to scheduled arrival date

Comments and Restrictions: No pets allowed. Taxes additional to basic rates

SUGARBUSH GOLF COURSE

The Sugarbush Golf Course is a Robert Trent Jones, Sr.–designed 6524-yard par-72 layout cut through Vermont mountain forest just north of Warren. Warren has a land area of 27,350 acres and is located in the Mad River Valley, where pioneers carved their farms out of hillsides beginning from the late 1700s. The town now has approximately 1100 people, and tourism is its main industry. The Sugarbush Golf Course was built to increase the year-round recreational enjoyment in this noteworthy ski resort area.

The Sugarbush Golf Course has rolling hills; tightly treed fairways; medium-sized, moderately fast, undulating greens; and relatively few bunkers. There are many blind shots caused by doglegs and the natural flow of the terrain. My favorite hole on this course is the 570-yard par-5 second, a blind dogleg right that winds downhill from an elevated tee. The left side of the fairway has deep rough, trees and drop-offs. The right side features rock outcroppings, trees and rough. On the tee shot you have to avoid hitting the ball out of bounds, then on your second shot, which is usually from a downhill lie, you have to reach a flat landing area approximately 150 yards from the green. The approach is slightly uphill to a medium-sized, rolling green with a trap to the front left.

A memorable par 3 at Sugarbush is the 182-yard eleventh, which plays from an elevated tee to a small green guarded by a pond and a trap to the front left. The shallow target is set in a wooded hillside, allowing no margin for error.

As you wend your way through the course, there are many beautiful vistas of the surrounding Green Mountains. You can walk the course, but you have to be in good shape to do it. The narrow fairways, trees, uneven lies, blind target areas, and strategically placed bunkers and tricky greens make it difficult to score here. But after playing Sugarbush, because of its challenge and beauty, you will want to come back again.

The Sugarbush Inn offers a choice of rooms or suites. Adjacent to the inn are 1- to 3-bedroom townhouses. Casual and formal meals are available at 3 restaurants at the inn and golf course. Recreational amenities include 11 tennis courts (6 Har-Tru, 5 red clay) with instruction available, and a swimming pool, saunas, Jacuzzi, and weight room are available at the nearby fitness center. Other activities including fishing, boating, hiking, bicycling, skiing, and camping are popular in this area. Sugarbush also has meeting and conference facilities for groups of up to 200 people.

A variety of special offers is available at Sugarbush, including tennis, golf, skiing, autumn leaf tour and other packages. *Tennis* magazine has rated Sugarbush one of the 50 greatest U.S. tennis resorts. Twenty-five additional courts, besides the 11 at the inn, are available to tennis players.

Recommended Golf Courses in Vermont

Within 1 Hour of Brattleboro:

Haystack Golf Course, Wilmington, (802) 464–8301, Semiprivate, 18/6549/72

Mount Snow Golf Club, West Dover, (802) 464–5642, (800) 451–4211, Resort, 18/6894/72

Within 1 Hour of Burlington:

Basin Harbor Club, Vergennes, (802) 475–2309, Resort, 18/6513/72

Stowe Country Club, Stowe, (802) 253–4893, Public, 18/6206/72

Williston Golf Club, Williston, (802) 878–3747, Public, 18/5604/69

Within 1 Hour of Montpelier:

Country Club of Barre, Barre, (802) 476–7658, Public, 18/6191/71

Within 1 Hour of Rutland:

Crown Point Country Club, Springfield, (802) 885–1010, Semiprivate, 18/6572/72

Killington Golf Course, Killington, (802) 422–6700, (800) 343–0762, Resort, 18/6327/72

Manchester Country Club, Manchester, (802) 362–3148, Private (accessible to local hotel guests), 18/6724/72

Proctor-Pittsford Country Club, Pittsford, (802) 483–9379, Public, 18/6052/70

Quechee Club, Quechee, (802) 295–6245, Private (accessible to residents of Quechee properties, guests). Highland: 18/6765/72. Lakeland: 18/6569/72

Woodstock Country Club, Woodstock, (802) 457–6674, (800) 448–7900, Semiprivate, 18/6001/69

Vermont: Useful Information

Vermont Travel Division, 134 State St., Montpelier, VT 05601, (802) 828–3239

Vermont Chamber of Commerce, Department of Travel and Tourism, P.O. Box 37, Montpelier, VT 05601, (802) 223–3443

National Forest Service, Forest Supervisor, Green Mountain National Forest, Rutland, VT 05701, (802) 773–0300, (800) 280–CAMP (national forest information and reservations)

Fish and Wildlife Division, Agency of Natural Resources, 103 South Main St., Waterbury, VT 05676, (802) 244–8711 (recreation information, fishing and hunting regulations)

Country Inns Along the Trail, Churchill House Inn, RR 3, P.O. Box 3265, Brandon, VT 05733, (802) 247–3300 (organizes inn-to-inn vacations)

Northeastern and Washington, DC Area

Course Name: LANDSDOWNE GOLF CLUB

Course Type: Resort
Resort: Landsdowne Conference Resort
Address: 44050 Woodridge Parkway
Leesburg, VA 22075
Phone: (703) 729–8400 (Golf Course)
(703) 729–8400,
(800) 541–4801 (Resort)
Fax: (703) 729–4096 (Resort)

GOLF COURSE

Director of Recreation: Bill Chandler
Course Length/Par (All Tees): Back 7057/72, Blue 6552/72, White 5954/72, Forward 5213/72
Course Slope/Rating (All Tees): Back 130/74.0, Blue 126/71.5, White 121/69.0, Ladies' Forward 134/75.0
Course Architect: Robert Trent Jones, Jr. (1991)
Golf Facilities: Full Pro Shop X, Snack Bar X, Lounge X, Restaurant X, Locker Room X, Showers X, Club Rental X, Club Repair No, Cart Rental X, Instruction X, Practice Green X, Driving Range X, Practice Bunker X, Club Storage X
Tee-Time Reservation Policy: Must be a resort guest, member or member of prearranged group outing to play the course. Hotel guests can reserve at time of confirmed reservation
Ranger: Yes
Tee-off-Interval Time: 7 to 10 min.
Time to Play 18 Holes: 4½ hrs.
Course Hours/Earliest Tee-off: 7 a.m.
Green and Cart Fees: $90 for 18 holes with cart Fri., Sat., Sun., holidays; $80 for 18 holes with cart weekdays
Credit Cards: All major cards
Season: Yr. round. Busiest season April to June
Course Comments: Cart mandatory. Yardage book available. Must be a resort guest, member or part of planned golf outing to play the course
Golf Packages: Available through resort. Rates not seasonal for individuals.
Seasonal packages for groups of more than 40
Discounts: None
Places to Stay Nearby: Must be a guest of Landsdowne or part of a golf outing to play the course. Colonial Inn of Leesburg (703) 777–5000; Carradoc Hall Inn (703) 771–9200, (800) 552–6702; Best Western Leesburg (703) 777–9400; Algonkian Regional Park (703) 352–5906
Local Attractions: Loudoun Museum, Morven Park, Old Stone Church, historic Leesburg tours, garden tours, seasonal festivals and crafts fairs, steeplechase horse racing, Algonkian Regional Park, Washington and Old Dominion Railroad Regional Park, Oak Hill, Oatlands Plantation Mansion, winery tours, Willowcraft Farm Vineyards, Manassas and Civil War sites, Washington, DC. County of Loudoun Visitor Bureau (703) 777–0519, (800) 752–6118
Directions: From Capital Beltway: Rte. 7 (Leesburg Pike) west 18 mi. Pass Ashburn Village on left, turn right on to Landsdowne Blvd., right onto Woodridge Pkwy. to golf course. From Dulles International (8 mi.): Rte. 28 (Sully Rd.) north to Rte. 7, west on Rte. 7, 4 mi., right onto Landsdowne Blvd., right onto Woodridge Pkwy. to golf course
Closest Commercial Airports: Dulles International, Washington, DC (20 min.); Baltimore–Washington International (1 hr.); Philadelphia International, PA (2 hrs.); Richmond International (2½ hrs.)

RESORT

Date Built: 1991
No. of Rooms: 305, including 14 executive suites
Meeting Rooms: 25. Capacity of Largest: 900 persons. Meeting Space: 45,000 sq. ft.
Room Price Range: $149 for 1-room, single or double occupancy, to $169 for 1-room, double occupancy, standard rate. Golf packages and other special rates available
Lounge: Stonewalls
Restaurants: Riverside Hearth, Potomac Grille, Fairways (seasonal)

Entertainment: For special events and groups

Credit Cards: All major cards

General Amenities: Meeting and conference facilities with audiovisual, food-service and secretarial-support capabilities

Recreational Amenities: 5 lighted tennis courts, squash, racquetball, volleyball, indoor and outdoor swimming pools, executive fitness center, bicycling, horseback riding, billiards, snooker

Reservation and Cancellation Policy: Credit card or cash deposit to hold reservation. 24-hr. cancellation prior to arrival date for full refund

Comments and Restrictions: Pets not allowed. Taxes additional to base rates

LANDSDOWNE GOLF CLUB

The Landsdowne Conference Resort is situated on 205 acres located within a 2267-acre multiuse development along the Potomac River in Virginia hunt country 25 miles northwest of Washington, D.C. The resort offers 305 deluxe guest rooms, including 14 suites; 45,000 square feet of total conference space, including a 124-seat tiered amphitheater and various meeting rooms; recreational amenities, including 5 lighted outdoor tennis courts, squash and racquetball courts, a men's and women's health club with Heartline exercise equipment, outdoor volleyball courts, indoor and outdoor swimming pools, whirlpools and massage treatment rooms. There are 2 restaurants, the Potomac Grille and Riverside Hearth, featuring regional American cuisine. And there is a tavern with billiards, snooker, a laser juke box and a large-screen television.

The restaurants overlook the 7040-yard par-72 Robert Trent Jones, Jr., golf course which was opened in 1991. The bentgrass greens are large, moderately fast and undulating. The fairways are generally bordered by mature trees and water comes into play on only three holes. The number-1-handicap hole is the 442-yard par-4 sixth, which plays straight and slightly uphill to a deep, narrow green protected by a huge bunker on the right. The tee shot has to be straight and must avoid three large bunkers on the left. This hole generally plays into the wind, which makes it extremely long. In fact, wind plays a major role on the entire golf course, especially the more open front nine.

A formidable par 5 on the front side is the 610-yard fifth, which plays straight to a deep green with small traps to the right front and left. Trees line the fairway on the left coming into the green. Your third shot is downhill, however, which should ease the pain on this hole.

The par-3-holes at Landsdowne tend to play long and tough. A beautiful par 3 is the 203-yard fifteenth, which is all carry over water to a large, crowned green with a trap to the left and forward. The only bail-out area here is to the left. If the wind is blowing toward you, as it often is, clearing the water is not easy.

The finishing hole is a 401-yard par 4 that plays to a large green 100 feet higher than the tee, adding considerable distance to the hole. The tee shot is steeply uphill and has to clear large bunkers to the left of the fairway landing area, which is well protected by trees. Many consider this the most difficult hole on the course, but others think that sixteen is equally difficult. This 417-yard dogleg left is well treed, and a stream borders the left fairway. The approach shot is severely uphill to a deep, three-tiered green well guarded by traps left and right. The back nine is almost a different course from the front in that it winds through woods and has some beautiful stone walls, streams and water hazards. There are some severe elevation changes on this side. I especially liked the 210-yard par-5 thirteenth, which plays down to a large, wide green banked and trapped in back with a severe drop-off on the left.

There is a variety of golf packages at Landsdowne and individual instruction is available from the staff. The conference center has a complete pro shop, restaurant and bar, and locker rooms and showers with sauna and steam rooms for ladies and gentlemen. A putting green and chipping and sand bunker practice area are located outside. The Potomac Grille has an excellent wine and beer list, as well as an excellent selection of Scottish single-malt whiskeys. The menu includes everything from deep-fried squid with parsley, lemon and red pepper rémoulade to barbecued baby-back ribs.

Memberships are available at the Landsdowne Golf Club, or you can play as part of an outing or as a regular guest of the resort. Landsdowne is convenient to Washington, Baltimore and Philadelphia, filling a need for quality, accessible golf in that area. The living quarters, or hotel rooms, are upstairs in the multistory Landsdowne Conference Center building, and the leisure areas, including the recreational facilities, are on the lower floors.

The operating theme of the Benchmark Organization, which manages Landsdowne, is "Living, Learning, and Leisure." These areas are separate entities within the facility. The conference and meeting area has a wide variety of facilities to meet every conceivable conference need. For inspiration, many of the meeting rooms are named for people such as David Sarnoff, William Faulkner and James Thurber. The quote from Sarnoff on the plaque next to his room: "What the human mind can conceive and believe, it can accomplish." Or from James Thurber: "It's better to ask some of the questions than know all the answers." Many of these concepts apply to golf.

Recommended Golf Courses in Virginia

Within 1 Hour of Washington, DC:

Fairfax:

Penderbrook Golf Club, Fairfax, (703) 383–3700, Public, 18/6152/71

Fredericksburg Area:

The Greens at Fredericksburg, Fredericksburg, (703) 786–8385, Public. No.1: 18/7155/72. No.2: 18/6790/72

Lee's Hill Golfers Club, Fredericksburg, (703) 891–0111, (800) 930–3636, Public, 18/6805/72

Meadow Farms, Locust Grove, (703) 854–9890, Public, 18/7005/72

Gainesville:

Virginia Oaks Golf and Country Club, Gainesville, (703) 551–2103, Public, 18/6925/72

Lorton:

Pohick Bay Regional Golf Course, Lorton, (703) 339–8585, Public, 18/6405/72

Reston:

Hidden Creek Golf Club, Reston, (703) 437–4222, Semiprivate, 18/6704/71

Reston National Golf Course, Reston, (703) 620–9333, Public, 18/6871/71

Richmond Area

Recommended Golf Courses in Virginia

Within 1 Hour of Richmond:

The Crossings, Glen Allen, (804) 261–0000, Public, 18/6619/72

Mill Quarter Plantation, Powhatan, (804) 598–4221, Public, 18/6944/72

River's Bend Country Club, Chester, (804) 530–1000, Semiprivate, 18/6671/71

Sycamore Creek Golf Course, Manakin Sahot, (804) 784–3544, Public, 18/6256,70

Western Virginia Area

Course Name: THE HOMESTEAD Cascades, Lower Cascades, Homestead Courses

Course Type: Resort
Resort: The Homestead
Address: U.S. 220
Hot Springs, VA 24445
Phone: (703) 839–5660 (Cascades)
(703) 839–5500,
(800) 542–5734 (VA),
(800) 336–5771 (outside VA) (Resort)
Fax: (703) 839–7656 (Resort)

GOLF COURSE

Director of Golf: Wayne Nooe

Head Professionals: Cascades: Barry Carpenter. Lower Cascades: Bobby Fry. Homestead: Don Ryder

Course Length/Par (All Tees): Cascades: Back 6566/70, Middle 6282/70, Ladies' Forward 5488/71. Lower Casades: Back 6619/72, Middle 6240/72, Front 4726/70. Homestead: Back 5957/71, Ladies' Forward 5150/72

Course Slope/Rating (All Tees): Cascades: Back 136/72.9, Middle 134/71.6, Forward 127/67.8, Ladies' Middle NA/76.3, Ladies' Forward 137/71.6. Lower Cascades: Back 127/72.2, Middle 124/70.4, Front 116/66.7, Ladies' Middle NA/74.6, Ladies' Forward 116/65.5. Homestead: Back 121/68.2, Forward 115/68.7, Ladies' Back NA/74.4, Ladies' Forward 115/70

Course Architects: Cascades: William S. Flynn (1924), Robert Trent Jones, Sr. (renovation, 1961). Lower Cascades: Robert Trent Jones, Sr. (1963). Homestead: Donald Ross (1892), William S. Flynn (renovation, 1924)

Golf Facilities: Full Pro Shop X, Snack Bar X, Lounge X, Restaurant X, Locker Room X, Showers X, Club Rental X, Club Repair X, Cart Rental X, Instruction X, Practice Green X, Driving Range X, Practice Bunker X, Club Storage X

Tee-Time Reservation Policy: Resort guests: At time of reservation at resort through hotel central starting system. Outside play: Up to 7 days in advance

Ranger: Yes

Tee-off-Interval Time: Cascades: 10 min. Homestead, Lower Cascades: 8 min.

Time to Play 18 Holes: Cascades: 5 hrs. Lower Cascades: 4 hrs., 15 min. Homestead: 4 hrs.

Course Hours/Earliest Tee-off: 7:04 a.m. 6 p.m. last tee-off in summer months Lower Cascades, Homestead

Green Fees: Cascades: $100 for 18 holes with cart. Homestead, Lower Cascades: $75 for 18 holes with cart. Homestead: $38 for 9 holes with cart

Cart Fees: $18 for 18 holes per person

Credit Cards: All major cards

Season: April through Nov.

Course Comments: Cart mandatory, or you may take a caddie and walk. Yardage book available. 9-hole rate on Homestead only after 5 p.m.

Golf Packages: Available through resort

Discounts: Through golf packages

Places to Stay Nearby: HOT SPRINGS: Cascades Inn (703) 839–5355. LEXINGTON: Historic Country Inns. Alexander–Withrow House, McCambeel Inn, Maple Hall (703) 463–2044. WARM SPRINGS: Inn at Gristmill Square (703) 839–2231. Staunton: Frederick House (703) 885–4220

Local Attractions: LEXINGTON: Virginia Military Institute, Washington and Lee University, Stonewall Jackson house. CHARLOTTESVILLE: University of Virginia. Monticello, Warm Springs pools, Staunton. Montpelier. Roanoke. Bath County Chamber of Commerce (703) 839–5409

Directions: U.S. Rte. 220 runs north and south through Hot Springs. The Homestead is 20 mi. from I–64 and 60 mi. from I–81. Take U.S. Rte. 220 exit from I–64, proceed north on Rte. 220 to resort

Closest Commercial Airports: Lewisburg, WV (1 hr.); Roanoke Municipal (1½ hrs.); Albemarle, Charlottesville (2 hrs.); Dulles International, Washington, DC (4½ hrs.)

RESORT

Date Built: 1766

No. of Rooms: 600 guest rooms, including 75 parlor suites

Meeting Rooms: 26. Capacity of Largest: 1000 persons. Meeting Space: 51,284 sq. ft.

Room Price Range: $263 to $337, single occupancy, peak season (mid-Apr. to early Nov.), including breakfast and dinner

Lounge: The View Lounge

Restaurants: Cafe Albert, Cascades Club, Casino, Dining Room, Grille, Lower Cascades Club, Sam Snead's Tavern, Ski Lodge Restaurant, Snack Bar

Entertainment: Disco music and dancing in Homestead Club, live orchestra music in the Dining Room, pianist in the Grille

Credit Cards: American Express, Master-Card, Visa

General Amenities: Babysitting services, shopping, movies, afternoon tea, tennis shop, photographer; full meeting and conference capabilities including audiovisual, food service and secretarial support; supervised children's playground, local tours

Recreational Amenities: Bowling, carriage rides, dancing, fishing, hiking, horseback riding, ice-skating (Olympic-sized rink), lawn bowling, skeet shooting, skiing; spa with baths, steam, sauna, massage and fitness center; swimming, 2 outdoor pools, 1 indoor pool; sand beach, warm springs pools; tennis including 15 Har-Tru and 4 all-weather courts with professional instruction; indoor games including table tennis, billiards, bridge, canasta, backgammon, checkers, chess, puzzles; archery, badminton, bowling

Reservation and Cancellation Policy: Credit card guarantee required to hold reservation. Cancellation must be made 14 days prior to arrival or up to 6 p.m. the day of arrival if reservation made inside of 14 days to avoid penalties

Comments and Restrictions: Men required to wear coat and tie in the dining room and jackets only in the Grille, Homestead Club and all public areas after 7 p.m. Modified American plan including breakfast and dinner optional. Infant to 12-yr.-old child in room with parents no charge. Additional charge for person 13 yrs. and up

THE HOMESTEAD

The Homestead, a 600-room national historic landmark hotel, is situated on 15,000 acres of land at 2500 feet above sea level in a beautiful valley of the Allegheny Mountains. The area was first noted for its warm-spring spas, and everyone from American Indians to Thomas Jefferson and 9 other presidents have stayed here. Originally valued for medicinal purposes, the springs became more and more valued as centers for pleasure and social activity. In 1760 the Homestead's status as a resort began officially, when Thomas Bullit in partnership with Andrew Lewis obtained a deed for the Hot Springs tract of some 300 acres. In 1876 the first hotel was built on the site. Over the years the hotel passed through a number of hands until in 1891 a group of financiers under the leadership of Chesapeake and Ohio Railway president M. E. Ingalls purchased the hotel and land including the Hot Springs. Subsequently the Warm Springs, Healing Springs and other parcels were added, creating today's Homestead Resort. The Ingalls family still owns and manages the resort.

Two of the golf courses, the Cascades, designed by William Flynn and opened in 1924, and the Lower Cascades, designed by Robert Trent Jones, Sr., and opened in 1963, are ranked among the best resort courses in the United States by *Golf Digest, Golf* magazine and other publications. The Homestead is steeped in golf tradition. Sam Snead grew up within walking distance of the Homestead and worked here before going on to win a record 84 PGA titles. Glenna Collett Vare, one of the greatest of all women golfers, defeated Virginia Van Wie 11 to 10, to win the Women's U.S. Amateur Championship at the Cascades course in 1928. The Cascades has been the site of many other major golf tournaments, including the Curtis Cup, the U.S. Women's Open, the State Amateur, the U.S. Senior Amateur, and the Men's U.S. Amateur. Sam Snead returned to the golf staff at the Homestead in 1975 after working for many years at the nearby Greenbrier in White Sulphur Springs, West Virginia.

The Cascades is just down the road from the spectacular Kentucky brick resort hotel, whose great entrance hall is 42 feet wide, 211 feet long, and 22½ feet high. A clock tower at the top of the hotel can be seen for miles around. The building of the Cascades was prompted in April, 1923, when some of the resort's directors were held up by slow play on the original Homestead Course. They decided to build another course and hired William S. Flynn, who had worked on Pine Valley, to design it. This was the first distinguished golf course Flynn designed himself. He had assisted Hugh Wilson with completion of the East Course at Merion in 1909 and worked on other projects. He then went on to design the Seaview Golf Club's Pines Course (9 holes) in Absecon, New Jersey; and the Shinnecock Hills Golf Course in Southampton, Long Island; and the Boca Raton Hotel North Course in Florida, with Howard Toomey. He also designed and remodeled numerous other courses, primarily in the Eastern United States.

The Cascades Course plays 6566 yards from the back tees and is a well treed, rolling, up-and-down course with very little water. The medium-sized, fast greens are well protected by traps and trees. The course makes you play every club in the bag and requires the ability to play from a variety of downhill, sidehill and uphill lies. The number-1-handicap hole is the 576-yard par-5 fifth, which is completely bordered by trees on the right from the tee to the small, narrow green protected by traps to the left and back. A pair of fairway bunkers guards the tee-shot landing area on the left, and if you are too far right you are likely to have a blind uphill and sidehill wood shot out of the rough. There are few flat spots on this fairway.

The ninth is a tough, 450-yard par 4 with a spectacular view from the highly elevated tee across a ravine and a valley to a plateaued landing area. Anything short on the tee shot leaves you a blind second shot to a medium-sized, round, undulating green that sits in a valley and is surrounded by trees and traps to the left, back and right. A pretty par 3 on the front nine is the 198-yard fourth, which plays from an elevated tee to large green with traps left and rear. A small fairway area is in front of the green, and an errant shot left, back or right will catch sand or trees.

Perhaps the most difficult par 4 on the course is the 476-yard par-4 twelfth, a dogleg left down a well-treed tight fairway to a long, narrow green with traps on both sides. The second shot is a wood or a long

iron that can catch any of the three fairway traps located approximately 50 to 75 yards from the green. After two more demanding par 4s comes the tough, 213-yard par-3 fifteenth, with a tee shot out of a tunnel of pines and straight to a deep, tiered green protected by traps on the left and right. There is also an overhanging tree on the right. After back-to-back par 5s, the Cascades closes with a beautiful par 3 playing 192 yards from an elevated tee over a small lake to an elevated green with traps to the left and right front.

Although the Cascades doesn't play overly long, the well-treed fairways, uneven lies, hills and well-trapped greens make this course a beautiful and difficult challenge. At the USGA's request the fairways were widened for the 1988 U.S. Amateur, but they are back to normal (tight) now. Treed alleyways of pine, oak, maple, hemlock, beech, and others can make this a trying experience.

The Lower Cascades is also a short drive from the main hotel and is a few miles from the Cascades Course. This Robert Trent Jones, Sr., layout plays 6663 yards from the back tees and was also the site of the 1988 U.S. Amateur, as well as many other national and state tournaments. The Lower Cascades is more open than the Cascades and has over 70 large Robert Trent Jones traps. It is best to be conservative here and put away your driver, especially on holes nine, ten, sixteen and eighteen, where tee-shot placement is more crucial than distance. On the ninth, a 413-yard par-4 dogleg left, you can cut the corner over the top with a 3-wood, for example, or you can play straight to the right side of the dogleg. When you get to this, or any green on the Lower Cascades, try to keep below the hole. These fast, sloping bentgrass greens are kept between 9 and 10 on the stimpmeter. The 450-yard par-4 third hole is probably the most difficult hole on the course. A dogleg right, with trees on the right, this hole is long and uphill to the contoured green.

Sam Snead, who still often plays this course, claims that he makes many of his bogeys on the 357-yard par-4 tenth, which is a dogleg left. He suggests a 3- or 4-wood or a 1-iron off the tee. The green, which is relatively flat, should not be hard to reach on the second shot as long as the tee shot is well positioned. The finishing hole is the 379-yard par-4 eighteenth, a dogleg left over a creek to a green protected by a trap on the left. Many golfers lay up before the creek—which is approximately 240 yards from the tee. The narrow, forward-sloping green is protected on the right by large walnut trees.

The Homestead course was originally designed by Donald Ross and was built in 1892. It is said to have the longest "continuously operating tee in America" and is still open for play. A shorter course than the other two, this one plays 5957 yards from the back and 5150 yards from the front tees. The Homestead was the first golf course in Virginia, and in 1909 William Howard Taft, America's first "golfing" president, played this venerable layout, which was redesigned in 1924 by William S. Flynn. A favorite hole here is the short, 298-yard par-4 third, which is straight downhill to a typically small, old-style green.

Each golf course has its own clubhouse, locker rooms, pro shop, golf equipment rentals, and putting greens. Individual and group instruction is available from the staff of 3 head professionals. A variety of golf, tennis and other packages is available at the Homestead, with the season being April through November. There is a driving range near the Cascades Inn, which is within 1500 yards of the Cascades Course and is a favorite place for golfers. The inn is an informal, 100-year-old establishment in the hamlet of Healing Springs. It has a dining room, glassed-in lounge, spacious lawns and a swimming pool.

The Homestead itself is a year-round *Mobil Travel Guide* Five-Star Resort and offers every activity under the sun in addition to its internationally recognized golf facilities. The "Springs of Virginia," once compared to Baden-Baden in Germany and Bath in England at the height of the spa heyday, are still here, and skiing, horseback riding, trout fishing, skeet and trap shoot-

ing, sporting clays, archery, lawn bowling, a health club/exercise spa, warm springs pools and swimming pools, 19 tennis courts and indoor games are available along with over 100 miles of hiking and riding trails. The various dining facilities offer elegant and informal cuisine and include dining facilities at the golf course. Dancing can be enjoyed in the dining room and Homestead Club. Within driving distance are numerous historical sites such as Thomas Jefferson's Monticello. And the countryside, including the Blue Ridge Mountains, provides some of the most beautiful landscapes in America.

The Homestead is one of the few resorts to receive *Golf* magazine's Gold Medal Award as one of the best golf resorts in America. This is truly a unique place. Where else can you go to visit a national historic landmark building with a men's pool supposedly designed by Thomas Jefferson, two top-ranked golf courses, and 15,000 acres of beautiful land where Woodrow Wilson spent his second honeymoon and John D. Rockefeller flipped dimes into the fountains?

Course Name: WINTERGREEN RESORT Stoney Creek, Devil's Knob Courses

Course Type: Resort
Resort: Wintergreen
Address: Route 664 West/P.O. Box 706 Wintergreen, VA 22958
Phone: (804) 325–2200, (800) 325–2200 (Resort)
Fax: (804) 325–6760 (Resort)

GOLF COURSE

Director of Golf: Mike Mayer
Head Professional: Devil's Knob: Lance Reynolds. Stoney Creek: Chris Warring. Golf Academy: Scott Ezell
Course Length/Par (All Tees): Stoney Creek: Championship 7005/72, Back 6740/72, Middle 6312/72, Forward 5500/72. Devil's Knob: Back 6576/70, Middle 6003/70, Forward 5101/70
Course Slope/Rating (All Tees): Stoney Creek: Championship 132/74, Back

126/72.6, Middle 121/71.6, Ladies' Forward 125/71. Devil's Knob: Back 126/72.4, Middle 119/69.8, Forward 118/68.6

Course Architects: Stoney Creek: Rees Jones (1988). Devil's Knob: Ellis Maples (1976)

Golf Facilities: Full Pro Shop X, Snack Bar X, Lounge X, Restaurant X, Locker Room X, Showers X, Club Rental X, Club Repair X, Cart Rental X, Instruction X, Practice Green X, Driving Range X, Practice Bunker X, Club Storage X

Tee-Time Reservation Policy: At time of registration or anytime with credit card guarantee. 48-hr. cancellation notice required for full refund

Ranger: Yes

Tee-off-Interval Time: 8 min.

Time to Play 18 Holes: 4½ hrs.

Course Hours/Earliest Tee-off: 7 a.m.

Green Fees: $68 for 18 holes Fri., Sat., Sun., holidays; $58 for 18 holes Mon.– Thurs. $40 for 9 holes Fri., Sat., Sun., holidays; $36 for 9 holes Mon.–Thurs.

Cart Fees: $16 for 18 holes per rider. $16 for 9 holes for 1 player

Credit Cards: American Express, Discover, MasterCard, Visa

Season: Stoney Creek: Year round. Devil's Knob: Mid-April to early Nov.

Course Comments: Walking limited. Can walk Stoney Creek Dec. 15 to March 15. Yardage book available. Wintergreen Golf Academy on site April to mid-Oct.

Golf Packages: Available through resort

Discounts: Seasonal (green fees lower Nov. 15 through March). Preferred lower rates to resort guests, property owners. 9-hole rates after 4:00 p.m.

Places to Stay Nearby: CHARLOTTES- VILLE: Sheraton Charlottesville (804) 971–5500, (800) 843–6664; Boars Head Inn (804) 296–2181. Lexington: Historic Country Inns: Alexander–Withrow house, McCampbellInn, Maple Hall— choice of three (703) 463–2044. LYNCHBURG: Holiday Inn (804) 847– 4424

Local Attractions: Homestead, Staunton, Natural Bridge, Charlottesville, Mon- ticello, Appomattox Court House, Sky- line Drive, Luray Caverns, Shenandoah National Park, wineries. Montpelier, Roanoke. Charlottesville/Albemarle Convention and Visitor's Bureau (804) 977–1783

Directions: From area north or east: I–64 west to exit 20 (Crozet, Rte. 250), 250 west to Rte. 151 south, turn left on Rte. 151 to Rte. 664 (14 mi. from 151), turn right on 664, Wintergreen is 4.5 mi. ahead

Closest Commercial Airports: Albemarle, Charlottesville (1 hr.); Lynchburg Mu- nicipal (1 hr.); Roanoke Municipal (1½ hrs.); Richmond International (2 hrs.); Dulles International, Washington, DC (3 hrs.)

RESORT

Date Built: 1975

No. of Rooms: 350 single-family rental homes and studios to 7-bedroom condo- miniums

Meeting Rooms: 17. Capacity of Largest: 650 persons. Meeting Space: 24,000 sq. ft.

Room Price Range: $85 for studio per night off season to over $550 for 7-bed- room home per night peak season. Golf and other packages available

Lounges: Cooper's Vantage Lounge, Gar- den Terrace Lounge, Grist Mill Lounge

Restaurants: Stoney Creek: Rodes Farm Inn, Verandah. Devil's Knob: Copper Mine, Garden Terrace, Devil's Knob Golf Clubhouse, Cooper's Vantage, Grist Mill, Trillium House

Entertainment: Live music at Cooper's Vantage Lounge

Credit Cards: American Express, Master- Card, Visa

General Amenities: Various children's programs at Camp Wintergreen for children 2½ to 12 yrs. old, teen outdoor adventure camp, babysitting, hayrides, bridge, natural history field trips, tennis and golf pro shops, seasonal activities, Mountain Inn shopping gallery, meeting and conference facilities with audio- visual and food services

Recreational Amenities: Stoney Creek: 2 swimming pools, 6 tennis courts with instruction; 16-acre lake for canoeing, swimming, fishing; equestrian center, bicycling and jogging paths. Devil's Knob: 19 tennis courts with pro shop, instruction, skiing, chairlift rides, exercise room and spa, 5 swimming pools

Reservation and Cancellation Policy: Advance deposit by check or money order equal to 1 night's rate plus tax required within 7 days of reservation date. Cancellation notice must be received 10 days prior to scheduled arrival date for deposit refund

Comments and Restrictions: No pets. Boarding facilities nearby. Nonparticipant package rates available. Maximum occupancy per unit limitations. Minimum age of 21 to rent accommodations. Reservations required for dinner at the Copper Mine, Garden Terrace, and Rodes Farm Inn restaurants. Taxes additional to basic rates

WINTERGREEN RESORT

The four-season Wintergreen Resort is situated on 11,000 acres of mountain and valley lands 43 miles southwest of Charlottesville. The resort, originally begun as a real-estate development in the 1970s, is fast accumulating recognition as an outstanding golf resort from a variety of sources. *Golf* magazine has awarded the resort its silver medal as one of the top golf resorts in America. In 1990 *Golf Digest* named the new Rees Jones Stoney Creek Golf Course the best new resort course. *Tennis* magazine has selected the Wintergreen as one of the "Top 50 Tennis Resorts" in the country. The American Hotel and Motel Association has awarded Wintergreen its Environmental Achievement Award for the resort's continuous effort to improve its environment through management and a variety of educational programs. Wintergreen's children's programs have earned it recognition from *Better Homes and Gardens* and *Family Circle* magazines as one of the top family resorts in the country. And it has received positive recognition for its conference and skiing programs and facilities.

At 3850 feet, Wintergreen's Devil's Knob, a 6576-yard Ellis Maples layout, is the highest golf course in Virginia. In addition to a fine test of golf, Devil's Knob offers 50-mile views of the Blue Ridge Mountains and the Shenandoah and Rockfish valleys below. Devil's Knob is normally open mid-April to mid-November, and the course features mountain laurel, fields of wildflower, rock outcroppings and surprisingly level playing conditions in addition to its views. The holes are generally well treed, with medium-sized to small, fast bentgrass greens with relatively few, but well-placed, bunkers and traps. There is a nice mix of short and long holes, doglegs and water holes, including the 600-yard, par-5 seventh, which is a double dogleg twice over water to a small, forward-sloping green guarded by traps left and right. This is considered the most difficult hole anywhere at Wintergreen.

The 166-yard par-3 eighth is a beautiful hole with a tee shot over a small lake to a shallow, kidney-shaped green that is trapped both front and back. The finishing hole on the front nine is a 402-yard par 4 that bends slightly toward a medium-sized green protected by a bunker on the left and trees left, back and front.

By now one is aware that just about every hole on this golf course is beautiful. The three finishing holes on the back nine start out with the 408-yard par-4 sixteenth, which drops almost 100 feet to the tree-lined fairway below. The second shot is to a shallow green protected in front by a trap on the left. An extremely accurate approach shot is required to avoid the trap yet hold the green. The 173-yard par-3 seventeenth plays from an elevated tee to a deep, forward-sloping green with two traps on the right, a stream in front and a large trap on the left. Even if you successfully reach the green on your tee shot, it is very easy to 3-putt. The final hole is a 430-yard par-4 dogleg right down a tree-lined fairway to a deep green protected by a trap on the left. A right fairway bunker guards the landing area at the knee of the dogleg. As with most holes at Devil's Knob, if your ball wanders on the tee shot or the approach, you will be penalized by traps, water or trees.

Devil's Knob has a total range of 1475 yards between the forward and back tees. Because of the altitude, the ball will probably carry 5 to 10 yards farther than you are accustomed to, and 30- to 40-foot changes in elevation usually require one club more or less than you would ordinarily use. The winds are tricky here, and because of the trees, traps and elevation changes, club selection and especially ball placement are extremely important. The greens are usually fast and slope toward the fairway so it is wise to stay below the hole.

Stoney Creek is a 7005-yard layout down in the valley over 3000 yards below Devil's Knob. After only a few years of operation, *Golf Digest* ranks Stoney Creek among the top 6 courses of any kind in the state of Virginia. Pleasing views of the Blue Ridge Mountains surround this golf course, which has moundings and a Scottish feel on the front nine. The back nine is much tighter, however, with tight fairways, elevated tees and well-trapped greens surrounded by pine, beech and oak forests. Though open, the front nine has creeks and lakes coming into play on eight of its holes. And if your shot is off the fairway and playable, you are not likely to have a flat lie. On the 440-yard par-4 tenth, for example, you have to hit the ball 245 yards off the tee to see the green on your approach shot. The greens have a variety of undulations with many more breaks than the greens on Devil's Knob. So it is important to approach the green from the proper angle to be in a position to score.

The Stoney Creek Course affords you the opportunity to play from any of four tee distances, ranging from 7005 yards from the championship tees to 5500 yards from the forward tees. From the championship tees and the shorter 6740-yard back tees there are a number of long and testing par 4s and par 5s. The number-1-handicap hole is the 575-yard par-5 thirteenth, a dogleg left to a deep, forward-sloping green with four traps right and three left.

The knee of the dogleg is guarded on the right by three bunkers, and trees line the fairway from tee to green. Two bunkers approximately 50 to 75 yards from the green guard the landing area to the right on the second shot. Depending on which tees you're playing, reaching the green on your second shot is extremely difficult because of the traps guarding the front of the green. There are more than 100 traps on this course, requiring you to be accurate, especially on the well-treed back nine.

The par 3s at Stoney Creek tend to be difficult because they have small to medium-sized greens with well-placed traps and water hazards. The beautiful 175-yard fifth hole plays over a lake to a shallow green edged in front by water and ringed by four traps in back. Often the tee shot is into the wind. The 181-yard eighth plays straight to a medium-sized green protected by two bunkers in front, a stream left and trees to the right. The 179-yard twelfth is down a tree- and stream-lined fairway to a wide but shallow, side-angled green with a trap in front and two in back. The beautiful 200-yard sixteenth has a tee shot from an elevated tee to a deep green, guarded left, right and back by traps, more than 100 feet below the tee.

The 450-yard par-4 finishing hole is an excellent way to end the round. A dogleg left, with a large pin oak tree guarding the landing area on the right, the second shot is to a medium-sized, heavily contoured green with a huge, 100-yard parallel waste bunker on the left running from the left of the green out along the left fairway. You have to nail two shots to get here in two.

Devil's Knob and Stoney Creek are two totally different but enjoyable golf experiences. Each course has its own clubhouse, men's and women's locker rooms, practice area, dining facilities and professional staff that provides individual and group instruction. Wintergreen offers the Wintergreen Golf Academy, which uses a variety of video-analysis and teaching techniques and provides professional instruction from April through October. Wintergreen also offers a variety of golf packages. Facilities in the valley, where Stoney Creek is situated, include the Verandah Restaurant, which overlooks the golf course from the 6000-square-foot clubhouse; indoor and outdoor swimming pools; and 6 tennis courts. Also in the valley is Rodes Farm Inn, another restaurant; stables for horseback riding; a 16-acre recreational lake for boating, fishing, and swimming; a shopping center; a medical center and residential real estate. This section of Wintergreen is made up of approximately 2000 acres.

The facilities on the mountain, where Devil's Knob is situated, includes over 24,000 square feet of meeting and banquet space, 350 rental homes and condominiums, 6 full-service restaurants, 3 lounges, and 2 seasonal restaurants, as well as indoor and outdoor pools, hot tubs, whirlpools, sauna, exercise rooms, shopping facilities and a variety of recreational activities including hiking, skiing, outdoor tennis, bicycling, and highly acclaimed children's programs at Camp Wintergreen. Short programs and more extensive daily sessions for young people ages 2½ to 17 range from babysitting services, nature camps, and "Kids Night Out" to "teen outdoor adventure camp." In addition to golf packages, a variety of family, tennis, and seasonal plans is offered.

More than 50 percent of Wintergreen's 11,000 acres has been set aside as permanent undisturbed forest. A full-time naturalist reviews all development plans for environmental and ecological impact. Also, an extensive year-round series of outdoor educational activities is offered at the resort, including a spring wildflower symposium, children's activities, and the popular "Fall Flight of the Raptors" program highlighting the hawk migration through the Shenandoah Valley.

If the golf options and varied activities at Wintergreen are not enough, many significant natural and historical sites are within easy reach of Wintergreen, including Monticello, Charlottesville, wineries, Montpelier, Lexington, Staunton, Natural Bridge, Roanoke and Appomattox.

Recommended Golf Courses in Western Virginia

Within 1 Hour of Harrisonburg:

Bryce Resort Golf Course, Basye, (703) 856–2124, Public, 18/6261/71

Caverns Country Club Resort, Luray, (703) 743–7111, Resort, 18/6452/72

Lakeview Golf Course, Harrisonburg, (703) 434–8937, Semiprivate. Lake/Peak: 18/6517/72. Peak/Spring: 18/6640/72. Lake/Spring: 18/6303/72

Shenandoah Valley Golf Club, Front Royal, (703) 636–4653, Semiprivate: No.1/No.2: 18/6121/71. No.2/No.3: 18/6330/71. No.1/No.3: 18/6399/72

Shenvalee, New Market, (703) 740–9930, Resort, 18/6595/71

Charlottesville Area:

Birdwood Golf Course, Charlottesville, (804) 293–4653, Semiprivate, 18/6820/72

Lake Monticello Golf Club, Palmyra, (804) 589–3075, Public, 18/69818/72

Royal Virginia Golf Club, Hadensville, (804) 457–2041, Public, 18/7106/72

Shenandoah Crossing Resort and Country Club, Gordonsville, (703) 832–9543, (800) 467–0592, Resort, 18/6192/72

Within 1 Hour of Lynchburg:

Hanging Rock Golf Club, Salem, (703) 389–7275, (800) 277–7497, Public, 18/6828/73

Olde Mill Golf Course, Laurel Fork (2 hrs. southwest of Lynchburg), (703) 398–2211, Public, 18/6833/72

Skyland Lakes Golf Course and Resort, Fancy Gap, (703) 728–4923, Public, 18/6364/71

Winton Country Club, Clifford, (804) 946–7336, Public, 18/6833/71

Williamsburg Area

Course Name: FORD'S COLONY
               COUNTRY CLUB
               White/Red, Blue/
               Gold Courses

Course Type: Semiprivate
Address: 240 Ford's Colony Drive
             Williamsburg, VA 23188
Phone: (804) 258–4130

GOLF COURSE

Head Professional: Scott Jones
Course Length/Par (All Tees):
   White/Red: Back 6755/72, Middle
   6237/72, Front 5614/72. Blue/Gold:
   Back 6787/71, Blue 6567/71, White
   6082/71, Forward 4986/71
Course Slope/Rating (All Tees):
   White/Red: Back 126/72.3, Middle
   122/70.2, Ladies' Forward 116/71.6.
   Blue/Gold: NA/NA
Course Architect: White/Red: Dan Maples
   (1985). Blue: Dan Maples (1988). Gold:
   Dan Maples (1992)
Golf Facilities: Full Pro Shop X, Snack
   Bar X, Lounge X, Restaurant X,
   Locker Room X, Showers X, Club
   Rental X, Club Repair X, Cart Rental
   X, Instruction X, Practice Green X,
   Driving Range X, Practice Bunker X,
   Club Storage X
Tee-Time Reservation Policy: Outside
   play: Up to 7 days in advance. Members
   have priority
Ranger: Yes
Tee-off-Interval Time: 8 min.
Time to Play 18 Holes: 4½ hrs.
Course Hours/Earliest Tee-off: 7 a.m.
Green and Cart Fees: Peak season: $95
   for 18 holes with cart weekends, holi-
   days; $85 for 18 holes with cart week-
   days. Lower rates Nov. to Mar.
Pull carts: Not allowed except for members
Credit Cards: American Express, Master-
   Card, Visa
Season: Year round. Busiest season April
   to Sept.
Course Comments: Cart mandatory
Golf Packages: Available through Ford's
   Colony
Discounts: Twilight rate after 2 p.m.

Places to Stay Nearby: Ramada Inn (804)
220–2800, (800) 492–2855; Best Western Williamsburg (804) 229–3003, (800)
528–1234; Days Inn historic area (800)
759–1166; Courtyard by Marriott (804)
253–6444, (800) 321–2211; Fort Magruder Inn and Conference Center (804)
220–2250, (800) 582–1010; Princess
Anne Motor Lodge (804) 229–2455,
(800) 552–5571; Williamsburg Hotel
and Motel Association (800) 446–9244

Local Attractions: COLONIAL WIL-
LIAMSBURG HISTORIC AREA: Brush–
Everard house, Bruton Parish Church,
capitol, historic trades shops, DeWitt
Wallace Decorative Arts Gallery, Gover-
nor's Palace, James Geddy house and
foundry, magazine and guardhouse,
Peyton Randolph house, Public Gaol,
Public Hospital of 1773, Raleigh Tav-
ern, Wetherburn's Tavern, Wythe house.
WILLIAMSBURG AREA: Abby Adrich
Rockefeller Folk Art Center, Bassett
Hall, Busch Gardens, Carter's Grove,
Mariner's Museum, NASA Langley
Visitors Center, College of William and
Mary, Yorktown, Jamestown settlement,
Water Country USA. Virginia Beach.
Colonial Williamsburg Foundation (800)
447–8679

Directions: From Colonial Williamsburg:
Richmond Rd. (Rte. 60) west to Olde
Towne Rd. (State Rte. 658). Turn south
(left), proceed 2 mi. to Long Hill Rd.,
then right 1½ mi. to the main entrance
on the left

Closest Commercial Airports: Richmond
International (1 hr.); Norfolk Interna-
tional (1 hr.); Dulles International,
Washington, DC (2½ hrs.)

FORD'S COLONY COUNTRY CLUB

Ford's Colony is an upscale country-
club real-estate development featuring 36
holes of golf within 2500 acres of scenic
woodland a few minutes from central
Williamsburg and its historic district.

All roads lead to the clubhouse at Ford's
Colony, which has an excellent restaurant
with extensive wine list upstairs; a complete pro shop; and the Men's Grill, a
formal lounge and a snack bar that serves

active golfers. A fitness center with tread-mill, stationary bicycles and Nautilus equipment is located here, as are men's and ladies' locker rooms and showers. On site are also 4 Har-Tru tennis courts and an outdoor lap pool. Magnificent views of the golf course are afforded by the clubhouse dining facilities and the surrounding patios.

The White/Red Course is 6755 yards with large, moderately fast, undulating bentgrass greens. The golf course is rolling, with well-placed, mature trees and strategically placed sand traps around the greens. A great hole on the front nine is the 402-yard par-4 fourth, which plays over water to a fairway that bends left along the water to a green guarded by water to the left, right and rear. Traps protect the green to the left, right and front. The tee shot is slightly uphill to a wide landing area, then down to the green. This course provides an excellent variety of holes, including doglegs left and right, water holes, and some long par 4s that are extremely challenging.

Water hazards appear on eight holes including the 569-yard par-5 eleventh, a dogleg left that plays down a treelined fairway cut by water approximately halfway to the green. The approach shot is uphill to a large green protected by three large, heavily lipped bunkers. Probably the most demanding hole on this side is the 475-yard par-4 sixteenth, a blind, sharp dogleg right that rolls up to the crest of a hill at the dogleg, then drops down 50 to 75 feet to a deep, left-to-right- and forward-sloping green with a huge bunker to the right and forward.

The Blue nine on the 6787-yard par-72 Blue/Gold Course has five holes with water hazards. The 217-yard par-3 eighth plays over water to a relatively small, forward-sloping green. A huge trap is to the right of the green, and a bank runs down to the water in front of it. The number-1-handicap hole on this course is the 538-yard par-5 fourth, which is well treed from the tee but opens up on the left side of the fairway on the second shot. Water cuts into the fairway on the right halfway to the green, and there is a huge right-fairway bunker just before

the water. A trap to the left could catch your second shot toward the green, which is slightly elevated and has a huge trap to the right.

The back nine has six holes with water hazards, large sand traps and large, undulating greens. A tough par 4 on this side is the eleventh, a 393-yard dogleg right, which plays from an elevated tee down a heavily wooded fairway to a large green trapped in back and front left. The tee shot has to clear a pond that borders the right side. A series of bunkers guards the left side of the fairway approximately 225 yards from the back tees.

There are club memberships at Ford's Colony, but the public can play both courses. Complete practice facilities are offered at Ford's Colony, and instruction is available from the staff of PGA professionals and assistants. In addition to its excellent golf courses, which have been sites for the Mid-Atlantic Professionals Tournament and other events, the dining room at the country club has been awarded the American Automobile Association's Four-Diamond Award, and the *Wine Spectator* has recently awarded Ford's Colony an Award of Excellence for having one of the top 100 wine lists in the world. The Ford's Colony wine cellars have more than 1000 wines to choose from.

The combination of the golf courses, excellent dining facilities, recreational amenities and a 768-square-foot country club meeting room seating 35 persons, makes Ford's Colony an ideal place for group meetings and conferences.

Course Name: **GOLDEN HORSESHOE GOLF COURSE**
              Gold, Green,
              Spotswood Courses

Course Type: Resort
Resort: Colonial Williamsburg
Address: P.O. Box 1776
              Williamsburg, VA 23187–1776
Phone: (804) 229–1000 (Golf Course)
              (800) 447–8679 (Central Hotel Reservations)

GOLF COURSE

Director of Golf: Del Snyder

Head Professional: Green Course: Glenn Byrnes

Course Length/Par (All Tees): Gold: Back 6700/71, Blue 6443/71, White 6179/71, Forward 5159/71. Green: Back 7120/72, Blue 6722/72, White 6244/72, Forward 5350/72. Spotswood 3745/62

Course Slope/Rating (All Tees): Gold: Back 137/73.1, Blue 134/72.1, White 131/71.1, Forward 120/66.2, Ladies' White 149/77.4, Ladies' Forward 130/70.4. Green: Back 132/74.9, Blue 128/70.4, White 124/70.1, Gold Forward 109/69.3, Ladies' White 126/74.4, Ladies' Forward 109/69.3. Spotswood: NA/NA

Course Architects: Gold: Robert Trent Jones, Sr. (1963). Green: Rees Jones (1991). Spotswood: Robert Trent Jones, Sr. (1963)

Golf Facilities: Full Pro Shop X, Snack Bar X, Lounge X, Restaurant X, Locker Room X, Showers X, Club Rental X, Club Repair Minor, Cart Rental X, Instruction X, Practice Green X, Driving Range X, Practice Bunker X, Club Storage X

Tee-Time Reservation Policy: Resort guests: At time of reservation. Outside play: Gold: Up to 2 weeks in advance. Green: Up to 1 month in advance with credit card guarantee

Ranger: Yes

Tee-off-Interval Time: 10 min.

Time to Play 18 Holes: 4 hrs., 45 min.

Course Hours/Earliest Tee-off: 7 a.m. (EDT) in season

Green and Cart Fees: Gold: $115 for 18 holes with cart. Green: $135 for 18 holes with cart

Credit Cards: All major cards

Season: Year round. Busiest April-May, Sept.-Oct.

Course Comments: Can walk anytime at full golf fee

Golf Packages: Available through resort

Discounts: Seasonal (Dec. to March 15). Twilight rate in summer

Places to Stay Nearby: Ramada Inn (804) 220-2800, (800) 492-2855; Best Western Williamsburg (804) 229-3003, (800) 528-1234; Days Inn historic area (800) 759-1166; Courtyard by Marriott (804) 253-6444, (800) 321-2211; Fort Magruder Inn and Conference Center (804) 220-2250, (800) 582-1010; Princess Anne Motor Lodge (804) 229-2455, (800) 552-5571; Williamsburg Hotel and Motel Association (800) 446-9244

Local Attractions: COLONIAL WILLIAMSBURG HISTORIC AREA: Brush–Everard house, Bruton Parish Church, capitol, historic trades shops, DeWitt Wallace Decorative Arts Gallery, Governor's Palace, James Geddy house and foundry, magazine and guardhouse, Peyton Randolph house, Public Gaol, Public Hospital of 1773, Raleigh Tavern, Wetherburn's Tavern, Wythe house. WILLIAMSBURG AREA: Abby Adrich Rockefeller Folk Art Center, Bassett Hall, Winthrop Rockefeller Archeological Museum, Busch Gardens, Carter's Grove, Mariner's Museum, NASA Langley Visitors Center, College of William and Mary, Yorktown, Jamestown settlement, Water Country USA. Virginia Beach. Colonial Williamsburg Foundation (800) 447-8679

Directions: East of Richmond (1 hr.): I-64, exit 56, follow signs

Closest Commercial Airports: Newport News/Williamsburg International (30 min.), Richmond International (1 hr.), Norfolk International (1 hr.)

RESORT

Date Built: 1937 (Williamsburg Inn)

No. of Rooms: Williamsburg Inn: 102. Governor's Inn: 200. Providence Hall: 43. Williamsburg Lodge: 315 guest rooms. Cascades Meeting Center: 88 executive suites. Motor House: 219 guest rooms. Colonial houses and taverns have additional accommodations

Meeting Rooms: Williamsburg Woodlands (Motor House): 3. Providence Hall House: 3. Commonwealth Hall: 1. Cascades Meeting Center: 10. Williamsburg Lodge and Conference

Center: 20. Capacity of Largest: Williamsburg Woodlands (motor house): 525 persons. Providence Hall House: 30 persons. Commonwealth Hall: 450 persons. Cascades Meeting Center: 350 persons. Williamsburg Lodge and Conference Center: 1300 persons. Meeting Space: Williamsburg Woodlands (motor house): 9000 sq. ft. Providence Hall House: 500 sq. ft. Commonwealth Hall: 5140 sq. ft. Cascades Meeting Center: 19,000 sq. ft. Williamsburg Lodge and Conference Center: 30,000 sq. ft.

Room Price Range: $69 at the Governor's Inn to $249 to $335 at Williamsburg Inn. Numerous seasonal rates and packages available

Lounges: Williamsburg Lodge, Garden Lounge

Restaurants: Williamsburg Inn: Regency Dining Room, Regency Lounge. Woodlands: Grill. Cascades: Dining Room. Williamsburg Lodge: Bay Room, Coffee Shop. Golf Courses: 2 clubhouse restaurants. Historic District: Clowning's Tavern, Christiana Campbell's Tavern, King's Arms Tavern, Shields Tavern, Wallace Gallery Cafe

Entertainment: Live music

Credit Cards: American Express, MasterCard, Visa

General Amenities: Hair-care salon, babysitting services, tours, garden tours, sports boutique in the Tazewell Club, shopping at Merchants Square; theater, classroom, banquet, conference, reception-style meeting facilities in the Williamsburg Lodge and Conference Center, Cascades Meeting Center; Woodlands, Providence Hall

Recreational Amenities: Tazewell Club Fitness Center with massage, whirlpool, steam room, saunas, lap pool, Life Cycle, Life Rower, Keiser and Nautilus equipment, aerobics, dance studio, swimming pool, 4 clay and 4 Har-Tru tennis courts, lawn bowling, croquet, badminton, miniature golf, bicycling, horseshoes, table tennis, jogging

Reservation and Cancellation Policy: 1 night's deposit required on credit card guarantee or check. 1-day advance notice of cancellation required for full refund

Comments and Restrictions: Pets allowed only in Governor's Inn. Taxes additional to base rates

GOLDEN HORSESHOE GOLF COURSE

Colonial Williamsburg is unique in that it has two excellent eighteen-hole championship golf courses and one excellent nine-hole executive course within walking distance of many significant historic sites, including the College of William and Mary, established in 1693 and the second oldest college in the United States (after Harvard); the Governor's Palace, a magnificent three-story structure built in 1706 and home of seven royal governors and the first two governors of the Commonwealth of Virginia—Patrick Henry and Thomas Jefferson; the capitol, which seated the House of Burgesses and the Council, the two houses of the legislature in colonial Virginia, and the General Court, the colony's highest judicial tribunal; and the Public Hospital, which opened in the fall of 1773 as the first public institution in British North American colonies devoted solely to the care and treatment of the mentally ill.

For 80 years Williamsburg was the political center of Virginia, one of England's largest, wealthiest, and most populous colonies. The historic area here was revived and restored beginning in 1926, when the Reverend Dr. W.A.R. Goodwin, rector of Bruton Parish Church, sought the help of John D. Rockefeller, Jr., in restoring the village, which began to fade after Richmond was named the capital by Thomas Jefferson during the American Revolutionary War. Williamsburg covers 173 acres of the 220-acre town laid out in 1699 by Royal Governor Francis Nicholson. Bisected by mile-long Duke of Gloucester Street, which has the College of William and Mary at one end and the capitol at the other, the historic area has 88 original structures, 50 major reconstructions and 40 exhibition buildings containing 225 rooms with furnishings from a 100,000-item collection. There are 90 acres of gardens and greens,

15 exhibition sites, 10 shops and 21 historic trade presentations. Museums include the DeWitt Wallace Decorative Arts Gallery, Abby Aldrich Rockefeller Folk Art Center, Bassett Hall, the Williamsburg home of Mr. and Mrs. John D. Rockefeller, Jr., and the Winthrop Rockefeller Archeological Museum.

Located just behind the Williamsburg Inn, winner of the *Mobil Travel Guide*'s highest rating, the Five-Star Award, is the Golden Horseshoe Golf Club, which includes the 6700-yard Gold Course designed by Robert Trent Jones, Sr., and opened in 1963. This beautiful, rolling layout spreads over 125 acres, whose features include a 5-acre lake, ravines and dense woodland valleys. Jones designed it around the existing land contours, utilizing depressions and elevated locations to achieve an interesting golf challenge. There are water hazards on seven holes, doglegs on six, and the bentgrass greens are small, moderately fast, undulating and usually elevated. The Golden Horseshoe Golf Course takes its name from an adventurous expedition led by Virginia governor Alexander Spotswood from Williamsburg over the Appalachian mountains in 1716. Upon their return to Williamsburg, Governor Spotswood presented each member of the expedition with a golden horseshoe. The excellent 3745-yard par-62 eighteen-hole executive course is named after Governor Spotswood. The same nine-hole venue is played twice from different tee positions. These courses are especially beautiful in spring, when the plum, crabapple and dogwood trees are in bloom.

The number-1-handicap hole on the Gold Course is the 411-yard par-4 fourth, which plays uphill over a tree-lined fairway to a deep green protected by traps to the left and right. Another difficult hole is the 497-yard par-5 second, which plays down a tree-lined fairway that slopes severely down to a large pond in front of an elevated green that is only 14 yards deep and is banked in back. If you hit a long tee shot, you can go for the hole, but you are likely to have a tricky downhill lie. Most players lay up to a flat landing area just in front of the pond, approximately 125 yards from the green. The front nine has two beautiful and difficult par 3s. The 190-yard third hole plays from an elevated tee over water down to a shallow, wide green with a small trap to its rear. The 207-yard seventh plays from an elevated tee over water to a medium-sized, three-tiered green guarded by traps to the left, right and rear.

The back nine is longer and more difficult than the front side. Included is the long, straight 631-yard par-5 fifteenth hole, which plays down a tree-lined fairway to a medium-sized green protected by five traps. No mortal reaches this green in two, and your third shot has to avoid the sand. There are another two scenic and difficult par 3s on this side. The 185-yard twelfth plays from an elevated tee over water to a wide, shallow, side-angled green well banked on the left. If your tee shot is to the right you are in the water, and if you land on the left bank you face a hazardous chip shot toward the water. The tee shot of the 160-yard sixteenth is from a beautiful, elevated tee to a large island green guarded by three traps. The finishing hole on the Gold Course is a dogleg left 442-yard par 4 whose tee shot is slightly uphill, with the second shot down to a narrow, deep green guarded by water and a trap on the left and another trap on the right. The course record from the back tees is a 67 by Jack Nicklaus, and Del Snyder, the director of golf at the Golden Horseshoe, holds the record from the 6443-yard regular tees with a 64. The Gold Course is a shotmaker's course with beautiful scenery, a variety of hazards, memorable holes and an opportunity to use every club in the bag. You'll want to play this course more than once.

The Green Course is a short golf-cart ride away from the Gold Course. It was designed by Rees Jones, the son of Robert Trent Jones, Sr., so the Jones family has designed all the courses here and with great success. *Golf Digest* named the Green Course one of the five best new resort courses in 1992. The Green Course is beautifully set in the woods with its rolling Rees Jones signature mounds reminiscent of his No. 7 course at Pinehurst. This 7120-

yard layout opened in 1991 and has its own 3000-square-foot clubhouse with pro shop, men's and women's locker rooms, a restaurant and magnificent views of the eighteenth hole from most vantage points in this three-story building. A large practice area and putting green are located here. The addition of the Green Course enables the resort to accommodate daily-fee golfers; resort guests; group outings, including those who utilize the resort's varied and extensive meeting and conference facilities; and, eventually, tournaments. This is a shot-maker's course routed to fit ravines, draws and rolling topography in this area. When you embark on your golf adventure here, each hole is a distinct and separate experience as you work your way through the woods and back to the clubhouse veranda.

The golf course was part of the Bassett Hall Plantation in the eighteenth century. Civil War redoubts of the Fort Magruder defense used in the Battle of Williamsburg in 1862 remain adjacent to the course. The property was included in the Bassett Hall property when John D. Rockefeller, Jr., acquired it in 1933. Appropriately, when the Golden Horseshoe Green Course opened October 28, 1991, Colonial Williamsburg's Fife and Drum Corps performed and the militia members fired a ceremonial artillery volley to celebrate its opening.

The Green Course has four tee distances ranging from 7120 to 5350 yards. Water comes into play on six holes, with two played directly over water. The bentgrass greens are large, moderately fast, slightly undulating and well guarded by traps. There are over 110 sand bunkers on this layout, and the mounded fairways tend to keep the ball funneled into the playing area, although it is always possible to kick the ball into the woods or to have uneven lies of varying proportions because of these mounds.

The number-1-handicap hole on the Green Course is the sixth hole, which plays 450 yards from the back tees, 427 from the blue, 402 from the white and 316 from the front tees. Mounds and trees line the fairway as you tee off to a landing area with bunkers on each side. The second shot is uphill to a green protected by traps left and right. From 110 yards into the green, there is a severe drop-off to the right side. Another tough hole on this side is the 538-yard par-5 eighth, a dogleg right that plays from an elevated tee over a gully to a landing area bordered by bunkers on the right. The second shot has to be kept to the left because of the narrow entrance to the green and a series of traps and bunkers that begins from 100 yards in. The green is deep and slopes forward and left to right, with two large traps to the left and two traps to the right.

The back nine plays somewhat longer than the front nine and has water hazards on four holes, including the 195-yard par-3 eleventh, which plays from an elevated tee over water to a green surrounded by an amphitheaterlike bank and a cathedral of magnificent trees. The combination of a series of pot bunkers to the rear of the green and water in front makes this a difficult par 3.

The finishing holes on the Green Course are quite formidable regardless of which tees you are playing from. The 466-yard par-4 fourteenth is a long dogleg left with a trap guarding the right side of the fairway on the tee shot. The second shot is onto an open, flat green that tilts slightly away from the fairway and is guarded by traps to the right and rear, with water on the left from 200 yards in. The 616-yard par-5 fifteenth is a long tree-lined dogleg right to a terraced green trapped rear and left. The 397-yard par-4 sixteenth is a sharp dogleg right whose fairway rolls down, then up to a well-trapped, forward-sloping green with a narrow entrance. The 220-yard par-3 seventeenth plays from an elevated tee over a ravine to a large right-to-left- and forward-sloping green with a huge bunker to the right and in front.

The finishing hole is a beautiful 531-yard par 5 with an elevated tee and a view to the well-trapped green and tree-framed clubhouse in the distance. From the back tees, the wide fairway is more than 200 yards away, and the tee shot must clear a stream in front of the fairway. The second shot is uphill toward a large green with well-placed bunkers beginning from approximately 150 yards in. The green is cut into a hill in an amphitheaterlike setting and slopes right to left and forward, with traps and pot bunkers on the left and right. The Green Course covers 250 acres and is a marvelous golf experience. You are likely to see deer, Canada geese, raccoon and a wide variety of birds while you are matching wits with this challenging new venue.

The clubhouse at the Golden Horseshoe overlooks the finishing hole on the Gold Course and has locker rooms, a complete pro shop, and the Clubhouse Grill and Terrace Restaurant, which provides an excellent view of the golf course and the Williamsburg Inn. A practice range and putting green are within walking distance. The Williamsburg Golf Plan is a golf package that includes play on the Golden Horseshoe and Spotswood courses, lodging in a Colonial Williamsburg hotel, meals, use of a cart and practice balls, a golf clinic for 8 or more persons and an admission ticket to the adjacent historic area. This package is available from early March until late November, but you should inquire about other packages. You can schedule your tee times when you register at the resort hotels, or you can call and reserve a tee time with a credit card guarantee if you are not staying there. Individual and group instruction is available from the PGA professionals and assistants.

The Williamsburg Inn has been named by *Golf* magazine as one of the twelve best golf resorts in America, and *Golf Digest* ranks the golf course among the best resort golf courses in America. Since it opened in 1937, the inn has accommodated numerous dignitaries, including Queen Elizabeth and several American presidents. The inn operates its own in-house upholstery shop and interior design studio, and no two guest rooms are decorated alike. In aggregate, Colonial Williamsburg has over 60,000 square feet of meeting and conference space in a variety of configurations ranging from Providence Hall House, a beautifully restored eighteenth century building with boardroom, library, dining room, garden room, sitting room, and bedrooms suitable

for smaller high-level meetings, to the more spacious Williamsburg Lodge and Conference Center, which can accommodate functions for up to 1300 persons. *Successful Meetings* magazine has awarded the Williamsburg Inn, Williamsburg Lodge and the Cascades its seventh consecutive Pinnacle Award for being an outstanding meeting facility.

In addition to golf and its historical, meeting, shopping, restaurant and general cultural amenities, Colonial Williamsburg provides a variety of recreational activities, including bicycling, jogging, tennis, lawn bowling, croquet, swimming, and other activities. The Tazewell Club Fitness Center offers a complete line of exercise and cardiovascular equipment, aerobic classes, whirlpool, steam room, sauna and 60-foot indoor lap pool.

When you walk down the streets of Colonial Williamsburg after a day of golf, a village that once hosted Patrick Henry, Thomas Jefferson, George Washington and other giants of American democracy, you are taken into another world. You should put Williamsburg and the Golden Horseshoe on your golfing itinerary.

Course Name: KINGSMILL RESORT
                 River, Plantation, Woods, Bray Links Courses

Course Type: Resort
Resort: Kingsmill Resort and Conference Center
Address: 1010 Kingsmill Road (Resort) 100 Golf Club Rd. (Golf Courses) Williamsburg, VA 23185
Phone: (804) 253–3906 (Golf Course) (804) 253–1703, (800) 832–5665 (Resort)

GOLF COURSE

Director of Golf: Archie Lemon
Head Professional: Woods: Tommy Highsmith. Teaching professional: Tim Polland
Touring Professional: Curtis Strange
Course Length/Par (All Tees): River: Back 6776/71, Middle 6003/71, Forward 4588/71. Plantation: Back 6590/72, Mid-

dle 6109/72, Forward 4875/72. Woods: Back 6784/72, Blue 6393/72, White 6030/72, Forward 5140/72. Bray Links: Back 705/27, Forward 569/27

Course Slope/Rating (All Tees): River: Back 126/73.4, Middle 119/69.5, Forward 109/65.7. Plantation: Back 120/70.5, Middle 115/69.3, Forward 108/68.2. Woods: Back 126/72.5, Blue 116/70.0, White 114/68.3, Forward 120/68.7. Bray Links: NA/NA

Course Architects: River: Pete Dye (1975). Plantation: Arnold Palmer and Ed Seay (1985). Woods: Tom Clark with Curtis Strange (1995). Bray Links: Ault, Clark and Associates, Ltd. (1989)

Golf Facilities: Full Pro Shop X, Snack Bar X, Lounge X, Restaurant X, Locker Room X, Showers X, Club Rental X, Club Repair Minor, Cart Rental X, Instruction X, Practice Green X, Driving Range X, Practice Bunker X, Club Storage X

Tee-Time Reservation Policy: Resort guests: At time of registration at resort. Members: 1 wk. in advance. Outside play: 1 day in advance. Members have priority

Ranger: Yes

Tee-off-Interval Time: River: 10 min. Plantation: 8 min.

Time to Play 18 Holes: 4½ hrs.

Course Hours/Earliest Tee-off: 7 a.m.

Green and Cart Fees: Outside play, peak season (Mar.-Sept.): $115 for 18 holes with cart

Credit Cards: All major cards

Season: Year round. Busiest seasons April through May, Oct. to early Nov.

Course Comments: Nonmembers have to take motorized cart. Golf schools on site

Golf Packages: Available through resort

Discounts: Seasonal (Dec. to early March)

Places to Stay Nearby: Ramada Inn (804) 220–2800, (800) 492–2855; Best Western Williamsburg (804) 229–3003, (800) 528–1234; Days Inn historic area (800) 759–1166; Courtyard by Marriott (804) 253–6444, (800) 321–2211; Fort Magruder Inn and Conference Center (804) 220–2250, (800) 582–1010; Princess Anne Motor Lodge (804) 229–2455,

(800) 552–5571; Williamsburg Hotel and Motel Association (800) 446–9244

Local Attractions: COLONIAL WILLIAMSBURG HISTORIC AREA: Brush–Everard house, Bruton Parish Church, capitol, historic trades shops, DeWitt Wallace Decorative Arts Gallery, Governor's Palace, James Geddy house and foundry, magazine and guardhouse, Peyton Randolph house, Public Gaol, Public Hospital of 1773, Raleigh Tavern, Wetherburn's Tavern, Wythe house. WILLIAMSBURG AREA: Abby Adrich Rockefeller Folk Art Center, Bassett Hall, Busch Gardens, Carter's Grove, Mariner's Museum, NASA Langley Visitors Center, College of William and Mary, Yorktown, Jamestown settlement, Water Country USA. Virginia Beach. Colonial Williamsburg Foundation (800) 447–8679

Directions: From north or south: I–95 to I–65 east, take exit 57A (Busch Gardens) and follow Rte. 199W to the first traffic light. Kingsmill entrance is on the left. From east or west: take I–64 to Williamsburg. Follow above directions

Closest Commercial Airports: Richmond International (1 hr.); Norfolk International (1 hr.); Dulles International, Washington, DC (3 hrs.); Raleigh/Durham (4 hrs.)

RESORT

Date Built: 1975

No. of Rooms: 365

Meeting Rooms: 9. Capacity of Largest: 500 persons. Meeting Space: 15,000 sq. ft.

Room Price Range: $105 for single guest room low season to $705 for 3-bedroom suite peak season (April to late Nov.). Golf, Busch Gardens, holidays and other packages are available

Lounge: Moody's Tavern

Restaurants: Bray Dining Room, Kingsmill Cafe, Peyton Grille

Entertainment: Live music in Moody's Tavern

Credit Cards: American Express, Diners Club, MasterCard, Visa

General Amenities: Supervised Kingsmill Kampers program (late May through Aug.) for young people ages 5 to 12; shopping at Tennis Pro Shops, Village shops, Market Place and nearby malls; Busch Gardens, complete meeting and conference facilities with audiovisual and food services

Recreational Amenities: Sports club including indoor and outdoor pools, Nautilus, aerobic exercise facilities, sauna, whirlpool, billiards/game lounge; marina with 86 boat slips, picnic and beach area, boat ramp, shower, and rest rooms; fishing, racquetball, jogging trails, tennis club with 13 Vel-Play tennis courts (2 lighted) with instruction available, fresh- and saltwater fishing, basketball

Reservation and Cancellation Policy: Credit card or an advance deposit for 1-night's lodging required to guarantee a room. Cash advance deposits and credit card guarantees refunded if cancellation received 72 hrs. prior to arrival date

Comments and Restrictions: No pets allowed. All packages sold on a space available basis. Certain packages may not be available for specific time periods. All rates based on European plan (no meals included). All rates subject to applicable state and county tax. Children under 18 stay free in the same room as parents (maximum 4 persons per room)

KINGSMILL RESORT

The Kingsmill Resort and Conference Center is a 365-room luxury resort within a 2900-acre residential property. The property is being developed by Anheuser–Busch along the James River in the historic Williamsburg region, midway between Richmond and Norfolk.

The resort features the 6776-yard Pete Dye–designed River Course and is the home of the PGA Tour's Anheuser–Busch Golf Classic, which was moved here in 1981. This course is heavily wooded, with small to medium-sized, moderately fast and undulating bentgrass greens. Water comes into play on half the holes, and there are more than 90 sand bunkers on the course.

Accuracy rather than distance is required at Kingsmill. Some holes, however, such as the 452-yard par-4 ninth, a slight dogleg left playing to a narrow but deep green protected by two bunkers on the right, also require distance. Even a big drive down the right side (to avoid the bunkers on the left) leaves a long iron to the green. Because most of the greens are elevated and usually heavily trapped, you often have to fly the ball into the green. Kingsmill's resident touring pro and two-time U.S. Open Champion Curtis Strange considers this one of the toughest holes on the course.

Another tough par 4 on the front side is the 437-yard fourth, whose tee shot plays over a stream. The second shot comes onto a wide, shallow, slightly elevated green protected by three traps in front and one in back. The golfer often has to come onto this green with a long iron or wood, making it difficult to hold. The 413-yard par-4 eighth is another challenge. If the tee shot is hit too far it will go through the fairway and down a bank on the left, and possibly into water below. The second shot is to a narrow, deep, undulating green with a very narrow entrance way protected by two traps. Two more traps flank each side of the green. If you miss to the right on the approach shot, there is a very severe drop-off.

The back nine is also challenging and features a nice run of three picturesque and difficult finishing holes. The 427-yard par-4 sixteenth is a dogleg right. The second shot has to avoid a cluster of traps beginning approximately 50 yards in front of a kidney-shaped green with a trap behind it. Reaching this green in two is a problem for many golfers. This is true on most of the par 4s on the River Course. The 179-yard par-3 seventeenth looks straightforward enough, but a variable wind can often be a factor. This is a beautiful hole, with the James River on the right. A narrow, deep green guarded by a large bunker on the right and two smaller traps on the left awaits you. The finishing hole is a 438-yard par 4 whose tee shot is over Moody's Pond to a narrowing fairway. A large tree on the left hinders a shot onto a narrow, deep green flanked by two traps on the left and a large trap on the right.

The 6590-yard par-72 Plantation Course, designed by Arnold Palmer and Ed Seay and opened in 1985, is also a fine test of golf. This golf course concludes with a 387-yard par 4, a dogleg left whose second shot is across Moody's Pond to a three-tiered green. A great place to practice your golf game at Kingsmill is the Bray Links Par Three, a nine-hole course with holes ranging from 54 to 109 yards and featuring an island green on the ninth hole and a double green on holes three and four.

The most recent addition to the Kingsmill golf venue is the Woods course, a 6784-yard par-72 layout designed by Tom Clark of Ault, Clark and Associates Ltd. with Curtis Strange, longtime Kingsmill resident and PGA touring professional. The Woods is woven through 200 acres of rolling Virginia woodlands cut by ravines. Water can come into play on six holes and strayed shots can roll into the woods, water or down into ravines. The fairways are ample and the greens are medium-sized with a variety of tricky indulations. The finishing holes on each side bracket a pond set below the small clubhouse. The 582-yard par-5 ninth requires three shots to reach a bulkheaded green bordered by water on the left and front. A strayed approach to the left or short will likely live with the fishes. The tough 462-yard par-4 eighteenth requires a long and accurate tee shot in order to set up an approach that will not be faded into the water on the right.

There is a full driving range and a short game area at the Woods. At present, there is a snack bar, modest locker room facilities and a small pro shop. In the future these amenities will likely be expanded.

The larger clubhouse serving the River and Plantation courses at Kingsmill includes all the amenities, such as locker rooms and showers, a complete bar and restaurant, and the Kingsmill Golf Pro Shop, which has been recognized as one of the best pro shops in the United States by *Golf Shop Operations* magazine. *Golf Digest* recognizes the golf course as one of the best resort golf courses in America,

and *Golf* magazine has awarded the resort its silver medal as one of the best golf resorts in the nation. There are approximately 1000 members, all property owners, at Kingsmill, and they have preferred tee times, but resort guests can reserve a time at the time of reservation. Outside play is allowed but only on 24-hour advance notice. Carts are required.

The staff of PGA golf professionals and assistants offers individual and group instruction. Golf packages are available through the resort. The courses get the heaviest use in April, May, October and early November. The Anheuser–Busch Golf Classic is held here in July. Lowest package rates are usually available from December to early March. Comprehensive golf schools for beginners, intermediate and advanced players are conducted at various times during the year Sunday through Friday and include resort accommodations; unlimited green and cart fees; welcome reception; Awards Banquet; complimentary range balls, bag storage, club cleaning; personal and group instruction; take-home "before and after" videotape; and free use of the sports club and tennis club facilities. The general policy at Kingsmill is not to add additional fees for use of the recreational and fitness facilities on site. For example, guests have free use of the tennis club, nine-hole Bray Links Par Three golf course, fitness center, racquetball courts, exercise classes, swimming pools, whirlpool, marina and private beach.

A variety of seasonal nongolf packages is also available, as is a supervised daily youth camp for children ages 5 to 12. This includes junior tennis and golf clinics, arts and crafts, storytelling, and fishing. Babysitting services are also available.

Meetings and Conventions magazine has awarded Kingsmill its Gold Tee Award for being an outstanding golf and conference center. Attractions beyond the resort such as Colonial Williamsburg, Virginia Beach, Busch Gardens, Yorktown, Jamestown, and nearby outlet malls add to the convenience and attractiveness of this award-winning golf hospitality center.

The Kingsmill Resort is a *Mobil Travel Guide* Four-Star and American Automobile Association Four-Diamond property, and is also a member of Preferred Hotels and Resorts Worldwide, a prestigious collection of the finest independent luxury hotels and resorts in the world. Among these hotels are La Valencia in La Jolla, California; the Peabody in Memphis, Tennessee; the Brown Palace in Denver, Colorado; and various others.

Course Name: THE TIDES INN
               Golden Eagle Course

Course Type: Resort
Resort: The Tides Inn
Address: King Carter Drive
               Irvington, VA 22480–0480
Phone: (804) 438–5501 (Golf Course)
               (804) 438–5000,
               (800) 843–3746 (Resort)
Fax: (804) 438–5222 (Resort)

GOLF COURSE

Head Professional: Jeff Winters
Course Length/Par (All Tees): Back 6963/72, Blue 6511/72, White 5985/72, Forward 5384/72
Course Slope/Rating (All Tees): Back 130/73, Blue 126/78.9, White 122/68.2, Ladies' Forward 121/69.9
Course Architects: George Cobb (1976), Buddy Loving (renovation, 1987)
Golf Facilities: Full Pro Shop X, Snack Bar X, Lounge X, Restaurant X, Locker Room X, Showers X, Club Rental X, Club Repair X, Cart Rental X, Instruction X, Practice Green X, Driving Range X, Practice Bunker X, Club Storage X
Tee-Time Reservation Policy: Resort guests: At time of confirmed reservation. Outside play: Flexible, call in advance
Ranger: As required
Tee-off-Interval Time: 10 min.
Time to Play 18 Holes: 4 hrs., 15 min.
Course Hours/Earliest Tee-off: 8:30 a.m.
Green Fees: Resort guests: $42 daily fee. Outside play: $58 for 18 holes
Cart Fees: $14 for 18 holes per person

Credit Cards: American Express, Master-Card, Visa
Season: Mid-March to Dec. Busiest season mid-April to June, Sept. to Nov.
Course Comments: Can walk except weekend mornings
Golf Packages: Available through the Tides Inn
Discounts: Resort guests, seasonal memberships. Twilight rate after 3 p.m.
Places to Stay Nearby: IRVINGTON: Tides Lodge (804) 438–6000, (800) 248–4337. NORFOLK: Omni International (804) 622–6664. VIRGINIA BEACH: Oceanside Holiday Inn (804) 428–1711, (800) HOLIDAY; Courtyard by Marriott (804) 490–2002, (800) 321–2211. WILLIAMSBURG: Ramada Inn (804) 220–2800, (800) 492–2855. Williamsburg Hotel and Motel Association (800) 446–9244
Local Attractions: Mary Ball Washington Museum and Library, Stratford Hall, shopping, antiquing, historic Christ Church, boating, fishing, Yorktown. Williamsburg. Jamestown. Norfolk. Portsmouth. Virginia Beach. Virginia Beach Tourism (800) 446–8038. Williamsburg Area Convention and Visitors Bureau (804) 253–0192. Norfolk Convention and Visitors Bureau (804) 441–5266, (800) 368–3097
Directions: From northern Virginia: I–95 to U.S. 17 south (Fredericksburg) to Saluda, Hwy. 33 east to Rte. 3 west (to Rappahannock River Bridge) to White Stone, left on Rte. 200 to Irvington and resort. From Richmond area (70 mi.): I–64 to exit 220 (Hwy. 33) to Saluda (follow above directions from Saluda). From Norfolk area (80 mi.): I–64 to U.S. 17 north to Saluda (follow above directions from Saluda)
Closest Commercial Airports: Richmond International (1 hr., 15 min.); Norfolk International (1½ hrs.); Newport News/Williamsburg International (1½ hrs.); Dulles International, Washington, DC (3 hrs.)

RESORT

Date Built: 1947

No. of Rooms: 111 singles, doubles, and semisuites

Meeting Rooms: 6. Capacity of Largest: 150 persons. Meeting Space: 6000 sq. ft.

Room Price Range: $130 to $226, double occupancy, modified American plan. Highest rates May through Oct. Golf, midweek, family vacation, golf widow and other packages available

Lounges: Chesapeake Club, Cap'n B's

Restaurants: Rappahannock Dining Room, Summer House (on pool deck), Cap'n B's (at Golden Eagle Golf Course)

Entertainment: Live music Mon., Wed., Fri., Sat., and Sun.

Credit Cards: American Express, Master-Card, Visa

General Amenities: Cruises, shopping and historic tours to Williamsburg, York-town; meeting and conference facilities with banquet-, theater- and conference-style rooms available; youth program with counselor from June to Aug., babysitting available

Recreational Amenities: Boating, charter fishing, outdoor saltwater pool, 4 all-weather and clay tennis courts, bicycling, croquet, game room, canoeing, paddleboats, marina for boats up to 130 feet; unlimited use of complete health and fitness facility with racquetball, aerobics, weight room, whirlpool, and steam room; shuffleboard

Reservation and Cancellation Policy: Personal check preferred to hold reservation. Cancellation must be made 4 days prior to arrival to avoid penalties

Comments and Restrictions: Full American plan available at additional per person fee. Gratuities and tax additional. Reduced rates for a 3rd person in parents' room. Children ages 4 and below free

THE TIDES INN

The Tides Inn is a family-owned and -operated resort that also happens to have, as *Golf* magazine put it, "the Toughest Golf Course No One's Ever Heard Of." It all began with Big Steve and Miss Ann. That is E. A. Stephens, a University of Virginia graduate and native of the Northern Neck in Upper Tidewater, Virginia, as is his wife, the former Ann Lee. In the early 1940s, while a Buick dealer in New Orleans, Stephens bought an abandoned farm on Carter's Creek near the Rappahonnock River. By 1947 he and his wife had opened their new inn, which included meals, rooms and other amenities at the daily rate of $16 per person. Today the Tides Inn has 111 rooms situated in the inn and the nearby Windsor House, Lancaster House, and Garden House. The resort is now owned by Big Steve's son Bob Lee Stephens and is very much a family business with an informal and personal touch. Bob Lee Stephens's sons Lee and Randy are involved in the management of the business, representing the third generation of Stephenses to do so.

A nine-hole golf course is within walking distance of the Tides Inn, and 5 minutes away is the 6963-yard George Cobb–designed Golden Eagle Golf Course, which opened in 1976 and is also owned by the Tides Inn. The Virginia State Amateur Championship has been hosted here, and the First Annual International Senior Women's Team Championship was held here in 1992. The Golden Eagle was cut out of a forest of oak, pine and cedar, has rolling fairways, and is riddled with more than 120 sand bunkers. The bentgrass greens are medium sized, fast and undulating. There are water hazards on seven holes. Lake Irvington, a centerpiece of this layout, is the primary source of the water. Each hole tends to be a separate, memorable experience, with no parallel holes. No real-estate development surrounds the course. And you can walk this course anytime except weekend mornings.

The number-1-handicap hole on the Golden Eagle is the 463-yard par-4 fifth, a dogleg left bordered on the left-hand side from tee to green by a lake. The tee shot is over the lake, so the strategic question is how much of the lake the golfer wants to cut without putting the ball in the drink. A big hitter can probably get the ball to within 170 yards of the hole. The approach shot is to a deep green with water on the left and two large traps on the right. The other tee distance options on this hole are 428, 412 and 360 yards from back to front, respectively. A long and well-bunkered par 5 on this side is the 571-yard sixth, which plays straight to a green completely surrounded by four traps. Five additional fairway bunkers are to be found in landing areas along the way to the hole. Another difficult par 4 is the 411-yard ninth, a dogleg right whose second shot is over a lake to a green fronted by water. Because the top tier of this green is on a severe angle, the pin placement is always on the lower, flatter level, making this a tough target.

The most difficult par 3 at the Golden Eagle is the 205-yard seventeenth, which plays uphill to a green surrounded by three traps. The tee shot has to reach the putting surface in the air, or else it will be stopped by a bank in front if it is short. The finishing hole is a 380-yard par-4 dogleg right that plays over a wide stream on the second shot to a deep, forward-sloping green in an amphitheaterlike setting. The putting surface is protected by two traps on the right and one on the left. Many of the holes at the Golden Eagle are affected by wind coming off the nearby Chesapeake Bay. This often makes the course play longer and more difficult than the yardage would indicate.

The clubhouse at the Golden Eagle has locker rooms and showers, a restaurant and bar, and a full pro shop whose staff provides individual and group lessons. A second grass tier has been added to the driving range. A practice green is available, but there are no practice bunkers at present. The Tides Inn offers reasonable golf packages, and the golf course can be played by guests for a flat daily fee. Cart fees are charged for each 18. The inn and the golf course are open mid-March through December with the busiest months on the golf course being mid-April through June and September through November. You can call anytime for a tee time.

The Tidewater Inn offers a variety of amenities in a down-home, friendly fash-ion. This includes access to their 127-foot yacht *Miss Ann,* 4 tennis courts, an air-conditioned game room, croquet, an Olympic-sized saltwater swimming pool, a nine-hole par-3 golf course adjacent to the inn; free use of sailboats, paddleboats and canoes; a supervised children's program during the summer months, free bicycle use, evening cocktail music and parlor games, dancing or movies, and unlimited use of a complete health and fitness facility. The resort operates on a modified American plan, and luncheons are available on an a la carte or prix fixe basis at Cap'n B's at the Golden Eagle golf course, aboard the resort's yachts, at the summer house adjacent to the pool and in the Rappahannock Dining Room.

The Tidewater Inn has meeting and conference facilities for small groups of up to 150 persons. There are 6 meeting rooms in banquet-, theater- or conference-style configurations, and a variety of organized activities for groups ranging from golf outings to banquets and cruises on the Chesapeake can be arranged.

While the Tidewater Inn's atmosphere is friendly and informal, hospitality is taken very seriously, and the inn and its staff have won awards and recognition to prove it. The resort has a *Mobil Travel Guide* Four-Star rating and an American Automobile Association Four-Diamond Rating. *Condé Nast Traveler* magazine has ranked the Tides Inn among the top 20 mainland resorts in the United States. The same publication also rated the Tides Inn among the 60 best travel experiences in the world.

Lancaster County, home of the Tides, is situated just north of the Rappahannock River and has evolved from a sedate rural farm and fishing area to a prime retirement area with approximately 11,000 residents. Nearby are the historic attractions of Williamsburg and Yorktown as well as the Chesapeake. For a unique and hospitable golf experience, visit the Tides Inn.

James River Country Club

The Museum at James River Country Club includes golf art and more than 1000 books. It also has a collection of early golf clubs, some dating back to the 1600s, golf balls and other equipment. The collection was assembled in the 1930s through the generosity of Archer Huntington, who also funded the collection's clubhouse display space. James River Country Club, 1500 Country Club Rd., Newport News, VA 23606, (804) 595–3327

Recommended Golf Courses in Virginia

Within 1 Hour of Williamsburg:

The Hampton's Golf Course, Hampton, (804) 776–9148, Public. Wood/Lakes: 18/6401/71. Lakes/Links: 18/6283/71. Woods/Links: 18/5940/70

Hell's Point Golf Club, Virginia Beach, (804) 721–3400, Public, 18/6966/72

Honey Bee Golf Club, Virginia Beach, (804) 471–2768, Semiprivate, 18/6075/70

Kiln Creek Golf and Country Club, Newport News, (804) 988–3220, Semiprivate, 18/6889/72

Newport News Golf Club at Deer Run, Newport News, (804) 886–7925, Public. Cardinal: 18/6624/72. Deer Run: 18/7081/72

Red Wing Lake Golf Course, Virginia Beach, (804) 437–4845, Public, 18/7080/72

Sleepy Hole Golf Course, Suffolk, (804) 538–4100, Public, 18/6695/71

Suffolk Golf Course, Suffolk, (804) 539–6298, Public, 18/6340/72

Tides Lodge, Irvington, (804) 438–6200, (800) 248–4337, Resort, 18/6586/72

Virginia: Useful Information

Virginia Division of Tourism, 901 E. Byrd St., Richmond, VA, 23219 (804) 786–2051, (800) VISITVA

Virginia State Chamber of Commerce, 9 S. 5th St., Richmond, VA 23219, (804) 644–1607

Department of Game and Inland Fisheries, 4010 West Broad St., Richmond, VA 23230, (804) 367–1000 (fishing and hunting regulations)

Department of Conservation and Recreation, Division of State Parks, 203 Governor St., Ste. 302, Richmond, VA 23219, (804) 225–3867, (800) 933–PARK

U.S. Forest Service, Southern Region, Information Office, 1720 Peachtree Rd. N.W., Atlanta, GA 30367-9002, (404) 347—2384, (800) 280–CAMP (information and reservations)

State Parks, Ticketron Reservation Center, P.O. Box 62221, Virginia Beach, VA 23462, (804) 786–1712 (general information) (804) 490–3939 (state park cabin reservations) (804) 490–3939

Course Name: SEMIAHMOO GOLF AND COUNTRY CLUB

Course Type: Resort
Resort: The Inn at Semiahmoo
Address: 9565 Semiahmoo Parkway
P.O. Box 790
Blaine, WA 98230–0790
Phone: (360) 371–7005 (Golf Course)
(360) 371–2000,
(800) 770–7992
Fax: (360) 371–5490 (Resort)

GOLF COURSE

Director of Golf: Brian J. Southwick

Course Length/Par (All Tees): Back 7005/72, Blue 6435/72, White 6003/72, Forward 5288/72

Course Slope/Rating (All Tees): Back 130/74.5, Blue 125/71.9, White 123/69.9; Ladies' White 131/75.5 Ladies' Forward 126/71.6

Course Architects: Arnold Palmer and Ed Seay (1986)

Golf Facilities: Full Pro Shop X, Snack Bar X, Lounge X, Restaurant X, Locker Room X, Showers X, Club Rental X, Club Repair X, Cart Rental X, Instruction X, Practice Green X, Driving Range X, Practice Bunker X, Club Storage X

Tee-Time Reservation Policy: Resort guests: 3 mos. in advance. Outside play: From 3 days in advance for Mon.– Thurs., from Fri. for weekend tee times

Ranger: Yes

Tee-off-Interval Time: 10 min.

Time to Play 18 Holes: 4 hrs., 15 min.

Course Hours/Earliest Tee-off: 6:30 a.m. to dark

Green Fees: Resort guests: $65 for 18 holes Fri., Sat., Sun., holidays, $62 for 18 holes Mon. through Thurs.; $45 for 9 holes weekends, $43 for 9 holes Mon. through Thurs. Outside play, peak season (May to Sept.): $70 for 18 holes Fri., Sat., Sun., holidays; $67 for 18 holes Mon. through Thurs.

Cart Fees: $14 for 18 holes per seat, $10 for 9 holes per seat

Pull Carts: $4.25 for 18 holes, $2.50 for 9 holes

Credit Cards: American Express, Master-Card, Visa

Season: Busiest season May to Sept. Open all year

Course Comments: Can walk anytime. Guests, members and property owners have tee-time priority

Golf Packages: Available through the resort. Highest rates April to Oct.

Discounts: Guests, members, and guests of property owners. Off-season, twilight

Places to Stay Nearby: BLAINE: Bay Side Motor Inn (360) 332–5288; Golden Tides Resort (360) 371–7333. BELLING-HAM: Best Western Heritage Inn (360) 647–1912, (800) 528–1234; Ramada Inn (360) 734–8830, (800) 228–2828; Resort at Sudden Valley (360) 734–6430. BED AND BREAKFASTS: Victoria Rose Bed and Breakfast (360) 332–8677; Circle F Bed and Breakfast (360) 733–2509

Local Attractions: Fishing, boating, What-com County Semiahmoo Park Museum, Victoria, Vancouver, San Juan Islands, bird watching, clamming. Vancouver, British Columbia. Vancouver Island. Blaine Visitor Center (360) 332–4544, (800) 371–5100

Directions: From Seattle (2 hrs.): North on I–5, exit 270 (Birch Bay Lynden exit), left on Birch Bay Lynden, 4½ mi. to Harbor View, turn right .3 mi. to Lincoln Rd., left to golf course

Closest Commercial Airports: Belling-ham International (30 min.); Vancouver International, British Columbia, Canada (1 hr.); Seattle–Tacoma International (2½ hrs.)

RESORT

Date Built: 1987

No. of Rooms: 200, including 12 suites, 40 rooms with fireplaces

Meeting Rooms: 11. Capacity of Largest: 448 persons banquet style. Meeting Space: 11,410 sq. ft.

Room Price Range: $175 to $300 for executive suites peak season (June to Oct.). Golf and other packages available year round

Lounges: Lobby Lounge, Packers

Restaurants: Packers Oyster Bar and Lounge, Stars, Pierside, Blue Heron Bar and Grill (at golf clubhouse)

Entertainment: Pianist in Stars Restaurant

Credit Cards: All major cards

General Amenities: Gift shop; meeting and conference facilities with audio-visual, banquet and catering facilities; supervised children's programs, babysitting service

Recreational Amenities: Boat cruises, charter fishing, bicycling, 2 tennis courts, 1 squash court, 2 racquetball courts, kayaking, volleyball, croquet, horseshoes, skiing, indoor/outdoor swimming pool; health club with indoor jogging track, weight and aerobics rooms, massage and tanning parlors, sauna, steam baths; 300-slip marina, hot-air balloon rides

Reservation and Cancellation Policy: Credit card will hold a reservation. 1 night's room-fee penalty if reservation not canceled 7 days before arrival

Comments and Restrictions: No pets. Discounts available to members of AARP, AAA, Canadian Automobile Association. Taxes additional to base rates

SEMIAHMOO GOLF AND COUNTRY CLUB

Located just below the Canadian border, approximately 45 miles south of Vancouver, British Columbia, Semiahmoo is part of an 1100-acre real-estate-development complex and resort facility located on Drayton Cove across from Blaine, Washington. The course itself was designed by Arnold Palmer and Ed Seay in 1987 and was named the best new resort course in America by *Golf Digest*.

The golf course measures 7005 yards from the back tees, with rolling fairways dotted with strategically placed bunkers and trees. In the background are residences of the development. The layout is relatively open, with medium-sized, fast, undulating, well-trapped greens. Water comes into play on six of the holes.

The number-1-handicap fourth hole at Semiahmoo plays 417 yards from the back tees and requires two relatively long and straight shots to a large, forward-sloping green protected by a huge trap on the left and one in front. Another tough hole is the 415-yard par-4 fourteenth, a dogleg to the right through a well-treed fairway. The green is large and forward sloping, and it has a large trap on the left.

Signature holes at Semiahmoo are the eleventh and twelfth holes, which wrap around water. The eleventh is a 371-yard par 4 whose tree-lined fairway narrows to 30 to 40 yards in the tee-shot landing area. Approximately 100 yards from the green large bunkers appear on the left and right, and the green itself is well guarded by two traps. Unless you are long off the tee, you will probably have to come in over water on the second shot and clear the trap in front of the green. The twelfth hole is a beautiful par 3 that measures 173 yards from the back tees and plays over water that cuts halfway into the fairway. Three traps protect a large green that slopes left to right toward the water.

Semiahmoo has a magnificent 26,000-square-foot clubhouse with full pro shop, locker room and showers, and restaurant facilities. Golf instruction, including individual, group, specialized swing clinics, corporate clinics and kids' clinic, is available. Practice facilities include a driving range and practice green. Golf packages are available year round, with the lowest-rate packages usually available from November through March. The golf course can be walked at any time, and nonguests can play the course.

Surrounding the golf course is a real-estate development with condominiums and homes. A few minutes away is the resort hotel, which is separated from the golf course and real-estate development by a mile-long land spit separating Drayton Harbor from Semiahmoo Bay. The area is excellent for fishing and boating. Victoria, British Columbia; the San Juan Islands;

and the Gulf Islands of Canada are within easy reach.

The 200-room inn and conference center at Semiahmoo has excellent views of the bay and harbor. Meeting facilities include a variety of theater, classroom, and conference options, and the 3 restaurants include Stars, for fine waterfront dining; Packers, an oyster bar and lounge that was formerly a salmon-canning room; and the Pierside family-style restaurant, on the water's edge. The fresh, local seafood; regional wines; and beers from regional microbreweries are a real treat. The inn also features recreation facilities, including indoor tennis, squash, an indoor track, racquetball, tanning booths, sauna, whirlpool, and a massage area, as well as a well-equipped exercise room.

When you step outside the inn and glance at it, it looks like a cannery. It formerly was the site of the Alaska Packers Salmon Cannery, where large 3-masted sailing ships of the Star Fleet brought salmon from Alaska for processing. Though the days of the tall ships have passed, the seafaring spirit is maintained by the nearby 300-slip marina and 5 miles of sandy beaches. More than 30 species of waterfowl, a resident population of harbor seals and numerous shore birds are wondrous to watch. Fish in the area include ling cod, rock fish, flounder, halibut, red snapper and salmon.

It has been over 200 years since Europeans came in contact with the Coast Salish Indians, which include the Semiahmoo. Today one of the finest golf-resort complexes in the Northwest stands on these old hunting and fishing grounds.

Recommended Golf Courses in Washington

Bellingham Area:

Eaglemont Golf Club, Mt. Vernon, (360) 424–0800, Semiprivate, 18/7006/72

Homestead Golf and Country Club, Lynden, (360) 345–1196, Semiprivate, 18/6927/72

Lake Padden Golf Course, Bellingham, (360) 738–7400, Public, 18/6675/72

Shuksan Golf Club, Bellingham, (360) 398–8888, Public, 18/6706/72

Sudden Valley Golf and Country Club, Bellingham, (360) 734–6435, (800) 734–6903, Semiprivate, 18/6553/72

Tri-Mountain Golf Course, Ridgefield, (360) 887–3004, Public, 18/6580/72

Seattle/Tacoma Area

Course Name: CLASSIC COUNTRY CLUB

Course Type: Public
Address: 4908 208th Street East
                       Spanaway, WA 98387
Phone: (206) 847–4440
Fax: (206) 846–9868

GOLF COURSE

Head Professional: Lorie Isaac
Course Length/Par (All Tees): Back 6793/72, White 6387/72, Gold 6008/72, Forward 5580/72
Course Slope/Rating (All Tees): Back 133/73.6, White 130/71.6, Gold 124/69.6, Forward 121/68.0. Ladies' Back 142/80.5, White 138/77.9, Gold 135/75.8, Forward 128/73.3
Course Architect: William Oberdorf (1991)
Golf Facilities: Full Pro Shop X, Snack Bar X, Lounge X, Restaurant X, Locker Room No, Showers X, Club Rental X, Club Repair X, Cart Rental X, Instruction X, Practice Green X, Driving Range X, Practice Bunker X, Club Storage No
Tee-Time Reservation Policy: Up to 9 days in advance for the public. Members have tee time reservation priority
Ranger: Yes
Tee-off-Interval Time: 10 min.
Time to Play 18 Holes: 4½ hrs.
Course Hours/Earliest Tee-off: 6 a.m.
Green Fees: $45 for 18 holes Sat., Sun., holidays; $30 for 18 holes weekdays. $25 for 9 holes Sat., Sun., holidays; $15 for 9 holes weekdays
Cart Fees: $23 for 18 holes, $15 for 9 holes per cart. Pull carts $5 for 18 holes, $3 for 9 holes
Credit Cards: All major cards

Season: Year round. Busiest June through Labor Day

Course Comments: You can walk anytime

Golf Packages: No

Discounts: Twilight. Seasonal Oct. through Apr. Junior, senior. "Pro shop selects your tee time" discounts

Places to Stay Nearby: TACOMA: Sheraton–Tacoma (206) 572–3200, (800) 325–3535. OLYMPIA: Ramada Inn Governor House (206) 462–1234, (800) 233–1234; Embassy Suites (206) 644–2500, (800) 362–2779. BELLEVUE: Hyatt Regency Bellevue (206) 462–1234, (800) 233–1234; Red Lion Inn Bellevue (206) 455–1300, (800) 547–8010. SEA–TAC: Seattle–Marriott Sea–Tac Airport (206) 241–2000, (800) 228–9290; Wyndham Garden Hotel (206) 244–6666, (800) WYNDHAM. SEATTLE: Alexis Hotel (206) 624–4844, (800) 426–7033; Doubletree Seattle Inn (206) 246–8220, (800) 222–TREE; Four Seasons Olympic (206) 621–1700, (800) 332–3442; Inn at The Market (206) 443–3600, (800) 446–4484

Local Attractions: BELLEVUE: Bellevue Art Museum, Bellevue Botanical Garden, Lake Hills Greenbelt, Rosalie Whyel Museum of Doll Art. OLYMPIA: The Capitol Group, Olympia Beer Co., State Capitol Museum. TACOMA: Children's Museum of Tacoma, Fort Lewis Military Museum, Lakewood Gardens, Point Defiance Park, Tacoma Art Museum, Washington State Historical Society Museum. PUYALLUP: Meeker Mansion, Van Lierop Bulb Farms. SEATTLE: See page 692

Directions: From Seattle (55 min.): Take I–5 south to Exit 127/Puyallup-Mt. Rainier. Proceed west on Hwy. 512 to Pacific Ave. Turn right (south) to 208th then left (east) to the golf course on the right. From Olympia (40 min.): Take I–5 north to Exit 127 then follow the directions above

Closest Commercial Airport: Seattle-Tacoma (45 min.)

THE CLASSIC COUNTRY CLUB

The Classic Country Club is a 6793-yard par-72 William Oberdorf–designed layout cut through woodlands one hour southeast of Seattle. The course features 62 sand bunkers and 32 grass bunkers, large, fast, undulating bentgrass greens and an occasional water hazard. The omnipresent trees can add difficulty to this easily walkable, country club-quality golf course.

Classic offers a variety of holes with the back tee distances ranging from 347 (No. 3) to 429 yards (No. 13) on the par 4s, from 134 (No. 15) to 209 yards (No. 4) on the par 3s, and from 530 (Nos. 7 and 14) to 581 yards on the par 5s. The scenic 134-yard par-3 eighth plays from an elevated tee over water to an ample green framed by bunkers. The 347-yard par-4 third, a dogleg right, requires you to position a longiron shot off the tee to the left in order to have a clear view to a slightly elevated green protected by three bunkers. A tree between the two bunkers to the right guards the green. The 581-yard par-5 finishing hole starts off with a blind tee shot from an elevated tee that must avoid water to the left of the landing area. The second shot is toward a well-bunkered double green shared with hole No. 12. Bunkers straddle the landing area from 100 yards in to the huge target.

Classic Country Club has a clubhouse with pro shop, locker rooms, full dining facilities, banquet space for 300, and outside deck and barbeque area. The practice area has a three-tiered tee area at its driving range which has flagged target greens. There are also putting and chipping greens and practice bunkers. Classic Country Club is rated one of the best golf courses in Washington by *Golf Digest*.

**Course Name: HARBOUR POINTE
                GOLF COURSE**

Course Type: Public
Address: 11817 Harbour Pointe Blvd.
              Mukilteo, WA 98204
Phone: (206) 355–6060,
              (800) 233–3128 (WA)

GOLF COURSE

Director of Golf and Head Professional: Mark Rhodes

Course Length/Par (All Tees): Back 6880/72, Blue 6487/72, White 6052/72, Gold 5460/72, Forward 4950/72

Course Slope/Rating (All Tees): Men's Back 138/73.3, Blue 136/71.6, White 128/70.4, Gold 118/67.0, Forward 111/64.5. Ladies' Back 150/79.9, Blue 148/77.9, White 140/76.5, Gold 129/72.4, Forward 121/69.3

Course Architect: Arthur Hills (first 9, 1989, second 9, 1990)

Golf Facilities: Full Pro Shop X, Snack Bar X, Lounge X, Restaurant X, Locker Room No, Showers No, Club Rental X, Club Repair X, Cart Rental X, Instruction X, Practice Green X, Driving Range X, Practice Bunker X, Club Storage No

Tee-Time Reservation Policy: Up to 7 days in advance. Prepayment required for booking a tee time in advance

Ranger: Yes

Tee-off-Interval Time: 9 min.

Time to Play 18 Holes: 4½ hrs.

Course Hours/Earliest Tee-off: Dawn to dusk

Green Fees: $45 for 18 holes Fri., Sat., Sun.; $40 for 18 holes Mon. to Thurs. $25 for 9 holes Fri., Sat., Sun.; $20 for 9 holes Mon. to Thurs.

Cart Fees: $25 for 18 holes

Credit Cards: MasterCard, Visa

Season: Year round

Course Comments: Can walk anytime

Golf Packages: None

Discounts: Juniors, seasonal for members only. Twilight rate 2½ hrs. from dusk ($12)

Places to Stay Nearby: EVERETT: Best Western Cascadia Inn (206) 258–4141, (800) 528–1234; Cypress Inn (206) 347–9099; West Coast Everett Pacific Hotel and Convention Center (206) 339–3333, (800) 426–0670; Marina Village Inn (206) 259–4040; Motel 6 (206) 347–2060. WHIDBEY ISLAND: Captain Whidbey Inn (206) 678–4097, (800) 366–4097; Fort Casey Inn (206) 678–8792; Coupeville Inn (206) 678–6668, (800) 247–6162

Local Attractions: Fishing, boating, camping, hiking, bicycling. EVERETT: Snohomish County Museum. COUPEVILLE: Island County Historical Museum. Whidbey Island. San Juan Islands. Everett Area Chamber of Commerce (206) 259–3164. Central Whidbey Chamber of Commerce (206) 678–5434. San Juan Islands Tourism (206) 468–3663. Island County Visitor Council (206) 678–4684

Directions: From Seattle (45 min.): I–5 north, exit 182 west to Hwy. 99, turn right on 99 to light, turn left onto Hwy. 525/Mukilteo Speedway 1 mi. to 2nd light, left onto Harbour Pointe Blvd., 1½ mi. to course on right

Closest Commercial Airport: Seattle–Tacoma International (1 hr.)

HARBOUR POINTE GOLF COURSE

The Harbour Pointe Golf Course, located 45 minutes northwest of Seattle on Puget Sound, was selected the best new public course in 1991 by *Golf Digest*. This 6880-yard par-72 Arthur Hills–designed layout has a variety of water hazards on the first nine holes, which are flat and wind through 28 acres of wetlands. The back nine is hilly and more tightly treed. The bentgrass greens at Harbour Pointe are large, moderately fast and undulating. Large traps strategically guard the greens. You have a choice of five tee distances, ranging from 6880 yards to 4950 yards on this fine golf course.

Shot placement, strategy and course management are important at Harbour Pointe. Because of the size of the greens, careful attention should be paid to pin placement, which is indicated by colored flags to select the depth and angle to come in from. The course starts out at a leisurely pace until you reach the 436-yard par-4 fifth hole, a long dogleg left to an elevated green with a bunker in front. The tee shot should be kept right-center but has to avoid a lateral water hazard on the right. The approach shot is all carry over the bunker in front of the green.

A beautiful and challenging par 3 on the front side is the 177-yard seventh, which plays from a slightly elevated tee over water to a deep, two-tiered green that is bordered by water to the rear and right. If you miss short, right or long you are likely to be in the water. The signature hole is the 394-yard par-4 eleventh which overlooks Puget Sound and Whidbey Island, and has a view of the Olympic Mountains in the distance. To your back is the Snoqualmie National Forest and the Cascade Mountain Range. The tee shot is downhill to a swale, and the approach shot is back uphill to a tiered green with bunkers to the right and rear.

Harbour Pointe is part of a 2000-acre planned community that is scheduled to include a mix of houses, apartments, condominiums, public parks, business and technology parks, public schools, religious institutions, marinas and retail shops. More than $3 million has been invested in the golf course, which covers 180 acres within this development.

At present, the clubhouse is modest, with pro shop and food facilities but no locker rooms and showers. A practice range, practice bunker and putting green are available. Group and individual instruction is available. You can walk the course anytime and make a tee-time reservation anytime in advance for the current year with prepayment. Reasonable twilight rates are available from 2½ hours before dusk.

Course Name: **KAYAK POINT GOLF COURSE**

Course Type: Public
Address: 15711 Marine Drive
Stanwood, WA 98292
Phone: (360) 652–9676,
(800) 562–3094

GOLF COURSE

Director of Golf: Elwin Fanning
Head Professional: Doug Fair
Course Length/Par (All Tees): Back 6719/72, Middle 6109/72, Forward 5409/72
Course Slope/Rating (All Tees): Men's Back 133/72.7, Middle 128/71.4, For-

ward 121/NA. Ladies' Back 144/NA, Middle 138/NA, Forward 129/72.6
Course Architects: Ron Fream, Peter Thomson, Michael Wolveridge and Terry Storm (1977)
Golf Facilities: Full Pro Shop X, Snack Bar X, Lounge X, Restaurant X, Locker Room X, Showers X, Club Rental X, Club Repair X, Cart Rental X, Instruction X, Practice Green X, Driving Range X, Practice Bunker X, Club Storage No
Tee-Time Reservation Policy: With prepayment (prepaying foursomes' green fees, limit 3 foursomes) anytime in advance; without prepayment 1 wk. in advance for weekdays. On site after your round weekends and holidays or by phone the Mon. prior to weekend or holiday desired
Ranger: Yes
Tee-off-Interval Time: 7 and 8 min.
Time to Play 18 Holes: 5 hrs.
Course Hours/Earliest Tee-off: 5 a.m. to dark
Green Fees: $27 plus tax for 18 holes Sat., Sun. holidays; $23 plus tax for 18 holes Mon. to Thurs. $14 plus tax for 9 holes Sat., Sun., holidays; $12 plus tax for 9 holes Mon. to Thurs.
Cart Fees: $25 plus tax for 18 holes per cart for 18 holes; $12.50 plus tax for 9 holes per cart
Credit Cards: MasterCard, Visa
Season: Year round. Busiest season April through Oct.
Course Comments: Can walk anytime
Golf Packages: None
Discounts: Seniors, juniors. Coupon book can be purchased for multiple rounds
Places to Stay Nearby: MARYSVILLE: Best Western Tulalip Inn (360) 659–4488, (800) 528–1234; Village Motor Inn (360) 659–0005. SEATTLE: Hotel Alternative (condominiums in Seattle/Bellevue area) (206) 867–9200, (800) 523–4356. Fax: (206) 885–4233; Alexis Hotel (206) 624–4844; Marriott's Residence Inn—Seattle Downtown/Lake Union (206) 624–6000; Best Western Airport Executive (206) 878–3300, (800) 528–1234; Doubletree Suites Hotel (206)

575–8220, (800) 528–0444; Holiday Inn, Seattle Sea–Tac (206) 248–1000, (800) HOLIDAY; Claremont Hotel (206) 448–8600; Four Seasons Olympic (206) 621–1700, (800) 332–3442; Inn at Virginia Mason (206) 583–6453, (800) 283–6453; Seattle Hilton (206) 624–0500, (800) 426–0535; Baker Guest Apartments (206) 323–9909. BED AND BREAKFASTS: Pacific Bed and Breakfast Agency (206) 784–0539; Washington Bed and Breakfast Guild (509) 548–6224

Local Attractions: Hunting, fishing, bingo, camping, hiking, boating. SEATTLE: Blake Island Marine State Park, Lake Washington Ship Canal and Hiram M. Chittenden Locks, Pike Place Market, Space Needle, Pacific Science Center, Pacific Arts Center, opera house, Pioneer Square District, Bagley Wright Theater, Seattle University, Kingdome, restaurants, art galleries, Seattle Art Museum, Museum of Flight, Museum of History and Industry, Queen Anne Hill, Woodland Park Zoo, Seattle Aquarium, University of Washington Arboretum, professional sports, theater, opera, music, seasonal festivals, Longacres Racetrack (horse racing), Seattle Children's Museum, wineries, ferry rides. Seattle/King County Convention and Visitors Bureau (206) 461–5800. Fax: (206) 461–5855

Directions: From Seattle: I–5 exit 199, west on Marine Dr. 13½ mi., follow signs. From Bellingham: I–5 south, exit 212, 532 west to Marine Dr., left on Marine Dr., 8 mi. to golf course

Closest Commercial Airports: Bellingham International (1 hr.), Seattle–Tacoma International (1½ hrs.)

KAYAK POINT GOLF COURSE

North of Seattle and approximately 15 miles west of I–5 is one of the best public golf courses in the United States. Carved out of a pine and fir forest with some dramatic changes in elevation, Kayak Point is a 6719-yard par-72 test that demands accuracy or you will be penalized virtually every time. Kayak Point covers 250 acres

and is situated within a 650-acre county park.

The course is extremely well maintained, and over $1 million has been invested in the clubhouse by Elwin Fanning, director of golf, and the lessor of the course from the County of Snohomish. Kayak Point's architect is Ron Fream (with Peter Thomson, Michael Wolveridge, and Terry Storm), who also designed Canyon Lakes Golf and Country Club, Kennewick, Washington; Mint Valley Municipal, Longview, Washington; Tapps Island Golf Club, Sumner, Washington; and many courses in California, Indonesia, Oregon and elsewhere.

The clubhouse is at the top of a hill and offers a view of magnificent pines and firs and beyond to the Cascade Mountain Range. The first hole, a par 4, starts off from an elevated tee and descends approximately 50 feet to the green almost 400 yards away. The fairway slopes to the right and is well protected by trees on each side. Virtually every hole on the course is lined with trees from tee to green, often making the fairways extremely narrow.

The second hole, a 549-yard par 5, starts off from an elevated tee. From the tee there is a dramatic 100-foot drop over a well-landscaped pond to a narrow, tree-lined fairway. You must get your drive out 175 yards to clear the pond and 225 to 250 yards to be in decent position. The second shot is straight down a tree-lined alley, and the third is onto a slightly elevated green with bunkers right-front and left-back. As with most of the holes, because of surrounding trees and banks on the side of the greens that will kick a ball into the woods or down a hill, there is little margin for error if you miss the green.

One of the most difficult holes on the course is the par-4 seventeenth, which plays 405 yards from the back tees. The tee shot is through a narrow, wooded chute and out onto a rolling fairway. The second shot comes up to an elevated green with a bunker on the right.

Among my favorite holes on the course is the par-4 seventh, which has a dramatic elevated tee that drops over 75 feet to a downward-sloping fairway whose landing area is a plateau with a view down to the green approximately 150 yards away. There is another drop of more than 75 feet to get to the green. A huge tree is positioned in the center of the fairway 100 yards from the tee. After negotiating this and avoiding the trees lining the fairway, you approach a large green that tilts slightly forward and drops off into trouble all around it.

In addition to tree-lined holes that demand great accuracy, there are several blind holes that make Kayak Point even more challenging. For example, on the front nine, both the eighth and ninth holes have blind tee shots. Although there are virtually no bunkers on the fairways, the accuracy required by narrow fairways and the likelihood of difficult lies on the sloped and rolling terrain require the golfer to play the course several times to get his or her bearings. While you are exploring the course, an abundance of wildlife might accompany you, including beavers, eagles, hawks, deer, squirrels and an occasional bear.

Course Name: McCORMICK WOODS

Course Type: Public
Address: 5155 McCormick Woods Drive Southwest Port Orchard, WA 98366
Phone: (206) 895–0130, (800) 323–0130 (WA)

GOLF COURSE

Head Professional: Ernie Taylor
Course Length/Par (All Tees): Back 7012/72, Championship 6632/72, Eagle 6155/72, Birdie 5758/72, Forward 5299/72
Course Slope/Rating (All Tees): Men's Back 145/74.5, Championship 138/72.7, Eagle 134/71.2, Birdie 129/69.3, Forward 127/67.1. Ladies' Back 157/81.1, Championship 149/78.6, Eagle 142/75.8, Birdie 136/73.4, Forward 132/70.5
Course Architect: Jack Frei (front 9, 1986, back 9, 1988)
Golf Facilities: Full Pro Shop X, Snack Bar X, Lounge Beer/Wine, Restaurant X, Locker Room X, Showers X, Club Rental X, Club Repair X, Cart Rental X, Instruction X, Practice Green X, Driving Range X, Practice Bunker X, Club Storage X
Tee-Time Reservation Policy: Up to 5 days in advance after 9 a.m. Property owners have priority
Ranger: Yes
Tee-off-Interval Time: 9 min.
Time to Play 18 Holes: 4 hrs., 45 min.
Course Hours/Earliest Tee-off: 6 a.m.
Green Fees: $45 for 18 holes Fri., Sat., Sun., holidays; $35 for 18 holes weekdays. $20 for 9 holes Mon.-Thurs. only
Cart Fees: $20 for 18 holes, $12 for 9 holes
Credit Cards: Discovery, MasterCard, Visa
Season: Year round. Busiest season April through Nov.
Course Comments: Can walk anytime. Yardage book available. Memberships available for property owners
Golf Packages: For tournaments of 16 or more
Discounts: Seniors (Mon., Tues., Wed.), seasonal rates (Nov. through Mar.), twilight
Places to Stay Nearby: PORT ORCHARD: Vista Motel (206) 876–8046. SILVERDALE: Silverdale on the Bay (206) 698–1000; Wilcox House (206) 830–4492. AIRPORT AREA: Best Western Airport Executel (206) 878–3300, (800) 528–1234; Embassy Suites Hotel (206) 227–8844, (800) EMBASSY; Seattle Marriott (206) 241–2000, (800) 228–9290. BED AND BREAKFAST: Ogle's Bed and Breakfast (206) 876–9170. See also Seattle listing on page 691

Local Attractions: Camping, fishing, boating. Port Orchard Chamber of Commerce (206) 876–3505
Directions: From Seattle (1 hr., 15 min.): Rte. 5 south to Hwy. 16, Hwy. 16 to Old Clifton/Tremont exit, turn left, 1.8 mi. to golf course
Closest Commercial Airport: Seattle–Tacoma International (45 min.)

MCCORMICK WOODS

Located within 90 minutes of Seattle, across Puget Sound, McCormick Woods is a 1298-acre planned residential and golf-course community. The 7012-yard par-72 golf course was designed by Jack Frei and created from the McCormick Tree Farm property, a 7800-acre parcel of forest land. Approximately half the total development acreage will have permanent open space, of which 125 acres includes the golf course; 400 acres will be left in a natural state, including lakes, ponds and wetlands. McCormick Woods Golf Course has been named one of America's top 75 public courses by *Golf Digest*, and the development has won a number of design awards, including Best Community Land Use Plan, Best Landscape Design, Best Planned Community and a special award for environmental sensitivity from the Seattle Master Builders Association.

The golf course is well treed, has rolling fairways and is bentgrass from the tees to hand-cut greens, which are large, moderately fast and undulating. Water comes into play on eight holes. Five tee distances are available to fit any golfer's game on this beautiful layout, which features fir, Japanese maple and cedar trees and a variety of animals such as deer, ducks, bobcats and more than 100 bird species. Though well treed, McCormick Woods is not overly tight. There are relatively few bunkers, but they are well-placed, as are the ponds, streams and trees. There is also a series of grass mounds throughout the course.

Two excellent holes on the golf course are the 235-yard par-3 fourth and the 398-yard par-4 fifth. The fourth plays over two ponds to a deep, undulating green guarded by a trap on the left, water in front and trees on the right. The fifth plays down a narrowing fairway with a pond and rows of trees protecting the landing area. The approach is to a narrow, deep green with a bunker on the left and a lake to the right. From these holes on a clear day you can see Mount Rainier in the distance.

The number-1-handicap hole at McCormick Woods is the par-4 third, which plays 427 yards from the back tees and doglegs slightly to the right down to a large green with water on the left. The green has three levels, front, center and middle, and is protected by a large bunker on the right. The hole requires a straight tee shot through the tree-lined fairway and a long accurate shot onto the well-protected green. The 575-yard par-5 ninth hole, a dogleg left with a blind tee shot, requires you to cut the edge of the trees on the left to get the ball down a steep hill to a flat landing area. The second shot is blind and uphill to a flat area inside the 150-yard mark. The green is a large double green shared with the eighteenth hole and is protected by bunkers both left and right.

One of the most difficult holes at McCormick Woods is the sixteenth, a straight 431-yard par 4 from the back tees. The fairway is undulating, with several mounds, and the green is large, slightly elevated and protected by a left-front bunker and a trap on the right. Eighteen is a beautiful 506-yard par 5. The fairway slopes from left to right in the tee-shot landing area, so you have to keep the shot left to avoid a large bunker on the right side of the fairway 200 to 250 yards from the tee. Trees to the left and a trap to the right narrow the fairway 50 yards from the green. A straight second shot is required, leaving a wedge downhill to the large double green shared with the ninth hole.

A practice driving range, putting green and practice bunker are available, as is instruction. A new clubhouse featuring MaryMacs Restaurant, a full pro shop, locker rooms and banquet facilities opened in 1995. McCormick Woods is a fine example of an excellently maintained, well-designed golf course that accommodates every level of the game.

Course Name: **PORT LUDLOW GOLF CLUB**
Tide, Timber, Trail Courses

Course Type: Resort
Resort: Port Ludlow Golf and Conference Center
Address: 9483 Oak Bay Road (Resort), 751 Highlands Dr. (Golf Course)
Port Ludlow, WA 98365

Phone: (360) 437–0272,
                  (800) 455–0272, (Golf Course)
                  (360) 732–2222,
                  (800) 732–1239 (Resort)
Fax: (360) 437–0971 (Resort)

GOLF COURSE

Director of Golf: Al Salvi
Head Professional: Michael Buss
Course Length/Par (All Tees): Tide/Timber: Back 6787/72, White 6262/72, Gold 5924/72, Forward 5598/72. Tide/Trail: Back 6683/72, White 6179/72, Gold 5776/72, Forward 5192/72. Timber/Trail: Back 6756/72, White 6249/72, Golf 5794/72, Forward 5112/72
Course Slope/Rating (All Tees): Tide/Timber: Back 131/72.7, White 124/70.3, Gold 121/68.8, Ladies' Forward 126/72.9. Tide/Trail: Back 138/73.1, White 128/70.7, Gold 123/69.2, Ladies' Forward 121/70.3. Timber/Trail: Back 138/73.6, White 128/71.4, Gold 123/69.2, Ladies' Forward 124/69.6
Course Architect: Tide/Timber: Robert Muir Graves (1975). Trail: Robert Muir Graves (1993)
Golf Facilities: Full Pro Shop X, Snack Bar Deli, Lounge Beer/Wine, Restaurant No, Locker Room Men's, Showers X, Club Rental X, Club Repair X, Cart Rental X, Instruction X, Practice Green X, Driving Range X, Practice Bunker X, Club Storage No
Tee-Time Reservation Policy: Resort guests: At time of room confirmation. Outside play: 1 wk. in advance. Property owners have priority
Ranger: Yes
Tee-off-Interval Time: 10 min.
Time to Play 18 Holes: 4½ hrs.
Course Hours/Earliest Tee-off: 7 a.m. to dark
Green Fees: Peak season (May to Oct.): $55 plus tax for 18 holes Fri., Sat., Sun., holidays; $50 plus tax for 18 holes Mon.-Thurs.
Cart Fees: $26 plus tax for 18 holes, $15 plus tax for 9 holes
Pull Carts: $3 plus tax for 18 holes

Credit Cards: American Express, MasterCard, Visa
Season: Year round. Summer rates May to Oct.
Course Comments: Can walk anytime. Memberships to property owners
Golf Packages: Available through resort
Discounts: Winter rates (Nov. to April). Twilight (May to Oct.)
Places to Stay Nearby: PORT TOWNSEND AREA: Bishop Victorian Guest Suites (360) 385–6122; Inn at Ludlow (360) 437–0411; Port Hadlock Inn (360) 385–5801, (800) 395–1595; Ravenscroft Inn (360) 385–2784; Manresa Castle (360) 385–5750, (800) 732–1281 (WA); Tides Inn (360) 385–0590, (800) VACTOWN; Port Townsend Motel and Spa (360) 385–2211, (800) VACTOWN. OLYMPIC NATIONAL PARK: Kalach Lodge (360) 962–2271; Lake Quinalt Lodge (360) 288–2571. BED AND BREAKFASTS: Old Consulate Inn (360) 385–6753; Starrett House Inn (360) 385–6059. See also Seattle listing on page 691
Local Attractions: Olympic National Park, camping, fishing, hiking, boating. PORT TOWNSEND: Victorian architecture, antiques; seasonal festivals and events such as antique shows, music festivals, boat festivals, crafts shows; wineries, Olympic Game Farm, Center for the Arts, Poulsbo (Scandinavian village). Port Townsend Chamber of Commerce, Tourist Information Center (360) 385–2722
Directions: From Seattle–Tacoma International Airport (45 min.): I–5 south, exit Hwy. 16 to Bremerton, Hwy. 3 toward Hood Canal Bridge, immediate right after taking bridge, Paradise Bay Rd., 6 mi. to golf course. Take ferry from downtown or north of Seattle. Ferries run about every 45 min.
Closest Commercial Airport: Seattle–Tacoma International (45 min.)

RESORT

Date Built: 1969
No. of Rooms: 180 guest rooms and 1- to 4-bedroom suites

Meeting Rooms: 12. Capacity of Largest: 325 persons banquet style. Meeting Space: 10,633 sq. ft.

Room Price Range: $60 for standard room to $359 for 4-bedroom suite peak season (May through Oct.). Off season (Nov. through April). Golf and other packages available year round

Lounge: Wreck Room Lounge

Restaurant: Harbormaster Restaurant

Entertainment: Tues. through Sun. during summer

Credit Cards: All major cards

General Amenities: Meeting and conference facilities with audiovisual and banquet services

Recreational Amenities: 7 outdoor tennis courts, 9–hole miniature golf course, outdoor swimming pool, 300-slip marina, horseshoes, basketball, croquet, volleyball

Reservation and Cancellation Policy: A deposit on all reservations equal to 1 night's room rate required 15 days from date reservation made. Notice of cancellation or shortened stay must be given at least 10 days prior to arrival date or deposit forfeited. Package rates must be paid in full prior to or on arrival

Comments and Restrictions: No pets allowed. Children under 12 yrs. stay free in parents' room. Taxes additional to base rates

PORT LUDLOW GOLF COURSE

Port Ludlow, a short ferry ride west of Seattle, features three nines, the Tide, Timber and Trail, designed by Robert Muir Graves and cut through virgin forest and also built on peat bogs. The original eighteen, the Tide and Timber, opened in 1975. The Tide nine wends its way through a real-estate development, but the Timber is more pristine, with less development. These nines have been ranked among the first 25 resort courses in America by *Golf Digest*. The Trail, also designed by Robert Muir Graves and opened in 1993, is the most difficult nine at Port Ludlow, largely due to its treelined fairways and many elevation changes.

There are also numerous elevation changes on the Tide/Timber eighteen. Strategy, careful club selection and accuracy are required if you want to score here. The fairways are well treed, and water comes into play on half the holes. The bentgrass greens, many of which are elevated, are generally large, moderately fast and undulating. Once you reach the green it is not difficult to three-putt because of their size and contours. The fifth green, for example, is 56 yards deep. Deep traps protect the greens, but there are virtually no fairway bunkers. The trees, land contours and water hazards keep you busy until you reach the putting surface.

The first hole gives you a flavor of what the rest of Port Ludlow will be like. This 404-yard par 4 is a slight dogleg left from an elevated tee. The tee shot is through a narrow opening flanked by hills to a fairway guarded by trees, with homes and condominiums in the background. The approach shot is to a medium-sized green guarded by a large bunker on the right and another to the rear.

A challenging hole is the 512-yard par-5 fifth, a double dogleg that bends right, then slightly left to a wide but shallow green. The tee shot should be to the left of center. If you are a big hitter and don't fade the ball, it is possible to hit it through the corner of the dogleg 255 yards away. On the second shot you might elect to lay up in front of a stream that cuts the fairway 75 yards from the green, or you can go for it. The green is protected by a large bunker at the right rear and another to the left front. My favorite hole on the Tide course is the 415-yard par-4 seventh, which plays straight down a tree-lined fairway to a very deep green protected by a large trap at the rear. A stream cuts the fairway approximately 130 yards from the green. A long hitter might elect to use a 3-wood or a long iron off the tee.

The Timber, which was built on a peat bog, features the 537-yard par-5 fourth, a sharp dogleg right that begins to turn 250 yards from the back tees. The first shot should be to the left side of the dogleg to see the green on the approach shot and to avoid the trees on the right side of the fairway. The second shot is to a long, wide green with huge bunkers to the rear and right front. The fairway is squeezed by trees on the right and a large bunker on the left, 100 yards from the green.

A beautiful par 3 on this side is the 171-yard eighth, which plays from an elevated tee all the way over water to a large green with a trap to the right rear. The finishing hole is a 497-yard dogleg-right par 5. The tee shot is to a narrow landing area guarded by trees. The second shot is to a large, wide green fronted by a huge trap and banked in back, with another large trap directly behind the green. Depending on pin placement, this hole provides a good opportunity for you to end your round with a birdie.

The new signature hole at Port Ludlow is the scenic 176-yard par-3 second on the new Trail nine. The tee shot is from a plateau with views of Port Ludlow Bay and, on a clear day, Mount Baker in Canada. The green is set approximately 75 feet below the tee and incoming winds off the bay can make this hole very difficult. It is a real pleasure to golf in this scenic and tranquil setting. You can walk the course anytime, and once you get there, you'll be in a world all you own. The Trail course is the most difficult to walk so many golfers take a cart if they are playing this new nine.

A driving range and practice green are available at Port Ludlow, and individual and group lessons are available. Golf packages are offered through the resort, whose peak season is May through October. Other recreational facilities include outdoor tennis courts, a swimming pool, marina and various games such as volleyball and croquet. Nearby are Olympic National Park and the Olympic Mountains, the historic port town of Port Townsend and other attractions. Seattle, Vancouver, and other islands can easily be reached by ferry.

In addition to the Port Ludlow Golf and Conference Center, you might want to consider the new Inn at Ludlow Bay, a 36-room 1920s-style facility featuring fireplaces and whirlpool tubs in your room plus spectacular views of the bay and the mountains.

Recommended Golf Courses in Washington

Seattle/Tacoma Area:

Alderbrook Golf and Yacht Club, Union, (206) 898–2560, Resort, 18/6312/73

Avalon Golf Club, Burlington, (206) 757–1900, (800) 624–0202, Public. North/West: 18/6597/72. West/South: 18/6576/72. North/South: 18/6771/72

Capitol City Golf Club, Olympia, (206) 494–5111, (800) 994–2582, Public, 18/6536/72

Cedarcrest Golf Course, Marysville, (206) 659–3566, Public, 18/5474/70

Dungeness Golf and Country Club, Sequim, (206) 683–6344, (800) 447–6826, Semiprivate, 18/6372/72

Gleneagles Golf Course, Arlington, (206) 435–6713, Public, 18/6002/70

Gold Mountain Golf Course, Bremerton, (206) 674–2363, (800) 249–2363, Public, 18/6749/72

Lake Spanaway Golf Course, Tacoma, (206) 531–3660, Public, 18/6810/72

Meadow Park Golf Course, Tacoma, (206) 473–3033, Public, 18/6093/71

Meriwood Golf Course, Lacey, (360) 412–0495, Public, 18/7170/72

Snohomish Golf Course, Snohomish, (206) 568–2676, Public, 18/6858/72

Riverside Country Club, Chehalis, (360) 748–8182, (800) 242– 9486, Public, 18/6155/71

Tumwater Valley Golf Course, Olympia, (360) 943–9500, Public, 18/7162/72

Willows Run Golf Club, Redmond, (206) 883–1200, Public, 18/6806/72

Whidbey Island:

Gallery Golf Course, Oak Harbor, (206) 257–6585, Public, 18/6326/72

Spokane Area/Eastern

Course Name: **INDIAN CANYON GOLF COURSE**

Course Type: Public
Address: Assembly Drive
West 4304 West Drive
(Mailing Address)
Spokane, WA 99204
Phone: (509) 747–5353

GOLF COURSE

Head Professional: Gary Lindeblad
Course Length/Par (All Tees): Back 6255/72, Middle 5943/72, Ladies' Forward 5355/74
Course Slope/Rating (All Tees): Men's Back 126/70.7, Middle 123/69.3, Forward 115/65.9. Ladies' Back 136/75.6, Middle 132/73.9, Forward 123/70.3
Course Architect: H. Chandler Egan (1935)
Golf Facilities: Full Pro Shop X, Snack Bar X, Lounge Beer/Wine, Restaurant No, Locker Room Limited, Showers Limited, Club Rental X, Club Repair X, Cart Rental X, Instruction X, Practice Green X, Driving Range X, Practice Bunker X, Club Storage No
Tee-Time Reservation Policy: From 1 day in advance Mon. through Fri., Sat. 6 a.m. in advance for following Sat., Sun., holiday tee times. Any time for out of county residents with credit card guarantee. MasterCard, Visa required
Ranger: Yes
Tee-off-Interval Time: 8 min.
Time to Play 18 Holes: 4½ hrs.
Course Hours/Earliest Tee-off: Sunrise to dark
Green Fees: Nonresidents: $22 for 18 holes, $16.75 for 9 holes
Cart Fees: Nonresidents: $22 for 18 holes per cart, $11 for 9 holes per cart
Pull Carts: $3 for 18 holes
Credit Cards: Cash or check for green fees. MasterCard, Visa for merchandise, carts, food
Season: April 1 to Nov. 1
Course Comments: Can walk anytime. 9-hole play only after 3 p.m. on weekends, holidays

Golf Packages: Available through local motels. Inquire at clubhouse
Discounts: County residents, juniors, twilight
Places to Stay Nearby: Courtyard by Marriott (509) 624–7600, (800) 321–2211; Holiday Inn Downtown (509) 838–6101, (800) HOLIDAY; Super 8 Motel (509) 535–0388, (800) 843–1991; Quality Inn Valley Suites (509) 928–5218, (800) 4–CHOICE; Red Lion Inn (509) 924–9000, (800) 547–8010; Ramada Inn Airport (509) 838–5211, (800) 228–2828; Best Western Trade Winds North (509) 326–5500, (800) 528–1234. BED AND BREAKFASTS: Washington Bed and Breakfast Guild (509) 548–6234 (reservation service)
Local Attractions: Riverfront Park, Wild Zoo, Cathedral of St. John the Evangelist, Turnbull National Wildlife Refuge, Grand Coulee Dam, Cheney Cowles Memorial Museum, Bing Crosby Library at Gonzaga University, Museum of Native American Indian Cultures, minor league baseball, Riverside State Park, skiing, boating, fishing, camping, hiking, horseback riding, white-water rafting, wineries, Lake Coeur d'Alene (ID), art galleries, Spokane River Centennial Trail, Manto Park and Botanical Gardens, apple orchards, seasonal festivals, theater, horse racing. Spokane Convention and Visitors Bureau (509) 747–3230, (800) 248–3230; Spokane Chamber of Commerce (509) 624–1393
Directions: From Spokane (4 mi.): 2nd Ave. west (1 way), turns into Sunset, follow Sunset to Assembly, turn right on Assembly to golf course
Closest Commercial Airports: Spokane International (5 min.), Seattle–Tacoma International (5 hrs.)

INDIAN CANYON GOLF COURSE

Spokane calls itself the Lilac City, but in the old days it was a rough fur-trapping and trading town. The city was named after the Spokanee Indians, who favored the Spokane River as a fishing grounds. Spokan means "the men who live in the country which grows the wheat" or "children of the sun," depending on whose interpretation you accept. The "e" was added to the city's name in 1891. Over time, after Indian wars that included Chief Joseph, who is buried at Nespolem on the nearby Colville Indian Reservation, and the ensuing frontier settlement, Spokane became the largest city between Minneapolis and Seattle.

Today, after reviving itself by hosting the 1974 World Exposition, the city is a prosperous town of over 175,000 with a diversified economy. Minutes from downtown the slopes of Mount Spokane rise 600 feet, and at the city's edge begins the vast rolling land of the rich Palouse Prairie, land that nurtures acres of winter wheat. Spokane is the gateway to 12 national parks and 15 national forests, and is home to 76 lakes and many white-water rivers. Water sports, hunting, fishing, skiing and other forms of outdoor recreation are popular here, including golf.

The Indian Canyon Golf Course is a rolling golf course punctuated by pine and fir trees. Although this layout is a relatively short 6255 yards from the back tees, it is difficult to get a flat lie, and the trees always seem to be in the way. Designed by H. Chandler Egan, the course was opened in 1935. Egan, a former U.S. Amateur champion, was one of the best early amateur golfers in America and designed many Pacific Northwest courses, including the Pacific Grove Golf Links in California and the Eastmoreland Golf Club in Portland, Oregon. In 1928 he revised the Pebble Beach Golf Links especially for the 1929 U.S. Amateur. Indian Canyon has small to medium-sized, undulating greens protected by one or two traps. Because of the large, mature trees that squeeze the fairways; small, tricky greens; and uneven fairway lies, Indian Canyon requires considerable finesse and accuracy to score.

The opening hole, which is one of two consecutive par 5s, is one of the more picturesque ones on the course. From an elevated tee there is a view of the city and the valley below. This hole plays 479 yards from the back tees and is sometimes converted to a par 4 for tournaments. Because of the tree-lined fairway, the challenge is to keep the ball in play. The small green has two traps on the right.

The number-1-handicap hole is the 438-yard par-4 fourteenth, a slight dogleg left that usually plays into the wind. The fairway is protected on both sides by trees, and generally the tee shot is played to the right center of a crowned fairway that slopes from left to right. The second shot is onto a large, deep green that slopes from back to front and is protected on the right front by a sand trap. Another difficult hole is the fifth, a straight, 403-yard par 4 made difficult by an uphill climb through a well-treed fairway. The tee shot is played to the left, and the second shot is onto a fast green with difficult undulations. The left side of the green is considerably lower than the right, so to be above the hole can mean three putts or more.

Indian Canyon has been the host to the Men's (1941, 1984) and Women's (1989) National Public Links, attesting to the excellent condition and challenging layout of the course. *Golf Digest* has rated it as one of the top 75 public courses in America. Be sure to add Indian Canyon to your golf itinerary.

Among the various tourist attractions in Spokane, you might consider visiting the Museum of Native American Indian Cultures, which features the artifacts of more than 3000 years of native Americans from Alaska to Peru. Spokane is also the birthplace of crooner Bing Crosby, who was a major benefactor of Gonzaga University, which he briefly attended. The Crosby Library at Gonzaga features an excellent book collection as well as Crosbyana, including gold records, an Oscar, and other memorabilia of Mr. Crosby, who died of heart failure on October 4, 1977, while on a golf course in Madrid, Spain.

Recommended Golf Courses in Washington

Spokane/Eastern Area:

The Creek at Qualchan Golf Course, Spokane, (509) 448–9317, Public, 18/6577/72

Downriver Golf Club, Spokane,
(509) 327–5269, Public, 18/6130/71

Hangman Valley Golf Course, Spokane,
(509) 448–1211, Public, 18/6904/72

Meadowwood Golf Course, Liberty Lake,
(509) 255–9539, Public, 18/6846/72

Wenatchee/Central Area

**Course Name: DESERT CANYON
GOLF COURSE**

Course Type: Resort
Address: 114 Brays Road
               Orondo, WA 98843
Phone: (509) 784–1111,
               (800) 258–4173
Fax: (509) 784–2701

GOLF COURSE

Head Professional: Brad Dally
Course Length/Par (All Tees): Back
  7293/72, Blue 6894/72, White 6181/72,
  Gold 5515/72, Forward 4899/72
Course Slope/Rating (All Tees): Back
  134/73.5, Blue 125/72.1, White
  114/69.1, Gold 106/67.2, Ladies' For-
  ward 115/70.6
Course Architect: Jack Frei (1993)
Golf Facilities: Full Pro Shop X, Snack
  Bar X, Lounge No, Restaurant X,
  Locker Room No, Showers X, Club
  Rental X, Club Repair No, Cart Rental
  X, Instruction X, Practice Green X,
  Driving Range X, Practice Bunker X,
  Club Storage X
Tee-Time Reservation Policy: Up to 7
  days in advance unless through hotels,
  then up to 90 days
Ranger: Yes
Tee-off-Interval Time: 10 min.
Time to Play 18 Holes: 5 hrs.
Course Hours/Earliest Tee-off: 6 a.m.
Green and Cart Fees: $55 for 18 holes
  Fri., Sat., Sun., holidays; $50 for 18
  holes weekdays
Credit Cards: MasterCard, Visa
Season: Year round. Busiest mid-May
  through mid-Oct.
Course Comments: Cart mandatory. 18-
  hole putting course on site

Golf Packages: For guests of on site golf
  villas (800) 560–7829, (509) 662–7184
Discounts: Seasonal from mid-Oct. to mid-
  May. Twilight
Places to Stay Nearby: CHELAN: Mary
  Kay's Whaley Mansion (509) 682–5735,
  (800) 729–2408; Westview Resort Motel
  (509) 682–4396. WENATCHEE: Best West-
  ern Heritage Inn (509) 664–6565, (800)
  528–1234; Red Lion Hotel (509) 663–
  0711, (800) 547–8010; Westcoast
  Wenatchee Center Hotel (509) 662–
  1234, (800) 426–0670
Local Attractions: WENATCHEE: North
  Central Washington Museum, Ohme
  Gardens County Park, Rock Beach
  Dam, Washington State Apple Commis-
  sion Visitor Center, Wenatchee National
  Forest, hiking, fishing, hunting, camping, boating, winter skiing. Wenatchee
  Area Chamber of Commerce, 2 S.
  Chelan, P.O. Box 850, Wenatchee, WA
  98807–0850 (509) 662–2116
Directions: From Wenatchee (35 min
  northwest): Take Hwy. 97 north 22 mi.
  to golf course on the right
Closest Commercial Airports: Wenatchee
  (45 min.); Yakima (2½ hrs.); Seattle-
  Tacoma International (3 hrs.); Spokane
  International (3½ hrs.)

DESERT CANYON GOLF COURSE

Desert Canyon is located on 480 acres
of desert-like terrain near the Cascade
Mountains along the Columbia River midway between Spokane and Seattle. The
course features large, fast, undulating
bentgrass greens. The course also has a
putting course with seven holes that border
or overlook a lake that has a bridge connecting hole No. 5's peninsula green to the
No. 6 teeing area, and a rock formation and
a waterfall in the area of No. 6, No. 13,
and No. 14. The championship course has
several desert-style waste bunkers, ravines,
sand bunkers, and mounds. Desert Canyon
is a strategic target layout that requires
course management skills to score.

One of the most memorable holes at
Desert Canyon is the 682-yard par-5 sixth
whose elevated tee overlooks the Wenatchee
Valley. Many golfers hit a 3-wood or long-

iron off the the tee to a target landing area then hit another 3-wood or long-iron to the next safe haven. This leaves anything from a 5- to a 9-iron into a small green guarded by a large pine 30 yards short and to the right of the target. The green, which is 170 feet below the tee, is bordered on the left by a 300-foot canyon.

The back nine, called The Lakes, has three strong finishing holes. The 574-yard par-5 sixteenth requires a drive that skirts a cluster of trees in the fairway. The second shot is a layup to a landing area in front of an 80-yard-wide canyon. The approach is over this abyss to a shallow green with a steep embankment behind it. The 231-yard par-3 seventeenth plays downhill to a 40-yard-deep, three-tiered hourglass-shaped green backed by a bunker. A waste area guards the front of the target. The eighteenth hole is a 412-yard par-4 whose tee shot plays downhill to an ample landing area. The approach must avoid a lake to the right and behind the green.

Desert Canyon has a double-ended driving range and two practice putting greens. It also has an interesting 18-hole putting course whose holes range in distance from 62 to 207 feet. Two-bedroom and three-bedroom on site villa golf packages are available. Desert Canyon is rated one of the best golf courses in Washington by *Golf Digest*.

Recommended Golf Courses in Washington

Walla Walla Area:

Canyon Lakes Golf Course, Kennewick, (509) 582–3736, Public, 18/6973/72

Veteran's Memorial Golf Course, Walla Walla, (509) 527–4507, Public, 18/6311/72

Wenatchee Area:

Leavenworth Golf Club, Leavenworth, (509) 548–7267, Semiprivate, 18/5711/71

Yakima:

Apple Tree Golf Course, Yakima, (509) 966–5877, Public, 18/6892/72

Washington: Useful Information

Travel Development Division, Department of Commerce and Economic Development, General Administration Bldg., Olympia, WA 98504, (360) 586–2088, (800) 544–1800

Seattle–King County Convention and Visitors Bureau, 800 Convention Plaza, Seattle, WA 98101, (206) 461–5800

Outdoor Recreation Information Office, 915 Second Ave., Rm. 442, Seattle, WA 98174, (206) 553–7460, (800) 280–CAMP (national parks and forest information, reservations)

Department of Fish and Wildlife, 600 Capitol Way North, Olympia, WA 98501, (360) 753–5700 (fishing and hunting regulations)

State Parks and Recreation Commission, 7150 Clearwater Ln., Olympia, WA 98504, (360) 753–2027 (recreation information)

Pacific Bed and Breakfast Agency, 701 N.W. 60th, Seattle, WA 98107, (206) 784–0539 (handles more than 200 rooms in Seattle area)

Travellors' Bed and Breakfast Reservation Service, P.O. Box 492, Mercer Island, WA 98040, (206) 232–2345 (handles over 500 rooms in Pacific Northwest, including Vancouver, Victoria)

Washington State Ferry Information (206) 464–6400, (800) 542–7052, (800) 542–0810

Course Name: THE GREENBRIER
Old White, Greenbrier,
Lakeside Courses

Course Type: Resort
Resort: The Greenbrier
Address: Route 60
White Sulphur Springs, WV
24986
Phone: (304) 536–7851 (Golf Course),
(304) 536–7862 (Starting
Times)
(304) 536–1110,
(800) 624–6070 (Resort)
Fax: (304) 536–7854 (Resort)

GOLF COURSE

Director of Golf: Robert Harris
Head Professional: Hill Herrick
Course Length/Par (All Tees): Old White:
Back 6640/70, Middle 6353/70, Forward
5658/70. Greenbrier: Back 6681/72,
Middle 6311/72, Ladies' Forward
5280/73. Lakeside: Back 6336/70,
Middle 6068/70, Forward 5175/70
Course Slope/Rating (All Tees): Old
White: Back 128/72.7, Middle 126/71.3,
Ladies' Forward 126/73.3. Greenbrier:
Back 136/73.7, Middle 133/71.7, La-
dies' Forward 123/72.5. Lakeside: Back
121/70.4, Middle 120/69.0, Ladies'
Forward 115/69.9
Course Architects: Old White: Charles
Blair Macdonald and Seth Raynor
(1913). Greenbrier: George O'Neil
(1924), Jack Nicklaus (renovation,
1978). Lakeside: Dick Wilson (1962)
Golf Facilities: Full Pro Shop X, Snack
Bar X, Lounge X, Restaurant X,
Locker Room X, Showers X, Club
Rental X, Club Repair X, Cart Rental
X, Instruction X, Practice Green X,
Driving Range X, Practice Bunker X,
Club Storage X
Tee-Time Reservation Policy: Resort
guests: At time of confirmed hotel
reservation. Outside play: On space-
available basis, call up to 3 days in
advance
Ranger: Yes
Tee-off-Interval Time: 8 min.

Time to Play 18 Holes: 4 hrs., 15 min.
Course Hours/Earliest Tee-off: 8 a.m.
Green Fees: Peak season (April to Oct.):
Resort guest: $90 daily fee. Outside
play: $175 daily fee
Cart Fees: $34 for 18 holes peak season
Caddies: $30 for single bag, $45 for double
bag
Credit Cards: All major cards
Season: Old White, Greenbrier: April
through Oct. Lakeside: Year round
Course Comments: Cart or caddy manda-
tory until 4 p.m.. Yardage book available
Golf Packages: Available through resort
Discounts: Green fees complimentary Dec.
through Feb., lower fees Nov. and March
Places to Stay Nearby: LEWISBURG:
General Lewis Inn (304) 645–2600;
Brier Inn (304) 645–7722; Fort Savan-
nah Motel (304) 645–3055, (800) 678–
3055. WHITE SULPHUR SPRINGS: Budget
Inn (304) 536–2121; Old White Motel
(304) 536–2441. BED AND BREAKFAST:
James Wylie House Bed and Breakfast
(304) 536–9444
Local Attractions: Monongahela National
Forest, Greenbrier River Trail, Greenbrier Forest State Parks, white-water
rafting, hiking, camping, fishing, horseback riding, boating, skiing. LEWISBURG:
North House Museum, Carnegie Hall,
crafts, antiques, historic district, Greenbrier Valley Theater. Lewisburg Visitors
Center (800) 833–2068. Greater Greenbrier Chamber of Commerce (304)
645–1000. White Sulphur Springs Convention and Visitor Bureau (800) 284–
9440
Directions: From I–64 E/W: White Sulphur
Springs exit, take Rte. 60 east/west (2½
mi.) to resort
Closest Commercial Airports: Greenbrier
Valley/Lewisburg (15 min.); Roanoke
Municipal, VA (1½ hrs.); Yeager, Charleston, (2 hrs.); Richmond International,
VA (4 hrs.); Dulles International, Washington, DC (5 hrs.); Pittsburgh International, PA (5 hrs.); Charlotte/Douglas
International, NC (5 hrs.)

RESORT

Date Built: 1910 (original hotel building)

No. of Rooms: 518 single, double rooms; 33 suites; 73 guest estate houses

Meeting Rooms: 30. Capacity of Largest: 2000 reception,1200 persons banquet style. Meeting Space: 70,000 sq. ft.

Room Price Range: From $164 to $260 per person modified American plan depending on season. Peak season April to Oct. Golf, tennis, Spa and Family Vacation and other packages available year round

Lounges: Tavern Room Lounge, Old White Club, Rhododendron Cocktail Lounge

Restaurants: Grille Room, Main Dining Room, Draper's Cafe, Ryder Cup Grille (seasonal), Porch, Tavern Room, Golf Club Dining Room

Entertainment: Live music in Old White Club, live music during dinner, contemporary DJ music in Tavern Room Lounge

Credit Cards: American Express, Diners Club, Discover, MasterCard, Visa

General Amenities: Babysitting services, children's programs, 30 shops, physician on site full time, movies, concerts, meeting and conference facilities with audiovisual and food services; Greenbrier Clinic providing diagnostic services

Recreational Amenities: 15 outdoor Har-Tru courts, 5 indoor Dynaturf courts; exercise/aerobics rooms, indoor and outdoor swimming pools, fishing, whitewater rafting, carriage rides, bowling, trap and skeet shooting, horseback riding, ice-skating, cross-country skiing, bicycling, croquet, shuffleboard, horseshoes, billiards, table tennis; jogging, hiking/fitness trails; spa and mineral baths

Reservation and Cancellation Policy: $175 deposit per room required to secure reservations Nov. through March. $400 deposit required April through Oct. Late arrival or early departure causes forfeiture of deposit, unless 7-day notice given Nov. through March, 15-day notice April through Nov.

Comments and Restrictions: Pets not permitted in the main hotel or guest houses. Rates and service charge do not include state tax. $125 charge for 3rd-person occupancy in same room, no charge if infant. No charge for children sharing parents' room. An individual partaking of alcoholic beverages has to be a club member which requires a nominal fee. Service charges added. Inquire or consult resort literature. Modified American plan (breakfast, dinner daily in Main Dining Room) included in rates

THE GREENBRIER

The Greenbrier is a five-star resort hotel beautifully situated on 6500 acres in the Allegheny Mountains of West Virginia, 250 miles southwest of Washington, DC. The resort began over 200 years ago as an informal spa where visitors came to "take the cure" from the white sulphur springs, believed to relieve the discomfort of rheumatism and other real or imagined maladies. The first permanent resort buildings were established in the early 1800s and included cottages that were privately owned by many of the socially prominent families who gathered here. Over the years The Greenbrier has received much attention. In his 1784 *Notes on the State of Virginia* Thomas Jefferson mentioned The Greenbrier's mineral waters before the resort became established. The Greenbrier became a social center for the aristocratic families of the South and hosted such dignitaries as Henry Clay, Andrew Jackson and many others. During the Civil War the resort narrowly averted being destroyed by Union troops, and it became the summer home of Robert E. Lee after the war.

By this time (1858) "Old White," the main building, had been built. This magnificent structure was 400 feet in length and had a dining room that could seat 1200 people. In 1869, the Chesapeake and Ohio Railway Co. extended its line through White Sulphur Springs and the resort, now part of the new state of West Virginia, began to rise again. In 1910, the C&O Railroad purchased the resort for $150,000, and a 250-room Georgian structure, the center wing of today's hotel, was constructed next to "Old White," which eventually had to be torn down. The Bath Wing, including the Roman-inspired indoor pool, was designed in 1912 by Harris and Richard of Philadelphia. At the time, the 100-by-42-foot Olympic-sized indoor pool at The Greenbrier was one of the largest in the world.

In 1930, the Cleveland firm of Small, Smith and Reeb was selected to design the North, South and Virginia wings and to modernize the central structure. This became essentially the 550-room hotel as it is known today. In the winter of 1941–42, at the start of World War II, The Greenbrier was used as an internment center for German and Japanese diplomats for some 6 months while moves were made to return them to their countries and to bring American diplomats home. In 1942 the United States Army purchased The Greenbrier and it became a military hospital. Virtually all of its furnishings were sold or removed to museums and other locales.

After the war the officers and directors of the C&O Railroad decided to repurchase the hotel, and in mid-April of 1948 a restored Greenbrier was reopened. Since then, various improvements and additions have been made without detracting from its historical tradition and charm. The 80-room West Virginia wing was completed in 1962, a conference complex was finished in 1974, the Old White Club was renovated in 1970, and the new Mineral Bath and Spa Building was opened in 1987. In 1974 The Greenbrier was listed on the National Register of Historic Places, and in 1990 it was designated a National Historic Landmark by the Department of the Interior. It is also included in the National Trust for Historic Preservation's short list of historic hotels of America.

The Greenbrier's golf tradition began in 1910, when the first nine of the Lakeside Course was completed. The course was refined when Charles Blair MacDonald built the Old White course, a 6250-yard eighteen-hole layout, in 1914. A few years earlier, MacDonald had designed the National Golf Links at Southampton, Long Island. The clubhouse at The Greenbrier was built in 1915 and has been expanded over the years. In 1914 the resort was open year round for the first time, and President Woodrow Wilson was among the first golfers to play MacDonald's Old White Course. That same year, John F. Kennedy's parents spent their honeymoon at The Greenbrier.

The Old White Course was officially opened with the West Virginia State Championship in 1914. It plays 6640 yards from the back tees and is par 70. This course is flatter than the Greenbrier but has smaller, well-trapped greens that can be especially difficult if you are putting from above the hole. Most of the greens slope forward. Position and strategy rather than length are extremely important here.

One of the most challenging holes on Old White is the 444-yard par-4 sixth, which is straight and well treed. Two long, straight shots are required to reach the putting surface, a small green protected by a large trap on the left and a bunker in front and slightly to the right, approximately 50 yards from the target. The sixteenth hole plays either 417 or 394 yards from the back tees, depending on which of two entirely separate greens are being used that day. The tee shot is a 185-yard carry over a large pond. The second shot has to carry a stream to reach an oval green protected by a trap to the left and another to the right. If the nearer green is used, the hole becomes a dogleg right and the approach shot is over dry land.

The first major golf tournament held at The Greenbrier was the 1922 United States Women's Championship, won by Glenna Collet, then 19 years old. Bobby Jones was one of the first golfers to play the second eighteen-hole course, designed and built by George O'Neil and opened in 1924. Initially this course was called the Number Three Course and was later renamed The Greenbrier Course. The Greenbrier, originally a 6721-yard par-72 layout, was redesigned by Jack Nicklaus in 1977. Woodrow Wilson, Glenna Collet, Bobby Jones and Jack Nicklaus are part of the parade of celebrities, dignitaries and immortal golfers who have walked these fairways. Others include Walter Hagen, Gene Sarazen, Joe DiMaggio, Babe Didrikson Zaharias, Babe Ruth, Bing Crosby, Arnold Palmer, Ben Hogan, Dwight D. Eisenhower, and of course, Sam Snead, who was the resort's professional for many years beginning in 1936 and today serves as head golf pro emeritus. Snead almost lost his job when he hit a 335-yard tee shot that struck Alva Bradley, then a member of the Chesapeake and Ohio Board of Directors, while he was on the green of the fifth hole at Old White. It was in 1959 that Snead shot his incredible 59 in the Greenbrier Open.

The Greenbrier Course is a 6681-yard, well-treed, rolling layout with strategic bunkers guarding moderately undulating bentgrass greens that vary in depth from 37 to 19 yards. Each hole is a separate and unique experience as the eighteen holes form a continuous blend of excellent and memorable golf. Water hazards appear on more than half the holes. The 176-yard par-3 eleventh, for example, plays directly over a stream to a wide, shallow, two-tiered green fronted by a huge sand bunker. There are also a variety of elevation changes on the course. The Ryder Cup matches were played on the Greenbrier in 1979 after Jack Nicklaus redesigned the course. PGA Senior tour events have been played here, and the West Virginia State Amateur Championship is always played here in July. In 1994 The Greenbrier course hosted the Solheim Cup Matches.

The number-1-handicap hole at the Greenbrier is the 456-yard par-4 sixth, which plays down a corridor of trees to a small, narrow green protected by a large bunker on the left. One of the most photographed holes at the Greenbrier is the beautiful 403-yard par-4 second. The tee shot on this hole has to be well positioned to avoid the out of bounds on the left and a large pond on the right. The approach shot is to a narrow, deep green with a sand trap on the left and a sand trap and water on the right.

The par-5 eighteenth is a strong finishing hole and can play from as far back as 637 yards from the back tees. The fairway is open compared to the other holes on The Greenbrier. The green is a double green shared with the eighteenth hole of the Lakeside course. It is well protected by five sand traps and rows of trees on each side of the fairway.

The Greenbrier's Old White and Greenbrier Courses are usually open April through October. The Lakeside Course is open year round, weather permitting. Carts or caddies are mandatory on all courses, and guests can reserve tee times when they make a reservation at the hotel. Nonguests pay a premium to play at The Greenbrier on a space-available basis. Peak-rate seasons are April through October, and golf fees are complimentary in December, January and February. A variety of golf and other packages is available through the resort.

The Lakeside Course is a 6336-yard par-70 layout designed by Dick Wilson and opened in 1962. Lakeside has more water than the other courses with water hazards on or near fifteen holes. The greens are medium sized to small, undulating and well protected by traps and water. Tee-shot placement, accurate approach shots and a strong short game are essential at Lakeside. One of the more difficult holes on this layout is the 430-yard par-4 sixth hole, which plays straight to a deep green protected by traps on each side. The tee shot is over a stream that winds along the left side of the fairway. Trees guard the right side all the way to the hole.

A challenging par 5 is the 575-yard fourth, which is tree-lined on the right and bordered by a stream and then trees on the left. The green is almost circular in shape and squeezed in front by trees and a bunker on the left and by a right-front bunker bordered by trees on the right.

The clubhouse at The Greenbrier has locker rooms and showers, the handy Ryder Cup Grille Room and the Golf Club Lounge. The Golf Club Sunday brunch accompanied by music from a jazz trio is a fixture at The Greenbrier. There is an excellent pro shop, and instruction is available from the staff of PGA professionals and assistants. The practice facilities include an ample driving range, practice greens and practice bunkers. *Golf* magazine ranks The Greenbrier among the top twelve golf resorts in America.

The Greenbrier has won numerous hospitality awards, including a Five-Star rating from the *Mobil Travel Guide* and a Five-Diamond rating from the American Automobile Association. The resort offers a full range of recreational activities including tennis, horseback riding, fishing, trap and skeet shooting, swimming, croquet, bicycling, mountain biking, falconry, white water rafting, hiking, billiards, bowling and winter sports such as skiing and ice-skating. The Greenbrier Spa, Mineral Baths and Salon, whose origins date back to 1778 and the use of white sulphur springs for therapeutic purposes, now includes whirlpool baths, steam, sauna, massage, Swedish shiatsu, nutrition counseling, spa cuisine and a range of exercise services, facilities and amenities including aerobic exercise, 2 Olympic-sized swimming pools, European facials, an exercise equipment studio and much more.

The Main Dining Room features continental and American cuisine; the Old White Club offers before- and after-dinner cocktails and dancing. Lighter fare is available at Draper's Cafe, the Tavern Room, and Golf Club, seasonally. You can experience a breakfast table that includes pan-fried brook trout, buckwheat cakes, hominy grits, Virginia ham and bacon, corn bread and biscuits, and you can select from the newly developed Greenbrier light cuisine, which is low in calories, fat and sodium. The 30,000-square-foot Greenbrier Clinic provides a full array of medical examinations, designed both for current evaluation and to give the returning guest advice on how to maintain good health. Opened in 1948, the clinic is one of America's first and finest medical facilities devoted exclusively to diagnostic and preventive medicine.

The Greenbrier's Conference Center provides 70,000 square feet of meeting space, 30 meeting rooms, and a 19,000-square-foot exhibit hall under one roof. The latest audiovisual and telecommunications equipment is available, as are the excellent food services of the resort. The resort has won numerous awards in recognition of its excellent meeting facilities and service including Gold Key, Gold Platter, Gold Tee and Hall of Fame awards from *Meetings and Conventions*; the Pinnacle Award from *Successful Meetings*; and the Award of Excellence and Paragon Award from *Corporate Meetings and Incentives*.

It has been a long time since colonial explorers followed rivers and animal paths to work their way through this region toward the Mississippi River and beyond. Henry Clay used to drop by on his way from Kentucky to Washington, then a grueling 4½ day trip by stage coach. The earlier nineteenth-century meetings of the Southern agrarian aristocracy have given way to an international clientele that seeks world-class amenities. Whether you are staying at the cottages, some of which date back to those less complicated frontier days, or at the main hotel, you will know that you have visited one of America's premier golf resorts.

**Course Name: HAWTHORNE VALLEY
                         GOLF COURSE**

Course Type: Resort
Resort: Snoeshoe Mountain Resort
Address: Route 219/P.O. Box 10
                       Snoeshoe, WV 26209
Phone: (304) 572–1000 (ext. 265,
                       Golf Course),
                       (304) 572–5252 (Resort)
Fax: (304) 572–5252 (Golf Course,
                       Resort)

GOLF COURSE

Head Professional: Daryl Boone
Course Length/Par (All Tees): Back 7044/72, Blue 6397/72, White 5976/72, Forward 4363/72
Course Slope/Rating (All Tees): Back 130/70.2, Blue 126/70.4, White 122/68.1, Forward 103/63.6
Course Architect: Gary Player (1993)
Golf Facilities: Full Pro Shop X, Snack Bar X, Lounge X, Restaurant X, Locker Room X, Showers X, Club Rental X, Club Repair X, Cart Rental X, Instruction X, Practice Green X, Driving Range X, Practice Bunker X, Club Storage X
Tee-Time Reservation Policy: Call anytime

Ranger: Yes
Tee-off-Interval Time: 10 min.
Time to Play 18 Holes: 4 hrs. 45 min.
Course Hours/Earliest Tee-off: 8 a.m.
Green Fees: $49 for 18 holes Fri., Sat., Sun., holidays; $43 for 18 holes weekdays. $27 for 9 holes anytime
Cart Fees: $14 for 18 holes, $10 for 9 holes per person
Credit Cards: All major cards
Season: May through Oct. Busiest Memorial Day weekend through Labor Day
Course Comments: Cart mandatory. Yardage book available
Golf Packages: Through resort
Discounts: Resort guests
Places to Stay Nearby: ELKINS: Econo Lodge (304) 636–5311, (800) 446–6900. LEWISBURG: General Lewis Inn (304) 645–2600. WHITE SULPHUR SPRINGS: The Greenbrier (304) 536–1100, (800) 624–6070; Old White Motel (304) 536–2441
Local Attractions: The National Radio Astronomy Observatory, Cranberry Glades Botanical Center, The Falls of Hills Creek, Beartown State Park, Watoga State Park, Droop Mountain, The Highland Scenic Highway, Pearl S. Buck Birthplace, Greenbrier River Trail, fishing, boating, hiking, horseback riding, camping, whitewater rafting
Directions: From I–68 (2 hrs.): Proceed south on Rte. 219 through Elkins to Rte. 66 (52 mi. south of Elkins) and east to resort. From I–64 (2 hrs.): Proceed north on Rte. 219 to Rte. 66 turnoff then drive east to resort
Closest Commercial Airports: Greenbrier Valley Airport, Lewisburg (11/2 hrs.); Roanoke Municipal, VA (3 hrs.); Pittsburgh International, PA (4 hrs.); Wheeling (4 hrs.)

RESORT

Date Built: 1974
No. of Rooms: The Inn at Snoeshoe: 150 rooms. Timberline Lodge: 50 rooms. Silver Creek Lodge: 240 unit condominium complex. Whistleplunk Village: 12 bedrooms, 48 condominium suites. The Mountaintop Lodge: 1- and 2-bedroom condominium suites
Meeting Rooms: 10. Capacity of Largest: 500 person ballroom. Meeting Space: 10,000 Sq. Ft.
Room Price Range: From $55 standard room to $142 for 4-bedroom at Silvercreek Lodge
Lounges: Whistleplunk Village, Yodeler's Pub
Restaurants: The Terrace, Brandi's, The Red Fox, Goodtime Bobby's, Yodeler's Pub, Cass Dinner Train, Hawthorne Valley Clubhouse, Just Because
Entertainment: music festivals, food festivals
Credit Cards: All major cards
General Amenities: Arcade, gift shops, Ski Barn, The General Store, Shirt Works store; meeting and conference facilities including audiovisual, banquet, and secretarial support
Recreational Amenities: Indoor heated swimming pools, jacuzzis, saunas, exercise rooms with Nautilus and other equipment; Har-Tru tennis courts, horseback riding, mountain biking center, winter skiiing, fishing, boating, hiking
Reservation and Cancellation Policy: Deposit must be made to hold reservation. Reservations made within 14 days of arrival must be guaranteed with a credit card. Deposit forfeited if 30 day cancellation notice not given
Comments and Restrictions: No pets. Nearest kennel 50 miles. Guests responsible for accomodations damage and must sign damage responsibility agreement

HAWTHORNE VALLEY GOLF COURSE

The Hawthorne Valley Golf Course is a Gary Player creation situated at 3050 to 3350 feet within Snoeshoe Mountain, a 11,000-acre year round residential and resort development in the Allegheny Mountain Range of Southeastern West Virginia. This property is adjacent to the dense woodlands of the Monongahela National Forest and offers a range of recreational activities including fishing, hunting, boating, hiking, mountain biking, horseback riding, and winter skiing.

The golf course, rated one of the best in West Virginia by *Golf Digest*, meanders through rolling meadows accentuated by huge grassy knolls, rock formations, and mountain lakes on its front nine. The most difficult hole on this side is the 445-yard par-4 second, a dogleg left whose tee shot requires a long carry over a waste area and a creek to reach a narrow landing area comprised of two tiers running parallel. The approach is to a deep, elevated, two-tiered green with a creek flowing below. Bunkers guard the rear of this tricky putting surface. The greens at Hawthorne Valley are large, bentgrass, quick, and have subtle undulations. Water hazards in the form of beautiful lakes, streams, and ponds can come into play on eleven holes. If you hit the fairway landing areas, you are likely to have a level lie, but errant shots that are playable will likely have uneven mountain lies.

The back nine is the more difficult side at Hawthorne Valley. Treelined holes, mountain streams, pronounced elevation changes and dry-laid rock-walled greens and tees add panache to the final nine. A memorable hole here is the 127-yard par-3 twelfth which plays from an elevated tee to a rock-fronted target 100 feet below. A creek runs at the base of the rocks, so it is better to be long than short. The toughest hole on this side is the 611-yard par-5 fourteenth, a marathon valley hole bordered by a stream, trees and then a mountain slope to the right. Two well-placed shots are required to set up an approach to a deep, elevated green with a bunker to its right, a downward slope to a stream on the left, and mature trees everywhere else.

Overlooking the Hawthorne Valley golf course is a large clubhouse with complete amenities including a grill room and pub. The practice area has a driving range with measured target flags, chipping and putting greens, and practice bunkers. The resort offers a variety of golf packages and accommodations ranging from standard hotel rooms to 4-bedroom condominiums.

Course Name:	**LAKEVIEW RESORT** **Lakeview,** **Mountainview Courses**
Course Type:	Resort
Resort:	Lakeview Resort and Conference Center
Address:	Highway 6/Box 88A Morgantown, WV 16505
Phone:	(304) 594–2011 (Golf Course) (304) 594–1111, (800) 624–8300 (outside WV) (Resort)
Fax:	(304) 594–9472 (Resort)

GOLF COURSE

Head Professional: Frank Sluchak

Course Length/Par (All Tees): Lakeview: Back 6760/72, Middle 6357/72, Forward 5432/72. Mountainview: Back 6447/72, Middle 6152/72, Forward 5385/72

Course Slope/Rating (All Tees): Lakeview: Back 130.1/72.8, Middle 124.9/70.9, Ladies' Forward 118/71.8. Mountainview: Back 119/70.7, Middle 116/69.4, Ladies' Forward 122/70.4

Course Architects: Lakeview: James Gilmore Harrison and Ferdinand Garbin (1954). Mountainview: Brian Ault (1985)

Golf Facilities: Full Pro Shop X, Snack Bar X, Lounge X, Restaurant X, Locker Room X, Showers X, Club Rental X, Club Repair X, Cart Rental X, Instruction X, Practice Green X, Driving Range X, Practice Bunker X, Club Storage X

Tee-Time Reservation Policy: Resort guests: At time of registration. Members 21 days in advance. Outside play: 10 days in advance

Ranger: Yes

Tee-off-Interval Time: 10 min.

Time to Play 18 Holes: 4½ hrs.

Course Hours/Earliest Tee-off: 7 a.m.

Green Fees: Resort guests: Lakeview: $37 for 18 holes Sat., Sun., holidays; $32 for 18 holes weekdays. Mountainview: $20 for 18 holes Sat., Sun., holidays; $18 for 18 holes weekdays. Outside play: Lakeview: $43 for 18 holes Sat., Sun., holidays; $38 for 18 holes weekdays. Mountainview: $21 for 18 holes

Cart Fees: $14 for 18 holes per person

Credit Cards: All major cards

Season: Lakeview: Year round, weather permitting. Mountainview: Late March to mid-Oct.

Course Comments: Cart mandatory. Yardage book available

Golf Packages: Available through resort

Discounts: American Lung Association cards on Mountain View, students, resort guests, seasonal (Nov. through March)

Places to Stay Nearby: Holiday Inn—Morgantown (304) 599–1680, (800) HOLIDAY; Hotel Morgan (304) 292–8401; Comfort Inn—Morgantown (304) 296–9364, (800) 221–2222; Euro-Suites Hotel (304) 598–1000, (800) 6–SUITES; Ramada Inn (304) 296–3431, (800) 543–8766 (WV); Days Inn (304) 598–2120, (800) DAYSINN

Local Attractions: West Virginia University, Cooper's Rock State Forest, Henry Clay Iron Furnace, Arboretum, Cook–Haven Pharmaceutical Museum, Monongahela Arts Center; Cheat Lake with fishing, water-skiing, swimming, boating; Coliseum, Martin Hall

Directions: From I–79: Hwy. 68 east to exit 10, take left, follow Lakeview Resort signs. From Baltimore/Washington, DC, area: I–68 to exit 10, follow Lakeview Resort signs

Closest Commercial Airports: Walter Hart, Morgantown (10 min.); Pittsburgh International, PA (1½ hrs.)

RESORT

Date Built: 1957

No. of Rooms: 191 rooms, 79 2-bedroom condominiums

Meeting Rooms: 23. Capacity of Largest: 600 persons banquet style. Meeting Space: 11,000 sq. ft.

Room Price Range: $79 for single room low season (mid.-Nov. through Apr.) to over $375 for governor's suite peak season (May to mid-Nov.). Golf, vacation and other packages available

Lounge: Off Broadway

Restaurants: Reflections-on-the-Lake, Grille

Entertainment: Dancing

Credit Cards: All major cards

General Amenities: Video gameroom, gift shops; meeting and conference facilities in theater, classroom, banquet settings with audiovisual and food services

Recreational Amenities: Lap pool, indoor cushioned running track, aerobic studio and classes; fitness center with Nautilus, Life Rower, Lifecycle, StairMaster, free weights, whirlpools, sauna, tanning beds, massage; 4 tennis courts, racquetball, indoor and outdoor swimming, miniature golf, hiking, fishing, boating, rock climbing, fitness trails, water-skiing

Reservation and Cancellation Policy: 1 night's room rental required 14 days prior to arrival for each reservation

Comments and Restrictions: On West Virginia University football weekends, 2-night minimum stay required, prepaid 30 days in advance. Taxes additional to base rates

LAKEVIEW RESORT

The Lakeview Resort and Conference Center features the 6760-yard par-72 Lakeview Course and the 6447-yard par-72 Mountainview layout. The Lakeview Course was designed by James Gilmore Harrison and Ferdinand Garbin. It features medium-sized, fast, undulating bentgrass greens with strategically located bunkers and tight fairways. There is a variety of elevation changes and slopes on these rolling fairways, which are plush and allow little roll. The course record at Lakeview, 67, is jointly held by Sam Snead, Jack Nicklaus and Orville Moody. *Golf Digest* rates the course one of the top five in the state of West Virginia.

Lakeview overlooks Cheat Lake, a major recreation area near Morgantown, home of the University of West Virginia. The front nine was built on the side of a mountain and requires careful course management. The number-1-handicap hole on the course is the 429-yard par-4 sixth hole, which has one of the tightest fairways at Lakeview. The fairway slopes left, often kicking balls into the adjacent woods and out of bounds. The green is elevated and undulating and is guarded by a bunker on the left. If you miss the green, you risk being out of bounds to the left or behind the putting surface.

The finishing hole at Lakeview is a monumental 620-yard uphill par 5 that plays up a tree-lined fairway to a green flanked by bunkers. The third shot is often blind, or a long iron or fairway wood. A par on this hole is a considerable achievement.

The Lakeview Course is open year round, weather permitting. The Mountainview Course, designed by Brian Ault and opened in 1985, is generally open from late March until mid-September and is an easier layout than Lakeview. The main clubhouse, locker rooms and pro shop for these courses are at the 191-room resort and conference center, which offers condominium accommodations. Another pro shop is located at the Mountainview Course clubhouse. Golf packages are available year round. The lowest rates are from early November to early April. A 2-night minimum stay is required on weekends.

The Lakeview Resort and Conference Center has 11,000 square feet of meeting and exhibit space, including 23 meeting rooms and banquet facilities for groups of up to 600 persons. Recreational facilities include a $2 million fitness and sports center with Nautilus, Life Rower, Lifecycle, StairMaster, free weights and other facilities. There are also on-site swimming pools, tennis courts, fitness trails, and access to Cheat Lake water sports such as boating, fishing, swimming and waterskiing.

Lakeview is easily accessible from nearby Morgantown and is less than a 2-hour drive from Pittsburgh.

Course Name: OGLEBAY
Speidel, Crispin Courses

Course Type: Public
Address: Oglebay Park
Wheeling, WV 26003
Phone: (304) 242–3000 (Golf Course)
(800) 624–6988
(Recreational Packages, Wilson Lodge Guest Rooms)
(304) 243–4090 (Cabin Reservations, Information)

(800) 633–9975 (From Canada, Wilson Lodge Guest Rooms)
(304) 243–4060 (Conference Planning Information)

GOLF COURSE

Head Professional: Karen Waiale
Course Length/Par (All Tees): Speidel: Back 7000/71, Blue 6555/71, White 6085/71, Forward 5515/71. Crispin: Back 5670/71, Forward 5100/71
Course Slope/Rating (All Tees): Speidel: Back 126/73, Blue 122/70.8, White 118/69, Ladies' Forward 120/72. Crispin: NA/NA
Course Architects: Speidel: Robert Trent Jones, Sr. (1971). Crispin: Emmet Devereaux (1930)
Golf Facilities: Full Pro Shop X, Snack Bar X, Lounge X, Restaurant No, Locker Room X, Showers X, Club Rental X, Club Repair X, Cart Rental X, Instruction X, Practice Green X, Driving Range X, Practice Bunker No, Club Storage X
Tee-Time Reservation Policy: Oglebay Park: Guests: 1 yr. in advance. Outside play: 60 days in advance. Credit card guarantee required for Fri., Sat., Sun., holidays
Ranger: Yes
Tee-off-Interval Time: 8 min.
Time to Play 18 Holes: 4 hrs., 45 min.
Course Hours/Earliest Tee-off: 7:15 a.m. to dark
Green Fees: $35 plus tax for 18 holes, $18 plus tax for 9 holes
Cart Fees: $24 plus tax for 18 holes, $13.50 plus tax for 9 holes
Pull Carts: $3.00
Credit Cards: American Express, Discover, MasterCard, Visa
Season: March 1 to Dec. 1
Course Comments: Can walk anytime. Yardage book available. Caddy Camp program. (Caddies June, July, Aug.)
Golf Packages: Available through resort
Discounts: Local residents, resort guests
Places to Stay Nearby: Oglebay Park Accommodations (800) 624–6988; Hampton Inn (304) 233–0440, (800)

HAMPTON; Best Western—Wheeling Inn (304) 233–8500, (800) 528–1234. BED AND BREAKFASTS: Yesterdays, Ltd. Bed and Breakfast (304) 233–2003; McClure House (304) 232–0300, (800) 862–5873

Local Attractions: Independence Hall, Oglebay Institute Mansion Museum, Victorian Wheeling House tours, historic district, Wheeling Suspension Bridge, fishing, hunting, factory outlets, Ohio River cruises, Stifel Fine Arts Center, horse racing at Mountaineer Park. MOUNDSVILLE: Grave Creek Mound State Park, Mountaineer Park, Lewis Wetzel Public Hunting and Fishing Area. Bethany. Wellsburg. Wheeling Tourist Information (800) 828–3097. Historic Bethany Information (304) 829–7285

Directions: I–70, exit 2A, Rte. 88 north to Oglebay Park, follow signs to golf course

Closest Commercial Airports: Wheeling (30 min.); Pittsburgh International, PA (1 hr.); Yeager, Charleston (3½ hrs.)

OGLEBAY

The Speidel Golf Course is a Robert Trent Jones, Sr., course located in 1500-acre Oglebay Park in the rolling hills of Wheeling, West Virginia. Oglebay was created from Waddington Farm, the summer estate of Colonel Earl Oglebay, an industrialist who willed the property upon his death in 1926 to the citizens of Wheeling "for recreational and educational purposes." The Crispin Course was the first golf course at Oglebay. It was designed by Emmet Devereaux, a golfer and huntsman who was born in New York City in 1861. He bought hunting dogs in the South in the spring, trained them on Long Island in the summer, sold them in Ireland in the autumn and spent winter hunting and golfing in the British Isles. One winter he measured British golf holes for C. B. MacDonald, who was then planning the National Golf Links of America on Long Island. Devereaux was a founding member of the National and went on to design the Congressional Country Club, Bethesda, Maryland; Leatherstock-

ing Country Club, Cooperstown, New York; and many others. The Crispin Course can still be played at Oglebay.

The Speidel Golf Course has been rated one of America's 75 best public golf courses by *Golf Digest* and is currently ranked the fifth best public or private golf course in the state of West Virginia by that publication. This 7000-yard layout features large, fast, undulating bentgrass greens that are well guarded by large traps. There are several elevation changes on this course, which demands shot placement, careful club selection and course management to score. Many of the fairways are well treed and uneven lies are common. There are water hazards on four holes.

Wind can also be a factor on the Speidel Course, especially in the spring and fall. The number-1-handicap par-4 tenth hole is long enough at 450 yards from the back tees, but a head wind can make the hole much more difficult. The tee shot on this dogleg left is from an elevated plateau and must avoid the large sand bunkers on the left side of the flat fairway landing area. The second shot is to a medium-sized green guarded by a large trap on the left.

Another challenging hole is the 590-yard par-5 fifth, which is fairly tightly treed. The tee-shot landing area is guarded by two traps on the right and another large bunker on the left. The second shot is generally a layup to the front of a large pond directly in front of the small green, which is guarded on the right by a trap. There is no room for error on the approach shot because it is out of bounds behind the green.

A picturesque par 3 is the 190-yard thirteenth, which plays from an elevated tee to a large green flanked by large traps left and right. This hole is especially scenic in the spring, when the surrounding crab apple trees are flowering.

There is a variety of accommodations within Oglebay Park. Wilson Lodge has 204 rooms and suite combinations including adjacent chalets, many with fireplaces and wet bars. There are also 2-, 4- and 6-bedroom cabins equipped with kitchens, baths, central heating, fireplaces. Year-round packages are available for golf, tennis, skiing and other activities.

Oglebay also has meeting and conference facilities that can accommodate groups of up to 700. There are dining facilities in a newly expanded multilevel restaurant in Wilson Lodge, and food is also available at the Hamm Clubhouse at the Speidel Golf Course and at other locales in the park. Among the other attractions at Oglebay are a 65-acre children's zoo, newly restored Waddington Gardens with thousands of flowers, Oglebay Mansion Museum, a nature center, picnic sites and entertainment at 2 lounges on the property. There is a busy calendar of events at Oglebay including a winter Festival of Lights that runs from November through February and attracts over 1 million people each year.

In addition to the Speidel and Crispin golf courses, there are a par-3 golf course and a miniature golf course here. Indoor and outdoor tennis and swimming, boating and fishing on Schenk Lake, horseback riding and skiing are also available.

Golf practice facilities at Oglebay include a driving range and practice green. The Oglebay Park Caddie Camp, which began in 1932, has won *Golf Digest*'s Junior Development Award (municipal winner) for innovative junior golf-development programs. The Oglebay program has 40 children caddying each summer and learning course maintenance. They receive free room and board in cabins on the park grounds and have a modest fee for expenses per week deducted from their caddy income. Karen Waiale's father used to run the caddy camp. She is now the head pro at Oglebay.

If you are interested in a challenging golf experience in a beautiful, family-oriented municipal park that looks more like an arboretum and cultural center, Oglebay is your place.

Recommended Golf Courses in West Virginia

Cacapon State Park Golf Course, Berkley Springs, (304) 258–1022, (800) 225–5982, Public, 18/6940/72

Canaan Valley State Park Golf Course, Davis, (304) 866–4121, (800) 622–4121, Resort, 18/6982/72

Glade Springs Resort, Daniels, (304) 763–2050, (800) 634–5233, Resort, 18/6941/72

Grandview Country Club, Beaver, (304) 763–2520, Semiprivate, 18/6834/72

Greenhills Country Club, Ravenswood, (304) 273–3396, Semiprivate, 18/6056/72

Locust Hill Golf Course, Charlestown, (304) 728–7300, Semiprivate, 18/7005/72

Pipestem State Park Golf Course, Pipestem, (304) 466–1800, Public, 18/6884/72

Tygart Lake Country Club, Grafton, (304) 265–3100, Semiprivate, 18/6210/72

Woodbridge Plantation Golf Club, Mineral Wells, (304) 489–1800, Semiprivate, 18/6806/71

Woods Golf Course, Hedgesville, (304) 754–7222 (Pro Shop), (304) 754–7977 (Resort), (800) 248–2222 (Resort), Resort, 18/6608/72

West Virginia: Useful Information

Division of Tourism and Parks, State Capitol Complex, Charleston, WV 25305, (800) 225–5982 (tourism, recreation information)

U.S. Forest Service, 200 Sycamore St., Elkins, WV 26241–3962, (304) 636–1800, (800) 280–CAMP (national forest information and reservations)

Division of Natural Resources, State Capitol Complex, Charleston, WV 25305, (304) 558–2771, (800) 225–5982 (fishing and hunting regulations)

Southern

Course Name: **BLACKWOLF RUN
Meadow Valleys,
River Courses**

Course Type: Public
Address: 1111 West Riverside Drive
Kohler, WI 53044
Phone: (414) 457–4446 (Golf Course)
(414) 457–8000, (800) 344–
2838 (American Club)
Fax: (414) 457–1684

GOLF COURSE

Director of Golf: Paul Becker
Course Length/Par (All Tees): Meadow
Valleys: Back 7142/72, Blue 6735/72,
White 6169/72, Forward 5065/72. River:
Back 6991/72, Blue 6607/72, White
6110/72, Forward 5115/72
Course Slope/Rating (All Tees): Meadow
Valleys: Back 143/74.7, Blue 138/73,
White 132/70.4, Ladies' Forward
125/69.5. River: Back 151/74.9, Blue
146/73.2, White 137/70.9, Ladies' For-
ward 128/70.7
Course Architect: Pete Dye (18 holes,
1988; 9 holes, 1989; 9 holes, 1990)
Golf Facilities: Full Pro Shop X, Snack
Bar X, Lounge X, Restaurant X,
Locker Room X, Showers X, Club
Rental X, Club Repair X, Cart Rental
X, Instruction X, Practice Green X,
Driving Range X, Practice Bunker X,
Club Storage X
Tee-Time Reservation Policy: American
Club guests: At time of room reserva-
tion. Outside play: Up to 14 days in ad-
vance. All tee times must be guaranteed
by a major credit card. A 48-hr. cancella-
tion notice required to avoid penalties·
Ranger: Yes
Tee-off-Interval Time: 10 min.
Time to Play 18 Holes: 4 hrs. 45 min.
Course Hours/Earliest Tee-off: 7 a.m.
Green and Carts Fees: American Club
guests: Meadow Valleys: $90 for 18
holes with cart. River: $123 for 18 holes
with cart
Credit Cards: American Express, Discover,
MasterCard, Visa

Season: Mid-April to Oct. Busiest season
Aug. through Sept.
Course Comments: Walking allowed any-
time. Yardage book available
Golf Packages: Available through the
American Club
Discounts: Early and late season up to mid-
May, from mid-Oct. Replays same day
Places to Stay Nearby: KOHLER: The
American Club (414) 457–8000, (800)
344–2838 MANITOWOC: Holiday Inn
(414) 682–5000, (800) HOLIDAY; Inn
on Maritime Bay (414) 682–7000, (800)
654–5353. SHEBOYGAN: Check-Inn
Fountain Park Motor Inn (414) 458–
4641; Harbor Inn (414) 452–2424;
Rochester Inn (800) 421–4667; Super 8
Motel (414) 458–8080. BED AND BREAK-
FAST: Yankee Hill Bed and Breakfast
(414) 892–2222
Local Attractions: KOHLER: Kohler Design
Center, Shops at Woodlake, Waelder-
house. GREENBUSH: Jung Carriage
Museum, Old Wade house. SHEBOYGAN:
John Michael Kohler Arts Center,
Sheboygan County Historical Museum,
Sheboygan Indian Mound Park, Kohler–
Andrae State Park, Jaycee Park, concerts,
theater, seasonal festivals. MANITOWOC:
Manitowoc Maritime Museum and
U.S.S. *Cobia*, Ruhr–West Art Museum,
Manitowoc Museum of Sculpture, Pine
River Dairy, Pinecrest Historical Vil-
lage. TWO RIVERS: Neshotah Park, Point
Beach State Forest, Rogers Street fish-
ing village, Old School, Woodland
Dunes Nature Center, fishing, camping,
hiking, boating, bicycling, skiing and
other winter sports, antiques. Sturgeon
Bay. Milwaukee. Sheboygan County
Planning and Resources Department
(414) 459–3060. Sheboygan Area Con-
vention and Visitors Bureau (414) 457–
9495
Directions: I–43 to exit 126, take Hwy. 23
west to County Rd. Y, take County Rd.
Y to Kohler, follow signs to golf course
Closest Commercial Airports: General
Mitchell International, Milwaukee (1 hr.,
15 min.); Chicago O'Hare International,
IL (3½ hrs.)

BLACKWOLF RUN

Blackwolf Run has two Pete Dye–designed eighteen-hole golf courses set on 400 acres adjoining a 500-acre wildlife sanctuary in Kohler, a village of fewer than 2000 people, 75 miles north of Milwaukee. These layouts are considered by many to be the best golf courses in Wisconsin. The facility was named after Black Wolf, chief of the Winnebago Indians and a well-known warrior in this region in the early 1800s. The 7142-yard Meadow Valleys Course is separated from the 6991-yard River Course by the Sheboygan River, which runs through the property for 7 miles. These two golf courses are completely different but equally challenging. Meadow Valleys has a 143 slope rating and a 74.7 course rating from the back tees. The River Course has a 151 slope rating and a 74.9 course rating.

The River Course at Blackwolf Run is a beautiful layout with sweeping panoramic views of the Sheboygan River Valley. The course has many elevation changes; a variety of large, fast, undulating bentgrass greens well protected by bunkers and water; water hazards on fourteen holes; and some intimidating, strategically placed fairway bunkers. There is a choice of four different tee distances ranging from 6991 to 5115 yards. The holes each have their own names, some of them foreboding, such as "Burial Grounds," "Gotcha," "Hell's Gate," "Blind Alley," and "Snapping Turtle."

There are many excellent golf holes at the River Course, which requires accuracy, strategic course management and consistency. The 419-yard par-4 fifth hole, "Made in Heaven," has a spectacular view from an elevated tee to a green that rises up from the landing area. The fairway is bordered on the right by the river and on the left by trees. The tee-shot landing area is protected by a large bunker on the right, 225 yards from the back tees. Both the tee shot and the approach shot should be kept to the left on this hole.

The ninth hole, "Cathedral Spires," is a beautiful par-4 dogleg right playing 337 yards from the back tees. Dye describes this hole in the yardage book:

A very, very short par-4, with such a dramatic setting. On August 5, 1989, standing there in the mud, I told Herb Kohler I thought this was the best hole I'd ever built. Why? Look closely. It has three fairways. The far left is safe. Skimming the big tooth aspen on the left yields a broader approach to the green but a long drive may roll you into a pot bunker. Straight at it on the right is for the high and mighty. Taking the latter course, even though the green has a lot of roll, may give you a chance of getting down in two. Or six.

From the tee you can see water to the left and water to the right. A pot bunker sits in the center of the fairway 250 yards from the tee, and two large bunkers guard the front of the green from 60 yards in. Water lines the right side of the shallow but wide putting surface. Another bunker is to the left rear.

My favorite par 3 on the River Course is the 205-yard thirteenth, "Tall Timber," which is a dogleg right from the two back tees. A river lined with willows borders the right fairway, and you have to clear these 60-foot-tall trees to reach a green that is more than 45 yards deep and fronted by two traps left and right with the river farther to the right. Occasionally fishermen work the river along this beautiful golf hole.

The finishing hole on the River Course, "Dyehard," is a long, 469-yard dogleg-left par 4 with water and trees on the left from the tee to a huge double green. The tee-shot landing area is protected on the right by a large bunker and on the left by heavy rough. The second shot is to an open entrance to the large green. This 23,000-square-foot double green is shared with the finishing hole on the Meadow Valleys Course.

Meadow Valleys' front nine is set on gently rolling terrain and is reminiscent of a Scottish-links course. The back nine reflects the overall influence of glaciers on the land, with deep ravines bordering a river valley. With its pot bunkers, huge sand traps, and plateaued greens, this course puts a premium on shot making. There are ten water holes, and the greens tend to be large, fast, undulating and well protected by water and sand. As an added touch, two flatbed railroad cars, one with wheels intact, serve as bridges over Weeden's Creek.

Meadow Valleys is another medley of tough, memorable and often diabolically beautiful Dye-inspired golf holes. The eighth hole, "Wet and Wild," is a scenic 240-yard par 3 that plays to a deep green backed by a bunker and bordered by water on the left. The variable winds can be a major factor on this hole and must be taken into consideration at all times. The next hole is the 462-yard par-4 "Deer Hunt," whose tee shot must avoid a huge bunker on the right. The second shot is down a fairway lined with traps on the left from 150 yards into a large green. On the right is water all the way to and around the back of the putting surface. There is little margin for error on the approach shot here.

The signature hole at Meadow Valleys is the 227-yard par-3 fifteenth, appropriately called "Mercy." The tee shot is from an elevated tee over an expansive ravine to a huge green. Unlike most of Dye's other courses, which feature small to medium-sized greens, the task of scoring only begins when you reach the large putting surfaces at Blackwolf Run.

The finishing hole is the long, 458-yard par-4 "Salmon Trap." The tee shot is to a landing area framed by trees, and the approach is over the river to the large double green. If your tee shot is not in the proper position, hitting the approach into the water becomes very simple.

Awaiting you after your round is a clubhouse that is almost as impressive as the golf courses themselves. This 40,000-square-foot structure is constructed of lodgepole pine logs, fieldstone and wooden shingles. The building has three banquet rooms, a conference room, a kitchen, men's and women's locker rooms, a pro shop, main dining room, bar, enclosed dining porch and several outdoor patios. Just outside the pro shop and to the right of the dining room is a handmade birchbark canoe in front of a beautiful tapestry that graces the wall. The canoe was made in northern Wisconsin in 1910.

Practice facilities at Blackwolf Run include a driving range, practice green and practice bunker. Instruction is available from the staff of professionals. The course is open to the public, and walking is allowed. Golf packages are available through the nearby American Club, which is a premier luxury resort hotel and conference center. Blackwolf Run is part of a development concept to make Kohler Village a business, hospitality and recreation center in Wisconsin. Kohler is synonymous with the Kohler Co., a leading manufacturer of plumbing products, furniture, generator sets and four-cycle engines. The company was founded in 1873 by John Michael Kohler. Today the company is one of the oldest and largest privately held companies in America. The company's headquarters are in Kohler, and Herbert V. Kohler, Jr., who was very involved in the development of the Blackwolf Run golf courses, has been its chairman and president since 1972. The Kohler Co. owns Blackwolf Run and the American Club, with its amenities.

The village of Kohler, incorporated in 1912, was one of the first planned communities in the United States. The American Club was built in 1918 as housing for immigrant Kohler Co. employees. Today it is an American Automobile Association Five-Diamond hotel, placing it among the top 50 hotels in the United States, and is on the National Register of Historic Places. The impressive interior of the American Club features handcrafted oak paneling, travertine counters, stained glass, crystal chandeliers and oriental rugs. Nine resort restaurants feature the finest American cooking and European continental cuisine, spa food and lighter fare. The American Club has received the International Food, Wine and Travel Writers Association Award of Excellence. Additional restaurants are located at the golf club, the Sports Core recreational complex, the River Wildlife Lodge on a 500-acre nature preserve, and in the village.

Recreational amenities available through the American Club include indoor swimming pools, indoor and outdoor tennis courts, racquetball courts, a running trail, a complete Nautilus circuit, Universal equipment, exercise bicycles, a treadmill, whirlpool, sauna and spa amenities including shiatsu and Swedish massage, herbal wrap, facials, fitness consultation, fitness classes and other features. Most of these recreational facilities are part of the American Club's Sports Core complex, set in a quiet woods near Wood Lake.

Meetings and Conventions and *Successful Meetings* magazines have recognized the American Club for its superior conference and golf facilities. There is over 21,000 square feet of conference space available for exhibits, meetings, parties, theatrical performances and dances. Among the rooms available are the 8000-square-foot Grand Hall of Great Lakes, which has the flexibility of being divided into five segments, or the Appley Theater, featuring 94 tiered seats with luxurious furnishings and high-tech audiovisual systems set in a modernized historic carriage house. The carriage house includes an excellent collection of Currier and Ives prints, lithographs, American oil paintings and other graphics spanning the seventeenth through early twentieth centuries and depicting mainly horse-and-carriage themes.

Another feature of the Kohler Village is the 500-acre private nature preserve, River Wildlife, which offers guests a variety of additional sporting opportunities including boating, fly fishing (the Sheboygan River is known for its excellent trout and salmon fishing), hiking, cross-country skiing, hunting and supervised trap-shooting range. On this site, with its wooded hills, grassy meadows and dramatic river banks, are nearly 30 miles of hiking and cross-country ski trails.

The American Club combines Old World charm and craftsmanship with amenities that meet the needs of the modern tourist. The interior of the American Club reflects its ethnic links to the immigrants who lived here but also reflects something resembling the rites of passage of American patriotism and assimilation. The Wisconsin Room, for example, honors the 30th state and includes 24 draw-ings of distinguished Wisconsinites. Two unique tapestries hang on either side of the entry stairs. One depicts the map of Wisconsin, with tiny, costumed figures representing the various ethnic groups and areas of the state in which they settled. The library hall in this hotel is adorned with portraits of distinguished Wisconsinites, from John Muir to Billy Mitchell. Each room honors famous Americans such as Mary Pickford, Ernest Hemingway, John James Audubon, Lou Gehrig and many others. Walter J. Kohler, a former governor of Wisconsin, definitely made it clear which side of the ocean he stood on.

One of Walter J. Kohler's credos is reflected in a quotation from John Ruskin, "Life without labor is guilt, labor without art is brutality." A considerable amount of hard work and artistic skill is reflected in the golf facilities at Blackwolf Run and the resort facilities at the American Club. Appropriately, it is rated one of the best golf resorts in America by *Golf* magazine. *Golf Digest* rates these the best golf courses in Wisconsin. Blackwolf Run will host the U.S. Women's Open in 1998. A must visit.

Course Name: GENEVA NATIONAL GOLF CLUB Palmer, Trevino Courses

Course Type: Semiprivate
Address: 1221 Geneva National Avenue South Lake Geneva, WI 53147
Phone: (414) 245–7011
Fax: (414) 245–6023

GOLF COURSE

Head Professional: Doug Nixon

Course Length/Par (All Tees): Palmer: Back 7171/72, Blue 6746/72, Copper 6138/72, Gray 5456/72, Forward 4904/72. Trevino: Back 7120/72, Blue 6710/72, Copper 6254/72, Gray 5650/72, Forward 5193/72

Course Slope/Rating (All Tees): Palmer: Back 140/74.9, Blue 136/72.8, Copper 131/70.0, Gray 128/71.4, Forward 122/68.4. Trevino: Back 135/74.2, Blue

132/72.3, Copper 128/70.4, Gray 128/70.2, Forward 123/69.9

Course Architects: Palmer: Arnold Palmer and Ed Seay (1991), Trevino: Lee Trevino (1991)

Golf Facilities: Full Pro Shop X, Snack Bar X, Lounge X, Restaurant X, Locker Room X, Showers X, Club Rental X, Club Repair X, Cart Rental X, Instruction X, Practice Green X, Driving Range X, Practice Bunker X, Club Storage X

Tee-Time Reservation Policy: Up to 14 days in advance with credit card guarantee

Ranger: Yes

Tee-off-Interval Time: 8 min.

Time to Play 18 Holes: 4½ hrs.

Course Hours/Earliest Tee-off: 7 a.m.

Green and Cart Fees: $85 for 18 holes

Credit Cards: American Express, Master-Card, Visa

Season: Mid-March through Oct. Busiest late May through Labor Day

Course Comments: Yardage books available. Carts mandatory. Private Gary Player Course available to members and on-site Inns of Geneva National. The Palmer and Trevino courses are open to the public Mon.–Thurs. Either the Palmer or Trevino course is open to the public Fri., Sat., Sun., holidays

Golf Packages: Inquire at pro shop. Available through Inns of Geneva National on site

Discounts: Prior to Memorial Day, after Labor Day

Places to Stay Nearby: The Abbey (414) 275–6811, (800) 558–2405; Interlachen Resort (414) 272–7333, (800) 225–5558; Lake Lawn Lodge (414) 728–7950, (800) 338–5253; Grand Geneva Resort and Spa (414) 248–8811, (800) 558–3417; Hilton Inn (414) 248–9181, (800) 445–8667. BED AND BREAKFAST: T. C. Smith Historic Inn Bed and Breakfast (414) 248–1097

Local Attractions: Lake Geneva, Big Foot Beach State Park, Clown Hall of Fame, Geneva Lake cruises, boating, fishing, swimming, horseback riding, hunting, camping, restaurants, shopping. Milwaukee. Lake Geneva Convention and Visitor's Bureau, 201 Wrigley Dr., Lake Geneva, WI 53147 (414) 248–4416

Directions: Four miles west of Lake Geneva on Hwy. 50

Closest Commercial Airports: General Mitchell International, Milwaukee (1 hr.); Chicago O'Hare International, IL (1½ hrs.)

GENEVA NATIONAL GOLF CLUB

Geneva National, located 75 miles northwest of Chicago in the Lake Geneva region of Southeastern Wisconsin, offers country club quality golf in a 1600-acre planned residential community. The terrain here features woodlands, hills, deep ravines, streams and ponds near Lake Como. Three brand-name golf architects were retained to add panache and quality to this development: Arnold Palmer, Gary Player, and Lee Trevino. The Palmer and Trevino layouts, both of which play from over 7000 yards from the tips, are open to the public; the Player course, a nine-hole layout that will eventually be eighteen holes, is open to club members and golfers who stay at the on-site Inns at Geneva National.

The 7171-yard Palmer Course can also be played from four other tee distances. Arnie says that "I set out to build a golf course that will accomodate the biggest championship in the world, and a week later can accommodate a family of average golfers." The course is set on rolling terrain that drops 300 feet from its highest point to two scenic holes along Lake Como, Nos. 16 and 17. The sixteenth is a 218-yard par 3 with the lake to your left and in full view behind the green. The tee shot is from an elevated tee down to a target protected by bunkers to its front left and right. The 573-yard par-5 seventeenth, a dogleg left bordered by the lake on the left, is reminiscent of the final hole at Pebble Beach. The 424-yard par-4 finishing hole climbs back up the hill toward the 56,000 square foot clubhouse, an imposing structure that has separate facilities for both the members and the public. The tee shot is to a concealed landing area and the approach is to a green well guarded by bunkers. The bentgrass greens at Geneva National tend to be large, subtly undulating, and moderately fast.

The Trevino Course, a 7120-yard layout, also has five tee distances to choose from. A more heavily wooded course, the Trevino requires an ability to work the ball from left to right, one of Lee Trevino's assets. The ball tends to break toward lake Como. The toughest hole on the front side is the 520-yard par-5 fifth, a dogleg right. The first shot is from an elevated tee to a landing area lined with trees. The second shot is usually a layup because the green is fronted by a creek that also borders the right side beginning approximately 100 yards from the target. Water hazards can come into play on seven holes on the Trevino Course including the difficult 608-yard sixteenth, the longest hole on the course. The tee shot landing area on this hole has bunkers to its left and out-of-bounds to the right. The hole is then narrowed by a pond on the right that cuts into the fairway approximately 100 yards from the green. The putting surface is shaped like a fist pointing a finger to the right. Bunkers guard the rear left and right sides and a pin placement tucked on the shallow shelf to the right can make the approach shot extremely difficult. The Trevino Course usually offers a variety of target paths to the hole. As Lee expains it "We need more courses that the regular player can play....If you miss a shot you should have a chance to recover."

The clubhouse has banquet facilities for up to 400 guests, and other amenities include locker room facilities, a quality pro shop, and a restaurant. The nearby Hunt Club Lodge also has a restaurant featuring such delicacies as Wisconsin venison medallions pan-seared with garlic cloves, pecans, and whole pearl onions, served with game glacé. The practice facilities at Geneva National includes a 100-yard-wide driving range with target flags and a short game area with putting greens that simulate the conditions on both the Trevino and Palmer courses. Within walking distance are the Inns of Geneva National which have suites starting at $225. A variety of golf packages including golf and accommo-

dations at The Inns are available. The Inns have vaulted ceilings, fieldstone fireplaces, private patios, and other comforts. All guests can enjoy private club privileges including tennis, swimming, sporting clays, hunting facilities, full dining options, and access to all three golf courses at any time.

Golf Digest has rated the Palmer and Trevino courses among the top 10 in Wisconsin.

Course Name: LAWSONIA
                Links, Woodlands
                Courses

Course Type: Public
Address: Wisconsin Highway 23
               Green Lake, WI 54941
Phone: (414) 294–3320,
               (800) 529–4453
Fax: (414) 294–3844

GOLF COURSE

Golf Director: Jeff Penkwitz

Course Length/Par (All Tees): Links: Back 6764/72, Middle 6466/72, Forward 5078/71. Woodlands: Back 6618/72, Middle 6186/72, Forward 5106/72

Course Slope/Rating (All Tees): Links: Back 130/72.8, Middle 128/71.5, Forward 115/65.2, Ladies' Middle 131/76.7, Ladies' Forward 114/68.9. Woodlands: Back 132/72.7, Middle 129/70.1, Forward 119/65.2, Ladies': Middle 137/75.6, Ladies' Forward 125/69.6

Course Architects: Links: William B. Langford (1930). Woodlands: Joe Lee and Rocky Roquemore (9 holes, 1983; 9 holes, 1991)

Golf Facilities: Full Pro Shop X, Snack Bar X, Lounge No, Restaurant X, Locker Room X, Showers X, Club Rental X, Club Repair X, Cart Rental X, Instruction X, Practice Green X, Driving Range X, Practice Bunker No, Club Storage X

Tee-Time Reservation Policy: Anytime in advance with credit card guarantee

Ranger: Yes

Tee-off-Interval Time: 8 min.

Time to Play 18 Holes: 4½ hrs.

Course Hours/Earliest Tee-off: 6 a.m.

Green and Cart Fees: Links: $50 for 18 holes with cart Fri., Sat., Sun., holidays, $48 for 18 holes Mon.-Thurs. Woodlands: $58 for 18 holes with cart Fri., Sat., Sun., holidays, $55 for 18 holes Mon.–Thurs.

Pull Carts: Available

Credit Cards: All major cards

Season: April to Oct. Busiest season July through Aug.

Course Comments: Cart mandatory Fri., Sat., Sun., holidays until 4 p.m. and until 2 p.m. on Woodlands Mon.–Thurs. 9-hole play available, except on Woodlands Fri., Sat., Sun., holidays. Golfers using a cart for 9 holes must play the Links course

Golf Packages: Available through local hotels and motels

Discounts: Season tickets. Seasonal and other specials. Twilight rates

Places to Stay Nearby: Roger Williams Inn (414) 294–3323. GREEN LAKE: Heidel House Resort and Conference Center (414) 294–3344; Four Seasons Motel (414) 294–3401; Bay View Motel (414) 294–6504. RIPON: Farmer's Daughter Inn (414) 748–2146 (farm)

Local Attractions: GREEN LAKE: Troster Arts and Crafts Center. OSHKOSH: Experimental Aircraft Association's Art Adventure Museum, Manufacturers Marketplace featuring outlet stores, Priebe Art Gallery, Paine Art Center and Arboretum, Oshkosh Public Museum, Grand Opera House. IOLA: Iola Mills Museum of Pioneer History, Hartman Creek State Park. RIPON: Ripon College, Center for the Arts, Ripon Foods Outlet Store, Little White Schoolhouse, Larson's famous Clydesdales, Farmer's Daughter dairy farm, seasonal festivals, camping, fishing, hiking, boating, skiing and other winter sports. Green Lake County Tourism (414) 294–4032. Green Lake Chamber of Commerce (414) 294–3231

Directions: Hwy. 23 just west of Greenlake, follow highway signs

Closest Commercial Airports: Oshkosh (45 min.); General Mitchell International, Milwaukee (1½ hrs.); Austin Straubel, Green Bay (1½ hrs.); Chicago O'Hare International (3 hrs.)

LAWSONIA

Victor Lawson, owner and publisher of the Chicago *Daily News* and founder of the *Associated Press*, and his wife Jessie visited the resort during the late 1800s and purchased 10 acres of land, where they built a summer cottage. By the early 1900s, they had built an estate, Lone Tree Farm, that covered 1074 acres with lake frontage of 2½ miles. Jessie Lawson supervised the estate and supervised the construction of water towers as well as bridges and stone walls. The property became a working cattle farm, and many workers lived on the property, which included a huge barn, still standing today, houses and other structures.

After the Lawsons died, the land was purchased by the H. O. Stone Co., which built the first eighteen-hole golf course (the Links), private homes and a hotel (now the Roger Williams Inn). The American Baptists purchased the property in 1943 and still own it. Today it is a year-round conference center and resort open to all races, creeds and denominations. Recreational facilities and activities include skiing and other winter sports, nature trails, fitness trails, hayrides, cookouts, an indoor competition swimming pool, wading pool, boating, bicycling, fishing, volleyball, tennis, and other activities. The Troster Arts and Crafts Center at Green Lake specializes in lapidary, ceramics and stained glass. Classes in ceramics, china decoration, lapidary work, stained glass, swimming, skiing, golf and other activities are offered at the resort.

The original 6764-yard Links Course was designed by William B. Langford and opened in 1930. Langford was born in 1887 in Austin, Illinois, suffered from polio as a child and took up golf as part of a rehabilitation program. He was a member of 3 Yale University NCAA championship golf teams from 1906 to 1908 and began as a golf-course architect after gaining a masters' degree in mining engineering at Columbia University. Langford eventually designed over 250 courses with his partner

Theodore J. Moreau, and he also owned and operated several daily-fee courses in the Chicago area. He was a strong promoter of public golf. Langford and Moreau designed Leathem Smith Lodge Golf Course, Sturgeon Bay; North Shore Acres Country Club, Kenosha; Our Country Club, Salem; Ozankee Country Club, Mequon; Spring Valley Country Club, Salem; and West Bend Country Club; all in Wisconsin. He died in 1977 at the age of 89.

Developed on 250 acres, the Links Course is an open, Scottish-style layout. Legend has it that a boxcar was buried beneath the seventh green and that dozens more were buried in the fairways. Supposedly sand was then poured over them to form huge bunkers. The Links has medium-sized, moderately fast, plateaued, multi-tiered greens, with steep bunkers protecting most of them. A series of strategically placed bunkers appear in the fairway landing areas and wind can be a factor on this open layout. *Golf Digest* has selected this layout one of America's 75 best public golf courses.

A memorable par 3 on the Links Course is the 161-yard seventh, which plays to the allegedly boxcar-supported elevated green 40 to 50 feet above the tee. The number-1-handicap hole is the 487-yard par-5 fifth, which plays to a green protected by two bunkers to the left and right and a third bunker to the right and forward. Many golfers have a good chance to reach the green in two on this one.

The 568-yard par-5 thirteenth is one of the most difficult holes on the course. The first shot is to a landing area well guarded by bunkers. The second is most likely to a landing area just before a deep gully that begins approximately 170 yards from an elevated green. The approach is over that abyss to a flat green with drop-offs to the rear and sides. Small, elevated greens; deep rough; and deep, snaking, large sand bunkers make the Links Course a challenging test of golf.

The Woodlands Course plays 6618 yards from the back tees. The course was carved out of woods and is much tighter than the Links, with some severe changes in elevation. The bentgrass greens are large, moderately fast, rolling and well bunkered. The fairways are also well bunkered, and it is not unusual to have a sidehill or downhill lie. Joe Lee and Rocky Roquemore designed this layout, whose first nine opened in 1983. The second nine was completed in 1991. Lee and Roquemore created three excellent courses at Disney World in Orlando; Doral's "Blue Monster" in Miami; and Cog Hill's Dubs Dread in suburban Chicago; as well as many other quality layouts.

The Woodlands Course starts out with a challenging 510-yard par 5, a double dogleg that bends left, then right to a large green protected by traps to the right, left and right front. The entire fairway is tree-lined and well guarded by a series of traps. The 341-yard dogleg-left par-4 second is a short but memorable hole. The first shot is to a landing area with a huge bunker to the right. The second shot is over a large quarry to a green with bunkers to the left and rear and fronted by the quarry. The tee shot must be kept right to avoid an oak tree guarding the left side of the fairway.

A beautiful par 3 on the front side, commonly called "The Cliff" hole, is the 168-yard third, which plays from an elevated tee to a well-trapped green 60 to 70 feet below. On the right is a scenic view of Green Lake. A challenging par 4 on the back nine is the 438-yard fourteenth, which is narrow, well-treed and long. The second shot must carry a deep gully to a large green guarded by a bunker to the left front. The combination of pine, maple, oak, elm and other trees in abundance, radical elevation changes, well-placed bunkers and panoramic views of Green Lake makes the Woodlands a challenging and beautiful golf experience.

The new clubhouse at Lawsonia has a pro shop, locker rooms and showers, restaurant and snack bar. No alcoholic beverages are served here, and no alcoholic beverages are allowed on the golf courses. Practice facilities include a driving range and putting green. Instruction is available. Golf packages are available through the on-site Roger Williams Inn and other hotels and motels in the area. Walking is allowed Monday through Thursday, and considering the quality of golf offered here, the fees are quite reasonable. Those staying at the Roger Williams Inn and nearby hotels and motels have access to the varied recreational amenities on the Green Lake conference-center property.

Course Name: UNIVERSITY RIDGE GOLF COURSE

Course Type: Public
Address: 7120 County Trunk Road
              Verona, WI 53593
Phone: (608) 845–7700
Fax: (608) 845–9639

GOLF COURSE

Director of Golf: Michael Urban
Head Professional: Brett Compton
Course Length/Par (All Tees): Back 6825/72, Blue 6402/72, White 5826/72, Forward 5005/72
Course Slope/Rating (All Tees): Back 142/73.2, Blue 139/71.2, White 128/68.4, Ladies' Forward 121/68.9
Course Architect: Robert Trent Jones, Jr. (1991)
Golf Facilities: Full Pro Shop X, Snack Bar X, Lounge X, Restaurant No, Locker Room X, Showers X, Club Rental X, Club Repair Off Site, Cart Rental X, Instruction X, Practice Green X, Driving Range X, Practice Bunker X, Club Storage No
Tee-Time Reservation Policy: Up to 5 days in advance. Anytime in advance for groups of 12 or more
Ranger: Yes
Tee-off-Interval Time: 9 min.
Time to Play 18 Holes: 4½ hrs.
Course Hours/Earliest Tee-off: 7 a.m.
Green and Cart Fees: $61 for 18 holes with cart, $46 for 18 holes walking
Credit Cards: American Express, MasterCard, Visa
Season: Apr. through Oct. Busiest July through Labor Day
Course Comments: You can walk anytime except Fri., Sat., Sun., holidays from Memorial Day weekend through Labor Day
Golf Packages: Inquire at pro shop

Discounts: Twilight. Junior, University of Wisconsin students
Places to Stay Nearby: VERONA: Grandview Motel (608) 845–6633. MADISON: Best Western (608) 244–2424, (800) 528–1234; The Edgewater Hotel (608) 256–9071; Holiday Inn East Towne (608) 244–4703, (800) HOLIDAY; Radisson Inn Madison (608) 833–0100, (800) 333–3333; Sheraton Inn and Conference Center (608) 251–2300, (800) 325–3535. BED AND BREAKFASTS: Annie's Bed and Breakfast (608) 244–2224; The Collins House Bed and Breakfast (608) 255–4230
Local Attractions: Madison Art Center, Madison Children's Museum, Henry Villas Park, Olbrich Botanical Gardens, State Capitol, State Historical Museum, The University of Wisconsin, Wisconsin Veteran's Museum, boating, fishing, hunting, bicycling, camping, and other recreation activities, Madison Muskies Midwest League baseball. Greater Madison Convention and Visitors Bureau, 615 E. Washington St., Madison, WI 53703 (608) 255–2537
Directions: From Madison (25 min. southwest): Take Park St. to Beltline (Rte. 1218) west. Exit southwest on Mineral Pt. Rd. Take a left south on M to PD and the golf course
Closest Commercial Airports: Madison (30 min.); General Mitchell Field, Milwaukee (2½ hrs.); Chicago O'Hare International (3½ hrs.)

UNIVERSITY RIDGE GOLF COURSE

The University Ridge Golf Course is a Robert Trent Jones, Jr. design that wends its way through 225 acres of meadows and woodlands south of Madison. The course has ample landing areas off the tees, but if you are not well-positioned, approach shots to the many elevated greens on the course will be difficult. If you stray the ball too far, difficult rough will take strokes from your score.

The front nine at University Ridge is an open links-style layout with rolling fairways and a stream and a pond that can come into play on four holes. The back nine has some abrupt elevation changes as it works its way through mature woodlands. Your round concludes with three strong holes beginning with the 533-yard par-5 sixteenth, a dogleg right whose downhill tee shot should be slightly faded around the corner to have a shot at reaching the green in two. The approach is uphill to a green fronted by a phalanx of grassy mounding and bunkers. A layup shot should be positioned to the left to take these obstacles out of play.

The next hole, a scenic 199-yard par 3, plays over a pond to a deep green protected by a bunker to its right and bordered by a grass mound to its left. The finishing hole is a tough uphill 413-yard par 4, a sharp dogleg left whose tee shot has to clear the bunkers and rough on the left in order to have a low-risk approach to the two-tiered green. Positioning on the tee shot, club selection, and proper calibration of pin position are critical to score well on this hole.

University Ridge is bentgrass from tee to green. Its putting surfaces are moderately fast, slightly undulating, and vary in size. The shorter holes tend to have smaller greens. The course is owned by the University of Wisconsin and is the home of its golf teams. The clubhouse is modest, but the pro shop is excellent. The practice area has a large driving range, putting and chipping greens, and practice bunkers. University Ridge was the site of the 1995 NCAA Men's Championship and will host the Women 's Championship in 1998. The course is rated among the best in Wisconsin by *GolfWeek* and *Golf Digest*.

Recommended Golf Courses in Wisconsin

Within 1¹/₂ Hours of Madison:

Abbey Springs Golf Club, Fontana-on-Geneva Lake, (414) 275–6111, Resort, 18/6466/72

Brighton Dale Golf Club, Kansasville, (414) 878–1440, Public. Blue Spruce: 18/6687/72. White Birch: 18/6977/72

Brown Deer Golf Course, Milwaukee, (414) 352–8080, Public, 18/6763/71

Country Club of Wisconsin, Grafton, (414) 375–2444, Public, 18/7108/72

Deertrack Golf Course, Oconomowoc, (414) 474–4444, Public, 18/6262/72

Devil's Head Resort and Convention Center, Merrimac, (608) 493–2241, (800) 472–6670, Resort, 18/6725/73

Dretzka Park Golf Course, Milwaukee, (414) 354–7300, Public, 18/6832/72

Evergreen Country Club, Elkhorn, (414) 723–5722, (800) 868–8618, Public. North/East: 18/6431/72. East/South: 18/6501/72. North/South: 18/6280/72

Grand Geneva Resort, Lake Geneva, (414) 248–2556, (800) 550–3417, Resort. Briar Patch: 18/6478/72. Brute: 18/6997/72

Ives Grove Golf Links, Sturtevant, (414) 878–3714, 18/6915/72

Johnson Park Golf Course, Racine, (414) 637–2840, Public, 18/6883/72

Kettle Hills Golf Course, Richfield, (414) 255–2200, Public. Ponds/Woods: 18/6787/72. Valley: 18/6455/72

Maplecrest Country Club, Kenosha, (414) 859–2887, Semiprivate, 18/6396/70

Mascoutin Golf Club, Berlin, (414) 361–2360, Semiprivate, 18/6821/72

Naga-Waukee Golf Course, Pewaukee, (414) 367–2153, Public, 18/6780/72

Oakwood Park Golf Course, Franklin, (414) 281–6700, Public, 18/6971/72

Old Hickory Golf Club, Beaver Dam, (414) 887–7577, Semiprivate, 18/6688/72

Petrifying Springs Golf Course, Kenosha, (414) 552–9052, Public, 18/5979/71

Pleasant View Country Club, Middleton, (608) 831–6666, Semiprivate, 18/6436/72

Quit-Qui-Oo Golf Club, Elkhart Lake, (414) 876–2833, Public, 18/6178/70

Rainbow Springs Golf Club, Mukwonago, (414) 363–4550, (800) 465–3631, Semiprivate, 18/6914/72

Reedsburg Country Club, Reedsburg, (608) 524–6000, Semiprivate, 18/6300/72

Rivermoor Country Club, Waterford, (414) 534–2500, Public, 18/6256/70

Riverside Golf Course, Janesville, (608) 757–3080, Public, 18/6508/72

Rock River Golf Course, Horicon, (414) 485–4990, Public, 18/6265/70

Spring Valley Country Club, Salem, (414) 862–2626, Public, 18/6450/70

Springs Golf Course, Spring Green, (608) 588–7707, Public, 18/6603/71

Trapper's Canyon Golf Club, Wisconsin Dells, (608) 253–7000, (800) 221–8876, Public, 18/6550/72

Central

Course Name: BROWN COUNTY

Course Type: Public
Address: 897 Riverdale Drive
Oneida, WI 54155
Phone: (414) 497–1731

GOLF COURSE

Head Professional: Jim Ostrowski
Course Length/Par (All Tees): Back 6749/72, Middle 6392/72, Ladies' Forward 5800/73
Course Slope/Rating (All Tees): Back 133/72.1, Middle 127/70.2, Ladies' Forward 121/72.7
Course Architect: Edward Lawrence Packard (1956)
Golf Facilities: Full Pro Shop X, Snack Bar X, Lounge X, Restaurant X, Locker Room X, Showers X, Club Rental X, Club Repair X, Cart Rental X, Instruction X, Practice Green X, Driving Range X, Practice Bunker X, Club Storage No
Tee-Time Reservation Policy: Call Mon. 6 p.m. prior for Sat., Sun., holiday tee times; 1 day in advance for Mon. through Fri. tee times
Ranger: Yes
Tee-off-Interval Time: 7 min.
Time to Play 18 Holes: 4 hrs., 45 min.
Course Hours/Earliest Tee-off: 5:45 a.m.
Green Fees: $16 for 18 holes daily; $10.50 for 9 holes daily. $2 reservation fee for advance tee times

Cart Fees: $22 for 18 holes per cart; $11 for 9 holes per cart
Pull Carts: $3 for 18 holes, $1.50 for 9 holes
Credit Cards: Cash or local check for golf fees. MasterCard, Visa for merchandise
Season: Mid-April to Nov. 1. Busiest season June through Aug.
Course Comments: Can walk anytime
Golf Packages: None
Discounts: Seniors, juniors, residents
Places to Stay Nearby: Radisson Inn (414) 494–7000, (800) 333–3333; Hampton Inn (414) 498–9200, (800) 426–7866; Embassy Suites (414) 432–4555, (800) 362–2779; Residence Inn by Marriott (414) 435–2222, (800) 331–3131; Motel 6 (414) 494–6730; Best Western Downtowner (414) 437–8771
Local Attractions: Bay Beach Amusement Park, Neville Museum, National Railroad Museum, Packer Stadium–Lambeau Field, University of Wisconsin—Green Bay, Bay Beach Wildlife Sanctuary, Triangle Sports Center, zoo; Brown County Parks with fishing, boating, camping, hiking, picnicking, skiing and other winter sports, hunting, and other recreational activities; Fox Valley Greyhound Park, Heritage Hill Living History Museum, Oneida Nation Museum, Green Bay Packer Hall of Fame. Green Bay Visitors and Convention Bureau (414) 494–9507
Directions: From Austin Straubel Airfield (5 min.): Take Rte. 172 west, right on Hwy. 54, first left on Overland Rd., right on Hwy. J, 2 mi. to golf course
Closest Commercial Airports: Austin Straubel, Green Bay (5 min.); General Mitchell International, Milwaukee (2½ hrs.); Chicago O'Hare International, IL (4½ hrs.)

BROWN COUNTY

Brown County Golf Course is a 6729-yard par-72 well-treed layout with rolling fairways and large, moderately fast bentgrass greens with minor undulations. Edward Lawrence Packard, a native of Northampton, Massachusetts, and architect of many golf courses in the United States and abroad, designed Brown County in the 1950s. He also designed the Stevens Point Country Club, the Wausau Golf Club, Baraboo Country Club, Peninsula State Park Golf Club and many other layouts in Wisconsin. The golf courses he designed at the Innisbrook Golf Club in Florida with his son, Roger, are among his more noteworthy works. Brown County is rated among *Golf Digest*'s list of America's 75 best public golf courses in the United States.

A challenging par 4 on the front nine at Brown County is the 438-yard ninth, a dogleg left down a tree-lined fairway to a large, wide, shallow green with two traps to the left. The corner of the dogleg is approximately 280 yards from the tee, and the second shot is over a stream cutting the fairway 130 yards from the green, which has a slightly uphill approach.

Holes eleven through thirteen provide a quality run of par 4s. The 442-yard dogleg-right eleventh plays to a landing area at the crest of a hill at the corner of the dogleg. The next shot is downhill to a large green with two bunkers to the left and one to the rear. The 399-yard twelfth starts with a tee shot over a creek to a narrow, tree-lined landing area. The second shot is to a deep, forward-sloping green with bunkers to the left and right. The 349-yard thirteenth is a tricky dogleg left. The tee shot is to a landing area to the right of a pond. The approach shot must avoid another pond that cuts into the fairway a bit in front of the putting surface and borders it to the right. A bunker guards the green on the left. The finishing hole is a 438-yard par-4 dogleg right, made longer and more difficult because it plays uphill.

Half the holes at Brown County are doglegs of one kind or another, making the course an interesting, varied and challenging venue. You can walk the course anytime, and the rates are quite low for golf of this quality.

The clubhouse has a pro shop, light-menu restaurant (open from mid-morning until early evening), locker rooms and showers. Practice facilities include a driving range, chipping green and practice bunker, and 2 putting greens. Lessons are available from the staff of professionals.

Course Name: SENTRYWORLD

Course Type: Public
Address: 601 North Michigan Avenue
                        Stevens Point, WI 54481
Phone: (715) 345–1600

GOLF COURSE

Head Professional: Bob Duncan
Course Length/Par (All Tees): Back 7055/72, Intermediate 6286/72, Club 5826/72, Forward 5197/72
Course Slope/Rating (All Tees): Back 144/74.5, Intermediate 135/71.8, Club 133/69.8, Ladies' Club 138/75.1, Ladies' Forward 130/71.6
Course Architect: Robert Trent Jones, Jr. (1982)
Golf Facilities: Full Pro Shop X, Snack Bar X, Lounge X, Restaurant X, Locker Room X, Showers X, Club Rental X, Club Repair X, Cart Rental X, Instruction X, Practice Green X, Driving Range X, Practice Bunker X, Club Storage X
Tee-Time Reservation Policy: Anytime after March 1. Credit card guarantee or deposit required to reserve tee time
Ranger: Yes
Tee-off-Interval Time: 10 min.
Time to Play 18 Holes: 4 hrs., 15 min.
Course Hours/Earliest Tee-off: 7 a.m.
Green and Cart Fees: $65 for 18 holes with cart (June to mid-Sept.). Total fee
Credit Cards: American Express, Master-Card, Visa
Season: Mid-April to Oct. Busiest season May to Sept.
Course Comments: Can walk anytime. Yardage book available
Golf Packages: Available (715) 345–1600
Discounts: Prior to June, after mid-Sept.
Places to Stay Nearby: Comfort Suites (715) 341–6000; Holiday Inn (715) 341–1340, (800) HOLIDAY; Best Western Royale Inn (715) 341–5110, (800) 528–1234; Super 8 Motel (715) 341–8888, (800) 848–8888; Budgetel Inn (715) 344–1900, (800) 428–3438; Trav-

eler Motel (715) 344–6455, (800) 341–8000

Local Attractions: University of Wisconsin—Stevens Point, Wisconsin Symphony Orchestra, Central Wisconsin Community Theater, Fine Arts Center, Museum of Natural History, Schmeeckle Reserve, Stevens Point Brewery. WAUSAU: Marathon County Historical Museum, Leigh Yawkey Woodson Art Museum, Wausau Insurance Companies, Grand Theater, Rib Mountain State Park, Hsu's Ginseng Garden. MARSHFIELD: Figi's Cheese and Gifts, Foxfire (botanical gardens), Upham Mansion, Wildwood Park and Zoo, New Visions Art Gallery. NEILLSVILLE: 1897 Jail Museum, Tufts Museum, WCCN's Wisconsin Pavillion. ONTARIO: Mill Bluff State Park. NECEDAH: Buckhorn State Park. FRIENDSHIP: Roche a Cri State Park, fishing, swimming, camping, hiking, boating, hunting, bicycling, skiing and other winter sports. Stevens Point Area Chamber of Commerce (715) 344–2556, (800) 236–4636

Directions: Hwy. 51 north to Stevens Point, exit Business 51, turn left on North Point to North Michigan, left to golf course

Closest Commercial Airports: Central Wisconsin (30 min.); Austin Straubel, Green Bay (1½ hrs.); General Mitchell International, Milwaukee (3 hrs.); Minneapolis–St. Paul International, MN (4 hrs.); Chicago O'Hare International, IL (5 hrs.)

SENTRYWORLD

Sentryworld was the brainchild of the late John Joanis, the former chairman of Sentry Insurance. A 14-handicapper, his dream was to have a world-class public golf facility near the Sentry Insurance headquarters in northern Wisconsin. Robert Trent Jones, Jr., was retained to design the course, and it opened in 1982 to wide acclaim. Over 300,000 geraniums and marigolds were planted on the course and it continues to be noted for its beauty as well as for the challenge it presents to any golfer. The course is situated on 180 acres adjacent to the world headquarters of Sentry Insurance.

In addition to its flowers, the 7055-yard par-72 layout is heavily treed with oak, maple and other varieties of trees, and it is well trapped, with 84 bunkers representing over 1.5 acres of sand. The rolling terrain is punctuated with strategic mounds on the fairways and around the greens, which are large, medium fast and undulating. Ponds, streams and bogs are a factor on at least half the holes. There are four tee distances to accommodate all levels of play.

Sentryworld starts out with three par 4s, each of which plays longer than 400 yards from the back tees. The first, a 430-yard dogleg left, is well protected by trees and two right-fairway bunkers. The green is guarded left and right-front by traps. The second hole is a narrow, tree-lined, 418-yard slight dogleg right to a narrow, deep green with traps to the left, right and right front. The third hole is a 406-yard dogleg right that has a large left-fairway trap at the turn to catch errant tee shots. The green is protected by a large trap to the left and one to the right, with water left and behind.

The fourth hole is a pretty 190-yard par 3 that plays to a large green protected left by a lake and right by a huge sand trap. The fifth hole is the number-1-handicap hole, a 526-yard par-5 dogleg left that bends around a lake and is well bunkered and treed on the right all the way into the hole. The second shot has to be hit down a narrow fairway to a green that is well protected by water to the left and three traps to the rear. The seventh hole is a tough 205-yard par 3 from the back tees, with trees to the right and two large traps protecting the green in front and one in the rear. The finishing hole on the front nine is a 511-yard par-5 dogleg left that is tightly treed most of the way to the green. The tee shot has to avoid a stream cutting the fairway from 230 to 270 yards out. The second shot must then negotiate another stream that winds in front of the green, which is trapped to the right and rear.

The signature hole on the back nine and the course is the famous 177-yard par-3 sixteenth flower hole that has 90,000 individual plants and annuals that are replaced every year, when a new floral design is created. The effort takes 20 people 10 days of 10-hour-a-day work, and the result is a beautiful lateral hazard. The large, three-tiered green is protected by two traps on the left and one on the right. This beautiful hole is followed by two difficult par-4 finishing holes. The 415-yard seventeenth is a dogleg right that is well protected by fairway trees into a long but shallow green guarded by water front and right and a trap to the rear. This hole requires a long, straight drive to the left center to have a clear shot onto the green without going into the water.

The 452-yard closing hole, a dogleg left, has three fairway bunkers on the right beginning 180 yards from a green protected by three traps to the left front, center front and right front. The tee shot over a small pond to the tree-lined landing area should put you in the left center of the fairway, but the second shot, usually a wood or a long iron, has to reach the green in the air. It is not easy to reach this green in regulation.

Sentryworld has been ranked by *Golf Digest* as one of the best public or private courses in the state of Wisconsin. The *Milwaukee Journal* has rated it number 2 in the state behind Blackwolf Run in Kohler. It is also ranked as one of the top 75 golf courses in America by *Golf Digest*, and it has been the site of the USGA Women's Public Links Championship (1986). The excellent golf-course design and maintenance as well as the natural beauty at Sentryworld makes the course a memorable golf experience.

Meeting and recreational facilities are offered within the Sentryworld complex, including 12 tennis courts, meeting and conference rooms, banquet facilities, restaurants, baseball diamonds, squash and racquetball courts and banquet facilities. Golf packages are available through local hotels. Information regarding packages and other amenities at Sentryworld can be obtained through the pro shop. Practice facilities, including a driving range, practice bunker and putting green, are excellent at Sentry-

world. The clubhouse includes a pro shop, restaurant, locker room and showers. Golf instruction is available from the staff of professionals.

Recommended Golf Courses in Wisconsin

Central:

Kettle Moraine Golf Club, Dousman, (414) 965–6200, Semiprivate, 18/6420/72

Lake Arrowhead Golf Course, Nekoosa, (715) 325–2929, Public, 18/6624/72

Mill Run Golf Club, Eau Claire, (715) 834–1766, (800) 260–3000, Public, 18/6065/70

New Richmond Golf Club, New Richmond, (715) 246–6724, Semiprivate, 18/6716/72

Northbrook Country Club, Luxemburg, (414) 845–2383, Semiprivate, 18/6190/71

Skyline Golf Club, Black River Falls, (715) 284–2613, Public, 18/6371/72

Sparta Municipal Golf Club, Sparta, (608) 269–3022, Public, 18/6544/72

North of Wassau:

Antigo Bass Lake Country Club, Antigo, (715) 623–6196, Semiprivate, 18/6184/71

Eagle River Golf Course, Eagle River, (715) 479–8111, Public, 18/6103/71

Forest Ridges Golf Course, Cable, (715) 794–2561, Resort, 18/6270/71

Hayward Golf and Tennis Center, Hayward, (715) 634–2760, Semiprivate, 18/6597/72

Nemadji Golf Course, Superior, (715) 394–9022, Public. East/West: 18/6701/72. North/South: 18/6362/71

Northwood Golf Course, Rhinelander, (715) 282–6565, Public, 18/6719/72

Peninsula State Park Golf Course, Ephraim, (414) 854–5791, Public, 18/6356/71

Spooner Golf Club, Spooner, (715) 394–9022, Semiprivate, 18/6407/71

Turtleback Golf and Country Club, Rice Lake, (715) 234–7641, Public, 18/6132/71

Voyager Village Country Club, Danbury, (715) 259–3911, Semiprivate, 18/6638/72

Wisconsin: Useful Information

Wisconsin Division of Tourism, P.O. Box 7606, Madison, WI 53707, (608) 266–2161, (800) 372–2737 (WI and neighboring states), (800) 432–TRIP (all other states)

Department of Natural Resources, P.O. Box 7921, Madison, WI 53707, (608) 266–2105 (fishing and hunting regulations)

U.S.D.A. Forest Service, Eastern Region, 310 W. Wisconsin Ave., Ste. 500, Milwaukee, WI 53203, (414) 297–3693, (800) 280–CAMP (information and reservations)

Course Name: JACKSON HOLE GOLF AND TENNIS CLUB

Course Type: Public
Address: 500 Spring Gulch Road
Jackson, WY 83001
Phone: (307) 733–3111
Fax: (307) 733–3442 (Call First to Notify)

GOLF COURSE

Head Professional: David Hardison
Course Length/Par (All Tees): Back 7168/72, White 6783/72, Ladies' Forward 6036/73
Course Slope/Rating (All Tees): Back 133/72.3, White 124/70.3, Ladies' Forward 125/73.2
Course Architects: Robert E. Baldock (1961); Robert Trent Jones, Sr., and Robert Trent Jones, Jr. (renovation, 1967)
Golf Facilities: Full Pro Shop X, Snack Bar X, Lounge X, Restaurant X, Locker Room X, Showers X, Club Rental X, Club Repair X, Cart Rental X, Instruction X, Practice Green X, Driving Range X, Practice Bunker X, Club Storage X
Tee-Time Reservation Policy: Call anytime
Ranger: Yes
Tee-off-Interval Time: 10 min.
Time to Play 18 Holes: 4½ hrs.
Course Hours/Earliest Tee-off: 7:30 a.m.
Green and Cart Fees: $73 for 18 holes with cart
Credit Cards: American Express, Master-Card, Visa
Season: April to Oct.
Course Comments: Can walk anytime. Memberships available
Golf Packages: None
Discounts: Group discounts, twilight rates
Places to Stay Nearby: See page 731
Local Attractions: See page 731. Jackson Hole Area Chamber of Commerce (800) 733–3316
Directions: 10 mi. north of Jackson on Hwy. 89, west at Gross Venture Junction to golf course

Closest Commercial Airport: Jackson Hole (5 min.)

JACKSON HOLE GOLF AND TENNIS CLUB

The Jackson Hole Golf and Tennis Club is beautifully situated in the shadow of the Grand Teton National Park in northwestern Wyoming. The Tetons rise sharply from a valley floor and have 6 different summits topping 12,000 feet. In an effort to preserve this area from commercial interests, John D. Rockefeller quietly bought up the land in the 1920s. Eventually, despite considerable local opposition, the 32,000 acres accumulated by Rockefeller and Forest Service lands were combined to form the Grand Teton National Park in the early 1950s. The Jackson Hole Golf and Tennis Club is on land formerly owned by the Rockefeller family's Rock Resorts. The Rockefellers still have property in the area, however, and can be seen trying to score on the 7168-yard par-72 layout.

The Jackson Hole Golf Course was originally designed by Robert E. Baldock and opened in the early 1960s. Laurance Rockefeller brought Robert Trent Jones, Sr., and Robert Trent Jones, Jr., in to redesign Jackson Hole in the late 1960s. Robert Trent Jones, Sr., had worked with Laurance Rockefeller on various Rock Resorts projects, such as Mauna Kea in Hawaii. The course is relatively flat, since it is located in the valley between the mountains. The bentgrass greens are medium-sized, fast, undulating, elevated and well protected by traps. The course is open but has strategically placed fairway bunkers, and water hazards come into play on eight holes. The course is at a 7000-foot altitude, and the ball tends to carry approximately 10 percent farther than one would normally expect. Many people like to walk the course, and walking is allowed anytime. Spruce, cottonwood, fir, aspen and other varieties of trees and plant life enliven this layout, as do deer, elk, moose and an occasional buffalo.

Two challenging and lengthy par 5s on the front nine are the 581-yard second and the 593-yard eighth. The second hole plays straight to a green fronted by an irrigation canal from the old ranch that used to occupy this land. On the right is a water hazard from tee to green. Most golfers have to lay up in front of the irrigation canal and hit a short iron to the green, which is protected by water on the right and front and bunkers to the left. The eighth hole is a slight dogleg right. The second shot is almost always a layup on this hole because of its length and the irrigation canal in front of the green, which has traps to its left and right.

An excellent par 4 on the back nine is the 364-yard twelfth, a dogleg to the right playing to a small green guarded by a large trap to the right and others on the left. The tee-shot landing area is protected by trees and a bunker on the right. The next hole, a 169-yard par 3, plays over a large pond to a forward-sloping green fronted by water and backed by a trap. Water also protects the green on the right side.

The clubhouse at Jackson Hole has an excellent restaurant, pro shop, locker rooms and showers. Individual and group instruction is available from the staff of professionals. The practice facilities include a large driving range, 2 putting greens and a practice bunker at what was the fifth hole on the original Baldock-designed course.

The Jackson Hole Golf Course is ranked among the best public and private courses in the state of Wyoming and has been listed among the top 75 public courses in America by *Golf Digest*. This was the site of the 1988 USGA Amateur Public Links Championship the 1993 U.S. Women's Amateur Public Links.

**Course Name: OLIVE GLENN GOLF
                AND COUNTRY CLUB**

Course Type: Public
Address: 802 Meadow Lane
               Cody, WY 82414
Phone: (307) 587–5551

GOLF COURSE

Head Professional: Vaughn P. Jenkins
Course Length/Par (All Tees): Back 6887/72, Middle 6515/72, Forward 5654/72

Course Slope/Rating (All Tees): Back 124/71.6, Middle 120/69.9, Ladies' Forward 120/71.2
Course Architects: Robert E. Baldock and Robert L. Baldock (1970)
Golf Facilities: Full Pro Shop X, Snack Bar X, Lounge X, Restaurant X, Locker Room X, Showers X, Club Rental X, Club Repair X, Cart Rental X, Instruction X, Practice Green X, Driving Range X, Practice Bunker X, Club Storage X
Tee-Time Reservation Policy: Up to 7 days in advance
Ranger: Yes
Tee-off-Interval Time: 10 min.
Time to Play 18 Holes: 4 hrs.
Course Hours/Earliest Tee-off: 6 a.m.
Green Fees: $21 for 18 holes, $13 for 9 holes
Cart Fees: $18 for 18 holes, $12 for 9 holes
Credit Cards: MasterCard, Visa
Season: April to Oct.
Course Comments: Can walk anytime
Golf Packages: None
Discounts: Juniors
Places to Stay Nearby: Best Western Sunset Motor Inn (307) 587–4265, (800) 528–1234; Holiday Motel (307) 587–4258; Irma Hotel (307) 587–4221; Super 8 (307) 527–6214. Wapiti Valley Lodges within 50 mi. of Cody on the way west to Yellowstone National Park: Pahaska Teepee (307) 527–7701, (800) 628–7791; Shoshone Lodge (307) 587–4044; Goff Creek Lodge (307) 587–3753; Absaroka Mountain Lodge (307) 587–3963; Bill Cody's Ranch Resort (307) 587–6271; Wise Choice Inn (307) 587–5004; Yellowstone Valley Inn (307) 587–3961, (800) 234–2902; Trout Creek Inn (307) 587–6288, (800) 341–8000. BED AND BREAKFAST: Caroline Lockhart's Bed and Breakfast Inn (307) 587–6074. There are many additional guest ranches and lodges on the way to Yellowstone from Cody and elsewhere. For additional information contact Cody Country Chamber of Commerce, P.O. Box 2777, Cody, Wyoming 82414, (307) 587–2297. Fax: (307) 527–6228

Local Attractions: Buffalo Bill Historical Center, Buffalo Bill Museum, Whitney Gallery of Western Art, Cody Firearms Museum, Plains Indian Museum, Buffalo Bill State Park, Old Trail Town, rodeos, Cody stampede, seasonal festivals, Plains Indian Pow Wow, fishing, white-water rafting, boating, hunting, winter sports including skiing, Shoshone River float trips, Yellowstone National Park, Buffalo Bill Dam, Shoshone National Forest, camping, hiking. Cody Country Chamber of Commerce (307) 587–2297

Directions: Grable Hwy. to Meadow Lane, 1 mi. to golf course

Closest Commercial Airports: Cody Regional (5 min.); Billings Logan International, MT (2 hrs.); Natrona International, Casper (4 hrs.)

OLIVE GLENN GOLF AND COUNTRY CLUB

Cody, Wyoming, is the home of the Olive Glenn Golf and Country Club, one of the best golf courses in the state. Cody, which has a year-round population of under 10,000 people, is just 52 miles east of the Yellowstone National Park in northwestern Wyoming. To the north are the Beartooth Mountains and Sunlight Basin, and the Absaroka Range and Wapiti Valley are to the west and the south respectively. In 1895 William F. "Buffalo Bill" Cody and two partners formed the Shoshone Land and Irrigation Co. in this area. Previously Cody had gained a reputation guiding parties of wealthy sportsmen and exploring the country of the Bighorn Basin. He was also noted for such other exploits as Indian scout, buffalo hunter, Wild West show performer and general impresario. More than 800 books have been written about him, and the town of Cody is named after him.

The 6887-yard par-72 Olive Glenn Golf Course was designed by Robert E. Baldock and his son, Robert L. Baldock, and opened in 1970. It is a rolling layout on the edge of the prairie, a transition point from the forests of Yellowstone to the west. The number-1-handicap hole on the course is the 466-yard par-4 first hole, which plays straight to a large green guarded by bunkers both left and right. The bentgrass greens at Olive Glenn are typically large, medium fast and somewhat flat. A few large traps guard each hole, and there are water hazards on half the holes.

The three finishing holes at Olive Glenn start with the memorable 165-yard par-3 sixteenth signature hole, which plays from a slightly elevated tee to a green protected in front by two bunkers and almost surrounded by water. The 424-yard par-4 seventeenth is a slight dogleg left to a deep green guarded by bunkers to the left and right. The approach shot has to carry a stream that cuts in front of the green approximately 50 yards from the putting surface. The 394-yard par-4 eighteenth begins with a tee shot over a stream. The second shot is to a deep green protected by traps to the left and right.

The clubhouse at Olive Glenn has a full-service pro shop, restaurant, snack bar, and locker-room and shower facilities. The Blue Room Restaurant at the Olive Glenn Golf and Country Club is a quality restaurant, and the Stage Coach Lounge is nearby. On site are 2 tennis courts, an indoor swimming pool, and a Jacuzzi. All club facilities are available with a paid round of golf and a cart. Practice facilities include a driving range, putting green and practice bunker. Green fees are extremely reasonable, and you can walk the course anytime.

The surrounding area includes many tourist attractions, such as guest ranches between Cody and Yellowstone National Park, the Buffalo Bill Historical Center in Cody, Grand Teton National Park and a variety of seasonal festivals, including the Plains Indian Pow Wow, rodeos and music festivals. This area is famous for its camping, fishing, boating, hiking, hunting, mountaineering and other recreational activities. The eastern gateway from Cody to Yellowstone was once called "the most scenic 52 miles in the United States" by Teddy Roosevelt.

Course Name: TETON PINES GOLF CLUB

Course Type: Resort
Resort: Jackson Hole Racquet Club Resort
Address: 3450 North Clubhouse Drive Jackson, WY 83001
Phone: (307) 733–1733 (Golf Course)
(307) 733–1005,
(800) 238–2223 (Resort)
Fax: (307) 733–2860 (Resort)

GOLF COURSE

Director of Golf: Bob Marshall
Head Professional: John D. Haines
Course Length/Par (All Tees): Back 7412/72, Blue 6878/72, White 6333/72, Forward 5486/72
Course Slope/Rating (All Tees): Back 137/74.2, Blue 125/71.0, White 118/68.2, Ladies' Forward 117/70.8
Course Architects: Arnold Palmer and Ed Seay (1987)
Golf Facilities: Full Pro Shop X, Snack Bar X, Lounge X, Restaurant X, Locker Room X, Showers X, Club Rental X, Club Repair X, Cart Rental X, Instruction X, Practice Green X, Driving Range X, Practice Bunker X, Club Storage X
Tee-Time Reservation Policy: Call anytime in advance. Credit card required to reserve more than 1 tee-off time
Ranger: Yes
Tee-off-Interval Time: 9 min.
Time to Play 18 Holes: 4 hrs.
Course Hours/Earliest Tee-off: 7 a.m.
Green Fees: Peak season (late June through Labor Day): Resort guests: $64 for 18 holes with cart. Outside play: $95 for 18 holes with cart
Cart Fees: $14 per person for 18 holes
Pull Carts: $3 for 18 holes
Credit Cards: American Express, Diners Club, MasterCard, Visa
Season: May to mid-Oct. Busiest season July through Labor Day
Course Comments: Peak season rates late June through Labor Day. Cart or caddy mandatory before 11:30 a.m. during peak season, weekends and holidays
Golf Packages: Available through resort

Discounts: Juniors
Places to Stay Nearby: Alpenhof Lodge (307) 733–3242, (800) 732–3244; Best Western Inn (307) 733–2311, (800) 842–7666; Rancho Aleare Lodge (307) 733–7988; Rusty Parrot Lodge (307) 733–2000, (800) 458–2004; Snow King Resort (307) 733–5200, (800) 522–5464; Spring Creek Resort (307) 733–8833, (800) 443–6139; Wort Hotel (307) 733–2190, (800) 322–2727. BED AND BREAKFASTS: Big Mountain Inn (307) 733–1981; Teton Tree House (307) 733–3333; Teton View (307) 733–7954; Wildflower Inn (307) 733–4710.
CONDOMINIUMS: Jackson Hole Property Management (307) 733–7945, (800) 443–8613; Teton Village Property Management (307) 733–4610, (800) 443–6840. Or contact central reservations for any accommodation. Jackson Hole Central Reservations (307) 733–4005, (800) 443–6931. Telex: 495–1490

Local Attractions: Grand Teton National Park, Bridger–Teton National Forest, town square, Jackson Hole Museum, Wildlife of the American West Art Museum, art galleries, National Elk Refuge, Yellowstone National Park, fishing, hunting, white-water rafting, boating, camping, hiking, horseback riding, restaurants, bicycling, mountaineering, hot-air ballooning, seasonal festivals, winter sports including skiing. Jackson Hole Area Chamber of Commerce (800) 733–3316

Directions: From Jackson Hole: Broadway 2 mi. south, turn right on Wyoming 22, go 5 mi. to Wyoming 390 north, take a right, resort 1½ mi. on the left

Closest Commercial Airports: Jackson Hole (30 min.); Salt Lake City International, UT (5½ hrs.); Billings Logan International, MT (6 hrs.)

RESORT

Date Built: 1988
No. of Rooms: 16 suites and 8 adjoining living rooms
Meeting Rooms: 2. Capacity of Largest: 34 persons.

Room Price Range: $275 to $635 per night for 2-bedroom suite. Golf and other packages available year round

Lounges: Teton Pines Bar

Restaurants: Teton Pines Restaurant

Entertainment: None

Credit Cards: American Express, Diners Club, MasterCard, Visa

General Amenities: Meeting and conference facilities for small groups

Recreational Amenities: 7 tennis courts, outdoor swimming pool, Jacuzzi, fly fishing, skiing

Reservation and Cancellation Policy: 2 nights' deposit within 2 weeks of reservation. Full refund of deposit made if 30-day cancellation notice given

Comments and Restrictions: No pets. Taxes additional to base rates

TETON PINES GOLF CLUB

The Teton Pines Golf Course is located a few miles from Jackson Hole in northwestern Wyoming near the Teton National Forest. Arnold Palmer and Ed Seay designed the 7412-yard par-72 layout, which was named the best new resort course of 1988 by *Golf Digest*. This rolling golf course was originally ranch land. The bentgrass greens here are moderately fast, undulating and well protected by large bunkers and water hazards, which come into play on half the holes. More than 42 acres of the course are covered by water. And there are magnificent views of the Teton Mountains.

There are four tee distances to choose from at Teton Pines, ranging from 7412 to 5486 yards, and each hole has its own name. The 634-yard par-5 seventh, the number-1-handicap hole on the course, is called "the Moose." This hole requires three long, accurate shots to a large, wide green with no sand bunkers. Because the course is at an elevation of more than 6000 feet, you should get approximately 10 percent more distance than you would get at sea level.

The last four holes at Grand Teton are challenging and memorable, starting with the 443-yard par-4 "Firehole." The tee shot is straight to a landing area protected by a huge bunker on the right. The approach shot has to carry a stream that runs in front of a deep green backed by a pond. The 202-yard par-3 sixteenth, called "Tramway," is all carry over water to a deep, left-to-right-angled green backed by a large bunker. The seventeenth, "Swan Song," is a short, 333-yard par 4 whose tee shot is over a small stream to a landing area just before a stream that cuts the fairway. On the right is another stream guarding the fairway on the tee shot. The approach shot is to a deep, right-to-left-sloped green.

"Rendezvous" is the 472-yard par-4 dogleg-right finishing hole. The tee shot is to a landing area just to the right of a huge sand bunker guarding the left side of the fairway. The approach shot is to a large green guarded on the left front and right front by two sizeable bunkers. The combination of length, water hazards and well-protected, challenging greens makes this an interesting course to play. Aspen, cottonwood, pine, willow and other trees, and wildlife such as sandhill cranes, eagle, osprey, blue heron, moose and others add to the attractiveness of this golf course in its beautiful Grand Teton setting.

The resort lodge offers 16 suites with king-sized beds, his and her bathrooms, sitting area, TV and deck. Or a master bedroom suite with a living room can be rented. A restaurant, fly-fishing ponds, outdoor swimming pool, Jacuzzi, tennis courts, and limited meeting space for approximately 20 persons are on site.

The clubhouse includes full pro shop, snack bar, bar, restaurant, locker rooms and showers. Practice facilities include a practice green, bunker and practice range. Individual and group instruction is available from the staff of professionals. Caddies are also available.

Recommended Golf Courses in Wyoming

Bell Knob Golf Club, Gillette, (307) 686–7069, Public, 18/7024/72

Buffalo Golf Club, Buffalo, (307) 684–5266, Public, 18/6684/71

Kendrick Golf Course, Sheridan, (307) 674–8148, Public, 18/6532/72

Riverton Country Club, Riverton, (307) 856–4779, Semiprivate, 18/7064/72

White Mountain Golf Course, Rock Springs, (307) 382–5030, Public, 18/7000/72

Wyoming: Useful Information

Wyoming Division of Tourism, I–25 at College Dr., Cheyenne, WY 82002, (307) 777–7777, (800) 225–5996

Wyoming State Museums and Historic Sites, 2301 Barrett Bldg., Cheyenne, WY 82002, (307) 777–7014 (recreation information)

Wyoming Recreation Commission, 2301 Barrett Bldg., Cheyenne, WY 82002, (307) 777–7695 (state parks)

State of Wyoming Game and Fish Commission, 5400 Bishop Blvd., Cheyenne, WY 82002, (307) 777–4600 (fishing and hunting regulations)

U.S. National Forest Service, Federal Center, Bldg. 85, Denver, CO 80225, (303) 236–9431, (800) 280–CAMP (national forest information and reservations)

U.S. National Forest Service, Federal Center, 324 25th St., Ogden, UT 84401, (801) 629–8600, (800) 280–CAMP (national forest information and reservations)

CANADA

Course Name: BANFF SPRINGS
Rundle, Sulphur,
Tunnel Courses

Course Type: Resort
Resort: Banff Springs Hotel
Address: Spray Avenue
Banff, Alberta T0L0C0
Phone: (403) 762–6833 (Golf Course)
(403) 762–2211,
(800) 268–9143 (Canada),
(800) 828–7447 (U.S.)
(Resort)
Fax: (403) 762–6830 (Resort)

GOLF COURSE

Head Professional: Doug Wood
Course Length/Par (All Tees): Rundle/
Sulphur: Back 6632/71, Middle
6391/71, Forward 5998/71. Rundle/Tun-
nel: Back 6443/72, Middle 6117/72,
Forward 5652/72. Sulphur/Tunnel: Back
6721/71, Middle 6420/71, Forward
5652/71
Course Slope/Rating (All Tees): Rundle/
Sulphur: Back 124/72, Middle 121/71,
Ladies' Forward 123/69. Rundle/Tunnel:
Back 122/71.5, Middle 118/70, Forward
NA/67.5. Sulphur/Tunnel: Back
124/72.5, Middle 121/71, Forward
NA/68.5
Course Architects: Rundle, Sulphur:
Stanley Thompson (1927). Tunnel: Bill
Robinson (1989)
Golf Facilities: Full Pro Shop X, Snack
Bar X, Lounge X, Restaurant X,
Locker Room X, Showers X, Club
Rental X, Club Repair X, Cart Rental
X, Instruction X, Practice Green X,
Driving Range X, Practice Bunker No,
Club Storage X
Tee-Time Reservation Policy: Call anytime.
48-hr. cancellation notice requested. At
least 1-wk. advance notice for large groups
Ranger: Yes
Tee-off-Interval Time: 7 and 8 min.
Time to Play 18 Holes: 4½ hrs.
Course Hours/Earliest Tee-off: 6 a.m.
Green and Cart Fees: Peak season (late
May through Sept.): Can$80 for 18

holes with cart, Can$41 for 9 holes with
cart
Credit Cards: All major cards
Season: May to mid-Oct.
Course Comments: Can walk, but have to
pay cart fee. Yardage book available
Golf Packages: Available through hotel
Discounts: Members, seasonal (May, Oct.).
Twilight rate (course is open until as
late as 10 p.m. in the summer); twilight
times after 3 p.m. from opening until
June and from mid-Aug. until closing;
from 5 p.m. June through mid-Aug.
Places to Stay Nearby: LAKE LOUISE: Chateau Lake Louise (403) 572–3511, (800)
268–9411; Post Hotel (403) 522–3989,
(800) 661–1586; Lake Louise Inn (403)
522–3791, (800) 661–9237. BANFF
AREA: Douglas Fir Resort (403) 762–
5591; Banff Park Lodge and Conference
Center (403) 762–4433, (800) 661–
9266; Banff Rocky Mountain Resort
(403) 762–5531, (800) 661–9563; Banff
Mountain Lodge (403) 762–2400, (800)
661–1367; Storm Mountain Lodge (403)
762–4155
Local Attractions: Whyte Museum of
Canadian Rockies, Banff National
Park, Luxton Museum, Natural History
Museum, Banff Centre of Fine Arts,
shopping, art galleries, buffalo pad-
docks, Vermillion Lakes Drive, Yoho
National Park, Kananaskis, Lake Louise,
Upper Hot Springs, Sulphur Mountain
Gondola, Cave and Basin Hot Springs,
Moraine Lake, Walter Phillips Gallery,
Parks Canada Museum, Cascade Rock
Gardens, Kootenay National Park, camp-
ing, fishing, hiking, horseback riding,
rafting, downhill and cross-country ski-
ing, mountain climbing, bicycling, boat-
ing, Radium Hot Springs, Fairmont Hot
Springs. Jasper. Banff National Park
(403) 762–3324. Banff Information
Centre (403) 762–4256
Directions: From Calgary (77 mi.): Hwy.
1 west to Banff, follow signs to Banff
Springs hotel and golf course
Closest Commercial Airports: Calgary
International (1 hr., 45 min.), Edmonton
International (5 hrs.)

RESORT

Date Built: 1888 (original hotel)

No. of Rooms: 846 guest rooms, including 278 deluxe rooms and 43 suites

Meeting Rooms: 55. Capacity of Largest: 1200 persons banquet style. Meeting Space: 107,000 sq. ft.

Room Price Range: Can$175 for standard, Can$275 for superior, Can$335 for deluxe peak season (mid-June to mid-Sept.). Golf packages and other reduced rates available year round

Lounges: Rundle Lounge, The Works, Ramsey Lounge, King Henry VIII Pub

Restaurants: King Henry VIII Pub, Waldhaus, Rob Roy, The Pavillion, Samurai, The Coffee House, Alberta Room, The Clubhouse

Entertainment: Dancing, music in Rob Roy Dining Room, piano in Rundle Lounge, live music in Alberta Room

Credit Cards: All major cards

General Amenities: 45 retail shops and boutiques, complete conference and meeting facilities with audiovisual and food services

Recreational Amenities: Fitness center with Nautilus equipment, masseuse, hot tubs, 1 indoor and 1 outdoor swimming pool; 5 tennis courts with tennis pro shop, instruction available; miniature golf, nearby skiing, boating, camping, hiking, fishing, horseback riding, hunting

Reservation and Cancellation Policy: Credit card or deposit of 1 night's stay required. Cancellation required 3 days in advance to avoid penalties

Comments and Restrictions: Taxes additional to base rates

BANFF SPRINGS

The Banff Springs Hotel bills itself as "a bastion of luxury in the wilderness," and it is. Situated among the snowcapped peaks of the Canadian Rockies and 77 miles from Calgary, Banff Springs is the crown jewel of the Canadian Pacific Hotel and Resort chain. It was near a long bend in the Bow River 80 miles west of Calgary that the Canadian Pacific Railway established Railroad Siding 29, a frontier outpost that would become known in 1883 as the town of Banff. William Cornelius Van Horne, then chairman of the Canadian Pacific Railway, masterminded the plan to bring tourists to the area by building a grand hotel. Bruce Price, father of etiquette emissary Emily Post and architect of Windsor Station in Montreal, designed the first building in the 1880s, which cost $250,000 and looked like a sixteenth-century French chateau. After various revisions, fires and additions, the hotel stands now as it was completed in 1928.

In 1927 the original eighteen-hole golf course (Rundle and Sulphur) was designed by the renowned Stanley Thompson, who had entered golf architecture in 1921. Thompson exhibited a degree of strategic design unprecedented in North America. Banff, which was officially opened by the Prince of Wales, and Jasper were two of his early triumphs. He also designed Digby Pines Golf Club, Digby, Nova Scotia; Capilano Golf and Country Club, West Vancouver, British Columbia; and many others. He was responsible for training a number of noteworthy assistants, including Robert Trent Jones, Sr., Howard Watson, C. E. Robinson, Norman Woods, Kenneth Welton, Robert Moote and Geoffrey S. Cornish.

A mile high in the Canadian Rockies, the original Rundle/Sulphur layout calls for extreme accuracy because of well-placed traps and optical illusions caused by the mountains towering all around the course. This often leads to incorrect distance estimates and poor club selection. In 1989 an additional nine, the Tunnel Course, was added to the resort. Because the course is located in Banff National Park, which is a game preserve, it is not unusual to have a deer or bear duck a fairway shot.

The number-1-handicap hole on the Rundle nine is the 514-yard par-5 seventh, which plays down a tree-lined fairway to a long, narrow green (40 yards by 10 yards) protected by four traps on the left and two traps to the right and back. The first shot has to clear a fairway trap on the left and approximately 190 yards from the tee. The second shot is to a target area in front of the green, or the ball can be run up onto the long green. A fairway trap is on the right, approximately 132 yards from the green. The most difficult hole on the Sulphur nine is the 429-yard par-4 fifth hole, which is treed from tee to green and has fifteen traps strategically placed along the way. The first shot is to the center, and the next shot, usually a long iron or a wood, has to be hit through a narrow entrance to the green trapped left and right from 105 yards in. The green is narrow and deep and slopes left to right and up toward the rear.

Both par 3s on Rundle are picturesque and challenging. The 171-yard fourth hole is aptly called the "Devil's Cauldron." The first shot is from an elevated tee across a glacial lake to a foot-shaped, 22-by-25–yard green that sits on a plateau, slopes forward and is banked all around. Four traps protect the green to the left, right front and rear. The 138-yard eighth hole is over water to a 28-yard-deep by 20-yard-wide green protected by large traps to the left and right. The tee shot is usually into a head wind, and the green has a ridge through the center from front to back, with the right side sloping toward the water. A beautiful and challenging par 3 on the Sulphur nine is the 220-yard first hole, which plays over water running from the right side of the tee to the green, which is large but well protected by three traps in back and one large trap to the left front.

In 1989, a new $3-million golf clubhouse was opened. The pro shop provides lessons, equipment and rentals. Locker rooms and showers are available, and food service includes complete breakfast, lunch and dinner menus. The hotel completed major renovations in the 1980s and recently built a new conference center at a cost of $23 million. This center has 107,000 square feet of meeting space, with a 250-seat audiovisual theater, saloon, restaurant, bowling alley and much more. The hotel itself is huge, with 846 guest rooms, and the resort in its entirety is ranked by *Golf* magazine as one of the best in North America. Canada's *Score* magazine rates Banff among Canada's top 10 public golf courses. Golf packages are available through the resort.

The area surrounding Banff is noted for its hot springs and natural beauty, including glacial blue lakes, blue-gray granite, fir, spruce and larch forests, wildflowers and wild animals including bison, elk, bear, moose, bighorn sheep, and others. The Canadian government began restricting these lands from overdevelopment in the 1880s, and a park system began to develop. Within a few hours' drive of Banff is a spectacular range of natural wonders and outdoor recreational attractions in Banff National Park, Waterton Lakes, Kootenay, Yoho, Jasper, the Lake Louise area and elsewhere.

Banff Springs provides one of the best golf experiences in North America in one of its most spectacular settings.

Course Name: JASPER PARK GOLF COURSE

Course Type: Resort
Resort: Jasper Park Lodge
Address: The Lodge Road/P.O. Box 40 Jasper, Alberta T0E1E0
Phone: (403) 852–3301, ext. 6157 (Pro Shop)
(403) 852–6090 (Tee-Times)
(403) 852–3301,
(800) 642–3817 (AB)
(800) 268–9143 (Canada, outside AB)
(800) 828–7447 (U.S.) (Resort)
Fax: (403) 852–5107

GOLF COURSE

Head Professional: Alan Carter

Course Length/Par (All Tees): Back 6598/71, Middle 6323/71, Ladies' Forward 6037/75

Course Slope/Rating (All Tees): Back NA/70.5, Middle NA/69.5, Ladies' Forward NA/73.4

Course Architect: Stanley Thompson (1925)

Golf Facilities: Full Pro Shop X, Snack Bar X, Lounge X, Restaurant X, Locker Room X, Showers No, Club Rental X, Club Repair X, Cart Rental X, Instruction X, Practice Green X,

Driving Range X, Practice Bunker No, Club Storage X

Tee-Time Reservation Policy: Resort guests: At time of reservation at resort. Outside play: Anytime in advance

Ranger: Yes

Tee-off-Interval Time: 8 min.

Time to Play 18 Holes: 4 hrs., 15 min.

Course Hours/Earliest Tee-off: 7 a.m.

Green Fees: Can$75 plus tax for 18 holes

Cart Fees: Can$32 plus tax for 18 holes

Pull Carts: Can$6.50 plus tax for 18 holes

Credit Cards: All major cards

Season: Late April to Oct. Busiest season June through Aug.

Course Comments: Can walk anytime. Yardage book available

Golf Packages: Available through resort.

Discounts: Twilight rate, varies by season

Places to Stay Nearby: Chateau Jasper (403) 852–5644; Jasper Inn (403) 852–4461, (800) 661–1933; Pyramid Lake Bungalows (403) 852–3491; Alpine Village (403) 852–3285

Local Attractions: Jasper Tramway, Athabasca Falls, Goat Lookout, Sunwapta Falls, Stutfield Glacier, Columbia Icefield, Marmot Basin, Mount Edith Cavell, Punchbowl Falls, Miette Hot Springs, Moiligne Canyon, Medicine Lake, Maligne Lake, Lake Beauvert, Lake Edith and Lake Annette, Patricia and Pyramid lakes, Whistler Mountain, seasonal events such as rodeo, fishing, boating, hunting, hiking, camping, bicycling, mountain climbing, horseback riding, skiing, ice-skating, tours. Jasper Park Chamber of Commerce (403) 852–3858. Fax: (403) 852–4932. Canadian Parks Service Information (403) 852–6161

Directions: From Edmonton (4 hrs.): Rte. 16 to Jasper, follow signs to resort

Closest Commercial Airports: Edmonton International (4 hrs.); Calgary International (4½ hrs.); Vancouver International, BC (9 hrs.)

RESORT

Date Built: 1923

No. of Rooms: 442 rooms and suites in the main lodge and cabins

Meeting Rooms: 13. Capacity of Largest: 835 persons banquet style. Meeting Space: 47,000 sq. ft.

Room Price Range: Can$316 for regular Can Pacific, Can$385 for Chateau deluxe, Can$485 for 1-bedroom Heritage premier suite peak season (mid-May to late Sept.). Lowest rates Jan. to late April, late Oct. to mid-Dec. Value season late April to late May, mid-Oct. Golf and other packages available

Lounges: Moose's Nook, Palisade Lounge, Emerald Lounge, Tent City, Spike Lounge

Restaurants: Beauvert Dining Room, Spike Lounge (at clubhouse), Edith Cavell Dining Room, Meadows Cafe, Moose's Nook, Emerald Lounge, Palisade Lounge

Entertainment: Tent City Night Club

Credit Cards: All major cards

General Amenities: Photographic services, supervised children's programs, 17 retail shops on site, meeting and conference facilities with audiovisual and food services

Recreational Amenities: Recreation center with table tennis, pool table, shuffleboard; health club with Universal gym, Monark 867 stationary bicycle, heated outdoor swimming pool; 4 hard-surface tennis courts, instruction available; sauna, whirlpool, board games, playground, riding stables, boating, fishing, bicycling; jogging, walking and hiking trails; white-water rafting, softball, basketball, croquet, ice-skating, skiing, sleigh rides, tobogganing

Reservation and Cancellation Policy: 1 day's deposit due within 30 days after booking by check, money order or credit card guarantee. Cancellation required 2 days prior to scheduled arrival date

Comments and Restrictions: Taxes and gratuities not included in basic prices. Modified American plan available

JASPER PARK GOLF COURSE

The Jasper Park Golf Course is a magnificent, 6598-yard par-71 Stanley Thompson layout set within the 1000-acre Jasper Park resort property in the Canadian

Rockies. David Thompson (no relation to Stanley), Canada's renowned fur-trade-era explorer and map maker, first passed this way in the early nineteenth century while looking for a western route through the Rockies. One of his men, William Henry, built a fur-brigade way station in this region, and 100 years later, when the railway arrived, a steady flow of visitors came to the region. Jasper National Park was founded in 1907 and is now a major year-round recreational center in the province of Alberta.

In an effort to attract tourists to this area and to generate railway business at the same time, in 1922 the Hotel Department of the Canadian National Railway took over what was then a rustic camp. New buildings were constructed, including Jasper Park Lodge, which at the time was one of the largest single-story log structures in existence. Stanley Thompson, designer of the Banff Springs Golf Club, the Capilano Golf and Country Club and many other golf courses in Canada, the United States and abroad, was commissioned to build a golf course, which opened in 1925. The course was built near the shores of Lake Beauvert and was cut through pine woods. The layout is approximately 3500 feet above sea level, with scenic views of the surrounding mountains and the lake. Many tee boxes on this course face a mountain peak in the distance. The layout flows in a clockwise direction through rolling, tree-lined fairways.

The fairway landing areas are reasonably generous, considering the predominance of trees, but the greens are small to medium-sized, usually slightly elevated, and well protected by artfully designed bunkers. Fairway bunkers provide an indication of the line of play, and they sometimes save balls from kicking into the woods. The greens are generally open in front, allowing a golfer to bump and run the ball onto the putting surface, but several holes have bunkers 20 to 30 yards from the front of the green, making accuracy and club selection on approach shots crucial.

The Jasper Park Golf Course provides a wide range of distances and strategies. For example, the par 5s range from 458

to 603 yards from the back tees. The par 3s vary from 138 yards to 240 yards, and the par 4s from 360 yards to a hefty 461 yards.

One of the more famous par 3s is the 231-yard ninth, which plays from an elevated tee to a deep, forward-sloping, well-banked green set up on a slight plateau below. Should you miss the green, the drop-offs around it slope to an arc of seven bunkers forming the pattern of a reverse question mark from the front left of the putting surface around to the top right in back of the target. The combination of a significant elevation drop from tee to green, prevailing left-to-right winds and the high altitude of the Canadian Rockies makes club selection and direction tricky here. Typically, the green is moderately fast, forward-sloping and has some subtle undulations.

The finishing hole at the Jasper Park Golf Course is a beautiful downhill hole, a par-4, 463-yard dogleg left. The tee shot should be played over a left fairway bunker to a landing area approximately 200 to 225 yards from the green. The approach shot is very tough, because it is likely to be a long iron or wood from a downhill lie to a narrow, deep green tightly guarded by large traps on both sides. Approximately 35 yards in front of the green is a large bunker that must be cleared to have a chance to reach the putting surface in regulation.

Jasper Park Lodge was rebuilt in the early 1950s after a fire destroyed the main lodge building. Rooms are available in this structure, which has a large window overlooking Lake Beauvert and the mountains beyond. There are 442 rooms and suites in the main lodge and the nearby cabins, including 9 of the original log cabins, along the lake. There are 8 restaurants and dining areas on the property and many recreational amenities are offered, including tennis courts, a fitness center, boating, swimming pools, riding stables, fishing, bicycling, hiking and jogging trails, saunas, whirlpools and a variety of games ranging from table tennis to shuffleboard. The resort becomes a center for winter sports such as skiing and ice-skating after the golf season. Golf, skiing and other packages are available through Jasper Park Lodge year round. The resort provides supervised children's programs from May to September for children 4 to 12 years of age. Also on the premises are a variety of retail shops.

There is also a variety of meeting and conference facilities for up to 1000 persons. *Meetings and Conventions* magazine has awarded Jasper Park Lodge its Golden Tee Award for outstanding golf and meeting amenities. The conference planning staff at Jasper Park Lodge can arrange everything from organized activities to music from local bagpipers.

There are many attractions within a short drive of Jasper Park Lodge, especially natural wonders such as Maligne Lake, Mount Edith Cavell, Athabasca Falls, Stutfield Glacier, and the 4200-square-mile Jasper National Park area, which is also a wildlife sanctuary. Black bear, grizzly bear, moose, elk, bighorn sheep, caribou, coyote, wolf, and a variety of birds and other species are likely to come across your path.

Golf magazine voted Jasper Park Lodge the number one resort course in Canada in 1989, and *Score*, Canada's leading golf magazine, rates it among Canada's top 25 public courses.

Course Name: KANANASKIS COUNTRY GOLF COURSE Mt. Kidd, Mt. Lorrette Courses

Course Type: Resort
Resort: The Lodge at Kananaskis
                      Hotel Kananaskis
                      Inn at Kananaskis
Address: Highway 40
                      Kananaskis Village, Alberta
                      T0L2H0
Phone: (403) 591–7070 (Golf Course)
                      (403) 591–7711,
                      (800) 528–0444 (Resort)
Fax: (403) 591–7770 (Resort)

GOLF COURSE

Director of Golf: Brian Bygrave
Head Professional: Wayne Bygrave
Course Length/Par (All Tees): Mt. Kidd: Back 7083/72, Blue 6590/72, White 6039/72, Forward 5539/72. Mt. Lorrette:

Back 7102/72, Blue 6643/72, White 6155/72, Forward 5429/72
Course Slope/Rating (All Tees): Mt. Kidd: Back 134/72.8, Blue 128/70.5, White 124/68.2, Forward NA/66.5, Ladies' White NA/74.5, Ladies' Forward NA/71.5. Mt. Lorrette: Back 137/74.1, Blue 131/72.1, White 127/69.8, Forward NA/64.5, Ladies' White NA/76, Ladies' Forward NA/72
Course Architect: Robert Trent Jones, Sr. (1983)
Golf Facilities: Full Pro Shop X, Snack Bar X, Lounge X, Restaurant X, Locker Room X, Showers X, Club Rental X, Club Repair X, Cart Rental X, Instruction X, Practice Green X, Driving Range X, Practice Bunker X, Club Storage X
Tee-Time Reservation Policy: Up to 60 days in advance
Ranger: Yes
Tee-off-Interval Time: 9 min.
Time to Play 18 Holes: 4½ hrs.
Course Hours/Earliest Tee-off: 6:30 a.m. to dark
Green Fees: Can$45 for 18 holes
Cart Fees: Can$26 for 18 holes (Can$13 per person)
Pull Carts: Can$5 for 18 holes
Credit Cards: American Express, Master-Card, Visa
Season: Early May to mid-Oct.
Course Comments: Can walk anytime. Yardage book available
Golf Packages: Spring and fall season through Kananaskis Lodge, Hotel of Kananaskis, Inn at Kananaskis
Discounts: Seniors, juniors (Mon. to Thurs. excluding holidays)
Places to Stay Nearby: Ribbon Creek Hostel (403) 591–7333; William Watson Lodge (facilities for seniors, handicapped) (403) 591–7711; Kananaskis Inn Best Western (403) 591–7500, (800) 372–9577; Kananaskis Guest Ranch (403) 673–3737; Mount Kidd RV Park (403) 591–7700; Rafter Six Ranch Resort (403) 673–3622; Kananaskis Village Resort Association (information, reservations) (403) 591–7555, (800)

332–1013 (AB), (800) 661–1064 (Canada outside AB)

Local Attractions: Canmore Nordic Centre, Peter Lougheed Provincial Park, Banff National Park, Kootenay National Park, Yoho National Park, Glacier National Park, Fairmont Hot Springs, Radium Hot Springs, Floc Lake, O'Hara, Nakiska Ski Resort (site of the 1988 Winter Olympics), Boundary Ranch, hunting, fishing, camping, hiking, boating, cross-country and downhill skiing, ice-skating, horseback riding, parks. Canada Information Services (403) 292–4401. Kananaskis County Tourism (403) 297–3362, Kananaskis Village Information Centre (403) 591–7555, Banff Information Centre (403) 762–1550, Canmore Visitors Centre (403) 678–5277

Directions: Travel west from Calgary or east from Banff on Hwy. 1 (TransCanada Hwy.) to Hwy. 40 (Kananskis Trail Exit). The golf course is approximately 15 miles south on Hwy. 40. Follow the signs

Closest Commercial Airports: Calgary International (1½ hrs.), Edmonton International (2½ hrs.)

RESORT:

Date Built: 1987

No. of Rooms: 324 guest rooms, 255 in the lodge, 69 rooms in the manor-style hotel

Meeting Rooms: 14. Capacity of Largest: 600 persons banquet style. Meeting Space: 26,650 sq. ft.

Room Price Range: Peak season (June through Sept.): Can$231 Canadian to Can$175 European plan. Lower winter rates. Golf, ski, fitness and other packages available year round

Lounges: Lodge: Bighorn Lounge. Hotel: Fireside Cocktail Lounge

Restaurants: Lodge: Peaks Dining Room, Bradys Market, Bighorn. Hotel: Escapade Dining Room, Fireside Lounge, Obsessions Lounge

Entertainment: Harp, piano music in hotel, live music in the Bighorn Lounge

Credit Cards: All major cards

General Amenities: 8 shops and boutiques, beauty salon and tanning parlor, helicopter tours, meeting and conference facilities with audiovisual and food services

Recreational Amenities: Hiking, fishing, boating, bicycling, climbing, hunting, river rafting, camping, horseback riding. Lodge: health club with indoor pool, sauna, massage, whirlpool, video game arcade, activities room, 6 tennis courts, cross-country and downhill skiing at Nakiska and Fortress Mountain, sleigh rides, ice-skating

Reservation and Cancellation Policy: Credit card or cash deposit required to hold reservation. 3-day cancellation notice required to avoid penalties

Comments and Restrictions: Taxes additional to base rates

KANANASKIS COUNTRY GOLF COURSE

The Kananaskis Country Golf Course is located in the scenic Kananaskis River Valley and is surrounded by the Canadian Rockies. Designed by Robert Trent Jones, Sr. in the early 1980s, the two eighteen hole courses wind gently along the river under the jagged peaks of Mt. Lorette and Mt. Kidd.

These beautiful golf courses feature large, moderately fast, undulating bentgrass greens. Large bunkers protect the greens as well as key fairway landing areas. There are water hazards on more than half the holes on these courses, which are generally open, but trees such as fir and poplar can easily come into play if the ball strays too much. Because of the high altitude, shots carry 10 to 15 percent farther than normal. Consistent with Robert Trent Jones's credo, it is not easy to par the holes on these courses, but getting a bogey is a reasonable expectation for the average golfer. There are four tee distances to choose from on both courses, enabling any golfer to find his or her comfortable golfing distance.

The Mt. Kidd course plays 7050 yards from the back tees. Wind can be a factor on this rolling layout, which lies in a valley framed by the mountains. One of the more memorable holes on this course is the 197-yard par-3 fourth, which plays from an elevated tee to a wide, shallow green approximately 30 feet below. Bunkers guard the front, right and rear of the target, and water almost completely surrounds the hole. There is usually a tail wind on this hole, making club selection and, of course, accuracy critical.

The finishing hole at Mt. Kidd seems a long march if you play from the back tees. This 642-yard par 5 plays straight to a large green guarded by three well-placed bunkers to the left, right and front. The tee shot is to a landing area just before a left-fairway bunker. The second shot must avoid a cluster of bunkers 180 yards from the green. The other tee distances on this hole are 576, 553 and 546 yards.

The Mt. Lorrette Course is also laced with water from the Kananaskis River and has expansive fairways, greens and bunkers. This layout plays 7102, 6643, 6155 and 5429 yards from each of the tee distances. The 412-yard par-4 first hole should have your undivided attention because it requires considerable accuracy, and strayed shots can quickly cost you strokes. The right side of the fairway is bordered by a stream, and the left side features two large ponds. Many golfers use a long iron off the tee to reach a landing area guarded by a pond on the left and water on the right. The approach is to a narrow, deep forward-sloping green with a bunker to the right front and a stream to the rear. Two well-placed shots are required to reach this green in regulation.

An excellent par 5 at Mt. Lorrette is the 523-yard dogleg-left fourteenth. The tee shot is to a landing area guarded by a pair of bunkers to the left. Another fairway bunker squeezes the fairway 90 yards from the green. To the far right is a stream that runs from tee to around the back of the green. Some golfers are tempted to go for the green on the second shot. The narrow, deep target is well bunkered to the left, right front, right and rear. Jones uses water, sand and the natural contours of the land to give you much to think about on this hole. And when one reviews the hole layouts for both

the Mt. Kidd and Mt. Lorrette courses, it is striking the variety of shapes and sizes that the hazards and the greens have. For example, some of the greens are deep and narrow (41 by 18 yards on Mt. Lorrette's 188-yard par-3 fifteenth) while others are rather small (24 by 25 yards on Mt. Kidd's 437-yard par-4 third). These variations add to the challenge of these golf courses.

A modern clubhouse is within easy walking distance of the first tee on both golf courses at Kananaskis. This facility features valet parking, club handling and storage, locker rooms, showers, a lounge, private function rooms and a full-service pro shop. Near the pro shop is the Robert Trent Jones Pavilion, a full-service tournament center available for groups of up to 300. Practice facilities include driving range, practice putting greens and practice bunkers. Individual and group lessons are available from the staff of professionals. The golf fees here are very reasonable considering the quality of the golf courses. Packages are available through the nearby Kananaskis Lodge, Hotel Kananaskis and the Inn at Kananaskis.

The Lodge at Kananaskis and the Hotel Kananaskis have more than 300 rooms, a variety of restaurants, live entertainment and recreational amenities including a health club, swimming pools, horseback riding, tennis and other activities. There are also meeting and conference facilities that can accommodate groups of 600 persons in a banquet setting. In the winter this area becomes a major skiing center, with cross-country and downhill facilities as well as other winter sports available. The surrounding areas provide ample hiking, fishing, boating, camping and other recreational opportunities.

Kam-Alta Golf Management runs the golf operation at Kananaskis. The operating philosophy is to provide a high level of service to the public at an affordable cost. You will find an excellent blend of beauty and challenge at Kananaskis. *Score* magazine, *Golf Digest* and *Golf* magazine rate these golf courses among the best public courses in Canada.

Course Name: WOLF CREEK
East, South, West Courses

Course Type: Public
Address: Highway 2/R.R. Site 10/Box 5
Ponoka, Alberta, Canada
T4J1R3
Phone: (403) 783–6050 (Tee Times)
(403) 783–6566 (Resort)

GOLF COURSE

Director of Golf: Ryan Vold
Head Professional: Clint Duff
Course Length/Par (All Tees): West/East:
Back 6516/70, Silver 5950/70, Blue
5691/70, Forward 4880/70. East/South:
Back 6818/70, Silver 6230/70, Blue
5933/70, Forward 5144/70. South/West:
Back 6730/70, Silver 6136/70, Blue
5684/70, Forward 4990/70
Course Slope/Rating (All Tees):
West/East: Back 138/74.0, Silver
131/71.0, Blue 127/70.0, Ladies'
Forward 117/70.0. East/South: Back
135/75.0, Silver 129/72.0, Blue
126/71.0, Ladies' Forward 117/70.0.
South/West: Back 139/74.0, Silver
132/71.0, Blue 127/70.0, Ladies' For-
ward 117/69.0
Course Architect: Rod Whitman (9 holes,
1984; 9 holes, 1985; 9 holes, 1991)
Golf Facilities: Full Pro Shop X, Snack
Bar X, Lounge X, Restaurant X,
Locker Room X, Showers X, Club
Rental X, Club Repair No, Cart Rental
X, Instruction X, Practice Green X,
Driving Range X, Practice Bunker X,
Club Storage X
Tee-Time Reservation Policy: Anytime
with credit card guarantee
Ranger: Yes
Tee-off-Interval Time: 9 min.
Time to Play 18 Holes: 4½ hrs.
Course Hours/Earliest Tee-off: 7 a.m.
Open until 11 p.m. in summer
Green Fees: Can$35 for 18 holes; Can$20
for 9 holes
Cart Fees: Can$24 for 18 holes
Credit Cards: American Express, Diners
Club, MasterCard, Visa
Season: Mid-April to Oct.

Course Comments: Can walk anytime.
Yardage book available. Golf school on
site
Golf Packages: Contact pro shop
Discounts: Through on site Wolf Creek Inn
(403) 782–4716
Places to Stay Nearby: Ponoka Stampeder
Inn (403) 783–5535; Riverside Motor
Inn (403) 783–4444. RED DEER: Black
Knight Inn (403) 343–6666, (800) 661–
6498; Great West Inn (403) 342–6567,
(800) 661–1854; Red Deer Lodge (403)
346–8841, (800) 662–7181
Local Attractions: Fort Ostell Museum,
fishing, boating, camping, hiking, hunt-
ing, skiing and ice-skating, horseback
riding. WETASKIWIN: Reynolds Museum,
Wetaskiwin and District Museum. RIM-
BEY: Pas-Ka-Poo Historical Park. RED
DEER: Old Court House, Red Deer and
District Museum Archives, Waskasoo
Park, Fort Normandeau, Kerry Wood
Nature Centre. DEVON: University of Alberta Devonian Botanic Garden, Clif-
ford E. Lee Nature Sanctuary.
Edmonton. Alberta Tourism (800) 661–
8888, (800) 222–6501. Edmonton Tour-
ism Visitor Center (403) 988–5455,
(403) 422–5505
Directions: Hwy. 2, 8 mi. southwest of
Ponoka
Closest Commercial Airports: Edmonton
International (1 hr.), Calgary Interna-
tional (1½ hrs.)

WOLF CREEK

Wolf Creek is an excellent and challenging Scottish-links-style 27-hole layout located on the wind-swept prairie of Alberta,
midway between Edmonton and Calgary.
The three nines were designed by Rod
Whitman, who apprenticed under Pete Dye.
His friend Ryan Vold, a member of the
Canadian Professional Golf Association
and director of golf at Wolf Creek, teamed
up with Whitman to build the course on the
Vold family ranch.

The Wolf Creek layout seems short,
with the back tees for the South/West
Course at 6730 yards and the other distances at 6136, 5684 and 4990 yards,
respectively. However, the advice on the

scorecard is to play the back tees only if you have less than a 6 handicap. Experience has shown that more than 130 bunkers (on 27 holes); tricky, large, fast, undulating bentgrass greens; unpredictable wind conditions and an abundance of well-placed trees and mounds can run up your score very quickly if you don't pay close attention to shot placement, club selection and strategy. Cattle skulls serve as 150-yard markers, sometimes foreshadowing formidable challenges ahead.

The 391-yard par-4 second hole, "Sod Wall," on the South Course is one of the difficult holes at Wolf Creek. The tee shot is through a tight, tree-lined chute to a landing area beyond a stream that cuts the fairway halfway to the hole. The approach is to a two-tiered green guarded by a sod-walled bunker directly in front and traps to the right, left and rear.

Another tricky par 4 is "Hank's Alley," the fourth hole whose tee shot is over a stream to a landing area guarded by the stream to the right. The approach is to a small green bordered by water on the left and to the rear. Shot making and position are crucial on this hole.

Many a story has been told about hole number nine and the 1990 Alberta Open, which is held at Wolf Creek annually. Two excellent pro golfers scored 12 and 14 respectively on this 445-yard par-4 dogleg left, called "Deception." The tee shot is to a landing area guarded by bunkers on the left. The approach is over a ravine to a small green that looks deceptively closer than it is. Surrounding the green are deep holes, sand bunkers and mounds.

One of the more difficult holes on the East Course is "The Gorge," a par-4 dogleg left playing 426 yards from the back tees. The tee shot must carry at least 175 yards to clear a gorge directly below. Trees line the left side of the fairway, so it is best to keep your drive to the right. The approach is to a medium-sized green surrounded by an arc of trees and guarded by a deep hole to the right.

The clubhouse at Wolf Creek is a 22,000-square-foot log structure with impressive 40-foot ceilings. Housed inside are banquet facilities; a restaurant featuring steaks, Barney burgers and Mexican barbecue; locker rooms, showers and a full-service pro shop. Practice facilities include driving range, putting green and practice bunker.

Ponoka is a major agricultural center in Alberta and features one of the best rodeos in North America in late June. Cowboys and Scottish-style golf—an odd but interesting combination. You won't be disappointed when you visit Wolf Creek. *Score* magazine ranks it among Canada's top 15 public golf courses.

Recommended Golf Courses in Alberta

Barrhead Golf Course, Barrhead, (403) 674–3050, Public, 18/6600/72

Coloniale Golf and Country Club, Beaumont, (403) 929–4653, Semiprivate, 18/7020/72

Cottonwood Golf and Country Club, De Winton, (403) 938–7200, Semiprivate, 18/6747/72

D'Arcy Ranch, Okotoks, (403) 938–4455, (800) 803–8810, Public, 18/6919/72

The Dunes Golf and Winter Club, Grandê Prairie, (403) 538–4333, Public, 18/6373/71

Goose Hummock Golf Club, Gibbons, (403) 921–2444, Resort, 18/6604/71

Henderson Lake Golf Club, Lethbridge, (403) 329–6767, Public, 18/6512/70

Heritage Pointe Golf and Country Club, De Winton, (403) 256–2002, Resort. Desert/Heritage: 18/6904/72. Heritage/Pointe: 18/7044/72. Pointe/Desert: 18/6936/72.

Ironhead Golf and Country Club, Wabamum, (403) 892–4653, Semiprivate, 18/6650/72

Lakeside Greens Golf and Country Club, Chestermore, (403) 569–9111, Semiprivate, 18/6725/72

Land-O-Lakes Golf Club, Coaldale, (403) 345–2582, Semiprivate, 18/6459/71

The Links at Spruce Grove, Spruce Grove, (403) 962–4653, Public, 18/6767/72

Medicine Hat Golf and Country Club, Medicine Hat, (403) 527–8086, Semiprivate, 18/6612/72

Paradise Canyon Golf and Country Club, Lethbridge, (403) 381–7500, Semiprivate, 18/6810/71

Pheasantback Golf and Country Club, Stettler, (403) 742–4653, Public, 18/6104/71

Ponoka Community Course, Ponoka, (403) 783–4626, Public, 18/6350/71

Redwood Meadows Golf and Country Club, Bragg Creek, (403) 949–3663, Semiprivate, 18/6943/72

Alberta: Useful Information

Travel Alberta, City Centre Bldg., 10155 102nd St., Department E, Box 2500, Edmonton, AB T5J2Z4, (403) 427–4321 (Edmonton), (800) 222–6501 (AB), (800) 661–8888 (outside AB)

Alberta Recreation and Parks, Standard Life Centre, 10405 Jasper Ave., Edmonton, AB T5J3N4, (403) 427–2280 (recreation information)

Alberta Forestry Lands and Wildlife, Fish and Wildlife Division, 9920 108th St., Edmonton, AB T5K2M4, (403) 427–3590 (fishing and hunting regulations)

BRITISH COLUMBIA

Course Name: CORDOVA BAY

Course Type: Public
Address: Cordova Bay Road
Victoria, British Columbia, Canada V8Y263
Phone: (604) 658–4444
Fax: (604) 658–4951

GOLF COURSE

Head Professional: Jim Goddard
Course Length/Par (All Tees): Back 6558/72, Middle 6186/72, Forward 5330/72
Course Slope/Rating (All Tees): Back NA/71, Middle NA/69, Forward NA/65, Ladies' Middle NA/76, Ladies' Forward NA/72

Course Architect: William G. Robinson (1991)
Golf Facilities: Full Pro Shop X, Snack Bar X, Lounge X, Restaurant X, Locker Room X, Showers X, Club Rental X, Club Repair X, Cart Rental X, Instruction X, Practice Green X, Driving Range X, Practice Bunker X, Club Storage X
Tee-Time Reservation Policy: Telephone in advance, credit card guarantee
Ranger: Yes
Tee-off-Interval Time: 8 min.
Time to Play 18 Holes: 4½ hrs.
Course Hours/Earliest Tee-off: 7 a.m. to dark (sunset at 10 p.m. June and July
Green Fees: Can$42 plus tax for 18 holes Sat., Sun., holidays; Can$39 plus tax for 18 holes Mon.-Fri.
Cart Fees: Can$22 plus tax for 18 holes, Can$12 plus tax for 9 holes (twilight only)
Credit Cards: American Express, MasterCard, Visa
Season: Year round. Busiest season April through Sept.
Course Comments: Can walk anytime
Golf Packages: Available. Inquire at pro shop
Discounts: Twilight. Juniors (18 and under)
Places to Stay Nearby: DOWNTOWN VICTORIA: Inn on the Harbor (604) 386–3451; Royal Scot Inn (604) 388–5403, (800) 663–7515; Empress Hotel (604) 384–7121, (800) 268–9411; Captain's Palace (604) 388–9191; James Bay Inn (604) 384–7151; Best Western Carlton Plaza (604) 388–5513, (800) 663–7241. BED AND BREAKFASTS: Beacon Hill (604) 388–4485; Huckleberry Inn (604) 598–8876; Prior House Bed and Breakfast (604) 592–8847
Local Attractions: Butchart Gardens, Fable Cottage Estate and Gardens, Maritime Museum, Mattick's Farm (shopping), Royal British Columbia Museum, Crystal Garden, Royale Theatre, Olde England Inn and Ann Hathaway's Cottage, Collector's Car Museum, Parliament buildings, restaurants, shopping, boating, fishing, camp-

ing, hiking, bicycling. Victoria Visitors Information Centre (604) 382–2127

Directions: 15 min. north of Victoria. North on Hwy. 17, east on Sayward Rd., follow signs to golf course. British Columbia Ferries (604) 386–3431

Closest Commercial Airports: Victoria International (12 min.), Vancouver International (3 hrs., including ferry ride)

CORDOVA BAY

One bleak November day, Jim Goddard, the club pro at the newly opened William Robinson–designed Cordova Bay Golf Course, took me around the eighteen-hole circuit. Despite occasional rain and 45 degree temperatures, the course was full, as it has been since it was transformed from farmlands and woods to a 6558-yard par-72 layout a few years ago.

The front nine is relatively open with little water, but sand traps protect large greens with subtle undulations. The number-1-handicap hole at Cordova Bay is the 453-yard par-4 fifth, which doglegs sharply to the left. The tee-shot target is at the turn of the dogleg, which then leaves you over 200 yards uphill to a large green protected by two traps. From this point on, the course starts to play much tougher.

The back nine is more rolling, with woodlands, water on six holes, and a rich array of fruit trees, wildflowers and newly planted sapplings. It was clear that having come over from Victoria's venerable Victoria Golf Club, Goddard had a great deal of pride in this new, privately owned public golf course, which is not too far from Cordova Bay and has magnificent views of Haro Strait.

The most difficult par 4 on the back nine is the 420-yard tenth hole whose tee shot is through a narrow chute, leaving a long second shot to a large, elongated, forward-sloping, elevated green with three traps protecting it and water crossing in front. My favorite hole at Cordova Bay is the 512-yard par-5 fourteenth, which doglegs left and is shaped somewhat like a hammer, with a very narrow opening on the tree-lined second shot. Some low-handicap players can go over the top and reach the green in two, but most mortals should play two straight shots and come onto the long, narrow green from right to left.

The combination of interesting doglegs; large, well-trapped greens; numerous water hazards; and well-placed fairway bunkers makes Cordova Bay a challenging golf experience.

Cordova Bay has a fine pro shop and restaurant but limited locker-room capacity in its new 5500-square-foot clubhouse. It has an excellent 20-station lighted and roofed driving range that plays 270 yards to the far fences and has strategically placed flags for targets. As newly planted trees mature and other subtle adjustments are made at Cordova Bay, it will be an increasingly difficult golf challenge but always pleasant. And you're only 30 minutes from downtown Victoria, one of the most beautiful cities in North America.

Course Name: GALLAGHERS CANYON

Course Type: Semiprivate
Address: 4320 Gallagher's Drive West Kelowna, British Columbia V1W3Z9
Phone: (604) 861–4240
Fax: (604) 861–1852

GOLF COURSE

Head Professional: Rod Cochrane
Course Length/Par (All Tees): Back 6823/72, Middle 6448/72, Forward 5574/72
Course Slope/Rating (All Tees): Back 136/73.5, Middle 133/71.7, Forward 125/67.7. Ladies' Forward 131/73.8
Course Architect: William G. Robinson and Les Furber (1980)
Golf Facilities: Full Pro Shop X, Snack Bar X, Lounge X, Restaurant X, Locker Room X, Showers X, Club Rental X, Club Repair X, Cart Rental X, Instruction X, Practice Green X, Driving Range X, Practice Bunker X, Club Storage X
Tee-Time Reservation Policy: Anytime in advance. Members only can reserve tee times on Sat. and Sun.
Ranger: Yes

Tee-off-Interval Time: 9 min.

Time to Play 18 Holes: 4½ hrs.

Course Hours/Earliest Tee-off: 6:30 a.m. to dark

Green Fees: Can$55 for 18 holes

Cart Fees: Can$26.32 for 18 holes. Can$13.16 for 1 person

Credit Cards: American Express, Master-Card, Visa

Season: Mid-March to mid-Nov.

Course Comments: Can walk anytime. Yardage book available

Golf Packages: Available. Group rates and hotels

Discounts: Juniors, guest of members, twilight

Places to Stay Nearby: Grand Okanagan Lakefront Resort and Conference Center (800) 66–RELAX; Lake Okanagan Resort (604) 769–3511, (800) 663–3273; Ramada Lodge Hotel (604) 860–9711; Hotel El Dorado (604) 763 7500. CONDOMINIUM RENTALS: Hawthorn Park (604) 661–6636; Okanagan Bed and Breakfast Association (604) 868–2700

Local Attractions: Okanagan College, bicycling, hiking, camping, boating, horseback riding, tennis; vineyards including Mission Hill, Chateau St. Claire, Gray Monk, Cedar Creek, Calona, Hainle; theater, symphony, restaurants, shopping, casino gambling; parks and gardens including Kasugai Gardens, Woodhaven Nature Conservancy Park, Okanagan Mountain Provincial Park, many others; British Columbia Orchard Industry Museum, Fraser Lake Trout Farm, Kelowna Historic Museum, orchard tours. Kelowna Chamber of Commerce (604) 861–1515

Directions: From Vancouver (4 hrs.): Coquihalla Hwy., follow signs to golf course when you get to Kelowna

Closest Commercial Airports: Ellison Field, Kelowna (15 min.), Vancouver International (4 hrs.), Calgary International, AB (6 hrs.)

GALLAGHERS CANYON

Canada's *Score* magazine ranks Gallaghers Canyon as one of the top public golf courses in Canada, and justifiably so.

Located in the hills overlooking Lake Okanagan and the city of Kelowna, Gallaghers Canyon is a 6823-yard par-72 layout approximately 4 hours east of Vancouver and slightly north of the United States border and the state of Washington. The course, whose rugged terrain overlooks both Gallaghers and Scenic canyons, was originally opened in 1980 and, after initial financial difficulties, revived by Angus MacKenzie, a Calgary oilman, who acquired the property. In 1990, the course was sold to Burrard International, which is involved in real-estate development in California and British Columbia.

Gallaghers Canyon was designed by William G. Robinson, who was born in Ontario, Canada, and began his golf-architecture career by studying landscape architecture at Pennsylvania State University and working for Robert Trent Jones, Sr.'s, firm during the summer. He also played on the Penn State golf team. After graduation, he worked for noted golf architect Geoffrey Cornish and in 1977 formed and became president of Cornish and Robinson Golf Course Designers Ltd. of Calgary, Alberta. He has designed many courses in the United States, Canada and abroad, including the Cranberry Valley Golf Club, Harwich, Massachusetts with Cornish; Sterling Farms Municipal, Stamford, Connecticut with Cornish; Stratton Mountain Golf Club, Stratton, Vermont, with Cornish; and Clairville Golf Club, Toronto, Ontario. Gallaghers Canyon was the site of the 1988 Men's Canadian Amateur Championship.

The vantage point from the elevated tee on the 434-yard par-4 first hole gives you a sense of the challenge and beauty that Gallaghers Canyon will provide. The fairway is protected by Ponderosa pines and plays straight to an elevated green protected by traps on the right. Another good par 4 is the 420-yard fifth which plays from an elevated tee straight through a tree-lined corridor to a green protected by two traps on the right and one on the rear. The fairway is downhill all the way, and it is possible to end up with a downhill lie on your second shot, which is to a medium-sized green that slopes from back to front. Don't be above the hole.

On the back side, the 550-yard par-5 twelfth hole, a double dogleg left then right, is a local favorite. Trees line the left fairway virtually all the way, and the right side is open at the outset but then is well-treed on the second shot, to a medium-sized green protected to the left and right front by traps. The most difficult hole on this side is the 443-yard fourteenth, which is long and straight with trees lining the entire fairway.

Because of the relatively mild climate of the Okanagan region of south central British Columbia, Gallaghers Canyon can be played from mid-March to mid-November. More than 40,000 rounds are played at Gallaghers Canyon per year, attesting to its growing popularity and recognition as one of Canada's finest public courses.

Course Name: **PEACE PORTAL GOLF CLUB**

Course Type: Public
Address: 16900 4th Avenue
P.O. Box 45888, Sunnyside
Mall Post Office
Surrey, British
Columbia V4A9N3
Phone: (604) 538–4818

GOLF COURSE

Head Professional: Wendyl Arnold

Course Length/Par (All Tees): Back 6363/72, Middle 6103/72, Ladies' Forward 5621/75

Course Slope/Rating (All Tees): Back 127/70.7, Middle 124/69.5, Ladies' Forward 133/73.5

Course Architects: Francis L. James (1928), Stan Leonard and Philip Tattersfield (renovation, NA)

Golf Facilities: Full Pro Shop X, Snack Bar X, Lounge X, Restaurant No, Locker Room X, Showers X, Club Rental X, Club Repair Limited, Cart Rental X, Instruction X, Practice Green X, Driving Range No, Practice Bunker X, Club Storage No

Tee-Time Reservation Policy: From Thurs. for Sat., Sun., holidays. Up to 7 days in advance for Mon.-Fri.

Ranger: Yes

Tee-off-Interval Time: 8 min.

Time to Play 18 Holes: 4½ hrs.

Course Hours/Earliest Tee-off: Dawn to dusk

Green Fees: Can$49 for 18 holes Sat., Sun., holidays; Can$39 for 18 holes weekdays

Cart Fees: Can$26 for 18 holes per cart

Credit Cards: American Express, MasterCard, Visa

Season: March to Oct.

Course Comments: Can walk anytime

Golf Packages: None

Discounts: Twilight

Places to Stay Nearby: WHITE ROCK: Best Western Pacific Inn (604) 535–1432; Bay Motor Inn (604) 531–5557; Breakaway Inn Motel (604) 535–1110; Cedar Lane Motel (604) 531–4473; Ocean Beach Hotel (604) 531–4550. SURREY: Surrey Inn (604) 588–9511; Happy Day Inn (604) 589–1033. VANCOUVER AIRPORT AREA: Executive Inn (604) 278–5555; Delta Pacific Resort and Conference Centre (604) 278–9611; Abercorn Inn Best Western (604) 270–7576

Local Attractions: Peace Arch Monument, White Rock Archives Museum, fishing, boating, camping. SURREY: British Columbia Transportation Museum, Canadian Museum of Flight and Transportation, Colebrook Trout Farm, Barnston Island, Arnold Mikelson Gallery, Serpentine Fen Bird Sanctuary. Vancouver Island. Vancouver. Vancouver Travel Infocentre (604) 683–2000; White Rock Travel Infocentre (604) 536–6844; Surrey Travel Infocentre (604) 581–7130

Directions: Hwy. 99 to 8th Ave. east turnoff, take 8th Ave. east to 172nd St., turn right on 4th St. to clubhouse on the right

Closest Commercial Airports: Vancouver International (40 min.); Seattle–Tacoma International, WA (3 hrs.)

PEACE PORTAL GOLF CLUB

Peace Portal is a heavily played and demanding 6363-yard course that has a rich history. Located just north of the American border above Blaine, Washington, Peace Portal was built in 1927 by Sam Hill, a Seattle lawyer who earlier had set up a saloon in the area to beat the Prohibition laws in the United States. Golf was added as an amenity to the basic liquor business, and Peace Portal eventually became one of Canada's best public golf courses. The course is hilly and well treed, with many undulations and valleys in its fairways. Water, in the form of ponds and the swiftly flowing Little Campbell River, which flows into Semiahmoo Bay, comes into play on five holes on the back nine.

The club is privately owned, but membership has been restricted to accommodate public play. Despite the arduous up-and-down nature of the course, most golfers walk the course, as is the hearty Canadian custom. My favorite hole at Peace Portal is the seventeenth, a par-4 slight dogleg right, 350 yards from the back tees. The tee box is beautifully manicured and stepped with railroad-tie bases and generous landscaping. Two ponds are on the left, the second extending over 100 yards along the fairway. The river crosses the fairway approximately 75 yards from the green. The elevated tee shot is through a narrow, well-treed gap, and ideally the shot should be played to the center of the fairway, with the second shot being a lofted club to the large, slightly elevated, forward-sloping green protected by a few trees but no traps.

The number-1-handicap hole at Peace Portal is the par-4 fifth hole, 461 yards from the back tees, a sharp dogleg right and well protected by trees along both sides of the rolling fairway from 350 yards in. The large green, which slopes from right to left and is slightly undulating, is visible from approximately 200 yards out. It is extremely difficult to reach this green, protected by trees on the left and two bunkers on the right, in regulation.

Most of the greens at Peace Portal are medium sized to large with subtle undulations and forward slopes. These can make the course difficult enough, but the strategic position of the mature trees and the hilly nature of the course make it more difficult than the yardage would indicate. As one club member graciously said after hitting his tee shot into the water on the seventeenth, "I have been a member of this club for 15 years, and I have never tired of playing the course."

Peace Portal has a clubhouse with bar, snack bar restaurant, full pro shop, locker rooms and showers. Throughout the clubhouse are wonderful framed photos of golf as it has evolved at Peace Portal over the years. Outside is a practice green and practice bunker but no driving range. Canada's leading golf magazine, *Score*, rates this golf course among Canada's top public courses. For an unpretentious round on a mature, traditional golf course, Peace Portal is your spot.

Course Name: RIVERSHORE GOLF COURSE

Course Type: Public
Address: Comp 1 Site 13 RR No. 2
               Kamloops, British Columbia
               VTC2J3
Phone: (604) 573–4622

GOLF COURSE

Head Professional: Barry McPhee
Course Length/Par (All Tees): Back 7007/72, Gold 6763/72, White 6347/72, Forward 5445/72
Course Slope/Rating (All Tees): Back 132/74, Gold 130/73, White 126/71, Forward 118/66, Ladies' White NA/76, Ladies' Forward 122/72
Course Architect: Robert Trent Jones, Sr. (1982)
Golf Facilities: Full Pro Shop X, Snack Bar X, Lounge X, Restaurant X, Locker Room X, Showers X, Club Rental X, Club Repair Limited, Cart Rental X, Instruction X, Practice Green X, Driving Range X, Practice Bunker X, Club Storage X
Tee-Time Reservation Policy: Call anytime in advance
Ranger: Yes
Tee-off-Interval Time: 7 and 8 min.

Time to Play 18 Holes: 4½ hrs.

Course Hours/Earliest Tee-off: 7 a.m. to dark

Green Fees: Can$42 for 18 holes; Can$22 for 9 holes

Cart Fees: Can$28 for 18 holes, Can$16 for 9 holes

Pull Carts: Can$4 for 18 holes

Credit Cards: American Express, Visa. Only Visa for green fees

Season: Feb. 15 to Nov. 1

Course Comments: Can walk anytime. Yardage book available. Memberships available. Busiest June-Sept.

Golf Packages: Available

Discounts: Juniors (18 and under), seasonal

Places to Stay Nearby: Kamloops Travelodge (604) 372–8202, (800) 255–3050; Stockman's Hotel (604) 372–2281, (800) 663–2837; Panorama Inn (604) 374–1515, (800) 663–3813; Coast Canadian Inn (604) 372–5201, (800) 663–1144; Best Western Kamloops Towne Lodge (604) 828–6660

Local Attractions: Harper Mountain, Kamloops Historical Museum and Archives, Secwepemc Cultural Native Centre, Tod Mountain Ski Area, Adams River Salmon Run, Roderick Haig-Brown Conservation Area, fishing, hunting, boating, camping, hiking, cross-country and downhill skiing, ice-skating. High Country Tourist Association (604) 372–7770. Kamloops Visitors and Convention Bureau (604) 374–3377

Directions: On Trans Canada Hwy., 15 mi. east of Kamloops, look for golf-course sign

Closest Commercial Airports: Fulton Field, Kamloops (45 min.); Vancouver International (4½ hrs.); Calgary International, AB (6 hrs.)

RIVERSHORE GOLF COURSE

Rivershore Golf Course is a 7007-yard par-72 Robert Trent Jones, Sr.-designed layout located in a real-estate development in the semidesert flatlands along the Thompson River in British Columbia. This is a Scottish-style-links layout with two lakes and 100 sand traps. The bentgrass greens are large, moderately fast and undulating. Water hazards appear on nine holes, and bunkers strategically protect both the greens and fairway landing areas. The course is owned and operated by the development's property owners, but it is open to the public.

The most difficult hole on the course is the 443-yard par-4 ninth, which plays straight to a medium-sized green with drop-offs to the front and to the right side. A pair of sand traps guard the putting surface, one to the right and another to the left. The tee shot is to a landing area guarded by a cluster of bunkers to the left approximately 230 yards from the back tees. The approach to the slightly elevated green generally plays longer than you would think.

An excellent par 5 on the front side is the 537-yard eighth. The tee shot is to a landing area guarded by two bunkers on the left. Downhill from this point is a spectacular view to a wide, very shallow (18 yards) green surrounded by traps and guarded in front by a pond that cuts halfway into the fairway from right to left. Most golfers lay up to the bottom of the hill and then hit a wedge to the green. A heroic shot is required to reach the green in two, and the penalties can be severe if you miss. Be sure to practice your sand game before you arrive at Rivershore.

The back nine begins with one of the most difficult par 4s on the course. This 408-yard slight dogleg left is bordered by water on the left from the tee to the front of the green. The ideal tee shot is a long iron up the left side, leaving a mid-iron to a narrow, deep green that becomes wider and more shallow the farther right you are. The approach from the left is over water and must avoid traps to the left, rear and right of the putting surface. As with most holes at Rivershore, accuracy off the tee is necessary to have a fighting chance of reaching this green in regulation.

The most difficult par 3 at Rivershore is the 224-yard seventeenth, which plays to a deep green guarded both left and right by traps. A river borders the fairway on the left from tee to green. Depending on wind conditions and pin placement, and considering the depth of the green, careful attention to club selection is required here as on most approach shots at Rivershore.

The finishing hole is a 528-yard par 5 bordered on the left by the river. The tee-shot landing area is guarded by a cluster of four traps on the right, beginning 252 yards from the back tees. The second shot is probably a controlled iron to the front of the three-tiered green, which is over 40 feet deep and guarded by two traps to the right. Depending on pin position and your short game, a par or a birdie should be a distinct possibility on this hole.

There are four tee distances to play from on this challenging golf course. This should enable any golfer to fit his or her game to the layout. Rivershore is approximately a 4½-hour drive northeast from Vancouver; nevertheless, it is quite popular, with in excess of 40,000 rounds a year played here. The clubhouse features a bar, restaurant, locker rooms, showers and a pro shop. Instruction is available at the nearby practice facilities, which include a driving range, practice green and sand bunker. You can walk Rivershore anytime. Rivershore is ranked among Canada's top 15 public courses by *Score* magazine.

Course Name: ROYAL COLWOOD GOLF CLUB

Course Type: Semiprivate
Address: 629 Goldstream Avenue
P.O. Box 7428 Depot D
Victoria, British Columbia
V9B5B8
Phone: (604) 478–9591

GOLF COURSE

Head Professional: Terry Yacyshen
Course Length/Par (All Tees): Back 6542/70, Middle 6234/70, Ladies' Forward 5912/74
Course Slope/Rating (All Tees): Back 130/71.0, Middle 127/69.6, Forward NA/68.5, Ladies' Middle NA/76, Ladies' Forward 135/74.5
Course Architect: A. V. Macan (1913)
Golf Facilities: Full Pro Shop X, Snack Bar X, Lounge X, Restaurant X, Locker Room No, Showers No, Club Rental X, Club Repair X, Cart Rental X, Instruction X, Practice Green X, Driving Range X, Practice Bunker X, Club Storage X
Tee-Time Reservation Policy: Members have priority, certain restricted times. Call 48 hrs. in advance. Singles can be accommodated
Ranger: No
Tee-off-Interval Time: 8 min.
Time to Play 18 Holes: 4 hrs., 15 min.
Course Hours/Earliest Tee-off: 7 a.m. to dark
Green Fees: Can$74 daily for 18 holes
Cart Fees: Can$26 plus tax for 18 holes
Pull Carts: Can$3.50 for 18 holes
Credit Cards: MasterCard, Visa
Season: Year round. Busiest season April through Sept.
Course Comments: Can walk anytime. Currently lockers only for members
Golf Packages: None
Discounts: Member/guest and reciprocal
Places to Stay Nearby: DOWNTOWN VICTORIA: Inn on the Harbor (604) 386–3451; Royal Scot Inn (604) 388–5403, (800) 663–7515; Empress Hotel (604) 384–7121, (800) 268–9411; Captain's Palace (604) 388–9191; James Bay Inn (604) 384–7151; Best Western Carlton Plaza (604) 388–5513, (800) 663–7241. BED AND BREAKFASTS: Beacon Hill (604) 388–4485; Huckleberry Inn (604) 598–8876; Prior House Bed and Breakfast (604) 592–8847
Local Attractions: Butchart Gardens, Fable Cottage Estate and Gardens, Maritime Museum, Maddox Farm (shopping), Royal British Columbia Museum, Crystal Garden, Royale Theatre, Olde England Inn and Ann Hathaway's Cottage, Collector's Car Museum, Parliament buildings, restaurants, shopping, boating, fishing, camping, hiking, bicycling. Victoria Visitors Information Centre (604) 382–2127.
Directions: From Victoria: Trans Canada Hwy. north/sign, left on Millstream (1½ mi.), left on Goldstream (800 ft.)
Closest Commercial Airports: Victoria International (30 min.), Vancouver International (3 hrs., including 1 hr., 45 min. ferry ride)

ROYAL COLWOOD GOLF CLUB

Royal Colwood is a beautiful, traditional golf course that must be played if you are lucky enough to be on Vancouver Island. This 6542-yard par-70 layout was designed by A. V. Macan and built on what was 240 acres of farmland that has now become an oasis in a residential community. Macan was born in Dublin in 1882, attended Trinity College in Dublin and earned a law degree at the University of London. He emigrated to Vancouver, where he established a law practice and became known as one of the best amateur golfers in the area. After World War I, in which he lost part of his leg below the knee, he remained a scratch golfer but became a golf architect and designed the Shaughnessy Golf and Country Club in Vancouver; the Colwood National Golf Club in Portland, Oregon; the California Golf Club of San Francisco; and many others before passing away in Victoria in 1964 at age 82.

Macan took considerable pride in holes eleven, twelve and thirteen at Royal Colwood. The twelfth is a 423-yard par-4 dogleg left with mature trees lining the fairway on both sides. The approach is to a large, fast green protected by a bunker on the right. This hole follows Macan's maxim that "all par fours should require two well-planned and played shots to the green." The Royal Colwood features mature trees and strategically placed traps, and it has water hazards on six holes. The layout seems naturally cut out of the woods and is very flat, making it quite easy and enjoyable to walk.

Royal Colwood is one of the few officially designated "royal" clubs in Canada, the others being Royal Ottawa, Royal Quebec and Royal Montreal. The Prince of Wales, who briefly was King Edward VIII and then the Duke of Windsor after his abdication, played Colwood several times before becoming a patron of the club and persuading his father, King George V, to change the name to Royal Colwood Golf Club. It was the then Prince of Wales who supposedly dubbed the sixteenth hole the "Cathedral" because of the magnificent firs that frame this beautiful 387-yard par 4.

The tee shot on this narrow hole should be positioned to the left, and the approach is over a bunker to an elevated green backed by another bunker.

One of the most challenging par 3s here is the 241-yard eleventh, which plays to a green flanked by two large traps. This is a golf course you will want to visit again after you have played it the first time.

More than 90,000 rounds of golf per year are played at Royal Colwood, which is open year round and stays open until 10 p.m. in July. The course is kept in excellent condition, and the climate in Vancouver makes the layout seem like a lush nature preserve.

Course Name: WESTWOOD PLATEAU GOLF AND COUNTRY CLUB

Course Type: Public
Address: 3251 Plateau Road
Coquitlan, British Columbia
V3E3B8
Phone: (604) 941–4236
Fax: (604) 552–0920

GOLF COURSE

Head Professional: Ron Woods
Course Length/Par (All Tees): Back 6770/72, Plateau 6355/72, Gryphon 5893/72, Banner 5514/72, Forward 5014/72
Course Slope/Rating (All Tees): Back 134/71.9, Plateau 129/69.9, Gryphon 127/67.6, Banner 122/66.0, Forward 109/63.9
Course Architect: Michael Hurdzan (1995)
Golf Facilities: Full Pro Shop X, Snack Bar X, Lounge X, Restaurant X, Locker Room X, Showers X, Club Rental X, Club Repair X, Cart Rental X, Instruction X, Practice Green X, Driving Range X, Practice Bunker X, Club Storage X
Tee-Time Reservation Policy: Up to 7 days in advance for the public. Up to 1 year in advance for out-of-town play with Can$10 surcharge
Ranger: Yes
Tee-off-Interval Time: 12 min.
Time to Play 18 Holes: 5 hrs.
Course Hours/Earliest Tee-off: 6:30 a.m.

Green and Cart Fees: Can$80 for 18 holes Fri., Sat., Sun., holidays; Can$70 for 18 holes weekdays
Credit Cards: All major cards
Season: March through Oct.
Course Comments: Can walk anytime at full golf fee. Can$10 credit awarded to walkers
Golf Packages: Contact pro shop or Golf Vancouver (800) 565–7302
Discounts: Twilight (4½ hrs. before dusk)
Places to Stay Nearby: VANCOUVER: Buchan Hotel (604) 685–5354; Four Seasons Hotel (604) 689–9333, (800) 689–9333, (800) 332–3442 (U.S.); Georgia Hotel (604) 682–5566, (800) 663–1111; Le Meridien-Vancouver (604) 682–5511, (800) 543–4300; Pan Pacific (604) 662–3223, (800) 937–1515; Sylvia Hotel (604) 681–9321; Wedgewood Hotel (604) 689–7777, (800) 663–0666; West End Guest House (604) 681–2889
Local Attractions: Capilano Suspension Bridge and Park, Deer Lake Park, Dr. Sun Yat-Sen Classical Chinese Garden, Harbour Centre Complex, Maritime Museum, North Shore Museum, Archives and Art Gallery, Stanley Park, University of British Columbia, Vancouver Art Gallery, Chinatown, English Bay, Granville Island, Robson Street, Vancouver Museum, Vandusen Botanical Gardens, professional sports including CFL football, NHL hockey, AAA professional baseball, NBA basketball, soccer, the arts, nightlife, casinos, restaurants, parks and gardens, beaches, shopping, boating, fishing. Vancouver Travel Info Centre, Box 492, 96 Plaza Level, Four Bental Centre, Vancouver, BC V7X1L3 (604) 683–2000
Directions: Westwood Plateau is 12 miles east of Vancouver
Closest Commercial Airports: Vancouver International (1 hr.); Seattle-Tacoma International (4½ hrs.)

WESTWOOD PLATEAU GOLF AND COUNTRY CLUB

Westwood Plateau Golf and Country Club is a Michael Hurdzan-designed 6770-yard par-72 gem that is the cornerstone of a planned residential community in a forested, mountain setting east of Vancouver. Four lakes and two streams can come into play on this course which has a variety of scenic vistas and elevation changes. The streams feed into a salmon spawning area and deer, coyote, bear, eagle, hawks, and other creatures roam the region. The opening holes at Westwood Plateau provide views of virgin forest, the middle holes have vantage points to the Strait of Georgia and Vancouver island to the west, and the last two holes afford southerly views of Mt. Baker and the Frasier Valley.

There are more than fifty bunkers on the golf course which has bentgrass tees and greens, rye fairways, and fescue rough. The large greens are somewhat flat, providing a safe haven for those who can successfully negotiate the route to the target. The greens on the par 5s tend to be the smallest and the par 3s have the largest putting surfaces on this scenic course. One of the more dramatic par 3s at Westwood Plateau is the 205-yard third which plays across a gorge up approximately 50 feet to a plateaued green cut into the side of a mountain. In front of the target is a large catch bunker and behind it is a pot bunker. It is better to be long on this hole than to risk being in the abyss. The 583-yard par-5 seventh, whose first shot plays downhill to a tight landing area framed by trees and rough, is one of the most difficult holes on the course. The second shot is down a fairway with bunkers on the right and a stand of trees to the left. Most golfers will take three shots to reach a green with three large bunkers to the left and a dropoff to the rear. The 456-yard seventeenth is one of the best par 4s on the course. The tee shot is down a steep hill to a landing area in front of a deep ravine that cuts the fairway 275 yards from the back tees. The approach is all carry to a green guarded left, right and rear by bunkers.

Westwood Plateau has a clubhouse that is near a large practice area including a nine hole golf course, three practice holes, a driving range, practice greens and practice bunkers. On the other side of the mountain, separating this facility from the new championship golf course, is a 35,000 square foot modern clubhouse with banquet, restaurant, pro shop, and other facilities. In 1995 *Golf Digest* rated Westwood Plateau one of the best two new public golf courses in Canada.

Course Name: WHISTLER
Nicklaus North,
Arnold Palmer
(Whistler Golf Club),
Robert Trent Jones, Jr.
(Chateau Whistler
Golf Club) Courses

Course Type: Resort
Resort: Chateau Whistler Resort
Address: Highway 99/4599 Chateau Boulevard/Box 100 Whistler Village, British Columbia V0N1B0
Phone: (604) 938–9898 (Nicklaus North), (604) 932–3280 (Arnold Palmer Golf Course), (604) 938–2092 (Robert Trent Jones, Jr. Golf Course), (604) 938–2010, (Resort), (800) 828–7447 (U.S.) (Resort)
Fax: (604) 938–2055 (Resort)

GOLF COURSE

Head Professionals: Nicklaus North: Rod Cochrane. Arnold Palmer: Brad White. Robert Trent Jones, Jr.: Greg McCullough

Course Length/Par (All Tees): Nicklaus North: Back 6908/72, Blue 6413/72, White 6004/72, Green 5489/72, Forward 4730/72. Arnold Palmer: Back 6397/72, Middle 5995/72, Forward 5343/72. Robert Trent Jones, Jr.: Back 6605/72, Blue 6185/72, White 5635/72, Forward 5075/72

Course Slope/Rating (All Tees): Nicklaus North: Back 138/73.5, Blue 133/71.3, White 125/68.7, Green 120/66.4, Forward 114/63.0. Arnold Palmer: Back NA/71.0, Middle NA/69.0, Forward NA/66.0, Ladies' Middle NA/74.5,

Ladies' Forward NA/70.0. Robert Trent Jones, Jr.: NA/NA

Course Architects: Nicklaus North: Jack Nicklaus (1995). Arnold Palmer: Arnold Palmer (1983), Robert Trent Jones, Jr.: Robert Trent Jones, Jr. (1992)

Golf Facilities: Full Pro Shop X, Snack Bar X, Lounge No, Restaurant No, Locker Room No, Showers No, Club Rental X, Club Repair X, Cart Rental X, Instruction X, Practice Green X, Driving Range X, Practice Bunker X, Club Storage No

Tee-Time Reservation Policy: Anytime in advance with credit card guarantee

Ranger: Yes

Tee-off-Interval Time: 9 min.

Time to Play 18 Holes: 4 hrs., 45 min.

Course Hours/Earliest Tee-off: 6 a.m. to dark

Green Fees: Nicklaus North: Can$108 for 18 holes Fri., Sat., Sun., holidays, Can$88 for 18 holes Mon.-Thurs. Palmer, Jones: Can$70 for 18 holes Fri., Sat., Sun., holidays, Can$60 for 18 Mon.-Thurs.

Cart Fees: Can$25 for 18 holes per cart

Pull Carts: Nicklaus North: free. Palmer, Jones: Can$4 for 18 holes

Credit Cards: American Express, MasterCard, Visa

Season: Mid-May to late Oct.

Course Comments: Can walk anytime. Yardage book available

Golf Packages: No

Discounts: Seasonal, twilight

Places to Stay Nearby: VILLAGE CENTER: Delta Mountain Inn (604) 932–1982; Tantalus Resort Condominium Lodge (604) 932–4146; Nancy Greene Lodge (604) 932–2221; Pension Edelweiss (604) 932–3641; Crown Resort (604) 932–2215; Whistler Village Inn (604) 932–4004; Glacier Lodge (604) 932–2882; Fireplace Inns (604) 932–3200; Whistler Resort Association (central booking service) (604) 932–4222. BED AND BREAKFASTS: Ski Whistler Bed and Breakfast Reservation Service (604) 932–2667

Local Attractions: Shops, restaurants, biking, boating, fishing, hiking, camping, hunting, horseback riding, swimming, skiing, ice-skating, Brandywine and Nairn falls, Whistler Historic Museum and Archives, Whistler and Blackcomb Mountain Ski areas. Whistler Resort Association (604) 932–3928; reservations (604) 932–4222, (800) 634–9622 (U.S.)

Directions: Hwy. 99, golf course on Hwy. 99 in Whistler

Closest Commercial Airport: Vancouver International (2 hrs.)

RESORT:

Date Built: 1989

No. of Rooms: 343 moderate, premiere, 1- and 2-bedroom suites, junior suites, deluxe suites, executive suites

Meeting Rooms: 10. Capacity of Largest: 550 persons banquet style. Meeting Space: 14,000 sq. ft.

Room Price Range: Can$350 for a standard room to Can$900 for 2-bedroom sites peak season (late Nov. to late April). Golf packages and other seasonal and reduced rates available

Lounges: Mallard Bar

Restaurants: La Fiesta, Wildflower, Mallard Bar

Entertainment: Live entertainment in Mallard Bar, La Fiesta (seasonally), piano music in Wildflower

Credit Cards: All major cards

General Amenities: 12 retail boutiques, babysitting services, meeting and conference facilities with audiovisual and food services

Recreational Amenities: Health club with cardiovascular fitness equipment and attendants, indoor/outdoor swimming pool, massage, whirlpools, sauna, steam; 3 outdoor tennis courts, instruction available; cross-country and downhill skiing, snowshoeing, sleigh rides, horseback riding, river rafting, fishing, boating, bicycling

Reservation and Cancellation Policy: Credit card guarantee to hold room, or 1 night's deposit can be mailed in. 1-wk. prior notice of reservation change or cancellation required to avoid penalties. 2-wk. notice required peak season

Comments and Restrictions: Taxes additional to base rates

WHISTLER

Whistler Village is approximately a 2-hour drive north on the Squamish Highway from Vancouver. In the old days the route between Squamish and Lillooet was used as a hunting trail by Indians. In 1873 surveyors for the Canadian Pacific Railway cut a trail from Squamish to Pemberton. The trail was used to drive cattle to market in Vancouver. As time went on the railroad came, settlers arrived, and later, in the 1960s, Whistler became a major ski destination. In the 1970s Whistler was made into a year-round resort, and Arnold Palmer was retained to build a golf course on a 126-acre site in the valley framed by the snow-capped peaks of Whistler, Blackcomb and other mountains.

There were some preliminary problems with bogs, underground streams and other quirks of nature on the property, but eventually those problems were solved, and a 6397-yard par-72 layout, also called The Whistler Golf Club, was opened in 1983. Since then *Score* magazine has recognized this golf course as one of Canada's top public golf courses and *Golf* magazine has named it one of the best golf resorts in North America. Canadian Pacific Railway, Whistler's owner, built Chateau Whistler Resort, a twelve-story, 343-room all-season luxury hotel at the base of Blackcomb and Whistler mountains. This is the largest resort hotel of its kind built in Canada since the turn of the century.

The Arnold Palmer course at Whistler is not long, but it has eight lakes and ponds; a winding river; a variety of medium-sized to large, fast, undulating bentgrass greens; and large bunkers well placed near putting surfaces and fairway landing areas. Accuracy, club selection and course management should be the watchwords here. And, of course, when you reach a sizeable Arnold Palmer–designed green, three putts are a possibility. No matter what your handicap, this layout should present an enjoyable challenge.

After a golfer-friendly 375-yard par 4 for the first hole, you are presented with a tough 410-yard par 4. The tee shot is to a landing area tightly protected by fairway bunkers on the left and right sides. The approach is uphill to an elevated green guarded by a large trap to the right and another to the rear. The number-1-handicap hole on Whistler is the 535-yard par-5 dog-leg right third, which dares you to cut the corner to have a shot at reaching the green in two. You can either go directly over the corner, which is bordered by a stream, or you can fade the ball around the dogleg. The approach is to a large green with two traps on each side and a lake to the left and rear.

The 225-yard par-3 fifth hole makes up for some of the shorter par 5s on the Whistler course. The tee shot is often into the wind, making this hole play like a short par 4. The large green is well guarded by traps to the left, rear and right. A combination of a tricky pin placement and a large rolling green could lead to three putts. Scott Staley, head professional at Whistler and holder of the course record (65), urges golfers to keep the ball down, especially on holes nine through thirteen, because of thermal winds that come up this valley from the coast and Squamish to the south.

The consensus is that the 391-yard par-4 thirteenth hole is the most difficult hole at Whistler. The tee shot on this sharp dogleg left is to a landing area that slopes slightly from left to right. The left corner is guarded by a large rock formation covered with spruce trees, so there is no chance for a big hitter to cut the corner. The wind is usually into the golfer's face, making it likely that the second shot will be long and blind to a green guarded by traps to the right, rear and left front. In the background is Blackcomb Mountain.

Clubhouse facilities are modest, with a pro shop and snack bar but no locker rooms, showers or dining facilities. However, a sizeable clubhouse is under construction. Golf instruction is available at Whistler, and golf packages are available through the resort. Practice facilities include a practice range, practice bunker and putting green.

The Robert Trent Jones, Jr., Course, opened in 1992, plays 6605 yards from the back tees, 6185 from the blue, 5635 from the white and 5075 from the forward tees. This course, which is privately owned and a five minute drive from the hotel, features rock faces, waterfalls and some dramatic elevation changes. The 210-yard par-3 eighth hole, for example, plays to a very small green with water on the left and a 20-foot-high granite rock face protecting the right. This course is open to both the public and resort guests.

The latest addition to the repertoire of golf courses available to hotel guests and the public is the Nicklaus North Course, a 6908-yard par-72 layout which opened in 1995. Approximately five miles from the resort, this course is a great walking venue featuring flat, treelined fairways along the lake. Water can come into play on fourteen holes and the wind is a factor on the back nine. A base of six feet of sand was set down before this golf course was built. There are 58 bunkers on the Nicklaus which offers five tee distances. The par 3s are among the most challenging holes on the course, especially the signature 226-yard seventeenth and the 225-yard twelfth which has an island green.

The rooms at Chateau Whistler, which range from 450 to 1200 square feet, feature alpine views, color television with in-house movies, rooms equipped for the handi-capped, full bathrooms, minibars and other amenities. The resort has 14,000 square feet of meeting space, including 2 grand ballrooms, and a variety of recreational facilities, including a fitness center with indoor/outdoor swimming pool, saunas, whirlpools, massage, steam, outdoor tennis courts with professional instruction available, and other activities such as horseback riding, fishing, boating and bicycling. In the winter Whistler becomes a major skiing destination. Skiers can choose from over 85 marked ski trails and challenging downhill slopes on 2 world-class mountains.

The Chateau Whistler was designed by the Musson Cattell Partnership and Downs

Archomboult. Canadian Pacific Hotels and Resorts has a tradition of developing landmark properties at the hub of key destinations in Canada. The "railway hotels" are known for their turn-of-the-century chateau designs. The interior of the chateau features 5-foot square columns of Squamish rock, green slate, expansive beamed ceilings, pecan paneling, Canadian folk art and Mennonite weavings. Canadian Pacific Hotels and Resorts is the largest single owner and operator of golf courses in Canada.

Recommended Golf Courses in British Columbia

Big Sky Golf and Country Club, Pemberton, (604) 894–6106, (800) 668–7900, Resort, 18/7001/72

Castlegar Golf Club, Castlegar, (604) 365–5006, (800) 666–0324, Public, 18/6677/72

Christina Lake Golf Club, Christina Lake, (604) 447–9313, Semiprivate, 18/6615/72

Crown Isle Golf Club, Courtenay, (604) 338–6811, (800) 668–3244, Semiprivate, 18/7024/72

Eagle Point Golf and Country Club, Kamloops, (604) 573–2453, Public, 18/6762/72

Fairmont Hot Springs Golf Club, Fairmont Hot Springs, (604) 345–6514, Resort. Mountainside: 18/6510/72. Riverside: 18/6507/71

Fairview Mountain Golf Club, Oliver, (604) 498–3521, Semiprivate, 18/6537/72

Fairwinds Golf and Country Club, Nanoose Bay, (604) 468–7666, Resort, 18/6120/71

Golden Golf and Country Club, Golden, (604) 344–2700, Semiprivate, 18/6540/72

Harvest Golf Club, Kelowna, (604) 862–3103, (800) 257–8577, Resort, 18/7104/72

Kelowna Springs Golf Club, Kelowna, (604) 765–8511, Resort, 18/6675/72

Kokanee Springs Golf Resort, Crawford Bay, (604) 227–9362, (800) 979–7999, Resort, 18/6755/71

The Lone Wolf Golf Club, Taylor, (604) 789–3711, Public, 18/6817/72

Meadow Gardens Golf Club, Pitt Meadows, (604) 465–5474, Semiprivate, 18/7041/72

Morningstar Golf Club, Parksville, (604) 248–8161, Semiprivate, 18/6725/72

Northview Golf and Country Club, Surrey, (604) 576–4653, Public. Canal: 18/7191/72. Ridge: 18/6900/72

Olympic View Golf Club, Victoria, (604) 474–3671, Public, 18/6573/72

Predator Ridge Golf Resort, Vernon, (604) 542–3436, Resort, 18/7156/73

Rossland Trail Country Club, Trail, (604) 693–2255, Semiprivate. Birchbank: 18/6413/71

Springs Golf and Country Club, Radium Hot Springs, (604) 347–6444, (800) 667–6444, Resort, 18/6680/72

Storey Creek Golf Club, Campbell River, (604) 923–3673, Public, 18/6695/72

Swan-E-Set Bay Resort and Country Club, Pitt Meadows, (604) 465–3888, Public. Resort Course: 18/7000/72

Trickle Creek Golf Resort, Kimberley, (604) 427–3389, Resort, 18/6896/72

British Columbia: Useful Information

Ministry of Tourism, Parliament Bldg., 1117 Wharf St., Victoria, BC V8V1X4, (800) 663–6000

Tourism Vancouver, Department AG91, Info Centre, Plaza Pavilion, Four Bentall Centre/P.O. Box 49296, 1055 Dunsmuir St., Vancouver, BC V7X1L3, (604) 683–2000, (800) 888–8835

National Parks Service, 220 Fourth Ave. SE/Box 2989 Station M, Calgary, AB T2P3H8, (403) 292–4401

Tourism Association of Vancouver Island, #302–45 Bastion Square, Victoria, BC V8W1J1, (604) 382–3551

British Columbia Bed and Breakfast Association, 810 West Broadway Ave./P.O. Box 593, Vancouver, BC V5Z4E2, (604) 276–8616

Extension and Information Branch, Ministry of Parks, 4000 Seymour Pl., 3rd Fl.,

Victoria, BC V8V1X5, (800) 663–6000 (recreation information)

Fish and Wildlife Branch, Ministry of Environment, Parliament Bldgs., Victoria, BC V8V1X5, (800) 663–6000 (fishing and hunting regulations)

MANITOBA

Course Name: WASAGAMING GOLF COURSE

Course Type: Public
Address: Riding Mountain National
              Park/Box 52
              Wasagaming, Manitoba
              R0J280
Phone: (204) 848–7445

GOLF COURSE

Head Professional: Jim Dudmon (General Manager)
Course Length/Par (All Tees): Back 6070/72, Ladies' 6070/75
Course Slope/Rating (All Tees): Back NA/69, Ladies' NA/73
Course Architect: A. W. Creed (9 holes, 1928), (9 holes, 1934)
Golf Facilities: Full Pro Shop X, Snack Bar X, Lounge X, Restaurant X, Locker Room No, Showers No, Club Rental X, Club Repair X, Cart Rental X, Instruction No, Practice Green X, Driving Range No, Practice Bunker X, Club Storage X
Tee-Time Reservation Policy: Up to 7 days in advance
Ranger: Occasionally
Tee-off-Interval Time: 7 min.
Time to Play 18 Holes: 4½ hrs.
Course Hours/Earliest Tee-off: Sunrise to sunset
Green Fees: Can$24 for 18 holes
Cart Fees: Can$28 for 18 holes, Can$17 for 9 holes
Pull Carts: Can$4 for 18 holes, Can$3 for 9 holes
Credit Cards: MasterCard, Visa
Season: May to mid-Oct.
Course Comments: Can walk anytime
Golf Packages: None
Discounts: Juniors, seasonal passes, twilight

Places to Stay Nearby: RIDING MOUNTAIN NATIONAL PARK: Lee's Holiday Bungalows (open mid-May to mid-Sept.) (204) 848–2511; Elkhorn Resort and Conference Center (204) 848–2802; McTavish's Motel (204) 848–7366; Doners Buffalo Resort (204) 848–2404; Manigaming Motel (204) 848–2459
Local Attractions: RIDING MOUNTAIN NATIONAL PARK: Camping, fishing, hiking, nature trails, boating, park theatre complex, crafts, horseback riding, bicycling, seasonal festivals, skiing, ice-skating, ice fishing and other activities. Wasagaming Chamber of Commerce (204) 848–2742. Riding Mountain National Park (204) 848–2811
Directions: From Winnipeg (175 mi.): Hwy. 16 west to Hwy. 10 to Riding Mountain National Park (65 mi. north of Brandon), golf course 3 mi. into the park
Closest Commercial Airport: Winnipeg International (3 hrs.)

WASAGAMING GOLF COURSE

Manitoba has a population of slightly over 1 million people living in a land area of over 250,000 square miles. The land is flat in this province, which is known as the "Home of Hudson's Bay" or "the Prairie Province." In the southwestern corner of Manitoba is an escarpment intersected by waterways that lead to the Riding Mountains, which rise to a height of over 2400 feet above the prairie. Situated approximately 175 miles northwest of Winnipeg, the capital of Manitoba, is 1150- square-mile Riding Mountain National Park, which is a major recreational area in the region. Camping, boating, fishing, skiing, hiking, bicycling and other activities take place within the park, including golf on its 6070-yard Wasagaming Golf Course.

This beautiful, hilly layout, with its many blind shots and sidehill, uphill, and downhill lies, provides an excellent test of golf and beautiful views of 9-mile-long Lake Clear and the surrounding forests. As you might imagine, Wasagaming requires course knowledge, accuracy, and an ability to manage a tight layout with small- to medium-sized greens well protected by bunkers. These greens are fast, undulating and tricky to read. The Wasagaming course was laid out over 50 years ago and has the design and feel of a traditional mountain course. There is only one tee distance for each hole.

The signature hole at Wasagaming is the 126-yard par-3 seventeenth, which plays from an elevated tee down 60 feet to a green cut into the side of a hill. To the rear of the green is a cluster of four bunkers, and in front is a creek. A swale running across the green makes putting difficult and certain pin placements can make this hole even more difficult.

Another memorable hole is the 350-yard tenth, a par 4 tightly treed on both sides. A creek crosses the fairway approximately 200 yards away but before you tee off you have to look through a periscope to see whether there are any golfers below you. The tee shot should be hit approximately 235 yards to reach a flat area. Otherwise you are likely to have a steep uphill lie on your approach to the smallest green on the course. This green is slick and slopes from front to back, and putts generally break toward the lake.

Wasagaming provides an interesting and varied test of golf. While there are many short holes, that doesn't necessarily reduce their difficulty, as finesse is required to score. The par 5s on the course are 521, 465, 530 and 550 yards respectively, and three par 4s are over 425 yards long.

The clubhouse at Wasagaming has a bar, restaurant and pro shop, but practice facilities and other amenities are limited. That doesn't detract from the beauty and challenge of this golf course, however.

Recommended Golf Courses in Manitoba

Clear Lake Golf Course, Onanole, (204) 848–5653, Public, 18/6070/72

Falcon Beach Golf Course, Whiteshell Provincial Park, Falcon Lake, (204) 349–2554, Public, 18/6937/72

Hecla Island Golf Course, Hecla Island, (204) 475–2354, Resort, 18/6679/72

The Links at Quarry Oaks, Steinbach, (204) 326–4653, Public, 18/7009/72

Minnewasta Golf and Country Club, Morden, (204) 822–4992, Public, 18/6582/72

Manitoba: Useful Information

Travel Manitoba, Department 267, 7th Fl., 155 Carlton St., Winnipeg, MB R3C3H8, (204) 945–3777, (800) 665–0040

Travel Information Centre, Rm. 101, Legislative Bldg., Broadway and Osborne, Winnipeg, MB R3C0V8, (204) 945–3777 (additional information)

Tourism Winnipeg, Convention Center, 375 York, Ste. 232, Winnipeg, MB R3C353, (204) 943–1970, (800) 665–0204

NEW BRUNSWICK

Course Name: ALGONQUIN GOLF COURSES Seaside, Woodlands Courses

Course Type: Resort
Resort: The Algonquin
Address: 184 Adolphus Street St. Andrews, New Brunswick E0G2X0
Phone: (506) 529–3062 (Golf Course) (506) 529–8823, (800) 268–9411 (Resort)
Fax: (506) 529–4194 (Resort)

GOLF COURSE

Head Professional: Lindon Garron
Course Length/Par (All Tees): Seaside: Back 6451/72, Middle 6131/72, Ladies' Forward 5926/74. Woodlands: 1920/31
Course Slope/Rating (All Tees): Seaside: Back 114/69.3, Middle 110/67.6, Ladies' Forward 127/74.5. Woodlands: 83/56.5
Course Architect: Seaside: NA (18 holes, 1894). Donald Ross (Redesign, 1921). Woodlands: Donald Ross (1921)
Golf Facilities: Full Pro Shop X, Snack Bar X, Lounge X, Restaurant X, Locker Room X, Showers X, Club Rental X, Club Repair X, Cart Rental X, Instruction X, Practice Green X,

Driving Range X, Practice Bunker No, Club Storage X

Tee-Time Reservation Policy: Call anytime

Ranger: Yes

Tee-off-Interval Time: 8 min.

Time to Play 18 Holes: 4 hrs.

Course Hours/Earliest Tee-off: 7 a.m.

Green Fees: Can$36 for 18 holes Fri., Sat., Sun., holidays, Can$34 for 18 holes Mon.-Thurs. Can$26 for 9 holes Fri., Sat., Sun., holidays, Can$24 for 9 holes Mon.-Thurs.

Cart Fees: Can$28 for 18 holes, Can$17 for 9 holes

Credit Cards: All major cards

Season: May 1 to Oct. 1. Busiest season July through Aug.

Course Comments: Can walk anytime. Yardage book available

Golf Packages: Available through resort

Discounts: Twilight. Resort guests. Seasonal, lowest season before May, after Sept.

Places to Stay Nearby: Best Western Shiretown Inn (506) 529–8877, (800) 528–1234; Rossmount Inn (506) 529–3351; The Walker Estate (506) 529–4210; Tara Manor Inn (506) 529–3304. BED AND BREAKFAST: Chamcook Forest Lodge Bed and Breakfast (506) 529–4778

Local Attractions: Lighthouses, fishing, hunting, boating, hiking, camping, historic buildings, gardens, Henry Phipps Ross and Sarah Juliette Ross Memorial Museum, Sheriff Andrews house and gardens, Fort and Block house, Church of England Cemetery, Charlotte County Courthouse, Greenock Church and other historic buildings, Huntsman Marine Science Center and Aquarium, Sunbury Shores Arts and Nature Center, bicycling, swimming, seasonal festivals, whale watching, cruises, lighthouses, salmon information and visitor center, bird watching. Saint John. St. Stephen. Campobello Island. St. Andrews Tourist Bureau (506) 466–4858

Directions: Rte. 127 to St. Andrews, to Reed Ave., take right on Reed to golf course, hotel is past golf course, turn left onto Harriet from Reed, at first intersection, turn right onto Prince of Wales

Closest Commercial Airports: Saint John (1½ hrs.); Bangor International, ME (2 hrs.); Boston Logan International, MA (8 hrs.); Dorval International, Montreal (12 hrs.)

RESORT:

Date Built: 1889

No. of Rooms: 248 guest rooms and suites

Meeting Rooms: 9. Capacity of Largest: 400 persons banquet style. Meeting Space: 18,462 sq. ft.

Room Price Range: Can$139 for standard queen to Can$549 for 2 bedroom. Golf packages and other specials available

Lounges: Library Bar, Dockside Pub

Restaurants: Dockside Pub, Greens Restaurant, Passamaquoddy Dining Room

Entertainment: Live music in Library, Dockside

Credit Cards: All major cards

General Amenities: Smoke and gift shop; meeting and conference facilities in banquet, reception, classroom, theater, board-room settings with audiovisual and food services

Recreational Amenities: 2 tennis courts, shuffleboard, bicycling, private beach; health spa with sauna, hot tub, aerobic classes, exercise room, weight equipment, rowing machines, StairMaster, treadmills, and free weights

Reservation and Cancellation Policy: 1 night's deposit required to hold reservation. Cancellation or changes required 48 hrs. prior to arrival date to avoid penalties

Comments and Restrictions: Provincial sales tax additional to basic rates

ALGONQUIN GOLF COURSES

The Algonquin Golf Courses sit on Passamaquoddy Bay in New Brunswick's St. Andrews, a resort town approximately 2 hours' drive northeast of Bangor, Maine. The 18-hole Seaside course was originally built in 1894 and later redesigned in 1921 by Donald Ross who also designed the 9-hole Executive Course.

The Seaside Course plays 6451 yards from the back tees, with views of the sea from thirteen of the holes. The course is open, with small, moderately fast greens with some undulations. A major variable is the wind, which can rapidly alter club selection and strategy on some of the holes. The Seaside Course hosted the Canadian Senior Men's Tournament in 1979 and the Canadian PGA Club Professional Tournament in 1989.

In the old golf tradition, each of the holes at Seaside has a name. The 429-yard par-4 first hole is called "Patience," possibly because it plays into the prevailing winds and might not be easy to reach in regulation. The tee shot should be to the left center of the fairway to avoid the overhanging trees that line the right side. The approach is downhill to a small, flat, circular green. Enough club has to be used to carry a soft area that usually slows balls hit in front of the green.

The par 3s at Algonquin are very challenging because of the wind and the small greens. The 189-yard third, for example, plays over a pond to a green protected by five traps. The target is only 18 yards by 20 yards wide. The green slopes forward, so any shot from above the hole tends to be quite tricky. This hole is called "the Stumps."

The tee distances on individual holes at Algonquin are quite varied and interesting. The par 4s range from 308 to 429 yards from the back tees, and the par 5s range from 478 to 556 yards. The par-4 finishing, or "Home," hole plays 422 yards and slightly uphill. On the right is a line of trees, and out of bounds is to the left. The first shot should clear a slight rise for you to have a mid-iron or long iron to the narrow, deep green. Two well-executed shots are needed to reach this target in regulation.

The Algonquin Resort originally opened in 1889 and has recently added 50 new guest rooms and suites. A new 15,000-square-foot convention center has been added, and improvements have been made to the tees, greens and fairways on the golf course. Golf packages are available through the resort and begin at approximately Can$200 for 1 night's accommodations, breakfast and 2 days of unlimited golf. The Algonquin is a pleasant course to walk, and the Woodland Course affords you an opportunity to work on your short game. Practice facilities include a driving range and putting green.

St. Andrews is noted for its historic buildings, fishing, lighthouses and natural beauty. Nearby are Saint John, Campobello Island and other sites.

Recommended Golf Courses in New Brunswick

Edmundston Golf Club, Edmundston, (506) 735–7266, Semiprivate, 18/6514/73

Mactaquac Province Park Course, Mactaquac, (506) 363–4139, Public, 18/7002/72

New Brunswick: Useful Information

Tourism New Brunwick, Box 12345, Fredericton, NB E3B5C3, (506) 453–2377, (800) 561–0123, (800) 422–4422 (in New Brunswick)

Fish and Wildlife Branch, P.O. Box 6000, Marine Forestry Complex, Fredericton, NB E3B5H1

Information for major cities: Fredericton (506) 452–9500; Moncton (506) 853–3333; Saint John (506) 658–2990

Interprovince Ferry Information (902) 794–5700

NEWFOUNDLAND AND LABRADOR

Course Name: TWIN RIVERS GOLF COURSE

Course Type: Public
Resort: St. Christopher's Resort
Address: Trans Canada Highway
Port Blanford, Newfoundland
A0C2G0
Phone: (709) 543–2203 (Golf Course)
(709) 543–2525 (Resort)
Fax: (709) 543–2201 (Resort)

GOLF COURSE

Head Professional: Robert Hussey
Course Length/Par (All Tees): Back 6546/71, Middle 6090/71, Forward 5326/71

Course Slope/Rating (All Tees): Back 128/71.9, Middle 120/69.7, Ladies' Forward 129/72.5

Course Architect: C. E. "Robbie" Robinson (9 holes, 1983), Doug Currick (9 holes, 1991)

Golf Facilities: Full Pro Shop X, Snack Bar X, Lounge X, Restaurant X, Locker Room X, Showers X, Club Rental X, Club Repair X, Cart Rental X, Instruction X, Practice Green X, Driving Range X, Practice Bunker No, Club Storage No

Tee-Time Reservation Policy: 24 hrs. in advance. Groups of 16 or more call earlier

Ranger: Yes

Tee-off-Interval Time: 8 min.

Time to Play 18 Holes: 4½ hrs.

Course Hours/Earliest Tee-off: 6:30 a.m. weekends, 7 a.m. weekdays

Green Fees: Can$35 plus tax for 18 holes Fri., Sat., Sun., holidays. Can$32 plus tax for 18 holes Mon.-Thurs.

Cart Fees: Can$27 plus tax for 18 holes per cart

Credit Cards: American Express, MasterCard, Visa

Season: Mid-May to mid-Oct.

Course Comments: Can walk anytime. Yardage book available

Golf Packages: None

Discounts: Twilight. Seasonal, lower rates before mid-June, after mid-Oct.

Places to Stay Nearby: St. Christopher's Resort (709) 543–2525. GANDER: Hotel Gander (709) 256–3981; Holiday Inn (709) 256–3981. ST. JOHN'S: Best Western Travellers Inn (709) 722–5540; Hotel Newfoundland (709) 726–4980; Radisson Plaza Hotel (709) 739–6404

Local Attractions: Terra Nova National Park. SALVAGE: Fisherman's Museum. GREENSPOND: Museum. ST. JOHN'S: Newfoundland Museum, Memorial University Botanical Garden, Arts and Culture Centre, Anglican Cathedral, Newfoundland Museum at the Murray Premises, boating, fishing, hiking, bicycling, bird watching, camping. Trinity. Terra Nova National Park (709) 533–2801. Department of Development, Tourism and Promotions Branch (800) 563–6353

Directions: From St. John's (2½ hrs.): Trans Canada Hwy. west, look for signs for Twin Rivers Golf Course

Closest Commercial Airport: Gander International (1 hr.)

TWIN RIVERS GOLF COURSE

The Twin Rivers Golf Course is a 6546-yard layout beautifully situated near the Terra Nova National Park in Atlantic Canada. The course was developed as part of an agreement between the Province of Newfoundland and Parks Canada, whereby the province would allocate land on the west coast of Newfoundland for the development of Gros Morne National Park, while in return Parks Canada would develop an eighteen-hole golf course for the province in one of its national parks.

C. E. "Robbie" Robinson designed the first nine, which opened in 1983. These holes meander through the forest of spruce and fir and stretch along the rugged terrain of the Northwest River. Doug Currick was retained to develop another nine, which was integrated with the original layout and opened in 1991. His holes are numbers four, six through eleven, fourteen and fifteen. This course is set amidst the scenic beauty of trees, rocks, rivers and ocean and is populated by wildlife including moose, bald eagles, salmon and others.

The fairways on Twin Rivers are well guarded by trees, bunkers and scenic water hazards. The large bentgrass greens are moderately fast and undulating. They have a variety of interesting shapes and sizes, and they are well protected by aesthetically pleasing but dangerous bunkers. The 212-yard par-3 eleventh, for example, has a deep, elevated green protected by three deep bunkers to the left and a pair to the right.

The eighth, a 175-yard par 3, is one of five beautiful river holes, the others being numbers thirteen, fourteen, fifteen and seventeen. The tee shot is from an elevated tee down to a small green 80 feet below. The back and right of the green are guarded by three traps. A stream guards the front.

The 521-yard par-5 tenth is one of two beautiful ocean holes on the course. The tee shot is over 180 yards of ocean to a landing area protected by bunkers on both sides. To the right is the Atlantic Ocean, and to the left are trees. The second shot is to a landing area also framed by bunkers. The approach is to a medium-sized green protected by two bunkers to the left. The prevailing wind on this hole in the summer is from left to right, toward the ocean.

Twin Rivers also has Scottish-style open holes. The 542-yard par-5 sixth, for one, is the longest par 5 on the course. The wind is generally against the golfer. The tee shot is to a landing area protected by bunkers to the right and left. The landing area on the second shot also has bunkers. The medium-sized green is guarded by bunkers to the right and left front. Arrayed in back of the green are a series of mounds.

Twin Rivers provides you with an excellent golf challenge that is also beautiful. The course is now managed by St. Christopher's Resort, a 90-room luxury-hotel complex that includes dining, fitness and other recreational facilities as well as easy access to the golf course.

Recommended Golf Courses in Newfoundland

Bally Haly Golf and Curling Club, St. John's, (709) 753–8053, Semiprivate, 18/5835/71

Newfoundland and Labrador: Useful Information

Department of Tourism and Culture, P.O. Box 8700, St. John's, NF A1B4J6, (709) 729–2830, (800) 563–6353. Fax: (709) 0057. Approved accommodations by the Newfoundland and Labrador Department of Development, (709) 729–3831

Marine Atlantic, P.O. Box 250, North Sydney, NS B2A3U3, (902) 794–5700. Fax: (902) 564–7480 (ferry information). Reservations from continental U.S.: (800) 341–7981

NOVA SCOTIA

Course Name: HIGHLAND LINKS

Course Type: Resort
Resort: Keltic Lodge
Address: Ingonish Beach
Cape Breton, Nova Scotia
B0C1L0
Phone: (902) 285–2600 (Golf Course)
(902) 285–2880 (Resort)
Fax: (902) 285–2859 (Resort)
Telex: 019 35117

GOLF COURSE

Head Professional: Joe Robinson
Course Length/Par (All Tees): Back 6596/72, Middle 6198/72, Ladies' Forward 5664/76
Course Slope/Rating (All Tees): Back 139/72, Middle 134/71, Ladies' Forward 127/73
Course Architect: Stanley Thompson (1941)
Golf Facilities: Full Pro Shop X, Snack Bar X, Lounge X, Restaurant No, Locker Room X, Showers X, Club Rental X, Club Repair X, Cart Rental X, Instruction X, Practice Green X, Driving Range No, Practice Bunker No, Club Storage No
Tee-Time Reservation Policy: Up to 1 day in advance. Anytime for those who live outside the region
Ranger: Yes
Tee-off-Interval Time: 8 min.
Time to Play 18 Holes: 5 hrs.
Course Hours/Earliest Tee-off: 6:30 a.m.
Green Fees: Can$38 for 18 holes peak season
Cart Fees: Can$27 for 18 holes per cart
Pull Carts: Can$5 for 18 holes
Credit Cards: MasterCard, Visa
Season: Mid-May to end of Oct.
Course Comments: Can walk anytime. Yardage book available
Golf Packages: Available through lodge
Discounts: Seasonal, lower rates before July, after Aug. Junior
Places to Stay Nearby: Keltic Lodge (902) 285–2880. CHETICAMP: Laurie's Motel (902) 224–2400; Park View Motel (902) 224–3232. SYDNEY: Best

Western Bretoner (902) 539–8101;
Cambridge Suites Hotel (902) 562–
6500; Keddy's Inn (902) 539–1110

Local Attractions: Cape Breton Highlands
National Park, Alexander Graham Bell
Museum, Margaree Salmon Museum,
Gaelic College at St. Ann's, fishing,
boating, swimming, camping, nature
trails, hiking. Nova Scotia Tourism
Information Centre (902) 424–5000;
Cape Breton Highlands National Park,
(902) 285–2691 (winter), (902) 285–
2535 (summer). Cape Breton Island
Tourism (800) 565–9464

Directions: Trans Canada Hwy. to Cabot
Trail. Follow Cabot Trail to Ingonish/
Cape Breton Highlands National Park.
Follow signs to Keltic Lodge and golf
course

Closest Commercial Airports: Sydney
(1½ hrs.), Halifax International (5 hrs.)

HIGHLAND LINKS

Highland Links is a beautiful Scottish-
links course located within Cape Breton
Highlands National Park in Nova Scotia,
approximately 5 hours northeast by automobile from Halifax. This is the land of rough
oceans, high cliffs, hearty seafarers,
Acadian cuisine, highland nature walks
and lilting speech. Cape Breton Highlands
National Park was created in 1936 as the
first national park in the Atlantic Provinces.
It covers 366 square miles and is a haven
for backpacking, picnicking, fishing and
other recreational activities.

Stanley Thompson designed the Highland Links, which opened in 1941. The
6596-yard par-72 layout stretches 2 kilome-
ters out to sea on the Middle Head Peninsula and inland to the rugged highlands of
Cape Breton. Thompson called the Highlands Links his "Na Beanntan agus a'
Mhuir"—mountains and ocean—course.
Each narrow, rolling fairway has its own
view of glen or highlands. The Highland
Links was designed to be played, enjoyed
and experienced on foot. Motorized carts
were first permitted on this wonderful
layout in 1996.

The Highland Links features small,
undulating greens and unforgiving rough.

Most of the sand bunkers are around the
holes. The changeable wind adds another
dimension of challenge and uncertainty to
this layout. The Clyburn River Valley meanders within the golf course, and marvelous
hillsides of maple, hemlock, and white pine
dot the landscape.

One of the more memorable holes on
the course is the 548-yard par-5 fifteenth,
called "Tattie Bogle." Tattie Bogle are po-
tato pits or hillocks, where potatoes are
planted and covered with thatch. The fairway is lined with trees from the tee to the
narrow, deep green protected by traps and
mounds to the left and right. The tee shot
should ideally be hit over a rise to the left,
approximately 250 yards from the back
tees, to have a view of the green. Most golfers get stuck below the hill and have to hit
a blind second shot to a landing area 50 to
100 yards in front of the green. That leaves
a wedge to reach the putting surface. When
you tee it up on this hole, the ocean is
directly ahead of you on the horizon
behind the green.

"Hame Noo," or "home now," is the finishing hole. It plays 409 yards to a tricky,
small, crowned green guarded by a large
trap to the left and another to the right. Ideally, the tee shot is hit to the left side to
have a good angle onto this putting surface.
Usually, as is the case with most of the
holes on the back nine, the wind is at your
back during the summer months. On the
front nine, the wind is usually into your
face.

One of the most difficult par 3s at the
Highland Links is the twelfth, "Cleugh," a
term used for a deep gully or ravine with
precipitous sides. This hole plays 227 yards
from the back tees to a deep green un-
guarded by sand bunkers. To the left is a
drop-off to the Clyburn River, and trees
guard the right side and back of the green.
One of the most scenic walks on this
course is the walk from the twelfth green
to the thirteenth tee, a 1/4-mile stroll along
the Clyburn River.

The Keltic Lodge, first opened in 1940,
is one of the best hotels in Cape Breton
and is convenient to the golf course. The
main lodge has 32 guest rooms and a

dining room, lounge and cocktail lounge. The nearby White Birch Inn has 40 guest rooms, and there are separate cottages with 2 or 4 bedrooms, private bath, sitting room and fireplace. Babysitting, laundry and other services are available. Recreational amenities include a heated swimming pool, national park hiking trails, tennis, salt- and fresh-water beaches and fishing. For further information or reservations, the Manager, Keltic Lodge, P.O. Box 70, Ingonish Beach, NS B0C1L0, (902) 285–2880, (800) 565–0000 (Canada), (800) 492–0643 (ME only), (800) 341–6096 (U.S., except AK, HI, ME).

Many golfers who have played courses in both the United States and Canada rate Highland Links one of the finest courses in North America. *Score* magazine rates it among the best public golf courses in Canada. Recent improvements include a new irrigation system, resodded tees and renovation of the course's original bunkers. Fewer than 20,000 rounds of golf are played here every year, and the reasonable green fee is a daily fee. Golf packages are available through the Keltic Lodge.

Recommended Golf Courses in Nova Scotia

Abercrombie Golf Club, New Glasgow, (902) 752–6249, Semiprivate, 18/6300/72

Ashburn Golf Club, Halifax, (902) 861–4013, Semiprivate, 18/6450/72

Ken-Wo-Country Club, Wolfville, (902) 681–5388, Semiprivate, 18/6308/70

Oakfield Country Club, Grand Lake, (902) 861–2658, Semiprivate, 18/6781/73

Paragon Golf and Country Club, Kingston, (902) 765–2554, Semiprivate, 18/6245/72

Pines Hotel Golf Course, Digby, (902) 245–4104, Resort, 18/6204/71

Nova Scotia: Useful Information

Nova Scotia Department of Tourism, P.O. Box 130, Halifax, NS B3J2M7, (902) 424–5000, (800) 565–7166 (Canada), (800) 492–0643 (U.S., Maine), (800) 341–6096 (U.S. except ME)

Farm and Country Vacations Guide, c/o Jane Reid Stevens, Secretary, Nova Scotia Farm and Country Vacation Association, Newport Station, Hunts County, NS B0N2B0, (902) 798–5864

Sports and Recreation Commission, P.O. Box 864, Halifax, NS B3J2V2, (902) 424–7512 (recreation information)

Information Officer, Department of Lands and Forests, 1701 Hollis St., P.O. Box 698, Halifax, NS B3J2T9, (902) 424–6608 (fishing and hunting regulations)

Marine Atlantic (902) 794–5700, (800) 341–7981 (U.S.) (interprovince ferry information)

ONTARIO

Course Name: ANGUS GLEN GOLF CLUB

Course Type: Public
Address: 4495 Major Mackenzie E. Markham, Ontario, L6C1N9
Phone: (905) 887–5157
Fax: (905) 887–9424

GOLF COURSE

General Manager and Head Professional: Kevin Thistle
Course Length/Par (All Tees): Back 7300/72, Blue 6835/72, White 6332/72, Forward 5721/72
Course Slope/Rating (All Tees): Back 143/76, Blue 137/73.4, White 131/71.1, Forward NA/NA
Course Architect: Doug Carrick (1994)
Golf Facilities: Full Pro Shop X, Snack Bar X, Lounge X, Restaurant X, Locker Room X, Showers X, Club Rental X, Club Repair X, Cart Rental X, Instruction X, Practice Green X, Driving Range X, Practice Bunker X, Club Storage X
Tee-Time Reservation Policy: Up to 1 month in advance
Ranger: Yes
Tee-off-Interval Time: 9 min.
Time to Play 18 Holes: 4 hrs. 45 min.
Course Hours/Earliest Tee-off: 7 a.m.
Green and Cart Fees: Can$100 for 18 holes

Credit Cards: American Express, Master-
Card, Visa
Season: Mid-Apr. to mid-Nov.
Course Comments: Cart mandatory.
Yardage book available
Golf Packages: Inquire at pro shop
Discounts: Group tournament rates
Places to Stay Nearby: MARKHAM:
Journey's End Motel (905) 477–6077.
TORONTO: See page 773
Local Attractions: Markham Museum.
TORONTO: See page 773
Directions: 25 miles north of Toronto.
Take Hwy. 401 east to Hwy. 404 north
to Hwy. 7 east to Kennedy North Exit.
Take Kennedy north to Mackenzie and
golf course
Closest Commercial Airport: Lester B.
Pearson International (1 hr.)

ANGUS GLEN GOLF CLUB

Angus Glen, situated 25 miles north of
Toronto, is a Doug Carrick-designed layout
that has quick, undulating, bentgrass
greens, ample fairways, and over one hundred bunkers. This site was formerly a 225-
acre farm where champion Aberdeen
Angus cattle and thoroughbred horses were
bred. Wind can affect play on several holes
at Angus Glen. It swirls in the well-treed
valley holes, No. 4 through No. 8, and it
blows across the open, links-style holes on
Nos. 11 through 17. Bruce Creek, wetlands,
and ponds can come into play on half the
holes.

Angus Glen begins with its longest par
4, a 475 yarder, the most difficult hole on
the course. The tee shot on this slight dogleg right plays to a landing area with a cluster of four bunkers to its left. The farther
left you position your drive, the better the
angle coming in to a deep green. This target is protected by a large bunker to its left
and a large pond that severely narrows the
entranceway to the green from the right
side. If your tee shot does not fully roll to a
flat area beyond the bunkers, you will have
a tricky downhill lie. A bailout miss to the
left front of the green leaves you in a swale
of thick rough. This tough opening hole's
other tee distances are 445, 391, and 353
yards. A scenic par 3 on the front side is

the 208-yard sixth which plays from an
elevated tee to a long, shallow, undulating
green that is bordered by a bunker to its
left, another to its front left, and a pond to
the right. A pin position to the rear of this
three-tiered target puts a premium on club
selection and accuracy. The first nine concludes with a solid 550-yard par 5 dogleg
left whose tee is perched on a dramatic
elevated escarpment. The opening shot is
down 50 feet and over wetlands to a landing area framed by five bunkers to its left
and another two to the right. The tiered
green can be reached in two if you clear
the bunkers on the left with a draw and get
a good roll thereafter. The second shot,
which is likely to be from a downhill lie,
must be bounced in from the left yet avoid
a cluster of bunkers 100 yards from the
green and another group of bunkers bracketing the entranceway to the target.

There are many tough and memorable
holes on the back nine. The 435-yard par-4
tenth has a landing area bordered by trees
to the left and wetlands that quickly cut in
behind the bunker on the right. The second
shot, the most difficult approach shot on
the course, is over the wetlands to a deep
left-to-right angled two-tiered green that is
guarded by three deep bunkers in front and
two more to its rear right. The round concludes with a 420-yard par 4, another hole
that requires strategic thinking, positioning,
proper club selection, and execution. This
severe dogleg left has wetlands to the left
of the landing area. The tee shot must be to
the left, but not in this hazard. It also must
not be long enough to reach Bruce Creek
which cuts the fairway 100 yards from the
green. A well-executed drive will leave you
with slightly over 110 yards to the green. A
safer shot farther to the right could leave
you with 200 yards to the deep, four sec-
tioned green with a bunker to its left and
water on the right.

The clubhouse at Angus Glen is a classic Victorian design with banquet rooms,
dining room, complete locker room amenities, and a quality, professionally-staffed
pro shop. The practice facilities includes a
tiered three-acre teeing area on its driving
range, eight target greens, and a practice

fairway. There is also a short game area that includes bunkers and chipping and putting greens. *Golf Digest* selected Angus Glen the best new public course in Canada in 1995. Douglas Carrick, its designer and a native of Toronto, became a partner with noted Canadian golf architect C. E. "Robbie" Robinson, then continued the practice after Mr. Robinson died in 1989. Angus Glen is an outstanding achievement by Mr. Carrick and his associates.

Course Name: **DEERHURST RESORT Highlands, Lakeside Courses**

Course Type: Resort
Resort: Deerhurst Resort
Address: Rural Route 4
Huntsville, Ontario POA1KO
Phone: (705) 789–2381 (Golf Course), (800) 461–4393, (705) 789–6411 (Resort)
Fax: (705) 789–1666 (Golf Course), (705) 789–2431 (Resort)

GOLF COURSE

Head Professional: Paul W. Kennedy
Course Length/Par (All Tees): Highlands: Back 7011/72, Blue 6506/72, White 6012/72, Forward 5393/72. Lakeside: Back 4667/65, Middle 4142/65, Forward 3737/65
Course Slope/Rating (All Tees): Highlands: Back NA/73.5, Blue NA/71.0, White NA/68.5, Forward NA/65.5. Lakeside: Back NA/63, Middle NA/60, Forward NA/60
Course Architects: Highlands: Robert Cupp and Thomas McBroom (1990), Lakeside: C. E. Robinson (NA). Renovated by Thomas McBroom (1988)
Golf Facilities: Full Pro Shop X, Snack Bar X, Lounge X, Restaurant X, Locker Room No, Showers No, Club Rental X, Club Repair X, Cart Rental X, Instruction X, Practice Green X, Driving Range X, Practice Bunker No, Club Storage X
Tee-Time Reservation Policy: Call anytime
Ranger: Yes
Tee-off-Interval Time: 9 min.
Time to Play 18 Holes: 4½ hrs.

Course Hours/Earliest Tee-off: 6 a.m.
Green and Cart Fees: Can$84 for 18 holes Fri., Sat., Sun., holidays; Can$79 for 18 holes weekdays
Credit Cards: All major cards
Season: May through Oct. Busiest July and Aug.
Course Comments: Only club members may walk the course
Golf Packages: Through resort
Discounts: Resort guests. Twilight, replays, seasonal
Places to Stay Nearby: Best Western Hidden Valley Resort Hotel (705) 789–2301, (800) 528–1234; Comfort Inn by Journey's End Motels (705) 789–1701; Grandview Inn (705) 789–4417, (800) 267–0525
Local Attractions: Huntsville Dyer Memorial, Maddill Church, Lions Lookout Park, Algonquin Provincial Park, hunting, fishing, boating, bicycling, camping, winter skiing, boating, Muskoka Pioneer Village. Huntsville Chamber of Commerce, 800 West St. N., Huntsville, ON, Canada P0A1K0 (705) 789–4771. Almaguin Nipissing Travel Association, Regional Information Centre, Seymour St. and North Bay Bypass, Box 351, North Bay, Ontario, P1B8H5 (705) 474–6634
Directions: Take Hwy. 400 north to Hwy. 11 to Huntsville. Turn right onto Hwy. 60 to Deerhurst
Closest Commercial Airport: Lester B. Pearson International, Toronto (2½ hrs.)

RESORT

Date Built: 1896
No. of Rooms: 370 guest rooms and suites
Meeting Rooms: 21. Capacity of Largest: 400 persons. Meeting Space: 22,000 sq. ft.
Room Price Range: From just under Can$99 for a standard room to approximately $400 for a 3-bedroom condominium. Packages available year round
Lounges: Cypress Lounge, Tee Bar, Pub
Restaurants: The Lodge, The Pub, Steamers
Entertainment: Live entertainment and stage shows
Credit Cards: All major cards

General Amenities: Meeting and conference amenities including audiovisual, food service and secretarial support; general store, beauty salon; children's program for ages 5 to 12 years, outdoor playground

Recreational Amenities: Spa, sauna, whirlpool, horseback riding, boating, fishing, 8 outdoor tennis courts, 4 swimming pools, 1 racquetball court, 3 squash courts, 4 indoor tennis courts, horseback riding, water skiing, winter snow mobiling, dog-sledding, hay rides, tobogganning, sleigh rides, cross-country skiing, snoeshoeing, Hidden Valley Highlands Ski Club nearby

Reservation and Cancellation Policy: One night deposit required to hold reservation. 7-day cancellation policy to receive full refund. Balance of planned room fee must be paid 7 days in advance of arrival

Comments and Restrictions: No pets

DEERHURST RESORT

Deerhurst Resort is situated in the Lake of Bays Resort Region at the western entrance to the 3000-square-mile Algonquin Provincial Park two and one half hours north of Toronto. The resort's Highlands course was carved out of rock and trees. This layout has many elevation changes and tight fairways lined with maple, oak, pine, poplar, birch, and other varieties. The Highlands is bentgrass from tee to green. Creeks, ponds, and granite outcroppings add striking beauty to this course.

There are many excellent and difficult holes on this golf course. A tough par 3 is the 231-yard eighth that plays from an elevated tee down several feet and three club lengths to a huge double green, bordered by mounds and shared with No. 17. Two pot bunkers guard the left side of this deep green. A swirling wind can add difficulty to this scenic hole. The other tee distances on No. 8 are 200, 131, and 126 yards. The par 3s average over 200 yards from the tips at Deerhurst Highlands.

One of the most difficult par 4s on the course is the 465-yard second which plays from an elevated tee down to a fairway more than 150 feet below. It takes a drive of over 200 yards from the back tees to reach the landing area. The approach is uphill through a corridor of trees to a deep, narrow green with a shelf to its rear. Framing the green are a series of mounds and a cathedral of trees.

The par 5s at Deerhurst are varied and memorable. The 601-yard dogleg left fifth is the longest hole on the course. The tee shot plays into the wind to a landing area guarded by bunkers to its left at the turn of the dogleg. The fairway is lined with a series of mounds of thick Scottish fescue that severely penalizes stray shots. The second shot is to a landing area inside 150 yards, but to the right of a pond that narrows the fairway beginning 130 yards from the green. The approach is to a deep green bordered by the pond and a bunker to its left and a cluster of bunkers to its right. Fescue mounds in this area add additional problems for errant shots.

The Highlands demand that you keep the ball in the landing areas because of the trees, mounded rough, and bunkers. The greens range in depth from 24 to 41 yards and many of them are narrow or sit at tricky angles relative to bunkers and other obstacles. Many of the putting surfaces have mounds or shelves that make positioning of approach shots extremely important here.

Deerhurst Resort, part of the venerable Canadian Pacific Chain, is set along Peninsula Lake and Sunset Bay. Lakeside, a good 4667-yard par-65 short course, is within walking distance of the lodge. This course, which was originally designed by "Robbie" Robinson and was renovated by Tom McBroom in 1988, has eight par 3s, 9 par 4s, and one par 5 with hole distances ranging from 106 to 460 yards from the back tees. The 1000-acre Deerhurst Resort is open year round and has, after a major renovation in the 1980s, a full range of activities and amenities ranging from golf, tennis, and water sports to skiing, dogsledding, and sleigh rides. Should you wish to hone your golf game in the winter, Deerhurst has an indoor practice facility.

Course Name: GLEN ABBEY GOLF CLUB

Course Type: Public

Address: 1333 Dorval Drive
Oakville, Ontario L6J4Z3

Phone: (905) 844–1800, (905) 844–1811 (Starting Times)

Fax: (905) 844–2035

GOLF COURSE

Head Professional: Grover Braund

Course Length/Par (All Tees): Back 7102/73, Blue 6618/73, White 6202/73, Ladies' Forward 5577/74

Course Slope/Rating (All Tees): Back 140/77, Blue 132/75, White 127/73, Forward 117/NA, Ladies' Forward NA/73.5

Course Architect: Jack Nicklaus (1976)

Golf Facilities: Full Pro Shop X, Snack Bar X, Lounge X, Restaurant X, Locker Room X, Showers X, Club Rental X, Club Repair X, Cart Rental X, Instruction X, Practice Green X, Driving Range X, Practice Bunker X, Club Storage X

Tee-Time Reservation Policy: Call anytime in advance, prepay with credit card

Ranger: Yes

Tee-off-Interval Time: 8 to 9 min.

Time to Play 18 Holes: 4½ to 5 hrs.

Course Hours/Earliest Tee-off: 7:30 a.m. to dark

Green and Cart Fees: Can$145 for 18 holes with cart

Credit Cards: American Express, MasterCard, Visa

Season: Late April to Oct. 31

Course Comments: Cart mandatory

Golf Packages: Available through tour companies, not at club

Discounts: Seasonal, spring, from mid-Oct.

Places to Stay Nearby: Holiday Inn (905) 845–7561, (800) HOLIDAY; Howard Johnson (905) 842–4780. TORONTO: Bradgate Arms (416) 968–1331; Bristol Place Hotel (416) 675–9444; Camberley Club Hotel (416) 947–9025; Crowne Plaza Toronto Centre (416) 597–1400; Four Seasons Hotel (416) 964–0411; Guild Inn (416) 261–3331; Hilton Hotel (416) 869–3456; Inn on the Park (416) 444–2561; L'Hotel (416) 597–1400; Markham Suites (416) 470–8500; Skydome Hotel (416) 360–7100; Sutton Place Kempinski Hotel (416) 924–9221; Toronto Marriott Eaton Centre (416) 597–7200; Toronto Prince Hotel (416) 444–2511; Westin Harbour Castle (416) 869–1600

Local Attractions: Canadian National Tower, Skydome, Metro Toronto Zoo, Kortright Centre for Conservation, harbor front, Ontario Place, Parliament buildings, Ontario Science Centre, restaurants, theater, art galleries, shopping, Allan Botanical Gardens, Art Gallery of Ontario and the Grange, Campbell House, Casa Loma, City Hall and Nathan Phillips Square, Hockey Hall of Fame, Marine Museum of Upper Canada, Royal Ontario Museum, Toronto Island Parks, professional hockey, baseball, football, Gray Line boat tours of Toronto, thoroughbred horse racing. Metropolitan Toronto Convention and Visitors Association (416) 368–9821, (800) 363–1990

Directions: Queen Elizabeth to Oakville/Dorval Dr. exit, north 1 mi. to golf course (20 mi. west of Toronto)

Closest Commercial Airports: Mount Hope, Hamilton (30 min.); Lester B. Pearson International, Toronto (30 min.)

GLEN ABBEY GOLF CLUB

Glen Abbey is a tough, Jack Nicklaus–designed golf course called home by the Royal Canadian Golf Association. The Canadian Open is held annually on this open, 7102-yard par-73 layout that features large, fast, undulating bentgrass greens. The other tee distances are 6618, 6202 and 5577 yards from back to front. Glen Abbey has no members, is fully open to the public and is the first golf course in Canada designed specifically for tournaments.

The upper level of the golf course, or front nine, has gently rolling fairways and three lakes. Water comes into play on the beautiful 156-yard par-3 third hole, which is all carry over a lake to a deep but narrow green guarded by two large traps to the left, another to the right and water below the banked putting surface. Supposedly more than 15,000 balls a year are fished out of this lake, but the tendency is to use too much club, leaving a nasty sand shot or chip shot back toward the green and the water.

Another memorable par 3 on this side is the 197-yard seventh hole, which plays over a lake to a small green well protected by three traps. Often the wind is blowing into the golfer's face on this challenging hole.

One of the more difficult par 4s at Glen Abbey is the 458-yard ninth. Ideally, the tee shot is to the left side of a fairway guarded by trees on both sides and a bunker to the right of the landing area. The approach is over the corner of a lake on the right to a medium-sized green fronted by water.

The upper nine was originally somewhat uninteresting flatland, but in excess of 1 million cubic feet of earth was moved at Nicklaus's direction to provide rolling contours and mounds to the fairway. Earth was also moved to create amphitheaterlike settings for spectators who come to see the Open and other events. It should be noted that Nicklaus has never won the Canadian Open, the only PGA tour event held outside the United States, but has finished second 7 times.

The back nine, which wends its way through a natural river valley, has some of the toughest and most memorable holes on the course. The 452-yard par-4 eleventh, for example, requires a 220-yard carry from the back tees to the fairway 120 feet below. To the left of the landing area are trees and to the right a pair of large bunkers. The approach must carry a broad stream, Sixteen Mile Creek, that fronts a small green protected by a bunker on the right. The next hole is the most difficult par 3 on the course. It plays 187 yards to a wide, shallow green fronted by Sixteen Mile Creek and guarded by three traps in front and another to the rear. There is not much margin for error on this one.

The 529-yard par-5 thirteenth again has the stream as a nemesis. The tee shot is over the stream to a landing area protected by traps on the right and the stream, which is now on the left, only to later cut back in front of the green beginning 120 yards from the putting surface. The approach is usually a layup in front of this stream and then a wedge to the narrow, deep green guarded by a trap and the stream in front. This is a very delicate approach shot because if you are short sand or water awaits you, and if you are long it is very tough to recover.

The 426-yard par-4 fourteenth is a slight dogleg right to a landing area flanked by the stream on the right and two bunkers and water on the left. The approach is to a deep, elevated green with a swale in the center. A longer shot than one would think is required to reach this green, and if you have to putt through the swale, a three-putt is likely.

The trilevel clubhouse at Glen Abbey is well set up for tournaments, banquets, business meetings and other activities. The Jack Nicklaus Room is a private suite used for small dinners, cocktail receptions and business meetings. There is also the Main Restaurant, the Glen Abbey Room and a cocktail lounge. On site are locker rooms, showers and a full pro shop. Just outside are a practice range, practice bunkers and putting green. Clinics, total immersion workshops and individual lessons, including video swing analysis, are available from the staff of professionals. Also at Glen Abbey is the Royal Canadian Museum and Golf Hall of Fame, a must-visit. A new golf museum is in the process of being built and a 19th hole, a 137-yard par 3 that will be located between the original No. 11 and 12 holes, will be added. This extra hole will enable renovations, approved by Jack Nicklaus, to be made to the course while keeping 18 holes in play.

The Glen Abbey Golf Club is a mere 20 miles west of Toronto in the suburb of Oakville. The 200-acre property was once owned by the Jesuits, hence the "Swinging Monk" golf logo. The mature oak, maple, willow, pine, spruce and other varieties of trees on this former estate, coupled with Jack Nicklaus's first design as an independent architect, make this a beautiful and unique golf experience.

Course Name: **LIONHEAD GOLF AND COUNTRY CLUB**
Legends, Masters Courses

Course Type: Public
Address: 8525 Mississauga Road
Brampton, Ontario L6V3N2
Phone: (905) 455–4900

GOLF COURSE

Director of Golf: Beth Boyd
Course Length/Par (All Tees): Legends: Back 7198/72, Gold 6845/72, Blue 6409/72, Forward 5730/72. Masters: Back 7035/72, Gold 6632/72, Blue 6222/72, Forward 5553/72
Course Slope/Rating (All Tees): Legends: Back 153/76.4, Gold 150/74.7, Blue 145/72.6, Forward 138/69.5. Masters: Back 146/75.0, Gold 142/73.2, Blue 137/71.1, Forward 131/60
Course Architect: Ted Baker (1991)
Golf Facilities: Full Pro Shop X, Snack Bar X, Lounge X, Restaurant X, Locker Room X, Showers X, Club Rental X, Club Repair X, Cart Rental X, Instruction X, Practice Green X, Driving Range X, Practice Bunker X, Club Storage X
Tee-Time Reservation Policy: 1 day to 1 mo. in advance, Credit card confirmation required
Ranger: Yes
Tee-off-Interval Time: 8½ min.
Time to Play 18 Holes: 5 hrs.
Course Hours/Earliest Tee-off: 6:30 a.m.
Green and Cart Fees: Legends: Can$130 for 18 holes with cart. Masters: Can$115 for 18 holes with cart
Credit Cards: American Express, Master-Card, Visa
Season: Mid-April to Nov.
Course Comments: Cart mandatory. Yard-age book available
Golf Packages: For group bookings of 30 or more
Discounts: Seasonal, twilight
Places to Stay Nearby: MISSISSAUGA: Delta Meadowvale (905) 821–1981; Hilton International—Toronto Airport Hotel (905) 677–9900; Novotel Hotel (800) 221–4542; Ramada Airport West (905) 624–1144. TORONTO: Bradgate Arms (416) 968–1331; Bristol Place Hotel (416) 675–9444; Camberley Club Hotel (416) 947–9025; Four Seasons Hotel (416) 964–0411; Guild Inn (416) 261–3331; Hilton Hotel (416) 869–3456; Inn on the Park (416) 444–2561; L'Hotel (416) 597–1400; Markham Suites (416) 470–8500; Sutton Place Kempinski Hotel (416) 924–9221; Toronto Prince Hotel (416) 444–2511
Local Attractions: Canadian National Tower, Skydome, Metro Toronto Zoo, Kortright Centre for Conservation, harbor front, Ontario Place, Parliament buildings, Ontario Science Centre, restaurants, theater, art galleries, shopping, Allan Botanical Gardens, Art Gallery of Ontario and the Grange, Campbell House, Casa Loma, City Hall and Nathan Phillips Square, Hockey Hall of Fame, Marine Museum of Upper Canada, Royal Ontario Museum, Toronto Island Parks, professional hockey, baseball, football, Gray Line boat tours of Toronto, thoroughbred horse racing. Metropolitan Toronto Convention and Visitors Association (416) 368–9821, (800) 363–1990
Directions: Hwy. 401 to Mississauga Rd., Mississauga 3 mi. north to country-club entrance
Closest Commercial Airport: Lester B. Pearson International, Toronto (20 min.)

LIONHEAD GOLF AND COUNTRY CLUB

Lionhead is a 36-hole Ted Baker–designed layout in Brampton, an easy 30-minute drive from Toronto. This $30-million facility features such amenities as a 3-acre bentgrass practice range; an $8-million, 33,000-square-foot modern clubhouse with 4 locker rooms; a 410-seat dining room; custom club fitting; a complete pro shop; a bar and restaurant and others. Lionhead calls itself "the Most Private Public Golf Facility in Canada" and is heavily geared to corporate and other meetings and functions.

Lionhead is set on 422 acres and has four tee distances to choose from, enabling this layout to comfortably accommodate all skill levels. The hand-cut bentgrass greens at Lionhead are large, moderately fast and undulating. Lionhead plays through contoured terrain with man-made lakes and ponds, the Legends through the Credit River Valley and the Masters through rolling, well-treed territory featuring oaks and other varieties of trees. The entire 36 holes is a beautiful mix of meadows, wetlands, and rolling hills with mature trees.

There are many memorable holes at Lionhead, including the 458-yard tenth at Legends, which plays from a cliff straight down a tight fairway. The second shot is all carry to an elevated green well protected by bunkers. Water in the form of streams, especially the Credit River, ponds and wetlands comes into play on at least half the holes at Lionhead. The greens and fairways are strategically bunkered, requiring you to be careful about positioning, club selection and course management. The course has relatively tight landing areas, and you have to be careful about how you come onto the greens to avoid bunkers or three-putt situations.

The Masters is a more forgiving course with wider landing areas, rolling hills and many bunkers. The 411-yard par-4 fourth hole on the Masters is one of the more difficult holes on the course. Position on the tee shot is crucial, and the shot has to avoid hitting a sand bunker on the right or being blocked by trees. The approach shot is from a plateaued landing area over a ravine to a two-tiered green with a drop-off to the woods on the left. A series of pot bunkers covers the incline up to the green from the ravine.

The finishing hole on the Masters is a memorable test of golf. The tee shot on this 443-yard par 4 must avoid the bunkers near the landing area on the right. The approach is usually a long iron to a green guarded by traps to the right front and the rear. There is a drop-off down a bank to the right of the green.

No matter which course you try, the well-placed bunkers, water hazards, strategically placed trees, and large, undulating greens at Lionhead will require you to care-

fully plot your strategy, position your shots and pay close attention to club selection.

It is the Lionhead Golf and Country Club's stated goal to become the number one golf course in Canada. If you are in the Toronto area, be sure to give this golf course a try. It is one of the bright new lights on Canada's golf horizon.

Course Name: NATIONAL PINES

Course Type: Semiprivate
Address: Huronia South Road
              Barrie, Ontario L4M4S7
Phone: (705) 431–7000,
              (800) 663–1549 (Canada)

GOLF COURSE

Head Professional: Jeff Boismier
Course Length/Par (All Tees): Back 7013/72, Gold 6617/72, Blue 6144/72, White 5496/72, Forward 4980/72
Course Slope/Rating (All Tees): Back 144/74.5, Gold 137/72.6, Blue 132/70.2, White 121/66.7, Forward 117/64.3. Ladies' Blue 134/75.8, White 126/72.2, Forward 117/69.4
Course Architect: Thomas McBroom (1992)
Golf Facilities: Full Pro Shop X, Snack Bar X, Lounge X, Restaurant X, Locker Room X, Showers X, Club Rental X, Club Repair X, Cart Rental X, Instruction X, Practice Green X, Driving Range X, Practice Bunker X, Club Storage Members Only
Tee-Time Reservation Policy: Up to 4 days in advance with credit card guarantee
Ranger: Yes
Tee-off-Interval Time: 10 min.
Time to Play 18 Holes: 4½ hrs.
Course Hours/Earliest Tee-off: 6:30 a.m. Fri., Sat., Sun., holidays; 7:30 a.m. weekdays
Green Fees: Can$60 plus tax for 18 holes Fri., Sat., Sun., holidays; Can$50 for 18 holes weekdays
Cart Fees: Can$15 for 18 holes per person
Credit Cards: American Express, MasterCard, Visa
Season: May through Oct. Busiest June through Sept.

Course Comments: Can walk anytime. Yardage book available

Golf Packages: Inquire at pro shop

Discounts: Twilight after 2 p.m.

Places to Stay Nearby: Best Western Royal Oak Inn (705) 721–4848, (800) 528–1234; Comfort Inn (705) 721–1122, (800) 221–2222; Holiday Inn Barrie (705) 728–6191, (800) HOLIDAY; Horseshoe Resort (705) 835–2790

Local Attractions: Lake Simcoe, fishing, boating, Barrie Raceway, Springwater Provincial Park, seasonal festivals, MacLaren Art Centre, Simcoe County Museum, Canadian Forces Base Borden Military Museum, winter skiing. Georgian Lakelands Travel Association, 66 Coldwater St. East, Orillia, Ontario, L3V1W5 (705) 325–7160

Directions: Hwy. 400 to Innisfil Beach Rd. Proceed east on Innisfil Beach Rd. 1¼ mi. to Huronia Rd. (County Rd. 54). Proceed on Rte. 54 (Huronia) 2 mi. to golf course

Closest Commercial Airport: Lester B. Pearson International, Toronto (1 hr.)

NATIONAL PINES GOLF AND COUNTRY CLUB

National Pines is a Thomas McBroom-designed parkland-style course set on 200 acres of rolling hills and mature trees just south of Barrie and one hour northwest of Toronto. Rated one of the best new courses by *Golf Digest* in 1993, National Pines is bentgrass from tee to green and has bluegrass rough. The fairways and green areas are well-bunkered and Lovers Creek and wetlands come into play on several holes.

National Pines eases you into the course with a 521-yard par 5 that plays 497, 470, 446, and 421 yards form its other tee distances. A slight dogleg left, the tee shot landing area is guarded by a bunker to the left and the second shot is toward a deep green protected by three bunkers to its left and another to its top right. After a short par 4 the course toughens up considerably with three of its most difficult holes, all par 4s. The 443-yard third plays to a narrow landing area bordered by wetlands to the right and trees to the left. The approach is to a narrow, long green angled from right to left and guarded by two bunkers to the right. The depth of approach becomes very shallow should you have to come in from the right. The necessity for solid tee shots in order to set up optimimum approach angle that will take obstacles such as bunkers out of play is a major consideration at National Pines. The 458-yard fourth is the most difficult hole on this course. The drive is to a narrow landing area squeezed by a bunker to the left and wetlands to the right. The approach is to a narrow, deep, two-tiered green bordered by wetlands to the right and guarded by a bunker on the left. The sixth hole, a slight dogleg right, plays 449 yards from the back tees to a tee shot landing area with a bunker and out of bounds to its right. The approach is to a narrow, deep green with two bunkers on the left.

A good hole on the back nine is the 361-yard par-4 fifteenth which forces you to choose between two fairway landing areas split by wetlands. There is little risk on the tee shot if you lay up to the left before the wetlands. But then your second shot must clear for bunkers to reach a shallow target just behind them. Should you venture to hit a 212-yard drive (or more) over the wetlands to the fairway on the right, the bunkers will be taken out of play and you will have a deeper landing to work with.

The clubhouse at National Pines, a member-owned club that recently made its facilities accessible to the public, is a modern, pine post-and-beam structure with banquet, dining, and other amenities. The practice area has a three-tiered tee area on its driving range which has seven target flags. Putting and chipping greens and practice bunkers are also available. Thomas McBroom, a native of Toronto and a former assistant to C. E. "Robbie" Robinson, is a bright young star in the golf architecture galaxy. You should try this course.

**Course Name: ROSELAND GOLF
AND CURLING CLUB**

Course Type: Public
Address: 455 Kennedy Drive West
                Windsor, Ontario N9G1S8
Phone: (519) 969–3810 (Pro Shop)

GOLF COURSE

Head Professional: Glenn Patterson
Course Length/Par (All Tees): Back
    6503/72, Middle 6176/72, Ladies' For-
    ward 6037/75. 9-hole course: 900/27
Course Slope/Rating (All Tees): Back
    119/72.0, Middle 116/69.3, Ladies' For-
    ward 123/73.1. 9-hole course: NA/NA
Course Architect: Donald Ross (1924)
Golf Facilities: Full Pro Shop X, Snack
    Bar X, Lounge X, Restaurant X,
    Locker Room X, Showers X, Club
    Rental X, Club Repair X, Cart Rental
    X, Instruction X, Practice Green X,
    Driving Range X, Practice Bunker X,
    Club Storage No
Tee-Time Reservation Policy: First come,
    first served Mon. to Fri. Call Wed. from
    9 a.m. for Sat., Thurs. 9 a.m. for Sun.
    and holiday tee times
Ranger: Yes
Tee-off-Interval Time: 8 min.
Time to Play 18 Holes: 5 hrs.
Course Hours/Earliest Tee-off: 6 a.m. to
    dark
Green Fees: Can$27 for 18 holes Sat.,
    Sun., holidays; Can$25 for 18 holes
    weekdays. Can$16.50 for 9 holes Sat.,
    Sun., holidays; Can$15.50 for 9 holes
    weekdays
Cart Fees: Can$28 for 18 holes per cart,
    Can$15 for 9 holes
Credit Cards: MasterCard
Season: March 15 to Nov. 15
Course Comments: Can walk anytime
Golf Packages: None
Discounts: Seniors (weekdays to 9 a.m.).
    Twilight rate after 6 p.m. weekdays, 4
    p.m. weekends and holidays
Places to Stay Nearby: Journey's End
    Motel (519) 972–1331, (800) 668–4200;
    Relax Inn (519) 972–1100, (800) 661–
    9563; Best Western Continental Inn
    (519) 966–5541; Holiday Inn (519) 253–

4411. PELEE ISLAND: Mill Point Lodge
Country Inn (519) 724–2223
Local Attractions: Art Gallery of Windsor,
    Hiram Walker Historical Museum,
    University of Windsor, Windsor City
    Market, Windsor Raceway, Pelee Island,
    Ojibway Park, Jackson Park, Olde Sand-
    wich, Victoria Avenue, fishing, boating,
    annual festivals. Tourist and Convention
    Bureau of Windsor and Essex County
    (519) 255–6530
Directions: From Toronto (3½ hrs.): Hwy.
    401 west, Detroit tunnel exit, to first set
    of lights (Cabana Rd.), left on Cabana to
    McGraw, left at McGraw, follow golf
    course sign, to stop sign (Kennedy Dr.),
    turn left on Kennedy. From Detroit (45
    min.): Cross Ambassador Bridge to
    Canada, take 3 east to Cabana Rd., turn
    left to golf course sign (McGraw St.),
    turn right to Kennedy Dr., left to golf
    course
Closest Commercial Airports: Windsor (10
    min.); Detroit Metropolitan, MI (1 hr.)

ROSELAND GOLF AND CURLING CLUB

The Roseland Golf and Curling Club is
a 6503-yard par-72 Donald Ross–designed
course that originally opened in 1924 and
was a privately owned club until the city of
Windsor purchased it in 1972. Today it is a
stop on the Canadian Professional Golf
Association Tour and is rated among the
top fifteen best public golf courses in
Canada by *Score* magazine.

Roseland is well treed with narrow fairways and small, moderately fast, undulating greens protected by many of the 68
sand bunkers on the course. Every effort
has been made to retain the original Ross
design.

The par 3s at Roseland are very challenging and include the 196-yard fourth
hole, which has a slightly elevated, forward-
sloping green protected by a large trap to
the left and another to the front and right.
A large walnut tree stands slightly to the
right of this green, providing another
obstacle to consider.

The three excellent and challenging
finishing holes at Roseland begin with the

167-yard par-3 sixteenth, which plays to a slightly elevated green guarded by traps to the left and to the right. The 423-yard par-4 seventeenth is tightly treed with a tee-shot landing area perhaps 35 yards wide. The approach is to a small green guarded to the right front by a bunker. A shelf is on the left side of the green, making the second shot tricky.

The finishing hole is rated the number-1-handicap hole on the course. This 450-yard par-4 dogleg left has a narrow fairway, considering the length of the hole. The approach shot is usually a long iron or fairway wood to a crowned green with traps to the left and right front. This elevated target is difficult to hold on the long second shot.

The clubhouse has banquet facilities, a curling rink, restaurant, bar, locker rooms and showers, and a pro shop. Nearby is a 900-yard nine-hole course, putting green and practice bunker. Group and individual instruction is available, and walking is allowed anytime on this quality municipal layout.

This is a very busy golf course because of its excellent design and reputation for high maintenance standards. Many people drive from the Detroit area, less than 1 hour away, to play here. For a memorable golf experience on a traditional Donald Ross layout, Roseland is worth a visit.

Recommended Golf Courses in Ontario

Barrie Area:

Hawk Ridge Golf Club, Orilla, (705) 329–4653, Public, 18/6675/72

Horseshoe Valley Resort, Barrie, (705) 835–2790, Resort, 18/6167/72

Monterra Golf Course, Collingwood, (705) 445–0231, Resort, 18/6581/72

Kingston:

Glen Lawrence Golf and Country Club, Kingston, (613) 545–1021, Semiprivate, 18/6584/71

London:

Forest City National Golf Club, London, (519) 451–0994, Public, 18/6850/72

Within 1 Hour of Toronto:

Blue Springs Golf Club, Acton, (519) 853–4434, Semiprivate, 18/6575/72

Carlisle Golf and Country Club, Carlisle, (905) 689–8820, (800) 661–4343, Public, 18/6557/72

Chestnut Hill Golf and Country Club, Richmond Hill, (416) 213–7456, Semiprivate, 18/7087/72

Hockley Valley Resort Golf Club, Orangeville, (519) 942–0754, 18/6391/70

Markham Green Golf and Country Club, Markham, (905) 294–6156, Semiprivate, 18/6538/71

Nobleton Lakes Golf Club, Nobleton, (905) 859–4070, Public, 18/7089/72

Osprey Valley Heathlands Golf Course, Alton, (416) 454–4653, Public, 18/6810/71

Peninsula Lakes Golf Club, Fenwick, (905) 892–8844, Public, 18/6750/72

Pheasant Run Golf Club, Sharon, (416) 898–3917, Public. Southern/Midlands: 18/6450/72. Midlands/Highlands: 18/6578/72. Highlands/Southern: 18/6350/72

Richmond Hill Golf Club, Richmond Hill, (905) 889–4653, Public, 18/6004/70

Royal Woodbine Golf Club, Etobicoke, (416) 674–4653, Semiprivate, 18/6545/72

Silver Lakes Golf and Country Club, Newmarket, (905) 836–8070, Semiprivate, 18/6910/72

St. Andrews Valley Golf Club, Aurora, (905) 727–7888, Public, 18/7304/72

Thunderbird Golf and Country Club, Ashburn, (905) 686–1121, Semiprivate, 18/6469/72

Whirlpool Golf Course, Niagara Falls, (416) 356–1140 (1½ hrs. from Toronto), Public, 18/6994/72

Within 1 Hour of Ottawa:

Brockville Country Club, Brockville, (613) 342–2468, Semiprivate, 18/6550/72

Eagle Creek Golf Club, Dunrobin, (613) 832–0728, Semiprivate, 18/7067/72

Kanata Lakes Golf and Country Club, Kanata, (613) 592–1631, Semiprivate, 18/6730/70

Loch March Golf and Country Club, Kanata, (613) 839–5885, Public, 18/6750/72

Upper Canada Golf Club, Morrisburg, (613) 543–2003, Semiprivate, 18/6922/72

Southampton:

Chippewa Golf and Country Club, Southampton, (519) 797–3684, Semiprivate, 18/6420/72

Windsor:

Kingsville Golf Club, Kingsville, (519) 733–6385, Public. Red/White: 18/6297/72. White/Gold: 18/6305/72. Red/Gold: 18/6518/72

Ontario: Useful Information

Ministry of Culture, Tourism and Recreation, 77 Bloor St. W, Toronto, ON M7A2E5, (416) 314–0944 (English, in Toronto), (416) 314–0956 (French, in Toronto), (800) 668–2746 (English, U.S. and Canada), (800) 268–3736 (French, Canada except YT, NT)

Fish and Wildlife Division, Ministry of Natural Resources, Whitney Block, Queen's Park, Toronto, ON 47A1W3, (416) 314–1177 (fishing regulations), (416) 314–2225 (hunting regulations)

Ontario Accommodation Directory (free copy), Ontario Travel, Queens Park, Toronto, ON M7A2R9 (800) 668–2746

Metropolitan Toronto Convention and Visitors Association, 207 Queen's Quay W, Ste. 590, P.O. Box 126, Toronto, ON M5J1A7, (416) 368–9521, (800) 363–1990

Ottawa Tourism and Convention Authority, 130 Albert, Suite 1800, Ottawa, ON K1P5G4, (613) 237–5150

Niagara Falls Visitor and Convention Bureau, 5433 Victoria Ave., Niagara Falls, ON L2G3L1, (905) 356–6061

Niagara Parks Commission, P.O. Box 150, Niagara Falls, ON L2E6T2, (905) 356–2241

PRINCE EDWARD ISLAND

Course Name: BRUDENELL GOLF AND COUNTRY CLUB

Course Type: Resort
Resort: Rod Brunnell Resort and Conference Center P.O. Box 67, Cardigan, Prince Edward Island C0A1G0
Address: Georgetown Road/Box 11 Cardigan, Prince Edward Island, C0A1G0
Phone: (902) 652–2342 (Golf Course), (902) 652–2332 (Resort)
Fax: (902) 652–2898 (Golf Course/ Government Office), (902) 652–2886 (Resort)

GOLF COURSE

Head Professional: Ron Giggey

Course Length/Par (All Tees): Back 6517/72, White 6037/72, Red 5662/69, Forward 5082/69

Course Slope/Rating (All Tees): Back 131/72, White 128/70, Red 116/68. Ladies' Red NA/73.5, Forward NA/70.5

Course Architect: Robbie Robinson (1968)

Golf Facilities: Full Pro Shop X, Snack Bar No, Lounge No, Restaurant No, Locker Room X, Showers X, Club Rental X, Club Repair Minor, Cart Rental X, Instruction X, Practice Green X, Driving Range X, Practice Bunker X, Club Storage X

Tee-Time Reservation Policy: Anytime

Ranger: Yes

Tee-off-Interval Time: 8 min.

Time to Play 18 Holes: 4½ hrs.

Course Hours/Earliest Tee-off: 6 a.m.

Green Fees: Can$34 for 18 holes

Cart Fees: Can$25 for 18 holes per cart

Credit Cards: All major cards

Season: May through Oct. Busiest July and August

Course Comments: Can walk anytime. Yardage book available

Golf Packages: Through the resort

Discounts: Lower rates up to mid-June, after Sept. Twilight

Places to Stay Nearby: BRACKLEY BEACH: Shaw's Hotel and Cottages (902) 672-2022. CHARLOTTETOWN: See page 781

Local Attractions: General P.E.I.: Victoria-by-the-Sea, Basin Head Fisheries Museum, Prince Edward Island National Park, Fort Amherst Port LaJoie National Historic Site, Lord Selkirk Pioneer Settlement, Acadian Museum of Prince Edward Island. CHARLOTTETOWN: See page 781

Directions: From Charlottetown (1 hr.): Drive east on Hwy. 1 to Hwy. 3 to golf course near Georgetown

Closest Commercial Airport: Charlottetown Municipal (1 hr.)

BRUDENELL GOLF AND COUNTRY CLUB

The Brudenell Golf and Country Club is a 6517-yard Robbie Robinson–designed layout located within the 1485-acre Brudenell River Provincial Park one hour east of Charlottetown. The course is set on 200 acres of former farmland overlooking the Brudenell River. Brudenell is bentgrass from tee to its large greens. There are a variety of blind tee shots here such as the first shot on the 490-yard par-5 fourth, a dogleg left with trees bordering the right side and most of the left. You may ascend to an observation tower to survey the scenic golf course and determine whether it is safe to tee off. From this vantage point you will note that water can come into play on many holes at Brudenell. The wind is also a factor here as it sweeps up the river from the Atlantic mid-morning, then dies down in the afternoon.

The toughest par 4 on the course is the 462-yard second, a slight dogleg left that plays uphill. The par 3s are scenic and memorable. The 163-yard fifth borders the river to the left making any pulled shot a disaster. The beautiful 143-yard tenth plays over a pond to a well-bunkered green. Behind the tee and to the left is the river.

Brudenell has a symmetrical six par 3s, 4s, and 5s. The longest par 3 is the 225-yard sixteenth, considered the most difficult hole to par on the course. Correct club selection and, of course, proper execution

of the tee shot is required to avoid the heavy rough, grassy mounds, and bunkers around the green. Bunkers, almost one hundred of them, add to the difficulty of this great golf course.

Other golfers at Brudenell will include international tourists as well as local farmers, fishermen, and town folk. This is a scenic walk through woodlands and along waterways. The local notoriously coarse red bunker sand has been replaced by more beneficent white sand. Near the modest clubhouse is a good practice range with distance signs. Nearby are putting and chipping greens.

Course Name: THE LINKS AT CROWBUSH COVE

Course Type: Public
Address: Highway 2/P.O. Box 204 Morell, Prince Edward Island, C0A150
Phone: (902) 961–2800
Fax: (902) 961–2257

GOLF COURSE

Head Professional: Steven Dowling
Course Length/Par (All Tees): Back 6903/72, Blue 6475/72, White 6004/72, Forward 4965/72
Course Slope/Rating (All Tees): Back NA/75, Blue 127/73, White 120/71, Forward 116/67
Course Architect: Thomas McBroom (1993)
Golf Facilities: Full Pro Shop X, Snack Bar X, Lounge X, Restaurant X, Locker Room X, Showers X, Club Rental X, Club Repair X, Cart Rental X, Instruction X, Practice Green X, Driving Range X, Practice Bunker X, Club Storage X
Tee-Time Reservation Policy: Anytime with a major credit card
Ranger: Yes
Tee-off-Interval Time: 10 min.
Time to Play 18 Holes: 4½ hrs.
Course Hours/Earliest Tee-off: 7 a.m.
Green Fees: Can$45 for 18 holes
Cart Fees: Can$25 for 18 holes per cart
Credit Cards: All major cards

Season: May through Oct. Busiest months July and Aug.

Course Comments: Can walk anytime

Golf Packages: Inquire at the pro shop

Discounts: Lower rates before May through mid-June, Oct. Twilight

Places to Stay Nearby: CHARLOTTETOWN: See page 781

Local Attractions: See page 781

Directions: From Charlottetown (20 mi.): Take Hwy. 2 east to golf course

Closest Commercial Airport: Charlottetown Municipal (30 min.)

THE LINKS AT CROWBUSH COVE

The Links at Crowbush Cove, one of the best new public golf courses in Canada, is set in the dunes of Lakeside in northeastern Prince Edward Island. Designed by Canadian Thomas McBroom, who also created the outstanding Barrie National Pines and Deerhurst Highlands (with Robert Cupp) in Ontario, this course offers ocean views from every hole, undulating bentgrass greens, pot bunkers, a mixture of wild and natural grasses, dunes anchored by marram grass, bayberry bushes and evening primrose, and wetlands. An Audubon conservation area, Crowbush Cove teems with wildlife including cormorants, wood ducks, mergansers, heron, and other creatures.

The first five holes at Crowbush Cove are lined with spruce, fir, birch, hemlock, and other trees, but then the course opens up and the variable ocean winds become more of a factor. Water in the form of wetlands, ponds, streams, and the Atlantic Ocean can come into play on more than half the holes. Almost one hundred bunkers add another level of difficulty to this course.

One of the most scenic holes at Crowbush Cove is the 565-yard par-5 eleventh which plays from an elevated tee one hundred feet above the fairway. A prevailing tailwind helps to shorten the hole, but the second shot is still usually a layup in front of a marsh that begins 150 yards from a small green. The approach is over a minefield of pot bunkers to a target guarded by sand bunkers to its right.

The round concludes with a short par 3 and a lengthy par 4. The 113-yard seventeenth plays toward the ocean and demands a knock-down shot to keep the ball from being buffeted to some unknown destination. The 464-yard eighteenth offers an elevated tee shot aided by a tailwind as you work your way from the ocean and back to the clubhouse. The second shot is usually a long-iron or fairway wood to an uphill green guarded by mounds and bunkers. This ample bentgrass putting surface is bisected by a swale.

Crowbush Cove adds to the convenient collection of quality public golf courses that includes Brudenell and Mill River in this region. This great walking course also has a spacious driving range with target greens, a practice bunker, and putting and chipping greens. The Links at Crowbush Cove is the site of the 1997 Canadian Amateur Golf Championship.

Course Name: MILL RIVER

Course Type: Public

Address: Highway 2/P.O. Box 399 O'Leary, Prince Edward Island C0B1V0

Phone: (902) 859–8873 (Golf Course) (902) 859–3555 (Resort)

Fax: (902) 859–2486, (800) 377–8339 (Resort)

GOLF COURSE

Head Professional: R. Mark Roberts

Course Length/Par (All Tees): Back 6830/72, White 6467/72, Red 6122/72, Forward 5400/72

Course Slope/Rating (All Tees): Back 134/71.0, White 127/68.5, Ladies' Red 131/74, Ladies' Forward 122/70.5

Course Architect: C. E. "Robbie" Robinson (1971). Graham Cooke (Renovation, NA)

Golf Facilities: Full Pro Shop X, Snack Bar X, Lounge X, Restaurant X, Locker Room X, Showers X, Club Rental X, Club Repair Minor, Cart Rental X, Instruction X, Practice Green X, Driving Range X, Practice Bunker X, Club Storage X

Tee-Time Reservation Policy: Up to 1 year in advance

Ranger: Yes

Tee-off-Interval Time: 8 min.

Time to Play 18 Holes: 4½ hrs.

Course Hours/Earliest Tee-off: 6:30 a.m.

Green Fees: Can$30 plus tax for 18 holes

Cart Fees: Can$25 for 18 holes per cart

Credit Cards: American Express, Debit, MasterCard, Visa

Season: May to end of Oct. Busiest season July through Aug.

Course Comments: Can walk anytime

Golf Packages: Available through resort

Discounts: Seasonal (May to mid-June, mid-Sept. to mid-Oct.). Weekly rates

Places to Stay Nearby: O'LEARY: Rodd's Mill River Resort and Conference Center (902) 859–3555. SUMMERSIDE: Best Western Linkletter Inn (902) 436–2157; Quality Inn Garden of the Gulf (902) 436–2295. CHARLOTTETOWN: The Charlottetown (902) 894–7371; Prince Edward Hotel and Convention Centre (902) 566–2222, (800) 828–7447

Local Attractions: CAVENDISH: Prince Edward Island Marine Aquarium, Ripley's Believe It or Not Museum, Royal Atlantic Wax Museum, amusement parks. ALBERTON: Alberton Museum, Prince Edward Island miniature railway. CHARLOTTETOWN: Confederation Centre of the Arts, Cameo Cabaret, MacKenzie Theatre, Holland College Centre of Creative Arts, MicMac Indian Village. KENSINGTON: Woodleigh, Prince Edward Island National Park, camping, charter boats, fishing, bicycling. PORT HILL: Green Park shipbuilding and historic house. Prince Edward Island Department of Tourism and Parks (902) 368–4444, (800) 565–0267

Directions: Hwy. 2, 40 min. west from Summerside to Trans Canada Hwy., to golf course, which is just off Hwy. 2

Closest Commercial Airport: Charlottetown Municipal (1½ hrs.)

MILL RIVER

Mill River is a 6830-yard par-72 tightly treed layout situated in western Prince Edward Island, midway between O'Leary and Alberton. The course was designed by C. E. "Robbie" Robinson and opened in 1971. The layout is beautifully situated on 300 acres of land, and water comes into play on six holes. The course has been rated one of the best public golf courses in Canada by *Score* magazine, and it has been the site of the Canadian Junior Men's Golf Championship.

The greens at Mill River are large, undulating and often tricky to read. Many are elevated. Probably the most memorable hole at Mill River is the 419-yard par-4 seventh, whose fairway is split by a chain of ponds running up the center from tee to green. There is very little room on either side of these hazards because of the tightly treed fairways. As a result, most golfers use irons off the tee.

The 365-yard par 4 finishing hole at Mill River is a dramatic dogleg left. The tee shot is toward the corner of the dogleg, which is protected and bunkers on the left. The approach is toward a green encircled by traps and fronted by a large pond.

Mill River is situated in Mill River Provincial Park. Rodd's Mill River Resort is on site, with dining facilities and accommodations. Nearby is a marina, tennis courts, camping, cross-country skiing and other recreational amenities. The resort also has convention facilities, an indoor swimming pool, squash courts and a Nautilus room. For further information about accommodations and golf packages contact Rodd's Mill River Resort, P.O. Box 399, O'Leary, Prince Edward Island C0B1V0, (902) 859–3555.

Prince Edward Island has a green-fee-card golf discount program for a variety of golf courses in the province. For further information contact Golf Prince Edward Island, P.O. Box 2653, Charlottetown, Prince Edward Island C1A8C3, (902) 566–1313.

Recommended Golf Courses in Prince Edward Island

Belvedere Golf and Winter Club, Charlottetown, (902) 892–7838, Semiprivate, 18/6372/72

Green Gables Golf Course, Cavendish, (902) 963–2488, Public, 18/6500/72

Stanhope Golf and Country Club, Stanhope, (902) 672–2842, Public, 18/6439/72

Prince Edward Island: Useful Information

Prince Edward Island Department of Tourism and Parks, Visitor Services Division, Box 940, Charlottetown, Prince Edward Island C1A7M5, (800) 565–0243 (ON, Quebec, NF), (800) 565–7421 (NB, NS), (902) 368–4444 (U.S. west of the Mississippi), (800) 565–0267 (U.S. east of the Mississippi), (800) 565–0267 (North America)

Marine Atlantic (902) 794–5700. Northumberland Ferries Ltd. (800) 565–0201 (from PE, NS, NB) (interprovince ferry information)

Department of the Environment, Fish and Wildlife Division, P.O. Box 2000, Charlottetown, PE C1A7N8, (902) 368–4683 (fishing and hunting regulations)

QUEBEC

Course Name: CARLING LAKE

Course Type: Semiprivate
Address: Route 327
Pine Hill, Quebec J0V1A0
P.O. Box 1120, Brownsburg,
Quebec J0V1A0 (Mailing
Address)
Phone: (514) 476–1212 (Golf Course)
(514) 533–9211 (Resort)
Fax: (514) 533–5813 (Golf Course)

GOLF COURSE

Head Professionals: André Gagnier, Jean Millaire
Course Length/Par (All Tees): Back 6691/72, Middle 6307/72, Forward 5352/72
Course Slope/Rating (All Tees): Back 126/72.5, Middle 122/71, Ladies' Forward 123/71.5
Course Architect: Howard Watson (1961)
Golf Facilities: Full Pro Shop X, Snack Bar X, Lounge X, Restaurant X, Locker Room X, Showers X, Club Rental X, Club Repair No, Cart Rental X, Instruction X, Practice Green X, Driving Range X, Practice Bunker No, Club Storage No

Tee-Time Reservation Policy: Up to 3 mos. in advance
Ranger: Yes
Tee-off-Interval Time: 8 min.
Time to Play 18 Holes: 5 hrs.
Course Hours/Earliest Tee-off: 6 a.m. weekends, 7 a.m. weekdays
Green and Cart Fees: Can$60 for 18 holes with cart Fri., Sat., Sun., holidays; Can$50 for 18 holes with cart weekdays
Credit Cards: American Express, MasterCard, Visa
Season: May to mid-Oct. Busiest June-Aug.
Course Comments: Cart mandatory
Golf Packages: None
Discounts: Replays
Places to Stay Nearby: ON SITE: Lake Carling Hotel (514) 476–1212. LACHUTE: Manoir La Lorraine (514) 562–5256; Motel Weldon (514) 562–2456. NEAR MT. TREMBLANT: Laurentians/Le Tremblant Club (800) 363–2413; Auberge Chateau Beauvallon (819) 425–7275; Mont Tremblant Resort (819) 425–8711, (800) 461–8711; Village Mont St. Sauveur (514) 227–4671; Hotel l'Eau à la Bouche (514) 229–2991; Le Chanticleer (800) 363–2420; Far Hills Inn (800) 567–6636. Laurentian Tourist Office and Central Reservations at more than 100 hotels, motels and condominiums (800) 363–5606. MONTREAL: Bonaventure Hilton International (514) 878–2332, (800) 268–9275; Ritz Carlton (514) 842–4212, (800) 363–0366; Meridien (514) 285–1450, (800) 361–8234; Four Seasons (514) 284–1110, (800) 268–6282; Best Western Hotel International (Dorval Airport) (514) 631–4811, (800) 361–2254; Holiday Inn Airport (Dorval Airport) (514) 739–3391, (800) 465–4329. BED AND BREAKFASTS: Bed and Breakfast lodging/central information (514) 252–3138
Local Attractions: LAURENTIANS: Skiing, ice-skating, restaurants, hiking, camping, fishing, boating, bicycling, antiquing. MONTREAL: Old Montreal, restaurants, shopping, Chinatown, Forum, Botanical Garden, Museum of Fine Arts, Olympic Stadium, McGill University, Indian Reserve, Mount Royal,

Montreal Symphony, Dow Planetarium, art galleries, museums, theater, Montreal Opera, ballet, Place des Arts, St. Lawrence River cruises, Japanese Garden, Chinese Garden, horse racing, curling, bicycling, horseback riding, fishing, boating, skiing, ice-skating. Greater Montreal Convention and Tourism Bureau (514) 844–5400, (800) 363–7777. Information on parks, animal reserves, reservations (418) 890–5349

Directions: From La Chute: Hwy. 327 north toward Arundel, golf course on the right near Pine Hill

Closest Commercial Airports: Dorval International, Montreal (1 hr.); Mirabel International, Montreal (1 hr.)

CARLING LAKE

Carling Lake is a beautiful and challenging 6645-yard layout designed by Howard Watson and situated in the Laurentians, approximately 1 hour northwest of Montreal near Pine Hill. Watson was born in Dresden, Ontario, in 1907 and attended the University of Toronto. He worked for Stanley Thompson and later, in 1930, with Robert Trent Jones, Sr., in the newly formed Thompson, Jones and Co. During the Depression, he worked at various jobs in addition to his work at Thompson and Jones, including stints as a greenskeeper and turf consultant. He served in World War II with the Royal Canadian Engineers, then formed his own firm, Canadian Golf Landscaping Ltd., in Quebec in 1949. He designed and remodeled many golf courses in Canada, the United States, the Caribbean and South America. Some of his courses include Don Valley Municipal in Toronto; Le Chanticleer Golf Club in Quebec; and the A. D. Dana Estate Golf Club in Stowe, Vermont.

Carling Lake was formerly a private club but is now open to the public. The course features mature trees; rolling fairways with some dramatic elevation changes; large, moderately fast, undulating bentgrass greens; strategically placed bunkers; and water hazards on four holes. Many of the greens are elevated.

The course starts off with a challenging par 4 that plays 398 yards from the back tees. The approach shot, slightly uphill, is to a narrow green. To the left front of the green is a sand trap, and another is farther forward and to the right. The tee-shot landing area is guarded by two fairway bunkers to the right.

A challenging par 3 on this side is the 227-yard eighth, which plays to a large green flanked by a huge trap on the left. In front of the green and slightly to the right are two additional bunkers. The next hole is a tricky 483-yard par 5 whose tee shot is from an elevated tee to an open landing area with a series of bunkers to the right. The second shot is uphill and over a tunneled fairway (the entrance road to the club runs underneath) and then down to a large, undulating area framed by trees, with a stream running in front and a pond to the right. If you are trying to reach the green on your second shot, these unseen obstacles await you on the other side of the aforementioned hill. If you lay up, your third shot is likely to be from a downhill lie.

There are seven par 4s, one par 3 and a par 5 on the back nine. The 573-yard par-5 fourteenth is a dogleg left with trees and a large fairway bunker at the right corner of the dogleg. Trees guard the left side of the fairway beginning approximately 160 yards from the elevated tee. The second shot is toward a deep green with traps on both sides.

The most difficult par 4 on the back nine is the 438-yard sixteenth, which plays from an elevated tee to a narrowing fairway with a small lake cutting into its right side beginning approximately 175 to 200 yards away. You are faced with the choice of playing up to the water and hitting a long shot to an elevated green protected by traps to the left and right or playing to a narrow landing area to the left of the lake.

The variety of holes; the many memorable natural points of reference such as hills, lakes and trees; and the beautiful rolling setting make Carling Lake an enjoyable place to play. It is also a good way to visit the Laurentians, whose 1-billion-year-old rock formations and surrounding hills provide one of the largest concentrations of down-hill ski areas in North America. The development of golf courses has helped make the Laurentians a year-round resort area within a short distance of Montreal. Summer activities such as fishing, boating, golf, camping and hiking are very popular here. There are many attractive French Canadian villages and towns in the region, with food and wine that will make you very happy. And in addition to Carling Lake, rated as one of Canada's top fifteen public golf courses by *Score* magazine, there are many other golf courses worth playing here.

The new 100-room Lake Carling Hotel is within walking distance of the first tee. This hotel features conference rooms; fitness facilities such as exercise equipment, indoor pool, sauna, and other amenities; and a restaurant and bar.

Course Name: GRAY ROCKS

Course Type: Resort
Resort: Gray Rocks
Address: Route 327/P.O. Box 1000
                St.-Jovite, Quebec J0T2H0
Phone: (819) 425–2771 (Golf Course)
                (514) 861–0187 (Montreal),
                (819) 425–2771, (800) 567–
                6744 (Resort)
Fax: (819) 425–3006 (Resort)

GOLF COURSE

Head Professional: Edward Eustace
Course Length/Par (All Tees): Back 6320/72, Middle 6152/72, Ladies' Forward 5750/73
Course Slope/Rating (All Tees): Back 119/69.4, Middle 118/68.7, Ladies' Forward NA/72
Course Architect: NA (9 holes, 1923), NA (9 holes, 1959)
Golf Facilities: Full Pro Shop X, Snack Bar X, Lounge X, Restaurant X, Locker Room X, Showers X, Club Rental X, Club Repair X, Cart Rental X, Instruction X, Practice Green X, Driving Range X, Practice Bunker X, Club Storage X
Tee-Time Reservation Policy: Resort guests: From time of hotel reservation. Outside play: Up to 48 hrs. in advance

for Sat., Sun., holidays; up to 7 days in advance Mon.-Fri.
Ranger: Yes
Tee-off-Interval Time: 8 min.
Time to Play 18 Holes: 5 hrs.
Course Hours/Earliest Tee-off: 5:30 a.m. (summer)
Green Fees: Peak season (July to early Sept.): Resort guests: Can$32 for 18 holes Sat., Sun.; Can$22 for 18 holes weekdays. Outside play: Can$40 for 18 holes Sat., Sun., holidays, Can$35 Mon.-Fri.
Cart Fees: Can$28 for 18 holes per cart
Credit Cards: All major cards
Season: May to late Oct., weather permitting
Course Comments: Can walk anytime. Yardage book available
Golf Packages: Available through resort
Discounts: Seasonal, twilight. Replay discounts for guests, weekly tickets for guests
Places to Stay Nearby: Hotel Le Petite Chateau (819) 425–8645; Auberge Mountain View (819) 425–3429. MONT TREMBLANT: Hotel Mont Tremblant (819) 425–3232
Local Attractions: Skiing, boating, fishing, hunting, camping, hiking, bicycling, tennis, restaurants, shopping, horseback riding, antiques. St.-Jovite Tourist Information (819) 425–8614. Mont Tremblant Tourist Information (819) 425–8671. Chamber of Commerce (819) 425–8441
Directions: From Montreal (1½ hrs.): Laurentian Auto Rte. (Hwy. 15) north to Hwy. 117. From outside Ste. Agathe: Hwy. 117 for 18 mi. (30 km) to first exit for St.-Jovite, turn right at first traffic light on 327 north to Gray Rocks
Closest Commercial Airports: Mirabel International, Montreal (1 hr.); Dorval International, Montreal (1½ hrs.); Uplands International, Ottawa, ON (2 hrs.)

RESORT

Date Built: 1906
No. of Rooms: 202 standard, superior at main inn, 24 rooms in Le Chateau, 56 1- and 2-bedroom condominiums in Village des Soleils

Meeting Rooms: 10. Capacity of Largest: 400 persons banquet style. Meeting Space: NA

Room Price Range: Can$140 per person with 2 meals. Peak rate season late July to mid-Aug. during golf season. Golf, ski and other packages available year round

Lounges: Thirsty Eagle, Sunset Room

Restaurants: Main Dining Room, Snack Bar

Entertainment: Dancing, piano and jazz music

Credit Cards: American Express, Enroute, MasterCard, Visa

General Amenities: Day-care services for children ages 1 to 6 yrs., youth ski programs, French lessons, babysitting services, children's programs (July and Aug.); meeting and conference facilities with audiovisual and food services

Recreational Amenities: Le Spa Fitness Center with indoor pool, sauna, whirlpool, Swedish massage, Nautilus, 14-station global gym, Concept II Rowing Ergometers, NordicTrack cross-country ski simulators, LifeCycle, Liferower, skiing and instruction (Snow Eagle Ski School), ice-skating, sleigh rides, water polo, 22 Har-Tru tennis courts and instruction, marina and beach on Lake Ouimet, riding stable and horseback riding, boating, swimming, lawn bowling, shuffleboard, croquet, volleyball, mountain bicycling

Reservation and Cancellation Policy: Deposit of Can$100 per person required by check or credit card. All cancellations subject to minimum fee of $10 per person. Notice of cancellation must be received 25 days prior to arrival date. Cancellation fee of $4 per day per person will be deducted from deposit. No refunds given for late arrivals, early departures or missed meals

Comments and Restrictions: No pets allowed. Children ages 2 to 6 yrs. pay 1/2 rate when staying in room with 2 persons paying full rate. Children ages 7 to 12 pay 3/4 rate when sharing a room with 2 persons paying full rate. Special rates for single parents staying with children. Daily rate reduced when staying more than 1 night

GRAY ROCKS

The Gray Rocks Inn is in the Laurentians, a forest-covered mass of Precambrian rock a few hours north of Montreal near St.-Jovite. George and Lucille Wheeler started this inn in 1906, after illness and other misfortunes forced them out of the arduous lumber business that originally drew them to this region. The inn is beautifully situated on Lake Ouimet and in the early days drew hunters, fishermen and other hardy souls. As the area grew more accessible by railroad, roads and air, it became more successful and more famous, and was even used as a location for several movies.

The first nine holes of the golf course were built in the 1920s as more demand for recreation was placed on the resort. The course was not easy to build because of the rocky terrain, but horses, plows, picks, shovels and heavy doses of dynamite were used to clear the land. In 1928 the fees were $1 a day, or $15 for the season. In 1959 today's front nine was completed. By this time Gray Rocks was a well-established year-round resort especially known for its skiing. Lucille Wheeler, a granddaughter of the original owners, won a bronze medal in skiing in the 1956 Olympics at Cortina, Italy, and later became the first North American to win the World Championship.

The 6320-yard Gray Rocks layout has blind shots, small greens, some dramatic elevation changes, occasional strategically placed bunkers and reasonably open fairways, even though much of the course was carved out of the pines, a combination that makes Gray Rocks a popular golf challenge. One of the more difficult par 4s at Gray Rocks is the 420-yard third, which starts with a tee shot slightly uphill to a target area just right of center. The second shot is to a forward-sloping, elevated green with a bunker to the front left. Depending on the wind, you might use anything from a fairway wood to a 6-iron on this approach shot. The most memorable hole on the course is the 150-yard par-3 fourteenth, which plays from a plateau to the smallest green on the course. This hole is on the steep side of a hill, "Sugar Peak," and there is no fairway. Some players run the ball onto the hill slope to the right and let it trickle onto the green.

The clubhouse at Gray Rocks includes a bar, restaurant, locker rooms and showers. Golf packages and golf instruction are available. The resort offers a variety of year-round recreational amenities, including downhill and cross-country skiing and instruction (organized ski programs have been held here since 1930), tennis, boating, horseback riding and numerous other activities.

Less than 100 years ago life in this rugged region could be beautifully stark. George and Lucille Wheeler lost some children to accidents and disease, and they both almost died of typhoid. Today the Gray Rock Inn is testimony to their determination and imagination in turning a faltering lumber business into an internationally known hospitality retreat. Gray Rocks was the first resort in the Laurentians. Now there are several resorts and over 5000 hotel rooms in what is one of the most beautiful and popular recreation areas in North America.

Recommended Golf Courses in Quebec

Within 1/2 Hour of Montreal:

Atlantide Club De Golf, Île-Perrot, (514) 425–2000, Semiprivate, 18/6000/72

Baie Missisquoi Golf Club, Venise-en-Quebec, (514) 244–5932, Public, 18/6357/72

Golf Le Mirage, Terrebonne, (514) 477–5854 (Arizona Course), (514) 477–4254 (Carolina Course), Semiprivate. Arizona: 18/6210/71. Carolina: 18/6708/71

Lachute, Lachute, (514) 562–5228, (800) 363–5583, Semiprivate. Course 1: 18/6264/72. Course 2: 18/6417/72

Le Cardinal, Laval, (514) 627–3077, Semiprivate, 18/6312/72

Le Chanticler Golf Club, Ste.-Adele, (514) 229–3742, Public, 18/6280/70

Le Chateau Montebello, Montebello, (819) 423–6341, Semiprivate, 18/6235/70

L'Esterele Golf Club, Prevost, (514) 228–4532, Resort, 18/6460/71

Owl's Head, Mansonville, (514) 292–3666, Resort, 18/6705/72

Royal Laurentien, St.-Faustin, (819) 326–2347, Semiprivate, 18/6108/71

Triangle d'Or, St.-Remi, (514) 454–3976, Semiprivate, 18/6367/72

Quebec: Useful Information

Tourism Quebec, Case Postale 2000, Quebec G1K7X2, (514) 873–2015, (800) 363–7777 (Canada, U.S.)

Laurentians Tourism, Maison du Tourisme des Laurentides, 14142 Rue de Lachapelle, R.R. 1, St.-Jérôme, Quebec J7Z5T4, (514) 436–8532

Ministere du Loisir, de la Chasse et de la Peche du Quebec, 150 Boul. St. Cyrille est., Quebec G1R4Y3, (418) 890–5349, (800) 462–5349 (Quebec), (418) 890–5349 (outside Quebec) (fishing and hunting regulations and provincial park lodging reservations)

SASKATCHEWAN

Course Name: WILLOWS GOLF AND COUNTRY CLUB Bridges, Island, Lakes, Xena Courses

Course Type: Semiprivate
Address: 303 21st Street E
Saskatoon, Saskatchewan
57K0C1
Phone: (306) 956–1100
Fax: (306) 664–4135

GOLF COURSE

Head Professional: Wade Hudyma
Course Length/Par (All Tees):
Island/Bridges: Back 6810/71, Blue 6351/71, White 5683/71, Forward 5235/71. Island/Lakes: Back 6839/71, Blue 6387/71, White 5679/71, Forward 5137/71. Island/Xena: Back 7032/71, Blue 6596/71, White 5857/71, Forward

5387/71. Bridges/Lakes: Back 6877/71, Blue 6412/72, White 5820/72, Forward 5314/72. Bridges/Xena: Back 7070/72, Blue 6621/72, White 5998/72, Forward 5564/72. Xena/Lakes: Back 7099/72, Blue 6657/72, White 5994/72, Forward 5466/72

Course Slope/Rating (All Tees): Island/Bridges: Back 126/74, Blue 122/71, White 116/68, Forward NA/66. Island/Lakes: Back 124/74, Blue 120/71, White 114/68, Forward NA/65. Island/Xena: Back 126/75, Blue 122/72, White 116/69, Forward NA/67. Bridges/Lakes: Back 128/74, Blue 124/71, White 118/68, Forward NA/66. Bridges/Xena: Back 130/78, Blue 126/72, White 120/69, Forward NA/68. Xena/Lakes: Back 128/75, Blue 124/72, White 118/69, Forward NA/67

Course Architect: Bill Newis (1991)

Golf Facilities: Full Pro Shop X, Snack Bar X, Lounge X, Restaurant X, Locker Room X, Showers X, Club Rental X, Club Repair X, Cart Rental X, Instruction X, Practice Green X, Driving Range X, Practice Bunker X, Club Storage X

Tee-Time Reservation Policy: Outside play: Up to 3 days in advance. Club members have priority

Ranger: Yes

Tee-off-Interval Time: 8 min.

Time to Play 18 Holes: 4½ hrs.

Course Hours/Earliest Tee-off: 5:30 a.m. peak season

Green Fees: Can$25 for 18 holes with cart Fri., Sat., Sun., holidays, Can$18 for 18 holes Mon.-Thurs.

Cart Fees: Can$22 per cart for 18 holes

Credit Cards: All major cards

Season: April to Oct. Busiest June, Sept.

Course Comments: Cart mandatory. Yardage book available

Golf Packages: None

Discounts: Juniors. Twilight rates

Places to Stay Nearby: Holiday Inn Saskatoon (306) 244–2311; Hotel Bessborough (306) 244–5521, (800) 667–8788; Saskatoon Inn (306) 242–1440, (800) 667–8789; Sheraton Cavalier (306) 652–6770, (800) 325–3535; Ramada Renaissance (306) 665–3322, (800) 268–9889; Country Inn and Suites by Carlson (306) 934–3900, (800) 456–4000

Local Attractions: Saskatchewan International Raceway, University of Saskatchewan, art galleries, antique shops, seasonal events including music festivals, rodeo, horse shows, crafts fairs, children's festival, Marquis Downs thoroughbred horse racing, Forestry Farm Park, Saskatchewan Place, Mendel Art Gallery and Civic Conservatory, Diefenbaker Centre, Western Development Museum. Saskatoon Visitor and Convention Bureau (306) 242–1206

Directions: Circle Dr. (Idlewild) to Lorne exit, south on Lorne to Cartright, left on Cartright, follow signs to development and golf course

Closest Commercial Airport: Saskatoon (5 min.)

WILLOWS GOLF AND COUNTRY CLUB

The "pocket pro" or yardage book for the Willows Golf and Country Club seems as thick as a dictionary, possibly because there are four new nine-hole courses on this layout and they can be played in any combination. The creation of these courses required 2.2 million square yards of earth to be moved to form a dunes-style golf course, designed by Bill Newis. What was formerly a flat hay field had become one of the best public golf facilities in Canada.

The Lakes Course, which has water hazards on six of its nine holes and plays 3453 yards from the back tees, is considered the most difficult nine among the four courses. The narrow, deep, well-bunkered greens on the Lakes, as well as the wind-swept, mounded and well-guarded fairways, make this side a solid golf challenge. The number-1-handicap hole is the 454-yard par-4 seventh, a sharp dogleg left. The tee shot is to a landing area just beyond the corner of the dogleg, which is guarded on left by a stand of poplar trees. The approach must avoid a water hazard to the right front of a deep, right-to-left-angled, two-tiered green with a huge trap to its right and mounds encircling the rest of the target. Length and accuracy are obviously essential on this hole, which plays 436, 409, and 392 yards from the other tee distances.

Another memorable hole at the Willows is the eighth hole on the Island nine. The tee shot on this 158-yard par 3 is all carry over water to a medium-sized island green with very little room around it for error. A small trap is to the left front and another to the right on this hole. The wind can also complicate club selection.

A tough par 4 on the Bridges Course is the 421-yard third hole, a dogleg left playing to a narrow, deep green protected by traps on either side. The tee shot must avoid a large bunker to the left and water to the right of the landing area. Club selection and accuracy on the approach shot are essential on this excellent golf hole.

The Xena nine features a long and challenging number-1-handicap hole, the 444-yard par-4 fifth. The tee shot is to a landing area straddled by large bunkers to the left and right. The approach is to a narrow, deep green that drops off sharply to the right. To the left is a large bunker, and almost directly behind the putting surface is a water hazard that can hurt you if you select the wrong club and carry the green.

The 33,000-square-foot clubhouse at the Willows Golf and Country Club is a two-story, southwestern-style structure with a reception area, pro shop, convention and seminar facilities, members lounge, locker rooms and showers, massage facilities, hair salon and restaurant with bar. A refurbished barn, one of the few remaining buildings from the original property, now serves as a multipurpose facility for outings and other functions.

The practice area includes a driving range measuring over 300 yards long with practice tees at both ends. There are also 2 large putting greens and a practice bunker

area. Instruction is available from the staff of professionals.

Reg Schafer, who grew up on a farm in Xena (the Xena course's namesake) before going on to become a successful businessman, conceived of and spearheaded this 457-acre development, which includes a residential community. The quality of the golf facility has been enhanced by constructing a 2½-million gallon reservoir and excellent irrigation system, planting over 4000 trees, constructing 8-foot concrete golf-cart pathways and adding other amenities. The Willows Classic, the Canadian Professional Golf Tour's only stop in Saskatchewan, was held here during the first year of operation.

Recommended Golf Courses in Saskatchewan

Cooke Municipal Golf Course, Prince Albert, (306) 763–2502, Public, 18/6319/71

Murray Municipal Golf Club, Regina, (306) 777–7739, Public, 18/6782/72

Waseksiu Lake Golf Club, Prince Albert National Park, Waseksiu, (306) 663–5302, Public, 18/6051/70

Saskatchewan: Useful Information

Tourism Saskatchewan, Saskatchewan Trade and Convention Centre, 1919 Saskatchewan Dr., Regina, SK S4P3V7, (800) 667–7538 (SK), (800) 667–7191 (Canada outside SK, U.S.). Fax: (306) 787–3872

Regina Convention and Visitors Bureau, Box 3355, Regina, SK S4P3H1, (306) 789–5099

Saskatoon Visitor and Convention Bureau, 310 Idylwyld Dr. N, Box 369, Saskatoon, SK S7K3L3, (306) 242–1206

Saskatchewan Parks and Renewable Resources, 3211 Albert St., Regina, SK S4S5W6, (306) 787–2700 (fishing and hunting regulations)

BAHAMAS, BERMUDA, CARIBBEAN

BAHAMAS

Course Name: BAHAMAS PRINCESS
Emerald, Ruby Courses

Course Type: Resort
Resort: Bahamas Princess Resort and Casino
Address: West Sunrise Highway
P. O. Box F-40207
Freeport, Grand Bahama Island
Phone: (809) 352–6721 (Golf Course)
(809) 352–9661,
(800) 223–1818 (Princess Tower)
(800) 223–1834 (Group Reservations)
(809) 352–6721 (Princess Country Club)
(809) 352–7811 (Princess Casino)
Fax: (809) 352–2542 (Princess Tower)
Telex: 297–30016 (Princess Tower)
297–30007 (Princess Country Club)

GOLF COURSE

Director of Golf: Jef Becker
Course Length/Par (All Tees): Emerald:
Back 6679/72, Middle 6402/72, Ladies'
Forward 5722/75. Ruby: Back 6750/72,
Middle 6385/72, Ladies' Forward
5622/74
Course Slope/Rating (All Tees): Emerald:
Back 121/72.3, Middle 118/71, Ladies'
Forward 121/73.1. Ruby: Back
122/72.4, Middle 118/70.8, Ladies'
Forward 120/72.4
Course Architects: Emerald: Dick Wilson
(1964). Ruby: Joe Lee (1966)
Golf Facilities: Full Pro Shop X, Snack
Bar X, Lounge X, Restaurant X,
Locker Room X, Showers No, Club
Rental X, Club Repair X, Cart Rental
X, Instruction X, Practice Green X,
Driving Range X, Practice Bunker X,
Club Storage X
Tee-Time Reservation Policy: Call anytime
Ranger: Yes
Tee-off-Interval Time: Emerald: 9 min.
Ruby: 8 min.

Time to Play 18 Holes: 4 hrs.
Course Hours/Earliest Tee-off: 7:30 a.m.
Green and Cart Fees: Resort guests: $60
for 18 holes with cart. Nonguests: $65
for 18 holes with cart
Credit Cards: All major cards
Season: Year round. Busiest season Nov.
through March
Course Comments: Cart mandatory
Golf Packages: Available through resort
Discounts: Seasonal (May through Oct.),
twilight
Places to Stay Nearby: LUCAYA:Quality
Atlantic Beach and Golf Resort (809)
373–1444; Radisson Lucaya Beach
Resort and Casino (809) 373–7777,
(800) 333–3333. TIMESHARING: Dundee
Bay Villas, Box F-2690, Freeport, (809)
352–4222; Lakeview Manor Club, Box
F-2699, Freeport, (809) 352–2283;
Ocean Reef Resort and Yacht Club,
Box F-898, Freeport, (809) 373–4661;
Timesales (Bahamas) Ltd., Freeport,
(809) 352–7039; Caribbean International
Realty, Freeport, (809) 352–8795
Local Attractions: Fishing, sailing,
snorkeling, tennis, horseback riding,
International Bazaar, Dolphin Experi-
ence, Grand Bahama Museum. LUCAYA:
Garden of the Groves, Rand Memorial
Nature Center, Lucayan National Park,
shopping, restaurants. Ministry of Tour-
ism (809) 352–8044. Grand Bahama
Island Promotion Board (809) 352–
7848, (809) 352–8356
Directions: From Freeport International
Airport: Airport road to east Mall Dr.
to West Sunrise Hwy., which goes into
property
Closest Commercial Airport: Freeport
International (10 min.)

RESORT:

Date Built: 1964, various additions since
then
No. of Rooms: 965. Princess Tower: 400
rooms, including 19 suites. Princess
Country Club: 565 rooms, including 4
suites, 2 villas
Meeting Rooms: 12. Capacity of Largest:
900 persons banquet style. Meeting
Space: 38,500 sq. ft.

Room Price Range: $125 to $140 per person for standard room peak season (mid-Dec. through early April). Golf and other packages, seasonal rates available

Lounges: Princess Tower: Sultan's Tent, Sultan's Court, La Trattoria Bar, Chic Charney Pool Bar. Princess Casino: King's Court, Casino Royal Theatre. Princess Country Club: Palm Pavilion, John B. Bar

Restaurants: Princess Tower: Morgan's Bluff, La Trattoria, Lemon Peel. Princess Casino: Crown Room, Garden Cafe. Princess Country Club: Guanahani's, Rib Room, Patio, John B.

Entertainment: Las Vegas–style revue at Casino Royal Theatre, live music and dancing, "Goombaya" show

Credit Cards: All major cards

General Amenities: Native cooking demonstrations, babysitting services, florist, meeting and conference facilities with audiovisual and food services, beauty parlor and barber shops, arts and crafts demonstrations, playground

Recreational Amenities: Casino gambling at Princess Casino including sports book betting; 12 tennis courts with pro shop, instruction; 2 swimming pools and hot tubs, table tennis; fitness center with exercise room, aerobics, massage, sauna; basketball, volleyball

Reservation and Cancellation Policy: Reservation deposit required. 14-day cancellation notice required to avoid penalties

Comments and Restrictions: No pets allowed. Government tax and resort levy additional. European and modified American plans available. Some restaurants, bars and entertainment may not be available during certain times of the year. Maximum of 4 persons in a double room. Taxes and service are additional

BAHAMAS PRINCESS

The semitropical Bahama Islands stretch 750 miles from 50 miles off the Florida coast to Inagua, 60 miles from Haiti. They were first "discovered" by Christopher Columbus in 1492 when he landed on Guanahani and renamed it San Salvador.

The British eventually took it over and governed it until 1973, when the Bahamas became an independent nation. During the interim, because of its strategic position as a natural barrier across the eastern gateway to the Gulf of Mexico, the Bahamas have hosted pirates, Confederate blockade runners, bootleggers, and, of course, the colonialists. More recently about 80 percent of the people vacationing in the Bahamas are from the United States. Among its main attractions are beautiful turquoise waters, white-sand beaches, 2000 cays, islets and various forms of recreation ranging from gambling to golf. Nassau and Freeport are the tourist destinations of choice.

Situated in Freeport on 2500 acres with tropical gardens and grottos is the Bahamas Princess Resort and Casino, which has almost 1000 rooms situated in its Princess Tower and the Princess Country Club. There are many recreational activities here, including tennis, swimming, the beach and water sports, fishing and a fitness center. The Emerald and Ruby golf courses provide an excellent venue for golf.

The 6679-yard par-72 Emerald Course was designed by Dick Wilson and opened in 1964. One of the more notable holes on this layout is the 532-yard par-5 ninth. The tee shot should be hit to the right center of the fairway just to the left of a large trap guarding the landing area. The second shot is to a green guarded by a large pond on the left and a trap to the right. A big hitter can try to cut the right edge of the pond to reach the green in two. Most golfers play to the right of the pond and hit a wedge to the green.

The Ruby Course was designed by Dick Wilson's associate, Joe Lee, and plays 6750 yards from the back tees. Water comes into play on five holes on this course, which is more tightly treed than the Emerald. The Arawak pines and lush foliage on this layout might lull you into thinking that you are visiting a botanical garden. You will awake, however, to the challenge of some excellent golf holes. The number-1-handicap hole on the course is the 423-yard par-4 ninth, whose tee shot is to a landing area guarded by bunkers on the left. The approach is to a green well guarded by traps on the left.

Perhaps a more difficult par 4 is the 404-yard thirteenth, a dogleg right that generally plays into the wind. The tee shot is to the left of a lake guarding the right side of the fairway. Your approach shot is over the lake to a well-bunkered, slightly elevated green. Careful gauging of wind conditions and accurate club selection are important on this hole.

Among the various diversions at the Bahamas Princess is the Princess Casino, with slot machines, minibaccarat tables, blackjack, dice, roulette and other games of chance. There are several restaurants, bars and entertainment venues, including a Las Vegas–style revue. The restaurants range from Guanahani's, which serves Bahamian specialties such as native grouper and barbecued spare ribs, to La Trattoria, which features Italian food in a casual atmosphere. Adjacent to the casino is a 12-acre international bazaar containing shops and restaurants from 36 countries on 5 continents.

Meeting facilities at the resort include more than 38,000 square feet of space in a variety of configurations such as theater, classroom, boardroom and banquet settings. Golf packages are available through the resort. Peak season is generally mid-December through March.

Recommended Golf Courses in the Bahamas

Abaco Island:

Treasure Cay Resort, Abaco Island, (305) 525–7711, (800) 327–1584, Resort, 18/6985/72

Eleuthera Island:

Cotton Bay Club, Rock Sound, (800) 334–3523, (809) 334–6101, Resort, 18/6594/72

Grand Bahama Island:

Fortune Hills Golf Course, Freeport, (809) 373–4500, Resort, 9/3250/36

Lucaya Golf and Country Club, Freeport, (809) 373–1066, Resort, 18/6824/72

New Providence Island:

Cable Beach Golf Club, Nassau, (809) 327–6000, (800) 432–0221, Resort, 18/7040/72

Carnival's Crystal Palace, Nassau, (809) 327–6200, (800) 377–8617, Resort, 18/6534/72

Divi/Bahamas Beach Resort and Country Club, Nassau, (809) 326–4391, (800) 367–3484, Resort, 18/6568/72

Paradise Island Golf Club, Paradise Island, (809) 326–3925, (800) 321–3000, Semiprivate, 18/6770/72

South Ocean Golf and Beach Resort, Nassau, (809) 362–4391, Resort, 18/6707/72

Bahamas: Useful Information

Bahamas Tourist Offices:

U.S. Bahamas Tourist Office, 255 Alhambra Circle, Suite 425, Coral Gables, FL 33134, (305) 442–4860

New Providence: Bahamas Ministry of Tourism, P.O. Box N3701, Market Plaza, Bay Street, Nassau, New Providence

BERMUDA

Course Name: CASTLE HARBOUR
               GOLF CLUB

Course Type: Resort
Resort: Marriott's Castle
               Harbour Resort
Address: Paytner Road
               Tuckers Town, Bermuda
Phone: (809) 293–2040,
               (800) 228–9290 (Resort)
Fax: (809) 293–1051(Golf Course),
               (809) 293–8288 (Resort)

GOLF COURSE

Director of Golf: Bruce Fraser
Course Length/Par (All Tees): Back 6440/71, Middle 5990/71, Ladies' Forward 4995/71
Course Slope/Rating (All Tees): Back 120/71.3, Middle 123/69.2, Ladies' Forward 116/69.2
Course Architect: Charles Banks (1932)

Golf Facilities: Full Pro Shop X, Snack Bar X, Lounge X, Restaurant X, Locker Room X, Showers X, Club Rental X, Club Repair Minor, Cart Rental X, Instruction X, Practice Green X, Driving Range No, Practice Bunker No, Club Storage X

Tee-Time Reservation Policy: Guests: At time of hotel reservation. Public: Up to 48 hrs. in advance

Ranger: Yes

Tee-off-Interval Time: 8 min.

Time to Play 18 Holes: 4½ hrs.

Course Hours/Earliest Tee-off: 8 a.m. in season (March to Nov.), 7:30 a.m. otherwise

Green Fees: $100 for 18 holes March to Nov., $60 for 18 holes at other times

Cart Fees: $21 for 18 holes per person

Credit Cards: All major cards

Season: Year round

Course Comments: Cart mandatory

Golf Packages: Available through resort

Discounts: Seasonal. Twilight rate during daylight savings time from 4:30 p.m.

Places to Stay Nearby: Southampton Princess Hotel (809) 238–8000; Fourways Inn Cottage Colony (809) 236–6517; Harmony Club (809) 236–3500; Princess Hotel (809) 295–3000; Ariel Sands Beach Club (809) 236–1010

Local Attractions: Bermuda Maritime Museum, Fort St. Catherine, Royal Naval Dockyard, Gibb's Hill Lighthouse, Bermuda's Botanical Gardens, Crystal Caves, shopping, Old Devonshire Church, Spittal Pond Nature Preserve, boat tours, Blue Grotto dolphin show, fishing charters; Bermuda Aquarium, Museum and Zoo; Springfield Library and Gilbert Nature Reserve. Hamilton. Bermuda Department of Tourism (800) 223–6106 (U.S.), (809) 292–0023 (Bermuda)

Directions: From Bermuda International Airport: Kindley Field Rd., over bridge to Blue Hole Hill, left at Harringtown Sound Rd., to hotel on the left

Closest Commercial Airport: Bermuda International (15 min.)

RESORT:

Date Built: 1931

No. of Rooms: 402 rooms, 27 suites

Meeting Rooms: 14. Capacity of Largest: 600 persons banquet style. Meeting Space: 9000 sq. ft.

Room Price Range: $220 to $340 peak season (mid-March to mid-Nov.). Lower rates, golf and other packages available on a seasonal basis

Lounges: Bay View Lounge, Golf Grill Pub, The Blossoms

Restaurants: Windsor, Mikado, Golf Grill

Entertainment: Live music, dancing, disc jockey

Credit Cards: All major cards

General Amenities: Children's program, meeting and conference facilities with audiovisual and food services

Recreational Amenities: Private marina, beach, boating, scuba diving, fishing and other water sports, 6 tennis courts with instruction available, health club with exercise room, saunas, massage, cruise boat, 3 outdoor swimming pools, motor bikes

Reservation and Cancellation Policy: Reservation deposit required 10 days prior to arrival date. Cancellation notice required 14 days to avoid penalties

Comments and Restrictions: No pets. Service charge and taxes additional to base rates

CASTLE HARBOUR GOLF CLUB

Charles Henry Banks, a native of Amenia, New York, where he was born in 1883, designed the Castle Harbour Golf Club and the nearby private Mid Ocean Club in Tuckers Town, Bermuda. Charles Blair MacDonald and Seth Raynor collaborated with him on the latter. Banks met Raynor after graduating from Yale in 1906 and while teaching at the Hotchkiss School in Salisbury, Connecticut, collaborated with Raynor on the Hotchkiss and other courses. After Raynor died in 1926, Banks completed some of Raynor's designs. Banks co-developed some excellent golf courses in the United States and elsewhere including the Yale University Golf Club in New Haven, Connecticut, with Charles Blair

MacDonald and Seth Raynor. Castle Harbour was the last golf course he designed before dying of a heart attack at age 48.

The Castle Harbour Resort was opened in 1931 by the Furness Witty Steamship Line to serve as an elegant stopover for passengers traveling between the United States and Great Britain. The 402-room hotel overlooks beautiful Harrington Sound. During the 1980s Marriott invested more than $60 million to restore the hotel and grounds to its former grandeur.

The 6440-yard par-71 golf course is quite hilly; has undulating, tricky greens whose putts tend to roll toward the ocean; and features a variety of well-placed bunkers. You have to hit landing areas and manage your game at Castle Harbour. The wind, which comes from the north in the winter and from the south-southwest in the summer, can also affect club selection and strategy. The 112-yard par-3 third, for example, might require anything from a 6-iron to a wedge off the tee.

The first hole and the finishing hole are two of the more memorable holes at Castle Harbour. The tee on the 330-yard first hole is set 85 feet above the fairway landing area and affords you magnificent views of the ocean and the golf course. The finishing hole is a 235-yard par 3 that plays to a deep, left-to-right-sloping green with a bunker to the back left and a pond to the right. Farther right is the beach and the ocean.

The Castle Harbour resort offers golf packages, a variety of restaurants, private marina, beach, tennis courts, swimming pools, boating and other water sports, a health club, cruise boat and a variety of other amenities. The resort has won a variety of meeting and hospitality awards including the American Automobile Association Four-Diamond Award, *Successful Meetings* magazine's Pinnacle Award, and *Meeting and Conventions* magazine's Gold Tee Award.

Recommended Golf Courses in Bermuda

Belmont Hotel Golf and Beach Club, Warwick, (809) 236–1301, Resort, 18/5777/70

Mid Ocean Club, Tuckers Town, (809) 293–0330, Semiprivate, 18/6547/71

Port Royal Golf Course, Southampton, (809) 234–0972, Public, 18/6565/71

Bermuda: Useful Information

Bermuda Dept. of Tourism, 310 Madison Ave., New York, NY 10017, (800) 223–6106

Bermuda Dept. of Tourism, Church St., Hamilton, Bermuda

DOMINICAN REPUBLIC

Course Name: **CASA DE CAMPO RESORT**
Teeth of the Dog, Links, La Romana Country Club Courses

Course Type: Resort
Resort: Casa De Campo
Address: P. O. Box 140
La Romana, Dominican Republic
Phone: (809) 523–3333 (Golf Course)
(305) 856–5405,
(800) 877–3643 (U.S. and Canada) (Resort)
Fax: (809) 523–8800 (Golf Course),
(809) 523–8548 (Resort)

GOLF COURSE

Director of Golf: Gilles Gagnon
Course Length/Par (All Tees): Teeth of the Dog: Back 6888/72, Middle 6057/72, Forward 5571/72. Links: Back 6461/71, Middle 5597/71, Forward 4521/71. La Romana Country Club: Back 7191/72, Blue 6661/72, White 6137/72, Forward 5176/72
Course Slope/Rating (All Tees): Teeth of the Dog: Back 140/74.1, Middle 129/70.1, Ladies' Middle 139/75.4, Ladies' Forward 130/72.9. Links: Back 124/70, Middle 116/66.3, Ladies' Middle 123/71.4, Ladies' Forward 113/65.7. La Romana Country Club: Back 144/74.5, Blue 137/73.2, White 126/69.8, Forward NA/NA, Ladies' White 141/75.6, Ladies' Forward 122/69.3
Course Architect: Teeth of the Dog: Pete Dye (1971). Links: Pete Dye (1976). La Romana Country Club: Pete Dye (1989)

Golf Facilities: Full Pro Shop X, Snack Bar X, Lounge X, Restaurant X, Locker Room X, Showers X, Club Rental X, Club Repair Minor, Cart Rental X, Instruction X, Practice Green X, Driving Range X, Practice Bunker X, Club Storage X

Tee-Time Reservation Policy: Up to 1 year in advance

Ranger: Yes

Tee-off-Interval Time: 8 min.

Time to Play 18 Holes: Teeth of the Dog: 4½ hrs. Links, La Romana Country Club: 4 hrs., 15 min.

Course Hours/Earliest Tee-off: 7:30 a.m., latest reserved tee time 4 p.m.

Green and Cart Fees: Teeth of the Dog: $100 for 18 holes with cart. Links: $70 for 18 holes with cart. La Romana is a private club. Guest of member: $75 for 18 holes

Credit Cards: American Express, MasterCard, Visa

Season: Year round

Course Comments: Cart mandatory. Casa de Campo Golf School. Caddies available, $10 for 18 holes plus tip

Golf Packages: Available through resort

Discounts: Twilight rate from 2:30 p.m.

Places to Stay Nearby: SANTO DOMINGO: Hotel Santo Domingo (809) 535–1511, (800) 223–6620; Santo Domingo Sheraton Hotel and Casino (809) 686–6666, (800) 325–3535; Hostal Palacio Nicolas de Ovando (809) 687–3101. PUNTA CANA: Bavaro Beach Resort (809) 682–2162; Club Mediterranean (809) 687–2767, (800) CLUB–MED

Local Attractions: Altos de Chavon artist colony, beach, boating, fishing, Church of St. Stanislaus, Museum of Archeology, shopping, polo matches, rodeos, seasonal festivals. SANTO DOMINGO: National Botanical Gardens, National Zoological Park, Plaza de la Cultura, National Aquarium, La Vega Vieja, Mt. Isabel de Torres, Parque de los Tres Ojos, Pico Duarte, Puerto Plata, Samana, San Pedro de Macoris. Sosua. Dominican Republic Department of Tourism (212) 768–2480; (305) 444–4592; 1464 Crescent St., Montreal, Quebec H3A2B6, (514) 933–9008

Directions: From Santo Domingo: New (Ocean) Rd. east to La Romana, follow signs to resort. From La Romana: Airport within the resort

Closest Commercial Airports: La Romana International (5 min.), Las Americas International, Santo Domingo (1½ hrs.)

RESORT:

Date Built: 1973

No. of Rooms: 950 villa rooms, including 268 casita rooms, 1- to 4-bedroom villas

Meeting Rooms: 9. Capacity of Largest: 320 persons banquet style. Meeting Space: 8900 sq. ft.

Room Price Range: $90 for villa room off season (early April to late Dec.) to $995 for 4-bedroom villa peak season (Christmas/New Year's). Golf and other packages available

Lounge: La Caña

Restaurants: Minitas Beach, Cafe El Patio, Lago Grill Restaurant, Tropicana, Cafe Del Sol, Casa Del Rio, La Piazzetta, Sombrero, El Pescador

Entertainment: Genesis disco music, dancing, mariachi music; live bands in La Caña

Credit Cards: All major cards

General Amenities: Children's camp for ages 5 to 13, babysitting services year round, meeting and conference facilities with audiovisual and food services

Recreational Amenities: Horseback riding, skeet shooting, 19 swimming pools, 13 Har-Tru tennis courts with instruction, beach and water sports, boating, jogging track; fitness center with free weights, Universal exercise machines, massage, squash and racquetball courts, sauna, Jacuzzi, polo, fishing

Reservation and Cancellation Policy: Varies by time of year. 1 night's deposit required to guarantee reservations Dec. 21 to Jan. 7. Must cancel by Nov. 30 to receive full refund. From mid-Jan. to mid-April 15-day advance notice of cancellation required. Other times and summer 3-day cancellation notice required

Comments and Restrictions: Taxes and service charges additional. Modified American plan and full American plan available

CASA DE CAMPO RESORT

The Casa de Campo Resort is probably the ultimate resort in the Caribbean and just about anywhere else. Situated on 7000 acres near the sugar-refining town of La Romana on the southeastern coast of the Dominican Republic, Casa de Campo began with the enthusiasm of Alvaro Carta and the Teeth of the Dog golf course, designed by Pete Dye. Dye also designed the Links Course and the private La Romana Country Club golf course. In the 1960s, Carta, an exiled Cuban, was an executive at Gulf+Western (now Paramount Communications), which then owned 400,000 acres of land in the region and was the driving force in developing Casa de Campo. Previously he had sold his sugar mill to Gulf+Western and joined the corporation as president of Gulf+Western Americas.

The Teeth of the Dog Golf Course, opened in 1971, plays 6888 yards from the back tees. Eight of its holes are along the ocean, and it is said that play is occasionally slowed because golfers bring their cameras with them to preserve their links and ocean memories for posterity. Wind is a major factor on this rolling layout, which has medium-sized, moderately fast Tif-dwarf Bermuda greens and a wide variety of pot and other forms of bunkers. The wind is likely to be less of a factor if you play in the afternoon.

The golf course was originally named Campo de Golf Cajuiles after the many cashew trees on the grounds, but the name was changed in deference to the sixteenth hole, a 185-yard par 3 that plays along the ocean over a massive waste bunker to a green with bunkers to the left and rear, and a dramatic drop-off on the right to jagged teethlike coral rocks and the ocean below. The wind tends to blow from left to right and into the golfer's face on this beautiful and treacherous golf hole.

Dye considers the 384-yard par-4 fifteenth one of the most difficult par 4s of its length that he has designed. The first shot is over a corner of the ocean to the fairway. Because the wind is usually in your face, this is not an easy fairway to hit. The next shot will no doubt be a mid-iron or a short iron to a green with a deep bunker to the right front and several bunkers to the left.

Holes five through eight and fifteen through seventeen play along the ocean. The ninth and eighteenth holes cross the resort's private international airport runway. If the ball strays at the Teeth of the Dog, you are likely to be in a bunker, the water, or very high elephant-grass rough. There are bailout areas should you decide to play defensively, but this will only make the course play longer and, ultimately, with more difficulty.

The 6461-yard Links Course is an excellent test of golf with smaller greens and tighter fairways than the Teeth of the Dog, but less wind because of its inland location. This course opened in 1976. The private La Romana Country Club course opened in 1989. You can play it at selected times or if you are the guest of a member. The Teeth of the Dog Course has been ranked among the world's 100 greatest courses by *Golf* magazine, which has also awarded Casa de Campo a gold medal for being one of the best golf resorts. *Meetings and Conventions* magazine awarded Casa de Campo its Gold Tee Award in 1991 for being an outstanding golf and meeting site. Only one other resort in the Caribbean won this award.

In 1982 the Cuban-American Fanjul family of West Palm Beach purchased Casa de Campo from Gulf+Western. Since that time various amenities have been added to make this a full-service resort. There are now 950 guest rooms including 268 casitas situated in one- and two-story clusters overlooking the Caribbean Sea. They were designed by Oscar de la Renta, a native of the Dominican Republic and an internationally known designer. Private villas with amenities such as pools and Jacuzzis are available throughout the site.

Recreational facilities include polo; shooting; tennis; swimming pools; water sports; horseback riding; fishing; a fitness center with Universal exercise machines; squash and racquetball courts; massage; sauna and other amenities. Dining facilities include a variety of restaurants and lounges offering everything from pineapple and banana milkshakes to fresh-caught ocean fish dishes. The resort has an executive conference center and meeting facilities for up to 500 people. Nearby is Altos de Chavon, an authentic replica of a sixteenth-century Spanish village, which is situated in cliffs overlooking the Chavon River. This village was constructed by hand by local artisans and is now a cultural center. It has a 5000-seat Grecian-style amphitheater that has hosted international stars such as Frank Sinatra and Julio Iglesias. The village is home to a school of design and features a variety of art galleries and crafts shops.

There is a golf school at Casa de Campo, and complete golf practice facilities along with a clubhouse, pro shop, locker room, showers and adjacent dining facilities are offered. Carts are mandatory on the courses and forecaddies are available to enhance your golf experience. Golf packages are available at Casa de Campo, which is a truly international golf setting in a beautiful locale. Pete Dye, who maintains a thatched hut compound beside the seventh hole of the Teeth of the Dog, plans to build a fourth course near Altos de Chavon.

Recommended Golf Courses in the Dominican Republic

Playo Dorado Golf Club, Puerto Plata, (809) 320–4340, Resort, 18/6650/72

Radisson Puerto Plata Resort Golf Course, Puerto Plata, (809) 586–3557, (800) 333–3333, Resort, 18/6730/72

Dominican Republic: Useful Information

Dominican Republic Tourist Office, 2355 Salzedo St., Suite 307, Coral Gables, FL 33134, (305) 444–4592, (800) 358–9594

Ministry of Tourism, Av. Mexico at Jacinto de la Concha, Santo Domingo, Dominican Republic, (809) 689–3655, (809) 689–3637

JAMAICA

Course Name:　HALF MOON GOLF CLUB

Course Type:　Resort
Resort:　　　Half Moon Golf, Tennis and Beach Club
Address:　　Route A1/P.O. Box 80 Montego Bay, Jamaica, West Indies
Phone:　　　(809) 953–3105 (Golf Course) (809) 953–2211, (800) 237–3237 (Resort)
Fax:　　　　(809) 953–2731 (Resort)

GOLF COURSE

Director of Golf: Attila Becsy
Resident Professional: Byron Bernard
Course Length/Par (All Tees): Back 7115/72, Middle 6582/72, Forward 5990/72
Course Slope/Rating (All Tees): Back NA/73.9, Middle NA/73.5, Ladies' Forward NA/70
Course Architect: Robert Trent Jones, Sr. (1961)
Golf Facilities: Full Pro Shop X, Snack Bar X, Lounge X, Restaurant X, Locker Room X, Showers X, Club Rental X, Club Repair X, Cart Rental X, Instruction X, Practice Green X, Driving Range X, Practice Bunker X, Club Storage X
Tee-Time Reservation Policy: Call anytime
Ranger: Yes
Tee-off-Interval Time: 9 min.
Time to Play 18 Holes: 4 hrs.
Course Hours/Earliest Tee-off: 7 a.m.
Green Fees: Resort guests: Half price unless on golf package. Outside play: $85 for 18 holes, $50 for 9 holes peak season
Cart Fees: $25 for 18 holes, $18 for 9 holes
Credit Cards: All major cards
Season: Year round. Busiest season Nov. 15 to April 15
Course Comments: Can walk anytime. Caddies mandatory, $12 for 18 holes, $7 for 9 holes
Golf Packages: Available through resort
Discounts: Resort guests, golf packages

Places to Stay Nearby: Round Hill (809) 952–5150; Wyndham Rose Hall (809) 953–2650; Holiday Inn Rose Hall (809) 953–2485; Richmond Hill Inn (809) 952–3859; Tryall Golf, Tennis and Beach Club (809) 952–5110, (800) 336–4571

Local Attractions: Shopping, fishing, boating, horseback riding, beaches and water sports. MONTEGO BAY: Rose Hall Great House, Greenwood Great House, Martha Brae River, Ocho Rios, Dunn's River Falls, Prospect Plantation Town, Golden Eye; Port Antonio. Negril. Mandeville. KINGSTON: Kings House, Institute of Jamaica, University of the West Indies, National Gallery, Bob Marley Museum, Royal Botanical Gardens, Archaeological and Historical Museum; night clubs, restaurants. Jamaica Tourist Board, Tourism Centre Building, New Kingston Box 360, Kingston 5, (809) 929–9200

Directions: From Donald Sangster International Airport (5 mi.): Hwy. A1 east to resort

Closest Commercial Airport: Donald Sangster International (15 min.)

RESORT:

Date Built: 1961

No. of Rooms: 220 rooms and 20 luxury villas

Meeting Rooms: 8. Capacity of Largest: 350 persons. Meeting Space: 7310 sq. ft.

Room Price Range: $210 per person to $660 for 2 persons peak season (Dec. 15 to April 15). Lowest rates during other months from $120. Golf and other packages available

Lounge: Cedar Bar

Restaurants: Seagrape Terrace, Sugar Mill, Il Giordino

Entertainment: Dancing, live entertainment

Credit Cards: All major cards

General Amenities: Babysitting, meeting and conference facilities with audiovisual and food services

Recreational Amenities: 13 tennis courts (7 lighted) with instruction available, 4 squash courts, bicycling, fishing, boating, scuba diving, beach and water sports, horseback riding, 39 swimming pools; fitness center with Nautilus equipment, aerobic instruction, massage, sauna

Reservation and Cancellation Policy: Reservation deposit required. 30-day cancellation notice required in season for full refund. 14-day cancellation notice required at other times

Comments and Restrictions: No pets. Service charges and taxes additional to base rates

HALF MOON GOLF CLUB

The Half Moon Golf Club is a challenging 7115-yard layout near Montego Bay in Jamaica. The course was designed by Robert Trent Jones, Sr., and opened in 1961. This beautiful layout has wide, rolling fairways with a variety of large palm, willow, rubber, coconut and other trees guarding them. Any ball that strays from the fairway is likely to be in trouble. Water hazards appear on seven holes, and there are well over 100 strategically placed bunkers on the course. An irrigation ditch that crosses several fairways can also cause problems. The wind off the nearby ocean adds to the difficulty of this challenging test of golf. Caddies assist you with club selection, reading the tricky greens and keeping your spirits up.

There are many difficult holes on the Half Moon Course, especially from the back tees. The 570-yard par-5 dogleg-left third hole is a true three-shot par 5 to a green well protected by traps. The 462-yard par-4 ninth plays straight into the wind. The tee-shot landing area is well guarded by bunkers, and the long approach is to a green guarded by traps to the left, right and rear. Very few golfers reach this green in regulation.

The Half Moon Golf, Tennis and Beach Club offers a variety of ocean-front hotel rooms, villas, cottages and suites beautifully situated on 400 acres of grounds covered by beautiful gardens and featuring recreational amenities such as swimming pools, tennis courts, a health club, nearby beaches, fishing, water sports, tours and other activities. The Sugar Mill Restaurant is one of the best restaurants in Jamaica and features seafood and other dishes.

There are other quality golf courses nearby in addition to Half Moon Bay. Golf packages are available through the resort hotel, which has been designated a Four-Diamond destination by the American Automobile Association and has won a variety of other culinary and hospitality awards.

Recommended Golf Courses in Jamaica

Caymanas Golf Club, St. Catherine, (809) 968–3003, Semiprivate, 18/6570/72

Constant Spring Golf Club, Kingston, (809) 924–1610, Semiprivate, 18/5474/70

Tryall Golf, Tennis and Beach Resort, Hanover, (809) 956–5681, Semiprivate, 18/6420/71

Upton Golf and Country Club, Ocho Rios, (809) 974–2528, Semiprivate, 18/6819/71

Wyndham Rose Hall Resort, Montego Bay, (809) 953–2650, Resort, 18/6991/72

Jamaica: Useful Information

Jamaica Tourist Board, 801 Second Ave., 20th Floor, New York, NY 10017, (212) 856–9727, (800) 233–4JTB

Jamaica Tourist Board, Tourism Centre Bldg., 2 St. Lucia Ave., Kingston 5, (809) 929–9200

Jamaica Tourist Board, Cornwall Beach, Montego Bay, Jamaica, (809) 952–4425

PUERTO RICO

Course Name: HYATT DORADO
               BEACH
               East, North,
               South, West Courses

Course Type: Resort
Resort: Hyatt Dorado
Address: Dorado Beach,
               PR 00646
Phone: (809) 796–8916 (Cerromar
               Beach)
               (809) 799–8961 (Dorado
               Beach)
               (809) 796–1234,
               (800) 233–1234 (Resort)
Fax: (809) 796–1234 (Resort)
Telex: 3859758

GOLF COURSE

Head Professional: East, West: Miguel Colon, Jr. North, South: Dave Hall

Course Length/Par (All Tees): East: Back 6985/72, Middle 6430/72, Forward 5805/72. West: Back 6913/72, Middle 6431/72, Forward 5883/72. North: Back 6841/72, Middle 6249/72, Forward 5547/72. South: Back 7047/72, Middle 6298/72, Forward 5486/72

Course Slope/Rating (All Tees): East: Back 127/72.0, Middle 122/70.2, Ladies' Forward 116/72. West: Back 127/72, Middle 122/70.2, Ladies' Forward 117/72. North: Back NA/NA, Middle 120/NA, Forward 114/NA. South: Back NA/NA, Middle 121/NA, Forward 113/NA

Course Architect: East: Robert Trent Jones, Sr. (1958). West: Robert Trent Jones, Sr. (1958). North: Robert Trent Jones, Sr. (1971). South: Robert Trent Jones, Sr. (1971)

Golf Facilities: Full Pro Shop X, Snack Bar X, Lounge X, Restaurant X, Locker Room X, Showers X, Club Rental X, Club Repair X, Cart Rental X, Instruction X, Practice Green X, Driving Range X, Practice Bunker X, Club Storage X

Tee-Time Reservation Policy: Resort guests: At time of reservation. Outside play: 2 days in advance

Ranger: Yes

Tee-off-Interval Time: 7 min. up to 10 a.m., 10 min. after 10 a.m.

Time to Play 18 Holes: 4 hrs.

Course Hours/Earliest Tee-off: 7:30 a.m.

Green Fees: Hotel guests: East, West: $80 for 18 holes. North, South: $60 for 18 holes. Outside play: East, West: $120 for 18 holes. North, South: $100 for 18 holes

Cart Fees: $20 for 18 holes per person

Credit Cards: All major cards

Season: Year round. Busiest season Dec. to Feb.

Course Comments: Cart mandatory

Golf Packages: Available through resort

Discounts: Twilight rate after 3 p.m.

Places to Stay Nearby: Hyatt Regency Cerromar Beach (809) 796–1234, (800)

228–9000. OLD SAN JUAN: Hotel El Convenio (809) 723–9020, (800) 468–2779. SAN JUAN: El San Juan Hotel and Casino (809) 791–1000, (800) 468–2818; Caribe Hilton International (809) 721–0303, (800) 445–8667; Sands Hotel and Casino (809) 791–6100, (800) 443–2009; Condado Beach Hotel (809) 721–6090, (800) 468–2775; Excelsior (809) 721–7400, (800) 223–9815

Local Attractions: Old San Juan, New San Juan, "El Camandante" Race Track, El Yunque Rain Forest, Luquillo Beach, Bacardi Rum Distillery, Camuy Caves, fishing, cock fighting, professional baseball, horseback riding, water sports, bicycling

Directions: From San Juan: Auto Pista Expressway (Hwy. 22) west to Dorado exit, drive through Dorado, resort on the right 1½ mi. from Dorado

Closest Commercial Airport: Luis Muñoz Marín International, San Juan (45 min.)

RESORT:

Date Built: 1958

No. of Rooms: 298 guest rooms and casitas

Meeting Rooms: 11. Capacity of Largest: 550 persons banquet style. Meeting Space: 15,500 sq. ft.

Room Price Range: $170 for guest room off season (June through Sept.) to over $610 Modified American Plan. Peak season late Dec. to mid-April

Lounges: Lobby Bar, Pool Bar, Casino Bar

Restaurants: Ocean Terrace Cafe, Su Casa, Surf Room, Golf Pro Shop, Beach Bohio

Entertainment: Nightly movies, gaming casino

Credit Cards: All major cards

General Amenities: Babysitting, handicapped rooms, barbershop, beauty shop; supervised activities program for children 3 to 15 yrs. available during summer months, spring break, Easter, Thanksgiving and Christmas holidays, and weekends throughout the year; children's menus, meeting and conference facilities with audiovisual and food services

Recreational Amenities: Beach, 7 tennis courts, volleyball, 2 swimming pools, charter fishing, boating; Spa Caribe Health Club with aerobics, aquarobics, Life Cycles, Liferowers, Powercise machines, massage, health programs, skin and body care; bicycling, jogging, aerobics, nature walks, table tennis, backgammon, cards, private gaming casino

Reservation and Cancellation Policy: Reservations must be secured with deposit within 14 days of verbal confirmation. Deposit refundable if cancellation received in writing at the hotel no less than 60 days prior to arrival during Christmas season, 21 days in winter season, 14 days otherwise

Comments and Restrictions: Room tax additional to base rates

HYATT DORADO BEACH

The 1000-acre Dorado Beach complex featuring the Hyatt Dorado Beach Hotel and the Hyatt Regency Cerromar Beach Hotel also has a veritable golf feast—four Robert Trent Jones, Sr.–designed golf courses. There are also many other recreational amenities, including 2 miles of ocean beach; swimming pools; tennis courts with a pro shop and instruction available; a private gaming casino (1 in each hotel); deep-sea fishing; a health spa with state-of-the-art fitness equipment including Life Cycles, Liferowers, Powercise machines, supervised health programs, skin and body care, massage, spa cuisine and other amenities; jogging; bicycling; and water sports such as windsurfing, water- skiing, scuba diving and snorkeling.

Two golf courses (East and West) are located at the Hyatt Dorado Beach and two (North and South) are at the Hyatt Regency Cerromar Beach. Guests of either hotel have reciprocal playing privileges on all four courses. The East and West Courses at the Dorado Beach Hotel are designed to challenge players at every skill level. They feature massive greens, a variety of sand traps, many water hazards and strategically placed coconut and citrus trees. There is a variety of doglegs, and a mixture of tropial rain forest and ocean views frame the airways.

The East Course, opened in 1958, is considered by many to be the most difficult layout at the resort. A few years ago Jones supervised the $2-million upgrading of this course and the North Course. The par-72 East Course plays 6985 yards from the back tees. There are water hazards on more than half the holes, and more than 80 sand bunkers protect the greens and fairway landing areas.

The most famous hole on the East Course is the 540-yard par-5 thirteenth, a double dogleg left, then right, which Jack Nicklaus has rated among the top ten holes in the world. The tee shot is over the corner of a pond to the left to a landing area beginning 220 yards from the back tees. If you can work the ball from right to left and hit long, it is possible to be within 250 yards of the green on your second shot. If you miss, however, you are likely to be in the water on the left or trees on the right, or you could be very far from the hole and to the far right. Most players follow the land route of the fairway and try to reach the green in regulation. The second shot toward the green has to avoid a large pond to the right that begins approximately 200 yards from the hole and runs up to the right side of a deep green with two large bunkers to the right and another large bunker and trees to the left. Trees guard the left side of a narrowing fairway from 200 yards into the green. A prevailing wind from the east is into the golfer's face on this hole, making it a very interesting challenge.

The ocean winds are also a major factor on the West Course, which plays 6913 yards from the back tees. There are also plenty of trees, sand and water on this layout, which has some very demanding par 3s. The 202-yard ninth hole, for example, is all carry over water to a deep, left-to-right-angled green with water to the left, rear and slightly front, and two large bunkers to the right with trees a bit farther back. There is virtually no margin for error on this beautiful but intimidating golf hole.

Abutting the East and West courses are the newer but compatible North and South layouts, which are convenient to the Hyatt Regency Cerromar Beach. Each set of courses has its own clubhouse with pro shop, locker rooms and showers, restaurant, lounge and practice facilities, which include a driving range, sand bunkers, chipping green and putting green. Instruction in the form of clinics and personal lessons is available from the staff of PGA professionals.

The par-72 North Course plays 6841 yards from the back tees and the par-72 South, 7047 yards. These courses are also well bunkered, with large greens. Water hazards appear on more than half the holes. They are also excellent courses to play. Golf packages are available through both hotels. *Golf* magazine has rated Hyatt Dorado Beach among the top 12 courses (Gold Medal Award) and the Hyatt Regency Cerromar Beach among the next 32 courses (Silver Medal Award) in the world. *Meetings and Conventions* magazine has awarded the Hyatt Dorado Beach Hotel a Gold Tee Award for its excellent golf and meeting capabilities. Both hotels have extensive meeting and conference facilities with audiovisual and food-service support services.

The Dorado Beach has 298 air-conditioned rooms, including casitas. This hotel was originally developed by Laurance Rockefeller, and the quality is excellent. The seven-story Hyatt Regency Cerromar Beach Hotel has 504 rooms and suites. In total, there are more than 6 restaurants featuring Spanish and Italian cuisines, and a variety of other fares. The resort also has a horticultural director who oversees hundreds of varieties of plants and a staff of 50 gardeners and landscapers. Another memorable item is the river pool, a $3-million, 1776-foot long, 4½-acre fresh-water swimming pool built in 1986.

Recommended Golf Courses in Puerto Rico

Bahia Beach Plantation, Rio Grande, (809) 256–5600, Public, 18/6695/72

Berwind Country Club, Rio Grande, (809) 876–3056, Semiprivate, 18/7011/72

Palmas del Mar, Humacao, (809) 852–6000, (800) 725–6270, Resort, 18/6803/72

Puerto Rico: Useful Information

Puerto Rico Tourism Company:

U.S. 575 Fifth Ave., New York, NY 10017, (212) 599–6262, (800) 223–6530

Tourism Information Center, Luis Muñoz Marín International Airport, Isla Verde, Puerto Rico (809) 791–1014

U.S. VIRGIN ISLANDS (St. Croix, St. John, St. Thomas)

ST. CROIX

Course Name: CARAMBOLA BEACH GOLF CLUB

Course Type: Public
Address: 72 Estate River
              P.O. Box 3031
              Kingshill, St. Croix, U.S.
              Virgin Islands 00851
Phone: (809) 778–5638

GOLF COURSE

Head Professional: Rob Walling (Golf Club Manager)
Course Length/Par (All Tees): Back 6843/72, White 6228/72, Gold 5687/72, Ladies' Forward 5424/73
Course Slope/Rating (All Tees): Back 131/72.7, White NA/69.8, Gold NA/67.4, Ladies' Forward 125/71.0
Course Architect: Robert Trent Jones, Sr. (1966)
Golf Facilities: Full Pro Shop X, Snack Bar X, Lounge X, Restaurant X, Locker Room X, Showers X, Club Rental X, Club Repair X, Cart Rental X, Instruction X, Practice Green X, Driving Range X, Practice Bunker X, Club Storage X
Tee-Time Reservation Policy: Resort guests: Up to 30 days in advance. Non-guests: Up to 24 hrs. in advance
Ranger: Yes
Tee-off-Interval Time: 8 min.
Time to Play 18 Holes: 4 hrs.
Course Hours/Earliest Tee-off: 7:30 a.m.

Green Fees: Peak season (Nov. to April): $55 for 18 holes, $35 for 9 holes
Cart Fees: $25 for 18 holes per cart, $16 for 9 holes per cart
Credit Cards: American Express, Master-Card, Visa
Season: Year round. Busiest season mid-Dec. through April
Course Comments: Cart mandatory
Golf Packages: Available through resort
Discounts: Seasonal (off season May through Oct.). Twilight rate from 3 p.m. peak season, otherwise 2 p.m.
Places to Stay Nearby: Villa Madeleine (809) 773–8141, (800) 548–4461; Hotel Caravelle (809) 773–0687, (800) 524–0410; Sprat Hall (809) 772–0305, (800) 843–3584; Waves at Cove Bay (809) 778–1805, (800) 545–0603
Local Attractions: Shopping, sailing, boating, scuba diving, snorkeling, fishing, horseback riding, Cruzan Rum Distillery, Davis Bay, St. George Village Botanical Gardens, Judith's Fancy, Whim Great House, Frederiksted. Sandy Point. Buck Island. St. John. St. Thomas
Directions: Follow Carambola signs from main gate of airport. From other areas: Call club and ask for directions
Closest Commercial Airport: Alexander Hamilton (15 min.)

CARAMBOLA BEACH GOLF CLUB

The Carambola Beach Golf Club features a 6843-yard par-72 Robert Trent Jones, Sr., golf course situated in a beautiful valley just inland from Davis Bay and the Caribbean Sea. The front nine of this course is short and requires well-placed, strategic golf shots. The back nine tends to play longer and a bit more difficult. The course features rolling fairways, large bunkers, a variety of doglegs and straightaway holes, and a nice mix of elevation changes and contours. Large, strategically placed bunkers guard the greens, and water comes into play on eight holes.

The few backbreaking holes on the back nine are the 477-yard par-4 thirteenth and the 593-yard par-5 fifteenth, which plays uphill to a heavily bunkered green. The two finishing holes are both memorable and excellent golf challenges. The 185-yard seventeenth plays over water to a wide, well-bunkered green. The 476-yard, par-4 eighteenth, a dogleg left, requires a big drive to reach the corner. The next shot is uphill to a well-bunkered green. Besides the golf challenge at Carambola, you will remember the beauty of the course and foliage such as bougainvillea, hibiscus, and mahogany trees framed by mountains and rain forests in the distance.

At this writing, the Carambola Beach Resort, originally developed by Laurance Rockefeller, is closed. You might check to see whether it has reopened.

Recommended Golf Courses in the U.S. Virgin Islands

Buccaneer Beach Hotel, Christiansted, St. Croix, (809) 773–2100, Resort, 18/6117/71

Mahogany Run, St. Thomas, (809) 775–5000, (800) 253–7103, Public, 18/6022/70

U.S. Virgin Islands: Useful Information

U.S. Virgin Islands Division of Tourism, 1270 Avenue of the Americas, New York, NY 10020, (212) 332–2222, (800) USVI–INFO

U.S. Virgin Islands Division of Tourism, 1 Tolbod St., St. Thomas, Box 6400, Charlotte Amalie, U.S. Virgin Islands 00804, (809) 774–8784

St. Croix, Box 4538, Christiansted, U.S. Virgin Islands 00822, (809) 773–0495

Customs House Bldg., Strand St., Frederiksted, U.S. Virgin Islands 00840, (809) 772–0357

St. John, Box 200, Cruz Bay, U.S. Virgin Islands 00830, (809) 776–6450

WEST INDIES (Nevis, St. Kitts, St. Lucia)

NEVIS

Course Name:　THE FOUR SEASONS RESORT NEVIS

Course Type:　Resort
Resort:　　　Four Seasons Resort Nevis
Address:　　 Pinney's Beach
　　　　　　 P.O. Box 565

　　　　　　 Charlestown, Nevis,
　　　　　　 West Indies
Phone:　　　 (809) 469–1111,
　　　　　　 (800) 332–3442 (U.S.),
　　　　　　 (800) 268–6282 (Canada)
　　　　　　 (Golf Course)
Fax:　　　　 (809) 469–1112

GOLF COURSE

Head Professional: David Porter
Course Length/Par (All Tees): Back 6766/71, Blue 6199/71, White 5623/71, Forward 5153/71
Course Slope/Rating (All Tees): Back 125/71.7, Blue 121/69.5, White 116/68.6, Ladies' Forward 117/69.3
Course Architect: Robert Trent Jones, Jr. (1991)
Golf Facilities: Full Pro Shop X, Snack Bar X, Lounge X, Restaurant X, Locker Room X, Showers X, Club Rental X, Club Repair X, Cart Rental X, Instruction X, Practice Green X, Driving Range X, Practice Bunker X, Club Storage X
Tee-Time Reservation Policy: Resort guests: At time of hotel reservation. Outside play: 24 hrs. in advance generally
Ranger: Yes
Tee-off-Interval Time: 10 min.
Time to Play 18 Holes: 4 hrs.
Course Hours/Earliest Tee-off: 7 a.m.
Green and Cart Fees: Resort guests: $100 for 18 holes with cart. Outside play: $125 for 18 holes with cart
Credit Cards: All major cards
Season: Year round. Busiest season mid-Dec. to mid-April
Course Comments: Cart mandatory
Golf Packages: Available through resort
Discounts: Resort packages
Places to Stay Nearby: Hermitage (809) 469–3477, (800) 223–9815 (U.S.), (800) 468–0023 (Canada); Nisbet Plantation Beach Club (809) 469–9325, (800) 344–2049 (U.S.); Golden Rock (809) 469–9373 (collect); Pinney's Beach Hotel (809) 469–5207
Local Attractions: Nelson Museum, Hamilton House, shopping, restaurants, Grove Park, St. John's Church, Eden Brown Estate, St. Thomas Anglican

Church, boating, deep-sea fishing, hiking, horseback riding, water sports. Charlestown. Nevis Tourism Office (809) 469–5521

Directions: From New Castle Airport (10 min.): Take main highway (coast road) toward Pinney's Beach and resort

Closest Commercial Airports: New Castle, Nevis (10 min.); Golden Rock, St. Kitts (30 min. by water launch)

RESORT:

Date Built: 1991

No. of Rooms: 196 rooms and suites

Meeting Rooms: 5. Capacity of Largest: 100 persons banquet style. Meeting Space: 5000 sq. ft.

Room Price Range: $550 for deluxe room to $3450 for 3-bedroom suite peak season (Jan. to mid-April). Golf packages and seasonal rates available. Lower rates late April to mid-Nov.

Lounges: Ocean Terrace, Library, Tap Room

Restaurants: Grill Room, Dining Room, Pool Cabana, Sports Pavilion

Entertainment: Live music, dancing

Credit Cards: All major cards

General Amenities: Supervised children's program for ages 3 to 12, beauty salon, boat cruises, island tours, meeting and conference facilities with audiovisual and food services; tours to St. Maarten, Anguilla, St. Barthelemy

Recreational Amenities: Tennis center with 10 courts (6 Har-Tru, 4 red clay), pro shop, instruction; health club with Lifecycles, StairMasters, treadmills, aerobics, sauna, whirlpool, massage; beaches with snorkeling, boating and other water sports; fishing, horseback riding, volleyball, croquet, shuffleboard, darts, pool tables, fresh-water swimming pool, wading pool, water sports staff and instruction

Reservation and Cancellation Policy: Deposit of 3-nights' room rate plus tax must be received by the resort within 21 days of booking. Deposits apply to the first 2 nights and the last night of the stay. If a stay is less than 3 nights, 1 night's deposit only is required. Advance deposits may be made by check or money order (payable to Four Seasons Resort Nevis), or by American Express, MasterCard or Visa. Payment may be sent to Four Seasons Resort Nevis, 122 E. 55th St., New York, NY 10022, Attn: Advance Reservations. For full refund, resort must be notified of cancellation 21 days prior to arrival date, or full amount forfeited

Comments and Restrictions: Service charges and taxes additional to base rates. No charge for children under 18 yrs. staying in parents' room. Modified and full American plan available. Airport and water transfers additional

THE FOUR SEASONS RESORT NEVIS

Four Seasons Resort Nevis is a new, 196-room hotel set on Pinney's Beach on Nevis, a 2-hour flight southeast of Miami, Florida. The resort features a 6766-yard par-71 Robert Trent Jones, Jr.–designed golf course that winds its way up the volcanic slope of 3232-foot Nevis Peak. This golf course features large, moderately fast Bermuda-grass greens that have subtle undulations and breaks that tend to head away from the mountain toward the nearby Caribbean Sea. There are 72 bunkers on the Nevis course, which has an excellent irrigation system and well-conditioned fairways and greens.

The signature hole on the golf course is the 663-yard par-5 fifteenth, which plays downhill to a deep, two-tiered green protected by two traps on the right and a trap on the left. The wind tends to be behind you on this marathon, which drops 200 feet from tee to green. The fairway is narrow, and most golfers feel fortunate to reach the green in three. The tee affords magnificent views of the western half of Nevis Island.

As you work your way through the golf course, it tends to become more thick and well protected by jungle-style foliage. The course opens up again on the two finishing holes. The seventeenth is a 419-yard par 4 cut by a stream approximately 260 yards from the back tees. A trap guards the left side of the tee-shot landing area. The approach is to a narrow, deep green guarded by a stream to its left.

At 445 yards, the eighteenth is a long par 4, but often you will have a 10-to-20 knot tail wind. The first shot is to a landing area squeezed by water on the left and a bunker to the right. The approach is to a medium-sized green guarded by two traps to the left front and another to the right. To the rear of the green is a beautiful view of the beach and the ocean.

Other recreational facilities at Nevis include the Sports Pavilion, which has a health club featuring Nautilus equipment, Lifecycles, StairMasters, treadmills and amenities including saunas, massage rooms and a unisex hair salon. Fitness programs including aerobics, aqua-aerobics, fitness walks and jogging are offered. There are 6 Har-Tru and 4 red-clay tennis courts, instructional programs and a fully equipped tennis pro shop. A variety of water sports such as snorkeling, windsurfing, water-skiing, deep-sea fishing and instructional programs are available. Other activities include horseback riding, croquet, volleyball, bicycling and horseshoes. Local shopping and touring excursions are easily arranged.

The rooms at the Four Seasons Resort Nevis are luxurious and oversized, between 550 and 2200 square feet with large verandas overlooking the ocean, Nevis Peak or the golf course. The 2 restaurants at the resort offer casual and formal dining. There is live entertainment, cocktail service is available in the hotel lounge, and an on-site night club is open evenings. The resort also offers 5000 square feet of meeting space, including audiovisual and banquet-support services.

A daily supervised youth program, "Kids for All Seasons," is offered from 9 a.m. to 6 p.m. for children ages 3 through 12. Lunch and dinner are served, and a variety of sports and other activities are offered.

The Four Seasons Resort Nevis offers a variety of golf, tennis and other packages. A 7-nights' luxury accommodation golf package includes a deluxe oceanfront room, unlimited golf for 2 with power cart, breakfast, a half-hour private lesson with a PGA professional, dinner including wine for 2 each evening in the dining room of the plantation-style Great House or in the Grill Room, a complimentary daily golf clinic and other amenities for approximately $3000 per person (double occupancy) peak season from mid-January through April. Inquire about the most recent packages offered.

Nevis was allegedly called "Our Lady of the Snows" by Christopher Columbus when he sighted it in 1493. The 36-square-mile island is separated from its sister island of St. Kitts by a 2-mile-wide channel. St. Kitts and Nevis became an independent nation in 1983. The northeast trade winds serve to modify Nevis's temperatures but can be tricky on the golf course.

After the time of Columbus, Nevis became a European health spa and producer of tobacco, cotton, ginger, indigo and sugar. Alexander Hamilton, secretary of the treasury under George Washington, was born in Charlestown, Nevis. The Four Seasons Resort and its excellent golf course enhance Nevis's reputation as "Spa of the Caribbean."

Recommended Golf Courses in the West Indies

St. Kitts:

Royal St. Kitts Golf Club, Frigate Bay, (809) 465–8339, Public, 18/6918/72

Barbados:

Sandy Lane Golf Club, St. James, (809) 432–1311, Resort, 18/6553/72

St. Maarten:

Mullet Bay Golf Club, Phillipsburg, (001-5995-52801), (800) 468–5538, Resort, 18/6300/70

Turks and Calicos Island:

Provo Golf Club, Providenciales, (809) 946–5991, Resort, 18/6217/72

West Indies: Useful Information

St. Kitts and Nevis Tourist Office, 414 E. 75th St., New York, NY 10021, (212) 535–1234, (800) 582–6208

St. Kitts and Nevis Dept. of Tourism, Pelican Mall, Bay Road, Basseterre, St. Kitts, (809) 465–4040

# MEXICO

BAJA SUR

Course Name: CABO DEL SOL GOLF CLUB

Course Type: Public
Address: Highway 1, Los Cabos, Mexico
Phone: 011–52–11–4–33149,
(800) 637–2226 (Golf Course),
(800) 386-2465 (Tee Times)

GOLF COURSE

Head Professional: Brad Wheatley
Course Length/Par (All Tees): Back 7037/72, Gold 6698/72, Blue 6252/72, White 5790/72, Forward 4696/72
Course Slope/Rating (All Tees): Back 137/74.1, Gold 130/72.1, Blue 124/69.6, Ladies' White 123/72.4, Forward 111/67.1
Course Architect: Jack Nicklaus (1994)
Golf Facilities: Full Pro Shop X, Snack Bar X, Lounge No, Restaurant No, Locker Room No, Showers No, Club Rental X, Club Repair Minor, Cart Rental X, Instruction X, Practice Green X, Driving Range X, Practice Bunker X, Club Storage X
Tee-Time Reservation Policy: At time of hotel reservation through travel agent or local resorts. Up to 7 days in advance otherwise
Ranger: Yes
Tee-off-Interval Time: 10 min.
Time to Play 18 Holes: 4 hrs. 15 min.
Course Hours/Earliest Tee-off: 7 a.m.
Green and Cart Fees: $115 plus tax for 18 holes with cart
Credit Cards: American Express, MasterCard, Visa
Season: Year round. Busiest late December through April
Course Comments: Cart mandatory
Golf Packages: Through resort hotels, travel; agents
Discounts: Seasonal, lowest rates June-Sept. Resort guests. Juniors
Places to Stay Nearby: Hyatt Hotel (on site) (800) 233–1234; Palmilla Resort (800) 637–2226, Fax: (714) 851–2498; Hotel Finisterra (714) 476–5555, (800) 347–2212; Melia San Lucas (800) 336–3542; La Jolla de Los Cabos (800) 455–CABO, 011–52–114–2–0811; Hotel Solmar (310) 459–9861, (800) 344–3349; Terrasol Beach Resort 011–52–114–3–1803, (800) 524–5104; Hotel Buena Vista Beach Resort (800) 752–3555; Westin Regina Resort 011–52–114–2–9000, (800) 228–3000, Hotel Cabo San Lucas 011–52–114–3–3457, (800) 733–2226, Fax: 011–52–114–4–0015; Hotel Twin Dolphins 011–52–114–30–0256; Pueblo Bonito Resort 011–52–114–3–1976; Cabo San Luca Country Club 011–52–114–3–1922, (800) 854–2314, Fax: 011–52–114–3–1119; Casa de Mar Hotel 011–52–114-4-0030, (800) 221–8808; Mexico Condo Reservations on the Beach (800) 262–4500

Local Attractions: Beaches, sport fishing, water sports including boating, surfing, snorkeling and others, whale watching, horseback riding, tennis, restaurants, night clubs, crafts, shopping
Directions: 20 minutes south of Los Cabos International Airport, off Hwy. 1
Closest Commercial Airports: Los Cabos International (20 min.), from San Diego (850 miles south, 2 hrs. by air)

CABO DEL SOL GOLF CLUB

Cabo del Sol, a formidable 7037-yard par-72 Jack Nicklaus design within an 1800-acre golf course residential development on the Sea of Cortez, has seven holes bordering the sea including three memorable finishing holes. The 445-yard par-4 sixteenth plays out of the foothills down to a deep green with the water on the horizon. The tee shot must carry and avoid bunkers to the right of the ample landing area. The next shot is downhill and must avoid severe dropoffs to the left, right and rear of the green. The tee shot on the 173-yard par-3 seventeenth is from a cliffside perch over the beach and down to a green cut into a hill and guarded by blackened rocks. To your right is the Bay of Whales and the white dots on the sand below are golf balls that didn't have the right stuff. The finishing hole is a spectacular 425-yard par-4 dogleg right that is bordered by the sea to the right. The bailout area on the approach shot is to the left of the green. A missed shot to the right will tumble toward the sea below.

The Bermuda grass greens at Cabo Del Sol are ample with few undulations. The most difficult hole here is the 460-yard par-4 fifth which plays down to the sea. You are required to decide how much of the surrounding arroyos you attempt to carry in order to reach a safe approach to the green. A conservative tee shot can easily leave you requiring a fairway wood to reach the target. The next two holes, beautiful par 3s that play along the water to your left, provide a scenic interlude before you match wits with the 436-yard par-4 eighth and the 467-yard par-4 ninth which takes you back to the clubhouse up the hill from the sea.

Cabo Del Sol has been the site of the Senior PGA Senior Slam of Golf event. In addition to Cabo Del Sol, a cluster of quality golf courses in this hot new tourist spot at the tip of the Baja peninsula include Nicklaus-designed nines at the Palmilla Resort, the Pete and Roy Dye-designed courses at Campo de Carlos, the Robert Trent Jones, Jr. courses at Melia Cabo Real and the Loreto Golf Course. In addition to golf, this region has long been noted for its world class sport fishing and seafood delicacies ranging form mahimahi to lobster. Year round over 300,000 tourists visit this area which has been made more accessible through road and air transport improvements. There are now a variety of resort hotels and other accomodations, night clubs, restaurants, shops and other diversions. Golf packages are available through the resort hotels or your travel agent.

Course Name: PALMILLA GOLF CLUB
Arroyo, Mountain,
Ocean Courses

Course Type: Resort
Resort: Hotel Palmilla
Address: Highway 1, Apartado Postal 52, San Jose del Cabo, Mexico
Phone: 011–52–114–2–0582, (800) 637–2226 (Reservations), (800) 286–2465 (Tee Times)
Fax: (714) 476–1648

GOLF COURSE

Head Professional: Brad Wheatley

Course Length/Par (All Tees): Arroyo/Mountain: Back 6939/72, Gold 6346/72, Blue 5888/72, White 5673/72, Forward 4856/72. Mountain/Ocean: Back 7114/72, Gold 6832/72, Blue 6439/72, White 5957/72, Forward 5169/72. Arroyo/Ocean: 6849/72, 6528/72, Blue 6145/72, White 5690/72, Forward 4979/72

Course Slope/Rating (All Tees): Arroyo/Mountain: Back 137/73.9, Gold 123/71.5, Blue 109/68.8, White 108/66.2, Ladies White 121/71.8, Ladies Forward 105/67.1. Mountain/Ocean: Back 139/74.9, Gold 125/72.9, Blue 112/70.2, White 110/67.7, Ladies White 124/73.4, Forward 109/68.8. Arroyo/Ocean: Back 136/73.4, Gold 123/71.2, Blue 110/68.8, White 108/66.3, Ladies White 121/71.9, Forward 106/67.8

Course Architect: Jack Nicklaus (1992)

Golf Facilities: Full Pro Shop X, Snack Bar X, Lounge No, Restaurant No, Locker Room No, Showers No, Club Rental X, Club Repair Minor, Cart Rental X, Instruction X, Practice Green X, Driving Range X, Practice Bunker X, Club Storage X

Tee-Time Reservation Policy: At time of confirmed reservation at the Palmilla Hotel. Up to 7 days in advance otherwise

Ranger: Yes

Tee-off-Interval Time: 10 min.

Time to Play 18 Holes: 4 hrs.

Course Hours/Earliest Tee-off: 7 a.m.

Green and Cart Fees: $100 for 18 holes peak season (Oct.-May)

Credit Cards: American Express, MasterCard, Visa

Season: Year round. Busiest Jan.-Mar. Inquire about lower seasonal rates

Course Comments: Cart mandatory

Golf Packages: Through resort, travel agents

Discounts: Seasonal, resort guests

Places to Stay Nearby: See page 809

Local Attractions: See page 809

Directions: From San Jose del Cabo International Airport take Hwy. 1 south to resort, off Hwy. 1

Closest Commercial Airports: San Jose del Cabo International Airport (15 min.). from San Diego (850 miles south, 2 hrs. by air)

RESORT

Date Built: 1956

No. of Rooms: 72 rooms

Meeting Rooms: 1. Capacity of largest: 200 persons, reception. Meeting Space: 2000 sq. ft.

Room Price Range: $130 to $515 European plan plus taxes and service. Golf and other packages available year round. Lowest rates June through Sept.

Lounges: La Cantina

Restaurants: La Paloma

Entertainment: Live music

Credit Cards: American Express, MasterCard, Visa

General Amenities: Massage, shopping excursions, dive shop, hotel fishing boat fleet, meeting facilities with business and food service support services

Recreational Amenities: 2 tennis courts, 2 paddle ball courts, shuffleboard, croquet, volleyball, horseback riding, beaches, deep-sea fishing, boating, surfing, snorkeling, scuba diving, bicycling, whale watching, water skiing, wind surfing

Reservation and Cancellation Policy: Deposit or credit card guarantee required to secure reservation.

Comments and Restrictions: Taxes and gratuities additional. No pets

PALMILLA GOLF CLUB

The Baja Peninsula is a long spit of rough, rocky desert terrain bordered by the Pacific Ocean to the west and the Sea of Cortez, also called the Gulf of California, to the east. At the end of this appendage, between La Paz, the state capitol, and the resort areas of Cabo San Lucas and San del Cabo, is a booming economic and recreational center that is becoming a significant golf destination. One of the jewels of this region is the Palmilla Golf Club featuring the Arroyo, Mountain and Ocean nines designed by Jack Nicklaus. On site is the 72-room Hotel Palmilla overlooking the Sea of Cortez. Above the hotel and the golf courses are the Sierra Laguna Mountains.

The Arroyo/Mountain Course was the first to open at his resort. This 6939-yard par-72 layout, which winds through rocky desert terrain and around arroyos in the foothills above the hotel, is a target layout by the sea. Virtually every hole offers a view of the ocean but it is the arroyos, desert landscape and the rocky terrain that you'll have to contend with. The tees on this Bermuda grass layout are often elevated and proved a clear view of the work at hand. And often you'll be offered a choice of whether to attempt the heroic shot or try a more conservative approach.

One of the most difficult and memorable holes on the Mountain nine is the 401-yard par-4 fifth, a dog-leg right whose tee shot must carry an arroyo to safely reach and island of green fairway surrounded by rocky desert and dropoffs. The second shot is over an arroyo to a target below and cut into a hill. In front of this green are large bunkers to keep poorly executed shots from disappearing into the abyss below. The Mountain nine is the tighter, more difficult nine. The Arroyo measures 3337 yards from the back tees, the Ocean 3512 yards and the Mountain 3602 yards. Although these nines can be played in any sequence, the course is usually set up to open with the easier Arroyo layout.

A good hole on the Arroyo nine is the 304-yard par-4 second which gives you the choice of playing two fairways. The lower fairway to the left offers a route to the green for big hitters but it is guarded by bunkers to the left and desert terrain farther left. The safer path is to the upper fairway on the right but that leaves a longer approach to the green. The putting surfaces here have subtle undulations and are tricky to read. But they usually have an entranceway that allows you to run the ball to the target. The trouble, in the form of bunkers and desert, is usually to the left and right and behind the target. A difficult par 3 on the Arroyo is the 243-yard eighth which offers a spectacular view of the Sea of

Cortez. The green, guarded by bunkers to its left and front, is 70 feet below the back tee.

Palmilla offers five tee distances and both the tees and fairway sprinkler heads are marked in meters and yards. The Ocean nine, which will open in the near future, provides another quality golf option here. Two of its holes, the 465-yard par-4 third and the 162-yard par-3 sixth are near the sea. The par 5s, the 533-yard fifth and the 500-yard ninth provide some relief from tough par 4s, the third and the 460-yard second, and the 235-yard par-3 fourth. Jack Nicklaus has provided a resort course that any golfer can enjoy but he has also created a challenging test for the low handicap golfer.

In the old, old days this area was a pirate hangout. In the old days Palmilla was a favorite fishing retreat where John Wayne, Bing Crosby and other celebrities chased marlin, sailfish and other varieties. In the late 1960s the Mexican government formed Fonatur, an economic development agency that targeted this region as a growth area. With the opening of the Transpeninsular highway in 1973 and the growth of tourism here, the Palmilla resort and its golf course real estate development are part of the wave of the future. The hotel, whose spacious rooms have no televisions or telephones, feature plantation windows, overhead fans, tile floors, large modern bathrooms and scenic views of the sea. The La Cantina bar serves up a splendid margarita and the LaPaloma restaurant provides fresh seafood such as mahimahi, sea bass and red snapper.

Nearby are the restaurants, sites and charms of San Jose de Cabo, Cabo San Lucas and Todos Santos.

COLIMA

Course Name: **ISLA NAVIDAD COUNTRY CLUB**

Course Type: Resort
Address: Manzanillo, Mexico
Phone: 011–52–364–1–8283

GOLF COURSE

Director of Sports Manmagement: Jabriel Garcia
Course Length/Par (All Tees): Back 7059/72, White 6541/72, Yellow 5934/72, Forward 5365/72
Course Slope/Rating (All Tees): NA/NA
Course Architect: Robert von Hagge (1993)
Golf Facilities: Full Pro Shop X, Snack Bar X, Lounge X, Restaurant X, Locker Room X, Showers X, Club Rental X, Club Repair X, Cart Rental X, Instruction X, Practice Green X, Driving Range X, Practice Bunker X, Club Storage X
Tee-Time Reservation Policy: Call anytime in advance
Ranger: Yes
Tee-off-Interval Time: 8 min.
Time to Play 18 Holes: 4 hrs.
Course Hours/Earliest Tee-off: 7 a.m.
Green and Cart Fees: $100 for 18 holes with cart
Credit Cards: American Express, MasterCard, Visa
Season: Year round. Busiest Dec.-Apr.
Course Comments: You may use the practice facilities for approximately $20
Golf Packages: Through resort hotels, travel agents
Discounts: Through resort hotels, travel agents
Places to Stay Nearby: See page 814
Local Attractions: See page 814
Directions: From Manzanillo Playa de Oro International Airport (30 min. north). Take Hwy. 200 north to turnoff to Isla Navidad just south of Melaque. Follow signs to resort and golf course
Closest Commercial Airports: Manzanillo Playa de Oro International (30 min.). From Mexico City (90 min. northwest by air)

ISLA NAVIDAD GOLF CLUB

A one hour drive north from Manzanillo is Isla Navidad. When you turn west off the main north-south road, Highway 200, and head west toward the Pacific, the land is quiet and undeveloped, only interrupted by an occasional fisherman's thatched-roof hut on a sandy knoll. And then you come upon the impressive stucco tile-roofed entrance gate to Isla Navidad, a 1,100-acre development featuring a Robert von Hagge–designed golf course served by a 20,000 square-foot clubhouse with complete amenities including locker rooms, showers, a full pro shop and a full service restaurant.

Brick cart paths wend through the rolling layout which features large, undulating Tifdwarf Bermuda greens, huge sculpted bunkers and an occasional water hazard. A new nine, added to the original 7,053-yard par-72 layout that opened in 1993, has water on every hole and is likely to be the most difficult of the three nines.

The original eighteen starts out with a 522-yard par 5 which plays straight to a deep green bordered by water to its left and banked knolls to its immediate right. The tee shot landing area is framed by water on the left and bunkers to the right. A series of mounds bordering the fairway increases the likelihood of uneven lies or odd kicks from errant shots, but the course is not penal or intimidating. The greens are fast with small shelves and subtle undulations. Grass swales around the greens and ample bunkers with local coarse sand require skill with a wedge.

Among my favorite holes on the front nine is the 208-yard par-3 third which plays from a slightly elevated tee toward a deep green framed by two large bunkers. On a summer morning the wind was coming in from left to right off the ocean, visible behind the green. To the far right is a sandy waste area much like Scottish dunes. After you come off this green and go to the next tee, deserted ocean beaches can be viewed as far as the eye can see. Calibrating the ocean wind is an important part of course management at Isla Navidad where an errant shot caused by poor club selection will leave you in a bunker, wiry rough or, occasionally, the water.

The 418-yard par-4 ninth is a great finishing hole beautifully set right below the clubhouse. The first shot is to an open landing area but the approach must negotiate a lake that begins on the right, 125 yards from the green, then cuts into the fairway in front of the target. This is a major obstacle if your tee shot has strayed to the right. To the left of the lake is a narrow entranceway to the green which is backed by three large bunkers.

The round concludes with the 433-yard par-4 eighteenth, the most difficult hole on the course. The tee shot is to a narrow landing area guarded by water to the left and bordered by grassy mounds on the right. A poor tee shot requires most golfers to approach this forward-sloping green with a long iron or wood, a dangerous proposition.

The long term plan for this development is to have a 200-room hotel, two marinas, a spa, shops and other amenities.

This is already one of the best golf facilities in Mexico.

Course Name: LA MANTARRAYA

Course Type: Resort
Resort: Las Hadas Resort
Address: Av. Vista Hermosa y Av. de los Riscos, 28200 Manzanillo, Mexico
Phone: 011–52–333–4–2000, (800) 272-1107 (Resort), 011–52–333–4–0000 (Golf Course)
Fax: 011–52–333–4–1950

GOLF COURSE

Director of Golf: Rafael Belmont
Course Length/Par (All Tees): Back 6468/71, Blue 5997/71, White 5535/72, Forward 4760/71
Course Slope/Rating (All Tees): Back NA/73.7, Blue NA/71.4, White NA/69.0, Ladies' Forward NA/69.1
Course Architects: Pete and Roy Dye (9, 1974; 9, 1984)
Golf Facilities: Full Pro Shop X, Snack Bar X, Lounge X, Restaurant X, Locker Room X, Showers X, Club Rental X, Club Repair X, Cart Rental X, Instruction X, Practice Green X, Driving Range X, Practice Bunker X, Club Storage X
Tee-Time Reservation Policy: At time of confirmed hotel reservation. Up to 7 days in advance otherwise
Ranger: In season

Tee-off-Interval Time: 8 min.

Time to Play 18 Holes: 4 hrs.

Course Hours/Earliest Tee-off: 7 a.m.

Green and Cart Fees: $90 for 18 holes plus tax, caddie (required) $16 for 18 holes

Credit Cards: American Express, Master-Card, Visa

Season: Year round. Busiest mid-Dec. through Easter holidays

Course Comments: Can walk the course but must take caddie in cart

Golf Packages: Through resort hotels, travel agents

Discounts: Seasonal, through reasort

Places to Stay Nearby: Club Maeva 011–52–333–3–2223, Fax: 011–52–333–3–0395; Club Santiago 011–52–333–3–0413; Sierra Radisson Plaza 011–52–333–3–2000, (800) 333–3333; Villas La Audiencia 011–52–333–3–0861; Plaza Las Glorias 011–52–333–3–0400, (800) 635–8483; Fiesta Mexicana 011–52–333–3–1100, (800) 325–2525

Local Attractions: Beaches, fishing, water sports including boating, surfing, snorkeling; seasonal festivals, restaurants, Mexican League professional baseball, shopping, crafts, horseback riding, tennis, tours. COLIMA 60 miles east of Manzanillo: provincial capitol, crafts and architectural center

Directions: From Manzanillo International Airport (30 min.). Take Hwy. 200 south toward Manzanillo. Take right at Peninsula de Santiago and follow signs to the resort

Closest Commercial Airports: Manzanillo International (Playa de Oro) Airport (30 min.). From Mexico City (90 min. northwest by air)

RESORT

Date Built: 1974

No. of Rooms: 220 rooms, including 41 suites

Meeting Rooms: Accommodates groups of up to 300 persons

Room Price Range: $155 to $265 for standard room. Peak season mid-Dec. through mid-April

Lounges: El Oasis, Coco Loco, Dona Albina, Disco Cartouch

Restaurants: El Terral, Legazpi, El Palmar

Entertainment: Live music, dancing

Credit Cards: American Express, Master-Card, Visa

General Amenities: Shopping arcade, meeting rooms with business and food services, tours arranged

Recreational Amenities: marina, 8 hard surface, 2 clay tennis courts; beach, 2 swimming pools, water sports including snorkeling, boating, fishing, scuba diving, horseback riding

Reservation and Cancellation Policy: Deposit required to guarantee reservations. 15 day cancellation policy

Comments and Restrictions: No pets. Taxes and gratuities additional

LA MANTARRAYA GOLF CLUB

Manzanillo, 180 miles south of Puerto Vallarta, was named for its beautiful fields of camomile (manzanillo in Spanish) by the Spanish explorer Cortez in 1531. With a population of over 75,000, Manzanillo ranks as one of Mexico's most important west coast ports, largely because it is the only one with rail connections to the interior. The Golden Strand which extends 10 miles north from Manzanillo to the Santiago Peninsula is dotted with hotels, beaches and restaurants culminating with Las Hadas (The Fairies), a self-contained white stucco luxury resort ensconced on the peninsula's southern slope. Within the Las Hadas resort, the creation of the multi-millionaire Antenor Patino and a location for the movie *10* with Dudley Moore and Bo Derek, is the Pete and Roy Dye–designed La Mantarraya golf course.

Water comes into play on eleven holes here and there is an abundance of waste bunkers, bunkers with coarse local sand, and well-placed palm, mango and other trees often appear in the wrong place at the wrong time. The wind off the nearby Pacific can also be a factor, varying according to season.

La Mantarraya has many excellent golf holes, most of which require strategic shot-making rather than distance. The course starts off with a difficult 395-yard par 4 (from the back tees), a dogleg left with a stream to the left and a pair of fairway bunkers bracketing the tee shot landing area. The approach shot is over the stream to a deep, undulating, slightly-elevated green. Next is a spectacular 175-yard par 3, the first of three par 3s on the front side. A long carry is required over water to reach the large green fronted by traps and with an unusual bunker in the middle of the putting surface. These two opening holes provide a good taste of the variety and challenge on this layout.

Among my favorite holes on the back nine is the 351-yard par-4 fourteenth with a stream that cuts in front of the tee and runs up the right fairway and out to the ocean on the horizon. An accurate tee shot, probably a long iron or a 3-wood, is required to set up a lefted approach to carry the stream which cuts in front of a forward-sloping, narrow green backed by bunkers. One of the most difficult par 5s on the course is the 521-yard fifteenth that has a tee shot landing area fronted and bordered on the right by a stream. The fairway then starts to narrow with intermittent palm trees and a waste bunker to the right. The medium-sized green is fronted by sand and protected to its rear by another bunker.

The most memorable hole at La Mantarraya is the 144-yard par-3 eighteenth whose tee is on a beautifully landscaped plateau looking out over the Pacific to an island green backed by a magnificent view of the resort as it juts out into the ocean. Rocks border the small target below and, as at the Dye-designed 17th at TPC Sawgrass, there is little margin for error. Both my caddie and I took a few extra shots off the tee at twilight on a warm June evening, just to enjoy this memorable experience. Local families strolled the golf course, some fished in the streams and others played on the adjacent public beach. And, as on many Mexican and Caribbean golf courses, there was a constant flow of local prospectors for looking for tourist gold, golf balls that can be resold for a king's ransom.

The rooms at the hotel have overhead fans, high ceilings, marble floors and are attended by employees in crisp, white uniforms. American-style fare such as hamburgers, corn flakes and eggs and bacon can be ordered here as well as gaspacho, grilled lobster, huevos rancheros and a rich variety of locally caught fresh seafood.

GUERRERO

Course Name: **ACAPULCO PRINCESS GOLF CLUB**
Acapulco Princess, Pierre Marques Courses

Course Type: Resort
Resort: Acapulco Princess
Address: Playa Revolchadero/AP1351 Acapulco, Mexico
Phone: 011–52–748–43100 (Golf Course)
(800) 223–1818 (Resort)
(800) 223–1834 (Resort, Group Reservations)
Fax: 011–52–746–9–7017 (Resort)

GOLF COURSE

Director of Golf: Wayne Sisson
Course Length/Par (All Tees): Acapulco Princess: Back 6355/72, Middle 6085/72, Forward 5400/72. Pierre Marques: Back 6855/72, Championship 6557/72, Regular 6112/72, Ladies' Forward 5197/73
Course Slope/Rating (All Tees): Acapulco Princess: Back 117/NA, Middle NA/NA, Forward 115/NA. Pierre Marques: Back NA/71.5, Championship 127/69.4, Regular NA/69.8, Ladies' Forward 116/72.9
Course Architects: Acapulco Princess: Ted Robinson (1991). Pierre Marques: Robert Trent Jones, Sr. (1967)
Golf Facilities: Full Pro Shop X, Snack Bar X, Lounge X, Restaurant X, Locker Room No, Showers No, Club Rental X, Club Repair X, Cart Rental X, Instruction X, Practice Green X, Driving Range X, Practice Bunker X, Club Storage X

:e-Time Reservation Policy: Resort guests: At time of reservation. Outside play: 1 day in advance

Ranger: Yes

Tee-off-Interval Time: 7 min.

Time to Play 18 Holes: 4 hrs., 20 min.

Course Hours/Earliest Tee-off: 7:35 a.m.

Green and Cart Fees: Resort guests: $63 for 18 holes with cart. Outside play: $84 for 18 holes with cart

Credit Cards: All major cards

Season: Year round. Busiest season mid-Dec. to March

Course Comments: Cart mandatory. Shower available at Pierre Marques clubhouse

Golf Packages: Available through resort

Discounts: Seasonal (March to Oct.)

Places to Stay Nearby: Pierre Marques 74–84–2000, (800) 223–1818; Las Brisas 74–84–1650, (800) 228–3000. Fax: 74–84–2269; Hyatt Continental Acapulco 74–84–0909, (800) 223–1818. OLD ACAPULCO: Playa Hermosa 74–84–1491

Local Attractions: Beaches, restaurants, shopping, Papagayo Park, nightclubs; water sports such as water-skiing, snorkeling and others; fishing, tennis, Fuerte de San Diego, Museo Historico de Acapulco, Old Acapulco, bull fights. OUTSIDE ACAPULCO: Taxco. Ixtapa/Zihuatanejo. State of Guerrero Department of Tourism (SEFOTUR) 74–84–7050. Secretaria de Turismo 74–85–1049, 74–85–1304

Directions: Take left from airport onto main road, 5 mi. to hotel on the left

Closest Commercial Airport: Juan N. Alvarez, Acapulco (5 min.)

RESORT:

Date Built: 1971

No. of Rooms: 1019, including guest rooms, condominiums, villas, junior suites, penthouses, 1-bedroom suites

Meeting Rooms: 19. Capacity of Largest: 17,167 sq. ft. Meeting Space: 34,500 sq. ft.

Room Price Range: $250 for single standard to $900 for 2-bedroom penthouse per room, modified American plan, peak season (mid-Dec. through March). Golf

and honeymoon packages and lower seasonal rates, European plan available

Lounges: Laguna, La Cascada, La Palma, Grotto, La Palapa, La Hacienda, Bar Le Gourmet

Restaurants: La Veranda, Chula Vista, La Posadita, La Princessa, El Jardin, La Gourmet, La Hacienda, Golf Snack Bar

Entertainment: Dancing and music in Tiffany disco bar

Credit Cards: All major cards

General Amenities: Sunday film show, babysitters, sightseeing tours, cruises, meeting and conference facilities with audiovisual and food service, pharmacy, souvenir shops, boutiques, jewelry stores and art stores on premises

Recreational Amenities: Beach; fitness center with aerobics classes, horseback riding, jogging track, sauna, 11 tennis courts with professional instruction available; 4 fresh-water pools, 1 salt-water lagoon with water slide, children's wading pool, off-site deep-sea fishing, scuba diving, water-skiing and other water sports

Reservation and Cancellation Policy: Deposit required to guarantee reservation. Must cancel by mid-Nov. for reservations during peak season to avoid penalties. 3-day notice at other times

Comments and Restrictions: Added-value government tax applies to all purchases. Modified American plan in peak season (mid-Dec. through Easter). European plan during off season. Some of the facilities may not be operating at all certain times of year

ACAPULCO PRINCESS GOLF CLUB

The Acapulco Princess resort is situated near Acapulco Bay, one of the world's most beautiful natural harbors. In the old days, Acapulco was a significant Spanish port, used as a base of operations for trade with Far Eastern and other clients. More recently, this area is known as a vacation retreat with beaches, a variety of restaurants, resort hotels and night life. In the 1950s, Acapulco was a town of 20,000 with an economy based largely on fishing.

Today it is one of Mexico's largest cities, with more than 2 million people.

The Acapulco Princess is a huge, pyramid-shaped structure flanked by 2 white towers and surrounded by 4580 acres of meticulously manicured gardens and grounds. A short walk from the hotel is the 6355-yard Ted Robinson–designed Acapulco Princess Course, which opened in 1991. This layout is flat and well treed, and has water hazards on more than half the holes. Most fairway landing areas are guarded by sand bunkers and water. The medium-sized to large greens are usually protected by two or three traps and an occasional pond.

The Acapulco Princess Course is a good example of low stress resort golf. The 350-yard par-4 dogleg-right sixth hole plays to a green guarded by two bunkers to the left. The tee shot is to a landing area to the right of a long pond and to the left of a fairway bunker. The 345-yard par-4 ninth is a slight dogleg left to a deep green framed by a horseshoe of water left, rear and right. To the left and left front are traps. A memorable par 3 on this layout is the 135-yard seventeenth, which plays over a pond to a deep green protected both front and rear by bunkers. The longest par 3 at the Acapulco Princess is the 210-yard third hole, which plays to a deep green flanked by two large traps. As you wend your way through this scenic layout, it is clear that your approach shots and short game are the key to scoring on the Princess.

A more formidable layout is the 6855-yard par-72 Robert Trent Jones, Sr.–designed Pierre Marques Course, which opened in 1967. This is a longer and more difficult course, partly because of the wind, trees, hilliness and water hazards. The number-1-handicap hole is the 549-yard par-5 sixth, which usually plays into the wind. The tee shot on this dogleg left is to a landing area guarded by traps to the left and right. The second shot is probably a layup to a pond that crosses in front of a green well guarded by traps to the front and right. The third shot is a wedge or more to the putting surface.

The three finishing holes at the Pierre Marques are memorable. The 396-yard par-4 sixteenth is a slight dogleg right to a green fronted by a pond. The first shot is to a landing area guarded by traps to the right. The approach must clear the water and avoid the traps guarding the rear of the green. The 148-yard par-3 seventeenth plays over water to a green surrounded by water in front and traps elsewhere. The last hole, a 421-yard par 4, has a tee shot over water, into the wind and uphill to a landing area guarded by a bunker on the right. The next shot is also uphill to a green well protected by traps.

You can stay at the Acapulco Princess or nearby Pierre Marques, a quieter hotel, and play these courses. The Princess has a variety of rooms ranging from standard guest rooms to penthouses that have wet bars and can accommodate receptions of up to 60 guests. Mexico's arts and handicrafts are tasteful elements in all these rooms. Recreational facilities at the resort include tennis, swimming pools, horseback riding, a fitness center and a variety of other activities. Nearby are beaches, water sports, fishing and boating opportunities. There is more than 34,000 square feet of meeting space at the Acapulco Princess, and *Meetings and Conventions* magazine awarded it a Gold Tee in 1991, the first year of that award, for its excellent meeting and golf amenities.

The Acapulco Princess is rated a Five-Diamond facility by the American Automobile Association. Its numerous restaurants offer a choice of French food in Le Gourmet, one of Acapulco's finest French restaurants, or you might enjoy Mexican cuisine at La Hacienda, which has barbecue specialties and steaks. In addition to the amenities at the hotel, there are the restaurants and night clubs of Acapulco to consider.

Golf packages are available through the resort. The peak season is mid-December through Easter. Instruction is available at both courses, and practice facilities include a driving range, practice bunkers and putting green.

Course Name: MARINA IXTAPA
GOLF CLUB

Course Type: Resort
Address: Paseo Ixtapa, Ixtapa, Mexico
Phone: 011-52-753-3-1500

GOLF COURSE

Head Professional: Charles McClain
Course Length/Par (All Tees): Back
6781/72, White 6300/72, Yellow
5740/72, Forward 5197/72
Course Slope/Rating (All Tees): NA/NA
Course Architect: Robert von Hagge
(1992)
Golf Facilities: Full Pro Shop X, Snack
Bar X, Lounge X, Restaurant X,
Locker Room X, Showers X, Club
Rental X, Club Repair X, Cart Rental
X, Instruction X, Practice Green X,
Driving Range X, Practice Bunker No,
Club Storage No
Tee-Time Reservation Policy: Call anytime
in advance
Ranger: Yes
Tee-off-Interval Time: 8 min.
Time to Play 18 Holes: 4 hrs.
Course Hours/Earliest Tee-off: 7 a.m.
Green and Cart Fees: $50 for 18 holes
with cart
Credit Cards: American Express, Master-
Card, Visa
Season: Year round. Busiest Nov.-Apr.
Course Comments: Cart mandatory
Golf Packages: Through resort hotels,
travel agents
Discounts: Twilight. Through resort hotels,
travel agents
Places to Stay Nearby: IXTAPA: Sheraton
Ixtapa Resort 011-753-3-1858, (800)
334-8484; Plaza Ixtapa 011-753-3-
1866; Westin Ixtapa 011-753-3-2121,
(800) 228-3000; Krystal Ixtapa 011-
753-3-0333, (800) 231-9860; Stouffer
Presidente Ixtapa 011-753-3-0018,
(800) HOTELS-1. ZIHUATANEJO: Villa
de Sol 011-753-4-3239, (800) 223-
6510; La Casa Que Canta 011-753-4-
2106; Hotel Villas Miramar 011-753
-4-2106. House, apartment, condominium rentals: Century 21, Av. Marina,
National 71G, Zihuatanejo, Mexico 011-
753-435-46; Elizabeth Williams, P.O.

Box 167, Zihuatanejo, Mexico 011-753-
4-2606, Fax: 011-753-4-4762
Local Attractions: IXTAPA: Beaches, shopping, crafts, boating, fishing, scuba diving, surfing, restaurants, night clubs,
horseback riding, tennis, tours, seasonal
festivals. ZIHUATANEJO: Museo Argueolo-
gia de la Costa Grande, restaurants,
beaches, water sports, restaurants, shopping, horseback riding, tours
Directions: Take Paseo Ixtapa (the ocean
road along the Playa del Palmar) to the
Ixtapa Marina, just north of central Ixtapa
Closest Commercial Airports: Ixtapa-
Zihuatanejo Airport (30 min.). From
Mexico City (1 hr. southwest by air)

MARINA IXTAPA

The 6781-yard par-72 Marina Ixtapa
golf course was designed by Robert von
Hagge and features several bunkers, grass
mounds and tricky grass indentations bordering the fairways and greens. Water can
come into play on eleven holes and
the ocean winds often add difficulty to this
challenging layout. The large greens have a
variety of shelves and undulations, making
it easy to three-putt if your approach shots
are not well executed. Von Hagge provides
a range of tee distances and hole designs to
make this course one that you will want to
play more than once.

The four finishing holes offer an excellent conclusion to a round at the Marina.
The 401-yard par-4 fifteenth is a dogleg
right cut by a diagonal channel approximately 100 to 150 yards from the back
tees. The tee shot should be played to the
left center in order to avoid the channel
and to elude the right bunker twenty yards
in front of the deep, forward sloping green.
The 396-yard par-4 sixteenth, the number
one handicap hole on the course, is a sharp
dogleg left bordered by a canal on the left
from tee to green.

The seventeenth is a 146-yard par 3
whose deep green is fronted by the canal.
The back tee position leaves you a fore-
shortened target area with more likelihood
of catching the water or any of the three
bunkers protecting the putting surface. The

lengthy 609-yard par-5 finishing hole is bordered by a canal on the left. The difficulty of the approach shot to the green depends on the quality of the two preceding shots. A huge bunker cuts the fairway 100 yards from a deep green guarded by water to the left and grassy mounds to the right. Another bunker protects the rear of the target.

Marina Ixtapa is within a new multimillion-dollar golf course real estate and development complex on the Pacific Ocean. The golf course is served by a two-story white stucco Spanish-style clubhouse with pro shop, restaurant, bar, golf cart and club storage facility. The Marina golf course has a practice putting green surrounding a swimming pool and a separate practice range with a small adjacent putting green.

JALISCO

Course Name: **MARINA VALLARTA GOLF CLUB**

Course Type: Semiprivate
Address: Paseo de la Marina Norte, KM 7.5 Carretera Aeropuerto, Puerto Vallarta, Mexico
Phone: 011–52–322–1–0545

GOLF COURSE

Head Professional: Tim Sulak
Course Length/Par (All Tees): Back 6701/71, Middle 6093/71, Ladies' Forward 5279/72
Course Slope/Rating (All Tees): Back 136/73.2, Middle 128/71.4, Forward 117/70.1
Course Architect: Joe Finger (1989)
Golf Facilities: Full Pro Shop X, Snack Bar X, Lounge X, Restaurant X, Locker Room X, Showers X, Club Rental X, Club Repair X, Cart Rental X, Instruction X, Practice Green X, Driving Range X, Practice Bunker X, Club Storage X
Tee-Time Reservation Policy: Call anytime
Ranger: Yes
Tee-off-Interval Time: 8 min.
Time to Play 18 Holes: 4 hrs. 15 min.
Course Hours/Earliest Tee-off: 7 a.m.

Green and Cart Fees: $80 for 18 holes including cart. Fee varies depending on hotel discounts
Credit Cards: American Express, MasterCard, Visa
Season: Year round. Busiest late Dec. through Apr.
Course Comments: Caddies mandatory. Walking allowed with caddy. Caddies paid on tips only basis
Golf Packages: Through resort hotels, travel agents
Discounts: Replays. Through resort hotel, travel agents
Places to Stay Nearby: Marriott Casa Magna (on site) 011–322–1–1004, (800) 228–9290; Fiesta Americana 011–322–4–2010, (800) FIESTA–1; Hyatt Coral Grand 011–322–2–5191, (800) 233–1234; Krystal Vallarta 011–322–2–0202, (800) 231–9860; Ramada Vallarta Beach Resort 011–322–4–1700, (800) 272–6232; Regina Vallarta 011–322–1–1100; La Jolla de Mismaloya 011–322–3–0660; Melia Puerto Vallarta 011–322–1–2000
Local Attractions: Restaurants, shopping, beaches, fishing, boating, scuba diving, snorkeling, seasonal festivals, bullfights, municipal market, crafts, tennis, horseback riding, art galleries, tours
Directions: From Puerto Vallarta Gustavo Diaz Ordaz International Airport take Hwy. 200/Ocean Hwy. south 5 min. to Marriott Casa Magna at the corner of Paseo de la Marina. Golf course is across from the beachfront hotel
Closest Commercial Airports: Puerto Vallarta Diaz Ordaz International Airport (5 min.). From Mexico City (90 min. northwest by air)

MARINA VALLARTA GOLF CLUB

Puerto Vallarta, a bustling international beach community of over 250,000 people, is situated on the dramatic Bahia de Banderas (Bay of Flags), the seventh largest bay in the world. Richard Burton and Elizabeth Taylor, not avid golfers, put this town on the map when they fell in love during the filming of *The Night of the Iguana* in the mid-1960s.

North of downtown Puerto Vallarta and just south of the airport is a string of beachside hotels, marinas and restaurants. The Marina Vallarta Golf Club, which features a 6,701-yard par-71 Joe Finger–designed layout, is within walking distance of the Marriott Casa Magna Hotel, an extravaganza with all the amenities of a self-contained resort. Patrons of the Marriott and other resort hotels can reserve tee times and store clubs at the Marina.

The Marina is an open resort-style course with large greens protected by two or three sizeable bunkers and bordered by mounds, swales and water hazards. The ocean breezes add another variable to consider when playing this course. The Bermuda grass greens are medium speed and in fairly good shape. Caddies are required whether you intend to walk this course or ride.

A good par 4 at the Marina is the 428-yard seventh whose tee shot plays to a genreous landing area with a bunker to the right. The approach shot is to a deep green bordered by two large bunkers and protected by an island of rough 30 yards in front of the green. My favorite par 4 on this side is the 439-yard fifth which has an open tee shot then a demanding approach shot to a deep, forward-sloping green guarded by water to its left and front and a large bunker to the right.

The most difficult par 3 on the course is the scenic 206-yard thirteenth which has the beach and the bay to your left, a water hazard to the right and a bunker to the immediate right of a deep, forward-sloping target with a small shelf in its right front quadrant. The left-to-right wind puts club selection and accuracy at a premium on this memorable golf hole. The round finishes with a 418-yard par 4. The tee shot is straight toward the distant mountains. To the right is a series of bunkers and to the left are homes, cactus and other desert vegetation. The approach shot is to a deep green with water to its left, a left front bunker which narrows the entranceway and a huge bunker to the right. A well-positioned tee shot is necessary to set up a birdie or par opportunity on this hole.

As you look south across the Bay of Flags from the Marina Vallarta Golf Course, you see the hotel district merge into the cobblestoned Old Town situated around the Rio Cuale. City Hall, the Chruch of Our Lady Guadalupe, the municipal market, Gringo Gulch (home of the expatriates), and shops selling folk art, jewelry and other delights should be included in your itinerary. South of the Rio Cuale is the Playa de los Muertos (Beach of the Dead Ones), the most popular and crowded beach in this region. Your hotel can arrange trips to bullfights, nearby jungles and waterfalls, or Mexican fiestas as well as cruises, fishing outings and other activities.

Recommended Golf Courses in Mexico

From the United States, dial 011–52 and the telephone number listed below:

Baja Sur

Baja Country Club, Ensenada, 667–30303, Semiprivate, 18/6834/72

Bajamar, Ensenada, 662–03300, Semiprivate, 18/6894/72

Real Del Mar Golf Club, Rosarito, 918–0066627, Semiprivate, 18/6403/72

Club Campestre de Tijuana, Tijuana, 6686–1401, Semiprivate, 18/6630/72

Baja Sur:

Campo de Carlos, Cabo San Lucas, 684–31922, Semiprivate, 18/7158/72

Loreto Golf Course, Loreto, 683–30408, Semiprivate, 18/6800/72

Campeche:

Club de Golf Playa Palmas, Campeche, 938–938–21858, Semiprivate, 18/6234/72

Chihuahua:

Club Campestre Chihuahua, Chihuahua, 14–180011, Semiprivate, 18/6851/72

Club Campestre Juarez, Ciudad Juarez, 61–77707, Semiprivate, 18/6846/72

Coahuila:

Club Campestre Saltillo, Saltillo, 84–37901, Semiprivate, 18/6543/72

Club Campestre de Torreon, Torreon, 111–135080, Semiprivate, 18/6800/72

Durango:

Centro Campestre Lagunero, Durango, 171–41194, Semiprivate, 18/6286/72

Guanajuato:

Club Campestre Celayense, Celaya, 461–21397, Semiprivate, 18/6480/72

Club Campestre Leon, Leon, 471–70521, Semiprivate, 18/6635/72

Guerrero:

Campo de Golf Ixtapa, Ixtapa, 753–31062, Semiprivate, 18/6898/72

Jalisco:

Club Deportivo Atlas de Guadalajara, Guadalajara, 36–890085, Semiprivate, 18/6742/72

San Isidro Club de Golf, Guadalajara, 36–332814, Semiprivate, 18/6663/72

Mexico (Federal District):

Club de Golf Campestre Del Lago, Mexico City, 5–849926, Semiprivate, 18/6580/72

Club de Golf Chiluca, Ciudad Lopez, 594–21700, Semiprivate, 18/6776/72

Club de Golf Campestre Del Lago, Col. Polanco, 557–6913, Semiprivate, 18/6590/72

Club de Golf Mexico, Tlalpan, 5–5732000, Semiprivate, 18/7142/72

Club de Golf Valle Escondido, Satelite, 5–8223422, Semiprivate, 18/6772/72

Mexico (State of):

Club de Golf Avandaro, Valle de Bravo, 5–6876645, Semiprivate, 18/6369/72

Club de Golf La Hacienda, Atizapan De Zaragoza, 5–3790033, Semiprivate, 18/7090/72

Club de Golf San Carlos, Edo. de Mexico, Mexico City, 721– 63793, Semiprivate, 18/6829/71

Coral Golf Club, Edo. de Mexico, Mexico City, 597–20277, Semiprivate, 18/6644/72

Rancho Avandaro Country Club, Valle de Bravo, 726–20003, Semiprivate, 18/6725/72

Morelos:

Club Campestre Lomas de Cocoyos, Cocoyoc, 735–61211, Semiprivate, 18/6724/72

Club Deportivo Cocoyoc, Cocoyoc, 735–61211, Resort, 18/5697/72 (two rounds, 9 hole course)

Club de Golf Los Tabachines, Cuernavaca, 731–43999, Semiprivate, 18/6742/72

Club de Golf Santa Fe, Cuernavaca, 739–12011, Semiprivate, 18/6888/72

Club de Golf San Gaspar, Cuernavaca, 731–90002, Semiprivate, 18/6879/72

Nuevo Leon:

Club Campestre Monterrey, Monterrey, 83–785818, Semiprivate, 18/6826/72

Club de Golf Valle Alto, Monterrey, 83–573203, Semiprivate, 18/6854/72

Oaxaca:

Campo de Golf Tangolunda, Huatulco, 958–10037, Semiprivate, 18/6851/72

Puebla:

Club Campestre El Cristo, Atlixco, 244–50295, Semiprivate, 18/6653/72

Club de Golf Puebla, Puebla, 224–31130, Semiprivate, 18/6795/72

Queretaro:

Club Campestre Queretaro, Queretaro, 463–62011, Semiprivate, 18/6863/72

Club de Golf Tequisquiapan, Tequisquiapan, 467–30092, Semiprivate, 18/6754/72

Quintana Roo:

Club de Golf Pok-Ta-Pok, Cancun, 988–31230, Semiprivate, 18/6721/73

Sinaloa:

Country Club de Culican, Culican, 671–42275, Semiprivate, 18/7212/72

El Cid Country Club, Mazatlan, 691–33333, Semiprivate, 18/6729/72

Tamaulipas:

Club Campestre Riviera Del Bravo, Nueva Ladero, 871–42334, Semiprivate, 18/6325/72 (two rounds, 9 hole course)

Club Campestre Reynosa, Reynosa, 892–21886, Semiprivate, 18/6640/72 (two rounds, 9 hole course)

Club Campestre Victoria, Victoria, 131–21110, Semiprivate, 18/6874/72

Sonora:

Country Club San Carlos, San Carlos, 622–60339, Semiprivate, 18/6829/72

Las Misiones Country Club, Garza Garcia, 83–780025, Semiprivate, 18/6751/72

Veracruz:

Club Campestre Coatzacalcos, Coatzacalcos, 921–40884, Semiprivate, 18/6224/72 (two rounds, 9 hole course)

Club Campestre Cordobes, Cordoba, 271–20144, Semiprivate, 18/6567/72 (two rounds, 9 hole course)

Club de Golf La Villa Rica, Veracruz, 293–350581, Semiprivate, 18/6213/70 (two rounds, 9 hole course)

Club de Golf de Xalapa, Xalapa, 281–76217, Semiprivate, 18/6874/72 (two rounds, 9 hole course)

Yucatan:

Club de Golf Yucatan, Merida, 992–47525, Semiprivate, 6605/72

Mexico: Useful Information

Mexican Government Tourism Office:

U.S. 405 Park Ave., Ste. 1002, New York, NY 10022, (212) 755–7261

1911 Pennsylvania Ave., NW, Washington, DC 20006, (202) 728–1750

70 E. Lake St., Ste. 1413, Chicago, IL 60601, (312) 565–2786

2707 N. Loop W, Ste. 450, Houston, TX 77008, (713) 880–5153

10100 Santa Monica Blvd., Ste. 224, Los Angeles, CA 90067, (310) 203–8191

2373 Ponce de Leon Blvd., Suite 710, Coral Gables, FL 33134, (305) 443–9160

Canada 1 Place Ville Marie, Ste. 2409, Montreal, Quebec H3B3M9, (514) 871–1052

181 University Ave., Ste. 1112, Toronto, ON M5H 3U7, (416) 364–2255

United Kingdom 7 Cork St., London W1X1OB, 01–734–1058

This index includes golf courses located at 617 sites in the United States, Canada, the Bahamas, Bermuda, the Caribbean and Mexico. More than 2,000 recommended courses in these regions are listed in the text.

Index

UNITED STATES
ALABAMA
Cambrian Ridge Golf Club, Greenville . . . 6
Canyon, Loblolly, Sherling, Short Courses
Grand National Golf Club, Opelika 8
Lake, Links, Short Courses
Kiva Dunes Golf Club, Gulf Shores 3
Lagoon Park Golf Course, Montgomery . . . 9
Lakewood Golf Club, Point Clear 4
Azalea, Dogwood Courses
ALASKA
Eagleglen Golf Course, Anchorage 13
ARIZONA
The Boulders, Carefree 16
North, South Courses
Gainey Ranch Golf Club, Scottsdale 19
Arroyo, Dunes, Lakes Courses
Grayhawk Golf Club, Scottsdale 21
La Paloma Country Club, Tucson 35
Canyon, Hill, Ridge Courses
Loews Ventana Canyon Resort, Tucson . . 37
Canyon Course
Loews Ventana Golf and Racquet
Club, Tucson 40
Canyon, Mountain Courses
Los Caballeros Golf Club, Wickenburg . . . 22
Sedona Golf Resort, Oak Creek 15
Starr Pass Golf Club, Tucson 42
Stonecreek, Paradise Valley 24
Superstition Springs Golf Club, Mesa . . . 26
Tournament Players Club (TPC) of
Scottsdale, Scottsdale 28
Desert, Stadium Courses
Troon North Golf Club, Scottsdale 30
Tucson National Resort and Spa, Tucson . 44
Gold, Green, Orange Courses
The Wigwam Resort, Litchfield Park 32
Blue, Gold, West Courses
ARKANSAS
Mountain Ranch Golf Course,
Fairfield Bay 47
CALIFORNIA
Ancil Hoffman Golf Course, Carmichael . . 50
Carmel Valley Ranch, Carmel Valley 60
Desert Dunes Golf Club, Palm Springs . . . 86
Desert Springs, Palm Desert 87
Greens, Palms, Valley Courses
Four Seasons Resort Aviara, Carlsbad . . . 98
Hunter Ranch Golf Course, Paso Robles . . 71
Indian Wells, Indian Wells 90

East, West Courses
Industry Hills Recreation and Conference
Center, City of Industry 79
Babe Didrikson Zaharias, Dwight D.
Eisenhower Courses
La Purisima Golf Course, Lompoc 72
La Quinta Golf Club, La Quinta 92
Dunes, Mountain Courses
The Links at Spanish Bay, Pebble Beach . . 62
Moreno Valley Ranch Golf Club,
Moreno Valley 81
Lake, Mountain, Valley Courses
Ojai Valley Inn and Country Club, Ojai . . 74
Pasatiempo, Santa Cruz 54
Pebble Beach Golf Links, Pebble Beach . . 64
Pelican Hill Golf Club, Newport Coast . . 83
Links, Ocean Courses
PGA WestJack Nicklaus Resort
Course, La Quinta 95
PGA WestTournament Players Club
Stadium Golf Course, La Quinta 95
Plumas Lake Golf Course, Marysville . . . 51
The Poppy Hills Golf Course,
Pebble Beach 67
Rancho La Costa, Carlsbad 100
North, South Courses
Sandpiper Golf Club, Goleta 77
Silverado Country Club, Napa . . . . . . \ . 56
North, South Courses
Singing Hills Country Club and Lodge,
El Cajon 103
Oak Glen, Pine Glen, Willow Glen Courses
Spyglass Hill Golf Course, Pebble Beach . . 66
Squaw Creek, Squaw Valley 52
Steele Canyon Golf Club, Jamul 105
Canyon, Meadow, Ranch Courses
Torrey Pines, La Jolla 106
North, South Courses
COLORADO
Arrowhead Golf Club, Littleton 110
Breckenridge Golf Club, Breckenridge . . 118
The Broadmoor Golf Club, Colorado
Springs 126
East, South, West Courses
Fox Hollow at Lakewood, Lakewood . . . 111
Canyon, Links, Meadows Courses
The Golf Courses at Hyland Hills,
Westminster 112
Blue, Gold, North, South Courses
Grandote Golf and Country Club, Laveta 129

eystone Ranch Golf Course, Keystone . 119
Marianna Butte Golf Course, Loveland . 114
Pole Creek Golf Club, Winter Park 122
Riverdale, Brighton 115
 Dunes, Knolls Courses
Sonnenalp Golf Club, Vail 123
Tamarron: The Cliffs, Durango 131
CONNECTICUT
Richter Park, Danbury 134
DELAWARE
Garrison's Lake Golf Club, Smyrna . . . 137
FLORIDA
Amelia Island Plantation, Amelia Island . 178
 Long Point, Oakmarsh, Oceanside,
 Oysterbay Courses
Arnold Palmer's Bay Hill Club,
 Orlando 154
 Challenger, Champion, Charger Courses
Bay Point Yacht and Country Club,
 Panama City Beach 186
 Club Meadows, Lagoon Legend Courses
The Champions at Summerfield, Stuart . 139
Colony West Country Club, Tamarac . . 140
Doral Golf Resort and Spa, Miami 141
 Blue, Gold, Green, Red, Silver,
 White Courses
Eastwood Golf Course, Fort Myers 197
Emerald Dunes, West Palm Beach 145
Gateway Golf and Country Club,
 Fort Myers 199
Golden Ocala Golf and Country Club,
 Ocala 157
The Golf Club at Marco Island,
 Marco Island 200
Grand Cypress Golf Club, Orlando . . . 158
 East, New, North, South Courses
Grenelefe, Haines City 163
 East, South, West Courses
Hunter's Creek, Orlando 165
Innisbrook Resort and Country Club,
 Tarpon Springs 190
 Copperhead, Island, Sandpiper Courses
Lely Flamingo Island Club, Naples . . . 202
Links at Key Biscayne, Key Biscayne . . 146
LPGA International, Daytona 174
The Palm Coast Resort, Palm Coast . . . 176
 Cypress Knoll, Matanzas Woods,
 Palm Harbor, Pine Lakes Courses
Pelican's Nest Golf Club, Bonita
 Springs 204
 Gator, Hurricane, Panther, Seminole Courses
PGA National Golf Club, Palm Beach
 Gardens 147
 Champion, Estate, General, Haig,
 Squire Courses
Sandestin Beach Hilton Golf and Tennis
 Resort, Destin 189

 Baytowne, Burnt Pine, Links Courses
Sawgrass Resort, Ponte Vedra Beach . . . 182
 East, Marsh Landing, Oak Bridge, South,
 TPC Stadium, TPC Valley, West Courses
Walt Disney World Resort, Lake
 Buena Vista 167
 Eagle Pines, Lake Buena Vista, Magnolia,
 Oak Trail, Osprey Ridge, Palm Courses
West Palm Beach Country Club, West
 Palm Beach 151
Windsor Parke Golf Club, Jacksonville . 185
World Woods, Brooksville 194
 Pine Barrens, Rolling Oaks, Short Courses
GEORGIA
Bull Creek Golf Course, Columbus 223
 East, West Courses
Callaway Gardens Golf Course and
 Resort, Pine Mountain 207
 Garden View, Lake View, Mountain
 View, Sky View Courses
Jones Creek Golf Club, Evans 218
Lake Lanier Islands Golf Club, Lake
 Lanier Islands 210
Osprey Cove Golf Club, St. Marys 225
Port Armor Club, Greensboro 220
Reynolds Plantation Golf Club,
 Greensboro 222
 Great Waters, Plantation Courses
Savannah Inn and Country Club,
 Savannah 231
The Sea Island Golf Club, St. Simons . . . .
 Island 226
 Marshside, Plantation, Seaside, Retreat,
 St. Simons Island Club Courses
Southbridge Golf Club, Savannah 233
Stone Mountain Park Golf Course,
 Stone Mountain 212
 Lakemont, Stonemont, Woodmont Courses
Stouffer Renaissance Pine Isle Resort, Lake
 Lanier Islands 213
White Columns Golf Club, Alpharetta . . 216
HAWAII
The Challenge at Manele, Lanai City,
 Lanai 256
The Experience at Koele, Lanai City,
 Lanai 258
Hapuna Golf Course, Kamuela, Hawaii . 236
Kapalua Golf Club, Lahaina, Maui 259
 Bay, Plantation, Village Courses
Kauai Lagoons Golf and Racquet Club,
 Kalapaki Beach, Lihue, Kauai 247
 Kiele, Lagoons Courses
Koolau Golf Course, Kaneohe, Oahu . . . 266
Ko Olina Golf Club, Ewa Beach, Oahu . . 267
Makena Resort, Kihei, Maui 263
 North, South Courses

Mauna Kea Golf Course, Kohala Coast,
Hawaii 240
Mauna Lani Resort Golf Courses, Kohala
Coast, Hawaii 237
North, South Courses
Poipu Bay Resort Golf Course, Koloa,
Kauai 250
Prince Course, Princeville, Kauai 251
Makai (Lakes, Ocean, Woods),
Prince Courses
Sheraton Makaha Golf Club,
Makaha, Oahu 269
Waikoloa Golf Club, Waikoloa, Hawaii . . 244
Beach, Kings' Courses
Wailea Golf Club, Maui 264
Blue, Emerald, Gold Courses
Wailua Municipal Golf Course,
Lihue, Kauai 255
IDAHO
Coeur d'Alene, Coeur d'Alene 274
Elkhorn Resort, Sun Valley 277
Quail Hollow Golf Club, Boise 273
Sun Valley, Sun Valley 279
ILLINOIS
Cantigny Golf Course, Wheaton 284
Hillside, Lakeside, Woodside Courses
Cog Hill, Lemont 287
No. 1, No. 2, No. 3, No. 4/Dubsdread
Eagle Creek, Findlay 302
Eagle Ridge, Galena 298
East, North, South, General Courses
Heritage Bluffs Public Golf Club,
Channahon 289
Kemper Lakes, Long Grove 290
Lick Creek Golf Course, Pekin 283
Pine Meadow Golf Club, Mundelein . . . 293
Prairie Landing Golf Club, West Chicago 295
The Rail Golf Course, Springfield 305
Ruffled Feathers Golf Club, Lemont . . . 296
Spencer T. Olin Community Golf Course,
Alton 300
INDIANA
Blackthorn Golf Club, South Bend 314
Brickyard Crossing, Indianapolis 307
Covered Bridge Golf Club, Sellersburg . 315
Eagle Creek Golf Course, Indianapolis . . 308
Eagle Creek, West Nine Courses
Golf Club of Indiana, Lebanon 310
Hulman Links Golf Course, Terre Haute . 317
The Legends of Indiana Golf Course,
Franklin 311
Otter Creek Golf Course, Columbus . . . 312
East, North, West Courses
Sultan's Run Golf Course, Jasper 316
IOWA
Amana Colonies Golf Course, Amana . . 321

KANSAS
Alvamar Golf Club, Lawrence 324
Buffalo Dunes Golf Course, Garden City . 325
Deer Creek Golf Club, Overland Park . . 326
Terradyne Resort Hotel and Country Club,
Andover 328
KENTUCKY
Griffin Gate Golf Course, Lexington . . . 330
Kearney Hill Golf Links, Lexington . . . 332
Lassing Pointe Golf Club, Union 333
LOUISIANA
The Bluffs on Thompson Creek,
St Francisville 336
MAINE
Sable Oaks Golf Club, South Portland . . 339
The Samoset Resort Golf Club, Rockport 340
Sugarloaf Golf Club, Carrabassett Valley . 342
Waterville Country Club, Waterville . . . 344
MARYLAND
Hog Neck Golf Course, Easton 346
Queenstown Harbor Golf Links,
Queenstown 347
Lakes, River Courses
MASSACHUSETTS
The Captain's Golf Course, Brewster . . . 350
Country Club of New Seabury,
New Seabury 352
Blue, Green Courses
Crumpin-Fox Club, Bernardston 355
Taconic Golf Club, Williamstown 357
MICHIGAN
Boyne Highlands Resort, Harbor Springs . 372
Donald Ross Memorial, Heather,
Moor Courses
Boyne Mountain Resort, Boyne Falls . . . 376
Alpine, Hemlock Executive, Monument
Courses
Dunmaglas Golf Course, Charlevoix . . . 379
Elk Ridge Golf Course, Atlanta 365
Grand Haven Golf Club, Grand Haven . . 387
Grand Traverse Resort, Grand Traverse
Village (Acme) 380
The Bear, Spruce Run Courses
High Pointe Golf Club, Williamsburg . . . 382
Lakewood Shores Resort, Oscoda 366
The Gailes, Resort Courses
The Orchards Golf Club, Washington . . 363
Rattle Run, St. Clair 361
Shanty Creek Schuss Mountain Resort,
Bellaire 384
Legend, Schuss Mountain, Shanty Creek
Courses
Thoroughbred Golf Club, Rothbury . . 389
Timber Ridge Golf Club, East Lansing . . 362
Treetops Sylvan Resort, Gaylord 367
Fazio, Jones, Smith Courses
Wilderness Valley Golf Resort, Gaylord . 370
Black Forest, Valley Courses

MINNESOTA
Bunker Hills Golf Course, Coon Rapids . 392
   East, North, West, Executive Courses
Edinburgh USA, Brooklyn Park 393
Majestic Oaks Country Club,
   Ham Lake 394
   Executive, Gold, Platinum Courses
The Pines, Nisswa 396
   Lake, Marsh, Woods Courses
MISSISSIPPI
Kirkwood National Golf Club,
   Holly Springs 401
Timberton Golf Club, Hattiesburg 402
MISSOURI
Lodge of the Four Seasons, Lake Ozark . 404
   Executive, Robert Trent Jones
   Championship, Seasons, Ridge Courses
Missouri Bluffs Golf Club, St. Charles . . 408
Tan-Tar-A Golf Club, Osage Beach . . . 406
   Hidden Lakes, Oaks Courses
MONTANA
Buffalo Hill Golf Club, Kalispell 411
   Cameron, Championship Courses
Eagle Bend Golf Club, Bigfork 412
   Lake, Ridge Courses
Whitefish Lake Golf Club, Whitefish . . 414
   North, South Courses
NEBRASKA . . . .
Shadow Ridge Golf Course, Omaha . . . 417
Woodland Hills Golf Club, Eagle 418
NEVADA
Dayton Valley Country Club, Dayton . . 424
Desert Inn Country Club, Las Vegas . . 420
Edgewood Tahoe Golf Course, Stateline . 425
The Golf Club of Genoa Lakes, Genoa . 427
Incline Village Golf Resort, Incline
   Village 428
   Championship, Executive Courses
The Legacy Golf Club at Green Valley,
   Henderson 422
NEW HAMPSHIRE
The Balsams Resort, Dixville Notch . . . 432
   Coashaukee, Panorama Courses
Bretwood Golf Course, Keene 435
   North, South Courses
The Country Club of New Hampshire,
   North Sutton 437
Eastman Golf Links, Grantham 439
Portsmouth Country Club, Greenland . . 440
Shattuck Inn Golf Course, Jaffrey 441
Sky Meadow Country Club, Nashua . . . 442
NEW JERSEY
Great Gorge Country Club, McAfee . . . 445
   Lake, Rail, Quarry Courses
Hominy Hill Golf Course, Colts Neck . . 447
Howell Park Golf Course, Farmingdale . 449

Marriott's Seaview Golf Resort,
   Absecon 451
   Bay, Pines Courses
NEW MEXICO
Cochiti Lake Golf Course, Cochiti Lake . 455
The Inn of the Mountain Gods,
   Mescalero 456
Pion Hills Golf Course, Farmington . . . 458
Santa Ana Golf Course, Bernalilo 460
   Coronado, Rio Grande, Tamaya
Taos Country Club, Rancho de Taos . . . 462
University of New Mexico Golf Course,
   Albuquerque 463
   North, South Courses
NEW YORK
Bethpage State Park, Farmingdale 467
   Black, Blue, Green, Red, Yellow Courses
Colgate University Seven Oaks Golf Club,
   Hamilton 478
The Concord Championship Golf Club,
   Kiamesha Lake 473
   Challenger, International, Monster Courses
En-Joie Golf Club, Endicott 476
Glen Oak Golf Course, East Amherst . . . 481
Leatherstocking Golf Club,
   Cooperstown 479
Montauk Downs State Park, Montauk . . 469
The Sagamore Golf Club, Bolton
   Landing 482
Saranac Inn Golf and Country Club,
   Saranac Inn 485
Saratoga Spa State Park, Saratoga
   Springs 488
   Championship, Executive Courses
Spook Rock Golf Course, Ramapo 471
NORTH CAROLINA
Bryan Park and Golf Club, Brown
   Summit 492
   Champions, Players Courses
Duke Golf Club, Durham 510
Linville Golf Club, Linville 513
Marsh Harbour Golf Links, Calabash . . 515
The Neuse Golf Club, Clayton 511
Oak Hollow Golf Course, High Point . . 494
Oyster Bay Golf Links, Sunset Beach . . 516
Pinehurst Resort and Country Club,
   Pinehurst 498
   Course Numbers 1, 2, 3, 4, 5, 6, 7, 8
Pine Needles Golf Course, Pinehurst . . . 504
The Pit Golf Links, Pinehurst 506
Talamore Golf Course, Southern Pines . . 508
Tanglewood Park, Clemmons 495
   Championship, Reynolds Courses
NORTH DAKOTA
Edgewood Golf Course, Fargo 520
Minot Country Club, Minot 521
Riverwood Golf Course, Bismarck 522

INDEX

OHIO
Avalon Lakes Golf Course, Warren 524
Blue Ash Golf Course, Blue Ash 525
Cook's Creek Golf Club, Ashville 527
Eaglesticks Golf Club, Zanesville 528
Shaker Run Golf Club, Lebanon 530
The Vineyard, Cincinnati 531
OKLAHOMA
Page Belcher Golf Course, Tulsa 536
Olde Page, Stone Creek Courses
Forest Ridge Golf Course, Broken Arrow 537
Karsten Creek Golf Course, Stillwater . . 538
OREGON
Eastmoreland Golf Course, Portland . . . 546
Heron Lakes Golf Course, Portland . . . 548
Great Blue, Greenback Courses
Pumpkin Ridge Ghost Creek Course,
Cornelius 550
Salishan Golf Links, Gleneden Beach . . 551
Sandpines Golf Course, Florence 553
Sunriver Resort Golf Course, Sunriver . . 541
Crosswater, North Woodlands, South Meadow
Courses
Tokatee Golf Club, Blue River 545
PENNSYLVANIA
Champion Lakes Golf Club, Bolivar . . . 564
Country Club of Hershey, Hershey 558
East, West Courses
Nemacolin Woodlands Resort,
Farmington 566
Links, Mystic Ridge Courses
Quicksilver Golf Club, Midway 568
Toftrees Resort, State College 562
Wyncote Golf Club, Oxford 556
RHODE ISLAND 571
SOUTH CAROLINA
Arcadian Shores Golf Club,
Myrtle Beach 591
Caledonia Golf and Fish Club,
Pawleys Island 592
Callawassie Island Club, Beaufort 580
Dogwood, Magnolia, Palmetto Courses
Dunes West Golf Course, Mount Pleasant 572
Heather Glen Golf Links, North
Myrtle Beach 593
One, Two, Three Courses
Heritage Golf Club, Pawleys Island 595
Kiawah Island Resort, Kiawah Island . . 573
Marsh Point, Ocean, Osprey Point, Turtle
Point Courses
The Legends Golf Club, Myrtle Beach . . 596
Heathland, Moorland, Parkland Courses
The Long Bay Club, Longs 598
Palmetto Dunes Resort, Hilton Head
Island 582
Fazio, Hills, Jones Courses at Palmetto
Dunes; Cupp, Hills Courses at Palmetto Hall

Sea Pines Resort, Hilton Head Island
Harbour Town, Ocean, Sea Marsh Cou.
Tidewater Golf Club and Plantation,
North Myrtle Beach . . . .
Wild Dunes, Isle of Palms . . . .
Harbor, Links Courses
Wild Wing Plantation, Conway . . . . .
Avocet, Falcon, Hummingbird, Wood Stork
Courses
SOUTH DAKOTA
Hillcrest Golf and Country Club,
Yankton 606
Meadowbrook Golf Course, Rapid City . 607
Willow Run Golf Course, Sioux Falls . . 608
TENNESSEE
Fall Creek Falls State Park Golf Course,
Pikeville 611
The Legends Club of Tennessee, Franklin . 612
North, South Courses
Springhouse Golf Club, Nashville 614
Stonehenge Golf Club, Fairfield Glade . . 615
TEXAS
Barton Creek, Austin 619
Crenshaw and Coore, Fazio, Lakeside
Courses
Four Seasons Resort and Club, Irving . . 625
Tournament Players Course
Hill Country Golf Club, San Antonio . . . 637
Horseshoe Bay Country Club,
Horseshoe Bay 622
Applerock, Ram Rock, Slick Rock Courses
Hyatt Bear Creek Golf and Racquet Club,
Dallas-Fort Worth Airport 628
East, West Courses
La Cantera Golf Club, San Antonio . . . 639
Pecan Valley Golf Course, San Antonio . 640
The Quarry, San Antonio 642
Timarron Golf and Country Club,
South Lake 631
Waterwood National Country Club,
Huntsville 632
The Woodlands, The Woodlands 635
North, TPC Courses
UTAH
Green Spring Golf Course, Washington . 645
Park Meadows Golf Club, Park City . . . 646
Sunbrook Golf Club, St. George 648
Valley View Golf Course, Layton 649
VERMONT
Gleneagles Golf Course, Manchester . . . 652
Rutland Country Club, Rutland 654
Stratton Mountain Country Club,
Stratton Mountain 655
Forest, Lake, Mountain Courses
Sugarbush Golf Course, Warren 658

INDEX

...olony Country Club,
...msburg 672
...Gold, Red/White Courses
...n Horseshoe Golf Course,
...liamsburg 673
...ld, Green, Spotswood Courses
...e Homestead, Hot Springs 663
...ascades, Homestead, Lower Cascades
Courses
...Kingsmill Resort, Williamsburg 678
  Bray Links, Plantation, River,
  Woods Courses
Landsdowne Golf Club, Leesburg 661
The Tides Inn, Irvington 682
  Golden Eagle Course
Wintergreen Resort, Wintergreen 667
  Devil's Knob, Stoney Creek Courses

WASHINGTON
Classic Country Club, Spanaway 688
Desert Canyon Golf Course, Orondo . . 700
Harbour Pointe Golf Course, Mukilteo . 689
Indian Canyon Golf Course, Spokane . . 698
Kayak Point Golf Course, Stanwood . . . 691
McCormick Woods Golf Course,
  Port Orchard 693
Port Ludlow Golf Course, Port Ludlow . 694
  Tide, Timber, Trail Courses
Semiahmoo Golf and Country Club,
  Blaine 686

WEST VIRGINIA
The Greenbrier, White Sulphur Springs . 702
  Greenbrier, Lakeside, Old White Courses
Hawthorne Valley Golf Course,
  Snowshoe 706
Lakeview Resort, Morgantown 708
  Lakeview, Mountainview Courses
Oglebay, Wheeling 710
  Crispin, Speidel Courses

WISCONSIN
Blackwolf Run, Kohler 713
  Meadow Valleys, River Courses
Brown County Golf Course, Oneida . . . 723
Geneva National Golf Club,
  Lake Geneva 716
  Palmer, Trevino Courses
Lawsonia Golf Course, Green Lake . . . 718
  Links, Woodlands Courses
Sentryworld Golf Course, Stevens Point . 724
University Ridge, Verona 721

WYOMING
Jackson Hole Golf and Tennis Club,
  Jackson 728
Olive Glen Golf and Country Club,
  Cody 729
Teton Pines Golf Club, Jackson 731

CANADA

ALBERTA
Banff Springs, Banff 737
  Rundle, Sulphur, Tunnel Courses
Jasper Park Golf Course, Jasper 739
Kananaskis Country Golf Course,
  Kananaskis Village 742
  Mt. Kidd, Mt. Lorrette Courses
Wolf Creek, Ponoka 745

BRITISH COLUMBIA
Cordova Bay, Victoria 747
Gallaghers Canyon, Kelowna 748
Peace Portal Golf Club, South Surrey . . 750
Rivershore Golf Course, Kamloops . . . 751
Royal Colwood Golf Club, Victoria . . . 753
Westwood Plateau Golf and
  Country Club, Coquitlan 754
Whistler, Whistler Village 756
  Arnold Palmer, Robert Trent Jones, Jr.
  Courses

MANITOBA
Wasagaming Golf Course, Wasagaming . 760

NEW BRUNSWICK
Algonquin Golf Courses, St. Andrews . . 761
  Seaside, Woodlands Courses

NEWFOUNDLAND AND LABRADOR
Twin Rivers Golf Course, Port Blanford . 763

NOVA SCOTIA
Highland Links, Cape Breton 765

ONTARIO
Angus Glen Golf Club, Markham 767
Deerhurst Resort, Huntsville 769
  Highlands, Lakeside Courses
Glen Abbey Golf Club, Oakville 771
Lionhead Golf and Country Club,
  Brampton 773
  Legends, Masters Courses
National Pines, Barrie 774
Roseland Golf and Curling Club,
  Windsor 776

PRINCE EDWARD ISLAND
Brudenell Golf and Country Club,
  Cardigan 778
The Links at Crowbush Cove, Morell . . 779
Mill River, O'Leary 780

QUEBEC
Carling Lake, Pine Hill 782
Gray Rocks, St.-Jovite 784

SASKATCHEWAN
Willows Golf and Country Club,
  Saskatoon 786
  Bridges, Island, Lakes, Xena Courses

BAHAMAS, BERMUDA, CARIBBEAN

BAHAMAS
Bahamas Princess, Freeport 791
  Emerald, Ruby Courses

INDEX

BERMUDA
Castle Harbour Golf Club,
Tuckers Town 793
DOMINICAN REPUBLIC
Casa De Campo Resort, La Romana . . . 795
La Romana Country Club, Links, Teeth
of the Dog Courses
JAMAICA
Half Moon Golf Club, Montego Bay . . . 798
PUERTO RICO
Hyatt Dorado Beach, Dorado Beach . . . 800
East, North, South, West Courses
U.S. VIRGIN ISLANDS
Carambola Beach Golf Club, Kings Hill,
St. Croix 803
WEST INDIES
Four Seasons Resort Nevis, Charlestown,
The Nevis 804

MEXICO
BAJA SUR
Cabo Del Sol, Los Cabos 8C
Palmilla Golf Club, San Jose del Cabo . . 81(
Arroyo, Mountain, Ocean Courses
COLIMA
Isla Navidad Country Club, Manzanillo . 812
La Mantarraya, Manzanillo 813
GUERRERO
Acapulco Princess Golf Club, Acapulco . 815
Acapulco Princess, Pierre Marques Courses
Marina Ixtapa Golf Club, Ixtapa 818
JALISCO
Marina Vallarta Golf Club,
Puerto Vallarta 819

About the Author

Robert McCord is an author, book producer, agent and publishing consultant who lives in New York City. Mr. McCord has written the *Golf Book of Days* and *The Golf Connoisseur.* He is an avid but high-handicap golfer.